LAND USE REGULATION

ASPEN CASEBOOK SERIES

LAND USE REGULATION

Cases and Materials

Fifth Edition

Daniel P. Selmi
Professor of Law
Fritz B. Burns Chair in Real Property
Loyola Law School

James A. Kushner
Professor Emeritus
Southwestern Law School

Edward H. Ziegler
Professor of Law
University of Denver Sturm College of Law

Joseph F. C. DiMento
Professor of Law
University of California, Irvine School of Law

John Echeverria
Professor of Law
Vermont Law School

Wolters Kluwer

Published by Wolters Kluwer in New York.

Wolters Kluwer Legal & Regulatory U.S. serves customers worldwide with CCH, Aspen Publishers, and Kluwer Law International products. (www.WKLegaledu.com)

To contact Customer Service, e-mail customer.service@wolterskluwer.com, call 1-800-234-1660, fax 1-800-901-9075, or mail correspondence to:

    Wolters Kluwer
    Attn: Order Department
    PO Box 990
    Frederick, MD 21705

Printed in the United States of America.

2 3 4 5 6 7 8 9 0

ISBN 978-1-4548-7754-7

Library of Congress Cataloging-in-Publication Data

Names: Selmi, Daniel P., author. | Kushner, James A., author. | Ziegler, Edward H., author. | DiMento, Joseph F., author. | Echeverria, John D., author.
Title: Land use regulation : cases and materials / Daniel P. Selmi, Professor of Law, Fritz B. Burns Chair in Real Property, Loyola Law School; James A. Kushner, Professor Emeritus, Southwestern Law School; Edward H. Ziegler, Professor of Law, University of Denver Sturm College of Law; Joseph F. C. DiMento, Professor of Law, University of California, Irvine School of Law; John Echeverria, Professor of Law, Vermont Law School.
Description: Fifth edition. | New York : Wolters Kluwer, 2017. | Series: Aspen casebook series | Includes bibliographical references and index.
Identifiers: LCCN 2017002326 | ISBN 9781454877547
Subjects: LCSH: Land use — Law and legislation — United States. | LCGFT: Casebooks.
Classification: LCC KF5698 .S45 2017 | DDC 346.7304/5 — dc23 LC record available at https://lccn.loc.gov/2017002326

About Wolters Kluwer Legal & Regulatory U.S.

Wolters Kluwer Legal & Regulatory U.S. delivers expert content and solutions in the areas of law, corporate compliance, health compliance, reimbursement, and legal education. Its practical solutions help customers successfully navigate the demands of a changing environment to drive their daily activities, enhance decision quality and inspire confident outcomes.

Serving customers worldwide, its legal and regulatory portfolio includes products under the Aspen Publishers, CCH Incorporated, Kluwer Law International, ftwilliam.com and MediRegs names. They are regarded as exceptional and trusted resources for general legal and practice-specific knowledge, compliance and risk management, dynamic workflow solutions, and expert commentary.

To the Hon. Manuel L. Real
—DPS

In memory of Solomon Kushner
—JAK

In memory of Hank Seney and John Batt
—EHZ

To all of my land-use students
—JFCD

To Carin
—JE

Summary of Contents

Contents

8. *The First Amendment and Other Constitutional Protections*   389

Preface to the Fifth Edition

For the fifth edition, the casebook welcomes two new authors and bids farewell to two others. Joining the book are Professor Joseph DiMento from the University of California at Irvine Law School and Professor John Echeverria from the Vermont Law School. Joe brings to the book a lengthy background in planning issues. In particular, his writings on the so-called "consistency doctrine" have been enormously influential. John is well-known nationally as a prolific scholar on the takings clause and on other constitutional questions raised by land use regulation.

Leaving us is founding author Professor James Kushner of Southwestern Law School. Jim leaves behind four editions of this casebook as well as a voluminous and remarkable legacy of publications in the land use and housing fields. Professor Edward Ziegler also has retired. Ed is well-known for his writing in the land use field, and in particular for his work as the principal editor of the national multi-volume treatise, Rathkopf's The Law of Zoning and Planning. Both have more than earned their retirements, and we wish them well.

When the casebook was initiated in 1989, the first edition of the book noted that one of its pedagogical goals was to emphasize very recent cases so as to place students squarely within the context of modern land use law. We wanted a book that exposed students to ongoing issues and to the lively political undercurrents of this dynamic field of law. With this fifth edition, we have undertaken a broad review of recent developments so as to continue to fulfill that goal.

Users will see that we have re-worked the takings chapters to consolidate all the takings issues into one chapter. The materials have also been expanded to better reflect the current debate over preferred directions for takings law. Additionally, the chapter on other constitutional law issues, particularly those arising under the First Amendment, has also been substantially revised.

The biggest change, however, has been the addition of a new chapter entitled "Confronting New Challenges: Smart Growth, Health, Climate Change, and Vulnerable Populations." In addition to an expanded set of materials directed to the continuing development of "smart growth" principles, the chapter captures some new issues bearing on land use that have emerged. These include the land use impacts of climate change, a subject that some local governments are addressing even if state governments (and now, perhaps, the federal government) try to ignore it. Other parts of this new chapter address the relationship between land use policies and the rise in obesity among the American population, the continuing disputes over local regulation of homes for individuals battling substance abuse, and the land use implications of responding to problems posed by homelessness. Finally, the chapter addresses state and local land use efforts directed at regulating sites that dispense marijuana, both for medical use and now increasingly for recreational use.

These new materials are topical and highly interesting to students. We believe that both professors and students will enjoy them.

Professor Echeverria gratefully acknowledges the valuable research assistance of James LaRock as well as the support of Vermont Law School librarians Cynthia Lewis, Christine Ryan, and Michelle LaRose.

Professor DiMento wishes to thank his research assistants Ian Deady and Ethan Mora, who were extraordinary in their commitments and professionalism, and Ms. Lisa Payne, faculty assistant, whose organizational skills kept all of the background resources available and provided superior production services. Librarians Lisa Junghahn, Christina Tsou, and Dianna Sahhar identified sources and resources that make for a comprehensive treatment. Writing casebooks in the digital world often requires the professional services of information technology staff; Joe Macavinta, Jose Diaz, and Enrique Morones were generous in their support. Enid Zhou provided essential citation assistance.

Professor Selmi wishes to thank Loyola Law School and the Fritz B. Burns Foundation for their generous support. He also wishes to thank Dan Martin, Director of the Law Library, and Caitlin Hunter, Reference Librarian, for their invaluable assistance. Finally, he thanks Mell Banez, Pam Buckles, and the other members of the Faculty Support Office who worked tirelessly on the project.

Acknowledgments

Abatzoglou, John T., Joseph F. C. DiMento, Pamela Doughman and Stefano Nespor, A Primer on Global Climate Change Science, in DiMento and Doughman (eds.), Climate Change: What It Means for Us, Our Children, and Our Grandchildren 15-31 (2d ed. 2014). Copyright © 2014 Massachusetts Institute of Technology. Reproduced by permission by The MIT Press. All rights reserved.

Beatley, Timothy. Ethical Land Use: Principles of Policy and Planning 3-4, 13-16 (1994). Copyright © 1994 The Johns Hopkins University Press. Reproduced by permission. All rights reserved.

Callahan, Denise G. West Chester Moratorium on Rehab Centers, Journal-News (April 28, 2016). Copyright © 2016 Cox Media Group. Reproduced by permission. All rights reserved.

Costonis, John J. Icons and Aliens: Law, Aesthetics, and Environmental Change 12-19, 76-79 (1989). Copyright © 1989 The Board of Trustees of the University of Illinois Press. Reproduced by permission. All rights reserved.

Fischel, William A. Why Are There NIMBYs?, 77 Land Economics 144 (2001). Copyright © 2001 The University of Wisconsin Press. Reproduced by permission. All rights reserved.

Gerrard, Michael. Whose Backyard, Whose Risk: Fear and Fairness in Toxic and Nuclear Waste Siting 99-107 (1994). Copyright © 1994 Massachusetts Institute of Technology. Reproduced by permission of The MIT Press. All rights reserved.

Gordon, Peter and Harry W. Richardson. Are Compact Cities a Desirable Planning Goal? 63 J. Am. Plan. Ass'n 232 (1997). Copyright © 1997 American Planning Association. Reproduced by permission. All rights reserved.

Hirsch, Werner Z. Law and Economics: An Introductory Analysis 6-7, 14-15, 22, 80-82 (3rd ed. 1999). Copyright © 1999 Elsevier, Ltd. Reproduced by permission. All rights reserved.

PART ONE

INTRODUCTION TO
LAND USE CONTROLS

1

■

The Regulatory Setting: Land, Ethics, Economics, and Participants

A. THE VITALITY OF CONTEMPORARY LAND USE REGULATION

Land use regulation is probably the area of law that most affects the quality of life in the United States. The design of communities and their development are complex subjects that are fraught with the vicissitudes of politics and factionalism. At various times, developers are pitted against current residents, environmentalists against advocates of growth, rich against poor, homeowners against renters, and automobile users against transit users and bicyclists. Business may even oppose business.

Land use law reflects the dynamic process of deciding how land is utilized. The field is rapidly evolving. In the past 30 years, for example, the United States Supreme Court has issued opinions that have markedly changed how local governments may condition the approval of new development. The courts are also grappling with the intersection between First Amendment rights, such as freedom of religion, and the ability of local governments to regulate the use of churches. The subjects of "sustainable development" and "smart growth" continue to receive public attention. In recent years, some public health researchers have linked land use decisions — in particular, decisions that require homeowners to use vehicles for almost all tasks — to the problem of obesity in American society. And new land-use related problems, ranging from homelessness to global warming, have emerged.

From the student's perspective, modern land use cases are exciting. They often include stories that are reminiscent of soap operas (or old-time melodramas), and the cast of characters is large. There are landowners and developers, neighbors who become involved in every aspect of their community's development, environmentalists concerned about the impacts of growth, civil rights activists seeking more

3

housing, inspectors and bureaucrats who are part of the local land use governmental machinery, regulatory bodies that are often controlled by elected or appointed officials with declared ideological agendas, and judges who must review local decisions.

A former speaker of the United States House of Representatives once uttered the oft-quoted phrase, "All politics is local." The land use stories from around the country certainly confirm this statement, for land use disputes are intensely political and occupy the center stage of local politics. The participants care deeply about the issues, and they demand a right to be heard.

The import of land use issues also varies widely. A few are extremely important to the future of a region, while others are much smaller in scope. To get a taste of modern land use, consider the following summaries of controversies that arose in 2016:

- A resident of LaGrange, Kentucky, sought a conditional use permit for a drive-in movie theater along a rural county road. The project's proponent cited the economic stimulus for the area and argued it would be an amenity that the "community can enjoy together." Opponents, however, vigorously opposed the project, which would have two screens and an 800-car parking lot. They said the traffic would overwhelm the road to the site. "I don't want to hear screams from a horror flick," said one opponent. The project applicant replied that at the drive-in the sound would only be heard in cars through a speaker system. Martha Elson, Opponents of Drive-in: "Stop the Show," The Courier-Journal (Louisville, Ky.) (Sept. 16, 2016).

- A county council member in Montgomery County, Maryland, introduced a bill aimed at "zombie foreclosures." Under the bill, buyers of foreclosed property would have 30 days in which to register their purchases with the state. If they did not do so, they would face a $1000 a day fine. The problem, said the councilperson, was that when lenders foreclose on properties, there can be delays in the formal transfer of title, and during that period authorities cannot identify who is responsible for the property, contributing to blight in some areas and reduced property values. Bill Turque, Fines Proposed for "Zombie Foreclosures," The Washington Post (Sept. 21, 2016).

- Two local councilpersons proposed a building moratorium on the construction of homes in so-called "paper subdivisions." According to the proponents, these are old, undeveloped subdivisions that were approved long ago but do not have comprehensive drainage or sewerage plans. However, local Habitat for Humanity officials opposed the moratorium, arguing that they build homes in such areas for the working poor because the land is more affordable there. Another councilperson found the timing of the proposal "troubling" in light of the homes lost in recent flooding. One of the proponents of the moratorium said the parish has 37 such paper subdivisions and that, on 21 of them, over 20,000 lots were available for building. Sara Pagones, Council Delays Taking Up Building Moratorium, Baton Rouge Advocate (Sept. 3, 2016).

- A church in Dover, Delaware has proposed a "village" of 15 tiny houses that would be located adjacent to Victory Church. The houses would rent for $200-$300 per month to people who have jobs but cannot afford permanent housing. Neighbors, however, opposed the project. One neighbor said the church had not talked to the neighbors about the plan, and people "are terrified of what is coming." Signs declaring "No Tiny Houses" have appeared in yards. Jerry Smith, Tiny House Village Opposed, The Wilmington News Journal (Aug. 31, 2016).

- Dyersville, Iowa is the home of the stadium built for and featured in the movie "The Field of Dreams." The Dyersville City Council voted to rezone the property from agricultural to commercial so that a youth sports complex with a number of fields could be built next to the Field of Dreams stadium. However, 23 neighbors opposed the plans to build a tournament baseball park on the 193-acre farm located next door. The litigation reached the Iowa Supreme Court, and 150 people watched the court proceedings in the Grand Theater in downtown Keoku. Free cookies were available. Kyle Munson, Field of Dreams at Bat Before Supreme Court in Wake of Author's Death, Des Moines Register (Sept. 21, 2016).

B. THE LAND RESOURCE IN AMERICA: DISTRIBUTION AND TRENDS

To understand the context in which the law of land use controls operates, the student must have some sense of the land resources of the United States and how that land is now used.

■ MAJOR USES OF LAND IN THE UNITED STATES, 2007
U.S. Department of Agriculture (2011)

Cropland. Total cropland includes land planted for crops (82 percent of total cropland), cropland used for pasture, and idled cropland (including acreage removed from production under Government programs, such as the Conservation Reserve Program). Total cropland increased in the late 1940s, declined from 1949 to 1964, increased from 1964 to 1978, and decreased again from 1978 to 2007. Between 2002 and 2007, total cropland decreased by 34 million acres to its lowest level since this series began in 1945.

Grassland Pasture and Range. The estimated acreage of grassland pasture and range increased by 27 million acres (almost 5 percent) between 2002 and 2007, partly offsetting a decline in this land-use type during 1945-97.

Forest-Use Land. Forest-use land in 2007 includes 127 million acres of grazed forests, but excludes an estimated 80 million forest acres in parks, wildlife areas, and other special uses. Forest-use land increased 20 million acres (3 percent) from 2002 to 2007, continuing a trend that became evident in 2002 and reversing an almost 50-year downward trend. The 14-percent decline in forest-use land between 1949 and 2002 was largely due to forest-use land reclassified to special-use areas.

Urban and Rural Residential Areas. Urban land acreage quadrupled from 1945 to 2007, increasing at about twice the rate of population growth over this period. Land in urban areas was estimated at 61 million acres in 2007, up almost 2 percent since

2002 and 17 percent since 1990 (after adjusting the 1990 estimate for the new criteria used in the 2000 Census). The Census Bureau estimates that urban area increased almost 8 million acres (13 percent) during the 1990s.

Special-Use Areas. Special-use areas include rural transportation, national/state parks, wilderness and wildlife areas, national defense and industrial areas, and farmsteads and farm roads. Over all 50 States, special-use areas have increased nearly threefold since 1959, including a fourfold increase in rural parks and fish and wildlife areas. Over 2002-07, special-use areas increased more than 16 million acres (6 percent).

Ownership. Nearly 60 percent (1.35 billion acres) of the land in the United States is privately owned. The Federal Government owns 29 percent (653 million acres), over a third of which is in Alaska. State and local governments own about 9 percent (198 million acres). About 3 percent (66 million acres) is held in trust by the Bureau of Indian Affairs. There were no major changes in these aggregate ownership statistics from 2002 to 2007. Foreign ownership accounted for about 1 percent (22 million acres) of U.S. land in 2007.

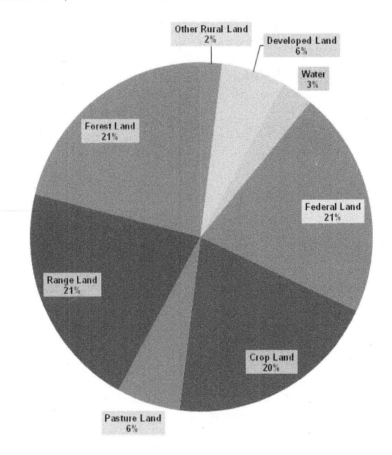

■ FIVE OF THE NATION'S ELEVEN FASTEST-GROWING CITIES ARE IN TEXAS
United States Census Bureau (May 19, 2016)

Georgetown, Texas saw its population rise 7.8 percent between July 1, 2014, and July 1, 2015, making it the nation's fastest-growing city with a population of 50,000 or more, according to estimates released today by the U.S. Census Bureau.

Georgetown is part of the Austin-Round Rock metro area, which crossed the 2 million population threshold in 2015 for the first time, according to statistics released earlier this year. This metro area is also home to Pflugerville, the nation's 11th fastest-growing large city. Austin itself added more people over the period (19,000) than all but seven other U.S. cities.

Texas was home to five of the 11 fastest-growing cities (New Braunfels, Frisco and Pearland were the others), and five of the eight that added the most people (Houston, San Antonio, Fort Worth and Dallas were the others).

New York remained the nation's most populous city and gained 55,000 people during the year ending July 1, 2015, which is more than any other U.S. city. New York City consists of five boroughs, each of which is a separate county equivalent of New York State. The five boroughs are Brooklyn, Queens, Manhattan, The Bronx and Staten Island. Queens (16,700), Brooklyn (16,000) and the Bronx (13,700) accounted for the bulk of New York's growth.

Denver joined the list of the 20 most populous cities in the United States, moving up two spots to 19th. It displaced Detroit, which fell from 18th to 21st. In addition, Seattle moved up two spots to 18th. Denver and Seattle were both among the nation's 11 top numerically gaining cities.

Among the 15 fastest-growing cities, the only one outside the South or West was Ankeny, Iowa, a suburb of Des Moines. It grew by 6.5 percent, ranking third. Ankeny completed a special census on Dec. 10, 2014, that showed the population to be 54,598. The 2015 estimate puts the population at 56,764. . . .

Other highlights:

- Aside from New York, each of the 15 cities that gained the highest number of people between 2014 and 2015 were in the South or West. Three were in California (Los Angeles, San Diego and San Francisco).
- California and Arizona each had two cities on the list of the 15 fastest growing cities.
- Of the 19,505 incorporated places in the United States, around 76 percent (14,804) had fewer than 5,000 people in 2015. Only about 3.9 percent (754) had populations of 50,000 or more.

Looked at a bit more broadly: Between 2010 and 2013, 51 percent of the population increase in the 52 major metropolitan areas — defined as areas with more than 1 million in population — was located in the southern part of the United States. Thirty percent took place in the West. Only 11 percent was in the Northeast, and 8 percent in the Midwest. http://www.newgeography.com/content/004240-special-report-2013-metropolitan-area-population-estimates (using Census Bureau data found at https://www.census.gov/popest/data/metro/totals/2013/) (last visited Sept. 24, 2016).

Two other recent demographic trends in the United States will impact future land use decisions:

1. Millenials, young adults born after 1980, have likely surpassed Baby Boomers (born 1946-1964) as the largest U.S. generation. They are the most racially diverse generation in American history. Many are still living at home, perhaps because of student debt.
2. The share of American adults who live in "middle class" households fell to 50 percent in 2015. For the previous 4 decades, those individuals were in the nation's economic majority. Also, the financial gap widened further between middle-and upper-income Americans. The latter hold 49 percent of U.S. aggregate income (up from 29 percent in 1970) and 7 times as much wealth as middle-income households. http://www.pewresearch.org/fact-tank/2016/03/31/10-demographic-trends-that-are-shaping-the-u-s-and-the-world/ (last visited Sept. 24, 2016).

Notes and Comments

1. *The Distribution of Land Ownership.* Most students undoubtedly understand that some land in the United States, such as the national parks, is owned by the federal government. You may be surprised, however, to learn how much of the nation's land is federally controlled:

> The federal government owns roughly 640 million acres, about 28% of the 2.27 billion acres of land in the United States. Four agencies administer 608.9 million acres of this land: the Bureau of Land Management (BLM), Fish and Wildlife Service (FWS), and National Park Service (NPS) in the Department of the Interior (DOI), and the Forest Service (FS) in the Department of Agriculture. Most of these lands are in the West and Alaska. In addition, the Department of Defense administers 14.4 million acres in the United States consisting of military bases, training ranges, and more. Numerous other agencies administer the remaining federal acreage.

Congressional Research Service, Summary, Federal Land Ownership: Overview and Data (Dec. 29, 2014). *See also* Quoctrung Bui and Margot Sanger-Katz, Why the Government Owns So Much Land in the West, N.Y. Times (Jan. 5, 2016) (discussing the history of federal land ownership).

Is this government ownership inconsistent with a private market economy that emphasizes individual home ownership and economic entrepreneurship? Some have vigorously argued that the federal lands should be sold off, at least in part. *See, e.g.,* Dale A. Oesterle, Public Land: How Much Is Enough?, 23 Ecol. L.Q. 521, 574 (1996) ("we should sell federal lands where commodity based uses predominate"). The issue has also been raised in the 2016 election. Do you agree?

2. *Transportation and Urban Development.* In his influential book Edge City: Life on the New Frontier (1991), journalist Joel Garreau documented the development of so-called "edge cities," large new cities just outside of the traditional urban centers. Garreau emphasized the relationship between "edge cities" and the

edge cities

transportation infrastructure, suggesting that cities are always created around the "state of the art" transportation device of the time. According to Garreau, "edge cities" result from a combination of the automobile, the jet plane, and the computer. *Id.* at 32. A 2011 book, Aerotroplis: The Way We'll Live Next, by John D. Kasarda and Greg Lindsay, takes the provocative position that in the twenty-first century cities will need to be spread around airports, and that economic and technological forces will lead to this result. Airports will shape development in this century, much like highways did the previous century, and railroads in the eighteenth century. *See also* National Center for Sustainable Transportation and U.C. Davis Institute of Transportation Studies, What Affects U.S. Passenger Travel? Current Trends and Future Perspectives (Feb. 2016).

Who should make the decisions about where the transportation infrastructure needed for development, such as expansions of the freeway system, is located? As you will see, while local government continues to make the most important decisions about individual developments, the money to build freeways, and the decisions about the location of those freeways, has been left largely in federal hands (although this is now changing somewhat).

3. *Regulating Land Use.* Do you see any need for local government to regulate land uses? In the introduction to his 1972 book Land Use Without Zoning, Professor Bernard H. Siegan cogently states his case opposing government intervention:

> For most people, home is where the major part of life is spent. . . . Its characteristics greatly influence the quality of one's life.
>
> For those concerned with the quality of life, housing and local environmental conditions merit the highest priority. I believe one means to achieve these objectives is to eliminate one of the principal barriers to production, zoning, and thereby allow the real estate market greater opportunity to satisfy the needs and desires of its consumers. My studies show that zoning is neither necessary to maintain or protect property values nor an aid to "planning" — its principal justifications. On the contrary, it has adverse effects on both. When it impedes the production of housing, it also impedes the achievement of better housing and housing conditions.

See also Timothy Sandefur, Cornerstone of Liberty: Property Rights in 21st Century America (2006) (arguing that any limitation on property use by regulation is a taking that requires compensation).

Based on your knowledge of how land is used in the United States, do you agree with these positions?

4. *Land Conversion.* The excerpt above from "Major Uses of Land" gives a static view of the types of major land uses. But changes are occurring daily, and you need to see the overall trend over time:

> By 1982, approximately 71 million acres of the lower 48 States had already been developed. Between 1982 and 2012, the American people developed an additional 44 million acres for a total of 114 million acres developed. Of all historic land development in the United States, excluding Alaska, over 37 percent has occurred since 1982. Much of this newly developed land had been existing habitats, including 17 million acres converted from forests.
>
> A projection that the U.S. population will increase from 310 million to 439 million between 2010 and 2050 suggests that land conversion trends like these will continue. . . .

Proposed Revisions to the U.S. Fish and Wildlife Service Mitigation Policy, 81 Fed. Reg. 12380, 12381 (Mar. 8, 2016).

5. *People on the Move.* For decades a larger trend was the expansion of housing in the suburbs and the deterioration of at least some large urban cities. Some observers, however, have concluded that the trend may be changing. Robert Lang and Jennifer LeFurgy, Boomburb "Buildout": The Future of Development in Large, Fast-Growing Suburbs, 42 Urban Affairs Review 533 (2007) (finding that more than half of the "boomburbs" — technically, incorporated areas with more than 100,000 residents that are not the largest city in their metropolitan areas — will be at the buildout point by 2020). Others have commented on the "decline of the suburb," and the Secretary of Housing in the Obama Administration has stated, "We've reached the limits of suburban development: People are beginning to vote with their feet and come back to the central cities." Still others cite increasing poverty in the suburbs. Elizabeth Kneebone and Natalie Holmes, U.S. Concentrated Poverty in the Wake of the Great Recession (Mar. 31, 2016) found at https://www.brookings.edu/research/u-s-concentrated-poverty-in-the-wake-of-the-great-recession (last visited Sept. 24, 2016).

However, recent census data has generated yet other views about the future of the suburbs. Laura Kusisto, More Americans Are Again Moving to Suburbs Than Cities, http://blogs.wsj.com/economics/2016/03/24/more-americans-are-again-moving-to-suburbs-than-cities/ (3/24/16), citing Jed Kolko, 2015 Population Winners: The Sunbelt and the Surburs, http://jedkolko.com/2016/03/23/2015-population-suburbs-sunbelt/ (last visited Sept. 24, 2016) (arguing that the suburbs continue to remain a favored destination).

What do you think? Is the suburban boom over or will it continue as the recession fully abates? What are the land use implications of each of these outcomes?

6. *Websites.* It will come as no surprise to you that a number of websites regularly follow developments in the land use, planning, and design field. A "top 10" list of websites in this general area for the year 2015 can be found at http://www.planetizen.com/node/83095/top-10-websites-2015 (last visited Sept. 24, 2016).

7. *The Importance of Land Use.* Consider the following statement about the importance of "land use":

> Land use is the human modification of the Earth's surface, which has strongly affected and will increasingly shape planetary functions . . . Looming sustainability problems such as climate change, increasing demand for food, accelerating urbanization, the ongoing biodiversity crisis and widespread changes in the structure and functioning of ecosystems with implications for the services they provide all indicate that research at the interface of humans and the environment will continue to be of utmost societal relevance . . . Land use is the key for understanding and potentially solving these sustainability challenges . . .

Daniel Muller and Darla K. Munroe, Current and Future Challenges in Land-Use Science, J. of Land Use Science, Vol. 9 No. 2, 133 (2014). The materials in the book are designed to provide you with insights into these types of broader issues.

C. LAND USE AS AN ETHICAL DECISION

A central theme of this text is the ethical dimension of land use regulation. The word "ethics" is used in a couple of different ways. In its narrowest sense, there are legal issues concerning ethics, such as when a decision maker has a conflict of interest in rendering a land use decision. There also exist questions regarding the ethics of developers. For example, they may bring litigation against opposing groups to intimidate them, suits known as "strategic lawsuits against public participation" (or "SLAPP" suits). Alternatively, developers may threaten to bring suits against public entities for damages, suits that pose the specter of heavy litigation costs. Opponents of growth have similar choices. Is it ethically justifiable for such opponents to institute litigation challenging *every* discretionary decision made by local government on a development project?

Here, however, we speak of an "ethic" on a broader level: as a value underlying the choice about how land is used. When we choose the uses to be allowed on property, those choices either serve or can conflict with an underlying land "ethic": a series of principles that govern our view of the proper role that property is to play in society. An important component of this ethic is the extent to which natural resources should be viewed as available for exploitation by the property owner, or whether those resources are subject to a broader public interest in them.

The following readings outline alternative views of land use ethics as reflected in how property rights are defined.

■ FRED BOSSELMAN, FOUR LAND ETHICS: ORDER, REFORM, RESPONSIBILITY, OPPORTUNITY
24 Envtl. L. 1439, 1440-1441 (1994)

I. INTRODUCTION

The term "land ethics" has found a prominent place in environmental literature ever since Aldo Leopold rather casually and cryptically coined it in the 1930s. If one defines the phrase to mean a system of thought that relates land to ideas of right and wrong, one can identify many prior systems which have achieved prominence at some time or place. . . .

I conclude that only a pluralistic process in which multiple land ethics are debated will be a satisfactory basis for the resolution of many of the current bitter conflicts over land in America. . . . The four land ethics discussed [below] play important roles in the United States today. This section briefly describes these roles.

A. ORDER

[The land policies of the semi-legendary King Arthur were] designed to protect the social order [and] continue to play an important role in the United States. Although class distinction in the United States never attained the rigidity of the English model, land policy in the United States has frequently been used to stabilize existing social relationships.

For example, federal tax policy creates a sharp distinction between home-owners, who receive interest deductions, and tenants, who do not. A new nationally supported system of mortgage commodification has increased the extent to which "homeowners" now hold in an almost tenurial relationship to the pension funds and similar institutions that dominate long-term investment. An Arthurian network of deed restrictions and local zoning protects many residential communities from disruptions in the social order. Gated communities increasingly resemble fortified castles.

B. REFORM

[Demands for reform like David Ricardo's in post-[W]aterloo England] are less shrill in the United States than in many other countries because the privileges attached to land ownership have never been as dramatic as those that prompted Ricardo's call for reform. Nevertheless, substantial privileges exist and have prompted demands for greater equity.

Reformers object that agricultural interests destroy the soil resource and pollute the environment while receiving cash subsidies, property tax abatements, and relief from responsibility for damages caused by pesticides. They question whether mining interests should continue to use the federal lands without making reimbursement to taxpayers. One noted law and economics scholar has characterized urban redevelopment cartels as "feudal."

C. RESPONSIBILITY

Modern [followers of John Muir] have substituted wetlands for Muir's Sierran peaks as the resource most in need of preservation. Moreover, the protection of wilderness has become well-accepted policy in Congress, and a growing recognition of the importance of biodiversity has placed emphasis on the need for preservation of a wide range of habitats. Perhaps the most dramatic recent success of the ethic of responsibility is the legislation imposing responsibility on those who have poisoned the land through careless use of toxic chemicals . . . .

Although those who attempt to model their activities on Muir's are but a small fraction of the population, Muir's influence goes far beyond those who follow directly in his footsteps. Many Americans honor his example intermittently or vicariously. For example, the Outward Bound movement has brought thousands of business executives into the wilderness as an educational experience, and groups like the Nature Conservancy allow people to honor their responsibility to nature vicariously through cash or land donations.

D. OPPORTUNITY

If utilitarians had worried that the entrepreneurial opportunity to create wealth out of land would be stifled by rigid controls, by the ability of privileged vested interests to avoid reform, and by the demands of preservationists for greater responsibility, the free-wheeling business climate of the 1980s proved their worries groundless. Legislation converted many savings and loan associations into governmentally insured entrepreneurial vehicles for the development of real estate that were often operated by developers with little regard for market needs. The result was a taxpayer bailout of unprecedented proportions and a record oversupply of commercial buildings, which may dampen new construction well into the twenty-first century.

Meanwhile, in residential real estate, Ricardo's idea that economic rent was the windfall of the gentry was transformed into the government-subsidized home-ownership movement—if you can't beat the gentry, join the gentry! Economists might classify land as just another asset, but the American public thought otherwise.

Landowners continue to be successful in amassing government subsidies for their activities (or inactivities), relying on the Jeffersonian mystique to hide the fact that most of the subsidies are being paid to large corporations. Congress has begun paying farmers to not farm in sensitive areas, and some landowners are seeking higher subsidies against losses in land value . . . .

VII. Conclusion

Each of the land ethics discussed in this article represents an important factor in the way Americans currently think about land. . . . Each will be an element of any public decisionmaking process having a major impact on land. The search for a new land ethic will continue, but in a democratic society the existence of multiple ethics must be accepted.

■ JOSEPH WILLIAM SINGER, THE OWNERSHIP SOCIETY AND TAKINGS OF PROPERTY: CASTLES, INVESTMENTS AND JUST OBLIGATIONS
Harv. Envtl. L. Rev. 309 (2006)

Conservatives argue for an expansive interpretation of the rights of owners with correspondingly narrow limits on the powers of government. This means that they have a large vision of which acts of ownership are self-regarding in nature; they view most property rights and their exercise as legitimately concerning the owner alone. If almost every exercise of a property right is viewed as a self-regarding act, then the state has no business interfering with it. Liberals argue for a more expansive realm for government regulation, and in so doing, they by necessity take a narrower view of the range of acts of ownership that are legitimately self-regarding in nature. How should we think about this issue? Scholars generally approach this question by identifying a decision procedure that provides guidance in choosing between the conflicting interests of the parties. This procedure may be based on balancing interests, comparing the costs and benefits of alternative legal rules, imagining what rules would be adopted in a suitable setting such as a social contract made by free and equal individuals, or by identifying fundamental human interests that should be protected as individual rights. I want to step back and consider how we think about this question before we apply a decision procedure. We approach the question of defining property rights partly by adopting conceptions of what ownership means. These conceptions are embodied in conscious or unconscious images that orient our thinking in particular directions and frame our analysis of the underlying policy question.

We can observe two common models of ownership in legal discussions about property and the relation between property owners and the government. The first image is that of a lord in a castle, and the second is that of an investor in a market economy. These two models of property focus on the rights of the owner, and they define those rights in different ways. I want to argue that there is a third model of property . . . The third model of property starts from the idea that owners have obligations as well as rights. The image that supports this notion is that of a citizen in a free and democratic society. This model of property as citizenship adjudicates

[handwritten margin note: conservatives v. liberals]

conflicts that arise between the castle model and the investment model. The first two models are well-known, although their implications are not well-understood. The last model is present in our law and political discussions about property, but it has been marginalized and suppressed.

■ ERIC T. FREYFOGLE, PROPERTY RIGHTS, THE MARKET, AND ENVIRONMENTAL CHANGE IN 20TH CENTURY AMERICA
32 Envtl. L. Rptr. 10254 (2002)

Over the past century, U.S. laws and regulations have increasingly re-embedded property rights in a communal order, aimed in important part at protecting the natural environment. Property law continues to recognize and protect individual rights, as it has for generations, but it recognizes other aims as well, and constraints on the market are pervasive. Aggregate calculations are hard to undertake, yet plentiful evidence suggests that these constraints have served not to contain economic growth, but to help fuel it, both by correcting the market's flaws in pricing and allocation and by fostering the kind of trust, social cohesiveness, and civic stability that any market needs to work well. In the ongoing drama of private property in America, the market is only one of the lead characters . . . .

Though the contemporary scene is distinctly messy, it is possible to identify six major themes or trends in contemporary landed property rights. Briefly stated, they are as follows:

- *[handwritten margin note: Rights reduced, protection increase]* Landowner rights to use land are increasingly tailored to the land and to the surrounding social context; that is, rights to use land are becoming more context-dependent. In a related shift, rights to use land intensively are being reduced, with corresponding increases in the protections landowners enjoy against disruptive land uses by neighbors.

- Old categories of private ownership versus public ownership are being blurred, with more instances of intermediate ownership forms that mix the categories. Increasingly, rights in a single piece of land are fragmented among various "owners," with some rights held by the prime user of the land while other rights are held by neighbors, private entities, and government bodies.

- Land use planning is taking place on larger spatial scales and covering rural lands, aimed chiefly (although not solely) at urban sprawl, quality-of-life issues, and various land use-related environmental problems.

- American law has made substantial progress toward a complex reconciliation of the unending conflict between the private owner's desire for clearly defined, stable property norms and the community's contrasting need to retain power to redefine ownership rights in light of shifting conditions and values. The reconciliation offers substantial protection for existing land uses but far less protection for landowner desires to devote land to new uses.

- Governments at all levels, from the most local to the national and even global, are becoming involved in the processes of defining and controlling land use rights, albeit with little consensus and much experimentation on how best to allocate power and responsibility among the various governing levels.

- In the vitally important rhetorical battleground over the meaning of private property, individualistic, commodity-focused images of ownership have gained prominence, and they have significantly impeded efforts to address rural land use problems, particularly land degradation caused by agriculture and other commodity-production activities. Though conservation advocates have been slow to develop alternative images of ownership—ones that draw upon organic, communal understandings of ownership—alternative images are emerging, thus joining the contest over private property as cultural emblem.

■ TIMOTHY BEATLEY, ETHICAL LAND USE: PRINCIPLES OF POLICY AND PLANNING
3-4, 13-16 (1994)

[T]he social allocation of land to different uses and activities is fundamentally and inextricably a problem of ethics. This is so because such land-use decisions have, both individually and cumulatively, tremendous social and environmental impacts. Land-use actions can destroy important elements of the natural environment, and today land development and urban growth are major causes of the loss of such areas as wetlands, habitat for endangered species, and forestlands, among others. Development patterns have much to do with the nature and extent of pollution generated by our society—ozone and carbon monoxide in urban areas due to land-use patterns that rely unduly on the automobile, nonpoint sources of water pollution generated by impervious surfaces, loss of natural vegetation, careless construction practices, and a variety of urban and rural uses such as underground storage tanks, landfills, and agricultural operations. . . . Land-use decisions have tremendous social and economic implications as well. Such decisions influence the distribution of basic goods and services in the society, including access to jobs, schools, transportation, and recreation facilities, among others. Land-use decisions also influence the distribution of *bads*, or hazards and threats to health and safety, including the extent to which individuals and families are placed at risk to cancer-causing toxic waste facilities; to floods, hurricanes, earthquakes, or other natural disasters; to hazardous air and water pollutants; or to dangerous traffic and road conditions. Land-use decisions, moreover, have the capability to isolate and segregate different social and economic groups, and to influence how people view themselves and the value of their lives.

In short . . . [a]ll decisions about the use of land, then, are inherently ethical judgments, inherently ethical choices. Land-use decisions and policies raise questions of right and wrong, good and bad. . . .

CENTRAL QUESTIONS IN LAND-USE ETHICS . . .

DEFINING THE RELEVANT MORAL COMMUNITY

To resolve dilemmas about land-use policy it is important to determine what the relevant moral community is. There are at least three dimensions to this question.

How far or even

The first is *geographical.* Are we, on the one hand, obligated to consider the effects of a land-use decision or policy on the immediate neighborhood or community? Or should we consider the interests and well-being of broader publics — say, of the residents of the surrounding region, state, or nation? ...

How far into the future

A second dimension to this question is *temporal.* Many land-use decisions and policies clearly have impacts that extend into the future. In considering whether to allow the destruction or degradation of some natural landscape, are we obligated to consider only the interests of the present human population? Or do we have an obligation to consider a much longer time frame, to factor into our moral calculations the effects of such an action on future generations? ...

Humans only.

A third dimension to the question of how to determine the relevant moral community is *biological.* Must we, when making land-use decisions, consider the interest and well-being of other forms of life? Some have argued that, morally, our only obligations extend to *Homo sapiens,* while others suggest that certain ethical obligations extend to all sentient life-forms. Still others argue that the moral community must include all forms of life, sentient and nonsentient alike, and that land-use and other societal decisions must reflect a certain level of ethical respect for this life.

Notes and Comments

1. *The Four Land Ethics.* Professor Bosselman argues that understanding the four land ethics is necessary if we are to realize why the current debates over land use are intemperate and ideological. Which of these four ethics best reflects your own personal understanding of the role that land is to play in American society? How did you form that view?

As you read the material in the book, you should consider whether land use laws serve one of the "ethics" identified by Professor Bosselman more than others.

Professor Bosselman also states that we need "ongoing conflict management systems to cope with regular conflicts between existing ethical systems." What kinds of systems might be designed for this purpose? Would they be legislative or adjudicatory? Or would they follow some other model, such as negotiation?

2. *The Significance of the Opportunity Ethic.* Wealth creation is perhaps the principal justification for a regime of private property rights. *See, e.g.,* Thomas W. Merrill, Private Property and the Politics of Environmental Protection, 28 Harv. J.L. & Pub. Pol'y 69, 72 (2004) ("Private property generates wealth. One reason for this is that private property creates vastly enhanced incentives for investing in improvements to resources. Another reason is that private property translates into longer time horizons in considering investments. A third is that private property leads to a much more efficient allocation of resources.").

How important is the "opportunity" land ethic to the American economy? Is it sufficiently central that greater restrictions on the ability to use land should be resisted on economic grounds? Or are there sufficient other outlets for entrepreneurial activities that the opportunity land ethic should play a less important role in land use law?

3. *Anthropocentric v. Ecocentric Land Ethics.* Professor Kristin Shrader-Frechette looks at another way of differentiating land use ethics:

Although both land-use ethics and the earlier land-reform ethics call for a new land philosophy and a new land practice, they are primarily *anthropocentric*. They demand a change in our behavior so as to prevent harm to humans. . . .

The two remaining land ethics, land-community ethics and land-rights ethics, however, are primarily nonanthropocentric or ecocentric. They issue moral imperatives, not for the sake of human well-being alone, but also for the good of the land (the entire biosphere) as a whole, apart from human interests. Although humans are included in the biosphere, presumably somewhat different actions might be mandated by an ecocentric or biocentric ethics that attempts to maximize the good of the whole biosphere, as opposed to an anthropocentric ethics that attempts to maximize the good of one subset of inhabitants (humans) of the biosphere.

Four Land Ethics: An Overview, in Lynton Keith Caldwell & Kristin Shrader-Frechette, Policy for Land: Law and Ethics, 57-58 (1993). *See also* Lynda L. Butler, The Resilience of Property, 55 Ariz. L. Rev. 847, 867 (2013) ("a homocentric view of the relationship between humans and nature . . . aggravates the adverse impacts of property use on the environment . . .").

Note how the types of ethics identified in this excerpt broaden the purposes that land use law would serve. Is it possible to blend the types of ethics identified in the excerpt?

4. *Land Use and Religious Belief.* For some, religious beliefs are important factors in making land use decisions. For example, some authors have traced the development of a "Judeo-Christian principle of stewardship," with its consequences for such issues as land ownership. *See* Peter W. Salsich, Jr., *Toward a Property Ethic of Stewardship*, in Charles Geisler & Gail Daneker (eds.), Property and Values: Alternatives to Public and Private Ownership (2000). Professor Salsich concludes that, while the principle of stewardship has "waxed and waned over the years," the ideal has survived and "is a consistent part of historical and current Judeo-Christian teachings." *Id.* at 36. He emphasizes that this principle would, for example, encourage the adoption of policies that could help a wide range of families obtain decent housing rather than maximizing advantages for families that do not need governmental assistance. *Id.*

5. *The Significance of the Muirian Ethic.* The developing understanding of ecology plainly calls into question the self-contained notion of traditional property law, including the "castle" mythology discussed in the Singer excerpt. For example, we now know that species require sufficient habitat for their survival, but this habitat may bear little relationship to the pattern of land ownership now extant. Should the right to use land in private ownership be changed to reflect this ecological knowledge? The late Professor Joseph Sax has described the significant implications that this "economy of nature" poses for traditional property law:

Assuming no compensation and a willingness to look anew at the nature of rights in land, what might property rights designed to accommodate both transformational needs and the needs of nature's economy look like? They would, at the least, be characterized by the following features:

1. Less focus on individual dominion, and the abandonment of the traditional "island" and "castle-and-moat" images of ownership.

2. More public decisions, because use would be determined ecosystematically, rather than tract by tract; or more decisions made on a broad, systemwide private scale.
3. Increased ecological planning, because different kinds of lands have different roles.
4. Affirmative obligations by owners to protect natural services, with owners functioning as custodians as well as self-benefitting entrepreneurs.

Property Rights and the Economy of Nature: Understanding *Lucas v. South Carolina Coastal Council*, 45 Stan. L. Rev. 1433, 1451 (1993).

By contrast, a libertarian view of property rights can take the opposite view. It would see land parcels as ecologically discrete, separate commodities rather than as part of an integrated whole. As a result, nature would not constrain land use. *See* Alexandra Klass, Property Rights on the New Frontier: Climate Change, Natural Resource Development, and Renewable Energy, 38 Ecol. L.Q. 63, 65 (2011) (contrasting the historical role of property rights, which created a structure for conveying property rights in natural resources to private parties to encourage development, with modern law, which limits property and resource development rights).

Which model seems more correct to you? Does the prospect of global warming reinforce the "Muirian ethic"?

6. *The "Bundle of Rights" Conception of Property?* As you can see from the excerpts presented above, defining property rights depends on how you view the nature of property. In Property Frames, 87 Wash. L. Rev. 449 (2010), Professors Jonathan Nash and Stephanie Stern investigate two ways of framing property: as a "bundle of rights" or as a "discrete asset." Under the bundle approach, property is seen as encompassing a "bundle of sticks," with each stick representing an individual right. The rights would include the right to use the property, the right to exclude others, the right to sell the property, etc. In contrast, in the "discrete asset" approach the property's owner has dominion over the asset. The authors conclude that the bundle approach has been largely, although not universally, accepted over the last century. *See also* Anna diRobilant, Property: A Bundle of Sticks or a Tree?, 66 Vand. L. Rev. 869 (2013).

Professor Richard Epstein, a strong defender of property rights, endorses the traditional conception of property ownership as a "bundle of sticks": "[T]his emphasis on the bundle of rights has been used by the advocates of strong property rights, like myself, to say that each stick in the bundle is entitled to equal protection. . . . [T]he set of rights found in the traditional bundle of property rights was far from arbitrary, as each stick in that bundle is needed to enhance the value of the whole." Richard A. Epstein, How to Create — or Destroy — Wealth in Real Property, 58 Ala. L. Rev. 741, 746 (2006). *See also* Jane B. Baron, Rescuing the Bundle-of-Rights Metaphor in Property Law, 82 U. Cin. L. Rev. 57, 60 (2013) (arguing that the "bundle-of-rights conceptualization remains useful" because it "helps to specify the legal relations of parties in both simple and complex property arrangements, to identify explicitly the normative choices implicit in those arrangements, to assess the quality of the human relationships that property entails, and to force the production of information pertinent to those issues.").

Is each stick in the "bundle" — exclusion, possession, use, development, and disposition — essential to achieving wealth creation? On the other hand, what if regulation interferes with one right but not the others? Is that a taking? If not, how far does interference with the "bundle of rights" have to go before a taking occurs?

7. *An Inherent Right to Develop Property?* A related question is whether the ownership of property includes an inherent right to develop that property. Professor Steven Eagle argues that "the existence of an inherent right of development" is implicit in recent Supreme Court decisions, which you will read in Chapter 7, that prohibit "'[e]xtortionate demands' for property or money as a condition for granting development permits." Steven J. Eagle, The Perils of Regulatory Property in Land Use Regulation, 54 Washburn L.J. 1, 21 (2014). Do you agree that such an inherent right exists? If so, how would you define the extent of that right?

8. *Defining the Extent of the Social Obligation.* Professor Laura S. Underkuffler suggests the need for recognition for the "social obligations" of ownership. She states:

> [W]e should develop an articulated social-obligation norm not only because it would rationalize an irrational situation, or even because it is a good idea; rather, we should do so because we must. Political, cultural, legal, and other realities leave us no choice. We no longer have the luxury of operating with the "mythology" of property as a free-standing, individually protective, socially acontextual entity. We must explicitly acknowledge property's other side.

Property As Constitutional Myth: Utilities and Dangers, 92 Cornell L. Rev. 1239, 1243 (2007). *See also* Joseph William Singer, Property as the Law of Democracy, 63 Duke L.J. 1287, 1304 (2014) ("Property law establishes a baseline for social relations compatible with democracy, both as a political system and a form of social life."). *Compare* Steven Eagle, A Prospective Look at Property Rights and Environmental Protection, 20 Geo. Mason L. Rev. 725, 749 (2013) (redefining underlying property rights means that "in effect all development rights cease to be well specified. They may stay with the individual, or they may be blocked by the state, but there is no process which prevents the alternation back and forth from one side to the other. It then becomes the classic rent seeking dynamic driving you to a social minimum.").

Do you agree with Professor Eagle that redefining underlying property rights to take into account a wider scope of concerns has unacceptable adverse effects? If you do not, what is the scope of this social-obligation norm?

Professor Beatley raises the difficulty of determining "what the relevant moral community is." Looking at this issue in the first sense that he discusses, the geographical sense, he asks whether one is obligated to consider the effects of a land use decision only on the immediate neighborhood or whether the residents of the region or perhaps the state also must be considered. Think about this issue in terms of standing to litigate a decision. Who should be allowed to challenge a local government decision? Only those living in the community? Or should other, non-community members be given such rights? As you will see in this book, the land use system now recognizes the rights of "third parties" in land use disputes to an extent unheard of 50 years ago.

9. *The Exclusion of "Undesirables."* Another critical aspect of the ethical questions raised by land use regulation is the relationship between regulation and discrimination. Professor Jerry Frug has charged that local control over land use has resulted in the exclusion of what he terms "the wrong kind of people" — those excluded to make a residential neighborhood seem desirable. Jerry Frug, The Geography of

Community, 48 Stan. L. Rev. 1047 (1996). Indeed, academics charge that this type of exclusion was a driving force in the suburbanization of the United States. As Professor Stacy E. Seicshnaydre summarized in The Fair Housing Choice Myth, 33 Cardozo L. Rev. 967, 991 (2012): "Local land-use decision-making proceeds from the assumption that we can — and perhaps even should — concentrate social and economic advantage by preserving socioeconomically homogeneous enclaves. In fact, socioeconomic homogeneity has been the bedrock of local land use policy since the 1920s." And in Ezra Rosser, The Ambition and Transformative Potential of Progressive Property, 101 Cal. L. Rev. 107 (2013), the author argues that even so-called "progressive property" theorists ignore the need for a "fresh start to correct for the problematic origins of property in the United States and the exclusionary effect of ownership rights. . . ."

Do you agree? Or do current land use patterns merely reflect existing consumer preferences, as we might expect in a market economy?

D. LAND USE AND ECONOMIC THEORY

As you are probably aware, a considerable body of literature has developed in the field known as "Law and Economics." *See, e.g.,* Richard Posner, Economic Analysis of Law (1998). These writings have attempted to examine the consistency between recognized legal principles and the overriding criterion of microeconomic analysis: the assurance of economically efficient outcomes. Much of this literature is directly relevant to land use, examining whether current land use rules either promote or hinder economic efficiency. Indeed, one of the seminal articles in the field addressed legal entitlements from the perspective of what was, in essence, a land use dispute. *See* Ronald Coase, The Problem of Social Cost, 3 J. L. & Econ. 1 (1960).

Examining land use from an economic perspective provides a useful counterpart to the viewpoint, discussed above, that land use is an "ethical" issue. In the excerpts discussed below, you will see how the economist views land use regulation. In particular, economic theory demonstrates how, at least from the standpoint of efficiency, the initial "entitlement" to land use rights is irrelevant. No matter which party initially holds that entitlement, the parties will reach an economically efficient outcome — an outcome that achieves the result at the lowest possible cost. First, though, a brief word about terminology.

The economic theory we are concerned with addresses how markets take negative externalities into account. These occur when the activity of one individual on land imposes a cost on another individual. For example, if a landowner runs a large pig farm on his or her property (in modern terminology, a "confined animal feeding operation," or "CAFO"), that operation could impose negative externalities on neighbors, such as noise or, most likely, bad smells. More prosaically, a church in a residential neighborhood can impose externalities if large numbers of cars use all the parking on a street.

A related problem here is the question of the so-called tragedy of the commons. This occurs when lands are available for use by the public. In a leading article by that title, the author reasoned that individuals using a common area for grazing would have an economic incentive to keep adding additional animals to their flocks. The reason would be that, while the owner could keep all the benefit from that additional animal, the costs imposed by its grazing on the commons would be spread throughout the other users of the commons. The result would be the destruction of the commons caused by each individual user acting in his or her own self-interest. *See* Garrett Hardin, The Tragedy of the Commons, 162 Science 1243 (1968).

The concepts of externalities and the tragedy of the commons plainly illustrate the function of much of land use regulation. It is a body of law intended in large part to avoid externalities and damage to common goods. It does so by granting entitlements to individuals who are allowed to undertake land uses. But the question remains whether, in dealing with externalities, the current land use system serves the overriding purpose of economic efficiency.

■ WERNER Z. HIRSCH, LAW AND ECONOMICS: AN INTRODUCTORY ANALYSIS
6-7, 14-15, 22, 80-82 (3d Ed. 1999)

The concept of property rights relates to the set of privileges and responsibilities accorded to a person in relation to the owning of property in general and real property in particular. These rights are determined by a long history of property laws, whether common laws or statutory laws. The right to property is the power to exclude others from or give them access to a benefit or use of the particular object. An elaborate system of property, liability, and inalienability rules exists to bolster an owner's claim to the property or good. Property rights to an unexplored area, such as the moon or the sea, are determined by international agreements entered into by bodies that have the power to enforce them. A mere individual without the coercive power of government could not hope to enforce a claim to, for example, the Atlantic Ocean.

The presence of property rights furnishes incentives to use resources efficiently. Given a legal system that enforces property rights, holders can have confidence that they will obtain returns from the use of property.

Under what conditions is a system of property rights efficient? The conditions include universality, exclusivity, and transferability. *Universality* implies that all resources should be owned by someone. *Exclusivity* is defined as the right to exclude people who might want to take part of the property. *Transferability* provides for voluntary exchanges that in general are value enhancing. . . .

[handwritten margin note: Universality / Exclusivity / Transferability]

Zoning is an area that lends itself more than some others to economic analysis. . . . [Z]oning involves the division of land into districts or zones having different regulations. These regulations impose legal constraints under which the land market must operate and rights and entitlements can be exchanged. The constraints are made in accordance with a comprehensive plan, ostensibly designed to promote the health, safety, and general welfare of the population. . . .

[handwritten margin note: Zoning]

Efficiency of resource allocation and equity in income distribution are major considerations. The efficiency issue arises because, in the presence of externalities, land use controls in general and zoning in particular are designed to improve resource allocation. A major task is to assess the extent to which zoning does or does not accomplish this objective.

The equity issue arises because of direct and indirect influences of zoning. Direct influences relate to zoning's reallocation of rights and entitlements, with the result that some parties gain and others lose. At the same time, there are indirect effects because zoning influences patterns of local government finance, which in turn affect the distribution of income or at least the ability of local governments to redistribute income. . . .

Microeconomic theory can offer some further helpful insights — for example, into the relation between zoning and negative externalities. According to economic theory, the separation of land uses increases the efficiency of property markets to the extent that it causes the price of the parcel of land to equal its true marginal product without causing the prices of equal parcels of land to differ. Thus, for a zoning ordinance to increase the efficiency of the local property market, it should remove any externalities that exist and yet do so without artificially constraining the supply of land in any given use. However . . . increasing efficiency of land use in this manner is not easy.

■ DAVID SCHLEICHER, CITY UNPLANNING
122 Yale L.J. 1670, 1680–91 (2013)

A. Economic Theory and Zoning

The initial justification for zoning was reducing nuisances. As Ronald Coase famously showed, nuisances are not caused by the tortfeasor alone; they are equally caused by the existence of an incompatible land use nearby.[23] By dividing cities into zones, each with permitted uses for land, local governments could reduce the incidence of nuisance administratively, rather than by relying on litigation. This reasoning was central to the Supreme Court's decision in Village of Euclid v. Ambler Realty Co., which upheld the constitutionality of zoning.

Whatever the merits of this view, it became clear that zoning regimes did far more than reduce traditionally justiciable nuisances. Particularly after World War II, zoning policy expanded from traditional height limits and "cumulative zoning" — which barred higher-intensity uses like heavy manufacturing from single-family areas but not vice versa — to more aggressive techniques that gave planners both more flexibility to condition approvals on meeting requirements set by the city and more ways to restrict building, including noncumulative zoning rules that assigned uses to specific areas . . . .

The idea that a government planner should decide the best uses for private real property may seem like an odd economic theory, but it has a basis in the economics of property law. Robert Nelson and William Fischel developed a theory of zoning to justify such comprehensive planning built around a government's ability to negotiate on behalf of all property owners in the jurisdiction.[28] Their thinking was explicitly Coasean. If landowners have an absolute right to build, and a landowner wants to

23. R.H. Coase, The Problem of Social Cost, 3 J.L. & Econ. 1, 2 (1960).
28. [William A.] Fischel, Economics of Zoning Laws, [A Property Rights Approach to American Land Use Controls (1985)] supra note 4, at 72-149; [Robert H.] Nelson, [Zoning and Property Rights: An Analysis of the American System of Land-Use Regulation (1977)] supra note 4, at 39-51. While Nelson and Fischel were extremely important in formalizing, developing, and extending the logic of collective property rights as a justification for zoning, some version of this idea had been the basis of economic thinking on zoning for many years . . . .

build something that has a negative effect on her neighbors, the transaction costs and collective action problems of getting all the neighbors together to pay the property holder not to build (or to build less) would be prohibitive. If, on the other hand, local governments, representing the interests of property holders in a city, have the ability to deny a landowner the right to build for any reason, the potential developer can simply pay the city for the right to build. The assignment of the right should not matter if transaction costs are low, as Coasean bargaining between the developer and the city should ensure that we get to the optimal amount of development. While both the Supreme Court's "exactions" doctrine and state laws on impact fees limit the ability of local governments to condition land-use decisions on unrelated conditions or cash gifts, local governments still can negotiate with developers over certain terms or let in only those developments they find appealing.

This view has been criticized on a number of practical, ethical, and legal grounds, but it still serves as the basic economic justification for the type of comprehensive zoning regimes we have in most local governments. Two criticisms stand out: representation and externalities. The community property-rights theory of zoning is dependent on the idea that local governments represent the collective interest of property holders. Some have challenged this, arguing that urban elections are not particularly responsive, but Fischel argues that this describes most small towns and suburbs (if not big cities) relatively accurately because "homevoters" — homeowners worried about the value of their houses — tend to dominate local elections.

Placing the defense of zoning in a suburban milieu raises the stakes of the second major problem with the community property-rights view: externalities. Small suburban governments may represent their homevoters, but they don't much care about people beyond their boundaries. Whatever effects development has on landowners and residents beyond the boundaries of a local government are excluded from consideration, and hence are undervalued in zoning decisions. While they have not been very specific about what form those externalities take, scholars have suggested that a number of ills result from local governments' failure to internalize externalities, including interlocal economic inequality and sprawl.

This defense of zoning, with its focus on suburban politics and development, was easy to integrate with the central theory of the economics of local government law: the Tiebout model. As famously argued by Charles Tiebout, local government services are provided at the efficient level because individuals can sort among the many local governments in a region to select their ideal package of services.[35] So too with capital, the story goes: there will be some local governments in a region that want new development, and so we need not worry about those governments that exclude it. Further, zoning solved one of the great internal problems in the Tiebout model. As Bruce Hamilton showed, in local governments funded by property taxes, the basic Tiebout model has no equilibrium.[36] Any time a city establishes a high level of services and taxes, it gives property owners an incentive to subdivide their property, allowing more residents to receive the average level of services in the city but pay a lower individual amount of property taxes. Zoning rules like minimum lot

35. Charles M. Tiebout, A Pure Theory of Local Expenditures, 64 J. Pol. Econ. 416 (1956).

36. Bruce W. Hamilton, Zoning and Property Taxation in a System of Local Governments, 12 Urb. Stud. 205, 210-11 (1975) (developing a Tiebout theory consistent with local zoning and property tax powers); see also Fischel, Homevoter Hypothesis, supra note 4, at 65-66 (discussing Hamilton's work).

requirements allow cities a way out of this problem by giving them a tool to fix the population.

However, what counted as a solution in the world of the Tiebout model also served as the basis for the most common critique of modern zoning. When cities engage in fiscal zoning, rich localities can avoid any responsibility to pay taxes for programs for the poor. When states and courts limit local zoning authority — such as in the Mount Laurel decisions in New Jersey and Massachusetts's "anti-snob" zoning laws — they often do so to stop localities from excluding poor residents.

The basic economic case against [zoning] is equally well known. Robert Ellickson laid it out in its classic form in a series of articles in the late 1970s and early 1980s.[39] Ellickson's central claim is that zoning regimes work as supply restrictions that serve to artificially boost the price of homes, harming those who want to buy into communities and holders of developable land. Local governments can be thought of as monopolists: their success in increasing the value of existing houses will turn on their degree of market power (i.e., how much people value their specific location or public services) and the behavior of other, similar towns. Ellickson also argued that the positive effects of zoning were substantially overstated. Although zoning regimes reduce nuisances, individuals operating in an unregulated land market have the ability and the incentives to address problems of negative externalities, and the "prevention costs," or the foregone gains from using property as landowners intended, could be quite large. Notably, he also argued that inclusionary zoning, or policies that require the building of low-income housing near high-income housing, has similar negative effects to ordinary growth controls as it serves as a tax on development and provides benefits only to a fortunate few. Ellickson suggested a reformulation of nuisance law, implemented by "nuisance boards" instead of courts, to replace zoning as the primary means of regulating land use.[44] Alternatively, the Takings Clause could be used to restrict excessive uses of the zoning power.[45] Richard Epstein, writing in a similar vein, argued that many zoning regimes, particularly those that bar development in currently undeveloped property, should be considered violations of the Takings Clause.[46]

Bernard Siegan's roughly contemporaneous critique was built around his in-depth analysis of Houston, a city without a zoning map and with more limited land-use regulations than other cities.[47] He argued that zoning distorted the property market by moving development away from its intended locations, increased the cost of housing, led to slower growth, and did little to reduce genuine nuisances. Instead, it was merely a means for the politically powerful to extract rents . . . .

39. See [Robert C.] Ellickson, Alternatives to Zoning [Covenants, Nuisance Rules, and Fines as Land Use Controls, 40 U. Chi. L. Rev. 681, 682 (1973)] supra note 5, at 695-705 (arguing that zoning is both inefficient and causes substantial inequity); [Robert C.] Ellickson, Irony of "Inclusionary" Zoning, [54 S. Cal. L. Rev. 1167, 1184-87 (1981)], supra note 5, at 1184-85 (arguing that inclusionary zoning will reduce the supply of affordable housing); [Robert C.] Ellickson, Suburban Growth Controls [: An Economic and Legal Analysis, 86 Yale L.J. 385, 400 (1977)] supra note 5, at 400.

44. Ellickson, Alternatives to Zoning, supra note 5, at 762-66.

45. Ellickson, Suburban Growth Controls, supra note 5, at 418-22. For similar reasons, Michelle White proposed taxing local governments that engage in excessive zoning. Michelle J. White, Suburban Growth Controls: Liability Rules and Pigovian Taxes, 8 J. Legal Stud. 207, 209-10 (1979).

46. See Richard A. Epstein, Takings: Private Property and the Power of Eminent Domain, at x, 130-34 (1985).

47. [Bernard H.] Siegan, [Land Use Without Zoning (1972),] supra note 5, at 91-129.

Notes and Comments

1. *Zoning and Efficiency: Point and Counterpoint.* Economic theory allows the evaluation of zoning against the principal norm offered by microeconomics: efficiency. A principal aim of zoning is to avoid land use conflicts that are nuisance-like in nature. Some economists, however, have concluded that zoning is not superior to the unregulated situation. In a leading article discussed in the City Unplanning excerpt, Professor Robert Ellickson sums up the "case against" zoning as follows:

> These locational decisions [imposed through zoning] unquestionably reduce the nuisance costs that would occur if land uses were randomly distributed. Nonzoning allocations, however, may also be better than random. Urban land markets automatically reduce nuisance costs far below the level that would be found with random land use distribution. Industrial plants are not attracted to prime residential areas; instead, they naturally congregate along railroad tracks, just where zoning is likely to put them. . . . It is difficult to disagree . . . that a nonzoning system seems to have allocated these uses as efficiently as any zoning scheme could have. Thus, even if a zoning system is more efficient than random land use, it does not necessarily follow that it reduces nuisance costs more than the market mechanism.

Alternatives to Zoning: Covenants, Nuisance Rules, and Fines as Land Use Controls, 40 U. Chi. L. Rev. 681, 693-94 (1973).

In turn, others have argued that, given the nature of environmental problems in today's world, ownership of land cannot fulfill the preconditions that economists set for a privatized solution to land use problems. Amy Sinden, The Tragedy of the Commons and the Myth of a Private Property Solution, 78 U. Colo. L. Rev. 533, 591-92 (2007). Are the practical difficulties of a private solution so large as to call for government regulation?

2. *Economic Analysis and Information.* To make an efficient decision, a consumer must have accurate information about the choice before her. One of the assumptions of microeconomic theory is that consumers have "perfect information" in making decisions. To the extent that they do not, government intervention may correct that imbalance.

Consumer choices, of course, have important implications for land use. For example, the materials set forth above in this chapter concerning the census show the great migration to the suburbs that has occurred and continues to occur. Consumers, presumably, are simply exercising their preference for cheaper housing in these areas and the amenities that go with it, and they are willing to put up with longer commutes to do so. What if, however, they are acting on flawed or incomplete information? *See* Mark S. Davies, Understanding Sprawl: Lessons from Architecture for Legal Scholars, 99 Mich. L. Rev. 1520, 1527 (2001) (suggesting "the possibility that consumer errors are contributing to sprawl" and that the field of "behavioral law and economics" may help scholars understand sprawl).

3. *Overregulation and Efficiency.* One of the key insights of economic theory is its tendency to look at "mid-points" rather than all or nothing alternatives. For example, the most efficient land use solution to a noise problem may not be to completely ban it at a given location. Rather, efficiency might dictate that noise should be slightly reduced, and the neighboring buildings should have double-paned windows. *See* William A. Fischel, A Property Rights Approach to Municipal

Zoning, 54 Land Econ. 64 (1978) (noting that "[e]mpirical investigations by several economists suggest that zoning tends to exclude land uses which have rather small effects on neighboring properties"). Given that land use is a political decision at the local level, are politicians more prone to less-efficient "all or nothing" solutions?

4. *Entitlements and the Coase Theorem.* As explained in the articles excerpted above, Coase's famous insight was that the parties would reach the same efficient solution through bargaining no matter which party to a land use dispute is given the initial "entitlement" or right to use. *See* Robert C. Ellickson, Order Without Law: How Neighbors Settle Disputes (1991) (noting "a central proposition of law and economics [the Coase Theorem] that portrays people as bargaining to mutual advantage from whatever starting points the legal system has bestowed on them"); William A. Fischel, Zoning Rules! The Economics of Land Use Regulation 227 (2015) ("Economic principles of an ordinary sort — the presence of conflicting uses of property (sometimes called 'externalities'), showed that the initial legal entitlements duly established . . . made no ultimate difference in how resources were actually deployed."). Does this conclusion mean that the law should be indifferent as to who receives such entitlements? What about considerations of equity? Or concerns about discrimination?

Consider, for example, the famous case of *Spur Indus., Inc. v. Del E. Webb Dev. Co.*, 494 P.2d 700 (Ariz. 1972). A developer built a retirement community next to a large agricultural feedlot. Then, after the noise and smells from the feedlot bothered the residents, the developer sued the feedlot owner on the grounds that the feedlot was a nuisance. The court held that the feedlot did constitute a nuisance. From a Coasian perspective, that should end the matter — the parties could then negotiate to reach an efficient solution. The court, however, ordered the developer to pay damages to the feedlot owners that would cover the expense of relocating. Arguably, the distributional effects of the initial legal entitlement drove the court's holding in this regard. *See generally* James E. Krier and Stewart J. Schwab, Property Rules and Liability Rules: The Cathedral in Another Light, 70 N.Y.U.L. Rev. 440, 447 (1995) (suggesting that both "efficiency" and "justice" bear on who should be awarded the initial entitlement).

5. *More Entitlements.* The land use system responds to externality problems, and the inability to reach Coasian bargains to resolve such problems, by legal mandates that entitle landowners to certain uses. The landowner has "monopoly" control over the uses on his or her property. But perhaps this system is too inflexible. In Property and Precaution, 4 J. Tort L. 1 (2011), Professor Lee Ann Fennell suggests that the entitlements create "veto powers" by landowners that act as strong impediments to efficient outcomes. She argues that by granting broader monopoly power to landowners than is actually useful to them, and making that power costless to retain, the system impedes efficient transactions. For example, consider a solar easement that a neighbor needs on the adjoining land. Professor Fennell's solution is that a local government could offer something like a property tax reduction to a household that agreed to make a solar easement available for later, unilateral purchase by the neighbor seeking to install the solar unit. The result would be a range of property entitlements, rather than the rigid entitlements now in effect.

The result would be more efficient. Do you believe such a system is workable? What problems would you foresee in implementing it?

6. *Land Use Regulation and Public Goods.* Another key concept in economic theory is that of "public goods," sometimes called "public services." If the developer of a good cannot legally protect it, others known as "free riders" may use it freely. Because of this problem, society may not produce such goods in the quantities that are needed. For example, a forest might play a role in a moderate climate, controlling runoff from a watershed or providing habitat for wildlife. However, because the owner cannot derive value from those services, he or she has no incentive to preserve the resource. The property's value does not reflect the value to the broader society. Joseph H. Guth, 9 Vt. J. Envtl. L. 431, 483 (2008).

Land use planning and regulation can be seen as a means of ensuring that public goods are produced in sufficient amounts. *See* Christopher J. Weber, Public Choice, Pigouvian and Coasian Planning Theory, 35 Urb. Studies 53, 54 (1998) ("Land-use planning produces several types of public goods . . . in its control of urban development. It reserves land for public utilities and social infrastructure: the market would underallocate. . . . It produces policies for minimizing external-ities (local spillover costs): . . . the market would undersupply such agreements largely because of the transaction costs of making and enforcing them . . .").

A 2005 article suggested that a large number of ecosystem public goods exist. James Salzman, Creating Markets for Ecosystem Services: Notes from the Field, 80 N.Y.U. L. Rev. 870 (2005) ("We have no shortage of markets for most ecosystem goods (such as clean water and supplies), but the ecosystem services underpinning these goods (such as water purification and pollination) are free. . . . [T]here are not direct price mechanisms to signal the scarcity or degradation of these public goods until they fail . . ."). *See also* Lynda L. Butler, The Resilience of Property, 55 Ariz. L. Rev. 847, 867 (2013) (citing "the failure of economic analysis to capture adequately the existence value of human and nonhuman species and of present and future generations"). Is government regulation or the creation of a "market" for these services the better solution?

7. *The Motives of Public Officials.* Supporters of land use regulation often assume that public officials administering the land use system will be motivated to serve the public interest. So-called "public choice theory," a form of economic theory, ques-tions this assumption. It theorizes that public officials and city administrators are motivated by the same types of incentives that motivate developers, and thus would seek to promote their own interests. Note, Phillip L. Fraetta, Contract and Conditional Zoning Without Romance: A Public Choice Analysis, 81 Fordham L. Rev. 1923 (2013); Steven J. Eagle, Reflections on Private Property, Planning, and State Power, 61 A.P.A. Planning & Envtl. L. 3, 8 (January 2009).

Do you agree? If so, how would your conclusion affect the design of the land use regulatory system?

8. *Implications of Economic Analysis.* Economic analysis is a tool that can be used to make judgments about whether various land use regulations produce gains in the public interest. It has also famously been used to build a model showing that, if local governments provide purely local public services and individuals move to the local government that best fits their preferences, then local services will be provided at an efficient level. Charles Tiebout, A Pure Theory of Local Expenditures, 64 J. Pol. Econ. 416 (1956); *see also* David Schleicher, The City as a Law and Economic Subject, 2010 Ill. L. Rev. 1507 (suggesting an alternative theory, "agglomeration

economics," positing that individuals and businesses make location decisions on the basis of where other individuals and businesses decide to locate).

As you read the materials in the book, economic analysis will suggest a preference for certain kinds of processes as well. For example, the economist would favor bargaining between parties that will result in a more optimal or efficient result. Thus, the economist would likely favor the recent trend in land use law, examined in detail in Chapter 10, toward the use of "development agreements" that result from bargaining between developers and local governments. *See* Donald C. Guy & James E. Holloway, The Recapture of Public Value on the Termination of the Use of Commercial Land under Takings Jurisprudence and Economic Analysis, 15 B.Y.U. J. Pub. L. 183, 217-218 (2001) (noting economists' preference for market-based solutions such as development agreements); Christopher Serkin, Local Property Law: Adjusting the Scale of Property Protection, 107 Colum. L. Rev. 883 (2007) (suggesting that local governments should be allowed to select various levels of property protection, and homeowners could choose the level of protection they want.)

E. THE PLAYERS IN THE REGULATORY PROCESS

One fundamental aspect of the current regulatory system is the location of governmental power. Unlike many other areas of modern law in which the federal government has played a key role, land use regulation remains principally a matter for local governments. It is critical for the student to recognize the implications of this institutional arrangement. For example, many important regulatory decisions in American society are entrusted to administrative agencies, often located at the state or federal level. Land use decisions, in contrast, are made by elected officials at the local level.

The following excerpt introduces you to the governmental jurisdictions that regulate land use at the local level.

■ ERIC DAMIAN KELLY, MANAGING COMMUNITY GROWTH: POLICIES, TECHNIQUES AND IMPACTS
8-11 (2d Ed. 2000)

Planning and land use control in the United States take place largely at the local government level (a small number of states are also heavily involved in planning . . .). The United States contains more than 3100 counties and 19,000 municipalities. Not all local governments are active in planning. Many municipalities are too small: 70 percent of the total (about 13,000) serve fewer than 2500 people; another 19 percent (about 3700) serve more than 2500 but fewer than 10,000. Few of the very small local governments are likely to be active in planning, although some certainly are. Virtually all municipalities with populations of more than 25,000 — numbering about 1000 — have some sort of land use controls.

Counties participate in the land use control system in some states. In other states counties have little or no land use authority. . . . Allowing for all those local governments that do not exercise such power, it is safe to estimate that well over 3000 local governments in the United States are involved in planning decisions, and perhaps as many as 10,000.

Having several thousand local governments involved in planning over the vast land area of the United States may not seem significant. In heavily populated and growing areas, however, virtually all local governments are likely to be involved in their own separate planning and land use decisions. . . .

As if the system of land use controls itself were not complicated enough, the task assigned to that system poses enormous difficulties. Through the planning process, a local government attempts to plan for the use of land within its jurisdiction. Most of that land is privately owned, and many landowners have no idea what they will do with their land in the future. Some are happy farming it now and have no plans to do anything else, although one or more of them may cheerfully sell out to a developer within a year or a decade. Other landowners may be holding the land primarily for investment. . . .

A local government must try to plan for the future of such land, even though its owners, who are more intimately familiar with it, have no plans, impractical plans, impossible plans, or plans that simply may change. Although some local planners would resolve that situation by simply dictating future land uses to private owners, residents of the United States relate closely to land, emotionally as well as financially and legally; and they generally resent perceived intrusions on their ownership rights. . . . Thus, although most responsible owners recognize the need for some system of controls as a part of creating an orderly society, the political burden of proof generally remains on the local government to demonstrate why a particular restriction is necessary and reasonable. The system itself thus remains, in most cases, largely a reactive one.

———————

As is true for all other types of lawyers, a critical issue for land use lawyers is understanding the background and make-up of the decision-making body as well as the motivations and backgrounds of others who participate in the process. Within the local government are various "players" that affect the outcome of a land use decision. The following note summarizes "who's who" at the local government level.

A Note on the Participants in the Land Use Process

City Councils and City Managers. The chief decision-making body at the local government level is the city or town council. Some localities have a mayor who is elected, while others hire a city manager to manage the municipal government. The number of individuals on the council can vary; the national average is six, but some councils are larger. The number of council members is proportional to the population of a city, but there is no national standard of proportion. Some cities elect city council members on a citywide basis; others divide the municipality into districts, with a single council member representing a geographical section of the city. The district method is most common in larger cities; however, two-thirds of cities who responded to a 2006 survey elected council members-at-large. The position of council member is usually part-time. *See generally* National League of Cities, Forms of Municipal Government, found at http://www.nlc.org/build-skills-and-net works/resources/cities-101/city-structures/forms-of-municipal-government (last visited Sept. 25, 2016).

Members of the council (which this note will call council members for convenience, but who are also known as aldermen, selectmen, freeholders, or commissioners) play the central role in land use decisions. The land use practitioner must always keep in mind that these are politicians; thus they are concerned with elections (and re-elections) as well with the "facts" of political life. A council member, for example, may be looking to seek higher elective office later, and thus may be building alliances with various political constituencies (although the vast majority of council positions are officially nonpartisan, not party affiliated). In general, council members receive relatively little remuneration for serving on the council.

Council members are, in general, well-educated. As of 2001, 75 percent of them had a college degree, and 40 percent of them had a professional or graduate degree. Councils draw heavily from the business, management, and professional occupations. Some council members may be lawyers, certainly, but in all likelihood others will have no legal training. *See generally* James H. Svara, Two Decades of Continuity and Change in American City Councils (2003). Almost all will have gotten their start by volunteering at the local level, often through local citizens groups or neighborhood councils. They care deeply about the community in which they live, but they may not always agree in their political viewpoints. For example, some members may be pro-growth, while others take a slow-growth stance.

The Planning Staff. The municipal staff is also critically important to the land use practitioner. There will be a planning director and a planning staff that will work on any development application made in that jurisdiction. The staff may have previously completed a general plan for the jurisdiction. The staff may also be divided up into specialties. For example, one member may handle subdivisions, while another specializes in commercial buildings.

The relationship between the council members and the staff bears attention. Since the council employs the planning director, in many instances it will have a great deal of respect for positions taken by the director. In other cases, local politics may have made the planning director less influential. Still, the planning director and department can be viewed as neutral; thus, their recommendation on a proposal can be critical. Also, courts may pay special attention to the conclusions and recommendations of the planning staff.

The Planning Commission. Most local jurisdictions also have planning commissions whose members are appointed by the council. In some municipalities, a council member and a commissioner may be responsible for a specific part of the jurisdiction. And in jurisdictions of any size, appointments to the planning commissioner are coveted. To gain an appointment, members usually must have engaged in community activity beforehand (again, perhaps as a member of a citizens group or a volunteer on city committees), and thus have acquired a reputation.

In general, planning commissioners view themselves as much more "neutral" than council members. They have far less of a political agenda, and they are likely to devote considerable time to studying land use proposals. They will see themselves as

E. The Players in the Regulatory Process   31

compiling the needed information for a sound decision, even if they know that (as is often the case) the council rather than the planning commission is the final decision maker.

The Municipal Attorney and the Zoning Administrator. The municipality will need legal advice, which is obtained from the city or town attorney. Larger jurisdictions will have a number of attorneys that work full-time for the city with offices at city hall. Smaller jurisdictions may have one attorney, or they may contract with an outside law firm for services. Given the increasingly complex legal issues that arise in land use disputes, the municipal lawyer's role is critical in advising the planning commissioners and council members.

Some jurisdictions also have a zoning administrator who may handle such matters as requests for certain permits. This person in all likelihood will be a city employee with considerable experience and savvy.

Other Governmental Organizations. Finally, as noted above, other governmental organizations may play a role in the decision-making process. For example, if a developer seeks subdivision approval, a water district, a sewage district, and a school district may review the proposal and comment on it. Moreover, approval of certain regional bodies may be necessary in addition to the municipal approval.

Finally, if the land in question is "unincorporated" (i.e., has not been annexed — made a part of a city), jurisdiction over a land use approval on that land will lie with the county. Once again, these decisionmakers are likely to be elected officials — county commissioners, supervisors, or the like. The counties are often larger geographic areas (with a number of cities in them). Accordingly, the elected officials may have larger concerns in mind than those of council members in a city. However, because land use disputes are often controversial, their wider jurisdiction may not translate into less attention given to the land use proposal.

Citizens Groups and Business Groups. As you will see later in this book, citizens have become vigorous participants in the land use approval process. Often they will organize into a specific group opposed to a particular project. In direct contravention may be other groups who express support for a project. For example, a local union may support a development because of the jobs it will bring, or housing advocates may support a proposal because it will bring low- or moderate-income housing.

One group stands out in influence: "neighborhoods." In one poll, council members cited this "interest group" as having far and away the largest influence on council decisions. *See, more generally,* Sarah F. Anzia, City Policies, City Interests: An Alternative Theory of Interest Group Systems (Aug. 2015) found at https://gspp.berkeley.edu/research/working-paper-series/city-policies-city-interests-an-alternative-theory-of-interest-group-system (last visited Sept. 25, 2016) (analyzing interest group influence at the local government level).

———————————

The land use approval process is, of course, part of a much larger process entailed in initiating, implementing, and completing a real estate project. You should be generally aware of the entire process. Consider the following eight-stage model of real estate development.

■ MIKE E. MILES, LAURENCE M. NETHERTON, & ADRIENNE SCHMITZ REAL ESTATE DEVELOPMENT: PRINCIPLES AND PROCESS
6 (5th ed. 2015)

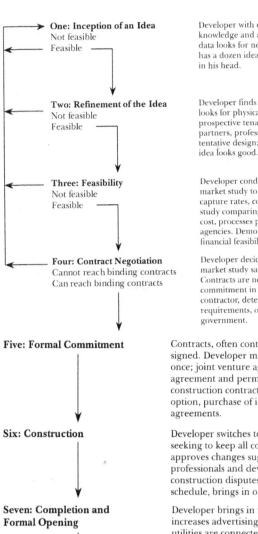

One: Inception of an Idea
Not feasible
Feasible

Developer with extensive background knowledge and a great deal of current market data looks for needs to fill, sees possibilities, has a dozen ideas, does quick feasibility tests in his head.

Two: Refinement of the Idea
Not feasible
Feasible

Developer finds a specific site for the idea; looks for physical feasibility; talks with prospective tenants, owners, lenders, partners, professionals; settles on a tentative design; options the land if the idea looks good.

Three: Feasibility
Not feasible
Feasible

Developer conducts or commissions formal market study to estimate market absorption and capture rates, conducts or commissions feasibility study comparing estimated value of project with cost, processes plans through government agencies. Demonstrates legal, physical, and financial feasibility for all participants.

Four: Contract Negotiation
Cannot reach binding contracts
Can reach binding contracts

Developer decides on final design based on what market study says users want and will pay for. Contracts are negotiated. Developer gets loan commitment in writing, decides on general contractor, determines general rent or sales requirements, obtains permits from local government.

Five: Formal Commitment

Contracts, often contingent on each other, are signed. Developer may have all contracts signed at once; joint venture agreement, construction loan agreement and permanent loan commitment, construction contract, exercise of land purchase option, purchase of insurance, and prelease agreements.

Six: Construction

Developer switches to formal accounting system, seeking to keep all costs within budget. Developer approves changes suggested by marketing professionals and development team, resolves construction disputes, signs checks, keeps work on schedule, brings in operating staff as needed.

Seven: Completion and Formal Opening

Developer brings in full-time operating staff, increases advertising. City approves occupancy, utilities are connected, tenants move in. Construction loan is paid off, and permanent loan is closed.

Eight: Property, Asset, and Portfolio Management

Owner (either developer or new owner) oversees property management (including re-leasing), reconfiguring, remodeling, and remarketing space as necessary to extend economic life and enhance performance of asset; corporate management of fixed assets and considerations regarding investor's portfolios come into play.

Figure 1-1
The Eight-Stage Model of Real Estate Development

Notes and Comments

1. *Other Players.* Of course these are not the only "players" in the land use field. For a famous, if now somewhat dated, look at the participants in the land use business, *see* Richard F. Babcock, The Zoning Game Revisited (1985). A recent, humorous "transcript" of proceedings before a fictional city is R. Marlin Smith, Proceedings Before the Planning and Zoning Board of the City of San Cibola, ALI-ABA Land Use Institute: Planning, Regulation, Litigation, Eminent Domain and Compensation, Aug. 25-27, 2005.

2. *The Lawyer's Role.* Many authors have produced lists of the "stages" of a development project. *See, e.g.*, Rick Daley, The Ten Stages of a Real Estate Development Project, The Practical Real Estate Lawyer 33 (Nov. 2011). This casebook is concerned with the part of the process in which a project applicant must secure government approvals for the development. More broadly, it is concerned with the types and effects of governmental regulations on property, and the rights of participants in the land use process.

3. *Administrative Law.* Because most land use decisions are made by governmental bodies, the lawyer practicing in this field must be aware of the general procedures that local government entities follow in making decisions. They must also be cognizant of the principles that courts apply in reviewing such decisions. Much of this body of law is covered in the law school course on administrative law.

F. ORGANIZATION AND THEMES OF THIS CASEBOOK

1. Organization: The Structure of the Book

The casebook is designed to provide the student with a comprehensive understanding of the law of land use regulation in a practical, contemporary context. The materials emphasize the theoretical foundation for modern regulation and touch on the most controversial and significant applications of land use law doctrine. In line with this approach, with the exception of a selected group of "classic" cases of which every student of land use must be aware, the cases selected for use in the book are mostly of very recent vintage. The goal is to put you in the midst of the currents of issues swirling through land use regulation as it is now practiced throughout the country.

At the outset, we urge you to spend a few minutes thinking about the overall structure of the book and how the five parts relate to each other. Part Two of the materials begins with the basic building blocks of public regulation. Thus, Chapter 2 covers zoning and its various permutations, while Chapter 3 is an overview of the administration of subdivision regulation. Chapter 4 deals with the financing of infrastructure, and Chapter 5 lays out the role that the comprehensive planning process plays in regulation. Together, these five chapters constitute the foundation of modern land use regulation. You will encounter variations on these tools as you confront issues covered in later chapters.

With the basic tools of land use regulation in mind, Part Three of the book turns to the limits of and on land use regulation, which take several different forms. First, Chapter 6 looks at the various doctrines that govern judicial review of local land use decisions. Issues include review of the procedures followed by local governments, the use and misuse of litigation (by opponents and proponents), and the availability of relief in the federal courts. Chapter 7 analyzes the most important constraint on local land use regulation — the Takings Clause. As you will see, the Supreme Court recently has been very active in this area, issuing a series of very important decisions. In Chapter 8, we turn to another set of constitutional limits that may not immediately strike you as related to land use: the limits found in the First Amendment's protections of freedom of speech and freedom of religion. Chapter 8 also briefly discusses the limits imposed by the Due Process and Equal Protection Clauses.

Finally, the last two chapters of this part look at limits of a different sort. Chapter 9 focuses on the restrictions that the regional, state, and federal governments place on local governmental control of land use. For example, in some rare instances state law or federal law may preempt local regulation. Chapter 10 then asks the student to step back and consider alternatives to the model of land use control that presently is dominant. Since the land use field may well be in a state of transition from a legislative or adjudicative model of land use controls to one based on bargaining, this chapter provides a critical bridge to the future.

Part Four of the book centers on emerging issues in land use regulation and the critical tradeoffs they entail. Chapter 11 covers a series of issues that are increasingly important and that have arisen as the link between them and land use regulation has become more apparent. For example, the chapter examines the relationship between land use and global warming, sustainability, and health. Chapter 12 isolates a particular emerging concern: the interplay between land use regulation and the supply of needed housing in a jurisdiction.

The last part of the book then turns to how the land use system effectuates specific policy objectives. Here you will especially encounter more cutting edge issues often seen in the daily newspaper. Chapter 13 examines those laws established to prevent discrimination and to ensure equal opportunity in the land development process. Chapter 14 focuses on environmental protection, with particular emphasis on how federal and state laws designed to protect the environment have affected the development of land. Chapter 15 addresses planning issues in redevelopment, emphasizing economic development and issues of anticompetitiveness in land planning regulation. Chapter 16 addresses the siting of unpopular land uses and the question of environmental justice, while Chapter 17 concludes the book by looking at how the land use system is used to protect aesthetic values.

2. Themes

While the casebook is organized in chapters that cover discrete topics, you will find certain themes in the materials that recur throughout the book. These themes create a different type of lens through which to examine the workings of land use regulation.

The Benefits and Dangers of Discretion. Perhaps the most obvious recurring theme is the benefits and dangers of the discretion that land use law confers on local government. Because of the need to identify the environmental harms and infrastructure costs generated by individual projects, land use regulation has evolved to establish legislative and administrative techniques for deciding whether to approve those projects. These techniques allow local governments to exercise a great deal discretion in making those decisions. In addition to authorizing the local gover ment to approve or reject the project, the land use regulatory system also allows t government to impose permit conditions, including conditions to mitigate identi- fied environmental harms or infrastructure needs, to alter the project and its site design, to mandate other improvements, and to require the developer to finance facilities. The authority to exercise this discretion is found in subdivision ordi- nances, laws establishing review procedures for site plans, and enactments subject- ing development to permitting requirements.

With the exercise of this type of vast discretion, however, comes the danger that this power will be used arbitrarily. Students must carefully consider whether such discretion is advisable and how the legal system can be structured to ensure that it is exercised properly.

The Dynamic Nature of Land Use Regulation. Another important theme is the dynamic nature of land use regulation. Almost every area comprising the field of land use regulation is undergoing changes. These changes reflect not only the rapidly evolving discipline of land use planning, but also the changes in law imposed by the courts on judicial review and the modification of procedures and standards by state legislatures. They also reflect the increasing recognition that land use inter- sects many local problems, from homelessness and panhandling to obesity in schoolchildren. All of this activity means that practitioners in this field must not only keep current on the law, they also must demonstrate flexibility in altering their techniques to reflect these changes. The ability to recognize trends and take advantage of rapidly changing circumstances becomes critical.

Land Use and the Difficulty of Attaining Prescribed Goals. Land use regulation is often asked to achieve goals that may be very difficult for communities to attain. For example, the land use regulatory process must secure sufficient housing for all segments of the community while, at the same time, providing environmental pro- tection and saving open space. If goals such as these are in conflict, as they often are, attaining them all is not possible.

In addition, the political nature of the regulatory process can impede rational efforts to attain goals. For example, the political positions adopted by local politi- cians during an election may greatly restrict their flexibility in solving problems. Additionally, state law may establish goals contrary to those held by the politician's political base of support. When that clash occurs, the outcome is quite predictable: the political position will prevail, perhaps to the detriment of larger society.

Finally, there are other, newer goals that have arisen: eliminating homelessness and combatting obesity. You need to decide whether the land use system is equipped to seriously address them.

The Tension Between Regulatory Methods and Constitutional Protections. Another broad theme in land use regulation is the tension between regulatory methods and constitutional protections. The recent United States Supreme Court cases on takings underscore the escalating conflict between constitutional restrictions and government's ability to effectively regulate land use and the development process. The trend is clearly toward more constitutional protection; increasingly, developers are going to court and finding a more attentive judiciary. At the same time, First Amendment rights, put at risk by actions such as municipal attempts to preserve historical church structures and to regulate adult businesses, are increasingly being litigated in the land use context.

The Third-Party Participation. Third parties such as citizen and environmental groups are key players in the development process. The range of interests represented by third parties varies widely. These parties include neighborhood residents, business associations, advocates for affordable housing, civil rights activists, construction trade unions, civic groups promoting democracy, environmental groups, and conservative public interest organizations seeking to preserve property rights.

When you read the materials in the casebook, you will see how the actions of these groups affect the development process, both directly through participation in a particular decision and indirectly through political activity. What is debatable is whether such participation is useful and should be encouraged, or is counterproductive and contributes only to economic inefficiency and delay. The materials in this casebook will put you in a position to make judgments about issues associated with this type of third-party participation.

The Cost and Consequences of Growth. As municipalities throughout the United States are now well aware, there is no "free lunch" associated with growth. Municipalities now strive to ensure that the costs of new developments are covered by tax-financed public or private sources, such as exactions imposed on the developer or assessments imposed upon the ultimate homeowner. It is also possible to analyze potential environmental effects caused by new development and to design measures to mitigate those effects. A well-accepted principle of growth management emphasizes the concept that the infrastructure to support new development—roads, schools, water, sewer services, and so forth—must be "concurrently available" with that new development. In other words, it is inappropriate to "build now" and let lagging infrastructure catch up later.

Sprawl, however, imposes other opportunity costs which may impede this goal of concurrency. For example, the approval of a particular type of development may constitute a "lost opportunity" to develop convenient public transit. The density of the project may be too low, or the design of the project too spread out, to locate transit conveniently to the development. Additionally, sprawl may also mean that new suburban employment centers are inaccessible for those individuals who live in the central city and who are most in need of access to employment.

As you consider the land use regulatory system, you must decide whether it adequately addresses the costs that such development imposes, and whether those costs call for significant changes in development patterns.

Regulation and Social Equity. Most land use observers would agree that the poor and minority groups are often the losers in the land use regulatory process. Their economic plight in many instances leaves them confined to the declining central city, without access to economic opportunities available in the wider region. In some cases, the land use regulatory system operates to exclude such groups from needed housing—so-called exclusionary zoning. In other instances, poor residents find that they are exposed to greater risks from facilities that have externalities associated with them, such as landfills and hazardous waste disposal operations. This perceived unfair allocation of risk has given rise to the environmental justice movement discussed in this book.

The Friction Between Urbanization and Environmentalism. The most fundamental part of the debate over contemporary land use regulation is whether to maintain and extend the pattern of suburban development so prevalent over the last quarter century or to pursue a more compact development pattern. Such a pattern, for example, might emphasize the planning of villages located near transit stations. It likely would emphasize so-called sustainable development, a concept that includes such features as maximizing recycling of solid wastes, using reclaimed water, and minimizing the use of toxic chemicals such as pesticides. Many of its features are termed "smart growth" in the recent literature.

Whether the movement toward sustainable development will result in extensive changes in how development occurs is a theme that recurs throughout the book, and it is one that the student must carefully consider.

Regionalism and the Appropriate Level of Government for Land Use Regulation. For some time, it has been apparent that the traditional model of land use regulation at the local level may no longer be appropriate in many circumstances. Problems are often insoluble at the neighborhood or municipal level; they require regional solutions. Another difficulty arises from the fact that cities compete for tax-generating development, such as large shopping malls, while seeking to exclude other uses, such as low and moderate income housing, that generate insufficient taxes to fund needed services and facilities. Moreover, as our concern over environmental protection has grown, environmentalists have increasingly argued that the current institutional arrangement for land use control, which is founded on local government jurisdictional boundaries, is inadequate to respond to the larger effects of development on ecosystems. In response, defenders of the status quo emphasize that the government closest to the people works best, and that moving the locus of land use authority away from local government would be undemocratic and would lead to ineffective bureaucracy at the state or regional level.

As you read the cases and other materials in this book, you must evaluate the pros and cons of situating land use regulatory authority primarily at the local level.

Regulation, Deregulation, and Economic Efficiency. An understanding of the land use regulatory process cannot be achieved without an appreciation for economics. Regulations can greatly affect the desirability of property by either increasing or decreasing the costs associated with development.

For example, "over-zoning" — the practice of zoning many more acres in a community for a single use, perhaps industrial, than is needed — may tend to reduce the price of such land and increase the community's attractiveness to industrial development. Alternatively, regulations that increase the size of home sites, reduce density by placing fewer homes on larger tracts, or increase the developer's obligation to fund infrastructure and mitigate environmental impacts, may tend to increase the cost of housing. The law of supply and demand is operative.

Any reform of the existing land use system must balance the need for affordable housing and for reasonable land prices that will attract developers against the need to ensure a high quality of life through the provision of adequate infrastructure and sufficient environmental safeguards. The tradeoff is inevitable — and difficult.

The Future: Evaluation and Reform. Ultimately, the land use regulatory process must be evaluated for its ability to achieve the societal objectives assigned to it. A realistic appraisal of the current law reveals that a majority of citizens in a given local jurisdiction may not favor many of the objectives that land use laws are designed to serve, such as ensuring adequate housing, assuring access to employment for the poor, or siting unwanted facilities. Can the land use system overcome the determined opposition of some individuals to these goals? Can it bring about housing for the poor, protection of natural resources, assurance of adequate infrastructure, and the siting of unpopular land uses such as landfills, incinerators, prisons, energy facilities, and homes for the disabled? If not, how can the system be reformed to achieve these goals?

These are the weighty questions that you must ponder as you encounter the materials ahead.

PART TWO

THE LAND USE REGULATORY TOOLS

2

Zoning

A. INTRODUCTION

1. In the Beginning: Euclidian Zoning

To serve her clients properly, the land use lawyer must be fully aware of the environment in which land use regulation takes place. Thus, for example, as the person who often heads a team of individuals working on a land use problem, the lawyer must fully understand the politics of the local government officials who must approve or disapprove a development. Most importantly, however, the lawyer must understand the legal tools of land use regulation, the fundamental building blocks found in both the ordinances of every local jurisdiction and the statutes of every state.

Fortunately, although they vary somewhat from jurisdiction to jurisdiction, the basic forms and functions of land use controls are relatively consistent throughout the country. The student must do more than recognize them, however; he or she must understand how they have evolved to the present and, based on that evolution, how they are likely to develop in the future. The historical context of land use regulation is important, for it offers fundamental insights into today's and tomorrow's land use regulatory system.

Although common law methods of controlling land uses through such mechanisms as covenants and nuisance law have existed for centuries, the chapter starts with the most famous zoning case, *Village of Euclid v. Ambler Realty*, 272 U.S. 365 (1926). In this decision, the United States Supreme Court upheld the constitutionality of a local government zoning ordinance even though it caused a large diminution in the property value of the plaintiff's property. Two years later in *Nectow v. City of Cambridge*, 277 U.S. 183 (1928), the Court handed down a decision demonstrating how a zoning regulation can go too far and be found unconstitutional. The Supreme Court then largely disappeared from the land use field for decades, surfacing in significant fashion only in the 1980s when it issued a series of rulings on the Takings Clause, discussed in Chapter 7. After *Village of Euclid* and *Nectow*, the state courts were left to sort out the huge volume of land use cases that arose throughout the ensuing decades, as the tentacles and forms of local land use regulation spread.

The *Village of Euclid* case is important for another reason: it introduces the student to the features of the classic zoning ordinance, often referred to as "Euclidian zoning." The theory behind this type of ordinance seems almost quaint in retrospect: the local government rationally decides which types of uses and densities should be allowed throughout the city, and it then passes a zoning ordinance implementing its conclusions. The local government thereafter will act largely as an observer while the operation of the ordinance shapes a rational development pattern throughout the jurisdiction.

*uses ;
densities*

2. The Need for Flexibility

This ideal, of course, was not fulfilled. For one thing, the economic interests affected by land use regulation are extraordinarily large, a fact clearly illustrated by the impact of the ordinance on the property in *Village of Euclid*. The existence of such large economic stakes makes it inevitable that a landowner will seek to change a zoning ordinance if it does not allow for the intensity or type of development the landowner wishes to pursue. Moreover, the concept of zoning plainly clashes with the celebrated American ideal of the individual entrepreneur, a person who recognizes an opportunity for a development, buys the land, and wants to build. The present zoning, however, may not allow the development. The power of these economic and entrepreneurial forces pushing for change in existing land use regulations means that flexibility in the system is necessary to accommodate change.

Other reasons besides the political need to accommodate the economic and entrepreneurial forces of land development support this need for flexibility. In particular, classic Euclidian zoning assumes that the zoning authorities can foresee how development will unfold in the jurisdiction and, based on that knowledge, will zone accordingly. That degree of foresight, however, rarely exists in a dynamic, constantly changing economy. Thus, the zoning map becomes less a plan for future development and more a hopeful but changeable model of future direction.

One example illustrates how unforeseen economic developments can require change in local land use regulation. Citizens in a given locality might theoretically agree that business and residential uses should be separated in the zoning ordinance; homes should not be subjected to the kinds of externalities often associated with businesses, such as noise from traffic, parking problems, employees coming and going during evening hours, and so forth. Technology, however, has in rapid-fire fashion brought us the Internet, electronic mail, Amazon, and computerized research, all of which allow individuals to work more easily from their homes. Indeed, air quality regulators vigorously promote the idea of "telecommuting" from home as a means of reducing air pollution. Or, perhaps, entrepreneurial homeowners may decide to supplement their income by using Airbnb to rent out a room on a daily basis to foreign visitors. These entrepreneurs may well find themselves in violation of local zoning laws that do not allow their businesses as a permitted use where they live.

In the decades after *Village of Euclid*, then, local jurisdictions attempted to introduce a measure of flexibility into their land use systems through a variety of regulatory devices. This chapter introduces those devices. The earliest flexibility devices were zoning amendments, variances from the zoning ordinance, and conditional use permits. Later, the local governments received permission from the courts to use floating zones and planned unit developments. All of the flexibility devices have the common characteristic of focusing closely on the individual impacts from a particular development or use, and specifically tailoring the land use device to those impacts. A fundamental purpose of this chapter is to familiarize the student with these devices. They are the basic tools of the land use lawyer's trade.

3. Flexibility and Discretion

In learning about how these devices work, however, the student soon encounters perhaps the most important underlying conundrum in the land use system: the question of how to give local governments sufficient discretion while, at the same time, constraining the exercise of that discretion to avoid arbitrary and inconsistent decision making. Flexibility in land use controls leads to a slippery slope; one person's valid zoning amendment or use permit is another's arbitrary change that conflicts with the overall land use regulatory pattern or smacks of political favoritism.

One means of controlling discretion is through judicial review, and Chapter 6 of this book examines the techniques that courts use to control judicial discretion. In the meantime, you must be aware that the concern over excessive local government discretion early on led to prohibitions against types of regulatory actions known as "spot zoning" and "contract zoning." In the case of spot zoning, certain zoning amendments are deemed illegal because they lack a comprehensive viewpoint and "single out" certain lands for quite different uses, while contract zoning is seen as an impermissible bargaining away of the local government's police power. The courts concluded that both spot zoning and contract zoning necessarily were enacted for the benefit of the individual landowner rather than in the public interest.

Spot zoning cases continue to appear regularly in the courts, but defining spot zoning in the abstract and "spotting" it (pardon the pun) in the real world are two very different undertakings. The case law on spot zoning sometimes seems a morass of cases that apply vague or quite different standards to reach inconsistent results, a state of affairs that puts a premium on the advocacy skills utilized by land use lawyers in each individual case.

4. The Rise of Bargaining

The slippery slope of "flexibility" grew even steeper in the last part of the twentieth century as development proposals became increasingly complex, and municipalities began to mitigate their impacts by negotiating various conditions imposed on the project. It is not a big step from negotiating marginal aspects of a proposal to negotiating a complete land use "deal" between a developer and a municipality. Furthermore, even though some aspects of a negotiated "deal" between a developer and a local jurisdiction can give cause for alarm, negotiated agreements are not necessarily a bad idea. Chapter 10 examines in more detail the "negotiation" model for land use decisions and allows you to draw conclusions about its efficacy. In the meantime, you must keep in mind that the greater the range of the negotiations, and the larger the number of conditions placed on individual projects as a result of the negotiations, the farther the land use system moves from its original moorings in the Euclidian model.

B. THE TRADITIONAL ZONING ORDINANCE

The most long-lasting (if not most important) legislative device for regulating land uses is the zoning ordinance. If you ask laypersons to explain what they understand the term "land use controls" to mean, they will likely mention zoning first. The exploration of zoning starts with what is probably the most famous American land use decision of the twentieth century, a decision that continues to have very important implications today.

■ VILLAGE OF EUCLID v. AMBLER REALTY
272 U.S. 365 (1926)

Mr. Justice SUTHERLAND delivered the opinion of the Court.

The Village of Euclid is an Ohio municipal corporation. It adjoins and practically is a suburb of the City of Cleveland. Its estimated population is between 5000 and 10,000, and its area from twelve to fourteen square miles, the greater part of which is farm lands or unimproved acreage. It lies, roughly, in the form of a parallelogram measuring approximately three and one-half miles each way. East and west it is traversed by three principal highways: Euclid Avenue, through the southerly border, St. Clair Avenue, through the central portion, and Lake Shore Boulevard, through the northerly border in close proximity to the shore of Lake Erie. The Nickel Plate railroad lies from 1500 to 1800 feet north of Euclid Avenue, and the Lake Shore railroad 1600 feet farther to the north. The three highways and the two railroads are substantially parallel.

Appellee is the owner of a tract of land containing 68 acres, situated in the westerly end of the village, abutting on Euclid Avenue to the south and the Nickel Plate railroad to the north. Adjoining this tract, both on the east and on the west, there have been laid out restricted residential plats upon which residences have been erected.

On November 13, 1922, an ordinance was adopted by the Village Council, establishing a comprehensive zoning plan for regulating and restricting the location of trades, industries, apartment houses, two-family houses, single family houses, etc., the lot area to be built upon, the size and height of buildings, etc.

The entire area of the village is divided by the ordinance into six classes of use districts, denominated U-1 to U-6, inclusive; three classes of height districts, denominated H-1 to H-3, inclusive; and four classes of area districts, denominated A-1 to A-4, inclusive. The use districts are classified in respect of the buildings which may be erected within their respective limits, as follows: U-1 is restricted to single-family dwellings, public parks, water towers and reservoirs, suburban and interurban electric railway passenger stations and rights of way, and farming, non-commercial greenhouse nurseries and truck gardening; U-2 is extended to include two-family dwellings . . . [The court then described zones U-3 through U-6, which gradually increase in intensity of use. For example, U-6 includes sewage disposal plants, scrap iron storage, and manufacturing and industrial uses not included in zones U-1 through U-5. A seventh class of uses is totally prohibited.]

Class U-1 is the only district in which buildings are restricted to those enumerated. In the other classes the uses are cumulative; that is to say, uses in class U-2 include those enumerated in the preceding class, U-1; class U-3 includes uses enumerated in the preceding classes, U-2 and U-1; and so on. In addition to the enumerated uses, the ordinance provides for accessory uses, that is, for uses customarily incident to the principal use, such as private garages. Many regulations are provided in respect of such accessory uses.

The height districts are classified as follows: In class H-1, buildings are limited to a height of two and one-half stories or thirty-five feet; in class H-2, to four stories or fifty feet; in class H-3, to eighty feet. To all of these, certain exceptions are made, as in the case of church spires, water tanks, etc.

The classification of area districts is: In A-1 districts, dwellings or apartment houses to accommodate more than one family must have at least 5000 square feet for interior lots and at least 4000 square feet for corner lots; in A-2 districts, the area must be at least 2500 square feet for interior lots, and 2000 square feet for corner lots; in A-3 districts, the limits are 1250 and 1000 square feet, respectively; in A-4 districts, the limits are 900 and 700 square feet, respectively. . . .

Appellee's tract of land comes under U-2, U-3 and U-6. The first strip of 620 feet immediately north of Euclid Avenue falls in class U-2, the next 130 feet to the north, in U-3, and the remainder in U-6. The uses of the first 620 feet, therefore, do not include apartment houses, hotels, churches, schools, or other public and semi-public buildings, or other uses enumerated in respect of U-3 to U-6, inclusive. The uses of the next 130 feet include all of these, but exclude industries, theatres, banks, shops, and the various other uses set forth in respect of U-4 to U-6, inclusive. . . . Annexed to the ordinance, and made a part of it, is a zone map, showing the location and limits of the various use, height and area districts, from which it appears that the three classes overlap one another; that is to say, for example, both U-5 and U-6 use districts are in A-4 area districts, but the former is in H-2 and the latter in H-3 height districts. . . .

The lands lying between the two railroads for the entire length of the village area and extending some distance on either side to the north and south, having an average width of about 1600 feet, are left open, with slight exceptions, for industrial and all other uses. This includes the larger part of appellee's tract. Approximately one-sixth of the area of the entire village is included in U-5 and U-6 use districts. That part of the village lying south of Euclid Avenue is principally in U-1 districts. The lands lying north of Euclid Avenue and bordering on the long strip just described are included in U-1, U-2, U-3 and U-4 districts, principally in U-2. . . .

Before proceeding to a consideration of the case, it is necessary to determine the scope of the inquiry. The bill alleges that the tract of land in question is vacant and has been held for years for the purpose of selling and developing it for industrial uses, for which it is especially adapted, being immediately in the path of progressive industrial development; that for such uses it has a market value of about $10,000 per acre, but if the use be limited to residential purposes the market value is not in excess of $2500 per acre; that the first 200 feet of the parcel back from Euclid Avenue, if unrestricted in respect of use, has a value of $150 per front foot, but if limited to residential uses, and ordinary mercantile business be excluded therefrom, its value is not in excess of $50 per front foot.

It is specifically averred that the ordinance attempts to restrict and control the lawful uses of appellee's land so as to confiscate and destroy a great part of its value. . . .

It is not necessary to set forth the provisions of the Ohio Constitution which are thought to be infringed. The question is the same under both Constitutions, namely, as stated by appellee: Is the ordinance invalid in that it violates the constitutional protection "to the right of property in the appellee by attempted regulations under the guise of the police power, which are unreasonable and confiscatory?" . . .

The ordinance now under review, and all similar laws and regulations, must find their justification in some aspect of the police power, asserted for the public welfare. The line which in this field separates the legitimate from the illegitimate assumption of power is not capable of precise delimitation. It varies with circumstances and conditions. A regulatory zoning ordinance, which would be clearly valid as applied to the great cities, might be clearly invalid as applied to rural communities. In solving doubts, the maxim *sic utere tuo ut alienum non laedas*, which lies at the foundation of so much of the common law of nuisances, ordinarily will furnish a fairly helpful clew. And the law of nuisances, likewise, may be consulted, not for the purpose of controlling, but for the helpful aid of its analogies in the process of ascertaining the scope of, the power. Thus the question whether the power exists to forbid the erection of a building of a particular kind or for a particular use, like the question whether a particular thing is a nuisance, is to be determined, not by an abstract consideration of the building or of the thing considered apart, but by considering it in connection with the circumstances and the locality. *Sturgis v. Bridgeman*, L. R. 11 Ch. 852, 865. A nuisance may be merely a right thing in the wrong place, — like a pig in the parlor instead of the barnyard. If the validity of the legislative classification for zoning purposes be fairly debatable, the legislative judgment must be allowed to control. *Radice v. New York*, 264 U.S. 292, 294.

There is no serious difference of opinion in respect of the validity of laws and regulations fixing the height of buildings within reasonable limits, the character of materials and methods of construction, and the adjoining area which must be left open, in order to minimize the danger of fire or collapse, the evils of overcrowding, and the like, and excluding from residential sections offensive trades, industries and structures likely to create nuisances. *See Welch v. Swasey*, 214 U.S. 91; *Hadacheck v. Los Angeles*, 239 U.S. 394; *Reinman v. Little Rock*, 237 U.S. 171; *Cusack Co. v. City of Chicago*, 242 U.S. 526, 529-530.

Here, however, the exclusion is in general terms of all industrial establishments, and it may thereby happen that not only offensive or dangerous industries will be excluded, but those which are neither offensive nor dangerous will share the same fate. But this is not more than happens in respect of many practice-forbidding laws which this Court has upheld although drawn in general terms so as to include individual cases that may turn out to be innocuous in themselves. *Hebe Co. v. Shaw*, 248 U.S. 297, 303; *Pierce Oil Corp. v. City of Hope*, 248 U.S. 498, 500. This inclusion of a reasonable margin to insure effective enforcement, will not put upon a law, otherwise valid, the stamp of invalidity. . . .

. It is said that the Village of Euclid is a mere suburb of the City of Cleveland; that the industrial development of that city has not reached and in some degree extended into the village and, in the obvious course of things, will soon absorb the entire area for industrial enterprises; that the effect of the ordinance is to divert this natural development elsewhere with the consequent loss of increased values to the owners of the lands within the village borders. But the village, though physically a suburb of Cleveland, is politically a separate municipality, with powers of its own and authority to govern itself as it sees fit within the limits of the organic law of its creation and the State and Federal Constitutions. Its governing authorities, presumably representing a majority of its inhabitants and voicing their will, have determined, not that industrial development shall cease at its boundaries, but that the course of such development shall proceed within definitely fixed lines. If it be a proper exercise of the police power to relegate industrial establishments to localities separated from residential sections, it is not easy to find a sufficient reason for denying the power because the effect of its exercise is to divert an industrial flow from the course which it would follow, to the injury of the residential public if left alone, to another course where such injury will be obviated. It is not meant by this, however, to exclude the possibility of cases where the general public interest would so far outweigh the interest of the municipality that the municipality would not be allowed to stand in the way.

We find no difficulty in sustaining restrictions of the kind thus far reviewed. The serious question in the case arises over the provisions of the ordinance excluding from residential districts, apartment houses, business houses, retail stores and shops, and other like establishments. . . . Upon that question this Court has not thus far spoken. The decisions of the state courts are numerous and conflicting; but those which broadly sustain the power greatly outnumber those which deny altogether or narrowly limit it. . . .

The decisions enumerated in the first group cited above agree that the exclusion of buildings devoted to business, trade, etc., from residential districts, bears a rational relation to the health and safety of the community. Some of the grounds for this conclusion are — promotion of the health and security from injury of children and others by separating dwelling houses from territory devoted to trade and industry; suppression and prevention of disorder; facilitating the extinguishment of fires, and the enforcement of street traffic regulations and other general welfare ordinances; aiding the health and safety of the community by excluding from residential areas the confusion and danger of fire, contagion and disorder which in greater or less degree attach to the location of stores, shops and factories. Another ground is that the construction and repair of streets may be rendered easier and less expensive by confining the greater part of the heavy traffic to the streets where business is carried on.

The matter of zoning has received much attention at the hands of commissions and experts, and the results of their investigations have been set forth in comprehensive reports. These reports, which bear every evidence of painstaking

Segregating: business, residential

consideration, concur in the view that the segregation of residential, business, and industrial buildings will make it easier to provide fire apparatus suitable for the character and intensity of the development in each section; that it will increase the safety and security of home life; greatly tend to prevent street accidents, especially to children, by reducing the traffic and resulting confusion in residential sections; decrease noise and other conditions which produce or intensify nervous disorders; preserve a more favorable environment in which to rear children, etc. With particular reference to apartment houses, it is pointed out that the development of detached house sections is greatly retarded by the coming of apartment houses, which has sometimes resulted in destroying the entire section for private house purposes; that in such sections very often the apartment house is a mere parasite, constructed in order to take advantage of the open spaces and attractive surroundings created by the residential character of the district. Moreover, the coming of one apartment house is followed by others, interfering by their height and bulk with the free circulation of air and monopolizing the rays of the sun which otherwise would fall upon the smaller homes, and bringing, as their necessary accompaniments, the disturbing noises incident to increased traffic and business, and the occupation, by means of moving and parked automobiles, of larger portions of the streets, thus detracting from their safety and depriving children of the privilege of quiet and open spaces for play, enjoyed by those in more favored localities, — until, finally, the residential character of the neighborhood and its desirability as a place of detached residences are utterly destroyed. Under these circumstance, apartment houses, which in a different environment would be not only entirely unobjectionable but highly desirable, come very near to being nuisances.

If these reasons, thus summarized, do not demonstrate the wisdom or sound policy in all respects of those restrictions which we have indicated as pertinent to the inquiry, at least, the reasons are sufficiently cogent to preclude us from saying, as it must be said before the ordinance can be declared unconstitutional, that such provisions are clearly arbitrary and unreasonable, having no substantial relation to the public health, safety, morals, or general welfare. *Cusack Co. v. City of Chicago, supra*, pp. 530-531; *Jacobson v. Massachusetts*, 197 U.S. 11, 30-31.

It is true that when, if ever, the provisions set forth in the ordinance in tedious and minute detail, come to be concretely applied to particular premises, including those of the appellee, or to particular conditions, or to be considered in connection with specific complaints, some of them, or even many of them, may be found to be clearly arbitrary and unreasonable. But where the equitable remedy of injunction is sought, as it is here, not upon the ground of a present infringement or denial of a specific right, or of a particular injury in process of actual execution, but upon the broad ground that the mere existence and threatened enforcement of the ordinance, by materially and adversely affecting values and curtailing the opportunities of the market, constitute a present and irreparable injury, the court will not scrutinize its provisions, sentence by sentence, to ascertain by a process of piecemeal dissection whether there may be, here and there, provisions of a minor character, or relating to matters of administration, or not shown to contribute to the injury complained of, which, if attacked separately, might not withstand the test of constitutionality. . . .

Under these circumstances, therefore, it is enough for us to determine, as we do, that the ordinance in its general scope and dominant features, so far as its provisions are here involved, is a valid exercise of authority, leaving other provisions to be dealt with as cases arise directly involving them. . . .

Decree reversed.

Mr. Justice Van Devanter, Mr. Justice McReynolds and Mr. Justice Butler, dissent.

Notes and Comments

1. *Euclidian Zoning.* The zoning ordinance at issue in *Village of Euclid* was typical of those adopted throughout the country at that time. It divided property into use, height, and area districts. This type of ordinance became known as "Euclidian Zoning," a reference to the *Village of Euclid* case. *See KCI Mgmt., Inc. v. Board of Appeal of Boston,* 764 N.E.2d 377, 381 (Mass. App. 2002) (referring to "this traditional Euclidian classification scheme that divides the city of Boston into residential, business, industrial, and other uniform zoning districts . . ."); John R. Nolon, The Law of Sustainable Development: Keeping Pace, 30 Pace L. Rev. 1246, 1251-1252 (Summer 2010) (term "Euclidian Zoning" is "a neat play on words because geometric shapes dominate zoning maps — districts tend to be rectangles, squares, or parallelograms — bounded by streets and property lines").

The traditional zoning ordinance has text accompanied by maps showing the classification scheme. *See Hatch v. Boulder City Council,* 21 P.3d 245 (Utah App. 2001) (finding zoning ordinance invalid because it failed to contain a map to accompany the text).

2. *Common Law Doctrines.* Zoning was certainly not the first legal control over land use. Two important common law doctrines, nuisance and restrictive covenants, were available to regulate land uses. Nuisance law involves a judicial determination as to whether one person's use of property has substantially impaired another's use and enjoyment of property. *See Schweihs v. Chase Home Fin., LLC,* 41 N.E.3d 1011, 1024, *appeal denied,* 48 N.E.3d 677 (Ill. 2016) ("The crux of the tort of private nuisance is to remedy wrongful behavior that *substantially* interferes with the use and enjoyment of one's property."); *44 Plaza Inc. v. Gray-Pac Land Co.,* 845 S.W.2d 576, 578 (Mo. App. 1992) ("a private nuisance is the unreasonable, unusual, or unnatural use of one's property which substantially impairs the right of another to enjoy his property"). Nuisance law continues to be used as a means of addressing land use disputes.

Another land use control mechanism is the restrictive covenant, which can prohibit certain types of land uses through deed restrictions. *See, e.g., Terry Weisheit Rental Properties, LLC v. David Grace, LLC,* 12 N.E.3d 930, 937 (Ind. Ct. App. 2014). A restrictive covenant is "a form of express contract between a grantor and a grantee in which the latter agrees to refrain from using his property in a particular manner." *Id.* An affirmative covenant requires a covenantor to do something — pay money, provide goods or services, or take some other action. *Wilkinson v. Chiwawa Communities Ass'n,* 180 Wash. 2d 241, 327 P.3d 614 (2014) (covenants did not prohibit short term vacation rentals of homes).

3. *Zoning and Nuisances.* What is the relationship between zoning and nuisance law? Is zoning merely another means of preventing nuisances on a prospective basis, or does it offer a useful analogy to justify a far more extensive land use regulatory system? In the *Village of Euclid* litigation, the National Conference on City Planning

filed an *amicus curiae* brief, authored by Alfred Bettman, that is generally credited with greatly influencing the final outcome. *See* Commentary, *Village of Euclid v. Ambler Realty:* The Bettman Amicus Brief, Am. Planning Ass'n, 56 Planning & Envtl. Law No. 3, p. 6 (Mar. 2006). The brief strongly argued the analogy between zoning and nuisance:

> What . . . is the relationship of zoning to the law of nuisances? . . . The law of nuisance operates by way of prevention as well as suppression. The zoning ordinance, by segregating the industrial districts from the residential districts, aims to produce, by a process of prevention applied over the whole territory of the city throughout an extensive period of time, the segregation of the noises and odors and turmoils necessarily incident to the operation of industry from those sections of the city in which the homes of the people are or may be appropriately located. The mode of regulation may be new; but the purpose and the fundamental justification are the same. . . .

Id. at 6.

4. *Zoning as a Legislative Act.* If zoning is a legislative act, a court would traditionally accord it a presumption of constitutionality. The court would defer to the legislative judgment, and the burden of proof would be on the party challenging a zoning ordinance. *Wrigley v. Harris*, 161 So. 3d 1114, 1116 (Miss. Ct. App. 2015) (Because the governing body's decision carries a presumption of validity, "the burden of proof is on the party asserting its invalidity."). The *Village of Euclid* opinion continues to be regularly cited by courts for this proposition. *Goldberg Cos., Inc. v. Richmond Heights City Council*, 690 N.E.2d 510, 514 (Ohio 1998) (the *Euclid* test is whether the ordinance is "clearly arbitrary and unreasonable, having no substantial relation to the public health, safety, morals, or general welfare"). As a practical matter, how important is this presumption in legal challenges to zoning ordinances? Furthermore, if a regulation substantially advances a legitimate state interest, it will survive a challenge alleging that it violates substantive due process and thus is unconstitutional. *See, e.g., Plaxton v. Lycoming County Zoning Hearing Bd.*, 986 A.2d 199, 205 (Pa. Commw. Ct. 2009) ("the party challenging the validity of provisions of the zoning ordinance must establish that they are arbitrary and unreasonable and have no substantial relationship to promoting the public health, safety and welfare").

5. *Justice Sutherland's Turnaround.* Although the constitutionality of zoning was settled in *Village of Euclid*, it was a close issue. The case was decided on rehearing after Justice Sutherland, who was considered a staunch defender of property rights, had earlier prepared a draft opinion that would have overturned the Euclid ordinance. A former Supreme Court law clerk has suggested that "talks with his dissenting brethren (principally [Justice] Stone, I believe) shook his [Sutherland's] convictions and led him to request a reargument, after which he changed his mind." Alfred McCormack, A Law Clerk's Recollections, 46 Colum. L. Rev. 710, 712 (1946). If you had dissented in *Village of Euclid*, what points would you have emphasized in your opinion?

6. *Zoning and Housing.* Justice Sutherland's opinion states that the "serious question in the case" arises over the provisions of the ordinance that exclude apartment houses and the like from residential uses. Why did this provision pose the most serious question in the case? Were you surprised by Justice Sutherland's attitude toward apartments ("very often the apartment house is a mere parasite")? What does this statement suggest about whether local governments have an obligation to

use their zoning power to ensure that all economic segments of the community can find housing? *See* Peter W. Salsich, Jr., Toward a Policy of Heterogeneity: Overcoming a Long History of Socioeconomic Segregation, 42 Wake Forest L. Rev. 459, 464-465 (2007):

> Justice Sutherland's derogatory reference to apartments (and by necessary implication, their occupants) as "mere parasite[s]" on residential neighborhoods in the Euclid decision has helped sustain an extreme reluctance of local governments, particularly in outlying suburbs, to permit the levels of density generally thought to be necessary to encourage developers to build housing for the lower half of the market, not to mention permitting scattered site deviations from the norm of single family-owned housing. As a result, restrictive local land use regulations increasingly are being identified as a major roadblock to affordable housing efforts throughout the country.

See also Christopher J. Tyson, Municipal Identity as Property, 118 Penn. St. L. Rev. 647, 686 (2014) ("The Court took what essentially amounts to a design issue and treated it as a substantive planning issue. This decision infused the Court's sanctioning of zoning with highly subjective value judgments, which ultimately set the stage for the housing development trends . . .").

7. *The* Nectow *Decision.* The *Village of Euclid* decision was an important victory for local governments that were adopting zoning ordinances. After the case was handed down, the obvious question was whether the Court would attempt to set further limits on the zoning power whose constitutionality was now generally confirmed. In *Nectow v. City of Cambridge*, 277 U.S. 183 (1928), part of plaintiff's land was put in an R-3 zone, which was restricted to dwellings, hotels, clubs, churches, and the like. It fronted on Brookline Street to the west, and on Henry Street, to the north. The land to the south was owned by Ford Motor Company, which operated an auto assembly factory there. There was also a soap factory and railroad tracks nearby. The lands beyond Henry Street to the north and beyond Brookline Street to the west were in a residential district and had some residences on them, while the land to the south and east was unrestricted. The result was that business and industry was excluded from this part of plaintiff's land, while the remainder of the tract was unrestricted.

A master assigned to the case found that the zoning did not promote the health, safety, convenience and general welfare, concluding that because of the adjacent industrial and railroad uses, the land was of little value for the limited uses permitted by the ordinance. The Supreme Court agreed. Although noting that the zoning determination should not be set aside unless it "has no foundation in reason and is a mere arbitrary and irrational exercise of government power," the Court nonetheless found that the master's finding was dispositive of the case. The Court particularly noted that the boundary line of the residential district, before reaching the plaintiff's property, ran along the streets. Thus, "to exclude the locus from the residential district requires only that such line shall be continued 100 feet further along Henry street and thence south along Brookline street." 277 U.S. at 188.

8. *The Reach of* Euclid. The importance of the *Euclid* decision to the development of the legal structure underlying land use controls cannot be overestimated. As one recent article summarized:

> In accepting the municipality's appeal in Village of Euclid v. Ambler Realty Co., the Court did much more than sanction the pecuniary loss suffered by Ambler Realty; it

endorsed a new form of urban planning that would revolutionize the American landscape. Modern residential zoning was constitutionally born. The Court ushered in a new era in the history of property—an era in which ownership was to mean something different from what it had meant in the preceding century. In post-Euclid America, ownership came primarily to signify security rather than freedom.

Nadav Shoked, The Reinvention of Ownership: The Embrace of Ownership and the Modern Populist Reading of Property, 28 Yale J. on Reg. 91, 95 (Winter 2011). After *Village of Euclid* and *Nectow*, how easy will landowners find it to challenge the constitutionality of zoning on their property? The *Nectow* decision illustrates how a zoning ordinance can be attacked on substantive due process grounds, but most challenges to such ordinances will fail.

After these first two zoning decisions, the Supreme Court largely abandoned the field of land use regulation for decades. As a result, land use law has largely been left to the state courts, which often undertake more rigorous scrutiny. A higher level of scrutiny is particularly evident when plaintiffs allege that land use ordinances exclude minorities or low- and moderate-income households, an issue discussed in Chapter 12 (dealing with securing a sufficient housing supply) and Chapter 13 (dealing with housing and discrimination).

While zoning is generally thought of as restricting uses on property, it usually does so by listing certain uses that are "permitted" on a property, thus excluding all others. What does it mean when zoning authorizes a "permitted use" on a particular piece of property, and how do we determine whether the use is "permitted"?

■ IN RE HOWARD CENTER RENOVATION PERMIT
99 A.3D 1013 (Vt. 2014)

SKOGLUND, J.

South Burlington School District (District) appeals from an environmental court decision approving Howard Center, Inc.'s application for interior renovations to an existing medical office to accommodate a new methadone clinic. The District contends the court erroneously concluded that . . . the clinic was a permitted "medical office" use under the South Burlington Land Development Regulations and therefore did not require site-plan or conditional-use review . . . We affirm.

The material facts are not in dispute. For a number of years, Howard Center has operated two out-patient clinics that provide medically supervised methadone and buprenorphine maintenance treatment for those with opioid dependence: one, which has operated since 2002, is located at the University Health Center (UHC) on South Prospect Street in Burlington, and the other, since 2011, at the office of the former Twin Oaks Counseling Service in South Burlington.

As part of a plan to relocate the Twin Oaks office and reduce the patient load at the UHC office, Howard Center entered into a lease for about 10,000 square feet of office space in an existing medical office on Dorset Street in South Burlington, and the following month submitted a building-permit application for interior renovation of the office space. The office is situated within one of several buildings on a 2.2–acre parcel and is part of a multi-unit, multi-use development. . . . The property lies within the City's Central District 2 (CD 2) zoning district, in which "Office, Medical" is a permitted use. Land Development Regulations (2012) (Regulations), app. C. The Regulations define the latter as "[a]ny establishment where human patients are examined and treated by doctors, dentists or other medical professionals but not hospitalized overnight." Regulations §2.02.

As the trial court found, Howard Center plans to use the renovated office for "the medication assisted treatment of patients suffering from opioid dependence. As part of this treatment, physicians and nurses will perform medical examinations and administer methadone or buprenorphine to the patients." A patient must be diagnosed with opioid addiction to receive treatment, which also entails mandatory individual and group counseling. The treatment of substance-abuse disorders in Vermont, the court noted, generally follows a "whole-patient approach," involving "the use of medication, in combination with counseling and behavioral therapies." Clinic staff will thus include several nurses and lab technicians, at least ten substance-abuse clinicians, case managers, and a consulting psychiatrist and psychologist — all under the direction of a licensed physician serving as the clinic's medical director.

The City's zoning administrator granted the renovation permit . . . because the proposal was solely for interior renovations of a permitted medical-office use and did not involve any "new use, change in use, or expansion of use" under the Regulations. Regulations §§14.03.A(1), 14.03.B(5). In response, the District — which administers a middle school and high school located approximately 500 and 1000 feet respectively from the proposed clinic — appealed the permit approval . . . to the South Burlington Design Review Board (DRB). The District questioned whether the methadone clinic qualified as a permitted use, but the DRB found that it "will involve . . . the examination and treatment of patients" and therefore involved no change of use from "office, medical." . . .

The District contends the trial court erred in concluding that the planned methadone clinic constitutes a permitted "medical office" use requiring no conditional-use or site-plan review under the Regulations. Our paramount goal in construing a zoning ordinance, like any statute, "is to give effect to the legislative intent." *In re Bjerke Zoning Permit Denial,* 2014 VT 13, ¶ 22, 195 Vt. __, 93 A.3d 82 (quotation omitted). "Thus, we construe an ordinance's words according to their plain and ordinary meaning, giving effect to the whole and every part of the ordinance." *In re Laberge Moto–Cross Track,* 2011 VT 1, ¶ 8, 189 Vt. 578, 15 A.3d 590 (mem.) (quotation omitted).

Because a "majority" of the staff at the clinic will provide mandatory substance-abuse and other behavioral counseling, the District maintains that it meets the definition of "social services" as an establishment providing "counseling for psychological problems," and therefore represents a new or additional use requiring conditional-use and site-plan review. The record evidence was clear and uncontroverted that the counseling therapies provided by the clinic are part of a patient's overall treatment plan, which generally entails a threshold medical diagnosis of opioid dependence, initial assessment and physical examination by medical staff, daily administration of methadone or buprenorphine administered by nursing staff, periodic testing to calibrate proper dosage, detect side effects, and monitor compliance, and coordination of care with other medical providers in the community — all under the supervision of an on-site physician.

In light of this evidence, we agree with the trial court that the clinic does not constitute a "social services" establishment — instead of or even in addition to a "medical office" — merely because treatment includes a counseling component.

Mental health counseling is an integral component of many medical specialties and practices providing integrated health-care services, and the record is devoid of any evidence of the City's intent to compel conditional-use or site-plan review under the "social services" rubric for each and every medical office that integrates patient counseling. See *In re Lashins,* 174 Vt. 467, 469, 807 A.2d 420, 423 (2002) (mem.) (observing that we prefer a "construction that implements the ordinance's legislative purpose, and, in any event, will apply common sense" to the construction) (quotation omitted).

To be sure, a substance-abuse or other free-standing clinic engaged in counseling without the extensive on-site medical personnel and treatment protocols provided by the Howard Center clinic might present a different question. As other courts in similar circumstances have concluded, however, the comprehensive methadone treatment provided by the clinic at issue *here* plainly constitutes a permitted medical-office use within the district, and did not require site-plan or conditional-use review under the Regulations . . . Accordingly, we find no basis to disturb the trial court's ruling.

Notes and Comments

1. *The Meaning of "Permitted Uses."* What does it mean when we say that a particular use of property is "permitted as of right" under the zoning ordinance? Courts often grapple with the plain meaning of a permitted use within the text of a zoning ordinance. *See, e.g., Fort v. County of Cumberland,* 761 S.E.2d 744 (N.C. App. 2014) (gun firing range was permitted by right as it was similar to the "recreation amusement" use in the ordinance); *Shilling v. Baker,* 691 S.E.2d 806 (Va. 2010) (spreading remains after cremation on property did not create a "cemetery"); *Marzulo v. Kahl,* 783 A.2d 169 (Md. Ct. App. 2001) (business of breeding and selling snakes was not "commercial agriculture"). Even if the use is permitted, the landowner must meet all other zoning requirements as well.

2. *A "Social Services" Office or a "Medical" Office?* To determine whether the landowner's use was a "permitted use" under the county zoning ordinance in *Howard Center,* the court had to characterize the activities that would be undertaken. Is this a pure question of law? Which contains the better characterization: the majority opinion, which concluded that the land use was a "medical office," or the school district, which argued it was a "social services" office? How did the school district frame its argument? Why did the court reject it?

If you agree that the issue here is a close one, should the court defer to the decision made by the local zoning board? If this had not been a permitted use, then the clinic would have to seek a conditional use permit, a land use device discussed later in this chapter. A conditional use permit is discretionary. Isn't the clinic the type of facility that might cause externalities, so a use permit is more appropriate so that local government could place conditions on the use? If so, do you think the clinic would have any difficulty obtaining one?

3. *"Nudist Club" or "Recreational Facility"?* In *Board of Supervisors of Madison County v. Gaffney,* 422 S.E.2d 760 (Va. 1992), the landowners operated a facility in which 170 paying members engaged in volleyball, frisbee, croquet, horseshoes, and the like. They did so in the nude. Would you characterize this as a "nudist club," a "private recreational area," or a "preserve and conservation area"? Only the latter was a

permitted use. And, in making your decision, would it be relevant that the activities on the property were undertaken in the nude? Does the power of the court to characterize land uses mean that judicial conceptions of morality can overtly dictate case outcomes? Judicial line drawing of a similar type is found in the adult zoning cases discussed in Chapter 8, which involve distinctions between "adult" and other movies, and taverns versus "topless" bars.

4. *The Standard Zoning Enabling Act.* Zoning ordinances throughout the United States tend to be remarkably similar in their features despite the fact that no overarching federal law dictates uniformity. This similarity is largely due to an unlikely source: the United States Department of Commerce. In the early 1920s, Herbert Hoover, who later became president of the United States, headed the department. Hoover in fact held progressive views and was particularly concerned with promoting home ownership and protecting residences from adverse urban impacts. To further these goals, he appointed the Advisory Committee on City Planning and Zoning.

The Advisory Committee drafted a Model Act, the "Standard Zoning Enabling Act," whose final version was published in 1924. This draft was intended to serve as a model for state legislation that would authorize the adoption of local zoning ordinances, and it set forth various concepts, which today are well known. The Standard Zoning Enabling Act struck a chord throughout the country and served as a unifying force for the development of modern land use regulation. Edward J. Sullivan, Recent Developments in Comprehensive Planning Law, 43 Urb. L. 823, 823 (2011) ("Approximately three-quarters of the states have adopted the 1926 Standard Zoning Enabling Act . . .").

5. *Sources of and Limits on Local Government Authority.* Traditionally, under American law local governments receive their authority from the state, through enabling legislation (such as, if enacted, the Standard Zoning Enabling Act). Absent such authority, local governments have no power to act. This limitation is reflected in a doctrine known as "Dillon's Rule," which requires courts to construe state grants of authority narrowly. *See, e.g., Sinclair v. New Cingular Wireless PCS, LLC,* 727 S.E.2d 40, (Va. 2012) (Under Dillon's Rule municipal corporations have only those powers that are expressly granted, those necessarily or fairly implied from expressly granted powers, and those that are essential and indispensable). Some cities and counties are so-called charter or home rule jurisdictions, set apart by the fact that they have their own charters pursuant to the particular state constitution. These jurisdictions have somewhat more power to act than other cities and counties that lack a charter. *See* Lynn A. Baker & Daniel B. Rodriguez, Constitutional Home Rule and Judicial Scrutiny, 86 Denv. U. L. Rev. 1337, 1338 (2009) (noting the contradiction between the idea that municipalities are best understood as creatures of state government and the idea of home rule which "accord[s] a sphere of authority—indeed, a *sovereignty* of sorts—to municipalities").

6. *No Permitted Uses?* Must a zone defined in a zoning ordinance authorize at least some permitted uses, or can all the uses require conditional use permits? In *Town of Rhine v. Bizzell,* 751 N.W.2d 780 (Wisc. 2008), the "B-2 District," entitled "Commercial Manufacturing or Processing," contained no permitted uses. The Wisconsin Supreme Court found that the ordinance was arbitrary and unreasonable, and thus facially unconstitutional. The court reasoned:

> Precluding any permitted use and then only providing generalized standards for obtaining a conditional use permit opens the door to favoritism and discrimination.

Under this scenario, a town, pursuant to the ordinance, may arbitrarily preclude any activity on the land in question because (1) there are no permitted uses as a matter of right; and (2) if obtaining a conditional use permit is completely within the discretion of a town, judicial review of a denial is significantly limited because of the non-specific nature of the conditional use standards. As a result, if such an ordinance was deemed acceptable, towns could preclude all uses at will and in a manner that virtually precludes any meaningful judicial review. Such a determination could open the door to abuse.

Id. at 802. Are you convinced? In this chapter, you will see that, over the decades, the trend has been away from permitted uses and toward discretionary permits. Is that trend constitutionally suspect under the reasoning of *Town of Rhine*?

7. *Home Occupations.* With the advent of electronic mail and the Internet, it is now possible for many individuals to work out of the home. This development, of course, has both environmental benefits and benefits for families. Such businesses, however, may run afoul of zoning laws that zone the property for residential use only. Local jurisdictions may respond by crafting "home business" zoning regulations. In *Sundberg v. Greenville Bd. of Adjustment*, 740 A.2d 1068 (N.H. 1999), a family member who did the paperwork (without salary) for the family welding supply business, which was operated from the family's mobile home, was "employed" within the meaning of the city's "customary home occupation" ordinance. Under that ordinance, such a "customary home occupation" could employ no more than two people. *See also Salton v. Town of Mayfield Zoning Bd. of Appeals*, 116 A.D.3d 1113 (App. Div. 2014) (upholding finding that petitioner was engaging in a "home occupation" as defined in the zoning ordinance by keeping exotic animals — three tigers and two leopards — on his property and allegedly collecting fees from people to view them).

8. *The Attack on Euclidian Zoning.* The primary thrust of traditional Euclidian zoning was to separate uses. Some critics have found that this idea behind zoning is responsible for much of the poor land use and urban sprawl so common in the late twentieth century. *See, e.g.*, Wayne Batchis, Enabling Urban Sprawl: Revising the Supreme Court's Seminal Zoning Decision Euclid v. Ambler in the 21st Century, 17 Va. J. Soc. Pol'y & L. 373, 374 (2010) ("The Supreme Court, however, gave its constitutional blessing to what we now know as urban sprawl. America has not been the same since."); James Howard Kunstler, Home From Nowhere, Atlantic Monthly, Sept. 1996, at 43 (finding that after World War II, the effects of zoning began to overshadow the historic elements of civic life); and Nicolas M. Kublicki, Innovative Solutions to Euclidian Sprawl, 31 Envtl. L. Rptr. 11001 (Aug. 2001) (cataloguing the effects of "Euclidian sprawl," including increased commuting costs, inefficient use of land, intensified sociological detachment of suburbanites, and exacerbation of the housing shortage).

Even more recently, some public health advocates have criticized suburban development as at least partly responsible for the epidemic of obesity that now plagues the United States. *See, e.g.*, Reid Ewing, Ross C. Brownson, and David Berrigan, Relationship Between Urban Sprawl and Weight of United States Youth, 31 Am. J. Prev. Med. 464, 472 (2006) (study concluding that "adolescents living in sprawling counties were more likely to be overweight or at risk of overweight than those in compact counties"); Allyson C. Spacht, Note, The Zoning Diet: Using Restrictive Zoning to Shrink American Waistlines, 85 Notre Dame L. Rev. 391 (2009) (arguing that "restrictive zoning to combat obesity is a valid exercise of the police power").

Do you agree with these criticisms? What about opposition from those who resist de-emphasizing single family homes? *See* Deborah M. Rosenthal, Breaking the Stranglehold of Single-Family Zoning: Strategies and First Steps Toward Modernizing Local Codes, Planning and Environmental Law (Feb. 2013) ("Every land use lawyer has witnessed the political wars that erupt at the slightest hint of reconfiguring single-family zones, even many subdivisions away from the irate homeowner.").

9. *New Urbanism.* Criticism of Euclidian zoning has resulted in support for what has become known as the "New Urbanism" school of planning, which attempts to center development around the creation of new neighborhoods with mixed-uses. *See* Michael Lewyn, New Urbanist Zoning for Dummies, 58 Ala. L. Rev. 257, 257-258 (2006) (policies favoring segregation of land uses "combined to create a pattern of land use often described as 'sprawl': low-density, automobile oriented development"). In S. Mark White & Dawn Jourdan, Neotraditional Development: A Legal Analysis, Land Use L. & Zoning Dig., Aug. 1997, at 3 the authors state:

> Responding to a perceived loss of community and the decline in quality of life occasioned by the automobile and urban sprawl, 'New Urbanism' and neotraditional development have challenged the assumptions of Euclidian zoning and conventional suburban development that residential and nonresidential uses must be separated, that streets should be wide and curvilinear, and that densities must be low.

Some new urbanists suggest that municipalities should turn from zoning to what are called "form-based" codes. These regulations emphasize control of the physical form of buildings rather than of their uses:

> Rather than prescribing development based on how a plot of land will be used — residential, say, or mixed-use commercial — the code defines the physical shape development should take in different parts of the city. That means buildings are considered in context of what's around them, regardless of what goes on inside.

Zach Patton, *The Miami Method for Zoning: Consistency over Chaos,* Governing (May 2016) at http://www.governing.com/topics/urban/gov-miami-zoning-laws.html?utm_term=The%20Miami%20Method%20for%20Zoning%3A%20Consistency%20Over%20Chaos&utm_campaign=The%20Miami%20Method%20for%20Zoning%3A%20Consistency%20Over%20Chaos%20&utm_content=email&utm_source=Act-On+Software&utm_medium=email (last visited Oct. 28, 2016). *See also* Richard S. Geller, The Legality of Form-Based Zoning Codes, 26 J. Land Use & Envtl. L. 35, 44 (2010). Form-based codes are keyed to a regulating plan that designates the appropriate form and scale (and therefore, character) of development, rather than only distinctions in land-use types. http://www.formbasedcodes.org (last visited Nov. 25, 2016). Does this idea of emphasizing form rather than use avoid the segregative effects of zoning while keeping its benefits? The website just cited includes a set of images contrasting how zoning and form-based regulation would approach regulating a block differently. So far, Miami has been the only large city to adopt the idea of a form-based code, known there as "Miami 21."

10. *Even More Goals for Zoning?* At the same time, zoning is now called upon to address new problems. For example, with the advent of Airbnb, HomeAway, and Flipkey, vacationers can now descend on what were otherwise single-family neighborhoods. This development, in turn, has brought pressure for more regulation,

often through zoning amendments. Charles Gottlieb, Residential Short-Term Rentals: Should Local Governments Regulate the "Industry"?, Planning and Environmental Law (Feb. 2013). Additionally, zoning is now called upon to advance a much wider variety of societal objectives. *See* John R. Nolon, Zoning's Centennial: The Need for Public Regulation of Land Use—The First Comprehensive Zoning Law (2016) at http://lawprofessors.typepad.com/land_use/2016/01/zonings-centennial-part-1-a-series-by-john-r-nolon.html (last visited Oct. 28, 2016) ("[Z]oning is used to achieve an impressive number of public objectives such as permitting transit oriented development, creating green infrastructure, preserving habitat, species, and wetlands, promoting renewable energy facilities, reducing vehicle miles traveled, and preserving the sequestering landscape."). Do such efforts place too much weight on zoning ordinances?

A Note on Nonconforming Uses

The Theoretical Conundrum. When local governments pass zoning ordinances or zoning amendments, they do not write on a clean "development slate." Existing land uses on the properties may exist, but the new zoning may not authorize those uses. In that situation, they are deemed "nonconforming" uses (that is, uses that do not conform to those allowed by the zoning ordinance). Nonconforming uses obviously disrupt the zoning plan that the ordinance seeks to implement. At the same time, however, landowners have legitimate expectations to continue use of their investments in the property.

The concept of nonconforming uses posed a considerable theoretical problem for the early proponents of Euclidian zoning. As we have seen above in this chapter, Euclidian zoning envisioned an orderly pattern of development in which various conflicting uses would be separated. The zoning theorists believed that nonconforming uses would naturally vanish over time. They erred in failing to recognize that the economics of the nonconforming use incentivizes the owner to maintain both the structure and the use.

Continuation of a nonconforming use after the adoption of a new zoning ordinance would jeopardize the benefits that the proponents of Euclidian zoning foresaw. They feared, however, that if zoning attempted to outlaw all pre-existing nonconforming uses, this prohibition would raise such significant constitutional questions that it might jeopardize the constitutionality of all zoning.

The compromise was to allow nonconforming uses to continue after the new zoning was passed but to restrict expansions of them and eventually to require their removal. *See* Edward M. Basset, Zoning, 115-116 (1936).

Nonconforming Uses: The Issues. The result of this compromise has been a steady stream of litigation over the validity of nonconforming uses. The following is a thumbnail sketch of a large and relatively intricate area of land use law.

(1) *Establishing Nonconforming Uses.* To obtain recognition of a valid nonconforming use, the landowner must establish that the use actually existed when the zoning restriction became effective. *See, e.g., Swan Creek Township v. Wylie & Sons Landscaping*, 859 N.E.2d 566, 570 (Ohio App. 2006) ("The party seeking to take advantage of a nonconforming use must demonstrate . . . that the use was lawful and that it antedated the institution of zoning"). A landowner cannot race to make expenditures before a regulatory action occurs so as to establish a nonconforming

use. *Hanchera v. Bd. of Adjustment*, 694 N.W.2d 641, 646 (Neb. 2005) ("good faith" required but lacking where use was established with knowledge of pendency of ordinance).

Nonconforming uses essentially become vested rights. Many states accord these uses constitutional protection, while in others statutes or local ordinances authorize the continuation of the nonconforming use. *See, e.g., Jones v. Town of Carroll*, 931 N.E.2d 535, 536 (N.Y. 2010) (nonconforming use is constitutionally protected); *Cicerella, Inc. v. Jerusalem Twp. Bd. of Zoning Appeals*, 392 N.E.2d 574, 577 (Ohio Ct. App. 1978) ("Any attempt by zoning legislation to deprive the owner of a pre-existing lawful use is generally regarded as an unconstitutional taking of property without compensation and without due process of law").

(2) *Scope of Nonconforming Uses*. As a general rule, the nonconforming use cannot be expanded or enlarged, nor can the structure in which it is being carried on be expanded. *See, e.g., Gorgone v. District of Columbia Bd. of Zoning Adjustment*, 973 A.2d 692 (D.C. App. 2009) (nonconforming use lost when "Chinese carry-out" restaurant replaced the prior use as a deli); *City of Okoboji v. Parks*, 830 N.W.3d 300, 301-02 (Iowa 2013) (nonconforming use of marina did not include use of facilities to service boat moored at the arena "on which alcohol is served or upon which entertainment, karaoke, abandon-ship parties, or howl-at-the-moon parties are provided"). *Compare Dovaro 12 Atlantic, LLC v. Town of Hampton*, 965 A.2d 1086 (N.H. 2009) (converting seasonal apartments into year-round condominium units was not a substantial change in the preexisting nonconforming use). However, some states allow the "natural expansion" of a pre-existing use, while others will allow a change to a "less offensive" nonconforming use. *See, e.g., Nettleton v. Zoning Bd. of Adjustment of the City of Pittsburgh*, 828 A.2d 1033, 1037 n.3 (Pa. 2003) ("the right to expand as required to maintain economic viability or to take advantage of increases in trade, is also constitutionally protected").

A land user with a valid nonconforming use is entitled to make normal repairs on the property. *See, e.g., Social Spirits, Inc. v. Town of Colonie*, 426 N.Y.S.2d 148 (Sup. Ct. App. Div. 1980) (restaurant retained nonconforming use status even though it remodeled its exterior and installed new electrical wiring, plumbing, and insulation); *Eddins v. City of Lewiston*, 244 P.3d 174 (Idaho 2010) (replacing an existing recreational vehicle with a new recreational vehicle in a manufactured home park constitutes a continuation of the nonconforming use). But where the owner removes every part of the structure except the foundation and the footings, the owner destroys the nonconforming use. *Motley v. Borough of Seaside Park Zoning Bd. of Adjustment*, 62 A.3d 908, 917 (N.J. App. Div. 2013).

(3) *Losing Nonconforming Uses*. To maintain the nonconforming use, the landowner must continue the use on the property, a rule that has generated legions of cases analyzing whether the use on the property has stopped. *See, e.g., Toys "R" Us v. Silva*, 676 N.E.2d 862 (N.Y. 1996) (nonconforming use status lapsed where, under a statute declaring that a nonconforming use lapses if discontinued during a two-year period, the warehouse was completely unused for 20 months and then used only slightly for the remainder of that period); *Cleveland MHC, LLC v. City of Richland*, 163 So. 3d 284 (Miss. 2015) (mobile home park did not lose its status as nonconforming on a lot-by-lot basis as existing mobile homes were removed from lots). Generally, the use is not lost simply because the property is conveyed to a new owner. *Duffy v. Milder*, 896 A.2d 27, 38 (R.I. 2004) (terming the rule "well-settled"). Nor is it lost because the owner fails to obtain a license needed to operate a business on the

property. *Guy v. Town of Temple*, 956 A.2d 272, 280-281 (N.H. 2008) (failure to obtain license for junkyard did not terminate nonconforming use).

One difficult situation that recurs involves the accidental destruction of the property through a fire or natural disaster. Some ordinances allow the property owner to replace the structure and continue the nonconforming use, within a certain time period. *Joubert v. City of New Orleans*, 30 So. 3d 186 (La. App. 2010) (neighbors had right to challenge whether nonconforming use could continue after delay in restoration in the aftermath of Hurricane Katrina); *Krill v. Board of Adjustment of the City of Bayonne*, 298 A.2d 308 (N.J. Sup. Ct. Law Div. 1972), *aff'd*, 313 A.2d 220 (N.J. Super. Ct. App. Div. 1973) (statute authorized repair of a building destroyed by fire without loss of nonconforming use status). Many other ordinances, however, terminate the nonconforming use where the fire or natural disaster has resulted in complete or substantial (as opposed to partial) destruction.

(4) *Eliminating Nonconforming Uses.* Courts often express the view that while nonconforming uses must be tolerated, the purposes of zoning require their elimination as soon as possible. *See, e.g., McKenzie v. Town of Eaton Zoning Bd. of Adjustment*, 917 A.2d 193, 198 (2007) ("It is well established both in this state and in others that a legitimate purpose of zoning is the reduction and elimination of nonconforming uses"); *King County Dept. of Dev. and Envtl. Services v. King County*, 305 P.3d 240, 245 (Wash. 2013) ("Nonconforming uses are disfavored, and . . . the doctrine is a narrow exception to the State's nearly plenary power to regulate land through its police powers.").

While nonconforming uses are protected against immediate prohibition by the local jurisdiction, they can be terminated after a sufficient period during which the investment in the property can be amortized. Many states follow the rule that the reasonableness of the amortization period is based on a balancing of public good against private loss. *See, e.g., City of Los Angeles v. Gage*, 274 P.2d 34, 44 (Cal. Ct. App. 1954) ("Use of a reasonable amortization scheme provides an equitable means of reconciliation of the conflicting interests in satisfaction of due process requirements"). A minority of courts find such amortization provisions unconstitutional on their face. *See Aristo-Craft, Inc. v. Village of Evendale*, 322 N.E.2d 309 (Ohio App. 1974). *See also McDowell v. Board of Adjustment of Twp. of Wall*, 757 A.2d 822, 829 (N.J. App. Div. 2000) ("a municipality may not take active steps to extinguish nonconforming uses . . . but instead must wait with 'fervent hope that they in time wither and die . . . '"). Much of the litigation in this area centers on the legality of the amortization period provided, with the outcome depending on the facts of the individual use to which the time period is applied. *See, e.g., Collins v. City of Spartanburg*, 314 S.E.2d 332 (S.C. 1984) (five-year amortization period for junkyard is reasonable).

For a lengthy discussion of protection of existing uses concluding that the justification for such protection is questionable, *see* Christopher Serkin, Existing Uses and the Limits of Land Use Regulations, 84 N.Y.U. L. Rev. 1222 (2009).

C. AMENDMENTS, SPOT ZONING, AND VARIANCES

The Euclidian zoning ordinance is legislative in nature, and a landowner who is not satisfied with the permitted uses on his or her property may seek a change in those uses by an amendment to the zoning ordinance. However, because zoning is to be "in accordance with a comprehensive plan," an amendment to the zoning ordinance that affects only a single parcel of property poses the distinct possibility of damaging or destroying the overall plan. The courts thus had to decide whether amendments to zoning ordinances would be treated with the deference generally accorded other legislation or examined more closely.

■ PLAINS GRAINS LIMITED PARTNERSHIP v. BOARD OF COUNTY COMMISSIONERS
357 Mont. 61, 238 P.3d 332 (2010)

Justice BRIAN MORRIS delivered the Opinion of the Court. . . .

I. THE INITIAL REZONE

Duane and Mary E. Urquhart and Scott and Linda Urquhart (Urquharts) sought a zone change from Agricultural (A-2) to Heavy Industrial (I-2) for 668 acres of land in the northeast portion of Cascade County. The Urquharts submitted their rezoning application on October 30, 2007, to allow for the construction and operation of SME's [Southern Montana Electric's] proposed coal-fired power plant, known as the Highwood Generating Station (HGS). SME changed its proposal for the HGS to a natural gas fired plant following the Department of Environmental Quality's revocation of SME's air quality permit. The Urquharts and SME participated jointly in the preparation of the application for rezoning. The Urquharts had agreed to sell the property to SME before the County approved the rezone.

The Urquharts' rezone application claimed that "the requested zoning to heavy industrial use is a prerequisite to the planned construction and operation of an electric generating station." The Cascade County Planning Department adopted and made public its initial Staff Report on November 19, 2007 (Staff Report). The Staff Report described the surrounding land uses as agricultural for more than twenty acres in every direction. Approximately 200 acres of the land fell within the boundaries of the Lewis and Clark Great Falls Portage National Historic Landmark. The Staff Report cited the Urquharts' attempt to "take advantage of the Tax Increment Financing mechanisms provided in state statutes" as the primary reason that the Urquharts had requested rezoning.

The Staff Report acknowledged that the construction and operation of the HGS would be "out of character with the existing agricultural land uses in the vicinity of the proposed rezoning." The Staff Report noted, however, that construction and operation of the HGS would not necessarily be "out of character with the land uses *allowed* under the existing A-2 zoning district." (Emphasis added). The Staff Report based this conclusion on the fact that the A-2 zone permitted electrical generation facilities through the special use permit process. As a result, the Staff Report determined that "the rezoning is not necessary to accommodate the HGS facility, as such a use is permissible with a special use permit." The Staff Report further noted that the actual construction of any structures or development of the property would require a zoning location-conformance permit.

SME submitted a letter on January 9, 2008, in response to the Staff Report and the Planning Board's report to the Commissioners. SME's letter contained eleven proposed "conditions" that were intended to address the Planning Board's comments. The SME letter contained, in pertinent part, an agreement by SME that "as a condition of rezoning to heavy industrial use, such use shall be solely for purposes of an electrical power plant."

Plains Grains claims to have been unaware of the SME letter until the Commission's public hearing on the proposed rezone on January 15, 2008. SME submitted an array of documentation at the public hearing, including a traffic impact study, a baseline noise study, a report on the health impacts of coal-fired power plants, a property appraisal report, and a landscape plan. The County adopted a resolution of intent on January 31, 2008, to rezone the Urquharts' property.

The resolution of intent incorporated by reference the eleven conditions offered in SME's letter. The County published notice of the resolution on four dates over the course of two weeks in February of 2008. The Commissioners met on March 11, 2008, to consider Final Resolution 08-22 to rezone the Urquharts' property from A-2 to I-2. The Commissioners adopted the Planning Board's report as their findings on the proposed rezone. More than 1900 citizens submitted comments on the proposed rezone. The Commission approved the motion to rezone. . . .

II. District Court Proceedings

Plains Grains filed a complaint on April 10, 2008. Plains Grains requested that the court set aside the County's approval of the rezone and requested that the court issue a writ of mandate, a writ of review before this Court, and a declaratory judgment. . . . Plains Grains . . . alleged that the zone change constituted impermissible spot zoning. SME and the Urquharts intervened on May 1, 2008.

Discussion . . .

Did the rezoning of 668 acres of land from Agricultural to Heavy Industrial constitute impermissible spot zoning?

We turn then to the merits of Plains Grains' spot zoning claim. Whether impermissible spot zoning has occurred presents a fact-specific inquiry that will vary from one case to the next. *Little* [*v. Bd. of County Comm'rs*], 193 Mont. 334, 346, 631 P.2d 1282, 1289. The presence of three conditions generally will indicate, however, that a given situation constitutes spot zoning, regardless of variations in factual scenarios. *Id.*

The first prong of the three-part *Little* test examines whether the requested use would differ significantly from the prevailing land uses in the area. *Id.* The second prong explores whether the area requested for the rezone would be "rather small" in terms of the number of landowners benefitted by the requested zone change. *Id.* Finally, the third prong analyzes whether the requested zone change would be in the nature of "special legislation" designed to benefit one or a few landowners at the expense of the surrounding landowners or the public. *Id.* A court must analyze the second and third prongs of the *Little* test in concert. *Boland v. City of Great Falls*, 275 Mont. 128, 134, 910 P.2d 890, 894 (1996). The number of landowners benefitted by the zone change speaks directly to the issue of whether the requested change constitutes special legislation in favor of one or a small number of landowners. *Id.*

We first must determine "whether the requested use differs from the prevailing use in the area." *North 93 Neighbors, Inc. v. Bd. of County Comm'rs*, 2006 MT 132, ¶ 65, 332 Mont. 327, 137 P.3d 557 (citing *Little*, 193 Mont. at 346, 631 P.2d at 1289). The

District Court acknowledged that there "unquestionably" would be a change from the current agricultural use to the proposed heavy industrial use represented by the HGS. The County cites *North 93 Neighbors* for the proposition that a court applying the first prong of the *Little* test may look to the land uses allowed under current zoning rather than the prevailing uses in the area. We analyzed the land uses allowed by current zoning in *North 93 Neighbors* only *after* we thoroughly had considered the existing uses in the area. Our conclusion that the prevailing uses were not significantly different from the proposed use was based on our consideration of both the prevailing uses *and* the uses allowed by current zoning. *Id.* Thus a court may consider the existing zoning in addition to prevailing uses. Nothing in *North 93 Neighbors* directs a court to consider what uses would be available under existing zoning in lieu of prevailing uses, as the County suggests.

We further distinguish *North 93 Neighbors* from the instant facts in that the proposed rezone in that case would have constituted merely an extension of existing zoning. We observed in *North 93 Neighbors* that "[e]xtending a preexisting zone classification to include a larger area does not constitute spot zoning." *North 93 Neighbors,* ¶ 67 . . . By contrast, the proposed rezone to facilitate construction of the HGS would create an island of heavy industrial zoning within a large area zoned for agricultural use.

Finally, the County's reliance on *North 93 Neighbors* fails because existing zoning adjacent to the proposed rezone in that case allowed for commercial use as of right. *North 93 Neighbors,* ¶ 66. Here, as Plains Grains points out, SME's proposed use would be allowed-if at all-only by the granting of a special use permit. The District Court applied the wrong test in rejecting the first prong of the *Little* spot zoning analysis. The District Court concluded that the requested use of the 668 acres for the proposed rezone would differ significantly from surrounding uses. SME does not challenge seriously this conclusion. Plains Grains has established the first prong of the *Little* test.

The second prong of the *Little* spot zoning test looks at whether the size of the parcel to be rezoned would be "relatively small." Consideration of the actual size of the parcel comprises only one element of this inquiry, but nonetheless constitutes a relevant factor. This Court determined in *Greater Yellowstone Coalition, Inc. v. Bd. of Comm'rs,* 2001 MT 99, 305 Mont. 232, 25 P.3d 168, that the County had engaged in impermissible spot zoning of a 323 acre parcel that comprised "a mere 2% of the District's 13,280 acres." *Greater Yellowstone Coalition,* ¶ 26. The 668 acres at issue in this case comprise a similarly small percentage of the land zoned for agriculture in Cascade County. The District Court acknowledged that Plains Grains "appears to have a compelling argument" with regard to the relatively small size of the area to be rezoned.

The number of landowners affected by the proposed rezone must be analyzed in concert with the third factor-whether the proposed zone change constitutes "special legislation." *North 93 Neighbors,* ¶ 68 (citing *Boland,* 275 Mont. at 134, 910 P.2d at 894). The number of landowners affected relates directly to whether the zoning constitutes special legislation designed to benefit one person. *North 93 Neighbors,* ¶ 68. This inquiry should focus on the benefits of the proposed rezone to surrounding landowners, not the benefits — financial or otherwise — that would accrue from the proposed development. *Boland,* 275 Mont. at 134, 910 P.2d at 894. The Urquharts' application for rezoning acknowledged that grain farming and cattle ranching constituted the predominant surrounding land uses. The Staff Report likewise confirms that agricultural production dominates the surrounding land uses.

The District Court found that "one landowner (be it viewed as either SME, the current deed holder, or the Urquharts, the applicants) will benefit at the expense of others." The court recognized that these costs constituted "not merely the location of a power plant in the 'Back 40' but the power lines, rail spurs, and other industrial detritus of a large, power generating facility." The court acknowledged that the impacts of this special legislation would be "imposed on some landowners by way of eminent domain." We agree. No discernible benefit for the rezone would accrue to the neighboring farmers and ranchers. The benefits of the rezone inure solely to the owners of the 668 acres, first the Urquharts and now SME.

The District Court based its determination that no spot zoning had occurred on its conclusion that the zone change "was in name only" and did not change the uses allowed under the existing Cascade County regulations. Our application of the *Little* factors reveals, however, that the rezoning of the HGS property constituted spot zoning. The requested heavy industrial use differs significantly from the current agricultural uses that dominate the surrounding area. The area to be rezoned is relatively small-both in absolute size and in terms of landowners affected. The proposed rezone smacks of "special legislation" in that the benefits would accrue to a single landowner to the detriment of the surrounding farmers and ranchers. *Little*, 193 Mont. at 346, 631 P.2d at 1289. . . .

We reverse the District Court's order granting summary judgment to SME and grant judgment in favor of Plains Grains on its spot zoning claim. . . .

Notes and Comments

1. *Two Types of Zoning Amendments.* An "amendment" to a zoning ordinance can take one of two forms: (a) the jurisdiction can amend the text of the zoning ordinance to create a new district, expand the uses allowed in a district, and so forth; (b) alternatively (or concurrently), it can amend the zoning map to change the zoning designations that apply to a specific piece of property.

2. *Defining Spot Zoning.* The term "spot zoning" is more easily defined than applied. Consider the following explanations of the term:

> Spot zoning results when a zoning ordinance creates a small island of property with restrictions on its use different from those imposed on the surrounding property. *Kane v. City Council of Cedar Rapids*, 537 N.W.2d 718, 723 (Iowa 1995).
>
> Spot zoning consists of zoning that "single[s] out a small parcel or perhaps even a single lot for a use classification different from the surrounding area and inconsistent with any comprehensive plan, for the benefit of the owner of such property." *Granger v. Town of Woodford*, 708 A.2d 1345, 1346 (Vt. 1998).
>
> Spot zoning is "a change in zoning applied only to a small area, which is out of harmony with comprehensive planning for the good of the community." *Hanna v. City of Chicago*, 771 N.E.2d 13, 23 (Ill. App. 2002) (*quoting Bossman v. Village of Riverton*, 684 N.E.2d 427 (Ill. App. 1997)).

3. *"Spotting" Spot Zoning.* How does the court determine whether the rezoning "furthers" the comprehensive zoning plan, and thus is legitimate, or constitutes

spot zoning and is invalid? In an early leading case, *Bartram v. Zoning Comm'n of the City of Bridgeport*, 68 A.2d 308 (Conn. 1949), the Connecticut Supreme Court stated:

> Action by a zoning authority which gives to a single lot or a small area privileges which are not extended to other land in the vicinity is in general against sound public policy and obnoxious to the law. It can be justified only when it is done in furtherance of a general plan properly adopted for and designed to serve the best interests of the community as a whole.
>
> The vice of spot zoning is in the fact that it singles out for special treatment a lot or a small area in a way that does not further such a plan.

Id. at 310-11.

4. *"Reverse" or "Inverse" Spot Zoning.* Spot zoning usually consists of a rezoning to a new use that is markedly different from surrounding uses. But "reverse" spot zoning is also a possibility. That offense occurred in *Riya Finnegan LLC v. Township Council of Twp. of South Brunswick*, 962 A.2d 484, 493 (N.J. 2008), in which the New Jersey Supreme Court stated:

> In the case of spot zoning, the owner of a particular parcel seeks to reap the benefit of a zoning decision, by special ordinance or by variance, which treats his or her property more favorably than the comprehensive plan would allow, to the detriment of the larger community or the immediate neighbors. In inverse spot zoning, it is the neighboring community that seeks to reap a benefit by imposing its particular view, contrary to the previously generated comprehensive plan, upon the specific parcel, to the detriment of the rights of that parcel's owner.

See Penn Street, L.P. v. East Lampeter Twp. Zoning Hg. Bd., 84 A.3d 1114 (Cmwlth Ct. Pa. 2014) (rejecting reverse spot zoning claim alleging that plaintiff's property "exists as a peninsula of R-Rural zoned land amidst a sea of commercially zoned [land]"); *In re Appeal of Realen Valley Forge Greenes Associates*, 838 A.2d 718 (Pa. 2003) ("reverse spot zoning" occurred where agricultural zone containing a golf course was surrounded by developed land).

5. *Spot Zoning in* Plains Grains? Are you convinced by the analysis in *Plains Grains*? Shouldn't the sheer size of the rezoning indicate that it is not spot zoning? *Compare Dockter v. Burleigh Bd. of County Comm'rs*, 865 N.W.2d 836 (N.D. 2015) ("[T]his tract of land consists of 311 acres, which was proposed to be divided into five to ten acre lots . . . which also militates against a claim that the rezoning change involves an individual lot singled out for discrimination, or different treatment."). If power plants are to be sited, given their externalities, aren't they better placed in agricultural areas? Moreover, if the use was allowed previously by special permit, doesn't that fact cut against the conclusion of spot zoning for a rezoning that changes the use to a permitted one?

6. *Spot Zoning and Invalidation.* Many courts treat "spot zoning" as a conclusion that requires invalidation of the ordinance. However, others hold that spot zoning is not illegal per se. *See Foothill Communities Coalition v. County of Orange*, 166 Cal. Rptr. 3d 627, 637 (App. 2014) (finding of spot zoning "does not end our analysis, however, as spot zoning may or may not be impermissible, depending on the circumstances."); *Etheridge v. County of Currituck*, 762 S.E.2d 289 (N.C. App. 2014) (finding spot zoning and then concluding, after a lengthy analysis, that the spot zoning had no reasonable basis). Does this "two-part" analysis make sense? By its

very nature, isn't spot zoning arbitrary and capricious? Shouldn't that end the matter? Note that in these cases that go on to determine reasonableness, a finding that spot zoning exists amounts to nothing more than a description, not a definition with *per se* legal consequences.

7. *Spot Zoning as an Incoherent Doctrine?* One author argues that the outcome of spot zoning challenges is simply unpredictable, given the criteria that the courts use to determine whether "spot zoning" occurred:

> The outcome of a spot zoning challenge may be no more predictable than a single bet at roulette, where red and black have roughly equal chances. The spot zoning doctrine is unpredictable because of the magnetic pull of conflicting policies. The first is that the amendment is a legislative act and entitled to presumptive validity if a connection with public health, safety, or welfare can be postulated. Contradictory pulls come from (1) judicial suspicion that a governmental regulation that focuses on a specific tract caters to a private interest, not the public interest; and (2) the [Standard Zoning Enabling Act's] formal requirement that zoning conform to a comprehensive plan. Accordingly, the spot zoning doctrine gets courts bogged down trying to decide justification on the facts of a particular zoning reclassification.

John Mixon and Kathleen McGlynn, A New Zoning and Planning Metaphor: Chaos and Complexity Theory, 42 Hous. L. Rev. 1221, 1231 (2006). Do you agree?

8. *Judicial Review of Rezonings.* Most courts follow the traditional approach to judicial review of legislative actions by a municipality. They presume that the rezoning is valid, place a heavy burden on the challenging party, and overturn the rezoning only if it is arbitrary and capricious. *See, e.g., Woll v. Monaghan Twp.*, 948 A.2d 933 (Pa. Commw. Ct. 2008 ("A zoning ordinance is presumed to be valid. . . . Therefore, one challenging the zoning ordinance has the heavy burden of establishing its invalidity.").

Setting forth a general rule about the facts that will support a rezoning is not possible. The following list of factors from the Illinois case of *Rodriguez v. Henderson*, 578 N.E.2d 57, 60 (Ill. App. Ct. 1991) can serve as a good general summary:

> (1) the existing uses and zoning of nearby property;
> (2) the extent to which property values are diminished by the particular zoning restrictions;
> (3) the extent to which the destruction of a plaintiff's property values promotes the health, safety, morals, or general welfare of the public;
> (4) the relative gain to the public as compared to the hardship imposed upon the individual property owner;
> (5) the suitability of the subject property for the zoned purposes;
> (6) the length of time the property has been vacant as zoned, considered in the context of land development in its vicinity;
> (7) the evidence or lack of evidence of community need for a proposed use.

The court also observed that whether the government has a comprehensive zoning plan for land use and development, and whether the ordinance is in harmony with it, are also relevant.

9. *The "Change or Mistake" Rule.* Small numbers of jurisdictions require a much greater showing to support a zoning amendment. They follow the rule that only a

mistake in the original zoning or a change in conditions subsequent to the enactment of the original ordinance can justify an amendment. *See, e.g., Howard County v. Dorsey*, 438 A.2d 1339, 1345 (Md. 1982). *See also Roundstone Dev., LLC v. City of Natchez*, 105 So. 3d 317, 320 (Miss. 2013) (following change or mistake rule because "a landowner should be able to rely upon a zoning plan to maintain the use and value of his property"); *Albuquerque Commons P'ship v. City Council of City of Albuquerque*, 184 P.3d 411 (N.M. 2008) ("The rule evidences a concern over the stability of zoning regulations and a landowner's right to rely on existing zoning rules.").

Another approach is presented in *Albuquerque Commons Partnership v. City Council of Albuquerque*, 184 P.3d 411 (N.M. 2008), which is discussed in Chapter 6. The court in *Albuquerque Commons Partnership* treats small-tract rezonings as quasi-judicial rather than quasi-legislative in nature.

The drafters of the Standard Zoning Enabling Act recognized that situations regarding particular properties would arise in which certain uses would cause unfairness. Accordingly, they built into the Act devices designed to provide relief in those situations. The devices are known as variances or "special exceptions," and virtually every local zoning ordinance includes them. However, because variances authorize actions otherwise disallowed by the zoning ordinance's provisions, they can be misused. Furthermore, courts have differed on whether variances should be given rarely or more generously. Consider the following variance decision in light of this background.

■ MARSHALL v. CITY OF PHILADELPHIA

97 A.3d 323 (Pa. 2014)

OPINION

JUSTICE MCCAFFERY.

In this zoning matter, we must determine if the Commonwealth Court applied an improper standard in reversing a zoning board's grant of a variance.

On November 8, 2010, the Archdiocese of Philadelphia ("Archdiocese") filed . . . for conversion of the Nativity B.V.M. Elementary School into a 63–unit, one-bedroom apartment complex for low income senior citizens, to be called Nativity B.V.M. Place. The school, in the Port Richmond section of Philadelphia, had been constructed in 1912 and operated by the Archdiocese in legal non-conformance with subsequently enacted zoning codes until 2008, when it had been closed due to declining enrollment and insufficient revenue. In 2009, the Archdiocese received funding under the Section 202 Supportive Housing for the Elderly program of the United States Department of Housing and Urban Development ("HUD") to convert the school to senior housing. . . .

On January 5, 2011, the ZBA held an evidentiary hearing . . .

The ZBA hearing ended with the members voting unanimously to grant the variances sought by the Archdiocese. . . .

[The Commonwealth Court overturned the variances.]

Under the Philadelphia Zoning Code, the ZBA is authorized to issue variances under certain circumstances, as follows.

§14–1801. Jurisdiction and Powers.

(1) The Zoning Board of Adjustment may, after public notice and public hearing: . . .

(c) authorize, upon appeal, in specific cases, such variance from the terms of this Title as will not be contrary to the public interest, where, owing to special conditions, a literal enforcement of the provisions of this Title would result in *unnecessary hardship,* and so that the spirit of this Title shall be observed and substantial justice done, subject to such terms and conditions as the Board may decide.

Phila. Zoning Code §14–1801(1)(c) (emphasis added).

Section 14–1802(1) of the Zoning Code sets forth specific criteria that the ZBA must consider in determining whether to grant a variance. This Court has "boiled down" the §14–1802(1) criteria into three key requirements: "(1) unique hardship to the property; (2) no adverse effect on the public health, safety or general welfare; and (3) . . . the minimum variance that will afford relief at the least modification possible." *East Torresdale Civic Association v. Zoning Board of Adjustment of Philadelphia County,* 536 Pa. 322, 639 A.2d 446, 447 (1994). The hardship must be unique to the property at issue, not a hardship arising from the impact of the zoning regulations on the entire district . . . In addition, the special conditions or circumstances forming the basis for the variance must not have resulted from the actions of the party seeking the variance. §14–1802(1)(d). The party seeking the variance bears the burden of proof. . . .

This Court has previously held that, in the context of use variances, "unnecessary hardship is established by evidence that: (1) the physical features of the property are such that it cannot be used for a permitted purpose; **or** (2) the property can be conformed for a permitted use only at a prohibitive expense; **or** (3) the property has no value for any purpose permitted by the zoning ordinance." . . .

[I]n establishing hardship, an applicant for a variance is *not required* to show that the property at issue is valueless without the variance or that the property cannot be used for any permitted purpose. . . .

Although a property owner is not required to show that his or her property is valueless unless a variance is granted, "[m]ere economic hardship will not of itself justify a grant of a variance.". . . . Particularly where a variance is sought in order to make a change from an existing use consistent with the zoning code to an inconsistent use, "the mere fact that the property would increase in value if a variance were granted, is not of itself a sufficient basis" upon which to find unnecessary hardship. . . .

[T]he Commonwealth Court determined that to establish unnecessary hardship in the context of an application for a use variance, "a property owner must demonstrate that the entire building is *functionally obsolete* for any purpose other than one not permitted under the relevant zoning ordinance." . . . The court then concluded that the Archdiocese had failed to present any evidence "demonstrating that it could not utilize the property [for] any of the several uses permitted in the R-10A Zoning District,"[1] and that the ZBA had "improperly found that a unique hardship existed." . . .

---

1. Under §14–205 of the Philadelphia Zoning Code, the permitted uses in an R–10A district were single family dwellings, residential related uses, and non-residential uses; duplexes and multi-family dwellings were *not* permitted uses. Residential related uses included professional offices in the dwelling

The Commonwealth Court's "functionally obsolete" standard appears to be merely a reiteration of the "practically valueless" standard, a standard for unnecessary hardship that we have repeatedly and explicitly rejected. . . .

The Commonwealth Court seems to have ignored the undisputed facts that the structure at issue was a century-old, legally non-conforming school building, which not only was already vacant but also was already in need of repair. The Archdiocese never suggested that the property was practically valueless . . . Rather, the Archdiocese grounded its unnecessary hardship argument on its assertion that the property could be conformed for a permitted use only at a prohibitive expense . . . [T]he ZBA was certainly entitled to infer that the building could not be used for any permitted purpose without major, prohibitively expensive renovation. . . .

[H]ere, the Archdiocese was awarded a grant of nearly ten million dollars from HUD's Supportive Housing for the Elderly program to fund the renovation of a building. . . . There is no question that withdrawal of the HUD funding to renovate the old building for senior housing would constitute a financial burden to the Archdiocese and also would negatively impact the mission of the Archdiocese's Catholic Health Care Services. Furthermore, the ZBA found that, "although the Subject Property served the community well for a long time as a school, the Subject Property can better serve the needs of the community as low income housing for seniors." . . .

We hold that the ZBA acted well within its discretion here in concluding that the Archdiocese had established unnecessary hardship and in granting the use variance for conversion of the property to low-income senior housing . . .

[On the issue of parking[2] the lower court] failed to grant proper deference to the ZBA with respect to its factual findings. Specifically, the court offered no support . . . for its legal conclusion that the Archdiocese must demonstrate that it was not feasible to "construct" the required number of parking spaces. While the meaning of "construct" in this context is not entirely clear, it is abundantly clear that the court gave no deference to the ZBA's findings that the Archdiocese's proposed parking arrangements "would not adversely impact the health, safety and welfare of the surrounding community," and "would not substantially or permanently injure the appropriate use of adjacent conforming properties." . . . The court also failed to mention the fact that the "No Parking" signs that the Archdiocese would petition the City to remove barred parking during school hours, and thus were indisputably no longer necessary or appropriate because the building is no longer used as a school. We hold that the ZBA did not abuse its discretion in accepting the Archdiocese's stated method as to how it would provide the necessary parking spaces.

Justice EAKIN, dissenting.

. . . At the evidentiary hearing before the Board, appellant only offered evidence demonstrating its proposed use would receive substantial federal funding and overwhelming support from the community; however, it did not submit any evidence related to the three methods of proving hardship enumerated in *Hertzberg*. While such funding for church-owned property is indisputably remarkable and

---

of the practitioner; places of worship; municipal art galleries, museums, and libraries; railroad stations; telephone exchange buildings; water or sewer booster substations; and day care facilities. Non-residential uses included art galleries, museums, or libraries; charitable institutions; club houses; fire stations; medical or surgical hospitals; police stations; rest, old age, nursing or convalescent homes, and nurseries; and water or sewage pumping stations.

2. Under . . . the Philadelphia Zoning Code, three parking places were required for every ten dwelling units in an apartment building containing 25 or more families in which occupancy was restricted to hose 62 years of age or older.

appellant's proposed use is certainly laudable, these particular points are inapposite to the case. The potential loss of federal monies if a variance is not granted does not constitute hardship, and the proposed socially salutary use does not carry the day. The question is not whether this would be a great use of the property — it is whether appellant proved other uses were uniquely impossible.

Because appellant presented no evidence relevant to "unique hardship," it failed to prove the need for a variance — a burden it was required to meet, not one the Board may assume has been shown.

Notes and Comments

1. *Safety Valves.* Variances are a staple of modern land use practice. They are intended to serve as "safety valves" where the strict application of Euclidian zoning causes unfairness to particular property owners. The origin of variances is traceable to Section 7 of the Standard Zoning Enabling Act, which empowers local "boards of adjustment":

> [t]o authorize upon appeal in specific cases such variance from the terms of the ordinance as will not be contrary to the public interest, where, owing to special conditions, a literal enforcement of the provisions of the ordinance will result in unnecessary hardship, so that the spirit of the ordinance shall be observed and substantial justice done.

Substantial parts of this section have been enacted in a majority of states.

A variance "runs with the land," and its benefit is available to the applicant's successors in title. *See, e.g., Campbell v. City of South Portland,* 123 A.3d 994 (Me. 2015) (finding that lot owner could use a dimensional variance granted 40 years before); *Amendola v. Zoning Bd. of Appeals,* 129 A.3d 743, 751 (Conn. App. 2015) (variance runs in perpetuity).

2. *Use and Area Variances.* Variances are broken into two general categories: use variances and area (sometimes called "bulk") variances. One court described the difference as follows:

> A use variance permits a use of land for purposes other than those proscribed the zoning ordinance. . . . An area variance does not involve a use prohibited by an ordinance, but concerns a deviation from specific requirements such as height limitations, setback lines, size regulations, and the like.

City of Johnston v. Christenson, 718 N.W.2d 290, 300 n.4 (Iowa 2006); *see also Ten Stary Dom Ptp. v. Mauro,* 76 A.3d 1236, 1243 (N.J. 2013) ("Provisions in a zoning ordinance that control the size and shape of a lot and the size and location of buildings . . . on a parcel of property are known as bulk or dimensional requirements."). Distinguishing between use and area variances, however, can be difficult. For example, would you consider a variance authorizing an increase in density to be a use variance or an area variance? How about a variance from parking requirements needed for a restaurant, which was an allowed use in the district? *Colin Realty v. Town of North Hempstead,* 21 N.E.3d 188 (N.Y. 2014) (area variance).

The distinction between use and area variances is significant, for the test for an area variance "generally is less onerous than the evidentiary showing required for a use variance." *Metropolitan Bd. of Zoning Appeals v. McDonald's Corp.,* 481 N.E.2d 141,

146 (Ind. App. 1985); *see Mendoza v. Licensing Bd. of Fall River*, 827 N.E.2d 180, 195 n.2 (2005) ("use variances should be particularly extraordinary because they inherently undermine the local zoning ordinance's division of uses"). Indeed, some states go so far as to prohibit the issuance of use variances. *See* Cal. Gov't Code §65906 (West 2011); Minn. Stat. Ann. §394.27, subd. 7 (West 2011).

3. *"Unnecessary Hardships."* In many states, an applicant for a use variance must demonstrate "unnecessary hardship," while an area variance requires a showing of "practical difficulties." *Trent v. German Twp. Bd. of Zoning Appeals*, 759 N.E.2d 421 (Ohio App. 2001). An early, leading decision concluded that to meet the "unnecessary hardship" test, an applicant must show:

> (1) [that] the land in question cannot yield a reasonable return if used only for a purpose allowed in that zone; (2) that the plight of the owner is due to unique circumstances and not to the general conditions in the neighborhood which may reflect the unreasonableness of the zoning ordinance itself; and (3) that the use to be authorized by the variance will not alter the essential character of the locality.

Otto v. Steinhilber, 24 N.E.2d 851, 853 (N.Y. 1939).

The unnecessary hardship test is most easily satisfied by a showing that the applicant's property has significant physical differences from other similarly situated properties. As the Pennsylvania Supreme Court put it, "Unnecessary hardship is established by evidence that the physical features of the property are such that it cannot be used for a permitted purpose or that the property can be conformed for a permitted use only at a prohibitive expense." *Allegheny West Civic Council, Inc. v. Zoning Bd. of Adjustment of the City of Pittsburgh*, 689 A.2d 225, 227 (Pa. 1997).

In contrast, the prospect of increased economic profit will not support the grant of a variance, as long as the owner can make a reasonable return from the permitted uses allowed by the ordinance. Furthermore, if the hardship is self-created, a variance cannot be granted. *See, e.g., City of Dallas v. Vanesko*, 189 S.W.3d 769, 774 (Tex. 2006) ("it was the way the Vaneskos chose to design their house that created the hardship . . . for there was nothing about this parcel of land which required a roof higher than what the zoning ordinance allowed"). The applicant may also need to prove that it cannot make a reasonable return on the property. *Surfrider Found. v. Zoning Bd. of Appeals*, 358 P.3d 664, 678 (Hawaii 2015) (although Permitting Director found that variance from shoreline setback on Waikiki Beach was necessary to "maintain economic viability" on the property, no financial data in the record supported that finding).

4. *"Practical Difficulties."* The other test often employed in variance decisions is whether the applicant has demonstrated "practical difficulties." In some states, the practical difficulties test is essentially treated as a restatement of the unnecessary hardship standard. *See, e.g., State v. Kenosha County Bd. of Adjustment*, 577 N.W.2d 813, 820 (Wis. 1998) ("this court has already decided that there is no significant distinction between the meaning of the two terms"). However, most others have assigned a separate meaning to the term. *See Walnut Acres Neighborhood Ass'n v. City of Los Angeles*, 185 Cal. Rptr. 3d 871, 872 (App. 2015) ("practical difficulties" is a "lesser standard" than "unnecessary hardship").

Most courts now hold that a person who purchases the land with notice of the zoning restrictions may still apply for a variance. *Richard Roeser Professional Builder, Inc. v. Anne Arundel County*, 793 A.2d 545 (Md. 2002).

5. *Analyzing* Marshall. What test did the Pennsylvania Supreme Court apply in determining whether "unnecessary hardship" was shown? How did that test differ from the one applied by the Commonwealth Court below? Did the applicant prove unnecessary hardship, or did the court just infer such proof? How did the dissent view the case differently from the majority?

The court seems to emphasize the funding procured by the applicant for the project. Was that funding relevant at all to the grant of the variance? Does the court's opinion suggest that it views variances as something more than just "safety valves"? Perhaps they are important means of adjusting land uses, in the same manner that a rezoning adjusts land uses.

6. *Variations on Variance Tests.* The New Hampshire Supreme Court has found that the definition of "unnecessary hardship" had become "too restrictive" in light of the constitutional rights of property owners. Accordingly, it adopted a new test for this term. Applicants must prove that:

> (1) a zoning restriction as applied to their property interferes with their reasonable use of the property, considering the unique setting of the property in its environment; (2) no fair and substantial relationship exists between the general purposes of the zoning ordinance and the specific restriction on the property; and (3) the variance would not injure the public or private rights of others.

Simplex Technologies, Inc. v. Town of Newington, 766 A.2d 713, 717 (N.H. 2001). Is this formulation an improvement? *Compare Cherrystone Inlet, LLC v. Board of Zoning Appeals of Northampton County,* 628 S.E.2d 324, 326 (Va. 2006) (applicant had to show that, without a variance, the zoning would interfere with all reasonable beneficial uses of the property).

7. *Impacts on Whom?* In *Jacoby v. Zoning Bd. of Adjustment,* 124 A.3d 694 (N.J. Super. 2015), a board of adjustment granted a variance allowing a 143.8-foot tall office building in a business zone which permitted a maximum height of 35 feet. Opponents of the building argued that the height of the building would dramatically affect the view of Palisades Cliffs, a natural area, from vantage points in both New York and New Jersey. The court found that the board erred in granting the variance by insufficiently considering its effects: "We have long recognized that a zoning board's duty to consider the 'surrounding neighborhood' encompasses more than just consideration of the municipality itself or the immediate vicinity of the structure." 124 A.2d at 464. Why was the board, a local agency, required to consider effects beyond its municipal border?

8. *Has the "Safety Valve" Ruptured?* Because variances authorize either uses or other deviations from the zoning ordinance not allowed on other properties, the variance power plainly raises the prospect of abuse and favoritism in the zoning process. *See, e.g., People ex rel. Fordham Manor Reformed Church v. Walsh,* 155 N.E. 575, 578 (N.Y. 1927) (warning by Chief Judge Cardozo that the variance power is "one easily abused"). This concern over municipal abuse of the discretion involved in granting variances has influenced judicial review of variance decisions. Courts have repeatedly warned that the burden on an applicant for a variance is a significant one. *See, e.g., Caruso v. Zoning Bd. of Appeals,* 130 A.3d 241, 250 (Conn. 2016) ("Zoning, by definition, restricts land use, and 'variance[s] must be reserved for unusual or exceptional circumstances.'") *Valley View Civic Ass'n v. Zoning Board of Adjustment,* 462 A.2d 637, 640 (Pa. 1983) ("The reasons for granting a variance must be substantial, serious and compelling.").

A 2004 survey of variances granted in North Carolina, however, paints a more favorable picture. David W. Owens, The Zoning Variance: Reappraisal and Recommendations for Reform of a Much-Maligned Tool, 29 Colum. J. Envtl. L. 279 (2004). The survey found that the most common variance request involved setbacks for structures. It also found that, while a "principal criticism of zoning variances is that they undermine the purpose and integrity of the land use plan and the zoning ordinance," that conclusion did not seem to hold in North Carolina (*id.* at 315), perhaps, in part, because the state's supreme court had outlawed use variances (*id.* at 310). Similarly, Professor William Fischel, who has done considerable scholarly work on land use and who served on the zoning board of adjustment in Hanover, New Hampshire, warned: "[E]ven the least sophisticated zoning boards have an asset that is almost never available to appellate judges or to statistical analysts: They know at least the neighborhood and usually the specific site from personal experience. Critics need to take that into account." William A. Fischel, The Evolution of Zoning Since the 1980s: The Persistence of Localism, http://papers.ssrn.com/sol3/papers.cfm?abstract_id=1686009 (2010) at 18 (last visited Nov. 11, 2016).

Is the concern over variances overblown?

D. FLEXIBILITY DEVICES

1. Use Permits

As zoning developed, other so-called flexibility devices arose as local governments and developers sought to lessen the rigidity of Euclidian zoning. *See* Tony Arnold, The Structure of the Land Use Regulatory System in the United States, 22 J. Land Use & Envtl. L. 441, 505 (2007) ("Traditional Euclidean zoning was supplemented, and perhaps even functionally supplanted to some degree, by flexible and advanced zoning techniques."). One such flexibility device is the conditional use permit.

■ UINTAH MOUNTAIN RTC, L.L.C. v. DUCHESNE COUNTY
127 P.3d 1270 (Utah Ct. App. 2005)

Before BILLINGS, P.J., BENCH, Associate P.J., and GREENWOOD, J.

OPINION

GREENWOOD, Judge:
***

BACKGROUND

Plaintiffs D. Brad Hancock, John D. Hancock, Tyson B. Hancock, and Beau D. Hancock own a small family farm (the Hancock Farm) located in Duchesne County,

Utah. In 2001, the Hancock family purchased a five-acre parcel of land (the Hancock Parcel) immediately adjacent to the Hancock Farm. Both the Hancock Farm and the Hancock Parcel are zoned A-5, which is an agricultural-residential zoning category with a five-acre minimum lot size.

Plaintiffs planned to establish a residential treatment center (Uintah RTC) on the Hancock Parcel, and formed Plaintiff Uintah Mountain RTC, L.L.C. for the purpose of operating Uintah RTC. Plaintiffs envisioned that Uintah RTC would house and treat young men between the ages of twelve and seventeen for low self-esteem, obesity, depression, attention deficit hyperactivity disorder, lackluster academic performance, and breakdowns in familial relationships, and also counsel those who had experimented with drugs or alcohol. Uintah RTC would not accept applicants with a history of violence or sexual offenses, or with any "significant criminal background." Initially, Uintah RTC was to be housed in an existing structure on the Hancock Parcel, which Plaintiff D. Brad Hancock was remodeling.

Plaintiff John D. Hancock conceived the idea of operating Uintah RTC after working as a counselor at a nearby residential treatment center, Cedar Ridge RTC. Cedar Ridge RTC is located in an area of Duchesne County also zoned A-5, and was granted a conditional use permit in 1997 to operate a residential treatment center.

In 2003, Plaintiffs submitted an application for a conditional use permit to the Duchesne County Planning Commission (the Planning Commission), seeking approval to operate Uintah RTC on the Hancock Parcel. The Duchesne County Code allows a "group home" in an A-5 zone as a conditional use. In order to obtain a conditional use permit for a group home, an applicant must complete a detailed application, *see* Duchesne County Code §17.40.020, and the Planning Commission must make certain findings in accordance with sections 17.52.050 and 17.52.053 of the Duchesne County Code.

The Planning Commission held public hearings regarding Plaintiffs' application, at which time Plaintiffs presented supporting documentary and testimonial evidence. A number of individuals who opposed Plaintiffs' application also attended the hearings, providing letters, news stories, and testimony in support of their position.

Based on the evidence presented, the Planning Commission determined, in compliance with section 17.52.050 of the Duchesne County Code, that (a) Uintah RTC would not be unduly detrimental or injurious to property or improvements in the vicinity and would not be detrimental to the public health, safety, or general welfare; (b) Uintah RTC would be located and conducted in compliance with the goals and policies of the Duchesne County General Plan and purposes of the zoning ordinance; and (c) the Hancock Parcel and the existing structure on the Hancock Parcel were of adequate size and dimensions to permit the conduct of Uintah RTC in a manner that would not be materially detrimental to adjoining or surrounding properties.

Additionally, the Planning Commission determined that Plaintiffs had met the special minimum conditions of section 17.52.053 of the Duchesne County Code, finding that (a) the location of Uintah RTC would be compatible with other land uses in the general neighborhood; (b) the site of Uintah RTC would be of sufficient size to accommodate the facility; (c) the site of Uintah RTC would be served by streets of sufficient capacity to carry the traffic expected to be generated by the facility; and (d) Uintah RTC, if otherwise in compliance with the conditional use permit, would not adversely affect other property in the vicinity or the general welfare of the county.

At the conclusion of the hearings, the Planning Commission unanimously approved the Plaintiffs' application for a conditional use permit, on the conditions that Plaintiffs (a) limit the number of young men residing in the facility at any one time to ten or, if required by the State of Utah, a number less than ten; (b) install an alarm system; (c) conduct monthly public relations meetings with neighbors; (d) provide a definition of "significant criminal background"; (e) show proof of liability insurance; and (f) comply with all other rules and regulations, including those contained within [Plaintiffs'] original application as well as applicable state and federal laws.

Subsequently, this decision was appealed to the County by neighbors who opposed the conditional use permit. Plaintiffs cross-appealed the Planning Commission's decision limiting the number of residents at Uintah RTC to ten.

The County affirmed the ten-resident limit on Uintah RTC, finding that Plaintiffs' application was incomplete, as "[n]o diagram was submitted for any number greater than ten," and "[n]o other evidence was presented to support a larger facility to accommodate 16 or 50 young men." The County also found that Plaintiffs presented "no evidence that the Planning Commission's limitation was arbitrary or capricious."

Regarding the neighbors' appeal, the County first denied Plaintiffs' request to dismiss the appeal on the basis that it was the product of "public clamor" — an insufficient basis for denying a conditional use permit. Turning to the merits of the appeal, the County determined:

> The Planning Commission's decision was not supported by the evidence, . . . there was insufficient evidence provided to address the issues of safety, traffic, and compatibility of the use to justify making the findings necessary to grant the conditional use. The area is clearly residential and agricultural, and from all that was presented we find that [Plaintiffs'] proposals are a commercial venture and not compatible with the area. . . . We agree [with the Planning Commission] that a single structure on five acres could be compatible to the area, but we disagree that this project could be compatible. It is clear that a single structure on five acres is inadequate for [Plaintiffs'] needs and that a larger project will be needed to be a viable venture. There has been nothing presented . . . to convince us that [Uintah RTC] is a viable project, nor could it be a compatible use in this area. We, therefore, overturn the decision of the [P]lanning [C]ommission and deny the conditional use permit. . . .

The district court affirmed. . . . The district court concluded that the denial of the conditional use permit in its entirety was not arbitrary and capricious because the decision was supported by substantial evidence. Further, contrary to Plaintiffs' argument, the court held that the denial was not based on mere public clamor, and referred to evidence received by the County in the form of a letter from Mr. Dale Cameron regarding the effect the treatment center would have on the surrounding properties. There was evidence presented to [the County] regarding safety concerns for these types of facilities. There was evidence presented regarding a nearby facility and some incidents that took place at that facility. It cannot be said from the evidence that the proposed facility would not be detrimental to the surrounding property. Therefore, the evidence supports [the County's] denial of the conditional use permit in its entirety.

Plaintiffs appeal. . . .

ANALYSIS

I. WHETHER THE COUNTY'S DECISION WAS ARBITRARY AND CAPRICIOUS

Plaintiffs argue that the County's denial of their application for a conditional use permit to operate a residential treatment facility of any size was arbitrary and capricious because it was not supported by substantial evidence. Specifically, Plaintiffs attack the County's findings under the Duchesne County Code that Uintah RTC (a) would not be "compatible to other land uses in the general neighborhood," Duchesne County Code §17.52.053(1); (b) would not "be served by streets of sufficient capacity to carry the traffic generated" by the facility, *id.* §7.52.053(3); and (c) would be detrimental to public safety and surrounding property, in violation of sections 17.52.050(1) and 17.52.053(4) of the Duchesne County Code. *See id.* §§17.52.050(1), .053(4).

We address these issues in turn, but first note a problem underlying each of them. It appears that the County upheld the Planning Commission's limitation of ten residents for Uintah RTC. However, it then examined the propriety of Plaintiffs' application for a conditional use permit assuming Plaintiffs would eventually desire a facility with a capacity for more than ten residents. This assumption was based on testimony of Plaintiffs that Uintah RTC would need between sixteen and fifty residents to be financially feasible. Indeed, the County stated: "It is clear that a single structure on five acres is inadequate for [Plaintiffs'] needs and that a larger project will be needed to be a viable venture." To the extent that the County's decision was based upon economic viability, it was improper. The Duchesne County Code does not include economic viability as a criterion for granting or denying a conditional use permit to operate a group home. Furthermore, the Duchesne County Code does not permit the County to deny an otherwise sufficient application for a conditional use permit based on the mere speculation that an additional, potentially expanded conditional use permit may be sought by Plaintiffs sometime in the future.

A. Compatible Use

Plaintiffs first argue that the County's determination that Uintah RTC would not be compatible with other uses in the general neighborhood was not supported by substantial evidence. We agree.

Section 17.52.053(1) of the Duchesne County Code requires, as a "special minimum condition" for a group home, that "[t]he location of the proposed use [be] compatible to other land uses in the general neighborhood." Duchesne County Code §17.52.053(1). In support of its conclusion that a residential treatment center would not be a compatible use, the County relied on "the submissions of the neighbors that the use in this area is single family dwellings on large lots with much open space." Accordingly, the County appears to have determined that Uintah RTC would not be compatible with other land uses in the general neighborhood because it is a commercial venture and "[t]his facility will need fences, parking, and attendant sheds and structures to house so many young men."

This conclusion is somewhat confusing given that earlier in its decision the County indicated that it agreed with the Planning Commission that a residential treatment center consisting of a single family residence on five acres would be in "keeping with the character of the neighborhood." Indeed, consideration of the structures that Uintah RTC may require seems more applicable to determining whether "the site is of sufficient size" under section 17.52.053(2), rather than determining whether it is a compatible use under section 17.52.053(1). *See* Duchesne County Code 17.52.053(2) (requiring "the site [be] of sufficient size to accommodate the proposed use together with all yards, open spaces, walls and fences, parking and loading facilities, [and] landscaping"). Considering this prong, the County found "[t]here is sufficient evidence on the record to support condition (2) regarding sufficient size."

We conclude, however, that the County's finding that Uintah RTC would not be a compatible use is not supported by substantial evidence. To the contrary, the evidence shows that in 1997 the County granted a conditional use permit to another facility, Cedar Ridge RTC, to operate a much larger residential treatment center in an area of Duchesne County also zoned A-5. Given the similarities in both neighborhood and use, it is unlikely that Cedar Ridge RTC would be a compatible use while Uintah RTC would not. *See Ralph L. Wadsworth Constr., Inc. v. West Jordan City,* 2000 UT App 49, ¶ 18, 999 P.2d 1240 (rejecting, as arbitrary and capricious, the city council's finding that the "appellants' proposed storage is much different than that of neighboring properties" because "the evidence shows that there are several other parcels near appellants' property which have outdoor storage areas similar to that proposed by appellants." (quotations omitted)). Therefore, the County's conclusion that Uintah RTC would not be a compatible use is not supported by substantial evidence.

B. Traffic

Plaintiffs next argue that the County's conclusion that Uintah RTC did not adequately address the issue of traffic was not supported by substantial evidence. We agree.

Section 17.52.053(3) of the Duchesne County Code mandates that "[t]he site shall be served by streets of sufficient capacity to carry the traffic generated by the proposed use." Duchesne County Code §17.52.053(3). Despite a thorough review of the record, we cannot find any evidence that supports the County's finding that traffic generated by the facility would be a problem. In fact, there is ample evidence in the record indicating that traffic for a ten-person facility would not be a problem. Furthermore, the County's decision is inconsistent on this issue. For example, at one point the decision notes that "[t]here is sufficient evidence in the record to support condition ... (3)[,] regarding streets sufficient to carry the traffic generated by ... a single residence structure on five acres with a maximum of 10 young men." However, the decision later concludes "there was insufficient evidence provided to address the issue[] of ... traffic." As Plaintiffs argue, it appears that the County's concerns with the traffic likely to result from a facility of more than ten persons generated its finding regarding traffic problems. Therefore, the County's decision regarding traffic was not supported by substantial evidence.

C. Public Safety and Welfare

Finally, Plaintiffs argue that the County's concern about safety aspects of the proposed use and its decision that Uintah RTC would adversely affect other property in the vicinity were not supported by substantial evidence. . . . Specifically, Plaintiffs claim that while there is evidence in the record to support the County's findings pursuant to these provisions, this evidence is nothing more than "public clamor," which is an insufficient justification to deny a conditional use permit. Again, we agree. . . .

In the instant case, the County determined that "there was insufficient evidence provided to address the issue[] of safety . . . to grant the conditional use." In making this conclusion, the County relied on its finding that

> the neighbors have also raised the issues of safety. No matter how you characterize it this is a facility for troubled youth, and troubled youth have their problems. There is evidence in the record that these types of facilities do have escapees and sometimes escapees cause injury to persons and property. We see no evidence in the record that these issues have been addressed in a manner that will be compatible with the permitted uses in this area.

This finding is the product of public clamor. The record before the County concerning this issue consists of submissions and comments from neighboring landowners, including letters raising safety concerns and news stories of other similar residential treatment centers that did have safety issues. However, there is no record evidence detailing actual safety issues with Uintah RTC. To the contrary, there are numerous safety requirements with which Uintah RTC must comply to obtain a license to operate a group home. In addition, proposed residents would not have histories of violence or significant criminal backgrounds, and the conditional use permit granted by the Planning Commission required Plaintiffs to carry sufficient liability insurance to cover damages caused by Uintah RTC. Moreover, it is undisputed that the site factors for Uintah RTC regarding safety (utilities, medical and law enforcement response time, fire protection, distance to the hospital) are either identical to or more favorable than the same site factors for Cedar Ridge RTC. Therefore, the County's decision to deny Plaintiffs' application for a conditional use permit for a ten-person residential treatment center was arbitrary and capricious because it was impermissibly "based solely on adverse public comment."[4] *Id.*

[The court then upheld the county's decision limiting Uintah RTC to ten students, finding that the applicant had only applied for a facility of that size.]

[W]e reverse the County's decision denying the conditional use permit in its entirety and affirm the County's decision to limit Plaintiffs' conditional use permit to ten residents. We reinstate Plaintiffs' conditional use permit, as granted, with all the conditions imposed by the Planning Commission.

WE CONCUR: JUDITH M. BILLINGS, Presiding Judge and RUSSELL W. BENCH, Associate Presiding Judge.

---

4. Although not based on public clamor, the record evidence supporting the County's determination that Uintah RTC would have an adverse effect on neighboring properties is similarly unpersuasive. The trial court identified a letter from Dale Cameron, a real estate appraiser, indicating a possible decrease in market values of surrounding properties, as sufficient evidence to support the County's decision on this factor. However, the County does not cite this letter in its decision. Moreover, this letter is of questionable probative value, given that Mr. Cameron admits that his conclusion is the product of speculation and that "[a]dditional research of this issue is needed."

Notes and Comments

1. *Use Permits v. Variances.* A variance differs conceptually from a special use. The latter involves a use that the zoning ordinance envisions to be proper under certain prescribed conditions. In contrast, a variance is a departure from the specific terms of the zoning ordinance. In other words, the variance allows the landowner to do something that the zoning ordinance forbids, while the special use permit allows a use that the ordinance authorizes. *See Texaco Refining and Marketing, Inc. v. Valente,* 571 N.Y.S.2d 328, 330 (Sup. Ct. App. Div. 1991) ("Unlike a variance, a special use permit does not involve a use of property forbidden by the zoning ordinance but instead constitutes a recognition of a use which the ordinance permits under stated conditions."). Because special use permits authorize uses that are envisioned in the zoning ordinance, while variances depart from the zoning ordinances, the standard for a variance is much more stringent. *Frigault v. Town of Richfield Planning Bd.,* 128 A.D.3d 1232, 1234 (App. Div. 2015).

2. *Special Uses, Conditional Uses, and Exceptions.* The zoning device used in the *Uintah Mountains* case is referred to by various names: a special use permit, a conditional use permit, or a special exception. A special use permit is required for certain uses that the zoning ordinance authorizes but that present special problems in certain locations because of the nature of the use:

> The uses for which a special exception is required are conceptualized generally as having some deleterious effects on surrounding uses or undeveloped land in the neighborhood — or, stated differently, may be said potentially not to promote the public safety, health, morals, welfare, and prosperity and, therefore, are not appropriate to be allowed as uses of right.

Montgomery County v. Butler, 417 Md. 271, 297, 9 A.3d 824, 839 (Md. 2010).

Because the use is potentially incompatible with other nearby uses, the applicant must obtain a permit. Examples of uses for which a special use permit is often required are gasoline stations, theaters, junk-yards, churches, day care centers, funeral homes, television transmission towers, and adult book stores. Each of these uses poses externalities that, if not controlled, can affect nearby properties. Some jurisdictions have even broader provisions, stating that any use not specifically permitted may be the subject of a special use permit.

Some ordinances provide for small deviations from allowable uses under the zoning ordinance through the granting of a minimal variance of exception. For example, such an approval might allow less than a 10 percent variation from the zoning ordinance, which the zoning administrator can approve without the cost and delay associated with a special use proceeding. Many jurisdictions, however, see the terms "special use," "conditional use," and "special exception" as interchangeable

3. *Accessory Uses.* Special uses must be distinguished from another zoning term, "accessory uses." These are uses that are incidental to the permitted use authorized by the zoning ordinance, and thus allowable as a matter of right. The Iowa Supreme Court defined "accessory use" as a use "often found in conjunction with the principal use" and "so common that the ordinance could not have intended to prevent its use." *City of Okoboji v. Okoboji Barz, Inc.,* 746 N.W.2d 56, 62 (Iowa 2008). For example, the courts have held that a "basketball backboard" is an accessory use and not a separate "building" under the applicable ordinance. *Dyno v. Village of*

Johnson City, 690 N.Y.S.2d 325 (A.D. 1999); *see also Eastern Service Centers, Inc. v. Cloverland Farms Dairy, Inc.*, 744 A.2d 63 (Md. Ct. Sp. App. 2000) (convenience store is an accessory use to a gas station). While accessory uses are usually minor, some interpretations of that term can be quite broad. For example, in *Henley v. City of Youngtown Bd. of Zoning Appeals*, 735 N.E.2d 433 (Ohio 2000), transitional apartments for homeless women and children were found to be an accessory use to the principal use of a church; thus, a convent could be converted to that use.

4. *Procedures for Use Permits.* The granting of a special use permit is an adjudicative decision, and the permit can be granted only after notice and hearing. Local ordinances typically assign the granting of such permits either to a board of adjustment or to the planning commission, with the possibility of an administrative appeal to the city council or other body. In granting a special use permit, the board or commission normally must make findings of fact and can place conditions on the permit to protect neighboring properties from such things as excessive noise or traffic.

To avoid the claim that the grant of a special use permits is an exercise of unbounded discretion and thus constitutes an invalid delegation of power, the board or commission must adhere to a set of legislatively prescribed standards. In most cases, however, the courts have approved the use of standards that are quite general. *See, e.g., Whittaker & Gooding Co. v. Scio Twp.*, 332 N.W.2d 527, 532 (Mich. Ct. App. 1983) (conditions "to protect the public interest . . . and the surrounding property, and to achieve the objectives of th[e] Ordinance"). Interestingly, in *RDNT, LLC v. City of Bloomington*, 861 N.W.2d 71, 76 (Minn. 2015), the Minnesota Supreme Court commented that the "absence of more express standards" makes a special use permit more vulnerable to a finding of arbitrariness.

5. *Conditions.* Special use permits typically are approved with conditions designed to ameliorate the impacts of the particular land use. These conditions can broadly relate to the operation of the site. *See 917 Lusk v. City of Boise*, 343 P.3d 41, 45 (Idaho 2015) (commission had authority to impose parking requirements beyond the ordinary minimum required). There are, however, limits on the power to condition. For example, the condition must relate to the use of the property, rather than merely regulating the owners of the property. *See Baughman v. Board of Zoning Appeals for Harrison Twp.*, 2002 WL 1773043 (Ohio App. 2002) (condition that any split or transfer of the property would nullify the permit exceeded the township's authority). Furthermore, the condition must concern the use allowed; the power to impose a condition does not allow the local government broad discretion to remedy any problem at the site. *See Curry Inv. Co. v. Board of Zoning Adjustment*, 399 S.W.3d 106 (Mo. App. 2013) (condition requiring removal of two nonconforming outdoor signs was unreasonable where the condition did not relate to special use criteria which applied to the allowed use, a pawn shop).

Evidence in the record must support the decision to deny the permit or impose the condition. *Gursline v. Board of Supervisors of Fairfield Twp.*, 123 A.3d 1142 (Commw. Ct. 2015) (no evidence in the record supported a conclusion that a natural gas well would be harmful to the health, welfare, and safety of the neighborhood). If the permittee violates the conditions, the permit can be revoked. *See, e.g., Malibu Mountains Recreation, Inc. v. County of Los Angeles*, 79 Cal. Rptr. 2d 25 (App. 1998) (revoking conditional use permit for tennis ranch).

In *The President and Directors of Georgetown College v. District of Columbia Bd. of Zoning Adjustment*, 837 A.2d 58 (D.C. App. 2003), the college submitted a "campus plan" as part of its application for a special exception. The Board of Zoning Adjustment approved but imposed nineteen conditions intended to alleviate impacts occurring off-campus. These conditions included: (1) a freeze of the University's enrollment at the year 1990 level, (2) a requirement of a "hotline" staffed on a 24-hour basis to receive complaints about student behavior, (3) a requirement that two students and two faculty members be on the board designed to handle neighbors complaints, and (4) a requirement that the university report violations of the code of student conduct to the student's parents or guardians, to the extent permitted by law. Are all of these conditions appropriate for this type of approval?

6. *The* Uintah Mountain *Application.* Why did the court overturn the county's conclusion that the proposed facility was not compatible with other uses in the neighborhood? Was the court's reasoning convincing when it rejected the county's determination because this was a "commercial venture" that would need fences, parking, etc.? Were you convinced by the court's comparison to the earlier Cedar Ridge facility, in which the county *had* granted a conditional use permit?

7. *The Neighbors' Veto Power?* The court in *Uintah Mountain* concluded that the findings regarding the risks posed by the facility were "the product of public clamor." How does a court tell the difference between "public clamor" and legitimate expressions of public opinion?

Some state statutes authorize written protests from neighboring landowners that, if they reach a minimum percentage, change the requirements for the vote needed to amend the ordinance. These provisions are traceable to Section 5 of the Standard Zoning Enabling Act, which declares:

> In case, however, of a protest against such change, signed by the owners of 20 percent or more either of the area of the lots included in such proposed change, or of those immediately adjacent in the rear thereof extending _____ feet therefrom, or of those directly opposite thereto extending _____ feet from the street frontage of such opposite lots, such amendment shall not become effective except by the favorable vote of three-fourths of all the members of the legislative body of such municipality.

As discussed in Chapter 16, a handful of statutes go even further, requiring the consent of certain neighboring land users before the zoning ordinance can be amended. Some courts have held that these types of provisions are an unlawful delegation of legislative power and therefore unconstitutional. *See Town of Gardiner v. Stanley Orchards, Inc.*, 432 N.Y.S.2d 335, 340 (Sup. Ct. 1980); *Williams v. Whitten*, 451 S.W.2d 535, 537-38 (Tex. Ct. App. 1970).

2. Floating Zones and Contract Zones

The system of Euclidian zoning was very much a visual process centering on the use of a zoning map. Landowners could look at the map, consult the text of the zoning ordinance, and determine the types of land uses allowed on a specific property. The system thus gave prospective notice to landowners of their rights at the time the local government adopted the system. At the same time, since the zoning map views the city as a whole, some assurance existed that the "benefits and burdens" of zoning were distributed for the good of the entire community.

The need for flexibility of uses on property, however, created pressure for case-by-case determinations of land uses on specific properties and led to new types of zoning devices. Consider carefully the extent to which the type of zoning in the next case, an important one in the evolution of land use law, is inconsistent with the principles implicit in Euclidian zoning.

■ RODGERS v. VILLAGE OF TARRYTOWN
96 N.E.2d 731 (N.Y. 1951)

FULD, Judge.

This appeal, here by our permission, involves the validity of two amendments to the General Zoning Ordinance of the Village of Tarrytown, a suburban area in the County of Westchester, within twenty-five miles of New York City.

Some years ago, Tarrytown enacted a General Zoning Ordinance dividing the village into seven districts or zones — Residence A for single family dwellings, Residence B for two-family dwellings, Residence C for multiple dwellings and apartment houses, three business districts and an industrial zone. In 1947 and 1948, the board of trustees, the village's legislative body, passed the two amendatory ordinances here under attack.

The 1947 ordinance creates "A new district or class of zone . . . [to] be called 'Residence B-B'", in which, besides one- and two-family dwellings, buildings for multiple occupancy of fifteen or fewer families were permitted. The boundaries of the new type district were not delineated in the ordinance but were to be "fixed by amendment of the official village building zone map, at such times in the future as such district or class of zone is applied, to properties in this village." The village planning board was empowered to approve such amendments and, in case such approval was withheld, the board of trustees was authorized to grant it by appropriate resolution. In addition, the ordinance erected exacting standards of size and physical layouts for Residence B-B zones: a minimum of ten acres of land and a maximum building height of three stories were mandated; set-back and spacing requirements for structures were carefully prescribed; and no more than 15% of the ground area of the plot was to be occupied by buildings.

A year and a half after the 1947 amendment was enacted, defendant Elizabeth Rubin sought to have her property, consisting of almost ten and a half acres in the Residence A district, placed in a Residence B-B classification. After repeated modification of her plans to meet suggestions of the village planning board, that body gave its approval, and several months later, in December of 1948, the board of trustees, also approving, passed the second ordinance here under attack. In essence, it provides that the Residence B-B district "is hereby applied to the [Rubin] property . . . and the district or zone of said property is hereby changed to 'Residence B-B' and the official Building Zone Map of the Village of Tarrytown is hereby amended accordingly [by specification of the various parcels and plots involved]."

Plaintiff, who owns a residence on a six-acre plot about a hundred yards from Rubin's property, brought this action to have the two amendments declared invalid and to enjoin defendant Rubin from constructing multiple dwellings on her property. . . .

While stability and regularity are undoubtedly essential to the operation of zoning plans, zoning is by no means static. Changed or changing conditions call for changed plans, and persons who own property in a particular zone or use district enjoy no eternally vested right to that classification if the public interest demands otherwise. Accordingly, the power of a village to amend its basic zoning ordinance in such a way as reasonably to promote the general welfare cannot be questioned.

The Tarrytown board of trustees was entitled to find that there was a real need for additional housing facilities; that the creation of Residence B-B districts for garden apartment developments would prevent young families, unable to find accommodations in the village, from moving elsewhere; would attract business to the community; would lighten the tax load of the small homeowner, increasingly burdened by the shrinkage of tax revenues resulting from the depreciated value of large estates and the transfer of many such estates to tax-exempt institutions; and would develop otherwise unmarketable and decaying property.

The village's zoning aim being clear, the choice of methods to accomplish it lay with the board. Two such methods were at hand. It could amend the General Zoning Ordinance so as to permit garden apartments on any plot of ten acres or more in Residence A and B zones (the zones more restricted) or it could amend that Ordinance so as to invite owners of ten or more acres, who wished to build garden apartments on their properties, to apply for a Residence B-B classification. The board chose to adopt the latter procedure. That it called for separate legislative authorization for each project presents no obstacle or drawback — and so we have already held. . . . Whether we would have made the same choice is not the issue; it is sufficient that the board's decision was neither arbitrary nor unreasonable.

As to the requirement that the applicant own a plot of at least ten acres, we find nothing therein unfair to plaintiff or other owners of smaller parcels. The board undoubtedly found, as it was privileged to find, that garden apartments would blend more attractively and harmoniously with the community setting, would impose less of a burden upon village facilities, if placed upon larger tracts of land rather than scattered about in smaller units. Obviously, some definite acreage had to be chosen, and, so far as the record before us reveals, the choice of ten acres as a minimum plot was well within the range of an unassailable legislative judgment.

The charge of illegal "spot zoning" — levelled at the creation of a Residence B-B district and the reclassification of defendant's property — is without substance. Defined as the process of singling out a small parcel of land for a use classification totally different from that of the surrounding area, for the benefit of the owner of such property and to the detriment of other owners . . . "spot zoning" is the very antithesis of planned zoning. If, therefore, an ordinance is enacted in accordance with a comprehensive zoning plan, it is not "spot zoning," even though it (1) singles out and affects but one small plot *see, e.g.,* Shepard v. Village of Skaneateles, supra, 300 N.Y. 115, 89 N.E.2d 619, or (2) creates in the center of a large zone small areas or districts devoted to a different use. . . . Thus, the relevant inquiry is not whether the particular zoning under attack consists of areas fixed within larger areas of different use, but whether it was accomplished for the benefit of individual owners rather than pursuant to a comprehensive plan for the general welfare of the community. Having already noted our conclusion that the ordinances were enacted to promote a comprehensive zoning plan, it is perhaps unnecessary to add that the record negates any claim that they were designed solely for the advantage of defendant or any other particular owner. Quite apart from the circumstance that defendant did not seek the benefit of the 1947 amendment until eighteen months after its passage, the all-significant fact is that that amendment applied to the entire territory of the village and accorded each and every owner of ten or more acres identical rights and privileges.

In point of fact, there would have been no question about the validity of what was done had the board simply amended the General Zoning Ordinance so as to permit property in Residence A and Residence B zones — or, for that matter, in the other districts throughout the village — to be used for garden apartments, provided that they were built on ten-acre plots and that the other carefully planned conditions and restrictions were met. It may be conceded that, under the method which the board did adopt, no one will know, from the 1947 ordinance itself, precisely where a Residence B-B district will ultimately be located. But since such a district is simply a garden apartment development, we find nothing unusual or improper in that circumstance. The same uncertainty — as to the location of the various types of structures — would be present if a zoning ordinance were to sanction garden apartments as well as one-family homes in a Residence A district — and yet there would be no doubt as to the propriety of that procedure. Consequently, to condemn the action taken by the board in effectuating a perfectly permissible zoning scheme and to strike down the ordinance designed to carry out that scheme merely because the board had employed two steps to accomplish what may be, and usually is, done in one, would be to exalt form over substance and sacrifice substance to form. . . .

The judgment of the Appellate Division should be affirmed, with costs.

Notes and Comments

1. *Floating Zones and Euclidian Zoning.* In *Bellemeade Co. v. Priddle*, 503 S.W.2d 734, 738 (Ky. 1973), the Kentucky Supreme Court noted that "a floating zone is differentiated from a fixed ('Euclidian') zone in that the latter is a specifically defined area under the zoning ordinance, while the boundaries of the former are undefined and it 'floats' over the entire district until by appropriate action the boundaries are fixed and it becomes anchored." *See also Campion v. Board of Alderman*, 899 A.2d 542, 554 (Conn. App. 2006) ("[A] floating zone is approved in two discrete steps — first, the zone is created in the form of a text amendment, but without connection to a particular parcel of property — and second, the zone is later landed on a particular property . . ."). They are also sometimes known as "overlay zones." *See Shageen v. Cuyahoga Falls City Council*, 2010 WL 625828 (Ohio App. 2010) ("the Special or Overlay Districts are 'floating zones' that 'hover' over the city until later action 'confines' them to particular areas").

Is the concept of a "floating zone" consistent with the underlying theory behind Euclidian zoning? Doesn't Euclidian zoning pre-suppose defined boundaries that can be examined in the zoning ordinance? Could a local government adopt a floating zone that would apply to the entire jurisdiction? *See Stefanoni v. Department of Economic & Community Dev.*, 70 A.3d 61 (Conn. App. 2013) (landowners sought approval of such a floating zone for affordable housing).

2. *Judicial Approval of Floating Zones. Rodgers* is the leading case upholding the concept of the floating zone. In another early decision, *Eves v. Zoning Board of Adjustment*, 164 A.2d 7, 11 (Pa. 1960), the Pennsylvania Supreme Court rejected the concept, reasoning that because floating zones await solicitation by individual landowners, "the development itself would become the plan, which is manifestly the

antithesis of zoning 'in accordance with a comprehensive plan.'" Similarly, the New Jersey Supreme Court initially rejected the technique. *Rockhill v. Chesterfield* Township, 128 A.2d 473 (N.J. 1957). Almost every state, however, has refused to follow *Eves* and *Rockhill*, often emphasizing the need for flexibility in the development process. *See, e.g., State ex rel. Zupancic v. Schimenz*, 174 N.W.2d 533, 537 (Wis. 1970) ("The virtue of allowing private agreements to underlie zoning is the flexibility and control of the development given to a municipality to meet the ever-increasing demands for rezoning in a rapidly changing area.").

3. *Form, Substance, and Means to the Same End.* The New York Court of Appeals in *Rodgers* notes that the village could have accomplished its zoning aims through two alternative actions: (1) amending the general zoning ordinance to permit garden apartments on any ten-acre plot of land in Residence A and B zones or (2) amending the ordinance to invite owners of ten or more acres to apply for a Residence B-B classification on their property. The court concluded that invalidating the floating zone "merely because the board had employed two steps to accomplish what may be . . . done in one would be to exalt form over substance." Do you see any difference in the two methods?

Could a city council pass an amendment to the zoning ordinance establishing and defining a "floating zone" and then delegate to an administrative body, such as the planning commission, the function of approving specific proposals that "anchor" the floating zone on a specific piece of property? Relatedly, does a local government act quasi-legislatively when it "anchors" a floating zone, or is its action quasi-judicial because it is focused on the specific property? *See Heithaus v. Planning and Zoning Comm'n of the Town of Greenwich*, 779 A.2d 750, 759 (Conn. 2001) ("Unlike the special permit, a floating zone is the product of legislative action.").

4. *Where's the Plan?* The court rejects plaintiff's spot zoning claim, concluding that the ordinances were enacted to promote a comprehensive zoning plan. How did the ordinance promote such a plan? Indeed, how can you have a comprehensive plan if you use a floating zone? If the adoption of a floating zone does not constitute spot zoning, what other grounds are available to attack a floating zone?

5. *The Further Evolution of Non-Euclidian Zoning.* The floating zone was an important step in the evolution of land use controls away from the strict application of the Euclidian model. Most significantly, floating zones depart from the traditional Euclidian concept that all uses must be mapped at the time the zoning district is created. Instead, they can be decided later, and the floating zone mechanism used to implement that decision. This process, in turn, led to other attempts that lead even further away from Euclidian zoning. Won't such flexibility in the regulatory system lead to bargaining between the public agency and the land owner as to the types of development that the zone will contain? *See* Stewart E. Sterk, Structural Obstacles to Settlement of Land Use Disputes, 91 B.U. L. Rev. 227, 251 (2011) ("Floating zones and planned unit developments provide municipalities with the flexibility to negotiate deals with developers over individual projects . . .").

3. Planned Unit Developments

If a floating zone for a single use is allowable, should it make any difference whether the zone allows for multiple, mixed uses? Do those uses have to be known in advance in a "two-step" process like the one outlined in *Rodgers*?

■ PETERS v. SPEARFISH ETJ PLANNING COMMISSION

567 N.W.2d 880 (S.D. 1990)

MILLER, Chief Justice.

Landmark Realty and Development Company (Landmark) and Spring Creek Ranch appeal the trial court's construction of a zoning ordinance and its decision that the Spearfish ETJ Planning Commission (Commission), the Spearfish City Council (City) and the Lawrence County Board of Commissioners (County) exceeded their authority and jurisdiction by approving a proposed planned unit development near Spearfish, South Dakota. We affirm.

FACTS

Landmark owns a 240-acre tract of land in Lawrence County, South Dakota. The land is located within the extraterritorial jurisdiction zoning area governed by the ETJ Planning Ordinances adopted by City and County and overseen by Commission. Landmark's property is zoned A-1, general agriculture.

As required by the ETJ Planning Ordinances, Landmark requested Commission's approval of a planned unit development (PUD), Spring Creek Ranch, to be constructed on the tract of land at issue in this appeal. The proposed PUD consisted of fifty-five single family residence estates, three clusters of single family attached residences containing twenty units, one bed and breakfast inn with six to eight guest rooms, and three to six duplex cabin units. The remainder of the tract was designated as "green space" for developing walking, biking, and cross-country skiing trails, with at least fifty percent of the green space slated as "open space," consistent with the requirements for PUDs. Commission recommended approval of the proposed PUD and, after reviewing the request, City and County approved the same. . . .

DECISION

The trial court concluded ETJ Planning Ordinance §4.10.1 was ambiguous. It interpreted the ordinance to limit residential density for PUDs in an A-1, general agriculture district to one dwelling per forty acres. Based on this interpretation, the trial court concluded Commission, City and County exceeded their authority and jurisdiction in approving the proposed PUD. We agree. . . .

ETJ Planning Ordinance §4.10.1 provides:

> A planned residential development, occupying three (3) acres or more shall be permitted in any A-1, PF or SRD District by special permit.
>
> The regulations established in this section are intended to provide optional methods of land development which encourage more imaginative solutions to environmental design problems, such as cluster planning. Residential areas thus established would be characterized by a unified building and site development program, open space for recreation, and the provision for commercial, religious, educational and cultural facilities which are integrated with the treatment. In order to accomplish these objectives the customary district regulations may be modified, provided that overall population densities do not exceed the densities of specific residential districts. . . .

Landmark and Spring Creek argue the emphasized language is unambiguous and a plain reading of the ordinance allows modification of the population density of A-1, general agriculture property to accommodate a PUD. In their brief on appeal, Petitioners argued that the emphasized language is ambiguous. However, in oral argument before this Court, Petitioners switched positions and suggested that the ordinance was unambiguous and a "plain reading" of the ordinance limits the population density of a PUD constructed on A-1, general agriculture property to one dwelling per forty acres.

Our review of ETJ Planning Ordinance §4.10.1 indicates the ordinance is ambiguous as to the meaning of "residential districts." "Residential districts" is not defined in §4.10.1. The term is not applied to A-1 general agriculture property anywhere in the comprehensive zoning plan other than the disputed final sentence of §4.10.1. The only other reference to "residential districts" in the ETJ Planning Ordinances is in §3.1.5(A) to describe suburban residential, rural residential and park-forest residential property. This reference does not pertain to or reference A-1, general agriculture property.

A plain reading of the term "residential districts" results in more than one reasonable definition and leads to more than one interpretation of ETJ Ordinance §4.10.1. The ordinance's language indicates that the customary district regulations may be waived for a proposed PUD but overall population density requirements may not. The ordinance does not make clear whether the population density for a proposed PUD is to be measured by the density governing the three districts which specifically allow PUDs (A-1, general agriculture, park forest, or suburban residential) or the three zoning districts specifically referred to as residential districts (suburban residential, rural residential, or park-forest residential) in other zoning ordinances. Absent an indication of which population density applies to a proposed PUD, the appropriate population density ranges from one dwelling per 7500 square feet in suburban residential districts to one dwelling per forty acres in A-1, general agriculture districts, depending on the understanding of the disputed ordinance. This wide range of possible population densities allowed by the ordinance's language results in an ambiguity. Any argument that the ordinance is not ambiguous belies the reality that the plain language of the ordinance results in more than one reasonable understanding of the PUD requirements. The trial court's conclusion ETJ Ordinance §4.10.1 was ambiguous as a matter of law was proper. Having determined the ordinance to be ambiguous, we must now determine the proper construction to be given to it. . . .

We agree with the trial court's construction of ETJ Planning Ordinance §4.10.1 that a PUD is subject to the population density limitations applicable to the district in which it is proposed. PUDs are allowed by special permit in three districts: A-1, park forest and suburban residential districts. Though the ordinance authorizing PUDs refers to "residential districts" as the basis for determining population density, PUDs are not allowed in all residential districts. A logical reading of the ordinance suggests that the population density limitations apply to those specific districts in which PUDs are allowed. The population density for a PUD is determined based on whether the PUD is proposed in an A-1, park forest or suburban residential district and limited to the population density for that specific district. Accordingly, Landmark's proposed PUD is limited to a population density of one dwelling per forty acres because of the property's status as A-1, general agriculture. . . .

Our interpretation is further supported by the fact that without population density limitations for PUDs in A-1, general agriculture districts, general agriculture districts would effectively be abolished. By removing the population density require-ments for agriculture districts, the very nature and customary uses of the districts become unpractical. The exception allowing for PUDs was not intended to abandon A-1, general agriculture districts, as evidenced by the zoning regulations specific recognition of the necessity of agriculture districts in the overall development and planning for the City and County. Our interpretation of ETJ Planning Ordinance §4.10.1 is consistent with the zoning purposes of both A-1, general agriculture dis-tricts and PUDs without sacrificing the purpose of one district at the expense of the other.

Despite the population density limitations currently affecting the proposed PUD in this case, Landmark and Spring Creek are not without a remedy. The dis-puted property may be rezoned as a residential district compatible with the popu-lation density necessary to support the PUD. . . . If City and County intended the PUD ordinances to replace the necessity of rezoning to higher population density districts in cases such as the Spring Creek development, we respectfully suggest the zoning ordinances be amended to so indicate. . . .

Affirmed.

SABERS, AMUNDSON, KONENKAMP, and GILBERTSON, JJ., concur.

Notes and Comments

1. *Flexibility Provided by PUDs.* A planned unit development (PUD) "is a zoning district in which a planned mix of residential, commercial, and even industrial use is sanctioned subject to restrictions calculated to achieve compatible and efficient use of land." *Brookview Properties, LLC v. Plainfield Plan Comm'n,* 15 N.E.3d 48, 50 (Ind. App. 2014). The use of PUDs marked a further large step away from the rigidity of Euclidian zoning. One court described it as allowing for a unified plan of develop-ment as an alternative to traditional zoning requirements. *Board of County Comm'rs of County of Boulder v. Hygiene Fire Protection Dist.,* 221 P.3d 1063, 1068 (Colo. 2009). However, the PUD concept unquestionably draws from such land use tools as special use permits and floating zones discussed earlier in this chapter.

The traditional zoning ordinance was directed at development on a lot-by-lot basis within the jurisdiction. In later decades, however, particularly after World War II, large-scale developments of subdivisions became the norm. Developers and local jurisdictions were faced with designing the future use of large tracts of undeveloped land. PUDs can be used for small pieces of property, but the flexibility that they provide makes them particularly suitable for large, mixed-use developments. *See, e.g,* *Woodland Manor Associates v. Keeney,* 713 A.2d 806 (R.I. 1998) (describing a PUD that included "various types of buildings to be combined as an integrated whole, with construction to occur in phases: phase 1, an apartment complex (Woodland Manor I); phase 2, a housing facility for the elderly (Woodland Manor II); phase 3, a nursing home (Coventry Health Center); and phase 4, a condominium complex (Woodland Manor III))."

2. *The Underlying Zoning.* Keep in mind that PUDs are part of an overall zoning ordinance, not an independent method of land use approval. Thus, it is perhaps unsurprising that the court in *Peters* viewed the PUD as constrained by the under-lying zoning. The Supreme Court of South Carolina in *Mikell v. County of Charleston,* 687 S.E.2d 326, 330 (S.C. 2009) reached much the same result, finding it "highly

implausible" that the County intended that a PUD could "completely vitiate the maximum density requirements set forth [for AG-10 Districts]."

3. *Benefits of PUDs.* In a leading case upholding the use of PUDs, *Cheney v. Village 2 at New Hope, Inc.*, 241 A.2d 81 (Pa. 1968), the Pennsylvania Supreme Court articulated the benefits of PUDs:

> [W]ith the increasing popularity of large scale residential developments, particularly in suburban areas, it has become apparent to many local municipalities that land can be more efficiently used, and developments more aesthetically pleasing, if zoning regulations focus on density requirements rather than on specific rules for each individual lot. . . . The ultimate goal of this so-called density or cluster concept of zoning is achieved when an entire self-contained little community is permitted to be built within a zoning district, with the rules of density controlling not only the relation of private dwellings to open space, but also the relation of homes to commercial establishments such as theaters, hotels, restaurants, and quasi-commercial uses such as schools and churches.

241 A.2d at 83. Other advantages may include lower costs as infrastructure costs are minimized and roads concentrated, additional open space for individual owners, and the inclusion of affordable housing.

PUDs also allow for increased environmental protection. *See Association of Rural Residents v. Kitsap County*, 4 P.3d 115, 119 n.3 (Wash. 2000) ("A PUD is essentially a mechanism which allows property owners the option of clustering or configuring lots in a plat to avoid development in sensitive areas, create open space, or achieve other environmental or aesthetic amenities."); Daniel R. Mandelker, Legislation for Planned Unit Developments and Master Planned Communities, 40 Urb. Law. 419, 421 (2008) (noting that PUDs can "provide usable open space by requiring common open space in return for 'clustering' housing elsewhere in the project"); John R. Nolon, An Environmental Understanding of the Local Land Use System, 45 Envtl. L. Rep. News & Analysis 10125, 10230 (2015) ("PUD provisions often require developers to mitigate the impacts of their projects by setting aside significant and usable open space . . .").

4. *Procedures for Approving a PUD.* How must a PUD be implemented? *See State ex rel. Marsalek v. Council of the City of South Euclid*, 855 N.E.2d 811 (Ohio 2006) (employing conditional use permit to establish PUD); *Peterson v. City of Clemson*, 439 S.E.2d 317 (S.C. Ct. App. 1993) (approving a two-step PUD process in which the city first adopts an ordinance permitting a PUD district and then later rezones a particular parcel of land pursuant to specific plans meeting the city's development regulations). Some decisions hold that a city cannot (1) pass an ordinance that amends the text of the zoning code to generally authorize a planned unit development district, and then (2) leave it to the planning commission to approve the specific location of the PUD. *Lutz v. City of Longview*, 520 P.2d 1374 (Wash. 1974).

5. *The Downside of PUDs: Arbitrariness, Non-Uniformity, or Spot Zoning?* Because PUDs can embrace a variety of uses in a development, they could be challenged on the basis that approval or denial of a PUD is a purely arbitrary decision by the local jurisdiction, one made without standards to guide it. In *Tri-State Generation & Transmission Co. v. City of Thornton*, 647 P.2d 670, 678 (Colo. 1982), the Colorado Supreme Court noted that the "same flexibility which is the primary virtue of a PUD ordinance also results in a loss of certainty and a concomitant concern with the

misuse and abuse of discretionary authority. Consequently, courts have generally required that standards be incorporated into a planned development ordinance in order to protect against arbitrary state action." What kind of standards could prevent this type of arbitrariness?

Another legal challenge to PUDs argues that mixing various uses violates the statutory requirement that zones be "uniform" in nature, a requirement that originates in Section Two of the Standard Zoning Enabling Act. The requirement "precludes case-by-case variance of regulatory requirements . . . in a given district." *MacKenzie v. Planning & Zoning Comm'n of the Town of Monroe*, 77 A.3d 904, 922 (Conn. App. 2013); *see Orinda Homeowners Committee v. Board of Supervisors*, 90 Cal. Rptr. 88 (Ct. App. 1970) (rejecting the claim). PUDs are also open to the charge of spot zoning. *See Citizens for Mount Vernon v. City of Mount Vernon*, 947 P.2d 1208, 1216 (Wash. 1997) ("if a planned unit development can be placed at any location within a city regardless of the underlying or surrounding zoning . . . it might raise issues of spot zoning and it might undermine the overall zoning plan"). For the most part, however, these potential challenges have not been successful.

6. *Bargaining and Contract Zoning.* As consideration of land uses on a case-by-case basis increased, such as when PUDs are used, it was inevitable that local municipalities and developers would engage in discussions about the conditions under which a particular land use would be approved. *See Palm Beach Polo, Inc. v. Village of Wellington*, 918 So. 2d. 988, 990 (Fla. App. 2006) (PUD "is an agreement between the land owner and the zoning authority, and the terms of development are negotiated between the parties in accordance with the conditions set forth in the governing ordinances."). Gradually, the types of conditions that municipalities required for such approvals became quite detailed, and cities sought to ensure the implementation of those conditions through a binding legal document. However, a long-standing principle of constitutional law stood in their way: many state constitutions had been interpreted to prevent cities from "contracting away" or "bargaining away" the police power.

Contract zoning issues arise when a local government enters into an agreement with a developer whereby the government extracts a performance or promise from the developer in exchange for its agreement to rezone the property, *City of White Settlement v. Super Wash, Inc.*, 198 S.W.3d 770, 772 n.2 (Tex. 2006) ("'Contract zoning' occurs when a governmental entity, such as a city, enters into a binding contract in which it promises to zone land in a certain way in exchange for a landowner's promise to use the land in a particular manner."). If the parties reach a formal agreement prior to the rezoning, third parties (perhaps neighbors) who challenge the rezoning can argue that the agreement constitutes illegal contract zoning. In the absence of specific statutory authority allowing such agreements, courts may find such actions illegal.

What is it about "bargaining" over land use approvals that might suggest that the outcome will not serve the public interest? Is it, as some courts conclude, a concern that reaching a bargain will short-cut otherwise required legislative procedures? *Dacy v. Village of Ruidoso*, 845 P.2d 793 (N.M. 1992). Or is the concern over the substance of the bargain? *See City of Knoxville v. Ambrister*, 263 S.W.2d 528 (Tenn. 1953) (rezoning agreements present opportunities for fraud and undue influence). If a court outlaws contract zoning, will the ruling mean that parties will not be able to bargain with the jurisdiction and reach agreements concerning the circumstances under which land use approvals and developments will occur? Or can creative law-yering overcome this "obstacle"?

7. *Bargaining and Development Agreements.* In recent years the practice of nego-tiating "development agreements" for both large- and small-scale developments has grown rapidly. Sean F. Nolon, Bargaining for Development Post-*Koontz*: How the Supreme Court Invaded Local Government, 67 Fla. L. Rev. 171, 199 (2015) ("[F]loat-ing zones, planned unit developments and developer agreements are a few examples of zoning instruments that rely on negotiation to create value for property owners and the community.") Development agreements are discussed in detail in Chapter 10. The law and economics literature discussed in Chapter 1 would encourage bargaining as a means of assuring efficiency. Assuming that the traditional concern over contract zon-ing has some merit, should the promotion of efficiency outweigh that concern?

4. Site Plan Review

As we have seen in the development of floating zones, PUDs and contract zoning, municipalities have utilized new zoning devices that expand their discretion to tailor the approval of developments with specific conditions that ameliorate adverse impacts. This recognition that individual developments pose idiosyncratic problems requiring a case-by-case examination also extends to permitted uses under zoning ordinances. Site plan review serves this review function.

■ SUMMA HUMMA ENTERPRISES, LLC v. TOWN OF TILTON
151 N.H. 75, 849 A.2d 146 (N.H. 2004)

DUGGAN, J.

The plaintiff, Summa Humma Enterprises, LLC d/b/a MB Tractor, appeals an order of the Superior Court (*Smukler, J.*) upholding the denial of its application to amend its site plan by the defendants, Town of Tilton and Town of Tilton Planning Board (board). We affirm. . . .

The plaintiff is a commercial business engaged in heavy equipment sales and service. The business is located approximately one-half mile west of the intersection of Interstate 93 and Route 3 in a commercial zoning district in Tilton. The plaintiff, seeking to install a ninety-foot flagpole to fly a 960 square-foot American flag, filed an application to amend its site plan with the board.

At a December 3, 2002 public hearing, the board reviewed the plaintiff's appli-cation. The board's regulations set forth the purposes served by site plan review, which govern the board's review of site plans. The purposes are:

> a. To provide for the safe and attractive development . . . of the site and to guard against such conditions as would involve danger or injury to health, safety, or prosperity by reason of:
> . . . . (3) Undesirable and preventable elements of pollution such as noise . . .
> b. To provide for the harmonious and aesthetically pleasing development of the municipality and its environs; . . . [and]

h. To include such provisions as will tend to create conditions favorable for health, safety, convenience and prosperity.

Based on these regulations, the board noted the following concerns with the plaintiff's site plan: (1) the required lighting of the flag at night; (2) a ninety-foot flagpole would exceed the zoning ordinance's height limitations on buildings; (3) the noise associated with the flag in windy conditions; (4) the safety concerns from ice falling or the pole itself falling; and (5) improper use of the flag for advertising.

The board directed several questions to the plaintiff's representatives, Chris Rice and Jason Kahn. Mr. Rice was unable to answer the board's questions about the size of the pole, the effect on the neighborhood of the required lighting and the potential noise.

In answering why a ninety-foot flagpole was required, Mr. Kahn first stated the purpose was to draw awareness to the flag. The board's minutes also reflect that "Mr. Kahn stated [the plaintiff] was trying to develop a brand presence. [The plaintiff] was trying to develop this brand as one identity and a 90 foot flag was one of his identities." In addressing the safety and noise concerns, Mr. Kahn stated that the manufacturer could provide information about the noise generated by flags flying in the wind and that the flagpole would be "fully engineered." He also stated that ice would not adhere to the flag and that the pole was tapered.

The board approved the proposal conditioned on a height restriction of fifty feet, the same height restriction in the town's zoning ordinance for buildings. The board imposed the height restriction based upon concerns about safety, noise and aesthetics.

The plaintiff appealed the board's decision to the superior court [which upheld the board]. . . .

The plaintiff first argues that the superior court erred in upholding the board's decision because there is no ordinance that precludes the installation of a ninety-foot flagpole. The plaintiff points to the zoning ordinance's specific height limitation for buildings to argue that the lack of a controlling statute or ordinance regulating the height of flagpoles precludes the board from denying the application to amend the site plan. We disagree.

Site plan review is designed to insure that uses permitted by a zoning ordinance are "constructed on a site in such a way that they fit into the area in which they are being constructed without causing drainage, traffic, or lighting problems." 15 P. Loughlin, *New Hampshire Practice, Land Use Planning and Zoning* §30.01, at 425 (2000). Site plan review is also "designed to assure that sites will be developed in a safe and attractive manner and in a way that will not involve danger or injury to the health, safety, or prosperity of abutting property owners or the general public." *Id.* §30.02, at 427. These purposes are "accomplished by subjecting the plan to the very expertise expected of a planning board in cases where it would not be feasible to set forth in the ordinance a set of specific requirements upon which a building inspector could readily grant or refuse a permit." *Id.*

Site plan review, however, is limited. It "does not give the planning board the authority to deny a particular use simply because it does not feel that the proposed use is an appropriate use of the land. Whether the use is appropriate is a zoning question." *Id.* §30.09, at 437. Nevertheless, the board has authority under site plan review to impose requirements and conditions that are reasonably related to land use goals and considerations within its purview. *See Nestor v. Town of Meredith*, 138 N.H. 632, 635, 644 A.2d 548 (1994); Loughlin, supra §30.09, at 438 (noting that the board "can and must condition approval upon installation of landscaping, curbing, and drainage facilities or other items which will make the proposed building fit into the area").

Here, the board approved the plaintiff's proposed flagpole with a fifty-foot height restriction. The board did not prohibit the plaintiff from using the property in a manner allowed by the zoning ordinance. Rather, it cited concerns with the safety, noise and aesthetics of the flagpole and conditioned the plaintiff's authorized use of the property to ensure that it was "developed in a safe and attractive manner" and would not involve "danger or injury to the health, safety, or prosperity of abutting property owners or the general public." Loughlin, *supra* §30.02, at 427. Where the role of site plan review is to ensure that uses permitted by the zoning ordinance are appropriately designed and developed, restricting the board's authority to the specific limitations imposed by ordinances and statutes would render the site plan review process a mechanical exercise. The planning board properly exercised its authority to impose conditions that are reasonably related to the purposes set forth in the site plan regulations; namely, the "safe and attractive development" of the site. Therefore, the superior court did not err in upholding the board's decision.

The plaintiff next argues that the superior court erred in upholding the board's decision because the board had no evidence regarding the potential noise created by the flag or the existence of safety concerns from the flagpole falling over or ice falling from it. We disagree.

Here, the superior court noted that the inquiry is "whether the [plaintiff] presented sufficient evidence to the board to sustain its burden and, if so, whether that evidence was sufficient to compel a finding in its favor." The only evidence presented to the board was the testimony of the plaintiff's representatives, Mr. Rice and Mr. Kahn. Mr. Rice was unable to address any of the board's concerns. Although Mr. Kahn stated that the manufacturer could provide information about the noise from the flag and the engineering of the flagpole, he did not provide any documentation addressing the noise, safety or lighting concerns. Based on this record, the superior court did not err in holding that "the board reasonably determined that the [plaintiff] failed to sustain its burden of addressing its concerns about safety, noise, and the effect on the area aesthetics of lighting [the flag and flagpole]." . . .

Affirmed.

BRODERICK, DALIANIS and GALWAY, JJ., concurred; NADEAU, J., dissented. NADEAU, J., dissenting.

I cannot join in today's holding, because I believe the planning board acted unreasonably in failing to afford the plaintiff a meaningful opportunity to address its concerns. . . .

In this case, the planning board meeting was held on December 3, 2002. The minutes of that meeting reflect that the board peppered the plaintiff and its representative with questions and voiced concerns regarding the noise, safety, and aesthetics of the plaintiff's flagpole. For example, board member Katherine Dawson "wondered if [the flag] wouldn't be noisy." Another board member, Michelle Jackson, noted, "she didn't feel the residents would want to see a flag the size of their homes or hear the noise it would make during windy conditions." Sandy Plessner, another board member, "asked what one would do if the flag became covered with ice and it were to get windy. [She] stated the ice could break off and fall to the ground." Ms. Dawson "stated the possibility existed for a flag pole to fall over in an ice storm." At the close of public comment, the board approved only a fifty-foot flagpole. The following day, the board issued its notice of decision. The superior court affirmed the ruling, noting that the plaintiff "failed to sustain its burden of addressing [the board's] concerns about safety, noise, and the effect on the area aesthetics."

I disagree with the superior court's ruling, as it ignores the reasons why the plaintiff failed to meet its burden the night of the board meeting in the first instance. First, at the time the plaintiff sought site plan approval, no zoning regulation prohibited the installation of a flagpole, nor had any restriction been enacted by the board limiting the height of flagpoles to fifty feet. Given that the plaintiff's proposal was not subject to any particular zoning or planning regulation, I cannot, unlike the majority, fault the plaintiff for being ill-prepared to answer the board's flagpole concerns the night of the meeting.

Second, especially when, as here, the concerns of the board are wholly speculative, the plaintiff should have been afforded more time to respond. To hold otherwise requires applicants for site plan review to anticipate and answer the whims of each board member in order to ensure that their proposals are approved. I find this result untenable, because the review process does not confer unfettered discretion upon local planning boards. . . .

As such, I would not penalize the plaintiff for being unable to answer the issues raised by the board members during the meeting. Rather, I believe the board should have afforded the plaintiff more time to respond to its concerns before acting upon the site plan. That the plaintiff may not have requested more time to redress the board's concerns is of no import. . . .

Notes and Comments

1. *Zoning, Site Plans, and Subdivisions.* The fact that a developer wants to build a structure that is a permitted use under the zoning ordinance does not necessarily mean that the development will go forward. It may still be subject to site plan approval under an ordinance like the one at issue in *Town of Tilton.* Even more significantly, if the development will subdivide land, it will likely be subject to extensive regulation under state subdivision laws, even though the use sought by the development is permitted under local zoning. Subdivision regulation is the subject of the next chapter in this casebook.

2. *The Purpose of Site Plan Approval.* Site plan approval affords the local jurisdiction an opportunity to undertake a detailed analysis of the precise features of the development project. The review focuses on such factors as building layout, placement of roads, and aesthetic features. *Prudential Ins. Co. of America v. Board of Appeals of Westwood,* 502 N.E.2d 137 (Mass. App. Ct. 1986) (site plans disclose "the specifics of the project, including the proposed location of buildings, parking areas, and other installations on the land"); *Mountain Valley Mall Associates v. Municipality of Conway,* 745 A.2d 481 (N.H. 2000) (site plan adequately dealt with parking, off-street loading of goods, pedestrian and wheelchair access, snow storage, and green space). Of course, once an applicant receives site plan approval, its development must conform to the conditions of that approval.

A local body acts in a quasi-judicial capacity in considering a site plan. *Willoughby v. Planning Bd. of the Twp. of Deptford*, 703 A.2d 668, 671 (N.J. Super. Ct. App. Div. 1997). As a result, it must accord due process to the applicant by giving him or her a fair hearing. Indeed, the hearing itself can become quite complex if the issues are contested. The result of the site plan evaluation is likely to be a series of additional conditions that the applicant must meet in order to build. Did the applicant receive a fair hearing in *Town of Tilton?*

3. *The Scope of Discretion I.* If opponents hotly contest approval of the development, it is critical for the applicant to determine the extent of the discretion that the site review ordinance gives to the local entity. In *Town of Tilton*, did the court correctly determine that the city retained power to regulate the height of the flagpole? What about the landowner's argument that — unlike the uses spelled out in a zoning ordinance — the height of the flagpole was not subject to other zoning restrictions? What about the fact that the zoning ordinance *did* regulate the height of buildings, but did not regulate the height of flagpoles? What if an airport is going to tear down buildings surrounding the airport — would that action trigger site review? The Vermont Supreme Court said no in *In re Burlington Airport Permit*, 103 A3d 153 (Vt. 2014), finding that the demolition was not a "change in use" that triggered site plan review.

4. *The Scope of Discretion II.* Are there other limits on the discretion that may be exercised under site review? In *CMB Capital v. Planning & Zoning Comm'n*, 4 A.3d 1256 (Conn. App. 2010), the commission denied an application for site plan approval in part because the chairman of the sewage authority had written that he had "concerns" about whether the sewage flow from the project would exceed design capacity. The court held that the commission could not deny the site plan based on this "preliminary" opinion. Rather, "the commission was required to grant the plaintiff's amended application on the condition that the plaintiff obtain approval from the authority." *Id.* at 1265. *See also Alesi v. Warren County Bd. of Comm'rs*, 24 N.E.2d 667, 677 (Ohio App. 2014) ("Although the Zoning Code allows the BOCC to determine the impact of a proposed site plan on local roadways, the BOCC exceeded its authority by requiring Pilot to submit another traffic-impact to ODOT — a state entity over which it has no control.").

What if the application meets the 8.3-foot setback requirement in the local ordinance but the planning board imposes a 30-foot setback to separate the proposed building from a neighbor? Does the planning board have authority to impose the greater setback? The court thought so in *Muldoon v. Planning Bd. of Marblehead*, 892 N.E.2d 353 (Mass. Ct. App. 2008). Do you agree if one purpose of the increased setback is to avoid "needlessly obliterating a major portion" of the neighbor's view?

5. *The Tension with Permitted Uses.* Many of the disputes over site review arise from the tension that exists between the concept of permitted uses under zoning ordinances, which allow a landowner to build as a matter of right, and the locality's retention of discretion under a site review ordinance. How far does the site review process intrude into the concept of a permitted use? Some courts have held that site review ordinances may not be used to deny a project that is a permitted use, while others disagree. *Compare Wesley Inv. Co. v. County of Alameda*, 198 Cal. Rptr. 872, 876 (Ct. App. 1984) ("The ordinances do not provide for an unbridled right to erect a retail store in a C-1 zone. Rather, the listing of permitted uses . . . is qualified by the provision . . . subjecting certain projects to site development review."); *GBT Realty Corp. v. City of Shreveport*, 180 So. 3d 458 (La. App. 2015) ("A municipality retains the

discretion to deny a site . . . plan submitted in accordance with use by right zoning, but that denial is subject to strict scrutiny.").

Could a local zoning code enact a site plan provision stating that "[n]o development shall be approved unless the plan . . . is compatible with the land uses surrounding the site"? Would that language give the local jurisdiction authority to deny a site plan on the grounds of incompatibility even though the site plan was for a permitted use? *See Colorado Springs v. Securecare Self Storage*, 10 P.3d 1244 (Colo. 2000) (upholding the denial of site plan for a service station on grounds of incompatibility with the surrounding neighborhood even though service stations were a permitted use in that zone). Does such a decision subvert the zoning for an area?

In *Richmond Co. v. City of Concord*, 821 A.2d 1059 (N.H. 2003), the New Hampshire Supreme Court upheld the denial of a site plan for a retail shopping center. The court upheld the denial, in part, on evidence that the shopping center would demolish all existing structures on the property, some of which had historical value. The project was consistent with the zoning on the property. Is this an appropriate use of a site plan ordinance?

6. *The Burden of Site Review.* Bearing in mind that the application for site review is for a permitted or otherwise approved use, consider the extent of the review summarized in *Trudy's Texas Star, Inc. v. City of Austin*, 307 S.W.3d 894, 897 (Tex. App. 2010):

> Once a site plan is filed, the applicant has 180 days to convince the City to approve it, although the deadline may be extended. The summary-judgment evidence reflects that site plan approval can be a tedious and somewhat unpredictable process. The filed plan is assigned to a team of City "reviewers" each of whom represent different areas of land use planning expertise (e.g., transportation, water quality, etc.). The reviewers are each required to provide "comments" — basically, objections or concerns regarding the site plan that, the record indicates, might or might not be based on any identifiable requirement of law — by a specified deadline. Once the reviewers generate comments, the applicant has the opportunity to address them, prepare an updated or amended site plan, and go through the review process again. This submission may elicit further comments and, depending on the applicant's ability or remaining desire to accommodate them, the process may continue for still more rounds of site plan updates and comments. Once the City reviewers' comments have been addressed to their satisfaction, the comments are deemed "cleared," denoting that the City is satisfied that any concerns have been resolved, and the site plan is approved. Once the site plan is approved, the site plan is "released" after the applicant posts security and the time for any appeal of the approval expires . . . Release of the approved site plan is the linchpin in the applicant's ability to obtain the remaining permits and approvals required to construct the improvement. A building permit may not be issued until the site plan is released.

See also State ex rel. Duncan v. Middlefield, 120 Ohio St. 3d 313, 314, 898 N.E.2d 952, 954 (2008) ("After Duncan's engineer submitted another site plan, the village engineer detailed over 150 items that were missing from the plan.").

Is this prudent regulation or bureaucracy run amuck?

3

Subdivision Regulation

A. INTRODUCTION

1. From Plats to Planning

A subdivision is a legal division of land, and the origins of subdivision law were largely concerned with accurately depicting the actual division of land. Originally, property divisions used "metes and bounds" property descriptions, a method that describes property by employing the geographical features of the area along with directions and distances. However, metes and bounds property descriptions generated mistakes and disputes, and they resulted in time-consuming and expensive property title searches and surveying in order to permit conveyances.

Modern subdivision review brought use of the so-called "platting" statutes. These allowed land transfer and recordation according to a plat (a map showing divisions of land) and parcel number. This newer process was much more accurate.

As land development procedures evolved, another large concern arose. Although communities typically adopted a vague, conceptual plan, usually in the form of a comprehensive zoning ordinance, individual subdivisions were often not well thought out. Gradually, the law responded by requiring increased planning and in-depth examination of proposed subdivisions. Contemporary subdivision review often generates a de facto specific community plan. This plan arises when the governing body first considers the type of uses and structures, as well as their relationship to the site, and then establishes planning criteria that the subdivision must meet.

2. The Purposes and Components of Substantive Review

Modern subdivision regulation has a number of purposes. The five central components of subdivision regulation are: (1) discretionary review to allow disclosure and mitigation of environmental harm; (2) assurance of the adequacy of infrastructure; (3) opportunity to shift the cost of development and infrastructure to the developer through the imposition of conditions on a subdivision and permit approval; (4) review to ensure compliance with planning and subdivision standards; and (5) assurance that the site is well planned, attractive, safe, and compatible with adjacent development.

The first component has become increasingly significant over the last 40 years. The process of subdivision review often uncovers adverse environmental impacts of a proposed project and identifies mitigation measures to alleviate those impacts. The subdivision review also is typically a trigger point for environmental review in those states that have environmental assessment laws, which are discussed in Chapter 14 of this casebook.

A second important function of subdivision review is its focus on whether the infrastructure is adequate to support the development. Infrastructure includes the public facilities and services necessary to service that development. The subdivision process should identify any problems in providing transit, reducing or managing traffic congestion, and providing water and sewer services, schools, parks, and libraries. Flood control and emergency services, including police and fire protection, also are typically addressed. The subdivision review process results in the local government imposing conditions on the approval of the subdivision that address site design and infrastructure, and the developer's obligations to fund or provide that infrastructure.

The subdivision review process has been successful in affording public officials the opportunity to undertake discretionary review of individual projects. These officials actively review the impacts of the project's design, impose mitigating conditions, order design modifications, and assign infrastructure costs to the developer. The perceived success of this discretionary process has spawned similar procedures for the review of site plans in cases not involving any subdivision approval, a topic discussed in Chapter 2.

In the next chapter, you will study another topic closely related to subdivision review: the issue of how infrastructure for a development can be financed. In particular, the chapter will focus on how municipalities assign the costs of new development through the application of permit conditions as well as through other, innovative financing techniques. By contrast, the current chapter focuses on how local governments undertake subdivision review and the scope of their review authority.

3. Timing and Vesting

One important problem posed by subdivision regulation concerns the timing of the review process, which may take several years to complete for large projects. Developers first seek tentative (or preliminary) approval of their subdivision tract. After review, the government will approve a tentative map that sets forth the proposed conditions of approval. The developer then responds to the problems and conditions identified, often altering the project to comply with those conditions. Finally, the developer seeks approval of a final subdivision map. Once that approval is received, the developer can seek building permits for the subdivision.

Both state and local standards, however, can change during this review period, as state legislatures or local governments adopt new or amended zoning, planning, or subdivision design criteria. To avoid these changes in the regulatory standards, developers may seek to acquire "vested rights" to complete their project or at least to avoid imposition of new development conditions. Conversely, until a local government completes the review of a proposed subdivision, it may not be aware of the seriousness of the environmental impacts or the infrastructure problems that the development presents and, based on this new awareness, it may seek to change the standards applicable to the development. Accordingly, local governments often prefer to withhold the vesting of any right to complete a development until late in the regulatory process.

The struggle for early or late vesting has occurred in every jurisdiction and will be reviewed in this chapter. As you will see, one legislative response has been the passage of so-called permit streamlining legislation. This legislation sets strict timetables in which local governments must complete their subdivision review process, often changing the common law vesting rules.

4. Efficiency, Politics, and Reform

Theoretically, the subdivision review process provides an effective mechanism for regulating the development of land. The process, however, was designed to achieve goals that may be difficult for communities to attain. For example, the credibility of the process may be threatened if politicians attempt to interfere, for political reasons, with the planning commission's or the planning board's exercise of its responsibilities.

The political interference may reflect a development policy that is quite different from the officially adopted plan and subdivision regulations in the particular jurisdiction. The technique of variances from subdivision standards, just like variances from zoning as described in Chapter 2, can be employed to depart from otherwise uniform planning requirements. Finally, the system of campaign contributions may cause citizens to question whether the regulatory outcome reflected the private interest of a developer rather than the public interest.

These situations raise ethical questions, and a central theme of this text is its focus on the ethical issues posed by land use regulation. Conflicts of interest comprise one type of ethical issue. In addition, there also exist questions regarding the ethical behavior both of developers and opponents of development. For example, a developer may threaten to bring bad faith litigation against opposing groups through the use of so-called "strategic lawsuits against public participation" or "SLAPP suits" (addressed in Chapter 6), or through litigation against the regulating agency threatening damage exposure and heavy litigation costs. At the same time, project opponents may oppose development of any sort on a particular property, in apparent disregard of the Fifth Amendment's limitation on the extent of government regulation, or they may litigate simply as a delaying tactic.

This chapter, as well as later chapters, will explore whether the subdivision system and the development process generally may be reformed to address such concerns. Such reforms might include increased specificity of the regulatory instruments, enhanced scrutiny in judicial review, or even deregulation of the land use control process.

Ultimately, the subdivision process must be evaluated for its ability to achieve specific societal objectives. Many of its objectives, such as protecting the environment or ensuring adequate housing, may be goals that are unpopular with the current democratic majority in the jurisdiction. Is it really possible for a planning commission to bring about housing produced for the poor, along with improved schools? Can a local government protect natural resources and, at the same time, ensure the availability of adequate infrastructure? You be the judge.

B. JURISDICTION AND DEFINITIONS

A threshold jurisdictional question in subdivision review is one of statutory interpretation. What is the definition of a "subdivision" that triggers subdivision review?

■ LOFTIN v. LANGSDON
813 S.W.2d 475 (Tenn. Ct. App. 1991)

LEWIS, Judge. . . .

Loftin purchased a large tract of land in the Rock Springs Community of Maury County in 1988. A farmhouse sat on the back of the property, and an easement for a driveway or lane ran from the public road to the highway. Although the deed showed the easement for this driveway to be 60 feet wide, only a narrow lane was passable at the time Loftin purchased the property.

In preparation of his plan to divide and resell a portion of the property, Loftin made major improvements to the land. He cleared the brush from much of the easement, and he graded and re-cherted the lane. To facilitate drainage, he dug ditches along both sides of the lane. He also installed a six inch water pipe along the length of the easement and made arrangements with representatives of the Duck River Electric Membership Corporation to have two poles and a power line installed on the property adjacent to the easement. Loftin made all of these improvements at great expense to himself in anticipation of realizing a higher profit when the property was sold.

Loftin divided this improved portion of his property into 18 separate tracts. He named the lane to the farm house Beasley Lane. Thirteen of the tracts ranged in size from 5.16 to 7.63 acres and fronted on Beasley Lane. Loftin planned to sell the tracts at auction on 9 June 1990.

Pursuant to this plan, he advertised the upcoming auction in the local newspaper, *The Daily Herald.* The ad displayed a map of the available tracts complete with roads and described the property as follows:

These tracts lay level to gentle rolling with plenty of good shade trees and are suitable for any style home. All tracts have good building sites, city water available, good building restrictions. These tracts are adjoining 20 tracts that were sold in December 1989 that have several very nice homes already built or under construction.

[Handwritten margin notes: "-18 tracts", "-Improved streets", "-Advertised in paper"]

Judy Langsdon, Director of Community Development for Maury County, became aware of Loftin's plans by reading the ad in the Sunday paper. Her attention was captured by the designation on the map of a road called Beasley Lane. Since she knew there was no road in that area by that name, she assumed that Loftin had constructed a new road. This action, she believed, brought Loftin's project under the Planning Commission's subdivision regulations.

After confirmation from the Maury County Road Superintendent that Beasley Lane was not a public right-of-way, Langsdon contacted Loftin and advised him that he could not proceed with his auction without prior approval from the Planning Commission. . . .

Loftin commenced this action on 1 June 1990. He asked the court for a declaratory judgment that his division and sale of the property did not constitute a subdivision under Tenn. Code Ann. §13-3-401(4)(B) and thus did not come under regulation by the Planning Commission. . . .

This action was heard on 8 June 1990. Both parties agreed that Planning Commission approval was necessary if the proposed division of the property required new street construction or utility construction. Both parties also agreed that the likely use for the property after the sale was residential. The parties agreed on very little else.

Langsdon's position was that substantial road improvements had been made to the "driveway/road" to make it useable to the thirteen lots which fronted on it. Therefore, road improvements were required for subdivision.

Loftin, on the other hand, contended that Beasley Lane had been in existence for at least 35 years and that, while he had graded and re-cherted it, he had not changed or relocated its route. He insisted that the lane was a private easement to which he would grant right of use to all those who chose to purchase property fronting on it. He compared Beasley Lane to private roads within a farm which are necessary to the farm's operations. When asked on cross-examination why the improved portion of Beasley Lane had ditches on both sides while the unimproved portion had none, Loftin replied that he didn't "think any ditches were required back then (when the lane was initially built)."

Loftin admitted that he put the water line in to make water available if the buyers wanted to hook onto it. He also admitted to negotiating with Duck River for the laying of power lines, but he insisted that future buyers could just as easily tie into existing power lines at the north and south ends of the property. When asked on cross-examination whether more power poles would have to be put along or near Beasley Lane "or the people along those thirteen lots couldn't tap on and get electricity to the property," Loftin answered, "Yes, I would suppose so. Yes."

In closing arguments Loftin maintained that the new utility construction which had already been accomplished on the property was not required. He insisted that the new property owners could drill a well rather than tap onto the new water line if they so chose. Langsdon argued at trial that in order to use the property to build houses, there would have to be a water main and an electric main available to the new buyers. These improvements to the land did not exist when Loftin purchased the land. Loftin had provided, or was in the process of providing, these improvements in order to make the land useable. Langsdon urged the court to consider the probable use of the land in determining whether utility construction was required.

Finding that the wording of Tenn. Code Ann. §13-3-401(4)(B) was "a little bit too imprecise" to grant Langsdon the relief she was seeking, the court issued a declaratory judgment in favor of Loftin. . . . The Tennessee law referred to by Langsdon is Tenn. Code Ann. §13-3-401(4)(B). This statute provides:

> "Subdivision" means . . . the division of a tract or parcel of land into two (2) or more lots, sites, or other divisions requiring new street or utility construction, or any division of less than five (5) acres for the purpose, whether immediate or future, of sale or building development, and includes resubdivision and when appropriate to the context, relates to the process of resubdividing or to the land or area subdivided.

In order to determine whether Loftin's division of property was a "subdivision," it is necessary for this Court to construe the meaning of this statute. . . .

Loftin would have us focus almost exclusively on the word "requiring." Even though he installed a water line, he argues that this action was not required since any purchaser could choose to dig a well instead of tapping onto this line. He further argues that his grading, resurfacing, and digging ditches along Beasley Lane was not required construction but was merely the clearing of an existing lane. While he admits that the purchaser will still have to add two power poles in order to supply power to these tracts, he insists that this would be "no greater construction of utilities" than would be required on the undisputed tracts which are also for sale. Furthermore, he testified that the reason no ditches were dug along the unimproved portion of the lane was because he did not "think any ditches were required [emphasis added] back then (when that portion was built)."

The essence of Loftin's argument appears to be: If the seller makes the improvements necessary for the division and sale of his property voluntarily before anyone tells him that those improvements are required, then the improvements are not required. Furthermore, since the improvements were not required, there is no reason for the seller to go before the Planning Commission to inquire as to whether or not the improvements are required. This argument leads ultimately to a "catch 22" which would render the statute meaningless when applied to any division of property over five acres in size and would defeat the intent of the legislation. Such a result is absurd. . . .

Loftin acknowledges that the purpose of his driveway/lane is to provide access to the subdivided lots from the public roadway. The purpose of Planning Commission regulations dealing with road construction is to insure that the roads are built in a manner such as will protect the health, safety, and welfare of the citizens. According to these regulations, the developer must have the road construction plans designed and sealed by a licensed civil engineer. These plans must show drainage tiles, ditches, grades, elevations, and the base and finish in detail. These plans must be approved before the developer can implement them. There is no evidence in the record that Loftin has taken any of the actions necessary to insure that his driveway/lane is safe, and under Loftin's proposed construction of the statute there is no governmental body with oversight to guarantee to the public that his driveway/lane is safe. Yet it is obvious that the intent of the legislature was that roadways traveled by the general public be safe.

Loftin admits that further utility construction is required if these buyers are to receive electricity on their lots from a public utility (only a minute percentage of our society produces its own alternative source of energy). Again, under his proposed construction of this statute, there is no one the public can look to for assurance that the poles have been set and the wires have been strung in a safe manner. The public would just have to take the large developer's word for it.

If one were to follow Loftin's reasoning, small developers (those offering lots of under five acres for sale) would be subject to planning commission regulations if utility or road construction were required, but large developers, who installed these conveniences of modern living before offering their lots for sale, would not be under such constraints. Such a construction of this statute would be absurd. . . .

The phrase Loftin asks us to construe says: "other division requiring new street or utility construction. . . ." Tenn. Code Ann. §13-3-401(4)(B). The phrase does not say: "new street or utility construction required *by a planning commission*." To add such a phrase to the statute would effectively amend the statute. . . .

This statute, like all statutes, must be applied in its present form unless doing so would result in "manifest injustice." There is no "manifest injustice" in applying this statute evenhandedly to large and small developers or in applying the statute in a manner that will further enhance the health, safety and welfare of the community. . . .

Loftin admits he made the road and utility improvements "to get the most money for (the land)." These improvements were "required" by the imperatives of the marketplace. These improvements were "required" within the ambit of Tenn. Code Ann. §13-3-401(4)(B). . . .

TODD, P.J., and CANTRELL, J., concur.

Notes and Comments

1. *Definitions and Interpretation.* The statutory language defining a subdivision is often critically important in a dispute over whether property has been subdivided. In *Loftin*, what is the correct interpretation of the word "required" in the statute defining coverage by the phrase "requiring new street or utility construction?" Does the court's interpretation of this phrase provide sufficient notice to developers as to whether they will be required to comply with the subdivision regulations?

2. *A Surprised Developer?* Was the developer in *Loftin* attempting to evade subdivision regulations by seeking to structure a project so that it would not come within the statutory definition, or was he genuinely surprised when the litigation was initiated? Look carefully at the proposed subdivision and the statutory definition of "subdivision" in reaching your conclusion. If you decide that this was an attempt to evade, would you see any ethical problems in advising a client to achieve that goal? *See also Nagle v. Snohomish County*, 119 P.3d 914 (Wash. Ct. App. 2005) (purchaser was aware he was buying a section of a larger parcel and thus not an innocent purchaser without notice of the illegal subdivision). More broadly, why did the developer oppose compliance with the subdivision laws in this instance?

3. *Evasion Techniques.* Some states define a subdivision as a division into five or more parcels. Would dividing a tract into four parcels without public approval be legal? What if each of the four parcels was subsequently subdivided into four more parcels, for a total of 16 parcels? *Manning v. Fox*, 198 Cal. Rptr. 558 (Ct. App. 1984) (the practice of "four-by-fouring" — that is, making a series of conveyances that individually do not trigger the statutory subdivision definition based on the number of lots created but which cumulatively exceed the standard — resulted in real estate licensing discipline).

What happens if local government and the developer settle litigation and the decree exempts a subdivision from applicable regulations? In *Trancas Property Owners Ass'n v. City of Malibu*, 41 Cal. Rptr. 3d 200 (Ct. App. 2006), a settlement would have exempted a subdivision from zoning, increased the zoning density, and blocked future zone changes in exchange for the developer agreeing to dedicate land for affordable housing. The court of appeals ruled the settlement invalid.

4. *Indirect Creation of Subdivisions.* Even if the landowner is not the immediate creator of the subdivision, compliance with the subdivision laws can be triggered. For example, in *Pratt v. Adams*, 40 Cal. Rptr. 505 (Ct. App. 1964), five or more partners or co-tenants sought judicial partition of a tract. The court ruled that a partition suit triggered the Subdivision Act, as the law simply requires that the actor "caused [the property] to be subdivided."

What if a will divides a tract, leaving it to more devisees than the minimum number exempted from the statutory subdivision definition? *See In re Sayewich*, 413 A.2d 581 (N.H. 1980) (subdivision regulation applies and requires approval to develop, or the court could order the entire tract sold and distribute the proceeds). The Maine Supreme Court held that a lease could create a new lot if it transferred a broad enough range of legal interests. *Horton v. Town of Casco*, 82 A.3d 1217, 1219 (Me. 2013) ("[I]t is the nature of the transferred interests, not the type of contract or instrument facilitating the transfer, that will determine whether a new lot is created.")

5. *Criminal Penalties.* Subdivision laws typically prohibit the sale, lease, or financing of any parcel of a subdivision until the recordation of an approved map in full compliance with the law, and any prior lot sale is void. *Black Hills Investments, Inc. v. Albertson's Inc.*, 53 Cal. Rptr. 3d 263 (Ct. App. 2007). Violation of subdivision laws can be a crime. In *McClellan v. State*, 933 P.2d 461 (Wyo. 1997), the court upheld three counts and rejected a claim of double jeopardy. It concluded that a $750 fine and three days imprisonment were within the permissible maximum of 30 days or $500 for each offense, and that the law allows a separate charge for each day of a violation following an illegal subdivision. *Compare Gallegos v. City of Las Vegas*, 957 P.2d 1159 (Nev. Ct. App. 1998). The Nevada subdivision statute covers the division of a parcel into two or more parts. The court, however, ruled that the repeated sale of individual parcels in the same year constitutes only one division even though portions of the parcels were transferred in 17 separate transactions.

6. *Relief for Purchasers from Unlawful Subdivisions.* To whom should the subdivision lot purchaser look for assurance that infrastructure is safely and effectively installed? Would the opportunity for tort recovery protect the public? Contrast the benefits and costs of a free market approach with those of subdivision review, which follows traditional public regulatory processes.

In one interesting case, a homeowner sued the developer of the "Holiday Harbor" subdivision in tort for failing to disclose that the subdivision was created on a former graveyard. *Hickman v. Carven*, 784 A.2d 31, 34 (Md. 2001) (plaintiff "dug a hole in her yard where a yucca plant had been and, about 12 inches below the surface, discovered some bones and a piece of metal that she believed to be a casket handle"). The court ruled that the 20-year statute of repose governing injuries after an improvement to realty did not apply to bar purchasers' action. *See also Kilgore Dev., Inc. v. Woodland Place, LLC*, 47 So. 3d 267 (Ala. Ct. Civ. App. 2009) (a purchase contract for the sale of 44 lots in a subdivision to a developer was illegal because it was executed prior to plat approval; thus, the purchaser was entitled to rescind).

7. *Consumer Protection.* Developers may default on obligations to complete infrastructure, leaving purchasers of home sites to cope with sewer system failure, low water pressure, flooding, and poor roads. Overreaching developers also may engage in false promises of community design and project amenities.

State legislation typically requires simultaneous compliance both with local planning requirements and marketing regulations administered by the state. State marketing regulation often requires developers to disclose plans as well as to file disclosure documents with a state real estate regulatory agency. Causes of action for misrepresentation or the failure to complete plans are often provided for, and remedies are authorized. These include public enforcement seeking injunctive relief against further development or marketing, and criminal sanctions for non-compliance or non-completion. *People v. Pacific Land Research Co.,* 569 P.2d 125 (Cal. 1977) (injunctive relief and restitution available in lawsuit by state). *See also Winant v. Bostic,* 5 F.3d 767 (4th Cir. 1993) (damages may be trebled but restitution is not available under North Carolina law where the developer made false promises of amenities such as a pool, a club, and exotic landscaping).

Congress has enacted the federal Interstate Land Sales Full Disclosure Act, 15 U.S.C. §§1701-20 (2006), requiring disclosure of terms, benefits, and amenities to purchasers, if the subdivision lot they purchased was marketed on an interstate basis.

8. *Ensuring Completion of Infrastructure.* In small subdivisions, building permits may issue only upon final inspection of the completed infrastructure, with emphasis on roads and utilities. Conditioning building permit issuance upon completion of all subdivision amenities in the case of large subdivisions, however, may be very costly for the developer. In that instance the developer cannot obtain a cash flow during an extended period of development. One technique used to ensure the completion of infrastructure is requiring the developer to post security or secure a performance bond. *Ponderosa Fire Dist. v. Coconino County,* 334 P.3d 1256, 1262 (Az. Ct. App. 2014) (performance bonds protect the public from bearing the costs of necessary subdivision improvements). *See also Parker v. Board of County Comm'rs of Dona Ana County,* 603 P.2d 1098 (N.M. 1979) (suspension of plat approval upon failure to complete road improvements).

C. THE PROJECT APPROVAL PROCESS

Apart from questions concerning the constitutional validity of subdivision conditions and exactions, a subject examined in Chapter 7, most subdivision litigation centers on the legality of the decision by the governmental entity to approve or deny the subdivision. The subdivision regulatory process is becoming increasingly sophisticated because of the technical nature of environmental and land planning, and the escalating complexities of legislative policies and procedures. These complexities can be further compounded by judicial interpretation. In some instances, particularly in small jurisdictions, the subdivision process may exceed the institutional capacity of the planning department and public officials to perform the tasks legally required.

Another fundamental problem you must consider is that to some degree the system seeks, through the utilization of a planning commission and a planning process, to override local "politics." In actuality, however, politics more frequently overrides the application of planning requirements, despite attempts by the legislature to provide rationality in the statutory scheme. The result is often a system with a veneer of rigor that places vast discretion in the hands of local government. When you review the following subdivision cases, ask whether local decisions and processes reflect both the potential rationality of the administrative process and planning expertise.

The following case addresses the administrative and judicial review standards in reviewing subdivision determinations.

■ BLUE RIDGE CO. v. TOWN OF PINEVILLE
655 S.E.2d 843 (N.C. Ct. App. 2008)

CALABRIA, Judge.

The Town of Pineville ("respondent") appeals from an order reversing respondent's denial of a subdivision application from Blue Ridge Company, L.L.C. ("petitioner"). . . .

I. FACTS

Petitioner owns 52.43 acres of undeveloped land in Mecklenburg County, in the Town of Pineville, North Carolina ("the property"). The property is adjacent to Lakeview Drive, the main street in a residential neighborhood of about fifty homes ("Lakeview Neighborhood") and the only means of access to the property. The property is zoned R-12. Petitioner applied to the Pineville Planning Board ("Planning Board") for approval of a 102 lot residential subdivision ("Netherby Subdivision").

Petitioner began the application process in August 2005 by submitting a sketch plan to the Planning Board which was approved on 22 September 2005. A preliminary plan was submitted in December 2005. Petitioner revised the preliminary plan twice in response to comments from respondent's staff. On 25 May 2006, the Planning Board unanimously denied the application.

Petitioner appealed the Planning Board's decision to the Town Council. The Town Council held a hearing, found that petitioner did not meet the requirements of the Town of Pineville Subdivision Ordinance section 6.150 ("section 6.150"), and denied the application. The Town Council based their denial on traffic and overcrowding of schools and noted that petitioner failed to show that additional students would not adversely affect the stability, environment, health and character of the neighboring area. Petitioner otherwise complied with the technical and safety requirements for subdivision plans. . . .

On 15 December 2006, Mecklenburg County Superior Court Judge Richard Boner found that petitioner complied with the objective technical and engineering standards set forth by respondent and denial of the petition was based on subjective requirements which did not provide petitioner with sufficient notice of what respondent expected. The trial court reversed the Town Council's denial of petitioner's application and remanded for a new hearing with respondent. In addition, the court ordered respondent to provide petitioner with any plans in existence at the time the application was filed for public facilities required for the subdivision and specific criteria regarding the environmental, health, and character of neighboring areas considered by the Town Council in determining whether the proposed sub-division complies with section 6.150.

Respondent appeals the trial court's order on the basis that respondent's decision to deny the subdivision was supported by competent, material and substantial evidence; the ordinance requirements are lawful and were lawfully applied; and respondent is under no obligation to instruct subdivision applicants before a hearing as to what and how they should present their application. Peti-tioner appeals on the basis that the subdivision plan should be approved without remanding for a new hearing.

II. STANDARD OF REVIEW

Appellate courts exercise review (1) to determine whether the trial court exercised the appropriate scope of review, and (2) if appropriate, deciding whether the court did so properly. The superior court judge sits as an appellate court on review pursuant to writ of certiorari of an administrative decision. If petitioner appeals the Town's decision on the basis of an error of law, the trial court applies *de novo* review; if the petitioner alleges the decision was arbitrary and capricious, or challenges the sufficiency of the evidence, the trial court applies the whole record test. If the trial court applies the whole record test, then the Town's findings of fact are binding on appeal if supported by substantial, competent evidence presented at the hearing. The superior court may apply both standards of review if required, but the standards should be applied separately to discrete issues.

Petitioner challenges the Town Council's decision as vague, arbitrary and capri-cious, unsupported by the record and claims the ordinance is void as a matter of law. The superior court determined that petitioner presented substantial evidence to support a finding that petitioner met the technical requirements for a subdivision plan, and the plan should have been approved. The superior court concluded that denial of the application was not supported by law because the subjective require-ments did not give petitioner notice of the Town Council's expectations for compliance.

The trial court applied the whole record test to the challenged findings and *de novo* review of the Town Council's ordinance. The trial court reviewed the evidence to determine petitioner met the technical requirements of the ordinance and reviewed *de novo* the legality of the general requirements. Therefore, we conclude the trial court conducted the proper scope of review.

III. DENIAL OF SUBDIVISION APPLICATION

First, we examine whether the trial court erred in reversing the Town Council's decision. Respondent argues its decision to deny petitioner's subdivision applica-tion was supported by competent, material and substantial evidence and should have been affirmed. . . .

"In reviewing a superior court order entered upon review of a zoning decision by a municipality, the appellate court must determine . . . whether the evidence before the Town Council supported the Council's action."

The Town Council denied petitioner's subdivision application on the basis it did not comply with general requirements outlined in the Town of Pineville, Subdivision Ordinance 6.150. The pertinent portions of section 6.150 are as follows:

Subdivision Ordinance
6.150. General Requirements

1. Consistency with adopted public plan and policies. All subdivisions of land approved under these regulations should be consistent with the most recently adopted public plans and policies for the area in which it is located. This includes general policy regarding development objectives for the area as well as specific policy or plans for public facilities such as streets, parks and open space, schools, and other similar facilities. Plans and policies for the community are on file in the offices of the Secretary to the Pineville Planning Board and in the offices of the Charlotte-Mecklenburg Planning Commission.
2. Conformity. All proposed subdivisions should be planned so as to facilitate the most advantageous development of the entire neighboring area. In areas with existing development, new subdivisions should be planned so as to protect and enhance the stability, environment, health and character of the neighboring area. . . .

Specifically, the Town Council found that the access route utilizing Lakeview Drive would add 1000 trips per day, increasing current traffic on that road by thirty percent, that homeowners and their children use the streets and sidewalks for bike riding and other recreational activities, that the Lakeview Neighborhood would triple in size from the construction of the Netherby Subdivision, that petitioner did not submit evidence as to the impact of the Netherby Subdivision on neighborhood schools, and that the "Netherby Subdivision does not protect the Lakeview Neighborhood from non-compatible encroachment."

When a subdivision ordinance requires several criteria for approval of a plan, failure to meet one requirement is a sufficient basis to deny approval. In order to determine whether petitioner failed to meet any of the requirements, it is necessary to examine each one.

A.   SCHOOL IMPACT

Petitioner contends the Town Council's denial of the application based on the impact on local schools was not supported by substantial and competent evidence. . . .

The ordinance expressly requires that subdivision plans conform with specific policy or plans for schools. Section 6.150(1) provides: "All subdivisions of land approved under these regulations should be consistent with the most recently adopted public plans and policies for the area in which it is located. This includes general policy regarding development objectives for the area as well as specific policy or plans for public facilities such as . . . schools. . . ."

The Town Council found that "[i]t is the policy of the Town of Pineville to have its children attend neighborhood elementary schools." This policy is not described in the General Requirements ordinance, nor is it outlined in the Future Land Use Plan. The only indication in the record of such a policy is in the form of a letter from a member of the School Building Solutions Committee dated 1 August 2006, and his testimony before the Town Council that same day, noting that

Charlotte-Mecklenburg Schools "wants Pineville's students to have neighborhood schools. . . . That's what this town wants, that's what the parents want. . . ." At the hearing, the Town Council received information that Pineville Elementary was currently over capacity and that

> [t]he staff feels that with the addition of a hundred and two lots-there is an equation that developers use to determine how many students will be in addition to existing neighborhoods. Currently, staff does not have that information of what it would be, but we just wanted to present that information to let you know there are other concerns. . . .
>
> Notwithstanding whether this letter sufficiently described the "most recently adopted public plans and policies for the area," this letter was not available to petitioner until the day of the hearing. The timeliness of the letter did not provide an adequate guiding standard for petitioner to follow.

Assuming *arguendo* such a policy was on file, since Pineville Elementary was considered over capacity at the time of the application, concern about children attending neighborhood schools would exist regardless of petitioner's proposed subdivision. *Woodhouse v. Board of Commissioners*, 261 S.E.2d 882, 888 (N.C. 1980) (Town's denial of application based on finding that fire fighting facilities would be outstripped is invalid since that problem would exist regardless of the proposed development).

Respondent also found that petitioner did not present evidence of the proposed subdivision's impact on schools. While that finding is supported by the record, the subdivision ordinance did not expressly require a school impact study. The Town Council is without authority to "deny a permit on grounds not expressly stated in the ordinance." We conclude respondent's finding that petitioner's application did not conform with section 6.150 on the basis of school impact is not supported by substantial and competent evidence.

B. TRAFFIC CONCERNS

Respondent found that "the design of the Netherby Subdivision does not encourage a safer nor easier flow of traffic." One goal and objective of the Land Use Plan is for subdivisions to be "designed in such a way to encourage a safer, easier flow of traffic." However, the finding that the subdivision does not encourage a safer flow of traffic is not supported in the record. Testimony presented to the Town Council indicates the thirty percent increase in traffic on Lakeview Drive would not impact the safety of the road. Don Spence, a consultant with Kublins Transportation Group, was retained by members of the Planning Board, Kevin Icard and Mike Rose, to examine the traffic conditions surrounding the area, and to measure the potential impact of traffic on the Lakeview Neighborhood. Spence testified that subdivisions consisting of a hundred lots "can produce approximately one thousand trips." Spence concluded that the "existing light traffic conditions combined with trip generation anticipated by the construction of Netherby at Regency Park will not exceed minimum traffic capacity standards." Spence testified that based on traffic volume, the additional trips would not create any "undue safety problems." Although the thirty percent increase was described as "significant," that standing alone is not sufficient to find that the Netherby Subdivision does not protect and enhance the stability, environment, health and character of the neighboring area.

The Town Council heard testimony from residents of Lakeview Neighborhood, stating that noise from the new subdivision would disturb the peace of the current neighborhood and cars must slow down to pass each other on the road, so the increase in traffic would not be safe. The residents did not rebut Spence's testimony with mathematical studies or any other factual basis to establish that the increase in traffic would adversely affect the community. *See Cumulus Broadcasting, LLC v. Hoke Cty. Bd. of Comm'rs,* 638 S.E.2d 12, 17 (N.C. Ct. App. 2006) (witness testimony in opposition to the granting of a permit relying solely upon their personal knowledge and observations is not enough to rebut quantitative data); *compare Howard v. City of Kinston,* 558 S.E.2d 221, 227-28 (N.C. Ct. App. 2002) (witness testimony that current traffic conditions result in near accidents involving children based on personal knowledge and observation supported a finding that an increase in traffic endangered health and safety of the neighborhood where expert testimony quantitatively confirmed witness' concerns); *see also Sun Suites Holdings LLC v. Board of Aldermen of Town of Garner,* 533 S.E.2d 525, 530 (N.C. Ct. App. 2000) ("[T]he expression of generalized fears does not constitute a competent basis for denial of a permit").

Here, a Lakeview resident testified there is currently "no concern of safety of traffic"; therefore, any conclusion that an increase in traffic would cause safety concerns is speculative and generalized in light of Spence's report showing that the increase in traffic would not create any safety problems. In addition, the residents' concerns seemed to be more about potential noise than about safety. Denial of a permit "may not be founded upon conclusions which are speculative, sentimental, personal, vague or merely an excuse to prohibit the use requested."

Respondent contends the increase in traffic affects conformity with the existing development. Section 6.150(2) provides: "All proposed subdivisions should be planned so as to facilitate the most advantageous development of the entire neighboring area. In areas with existing development, new subdivisions shall be planned so as to protect and enhance the stability, environment, health and character of the neighboring area. . . ."

"The general rule is that a zoning ordinance, being in derogation of common law property rights, should be construed in favor of the free use of property." N.C. Gen. Stat. §160A-371 provides that "[w]henever [a subdivision] ordinance includes criteria for decision that require application of judgment, those criteria must provide adequate guiding standards for the entity charged with plat approval."

The criteria characterized as the "most advantageous development" is vague. One goal and objective of respondent's Land Use Plan is to encourage development of single family homes in the Town of Pineville, "[t]he low percentage of single family homes . . . limits the growth potential of the Town." Petitioner's subdivision plan provides for single family homes; therefore, it would appear the Netherby Subdivision would be an advantageous development. . . .

IV. REMAND

Both petitioner and respondent argue the trial court's order to remand for a new hearing was in error. . . .

Respondent argues Pineville is under no obligation to provide petitioner with specific criteria to be used to determine whether the subdivision plan met the requirements of its ordinance. Petitioner contends because the technical requirements were met, it is *prima facie* entitled to a subdivision permit without remand. . . .

N.C. Gen. Stat. §160A-371 requires that "[w]henever [a subdivision] ordinance includes criteria for decision that require application of judgment, those criteria must provide adequate guiding standards for the entity charged with plat approval." Town boards must employ "specific statutory criteria which are relevant." The trial court remanded for clarification of subjective criteria in the town ordinance which is consistent with insuring "procedures specified by law in both statute and ordinance are followed." This is a reasonable action for a trial court to take and we conclude there was no error. . . .

Notes and Comments

1. *The Basis for the Denial.* How would you have advised the town? Would a more specific ordinance or more particularized subdivision regulations have altered the outcome? Does the town's choice of expert witness make a difference?

In *Oldham Farms Dev., LLC v. Oldham County Planning & Zoning Comm'n*, 233 S.W.3d 195 (Ky. Ct. App. 2007), the court upheld the denial of an application to subdivide 271 acres of real property into 446 residential lots. The landowner's application failed to meet certain requirements set out in county subdivision regulations regarding traffic flow, as certain roads adjoining or adjacent to the proposed subdivision were inadequate to sustain the expected average daily traffic generated by the new residences. A traffic engineer with 30 years of professional experience stated that the landowner's subdivision plan violated both the spirit and intent of the county's traffic regulations. Is *Oldham Farms* consistent with *Blue Ridge*?

2. *Road Congestion Standards?* Rather than characterizing the increase in traffic as significant, should the town have set out specific standards for road congestion, setting up levels of service such as the time it takes for vehicles to clear intersections?. For example, level A would mean there is no delay for waiting vehicles to cross the intersection with a signal, etc., so that level D might be two signal changes for waiting vehicles to clear the intersection. The town could require a traffic study to demonstrate that congestion is no greater than a B or C level. Would such an objective standard result in a different outcome?

3. *Treatment of Other Subdivisions.* Can a jurisdiction deny a subdivision based on impacts or conditions that exist off the subdivision site? In *Garipay v. Town of Hanover*, 351 A.2d 64 (N.H. 1976), a town denied a subdivision based on a finding that the off-site access road would be inadequate to handle the proposed 49 homes. The subdivision would be located at the top of a hill, and the road was described as narrow, steep and winding, with a grade that at times exceeded 15 percent and at least one horseshoe bend. The town police chief expressed reservations about the department's ability to respond to an emergency in the area in wintertime. Eighteen homes existed at the top of the hills, and the steepness of the road required the residents to leave their cars at the foot of the hill during winter.

The pertinent statute authorized the town to promulgate regulations that "provide against such scattered or premature subdivision of land as would involve danger or injury to health, safety, or prosperity by reason of the lack of . . . transportation . . . or other public services . . ." The applicant challenged the denial, arguing that the statute precluded the town from considering off-site factors. Do you agree?

See Alpenhof, LLC v. City of Ouray, 297 P.3d 1052, 1056 (Colo. Ct. App. 2013) ("Alpen-hof's interpretation [of the subdivision law] would leave the city powerless to protect the public. . . . from a flooding hazard . . ."). Did the denial in *Garipay* violate equal protection, in that the existing homes at the top of the hill had been approved earlier? *See Campo Grandchildren Trust v. Colson,* 834 N.Y.S.2d 295 (Sup. Ct. App. Div. 2007) (zoning board of appeals abused its discretion in denying subdivision approval since, several years earlier, it had approved a similar subdivision and variance application submitted by owner's predecessor-in-interest); *Town of Hollywood v. Floyd,* 744 S.E.2d 161, 168 (S.C. 2013) (developers failed to show that the planning commission treated them differently than other similarly situated developers in the subdivision application process).

Some jurisdictions require that, in making a decision on a subdivision appli-cation, the local governmental entity must restrict its evaluation to "on-site" crite-ria — that is, considerations stemming solely from the proposed site itself. For example, a planning commission might be foreclosed from considering local school overcrowding as a basis for denying a residential subdivision. *Cf. Steel v. Cape Corp.,* 677 A.2d 634 (Md. Ct. Spec. App. 1996) (a rejection of zoning, based on inadequacy of school capacity, resulted in a taking). The majority of jurisdictions do not require such a restriction.

4. *Standards of Judicial Review of Subdivision Approvals.* Subdivision approval involves a discretionary administrative determination focused on a particular parcel and a proposed development. In comparison, a legislative matter typically sets policy on a prospective basis. As an administrative determination, subdivision approval must conform to certain standards established by statute, ordinance, or regulation that are designed to aid judicial review of administrative or "quasi-judicial" deci-sions. These are decisions in which the local agency engages in fact finding regard-ing that specific parcel. *See, e.g., Regan v. Pomerleau,* 107 A.3d 327, 33 (Vt. 2014) (language relied upon by petitioners challenging a subdivision "provides no clear, specific, and enforceable standards to determine compliance . . ."); *Sansom v. Board of Supervisors of Madison County,* 514 S.E.2d 345 (Va. 1999) (upholding denial of a subdivision application under an ordinance prohibiting land disturbances within 50 feet of a "substantial surface drainage course").

Challenges typically allege that the decision is arbitrary or capricious, is not supported by substantial evidence, or reflects an error of law. *See, e.g., Whitesell v. Kosciusko County Bd. of Zoning Appeals,* 558 N.E.2d 889 (Ind. Ct. App. 1990) (no *de novo* judicial review or substitution of court's decision for that of the planning commission and the board of zoning appeals).

5. *Findings.* Decisions must be based on findings that are supported by substantial evidence in the record and that communicate the reasons for the denial. *Crown Point Dev.,Inc. v. City of Sun Valley,* 156 P.3d 573 (Idaho 2007) (invalidating denial of preliminary plat for fifth phase of subdivision for failure of findings that did not determine any facts, but rather were only recitations of evidence). One purpose of findings is to alert the project applicant to the specific reasons for denial so that the applicant may determine whether she can alter the project to eliminate the deficiency. *See Plan Comm'n of Harrison County v. Aulbach,* 748 N.E.2d 926, 937 (Ind. Ct. App. 2001) ("it was the Plan Commission's duty . . . to furnish the Devel-opers with all of the specific and concrete reasons for disapproval so that the Devel-opers could amend their plat to comply with the applicable ordinances"). Another reason for findings is to aid the applicant in appealing to a court and, thereafter to

aid the court in judicial review. *Advantage Dev., Inc. v. Board of Supervisors of Jackson Township*, 743 A.2d 1008 (Pa. Commw. Ct. 2000) (applicants have a right to a denial letter describing the requirements that have not been met so they can effectively appeal the denial to a court).

Other than raising technical violations, most challenges to subdivision approvals allege adverse environmental impacts, inadequacy of supporting infrastructure, or adverse effects on adjacent properties. Is the decision whether an approval was arbitrary or capricious akin to the application of the test for a violation of substantive due process? Is the court faced with a Hobson's choice: either excessively deferring to the administrative agency or substituting its judgment for that of the planning agency?

6. *Comparing Site Plan Review.* The central benefits of subdivision review derive from the opportunity for a discretionary review of the project to consider site design, environmental impacts, and effects on infrastructure capacity. Subdivision review provides an opportunity to require modifications of the plat and to impose exactions, such as requiring developers to finance facilities, pay impact fees, or dedicate land for facilities. Where property can be developed without subdividing, however, the development is not subject to the subdivision review process. The possibility that large projects with significant impacts akin to those of subdivisions would avoid this type of review prompted many communities to adopt site plan ordinances, discussed in Chapter 2.

Is subdivision review necessarily subjective and discretionary, or does the obligation for compliance with all laws and regulations ensure objectivity in the review process? The next case, *Burrell v. Lake County Plan Commission*, places the administrative subdivision review process in the context of overall land use planning controls.

■ BURRELL v. LAKE COUNTY PLAN COMMISSION
624 N.E.2d 526 (Ind. Ct. App. 1993)

SHARPNACK, Chief Judge.

This case concerns the denial of approval by the Lake County Plan Commission (Commission) to the preliminary subdivision plan submitted by Donald and Alice Burrell. The Burrells petitioned the trial court for a writ of certiorari to reverse the denial of plan approval and the trial court, after remanding for findings of fact by the Commission, denied relief and affirmed the Commission action. The Burrells now ask us to reverse the trial court and the Commission. . . .

In 1990, the Burrells filed an application with the Commission for subdivision approval of Rainbow Estates, a residential subdivision to be developed on their property in Lake County, Indiana. The Commission granted tentative approval for the subdivision [and] a public hearing on the Burrells' application for preliminary plan approval was held during the Commission's regular meeting of February 5, 1991. The Burrells' application was denied, consistent with the requirements of the applicable ordinance, based on the Commission's conclusion that the subdivision would have an adverse effect on the health, safety, and general welfare of the community. The Commission made no findings of fact in support of its conclusion. . . .

[T]he Burrells contend that the Commission's findings are not supported by substantial evidence. . . .

In our review of the Burrells' claim that the Commission's findings are not supported by substantial evidence, we may vacate the decision of the Commission "'only if the evidence, when viewed as a whole, demonstrates that the conclusions reached by the [Commission] are clearly erroneous.'" . . .

At the public hearing on the Burrells' proposed subdivision, the Commission heard a presentation in support of the Burrell's application and received the Commission staff recommendation that the application be approved, as the staff found that the proposed subdivision was "in compliance with the Comprehensive Plan of Lake County and [met] all the requirements of [the Ordinance]." The Commission also received evidence from remonstrators which included an affidavit from an engineer, Rowland Fabian. The remonstrators presented their position, along with supporting documentation, that the existing surface water drainage problem was unacceptable and that the proposed development would increase the problem. The engineer's affidavit discussed, inter alia, alleged deficiencies in the Burrells' plan, risks of leaching and biological contamination from the septic system for the subdivision, the existing excess surface water and flooding problem in the area, and his opinion that the development would contribute to drainage and soil erosion problems in the area. In March, 1992, pursuant to the trial court's instruction, the Commission entered findings in support of its conclusion that the Burrell's proposed subdivision would have an adverse effect on the health, safety, and general welfare of the community.[8]

The substantial evidence test is not a test of our agreement with the Commission's findings. Instead, our inquiry focuses on whether the Commission's decision

---

8. The Commission made the following findings: "The Plan Commission now finds that the report submitted to the Lake County Plan Commission on January 31, 1991 by Fabian Engineers, Inc. of Hammond, Indiana, describes in Paragraphs 3, 4, 5, 6, 7, and 8 of [sic] the inadequacies of the proposed development, specifically the lack of mathematical computations to support the conclusions that the project, as currently contemplated, is consistent with good engineering practices and will not cause damage to areas in and around the project within one mile; also

That none of the mathematical computations or procedures found and inferred in the State Board of Health Bulletin SE13 of 1988, specifically pages 41 to 46 and 47 to 50 of that manual, have been provided to the Lake County Plan Commission for review regarding this project; also

That even without engineering computations, the following general observations can be made regarding the pending proposal before the Lake County Plan Commission; to-wit

    a. That at proposed construction density, no septic system other than a mound system can operate effectively in the soils and topography in question. However, even a mound system is highly questionable and presents a substantial risk of leaching which would result in the biological contamination of both the subdivision and the surrounding areas;

    b. That as the area is currently developed, there is already substantial surface water runoff and flooding during normal rains, and during heaving [sic] rains the area around 129th and Tyler Street is subject to excessive water runoff and flooding.

    c. That any further development which reduces the existing capacity of the ground to retain surface water (such as the construction of new roadways, large homes, expansive driveways, tennis courts and the like), or the reduction of existing vegetation and trees in the area can only add to the existing problems, further overload the surface water drainage system and contribute to increased soil erosion and related problems of the area.

    d. That there is a substantial probability that leaching from the project could result in the biological contamination of any and all of the retention ponds, detention ponds and wetland areas located in the watershed in and about the project; . . .

(Record pp. 298-299). Although we agree with the Burrells that the Commission's findings consist almost entirely of verbatim portions of the engineer's affidavit submitted by Rowland Fabian, the Burrells cite no authority for the proposition that the adoption of portions of the Fabian affidavit vitiates the findings.

is founded on "a reasonably sound basis of evidentiary support." Additionally, we should sustain the Commission's decision if it is correct on any of the grounds stated for disapproval of the plan.

In their argument on this issue, the Burrells dispute the accuracy of the Fabian affidavit, much of which was adopted in the Commission's findings, and question Fabian's expertise. In his affidavit, Fabian states that he is a registered professional engineer and land surveyor in the State of Indiana with over forty years of experience. He further states that in the preparation of his affidavit be reviewed the plans and plats associated with the proposed development, soils studies, U.S. Coast and Geodetic Survey Quadrangle Maps for the area, a federal manual on wetlands conservation, aerial photography of the area, and that he made a personal walking inspection of the project site and surrounding area. In an administrative proceeding involving technical or scientific evidence such as in this case, it is not our task, nor is it within our area of expertise, to determine the credibility or weight to be given technical evidence such as that found in the Fabian affidavit. Our role, instead, is to determine whether the evidence before the Commission *taken as a whole* provides a reasonable evidentiary basis for the Commission's determination, and we conclude that it does.

The Commission received evidence from the remonstrators in a variety of forms at the hearing on the Burrells' plan. This evidence included oral testimony; a video-tape of the area accompanied by oral explanation; and a three-ring binder containing, among other things, an aerial photograph of the proposed development area and surrounding area, photographs depicting flooding in the area, a photocopy of §V(B) of the applicable subdivision ordinance (discussed *supra*), the engineer's affidavit by Rowland Fabian and accompanying attachments, photocopies of newspaper articles describing flooding and sewage disposal problems in Lake County, and a copy of a street and drainage plan that included soils report information. Our review of this evidence leads us to the conclusion that the Commission's findings are supported by substantial evidence of probative value. . . .

With reference to the Commission's findings regarding risks of leaching and biological contamination from the septic system for the subdivision (findings "a" and "d"), the Commission had before it the engineer's affidavit from Rowland Fabian. Additionally, attached to the Fabian affidavit was a letter from a Purdue University extension agronomist that discussed septic system design in difficult soils and referenced publications forwarded to Fabian dealing with issues of septic system design and installation. Although, as noted by the Burrells, the extension agronomist wrote:

> Whether or not homes in a development with 'small' lot sizes would have a high percentage of successfully operating systems depends on many factors, including the ability to lower seasonal water tables. It is probably impossible to give more than an impression or an estimate of risk without a thorough evaluation of the site and proposed development.

[I]n the next paragraph, he wrote: "However, if the majority of soils in the area are Morley, Pewamo, Wallkill and Carlisle then the area has a high risk of waste disposal problems." The street and drainage plan submitted to the Commission by remonstrators reveals that a significant percentage of the Burrells' property consists of these four problematic soils. With reference to the Commission's findings regarding both existing and anticipated flooding, bad drainage, and excessive surface water (findings "b" and "c"), the Commission had before it the Fabian affidavit, a street and drainage plan, photographs of flooding in the area, photocopies of newspaper articles regarding flooding in the county, and a videotape of the area accompanied by oral explanation.

We conclude that the Commission was presented with substantial evidence that the proposed subdivision presented significant risks of septic system leaching, as well as increased flooding and drainage problems. . . .

The Commission had a reasonable evidentiary basis on which to conclude that the subdivision would have an adverse effect on the health, safety, and general welfare of the community, a conclusion from which denial of the preliminary plan must follow under the Ordinance. . . .

Notes and Comments

1. *Regulatory Criteria and Subdivision Approvals. Burrell* stands for the proposition that a subdivision must meet all requirements established through subdivision regulation, zoning, or the comprehensive plan. *See also Board of County Comm'rs of Routt County v. O'Dell*, 920 P.2d 48 (Colo. 1996) (sustaining denial of plat in the face of environmental threats and declaring that the burden is on the applicant to present alternative development proposals that might have a lesser impact); Cal. Gov't Code §66473 (West 1997) (a plat application should be denied unless it complies with all standards, including any adopted comprehensive plan.) *But see Carruthers v. Board of Supervisors of Polk County*, 646 N.W.2d 867 (Iowa Ct. App. 2002) (board has the flexibility to disapprove or condition a plat for reasons not spelled out in so many words in statutes and governing ordinances, and the board must balance the interests of the owner and the possible burden on public improvements). Of course, if the jurisdiction repeatedly raises new objections to the subdivision, it can be found in bad faith and its denial of the subdivision overturned. *Honey Brook Estates, LLC v. Board of Supervisors of Honey Brook Township*, 132 A.3d 611 (Pa. Commw. Ct. 2016).

The correlative rule is that when a subdivision application complies with all regulations, it must be approved. *South E. Property Owners Ass'n v. City Plan Comm'n of the City of New Britain*, 244 A.2d 394 (Conn. 1968); *Furlong Co. v. City of Kansas City*, 189 S.W.3d 157 (Mo. 2006) (preliminary plat application becomes ministerial after officials determine that the plat conforms to zoning and subdivision regulations); *Broward County v. G.B.V. Int'l, Ltd.*, 787 So. 2d 838 (Fla. 2001) (if a developer satisfies its initial burden to show that a plat application meets statutory criteria, the burden shifts to the planning commission to show by competent, substantial evidence that the application does not meet the standards and is adverse to public interest).

The *Burrell* decision also demonstrates the need for comprehensive, formally adopted subdivision regulations setting forth the basis on which a project can be denied. An alternative to such action is the approval of a project generating unacceptable impacts where that approval is conditioned on modifications that would mitigate those impacts. *Miles v. Planning Bd. of Millbury*, 558 N.E.2d 1150 (Mass. App. Ct. 1992. Some jurisdictions require that local governmental agencies or legislative bodies reviewing subdivisions impose mitigating conditions rather than deny a plat. *See, e.g., Kohr v. Lower Windsor Township Bd. of Supervisors*, 910 A.2d 152 (Pa. Commw. Ct. 2006).

2. *Lawyering* Burrell. Examine, item by item, the various pieces of evidence put into the record by the opponents of the subdivision: The Fabian affidavit, the

videotape of the area, the "three-ring binder" containing photographs, the newspapers articles, the drainage plan, etc. For each item, ask yourself what purpose it served in building the case against the subdivision. Was that opposition well-organized? Did you find that evidence convincing?

In the litigation, the Burrells "dispute the accuracy of the Fabian affidavit." What test on judicial review was the court applying in reviewing that affidavit? How likely was that argument to prevail under that standard of review? Did the Burrells generally have a good chance of prevailing on appeal? Should they have even brought the case? *See, e.g., Dugan v. Liggan,* 121 A.D.3d 1471, 1473 (2014) ("While petitioners proffered opinions from their experts, who reached differing conclusions on various issues, the Department was free to rely upon one expert's opinion over the other" in deciding a subdivision application).

3. *Subdivisions and PUDs.* As discussed in Chapter 2, the use of a planned unit development (PUD) allows implementation of so-called "New Urbanism," a development concept calling for higher density mixed-use with pedestrian friendly streets and walks, and mixed uses in districts that include different housing types. It also allows mixed commercial and employment centers so important for modern transit villages and creatively planned subdivisions. *See* Peter Calthorpe, The Next American Metropolis: Ecology, Community, and the American Dream (1993); Andrés Duany et al., Suburban Nation (2000). Like subdivision and site plan ordinances, the PUD provides an alternative mechanism for addressing environmental and infrastructure problems. The regulatory scheme under PUD ordinances bears similarity to the site plan and subdivision process.

4. *Architectural Design and Consistency with Renderings.* The decision in *Frankland v. City of Oswego,* 517 P.2d 1042 (Or. 1973), illustrates a problem that can arise during subdivision and other types of project review. The final developed project may depart from the description of the project or the design concept and sketches, or renderings, submitted to support an application. At the preliminary stages of the review process, the developer in *Frankland* submitted sketches that presented a melange of "garden apartment" buildings varying in height and building shapes with many architectural details. The sketches presented a "woodsy" appearance in which the project appeared well-integrated with the surrounding forest. However, the developer later constructed large, monolithic apartment houses of uniform height. The Oregon court ruled that the sketches submitted became part of the PUD plan, thus committing the developer to the architectural design and building configuration depicted.

One lesson from *Frankland* is that a local government's subdivision ordinance will want to clarify the relationship between preliminary plans and the actual approval. As to the unattractiveness of the final subdivision, communities may wish to enact aesthetic control ordinances requiring final plans to conform to community standards for beauty and aesthetics. *See* Chapter 17 for a discussion of aesthetic regulation. Another alternative is the enactment of form-based zoning that can depict building and facade design, materials, and colors, as well as building and street design and scale. *See, e.g.,* Richard S. Geller, The Legality of Form-Based Zoning Codes, 26 J. Land Use & Envtl. L. 35 (2010) (endorsing the device and arguing that courts will uphold a fairly debatable legislative decision to adopt a form-based code that improves aesthetics, reduces pollutants, uses government resources more efficiently, and improves health and safety).

5. *Subdivisions, Zoning, and Master Planning.* In *Board of County Comm'rs of Cecil County v. Gaster,* 401 A.2d 66 (Md. 1979), the developer submitted a preliminary plat

application for a residential subdivision calling for 408 single-family detached lots on 174.3 acres, or 2.3 units per acre. The officially adopted master plan, however, called for a density at one dwelling unit per acre, together with planning standards for adequate roads, schools, and other facilities and services. The highest court in Maryland, the court of appeals, ruled that consistency was required between the subdivision, the subdivision regulations, and the master plan. The court emphasized that failing to require consistency would leave to the discretion of the developer whether the community would be designed with adequate schools, fire protection, parks, playgrounds, and other public facilities. This so-called "consistency" requirement with plans is addressed in more detail in Chapter 5 of this book.

The decision in *Gaster*, just as in *Burrell*, instructs that, in order to assure that subdivisions are well planned and served by adequate facilities and services, the jurisdiction's comprehensive plan should set forth the community's standards of service and facility capacity, as well as policies for imposing the costs of service delivery and facilities installation. The court in *Gaster* emphasized that zoning cannot fulfill this need, as it typically simply calls for a projected use.

D. VESTED RIGHTS TO DEVELOP

The subdivision review process involves review at various stages, such as the initial sketch plan review, the formal tentative or preliminary tract map review, and the final subdivision map review. Accordingly, the process may take many years, particularly where a large project is undertaken in phases. During that time, plans, statutes, and subdivision regulations may undergo substantial modification due to changes in the city's development policies.

This possibility of modification poses a significant problem for developers. They seek predictability in their investments and would like to have standards finalized and "locked in" at an early point so that financing and profitability can be forecast. In contrast, local communities prefer to retain the flexibility of imposing conditions at a later stage in the development process, in case new environmental impacts or infrastructure problems are identified at that point. The following case addresses the issue of when rights to a subdivision vest.

■ BOARD OF SUPERVISORS OF PRINCE GEORGE COUNTY v. MCQUEEN
752 S.E.2d 851 (Virginia 2014)

Opinion by Justice Elizabeth A. McClanahan.

I. Background

A. THE CLO ORDINANCE

The County's Board of Supervisors (the Board) in 2007 adopted a new zoning ordinance that included a set of provisions, entitled collectively the "CLO Cluster Overlay District" (hereinafter, the "CLO Ordinance"), permitting the development of cluster subdivisions.[1] CLO Ordinance §§90–332.2 through –332.16. A cluster subdivision proposed in accordance with the standards contained in the CLO Ordinance was a "permitted use by-right." CLO Ordinance §90–332.4(A). The standards consisted of categories of both general and specific requirements. CLO Ordinance §§90–332.6 through –332.14. The four general standards, which are implicated here, pertained only to minimum acreage, the provision of water and sewer, the exclusion of conservation areas, and the number of dwelling units allowed per acre. CLO Ordinance §§90–332.6.

In the application process for developing a cluster subdivision, the applicant was required to meet with the zoning administrator to review the requirements for a proposed cluster subdivision, arrange a site visit, and prepare a "property resource map" of the proposed site depicting such items as, for example, total acreage, slope percentages, flood plains, historic structures and woodlands. CLO Ordinance §90–332.16(A). The applicant was then required to submit a preliminary plat in accordance with the County's subdivision regulations.[2] CLO Ordinance §90–332.16(B). Finally, upon the County's approval of the preliminary plat, the applicant was required to submit a final plat in accordance with the County's subdivision regulations. CLO Ordinance §90–332.16(C).

B. MCQUEEN'S PROPOSED DEVELOPMENT

McQueen . . . initiated plans to develop his property as a cluster subdivision. In early May 2008, McQueen and his engineer "met informally" with Pamela Thompson (Thompson), the Deputy County Administrator and Interim Director of Planning, to review the requirements for such use of McQueen's property. McQueen's attorney subsequently submitted an "application" letter to Thompson describing in general terms McQueen's proposed development of "approximately 250 clustered residential dwellings," and "request[ing] a formal meeting" as required under CLO Ordinance §90–332.16(A).

McQueen, his engineer, and attorney, then met with Thompson on May 23, 2008. McQueen presented Thompson with a document consisting of a combined resource map and draft of a preliminary plat of McQueen's proposed development, and the four of them reviewed it that day. It was only after the May 23rd meeting, McQueen's engineer confirmed, that "we put together a formal submittal of the preliminary plat for the [C]ounty," which, he acknowledged, was filed on July 1. He further indicated that the draft of the preliminary plat "could have changed" between May 23rd and July 1.

After the May 23rd meeting, McQueen expected to receive "an approval letter within days" from Thompson. When that did not occur, McQueen filed a declaratory judgment action seeking a determination whether he was entitled to develop his property "by right" or only pursuant to a special exception. Shortly thereafter, McQueen nonsuited the action upon receiving a "compliance letter" from Thompson around June 19th.

---

1. The CLO Ordinance was described as "offer[ing] an alternative to conventional subdivision development by allowing for compact clusters of housing units rather than spaced lots that encompass the entire property." CLO Ordinance §90–332.2.

2. The following additional items were also required to accompany the preliminary plat under CLO Ordinance §90–332.16(B): notation on the plat of all conservation and open space areas; deed restrictions and covenants that would apply to private streets, public services, open space, and cluster subdivision lots; and the location of the building lots to be conveyed.

C.   THOMPSON'S COMPLIANCE LETTER

In the compliance letter, Thompson recited the four general standards set forth in CLO Ordinance §90–332.6 and indicated that McQueen's property met those standards. Thompson then stated, "[p]lease let this letter serve as notice that your property does meet the provisions of the CLO *[O]rdinance for by-right development* in Prince George County." (Emphasis added.) Thompson also advised that McQueen would "need to meet all other applicable provisions of federal, state, and local codes." In addition, she explained, "[o]nce final approval of the proposed development is obtained through the CLO [O]rdinance you will need to obtain Site Plan Approval and a Land Disturbance Permit prior to beginning any work on the site." According to Thompson, the letter was not required by the CLO Ordinance, and it did not approve a specific project.

D.   MCQUEEN'S PRESENT DECLARATORY JUDGMENT ACTION

Several months after Thompson issued the compliance letter, the Board repealed the CLO Ordinance. In response, McQueen filed this declaratory judgment action against the County and the Board (collectively, "the County"). McQueen sought a declaration that he obtained a vested right under Code §15.2–2307 to develop his property "as a by-right cluster subdivision" in accordance with the terms of the CLO Ordinance.

Under Code §15.2–2307, a landowner may establish a vested right in a land use when he "(i) obtains or is the beneficiary of a significant affirmative governmental act which remains in effect allowing development of a specific project, (ii) relies in good faith on the significant affirmative governmental act, and (iii) incurs extensive obligations or substantial expenses in diligent pursuit of the specific project in reliance on the significant affirmative governmental act." The statute does not define what constitutes a significant affirmative governmental act. Instead, it provides a list of seven acts "deemed to be significant affirmative governmental acts."[3] *Id.* The list is non-exclusive, however, as the statute expressly provides that the list is "without limitation." *Id.* At the time Thompson issued the compliance letter, the statute listed acts one through six; the seventh act was added by legislative amendment in 2010. *See* 2010 Acts ch. 315.

McQueen asserted that Thompson's compliance letter constituted a significant affirmative governmental act, that he relied in good faith on that act, and that he incurred extensive obligations and substantial expenses in diligent pursuit of developing his property as a cluster subdivision. Therefore, McQueen concluded, he met the three elements set forth in Code §15.2–2307 for the vesting of a right to use his property for that purpose.

As to the first statutory element, McQueen acknowledged that the compliance letter did not represent any one of the six significant affirmative governmental acts listed in Code §15.2–2307 at that time. Rather, McQueen contended, the letter constituted a significant affirmative governmental act under this Court's case law,

---

3. The seven "deemed" significant affirmative governmental acts in Code §15.2–2307 consist of the following: (i) accepting proffers related to a zoning amendment; (ii) approving a rezoning application, (iii) granting a special exception or use permit, (iv) approving a variance, (v) approving a preliminary subdivision plat, site plan or plan of development, (vi) approving a final subdivision plat, site plan or plan of development, and (vii) issuing a written order, requirement, decision or determination regarding the permissibility of a specific land use that is no longer subject to appeal and that is no longer subject to change or reversal under Code §15.2–2311(C).

citing *Board of Supervisors v. Crucible, Inc.*, 278 Va. 152, 158–61, 677 S.E.2d 283, 286–87 (2009) (applying the "without limitation" provision of the statute). . . .

II. ANALYSIS

We agree with the County that this case is controlled by *Crucible*. Similar to McQueen and his proposed cluster subdivision, the plaintiff in *Crucible* sought confirmation from the Stafford County zoning administrator that its proposed security training facility met the definition of a "school" under the local zoning ordinance in an A–1 zoning district. If it met the definition, the facility could be constructed "on a 'by right' basis, i.e., without additional discretionary approval by the County." 278 Va. at 156, 677 S.E.2d at 285. . . .

After meeting with the zoning administrator, the plaintiff in *Crucible* received a letter, titled "'Zoning Verification,'" in which the zoning administrator stated that plaintiff's proposed facility "'would be classified a "school" by definition in the Stafford County Zoning Ordinance,' and that the '[v]erification is valid as of [the date of the letter] and is subject to change.'" 278 Va. at 156, 677 S.E.2d at 285. However, before the plaintiff obtained approval of a site plan for the proposed facility, the Stafford County Board of Supervisors adopted a zoning ordinance that required a conditional use permit for locating a school in an A–1 zoning district. *Id.* . . .

[This] Court . . . explained that "[t]he alleged significant affirmative governmental act should be interpreted according to the plain meaning of the language used in the act" and "the evidence to support the claim to [vested land use] rights must be clear, express, and unambiguous." *Id.* (citing *Hale v. Board of Zoning Appeals*, 277 Va. 250, 274, 673 S.E.2d 170, 182 (2009)). Evidence of "only a future expectation" that the landowner will be allowed to develop his property in accordance with a current zoning classification under the ordinance is therefore insufficient to establish a vested property right in the continuation of the property's existing status. *Id.* (quoting *Hale*, 277 Va. at 271, 673 S.E.2d at 180). Furthermore, "statements of the zoning board's general support of the plan and informal assurances of future approval are not enough to constitute a significant affirmative governmental act." *Id.* . . .

[T]he Court concluded that the statement of zoning classification contained in the zoning administrator's verification letter to the plaintiff was not a significant affirmative governmental act. *Id.* at 161, 677 S.E.2d at 288. The Court reasoned that, "[a]ccording to the plain meaning" of the language in the verification letter, the zoning administrator did not "affirmatively approve" the plaintiff's project, and made "no commitment" to it. *Id.* at 160, 677 S.E.2d at 287. "The zoning administrator simply answered the question concerning the classification of [plaintiff's] project according to the Stafford County Zoning Ordinance in place on the date the request was made," and added that "the verification was subject to change." *Id.*

Like the "verification letter" for the proposed project in *Crucible,* the "compliance letter" in this case did not affirmatively approve McQueen's proposed development of a cluster subdivision. Nor did it make any commitment to McQueen regarding this project. Rather, the compliance letter confirmed that McQueen's proposed development met the general standards for a cluster subdivision. By definition, such confirmation was essentially limited under CLO Ordinance §90–332.6

to a determination of whether the proposal met the requirements for minimum tract size and maximum number of residential units per acre — a simple mathematical calculation. Because McQueen's proposal complied with those standards, Thompson advised McQueen in the compliance letter that he was entitled to pursue his project as a matter of right, i.e., without discretionary approval by the County. That, of course, was far short of the "clear, express, and unambiguous" approval of, or commitment to, a specific plan of development by McQueen as required for the creation of a vested development right.[6] *Crucible,* 278 Va. at 160, 677 S.E.2d at 287. . . .

Reversed and final judgment.

Notes and Comments

1. *The Competing Interests.* What are the competing interests at stake in determining whether a right to build a development has vested? Does the Virginia vesting statute adequately balance those interests? Does the developer have predictability? What is a "significant affirmative governmental act"? Does the statutory definition of the term supply sufficient guidance?

2. *Tests for Vesting.* While state statutes often address vesting, as occurred in *McQueen,* state courts also have employed a variety of common law tests to determine when rights have vested. Many of those tests, which apply variously to zoning changes and to subdivisions, were catalogued by the Utah Supreme Court in *Western Land Equities v. City of Logan,* 617 P.2d 388 (Utah 1980). They include:

a. Zoning Estoppel, which inquires whether there has been "substantial reliance" by the landowner before a zoning change is made. In turn, courts apply various formulations to determine "substantial reliance." For example, the "set quantum" test, which measures the change in position quantitatively, and the "proportionate" test, which determines the percentage of money spent or obligations incurred before the zoning change as compared with the total cost. Do these tests supply certainty and predictability, or do they almost guarantee litigation to determine their applicability?

b. The Balancing Test, which weighs the owner's interest in developing the property and the reasonableness of the proposed use against the interests of the public health, safety, morals, or general welfare. Are courts equipped to apply this test? Is it a test that is appropriate for the judicial function?

c. The Time of Application Test, which creates a vested right at the time of application for a building permit. Does this test constitute an acceptable "middle ground" which is a good compromise?

d. The "Substantial Change in Position" Test, which declares that a permittee gains a vested right only through a substantial change in position in reliance on the permit. Does that test put the subdivider in too much jeopardy of a changed political climate in the local jurisdiction which results in new regulations?

---

6. The first governmental approval required under the CLO Ordinance was an approval of the landowner's preliminary plat of a proposed cluster subdivision. CLO Ordinance §90–332.16(B). With the filing of the preliminary plat, the landowner was, for the first time, required to account for the numerous specific standards for the project under the CLO Ordinance along with the County's subdivision regulations. McQueen did not file his preliminary plat with the County until several days after Thompson issued the compliance letter. Thus, the letter could not have been interpreted as some implied approval of the plat. Nor did Thompson make any mention of an earlier draft of the preliminary plat in her letter.

Which of these tests would you adopt? Do you have a better idea?

3. *The Developer and the Community.* How should the balance be struck between the developer's concerns and those of the community? Once a preliminary subdivision plan is approved, the developer then proceeds to spend significant sums of money on the final plan. *See HJS Development, Inc. v. Pierce County,* 61 P.3d 1141 (Wash. 2003) (after receiving preliminary plat approval, an owner or developer may proceed to prepare detailed engineering drawings, conduct improvements, and prepare the final plat in compliance with the terms and conditions of the preliminary plat). The developer has distinct investment-backed expectations, and last minute regulatory changes can result in a substantial increase in cost that may make the project uneconomic.

4. *Late Vesting and the* Avco *Decision.* On the other hand, the infrastructure and environmental concerns over development are significant and can lead to important changes in regulatory enactments. In *Avco Community Developers v. South Coast Regional Comm'n,* 553 P.2d 546 (Cal. 1976), a leading decision in the area, the California Supreme Court opted for late vesting. The developer had obtained subdivision approval, spent over $2 million, and incurred another $740,468 in liabilities for developing a 74-acre tract. The tract was part of a 5234-acre area on which the developer wanted to build 18,925 residential units. The improvements made to the property included grading pursuant to a grading permit and the installation of utilities. Before the developer had sought a building permit, however, the state adopted coastal zone legislation requiring developers to obtain a coastal commission permit.

The developer claimed a vested right to complete the subdivision and, alternatively, argued estoppel premised on a development agreement. The court held that a developer that had not even sought a building permit could not be vested merely because it previously received permission to subdivide. Just as zoning does not provide a vested right to complete a project, the court observed that the government makes no representation that a developer will be exempt from laws in effect at the time of application for a building permit. The court concluded that a vested right can only be acquired where a developer has performed substantial work and incurred substantial liabilities in good faith reliance upon a building permit issued by the government. The permit must be based on approval of the plans for the specific buildings to be built.

In *Avco,* the developer had never applied for permits for specific buildings. In addition, if the developer's rights had vested with subdivision approval, the project could sit for years, exempting it from future zoning changes for an indefinite period. Is the vesting rule in *Avco* equitable?

5. *Preliminary and Final Subdivision Maps.* As addressed above in this chapter, many state subdivision laws require local government approval of a preliminary subdivision tract map. Then, after the developer has revised the project to comply with the conditions on the preliminary map, the developer files a final subdivision map. Should vesting be tied to the map process? If so, when should vesting apply — after the preliminary map, or not until the final map is filed?

6. *Equitable Estoppel.* Some jurisdictions, in addition to recognizing statutory or judicial vesting, rule freezes or grandfathering, may apply zoning estoppel. As discussed in note one, his doctrine generally applies to situations where a developer reasonably relies on a representation by the government and undertakes a substantial investment. *Congregation Etz Chaim v. City of Los Angeles,* 371 F.3d 1122 (9th Cir. 2004) (construction undertaken pursuant to a permit); *Mayor of City of*

Clinton v. Welch, 888 So. 2d 416 (Miss. 2004) (city estopped from ordering tree house removal following verbal approval of building inspector, expenditure of several thousand dollars, and no city action in five years). In *Exeter Building Corp. v. Town of Newburgh*, 47 N.E.3d 71 (N.Y. Ct. App. 2016), the New York Court of Appeals held that the reliance was not reasonable where the town had warned the landowners of a proposed rezoning on the property. And a recent California case emphasized that equitable estoppel can be invoked only in extraordinary cases. *Schafer v. City of Los Angeles*, 188 Cal. Rptr. 3d 655, 665 (Ct. App. 2015).

7. *Rule Freezes.* Another response to the vesting issue for subdivisions is to enact a "rule freeze" at some point in the development process. In *Weyerhaeuser v. Pierce County*, 976 P.2d 1279, 1283 (Wash. 1999), the court summarized the principle: "[D]evelopers filing a timely and complete land use application obtain a vested right to develop land in accordance with the land use laws and regulations in effect at the time of application." Thus, in *Kaufman & Broad Central Valley, Inc. v. City of Modesto*, 30 Cal. Rptr. 2d 904 (Ct. App. 1994), the statute protected the developer from very large increases in development fees adopted by the city after the tentative map stage but before the developer applied for building permits.

This type of "vesting tentative map" legislation can require the subdivider to submit specific building plans at the time of application for a vesting tentative tract. Developers, however, frequently do not want to undertake architectural costs for the entire subdivision at the time of subdivision approval. They may prefer to wait until the projected market demand warrants such action. As a result, in those jurisdictions that might require early architectural submissions, some subdividers will continue to operate under the uncertainty of the common law late-vesting rule followed in that state, foregoing the legislative early vesting opportunity.

8. *Development Agreements.* Yet another response to the vesting problem is to enter into a contract, known as a development agreement, that "locks in" the fee requirements applicable to a development. Specifically authorized by some state legislatures, the development agreement provides an enforceable arrangement between a regulating authority and the developer. Development agreements are examined in Chapter 10.

E. STREAMLINING AND DEVELOPMENT STANDARDS

The length of the permit process has led numerous jurisdictions to adopt so-called streamlining legislation. The legislation sets deadlines for public agencies to act. The following case offers a typical illustration of streamlining legislation. Note that, although the effect of streamlining laws often arises in the subdivision review process, these laws apply more broadly to a wide variety of development approvals.

■ GAUGHEN LLC v. BOROUGH COUNCIL OF BOROUGH OF MECHANICSBURG
128 A.3d 355 (Pa. Commw. Ct. 2015)

OPINION by Senior Judge JAMES GARDNER COLINS.

On November 26, 2008, plaintiff Gaughen LLC (Developer) submitted a land development plan to the Borough Manager of the Borough of Mechanicsburg

(Borough) seeking approval for a five-unit apartment complex under the Borough's Subdivision and Land Development Ordinance (SALDO). . . .

Section 22–402 of the Borough's SALDO provided:

Submission of Plan, Time Limits and Public Hearings.

1. Preliminary and final plans for all proposed subdivisions of land within the Borough shall be filed with the Planning Commission through the Borough Manager.

2. *No application shall be considered as filed for the purpose of this Chapter unless the same conforms in every respect to the requirements of this ordinance. The acceptance of an application by a Borough official does not waive the requirement that it conforms in every respect to this ordinance.*

3. *Preliminary and final plans shall each be acted on by the Borough Council and the decision shall be in writing and shall be communicated to the applicant or mailed to him at last known address within 90 days from the date such application is filed in the office of the Borough Manager.*

4. It is the intent of these regulations to provide for complete and thorough review of all proposed subdivisions. Therefore, an extension of time of 20 days may be requested from the subdivider in the case of subdivisions or land developments which, in the opinion of the Planning Commission, will require additional review time. Efforts will be made to request and obtain such extension at the time of the submission of the preliminary or final plan. However, an extension may be requested at any time during the review process.

(SALDO §22–402) (emphasis added).

. . . Section 22–403 of the SALDO, governing preliminary plans, stated:

11. Failure of the Borough Council to act on the preliminary plan submission and to notify the applicant of its action within 90 days of their receipt of said submission shall constitute an automatic approval.

On December 10, 2008, the Borough engineer issued a memorandum that noted that Developer's plan did not comply with certain provisions of the Borough's Zoning Ordinance, SALDO, and Stormwater Ordinance. . . .

The Mechanicsburg Planning Commission (Planning Commission) met in a regularly scheduled meeting on December 10, 2008, and discussed Developer's plan and some of the Borough engineer's comments. . . . The minutes of that meeting show that two of the Borough engineer's comments concerning SALDO compliance were discussed and that the Borough engineer withdrew one of those comments. . . . The Planning Commission Chairman asked Developer if it wanted to withdraw the plan based on zoning issues discussed at the meeting, and the Planning Commission tabled the plan at the request of Developer's engineer . . . In January 2009, Developer's engineer met with the Borough engineer and Borough officials to discuss issues concerning the plan. . . . Developer submitted no revised plan to the Borough . . .

The 90–day period from November 26, 2008, the date that Developer submitted its plan, ended on February 24, 2009. The Borough Council did not act on Developer's plan on or before February 24, 2009. The Borough never notified Developer that it considered Developer's application to be incomplete or not filed. . . . On February 18, 2009, the Borough sent Developer a letter representing that Developer's application date was December 10, 2008 and that the deadline for the Borough to act on the plan was March 10, 2009, and advising that the Borough Council would take action on the plan at its March 3, 2009 meeting unless Developer offered an extension of the review period . . .

[O]n February 25, 2009, Developer's engineer signed and faxed the Borough an extension of time until June 10, 2009 to act on the plan . . .

No further extension was granted by Developer, and on June 2, 2009, the Borough Council voted to deny Developer's plan. On June 9, 2009, the Borough notified Developer that the plan was denied, stating as the reasons for the denial each of the Zoning Ordinance, SALDO, and Stormwater Ordinance comments in the Borough engineer's December 10, 2008 memorandum, including the SALDO comment withdrawn at the Planning Commission meeting, and six deficiencies noted by Cumberland County's planning commission. . . .

On December 1, 2009, Developer filed a mandamus action seeking a deemed approval, contending that the plan was deemed approved under the Borough's SALDO because the Borough Council failed to act by February 24, 2009 and, alternatively, that the plan was deemed approved under the MPC because Developer did not agree to the February 25, 2009 extension and the Borough Council failed to act by March 10, 2009, the 90th day after the Planning Commission's first meeting on the plan. . . .

In this appeal, there is no dispute that Developer's plan was deemed approved on February 24, 2009, if the plan was "filed" under the SALDO on November 26, 2008, the date that it was filed with the Borough Manager. . . . There is no dispute the 90–day period from November 26, 2008 expired on February 24, 2009, and that the Borough Council neither acted on Developer's plan nor obtained any extension of time until after February 24, 2009. Rather, the trial court ruled that the SALDO deadline did not apply because Developer's plan was never validly filed under the SALDO, given Section 22–402(2) of the SALDO, providing that "[n]o application shall be considered as filed for the purpose of this Chapter unless the same conforms in every respect to the requirements of this ordinance" and that "acceptance of an application by a Borough official does not waive the requirement that it conforms in every respect to this ordinance." SALDO §22–402(2).

Developer does not dispute that its plan failed to fully comply with all requirements for approval under the SALDO, but argues that Section 22–402(2) only required conformity with filing requirements before a plan may be considered "filed" and the 90–day deadline begins to run, and contends that it complied with all filing requirements when it submitted its plan on November 26, 2008 because it paid the required filing fee and submitted the required number of copies of the plan. Developer also argues that the Borough was barred from asserting that the plan was not filed on November 26, 2008 because the Borough reviewed the plan, treated it as filed, and never asserted that the plan was incomplete or not filed until after the review period expired.

We agree with Developer that Section 22–402(2) requires conformity only with the SALDO's formal filing requirements before a plan may be considered filed, and that it does not require conformity with all substantive SALDO requirements as a prerequisite to filing . . . Section 22–402(2) is ambiguous and unclear as to its meaning. It states that an "application" is not filed unless it "conforms in every respect to the requirements of this ordinance" and "conforms in every respect to this ordinance," SALDO §22–402(2), not that a plan must meet all requirements for approval under the SALDO before it may be considered filed. Moreover, as the trial court noted (Trial Court Rule 1925 Opinion at 5), the SALDO does not set forth any requirements for an "application." . . .

Construing Section 22–402(2) as requiring that a plan be in conformity with all substantive requirements for approval under the SALDO before it can be considered filed and the deadlines for action on it can run is contrary to the purpose of both filing requirements and deemed approval provisions. The purpose of filing requirements for a land use application is to ensure that the municipality has the material that it needs to conduct a meaningful review and make a determination whether the applicant's plan complies with its ordinance, not to prevent the filing of applications for plans that do not meet all ordinance requirements for approval . . .

Moreover, construing the deadline for deemed approval as running only where the substantive requirements for approval are satisfied is inconsistent with the nature of a deemed approval. The merits of the application are irrelevant to a deemed approval . . . Deemed approvals are disfavored precisely because they can result in approvals of land uses that do not comply with local ordinances. . . . Accordingly, construing the SALDO's deemed approval provisions as operating only where the plan meets all requirements for approval under the SALDO is not a reasonable interpretation of the ambiguous language of Section 22–402(2). . . .

Our conclusion that Section 22–402(2) requires conformity only with the SALDO's filing requirements, however, does not resolve the issue of whether Developer's plan was validly filed under the SALDO. Contrary to Developer's contentions, the SALDO's filing requirements were not limited to a filing fee and a required number of copies of documents labeled as a "plan."

We need not resolve [this issue], however, because we agree with Developer that the Borough is barred from asserting that filing deficiencies in Developer's plan prevented the SALDO deadlines from running.

This Court has repeatedly held that acceptance or review of a land use application without asserting that it is incomplete bars a municipality from defending against deemed approval on the ground that the application was never validly filed. . . . If an application does not satisfy the municipality's filing requirements, it is the municipality's duty to notify the applicant that its application is rejected as incomplete and will not be considered. . . . If the municipality notifies the applicant that the application is rejected as incomplete and offers to return the filing fee, the deadlines for action on the application do not run and no deemed approval can occur. . . . If, however, the municipality treats the application as filed, deficiencies in the application do not prevent deemed approval deadlines from running . . .

Accordingly, where a municipality does not advise the applicant that its application has been rejected and will not be considered, the municipality cannot later defeat a deemed approval by arguing that the deadline for action did not run because the application was not properly filed. . . .

Here, the Borough did not reject Developer's plan as not validly filed. Although the Borough notified Developer of deficiencies in the plan, it did not state that the plan was not filed because it was incomplete or advise Developer that these deficiencies prevented the plan from being filed. . . . At no time did the Borough ever attempt to return Developer's application fee. Instead, it treated the plan as filed and proceeded to review the plan on the merits, raising the assertion that Section 22–402(2) prevented the plan from being filed under the SALDO only after Developer asserted a deemed approval. Nor did the Borough show that the plan became complete at a date later than November 26, 2008 and that its acceptance and treatment of the plan as filed therefore related to a date other than November 26, 2008 . . . Because the Borough chose to accept and treat Developer's plan as filed and raised its defense under Section 22–402(2) only after the fact, deemed approval cannot be denied on the ground that Developer's submission of the plan on November 26, 2008 did not constitute filing of the plan under the SALDO. . . .

The Borough argues that this rule does not apply because its SALDO did not require it to reject incomplete applications and expressly provided that "acceptance of an application by a Borough official does not waive the requirement that it conforms in every respect to this ordinance." SALDO §22–402(2). We do not agree . . .

Section 22–402(2)'s language that "acceptance of an application by a Borough official does not waive" the SALDO's requirements is inapplicable here. Such a non-waiver provision protects the Borough against the claims that an initial erroneous acceptance of a filing prevents the Borough from rejecting an application when it discovers that the application is incomplete, and also protects against claims that acceptance of an application bars the Borough from denying an application for noncompliance with SALDO provisions. Thus, under Section 22–402(2), the initial acceptance of Developer's plan would not have prevented the Borough from rejecting the plan as invalidly filed when it received its engineer's comments on December 10, 2008. The Borough could therefore have notified Developer in December 2008 that the plan was incomplete and would not be considered because of the deficiencies noted by the Borough engineer, and tendered the application fee. Had the Borough done so, neither the SALDO deadlines nor the MPC deadlines would have run and no deemed approval could have occurred . . . Likewise, the initial acceptance of the plan as filed did not waive the Borough Council's right to timely deny the plan based on the deficiencies noted in the Borough engineer's letter.

The Borough's conduct, however, was not the mere "acceptance of an application by a Borough official" to which Section 22–402(2) applies. Rather, the Borough chose to treat Developer's plan as filed and proceeded to review it after it knew of the possible deficiencies that could be grounds from rejecting the plan as incomplete . . .

We therefore reverse the trial court's denial of Developer's post-trial motion and remand this case to the trial court for the entry of judgment in mandamus in favor of Developer on its claim for deemed approval under the Borough's SALDO.[7]

Notes and Comments

1. *Permit Streamlining and Automatic Approvals.* Most states have enacted permit streamlining legislation designed to speed up the delay caused by development review. The legislation typically sets a maximum time for taking action on applications, holding hearings, rendering decisions, and notifying applicants. Streamlining laws apply to a wide variety of land use approvals, including subdivisions.

---

7. Developer asserts that it is entitled not only to deemed approval, but also to damages and issuance of permits. Only the issue of deemed approval under the SALDO is before us in this appeal. . . . We note, however, that to the extent that permits have been denied based on zoning issues, the deemed approval here will not entitle Developer to proceed with its project or obtain those permits. A deemed approval under a SALDO does not exempt a land use plan from zoning ordinance requirements or compel the granting of zoning variances. . . .

In many cases, the statute provides that projects may be "deemed approved" if action is not timely taken. Such "deemed approved" legislation appears fair when considered against unconscionable local delay. It could, however, result in the automatic approval of projects that will cause significant, adverse environmental impacts or require infrastructure beyond local supply capacity.

2. *The* Mechanicsburg *Holding.* Did the court reach the correct result? What authority requires the local government to notify an applicant that its application was inadequate? Why didn't the borough's conduct here amount to such a notification?

3. *"Deemed Approved" Avoided.* The harshness of deemed-approved permit streamlining has caused some courts to evade its impact. The easiest cases are those in which the statutory language does not clearly call for an automatic approval. *Nyack Hosp. v. Village of Nyack Planning Bd.,* 647 N.Y.S.2d 799 (Sup. Ct. App. Div. 1996) (although village failed to act on final site plan application after 62 days in violation of statute, the application is not approved by default as the state Village Law did not explicitly provide for default approval of site plans).

4. *Substantial Compliance.* Some courts avoid a default by finding substantial compliance with the streamlining statute. *See, for example, Board of Aldermen of Newton v. Maniace,* 711 N.E.2d 565 (Mass. 1999) (finding that the filing of the result of a city board's vote was sufficient to prevent the project from being automatically approved even though the plaintiff alleged irregularities in that filing); Frank C. Huntington & William J. Connolly, Equitable Considerations in Statutory Construction: *Board of Aldermen of Newton v. Maniace,* Boston Bar J. (March/April 2000) ("it seems likely that the majority [in *Maniace*] was motivated, at least in part, by a sense that constructive approval was too severe a penalty to impose on a local board for what was, at worst, a mere technical violation of the statute").

5. *"Vested Rights" Short of Deemed Approved.* While a streamlining statute can result in an automatic approval, its violation can also result in a "lesser" vested right — the local government can only apply the requirements in effect at that time. Thus, as the court held in *Norco Constr., Inc. v. King County,* 649 P.2d 103 (Wash. 1982), "Not only is the County's discretion limited by the procedure [time limits] of the statute, it is also limited by the land use restrictions that existed at the time the statutory time period had run." *See also The Village of Tiki Island v. Premier Tierra Holdings, Inc.,* 464 S.W.3d 435 (Tex. Ct. App. 2015) (applicant had "vested right" to have its application reviewed under the rules in effect when it filed its plat application).

6. *Multiple Submissions.* Applying streamlining provisions can be difficult where there have been multiple applications or submissions of information to the reviewing agency. In *Advantage Dev., Inc. v. Board of Supervisors of Jackson Township,* 688 A.2d 759 (Pa. Commw. Ct. 1997), Pennsylvania's intermediate appellate court ruled that in complex subdivision proceedings where multiple revised plans are submitted, each new submission does not create a clear legal right to another decision within the 90-day statutory period. Where the board of supervisors ultimately rejected the first final plan, the subdivision was not to be deemed approved because the board did not specifically reject a revised final plan.

7. *Remedies for Violations of Streamlining Laws.* What are the remedies available to a developer who believes that a public agency has missed a mandatory deadline and thus rendered the project automatically approved, but the agency refuses to acknowledge its error? The obvious remedy is a mandamus action ordering the project approved. *See State ex rel. Aspen Group, Inc. v. Washington County Bd. of Comm'rs,*

946 P.2d 347 (Or. Ct. App. 1997) (allowing plaintiff to recover statutory attorney's fees as well). But the delay may also cost the developer money. Is a damage remedy also appropriate? Some courts have said yes. *Schillerstrom Homes, Inc. v. City of Naperville*, 762 N.E.2d 494 (Ill. 2001).

8. *Waiving the Streamlining Protections.* To what extent can rights under the streamlining laws be avoided by voluntary waiver? Courts may apply the common law waiver doctrine in which an applicant waives its right to a decision within a specific period and agrees to an extension of that period. *Bickel v. City of Piedmont*, 946 P.2d 427 (Cal. 1997). In response to *Bickel*, the state legislature amended the statute to eliminate common law waiver. Cal. Gov't Code §65940.5 (West 2016). *See also Kauai Springs, Inc. v. Planning Comm'n of Cty. of Kauai*, 324 P.3d 951 (Haw. 2014) (applicant can "assent" under the ordinance to waiving the deadline as long as the assent occurs prior to the deadline).

9. *The Vesting and Streamlining Problem in Perspective.* You have now been exposed to the vesting "problem," the policy issues involved, and a variety of proposed solutions. What solution would you recommend? When should vesting occur? If early in the process, should the vesting encompass an actual right to construct, or just to prevent any later regulatory changes? If a timetable is violated, what should the remedy be: mandamus only, or damages and attorney's fees as well? Finally, should the courts recognize a right in the applicant to waive the timetable?

F. CONTROLLING GROWTH

The materials above focus on the approvals needed for an individual subdivision, the standards that apply to a subdivision, streamlining requirements, and the evidence needed to support the public agency's decision to approve or deny. As large-scale growth threatened to overwhelm local jurisdictions and greatly change their characteristics, cities began to re-examine the subdivision review process. Some sought to delay or control the growth in the jurisdiction. The following case is one of the first to address this issue, and it had a significant impact on how courts in other states viewed similar ordinances.

As you read the case, pay special attention to the process followed by the Town of Ramapo in enacting the ordinance and the way in which it was structured. At the time that the town was drafting the ordinances at issue, the town and its lawyers were entering uncharted legal territory.

■ GOLDEN v. PLANNING BOARD OF THE TOWN OF RAMAPO
285 N.E.2d (N.Y. 1972)

SCILEPPI, Judge.

Experiencing the pressures of an increase in population and the ancillary problem of providing municipal facilities and services, the Town of Ramapo, as early as 1964, made application for grant under section 801 of the Housing Act of 1964 (78 U.S. Stat. 769) to develop a master plan. The plan's preparation included a four-volume study of the existing land uses, public facilities, transportation, industry and commerce, housing needs and projected population trends. The proposals appearing in the studies were subsequently adopted pursuant to section 272-a of the Town Law, Consol. Laws, c. 62, in July, 1966 and implemented by way of a master plan. The master plan was followed by the adoption of a comprehensive zoning ordinance. Additional sewage district and drainage studies were undertaken which culminated in the adoption of a capital budget, providing for the development of the improvements specified in the master plan within the next six years. Pursuant to section 271 of the Town Law, authorizing comprehensive planning, and as a supplement to the capital budget, the Town Board adopted a capital program which provides for the location and sequence of additional capital improvements for the 12 years following the life of the capital budget. The two plans, covering a period of 18 years, detail the capital improvements projected for maximum development and conform to the specifications set forth in the master plan, the official map and drainage plan.

Based upon these criteria, the Town subsequently adopted the subject amendments for the alleged purpose of eliminating premature subdivision and urban sprawl. Residential development is to proceed according to the provision of adequate municipal facilities and services, with the assurance that any concomitant restraint upon property use is to be of a "temporary" nature and that other private uses, including the construction of individual housing, are authorized.

The amendments did not rezone or reclassify any land into different residential or use districts, but, for the purposes of implementing the proposals appearing in the comprehensive plan, consist, in the main, of additions to the definitional sections of the ordinance, section 46-3, and the adoption of a new class of "Special Permit Uses," designated "Residential Development Use." "Residential Development Use" is defined as "The erection or construction of dwellings or any vacant plots, lots or parcels of land" (§46-3, as amd.); and, any person who acts so as to come within that definition, "shall be deemed to be engaged in residential development which shall be a separate use classification under this ordinance and subject to the requirement of obtaining a special permit from the Town Board" (§46-3, as amd.).

The standards for the issuance of special permits are framed in terms of the availability to the proposed subdivision plat of five essential facilities or services: specifically (1) public sanitary sewers or approved substitutes; (2) drainage facilities; (3) improved public parks or recreation facilities, including public schools; (4) State, county or town roads — major, secondary or collector; and, (5) firehouses. No special permit shall issue unless the proposed residential development has accumulated 15 development points, to be computed on a sliding scale of values assigned to the specified improvements under the statute. Subdivision is thus a function of immediate availability to the proposed plat of certain municipal improvements; the avowed purpose of the amendments being to phase residential development to the Town's ability to provide the above facilities or services.

Certain savings and remedial provisions are designed to relieve of potentially unreasonable restrictions. Thus, the board may issue special permits vesting a present right to proceed with residential development in such year as the development meets the required point minimum, but in no event later than the final year of the 18-year capital plan. The approved special use permit is fully assignable, and improvements scheduled for completion within one year from the date of an application are to be credited as though existing on the date of the application. A prospective developer may advance the date of subdivision approval by agreeing to provide those improvements which will bring the proposed plat within the number of development points required by the amendments. And applications are authorized to the "Development Easement Acquisition Commission" for a reduction of the assessed valuation. Finally, upon application to the Town Board, the development point requirements may be varied should the board determine that such a variance or modification is consistent with the on-going development plan.

The undisputed effect of these integrated efforts in land use planning and development is to provide an over-all program of orderly growth and adequate facilities through a sequential development policy commensurate with progressing availability and capacity of public facilities. While its goals are clear and its purposes undisputably laudatory, serious questions are raised as to the manner in which these ends are to be effected, not the least of which relates to their legal viability under present zoning enabling legislation, particularly sections 261 and 263 of the Town Law. The owners of the subject premises argue, and the Appellate Division has sustained the proposition, that the primary purpose of the amending ordinance is to control or regulate population growth within the Town and as such is not within the authorized objectives of the zoning enabling legislation. We disagree.

In enacting the challenged amendments, the Town Board has sought to control subdivision in all residential districts, pending the provision (public or private) at some future date of various services and facilities. A reading of the relevant statutory provisions reveals that there is no specific authorization for the "sequential" and "timing" controls adopted here. That, of course, cannot be said to end the matter, for the additional inquiry remains as to whether the challenged amendments find their basis within the perimeters of the devices authorized and purposes sanctioned under current enabling legislation. Our concern is, as it should be, with the effects of the statutory scheme taken as a whole and its role in the propagation of a viable policy of land use and planning.

Of course, zoning historically has assumed the development of individual plats and has proven characteristically ineffective in treating with the problems attending subdivision and development of larger parcels, involving as it invariably does, the provision of adequate public services and facilities. To this end, subdivision control (Town Law, §§276, 277) purports to guide community development in the directions outlined here, while at the same time encouraging the provision of adequate facilities for the housing, distribution, comfort and convenience of local residents (*Village of Lynbrook v. Cadoo*, 252 N.Y. 308, 314, 169 N.E. 394, 396). It reflects in essence, a legislative judgment that the development of unimproved areas be accompanied by provision of essential facilities. And though it may not, in a definitional or conceptual sense be identified with the power to zone, it is designed to complement other land use restrictions, which, taken together, seek to implement a broader, comprehensive plan for community development.

It is argued, nevertheless, that the timing controls currently in issue are not legislatively authorized since their effect is to prohibit subdivision absent precedent or concurrent action of the Town, and hence constitutes an unauthorized blanket interdiction against subdivision.

It is, indeed, true that the Planning Board is not in an absolute sense statutorily authorized to deny the right to subdivide. That is not, however, what is sought to be accomplished here. The Planning Board has the right to refuse approval of subdivision plats in the absence of those improvements specified in section 277, and the fact that it is the Town and not the subdividing owner or land developer who is required to make those improvements before the plat will be approved cannot be said to transform the scheme into an absolute prohibition any more than it would be so where it was the developer who refused to provide the facilities required for plat approval. Denial of subdivision plat approval, invariably amounts to a prohibition against subdivision, albeit a conditional one . . . and to say that the Planning Board lacks the authority to deny subdivision rights is to mistake the nature of our inquiry which is essentially whether development may be conditioned pending the provision by the municipality of specified services and facilities. Whether it is the municipality or the developer who is to provide the improvements, the objective is the same — to provide adequate facilities, off-site and on-site; and in either case subdivision rights are conditioned, not denied. . . .

[T]hough the issues are framed in terms of the developer's due process rights, those rights cannot, realistically speaking, be viewed separately and apart from the rights of others "'in search of a [more] comfortable place to live.'" (*Concord Twp. Appeal*, 439 Pa. 466, 474, n.6, 268 A.2d 765, 768). . . .

There is, then, something inherently suspect in a scheme which, apart from its professed purposes, effects a restriction upon the free mobility of a people until sometime in the future when projected facilities are available to meet increased demands. Although zoning must include schemes designed to allow municipalities to more effectively contend with the increased demands of evolving and growing communities, under its guise, townships have been wont to try their hand at an array of exclusionary devices in the hope of avoiding the very burden which growth must inevitably bring . . . Though the conflict engendered by such tactics is certainly real, and its implications vast, accumulated evidence, scientific and social, points circumspectly at the hazards of undirected growth and the naive, somewhat nostalgic imperative that egalitarianism is a function of growth.

Of course, these problems cannot be solved by Ramapo or any single municipality, but depend upon the accommodation of widely disparate interests for their ultimate resolution. To that end, State-wide or regional control of planning would insure that interests broader than that of the municipality underlie various land use policies. Nevertheless, that should not be the only context in which growth devices such as these, aimed at population assimilation, not exclusion, will be sustained. . . .

Hence, unless we are to ignore the plain meaning of the statutory delegation, this much is clear: phased growth is well within the ambit of existing enabling legislation. And, of course, it is no answer to point to emergent problems to buttress the conclusion that such innovative schemes are beyond the perimeters of statutory authorization. These considerations, admittedly real, to the extent which they are relevant, bear solely upon the continued viability of "localism" in land use regulation; obviously, they can neither add nor detract from the initial grant of authority, obsolescent though it may be. The answer which Ramapo has posed can by no means be termed definitive; it is, however, a first practical step toward controlled growth achieved without forsaking broader social purposes.

The subject ordinance is said to advance legitimate zoning purposes as it assures that each new home built in the township will have at least a minimum of public services in the categories regulated by the ordinance. The Town argues that various public facilities are presently being constructed but that for want of time and money it has been unable to provide such services and facilities at a pace commensurate with increased public need. It is urged that although the zoning power includes reasonable restrictions upon the private use of property, exacted in the hope of development according to well-laid plans, calculated to advance the public welfare of the community in the future, the subject regulations go further and seek to avoid the increased responsibilities and economic burdens which time and growth must ultimately bring.

What we will not countenance, then, under any guise, is community efforts at immunization or exclusion. But, far from being exclusionary, the present amendments merely seek, by the implementation of sequential development and timed growth, to provide a balanced cohesive community dedicated to the efficient utilization of land. The restrictions conform to the community's considered land use policies as expressed in its comprehensive plan and represent a bona fide effort to maximize population density consistent with orderly growth. True other alternatives, such as requiring off-site improvements as a prerequisite to subdivision, may be available, but the choice as how best to proceed, in view of the difficulties attending such exactions . . . cannot be faulted.

Perhaps even more importantly, timed growth, unlike the minimum lot requirements recently struck down by the Pennsylvania Supreme Court as exclusionary, does not impose permanent restrictions upon land use (*see National Land & Inv. Co. v. Easttown Twp. Bd. of Adj.*, 419 Pa. 504, 215 A.2d 597, *supra; Concord Twp. Appeal*, 439 Pa. 466, 268 A.2d 765, *supra*). Its obvious purpose is to prevent premature subdivision absent essential municipal facilities and to insure continuous development commensurate with the Town's obligation to provide such facilities. They seek, not to freeze population at present levels but to maximize growth by the efficient use of land, and in so doing testify to this community's continuing role in population assimilation. In sum, Ramapo asks not that it be left alone, but only that it be allowed to prevent the kind of deterioration that has transformed well-ordered and thriving residential communities into blighted ghettos with attendant hazards to health, security and social stability — a danger not without substantial basis in fact.

The proposed amendments have the effect of restricting development for onwards to 18 years in certain areas. Whether the subject parcels will be so restricted for the full term is not clear, for it is equally probable that the proposed facilities will be brought into these areas well before that time. Assuming, however, that the restrictions will remain outstanding for the life of the program, they still fall short of a confiscation within the meaning of the Constitution.

An ordinance which seeks to permanently restrict the use of property so that it may not be used for any reasonable purpose must be recognized as a taking . . . An appreciably different situation obtains where the restriction constitutes a *temporary* restriction, promising that the property may be put to a profitable use within a reasonable time. . . .

Without a doubt restrictions upon the property in the present case are substantial in nature and duration. They are not, however, absolute. The amendments contemplate a definite term, as the development points are designed to operate for a maximum period of 18 years and during that period, the Town is committed to the construction and installation of capital improvements. The net result of the ongoing development provision is that individual parcels may be committed to a residential development use prior to the expiration of the maximum period. Similarly, property owners under the terms of the amendments may elect to accelerate the date of development by installing, at their own expense, the necessary public services to bring the parcel within the required number of development points. While even the best of plans may not always be realized, in the absence of proof to the contrary, we must assume the Town will put its best effort forward in implementing the physical and fiscal timetable outlined under the plan. Should subsequent events prove this assumption unwarranted, or should the Town because of some unforeseen event fail in its primary obligation to these landowners, there will be ample opportunity to undo the restrictions upon default. . . .

In sum, where it is clear that the existing physical and financial resources of the community are inadequate to furnish the essential services and facilities which a substantial increase in population requires, there is a rational basis for "phased growth" and hence, the challenged ordinance is not violative of the Federal and State Constitutions. . . .

Notes and Comments

1. *The Significance of* Ramapo *'s Planning.* The New York Court of Appeals emphasizes the comprehensive planning efforts that preceded the adoption of the *Ramapo* ordinance. What is the legal significance of these efforts? How did they seem to affect the court?

In *Rancourt v. Town of Barnstead*, 523 A.2d 55 (N.H. 1986), the plaintiff attacked the evidentiary basis for the provision in the town's master plan for a 3 percent annual growth rate. The town offered two exhibits as support for the measure: a state projection of growth for the town and a questionnaire distributed to the town's residents asking them what the "ideal" growth rate would be. The court overturned the measure, finding that the evidence did not constitute a "solid, scientific, statistical basis for the recommended three percent growth rate." *Id.* at 59.

An article by Professor John R. Nolon discusses the context of the Ramapo plan. John R. Nolon, The Contemporary Relevance of *Golden v. Ramapo*, Am. Bar Assn. Section of State and Local Gov't Law, State and Local Law News, vol. 26, No. 1, Fall 2002, at 1. The article notes that, at the time, the Ramapo plan's "inventions were sophisticated, controversial, and legally dubious." The article cites the city's "investment in comprehensive planning" as supporting the idea that "land-use laws that conform to objectives contained in adopted master plans are highly successful in overcoming legal challenges." *See also Beck v. Town of Raymond*, 394 A.2d 847, 852 (N.H. 1978) (growth controls "should be the product of careful study and should be reexamined constantly with a view toward relaxing or ending them").

2. *Authority for Enactment of Growth Management Programs.* The Ramapo growth control plan was implemented by requiring a "special permit." How was the ordinance able to control subdivisions in this manner? The court finds that control or regulation of population growth was not an "authorized objective" of the New York zoning enabling legislation. If growth control was not a zoning objective, how could the court uphold the ordinance? You should closely examine the argument made by the town, centering on its authority to control subdivisions, that the court accepted in upholding the growth control ordinance.

The *Ramapo* court's decision can be read as suggesting that restrictions on the "rate" or "pace" of growth are unauthorized by the New York zoning enabling statute. The impact of this point has not been significant, since local infrastructure controls nearly always operate by limiting residential subdivision development and can be supported by the delegated authority for regulating subdivisions.

3. *The Principle of Concurrency.* Requiring that infrastructure be available to support subdivisions is a concept known as "concurrency." This concept "endeavor[s] to achieve the orderly sequencing of development within a community." James H. Wickersham, The Quiet Revolution Continues: The Emerging New Model For State Growth Management Statutes, 18 Harv. Envtl. L. Rev. 489, 510 (1994). Concurrency "is a legislative-enacted growth management tool for ensuring the availability of adequate public facilities and services to accommodate development." Ronald L. Weaver, Concurrency, Concurrency Alternatives, Infrastructure, Planning and Regional Solution Issues, 12 U. Fla. J.L. & Pub. Poly. 251 (2001). The concept is a basic one:

> [A] developer applying for a building permit must show the local governing body that the demands of the proposed development will not exceed the maximum capacity of public facilities. If the local government determines that the existing public facilities cannot sustain the additional development, then the application for a permit to build will be denied.

Adam Strachan, Note, Concurrency Laws: Water as a Land-Use Regulation, 21 J. Land Resources & Envtl. L. 435 (2001).

A few states have enacted statutes requiring concurrency. Are concurrency measures really "growth control" measures? One book on the subject, addressing Florida's then-existing concurrency requirement, has stated: "Critics point out that the concurrency requirements, coupled with inadequate state funding for infrastructure, are encouraging development in rural and exurban areas where excess road capacity exists, contrary to state goals discouraging urban sprawl." Arthur C. Nelson & James B. Duncan, Growth Management Principles and Practices 97 (1995).

4. *No "Right to Sewers."* The *Ramapo* court notes that, if a developer does not want to wait until the town provides the infrastructure for its development, the developer has the option of providing that infrastructure. Note that there is no "right to sewers"; a developer does not have the right to insist that a local jurisdiction engage in deficit financing to pay for infrastructure. On the other hand, some courts have held that cities acting as public utilities cannot deliberately refuse to serve customers as a means of controlling growth. *See, e.g., Brennan Woods Ltd. P'ship v. Town of Williston*, 782 A.2d 1230 (Vt. 2001) (municipality may allocate capacity of the sewer system, but the allocation may be used to control population and density only "where decisions are based on the load to the sewer system. . . ." Decisions cannot "be based on growth limits in the town plan"); *Robinson v. City of Boulder*, 547 P.2d 228 (Colo. 1976) (city could only refuse to serve a new development outside its boundaries for utility-related reasons, not for planning reasons).

5. *The* Ramapo *Plan Abandoned.* The *Ramapo* program proved to be unsustainable. During the later 1970s, as growth slowed significantly, Ramapo began to follow the program less strictly. For example, it sometimes accepted financial contributions from builders who failed to accumulate the required number of points. The town also fell behind in its capital improvement program. The program also imposed significant administrative costs and burdens on the town. The principal

parts of the program ultimately were rescinded in 1983. *See* Ramapo Marks End of Controlled Growth, Journal News (Rockland County, N.Y.), July 11, 1983, at 1.

Today, the town of Ramapo has a population of about 110,000 people and continues to be, by most standards, a low-density community. Los Angeles has three times the net residential density of Ramapo. As a place to live, Ramapo, like its surrounding communities, is awash in the sea of metropolitan New York City sprawl.

6. *Exclusionary Zoning, Growth Management Programs, Regional Sprawl, and Sustainable Development.* Local growth management programs, of course, are adopted to address quality of life issues within a particular community. Within that community, land use controls as in Ramapo may attempt to deal, at least in part, with the internal problems of scattered, haphazard, and inappropriate development. What about the problems of regional sprawl? Local zoning and growth management programs are almost by definition low density and exclusionary in nature. What happens to the people and developments that are excluded from a community as a result these programs?

There are only two ways to grow, either up or out. The American paradigm of local control of land development through exclusionary and low-density zoning regimes is increasingly recognized as a significant cause of ever-expanding regional sprawl in this country. *See* Edward H. Ziegler, Urban Sprawl, Growth Management, and Sustainable Development in the United States: Thoughts on the Sentimental Quest for a New Middle Landscape, 11 Va. J. Soc. Pol'y & L. 26 (2003) (discussing and citing authorities on how local zoning and growth management contribute to regional sprawl).

Although it may be counterintuitive, critics of sprawl point out that "high density" is actually "Green Development." This assertion rests on the lower resource, energy, transportation, and environmental costs associated with higher-density development. A low-density built environment of detached single-family homes, with all land uses grouped as isolated, automobile-dependent pods of development, consumes an enormous amount of resources and energy to build, maintain, and operate. Presently, it is dependent on the plentiful supply of cheap fossil fuels, particularly oil. Is that model sustainable in the future?

4

Infrastructure

A. INTRODUCTION

1. The Underappreciated Subject

Infrastructure is perhaps the most unsexy, most essential, and least appreciated aspect of land use law and policy. Infrastructure has no formal, fixed definition. Generally speaking, it refers to all those things outside private homes, commercial businesses, and government offices that are necessary to make those spaces useful. Infrastructure includes roads, bridges, sidewalks, water and sewer lines, water wells, sewage treatment and pumping facilities, flood control structures, parks, bike paths, schools, hospitals and other health care facilities, police and fire stations, libraries, transit facilities, telephone lines and equipment, gas distribution systems, and fiber optic conduits. While infrastructure is typically thought to be physical in nature, the term can encompass various services, such as child care, education, and social services programs. The relative magnitude and quality of infrastructure in different locations have an enormous influence on the utility, and hence the value, of land for different purposes. Infrastructure is an unavoidable topic in a land use course because basic infrastructure is necessary to make productive use of land.

2. Who Should Pay?

The issue of *who* should pay for infrastructure presents a fundamental threshold issue. However one defines it, infrastructure is expensive. For example, the new Tappan Zee Bridge across the Hudson River in New York, now under construction, has as estimated price tag of $3.9 billion. *See* Joseph Berger, Braving the Elements Atop the New Tappan Zee Bridge. The New York Times (January 8, 2016) at http://www.nytimes.com/2016/01/10/nyregion/braving-the-elements-atop-the-new-tappan-zee-bridge.html (last visited Nov. 11, 2016). DC Metro, after years of neglect in maintaining the subway system in Washington, D.C., has launched a huge rebuilding effort that officials cannot even put a price tag on yet. *See* Paul Duggan, *Metro Will Shut Down Sections of Lines for Year-Long Subway Repair Work*, The Washington Post (May 6, 2016) at https://www.washingtonpost.com/local/trafficandcommuting/metro-armageddon-is-coming-a-year-of-shuttered-sections-massive-repairs/2016/05/06/9a7160d0-12e6-11e6-93ae-50921721165d_story.html (last visited Nov 11, 2016).

The question of who should pay is made more significant by the general understanding that the United States is woefully behind the eight ball in terms of investing in infrastructure, in particular in necessary upkeep and repairs. *See* generally Move: Putting America's Infrastructure Back in the Lead 9-17 (2015) (providing vivid illustrations of the practical consequences of the United States' deteriorated infrastructure). President Barack Obama made decrying the decrepit state of America's infrastructure a hallmark of his presidency. *See* Barack Obama Speech on Infrastructure and the Economy (July 25, 2013) at https://www.whitehouse.gov/photos-and-video/video/2013/07/25/president-obama-speaks-infrastructure-and-economy (last visited Nov 11, 2016). According to the 2013 edition of the American Society of Civil Engineers' "Report Card" on U.S. Infrastructure, the "cumulative GPA" for infrastructure was a low D+, with grades in individual sectors ranging from a high of B- for solid waste to a low of D- for inland waterways and levees. *See* 2013 Report Card for America's Infrastructure, http://www.infrastructurereportcard.org/a/#p/home (last visited Nov 11, 2016). Schools, transit, roads, aviation, wastewater hazardous waste, drinking water, and dams each received a D. The report estimated that it would take an expenditure of $3.6 trillion by 2020 to attain a state of "good repair" (i.e., a B) in each of the categories studied in the report. Some dispute the objectivity of the report card, and question whether the situation is as dire as the Civil Engineers assert. *See* James Pethokoukis, Actually, America Doesn't Have a Trillion-Dollar Infrastructure Crisis, A. Eideas (November 4, 2013) (http://www.aei.org/publication/actually-america-doesnt-have-a-trillion-dollar-infrastructure-crisis/) (last visited Nov 11, 2016). There is little doubt the present and future price tag for domestic infrastructure is substantial.

3. The Basic Choice: Taxpayers or Users?

The basic choice for covering these costs is either to look to taxpayers or to users. *See* Julie Kim, New Cities Foundation, Handbook on Urban Infrastructure Finance, 9 (2016). Assigning the cost to taxpayers treats infrastructure as a common responsibility of citizens and seeks to spread the financial responsibility for infrastructure as widely as the tax system will allow. By contrast, imposing the cost of infrastructure on users places the financial burden on those whose activities create particular burdens on the infrastructure system or who are specially benefited by investments in infrastructure. A moment's thought reveals that the choice of who pays can become considerably more complicated than a simple binary choice between taxpayers and users. On the taxpayer side, the cost of infrastructure may be borne by federal, state or local taxpayers, and the collected revenues can be and frequently are transferred from one level of government to another. It does not take an advanced degree in political science to recognize that local officials will be more inclined to spend more on infrastructure if a major portion of the cost is covered by some other level of government. On the user side, the cost of new infrastructure may be imposed on developers initially, but the particular circumstances of each project and real estate market will determine whether these costs are absorbed by the developer or transferred to the owners of the property slated for development or to purchasers of units in the development.

No definitive theory or body of data can resolve the issue of how to allocate the cost of infrastructure within a community. Making all land users "carry their own" weight in terms of infrastructure cost has a certain logical appeal. However, a strict policy of cost internalization could have deleterious social consequences. For example, it is generally recognized that families with school-age children impose substantial costs on local governments; but imposing extra fees on development that can accommodate families because educating children is expensive would have obvious adverse consequences for the community as well as the families. On the other hand, imposing a relatively light financial burden on commercial enterprises because they may impose fewer costs on the municipality may be perceived as inequitable.

B. TAX INCREMENT FINANCING

One of the most important contemporary tools for financing infrastructure — and one of the most controversial — is tax increment financing. The following two state court cases illustrate the kinds of challenges that are brought against the use of this infrastructure financing technique.

■ BOARD OF DIRECTORS OF THE INDUSTRIAL DEVELOPMENT BOARD OF THE CITY OF GONZALES, LOUISIANA, INC. v. ALL TAXPAYERS, PROPERTY OWNERS, CITIZENS OF THE CITY OF GONZALES
938 So.2d 11 (Mo. 2006)

Justice KIMBALL

In this case we are called upon to determine whether the use of public funds pursuant to our tax increment financing laws to finance a private retail development is unconstitutional. Because we find the economic development project at issue does not violate the constitutional prohibition against the loan, pledge or donation of public property or the equal protection provisions of the federal and state constitutions, we affirm the judgment of the court of appeal.

FACTS AND PROCEDURAL HISTORY

To promote economic development, various entities of the City of Gonzales and the State of Louisiana made a decision to enter into several agreements and to issue tax increment revenue bonds to effectuate a project resulting in a Cabela's Retail Center and a Sportsman Park Center. Thus, the project involves the use of Tax Increment Financing as provided in La. R.S. 33:9038.1 *et seq.* (the "TIF Act").

On April 25, 2005, the governing authority of the City of Gonzales (the "City") adopted an ordinance creating an economic development district within the City, which was named the "Gonzales Economic Development District No. 1" (the "District."). The District, which encompasses a 233–acre tract of land, is a political subdivision of the state pursuant to La. R.S. 33:9038.2. Additionally, in furtherance of its goals to secure funding for economic development projects, the governing authority of the City sought a rededication of taxes previously authorized. On April 23, 2005, a special election was held wherein the voters of the City approved the rededication of the one percent sales and use tax previously authorized on September 10, 1966, and the one-half percent sales and use tax previously authorized on April 1, 1989, for use by economic development districts created pursuant to the TIF Act to promote economic development in the City through the use of incremental increases in sales and use tax collected within the boundaries of the districts in addition to the previously authorized uses of the sales and use taxes. Thereafter, several resolutions authorizing governmental entities to enter into various agreements with private entities to carry out and fund the project were passed.

The parties to the agreements are Cabela's Retail LA, LLC ("Cabela's"), Carlisle Resort, LLC ("Carlisle"), the Louisiana Department of Revenue ("State of Louisiana" or the "State"), the District, the City, and the Industrial Development Board of the City of Gonzales, Louisiana, Inc. (the "Board"). The agreements, or project documents, include a "Cooperative Endeavor Agreement," a "Trust Indenture," a "Lease Agreement with Option to Purchase," and a "Public Facilities Management Agreement." These project documents set forth the terms of the project, which will result in the following: (1) the acquisition of approximately 49.22 acres of real estate (the "Cabela's Property"); (2) the acquisition, development, construction and equipping of a Cabela's retail outlet and related infrastructure (the "Cabela's Retail Center") to be operated by Cabela's; (3) the construction of related public improvements and infrastructure needed to support the Cabela's Retail Center and the remaining portion of the Cabela's Property within the District; (4) the construction of a museum; and (5) the development and construction of related public improvements and infrastructure needed to support the remaining approximate 48.5 acres within the District constituting the Sportsman Park Center (collectively, subsections (1) through (5) shall be referred to as the "Project").

Generally, the Cooperative Endeavor Agreement ("Agreement") provides that Cabela's will acquire 49.22 acres of property in the District from Carlisle and will construct, furnish and equip a 165,000 square foot retail facility, which will specialize in hunting, fishing, camping and outdoor gear. Cabela's also expects to cooperate with Carlisle in the development of other real estate in the District for complimentary retail and commercial ventures. Upon issuance of the bonds, Cabela's will transfer title of the Cabela's property and facilities to the Board. The Board will then enter into an agreement to lease the property and facilities to Cabela's, and the lease will contain an option to purchase. Cabela's will manage and maintain the Cabela's Retail Center, including the museum, pursuant to an agreement executed between Cabela's and the Board. Additionally, the Agreement states that Carlisle will develop 48.5 acres of its real estate as a Sportsman Park Center, which is located adjacent to the Cabela's Retail Center and within the District, for purposes of attracting certain complimentary retail and commercial ventures.

In order to finance the Project, the Board will issue tax increment revenue bonds in an amount not to exceed $49,875,000, which will be purchased by Cabela's and Carlisle. Specifically, the bonds will be purchased on a "pay-as-you-go" basis, and Cabela's will purchase up to $42,375,000 of the bonds while Carlisle will purchase up to $7,500,000 of the bonds. Proceeds of the bonds will be advanced by Cabela's and Carlisle to the Board or the City on a pro-rata basis when needed to fund the construction to be paid with proceeds of the bonds. The payment of the bonds is secured by the annual pledged state increment, which amounts to 1.50% of State sales and use tax collected within the District up to a maximum total amount of $10,500,000, and the annual pledged local increment, which amounts to 1.50% of the City sales and use tax collected within the District. . . .

On July 27, 2005, the Board filed a Petition for Motion for Judgment pursuant to the Bond Validation Act seeking a judicial declaration of the validity and legality of the Project, the project documents and the bonds. . . . The Board also asked the court to issue a permanent injunction against any person's institution of an action or proceeding contesting, among other things, the legality and validity of the bonds, the project documents, the pledges of revenue, and the legality and validity of the TIF Act and the Act's authorization of the project documents and transactions contemplated thereby.

On August 16, 2005, two Ascension Parish residents and sporting goods business owners of Ascension Parish, C.J. Hebert and Carl Singletary, filed a response to the Board's motion for judgment in which they asserted a peremptory exception of no cause of action. . . .

LAW AND DISCUSSION

Defendants' primary complaint in this court is that the Project and the TIF Act, to the extent it authorizes this Project, amounts to an unconstitutional donation of public funds to a private entity in violation of La. Const. art. VII, §14. They also contend the Project violates the Equal Protection Clauses of the federal and state constitutions. At the outset, we note that defendants do not challenge the use of public funds for development and construction of the museum or the infrastructure needed for the Project. Rather, they object to the donation of public funds to a private retailer for its use in the development, construction and equipping of a retail store.

Tax increment financing is a tool used to finance the redevelopment of economically depressed areas without causing any additional tax burden on local taxpayers. Alan C. Weinstein & Maxine Goodman Levin, *Tax Increment Financing, in* 6 ZONING AND LAND USE CONTROLS, ch. 33B, p. 33B–3 (Eric Damian Kelly, ed., Matthew Bender & Co. 2006). This type of financing originated in California in 1952 as a means to provide local matching funds for federal grants. *Id.* As funds for redevelopment became scarce, other states passed tax increment financing laws as the primary funding vehicle for local redevelopment projects. *Id. See also* John Grand, Comment, *Tax Increment Financing: Louisiana Goes Fishing for New Business,* 66 La. L. Rev. 851, 854–55 (2006). Presently, almost every state has enacted tax increment financing laws. J. Drew Klacik & Samuel Nunn, *A Primer on Tax Increment*

Financing, in TAX INCREMENT FINANCING AND ECONOMIC DEVELOPMENT: USES STRUCTURES, AND IMPACTS, ch. 2 (Craig L. Johnson & Joyce Y. Man, eds., State Univ. of New York Press 2001).

In Louisiana, tax increment financing is authorized by the state's Cooperative Economic Development Law. La. R.S. 33:9020. The Cooperative Economic Development Law was passed to aid local governmental subdivisions in alleviating the conditions of unemployment, underemployment, and other forms of economic distress presently existing in their areas. La. R.S. 33:9021. In passing this Law, the legislature found that while economic development serves the public interest, it is not solely a public purpose because successful economic development also serves the private interests of business and industry. *Id.* The legislature further found that public-private partnerships that take advantage of the special expertise of the private sector are among the most effective programs to encourage and maintain economic development, and that it is in the best interest of the State and its local governments to encourage, create, and support public-private partnerships. *Id.*

The TIF Act allows both ad valorem tax increment financing and sales tax increment financing. The instant case involves sales tax increment financing pursuant to La. R.S. 33:9038.4, which authorizes the District to issue revenue bonds to finance economic development projects. The bonds are payable "from revenues generated by economic development projects with a pledge and dedication of up to the full amount of sales tax increments annually to be used as a guaranty of any shortfall. . . ." La. R.S. 33:9038.4(A)(1). A "sales tax increment" is defined as:

> that portion of the designated sales tax, hereinafter defined, collected each year on the sale at retail, the use, the lease or rental, the consumption and storage for use or consumption of tangible personal property, and on sales of services . . . from taxpayers located within an economic development district which exceeds the designated sales tax revenues and hotel occupancy taxes, occupancy taxes, or similar taxes so designated that were collected in the year immediately prior to the year in which the district was established.

[handwritten margin note: increasing the prior yrs sales tax]

La. R.S. 33:9038.4(A)(2). In the instant case, there was no sales tax collected within the boundaries of the District in the year immediately prior to the year in which the District was established. Consequently, the sales tax increment consists of all the sales taxes that will be collected within the District.

The statute directs that the revenue bonds be issued to finance all or part of an economic development project. . . . La. R.S. 33:9038.4(M) provides:

> For the purposes of this Section, the term "economic development project" shall mean and include, without limitation, any and all projects suitable to any industry determined by the local governmental subdivision or, as appropriate, the issuers of revenue bonds, to create economic development. Economic development projects shall include, without limitation, public works and infrastructure and projects to assist the following industries within the meaning of Article VI, Section 21 of the Louisiana Constitution:
>
> (1) Industrial, manufacturing, and other related industries.
> (2) Housing and related industries.
> (3) Hotel, motel, conference facilities, and related industries.
> (4) Commercial, retail, and related industries.

(5) Amusement, places of entertainment, theme parks, and any other tourism-related industry.

(6) Transportation-related industries.

(7) Hospital, medical, health, nursery care, nursing care, clinical, ambulance, laboratory, and related industries.

(8) Any other industry determined by the local governmental subdivision or issuer of revenue bonds, as appropriate, whose assistance will result in economic development.

Thus, subsection (M) provides that an "economic development project" includes without limitation any project in any industry that a local governmental subdivision determines will create economic development. The subsection goes on to illustrate that economic development projects shall include without limitation public works and infrastructure and projects to assist commercial and retail industries within the meaning of La. Const. art. VI, §21. Generally, La. Const. art. VI, §21, entitled "Assistance to Local Industry," provides that in order to induce and encourage the location of industrial enterprises that would have economic impact upon the area and thereby the state, the legislature may authorize any political subdivision to issue bonds to finance the acquisition and improvement of industrial plant sites and other property necessary to its purposes and to then lease the property. The plain language of La. R.S. 33:9038.4(M) clearly indicates the legislature intended a broad interpretation of type of project that could be financed by bonds secured by sales tax increments. . . .

Defendants argue that the Project at issue is outside the scope of the type of "economic development project" contemplated by the TIF Act because it goes beyond "assisting" the development of private business and results in a direct hand-out to private business. We disagree with this view. As explained above, the TIF Act allows the public financing of any project in any industry that the local governmental subdivision has determined will create economic development. Here, the District has decided that the Project outlined in the Agreement will create economic development. The second sentence of the definition provided by La. R.S. 33:9038.4(M), which provides that economic development projects shall include without limitation public works, infrastructure and projects to assist commercial and retail industries, illustrates the types of projects and industries that may be induced and encouraged, as contemplated by La. Const. art. VI, §21, by the public financing but is not an exhaustive or exclusive list of the allowable projects. In light of the plain and broadly inclusive language utilized in the statute, we conclude that the legislature intended the TIF Act to be utilized for a project such as the one presented in this case.

Finding that the Project is authorized by the TIF Act, we now turn to defendants' allegation that the Project's financing structure amounts to an unconstitutional loan, pledge, or donation in violation of La. Const. art. VII, §14. At the outset, we recognize that in the exercise of the legislative power of the state, the legislature may enact any legislation that the state constitution does not prohibit. . . . [T]he question is whether the constitution limits the legislature, either expressly or impliedly, from enacting the statute at issue.

As with any challenge that alleges a constitutional violation, the starting point of our analysis must be the constitutional provision itself. La. Const. art. VII, §14(A) provides:

> Except as otherwise provided by this constitution, the funds, credit, property, or things of value of the state or of any political subdivision shall not be loaned, pledged, or donated to or for any person, association, or corporation, public or private. Except as otherwise provided in this Section, neither the state nor a political subdivision shall subscribe to or purchase the stock of a corporation or association for any private enterprise. . . .

The constitutional provision at issue prohibits the loan, pledge or donation of public property. La. Const. art. VII, §14(A). Because it does not define loan, pledge or donation, we must first determine exactly what the constitution intends to prohibit in Article VII, §14(A).

The term donation, as used in La. Const. art. VII, §14(A), is plain and unambiguous. The generally understood meaning of a donation is an act whereby one gratuitously gives something to another. The term donation contemplates giving something away. It is a gift, a gratuity or a liberality. We find that, essentially, the constitutional provision at issue seeks to prohibit a gratuitous alienation of public property. . . .

Similarly, the constitutional prohibition against loaning public property also contemplates giving away public funds. . . .

The underlying concept underlying the prohibition of the loan and donation of public funds is one of gratuitous intent. . . .

Applying these principles to the facts of the instant case, we conclude the Project does not constitute a prohibited loan, pledge or donation of public funds. The project documents clearly state that the bonds are not secured by the full faith and credit of the state or of any political subdivision. The documents clearly reveal that both the State and the City have not entered into the obligations at issue gratuitously. Clearly, both parties expect to receive something of value in return for the performance of their obligations. As evidence of the non-gratuitous intent of the public parties, the Agreement contains a provision that states unequivocally:

> The City and State have determined that the Project serves a public purpose and that, based solely on financial projections and other information provided to it by the [District], the Annual Pledged Local Increment and the Annual Pledged State Increment pledged and dedicated hereby, collectively is less than the financial benefits to be received by each as a result of the Project.

Additionally, the Agreement also contains a provision wherein the State's expectations are specified as follows:

> The State hereby acknowledges that there is a reasonable expectation that the Project will result in economic development within the State which will exceed the value of the obligations of the State contained herein thereby serving a public purpose.

In the absence of any other evidence, these statements, standing alone, would be insufficient to allow us to conclude a non-gratuitous intent on the parts of the State and the City. Taken as parts of the Agreement and related documents as a whole, however, they provide insight into the intent of the parties, and reveal that neither the State nor the City intend to enter into a gratuitous contract with Cabela's and Carlisle.

Furthermore, the property comprising the District is not currently providing the State and the City with any sales tax revenues. If the Project is successful, significant sales tax revenues will be generated. Although the State and the City have each pledged 1.50% of their portion of the sales taxes collected within the District, the State sales tax rate is 4% and the City sales tax rate is 2%. Thus, from the beginning of the Project, it appears that 2.50% the sales taxes collected by the State and 0.50% of the sales taxes collected by the City are not pledged to finance the bonds. Consequently, it seems that from the first sale made at the Retail Center, the State and the City will collect sales tax revenues that are not pledged to finance the bonds. These revenues would not otherwise have been collected without the cooperation of the parties to the Project.

The non-gratuitous nature of the Project is also plainly demonstrated by the obligations imposed by the project documents upon Cabela's and Carlisle in exchange for the State's and City's participation in the Project. In exchange for the obligations undertaken by the public parties, Cabela's will acquire the 49.22 acres upon which its Retail Center will be built. It will then construct, furnish and equip the retail center. When the bonds are issued, Cabela's will transfer title of the property and facilities located on the property to the Board, which will then lease the property and facilities to Cabela's.

For its part, Carlisle is obligated to develop 48.5 acres of its property located adjacent to the Cabela's Retail Center for purposes of attracting complimentary businesses, such as restaurants, movie theaters, hotels, water parks, and other retail businesses. Carlisle must complete development of the entire Sportsman Park Center by September 30, 2009.

The Agreement provides that Cabela's and Carlisle agree that they will have "no recourse against the State, the City, the [Board], the [District] or any portion of the Project in the event the Annual Pledged State Increment and the Annual Pledged Local Increment shall be less than the debt service on the Bonds, or for any other matter arising from or relating to the Bonds and Cabela's [and Carlisle] . . . shall indemnify, defend and hold harmless the State, the City, the [Board] and the [District] from any and all such claims." Cabela's and Carlisle are financing the Project up front with the purchase of the bonds. Thus, from the outset, Cabela's and Carlisle will be risking an appreciable amount of their own assets. Additionally, the bonds are payable solely from the Annual Pledged State and Local Increment, which means that if the Project generates low sales, payments on the bonds may not be made. Furthermore, the Agreement provides that Cabela's will be responsible for financing the completion of the retail center for all amounts in excess of the proceeds of the bonds if the bond proceeds are insufficient to cover the expenses for the retail center. This provision also places Cabela's finances at risk, especially for overages or if an unexpected event occurs during the completion of the Center because Cabela's would be required to complete the Retail Center regardless of the availability of bond proceeds.

Under the Agreement, Cabela's is obligated to ensure that the Retail Center remains in continuous operation until the Annual Pledged State Increment has been paid in full or a period of five years has elapsed, whichever is longer. Furthermore, Cabela's and Carlisle are obligated to use reasonable best efforts to purchase materials and equipment from businesses located in the City. It is also obligated to use reasonable efforts to employ residents of the City. It is anticipated these provisions will stimulate the local economy and undoubtably constitute one of many reasons the State and City have elected to participate in the Project.

The State's contribution of the Annual Pledged State Increment is contingent upon Cabela's employment of at least 300 full- and part-time workers at the prevailing wage rate and with the health insurance benefits typically provided to Cabela's employees. If Cabela's hires only between 200 and 300 employees, it waives receiving payment on the bonds in the amount of $5,000 for each job it failed to create. If it hires fewer than 200 employees, the State's payment of its Increment shall cease. These provisions indicate that the Project will bring important and substantial employment opportunities for the citizens of Louisiana, a benefit that surely motivated the State's and the City's decisions to participate in the Project.

The management agreement generally provides that Cabela's will be responsible for managing the public facilities, including the museum, which shall include maintenance and repairs, with the obligation to expend its own funds for the proper maintenance and repair. Cabela's is obligated to keep accurate account of its expenditures, to operate the museum pursuant to specified guidelines, and to employ personnel to properly maintain the public facilities. In exchange for these duties, Cabela's will be entitled to recover its actual costs arising out of the operation, maintenance and repair of the public facilities, with payment of these costs plus interest being deferred until Cabela's exercises its option to purchase the property in accordance with the lease agreement.

The lease agreement also mandates that Cabela's perform several obligations. Cabela's is obligated to pay rent equal to the actual amount of ad valorem taxes that would be owed if Cabela's itself owned the premises. Additional rents, in the form of all costs for insurance, maintenance, and improvements, are provided for by the lease agreement. Specifically, Cabela's must purchase builders' risk insurance, general liability and property damage insurance during the period of construction, and property damage and comprehensive general public liability insurance upon completion. In addition to the rents discussed above, Cabela's will pay personal property taxes on the equipment and inventory located on the premises. Cabela's will also indemnify the lessor against all liability, claims and suits connected with its use and management of the premises. The lease further provides that Cabela's will contract and pay for all utility services supplied to the premises. Regarding maintenance, the lease obligates Cabela's, at its cost, to repair, maintain and replace all necessary capital improvements to the leased premises. Additionally, Cabela's, at its cost, must make all other necessary and routine maintenance and repairs to the leased premises that are not otherwise provided for in the Management Agreement.

The lease agreement provides Cabela's an option to purchase the leased premises at the earlier of the expiration or payment in full of the Cabela's bonds. The purchase price of the leased premises would be the fair market value of the leased premises on the date Cabela's exercises its option to purchase. Cabela's would be allowed to take as a credit against the purchase price an amount equal to (1) the amount it paid for the property before it was transferred to the Board; (2) all rent paid by Cabela's to the Board during the lease term; (3) all additional rent paid by Cabela's during the lease term; (4) $2,500 for each full-time job and $1,250 for each part-time job created by Cabela's at the Retail Center; (5) $1,900,000 for each year that Cabela's operated the Retail Center during the Lease; and (6) any amount owed to Cabela's, including the Accrued Management Compensation provided for by the Management Agreement. It is stipulated that in the event these purchase price offsets exceed the purchase price, Cabela's will waive any right to collect the excess from the Board. If the purchase price exceeds the offsets, Cabela's will pay the Board the difference.

As detailed above, the management and lease agreements impose significant obligations upon Cabela's. Cabela's must pay a definite and substantial rent to the Board. The fact that the additional rents will be paid directly to third parties who provide the services appears insignificant because the Board, as owner, will receive the benefit of the payments and will not incur any administrative costs in paying the bills itself as it would if the payments were made directly to it. Furthermore, the management of the public facilities imposes upon Cabela's actual and appreciable obligations. Likewise, the fact that Cabela's will be paid a deferred management fee in the form of additional credits should it exercise the option to purchase does not negate Cabela's obligation to provide actual maintenance and repair services to the property.

The existence of the purchase price offsets that could conceivably result in no money exchanging hands if and when the property is sold to Cabela's does not negate the existence of the obligations imposed upon Cabela's during the terms of the lease agreement to render it a gratuitous contract. First, it is not certain that Cabela's will exercise its option to purchase the property and collect the offsets. Practically speaking, it is doubtful that Cabela's will exercise the option to purchase if the Project is not a long-term success. Even if Cabela's does choose to exercise the option to purchase, it is obligated to perform varied and substantial duties during the life of the assorted agreements. These reciprocal obligations on the part of Cabela's are not somehow retroactively diminished when the option to purchase is exercised, rendering a once-onerous contract a newly gratuitous contract. Furthermore, the purchase price offset for each job created by the Project is well below the expenses and costs of each employee hired and retained by Cabela's. Although Cabela's will receive a $2,500 credit for each full-time job it creates at the Retail Center, it will undoubtedly pay far more in salary, benefits, training, and expenses for that full-time employee.

In light of real and substantial obligations undertaken by Cabela's in exchange for the tax increment financing we conclude the financing scheme of the Project is not gratuitous on the part of the parties. Consequently, we do not find that the Project includes a loan or donation of public funds to a private retailer in violation of La. Const. art. VII, §14(A). Similarly, the Project does not constitute a prohibited pledge of public funds. . . .

Defendants' reliance on the fact that the legislature has made six unsuccessful attempts to amend the constitution to include economic development and/or industrial projects as an exception to §14(A) is misplaced. This particular Project, while certainly an economic development project, does not envision a prohibited loan, pledge or donation of public property so an economic development exception, even if it did indeed exist, would be unnecessary. Such an exception would allow a public entity to enter into an agreement to donate, or give away, public funds for purposes of economic development with no reciprocal obligations imposed upon the other party in exchange for the public funds. This is not the case presented here. . . .

Defendants also challenge the constitutionality of the TIF Act and the Project on equal protection grounds. They argue that there is no rational basis for the handout of public funds to Cabela's, a private retailer, to the detriment of other previously existing retailers. Defendants contend that they have already borne the costs of acquiring their buildings and equipping their stores, while the public will bear similar costs for Cabela's. They assert this disparity will result in an unfair advantage for Cabela's.

As an initial matter, we note that defendants' businesses have not attempted to avail themselves of the provisions of the TIF Act and, consequently, have not been denied tax increment financing. Nonetheless, it is settled that "[u]nder the Equal Protection Clause of the Fourteenth Amendment to the United States Constitution, in areas of social and economic policy, a statutory classification which does not proceed along suspect or semi-suspect lines, nor infringe on fundamental rights, need only be rationally related to a legitimate governmental interest." When an economic regulation is challenged as being violative of the Equal Protection clause, "this court may not sit as a super-legislature to judge the wisdom or desirability of legislative policy determinations made in areas that neither affect fundamental rights nor proceed along suspect lines. In the local economic sphere, it is only the invidious discrimination, the wholly arbitrary act, which cannot stand consistently with the Fourteenth Amendment. . . ."

In the instant case, we find defendants have failed to establish the existence of an equal protection violation. The TIF Act, a measure concerned with economic regulation, was enacted to promote economic development, which serves private businesses as well as the public interest. As such, it is rationally related to legitimate governmental interests. The Act does not result in arbitrary discrimination. Similarly, defendants have not shown that the Act fails to serve a legitimate government purpose. The promotion of economic development, which ultimately serves the public as a whole, is a legitimate governmental goal. For all these reasons, we reject defendants' constitutional challenges based on equal protection arguments.

CONCLUSION

For all the above reasons, we find that neither the TIF Act, as applied in this case, nor the Project at issue violate La. Const. art. VII, §14(A). Similarly, we find defendants did not prove the existence of an equal protection violation. Therefore, we reject the constitutional challenges presented by defendants and affirm the judgment of the court of appeal.

AFFIRMED.

Justice TRAYLOR, dissenting, joined by Justice KNOLL.

I respectfully dissent from the majority's finding that the financing structure set forth in this proposed development project is a constitutionally permissible use of public funds by a governmental entity. Moreover, I agree with defendants' proposition that the Project's financing structure amounts to a donation of public funds in violation of Article VII, Section 14(A) of the Louisiana Constitution which prohibits the loan, pledge or donation of anything of value belonging to the state or a political subdivision. . . .

The words contained in Article VII, Section 14(A) of the Louisiana Constitution are clear and unambiguous. Interpreting the words, using their ordinary meaning, it is clear that this constitutional provision prohibits the loan, pledge or donation of anything of value belonging to the state or political subdivision.

I find no ambiguity in this provision, for the meaning is easily ascertained from the plain language of the provision. . . .

The majority opines that our prior jurisprudence is "neither persuasive nor particularly applicable." I disagree with this conclusion. . . . [T]he key factor in determining whether Article VII, Section 14(A) is violated is whether the consideration given to the Board, under this agreement, is sufficient to find that the Board's corresponding use of public funds and property does not amount to a loan, pledge or donation in violation of Art. VII, Section 14(A). To find this agreement complies with the constitution would be inconsistent with this court's existing jurisprudence regarding Article VII, Section 14(A).

The majority finds the agreement between the Board and Cabela's constitutional, permissible and authorized by the TIF statutes. I agree that the TIF statutes were adopted to encourage cooperative endeavors between public and private entities to facilitate economic growth. In fact, as the majority notes, TIF statutes were enacted in response to the scarcity of funds for redevelopment projects in blighted areas. Louisiana's TIF statute certainly allows the Board to use public funds and property, however, the use of the public funds and property must be in compliance with the constitution. I do not believe that the use of public funds to wholly finance a private for-profit business, at the expense of small business owners and tax payers, was one of the envisioned uses of the TIF statute. . . .

An examination of this proposed financing agreement reveals that the Board is attempting to enter into an agreement with terms and effects which are constitutionally impermissible. Under the proposed financing structure, the Board purchases land from a private entity; issues bonds; and uses public funds to repay the bonds. In return, Cabela's pledges to encourage other businesses to relocate to the area and provides that it will pay "rent" for its use of the land. The categorization of certain payments as "rent" is deceptive and illusory. Under the lease agreement Cabela's agrees to pay property taxes on the land to the tax official for the parish. Cabela's also agrees to pay maintenance cost, insurance premiums and improvement cost. Significantly, these payments are made to third parties and not to the Board. As the majority points out, Cabela's will "expend its own funds for the proper maintenance and repair" of the building. However, the payments made to the third parties, for insurance and maintenance cost will be credited to Cabela's in the event it exercises its option to purchase. Cabela will also be compensated handsomely to undertake management responsibilities under the Agreement with a salary of $1.9 million per year for those services. In addition, this management fee will also be credited to Cabela's in the event it exercises its option to purchase. This sum could amount to as much as $57,000,000 should the lease extend to the full thirty year bond period, more than the initial bond amount. Cabela's also states that its facility will employ residents of the community. However, Cabela's is not inextricably bound to employ Gonzales residents, Cabela's must only "use reasonable efforts to employ residents of the City." The creation of jobs in our communities is paramount to uplifting the economy and is valuable consideration. However, the substantial credit Cabela's receives for employing workers negates any altruistic motive on the part of Cabela's.

An examination of the financing structure suggests that the Board, and the Board alone, is bearing all the financial burden of financing this privately owned enterprise, an act specifically prohibited by Article VII, Section 14(A). The financing scheme appears more akin to a disguised donation of public lands and funds rather than a lease agreement, and should Cabela's elect not to exercise its option to purchase, would amount to a loan of public funds and property. The majority opines that Cabela's is taking a great risk in developing its store in this area and promises to promote the local economy. I cannot see how Cabela's is taking any greater risk than any other business owner. A local business owner is more apt to employ local employees and have greater ties to the community. That same local business owner is not receiving credits for its business expenses nor is it being paid a "management fee" of $1.9 million dollars per year to engage in a for-profit business. When the benefits of the public entity are weighed against that received by the private entity, it is unimaginable how this financing structure amounts to anything other than a loan or donation of public property and funds. This financing structure uses public funds and property in a manner prohibited by Article VII, Section 14(A) of the Louisiana Constitution.

■ STE. GENEVIEVE SCHOOL DISTRICT R–II v. BOARD OF ALDERMEN OF THE CITY OF STE. GENEVIEVE
66 S.W.3d 6 (Mo. 2006)

Judge HOLSTEIN

The Ste. Genevieve school district and Mikel A. Stewart, an individual, appeal a trial court order dismissing their joint petition for declaratory judgment based on lack of standing and failure to state a claim upon which relief can be granted. After the court of appeals issued an opinion, the case was transferred to this Court. The judgment of the trial court is reversed, and the case is remanded.

I. FACTS

In 1992, the City of Ste. Genevieve created a Tax Increment Financing ("TIF") Commission pursuant to Missouri's Real Property Tax Increment Allocation Redevelopment Act. The commission recommended that the city establish a redevelopment area and approve a redevelopment project plan within it entitled the "Redevelopment Plan for Valle Springs Tax Increment Financing District." The city subsequently adopted ordinances embodying both recommendations and established the proposed redevelopment area and redevelopment plan.

The commission acted again in 1997, recommending that the boundaries of the pre-existing redevelopment area be enlarged to include three new redevelopment project areas (RPA 2, RPA 3, and RPA 4) and that the redevelopment plan be amended to provide for additional projects within these three new areas. Specifically, the plan called for the use of TIF revenues to pay for improvements in the water, storm water and sanitary sewer systems in RPA 3. All these changes were also adopted by city ordinance.

The city then solicited proposals for the redevelopment of part of RPA 3. Golden Management, Inc., submitted a proposal for the redevelopment of the Pointe Basse Plaza, a shopping center located in RPA 3. Golden's proposal called for TIF revenues to be used for property acquisition, site preparation, the relocation of utilities, road and traffic signal improvements, the relocation of some tenants of

Pointe Basse Plaza, and parking lot improvements to the shopping center. These improvements were in addition to the improvements already proposed for RPA 3. The proposal increased the overall costs associated with RPA 3 by over 360 percent adding well over $1,000,000 to the project's costs.

The city decided not to reconvene the TIF commission, which would have required the appointment of commission members by both the city and the Ste. Genevieve school district. Instead, the city adopted an ordinance that amended the overall redevelopment plan to embody the changes in RPA 3 proposed by Golden and that directed the city mayor to execute a redevelopment agreement with Golden. The ordinance also authorized the issuance of TIF notes to fund the cost associated with the redevelopment of Pointe Basse Plaza.

The Ste. Genevieve school district and Mikel A. Stewart then filed a petition for declaratory judgment, arguing that the city was without authority to amend the redevelopment project without reconvening the TIF commission. If the TIF commission had been reconvened, the Ste. Genevieve school district would have been able to appoint a certain number of members to the commission. Part of the property taxes abated by the redevelopment project would otherwise have gone to the school district. Stewart, according to the petition, is the superintendent of the Ste. Genevieve School District and is also a taxpayer of both the school district and the city. Originally, only the city was named as a defendant in the declaratory judgment action. However, Stewart and the school district later added Golden as a defendant.

The city and Golden filed motions to dismiss the action, claiming that both plaintiffs lacked standing to sue and that the petition failed to state a claim upon which relief could be granted. The trial court ruled that neither plaintiff had standing and, even if either one had standing, the petition failed to state a claim.

II. STANDING

Both Stewart and the school district have standing to bring the declaratory judgment action at issue in this case. . . .

The school district has a legally protected interest, conferred by statute, in appointing members to the TIF commission. Its power to appoint members to the commission is given in the very same statute that grants municipalities the power to use tax increment financing to fund redevelopment projects like this one.

The district also has standing because the city's actions, if improper, would unlawfully deprive the district of tax revenue. Under Missouri law, a school district that is threatened with the imminent unlawful deprivation of part of its funds has standing to seek a declaratory judgment challenging the statutory interpretation that would lead to the deprivation.

The very nature of TIF financing is that it funds the redevelopment of a particular parcel of property by abating increases in the property taxes on that parcel for a period of time determined by the costs of the redevelopment project. *See generally* sec. 99.845. This abatement applies both to taxes imposed by the municipality that authorizes the redevelopment project and to taxes imposed by any other taxing district, like a school district, in which the property is located. *Sec. 99.845.* If the city's amendment of the redevelopment plan without reconvening the TIF commission was unauthorized, the school district will be unlawfully deprived of tax funds to which it would otherwise be entitled.

The taxpayer, Stewart, also has standing to bring the declaratory judgment action, although his right to do so is less clear than the right of the school district. He has standing under his status as a taxpayer of the city and of the school district. A taxpayer has standing to challenge an alleged illegal expenditure of public funds, absent fraud or compelling circumstances, if the taxpayer can show either a direct expenditure of funds generated through taxation, an increased levy in taxes, or a pecuniary loss attributable to the challenged action of the municipality.

Missouri courts allow taxpayer standing so that ordinary citizens have the ability to make their government officials conform to the dictates of the law when spending public money. In this case, both the city and the school district will suffer a pecuniary loss from the transaction. Because the TIF Financing in this case abates increases in property tax, both the city and the school district will be unable to collect property taxes revenues that they otherwise would have collected. Because the redevelopment project costs the district and the city future tax revenue, the taxpayer has standing to seek a declaratory judgment. . . .

III. FAILURE TO STATE A CLAIM

In this case, the pleading asserts that the Real Property Tax Increment Allocation Redevelopment Act requires the city to reconvene the TIF commission before the city can make an amendment to the redevelopment plan that substantially alters the cost and scope of an individual redevelopment project and that the amendment occurred here without reconvening the commission.

Section 99.825 states that after the adoption of an ordinance approving a redevelopment area or projects, no amendments can be made by the city that (1) alter the exterior boundaries of the redevelopment area, (2) affect the general land uses established in the redevelopment plan, or (3) change the nature of the redevelopment project without complying with the full procedures that are required when a redevelopment area or project is originally proposed. These procedures include the use of the TIF commission, with a certain number of members appointed by the school district and other taxing districts in which the property is located, and the holding of public hearings and the issuance of recommendations by the commission. *Sec. 99.820.2.*

The amendment to the redevelopment plan, if proven, changes the nature of the redevelopment project. When interpreting a statute, courts must give effect to the intent of the legislature as it is expressed in the words of the statute. Absent a definition provided in the statute, the court must follow the plain and ordinary meaning of the words themselves. There is no room for construction where a statute is clear and unambiguous.

Looking at the language of sec. 99.825, the amendment in this case is a change in the nature of the redevelopment project. The term "nature" is somewhat ambiguous. It not only refers to "the essential characteristics of and qualities of a person or thing," as argued by the city and Golden, but also refers to "the distinguishing qualities or properties of something." *Webster's Third New International Dictionary* 1507 (1981).

Under either definition, the amendment changes the nature of the project. It increases the cost of the project by over $1,000,000, a 360% change. It also changes the entire focus of the project. Before the amendment, RPA 3 consisted of water, storm water, and sanitary sewer system improvements. After the amendment, the project consists of a massive redevelopment of a shopping center, extensive parking lot work, and even moving several of the shopping center's current tenants. It is difficult to imagine what would constitute a change in the nature of a redevelopment project if the alterations made by the amendment in this case do not. . . .

Accepting the allegations of the petition as true, the amendment in this case constitutes a change in the nature of the project.

Notes and Comments

1. *The Rise of Tax Increment Financing.* As noted in the *City of Gonzalez* case, the concept of TIF financing originated in California in the 1950s, primarily as a tool to promote urban redevelopment projects. For many years this tool was little used and not widely recognized. However, particularly after federal economic development funding dried up in the 1970s, states started to embrace the TIF mechanism with enthusiasm. Today, tax increment financing "is the most widely used local government program for financing economic development in the United States." Richard Briffault, The Most Popular Tool: Tax Increment Financing and the Political Economy of Local Government, 77 U. Chi. L. Rev. 65 (2010). The number of TIF districts across the country reach "into the thousands" and in some communities a significant fraction of the total land area is included in TIF districts. *Id.* at 70-71. Every state in the nation, other than Arizona, has enacted one or more statutes authorizing and fixing sideboards for the use of TIF financing.

2. *The Allure of TIF Financing.* For perennially cash-strapped communities, led by elected leaders responsive to voters' objections to tax hikes, TIF has an almost magical allure. The basic idea is that new tax revenues within a circumscribed area are dedicated to paying for infrastructure and other expenses associated with the new development. The new development, in turn, hopefully expands the tax base and encourages further development that expands the tax base even more. While TIF financing can be structured to pay for improvements on a pay as you go basis, the more usual practice is to use projected increases in tax revenues from an expanded tax base to support the issuance of bonds that provide the cash to pay for improvements upfront. TIF financing dedicates, or perhaps more accurately diverts, future tax revenues to repayment of the bonds; however, it does not result in any tax increase on existing taxpayers.

As described by one proponent of this approach:

> TIF financing is a win-win-win situation for the city, the private developer, and the taxpayers. City officials can claim credit for the new private development, an increased tax base, and the public improvements. The private developer obtains public improvements that enhance the value of the project, and would not have been feasible for the developer to finance privately, along with wholehearted city support for its project, which can prove useful in expediting the requisite land use approvals. Taxpayers benefit from the new public works and private development being added to the tax rolls.

George Lefcoe, Competing for the Next Hundred Million Americans: the Uses and Abuses of Tax Increment Financing, 43 Urb. Law. 427, 437 (2011). *See also* Richard

Briffault, *supra* (explaining that TIF "succeeds" in political terms because "it, like local government more generally, is highly decentralized; reflects and reinforces the fiscalization of development policy; plays off the fragmentation of local governments and the resulting interlocal struggle for investment; and fits well with the entrepreneurial spirit characteristic of contemporary local economic development.")

3. *Criticisms of TIF Financing.* Despite the popularity of TIF financing, and a general recognition of its capacity to help facilitate valuable economic development under certain circumstances, TIF financing has its critics. It is commonly contended that TIF financing is too often wasted on projects that: (1) "fail to achieve public goals," because the financing is used to support projects that fail to bring hoped-for investment or that harm the community in other ways; (2) "enrich special interests at the public's expense," by conferring unreasonable subsidies on politically connected developers while siphoning off tax revues needed for schools and parks and other public purposes; and (3) "encourage development in areas where it is needed least," by making TIF financing available not only in areas in financial distress but in areas where private development can thrive on its own, including on previously undeveloped tracts of land. Rob Kersh & Phineas Baxandall, U.S. PIRG Educational Fund, The Need for Increased Transparency and Accountability in Local Economic Development Subsidies 1-2 (2011).

These critiques of the outcomes of using TIF financing are typically paired with criticisms of the process used to allocate TIF financing, including that: (1) TIF financing "often lacks transparency," because the public has not been given data on project costs and benefits to permit evaluation of whether a particular TIF project makes sense; (2) TIF financing "often lacks accountability," because government champions of the use of this tool are under no obligation to report to the public if the goals of the project were met; and (3) "TIF [financing] can create 'slush funds' that lack public oversight and accountability," because in some jurisdictions TIF funds can be spent at the discretion of mayors or other public officials. Id. at 2.

Tellingly, the critics of TIF financing tend to span the political spectrum. For a criticism of TIF financing from a libertarian perspective see Stephen J. Eagle, The Perils of Regulatory Property in Land Use Regulation, 54 Washburn L. J. 1, 37-39 (2014) ("There are many justifiable criticisms of TIF financing, including: prosperous suburbs use TIF to lure jobs from less well-off communities; TIF projects don't confront seriously blighted urban areas, but rather support projects in the best commercial districts that could qualify; TIF often is used to subsidize retail development for the property and sales taxes it will bring, displacing sales and tax revenues from other locations; TIF projects drain property tax revenues from schools and counties; local governments sometimes confer excessive TIF-funded benefits to attract private redevelopers; and many local governments hide or neglect to gather information that would reveal whether TIF projects are successful." Finally, "[s]cant public reporting of TIF expenditures and revenues, 'guided by the invisible hand of lobbyists, political action committees and campaign contributions,' does nothing to allay suspicions of favoritism and corruption.")

4. *Interlocal Conflicts.* One of the more serious problems associated with TIF financing is the conflicts it can set up between and within communities. Neighboring communities may use offers of TIF financing to compete with each other for large commercial developments promising large property tax receipts, with the result that one community wins at the expense of its neighbor at a cost to the region as a whole. As illustrated by the *Ste. Genevieve School District* case, in some instances the

government entity offering the TIF financing can compel other taxing jurisdictions to forego anticipated tax receipts. Political leaders seeking to serve their constituents by promoting development might logically be expected to go overboard in promoting TIF financing if they can use it to impose the cost of subsidizing development on other political jurisdictions. How might a state legislature interested in ensuring greater political accountability police such practices?

C. EXACTIONS, SPECIAL ASSESSMENTS, AND OTHER FINANCING TECHNIQUES

1. *Exactions*

So-called "exactions" represent a mirror image of TIF financing insofar as TIF financing channels tax revenues to benefit particular development projects and specific developers. By contrast, exactions impose special responsibilities on particular developers to pay for infrastructure needed to support their development or to address impacts associated with their projects. While municipal officials support the use of both types of financing, exactions more clearly represent "new" additions to a municipality's assets, whether the exaction is in the form of cash or real property interests. On the other hand, developers tend to enthusiastically embrace the benefits conferred on them by TIF financing, but aggressively resist the burdens imposed on them through exactions.

An exaction is typically imposed in connection with a grant of permission to proceed with development, such as a zoning or subdivision approval. State statutes prescribe the types of exactions that local governments can impose. Two examples from different parts of the country are set forth below.

■ THE CALIFORNIA MITIGATION FEE ACT — CALIFORNIA GOVERNMENT CODE §66000

The California Mitigation Fee Act, enacted in 1987, defines a "fee" as "a monetary exaction other than a tax or special assessment, whether established for a broad class of projects by legislation of general applicability or imposed on a specific project on an ad hoc basis, that is charged by a local agency to the applicant in connection with approval of a development project for the purpose of defraying all or a portion of the cost of public facilities related to the development project." Cal. Govt. Code §66000.

The California act sets forth specific steps and standards a local government must meet in order to justify the imposition of a "fee" within the meaning of the act:

> (a) In any action establishing, increasing, or imposing a fee as a condition of approval of a development project by a local agency, the local agency shall do all of the following:
> (1) Identify the purpose of the fee.
> (2) Identify the use to which the fee is to be put. If the use is financing public facilities, the facilities shall be identified. That identification may, but need not, be made by reference to a capital improvement . . . , may be made in applicable

general or specific plan requirements or may be made in other public documents that identify the public facilities for which the fee is charged.

(3) Determine how there is a reasonable relationship between the fee's use and the type of development project on which the fee is imposed.

(4) Determine how there is a reasonable relationship between the need for the public facility and the type of development project on which the fee is imposed.

(b) In any action imposing a fee as a condition of approval of a development project by a local agency, the local agency shall determine how there is a reasonable relationship between the amount of the fee and the cost of the public facility or portion of the public facility attributable to the development on which the fee is imposed.

Cal. Govt. Code §66001

■ VERMONT IMPACT FEE LEGISLATION —
24 V.S.A. §5203

Vermont has enacted similar legislation "to enable municipalities to require the beneficiaries of new development to pay their proportionate share of the cost of municipal and school capital projects which benefit them and to require them to pay for or mitigate the negative effects of construction."

Specifically, the legislation provides that:

(a) A municipality may levy an impact fee on any new development within its borders provided that it has:

(1) . . . adopted a capital budget and program pursuant to chapter 117 of this title. The plan or capital budget and program may include:

(A) indication of locations proposed for development with a potential to create the need for new capital projects;

(B) standards for level of service for the capital projects to be fully or partially funded with impact fees;

(C) proposed locations and project lists, cost estimates and funding sources;

(D) timing or sequence of development in the identified locations; and

(2) developed a reasonable formula that will be used to assess a developer's impact fee. The formula shall reflect the level of service for the capital project to be funded and a means of assessing the impact associated with the development such as square footage or number of bedrooms. The level of service shall be either:

(A) an existing level of service;

(B) a state or federal standard; or

(C) a standard adopted as part of a town plan or capital budget.

(b) The amount of an impact fee used to fund a capital project shall be determined according to a formula developed under subsection (a) of this section. The fee shall be equal to or less than the portion of the capital cost of a capital project which will benefit or is attributable to the development and shall not include costs attributable to the operation, administration or maintenance of a capital project. The municipality may require a fee for the entire cost of a capital project that will initially be used only by the beneficiaries of the development so assessed. In this case, if the project will be used by beneficiaries of future development the municipality shall establish a formula consistent with the formula developed under subsection (a) of this section to require that beneficiaries of future development pay an impact fee to the owners of the development on which the impact fee has already been levied.

(c) In determining the amount of a fee that will be used to fund a capital project, the municipality may account for:

(1) the cost of the existing or proposed facility;

(2) the means, including state or federal grants and fees paid by other developers, by which the facility has been or will be financed;

(3) the extent, if any, to which impact fees should be offset to account for other taxes or fees paid by the developer that will cover the cost of the capital project;

(4) extraordinary costs incurred by the municipality in serving the new development;

(5) the time-price differential inherent in fair comparisons of amounts paid at different times.

(d) In determining the amount of the impact fee to compensate the municipality for expenses incurred as a result of construction, the municipality shall project the expenses that will be incurred. If the actual expense incurred is less than the fee collected from the developer, the municipality shall refund the unexpended portion of the fee within one year of the termination of construction of the project.

Notes and Comments

1. *State Litigation.* Application of different state statutes across the country has given rise to voluminous litigation interpreting and enforcing these measures. *See, e.g. Cresta Bella, L.P. v. Poway Unified School District,* 160 Cal. Rptr. 437 (Cal. Ct. App. 2013) (holding that school impact fees based on demolished and then reconstructed square footage included in new apartment complex were invalid under the Mitigation Fee Act); *Robes v. Town of Hartford,* 636 A.2d 342 (Vt. 1993) (developers failed to sustain their burden of proving unreasonableness of an impact fee imposed on new developments to finance future expansion of town's sewage capacity). *See also Treisman v. Town of Bedford,* 563 A.2d 786 (N.H. 1989) (holding a condition placed on a rooftop helipad permit to be in excess of statutory authority where the condition required that police and fire protection employees be allowed to use privately owned helicopters).

2. *Constitutional Litigation.* The higher-profile litigation relating to development exactions has involved constitutional "takings" claims under the Fifth Amendment to the U.S. Constitution. *See Koontz v. St. Johns River Water Mgmt. Dist.,* 133 S.Ct. 2586 (2013); *Dolan v. City of Tigard,* 512 U.S. 374 (1994); and *Nollan v. California Coastal Comm'n,* 483 U.S. 825 (1987). These cases are excerpted and discussed in detail in Chapter 7 addressing takings.

2. Special Assessments

■ STRAUSS V. TOWNSHIP OF HOLMDEL
711 A.2d 1385 (N.J. Super. L. 1997)

Judge of Superior Court LOCASIO

Plaintiffs represent approximately 137 property owners who reside in two separate subdivisions, the Estates of Holmdel and the Hills of Holmdel, which were approved for construction in sections in 1963, 1965, 1970 and 1972. Because there were no sewer trunk lines available, nor any plans to install trunk lines in the vicinity, the developers were not required to install sewer lines as a condition of approval, and therefore the houses were built with septic tanks.

Late in 1989, the septic systems began experiencing such serious failures that neither the repair, nor the reconstruction, of the systems was practicable. Because a nearby trunkline was, by then, under construction, making the installation of sewer lines into the Estates of Holmdel and the Hills of Holmdel feasible, defendant Holmdel Township decided, in June 1990, to extend the sewer lines into these developments.

On October 22, 1990, a sewer assessment ordinance, providing for the construction of sewer lines into the subdivisions, was introduced by defendant's township committee; a public hearing on the ordinance was held on November 26, 1990. After the ordinance's unchallenged adoption, bonds were sold to finance the project. A bonding ordinance was passed on December 17, 1990, and published on December 20, 1990, which provided for the issuance of $4,100,000 in bonds and, in order to offset a portion of the sewer installations costs, directed the levy of a special assessment on plaintiffs' properties, in accordance with the sewers' resultant increase in the value of each lot. Any amounts not paid, by those lot owners who received the benefit, would be paid by the township.

The installation of the sewer lines was completed in July, 1993 at a total cost of $2,755,986.00. Pursuant to N.J.S.A. §§40:56-1-89, a Sewer Assessment Commission was established which, after an investigation, which included a real estate appraisal, site visits, and consideration of comments made at a May 17, 1995 public hearing, concluded that this improvement resulted in a benefit of $14,700 per lot. The Commission's report was confirmed by a resolution of the township committee on September 11, 1995.[1] Plaintiffs filed their amended complaint, challenging this assessment, on October 11, 1995. Defendants now move for summary judgment as to count I, alleging equal protection violations, and court II, alleging negligence.

I ...

The Equal Protection Clause of the United States Constitution, made applicable to the states by the Fourteenth Amendment to the United States Constitution, requires "all persons similarly situated be treated alike and that no State ... shall deny to any person within its jurisdiction the equal protection of the laws." ...

[P]laintiffs contend that defendant's conduct fails to meet the "rational basis" standard which, in order to withstand constitutional attack, requires the regulation to be rationally related to a legitimate governmental objective. The rational basis test requires that the regulation (1) not be arbitrary or capricious and (2) have a rational basis in relation to the specific objective to be obtained. ...

Furthermore, a municipal ordinance, like all legislation, is entitled to a strong presumption of constitutionality. ... "The burden of demonstrating that a statute contravenes the equal protection clause is extremely formidable, as is attested by the long trial of failure." ...

---

1. Ultimately, the residents of the Estates of Holmdel and the Hills of Holmdel contributed $2,013,900 of the total cost of the sewer installation project, and the township absorbed the balance of $742,086. Had the township not absorbed this balance, the cost to the homeowners would have amounted to approximately $20,116 per lot.

When conducting an equal protection analysis under Article 1, Paragraph 1 of the New Jersey Constitution, the Court has employed a balancing test, which requires the Court to consider (1) the nature of the affected right, (2) the extent to which the governmental restrictions intrude upon it, and (3) the public need for the restriction. . . .

In the instant action, an analysis of the Equal Protection Clause of the United States Constitution and of the New Jersey Constitution yields the same result. A governmental entity may levy special assessments against properties which will benefit from a local improvement, including "the construction . . . of a sewer or drain in, under or along a street, alley or public highway, or portion thereof, or in, under or along any public or private lands." N.J.S.A. 40:56-1. Here, plaintiffs concede that, because the sewer lines increased the value of each home in question, their installation constitutes an improvement and not a service.

It is well-settled that the decision of whether particular improvements should be undertaken as a general improvement, for which the whole township would pay, or a local improvement, for which the specifically benefited property owners will pay to the extent they will be benefited, rests within the sound discretion of the municipality. . . .

Plaintiffs contend that the township's decision to levy a special assessment was arbitrary and capricious because the facts of this case are indistinguishable from previous situations where the township paid for sewers out of general funds. However, important distinctions exist between the Estates of Holmdel and Hills of Holmdel and the three other projects which the township financed.

The first of these three projects, Old Mannor and Newstead, were sewered in the 1960's at a time when the township was not facing the growing population and anticipated sewer costs it is facing today. The second of these three projects, located on Alloco Drive, was a relatively simple, single street project, costing approximately $120,000, which did not require the construction of a pump station because the nearest trunk line was located downhill from the development. In addition, at the time that the Alloco Drive project was approved, the township was in a period of intense development, so developers' connection fees and additional user fees, were generally sufficient to cover the costs of the sewers. The North Beers Street project, the third financed by the township, which cost only $100,000, was, like the two other projects, much less complex than the Estates of Holmdel and Hills of Holmdel. Conversely, the Estates of Holmdel and the Hills of Holmdel are characterized by numerous very hilly streets, rolling terrain, streams, flood plains, steep slopes, and wetlands. While other areas in the township may have some of these characteristics, they generally do not have the severe changes in topography which typify the Estates of Holmdel and the Hills of Holmdel. These distinctions in size and topography are what make a sewer system in the Hills of Holmdel and the Estate of Holmdel more complex and more expensive than the other projects financed by the township.

Plaintiffs also argue that they are being treated differently than those residents who live in developments where the developers were required to install sewers as a condition for approval. However, in all likelihood, the cost of installing those sewers was passed on to the residents of those developments in the purchase price of their homes. Therefore, the residents of those other developments have paid for their sewers in much the same way that the residents of the Estates of Holmdel and the Hills of Holmdel, by virtue of defendant's sewer assessment, have paid for theirs.

The township contends that it was looking toward the future when it decided to levy a special assessment upon plaintiffs. Because a large portion of the township is still un-sewered, if the township now sets a precedent by absorbing a large portion of the sewer costs, it will be using township tax monies to install sewer systems in various different neighborhoods. The township's only option, in paying for future sewers, is to increase taxes and sewer rates, or levy special assessments. To increase taxes and sewer rates for the entire town, in order to benefit only one certain group of citizens, would not be fiscally responsible to the remaining portions of the township. Plaintiffs are seeking to have all the residents of the township pay for a sewer system which benefits only them. This is unfair to the other taxpayers of the township. The township has a duty to be fiscally responsible to all its citizens. . . .

For the aforesaid reasons this court concludes that (1) because sewer lines were not readily available to this section of the township when the subdivisions were originally constructed, the township had a rational basis for not requiring the developer to install sewer lines, and (2) because of the complexity and the higher costs associated with now constructing sewers in the subdivisions, a rational basis exists for the township's decision to levy a special assessment against those directly benefited by the sewers. Because plaintiffs have not demonstrated facts sufficient to overcome the presumption of constitutionality, these decisions of defendant Holmdel are neither arbitrary nor capricious.

Therefore, this court finds that the township has not violated plaintiff's equal protection rights provided by the United States and New Jersey constitutions. Accordingly, defendant township's motion for summary judgment on count I is granted.

Notes and Comments

1. Special Assessments Distinguished. Traditionally, special assessments have been used to pay for improvements that benefit homeowners and other property owners throughout a district, such as a new park or fire station, or to establish public water or sewer service. The rationale for special assessments is that they place the burden of paying for improvements on those most directly benefited by them. Assessments can be a hardship for those on low or fixed incomes, and they can aggravate the impact of rising real property taxes on homeowners of modest means. Developers generally prefer assessment district financing over impact fees, because assessment districts allow them to directly pass on the costs to new residents. By contrast, if impact fees are used, the developer may not be able to pass them on to buyers as part of the sales price if the real estate market is "soft" and price competition between builders is keen.

2. The Mechanics of Special Assessments. Landowners in a particular neighborhood typically petition the city to designate the neighborhood as a special assessment district or, as illustrated by the *Strauss* case, the municipality decides to create the district on its own initiative. The city then sells bonds to undertake capital improvements funded by annual assessments imposed on all those benefited in the district. For example, the city may charge an assessment over a ten-year period based on the front footage of each property or the assessed value of each parcel. *See City of Boca Raton v. State,* 595 So. 2d 25 (Fla. 1992) (property assessed must receive a special benefit from the service provided, and the assessment must be reasonably apportioned among the specially benefited properties).

3. Potential Takings Issues? Because a special assessment is not imposed as a condition of issuance of a development approval, the *Nollan/Dolan* exactions analysis does not apply. Traditionally, courts have rejected claims that special assessments amount to compensable regulatory takings. *See Houck v. Little River Drainage Dist.*, 239 U.S. 254, 264-65 (1915) (municipal special assessments constitute an unlawful taking only if there is a flagrant abuse tantamount to a "confiscation of property"); *Branch v. United States*, 69 F.3d 1571 (Fed. Cir. 1995) (*per se* taking analysis held not applicable to taxes or special assessments); *Roedler v. Department of Energy*, 255 F.3d 1347 (Fed. Cir. 2001) (rejecting takings claim based on assessment of user fee on nuclear utility rate payers for disposal of spent nuclear fuel since assessment reasonably related to consumption and fees generated had not been used for some other purpose). *See also Blumenthal Inv. Trusts v. City of West Des Moines*, 636 N.W. 2d 255 (Iowa 2010) (holding that private paving agreement, as an alternative to assessment agreement, related to paving of street to ensure construction of public improvements for development of area did not violate developer's due process rights). *See generally* R. Lisle Baker, *Using Special Assessments as a Tool for Smart Growth: Louisville's New Metro Government as a Potential Example*, 45 Brandeis L. J. 1 (2006); Andrew Painter, Community Development Authorities, 45 U. Rich. L. Rev. 81 (2010).

4. Facilities Benefit Assessment Districts. In *J.W. Jones Companies v. City of San Diego*, 203 Cal. Rptr. 580 (Ct. App. 1984), the county sought to plan for adequate infrastructure in a generally undeveloped area and to shift the primary burden of financing facilities to developers and new residents. The financing device created to implement the county's comprehensive plan was a Facilities Benefit Assessment (FBA). The area in question envisioned 23,130 residential units and 698 acres of commercial and industrial uses. Based on an estimate of $55 million needed for streets and parks, nearly $27 million would be charged to the developer and approximately the same amount would be raised through the FBA. The remaining amount, just under $2 million, would be paid by the city and other sources.

The developer made several legal challenges to the FBA. As the charge was imposed to recoup the cost of public improvements made to specially benefit the property, the court found that the FBA was not a tax or assessment subject to Proposition 13, which would have required supermajority referendum approval by voters. The court also rejected an equal protection claim based on the exemption of already developed properties, concluding that such properties were not similarly situated insofar as they did not generate the need for the new proposed facilities. All undeveloped properties were treated similarly with an FBA assessment.

The FBA differed from the traditional special assessment in several respects. First, the traditional assessment is charged to properties specially benefited on the basis either of (1) an allocation to owners based on the front footage of the parcel in relation to the total frontage in the benefited district, or (2) the percentage of assessed valuation of each parcel. Under the FBA, the assessment was equally divided between each dwelling unit. Second, under the traditional special assessment, payments are made annually over a period, such as ten years, to service bonds sold to finance the facility. Under the FBA, the assessment was paid at the time of building permit application. By comparison, if the financing technique is an impact fee, the fee might be due upon subdivision approval. Thus, under the FBA, the developer could await market demand for units and avoid the higher carrying costs associated with impact fees.

Third, unlike the traditional special assessment, the FBA scheme did not consider the location of an assessed parcel; thus, proximity and contiguity to the facility are not essential. Finally, under the traditional special assessment, all benefited properties are equitably assessed for the benefit enjoyed. Under the FBA, developed properties were exempt.

The FBA was similar to the traditional special assessment in one respect: funds collected are earmarked and spent solely for the purpose for which the assessment was imposed. Both were enforced through lien foreclosure.

Would the developer and future residents prefer infrastructure financing by FBA or special assessment? Knowledge that they have to pay an annual assessment in addition to property taxes and mortgage payments may upset future homeowners, who may not realize that the price of their home, and thus their monthly mortgage payments, are lower because of the assessment. In addition, the income tax consequences of an assessment may be different from those of a mortgage. From the developer's standpoint, the FBA is superior. It is paid on a per dwelling basis as building permits are sought, while under the traditional special assessment, the assessments for each parcel come due annually regardless of the pace at which the project is actually constructed.

3. Other Financing Techniques

Still other financing techniques are used at the local level with the goal of maintaining and improving the community.

Business Improvement Districts. A variation on the special assessment district is the Business Improvement District, or "BID." BIDs are typically undertaken as a mini-redevelopment strategy to enhance the attractiveness of commercial districts. Rather than placing the administration within an existing or newly created governmental service district, BIDs are typically administered by private, nonprofit boards made up of district business owners. BIDs allow businesses in a specific neighborhood to expand upon the services provided by government.

For example, the BID might be used to provide additional security, valet parking, maintenance, expansion of public pedestrian spaces, installation of attractive lighting, or widening of sidewalks for landscaping and outdoor cafes and dining. The BID also might be used for the "calming" of streets, that is, strategies to reduce automobile traffic. In Europe, traffic calming is often initiated to make streets available for pedestrians. Suzanne H. Crowhurst Lennard & Henry L. Lennard, Liveable Cities 98 (1987) (Dutch transportation policy called a "Woon-erf" is not so much an auto-free policy as a traffic reduction or calming scheme often calling for the mixed use of streets by pedestrians, children, and residents' automobiles); Eran Ben-Joseph, *Changing the Residential Street Scene: Adapting the Shared Street (Woonerf) Concept to the Suburban Environment,* 61 J. Am. Plan. Ass'n. 504 (1995). *See also* Donald Appleyard, Liveable Streets (1981).

BIDs are often authorized by statute. *See, e.g.,* Cal. Sts. & High. Code §§36601-36670 (West Supp. 2015). In *Foote Clinic, Inc. v. City of Hastings,* 580 N.W.2d 81 (Neb. 1998), the court ruled that BIDs were legally authorized. It concluded, however, that the BID at issue violated state law by failing to specifically set forth the improvements to be made in the district and the estimated costs of those improvements. The Nebraska court ruled that assessment ordinances are to be strictly construed with doubts resolved in favor of the taxpayer. *See also Kessler v. Grand Cent. Dist. Mgmt. Ass'n*, 158 F.3d 92 (2d Cir. 1998) (BID district not subject to one-person, one-vote equal protection requirement, sustaining a weighted voting system that guaranteed majority representation by property owners). *See generally* Richard Briffault, *A Government for Our Time? Business Improvement Districts and Urban Governance*, 99 Colum. L. Rev. 365 (1999); David J. Kennedy, *Restraining the Power of Business Improvement Districts: The Case of the Grand Central Partnership*, 15 Yale L. & Pol'y Rev. 283 (1996) (BIDs can be used to generate profits for business and cause gentrification, which may result in displacing or excluding the less wealthy and which may adversely affect adjacent areas or the larger community without participation from citizens or area residents); Daniel R. Garodnick, Comment, *What's the BID Deal? Can the Grand Central Business Improvement District Serve a Special Limited Purpose?*, 148 U. Pa. L. Rev. 1733 (2000). Can a BID directed to commercial uses in a district exempt residential dwellings from assessments? *2nd Roc-Jersey Assocs. v. Town of Morristown*, 731 A.2d 1 (N.J. 1999) (sustaining special improvement district statute exempting residential properties).

Tax Abatements. Another approach to municipal financing of infrastructure involves so-called tax abatements, when municipalities reduce or forego taxes for some period of time, typically with the goal of encouraging developers and business to make improvements to property or to locate a project in a distressed or blighted area. *See, e.g.*, N.J.S.A. 40A:21-1 et seq. (five-year exemption and abatement law); and N.J.S.A. 40A:20-1 et seq. (long-term tax exemption law); Texas Tax Code §312.002. Critics lodge many of the same complaints about tax abatement programs that they make about other programs designed to spur investment by conferring special financial benefits on businesses: the programs lack transparency, they may be unduly influenced by the political agendas of local officials, and it is questionable whether they produce net long-term gains for the community. *See* Office of the State Comptroller, State of New Jersey, A Programmatic Examination of Municipal Tax Abatements (2010) found at http://www.nj.gov/comptroller/news/docs/tax_abatement_report.pdf (last visited Nov. 11, 2016).

Enterprise Zones. A final municipal finance strategy is the so-called enterprise zone, in which a municipality theoretically adopts a program of deep deregulation of businesses with the goal of stimulating economic activity in a depressed area of the community. Originally based on a concept developed in Great Britain, the idea has been championed by political conservatives in the United States and embraced by many states. *See* Richard Briffault, *The Rise of Sublocal Structures in Urban Governance*, 82 Minn. L. Rev. 503, 509-511 (1997). In practice, enterprise zones are often far different from the theoretical regulation-free environments envisioned by their early champions; instead, they commonly offer extensive government assistance in the form of tax abatements, loans and land assembly. *Id.*

D. PRIVATIZATION OF INFRASTRUCTURE

A Note on the Privatization of Infrastructure

Most citizens ordinarily give little thought to how infrastructure is owned and by whom it is managed. A great deal of infrastructure is and has long been privately owned and managed (subject to public regulation), such as traditional telephone lines and equipment. Other infrastructure, including roads, sidewalks, and public parks, are typically publicly owned and managed. But certain types of infrastructure can be either public or private. In recent decades, there has been robust debate about whether some infrastructure should be converted from public to private ownership.

The case for privatization of infrastructure rests in part on faith in free markets to allocate financial resources efficiently. With privatization, says Chris Edwards of the Cato Institute, "investment is less likely to flow to uneconomical projects that are chosen for political or ideological reasons." Chris Edwards, Take the Public-Private Road to Efficiency (February 20, 2013) at http://www.wsj.com/articles/SB10001424127887323478004578304372344816256 (last visited Nov. 11, 2016). Thus, the argument proceeds, privatization should help ensure that expenditures on infrastructure are not made wastefully, and should make it easier to attract private capital to finance the construction of infrastructure. Moreover, private enterprise is thought to be better than government at project and financial management; thus, "[p]rivate infrastructure is also more likely than government projects to be completed on-time and on budget." *Id.*

Compared to other parts of the world, the United States has been relatively slow to join the privatization bandwagon. Starting in the 1960s, Spain and France constructed their versions of interstate highway systems using a system of private concessions. In the 1980s, Australia embraced privatization, and in the 1990s, it spread to Latin America (notably Argentina, Brazil, Chile, Colombia, Mexico, and Peru) and more recently to Africa and the Middle East. Robert W. Poole, Jr., Reason Foundation, Annual Privatization Report 2015: Transportation Finance. Nonetheless, the United States has seen some major private infrastructure investment projects, such as the Dulles Toll Road outside Washington, D.C. and others.

The privatization agenda is often promoted under the banner of so-called "public-private partnerships," a phrase that is positive-sounding but turns out to have almost no meaning. *See* U.S. PIRG Education Fund, Private Roads, Public Costs at 5 (2009) at http://www.uspirg.org/reports/usp/private-roads-public-costs (last visited Nov. 11, 2016) ("The term public-private partnership is particularly ubiquitous, and woefully imprecise."). Even the most unambiguously governmental road project involves a public-private partnership in the sense that after designing the roadway, government officials typically enlist private contractors to lay down the pavement and do other work on the road. Under the purest form of privatization, a private firm acquires the right to all the benefits and bears all the financial risks associated with the project for the duration of the concession; if the traffic or toll revenues are less than projected, the concessionaire, not the government, suffers the loss. Under another familiar type of public-private partnership, a private firm will take over, for a fixed fee, various management responsibilities, but the benefits and risks of ownership are left with the public sector. Under this approach, the concessionaire is paid an "availability payment," meaning the private firm will be paid irrespective of traffic levels or the toll revenues. The responsibility for designing, building and even operating the roadway may be placed on the private firm, but the firm is guaranteed payment so long as it successfully performs.

Privatization—especially the extreme version—has its critics; it may involve either the leasing of existing toll roads to a private firm, or enlisting a private firm to construct a new road. First, critics contend that, "by privatizing roadways, officials hand over significant control over regional transportation policy to individuals who are accountable to shareholders rather than the public." *Id.* at 1. A contract governing the creation of a roadway concession will typically include a "non-compete" clause designed to prevent government officials from launching new initiatives (for example, building a new roadway, or promoting mass transit) that would draw demand from the private road; local governments may even be subject to claims for monetary "compensation" for breaching such clauses. While such clauses may be defensible in a narrow business sense, they constrain public policy choices in the transportation sector, possibly for an extended period. Second, critics contend that "[t]he upfront payments that states receive are often worth far less than the value of future toll revenue from the road." *Id.* Lastly, critics contend that private investors necessarily have higher costs than government, both because they generally do not enjoy the same tax advantages as local governments and because they have to pay a reasonable return to their investors, driving up the cost of public private partnerships. *Id.* at 23.

An overarching problem with public-private partnerships is that they tend to be very long term, creating a sometimes irresistible temptation for local officials to seek to secure short term political advantages at the cost of long-term public sacrifices that benefit private investors:

> Privatization of roads offers elected officials political benefits beyond the ability to avoid potentially unpopular tax increases to pay for transportation. In the short term, privatization promises a huge budget windfall, especially for privatization of existing roads, which creates budget slack and an ability to dedicate resources to other favored projects. New private roads offer special opportunities for credit-taking and ribbon cutting ceremonies. In either case, the long-term financial downside, particularly the loss of toll funds and rising toll rates paid by drivers, often is overshadowed by the short-term windfall.

Id. at 12.

Even privatization critics acknowledge the potential for offsetting efficiencies. A Congressional Budget Office study concluded, based on an admittedly small sample of projects, that public-private partnerships "have built highways slightly less expensively and slightly more quickly, compared with the traditional public-sector approach." Congressional Budget Office, Using Public-Private Partnerships to Carry out Highway Projects, vi (2012). Public-private partnerships also inevitably impose additional oversight costs on local governments. *See* U.S. Government Accountability Office, *Federal-Aid Highways: Increased Reliance on Contractors Can Pose Oversight Challenges for Federal and State Officials*, Report to the Chairman, Committee on Transportation and Infrastructure, House of Representatives, January 2008.

E. INFRASTRUCTURE AND THE ENVIRONMENT

1. Green Infrastructure

There is growing interest in the alternative of "green infrastructure." As defined by the Environmental Protection Agency, green infrastructure "is an approach to wet weather management that uses natural systems — or engineered systems that mimic natural processes—to enhance overall environmental quality and provide utility services." US EPA, Green Infrastructure, at https://www.epa .gov/green-infrastructure (last visited Nov. 11, 2016). Green infrastructure is often said to stand in contrast to "grey infrastructure," which refers to the familiar hard, engineered structures for handling storm water, such as gutters, storm sewers, tunnels, culverts, detention basins, and related systems.

The arsenal of green infrastructure is extensive, including green roofs, tree planting, rain barrels and cisterns, bioswales and rain gardens, and permeable pavements. The basic concept underlying green infrastructure is to use natural processes to improve water quality and handle large quantities of water by restoring the hydrologic function of the landscape, managing storm water at its source, and reducing the need for additional engineered solutions. Environmental Protection Agency, Green Infrastructure Opportunities that Arise During Municipal Operations, 1 (2015). "An important objective of green infrastructure is to reduce storm water volume, which improves water quality by reducing pollutant loads, streambank erosion, and sedimentation." *Id.*

Equally important, green infrastructure offers the promise of saving money. Green infrastructure may be cheaper to install than grey infrastructure because it is on site and seeks to take advantage of the natural capacity of the landscape to direct and absorb storm water. As stated in an EPA report:

> Traditional approaches to storm water management involve conveying runoff off-site to receiving waters, to a combined sewer system, or to a regional facility that treats runoff from multiple sites. These designs typically include hard infrastructure, such as curbs, gutters, and piping. LID-based designs, in contrast, are designed to use natural drainage features or engineered swales and vegetated contours for runoff conveyance and treatment. In terms of costs, LID techniques like conservation design can reduce the amount of materials needed for paving roads and driveways and for installing curbs and gutters. Conservation designs can be used to reduce the total amount of impervious surface, which results in reduced road and driveway lengths and reduced costs. Other LID techniques, such as grassed swales, can be used to infiltrate roadway runoff and eliminate or reduce the need for curbs and gutters, thereby reducing infrastructure costs. Also, by infiltrating or evaporating runoff, LID techniques can reduce the size and cost of flood-control structures.

Environmental Protection Agency, Reducing Stormwater Costs Through Low Impact Development (LID) Strategies and Practices, 9 (2007). At the same time, green infrastructure can reduce costs by reducing storm water flows and resulting downstream floods and flood damage. Environmental Protection Agency, Flood Loss Avoidance Benefits of Green Infrastructure for Stormwater Management (2015) (concluding, based on a modeling exercise, that annual flood damage to buildings and their contents, and associated income loss, can be reduced by over $100 million by incorporating green infrastructure into new development and redevelopment).

2. Climate Change and Infrastructure

The Changing Environment and Infrastructure. A new and important set of infrastructure issues has been brought to the fore by climate change. Since the launch of the Industrial Revolution, the burning of fossil fuels has increased the concentration of carbon dioxide in the atmosphere by more than 40%. U.S. Global Change Research Program, Third National Climate Assessment (2014) at http://nca2014 .globalchange.gov/ (last visited Nov. 11, 2016). Due to the so-called "green-house effect," this air pollution has led to an increase in U.S. average temperature from 1.3F to 1.9F since 1895, with most of the increase occurring since 1970. *Id.* As of the time this book was being written, in the summer of 2016, this year was on track to be the hottest year in history. *See* Andrea Thompson, First Half of 2016 Blows Away Temp Records, Climate Central (July 19, 2016) ("The first half of 2016 has blown away temperature records, capped off by a record hot June, once again bumping up the odds that 2016 will be the hottest year on record globally, according to data released Tuesday."). Even with aggressive mitigation efforts, the level of greenhouse gases is projected to increase in the future, producing still higher temperatures. But climate change and its impacts are already upon us. As stated on the U.S. Global Change Research Program website at http://www.globalchange.gov/climate-change (last visited Nov. 11, 2016): "Climate change is happening now. The United States and the world are warming, global sea level is rising, and some types of extreme weather events are becoming more frequent and more severe. These changes have already resulted in a wide range of impacts across every region of the country and many sectors of the economy."

Impacts on Infrastructure. A changing climate has profound implications for the condition of existing infrastructure facilities, the work of maintaining and repairing infrastructure, and the processes of designing and constructing new infrastructure. Indeed, as one commentator has put it, the entire infrastructure system "is placed at risk by global climate change." George E. Wannier, Infrastructure, Chapter 6, in The Law of Adaptation to Climate Change: U.S. and International Aspects, 173 (2012). He continues, "As sea levels and temperature rise, storms become more severe, and precipitation changes dramatically from region to region, the world we built for ourselves, and more specifically the links we have built to tie us together as a society, will be pressured — to crack, bend, or disappear beneath a changing planet." *Id.*

The U.S. Department of Transportation has compiled an informative list of "notable potential impacts" to the transportation sector from climate change:

- More frequent/severe flooding of underground tunnels and low-lying infrastructure, requiring drainage and pumping, due to more intense precipitation, sea level rise, and storm surge.
- Increased numbers and magnitude of storm surges and/or relative sea level rise that potentially shortens infrastructure life.
- Increased thermal expansion of paved surfaces, potentially causing degradation and reduced service life, due to higher temperatures and increased duration of heat waves.
- Higher maintenance/construction costs for roads and bridges, due to increased temperatures, or exposure to storm surge.
- Asphalt degradation and shorter replacement cycles, leading to limited access, congestion, and higher costs,due to higher temperatures.
- Culvert and drainage infrastructure damage due to changes in precipitation intensity, or snow melt timing.

- Decreased driver/operator performance and decision-making skills due to driver fatigue as a result of adverse weather.
- Increased risk of vehicle crashes in severe weather.
- System downtime, derailments, and slower travel times due to rail buckling during extremely hot days.
- Reduced aircraft performance leading to limited range capabilities and reduced payloads.
- Air traffic disruptions due to severe weather and precipitation events that impact arrival and departure rates.
- Reduced shipping access to docks and shore equipment and navigational aid damage.
- Restricted access to local economies and public transportation.

U.S. Department of Transportation Climate Adaptation Plan: Ensuring Transportation Infrastructure and System Resilience, 7 (2014).

The potential consequences of climate change for the nation's infrastructure systems are readily predictable and deeply disturbing. Keeping the roads in decent shape and the trains running is hard enough in a static world; adding higher temperatures, more extreme weather events, and greater variability and unpredictability to the weather will make the challenges much greater. Sea level rise will require the abandonment of some transportation routes and render some existing ports unusable. With time and sufficient financial resources, society can work around many of these problems. But the big questions are how much social and economic dislocation will climate change produce, and what other national and worldwide social and economic objectives may need to be shelved in order to address infrastructure problems created by climate change.

Possible Actions. The threat posed by climate change to our infrastructure systems is receiving attention at the highest level of government. In President Barack Obama's 2013 "Climate Action Plan," in the section on climate adaptation, the first-stated priority is "Building Stronger and Safer Communities and Infrastructure." The plan explains that even as the nation (and the world) must take steps to reduce carbon pollution, the nation must "also prepare for the impacts of a changing climate that are already being felt across the country." *Id.* at 5. The plan committed the administration to "help[ing] state and local governments strengthen our roads, bridges, and shorelines so we can better protect people's homes, businesses and way of life from severe weather." *Id.*

Specifically, the Plan calls for federal agencies to:

> identify and remove barriers to making climate-resilient investments; identify and remove counterproductive policies that increase vulnerabilities; and encourage and support smarter, more resilient investments, including through agency grants, technical assistance, and other programs, in sectors from transportation and water management to conservation and disaster relief.

Id. at 12-13. In addition, the Plan directs federal agencies "to ensure that climate risk-management considerations are fully integrated into federal infrastructure and natural resource management planning." Other steps include: (1) establishment of a task force of state, local, and tribal officials to provide advice on what actions the federal government can take to better support local preparedness and resilience-building efforts (the recommendations of the task force, issued in November 2014, are available at https://www.whitehouse.gov/sites/default/files/docs/task_force_report_0.pdf (last visited Nov. 11, 2016)); (2) providing "targeted support and assistance to help communities prepare for climate-change impacts;" and (3) promoting the development of new standards and codes that will produce "consistently safe buildings and infrastructure," as well as increased climate resilience of federal facilities and infrastructure.

National policies addressing the climate threat to infrastructure are particularized in different agency climate adaptation plans. For example, in 2014, the U.S. Department of Transportation issued a climate adaptation plan that focused on coping with the effects of climate change on transportation infrastructure. Recognizing that the national transportation system includes different modes (e.g., roads, waterways, transit, airports, and so forth) the plan lays out a three-part strategy, including: (1) enhancing the resilience of existing infrastructure; (2) incorporating projected climate change into the planning and design for new facilities; and (3) enhancing the resilience of the entire transportation system by recognizing important interdependencies between the different modes and creating redundant infrastructure facilities. U.S. Department of Transportation Climate Adaptation Plan: Ensuring Transportation Infrastructure and System Resilience 8 (2014). One of the most notable features of transportation infrastructure is that is it "inherently long lived," both in the sense that transportation facilities tend to be durable, but also in the sense that individual project decisions can influence the shape of a transportation network over the long term. *Id.* at 15. As a result, coping with the risks of climate change, and the associated uncertainties, is especially important in transportation planning.

Responding to Climate Disasters. Climate change projections are also influencing national disaster recovery efforts. In October 2012, Hurricane Sandy struck the coast of the northeastern United States, leaving 650,000 homes damaged or destroyed, forcing the permanent or temporary closure of hundreds of thousands of businesses, creating widespread and long-lasting power outages, and destroying and degrading transportation and other types of infrastructure. *See* Department of Housing and Urban Development, Hurricane Sandy Rebuilding Task Force, Hurricane Sandy Rebuilding Strategy (2013). The Rebuilding Task Force appointed in the aftermath of the storm crafted a strategy to guide rebuilding in the affected areas and also to establish a template for dealing with similar future events, which are projected to increase in frequency and intensity in coming decades. A centerpiece of the new strategy is to promote resilient rebuilding based on careful evaluation of future risk, especially sea level rise, using the latest climate science. As the task force report stated, "It is vital that science-based tools and the best available data are used to better anticipate community vulnerabilities for future disasters and to adopt measures that will reduce future human, economic, and environmental costs." *Id.* at 40.

Some experts have questioned how effectively the joint federal-state-local response to Hurricane Sandy implemented this forward-looking approach. *See* Rob Young, A Year After Sandy: The Wrong Policy on Rebuilding the Coast, Environment 360 (October 31, 2013) at http://e360.yale.edu/feature/a_year_after_sandy_the_wrong_policy_on_rebuilding_the_coast/2705/ (last visited Nov. 11, 2016) ("Since Hurricane Sandy hit the U.S. East Coast a year ago, federal, state, and local governments have made an important de facto policy decision without any debate, discussion, or national plan. It is this: We will attempt to hold the nation's shorelines in place using whatever means possible and whatever the cost. We will do this despite the undisputed scientific fact that sea levels are rising and coastal erosion along these shores will only increase in the future.") At the very least, it is progress for government officials to acknowledge the *need* to rebuild higher and better in anticipation of the storm next time.

As pointed out at the beginning of this chapter, much of the debate about infrastructure centers on the issue of who will pay for it. Climate change will create a demand for special kinds of infrastructure, such as coastal defense structures in the face of rising seas, which will present new versions of the "who pays" question, as illustrated by this case from New Jersey.

■ BOROUGH OF HARVEY CEDARS v. KARAN
214 N.J 384 (2013)

Justice ALBIN

When a municipality takes private property for a public use, the property owner is entitled to "just compensation" under our State and Federal Constitutions. In this case, as part of a massive public-works project, the Borough of Harvey Cedars exercised its power of eminent domain to take a portion of the beachfront property of Harvey and Phyllis Karan to construct a dune that connects with other dunes running the entire length of Long Beach Island in Ocean County. The dunes serve as a barrier-wall, protecting the homes and businesses of Long Beach Island from the destructive fury of the ocean.

That the Karans are entitled to "just compensation" for the taking of a portion of their property for this public project is not in question. Instead, the focus here is on how to calculate "just compensation" when the taking of a portion of the property for a public project may lessen in part and enhance in part the value of the remaining property.

At a condemnation trial, the court permitted the Karans to introduce evidence of the loss in value to their home caused by the dune obstructing their oceanfront vista. The trial court, however, denied Harvey Cedars the opportunity to show that the dune enhanced the value of the Karans' property by protecting it from the damage and destruction that is wrought by powerful storms and ocean surges. Based on our state-law jurisprudence, the court determined that only special benefits, not general benefits, flowing from a public project can be considered in calculating the enhanced value to the remaining property. In the court's view, the storm protection afforded by the project is a general benefit because the dunes not only protect all property owners in Harvey Cedars but also presumably add value to their property. Accordingly, the court did not allow the jury to consider evidence that the dunes — constructed at public expense to protect the island's homes from minor and catastrophic storms — enhanced the value of the Karans' property. The jury awarded the Karans $375,000 in damages, premised mostly on the loss of their oceanfront view. The Appellate Division affirmed.

We now conclude that when a public project requires the partial taking of property, "just compensation" to the owner must be based on a consideration of all relevant, reasonably calculable, and non-conjectural factors that either decrease or increase the value of the remaining property. In a partial-takings case, homeowners are entitled to the fair market value of their loss, not to a windfall, not to a pay out that disregards the home's enhanced value resulting from a public project. To calculate that loss, we must look to the difference between the fair market value of the property before the partial taking and after the taking. In determining damages, the trial court did not permit the jury to consider that the dune would likely spare the Karans' home from total destruction in certain fierce storms and from other damage in lesser storms. A formula — as used by the trial court and Appellate Division — that does not permit consideration of the quantifiable benefits of a public project that increase the value of the remaining property in a partial-takings case will lead to a compensation award that does not reflect the owner's true loss. Compensation in a partial-takings case must be "just" to both the landowner and the public. A fair market value approach best achieves that goal.

Because that approach was not followed in this case, we reverse the judgment of the Appellate Division and remand for a new trial.

I.

THE BEACH- AND STORM–PROTECTION PROJECT

The backdrop to this case is a beach-restoration and storm-protection project on Long Beach Island funded by federal, state, and local governments. This massive public project — carried out by the U.S. Army Corps of Engineers and the New Jersey Department of Environmental Protection — provides vital protection to the island's residents from beach erosion and storms that threaten homes and businesses with damage and destruction. One part of the project involves the pumping of massive amounts of sand onto the beach to extend the shoreline seaward by 200 feet. Another part involves beach nourishment every seven years over a period of fifty years to battle beach erosion. The last part of the project calls for the construction of dunes along the entire length of the island sufficient to hold back storm-triggered waves capable of destroying or seriously damaging homes and businesses. The dune seaward of the Karans' property is designed in the form of a trapezoid — twenty-two feet high and thirty feet wide at the top — and was built to replace an existing sixteen-feet-high dune.

The dune-construction project required the securing of easements on properties bordering the ocean. The responsibility and cost of acquiring those easements fell to the municipalities on Long Beach Island. One such municipality is the Borough of Harvey Cedars.

The Borough's obligation was to secure eighty-two perpetual easements over the portions of private beachfront properties closest to the ocean on which the dunes would be built. The Borough acquired sixty-six easements by voluntary consent of the property owners. However, the owners of sixteen beachfront properties, including the Karans, did not consent. As a result, in July 2008, the Borough adopted an ordinance authorizing it to acquire easements over those sixteen properties through its statutory powers of eminent domain.

The Borough and the Karans could not agree on a figure representing just compensation for a perpetual dune easement over the seaside portion of their property. The Karans rejected the Borough's offer of $300 as compensation for both the land taken and any devaluation of the remaining property.

The Karans' single-family, beachfront home sits on 11,868 square feet of land in Harvey Cedars. Constructed in 1973, the house is anchored on pilings and has three stories, with the upper two floors containing the dining and living quarters. These two floors open onto exterior decks, which had provided a panoramic view of the beach and ocean. The first level consists of a two-car garage and storage area for the heater, HVAC, and utility equipment.

To construct the twenty-two-foot dune, the Borough sought a perpetual easement over a strip of 3,381 square feet of the Karans' land nearest to the ocean. The easement covers more than one quarter of the Karans' property. The Karans claim that the newly constructed dune, standing between their home and the ocean, obstructs their view of the beach.

THE EMINENT DOMAIN ACTION

[After determining as matter of law that the financial benefits of the storm-protection project "were shared — even though in differing degrees — by the larger community of Harvey Cedars" and therefore were "general benefits," the trial court submitted the "just compensation" award to a jury, which returned an award of $375,000. The Appellate Division affirmed, agreeing with the trial court that storm protection afforded to the Karans' property was a general benefit that could not be considered in calculating the amount of just compensation due the Karans. The Supreme Court granted the Borough of Harvey Cedar's petition for certification.] . . .

IV.

The question before us solely concerns an issue of law — how to compute "just compensation" in a partial-takings case. Because our standard of review is de novo, we owe no deference to the legal conclusions reached by the trial court and Appellate Division.

We begin with some basic principles of law governing the case before us. The right to "just compensation" when the government takes property for a public use is one of the essential guarantees of both the United States and New Jersey Constitutions. This fundamental right is of ancient origin, predating the founding of our Republic, and is found even in the text of the Magna Carta.

Our State Constitution also specifically guarantees "just compensation" for a municipality's taking of an easement on private property for a public use. The Eminent Domain Act, N.J.S.A. 20:3-1 to 50, also makes clear that in the case of a partial taking of property, such as the acquisition of an easement by a municipality, a landowner is entitled to compensation not only for the property taken but also for "damages, if any, to any remaining property."

When an entire piece of property is acquired by the State or a municipality by the power of eminent domain, the landowner is entitled to just compensation measured by "the fair market value of the property as of the date of the taking, determined by what a willing buyer and a willing seller would agree to, neither being under any compulsion to act." The landowner whose property is taken in its entirety for a public use is not entitled to enhanced compensation because the taking will benefit his neighbors or increase the value of their homes. Had Harvey Cedars taken the whole of the Karans' property for the construction of a dune, no one would argue that — because of the future benefits that their neighbors would enjoy from the public project — the Karans would be entitled to more than the fair market value of their property, 1.9 million dollars.

However, our partial-takings jurisprudence, from its earliest beginnings, has not necessarily reflected the straightforward fair market value approach that is evident in total-takings cases. To find the source of the special/general benefits dichotomy, we must look back, understanding that "a page of history is" sometimes "worth a volume of logic."

[The Court's extensive discussion of court precedent discussing the distinction between general and special benefits is omitted.]

Today, the terms special and general benefits do more to obscure than illuminate the basic principles governing the computation of just compensation in eminent domain cases. The problem with the term "general benefits" is that it may mean different things to different courts. To some courts, the term "general benefits" is a surrogate for speculative or conjectural benefits. To other courts, general benefits are any benefits shared in common with a landowner's neighbors or community.

The fair-market considerations that inform computing just compensation in partial-takings cases should be no different than in total-takings cases. They are the considerations that a willing buyer and a willing seller would weigh in coming to an agreement on the property's value at the time of the taking and after the taking. In weighing the impact of a public project on the remainder property in a partial-takings case, a willing buyer and willing seller would likely consider benefits to the remainder that are not speculative or conjectural and that are not projected into the indefinite future. Our courts already perform the gatekeeping role of shielding the jury from speculative evidence in valuing just compensation in condemnation cases. For example, our courts do not permit the mere possibility of a zoning change to go before a jury in considering the highest and best use of property taken by eminent domain.

In short, just compensation should be based on non-conjectural and quantifiable benefits, benefits that are capable of reasonable calculation at the time of the taking. Speculative benefits projected into the indefinite future should not be considered. Benefits that both a willing buyer and willing seller would agree enhance the value of property should be considered in determining just compensation, whether those benefits are categorized as special or general.

We need not pay slavish homage to labels that have outlived their usefulness. . . .

V.

We find that the Appellate Division's use of the general-benefits doctrine in this case is at odds with contemporary principles of just-compensation jurisprudence. The jury was barred from hearing evidence about potentially quantifiable benefits arising from the storm-protection project that increased the value of the Karans' home. Just compensation does not entitle a landowner to a windfall from a partial taking of property.

Harvey Cedars condemned a portion of the seaside, oceanfront property of the Karans to acquire a permanent easement for the construction and maintenance of a twenty-two-foot dune to replace an existing sixteen-foot dune. The new dune was part of a much larger shore-protection project to benefit all the residents of Harvey Cedars and Long Beach Island. Unquestionably, the benefits of the dune project extended not only to the Karans but also to their neighbors further from the shoreline. Yet, clearly the properties most vulnerable to dramatic ocean surges and larger storms are frontline properties, such as the Karans'. Therefore, the Karans benefitted to a greater degree than their westward neighbors. Without the dune, the probability of serious damage or destruction to the Karans' property increased dramatically over a thirty-year period.

A jury evidently concluded that the Karans' property decreased in value as a result of the loss of their panoramic view of the seashore due to the height of the dune. A willing purchaser of beachfront property would obviously value the view and proximity to the ocean. But it is also likely that a rational purchaser would place a value on a protective barrier that shielded his property from partial or total destruction. Whatever weight might be given that consideration, surely, it would be one part of the equation in determining fair market value. Although, in determining the fair market value of the Karans' property, the jury was instructed to consider all features that enhanced and diminished the property's value, the jury also was told to disregard "general benefits produced by the dune project which [the Karans] may enjoy in common with other property owners in the area to reduce the value." This charge distorted the fair-market valuation of the property by artificially withholding a key component of the analysis. . . .

The Karans argue that they should not be made to pay twice for storm-damage protection afforded by a public project, once by their taxes and again by deducting the enhanced value of their home from the damages. However, that argument is far-fetched when the actual numbers are considered. The Harvey Cedars shore-protection project cost twenty-five million dollars, with the federal government bearing most of the cost, with the State bearing a lesser amount, and with the municipality pitching in one million dollars. Tens of millions of taxpayers contributed to the shore-protection project that shields the Karans' property from destruction. Because the Karans occupy frontline ocean property, the benefits afforded to them are much greater than to others. The portion of the Karans' taxes that goes to support the project may be infinitesimal compared to the value added to their home by the dune protection. Of course that value — whatever it may be — is ultimately a jury issue. If one accepted the Karans' argument, it would be permissible for landowners to receive a jury award of $375,000 for a dune's obstruction of their oceanfront view without having to offset any amount if the dune hypothetically increased the value of their home by the same $375,000. . . .

VI.

The historical reasons that gave rise to the development of the doctrine of general and special benefits no longer have resonance today. We are not dealing with railroads armed with eminent-domain powers taking land to lay tracks and calculating that the property owner is owed nothing because of benefits that may come in the indefinite future from commerce and population growth. Disallowing the deduction of those "benefits" is warranted because "just compensation" must be determined at the time of the taking and must be quantifiable.

Speculative or conjectural benefits conferred on a property owner whose land is partially taken by a public project should not offset a condemnation award because such benefits would not factor into a calculation of fair market value. On the other hand, reasonably calculable benefits — regardless of whether those benefits are enjoyed to some lesser or greater degree by others in the community — that increase the value of property at the time of the taking should be discounted from the condemnation award.

We cannot devise a perfect means for compensating a property owner whose land is partially taken as part of a public project. We can only ensure that every person will receive just compensation, as promised by our State and Federal Constitutions. Using fair market value as the benchmark is the best method to achieve that result. . . .

The Borough should not have been barred from presenting all non-speculative, reasonably calculable benefits from the dune project — the kind that a willing purchaser and willing seller would consider in an arm's length transaction. Those benefits are part of the fair-market equation, regardless of whether they are enjoyed by others in the community. The jury in this case should have been charged that the determination of just compensation required calculating the fair market value of the Karans' property immediately before the taking and after the taking (and construction of the twenty-two-foot dune).

The trial court's charge required the jury to disregard even quantifiable storm-protection benefits resulting from the public project that increased the fair market value of the Karans' property. In short, the quantifiable decrease in the value of their property — loss of view — should have been set off by any quantifiable increase in its value — storm-protection benefits. The Karans are entitled to just compensation, a reasonable calculation of any decrease in the fair market value of their property after the taking. They are not entitled to more, and certainly not a windfall at the public's expense.

VII.

For the reasons expressed, we reverse the judgment of the Appellate Division, vacate the condemnation award, and remand to the trial court for proceedings consistent with this opinion.

5

The Role of Planning

A. INTRODUCTION

1. The Allure of Planning

Since the advent of modern zoning in the twentieth century, the notion has existed that a planning process resulting in a plan (variously denominated a "master," "general," or "comprehensive" plan) will take place prior to the adoption of zoning. As discussed in Chapter 2, the Standard Zoning Enabling Act served as the model for the first zoning ordinances in many municipalities, and the link between planning and zoning was expressly recognized in the Act. It declared that zoning must be "in accordance with a comprehensive plan."

Furthermore, the concept that zoning must be comprehensive in nature and based upon rational planning is reflected in the seminal *Village of Euclid v. Ambler Realty* opinion upholding the constitutionality of zoning. As we have seen, in that decision the Supreme Court first quoted from an Illinois decision which observed that the exclusion of businesses from a residential district "is part of the general plan by which the city's territory is allotted to different uses." 272 U.S. 365, 392 (1926) (quoting *City of Aurora v. Burns*, 149 N.E. 784, 788 (Ill. 1925)). The Court also referred to "investigations" and "comprehensive reports" of various "commissions and experts," reports that the Court found "bear every evidence of painstaking consideration." 272 U.S. at 394. In effect, the Court described a planning process.

The idea that planning can provide solutions to particular societal problems has always strongly attracted legislative bodies, in part because it allows legislators to claim that, by establishing a planning process, they have "done something" in response to the problem. As one study of the planning profession summarized, "[c]onfidence in the efficacy of rational intervention had long been part of the reform tradition that developed earlier in the century and was institutionalized by the federal administration as part of Roosevelt's New Deal." Charles Hoch, What Planners Do: Power, Politics, and Persuasion 36 (1994); *see also* Robert Fishman (ed.), The American Planning Tradition (2000). Thus, it is not surprising that, during the same time period that the U.S. Department of Commerce produced the Standard Zoning Enabling Act, the department also issued the Standard Planning Enabling Act.

The attraction to planning has increased in recent decades, although its importance and acceptance by lawmakers has oscillated. When widespread concern over environmental degradation, such as diminishing open space and poor air and water quality, arose around 1970, planning was seen as a long-term solution to those ills. Thus, the federal Clean Air and Clean Water Acts include numerous provisions calling for the adoption of plans, and many states require the preparation of plans for critical land use areas, such as the coastal zone. And recent federal legislation requires planning for the national forests and other federally managed lands.

2. The Rise of the Consistency Doctrine

Because planning and zoning both concern how land should be used, it seems logical that some connection would be required between the two. However, as illustrated in *Wolf v. City of Ely*, an Iowa decision included in this chapter, most courts have rejected the argument that the language in the Standard Zoning Enabling Act requires that adoption of a separate planning document precede zoning. Planning and later regulatory implementation through tools such as zoning were not linked, with the result that plans rarely had any actual effect on land use decisions.

In the last 40 years, however, a growing number of jurisdictions have reemphasized the concept of planning and, at the same time, altered this traditional relationship between planning and zoning. Many states have adopted statutory provisions requiring local jurisdictions to adopt comprehensive master or general plans. These statutes can be quite precise about the required content of the plan, a development illustrated in this chapter by the California case *Twain Harte Homeowners Ass'n v. County of Tuolumne*.

In addition, significant numbers of states have adopted statutes requiring zoning, subdivision, and other regulatory controls to be "consistent" with the comprehensive general plan adopted by the local jurisdiction. These consistency statutes often have been accompanied by statutory provisions expanding the breadth of the local plan's contents, with the result that planning now encompasses a wide variety of subjects, ranging from economic development to use of natural resources, and climate change. The push for consistency statutes did not result from uniformity of academic opinion on the subject; there was and remains vigorous debate over whether this linkage is a good idea. But the *results* of using traditional land use controls without any link to a separate planning process were almost universally criticized, and this criticism bolstered arguments that planning and regulatory decisions such as zoning should be linked through consistency requirements.

These statutory requirements requiring linkage led in turn to litigation over the meaning of "consistency." The principal question is how closely the regulatory mechanism, whether it is zoning or regulation of a subdivision, must follow the general plan. Is "strict" consistency required, or does the local governmental body have discretion to determine what type of development will be consistent?

The Arizona Supreme Court's decision in *Haines v. City of Phoenix*, which you will read in this chapter, squarely addresses the meaning of consistency. Does the court interpret the statutes in this jurisdiction correctly? Is "strict" or "loose" consistency best to promote the goals of comprehensive planning?

3. The Efficacy of Consistency Requirements

The consistency statutes, which state legislatures began to enact in the early 1970s, have now been in place for a sufficient time to allow the drawing of some conclusions about their usefulness. The consistency requirement ideally allows planning to take place in an environment separated from the day-to-day political concerns that often permeate local regulatory decisions about land use. The theory is that once local governments have undertaken a planning process, made choices about the future course of land use in their jurisdiction, and adopted a plan to reflect those choices, they can then begin the process of implementing the plan. The integrity of the completed planning process will serve to ensure the rationality of zoning, subdivision, and other development decisions that the jurisdiction will make.

However, the reality of the planning process often has not lived up to this ideal. If the general plan is the vehicle that drives regulatory decisions "on the ground," then it is quite difficult to divorce the planning process from the politics that is part of day-to-day development decisions. Thus, in some instances the process of adopting the general plan has itself given rise to intense political controversy over growth policies in the local jurisdiction. In response, one tendency of the planners has been to deflect the political firestorm by adopting a plan that is either vague on key policy decisions or that includes policies designed to please all concerned factions. Over the long term, however, this solution pleases almost no one.

Another outcome of the consistency requirements has been to transform the problem of "spot zoning" into one of "spot planning." If the plan, rather than the zoning ordinance, is the critical force in the regulatory decision about the land use allowed on a specific property, and the plan's map calls for one type of use while the landowner wants another, the "answer" from the landowner's point seems simple — request the local jurisdiction to amend the plan map. *See* David Zahniser, "L.A. Votes to Resurrect Partially Built Hollywood Target," Los Angeles Times (May 4, 2016), reporting that the Los Angeles City Council unanimously voted to revise the planning and zoning rules that govern a Sunset Boulevard site, changing the height rules for the area. The project previously had been successfully challenged in court.

Promoters of the plan see parcel-specific amendments as undermining the achievement of the plan's overall policies, while development interests decry the bureaucracy involved. In their view, it now takes two steps to get a development approved — a plan change and then a later zone change, subdivision approval, or other type of permit approval — rather than the one step that was needed before the consistency requirement became effective.

Despite these criticisms, planning and consistency requirements continue to have considerable support, and planning has achieved some notable successes, particularly in the case of plans addressing specific regional problems or areas of critical concern, such as coastal zones. For example, the plan prepared and implemented by the San Francisco Bay Conservation and Development Commission has helped in attaining its prime objective of preventing the continued filling of San Francisco Bay. In 1965, when the planning process started, almost one-third of the original bay had been filled, but since the plan was completed and implemented, almost no further filling has occurred. "Before 1965, an average of about 2300 acres of the bay were being filled each year. Now only a few acres are filled annually — all for critical water-oriented needs. Even this small loss of water area is being mitigated by opening diked areas. As a result, the Bay is now larger than it was when BCDC was established." San Francisco Bay Conservation and Development Commission at http://www.bcdc.ca.gov/aboutus/ (last visited Nov. 6, 2016). These types of outcomes breed hope that, given the right circumstances, planning can be a success.

In Chapter 9 we address the federal Coastal Zone Management Act. Its application also has raised questions of consistency, across jurisdictions. Section 307(c)(1) of the Coastal Zone Management Act (CZMA) provides that: "[e]ach Federal agency conducting or supporting activities directly affecting the coastal zone shall conduct or support those activities in a manner which is, to the maximum extent practicable, consistent with approved state management programs." In *Secretary of the Interior v. California*, 464 U.S. 312 (1984), the Supreme Court addressed whether outer continental shelf (OCS) oil leases granted by the Department of the Interior are subject to review for consistency with the state management plan under CZMA to determine whether they "directly affect" the state coastal management plan. The court concluded that:

> A broader reading of §307(c)(1) is not compelled by the thrust of other CZMA provisions. First, it is clear beyond peradventure that Congress believed that CZMA's purposes could be adequately effectuated without reaching federal activities conducted outside the coastal zone. Both the Senate and House bills were originally drafted, debated, and passed, with §307(c)(1) expressly limited to federal activities in the coastal zone. Broad arguments about CZMA's structure, the Act's incentives for the development of state management programs, and the Act's general aspirations for state-federal cooperation thus cannot support the expansive reading of §307(c)(1) urged by respondents.

464 U.S. at 332.

4. Toward Sub-area and Neighborhood Plans

Urban planning has also seen the movement toward smaller planning areas. Many communities now utilize a general comprehensive plan for future growth that, among other things, addresses land use goals and policies but leaves much of the detail to sub-area or neighborhood plans. This trend is especially relevant in municipalities of hundreds of square miles, very different environmental challenges, and large populations.

These sub-area plans focus on the specific problems and land use issues in the particular area and establish a set of goals and policies for future land use and development in the area. The plans are typically formulated with extensive participation by area residents and business owners and usually reflect their values and concerns — which incidentally may not be those of the larger regime. These plans also may address concerns related to capital improvements, infrastructure, public facilities and human services, as well as concerns related to the environment, crime, parks, recreation, design and architecture, traffic, parking, and transit. Plans often provide short- and long-term strategies for addressing these concerns. Neighborhood plans also may provide specific policies and guidelines for future land use and development.

By ordinance, sub-area plans may be "advisory only" or they may be the "governing law" controlling approval of development applications in the area, especially where local elected officials treat their districts as fiefdoms. These districts that provide more detailed standards for development approval are often created to implement the goals and policies of these sub-area plans. Special zoning districts also may address the particular procedures for obtaining development approval in the planning area. *See generally* Edward Ziegler, Shaping Megalopolis: The Transformation of Euclidean Zoning by Special Zoning Districts and Site-Specific Development Review Techniques, 15 Zoning & Plan. L. Rep. 57 (1992).

5. Emerging Issues in Planning

As plans become increasingly important, new legal issues involving plans will arise, and old ones will be revisited. One important issue is whether a plan can affect a taking of private property, requiring compensation under the Fifth Amendment. In general, courts have traditionally held that planning, in and of itself, does not affect a taking. Their logic is simple: if the plan is not linked to an actual decision on development, the plan has no actual regulatory effect and thus cannot "take" property in the constitutional sense. But if a consistency requirement is in place and the plan becomes the key document and "governing law" in local development decisions, the argument that the plan actually and directly affects property becomes much stronger.

To date, most courts have continued to find that "planning," even in a strong consistency jurisdiction, does not effect a taking, a line of decisions that gives some breathing room to the planning process. *See* the Planning and Takings section in notes below. This conclusion can sit within a general respect for the importance of the comprehensive plan. In *Rainbow River Conservation, Inc. v. Rainbow River Ranch, LLC*, 189 So.3d 312 (Fla. Dist. Ct. App. 2016), the court recognized the plan as similar to a constitution for all future development but addressed it in a challenge to a settlement order entered into under Florida's Bert Harris Act. That act was a version of property rights legislation passed in recent years in several jurisdictions. It provided that "when a new law, rule, regulation, or ordinance of the state or of a political entity in the state, as applied, unfairly affects real property" the government must compensate if the owner's property or vested interest is "inordinately burdened by the government action."

The court explained the importance of the Local Government Comprehensive Planning and Land Development Regulation Act in promoting a broad view of the public interest and active citizen participation as engaged in by the intervenors in the settlement action. It then addressed the consistency versus property rights tension:

> Intervenors argued below, and on appeal, that a Bert Harris Act settlement agreement can never authorize development inconsistent with the local government's existing comprehensive plan because this would violate the Growth Management Act. *See*

§163.3194(1)(a), Fla. Stat. (2012) (providing that once a comprehensive plan has been adopted, "all development undertaken by, and all actions taken in regard to development orders by, governmental agencies in regard to land covered by such plan" must be consistent with that plan). We reject this argument because it is inconsistent with the plain language of the Bert Harris Act, which expressly authorizes settlement agreements that make an "adjustment of land development or permit standards or other provisions controlling the development or use of land" and include provisions for the issuance of "development order[s], a variance, special exception, or other extraordinary relief" even when the relief "would have the effect of contravening the application of a statute as it would otherwise apply to the subject real property. . . ." §70.001(4)(c) 1., (4)(c)9., (4)(d)2., Fla. Stat. (2012). . . . There may be a case where the public interests protected by the Growth Management Act can only be protected with a circuit court order that requires the local government to process a comprehensive plan amendment through the ordinary process, before implementation of a settlement agreement. However, the Legislature clearly contemplated that, [in some cases], the public interests served by the Growth Management Act could be satisfied by other means at the circuit court's disposal.

189 So. 2d at 316.

In the end, any determination about the efficacy of planning necessarily must return to many of the concerns raised in Chapter 1 about the political environment in which land use decisionmaking takes place and the role of governmental discretion in making land use decisions. In a book on planning, the authors noted the debt that current laws have to the Standard Zoning Enabling Act and the Standard City Planning Enabling Act. They then commented that "[o]ne of the fundamental concepts included in the system was that of removing planning from politics." Eric Damian Kelly and Barbara Becker, Community Planning 21 (2000). Others believe that all planning is essentially political, whether the decisions are made by elected officials or a professional planning staff. The student must decide whether it is possible — or even desirable — to create or separate a "rational" planning process for land use from the more overtly political process involved in formulating plans, enacting zoning and land development codes, and, very often, in making specific land use regulatory decisions.

If you decide that this separation is both possible and a worthy goal, ponder also the possibility that planning may become so specific and rigid that it will result in unfairness to individual landowners, and thus give rise to the same demands for "flexibility" that we examined in Chapter 2 with respect to zoning. But if the plan is too flexible, has the consistency requirement really brought any improvement in land use decisionmaking, or has it just added another layer of bureaucracy?

During an economic recession, development activity drops off, and planning may be perceived as an unnecessary burden standing in the way of needed new development and economic activity. Much new development in our metropolitan areas in the years ahead is expected to be multi-unit and higher density housing through infill and redevelopment. Large-scale suburban housing developments at the urban fringe may be harder to finance and market in this country. Is this a reason to abandon planning? Or does this change only increase the need for thoughtful and integrated planning for housing, transportation and jobs in our urban core areas and, perhaps, for regional and state planning as we study Chapter 9?

These questions lie at the core of the modern emphasis on planning as a predicate for regulatory approvals.

B. LAND USE PLANNING IN PERSPECTIVE

Behind the relatively simple idea of separating land uses through the adoption of a zoning ordinance was a set of assumptions regarding the role of government and the rationality of decision-making processes. Some of these assumptions were utopian, but their influence continues to be felt in land use law today.

The first of the following two excerpts demonstrates how planning was viewed at the outset of modern land use regulation, while the second addresses the same question at a later date.

■ UNITED STATES DEPARTMENT OF COMMERCE, A STANDARD CITY PLANNING ENABLING ACT
(1928)

SEC. 6. GENERAL POWERS AND DUTIES

It shall be the function and duty of the commission to make and adopt a master plan for the physical development of the municipality, including any areas outside of its boundaries which, in the commission's judgment, bear relation to the planning of such municipality. Such plan, with the accompanying maps, plats, charts, and descriptive matter, shall show the commission's recommendations for the development of said territory, including, among other things, the general location, character, and extent of streets, viaducts, subways, bridges, waterways, water fronts, boulevards, parkways, playgrounds, squares, parks, aviation fields, and other public ways, grounds and open spaces, the general location of public buildings and other public property, and the general location and extent of public utilities and terminals, whether publicly or privately owned or operated, for water, light, sanitation, transportation, communication, power, and other purposes; also the removal, relocation, widening, narrowing, vacating, abandonment, change of use or extension of any of the foregoing ways, grounds, open spaces, buildings, property, utilities, or terminals; as well as a zoning plan for the control of the height, area, bulk, location, and use of buildings and premises. . . . The commission may from time to time amend, extend, or add to the plan.

SEC. 7. PURPOSES IN VIEW

In the preparation of such plan the commission shall make careful and comprehensive surveys and studies of present conditions and future growth of the municipality and with due regard to its relation to neighboring territory. The plan shall be made with the general purpose of guiding and accomplishing a coordinated, adjusted, and harmonious development of the municipality and its environs which will, in accordance with present and future needs, best promote health, safety, morals, order, convenience, prosperity, and general welfare, as well as efficiency and economy in the process of development; including, among other things, adequate provision for traffic, the promotion of safety from fire and other dangers, adequate provision for light and air, the promotion of the healthful and convenient distribution of population, the promotion of good civic design and arrangement, wise and efficient expenditure of public funds, and the adequate provision of public utilities and other public requirements.

In the following article, the author describes the variety of plans that local governments have produced.

■ WILLIAM C. BAER, GENERAL PLAN EVALUATION CRITERIA: AN APPROACH TO MAKING BETTER PLANS
63 J. Am. Plan. Ass'n 329 (1997)

The Plan as Vision. . . . Simply put, the vision plan is an elegant attempt to publicly propose a "What if?" — to stimulate thought and elicit comment. Appropriate criteria pertain to communicating the vision in an empathetic, visceral and stimulating way that touches not just the mind, but the soul. . . .

The Plan as Blueprint. There was a tendency in the early days of planning to believe that a vision plan could readily be converted to a blueprint plan. The early term "Master Plan" nicely captures the underlying blueprint sentiment. The physical orientation of a Master Plan as blueprint was reflected in Bassett's (1938) early call to limit the scope of the plan to what can be shown on a municipal map: elements like streets, sidewalks, street trees, parks, lakes, public building sites, and the general districts for which private land should be zoned. . . .

Unfortunately, this approach produced few plan successes in the "real world." Often it was the zoning ordinance that was really the blueprint, while the general plan, if there was one, was strictly advisory. . . .

The Plan as Land Use Guide. The general plan as land use guide appeared in the 1950s. Although there were variants, it took a middle of the road approach to what a plan might be. . . .

The plan was a vision of the future, but not a blueprint; a policy statement, but not a program of action; a formulation of goals, but not schedules, priorities, or cost estimates. It was to be uninhibited by short-term practical considerations. . . .

The Plan as Remedy. The alternative to the plan as vision is the plan as remedy: the cure for an existing problem. Urban slums and the promise of federal moneys for their renewal in the 1950s provided such an alternate route to plan reconceptualization. Redevelopment plans were one result. Unlike general plans, redevelopment plans were short-range and specific, aimed at remedying the problems of slum housing, not at building new housing in the suburbs. The appropriate criteria here were largely federally determined, and were in the form of hurdles to surmount, or tests to pass, in order to receive a grant of funds: Local governments had to demonstrate their need for renewal by producing a comprehensive description of slum problems, and demonstrate their administrative and financial capacity to respond effectively by citing a Workable Program that called for a general plan, building codes, financial capacity — and, for the first time — citizen participation in governance. . . .

Process, not Plans. Beginning in the 1960s, planning as an ongoing process, rather than merely making particular plans, was widely embraced as the profession's true purpose. As Altshuler noted, a common planning principle held that "planning is more important than any plan." Moreover, the technical and factual underpinnings of physical plans were deemed insufficient. The city was no longer thought of as simply an artifact to be shaped by criteria for physical design; it was viewed as a mechanism of inter-related parts to be selectively transformed by applying criteria derived from systems theory. The social sciences were introduced to equip planners with more understanding of urban cause-effect relationships. Modeling urban processes, not drawing up a blueprint, was the key component shaping the criteria for this system.

Two other facets of a process orientation were citizen participation and planner advocacy for the poor. These concerns, too, introduced their own criteria. And in broadening the planner's perspective, social science also cast doubt on the validity of traditional planning criteria. There was no unitary "public interest," the social sciences reported, nor any possibility of rationalism and comprehensiveness. . . . Planning's legitimacy could be bestowed only by a participatory or advocacy process. . . .

Plans as Pragmatic Action. Discussion about plans during the 1970s tended toward the pragmatic. The American Law Institute's (1976) extensive Model Land Development Code, directed toward revising the enabling laws for planning, provided a streamlined framework for subdivision, zoning, and redevelopment. Its implicit criteria were procedural, focusing on how to mesh these assorted devices, but paying less heed to concern for the plan as overall direction-setter for development. . . .

Plans as Responses to State and Federal Planning Mandates. During the 1970s, state-wide plans came into being, often triggered by environmental concerns. . . . Most recently, in this vein, habitat conservation plans (HCPs) have introduced substantive criteria based on biodiversity and ecology.

Notes and Comments

1. *The Role of the Planning Commission.* Like the Standard Zoning Enabling Act discussed in Chapter 2, the Standard City Planning Enabling Act was drafted under the auspices of the federal Department of Commerce. Although not nearly as influential as the model act for zoning, the planning act included provisions that have influenced the adoption of state planning legislation. The act calls for the planning commission, rather than the local city council or body of elected officials, to adopt the plan. Why do you think this choice is recommended? What does it say about whether the drafters of the act envisioned the planning process as political in nature or as involving the application of expertise?

2. *Blueprint and Vision Plans.* Is it possible for a local government to create a blueprint plan — that is, one that is precise in terms of what land uses are envisioned for particular properties — and then actually to follow the plan when specific land use decisions, such as rezoning and subdivision approvals, are made? Does the inherently political nature of local governmental control of land use make the implementation of a plan impossible?

Is a blueprint plan even advisable? If the plan is that specific, does it usurp the function of zoning and subdivision regulation, so that the end result is simply more process before decisionmaking?

What are the benefits of creating a vision plan? Can we expect that, if all the various segments of a community are involved in creating a vision plan, the local elected officials will implement the plan's vision when they later make decisions about specific developments? Consider that in many large American cities it will seldom be the case that all segments of the city can actually participate — many will be constrained by time, financial need, or language.

3. *"Process, Not Plans."* The concept of process as the most important feature of planning has led some commentators, as the Baer article notes, to conclude that there is no single "public interest" with which the plan could be identified. Thus, the plan becomes, as the article indicates, a "side-show." Can planning processes based on rationalism reach generally accepted conclusions about land uses?

4. *The Possible Functions of a Plan.* In a classic article on the subject of planning, Professor Charles Haar suggests several functions that the general plan may perform: (1) as a device for serving "notice" on public and private parties as to the probable outcome of their development proposals; (2) as a basis for internal coordination of various governmental actions and programs; (3) as a "framework" for coordinating various land use regulatory devices; (4) as an actual control on private activities upon land; and (5) as a safeguard against arbitrary regulatory action. Charles Haar, The Master Plan: An Impermanent Constitution, 20 Law & Contemp. Probs. 353 (1955). In *Bell v. City of Elkhorn*, 364 N.W.2d 144, 147 (Wis. 1985), the Wisconsin Supreme Court stated that the objectives sought through the development of a comprehensive plan include the following:

> (1) improving the physical environment of the community; (2) promoting the public interest; (3) facilitating the implementation of community policies on physical development; (4) effecting political and technical coordination in community development; (5) injecting long-range considerations into the determination of short-range actions; and (6) bringing professional and technical knowledge to bear on the making of political decisions concerning the physical development of the community.

Which of these rationales for the plan do you find realistic and sufficient to justify the often considerable expenditure of resources needed to prepare a plan?

5. *Planning as a Meaningful (or Meaningless) Exercise.* Examples of unimplemented and now "dead" shelf plans are legion throughout the country. In some cases this is the original objective, as city officials, intent on continuing existing and often ad hoc and discretionary development policies, direct citizen discontent into multi-year study projects and plans that are later simply ignored and forgotten. But if one accepts planning as meaningful, plans are the starting point. They have to be implemented. Consider the reasoning of the Oregon Supreme Court in *Baker v. City of Milwaukie*, 533 P.2d 772, 776 (Or. 1975):

> If that plan is to have any efficacy as the basic planning tool for the City of Milwaukie, it must be given preference over conflicting prior zoning ordinances. To hold otherwise would allow a city to go through the motions and expense of formulating a

comprehensive plan and then relegating that document to oblivion through continued reliance on the older zoning ordinances.

Is planning a wasteful exercise if the law does not require that zoning ordinances, subdivision maps, and other regulatory approvals must conform to the plan? Circumstances change and so do plans. Ideally, plans provide an intelligible framework for analysis and decision. There is increasing evidence of the potential for urban planning to achieve its goals related to development of the built environment. *See* Nathan Blackburn, Planning Ahead: Consistency with a Comprehensive Land Use Plan Yields Consistent Results for Municipalities, 60 Okla. L. Rev. 73 (2007).

6. *Citizen Participation.* How important is citizen participation to the preparation of the plan? Can we expect citizens to devote the time needed to participate in the plan preparation, or will they only be galvanized into action when a specific development proposal becomes a subject for debate? Will local participants likely reflect the values and interests of their own neighborhood or of the larger community or region? Who balances larger regional and national interests in the local planning process?

Must plans be "democratic," and thus involve extensive citizen participation? Some analysts say they are better viewed as technical documents, in which planning experts put their knowledge to work to solve planning problems. *See Creative Displays, Inc. v. Florence,* 602 S.W.2d 682, 683 (Ky. 1980) (Kentucky Supreme Court invalidates a county comprehensive plan for failure of the county planning commission to hold public hearings prior to adoption).

7. *Citizen Participation and Consistency with Plans.* On the argument that planning promotes participation by locals on important municipal issues, consider the debate on whether the plan can be changed by initiative or referendum, seen by some as the ultimate form of participation. Cases on what is pejoratively called "ballot box planning" are addressed in Chapter 10. More recently in Florida, *see City of Riviera Beach vs. Riviera Beach Citizens Task Force,* 87 So. 3d 18 (Fla. App. 2012) where a ballot referendum to limit uses of a marina owned by the public was found not to be a comprehensive plan amendment. Florida Statute Section 163.3167(12) prohibits a referendum process involving a comprehensive land use change affecting five or fewer parcels of land. The court found that the "ballot did not involve a comprehensive plan amendment, rendering section 163.3165(12) inapplicable." Multiple uses were allowed for the waterfront parcels at issue, and the prohibition of one use among many with respect to a particular parcel does not involve or require a comprehensive plan amendment. *Id.* at 23-4.

8. *Planning and Bargaining.* As you will see in Chapter 10, one of the key developments in land use law over the past three decades has been the increased use of bargaining between cities and developers as a means of making land use decisions. *See* Daniel Selmi, The Contract Transformation in Land Use Regulation, 63 Stan. L. Rev. 591 (2011). In Planning and the Law, 20 Vt. L. Rev. 657 (1996), Professor Mandelker posited that a key issue in land use planning is the tension between the need for flexibility to make decisions and the need to limit discretion. He continued:

> These two needs are often difficult to reconcile. A city council must deal with a dynamic political environment and must engage in political bargaining in which outcomes are unpredictable. Notice that a "political bargaining in which outcomes are

unpredictable" requires flexibility and the discretion to shape decisions to problems and opportunities as they arise. A binding comprehensive plan can impede this kind of bargaining by limiting the discretion of decision-makers.

Id. at 657-658. Are comprehensive planning and bargaining inherently irreconcilable? *See* Patricia Salkin and Amy Lavine, Community Benefits Agreements and Comprehensive Planning: Balancing Community Empowerment and the Police Power, 18 J. L. & Pol'y 157 (2009). On the challenges of finding an empirical answer to the question, *see* Nicholas J. Marantz, "What Do Community Benefits Agreements Deliver? Evidence From Los Angeles." Journal of the American Planning Association (2015) 81(4), 251-67.

9. *Plans and New Media and Technology.* Can you think of how societal developments today with respect to new media and technology may affect planning over the next 20 years?

Planners are making imaginative uses of tools such as the Internet and computer-generated drawings, to visualize planning efforts and to make a wide variety of data and services available to the public. Developers and citizens involved in the development process also are finding innovative uses for the Internet in pursuing their interests. City council and planning commission agenda and decisions are readily posted online; meetings can be attended virtually, citizen sentiment can be tapped electronically. *See generally* Patricia Salkin, From Bricks and Mortar to Mega-Bytes and Mega-Pixels: The Changing Landscape of the Impact of Technology and Innovation on Urban Development, 43 Urb. Law. 11 (2011).

10. *Planning Legitimacy and Efficacy.* The Communist Bloc of countries centered their economies on a model of economic planning, and that effort failed. Are land use plans doomed to the same fate? *See* Andrew Morris and Roger Miner, The Destructive Role of Land Use Planning, 14 Tul. Envtl. L.J. 95, 96-97 (2000). Or will extensive public participation in plan development give them a legitimacy that was not present in the economic planning efforts of the Communist countries? Legitimacy, of course, is something different from "efficacy;" and "legitimacy," in this context, may come at considerable cost. Some proponents of sustainable development, for example, are highly critical of local urban planning in this country, arguing that regional, national, and global needs often are compromised by local parochial interests sometimes referred to as NIMBY ("not in my backyard") that tend to dominate the local urban planning and development process in nearly every community. *See* Edward H. Ziegler, Urban Sprawl, Growth Management, and Sustainable Development in the United States: Thoughts on the Sentimental Quest for a New Middle Landscape, 11 Va. J. Soc. Pol'y & L. 26, 53-54 (2003).

11. *Planning for Smart Growth and Sustainable Development.* The most significant change in urban planning theory since the 1920s has been the view that metropolitan sprawl in this country is no longer desirable or sustainable. Many voices in both the planning profession and in the development community under the banners of smart growth, new urbanism, and sustainable development now believe that traditional, low-density Euclidian zoning needs to be reformed to promote higher density, mixed use, and less automobile-dependent development. In Chapter 11 we address the meanings, goals, and tools to promote these types of development.

C. THE FORM AND CONTENT OF THE GENERAL PLAN

All regulatory efforts embody planning to some degree. Even a poorly executed zoning ordinance does "plan" for land uses on that property. A critical question, however, is whether a municipality must prepare a master or general plan that is separate from the zoning ordinances that it adopts, or whether the plan can be found within those ordinances. As you can see from the case below, although the Standard Zoning Enabling Act raised this question in the 1920s, courts today continue to consider it.

■ WOLF v. CITY OF ELY
493 N.W.2d 846 (Iowa 1992)

ANDREASEN, Justice.

The City of Ely adopted a zoning ordinance in 1978. The district court declared the ordinance invalid because it was not adopted in accordance with a comprehensive plan. Upon review we affirm the district court's declaratory judgment.

I. BACKGROUND.

John and Pat Wolf own three connecting parcels of land in or adjacent to the City of Ely that have been identified as parcels A, B and C. The Wolfs operate a salvage or junkyard on their property. Parcel A is located in an area that was zoned manufacturing; parcel B is located in an area zoned commercial; and parcel C is located in an area zoned residential or agricultural. . . .

The Wolfs filed the present action on April 9, 1990, seeking a court judgment declaring the entire zoning ordinance invalid and their use of their property (parcels A, B and C) lawful. The Wolfs allege the entire zoning ordinance is invalid [because] . . . it was not adopted in accordance with a comprehensive plan. . . .

III. COMPREHENSIVE PLAN.

. . . Iowa Code section 414.3 requires that zoning regulations "shall be made in accordance with a comprehensive plan." The requirement of a comprehensive plan is found in the zoning law of those states that have taken the standard state zoning enabling act as their model. The act did not define the term comprehensive plan.

A majority of courts in states where zoning must be "in accordance with a comprehensive plan" hold a plan external to the zoning ordinance is not required. 2 *The American Law of Real Property*, Planning and Zoning §12.02 (1991). However, an increasing number of legislatures specifically require that a plan be adopted. *Id.* The "comprehensive plan" requirement was imposed to prevent piecemeal and haphazard zoning. Standard State Zoning Enabling Act (United States Department of Commerce, §3 n.22 (1922)). The word "plan" connotes an integrated product of a rational process; the word "comprehensive" requires something beyond a piecemeal approach. . . .

Iowa Code section 358A.5, relating to county zoning, contains the identical requirement. In discussing this requirement, we stated: "If the Board gave full consideration to the problem presented, including the needs of the public, changing conditions, and the similarity of other land in the same area, then it has zoned in accordance with a comprehensive plan." *Montgomery v. Bremer County Bd. of Supervisors*, 299 N.W.2d 687, 695 (Iowa 1980). The Iowa Court of Appeals commented, "nothing in Chapter 358A requires a county to reduce a comprehensive plan to written form." *Webb v. Giltner*, 468 N.W.2d 838, 840 (Iowa App. 1991). The comprehensive plan requirement is intended to ensure the county board acts rationally rather than arbitrarily in exercising their delegated zoning authority. *Id.* . . .

Prior to the adoption of the 1978 zoning ordinance, Ely had established a planning and zoning commission. Under a 1976 ordinance, the Ely planning and zoning commission had authority to make such surveys, studies, maps, or plans which the commission believed bears a relation to the general comprehensive plan. The ordinance provided . . . that after adoption of a comprehensive plan by the commission an attested copy of the plan shall be certified to the council. The council could then approve the plan, and it would constitute the City's comprehensive plan. . . .

Contrary to the statutory and ordinance requirements, no comprehensive plan was developed by the commission and appropriately presented to the council. At trial, Thomas M. Tjelmeland, the mayor of Ely, admitted he was unaware of any written criteria used in development of the 1978 zoning ordinance. He testified the comprehensive plan consisted of the City's zoning ordinance combined with its zoning map. There were no other documents that he relied upon in interpreting the zoning ordinance.

A councilman of the City testified that no single person had been designated as administrative officer responsible for the administering of the zoning ordinance. The mayor and members of the Ely council would bring zoning matters to the entire council on an ad hoc basis. The councilman further testified that, in making decisions as to whether a specific use is allowed in a specific zone, he just listened, and if he thought it was right, he would go along with it. He had not heard of a comprehensive zoning plan.

The City offered evidence that, in June of 1975, the Linn County Regional Planning Commission (county commission) prepared a housing and community development study and a Linn County regional land use policy plan. The study recommended Ely and other nonmetropolitan cities use the plan as a guide for future growth and development. Although mayor Tjelmeland represented the City of Ely on the county commission, he testified he was unaware of any studies conducted when the 1978 zoning ordinance was drafted. He was unaware of any writing that set forth any proposed or future land use. He testified the 1975 regional housing and land use policy plans were not used in any of Ely's planning or zoning decisions.

The 1978 zoning ordinance was developed by combining different sections and provisions of two or more "model" municipal zoning ordinances. Throughout the ordinance, specific provisions of the model ordinances were deleted, marked "omit" or additional provisions were added in long-hand. . . .

At least two, and possibly four, different zoning maps have been identified as the official city zoning map. The City offered a crayola-colored zoning map as the official zoning map. This map was different than the zoning map identified as Ely's official zoning map in the first trial in 1989. One of the maps indicates the Wolfs' "tract C" was agricultural; the other indicates it was residential. The City acknowledges the 1978 zoning ordinance and zoning map have not been officially amended, changed, modified, or repealed.

Ely's zoning ordinance and zoning map do not suggest an integrated product of rational planning. The ordinance contains glaring omissions and serious structural problems. Although a significant portion of the land within the city limits is identified as agricultural land, the zoning ordinance makes no provisions regulating its use. Some words and terms that are defined in the ordinance are not used later in the ordinance. Extensive provisions relating to mobile homes are included in the definition section. Under the ordinance provisions, mobile homes are permitted only in an approved mobile home park. However, a mobile home park is not a permitted use or special use in any of the seven districts. Junkyards are specifically defined, although they are not a permitted use or special use in any of the districts. In one part of the zoning ordinance, the City prohibits fences of over five feet; in another part it requires a six-foot fence. The ordinance has twenty-eight separate parking classes for off-street parking, although the population of Ely was 275 in 1970 and 425 in 1980.

The structural problems in the zoning ordinance obviously arose from a careless combining of two or more model ordinances. Although such a clip-and-paste ordinance could produce a valid ordinance if carefully and rationally prepared, here the structure and content of the ordinance suggests a careless and irrational process was employed.

Other evidence demonstrates the City's failure to adopt the zoning ordinance in accordance with a comprehensive plan. Studies and plans developed by the county commission in 1975 were not considered by the council. The Ely Planning Commission failed to comply with the City ordinance requirement that a comprehensive plan be certified to the council as an attested copy of the plan. Although city records indicate the commission had presented a proposed zoning ordinance and zoning map in 1977, the records do not identify the proposed ordinance and map. Because the official zoning map was not clearly identified, there was confusion as to the limitation of uses to be applied to certain parcels of land. Amendments or changes to the ordinance and zoning map were reported in the city records, but council approval was made by resolution, contrary to ordinance and statutory requirements. . . .

. . . We, like the district court, find the City failed to comply with the requirement that zoning regulations be made in accordance with a comprehensive plan.

Notes and Comments

1. *"In Accordance with a Comprehensive Plan."* The Standard Zoning Enabling Act requires that all zoning be "in accordance with a comprehensive plan." The *Wolf* court interprets this phrase as not requiring a plan that is separate from the zoning ordinance. This interpretation, that the comprehensive plan and the zoning ordinance may be one and the same, is sometimes referred to as the "unitary" view. Embraced by almost all state court decisions on point is the conclusion that a separate plan is not required by this type of "in accordance with" language. *See, e.g., Apple Group, LTD. v. Granger Twp. Bd. of Zoning Appeals, et al.,* 41 N.E.3d 1185 (Ohio 2015) ("[w]e agree with those appellate courts that have considered the issue and have held that a comprehensive plan need not be set forth in a separate document and may be included in the township's zoning plan"); *Heithaus v. Planning and Zoning Com'n of Town of Greenwich,* 779 A.2d 750 (Conn. 2001); *Bogan v. Sandoval County Planning and Zoning Comm'n,* 890 P.2d 395, 404 (N.M. Ct. App. 1994) ("a comprehensive plan may

be found within the [zoning] ordinance itself where a comprehensive plan has not been enacted and . . . the plan need not even be in the form of a document").

2. *A Historical Dispute.* Most courts and commentators addressing the meaning of the "in accordance with a comprehensive plan" language have concluded that the drafters of the Standard Zoning Enabling Act were not referring to a separate plan. *See, e.g., State of Missouri ex rel. Chiavola v. Village of Oakwood,* 886 S.W.2d 74, 80 (Mo. Ct. App. 1994) (citing the notes accompanying the 1926 version of the Standard Zoning Enabling Act). However, this position may be in error in light of unpublished materials from the time the Act was drafted as well as other published materials at the time: "This historical backdrop suggests that preparation of an independent plan or study should be a condition precedent to the adoption of a zoning ordinance." Stuart Meck, The Legislative Requirement That Zoning and Land Use Controls Be Consistent with an Independently Adopted Local Comprehensive Plan: A Model Statute, 3 Wash. U. J.L. & Pol'y 295, 304 (2000).

3. *A Comprehensive Zoning Plan.* Apart from the separate plan issue, when is a zoning ordinance not sufficiently "comprehensive" to meet the statutory requirement that it be in accord with a "comprehensive plan"? A number of court decisions have held local zoning schemes invalid that failed to zone lands in a comprehensive fashion, often creating only one zoning district, such as allowing agricultural or some residential uses, but then allowing all manner of commercial and other uses by special permit or rezoning. *See, e.g., Hardin County v. Jost,* 897 S.W.2d 592 (Ky. App. 1995) (holding that this type of regulatory scheme is not zoning in accordance with a comprehensive plan); *Rockhill v. Chesterfield Tp., Burlington County,* 128 A.2d 473 (N.J. 1957) (to the same effect); *Town of Hobart v. Collier,* 87 N.W.2d 868 (Wis. 1958) (same). *See also Trail Mining, Inc. v. Village of Sun,* 619 So. 2d 118, 120 (La. Ct. App. 1993) (a single, prohibitive zoning regulation restricting gravel mining "does not comply with the comprehensive plan requirement").

4. *The Reasoning in* Wolf. If a separate plan is not required, why did the *Wolf* court pointedly note that the 1976 ordinance gave the planning commission the authority to prepare a separate plan, but that the commission did not do so? Even if a separate general plan is not required for zoning to be "in accordance with a comprehensive plan," the preparation of such a plan can help a municipality convince a court that its zoning meets this statutory requirement. Note also the *Wolf* court's emphasis on the fact that no other studies were conducted when the 1978 zoning ordinance was drafted.

In an influential 1968 decision, the New York Court of Appeals discussed the requirement that zoning be "in accordance with a comprehensive plan." It concluded that the master plan was relevant to determining whether this requirement was met:

> [T]he "comprehensive plan" requires that the rezoning should not conflict with the fundamental land use policies and development plans of the community. These policies may be garnered from any available source, most especially the master plan of the community, if any has been adopted, the zoning law itself and the zoning map.

Udell v. Haas, 235 N.E.2d 897, 902 (N.Y. 1968) (citations omitted). *See also Rayle v. Town of Cato Bd.,* 679 N.Y.S.2d (N.Y. App. Div. 2002) ("The court may satisfy itself that the municipality has a well-considered plan and that authorities are acting in the public interest to further it by examining all available and relevant evidence of the municipality's land use policies").

Even if a separate plan is not required, the preparation of a land use plan or supporting planning studies may in a later lawsuit serve as strong evidence that a city is acting in a particular zoning case to promote the general welfare. Numerous court decisions make clear that the court's ruling upholding a city's zoning action was favorably influenced by the city's prior planning activities and studies. *See* 1 Edward H. Ziegler, Rathkopf's The Law of Zoning and Planning, ch. 1 at 1.42 (4th ed. 2005 and Supp. 2012).

Without a separate plan, how can a plaintiff's lawyer ever argue that a zoning action, such as a rezoning to allow a fast food drive-through restaurant, is not in accordance with the city's comprehensive "zoning" plan? Can a plan actually be inferred from analysis of the zoning map and code and the actual land development within the city? What role could an expert planning witness play in such a case?

5. *Legal Effect of Plan If Adopted.* Though a separate plan may not be required by statute, if a city prepares and adopts a separate plan, what is the legal effect of such a plan? Almost all court decisions hold that an adopted plan that is not required and made the "governing law" by state statute or local ordinance is "advisory" only and not legally binding or controlling with respect to a city's zoning actions. *See, e.g., Nestle Waters North America, Inc. v. Town of Fryeburg*, 967 A.2d 702 (Me. 2009); *B.J. Alan Co. v. Congress Bd. of Zoning Appeals*, 124 Ohio St. 3d 1, 918 N.E.2d 501 (2009). *See also* 1 Edward H. Ziegler, Rathkopf's The Law of Zoning and Planning, ch. 14 at 14.22 (4th ed. 2005 and Supp. 2012).

Adoption of a separate plan in this situation and compliance with the plan may be evidence of the reasonableness of zoning action, but the plan is not "the law," and the provisions of the zoning ordinance are typically held to control the legality of the zoning action. *See, e.g., W&G McKinney Farms, L.P. v. Dallas County Bd. of Adjustment*, 674 N.W.2d 99 (Iowa 2004); *CACO Three, Inc. v. Board of Sup'rs of Huntington Tp.*, 845 A.2d 991 (Pa. Commw. Ct. 2004).

In recent years an increasing number of states have adopted statutes that authorize or require the preparation of a separate general plan. Many of these statutes set forth the requirements of the plan in considerable detail. As you read the following statute, which is representative of those adopted in many states, note especially the variety of different issues — including some only tangentially related to land use — that the plan must address.

■ NEW JERSEY STATUTES ANNOTATED
§40:55D-28

a. The planning board may prepare and, after public hearing, adopt or amend a master plan or component parts thereof, to guide the use of lands within the municipality in a manner which protects public health and safety and promotes the general welfare.

b. The master plan shall generally comprise a report or statement and land use and development proposals, with maps, diagrams and text, presenting, at least the following elements (1) and (2) and, where appropriate, the following elements (3) through (16):

(1) A statement of objectives, principles, assumptions, policies and standards upon which the constituent proposals for the physical, economic and social development of the municipality are based;

(2) A land use plan element (a) taking into account and stating its relationship to the statement provided for in paragraph (1) hereof, and other master plan elements provided for in paragraphs (3) through (14) hereof and natural conditions . . . (b) showing the existing and proposed location, extent and intensity of development of land to be used in the future . . . and stating the relationship thereof to the existing and any proposed zone plan and zoning ordinance; (c) showing the existing and proposed location of any airports and the boundaries of any airport safety zones . . . and (d) including a statement of the standards of population density and development intensity recommended for the municipality;

(3) A housing plan element . . . including, but not limited to, residential standards and proposals for the construction and improvement of housing;

(4) A circulation plan element showing the location and types of facilities for all modes of transportation required for the efficient movement of people and goods into, about, and through the municipality, taking into account the functional highway classification system of the Federal Highway Administration and the types, locations, conditions and availability of existing and proposed transportation facilities, including air, water, road and rail;

(5) A utility service plan element analyzing the need for and showing the future general location of water supply and distribution facilities, drainage and flood control facilities, sewerage and waste treatment, solid waste disposal and provision for other related utilities, and including any storm water management plan required. . . .

(6) A community facilities plan element showing the existing and proposed location and type of educational or cultural facilities, historic sites, libraries, hospitals, firehouses, police stations and other related facilities, including their relation to the surrounding areas;

(7) A recreation plan element showing a comprehensive system of areas and public sites for recreation;

(8) A conservation plan element providing for the preservation, conservation, and utilization of natural resources, including, to the extent appropriate, energy, open space, water supply, forests, soil, marshes, wetlands, harbors, rivers and other waters, fisheries, endangered or threatened species wildlife and other resources, and which systemically analyzes the impact of each other component and element of the master plan on the present and future preservation, conservation and utilization of those resources;

(9) An economic plan element considering all aspects of economic development and sustained economic vitality, including (a) a comparison of the types of employment expected to be provided by the economic development to be promoted with the characteristics of the labor pool resident in the municipality and nearby areas and (b) an analysis of the stability and diversity of the economic development to be promoted;

(10) An historic preservation plan element: (a) indicating the location and significance of historic sites and historic districts; (b) identifying the standards used to assess worthiness for historic site or district identification; and (c) analyzing the impact of each component and element of the master plan on the preservation of historic sites and districts; . . .

(12) A recycling plan element which incorporates the State Recycling Plan goals . . . and;

(13) A farmland preservation plan element, which shall include: an inventory of farm properties and a map illustrating significant areas of agricultural land; a statement showing that municipal ordinances support and promote agriculture as a business; and a plan for preserving as much farmland as possible in the short term by leveraging monies made available . . . through a variety of mechanisms including, but not limited to, utilizing option agreements, installment purchases, and encouraging donations of permanent development easements. . . .

(15) An educational facilities plan element . . .

(16) A green buildings and environmental sustainability plan element, which shall provide for, encourage, and promote the efficient use of natural resources and the installation and usage of renewable energy systems; consider the impact of buildings on the local, regional and global environment, allow ecosystems to function naturally; conserve and reuse water; treat storm water on-site; and optimize climactic conditions through site orientation and design.

In the next case, a court considers whether the local jurisdiction has complied with planning requirements that are similar to those in the New Jersey statutes.

■ TWAIN HARTE HOMEOWNERS v. COUNTY OF TUOLUMNE
188 Cal. Rptr. 233 (Ct. App. 1982)

Morony, Associate Justice.

Statement of the Case

This appeal arises out of challenges to the sufficiency of the Tuolumne County General Plan. . . .

"The Planning and Zoning Law (Govt. Code, tit. 7, div. 1, commencing with §65000) require[s] . . . that the board of supervisors of each county adopt a general plan for the 'physical development' of the county, pursuant to section 65300; that the plan be prepared and adopted according to standards established in section 65300.5 and 65301; and that it include each of nine 'elements' enumerated and described in section 65302." (*Camp v. Board of Supervisors* (1981) 123 Cal. App. 3d 334, 340, fn. omitted, 178 Cal. Rptr. 620.)[1] . . .

---

1. Except where otherwise indicated, statutory citations are to provisions of the Government Code as they read in 1980.

Section 65302 provided in pertinent part as follows:

The general plan shall consist of a statement of development policies and shall include a diagram or diagrams and text setting forth objectives, principles, standards, and plan proposals. The plan shall include the following elements: (a) A land use element. . . . (b) A circulation element. . . . (c) A housing element. . . . (d) A conservation element . . . (e) An open-space element. . . . (f) A seismic safety element. . . . (g) A noise element . . . (h) A scenic highway element. . . . (i) A safety element. . . .

DISCUSSION . . .

2. THE GENERAL PLAN

a. Land Use Element

Appellant contends that the general plan fails to meet statutory requirements in several of its elements. Initially, appellant contends that the land use element of the general plan does not comply with statutory requirements of Government Code section 65302, subdivision (a).

Section 65302, subdivision (a), provided in 1980 that a general plan mandated by section 65300: . . .

> shall include . . . [¶] A land use element which designates the proposed general distribution and general location and extent of the uses of the land for housing, business, industry, open space, including agriculture, natural resources, recreation, and enjoyment of scenic beauty, education, public buildings and grounds, solid and liquid waste disposal facilities, and other categories of public and private uses of land. *The land use element shall include a statement of the standards of population density and building intensity* recommended for the various districts and other territory covered by the plan. . . . (Emphasis added.)

The initial task faced by this court in determining the adequacy of the land use element is to determine the meaning of the terms "population density" and "building intensity." These terms are not defined in the relevant statutes, regulations or guidelines. The parties have cited no authority to assist this court in determining what the statute requires in this regard.

The general plan states "densities" for "urban residential" uses in terms of the maximum number of "dwelling units per gross acre." With respect to non-urban designations of "residential/agricultural," and "resource" lands, densities are stated in terms of minimum lot sizes. No densities are provided for areas designated "commercial," "open space," "industrial," "park and recreation," or "public/institutional/school." . . .

The County contends in the instant case that the measurement of dwelling units per acre meets the requirement for a statement of standards for population density and that the omission of a statement of population density for "commercial," "industrial" and "open space" land use designations reflects the fact that no residential development is permitted on those lands.

In a planning context, statements of population density might reasonably be related to residency rather than to the extent of intensity of use of all classifications.

For census purposes "population density" has been calculated as "the number of persons per square mile of land area . . ." and "[e]ach person enumerated was counted as an inhabitant of his usual place of abode. . . ." (U.S. Dept. of Commerce, Bureau of the Census, 1970 Census Users' Guide (Oct. 1970) at p. 93.) Cases in the zoning context have referred to measures of population density in terms of numbers of people per dwelling unit. (*See Village of Belle Terre v. Boraas* (1973) 416 U.S. 1, 19, 94 S. Ct. 1536, 1546, 39 L. Ed. 2d 797 (dis. opn. of Marshall, J.).) The term "population density" has also been used to refer to maximum numbers of people living in a residential development. (*See, e.g., Trinity Episcopal School Corporation v. Romney* (S.D.N.Y. 1974) 387 F. Supp. 1044, 1080.). . . .

It could be argued that in the planning arena standards of population density might most usefully be stated in terms of dwelling units per acre where some relationship between an average number of people per household has been established and where distinctions based upon factors such as the size and type of dwelling (e.g., single family residences, multiple family residential, mobile home) are supported in the plan.

Nevertheless, we cannot believe that the Legislature intended the terms "population density" and "building intensity" to be synonymous. . . .

It appears that the reasonable interpretation of the term "population density" as used in Government Code section 65302 is one which refers to numbers of *people* in a given area and not to dwelling units per acre, unless the basis for correlation between the measure of dwelling units per acre and numbers of people is set forth explicitly in the plan.

In the instant case, no statement relating dwelling units to numbers of people is presented in the general plan. Thus, we conclude that appellant's land use element is deficient insofar as it lacks an appropriate statement of standards for population density based upon numbers of people.

With respect to the requirement that the land use element must contain a "statement of the standards of . . . building intensity recommended for the various districts and other territory," there is no statement of building intensity for uses designated in the plan as "commercial," "residential/agricultural," "open space," "industrial," "park and recreation" or "public/institutional/school." At most, the "urban residential" designation with its statement of maximum dwelling units per acre is the only land use designation with any building intensity standard. Minimum lot sizes set for "residential/agricultural" and "resource" areas are not sufficient as a statement of a building intensity. Nor are general use captions such as "commercial-neighborhood," "commercial-shopping center," "commercial-visitor serving," "light industrial" and "heavy industrial," which provide only the vaguest picture of the intensity of development to be permitted in those areas and provide no standards at all as to possible restrictions such as height or size limitations, restrictions on types of buildings or uses to be permitted within a designated area. We therefore conclude that the land use element of the Tuolumne County general plan does not comply with the requirements of Government Code section 65302 as it fails to set forth an adequate statement of standards of population density and building intensity recommended for the various districts and other territory covered by the plan.

b. Circulation Element

Appellant further contends that the general plan is deficient for its failure to comply with the mandates of Government Code section 65302, subdivision (b) which requires in pertinent part that the plan include "[a] circulation element consisting of the general location and extent of existing and proposed major thoroughfares, transportation routes, terminals, and other local public utilities and facilities, *all correlated with the land use element of the plan.*" (Emphasis added.) . . .

Insofar as the Tuolumne County General Plan is concerned, the circulation element is contained in chapter VI: 2-3 and VI: 5 and on the display map which outlines existing and proposed roads designated as "arterial," "major collector," or "minor collector."[9] . . .

In the present case it can be seen that the circulation element does not attempt to describe or discuss the changes or increases in demands on the various roadways or transportation facilities of the County as a result of changes in uses of land which will or may result from implementation of the decision system and the general plan. As stated in a letter from several individuals commenting upon the draft general plan, "The [MEIR] and the MDGP do not address the important issues such as the demographic center of the county, the population centers, the movement habits of users or the traffic counts of the main roads and intersections." Although the Government Code does not explicitly require that a circulation element contain an inventory and data analysis followed by a locally derived program to solve problems identified in the inventory, and we do not so hold, it seems apparent from a review of the general plan [and] the supporting . . . documentation that there is no way to determine whether in fact the circulation element is correlated with the proposed land use element.

. . . The requirement of Government Code section 65302, subdivision (b) is that the land use element be correlated with the circulation element. The Tuolumne County general plan does not comply with the statutory requirements in this regard. . . .

FRANSON, Acting P.J., and ANDREEN, J., concur.

Notes and Comments

1. *Advising the County on Remand.* What legal advice would you give to the county concerning the specific steps that it must take to cure the plan's deficiencies? How would you justify each step that you recommend?

2. *The Contents of Plans.* Anderson, in Guidelines for Preparing Urban Plans 11 (1995), identified four parts to the "Typical Organization of a Long-Range Urban

---

9. In its entirety, the textual portion of the transportation-circulation element of the general plan provides as follows:

TRANSPORTATION/CIRCULATION [policy]

7 The street and highway network in the county will be classified according to the function they are intended to serve. The following four functional classifications will be used in Tuolumne County:

> *Arterial*—serves statewide and interstate travel. Primarily federal and state highways.
> *Major Collector*—serves intraregional travel. Average travel distances are shorter than on arterial routes.
> *Minor Collector*—collects traffic from local roads and channels it to major collectors or arterials. Serves to link locally important traffic generators.
> *Local Roads*—provide access to immediately abutting land uses or rural areas. Provide service over relatively short distances compared to collectors and arterials.

8 The County of Tuolumne will ensure that both its existing and proposed street configurations serve the ultimate functions they are intended to serve by protecting their alignments from encroachment. 9 The County of Tuolumne will encourage the development of a balanced transportation system, including public transit as well as privately operated vehicles.
   Scenic corridors along scenic routes in the county will be preserved. . . .

TRANSPORTATION/CIRCULATION [implementation]

G Adopt the functional street and highway classification indicated on the General Plan maps. H Ensure that rights-of-way for future streets are protected from encroachment by current development.
I Designate as scenic routes those roads and highways listed in Appendix F. The appendix also indicates the scenic features and implementation recommendations associated with each scenic route.

General Plan": (1) background material, including a summary of present conditions, assumptions concerning the future, projections of growth or change, and current and emerging issues; (2) goals and general policies; (3) an overview of the major plan proposals; and (4) inclusion of the specific elements in the plan. In *Town of Jonesville v. Powell Valley Village Ltd. P'ship*, 487 S.E.2d 207 (Va. 1997), the Virginia Supreme Court emphasized that under Virginia law, prior to a plan's adoption "a local governing body must conduct studies covering a wide range of factors including existing land use and development, trends and growth, population, employment and economic factors, public facilities, transportation facilities, and housing needs."

3. *Statutes and Types of Plans.* Recall the Baer article in which he outlined various types of plans (e.g., vision plans, blueprint plans) that local jurisdictions might produce. Do the statutes set forth above assume that the plan will be one of these types? Do the statutes preclude the adoption of certain types of plans — that is, preclude the adoption of a vision plan, for instance?

4. *Internal Plan Consistency.* The preparation of a comprehensive general plan requires tradeoffs among the various resources and interests implicated by the plan. The political difficulty of making such tradeoffs may lead to plans with internally conflicting policies. For example, the plan may promise to preserve open space or agriculture land while, at the same time, calling for a level of building within the jurisdiction that is inconsistent with either. Some states try to avoid this problem by explicitly providing that the jurisdiction's general plan must be internally consistent. For example, Rhode Island requires that the comprehensive plan "must be internally consistent in its policies, forecasts, and standards." R.I. Gen. Laws §45-22.2-6.

Could a local jurisdiction adopt elements of a plan that are in conflict but then render them internally consistent by including a clause in the plan which states that, in the event of such internal conflict, the land use element of the plan is to take precedence over all other elements? In *Sierra Club v. Kern County Bd. of Supervisors*, 179 Cal. Rptr. 261 (Ct. App. 1981), the court found such a clause invalid.

A related issue is whether each individual element of the plan must be internally consistent. *See Concerned Citizens of Calaveras County v. Calaveras County Bd. of Supervisors*, 212 Cal. Rptr. 273, 278 (Ct. App. 1985) ("[t]he first problem with the Calaveras County General Plan is that its circulation element is internally inconsistent on its face and therefore incomprehensible").

5. *Interjurisdictional Plan Consistency.* A somewhat related issue comes from interjurisdictional planning authorities. In *City of Malibu v. California Coastal Comm'n*, 121 Cal.App.4th 989 (2004). The court addressed a long standing tension as Malibu, which sits in the California Coastal Zone, in the court's words tried to "escape from the California Coastal Commission's 'local coastal program' for the city.". . . . Here is how the court described the controversy:

> The California Coastal Act requires cities within the coastal zones to develop a "local coastal program" (LCP) to guide their development. With an LCP in place, Malibu shoulders the burden of processing coastal development permits; otherwise, the responsibility rests with the California Coastal Commission (the Commission). In 2000, a full nine years after the City of Malibu incorporated, it had not implemented an LCP, thus forcing the Commission to continue processing coastal development permits for the city.

In September 2000 . . . Assembly Bill No. 988 . . . directed the Commission to write an LCP for Malibu, and in September 2002, the Commission did so. The next month, voters qualified on their local ballot a referendum on the LCP.

With the referendum pending, Malibu declared the Commission's LCP did not take effect, and argued that the Commission continued to be responsible for processing development permits. The Commission argued Malibu voters could not subject the Commission's acts to a referendum, that the LCP was enforceable, and Malibu was henceforth responsible for processing permits. . . .

The parties agree the LCP would be subject to a referendum if Malibu had drafted it . . . They disagree, however, on whether Malibu's local voters can put the Commission's LCP to a referendum. Malibu argues the LCP enacts laws local to Malibu (even if they are part of a statewide scheme) to which the fundamental right of referendum applies, regardless of who wrote it. The Commission argues, in contrast, that the Legislature may withdraw the right of referendum and did so here. . . . We conclude the Commission has the better argument. . . .

. . . The voters of Malibu are not without recourse . . . but these remedies are in the political, not judicial arena. . . . Malibu can petition the Commission to amend the LCP more to Malibu's liking. We suppose Malibu can even lobby the Legislature to regain the power to draft a new LCP, and with it the attendant right of referendum. But . . . such remedies are political, not judicial.

6. *The Scope, Costs, and Goals of the Planning Effort.* The New Jersey statute reproduced above allows a city to undertake an extensive planning effort. In one sense, a broad statute like this one allows a city to tailor its planning efforts to its individual circumstances. Small, rural cities will plan much differently from larger, urban cities. This is likely to be true not simply because of their obvious differences. The costs to a city of planning and zoning may be substantial and may be perceived as limiting planning efforts and as prohibiting complex and labor intensive forms of regulation, such as routine site-plan review, impact studies, and transfer of development rights programs. Some court decisions have allowed cities to adopt regulations to recoup from applicants the cost of development review. *See Area Plan Com'n of Evansville v. Evansville Outdoor Advertising, Inc.,* 789 N.E.2d 96 (Ind. Ct. App. 2003) (upholding schedule of administrative fees); *Neighbors For Livability v. City of Beaverton,* 35 P.3d 1122 (Or. Ct. App. 2001) (upholding payment of costs of engineering reports and authorizing city to retain consulting engineer at applicant's expense).

The scope of the plan raises the question of whether local planners can meaningfully address the topics authorized. These may range from economic development to recycling to farmland preservation. But if this kind of planning can be meaningfully carried out, perhaps there are other, broader topics that plans should address. For example, some authors have argued that planners have paid insufficient attention to health or race. *See* Charles Hoch, Racism and Planning, 59 J. Am. Plan. Inst. 451 (1993), and David Troutt, Katrina's Window: Localism, Resegregation, and Equitable Regionalism, 55 Buff. L. Rev. 1109 (2008). To what extent can planning address problems of racism? Does it depend largely on the type of plan (e.g., vision plan, blueprint plan, etc.) that the jurisdiction adopts? Some state court decisions have limited the powers conferred by a zoning enabling statute to addressing "land use" problems and not for addressing general social, cultural, or economic problems. *See De Sena v. Gulde,* 265 N.Y.S.2d 239 (N.Y. Sup. Ct. 1965) (rezoning cannot be justified by fear of racial rioting); *San Telmo Associates v. City of Seattle,* 735 P.2d 673 (Wash. Sup. Ct. 1987) (impact fee for low-income housing).

Can zoning address the problems of housing affordability, regional food security, gas prices, infrastructure costs, public health, social justice, and global warming? How about world poverty and illiteracy? Should intangible quality-of-life issues such as a sense of place, identity, and community spirit be an important part of planning? We take up some of these questions in Chapter 11, in the treatment of planning goals for smart growth and new urbanism, and in Chapter 17.

7. *Planning and Federal Lands.* The emphasis on detailed land use planning, evident in the statutes and case you just read, extends beyond the local level. Congress has required federal land management agencies to engage in planning processes to decide the uses of those lands. *See* George Cameron Coggins, The Developing Law of Land Use Planning on the Federal Lands, 61 U. Colo. L. Rev. 307 (1989); and Chapter 9, infra.

D. CONSISTENCY REQUIREMENTS

States that require the adoption of separate general plans often make the plan the primary land use document by requiring that zoning, subdivision maps, and other regulatory approvals conform in some manner to the general plan. Such consistency requirements, however, differ markedly from state to state. Consider the following statutes.

■ CALIFORNIA GOVERNMENT CODE §65860
(West 2016)

65860. (a) County or city zoning ordinances shall be consistent with the general plan of the county or city by January 1, 1974. A zoning ordinance shall be consistent with a city or county general plan only if both of the following conditions are met:

(1) The city or county has officially adopted such a plan.
(2) The various land uses authorized by the ordinance are compatible with the objectives, policies, general land uses, and programs specified in the plan.

(b) Any resident or property owner within a city or a county, as the case may be, may bring an action or proceeding in the superior court to enforce compliance with subdivision (a). Any such action or proceeding shall be governed by Chapter 2 (commencing with Section1084) of Title 1 of Part 3 of the Code of Civil Procedure. No action or proceeding shall be maintained pursuant to this section by any person unless the action or proceeding is commenced and service is made on the legislative body within 90 days of the enactment of any new zoning ordinance or the amendment of any existing zoning ordinance.

(c) In the event that a zoning ordinance becomes inconsistent with a general plan by reason of amendment to the plan, or to any element of the plan, the zoning ordinance shall be amended within a reasonable time so that it is consistent with the general plan as amended.

(d) Notwithstanding Section 65803, this section shall apply in a charter city of 2,000,000 or more population [i.e. Los Angeles] to a zoning ordinance adopted prior to January 1, 1979, which zoning ordinance shall be consistent with the general plan of the city by July 1, 1982.

◼ RHODE ISLAND GENERAL LAWS §45-24-30
(Lexis 1999)

(a) Zoning regulations shall be developed and maintained in accordance with a comprehensive plan prepared, adopted, and as may be amended, in accordance with chapter 22.2 of this title. . . .

◼ NEW JERSEY STATUTES ANNOTATED §40:55D-62
(West Supp. 2016)

(a) The governing body may adopt or amend a zoning ordinance relating to the nature and extent of the uses of land and of buildings and structures thereon. Such ordinance shall be adopted after the planning board has adopted the land use plan element and the housing plan element of a master plan, and all of the provisions of such zoning ordinance or any amendment or revision thereto shall either be substantially consistent with the land use plan element and the housing plan element of the master plan or designed to effectuate such plan elements; provided that the governing body may adopt a zoning ordinance or amendment or revision thereto which in whole or part is inconsistent with or not designed to effectuate the land use plan element and the housing plan element, but only by affirmative vote of a majority of the full authorized membership of the governing body, with the reasons of the governing body for so acting set forth in a resolution and recorded in its minutes when adopting such a zoning ordinance. . . .

◼ ME. REV. STAT. ANN. TIT. 30-A §4352
(West 2016)

2. Relation to comprehensive plan. A zoning ordinance must be pursuant to and consistent with a comprehensive plan adopted by the municipal legislative body . . .

Consider also the following section from model legislation produced by the American Planning Association's "Smart Growth" project.

◼ 8-104 CONSISTENCY OF LAND DEVELOPMENT REGULATIONS WITH LOCAL COMPREHENSIVE PLAN

(1) Land development regulations and any amendments thereto, including amendments to the zoning map, and land-use actions shall be consistent with the local comprehensive plan, provided that in the event the land development regulations become inconsistent with the local comprehensive plan by reason of

amendment to the plan or adoption of a new plan, the regulations shall be amended within [6] months of the date of amendment or adoption so that they are consistent with the local comprehensive plan as amended.

    a. Except as provided in paragraph (1) above, any land development regulations or amendments thereto and any land-use actions that are not consistent with the local comprehensive plan shall be voidable to the extent of the inconsistency. . . .

(3) The local planning agency shall find that proposed land development regulations, a proposed amendment to existing land development regulations, or a proposed land-use action is consistent with the local comprehensive plan when the regulations, amendment, or action:

    a. furthers, or at least does not interfere with, the goals and policies contained in the local comprehensive plan;
    b. is compatible with the proposed future land uses and densities and/or intensities contained in the local comprehensive plan; and
    c. carries out, as applicable, any specific proposals for community facilities, including transportation facilities, other specific public actions, or actions proposed by nonprofit and for-profit organizations that are contained in the local comprehensive plan.

Notes and Comments

1. *Consistency Required by Local Ordinance.* If no state statute requires that zoning or other approvals be consistent with the master or general plan, could a local government adopt such a requirement voluntarily? This is not an uncommon practice. In *Board of County Commissioners of Larimer County v. Conder*, 927 P.2d 1339 (Colo. 1996), the county first adopted a master plan, which was advisory only in the state. It then, however, included a requirement of compliance with the master plan in its subdivision regulations and denied a subdivision application on that ground.

The Colorado Supreme Court concluded that, under the Colorado Local Government Land Use Control Enabling Act of 1974, the county had the authority to incorporate master plan density provisions into its subdivision regulations. The master plan provisions at issue, however, "must be drafted with sufficient exactitude so that proponents of new development are afforded due process, the county does not retain unfettered discretion, and the basis for the county's decision is clear for purposes of reasoned judicial review." *Id.* at 1351. *See, e.g., West Bluff Neighborhood Ass'n v. City of Albuquerque*, 50 P.3d 182 (N.M. Ct. App. 2002) (finding that city may voluntarily adopt a consistency requirement but did not do so in this case); *Archers Glen Partners, Inc. v. Garner*, 933 A.2d 405 (Md. Ct. Spec. App. 2007) (upholding denial of a subdivision on the basis of inconsistency with master plan where the consistency requirement was adopted by ordinance rather than compelled by statute).

Even if the plan is binding, the more general provisions or purposes of the plan cannot override clearly and specifically applicable zoning ordinance provisions that are arguably compatible with the plan. *See Lakeside Indus. v. Thurston County*, 119 Wash. App. 886, 83 P.3d 433 (Div. 2 2004) (county commissioners lacked legal authority to apply plan's general purpose to deny special permit specifically allowed by zoning code).

2. *Statutory Approaches to Consistency.* Consider the statutory consistency requirements that you read. Are they sufficiently clear so that city officials can implement them? Is it better to define the term "consistent" or to leave it to local governments to interpret?

The New Jersey approach allows an approval that is not consistent but imposes voting and findings requirements. Is it better to allow inconsistencies, as New Jersey does, as long as the local officials fully face the inconsistency?

Are courts in that state more likely to apply a "tighter" interpretation of consistency because they know that local officials can approve projects even if they are not consistent with the plan? *See, e.g., Willoughby v. Planning Bd. of Twp. of Deptford*, 740 A.2d 1097, 1100 (N.J. Sup. App. Div. 1999) (reversing trial court, finding that the project was not consistent, and noting that such a finding "merely triggers two procedural requirements: a majority vote of the full authorized membership of the governing body and a statement of reasons"). The court specifically noted that the statute "does not require amendment of the master plan before an inconsistent ordinance is adopted." Will courts require local governments to fully recognize the inconsistency before they will uphold an action taken inconsistent with the plan? *See Willoughby v. Wolfson Grp., Inc.*, 753 A.2d 162 (N.J. Sup. App. Div. 2002) ("before adopting a zoning amendment inconsistent with the master plan, the governing body must expressly recognize the inconsistency. This will give effect to the significance the Legislature attached to the master plan"). Considerable judicial deference, however, is likely, as is shown to even amendments to the plan. *See Powerhouse Arts Dist. Neighborhood Ass'n v. City Council of City of Jersey City*, 413 N.J. Super. 322, 994 A.2d1054 (App. Div. 2010) (arbitrary and capricious standard applicable to plan amendments).

3. *What Must Be Consistent?* Local governments make a wide variety of land use decisions. They approve rezonings, subdivisions, variances, use permits, planned unit developments, site plans, etc. If a state has a consistency requirement, which of these decisions are subject to it? The answer will turn on the particular statutory language and on judicial interpretation. Consistency requirements have been applied in various jurisdictions to zoning classifications, density and intensity restrictions, growth caps, subdivision approvals, public works projects, levels of service requirements, sale of municipal assets, conditional use permits, and even variances and individual building permits. *See* 1 Edward H. Ziegler, Rathkopf's The Law of Zoning and Planning, ch. 14 at 14.29 (4th ed. 2005 and Supp. 2012). In *Graves v. City of Pompano Beach*, 74 So. 3d 595 (Fla. Dist. Ct. App. 2011), the court found under Florida law that a plat approval of a development order must be consistent with the local comprehensive plan.

The same issue can arise with a sub-area or neighborhood plan that is intended to implement the general plan. *See Napa Citizens for Honest Government v. Napa County Bd. of Supervisors*, 110 Cal. Rptr. 2d 579 (Ct. App. 2001). The court of appeal first held that the consistency doctrine requires the specific plan to "recite goals and policies that are consistent with those set forth in the County's General Plan." *Id.* at 606.

According to the court, "The proper question is whether development of the Project Area under the Updated Specific Plan is compatible with and will not frustrate the General Plan's goals and policies." *Id.* Is the difference between the two plans a clear one? Presumably, the goals of a subarea plan will be implemented by the specific standards of the zoning code.

4. *The Influence of the Plan.* If a jurisdiction has not adopted a requirement that zoning must be consistent with the general plan, should the plan be taken into account in determining whether a rezoning is arbitrary or capricious? Or does the fact that the legislature has not adopted a consistency requirement mean that a separate, comprehensive plan is irrelevant to all zoning decisions? In *Board of County Commissioners of Johnson County v. City of Olathe*, 263 Kan. 667, 952 P.2d 1302 (1998), the Supreme Court of Kansas commented that cities "are not bound by their comprehensive plans in making these rezoning decisions," but it "urged that the plans not be overlooked when changes in zoning are under consideration." *Id.* at 1313 (citing *Taco Bell v. City of Mission*, 234 Kan. 879, 894, 678 P.2d 133 (1984)). The court, however, then posed the question whether "this seeming disregard for both the City's officially adopted comprehensive plan and the airport compatibility plan tip the scales toward a finding of unreasonableness [of the rezoning]"? The court concluded that the rezoning was not unreasonable, citing the presumption that the zoning authority acted reasonably.

Did the court give too much deference to the city? What is the point of preparing a plan if a rezoning is flatly inconsistent with that plan but is nevertheless approved?

5. *Overriding the Zoning Ordinance?* If there is no binding consistency provision in a statute or ordinance, may a city, nevertheless, treat the plan as overriding the "governing law" of a zoning ordinance? *See, e.g., In re Approval of Request for Amendment to Frawley Planned Unit Dev.*, 638 N.W.2d 552 (S.D. 2002) (plan that was not legally binding did not override zoning provision for planned development); *Caco Three, Inc. v. Board of Sup'rs of Huntington Tp.*, 845 A.2d 992 (Pa. Commw. 2004) (subdivision ordinance controlled approval not plan which was only abstract recommendation).

In *Urrutia v. Blaine County*, 2 P.3d 738 (Idaho 2000), the court overturned the County Board's denial of a subdivision based solely on noncompliance with the comprehensive plan. The subdivision ordinance required that the land subdivided "shall conform to the Comprehensive Plan," but there was no statutory consistency requirement. The court first observed that the board "may . . . refer to the comprehensive plan as a general guide in instances involving zoning decisions." *Id.* at 743. However, "a more specific analysis, resulting in denial of a subdivision application based solely on non-compliance with the plan elevates the plan to the level of legally controlling zoning law." *Id.* Thus, the Board erred in relying completely on the comprehensive plan. *Id.* Also, in *In re Jerome Ct. Bd. of Comm'rs*, 281 P.3d 1076, 1094 (Idaho 2012), the court rejected a challenge to a Concentrated Animal Feeding Operation. Quoting an earlier opinion it concluded: "A comprehensive plan is not a legally controlling zoning law, it serves as a guide to local government agencies charged with making zoning decisions. The in accordance with language . . . does not require zoning decisions to strictly conform to the land-use designations of the comprehensive plan." *See also RDNT, LLC v. City of Bloomington*, 861 N.W.2d 71, 82 (Minn. 2015) (Anderson, J. concurring) ("[u]sing the comprehensive plan as a tool for specific zoning decisions invites, rather than minimizes, arbitrary and discriminatory municipal practices").

In John Baker and Edward Sullivan, *Father Does Not Know Best: A Response to Justice Anderson's Concurring Opinion in RDNT, LLC v. City of Bloomington*, 38 No. 9 Zoning and Planning Law Reports NL1 (2015), the authors critiqued judicial influence where comprehensive plans are not regarded as binding law:

> Because a comprehensive plan is a community's vision of its future, it embodies policy judgments, which courts should be especially reluctant to override. If cities and counties effectively lose the authority to base land-use decisions on whether the proposed use is consistent with a comprehensive plan, or if courts override local governments' reconciliation of competing policy objectives in the plan, it may have the practical effect of substituting the court's own value judgments for those of the community's elected representatives. That is because a failure to defer will create a vacuum that will be filled by the judges' own premises and assumptions about the kinds of places that would be appropriate for certain developments.

6. *Plans as Law Without Detailed Zoning Standards.* Zoning ordinances may require, as a standard for development approval, that an application be consistent with a city's governing sub-area or neighborhood plan. To what extent can a city substitute a plan's goals, policies, and guidelines for more conventional zoning standards? Are there limits to how flexible a plan's policy guidelines can be as standards for decision in zoning cases? *See, e.g, Hardin County v. Jost*, 897 S.W.2d 592 (Ky. Ct. App. 1995) (invalidating on vagueness and statutory grounds a zoning scheme based on numerical scores derived from a growth guidance assessment applied to individual applications); *Kosalka v. Town of Georgetown*, 752 A.2d 283 (Me. 2000) (invalidating "conserve natural beauty" as decisional standard); *Peterson Outdoor Advertising v. City of Myrtle Beach*, 489 S.E.2d 630 (1997) (invalidating "unsightly and inharmonious development" as approval standard). Are these cases where courts have overlooked the benefits of flexibility and discretion? If standards like these are upheld, have we abandoned the "rule of law" in land use regulation?

Even if it is clear from the statute that the state has adopted some form of consistency requirement, applying that requirement may not be simple. Particularly troublesome are situations in which the general plan is incomplete, a fact pattern that arose in the following case. But even if the plan is complete, the court must determine how much deference it should accord to a city's determination that a land use decision is consistent with it.

■ HAINES v. CITY OF PHOENIX
727 P.2d 339 (Ariz. App. 1986)

OPINION

HATHAWAY, Chief Judge.

Appellant contests the trial court's granting of summary judgment in affirmance of the City of Phoenix's (city) authority to rezone the parcel in controversy. . . .

On January 1, 1974, Arizona's Urban Environment Management Act (act) became effective. Laws 1973, Chapter 178; A.R.S. §9-461 et seq. The act requires municipalities to adopt long-range, general plans for urban development. A.R.S. §9-461.05(A). The act also authorizes specific plans. A.R.S. §9-461.08. The act requires municipal zoning ordinances be consistent with the general plans. §9-462.01(E). On July 3, 1979, the city adopted two plans — the Phoenix Concept Plan 2000 and the Interim 1985 Plan. It is disputed whether these plans are general or specific plans as defined by the statute.

This action arose from the Phoenix City Council's granting of a "height waiver" for a highrise office project that is proposed to be constructed by appellee Adams Group on 14.48 acres of land on Central Avenue between Glenrosa and Turney avenues in Phoenix. The property was zoned C-2H-R (intermediate commercial highrise) and subject to a 250-foot highrise limitation. The 1985 plan also limits to 250 feet buildings in the area in which this parcel is located.

On July 29, 1983, the Adams Group submitted an application to amend the city zoning ordinance to permit a building on the parcel in excess of the 250-foot height limitation. The rezoning application was heard by the planning commission on November 16, 1983. That body recommended denial by a 3 to 2 vote. Pursuant to §108-J.1 of the city zoning ordinance the Adams Group requested the city council to hold a public hearing on the application and not to adopt the planning commission's recommendation. Two hearings were held, on December 19, 1983 and February 6, 1984. On February 6, the city council approved a rezoning which allowed the Adams Group to erect a 500-foot building. Appellant then filed this action alleging the city council's action is inconsistent with the general or specific plans and therefore is in violation of A.R.S. §9-462.01(E). Appellees argue that the city had not adopted either a general or specific plan at the time of the city council action and the only issue before the city council was whether there was compliance with §412-B.2-F(1) of the Phoenix Zoning Ordinance, permitting height amendments.[1] . . .

I. HAS THE CITY ADOPTED A GENERAL OR SPECIFIC PLAN?

The act does not establish a timetable for the adoption of a general plan. Therefore, if the city was found not to have a general plan at this time, it would not be in violation of the act absent a showing of bad faith.

A.R.S. §9-461(1) states a general plan means:

. . . [A] municipal statement of land development policies, which may include maps, charts, graphs and text which set forth objectives, principles and standards for local growth and redevelopment enacted under the provisions of this article or any prior statute.

A.R.S. §9-461(5) states a specific plan means:

. . . [A] detailed element of the general plan enacted under the provisions of this article or a prior statute.

---

1. We note that subsequent to the filing of this action on October 2, 1985, the city adopted a plan it acknowledges is a general plan. General Plans for Phoenix 1985-2000. That plan, however, is irrelevant to the current dispute.

It is clear that both the Concept Plan 2000 and the Interim Plan 1985 meet the definition for a general plan. Additionally, Interim Plan 1985 could be viewed as a specific plan for the implementation of the general plan pronounced in Concept Plan 2000. Concept Plan 2000 establishes the policy of dividing the city into villages, each containing a core, gradient and periphery. Interim Plan 1985 establishes specific criteria for the implementation of that policy in the Encanto Area in which this dispute occurred. Additionally, there is not any evidence that these two plans were not adopted under the provisions of the article pursuant to A.R.S. §9-461.06. The real debate concerns A.R.S. §9-461.05, which enunciates the scope of a general plan.

A.R.S. §9-461.05(C) and (D) require the general plan to contain nine district elements. Those elements are:

1. A land use element.
2. Circulation element.
3. Conservation element.
4. Recreation element.
5. Public services and facility element.
6. Public buildings element.
7. Housing element.
8. Conservation rehabilitation and redevelopment element.
9. Safety element.

A review of the two plans establishes that some of the above-required elements have not been addressed by either Concept Plan 2000 or Interim Plan 1985. The question before this court, therefore, is whether the missing elements negate Concept Plan 2000 and Interim Plan 1985 as general or specific plans or are irrelevant to the existence of a plan and establish only that the city's plans are presently incomplete. We find the latter course of reasoning applies.

While these plans are probably not satisfactory in their completeness, they are clearly plans according to the statutory definition. Appellees' reasoning would permit the city to perpetually avoid urban planning by leaving out any element or any subdivision of an element defined in §9-461.05. This would produce the untenable result of the slightest omission causing the city to have no plan. Additionally, appellees argue that Concept Plan 2000 stated it was only the beginning of the development of a general plan and argue it cannot be interpreted to be a general plan. A rose by any other name, however, still smells as sweet, and the city cannot avoid implementation of the statute by creating a plan and then stating it is not one. Concept Plan 2000 and Interim Plan 1985 fit the statutory definitions and are therefore general and specific plans as defined by A.R.S. §9-461(1, 5).

II. Was the Rezoning in Conformity with the Plan?

A. Applicability of A.R.S. §9-462.01(E). A.R.S. §9-462.01(E) states:

All zoning ordinances or regulations adopted under this article shall be consistent with the adopted general or specific plans of the municipality. . . .

B. Is the amendment consistent with the general and specific plan? Normally the level of judicial review of a zoning ordinance or amendment is the rational basis test. . . . Under the rational basis test if the court can hypothesize any rational reason why the legislative body made the choice it did, the statute or ordinance is constitutionally valid. . . .

. . . Appellant argues instead that, due to the statute, there be no presumption of legislative validity and the city council be required to make written findings and articulate reasons for any deviation from the general plan. There is support for this approach. *See Roseta v. County of Washington*, supra, and *Love v. Board of County Commissioners of Bingham County*, 105 Idaho 558, 671 P.2d 471 (1983).

We, however, reject both of the above approaches. By the enactment of §9-462.01(E), the legislature has provided a standard by which to review zoning decisions in addition to the usual constitutional standard. That standard is consistency with the general plan. In our review, however, we will not substitute our judgment for that of the duly elected legislative body, the city council. Therefore our review will consist of viewing the record that was before the city council and determining if, from that evidence, the council could have decided that despite the deviation from the letter of the plan there was consistency. The burden of proof will still be on the plaintiff to show inconsistency.

Consistency has been defined as "basic harmony." J. DiMento, the Consistency Doctrine and the Limits of Planning (1980). *See also* Op. Ky. Att'y Gen. 68-558 (1968). Therefore in the current situation if from the evidence before it the city council could have determined that the rezoning was in basic harmony with the general plan, the rezoning is valid. Of course in cases where the rezoning does not deviate from the general plan, rational basis review will still be utilized.

This rezoning did deviate from the general plan in that it surpassed by a large margin the 250-foot height restriction. The plan, however, has other goals for that area. The plan does provide that gradient areas where this proposed building lies will have some concentrations of landuse in sub cores. Also there is a provision for commercial development of the Central Avenue corridor. The building height restrictions are only stated in precatory language. Additionally, the plan provided for open space in the gradient, encouragement of landscaping, areas for people to enjoy and commercial development. The city council had before it evidence that this building would be commercially beneficial, would provide open spaces and recreational areas, landscaping, etc. The council also heard testimony that the developer could build two 20-story buildings which would leave less open space and less potential recreational areas. In viewing the above evidence, we cannot say the city council was wrong in finding the rezoning in basic harmony with the general plan. We do not need specific findings by the council to come to this conclusion since we have viewed the same evidence the council viewed. Certainly written findings would be preferable, but they are not mandatory. . . .

Notes and Comments

1. *Three Possible Interpretations.* Consider three possible interpretations of the consistency requirement:

1. Because the city has not yet adopted a plan that fully complies with the statutory requirements, the question of the consistency of zoning with that plan cannot arise;

2. Because the city has not yet adopted a plan that fully complies with the statutory requirements, no zoning ordinances can be legally found consistent with that plan; and

3. Because the city has not yet adopted a plan that fully complies with the statutory requirements, the city's zoning ordinances need only be consistent with the parts of the plan which the city has already adopted.

Which of these three interpretations did the Arizona court adopt? Which is the superior interpretation? *Compare* with *Haines* the decision in *Camp v. Mendocino County Bd. of Supervisors*, 176 Cal. Rptr. 620 (Ct. App. 1981). In that case, the court invalidated the approval of two subdivisions on the grounds that, because the county's general plan did not have the contents required by statute, the county could not find the subdivisions consistent with the plan. *See also Heine Farms v. Yankton County*, 649 N.W.2d 597 (S.D. 2002). South Dakota defines a "zoning ordinance" as "any ordinance adopted by the board to implement the comprehensive plan." S.D.C.L. §11-2-1(10). It also separately defines the "comprehensive plan," and the County had none. The South Dakota Supreme Court held:

> Obviously, the Yankton County Commission could not enact a zoning ordinance implementing the goals, policies and objectives of a comprehensive plan for the development of the County if there was no comprehensive plan setting forth those goals, policies, and objectives.

649 N.W.2d at 602.

2. *"Strict" or "Loose" Consistency I.* How strict should the consistency requirement be? Did the holding in *Haines* "gut" the consistency requirement, or is flexibility in its operation needed if plans are to function properly? If a "strict" consistency requirement is adopted, would that interpretation mean that plans would become overly specific (as a substitute for detailed zoning standards) or would plans become even more flexible and discretionary in response to a strict consistency requirement? In *Save Our Heritage Org. v. City of San Diego*, 187 Cal. App. 4th 163 (Ct. App. 2015), the city sought to restrict auto access to central areas of a historic park and to build an additional access bridge. The court concluded that the project to revitalize the city's historic Balboa Park did not adversely affect the applicable land use plan, even if it violated certain policies. "The mere fact the Project had some elements that conflicted with a few of the policies embodied in the applicable land use plans does not preclude the City from finding the Project as a whole was consistent with the objectives, policies, general land uses, and programs specified in the applicable plans." *Id.* at 772.

A Mississippi case similar to *Haines* is *Hall v. City of Ridgeland*, 37 So. 3d 25 (Miss. 2010), wherein the Supreme Court of Mississippi upheld the grant of a conditional use permit for a 13-story office building in a commercial zone near a major highway where that zone otherwise allowed only buildings no more than four stories in height. The court rejected a spot zoning claim by neighbors and found that the permit was consistent with the intent of the city's comprehensive zoning plan (as implied in the zoning scheme) since the zoning scheme expressly allowed tall buildings (without height restriction) by a conditional use permit in that zone. The court further ruled that otherwise applicable MBA (maximum building area) and FAR (floor area ratio) limitations on office buildings in that zone were impliedly not intended (as construed by the city) to apply to really tall buildings in that zone. To do so, as the developer argued, could "hamstring the design of any building in Ridgeland in excess of four stories to a slender, toothpick like, unattractive, non-functional building." *Id.* at 40. In rejecting the neighbors' claim, the court's opinion noted that the developer's experts testified about the building's contributions to "sustainable development."

3. *"Strict" or "Loose" Consistency II.* Does a project have to be consistent with each policy in the general plan in order for a finding of consistency to be sustained, or must it just be consistent with the majority of those policies? In *Families Unafraid to Uphold Rural El Dorado County et al. v. El Dorado County Bd. of Supervisors,* 74 Cal. Rptr. 2d 1 (Ct. App. 1998), a low-density residential project was plainly inconsistent with the land use designation in the proposed general plan. (A statute required consistency with the draft plan.) The county argued, however, that "inconsistency with simply one general plan policy should not be enough to scuttle a project" and attempted to show other ways in which the project was consistent. The court of appeal overturned the approval, concluding that "the nature of the policy [in the plan] and the nature of the inconsistency are critical factors to consider" but that "the land use policy at issue here is fundamental." 74 Cal. Rptr. 2d at 17.

Similarly, in *Jaqua v. City of Springfield,* 91 P.3d 817 (Ore. App. 2004), an Oregon court held that city ordinances amending the zoning plan governing a residential area to facilitate construction of a needed hospital and supporting commercial development violated the general plan's limited authorization for "auxiliary" uses on land designated for residential use. The court ruled that locating a regional hospital and related commercial uses on 66 acres of a 180-acre residential zone was not simply a mere adjunct or supplement to the residential uses within the zone, but would change the primary use in the area from residential to commercial. Was the problem the size of the tract involved? Was it that the hospital would serve people from beyond the immediate neighborhood? For another example of a court closely scrutinizing and interpreting policies in a plan, *see Cathedral Park Condo. Committee v. District of Columbia Zoning Comm'n,* 743 A.2d 1231 (D.C. Ct. App. 2000).

In *Naraghi Lakes Neighborhood Preservation Ass'n v. City of Modesto* 204 Cal. Rptr. 3d 67 (2016), the court concluded: "As has been accurately observed by one court: 'It is beyond cavil that no project could completely satisfy every policy stated in [a city's general plan], and that state law does not impose such a requirement'" [citations omitted]. The case involved application of general plan provisions addressing the size of a shopping center project adjacent to an established neighborhood.

4. *Timing of Rezoning for Consistency?* The plan itself may provide for the timing and phasing of zoning changes necessary to implement the plan. Where this is not the case, difficult issues of deference to the city's judgment on plan interpretation and implementation can arise. What if a proposed rezoning will be consistent with the comprehensive plan? Does the developer have a right to demand that the local government rezone the property so it is consistent with that plan? This was one of the issues raised in *Hougham v. Lexington-Fayette Urban County Gov't,* 29 S.W.3d 370 (Ky. Ct. App. 2000). The landowner sought approval of a rezoning that was consistent with the plan, but the County denied the change on the basis of objections by the neighbors. The court upheld the denial, reasoning that "just because the zone

change request complies with the comprehensive plan . . . does not mean the zone request *must* be granted. . . ." *Id.* at 372.

Numerous court decisions uphold a city's reasonable denial of a "consistency" rezoning request when denial is otherwise supported by the policies of the plan. *See, e.g., Coucoulas/Knight Properties, LLC v. Town of Hillsborough,* 683 S.E.2d 228 (N.C. Ct. App. 2009) (consistency of rezoning does not compel approval); *Borsuk v. Town of St. John,* 820 N.E.2d 118 (Ind. 2005) (traffic problems required further road construction); 739 So. 2d 115 (Fla. App. 1999); and 1 Edward H. Ziegler, Rathkopf's the Law of Zoning and Planning, ch. 14 at 14.17 (4th ed. 2005 and Supp. 2016) (citing cases).

Similarly, in *Bergstol v. Town of Monroe,* 790 v. N.Y.S.2d 460 (App. Div. 2005), a New York court held that an existing zoning classification is not per se invalid based on inconsistency with the uses contemplated for the area in a legally binding comprehensive plan. Court decisions generally accord a city reasonable discretion in both plan interpretation and phasing and timing of plan implementation and recognize that zoning controls the details of plan implementation. *See, e.g., United Outdoor Advertising Co. v. Business Transp. & Housing Agency,* 746 P.2d 877 (Cal. App. 1986) (holding that general plan designations are "broad and temporary" and "amount only to a possibility of future rezoning . . . the circle on the general plan no more represents the precise boundaries of a present and future commercial area than the dot or square on a map of California represents the exact size and shape of Baker or any other community").

At some point in time, courts may grant an owner a mandamus remedy to force the city to reconcile a clear plan conflict. *See, e.g., Mendota Golf v. City of Mendota Heights,* 708 N.W.2d 162 (Minn. 2006).

5. *The "Shall-Should" Distinction.* In some cases, general or comprehensive plans contain "goals" as required by statute, but the goals are phrased in precatory language: "could" or "should" rather than "shall." Does this make a difference in determining whether a development is consistent with the plan? It did in *Haines* and certainly did in *Adelman v. Town of Baldwin,* 750 A.2d 577, 584 (Me. 2000), in which the court concluded:

> These sections do not mandate action but merely suggest recommended conduct. Three of the four terms use the permissive term *should,* but none of the sections use the mandatory language such as *must* or *shall.*

Plans may be purposely drafted to provide the city with flexibility and discretion. In *Monogios and Co. v. City of Pendleton,* 94 P.3d 118 (Ore. 2004), an Oregon court upheld the grant of a conditional use permit for the development of a city park that was to be less than the minimum size of 30 acres as provided in the comprehensive plan. The court found that the city council's interpretation of its own plan as merely a classification system for parks and not a set of mandatory approval criteria was not inconsistent with the express language of the plan or its apparent purpose or policies; the reference to minimum park size was only "aspirational."

Too much flexibility can undermine the integrity of a comprehensive plan and zoning scheme. Consider, for example, the situation where a client asks for your opinion as to the maximum residential densities allowed on her 40 acres of land under a planned development ordinance that incorporates and makes applicable the density provisions of the comprehensive plan. For this applicable planning area the plan provides in relevant part; "For this entire planning area the residential densities should be primarily low-to-medium residential densities — defined as no more than 6 residential units per acre." Some of the surrounding land in the planning area is undeveloped parkland and wetlands and some nearby tracts of land in the planning area are developed at low densities of 1-2 units per acre. What is the maximum density the plan may allow on your client's land? Could you possibly argue the plan allows 20 or more residential units per acre on your client's land?

6. *"Spot Planning."* If general plans are going to be amended on a piecemeal, "lot by lot" basis, amendments of this type might be labeled "spot planning." This technique is the planning equivalent of spot zoning, a topic discussed in Chapter 2 of this casebook. "Spot planning" means "the process of designating a small island of land for a use different from that permitted in the larger area." Joseph F. DiMento, Taking the Planning Offensive: Implementing the Consistency Doctrine, 7 Zoning & Plan. L. Rep. 41, 46 (1984).

In *Dayton v. City and County of Honolulu*, 462 P.2d 199, 209 (Haw. 1969), the Hawaii Supreme Court held that the procedural safeguards applicable to the original adoption of the plan must be followed for amendments to the plan. The court then continued:

> The record in this case shows that the county failed to follow a course of conduct consistent with the safeguards that are required in the initial adoption of the general plan. These safeguards require that alterations in the general plan must be comprehensive and long-range. More specifically, if the city believes the general plan of 1964 is obsolete, then comprehensive updating of the 1964 plan's studies . . . is in order . . . .

Id. Does the *Dalton* decision outlaw "spot planning"? *See also Price v. Payette County Bd. of County Commissioners*, 958 P.2d 583, 587 (Idaho 1998) ("Although these procedures [a plan amendment and a rezoning] can be done in tandem, the Board should deliberate first on the proposed amendment to the Comprehensive Plan, and consider whether or not a general type of growth should be permitted in a particular area; then, once the Board has made that determination, the Board should decide the appropriateness of a rezone within that area."). Spot planning is not per se illegal but may be challenged on statutory or constitutional due process grounds. *See, e.g., King County v. Central Puget Sound Growth Mgmt. Hearings Bd.*, 14 P.3d 133 (Wash. 2000) (invalidating plan change in agricultural area where land did not have poor soil and was suitable for agricultural use).

7. *The Standard of Judicial Review.* The standard that courts use to review local government determinations of consistency is important to practitioners. A 1987 Florida court of appeal decision took an approach that was deferential to the local government's consistency determination. In *Southwest Ranches Homeowners Ass'n, Inc. v. County of Broward*, 502 So. 2d 931 (Fla. Dist. Ct. App. 1987), plaintiffs challenged the determination by Broward County that a sanitary landfill and resource recovery plant was consistent with the county's general plan. After rejecting a standard of "strict adherence" to the plan, the court found that the facility was consistent with the plan:

> The Association also contends that the proposed waste disposal facility will be incompatible with the low-intensity agricultural character of the surrounding

environment. While there may be some truth in this statement, we note that the proposed use by the County, while being more "intensive" than previous zoning allowed, does not involve a higher population density of use. . . . The area in question is already the location of a high-density use, the Broward Correctional Institution. Certainly the prison facility could also be seen as incompatible with the norms set forth in the agricultural designation of the comprehensive plan. While we do not believe that one inconsistent use justifies another, we do believe this factor weakens the Association's contention that the area cannot support isolated high-intensity uses without losing its essentially agricultural character.

Id. at 938-39.

Is the court correct that one or two "isolated" high-intensity uses will not undermine the plan? *See also City of New Smyrna Beach v. Barton*, 414 So. 2d 542 (Fla. Dist. Ct. App. 1982) (applying a "fairly debatable" standard to the review of a consistency determination by the local government).

Other courts apply a similar deferential "reasonable interpretation" standard or "substantial compliance" test in their review of consistency determinations. *See, e.g., Trail v. Terrapin Run, LLC*, 403 Md. 523, 943 A.2d 1192 (2008) (reasonably in harmony with); *Goos RV Center v. Minnehaha County Comm'n*, 764 N.W.2d 704 (2009) (same). *In Mark Latham Excavation, Inc. v. Deschutes County*, 281 P.3d 644. 651 (Or. Ct. App. 2012), a case involving county interpretation of consistency with state planning goals, the Court of Appeals of Oregon concluded:

[T]he standard of review is highly deferential to the county. Although petitioner's interpretation of the PTMG Program to Meet the Goal (PTMG) [a legislative enactment to accomplish statewide land use goals] and land use regulations is certainly plausible, the issue remains whether the county's interpretation is plausible. The existence of a stronger or more logical interpretation does not render a weaker or less logical interpretation "implausible" . . . Petitioner's argument that its interpretation of the PTMG makes sense and is better than the county's interpretation cannot alone carry the day.

The case involved interpretation of Goal 5, a statewide planning goal enacted to "protect natural resources and conserve scenic, historic, and open space resources" in the face of a mining permit. We address Oregon's state-wide planning framework in Chapter 9. Also in Oregon, the court took a deferential approach to the city's interpretation of "foredune" involving an area wherein a landowner could build. *Rundell v. City of Bandon*, 275 P.3d 1010 (Or. Ct. App. 2012).

8. *Planning and Takings (Again).* Traditionally, the adoption of a master plan could not result in a taking of property under the Fifth Amendment, since the plan had no force or effect. *See, e.g., Cochran v. Planning Bd. of the City of Summit*, 210 A.2d 99 (N.J. Super. Ct. Law Div. 1965) (adoption of a master plan not implemented by further legislative action could not constitute a taking).

Does the plan's ability to effect the development of property through a strong consistency requirement now mean that the adoption of a general plan can effect a "taking" of private property, and thus require compensation? *See, e.g., Sproul Homes of Nevada v. Nevada Dep't of Highways*, 611 P.2d 620, 621 (Nev. 1980) ("It is well-established that the mere planning of a project is insufficient to constitute a taking for which an inverse condemnation action will lie.").

In the following excerpt you will see how the court interprets several issues raised by the consistency doctrine.

■ AVENIDA SAN JUAN PARTNERSHIP v. CITY OF SAN CLEMENTE

201 Cal.App.4th 1256, 135 Cal. Rptr. 3d 570 (2011)

OPINION

RYLAARSDAM, Acting P. J. —

. . .

FACTS

1. BACKGROUND

The subject parcel consists of an undeveloped 2.85 acres on a slope that fronts Avenida San Juan. When the owners bought it in 1980, the zoning allowed six dwellings per acre.

In the early 1980's the owners wanted to develop four houses on the property. Their plans were well within the existing land use restrictions. The City approved plans to subdivide the property allowing for four single family lots. These lots would be connected to the street by a cul-de-sac road. Construction of the road required considerable grading, but the City specifically found that there were no geological obstacles to developing the property with four residences. A city resolution at the time stated that "'all competent evidence before the City Council indicates that the site is developable without danger to adjacent properties.'"

Opposition arose in the neighborhood. In 1983 a landslide occurred in the Verde Canyon area, which is generally located to the southwest of the subject parcel and lies behind the homes which front the southern side of Avenida San Juan. The landslide did not involve the subject parcel. Even so, a group of neighbors petitioned the City to make the subject parcel open space. The City attorney at the time, however, opined that rezoning the parcel as open space would be a compensable taking. The City engineer said there was no reason to reconsider the tentative parcel map approval already given. The property remained zoned six houses per acre. However, the owners did not develop it at the time.

2. THE 1993 AND 1996 RVL RESTRICTIONS

In 1993, the City amended its general plan to create the RVL zoning and impose it on several properties, including the subject property. All parcels surrounding the subject property, however, were zoned RL. RVL zoning in San Clemente allows only one residence for every 20 acres. RL zoning allows four dwellings per acre.

The City did not get around to formally rezoning the property from "R-1-B-1" to the one-dwelling-per-20 acres RVL until 1996. In mid-February of that year the City approved changing the zoning for a variety of properties to correspond to the 1993 amended general plan.

The general plan states that the purpose of RVL zoning is to preserve open space in canyons. RVL zoning, under the terms of the City's ordinance, is intended to apply to cases of "significant acreage." The subject parcel is 2.85 acres. It is not a canyon. It is a slope. The ordinance says nothing about slopes.

The ordinance specifically recites that the purpose of RVL zoning is to "preserve currently undeveloped canyons which are either geologically unstable, or aesthetic open-space, or biological resources." There is no dispute that the parcel does not contain "any sensitive biological resources."

3. THE 2006 VARIANCE APPLICATION AND 2007 DENIAL

None of the partners in the partnership actually found out about the down-zoning from R-1-B-1 to RVL until 2004. That year they hired a civil engineer to help them once again try to develop the property.

In early September 2006 the owners submitted a development application to build four dwellings on the 2.85 acres. Specifically, the application sought a general plan amendment, zoning amendment, tentative parcel map, site plan permit, conditional use permit, and variance.

Some five months later, in February 2007, the city planning commission recommended denial of the application. The owners sought review by the city council. At a meeting of the city council on July 24, 2007, a resolution was approved denying the application.

4. THE ENSUING LITIGATION . . .

Judge McEachen specifically rejected the City's various reasons for zoning the property RVL, finding the parcel is not a canyon, as the City claimed, and there was no evidence of "negative geotechnical data." In fact the court noted that the land's "stability" was shown by a nearby cliff that faces the street without a retaining wall, and there was nothing unusual about the parcel's topography. The vegetation was the same chaparral and brush that is typical of all of Southern California. The trial court found the real reason for the RVL zoning was the City's desire to keep the property as open space.

Judge McEachen also specifically found "bad faith" in the City's handling of the owners' 2006 development application. He wrote: "Even though Plaintiff asked for a general plan amendment and a zoning amendment, the denials were all illogically 'based' on the fact that the application did not comply with the general plan and zoning ordinances." In essence, the City never gave any serious consideration to the owners' application. Under the heading "City's Bad Faith Handling of Plaintiff's 2006 Development Application," he wrote:

> With the September 1, 2006 application, Plaintiff submitted a proposed tentative parcel map which is substantially similar to Tentative Parcel Map 82-832 [(the one conditionally approved back in 1983)]. However, the application was rejected first by Mr. Nicholas [(an associate City planner)], then by the City's Planning Commission, then by the City Council. Even though Plaintiff asked for a general plan amendment and a zoning amendment, *the denials were all illogically 'based' on the fact that the application did not comply with the general plan and zoning ordinances.* Also, Mr. Nicholas wrote in at least two reports that since his recommendation to deny the application was based on its nonconformity to the general plan and zoning ordinances, 'staff did not complete any further review,'

meaning no real investigation occurred. Therefore, City had zero evidence for a finding that the proposed development was somehow physically unsuitable."

Judge McEachen further found that the City's land use officials had ignored the City's own ordinances which seek to promote cooperation with local landowners so as to come to a balanced accommodation of interests.

The judge elaborated on the City's underlying purpose to keep the property open space: "City targeted the Property for the stated purpose of 'protecting open space,' thus forcing Plaintiff to bear a public burden which should be borne by the public as a whole. Although City retained the authority to further amend the general plan and zoning ordinances, it held fast to its RVL zoning decision, instead of correcting this injustice." . . .

. . . .

THE WRIT OF MANDATE

Since the modified judgment gives the City the choice of complying with the earlier writ of mandate issued by Judge Stock we review the core conclusion of that writ, namely that the downzoning of the subject property, and later refusal to change that zoning, was arbitrary and capricious.

The "rezoning of property, even a single parcel, is generally considered to be a quasi-legislative act" thus "subject to review under ordinary mandamus." The standard for review of a quasi-legislative act is whether the action was "arbitrary or capricious or totally lacking in evidentiary support." . . .

Here, the trial court . . . found the downzoning, embodied in the both the 1993 general plan amendment and the 1996 zoning ordinance, and the City's 2007 refusal to consider rezoning the property, to be arbitrary and capricious. We agree. . . .

In the present case, there is no need to rest the determination on either Judge McEachen's finding of bad faith on the part of the City or the more rigorous form of review advocated by Justice Mosk in his concurrence in Ehrlich. Here, there is no question that the owners' parcel is a one-house-per-20-acre island in a two-to-six house-per-acre sea. Zoning maps in the record readily provide substantial evidence of spot zoning. Exhibit 6 is a color photo that shows higher density development on Avenida San Juan encircling the subject property. Even more telling is the City's own general plan map showing the applicable zoning. The subject parcel is a small RVL spot surrounded by denser land uses. Moreover, Judge McEachen personally visited the site and found that "There is nothing unusual about the Property's topography." . . .

In its reply brief, the City asserts its discriminatory downzoning and refusal to meaningfully consider the owners' 2006 development application was justified because the property is on a slope. Therefore the project requires high retaining walls and what the City characterizes as a "'tunnel-like'" access road.

The topography, or "slope," argument fails for several reasons. First and most basically, the topography rationale in this case does not support discriminatory treatment. Much of the City of San Clemente reflects the same topography, with many houses already built on slopes in the area. Judge Stock's statement of decision specifically found there were no "unique facts" calling for the parcel to remain a land-locked island. The City's community development director testified that almost all of San Clemente is on hilly terrain. As exhibit 6 shows, Avenida San Juan itself was carved out of a sloping terrain. The City obviously has no problem with slopes as distinct from canyons. Its own RVL zoning ordinance makes no mention of slopes in regard to RVL zoning.

Second, topography by itself was not a reason to deny the owners' various applications that would have allowed the City to make an exception to the imposition of RVL (one-house per 20 acres) on the subject parcel. The record is full of pictures of houses in San Clemente with high retaining walls. Any disruption from grading would necessarily be temporary and subject to reasonable restrictions to ameliorate any disruption to the neighbors. As Judge McEachen observed, the matter of retaining walls and excavation necessary for the cul-de-sac road were matters that might have been ironed out to "cure" those "specific concerns." Judge McEachen found that the City ignored its own ordinance requiring the City planning department to cooperate with local landowners so as to achieve a balanced accommodation of interests. And as the City itself recognizes in its opening brief, the specifics of the owners' application received "no detailed review." The arbitrariness of the City's denial is shown by its refusal to consider measures to "cure" the impact of grading or retaining walls.

Even under the City's 1993 general plan amendments, there were only two points of concern (called "opportunities and constraints" in the text) under the heading of "topography." The first was the "potential of increased susceptibility of erosion on steep slopes that have been *improperly graded*." (Italics added.) The second was the simple preservation of "the appearance of the natural hillsides and vegetation." Both of these "constraints," of course, could be addressed by reasonable mitigation measures. Likewise, language in a 1996 general plan amendment concerning the "[m]aintenance and restoration of significant natural systems and resources" including "steep slopes," is susceptible to address by reasonable mitigation measures. The 1996 language was framed in the context of allowing development compatible with the preservation of steep slopes, but requiring it to "comply with the Aesthetic Resources Element" including such "[m]aintenance."

Most fundamental, though, is the contradiction between the basic purpose of RVL zoning under the City's general plan and zoning laws, which is to preserve canyons, and this property, which, like much of the rest of the City, is on a slope. By its very terms, the rationale for the City's RVL zoning — protection of canyons — does not apply to the parcel here. This parcel, in this neighborhood, was being singled out for discriminatory treatment independent of the reason for RVL zoning in the first place. . . .

The trial court's conclusion in granting the writ of mandate that the subject parcel was arbitrarily and capriciously downzoned must therefore be affirmed.

[The court of appeal's discussion of the takings claim is omitted].

Notes and Comments

1. *The Court's Approach.* What level of judicial scrutiny is the court applying when it finds that the articulation of the relationship between the protection of slopes and protection of open spaces in canyons is arbitrary and capricious? If the local government concludes that the rezoning carries out the purposes of the general plan,

how much deference should a court give to that conclusion? The court also finds that the rezoning was "embodied in the both the 1993 general plan amendment and the 1996 zoning ordinance." Is the court mixing the plan with the measure, zoning, that implements the plan?

2. *The Use of the General Plan.* Consider how the court used the general plan in this case to reach its holding. Is the court applying a pure consistency analysis? If not, how exactly is it using the plan? Note also how the court concludes that the two "constraints" could have been dealt with by mitigation measures. How does that fact play into its conclusions?

3. *Discriminatory Treatment.* Do you agree with the court that the parcels here were singled out for discriminatory treatment? If so, what would you have advised the city attorney to do differently in counseling her client?

4. *Takings.* In an omitted part of this lengthy opinion, the court finds that a taking of plaintiff's property occurred. We address takings in Chapter 7.

E. REMEDIES FOR INCONSISTENCY

If a court does find that a development is inconsistent with the general plan, what should the remedy be? The following case may surprise you.

■ PINECREST LAKES, INC. v. SHIDEL
795 So. 2d 191 (Fla. App. 4 Dist. 2001)

FARMER, J.

The ultimate issue raised in this case is unprecedented in Florida. The question is whether a trial court has the authority to order the complete demolition and removal of several multi-story buildings because the buildings are inconsistent with the County's comprehensive land use plan. We conclude that the court is so empowered and affirm the decision under review.

Some twenty years ago, a developer purchased a 500-acre parcel of land in Martin County and set out to develop it in phases. Development there is governed by the Martin County Comprehensive Plan (the Comprehensive Plan). Phase One of the property was designated under the Comprehensive Plan as "Residential Estate," meaning single-family homes on individual lots with a maximum density of 2 units per acre (UPA). The Comprehensive Plan provides that

> [w]here single family structures comprise the dominant structure type within these areas, new development of undeveloped abutting lands *shall be required* to include compatible structure types of land immediately adjacent to existing single family development. . . .

Phases One through Nine were developed as single-family homes on individual lots in very low densities.

The subject of this litigation, Phase Ten, is a 21-acre parcel between Phase One and Jensen Beach Boulevard, a divided highway designated both as "major" and "arterial." Phase Ten was designated by the Comprehensive Plan as "Medium Density Residential" with a maximum of 8 UPA. . . .

[T]he developer sought to develop 136 units in two-story buildings, with a density of 6.5 UPA. The County's growth management staff recommended that the County Commission approve this second revised site plan for Phase Ten. Following a hearing at which a number of people objected to the proposal, including Shidel, the County Commission approved the Revision and issued a Development Order for Phase Ten permitting the construction of 19 two-story buildings.

Claiming statutory authority, Shidel and another Phase One homeowner, one Charles Brooks, along with the Homeowners Associations for Phases One through Nine, then filed a verified complaint with the Martin County Commission challenging the consistency of the Development Order with the Comprehensive Plan, requesting rescission of the Development Order. In response to the verified complaint, after a hearing the County Commission confirmed its previous decision to issue the Development Order.

Shidel and Brooks then filed a civil action in the Circuit Court against Martin County under the same statutory authority.[5] They alleged that the Development Order was inconsistent with the Comprehensive Plan. . . .

In granting [injunctive] relief, the court found that the developer had acted in bad faith. Specifically, the court found that the developer continued construction during the pendency of the prior appeal and continued to build and lease during the trial—even after losing on the consistency issue. The court found that the developer "acted at [its] own peril in doing precisely what this lawsuit sought to prevent and now [is] subject to the power of the court to compel restoration of the status prior to construction." The relief awarded was:

1. the Court permanently enjoined Martin County from taking any further action on the subject Development order for Phase Ten, other than to rescind it;
2. the Court permanently enjoined developer and its successors in interest from any further development of Phase Ten under the subject Development Order; and
3. the Court ordered developer to remove all apartment buildings from Phase Ten either through demolition or physical relocation by a date certain.

When the Final Judgment was entered, five of the eight-unit buildings had been constructed in Phase Ten (Buildings 8-12). Buildings 11 and 12 had already received their CO's, and fifteen of their sixteen units were actually occupied. Building 10 was fully completed and was awaiting final inspection as of the date the remedies stage of trial began. Buildings 8 and 9 were 50% and 66% completed respectively, also as of that date. . . .

[The court first found that the development was not consistent with the Comprehensive Plan.]

5. *See* §163.3215(1), Fla. Stat. (1995) ("Any aggrieved or adversely affected party may maintain an action for injunctive or other relief against any local government to prevent such local government from taking any action on a development order . . . which materially alters the use or density or intensity of use on a particular piece of property that is not consistent with the comprehensive plan adopted under this part.").

II. Remedy of Demolition

Developer challenges what it terms the "enormity and extremity of the injunctive remedy imposed by the trial court." It argues that the trial court's order requiring the demolition of 5 multi-family residential buildings is the most radical remedy ever mandated by a Florida court because of an inconsistency with a Comprehensive Plan. Specifically, the contention is that the trial judge failed to balance the equities between the parties and thus ignored the evidence of a $3.3 million dollar loss the developer will suffer from the demolition of the buildings. The court failed to consider alternative remedies in damages, it argues, that would have adequately remedied any harm resulting from the construction of structures inconsistent with the Comprehensive Plan. Developer maintains that the trial court erroneously failed to give meaningful consideration to the traditional elements for the imposition of injunctive relief. It contends that the trial court proceeded on an erroneous conclusion that where an injunction is sought on the basis of a statutory violation, no proof is required as to the traditional elements for an injunction. . . .

[W]hen the Legislature provides for an injunction in these circumstances, it has deliberately made the new public duty and its corresponding right of enforcement an integrated statutory prescription. By specifying that the public interest requires that a certain duty be vindicated in the courts and not primarily within other branches of government, the Legislature is well within its powers. Surely the Legislature's primary role in defining public policy under the constitution is broad enough to enable it to specify a legal remedy in an enactment, regardless of whether the traditional judicial restrictions on that remedy in other, non-statutory contexts would limits its usage. As the author of the primary duty, the Legislature alone shapes the form of its effectuating mechanism.

In section 163.3215, we think the Legislature has constructed such a statute. The statute leads off with a declaration that:

> Any aggrieved or adversely affected party may maintain an action for injunctive or other relief against any local government to prevent such local government from taking any action on a development order, as defined in s. 163.3164, which materially alters the use or density or intensity of use on a particular piece of property that is not consistent with the comprehensive plan adopted under this part.

From the plain and obvious meaning of this text we discern only two elements to the granting of an injunction against the enforcement of a development order: (a) the party is affected or aggrieved by (b) an approved project that is inconsistent with the Comprehensive Plan. In short, the existence of an affected neighbor is all that is necessary for the issuance of an injunction against a proposed land use that is inconsistent with the Comprehensive Plan.

We note that the statute does not say that the affected/aggrieved party bringing the action "creates a presumption of irreparable injury" by showing an inconsistency with the Plan. . . . When the Legislature wants to make a lesser intrusion on traditional equitable jurisdiction, it obviously knows how to do so. Here the statutory text makes the injunction the first and preferred remedy to alleviate the affects [sic] of [an] inconsistent land use. Hence, we read the statute to make the injunction the presumed remedy where the conditions prescribed are shown.

We disagree with the developer's contention that this statute was meant to create mere discretion in the court to issue an injunction. If injunctive relief is the specified, primary remedy to correct a violation of a public duty and to vindicate the right of a person affected by the violation of that duty, it can properly be deemed a rule that the Legislature has created, not a grant of discretion. Here the Legislature has devised an entire statutory scheme to insure that all counties have a Comprehensive Plan for the development of land within their respective jurisdictions. The scheme creates mandatory duties to have a plan, mandatory duties to have the plan approved by the state, and once approved mandatory duties to limit all developments so that they are consistent with the plan's requirements. At the end of all these mandatory duties — all these *shalls* — comes a new relaxation of the requirements on standing for citizen suits to enforce comprehensive land use plans and providing for the issuance of injunctions when an inconsistency affects another land owner. Judicial construction of that sole remedy as discretionary strikes us as remarkably inconsistent with not only the text of the statute itself but also with the purpose of the entire legislative scheme.

Developer lays great stress on the size of the monetary loss that it claims it will suffer from demolition, as opposed to the much smaller diminution in value that the affected property owner bringing this action may have suffered. It contends that a $3.3 million loss far outweighs the evidence of diminution in the value of Shidel's property, less than $26,000. Its primary contention here is that the trial judge erred in failing to weigh these equities in its favor and deny any remedy of demolition. Instead, as developer sees it, the court should have awarded money damages to eliminate the objector's diminution in value. . . .

Section 163.3215 says nothing about weighing these specific equities before granting an injunction. If the Legislature had intended that injunctive enforcement of comprehensive plans in the courts be limited to cases where such imbalances of equities were not present, we assume that it would have said so. As important, such balancing if applied generally would lead to substantial non-compliance with comprehensive plans. We doubt that there will be many instances where the cost of the newly allowed construction will be less than any diminution resulting from an inconsistency. Entire projects of the kind permitted here will frequently far exceed the monetary harms caused to individual neighbors affected by the inconsistency. In other words, if balancing the equities — that is, weighing the loss suffered by the developer against the diminution in value of the objecting party — were required before demolition could be ordered, then demolition will never be ordered.

Moreover it is an argument that would allow those with financial resources to buy their way out of compliance with comprehensive plans. In all cases where the proposed use is for multiple acres and multiple buildings, the expenditures will be great. The greater will be its costs, and so will be a resulting loss from an after-the-fact demolition order. The more costly and elaborate the project, the greater will be the "imbalance in the equities." The more a developer is able to gild an inconsistency with nature's ornaments — trees, plants, flowers and their symbiotic fauna — the more certain under this argument will be the result that no court will enjoin an inconsistency and require its removal if already built.

In this case the alleged inequity could have been entirely avoided if developer had simply awaited the exhaustion of all legal remedies before undertaking construction. It is therefore difficult to perceive from the record any great inequity in requiring demolition. Shidel let the developer know when it was just beginning construction of the first building that she would seek demolition if the court found the project inconsistent. When developer decided to proceed with construction in spite of the absence of a final decision as to the merits of the challenge under section 163.3215, the developer was quite able to foresee that it might lose the action in court. It could not have had a reasonable expectation that its right to build what it had proposed was finally settled. It may have thought the decision to build before the consistency question was settled in court a reasonable "business decision," but that hardly makes it inequitable to enforce the rule as written. . . .

We therefore affirm the final judgment of the trial court in all respects.

GUNTHER and GROSS, J.J., concur.

Notes and Comments

1. *The Developer's Nightmare.* What was the developer's mistake? It proceeded on the basis of a government approval, and there was no court order enjoining it from building. As a practical matter, does this decision mean that developers should not build whenever someone challenges the approval of their development on grounds of inconsistency with the comprehensive plan? In any event, lenders often are reluctant to fund a project if litigation is pending against it.

Will this decision mean that challengers will bring marginal consistency cases knowing that merely filing the suit will delay the development? From the plaintiff's perspective, delay may ultimately kill the project if the economics of it change over time.

2. *Bad Faith and Balancing.* The trial court found that the developer acted in "bad faith" by continuing construction during the pendency of the trial, even after losing on the consistency issue. How does this action show "bad faith" when part of it took place before the trial court had ruled against the developer on the consistency claim? On the other hand, if the court refuses the demolition remedy, doesn't the consistency requirement become meaningless in this case?

Normally, courts "balance the equities" when they grant injunctive relief. Why was no balance against demolition presented here? How would a court weigh the social benefits of granting injunctive relief? Destruction orders in zoning enforcement have become almost routine. Violations of zoning code provisions are generally considered nuisances per se and are often remedied by injunctive relief. *See Virginia City v. Estate of Olsen,* 201 P.3d 115 (Mont. 2009) (ordering removal of entire house); 4 Edward H. Ziegler, Rathkopf's The Law of Zoning and Planning, ch. 65 at 65.13 (4th ed. 2005 and Supp. 2016).

3. *The Remedy for Lack of Consistency.* What is the appropriate remedy if a court finds that a zoning ordinance or other enactment is not consistent with the general plan? If a zoning ordinance in a jurisdiction with a consistency statute is inconsistent with the plan in existence at the time of the ordinance's adoption, is that ordinance invalid *ab initio*? Or may the jurisdiction "cure" the deficiency by amending the general plan to eliminate the inconsistency? *See Lesher Communications, Inc. v. City of Walnut Creek,* 802 P.2d 317, 324-335 (Cal. 1990) ("A zoning ordinance that conflicts with a general plan is invalid at the time it is passed. The court does not invalidate the ordinance. It does no more than determine the existence of the conflict. It is the preemptive effect of the controlling state [consistency] statute . . . which invalidates the ordinance.").

If the plan is simply incomplete, rather than in actual conflict with the zoning ordinance, should the result be different? *See Lazy Mountain Land Club v. Matanuska-Susitna Borough Bd. of Adjustment and Appeals*, 904 P.2d 373, 379 n.22 (Alaska 1995) ("We do not hold that all zoning decisions made in the past that were prior to the adoption of a comprehensive plan are invalid. For example, where the municipality has subsequently adopted a comprehensive plan, and the preexisting zoning ordinance rationally complies with that plan, the landowner is not prejudiced and any defect is cured"). Broad injunctive relief against a local government also has been sanctioned by courts when necessary to effectuate statutory comprehensive plan and consistency requirements. *See* 1 Edward H. Ziegler, Rathkopf's The Law of Zoning and Planning, ch. 14 at 14.24 (4th ed. 2005 and Supp. 2016).

A Final Thought on Planning and Land Use Regulation. Might it be that the ultimate effect of reliance on planning and, more specifically, on adoption of a consistency doctrine turns on the underlying culture of the land use jurisdiction? Planning and regulation based on planning are tools that can, on the one hand, solidify an orientation toward rational, information-based decisionmaking. On the other hand, these tools are amenable to application in non- or loose-consistency jurisdictions, with use of a "substantial compliance" test, relying on post-decision record making, and with selective goal or plan provision application.

PART THREE

THE LIMITS OF CURRENT LAND USE REGULATION

6

Judicial Review of Land Use Decisions

A. INTRODUCTION

1. The Role of the Courts in Land Use

Although the vast majority of disputed land use decisions proceed to amicable (or, at least, final) resolution at the local government level, judicial review of land use decisions nonetheless plays a vital role in the land use process. The courts' influence is felt at several levels during the decision-making process. First, project proponents recognize that even if they prevail before the local government, litigation challenging the approval can delay the actual implementation of the project for several years, a prospect that can be economically devastating. Opponents of projects often see litigation as just another step in a long battle, perhaps not initially recognizing how expensive it will be. Opponents also may not realize that litigation probably will not produce a definitive outcome, for even if the opponents prevail in court, the project's sponsor usually can institute new proceedings before the local agency. Finally, local politicians and planning officials may dislike the stigma of a court finding that they have violated the law. They may fear even more the prospect of a court judgment assessing substantial monetary damages against the community and possibly community leaders themselves–liability which may or may not be covered by insurance policies. Their fear of a future adverse ruling can influence how local elected officials and their professional planning staff approach the consideration of a development.

The courts are thus a key player in the local land use process. From the perspective of the practicing lawyer representing a client in the approval process before a local jurisdiction, the prospect of judicial review requires a balancing act. The possibility of future litigation cannot be the ultimate focus of the lawyer's presentation at the local agency level; he or she must principally shape the presentation to convince the local elected officials of the rightness of their position. However, the lawyer cannot afford to forget that, if the decision ultimately is tested in a court, that test will often occur on the basis of the administrative record developed before the local government. Thus, the possibility of judicial challenges must always be kept in mind during the approval process.

This chapter examines issues that relate to how courts conduct judicial review. In many cases, that review will center on the fairness of the procedures followed by local governments. Some of these procedural requirements have constitutional origins. For example, a neighbor opposing a land use decision may be able to claim a procedural due process right to personal notice before the city or county can act. Generally, however, the procedural mandates originate in statutes or local ordinances, and the issues in litigation over them are somewhat mundane: Did the city publish notice of its proposed action in timely fashion? Did the city make all the required documents available before its decision? Was the hearing conducted properly? Did the city follow the state's "open meeting" law? Was the city required to make findings explaining its decision, and if so, were they adequate? Was there sufficient evidence in the record before the city to support the findings? And, ultimately, if the local government did make a procedural error, does that error rise to such a level that the court should invalidate the approval? Issues like these are the grist of much of the practical lawyering in land use litigation.

Other legal challenges to land use regulations focus less on process and more on whether the decision violates certain substantive legal rights. Thus, property owners may claim that a land use regulation restricts speech or freedom of religion in a way that violates the First Amendment. Other litigants may assert that a land use law or decision violates the Due Process Clause or the Equal Protection Clause. Or litigants may seek "just compensation" from government defendants on the theory that a regulation is so burdensome that it amounts to a "taking" under the Fifth Amendment. Such challenges are commonly mounted under the federal constitution, but they may equally well be brought under parallel constitutional provisions included in state constitutions. These types of constitutional challenges to land use regulation are discussed in detail in Chapters 7 and 8.

2. Fairness in Local Procedures

One aspect of the agency's decision making emphasized in this chapter is the issue of fairness to the project applicant and to others appearing before the agency. The underlying question that must be determined is whether bias or a conflict of interest has so impaired a decision maker's ability to impartially consider issues that a court should intervene.

Consider the hypothetical (but certainly realistic) scenario of a local politician who runs for mayor on an anti-growth platform in a vigorously contested election. After taking office, the mayor must preside over public hearings concerning development projects that the mayor has vigorously opposed during the election. Should the mayor be allowed to participate in the decisions on these projects? The election events would indicate that she has reached some judgments about the issues, but these judgments were precisely the reasons why the citizens of that city elected her. Or consider a mayoral candidate who runs on a pro-growth platform and whose campaign is largely and generously funded by real estate interests who wish to develop property within the jurisdiction. Do their contributions taint the development approval process to such an extent that the mayor should disqualify herself from participating?

The answers to these questions lie partly in the nature of the decision that the local government is making. Here, the student must consult the field of administrative law, which offers two important models of how agencies may act: either in a "quasi-legislative" capacity or a "quasi-judicial" capacity. If the local decision-making body is setting prospective rules for a variety of individuals, that action has the earmarks of legislating. In such instances, the courts are very cognizant of separation of powers. They give a large amount of deference to the decision, overturning it only if no rational basis exists to support it. For example, as we have seen in Chapter 2, Euclidian zoning originally was conceived of as a legislative activity; city politicians look at the future of a city as whole and establish land uses for the jurisdiction according to a "comprehensive plan."

The legislative model, however, bears little relationship to the reality of many land use decisions, which are much narrower in focus and are judicial in nature. For example, the granting of a conditional use permit adjudicates the terms and conditions to be imposed on a specific project. Indeed, many decisions adopting zoning amendments have the characteristics of adjudication. They come before the local decision-making body at the instigation of applicants who have a development proposal in mind for a specific, often relatively small parcel of property. The decision involves the presentation of evidence by the project applicant and perhaps the presentation of countering evidence by project opponents seeking to block the development.

Courts traditionally have treated these types of rezonings as legislative. However, in *Albuquerque Commons Partnership v. City of Albuquerque*, a principal case in this chapter, the court departed from this line of precedent. Focusing on how localities *actually* decide such questions, the court held that certain zoning decisions should be treated as quasi-judicial for purposes of judicial review.

The logic of this decision has considerable appeal. It seems to offer the potential of imposing increased rationality and fairness upon a local land use process that can be chaotic, overtly political, and often unfair in one sense or another to concerned parties. But the decision has vast practical ramifications and raises a host of difficult issues. Local governments (and later courts on judicial review) must decide which types of decisions are judicial and which still retain a legislative character. If a decision is judicial, the decision-making process must exhibit much more formality. The decision maker will have to be impartial, the evidentiary procedures followed at the hearing will be more structured, and the decision will be in writing and address the issues raised by the parties. The implications of treating certain zoning decisions as quasi-judicial thus are numerous and significant. For example, do opponents of a project now have a right to cross-examine witnesses in a hearing before the city council?

Consider again our hypothetical mayor who has been elected on an anti-growth (or pro-growth) platform. If the mayor is legislating, then the concern over decision-making fairness disappears. Politicians do not have to be "fair" in taking policy positions; they are elected *because of* those positions. Democracy is largely about vigorously debating opposing positions during an election and then implementing the winner's positions during the ensuing term of office. If the mayor is adjudicating, however, prejudgment of the matter is likely fatal. The impartiality of the decision maker is the most fundamental attribute of a fair procedure during adjudication, and in this hypothetical the mayor is anything but impartial.

These types of implications have given other courts pause. The majority of states continue to treat all zoning decisions as legislative in nature, no matter how small and how specific the particular decision. Nonetheless, the debate about the appropriate approach continues. From the student's perspective, the case serves as a very useful vehicle from which to examine the fundamental nature (and fairness) of the local land use decision-making power and how the large discretion inherent in that power should be constrained.

3. Reviewing the Substantive Decision

In addition to their focus on the decision-making process of the local government, the courts will also review the substance of the local land use decision. Whether the decision is viewed as legislative or judicial, the court will scrutinize that decision in light of the evidence that supports it. The test for reviewing the substance of the local government's decision may be whether the decision is "arbitrary or capricious," or an "abuse of discretion," or perhaps whether it has a "rational basis." The court's focus is on the reasoning that underlies the decision, given the evidence upon which it rests. The underlying purpose of the judicial function is always the same: to determine whether the agency's discretion was exercised reasonably under the circumstances.

Here another important ethical component to land use decision making must be considered: the effect of campaign contributions on local decision making. If local governments are exercising legislative powers, then citizens have constitutional rights to make campaign contributions to those running for office. But when local government elected officials also decide applications for important development approvals, the campaign contribution can appear to be an attempt to indirectly purchase influence.

Interestingly, issues regarding contributions rarely make it to the courts. One reason is that, in most instances, it is hard for a plaintiff to convincingly show that a contribution directly affected a vote. Another reason is that contributions implicate constitutionally protected First Amendment rights. Nonetheless, campaign contributions can cast doubt on the fairness of the decision-making process, and you will consider this matter in the chapter's materials.

4. The Role of Neighbors and Project Proponents

The chapter then moves its focus away from judicial review of the procedures used, and of the substantive decision, to the specific roles that two particular groups play in that decision-making process: neighbors and project proponents. One of the most important developments in the last 40 years of land use law has been the rise in influence of citizen groups. Many important land use decisions at the local level now have three players actively involved: (1) the project proponent; (2) citizens groups, who very often are neighbors concerned about the potential impacts from the proposed project; and (3) the local jurisdiction, particularly its planning staff.

The chapter examines the fundamental question of the weight that the decision-making process should accord to the views of these neighbors. Logically, if the decision is legislative in nature, it can be made for purely political reasons. For example, if a large neighborhood group opposes a project, a politician should be able to count potential votes and reflect that tally by voting "no." But other parties, most notably the project proponents, have a vital stake in the decision; after all, it is *their* land at issue. Furthermore, even if a decision is legislative, state statutes may impose limits on local government discretion.

Most courts conclude that neighborhood opposition to a project is relevant only if it is "factually based." The line between purely political statements and statements based on fact, however, is hard to draw. Consider, for example, the prototypical case of an application for a group home for troubled teenagers in a residential neighborhood. If approved, the home could adversely affect the value of nearby properties, and the neighbors have concerns over their personal safety. When are the neighbors' fears over this project legitimate "facts" for the city's consideration, as opposed to "irrational prejudice" that must be ignored?

And there is a final question: should the motivations of the opponents matter? In one principal case that you will read in this chapter, *Grant County Concerned Citizens v. Grant County Bd. of Adjustment*, the neighbors drill a well and then claim that, under the pertinent law, the existence of this well prevents the county from approving a nearby concentrated animal feeding operation. The court has to grapple with whether the motivation for the well should matter to its decision.

5. The Federal Courts and Local Land Use Decisions

Finally, no examination of the role that the courts play in reviewing local land use decisions would be complete without an assessment of where the federal courts fit in. For the most part, land use decisions involve only questions of state law over which the federal courts have no jurisdiction. But if a municipality's violation of law can be framed constitutionally as the failure to afford procedural or substantive due process, or the taking of property without compensation, the landowner may seek relief in federal court under Section 1983 of the federal Civil Rights Act.

A developer often views a federal court as a potentially more hospitable forum for claims than the state court, but federal courts are unquestionably leery of adjudicating land use disputes. Well aware of the sheer volume of local land use decisions, they fear inundation if the door to the federal courthouse swings open too widely for such cases. Thus, the procedural roadblocks to federal land use litigation under Section 1983 are formidable. Moreover, even when the federal court is willing to consider the case on the merits, plaintiffs have a difficult time prevailing. The Seventh Circuit's 2014 decision in *CEnergy-Glenmore Wind Farm v. Town of Glenmore*, a principal case in this chapter, is representative of the trend. The court is quite upfront about avoiding a situation where many land use cases will land in federal court. Still, plaintiffs keep trying to push the federal door open more widely, and they may yet succeed.

B. FAIRNESS IN THE DECISION-MAKING PROCESS

The procedural requirements that a local agency must follow in making a land use decision constitute fertile grounds for litigation challenging the agency's decision. Courts are experts in procedure, and they will insist that local agencies follow the procedures prescribed both by state law as well as by their own local ordinances.

The following case presents a complex tangle of facts and statutory requirements relating to an applicant's hearing before a local government. It will challenge your analytic abilities. As you read the case, first make sure that you fully understand the various actions that the town did take. Then examine the applicable statutes closely to determine whether those actions were proper. You should also note that lawyers representing clients in proceedings like this one must make snap decisions about such questions as whether continuances are allowable and whether to object to testimony or actions taken by opposing parties.

■ FRITO-LAY, INC. v. PLANNING AND ZONING COMMISSION OF THE TOWN OF KILLINGLY
206 Conn. 554 (1998)

Before ARTHUR H. HEALEY, CALLAHAN, GLASS, COVELLO and SANTANIELLO, JJ. ARTHUR H. HEALEY, Associate Justice.

The plaintiff, Frito-Lay, Inc. (Frito-Lay), appealed to the Superior Court from the denial of its application for a special permit and site plan approval (application) by the named defendant, planning and zoning commission of the town of Killingly (commission). . . .

. . . Frito-Lay is, and has been at all times relevant, the record owner of real estate in Killingly, upon which is situated a food processing facility and office. These premises are located in an industrial district as defined in the Killingly zoning regulations (regulations). After some discussions with Killingly town officials, Frito-Lay filed an application for a special permit on November 26, 1984, which was later supplemented by a site plan. This application explicitly proposed "new construction" of a wood chip burning electric "co-generation plant" and this proposed facility included, inter alia, a boiler, generator, silo and chimney.

The commission formally accepted Frito-Lay's application at its regular meeting of December 10, 1984. See General Statutes §8-7d(c). Thereafter, a public hearing was set by the commission for January 14, 1985. This public hearing was duly noticed and held on January 14, 1985. At that hearing, the commission heard testimony, received other evidence and heard oral argument for and against the application. The chairman of the commission specifically declared the public hearing closed at the end of the meeting of January 14, 1985. At that time, Frito-Lay's application was tabled to the commission's next regular meeting on February 11, 1985, pending the receipt of certain information required by the commission.

At its regular meeting of February 11, 1985, the commission, during its "Citizens' Participation"[4] item on its agenda, heard comments on the Frito-Lay

4. At that time, commission chairman Vincent Baiocchetti said: "All right, the next item on our agenda is Citizens' Participation. It is during this portion of the meeting that any taxpayer or resident of

application. The trial court found that "fourteen citizens voiced opinions during the course of the meeting on the plaintiff's application." A close examination of the transcript of the remarks made during the "Citizens' Participation" portion discloses that most of those speakers did not view the application with favor. Richard Cunneen, who later intervened and ultimately became a party defendant, was one of the citizens who spoke. After this portion of the meeting was over, commission chairman Vincent Baiocchetti addressed William Walker, Frito-Lay's plant engineer who was present, and told Walker that he had some questions to ask him.[6] Walker responded not only to the chairman's question, but also to a large number of questions from other members of the commission. At the end of this meeting, the commission voted unanimously to table the application until its next meeting on March 11, 1985.

At the outset of the meeting of March 11, 1985, the town planner, Richard Hubbard, announced that Frito-Lay would not be present that night due to a fatality at its plant and that Frito-Lay had requested an extension until the end of March. The commission determined that a special meeting would be held on March 26, 1985, and, therefore, that no action would be taken that night. Thereafter, the "Citizens' Participation" portion of the agenda preceded the other business of the meeting, as it had on January 14, 1985, and on February 11, 1985. At the "Citizens' Participation" portion, nine persons spoke on the Frito-Lay matter.

On March 26, 1985, the commission held a special meeting.[8] At the outset of this meeting, Baiocchetti, before opening "Citizens' Participation," said that the commission was "limiting discussion based on the information that [had] been gathered at the public hearing, so any comments that the citizens want[ed] to make regarding Planning and Zoning *should not, should not* relate to the matter before us this evening."[9] (Emphasis in original.) This immediately met with a demurrer from a prospective speaker. She was told by the chairman that anything she said "relative to the issue before [the commission that night would] carry no

---

the Town of Killingly may speak on any issue regarding Planning and Zoning. It need not be on the agenda for tonight. As the size of the crowd here, I'm sure there are a few people that want to make comments. I'll ask you to hold your comments to a maximum of three minutes. This is not an opportunity for discussion, arguments, back and forth, it's for you to say what you have to say, that's essentially it. Please state your name, your address, raise your hand, I'll recognize you, we'll go from there. Yes, sir?"

6. At that time, commission chairman Baiocchetti said to William Walker: "Mr. Walker, since you're the rep, and you're the man bearing the brunt of all this, there are some questions that I have, and it may answer some other questions, it may generate some others. In my business, I'm in a situation where I run into a lot of technical people, I asked a few questions of one person. Would it technically be feasible to take the plant exhaust, with the potato and hot oil odors, and use this air for boiler combustion air, as you can tell from what you've heard tonight and other nights, people aren't really opposed to this woodchip idea, what they're really opposed to is the smell, that's been coming, the smell and noise that's been coming since the plant began. That's really been generated, I think, most the aggravation that you're hearing from most of the people. Would it be possible to do this thing, I think it's my understanding that if you're able to do that, you would eliminate the odor completely, by burning it." Later, during this portion, Baiocehetti said to Walker: "Ok. Now, you've heard the comments that were brought out this evening, are there any in particular that you would like to address, or that you've addressed already, I guess you've already addressed them, of course." Walker did respond with observations. Thereafter, there followed more questions from commission members and responses to them by Walker.

8. This was noticed as a "special meeting" of the commission and the Frito-Lay application was the sole item noticed in the publication for the special meeting.

9. Baiocchetti's entire opening remarks were: "Up to Citizens' Participation. At this time in the meeting, we open the meeting to citizens' participation relative to any matter regarding Planning and Zoning. I'd like to state that, we are limiting discussion based on the information that has been gathered at the public hearing, so any comments that the citizens want to make regarding Planning and Zoning *should not, should not* relate to the matter before us this evening. Ok, anyone have anything they'd like to bring up, Planning and Zoning?" (Emphasis in original).

weight because [the commission had] already taken testimony." This woman, however, did speak on the Frito-Lay matter. Attorney Gregory Sharp, representing Cunneen, also spoke, as did Cunneen himself. Despite further statements by the chairman that the commission could accept "no more testimony" because the hearing had been closed in January, that that hearing had been "irrevocably closed," that the commission was not taking "any evidence at this point" and that the commission was "following state statutes exactly," fourteen citizens still spoke on Frito-Lay's operations and the great majority was opposed to its operations. During the "Citizens' Participation" portion, counsel for Frito-Lay, citing the opening statement of the chairman, objected to Sharp's proposal to speak, although he also said that he had no objection to members of the public speaking. After all of the members of the public had spoken, the chairman asked if anyone from Frito-Lay wished to make a comment. Walker indicated that, given the chairman's earlier ruling, Frito-Lay had elected not to comment.

Immediately thereafter, the chairman closed "Citizens' Participation" and the commission itself discussed the Frito-Lay application. That same evening, the commission voted to deny the Frito-Lay application by a vote of three to two. The reasons given for its denial were: (1) the application did not meet the requirements of §720.4(c) and (e)[11] of the Killingly zoning regulations; and (2) "the surrounding community has lost faith in Frito-Lay, Inc., due to past performance . . . promises have been made to the community prior to the construction of the facility which were not kept, which resulted in a loss of confidence in Frito-Lay's ability to do what it says it will do." Frito-Lay thereafter appealed to the Superior Court.

At the hearing on the appeal before the Superior Court, Frito-Lay claimed that the commission: (1) either failed to act within the statutory time frame or conducted multiple public hearings, which it claimed invalidated any purported commission action, thus resulting in the automatic approval of its application pursuant to General Statutes §§8-3c[13] and 8-7d;[14] (2) acted improperly from the outset in

11. Section 720.4(c) and (e) of the Killingly zoning regulations provide:

720.4 REVIEW OF SITE AND ARCHITECTURAL PLANS

The Commission shall review all plans in order to determine that the proposed use or the proposed extension or alteration of an existing use is in accord with the public health, safety and welfare after taking into account, where appropriate . . .
c. The nature of the surrounding area and the extent to which the proposed use or feature will be in harmony with the surrounding area or will serve as a transition between unlike areas and will protect property values and preserve and enhance the beauty of the area. . . . e. The avoidance of potential nuisance.

13. General Statutes §8-3c provides:

SPECIAL PERMITS AND EXCEPTIONS. HEARINGS. FILING REQUIREMENTS. The zoning commission or combined planning and zoning commission of any municipality shall hold a public hearing on an application or request for a special permit or special exception, as provided in section 8-2. . . . At such hearing any party may appear in person and may be represented by agent or by attorney. Such commission shall decide upon such application or request within the period of time permitted under section 8-7d. . . .

14. General Statutes §8-7d provides:

HEARINGS AND DECISIONS. TIME LIMITS. DAY OF RECEIPT. (a) Except as provided in subsection (b) of this section, in all matters wherein a formal petition, application, request or appeal must be submitted to a zoning commission, planning and zoning commission or zoning board of appeals under this chapter and a hearing is required on such petition, application, request or appeal, such hearing shall commence within sixty-five days after receipt of such petition, application, request or appeal and shall be completed within thirty days after such hearing

requiring an application for a special permit; and (3) acted illegally, arbitrarily or in abuse of its discretion in that the grounds assigned for its denial were not reasonably supported by the record. The Superior Court rejected all of these claims. . . .

We turn first to the issues encompassed by Frito-Lay's claim that its application must be granted as a matter of law because of the commission's failure to adhere to the mandatory time limits set out in §8-7d(a). We do not agree. . . .

. . . There is no question that more than sixty-five days had elapsed from January 14, 1985, to March 26, 1985, when the commission rendered its decision. Having requested this continuance beyond what would have been sixty-five days from January 14, 1985, Frito-Lay has no complaint about extending the sixty-five day limit. Although the record does not indicate that Frito-Lay was represented by counsel until March 26, 1985, as a corporate entity, it was, as much as any individual, chargeable with knowledge of the law. *M & L Homes, Inc. v. Zoning & Planning Commission*, 187 Conn. 232, 244-45, 445 A.2d 591 (1982). Frito-Lay's action in obtaining the extension to March 26, 1985, was a valid waiver of its right to require the defendant commission to make its decision under the statute within sixty-five days after the completion of the hearing of January 14, 1985. See General Statutes §§8-7d, 8-3c.

Ordinarily, this fact pattern, with the time for decision properly extended beyond the mandatory sixty-five day limit at the request of the applicant, would settle this phase of the matter. Frito-Lay, however, also contends that, the commission's disregard of the mandatory hearing procedures made the commission's March 26 vote, after the illegal proceedings of February 11, 1985, March 11, 1985, and March 26, 1985, a nullity. This alleged illegality of continuing to hold hearings after the close of the public hearing on January 14, 1985, it asserts, so tainted the proceedings that it resulted in the inability of the commission ever to render a valid decision within the sixty- five day limit. Thus, it maintains that its consent on March 11, 1985, to extend the time limit does not end this issue, but rather, under the circumstances, requires the automatic granting of its application.

Frito-Lay's claim requires that we examine, as the trial court did, the hearings of February 11, 1985, March 11, 1985, and March 26, 1985, to determine their legal significance in this context.

There is no dispute that the commission properly noticed and held a public hearing on the Frito-Lay application on January 14, 1985, and that, at the end of that

---

commences. All decisions on such matters shall be rendered within sixty-five days after completion of such hearing. The petitioner or applicant may consent to one or more extensions of any period specified in this subsection, provided the total extension of any such period shall not be for longer than the original period as specified in this subsection, or may withdraw such petition, application, request or appeal.

(b) Whenever the approval of a site plan is the only requirement to be met or remaining to be met under the zoning regulations for a proposed building, use or structure, a decision on an application for approval of such site plan shall be rendered within sixty-five days after receipt of such site plan. The applicant may consent to one or more extensions of such period, provided the total period of any such extension or extensions shall not exceed two further sixty-five day periods, or may withdraw such plan.

(c) For purposes of subsection (a) or (b) of this section, the day of receipt of a petition, application, request or appeal shall be the day of the next regularly scheduled meeting of such commission or board, immediately following the day of submission to such board or commission or its agent of such petition, application, request or appeal. . . .

hearing, the chairman declared the public hearing closed. *See* General Statutes §8-3c, 8-7d. . . . That hearing could properly have been continued and "completed within thirty days after [it] commence[d]," but it was not. We, therefore, must consider the legal effect of the "hearings" of February 11, March 11, and March 26. . . . Our cases consistently recognize the generally adversarial nature of a proceeding considered a "hearing," in which witnesses are heard and testimony is taken. . . . Applying proper principles to the record before us, what occurred on February 11, March 11 and March 26 were "hearings" on the Frito-Lay application, albeit without any sanction in the enabling zoning statutory scheme. After the hearing of January 14, 1985, was held and closed on that date, there could be no further "hearings" on Frito-Lay's application that would be permitted under the enabling statutory scheme on zoning. . . .

Even extending fair deference to the trial court's observation, which, like this court, did not hear testimony or take any evidence, we go on to examine its determination of the effect of what occurred at the post-January 14 hearings especially as to the lengthy "Citizens' Participation." . . . First, neither the trial court nor the defendants point to any statutory or other legal basis for allowing the "Citizens' Participation" phase of any of these three meetings on the Frito-Lay application, once the hearing of January 14, 1985, which was the time and place for such participation, was closed. There is no such basis, and such "Citizens' Participation" constituted a "hearing" on each occasion. Such participation prominently articulated concerns about the noise, odor, traffic problems and the lack of Frito-Lay's credibility, all matters that, in practical terms, addressed Frito-Lay's current application on the merits.

On March 26, 1985, an attorney for a resident "intervened," argued against granting the application, and introduced a photo of the Frito-Lay plant as an exhibit. The trial court observed correctly that commission members may legitimately utilize their personal knowledge in reaching a decision. *See, e.g., Burnham v. Planning & Zoning Commission*, 189 Conn. 261, 267, 455 A.2d 339 (1983). That, however, is not an acceptable explanation for the trial court's determination that "much, if not all," that was said about Frito-Lay's "existing operations" was common knowledge within Killingly, "as well as immaterial to the application." It was hardly "immaterial," especially given the second ground for denying the application, i.e., the community had lost faith in Frito-Lay "due to past performances," its "failure" to keep promises it made before its existing facility was constructed and the resulting loss of confidence in its ability "to do what it says it will do." Even assuming that much of this was common knowledge, these comments were made at hearings not authorized by law. . . .

On March 11, 1985, nine citizens spoke to the Frito-Lay matter during the "Citizens' Participation" portion of the meeting. No Frito-Lay representative attended that meeting because of an accident that had occurred at the plant that day. The trial court's memorandum of decision quotes at length from what it characterizes as the "testimony" of the defendant Cunneen himself given at this meeting about his conversations with "several areas of New England and New York State that have wood-burning facilities" and noted problems that they were having with such facilities. The trial court then observed that "[Cunneen's] testimony was echoed by other concerned residents." What occurred constituted a "hearing," again with no legal sanction.

On March 26, 1985, another "hearing," again without statutory sanction, took place on the Frito-Lay application. Not only did fourteen persons speak to it under the "Citizens' Participation" portion of that meeting, but that included, certainly for practical purposes, the intervention into the proceedings of an attorney representing Cunneen, who spoke, over the objection of Frito-Lay's counsel, against the application and introduced an exhibit. . . .

We do not agree with the defendants' argument that, at the March 26, 1985 hearing, Frito-Lay waived its right to object to any of the citizens' comments because its counsel listened without objection while "citizens made their point about the [Frito-Lay] facility," but only objected when Attorney Sharp began to speak. This is so for two reasons. First, Frito-Lay was entitled to rely on the chairman's statements that such remarks would and could not be considered by the commission. In this connection, we should state that, despite the multiple hearings after January 14, 1985, the entire record would support the view that the commission had maintained an open mind without having made any prejudgment on the Frito-Lay matter . . . Second, Frito-Lay fairly viewed this as a "hearing" beyond the thirty day limit and this was consistent with its position that its consent went only to the extension of the sixty-five day limit for decision and not to any new hearing. We also do not agree with the defendants' contention that Frito-Lay waived its opportunity to rebut "any new submissions" at the March 26, 1985 meeting. At that time, after all the speakers had concluded, the commission chairman asked Walker if he wished to respond. Walker, with counsel present, declined to do so. Here again, Frito-Lay was entitled to rely on the chairman's statements that what had occurred would and could not be considered. . . .

Having held that the post-January 14, 1985 hearings were illegal, we turn now to the relief requested by the plaintiff. Despite these statutory violations, the commission did render its decision within the sixty-five day statutory time limitation which started from January 14, 1985, and which had been properly extended. General Statutes §§8-3c, 8-7d. We do not believe that the automatic approval of an application, which we have said was mandated in such a case as *Vartuli*, where the zoning authority did not render its decision within the sixty-five day limitation, is also mandated in this case because of the failure to observe the thirty day limitation. "A statute should be interpreted according to the policy which the legislation seeks to serve." *Aaron v. Conservation Commission*, 183 Conn. 532, 538, 441 A.2d 30 (1981); see 2A J. Sutherland, Statutory Construction (4th Ed.) §§56.01 through 56.02. Section 8-7d requires "*a hearing*" and that "*such hearing* . . . shall be completed within thirty days after such hearing commences. . . ." (Emphasis added.) Section 8-3c provides that "[s]uch commission shall *decide* upon such application . . . within the period of time permitted under section 8-7d [the sixty-five day limitation]. . . ." (Emphasis added.) Moreover, §8-7d provides: "All *decisions* on such matters shall be rendered within sixty-five days after completion of such hearing." (Emphasis added.) There is no dispute at all that the commission properly advertised and held "a public hearing"; *see* General Statutes §8-3c; on January 14, 1985, and that it was formally closed on that date. At that time, the "hearing" requirement imposed by statute and the commendable policy of holding "a public hearing" for providing a public forum for citizen input had been satisfied. The commission, however, went further and held additional hearings after January 14, 1985. We do not read this statutory departure by the commission as requiring automatic approval as that does not present the need that this applicant, unlike those relying upon the sixty-five day limitation, "know with certainty that a definite course of statutory action has been taken by a commission, setting in motion clear avenues of appeal." *Carpenter v. Planning & Zoning Commission*, 176 Conn. 581, 597, 409 A.2d 1029 (1979), quoted in *Merlo v. Planning & Zoning Commission*, 196 Conn. 676, 684, 495 A.2d 268 (1985). In addition, we do not believe that the legislature intended automatic approval of the scenario presented to us. Given this view, we have determined that because the commission did act illegally, we should go no further than to sustain Frito-Lay's appeal and remand this entire matter to the commission for a new hearing in accordance with law.

Notes and Comments

1. *Sorting Out the Frito-Lay Events.* This case raises a number of procedural questions that involve the interplay between the statutory requirements set out in General Statutes Section 8-7d and the Planning and Zoning Commission's consideration of the application. You should carefully evaluate the following questions, bearing in mind that during these proceedings, the attorneys involved (and, where attorneys were not present, the other representatives of interested parties) were required to make quick decisions about courses of action that ultimately affected the outcome of the litigation:

   a. Did the Planning and Zoning Commission meet the statutory requirement that it complete the hearing within 30 days after the hearing commences? Did it render a decision within the time required?
   b. When did the "public hearing" end? How can the February 11, March 11, and March 26 proceedings be part of a "public hearing" when the Planning and Zoning Commission expressly closed the public hearing at the end of the January 14 meeting?
   c. Why couldn't the Planning and Zoning Commission validly argue that it simply disregarded the information presented at the hearings after January 14 because the "public hearing" had already closed?

2. *Citizens Participation.* The "citizens participation" part of the Planning Commission's proceedings gave rise to much of the defendant's legal difficulties in the case. Many of the comments received at that hearing concerned noise, odor, traffic and Frito-Lay's alleged "lack of credibility." These issues bear directly on the permit application and upon the commission's second ground for denying the application: Frito-Lay's "failure to keep past promises." Do these facts support an argument by Frito-Lay that the hearing was not really completed on January 14?

   Consider how, if you were the commission's lawyer, you could avoid having the commission hear information about the Frito-Lay application during the "citizens participation" periods that took place after the hearing was supposedly closed. For example, you could attempt to instruct the Commissioners that they must disregard any statements concerning the application that were made during the "public participation" period. Alternatively, perhaps the safest course legally is not to hold such a "citizens participation" proceeding while the application is pending. But both courses of action, of course, will not please the citizens of that city who oppose the project. What would you do?

On the other hand, Frito-Lay's representative responded to some of the public comments, and even at the March 26 public hearing, its counsel objected *only* to comments by an attorney, not to comments from the citizens. Why doesn't this partial objection to those comments constitute a waiver of any objection to a continuation of the hearing?

3. *Permit Streamlining.* As discussed in Chapter 3 in the context of subdivision regulation, some states have adopted stringent time limits requiring governmental agencies to act on applications within a set period of time. In *Frito-Lay* the court rejects the "automatic approval" remedy sought by Frito-Lay. Was the remedy that the court chose (a new hearing rather than automatic approval) consistent with the statute? The court concludes that, in this type of situation, the applicant does not need to "know with certainty" that a definite course of action was taken within the statutory period. But if that type of certainty isn't the purpose of the time limits in the statute, what is the purpose of those limits?

4. *Procedural Errors.* The issues most commonly litigated in cases where plaintiffs seek judicial review of land use decisions involve allegations of procedural error, such as those brought in the *Frito-Lay* case. *See, e.g., Roncari Indus., Inc. v. Planning and Zoning Comm'n of the Town of Windsor Locks*, 912 A.2d 1008, 1015 (Conn. 2007) ("It is well established that compliance with [the statute] that requires the filing of a copy of the proposed zoning amendment with the town clerk at least ten days before the public hearing is a prerequisite to the commission's exercising its jurisdiction, and failure to comply . . . renders the commission's zoning amendment invalid.").

Here are some other examples of typical claims of procedural error made in land use cases:

- A board of zoning appeals did not violate due process by limiting public comments to one minute and requiring the comments to pertain to specific factors at issue. *Guenther v. Sheffield Lake Zoning Bd. of Appeals*, 42 N.E.3d 816 (Ohio Ct. App. 2015)
- A statute required the board to submit a revised proposed ordinance to the County Commission at least 45 days prior to the permit hearing. Where the board failed to do so, its action was invalid. *Kohr v. Lower Windsor Twp. Bd. of Supervisors*, 867 A.2d 755 (Pa. Commw. Ct. 2005).
- A statute required that notice of a public hearing be published "once each week for two successive weeks." The township published the notice twice during the same calendar week: Monday June 26 and Saturday July 1. As a result, the township's new zoning ordinance was invalid. *Stassi v. Ransom Twp. Zoning Hg. Bd.*, 54 Pa. D. & C. 4th 303 (Ct. Common Pleas 2001). *See also Coleman v. City of Key West*, 807 So. 2d 84, 85 (Fla. Ct. App. 2002) ("Although a tropical storm is an excellent reason to cancel a hearing, it is not a valid reason for noncompliance with the notice requirements.").
- A city's publication of notice in a newspaper did not give plaintiff sufficient notice of a rezoning where the statute required "due notice" to interested parties. *City of Bloomington v. Underwood*, 995 N.E.2d 640, (Ind. Ap. 2013).

5. *Arbitrary Decisions.* Plaintiffs also may argue that the substance of the land use decision was illegal (rather than just challenging the procedures followed or the evidentiary support for the decision). The court reviews such substantive claims under various standards of review; the most common test is whether the decision

is arbitrary, capricious, or an abuse of discretion. *See, e.g., Tinseltown Cinema v. City of Olive Branch,* 158 So. 3d 367, 375 (Miss. 2015) ("[T]his case centers on the Board's denial of a site-plan application approximately one month after the Board had approved nearly the same plan. We find that the Board's decision was arbitrary. . . ."). This type of substantive review is closely related to constitutional challenges based on substantive due process, a subject discussed in Chapter 8.

Another issue that arises in local government matters, albeit somewhat infrequently, is a basic one of open government: must local decision makers deliberate over land use decision in public, or can they retreat beyond "closed doors"? This issue is governed by state "open meetings" acts.

■ CHEYENNE NEWSPAPERS, INC. v. BUILDING CODE BOARD OF APPEALS
222 P.3d 158 (Wyo. 2010)

VOIGT, Chief Justice.

Cheyenne Newspapers, Inc. (the Newspaper), appeals from a summary judgment granted by the district court in favor of the Building Code Board of Appeals of the City of Cheyenne (the Board), declaring that certain Board action did not violate the Wyoming Public Meetings Act, and that such action, therefore, was not null and void. . . .

ISSUES

1. Are quasi-judicial deliberations following a contested case hearing under the Wyoming Administrative Procedures Act (WAPA) subject to the Wyoming Public Meetings Act (the Act)?
2. Did the Board take any action that must be considered null and void when it met in private to deliberate on a contested case hearing and then voted on its decision in a public meeting?

FACTS

The Board was created by an ordinance of the City of Cheyenne, a municipality duly incorporated by the State of Wyoming. Board procedures are governed by rules promulgated in 1997. In 2008, the City of Cheyenne's Historic Preservation Board denied permits to demolish six houses in an historic district. The homeowners appealed to the Board. The Board conducted a public contested case hearing on June 27, 2008, during which hearing the parties were represented by counsel, witnesses were heard, and exhibits presented. At the close of the hearing, the Board retired to deliberate in private. These private deliberations, which the Board characterized as "quasi-judicial" rather than "executive session," extended into a meeting on July 2, 2008. The Board then convened a public meeting on July 14, 2008, during which it discussed its prior deliberations and then voted to adopt a draft decision affirming the denial of the demolition permits.

On July 8, 2008, the Newspaper filed in the district court a Petition for Injunction, seeking an order prohibiting the Board from entering a decision prior to deliberating in a public meeting. Because the Board issued its decision before the Newspaper's petition was heard, the Newspaper on July 16, 2008 filed an Amended Complaint, seeking instead an order declaring the Board's action to be "null and void as not in conformance with the Wyoming [Public] Meetings Act." . . .

DISCUSSION . . .

The instant case focuses upon the language of Wyo. Stat. Ann. §16-4-403(a) (LexisNexis 2009), which reads as follows:

> (a) All meetings of the governing body of an agency are public meetings, open to the public at all times, except as otherwise provided. No action of a governing body of an agency shall be taken except during a public meeting following notice of the meeting in accordance with this act. Action taken at a meeting not in conformity with this act is null and void and not merely voidable.

The following definitions found in Wyo. Stat. Ann. §16-4-402(a) (LexisNexis 2009) are relevant to the issues presented:

> (a) As used in this act:
>
> (i) "Action" means the transaction of official business of an agency including a collective decision of a governing body, a collective commitment or promise by a governing body to make a positive or negative decision, or an actual vote by a governing body upon a motion, proposal, resolution, regulation, rule, order or ordinance;
> (ii) "Agency" means any authority, bureau, board, commission, committee, or subagency of the state, a county, a municipality or other political subdivision which is created by or pursuant to the Wyoming constitution, statute or ordinance, other than the state legislature and the judiciary;
> (iii) "Meeting" means an assembly of at least a quorum of the governing body of an agency which has been called by proper authority of the agency for the purpose of discussion, deliberation, presentation of information or taking action regarding public business[.]

The nature of the administrative proceedings in this case leads us to single out one other statute that must be addressed. Wyo. Stat. Ann. §16-3-110 (LexisNexis 2009), which is part of the WAPA, reads as follows:

> A final decision or order adverse to a party in a contested case shall be in writing or dictated into the record. The final decision shall include findings of fact and conclusions of law separately stated. Findings of fact if set forth in statutory language, shall be accompanied by a concise and explicit statement of the underlying facts supporting the findings. Parties shall be notified either personally or by mail of any decision or order. A copy of the decision and order shall be delivered or mailed forthwith to each party or to his attorney of record.

The answer to the first question — whether the quasi-judicial deliberations following a contested case hearing under the WAPA are subject to the Act — can readily be answered by application of the rules of statutory construction to the Act. The starting point, of course, is the mandate in Wyo. Stat. Ann. §16-4-403(a) that "[a]ll meetings of the governing body of an agency are public meetings. . . ." First, it is logical to ask whether the Board is an "agency" under Wyo. Stat. Ann.

§16-4-402(a)(ii) because, if it is not, the Act does not apply. We would be hard-pressed to find any ambiguity in that statutory subsection, and equally hard-pressed to say that the Board is not an "agency" under the definition. The Board is a "board" created by an ordinance of the City of Cheyenne, which is a municipality. Next, we should ask whether a "meeting," as defined in Wyo. Stat. Ann. §16-4-402(a)(iii), took place. Once again, the statute is clear, and there is no factual dispute; the Board met to discuss and deliberate the appeal from the action of the City's Historic Preservation Board. Surely, no one could argue that such was not "public business," and there has been no suggestion that fewer than a quorum of the members was present.

The Board attempts to "hang its hat," at least in part, on the contention that it is not a "governing body" under the Act. Noting that the phrase "governing body" is not defined in the Act, it points out that, under Wyo. Stat. Ann. §15-1-101(a)(vi) (LexisNexis 2009), "governing body" is defined as "the council or commission constituting the elected legislative body of any city or town including the mayor who is the presiding officer." The Board also directs the Court to Wyo. Stat. Ann. §35-10-201(b) (LexisNexis 2009), where "governing body" is defined as the city council or the board of county commissioners. We find these statutory references to be unhelpful, at best, and misleading, at worst. Wyo. Stat. Ann. §15-1-101(a)(vi) defines the phrase solely for the purposes of Title 15, which contains the statutory authority for cities and towns in Wyoming. Wyo. Stat. Ann. §35-10-201(b) defines the phrase solely for the purposes of Article 2 of Title 35, which provides for the regulation of fireworks.

Generally speaking, a "governing body" is the "group . . . having ultimate control." *Black's Law Dictionary* 764 (9th ed. 2009). In the instant case, the group having ultimate control over the Board's decisions is the Board. It is not the city council. Furthermore, to define "governing body" in Wyo. Stat. Ann. §16-4-402(a)(iii) to limit it to the city council in all matters municipal would render the definition of "agency" in subsection (ii) of that statute less than meaningless; it would make it nonsensical. Simply put, if the legislature had intended to limit application of the Act to city councils and boards of county commissioners, it would have said so. Instead, it unambiguously included all of the entities listed in the definition of "agency."

So far, then, we have concluded that the Board is subject to the Act. The next question is whether quasi-judicial deliberations after a WAPA contested case hearing may be closed to the public. The answer is "no." Wyo. Stat. Ann. §16-4-403(a) mandates that all meetings of the governing body of an agency are public meetings, "except as otherwise provided." Under the Act, the only provision for closed meetings is for executive sessions as described in Wyo. Stat. Ann. §16-4-405 (LexisNexis 2009), which does not include quasi-judicial deliberations after a WAPA contested case hearing. In fact, the legislature in 1995 amended the definition of "meeting" to include "discussion, deliberation, presentation of information." Act of July 1, 1995, ch. 110, sec. 1, §16-402(a)(iii), 1995 Wyo. Laws 207, 208. The Act now clearly intends that an agency's deliberations occur during a public meeting. . . .

The conclusion that the quasi-judicial deliberations of an agency after a contested case hearing pursuant to the WAPA are not exempt from the Act does not answer the second question presented to the Court, which is whether some action was taken by the Board that the Court must declare to be null and void. In that regard, we find the facts of this case to be much like those in *Mayland v. Flitner*, 2001

WY 69, 28 P.3d 838 (Wyo. 2001). In *Mayland*, a board of county commissioners entered into executive session in violation of the Act, but took no action during that meeting that this Court found should be considered void. *Id.* at ¶ 31, 28 P.3d at 849. Instead, as in this case, the commissioners took action only later at an appropriately called public meeting. In other words, although the first sentence of Wyo. Stat. Ann. §16-4-403(a) was violated when the private meeting took place, the second sentence was not violated because the agency's action took place at a public meeting. Thus, the third sentence, wherein the action is declared null and void, does not apply.

Conclusion

The Board violated Wyo. Stat. Ann. §16-4-403(a) by deliberating at a closed meeting, but the agency action took place at a public meeting, so that agency action is not null and void.

Burke, Justice, concurring in part and dissenting in part.

The Wyoming Public Meetings Act provides that no "action" by a governing body of an agency shall be taken "except during a public meeting." Wyo. Stat. Ann. §16-4-403(a) (LexisNexis 2009). The term "action" is broadly defined to include "a collective decision of a governing body, a collective commitment or promise by a governing body to make a positive or negative decision, or an actual vote by a governing body upon a motion, proposal, resolution, regulation, rule, order or ordinance." Wyo. Stat. Ann. §16-4-402(a)(i). Any "action" not taken during a public meeting is "null and void." Wyo. Stat. Ann. §16-4-403(a).

It is undisputed that the Board in this case met and deliberated during a closed meeting. The majority holds that the Act requires an agency to deliberate only during a public meeting, but further concludes that deliberation alone is not an "action" rendered null and void when an agency deliberates in a prohibited meeting. I may agree that this interpretation is mandated by the plain language of the Act, but I do so reluctantly because of the practical result: the Board violated the Act, but there is no meaningful remedy available for the public.

More significantly, when analyzed under the appropriate standard of review, the record in this case fails to establish that the Board did not take action during its private meeting. There is no transcript or recording of the meeting . . .

According to the transcripts of the public meetings, on July 2, 2008, the Board passed a motion "that we go into closed deliberation." Later, during the public meeting held on July 14, 2008, the hearing examiner explained that the Board "conducted a four (4) hour meeting in this matter and then we retired to deliberate." He stated that he "began to draft our written opinion" after the private deliberations. The "opinion" was nineteen pages long, was complicated enough to include twenty-eight footnotes, and dealt with difficult and controversial issues. Even so, the Board's discussion at the open meeting was quite brief, consisting almost entirely of the hearing examiner's explanation of a few select findings and conclusions in the draft decision. After this brief discussion, the Board voted unanimously to uphold the Historic Preservation Board's decision. The decision was signed immediately after the vote, with one Board member suggesting that it would be signed and finished in "like seven minutes."

This information is insufficient to establish that the Board did not take any action during the closed meeting. To the contrary, the Board's perfunctory discussion during the public meeting, its unanimous vote on the question, and its immediate adoption of the written decision, all suggest that the Board did more than just deliberate during the closed meeting. It is fair to infer that the Board reached its decision during the closed meeting, and did little more than ratify the prior decision during the public meeting. . . .

Notes and Comments

1. *State Open Meeting Acts.* Acts like the one at issue in *Cheyenne Newspapers* (also known as "Sunshine Acts") generally presume that all proceedings of local decision makers are open to the public except for certain specified proceedings where secrecy is clearly called for (for example, consultation with a lawyer over litigation). Where a dispute does arise, the courts usually interpret the state open meeting laws broadly to require that meetings be open to the public. Did the court violate this "broad interpretation" approach in *Cheyenne Newspapers*? Is the Act meaningful if the agency can hold private discussions but then "act" on the record? What about the timing of when the opinion was drafted?

2. *Violations.* Determining whether a violation has occurred requires a close reading of the state's open meeting act. For example, such acts require that "meetings" be held publicly. Thus, a building inspector acting alone could not violate the state's open meeting act. *Plourde v. Habhegger*, 720 N.W.2d 130, 133 (Wis. Ct. App. 2006). Similarly, a private non-profit corporation that provided economic development services to a city was not subject to the state open meetings law even though it received 63 percent of its funding from public sources. *Frederick v. City of Falls City*, 857 N.W.2d 569, 579 (Neb. 2015). In *Citizens Alliance for Property Rights Legal Fund*, 359 P.3d 753 (Wash. 2015), the Washington Supreme Court parsed several phrases in the state's open meeting act — "Committee thereof," "Acts on behalf of," and "meeting" — to conclude that meetings of a team addressing an update of critical area land use ordinances did not violate the law. Three elected members of the county council attended.

3. *The "Litigation" Exception.* Most open meetings acts contain exceptions for litigation. The word "litigation," however, may have a broader meaning than you would immediately recognize. In *Kearns-Tribune Corp. v. Salt Lake County Comm'n*, 28 P.3d 686 (Utah 2001), the county commission went into closed session to discuss possible courses of action with respect to an annexation petition pending before a boundary commission. In the closed session, the county commission ultimately decided to appear before the boundary commission and send a letter. The court found that the "litigation" exception applied because the role of the boundary commission was "essentially one of resolving disputes between competing parties, the petitioner and the protesting party." Are you convinced?

The litigation exception certainly allows municipal bodies to meet in private to discuss settlements of pending lawsuits. However, in *Trancas Property Owners Ass'n v. City of Malibu*, 41 Cal. Rptr. 3d 200 (2006), the court held that a settlement agreed to in closed session violated the open meetings law because, as part of the settlement, the city agreed to take certain action that required a public hearing. The city was not excused even though it held the public hearing later. By contrast, the Pennsylvania

Supreme Court concluded that four meetings held with separate parties engaged in litigation with the township over a quarry were not "deliberations" within the meaning of the open meetings act. Instead, they were merely "fact-finding." *Smith v. Town of Richmond*, 82 A.3d 407 (Pa. 2013).

Could town officials go into executive session with their counsel to discuss the drafting of a moratorium ordinance and then validly invoke an exception to the open meeting requirement for "consultations between a body or agency and its attorney concerning the legal rights and duties of the body or agency"? What if the officials announced that the purpose of the session was "Consultation with Legal Counsel" while the open meeting law required the board to disclose "the precise nature of the business of the executive session"? The Maine Supreme Court affirmed the board's action in *Hughes Bros, Inc. v. Town of Eddington*, 130 A.3d 978 (Me. 2016). Do you agree?

4. *Electronic Meetings.* Before a conservation zoning overlay ordinance was adopted, members of the city council exchanged a variety of e-mails, some of which copied the entire council. Did the exchanges constitute a "meeting" in violation of the open meetings law? The Tennessee Court of Appeals thought not, finding that it was neither an intentional nor inadvertent "convening . . . for which a quorum is required." The Tennessee law, however, also stated that a violation can occur if electronic communication is "used to decide or deliberate public business." The court found that some of the e-mails constituted "deliberation," as the e-mails weighed arguments for and against the ordinance. *Johnston v. Metropolitan Gov't of Nashville and Davidson County*, 320 S.W.3d 299 (Tenn. Ct. App. 2009). The Hawaii Supreme Court found a violation of that state's open meetings law when members of a board circulated 14 memoranda among themselves. In addition to other facts, the court found it significant that the memoranda explicitly sought a commitment to vote. *Kanahele v. Maui County Council*, 307 P.3d 1174, 1201 (Haw. 2013).

5. *Site Visits.* Before deciding on an application for a subdivision approval, the board of commissioners held a "site visit" to the property. While the public was given proper notice of the visit and was allowed to go to the property when the board was there, they were kept away from the board members. Was the conduct of the visit sufficient to comply with the open meeting law? The Supreme Court of Ohio decided it was not. The court thought that the notice of the visit had to inform the public whether the meeting "is being held in order to conduct additional evidence gathering, or merely to confirm what an agency has already decided based upon evidence in the record." The court also said that the public "must be given the opportunity to accompany the hearing body, close enough to hear what is being said." *Noble v. Kootenai County*, 231 P.3d 1034, 1040 (Idaho 2010). Do both parts of the court's holding make sense? *See also WSG Holdings, LLC v. Bowie*, 57 A.3d 463, 480 (Md. 2012) (site visit was a "meeting" where "the visit . . . was not merely observatory, but participatory and influential").

6. *Remedies for Open Meeting Act Violations.* As you saw in *Cheyenne Newspapers*, even if the open meeting law is violated, the remedy may not necessarily be the invalidation of any enactment thereafter passed. Other remedial options may exist. In *Manning v. City of East Tawas*, 593 N.W.2d 649 (Ct. App. Mich. 1999), the city council violated the Open Meeting Act by holding a closed session and then withholding the minutes of the meeting. The act required their disclosure. The court of appeal held that, where a closed session concerned matters that were both exempt and

nonexempt from the public meeting requirements, as a remedy the trial court could "redact" portions of the closed session minutes and release those to the public. Under the act, the city council was also able to "reenact" its decision, and thus avoid the remedy of having its actions declared invalid by reason of the violation of the act.

The Minnesota Open Meetings Law declares that if a person has intentionally violated the law "in three or more actions brought under this chapter," the person "shall forfeit any further right to serve on such governing body." Minn. Stat. 13D.06, subd. 3. Could an intentional violation occur where the local officials relied on the advice of counsel? In *Brown v. Township*, 723 N.W.2d 1 (Minn. Ct. App. 2006), the court found that, while reliance would normally be reasonable, it was unreasonable in this case where the lawyer involved also represented one of the decision makers, who was personally involved in the land use dispute.

A Note on Standing and Exhaustion of Administrative Remedies

Standing to Challenge Local Decisions: General Principles. Who can challenge local land use decisions? Zoning enabling statutes typically authorize judicial review on behalf of "persons aggrieved." *See, e.g.*, Iowa Code §335.18 (2011) ("[a]ny person or persons, jointly or severally, aggrieved by any decision of the board of adjustment under the provisions of this chapter, or any taxpayer, or any officer, department, board or bureau of the county . . ."). The Supreme Court of Alaska has defined an "aggrieved" person as "one that is adversely affected." *Griswold v. City of Homer*, 252 P.3d 1020, 1028 (Alaska 2011).

Often, the state law will require the plaintiff to show some sort of "particularized" injury, one that is "special and different from the concerns of the rest of the community." *Standerwick v. Zoning Bd. of Appeals*, 849 N.E.2d 197, 208 (Mass. 2006); *Massey v. Butts County*, 637 S.E.2d 385 (Ga. 2006) (landowner lacked standing to challenge the issuance of a building permit to a neighbor for a barn because he did not show "special damage" rather than damage common to all property owners similarly situated). *See, e.g.*, Paul D. Wilson, "I Don't Live Next Door, But I Do Drive By on the Nearby Highway": Recent Developments in the Law of Standing in Court Cases Challenging Land Use Permits, 39 Urb. Law. 711 (2007).

Many states adopt general standing tests traceable to United States Supreme Court decisions. In *Sierra Club v. Morton*, 405 U.S. 727, 733 (1972), the Court summarized the principles:

> [I]n Association of Data Processing Service Organizations, Inc. v. Camp, 397 U.S. 150 . . . and Barlow v. Collins, 397 U.S. 159, we held . . . that persons had standing to obtain judicial review of federal agency action under [the Administrative Procedure Act] where they had alleged that the challenged action had caused them "injury in fact," and where the alleged injury was to an interest "arguably within the zone of interests to be protected or regulated" by the statutes that the agencies claimed to have violated.

In *Lujan v. Defenders of Wildlife*, 504 U.S. 555, 560-61 (1992), the court elaborated:

> [T]he irreducible constitutional minimum of standing contains three elements. First, the plaintiff must have suffered an "injury in fact" — an invasion of a legally protected interest which is (a) concrete and particularized . . . and (b) "actual or imminent, not 'conjectural' or 'hypothetical.'" . . . Second, there must be a causal connection

between the injury and the conduct complained of-the injury has to be "fairly . . . trace[able] to the challenged action of the defendant, and not . . . th[e] result [of] the independent action of some third party not before the court." . . . Third, it must be "likely," as opposed to merely "speculative," that the injury will be "redressed by a favorable decision." *Id.*, at 38, 43, 96 S. Ct., at 1924, 1926.

This test, or close variations of it, often appears in the state courts' jurisprudence on standing. *See, e.g., Carnival Corp. v. Historic Ansonborough Neighborhood Ass'n,* 753 S.E.2d 846, 850 (S.C. 2014); *Templeton v. Town of Boone,* 701 S.E.2d 709, 712 (N.C. Ct. App. 2010). Under the test, the injury that a plaintiff claims can be aesthetic or environmental. *See, e.g., Pye v. United States,* 269 F.3d 459 (4th Cir. 2001) (aesthetic concerns over a historic district are sufficient to constitute injury in fact, citing *Sierra Club v. Morton*).

Residents' Standing. One issue that recurs in land use cases is how close must the plaintiffs live to the property that is the subject of the land use decision. Some statutes actually define an "aggrieved person" as including persons within a specified distance from any portion of the land involved in the dispute. In a 2013 case, the Maryland Court of Appeals observed that "where standing to challenge a rezoning action was at issue . . . proximity is the most important fact to be considered." *Ray v. Mayor and City Council of Baltimore,* 59 A.3d 545, 550 (Md. 2013). The court divided potential plaintiffs into categories. Residents who live 200 to 100 feet away from the subject property are "almost" *prima facie* "aggrieved," while "protestants who lived more than 1000 feet from the rezoning site have repeatedly been denied standing." *Id.* at 555. *See also George v. Timberlake Associates,* 739 A.2d 1207, 1208 (Vt. 1999) ("Because they owned property in the 'immediate neighborhood' of the project under site plan review, petitioners were 'interested person[s]' with standing to challenge the planning commission's decision"); *Johnson v. Blaine County,* 204 P.3d 1127, 1131 (Idaho 2009) ("Johnson owns land adjoining the proposed development. He may be adversely affected by the approval of a development that would have higher housing densities . . .").

Sufficient Injury. In addition to proximity, standing in land use cases also will depend on an allegation of sufficient injury. As the New York Court of Appeals put it in a 2014 decision, "In land use matters . . . petitioner 'must show that it would suffer direct harm, injury that is in some way different from that of the public at large.' . . ." *Association for a Better Long Island, Inc. v. N.Y. State Dept. of Envtl. Conservation,* 11 N.E.3d 188, 192 (N.Y. 2014). *See, e.g., Butters v. Hauser,* 960 P.2d 181 (Id. 1998) (neighboring landowner had standing to challenge ordinance amendment and conditional use permit authorizing a radio transmission tower because "the tower looms over her land" and, allegedly, the tower caused problems with her phones and compact disc player. *Compare Concerned Citizens for the Preservation of Watertown v. Planning and Zoning Comm'n,* 984 A.2d 72, 75 (Conn. Ct. App. 2009) (organization did not have standing to challenge the denial of an application to amend the town zoning regulations where "plaintiff did not present any evidence that the commission's decision specially and injuriously affected its specific personal or legal interest").

Plaintiffs must be prepared to prove the injury. Thus, in a 2015 Idaho Supreme Court case, plaintiffs sought to challenge a land use decision as violating the state open meetings law because it was made in a meeting that started at an earlier time than the time listed in the notice. Plaintiffs lacked standing because they made no attempt to even attend the meeting and only had their comments read into the record. *Arnold v. City of Stanley*, 345 P.3d 1008 (Idaho 2015). Similarly, a 2015 Pennsylvania decision found that a plaintiff lacked standing to challenge a variance allowing a sign to be digitalized where, although the plaintiff could see the sign, "she did not explain how illuminating the proposed sign would cause her injury or to what extent its illumination would affect her." *Armstead v. Zoning Bd. of Adjustment of Philadelphia*, 115 A.3d 390, 398 (Pa. Commw. Ct. 2015).

Economic Injury. An applicant, of course, will have standing to challenge a denial of its project because of the economic injury it will suffer from the denial. However, where the third party is an entity that is a competitor of a successful project applicant, that party may have difficulty showing the requisite interest to support standing. As the New Hampshire Supreme Court put it in rejecting a competitor's standing to challenge a variance, "An appeal of a ZBA [Zoning Board of Appeals] decision is not a weapon to be used to stifle business competition." *Hannaford Bros. Co. v. Town of Bedford*, 64 A.3d 951, 957 (N.H. 2013).

Thus, in *Oceanport Indus., Inc. v. Wilmington Stevedores, Inc.*, 636 A.2d 892, 906 (Del. 1994), the plaintiff stevedoring company did not have standing to contest the issuance of permits for a bulk transfer facility that were issued to a competing company. The statutes that plaintiff alleged to be violated were "designed to protect the environment, not economic interests." *Compare Save the Plastic Bag Coalition v. City of Manhattan Beach*, 254 P.3d 1005 (Cal. 2011) (association of plastic bag manufacturers had standing to challenge ban on distribution of plastic bags at point of sale). In *Kroenlein v. Eddington*, 35 P.3d 1207 (Wyo. 2001), the Wyoming Supreme Court drew the following distinction: "[A] party does not have standing to contest issuance of a liquor license by virtue of the party's status as a competitor. . . . A party does have standing as a resident even though he or she is a competitor. . . ."

Associational Standing. A citizen's organization may obtain standing either by showing that the organization itself has suffered injury or that its members have been injured. Courts have found standing where an association alleged that its members breathed the air near a proposed major expansion of a mill (*In re International Paper Co.*, 363 A.2d 235 (Me. 1976)); where members' views would be blocked by the challenged development, which would lower the members' property values (*Edgewater Beach Owners Ass'n, Inc, v, Walton County*, 833 So. 2d 215 (Fla. Ct. App. 2002)); and where the members would be subject to airplane and helicopter traffic from a nearby airbase (*Glengary-Gamlin Protective Ass'n, Inc. v. Bird*, 675 P.2d 344 (Idaho Ct. App. 1983)).

Thus, an association had standing to challenge a wind energy facility in Wyoming where one member of the association owned property bordering the facility, while another lived "near" the facility and complained about construction vehicles causing traffic and safety issues. *Northern Laramie Range Found. v. Converse County Bd. of County Comm'rs*, 290 P.3d 1063 (Wyo. 2012). A trade organization, such as a building association, also will have standing if its members will be individually harmed. *See, e.g., Miss. Manufactured Housing Ass'n v. Board of Alderman of the City of Canton*, 870 So. 2d 1189 (Miss. 2004) (manufactured housing association had standing to challenge a zoning ordinance that restricted manufactured housing where the ordinance would have an adverse economic impact on members who sold manufactured homes in the jurisdiction.)

Public Agencies. Public agency plaintiffs, such as municipalities seeking to challenge decisions by their neighbors, also must show they are aggrieved. In a major 2013 case, the Pennsylvania Supreme Court found that municipalities had standing to challenge a state law that preempted regulation of certain oil and gas operations associated with fracking. The court held that the aggrievement was interference with the municipalities' duties to protect the environment. *Robinson Twp., Washington County, PA v. Commonwealth of Pennsylvania*, 83 A.3d 901 (Pa. 2013). *See also City of Hickory Hills v. Village of Bridgeview*, 367 N.E.2d 1305 (Ill. 1977) (city had sufficient interest to sue and thus was a "person aggrieved" where it was required to furnish sewer and water facilities for the development in question).

Housing Litigation. In *Warth v. Seldon*, 422 U.S. 490 (1975), the Supreme Court held that a variety of plaintiffs, including a developer of low cost housing as well as private individuals who sought to live in such housing, had no standing to challenge the exclusionary zoning practices of a municipality. The Court found that they did not allege demonstrable, particularized injury. *See, e.g., Taliaferro v. Darby Twp. Zoning Bd.*, 458 F.3d 181, 190 (3d Cir. 2006) ("Appellants have failed to allege an injury in fact that is concrete, particularized, or actual in order to confer standing upon them in regard to a denial of equal treatment as a result of the Appellees' alleged conspiracy to block the construction of residential housing . . ."). However, in *Village of Arlington Heights v. Metro. Housing Dev. Corp.*, 429 U.S. 252 (1977), a case that came down two years after *Warth*, the Supreme Court found that both a developer of low cost housing and private individuals alleging that they were eligible for such housing had standing to challenge a zoning ordinance that prevented the construction of the housing on a specific parcel of land.

The courts of several large states have proved more willing than the U.S. Supreme Court to confer standing on plaintiffs in housing litigation. *See, e.g., Southern Burlington County N.A.A.C.P. v. Township of Mount Laurel* (reproduced as a principal case in Chapter 12). In *Stocks v. City of Irvine*, 170 Cal. Rptr. 724 (Ct. App. 1981), the court rejected *Warth* and concluded that nonresidents had standing to sue. It also noted that under the *Warth* test, the more restrictive a city's zoning becomes, the less likely a builder will propose a project and thus have standing.

Exhaustion of Administrative Remedies. Students also should be aware of a related principle that affects the right to judicial review of local land use decisions: the plaintiff must pursue all administrative procedures to their completion before a court will review the agency's actions. This principle, known as the doctrine of exhaustion of administrative remedies, is a fundamental tenet of administrative law and is covered in courses on that subject. For example, if the zoning administrator denies an applicant's request for permission to develop, but under state law or local ordinance the applicant may appeal the denial to a board of zoning appeals, he or she must take that administrative appeal.

The principal purpose of the exhaustion requirement is to allow local agencies to fully exercise their discretion and utilize their expertise before judicial review occurs. *See, e.g., Foutz v. City of South Jordan*, 100 P.3d 1171, 1174 (Utah 2004). (Exhaustion requirement evidences a legislative intent "to recognize the authority granted to municipal decision-making bodies.") In the absence of such an appeal, any request for judicial relief will ordinarily fail. *See, e.g., Queen Anne's Conservation, Inc. v. The County Commissioners of Queen Anne's County*, 855 A.2d 325 (Md. 2004) (litigation must be dismissed where plaintiff failed to appeal approval of development rights and responsibilities agreement to County Board of Appeals); *Borden v. Planning & Zoning Comm'n. of the Town of North Stonington*, 755 A.2d 224 (Conn. Ct. App. 2000) (abutting landowner required to exhaust administrative remedies by appealing planning and zoning commission approval to town zoning board of appeals). Exhaustion of administrative remedies is more fully discussed in Chapter 7.

C. JUDICIAL CONTROL OF LOCAL DISCRETION

The overarching question that the courts face is how to control local discretion while, at the same time, appropriately deferring to legislative decisions made by local elected officials. *See* Daniel R. Mandelker, Model Legislation for Land Use Decisions, 35 Urb. Law. 635 (Fall 2003) (noting that the Standard Zoning Enabling Act, published decades ago, "did not contemplate the extensive use of discretion that occurs today"). A key question is the scope of review that the court will apply to rezoning decisions.

■ ALBUQUERQUE COMMONS PARTNERSHIP v. CITY COUNCIL OF ALBUQUERQUE
184 P.3d 411 (N.M. 2008)

Bosson, Justice.

In *Miller v. City of Albuquerque,* 89 N.M. 503, 554 P.2d 665 (1976), this Court held that when a zoning authority rezones a piece of property to a more restrictive use (known as "downzoning"), the zone change must be justified by either a change in the surrounding community or a mistake in the original zoning. We later reaffirmed this rule in *Davis v. City of Albuquerque,* 98 N.M. 319, 648 P.2d 777 (1982), and applied it to a rezoning pursuant to a sector plan. In this case, the City of Albuquerque adopted a new sector plan that restricted the uses on Petitioner's property. Petitioner argues, and the district court agreed, that, in adopting this sector plan, the City downzoned Petitioner's property without complying with *Miller* and in violation of Petitioner's procedural due process rights. A jury also agreed with Petitioner and awarded damages under 42 U.S.C. §1983. . . .

From 1987 to 1998, Petitioner Albuquerque Commons Partnership ("ACP") held a long-term ground lease for the old St. Pius High School site in Albuquerque, located north of the Winrock Shopping Center. This property is part of an approximately 460-acre area designated by the City's Comprehensive Plan as the Uptown Sector, one of several urban centers in the city. When ACP leased the 28-acre parcel from the Archdiocese of Santa Fe, the zoning was governed by the 1981 Uptown Sector Plan, under which the majority of the 460 acres, including ACP's property, was zoned SU-3, with the periphery being zoned either SU-2 or R-1. "SU-3 zoning provides suitable sites for high-intensity mixed uses — commercial, office, service, and residential." . . .

From the time the City adopted the 1981 Uptown Sector Plan until it passed the 1995 amendments that are the subject of this suit, the City approved several suburban retail projects within the same area . . . The City also approved a zone change allowing Toys R Us to demolish office space and replace it with a new stand-alone "medium box" retail building. As we shall see, these projects would not have been allowable under the 1995 Uptown Sector Plan amendments.

In 1991, ACP decided to sell its leasehold, selecting Opus Southwest Corporation ("Opus") to assume development of the property. . . .

[O]n September 30, 1994, Opus submitted its . . . site plan . . . proposing a smaller, 17.90-acre low-density "big-box" retail project. This project was to be located entirely within the SU-3 zone and would not require any zone map amendments. . . . The Planning Department's initial reports to the EPC on the project stated that the retail uses were allowed by the 1981 Uptown Sector Plan. . . .

On February 6, 1995, the City Council passed a resolution placing a four-month moratorium on all development within the Uptown Sector. . . .

The [subsequently] proposed revisions split the existing SU-3 zone into two new sub-zones: the "Intense Core" and the "Outside of Intense Core," separated by the Loop Road. Though the zoning classification remained the same for the entire area, additional regulations applicable only to the Intense Core were significantly more restrictive than those under the 1981 Uptown Sector Plan or in the Outside of Intense Core. The newly-proposed Intense Core regulations prohibited free-standing retail, imposed limitations on the size of retail buildings, and required mixed uses, with retail comprising no more than 10 percent of space built on a site. Additionally, the Intense Core regulations required a specific density of uses, structured parking, and, significantly, construction of an entire project at once, without phasing to match construction demand. In contrast, the Outside of Intense Core regulations allowed retail uses to continue at existing density. Retail was limited to 10 percent of new space, but "redevelopment/ replacement of existing space" was exempted.

ACP's leased property was located entirely within the Intense Core zone. Only two other property owners owned land in the Intense Core, and ACP's property made up two-thirds of the affected land. Further, though all three tracts of land were vacant, only ACP had a pending site plan submitted to the City. As a practical matter, therefore, the new regulations affected primarily ACP. . . .

The City Council then held two public hearings on the 1995 Uptown Sector Plan and on June 19, 1995, the Council voted 7-0 in favor of adopting the amended sector plan. . . . Pursuant to the City's adoption of the 1995 Uptown Sector Plan, the EPC voted to defer consideration of Opus' site plan indefinitely because it did not comply with the revised sector plan. . . .

DISCUSSION . . .

NEW MEXICO LAW ON REZONING: DOWNZONING AND THE *MILLER* RULE

New Mexico courts use the term "downzoning" to describe rezoning to a more restrictive use. The term as it has been employed by our courts is essentially a term of art that implies a rezoning action instituted by someone other than the land-owner—most often the municipality itself—that is directed at a single parcel or a small number of parcels within a larger zone area, and that expands the restrictions on the use of the property. *See Commons II*, 2006-NMCA-143, ¶ 68, 140 N.M. 751, 149 P.3d 67 ("'Downzoning' is an informal word of art that almost never appears in the statutes or ordinances.") . . . Such a targeted rezoning action is also called a "piecemeal rezoning" and stands in contrast to a "comprehensive rezoning," which "affect[s] a substantial portion of land within the zoning jurisdiction belonging to many landowners."

New Mexico courts have often used the term "downzoning" as shorthand for those actions that require justification pursuant to the "change or mistake" rule and the zoning authority's own regulations for zoning amendments, which in this case are contained in the City's Resolution 270-1980. The "change or mistake" rule, adopted by this Court in *Miller* and reaffirmed in *Davis*, dictates that the proponent of a zoning change, in this instance the City, must show that such a change is justified due to either a change in conditions in the community or a mistake in the original zoning. . . . The rule evidences a concern over the stability of zoning regulations and a landowner's right to rely on existing zoning rules. [W]hile a property owner does not have a vested right in a particular zoning classification, before a piecemeal zoning change is implemented, due consideration must be given to whether such a change is justified, particularly when the zoning authority and not the landowner seeks to rezone a piece of property. . . .

Also applicable to zoning amendments are the City's own rules and policies set forth in Resolution 270-1980. . . . Resolution 270-1980 tracks the change or mistake rule. . . . The Resolution also recognizes an additional criterion that can justify a zoning amendment, stating that the proponent of the change may show that "a different use category is more advantageous to the community, as articulated in the Comprehensive Plan or other City master plan, even though (1) or (2) above do not apply." . . .

The enhanced procedures that are required to accompany proposed zoning changes directed at a small number of properties constitute the primary protection for the landowner. . . . Therefore, without adopting any absolute standards or mechanical tests, we recognize that a municipality may be able to justify an amendment that downzones a particular property by demonstrating that the change is "more advantageous to the community, as articulated in the Comprehensive Plan or other City master plan." The proof in such a case would have to show, at a minimum, that "(1) there is a public need for a change of the kind in question, and (2) that need will be best served by changing the classification of the particular piece of property in question as compared with other available property." *Fasano v. Bd. of County Comm'rs of Washington County*, 264 Or. 574, 507 P.2d 23, 28 (1973).

QUASI-JUDICIAL VERSUS LEGISLATIVE ZONING DECISIONS

The essence of ACP's challenge to the 1995 Uptown Sector Plan Intense Core restrictions is that ACP's property was singled out for a downzoning and the City failed to follow the proper procedures or comply with the requisite criteria in adopting those amendments. The nature of a particular zoning action as either legislative or quasi-judicial is determinative of the procedures that the zoning authority is required to follow in implementing that action. . . . [W]hile we use the labels "legislative" and "quasi-judicial" for the sake of convenience, the real question here is whether the City's adoption of the 1995 Uptown Sector Plan amendments was fair overall, affording ACP adequate due process of law.

The Court of Appeals aptly explained the differences between legislative and quasi-judicial actions as follows:

> [L]egislative action reflects public policy relating to matters of a permanent or general character, is not usually restricted to identifiable persons or groups, and is usually prospective; quasi-judicial action, on the other hand, generally involves a

determination of the rights, duties, or obligations of specific individuals on the basis of the application of currently existing legal standards or policy considerations of past or present facts developed at a hearing conducted for the purpose of resolving the particular interest in question.

Commons II, 2006-NMCA-143, ¶ 36, 140 N.M. 751, 149 P.3d 67. Small-scale zone changes to which the *Miller* rule and Resolution 270-1980 apply are necessarily quasi-judicial, not legislative, in nature. . . . Further . . . , such changes . . . require specific factual findings relating to the affected properties. . . .

Characterization of a zoning action as quasi-judicial carries with it important procedural consequences. Thus, when a zoning authority initiates a proposal to downzone a particular property, the zoning authority must afford enhanced procedural protections to landowners whose properties are the subject of the zone change. . . . Quasi-judicial zoning matters are not politics-as-usual as far as the municipal governing body is concerned. In such proceedings, the council does not sit as a mini-legislature . . . but instead must act like a judicial body bound by "ethical standards comparable to those that govern a court in performing the same function." *High Ridge Hinkle Joint Venture v. City of Albuquerque*, 119 N.M. 29, 40, 888 P.2d 475, 486 (Ct. App. 1994).

Therefore, in addition to the right to individual notice, interested parties in a quasi-judicial zoning matter "are entitled to an opportunity to be heard, to an opportunity to present and rebut evidence, to a tribunal which is impartial in the matter — i.e., having had no pre-hearing or ex parte contacts concerning the question at issue — and to a record made and adequate findings executed." *Fasano*, 507 P.2d at 30. The burden is on the proponent of the zone change to establish that the change is justified. *See South of Sunnyside Neighborhood League v. Bd. of Comm'rs of Clackamas County*, 280 Or. 3, 569 P.2d 1063, 1071 (1977) (en banc). While the specific procedures employed "must adhere to fundamental principles of justice and procedural due process," they are not required to comport with the same evidentiary and procedural standards applicable to a court of law. . . . The issue is one of procedural fairness and predictability that is adaptable to local conditions and capabilities. The use of terms such as cross-examination, fair and impartial tribunal, and the like, need not be interpreted in the same sense as it might be in an attempt to reform the judicial process. . . . In New Mexico, justification for small-scale zone changes is governed by the criteria set forth in *Miller* and in the municipality's own policies and procedures, which in this case are contained in Resolution 270-1980.

Regardless of the justification, the decision-making body should provide "a clear statement of what, specifically, [it] believes, after hearing and considering all the evidence, to be the relevant and important facts upon which its decision is based," and a full explanation of why those facts lead it to the decision it makes. *South of Sunnyside Neighborhood League*, 569 P.2d at 1076. This is critical for facilitating meaningful judicial review of the action . . .

THE CITY'S ARGUMENTS

[O]n advice of counsel, the City adopted the 1995 Uptown Sector Plan amendments in the form of a legislative proceeding, thereby limiting evidence, preventing cross-examination, and making no effort to provide ACP with an impartial tribunal by limiting *ex parte* contacts on the part of the council members.[3] Apart from the broad and conclusory "whereas" points set forth in the ordinance adopting the 1995 Uptown Sector Plan, the City made no findings at all . . .

ADOPTION OF THE 1995 UPTOWN SECTOR PLAN INTENSE CORE RESTRICTIONS WAS NOT A LEGISLATIVE ACT

[T]he Court of Appeals correctly observed that a downzoning does not necessarily occur, requiring quasi-judicial process, simply because only a small number of properties are impacted by the decision or "a particular parcel is in the mind of the zoning authority when it takes action." . . . That statement is true as far as it goes, although the narrower the focus of the zoning action, the more likely it is that *Miller* will be implicated. By the same token, the fact that policy decisions are involved does not necessarily mean that a zoning action does not effect a downzoning. "Large-scale decisions of specific applicability frequently, if not inevitably, require of the decision-maker both the creation and the application of policy." *Neuberger v. City of Portland*, 288 Or. 155, 603 P.2d 771, 776 (1979). Nor is a rezoning, that applies to more than a single parcel, necessarily legislative. . . . When a zoning action is *specifically designed* to affect a relatively small number of properties *and* does not apply to similarly situated properties in the surrounding area or city-wide, that action is quasi-judicial, not legislative. . . .

The 1995 Uptown Sector Plan Intense Core restrictions, did not apply city-wide, or to the other five urban centers in the city, or even throughout the Uptown SU-3 area. Rather, the restrictions were confined to only a small portion of the Uptown sector, comprising about six percent of the total area and affecting only three landowners, by far the largest being ACP. . . .

Further, it appears that the 1995 Uptown Sector Plan amendments were not simply designed "to clarify and strengthen the [1981 Uptown Sector Plan]," as the Court of Appeals held. . . . The plain language of the 1981 Uptown Sector Plan, the City's own construction of the 1981 Uptown Sector Plan, and prior City approvals under that plan treated *all* of the SU-3 zone in Uptown as a "suburban commercial" center with shopping centers and restaurants that could be built "to virtually any intensity." Indeed, as stated earlier, an initial staff report on the second site plan submitted by Opus acknowledged that "the zoning on this site plan allows the proposed retail uses." Moreover, the amendments, by not placing limitations on retail uses for redevelopment or replacement of existing developments, were tailored to affect only ACP — the only property owner in the Uptown sector with a pending site plan — while exempting existing businesses. . . .

The very fact that the City postponed a decision on ACP's proposal while it rushed the sector plan amendments through a legislative process leads to a fair inference that the 1995 Uptown Sector Plan was meant to *change* the former sector plan, not simply clarify it. . . .

---

3. As an example of the legislative-type lobbying that accompanied the passage of the 1995 Uptown Sector Plan amendments, Ron Nelson, President of the Uptown Association, called Councilor Vicki Perea after she had proposed amendments to the 1995 Uptown Sector Plan that would have eased the impact on ACP. Mr. Nelson encouraged Councilor Perea not to make amendments that would allow the Opus Plan to proceed and stated his belief that if she worked at it, Councilor Perea could get the four votes needed to pass the amendments favored by the Uptown Association. Councilor Perea then withdrew her proposed amendments. Such contacts and influence are common and appropriate in the normal legislative functioning of a city council. However, when a council sits in a quasi-judicial capacity, as it must to effect a downzoning, its members must be insulated from such contact. . . .

Regardless of how the City tries to construe its actions, substantial evidence at trial showed that the 1995 Uptown Sector Plan Intense Core restrictions were directed specifically towards ACP and were not public policy matters of a general character. Those changes amounted to a downzoning of ACP's property. . . . Thus, the City's adoption of the 1995 Uptown Sector Plan was the type of zoning action that New Mexico courts, as well as courts from other jurisdictions, have traditionally viewed as quasi-judicial in nature primarily because of the disparate impact on only a small number of landowners. . . .

The City has failed to show that the adoption of 1995 Uptown Sector Plan amendments was legislative in nature, or that because the amendments were text amendments they did not rezone ACP's property. There is no legitimate justification for the City's failure to afford the proper procedural protections or comply with the standards set forth in *Miller* and Resolution 270-1980. We hold that the City's decision lacked procedural fairness and did not comport with due process of law.

Notes and Comments

1. *Due Process and the Legislative-Adjudicative Distinction.* The distinction between quasi-legislative acts and quasi-adjudicative acts is fundamental to constitutional and administrative law. In *LC&S, Inc. v. Warren County Area Plan Comm'n*, 244 F.3d 601, 602-603 (7th Cir. 2001), Judge Posner opened his opinion with a discussion of the differences between the procedural rights associated with legislating as opposed to adjudicating:

> "Legislative due process" seems almost an oxymoron. Legislation is prospective in effect and, more important, general in its application. Its prospective character offers further, and considerable, protection to any individual or organization that might be the legislature's target by imposing costs on all others who are within the statute's scope. The prospect of such costs incites resistance which operates to protect what might otherwise be an isolated, vulnerable, politically impotent target of the legislature's wrath or greed. . . . The right to notice and a hearing, the essence of [due process], are substitutes for the prospectivity and generality that protect citizens from oppression by legislators and thus from the potential tyranny of electoral majorities. . . .

What is the test for determining whether an action generally will be deemed quasi-adjudicative or quasi-legislative? What are likely to be the most important facts in determining whether the approval of a specific zoning amendment is deemed quasi-legislative or quasi-judicial? Consider the discussion of the Supreme Court of Connecticut in *Jewett City Savings Bank v. Town of Franklin*, 907 A.2d 67, 70 (Conn. 2006):

> A zoning commission's legislative decision is a policy decision that involves the exercise of broad discretion. *See Malafronte v. Planning & Zoning Board*, 155 Conn. 205, 209, 230 A.2d 606 (1967) ("[t]he discretion of a legislative body, because of its constituted role as a formulator of public policy, is much broader than that of an administrative board, which serves a quasi-judicial function"). Conversely, a zoning commission acts in an administrative capacity when its function is "to determine whether [a] proposed use is one which satisfies the standards set forth in the [zoning] regulations and the statutes." (Internal quotation marks omitted.)

The Maryland Court of Special Appeals also explained the difference: Adjudicative facts usually answer the questions "of who did what, where, when, how, with what motive or intent," while legislative facts "do not concern the immediate parties but are general facts." *Armstrong v. Mayor and City Council of Baltimore*, 906 A.2d 415, 423 (Md. Ct. Sp. App. 2006).

Are these formulations helpful?

2. Fasano *and Its Progeny I.* The leading case adopting a rule that small-tract rezonings are quasi-adjudicative is *Fasano v. Board of County Comm'rs*, 507 P.2d 23 (Or. 1973). A cornerstone of that decision was the court's finding that the zoning change must be proved to be in conformance with the jurisdiction's comprehensive plan. The court adopted a kind of "sliding scale" test: as the degree of zoning change increases, the burden of showing that the potential impact upon the area was carefully considered and weighed will also increase.

Both the *Fasano* decision and the much newer *Albuquerque Commons Partnership* decision are premised on the concept that certain types of rezonings are not really legislative in nature, and thus not deserving of the normal judicial deference given by the courts to legislative actions. Do you agree? Or is there something wrong — to use the term in *Albuquerque Commons Partnership* — with allowing "politics as usual" for such decisions? What do you make of the lobbying described in footnote 3 of the case?

3. Fasano *and Its Progeny II.* The *Fasano* holding has received some support. The most notable recent decision is the Florida Supreme Court's holding in *Board of County Comm'rs of Brevard County v. Snyder*, 627 So. 2d 469 (Fla. 1993). *See also Louisville and Jefferson County Planning Comm'n v. Schmidt*, 83 S.W.3d 449, 455 (Ky. 2002) ("While zoning is an inherently legislative power . . . it may at times be legislative in nature and at other times adjudicatory in nature, depending upon the nature of the zoning change"); *Anne Arundel Co. v. Bell*, 113 A.3d 639, 649 (Md. 2015) ("the piecemeal zoning process is decided unlegislative in nature"); *Quaker Court Ltd. Liab. Co. v. Board of County Comm'rs of the County of Jefferson*, 109 P.3d 1027, 1031 (Colo. Ct. App. 2004) (some site-specific rezonings are "considered quasi-judicial for purposes of judicial review"). Most states, however, have rejected the *Fasano* rule and continue to treat all rezonings as legislative in nature. *Childs v. Hancock County Bd. of Supervisors*, 1 So. 3d 855, 859 (Miss. 2009) ("The classification of property for zoning purposes is a legislative rather than a judicial matter"); *Cabana v. Kenai Peninsula Borough*, 21 P.3d 833, 836 (Alaska 2001) ("[W]e have chosen . . . to treat small-scale rezonings as legislative decisions"). *See* Charles L. Siemon and Julie P. Kendig, Judicial Review of Local Government Decisions: "Midnight in the Garden of Good and Evil," 20 Nova L. Rev. 707, 729-730 (1996) (estimating that, as of that time, the *Fasano*-type approach was used in a maximum of 15 states).

The reasoning in these opinions varies. For example, in *Margolis v. District Court*, 638 P.2d 297, 304 (Colo. 1981), the Colorado Supreme Court stated:

> It appears only logical that since the original act of zoning is legislative, the amendatory act of rezoning is likewise legislative even though the procedures may entail notice and hearing which characterize a quasi-judicial proceeding. Essentially, the city council ultimately amends the zoning ordinance or denies the amendment, a legislative function.

See also Hampton v. Richland County, 357 S.E.2d 463, 467 (S.C. Ct. App. 1987) (treating the rezoning of a single tract as anything other than a legislative act would invite countless challenges to the rezoning of single tracts, and the zoning body's authority to take legislative action "would likely be debased"); *Petersen v. Riverton City*, 243 P.3d 1261, 1265 (Utah 2010) (adjudicative actions such as deciding variances "are not of the same character as the Petersens' request to amend an existing zoning ordinance . . .").

Are these convincing reasons for rejecting *Fasano*?

One noted scholar has stated that the political nature of land use disputes argues against treating them as quasi-judicial. Michael Asimow, Due Process in Local Land Use Decision Making, 31 SPG Admin. & Reg. L. News 15, 16 (Spring 2006) ("[W]e delude ourselves if we think that heavily politicized land use planning disputes can be treated like the sort of judicialized trials that are mandated in other [procedural due process] contexts"). Do you agree? Or is the political nature of land use disputes precisely why the *Fasano* holding was a good one?

4. *The Consequences of Adjudicating.* The determination that a zoning decision is quasi-adjudicative has important effects both on local governments and on courts undertaking judicial review. In practical terms, such a decision raises a host of issues regarding the procedures that the local government now must follow (issues that have been and will continue to be the subject of litigation):

a. Opposing parties may now insist that they have a right to call witnesses under oath and to cross-examine witnesses for the applicant.

b. Decision makers such as members of a city council will likely be barred from meeting, outside of the hearing process, with proponents or opponents of zoning changes that are quasi-adjudicative.

c. If the parties to a quasi-judicial zone change are entitled to an "impartial decision maker," does *Fasano* mean that decision makers who have accepted campaign contributions cannot vote on the matter?

d. The local government probably will have to formalize its hearing procedures, such as by keeping a verbatim transcript of all zoning hearings.

e. Finally, the local government decision makers will likely have to adopt "findings of fact" for every quasi-adjudicative zone change.

See, e.g., Guilford Fin. Services, LLC v. City of Brevard, 563 S.E.2d 27, 41 (N.C. Ct. App. 2002) (setting forth the "essential elements" of a fair trial as (1) the party whose rights are being determined must be given the opportunity to offer evidence, cross-examine adverse witnesses, inspect documents, and offer evidence in explanation and rebuttal; (2) findings must be based on sworn statements; and (3) findings of fact must be supported by competent, material and substantial evidence).

The right to cross-examine, however, is not unlimited. In *People ex rel. Klaren v. Village of Lisle*, 781 N.E.2d 223, 235 (Ill. 2002), the Illinois Supreme Court emphasized that "a municipality may reasonably restrict the right of cross-examination based on subject matter." Considerations include the complexity of the issue, whether the witness possesses special expertise, whether the testimony reflects a matter of taste or personal opinion or concerns a disputed issue of fact, and "the degree to which the witness's testimony relates to the factors to be considered in approving the proposal." *Id.* at 236. *See also Carrillon Cmty. Res. v. Seminole County*, 45

So. 3d 7, 10 (Fla. Ct. App. 2010) (rejecting assertion that all participants in quasi-judicial proceedings should be allowed to cross-examine witnesses). Nor is strict adherence to the rules of evidence required. *Bulloch County Bd. of Commissioners*, 773 S.E.2d 37, 39 (Ga. Ct. App. 2015).

5. *Small Tract Plan Amendments.* The adoption of comprehensive general plans, like comprehensive zoning ordinances, is a quasi-legislative act. *Friends of Frederick Co. v. Town of New Market*, 120 A.3d 769, 780 (Md. Ct. App. 2015). But if the jurisdiction follows *Fasano*, how should it treat small plan amendments? The Florida Supreme Court addressed this issue in *Coastal Dev. of North Florida, Inc. v. City of Jacksonville Beach*, 788 So. 2d 204 (Fla. 2001). The court treated the amendment as legislative. It reasoned that, because the comprehensive plan is a fundamental policy decision, "[a]ny proposed change to that established policy likewise is a policy decision." *Id.* at 209. It distinguished small zoning changes on the ground that "a proposed zoning change . . . must be consistent" with the future land use map, "thus requiring policy application instead of policy reformulation." *Id.* Are you convinced? If a state has a consistency statute, under this logic wouldn't all zone changes — large or small — be subject to the plan, and thus "policy application"? *See* Bernard R. Appleman, Can Florida's Legislative Standard of Review for Small-Scale Land Use Amendments Be Justified?, 24 UCLA J. Envtl. L.& Pol'y 305 (2005-06) (criticizing *Coastal*).

6. *Ex Parte Contacts.* In some cases, the jurisdiction has unquestionably acted in a quasi-judicial manner, such as when it is granting subdivision approvals or conditional use permits. In those cases, are city council members free to receive ex parte telephone calls from constituents? In a post-*Fasano* Oregon case, *Neuberger v. City of Portland*, 607 P.2d 722 (Or. 1980), the Oregon Supreme Court held that *Fasano* "should not be read as adopting a mechanical rule that any ex parte contacts touching on a matter before a tribunal acting in a quasi-judicial capacity renders the tribunal, or its affected members, unable to act in that matter." *Id.* at 725. The issue, said the court, is not whether there were any ex parte contacts, but whether there was bias. More recently, an Oregon court of appeals found that *Fasano* called for a "high bar for disqualification" and cited Oregon courts as "repeatedly emphasiz-[ing] the unique political nature of elected, local officials making adjudicatory decisions." *Columbia Riverkeeper v. Clatsop County*, 341 P.3d 790, 808 (Ore. Ct. App. 2014). Do you agree?

7. *Should the Courts Intervene?* The *Fasano* holding is premised on concerns about the legitimacy of small tract rezonings when they are treated as legislative in nature. But even if you assume that there are valid concerns about the appropriateness of treating small tract rezonings in the same fashion as other types of legislative decision making at the local government level, you must consider whether a judicially crafted solution — treating such decisions as quasi-adjudicative — is the best response. Are state legislatures better equipped to consider and respond to such problems? What would you suggest?

The nature of such a legislatively devised procedure drove the decision in *Alford v. Boston Zoning Comm'n*, 996 N.E.3d 883 (Mass. Ct. App. 2013). In that case, plaintiffs challenged the approval of an Institutional Master Plan (IMP) for Boston College. They argued that the approval was quasi-judicial and, based on that contention, that the approval violated several procedural restrictions, including *ex parte* communications outside of the hearing process. They cited *Mullin v.*

Planning Bd. of Brewster, 456 N.E.2d 780 (Mass. Ct. App. 1983), in which the court held that the approval of a planned unit development was quasi-adjudicatory.

The court rejected the argument, in part because the IMP process was designed to *avoid* the previous situation in which Boston's numerous universities and hospitals had to seek individual use permits for expansions or changes. The court also found it significant that the procedures for the IMP process allowed unsworn statements by interested parties.

8. *The Assault on the Presumption.* As noted in the discussion on zoning in Chapter 2, the courts have traditionally accorded land use regulations a strong presumption of validity. *See, e.g., Harris Bank of Hinsdale v. County of Kendall,* 625 N.E.2d 845, 848 (Ill. 1994) ("A zoning ordinance is presumptively valid, the party contesting the zoning ordinance has the burden of proof, and the party may overcome the presumption of validity only by clear and convincing evidence."). Can *Fasano* be seen as a means of lessening or abolishing the presumption in a large segment of land use cases? Other commentators have suggested that the presumption should be reconsidered. *See* Daniel R. Mandelker & A. Dan Tarlock, Shifting the Presumption of Constitutionality in Land-Use Law, 24 Urb. Law. 1 (1992) (arguing that the traditional presumption should be changed).

If the assault on the presumption of validity is successful, will the amount of litigation over land use decisions become excessive? Will there be any real difference in the outcomes of the litigation? In how local governments approach their land use decision making?

9. *Findings.* Another vehicle employed by some courts to police the rationality of land use decisions is the requirement that local governments make findings to explain their quasi-adjudicatory decisions. *See Anderson House LLC v. Mayor and City Council of Rockville,* 939 A.3d 116, 127 n.17 (Md. 2008) (piecemeal zoning requires "[w]ritten findings of fact and conclusions of law explicating the reasons for the body's decision, expressed in terms of the statutory factors applying to the type of decision . . .").

In *Topanga Ass'n for a Scenic Community v. County of Los Angeles,* 522 P.2d 12 (Cal. 1974), the California Supreme Court ruled that a city or county "must set forth findings to bridge the analytic gap between the raw evidence and ultimate decision or order." *Id.* at 17. The court declared that such findings "direct the reviewing court's attention to the analytic route the administrative agency traveled from evidence to action." According to the court, such findings (1) conduce the administrative body to draw legally relevant subconclusions supportive of its ultimate decision; (2) facilitate orderly analysis and minimize the likelihood that the agency will randomly leap from evidence to conclusions; (3) allow the reviewing court to trace and examine the agency's mode of analysis; (4) enable the parties to determine whether and on what basis they should seek judicial review; and (5) serve a "public relations" function by helping to persuade the parties that administrative decision making is careful, reasoned, and equitable. *Id.* at 18-19. Another obvious purpose of findings is to aid the court in judicial review. *Broward County v. G.B.V. Int'l, Ltd.,* 787 So. 2d 838, 846 (Fla. 2001) ("We note the Commission did little to facilitate judicial review or to bolster its own decision; it made no findings, stated no formal reason for its decision, and issued no written order.").

Which of these separate functions that the findings requirement allegedly serves are realistic, and which are more theoretical than practical?

10. *Litigating a Findings Case.* In *Parsons v. District of Columbia Bd. of Zoning Adjustment*, 61 A.3d 650 (D.C. Ct. App. 2013), the court remanded a decision so the board could state findings of fact and conclusions of law. From the plaintiff's perspective, why would it be worth expending resources to bring a case in which the allegation is that the findings were insufficient? Presumably, the city would merely readopt its decision with new findings that meet the legal requirements. Or can you think of other strategic reasons that might justify such litigation? Note that in *Levi Family P'ship, L.P. v. City of Los Angeles*, 193 Cal. Rptr. 3d 584, 590 (Ct. App. 2015), the court held that the *Topanga* decision, discussed in the previous note, does not bar the agency from stating findings in the language of the ordinance and does not oblige the agency to support them with sub-findings. Does that decision tell you anything about how courts view cases challenging the adequacy of findings?

Can a city on remand adopt legally adequate findings? Or are the proceedings vitiated such that the entire hearing process must be re-started?

11. *Distracted Decision Makers.* Procedural due process assumes that the decision maker will consider and decide the evidence. But what does it mean to "consider" the evidence? In an unpublished California decision, the Court described the "hearing" as follows:

> [E]ight council members — three of whom were absent — were not in their seats. Only two council members were visibly paying attention. Four others might have been paying attention, although they engaged themselves with other activities, including talking with aides, eating, and reviewing paperwork.
>
> One minute into LSHS's presentation, a council member began talking on his cell phone and two council members, one of whom had been paying attention when the hearing opened, started talking to each other. A minute later, two other council members struck up their own private conversation. Three minutes into his presentation, LSHS's counsel complained "it doesn't appear that too many people are paying attention," an observation the videotape verifies, as only a few council members were sitting in their seats not talking to others.

Lacy St. Hospitality Serv., Inc. v. City of Los Angeles, 22 Cal. Rptr. 3d 805, 808 (Cal. Ct. App. 2004). The hearing was quasi-judicial. Did the decision makers give the applicant a fair hearing?

D. ETHICS AND FAIRNESS

Given the economic interests at stake in local land use decisions, as well as the fact that those decisions can shape an area for the foreseeable future, it should not surprise you that important ethical questions can arise in the land use process. One set of issues revolves around the question of whether political campaign contributions skew the local decision-making process. Another involves the ethical obligations that lawyers and planners involved in the process may have toward their clients and toward the public.

■ VILLAGES, LLC v. ENFIELD PLANNING AND ZONING COMMISSION

89 A.3d 405 (2014), appeal dismissed as improvidently granted, 127 A.3d 998 (2015)

LAVINE, J.

The record discloses the following facts and procedural history. On or about May 21, 2009, the plaintiff filed an application for a special use permit and an application for an open space subdivision consisting of thirty-eight residential housing lots situated on sixty-four acres of land in an R–44 residential district in Enfield. In Enfield, an open space subdivision in an R–44 district is permitted only by special use permit. . . . The commission denied both applications.

The plaintiff appealed from the denials to the trial court. . . .

The court found that . . . the plaintiff's allegations of bias and ex parte communication arose from the actions of Lori Longhi, a member of the commission. More specifically, the court found that Longhi took part in the hearing on the plaintiff's applications, played a significant role in the deliberations, and voted to deny the plaintiff's applications. Longhi had been a social friend of one of the plaintiff's owners, Jeannette Tallarita, and her husband, Patrick Tallarita, a former mayor of Enfield. There was a falling out among the friends, and the court found that Longhi was biased against Patrick Tallarita, who represented the plaintiff at the hearing before the commission. The court also found that Longhi engaged in an ex parte communication regarding the applications.

The court found two instances that gave rise to the plaintiff's claim of bias on Longhi's part. Prior to the events at issue here, Longhi accused Tallarita of using his influence as mayor to affect the outcome of commission decisions. Longhi's accusation led to the end of their social relationship. The plaintiff did not bring this matter to the attention of the commission prior to the public hearing, as Tallarita did not want to anger members of the commission . . . Because the plaintiff in the present case failed to raise Longhi's bias predicated on her falling out with Tallarita prior to or during the commission's hearing, the court found that the commission had no opportunity to rebut a claim of bias and held that the plaintiff could not raise the claim on appeal in the trial court.

The court, however, found that an incident in which Longhi stated that "she wanted [Tallarita] to suffer the same fate of denial by the commission that she had suffered" was a different matter. At trial, Anthony DiPace testified that Longhi had stated to him that the commission, when it previously considered an application that she had submitted, had "screwed her" and treated her unfairly when it denied that application. She was unhappy with Tallarita, who was then mayor, because he did not intervene on her behalf. She stated in the presence of DiPace that she wanted Tallarita to suffer the same fate, i.e., that the commission deny the plaintiff's applications. Tallarita did not become aware of Longhi's statement regarding the fate of the plaintiff's applications until after the commission had closed the public hearing. The court found that Longhi's comments were blatantly biased toward Tallarita and should not be tolerated. The court also found that it had not been possible for the plaintiff to bring Longhi's comments regarding Tallarita to the attention of the commission because he learned of them after the hearing had closed and the commission had denied the plaintiff's applications.

Credibility was a deciding factor in the court's decision regarding Longhi's ex parte communication. Tallarita, DiPace, and Bryon Meade testified during the trial. The court found that each of the men was a credible witness. Longhi also testified at trial, but the court found that her testimony was filled with denials of the allegations and concluded that her "comments did not ring true." The court found that Meade, a representative of the Hazardville Water Authority, testified with confidence that Longhi had met with him in person regarding the plaintiff's applications during the first week of October, 2009. Longhi testified, however, that Meade must have been confused because she met with him regarding another property. The court stated that Longhi's testimony was just not credible. . . .

In adjudicating the plaintiff's appeals, the court reviewed the transcript of the commission's October 15, 2009 meeting when it considered the plaintiff's applications. It found that the transcript was twenty-three pages long and that Longhi's comments appeared on every page but one, and that on most pages, Longhi's comments were the most lengthy. Her comments raised many negative questions about the plaintiff's applications. Moreover, in offering her comments, she cited her experience as an appraiser. The court found that Longhi dominated the meeting and that she intended to have a major effect on the commission's deliberations and subsequent votes. The court found clear and egregious bias on Longhi's part, and that her impact on the commission's deliberations and votes alone were reason to sustain the plaintiff's appeal.

Longhi's ex parte communication related to the issue of whether there was sufficient water pressure to furnish the fire department with enough water to extinguish a fire at the subdivision. After reviewing the transcript of the October 15, 2012 hearing, the court found that Longhi's arguments regarding the fire flows and water pressure were "intense" and were matters that she had discussed with Meade. The court also found that she expressed her concerns in a negative manner. In addition, it found that the commission's discussion concerning fire flow and water pressure was substantial and that those issues were the reason that the plaintiff's applications were denied. . . .

"A claim of bias must be raised in a timely manner. . . ."

We agree the bias predicated on the demise of the Longhi–Tallarita friendship alone was waived by the plaintiff. The record before the trial court and this court is devoid of any fact other than that Longhi and Tallarita were no longer on friendly terms. Without more, any claim of bias on Longhi's part, would have amounted to speculation. . . . We cannot say the same, however, with respect to Longhi's statement regarding the fate of the plaintiff's applications made to DiPace.

The timing and subject of the statements Longhi made to DiPace remove that incident of bias from the ambit of the *Moraski* waiver rule. DiPace testified that in his presence, in 2006 or 2007, Longhi stated with respect to an application before the commission that she was "being screwed over by the town." Longhi, according to DiPace's testimony, was angry because Tallarita was not helping her and that she hoped "someday that he would get screwed over by the town." At trial, Tallarita testified that DiPace told him about Longhi's statements after the commission had denied the plaintiff's applications. Once the public hearing had been denied, there was no avenue, other than on appeal, for the plaintiff to raise Longhi's bias. More importantly, Longhi's statements that DiPace heard were related directly to the applications being considered by the commission. Those statements demonstrated that she had prejudged the plaintiff's applications before the commission. . . .

II

The commission's second claim is that the court's findings that a member of the commission engaged in an ex parte communication with respect to the plaintiff's applications and that the plaintiff had not waived its claim by failing promptly to bring said communication to the attention of the commission are clearly erroneous. We disagree. . . .

The court found that Longhi met with Meade of the Hazardville Water Company in early October, 2009. The commission claims that the court's finding is clearly erroneous because Longhi testified that Meade must be confused because she met with him at another time with respect to another property. The court found that Meade testified with confidence about the incident and that Longhi was not a credible witness.

We have reviewed the transcript of Meade's testimony in the trial court. On direct examination, Meade testified, in part, as follows:

A. Yes, I was contacted by [Longhi].
Q. And do you recall about when that occurred?
A. Early October of 2009. Probably the first week, I don't know the exact date.
Q. Okay. And do you recall what she was contacting you about in relation to the subdivision?
A. Well, the meeting — I don't have a real clear recollection of the meeting, but I did put it in writing in an e-mail to Dave Frederick what it was about. And after reading the e-mail that I wrote it refreshed my memory that it had to do with fire flows and water pressures for the development.

On cross-examination, Mead testified, in part, as follows:

Q. Do you have a specific recollection of being in a conference room on that matter?
A. I have so many meetings with so many people I don't. The recollection is not real clear because I deal with a lot of developers and things. But what refreshed my memory was looking through my file on that project, and I did write the e-mail that I had the meeting. So you know, I wouldn't put something in. . . .

On the basis of our review of the record, we conclude that there was evidence in the record, to support the court's finding that Longhi spoke with Meade about the plaintiff's application in early October, 2009. . . .

We conclude, therefore, that the court's finding that the plaintiff had not waived the claim of ex parte communication was not clearly erroneous.

III

The commission's third claim is that the court's findings that the bias of one member of the commission deprived the plaintiff of a fair, honest, and legal determination and that the commission had not sustained its burden to demonstrate that the ex parte communication was harmless were clearly erroneous. We do not agree. . . .

It is well settled that that "[a]n ex parte communication raises a rebuttable presumption of prejudice. Once the plaintiff has shown that an improper ex parte communication has occurred, the burden of showing that the communication was harmless shifts to the party seeking to uphold the validity of the zoning commission's decision." *Daniel v. Zoning Commission,* supra, 35 Conn. App. at 597, 645 A.2d 1022.

In this case, the plaintiff met its burden to prove that Longhi had an ex parte communication with Meade regarding its applications. . . .

The commission's argument on appeal here is that the plaintiff failed to present any evidence that Longhi's comments influenced the votes of the other members of the commission. We disagree. The court reviewed the transcript of the hearing the commission held on October 15, 2009, to consider and vote on the plaintiff's applications. It found that Longhi had actively participated in the discussion and, in fact, dominated the discussion. On the basis of our review of the record, we conclude that the court's finding that Longhi influenced the other members of the commission was not improper. In conclusion, the plaintiff did not receive the fair hearing to which it was entitled, and we thus affirm the judgments of the trial court.

Notes and Comments

1. *Prejudgment and Adjudicative Actions.* If the decision by the local government is legislative in nature, no requirement exists that the decision makers be impartial. Thus, city council members are free to meet ex parte with one side to a disputed land issue, plot strategy, announce their position publicly, and seek to influence other votes on the council. These types of political activities are considered a routine and even a commendable part of the political process.

In contrast, where the decision of the local government is quasi-judicial in nature, a quite different model of procedure applies. Due process guarantees the parties a right to a fair hearing. As a California appellate court put it, "when functioning in such an adjudicatory capacity, the city council must be 'neutral and unbiased.' . . ." *Woody's Group, Inc. v. City of Newport* Beach, 183 Cal. Rptr. 3d 318, 324 (Cal. Ct. App. 2015). The *Villages* case illustrates two types of potential violations: bias and ex parte contacts related to the merits of the matter before the local body.

As to ex parte contacts, the key is disclosure. Courts may not be willing to invalidate proceedings on the basis of an ex parte contact if the contact is disclosed to the other parties and they are given a chance to respond. *See McPherson Landfill, Inc. v. Board of County Commissioners of Shawnee County,* 49 P.3d 522, 533 (Kan. 2002) ("With respect to the ex parte communications [regarding a use permit for a landfill] . . . the parties must be informed of the evidence submitted for consideration and must be provided an opportunity to respond and rebut the evidence."). Other courts look for prejudice before invaliding the decision. *Fitandes v. City of Saco,* 113 A.3d 1088 (Me. 2015) (city planner inappropriately sent an email to Zoning Board of Appeal, not part of the record, in which he disparaged the plaintiff, but there was no evidence of bias on the part of the Board).

Furthermore, conflicts of interest or bias on the part of the decision maker may invalidate the decision. Thus, a decision maker may be disqualified if he or she has a financial or personal interest that may be directly affected by the decision or has prejudged the issues, as evidenced by statements made before the matter was decided. *See G.L. v. State Ethics Comm'n,* 17 A.3d 445 (Pa. Commw. Ct. 2011) (after restaurant project was approved, petitioner became involved in working on the project and signed the documents that essentially established that the restaurant's final plans complied with all the conditions placed on the project, thereby engaging in official business on which he had a conflict of interest).

Finally, the normal rules of ethics apply regarding attorneys who may have conflicts of interest. *See Kane Properties, LLC v. City of Hoboken*, 68 A.3d 1274 (N.J. 2013) (attorney who represented party earlier in land use proceeding acted improperly by failing to fully recuse himself when he later became city attorney).

2. *Close Calls.* Situations in which allegations of prejudgment or bias can arise are manifold and often require the courts to make close judgment calls. For example, in *Marris v. City of Cedarburg*, 498 N.W.2d 842, 848 (Wis. 1993), the chairperson of a city board of zoning appeals, which was considering a claim of nonconforming use status, declared that the applicant's position was a "legal loophole" in need of "closing" and suggested that the members of the board "get [the applicant] on the Leona Helmsley rule." (The "Leona Helmsley rule" presumably had to do with the late Ms. Helmsley's well-publicized tax problems. *See United States v. Helmsley*, 760 F. Supp. 338 (S.D.N.Y. 1991), *aff'd*, 963 F.2d 1522 (2d Cir. 1992); Leona Helmsley Is Found Guilty of Evading Taxes, Wall St. J., Aug. 31, 1989.) The court found that "[t]aken together, these statements overcome the presumption of honesty and integrity that would ordinarily be applied" and that the phrase "get her" constituted prejudgment and a desire to prosecute. *Id.* at 849.

What if an official running for office states that he is "absolutely against" a proposal and, after the election, the proposal comes up for a vote? Does that automatically disqualify the official? The court thought not in *Davisco Foods Int'l, Inc. v. Gooding County*, 118 P.3d 116 (Idaho 2005). The court found it significant that the statement was made three years before and was included in an article in which the official was not directly quoted.

In another case, the trial court found that a council member "took it upon himself to further the cause of one party over another in his unabashed affinity for Champlin's position and disdain for that of the town's. In tandem his statements to town officials concerning Champlin's entitlement to expansion and his criticism of the town and its residents for what he perceived as their naivete in resisting development" overcame his presumed status as an honest negotiator. *Champlin's Realty Associates v. Tikoian*, 989 A.2d 427, 445 (R.I. 2010). Perhaps the outcome is correct. On the other hand, decision makers are entitled to react to the evidence. If you were appearing before an official like this one, wouldn't you rather have an idea of those reactions during the hearing?

3. *In the Family.* Issues arising from familial, employment, or social relationships often form the basis of ethics disputes. In *De Paolo v. Town of Ithaca*, 288 A.D.2d 68 (N.Y. Ct. App. 1999), Cornell University sought and received zoning approvals to implement a new cooling system on the campus. According to the plaintiff, four members of the town board had undisclosed conflicts of interest. One board member and the spouse of another were employees of Cornell. Another board member was a graduate student. The fourth board member was married to a Cornell retiree. The court held that there was no conflict of interest. Among other things, neither of the employees' work involved the cooling project. Are you convinced?

Compare Randolph v. Brigantine Planning Bd., 963 A.2d 1224, 1233 (N.J. Super. A.D. 2009). Here the chairwoman of the board owned a house with and lived with Doran, an engineer whose employee reviewed applications for the board. The court held that a conflict existed because "a citizen could perceive that [the chair-woman's] relationship with Doran could impair her independent judgment when considering" the advice of Doran's employee. Does this outcome seem correct to you? Finally, in *Haggerty v. Red Bank Borough Zoning Bd. of Adjustment*, 897 A.2d 1094 (N.J. Super. App. Div. 2006), the vice-chair of the board of adjustment was the acting chairperson of a hearing. Her father was "of counsel" to the applicant's law firm, although he did not personally appear or act in the matter. Should this be enough to disqualify the chair? The court held disqualification was mandated, noting that the acting chairperson's "independent status does not sever her family ties and thereby eliminate the conflict," and rejecting the trial court's conclusion that the conflict was "remote and speculative."

4. *Participating in an "Individual Capacity."* In *Rehoboth Art League, Inc. v. Board of Adjustment*, 991 A.2d 1163 (Del. 2010), an applicant sought to demolish a building and replace it. The decision came before the Board of Adjustment. During the proceeding, a town commissioner participated in his "individual capacity as a property owner," opposing the application but explaining that his views did not represent those of the town. After the application was denied, the applicant complained that its due process rights were violated because the town commissioner had the right to approve and remove members of the Board of Adjustment. What would you hold?

5. *Structural Bias.* Some observers have long suggested that local zoning boards are inherently biased in favor of development by virtue of the individuals appointed to those boards (*e.g.*, realtors, who might favor development as a means of furthering their economic interests). A recent study found that, "while some individual boards may be tilted toward development interests, overall the data suggests that there is only partial bias in that direction." Jerry L. Anderson and Erin Sass, Is the Wheel Unbalanced? A Study of Bias on Zoning Boards, 36 Urb. Law. 447, 467 (Summer 2004). It found that "direct influence positions" (e.g., "jobs that are likely to be directly impacted by zoning decisions") amounted to about 30 percent of the membership. *Id.* at 466. Is that number so large that statutory reform is necessary?

6. *Lobbying or Illegal "Political Activity"?* In *In re Convery*, 765 A.2d 724 (N.J. 2001), Convery represented a developer seeking zoning approvals from a township. He was a former mayor of that township and knew the political players. Convery took a series of political actions, including offering to help a politician's son obtain permanent employment with the county if the father and son would help obtain favorable votes from two zoning board members. The New Jersey Supreme Court upheld discipline imposed upon Convery for his actions.

Where, exactly, did the lawyer go "over the line" in his advocacy? Is what he did any different from the normal "exchange of favors" that is part and parcel of political life? Was the core of the ethical violation that the proceeding was a quasi-judicial one? If so, would the outcome have been different if the client had sought a rezoning?

7. *Contributions and Influence.* Do you think that local council members are actually influenced by campaign contributions? Or is it a case of developers and others contributing to politicians who already hold beliefs and attitudes toward development that are similar to theirs? You should know that, at the local government level, campaign contributions by development interests can constitute a significant percentage of all the contributions given to local candidates. Is there any way to really tell what influence the contributions have?

8. *Disclosure vs. Disqualification.* One case to directly raise the issue of the effect of campaign contributions was the California Supreme Court's decision in *Woodland Hills Residents Ass'n v. City Council*, 609 P.2d 1029, 26 Cal. 3d 938 (1980). The plaintiff, a homeowner's association, challenged the city's approval of a subdivision, contending that certain council members should have been disqualified from voting on the subdivision because the developer had made political contributions to campaign committees controlled by the council members. The plaintiffs argued that they were denied a "fair hearing" within the meaning of the applicable statute because the campaign contribution inevitably results in an appearance of bias.

The court rejected the claim, first noting that to disqualify a city council member because the developer made a constitutionally protected campaign contribution "would threaten constitutionally protected political speech and associational freedoms." 609 P.2d at 1033. The court also held that the state had opted for disclosure of campaign contributions, through the passage of the state Political Reform Act, rather than disqualification when a matter involving the donor comes before the local body. The fundamental policy question that you must consider is whether disclosure is an adequate means of ensuring that the subsequent land use decision is fair and in the public interest.

As the court indicates, there are also constitutional implications that arise from issues concerning campaign contributions. *See, e.g., Citizens United v. Federal Election Comm'n*, 130 S. Ct. 876 (2010). The complex issues raised by the cases are left to courses in Constitutional Law or Election Law.

Would a nonprofit organization be able to withhold the identity of contributors to its litigation fund? The court found that identity irrelevant in *Matthews v. City of Maitland*, 923 So. 2d 591 (Fla. Ct. App. 2006), rejecting the city's argument that the funding sources were competitors of the developer. It thought that compelled disclosure "would create a chilling effect on [citizens'] rights to organize and associate." *Id.* at 595. Do you agree?

9. *Political Retribution.* Can a plaintiff successfully allege, in a civil rights action brought in federal court, that its application for a development approval was denied because of political views? In *Brady v. Town of Colchester*, 863 F.2d 205 (2d Cir. 1988), plaintiff purchased a building, which it leased to the Borough of Colchester, a political entity controlled by Democrats. The Town of Colchester, however, was controlled by Republicans, and the town refused to issue an occupancy permit for the building. The court of appeal held that this action could violate due process and equal protection. *See also Paeth v. Worth Twp.*, 737 F. Supp. 2d 740 (E.D. Mich. 2010) (affirming two jury awards, one of which totaled $275,000 and which was based on the claim that "the defendant retaliated against the plaintiffs for exercising their right under the First Amendment to access the courts of the State of Michigan when they challenged the decision of the Worth Township Zoning Board of Appeals that denied the plaintiffs' application for a variance . . ."); *Paterek v. Village of Armada, Michigan*, 801 F.3d 630 (6th Cir. 2015) (retaliation cause of action found when defendants responded to plaintiff's speaking out by issuing tickets and firing plaintiff from his position on the Downtown Development Authority).

Is it retaliation if an elected official refuses to meet in person with an individual who has sued the town? The Second Circuit thought not in *Tuccio v. Marconi*, 589 F.3d 538, 541 (2d Cir. 2009) ("It does not follow . . . that government officials are compelled by law to behave with a litigation adversary exactly as they would if the person were not a litigation adversary."). The court warned, though, that the officials could not effectively deny him access to permits or opportunities to do business with the town.

E. THIRD-PARTY OPPOSITION TO DEVELOPMENT: NEIGHBORS' RIGHTS AND DEVELOPERS' RESPONSES

As you have seen in previous cases, much of the litigation in the land use area is brought by neighbors, citizens groups, and other parties who oppose a particular development or otherwise are challenging action (or inaction) taken by a local government. The next case focuses on the rights of such "third parties." Many have charged that the land use system is now so complicated that opposition to development can effectively block almost any large project, a subject that we return to in the discussion of the "not in my backyard" syndrome in Chapter 16. As you consider the following materials, try to determine how the legal system should structure the rights of third parties to participate in such decisions and to challenge them in court.

■ GRANT COUNTY CONCERNED CITIZENS v. GRANT COUNTY BOARD OF ADJUSTMENT
866 N.W.2d 149 (S.D. 2015)

GILBERTSON, Chief Justice.

FACTS AND PROCEDURAL HISTORY

On December 18, 2012, Teton filed an application with the Grant County zoning officer for a conditional use permit to construct and operate a Class A CAFO [Concentrated Animal Feeding Operation] in Grant County. In the application, which was available for public review, Teton indicated that the CAFO would house 6,616 swine larger than 55 pounds (referred to as "finisher" swine in the ZOGC [Zoning Ordinance for Grant County]) and 1,200 swine smaller than 55 pounds (referred to as "nursery" swine in the ZOGC).

The Board scheduled a hearing for January 14, 2013, to consider Teton's application. In compliance with section 504(2) of the ZOGC, Grant County's zoning officer published notice of the hearing "once ten (10) days prior to the hearing in a paper of general circulation in the area affected." The published notice mistakenly reversed the number of finisher and nursery swine listed in the application, instead reporting the CAFO would house no more than 6,616 swine smaller than 55 pounds and 1,200 swine larger than 55 pounds. However, the published notice did indicate the correct number of total swine and that the CAFO was categorized as a Class A CAFO — the largest classification, consisting of 2,000 or more "animal units."[3]

---

3. An "animal unit" is a unit of measurement utilized by the ZOGC in order to uniformly apply the CAFO regulations to varying types of livestock. One head of "feeder or slaughter cattle" equals one

The scheduled hearing took place on January 14, 2013. The Board addressed the error in the published notice at the beginning of the hearing, but the record does not indicate that any concerns were raised or objections noted at that time. Approximately 200 people attended the hearing. After Teton presented its information to the Board and answered questions from the Board's members, the Board opened the hearing to public comment. Every member of the public present who wished to comment—whether an opponent or a proponent—was allotted five minutes to speak. Although Teton anticipated using a road jointly maintained by Melrose and Big Stone Townships, it failed to directly notify Melrose Township of the hearing. Nevertheless, at least one individual who spoke at the hearing indicated the Township was aware of the hearing and had discussed the proposed CAFO.

Opponents of the application, including Kathy Tyler (Tyler's wife) and other members of GCCC [Grant County Concerned Citizens], raised several substantive concerns with Teton's application. Mrs. Tyler informed the Board that if Teton's application was approved, the CAFO would be located—in violation of the ZOGC—within 2,640 feet of a newly constructed well on the Tyler property. In response, one of Teton's representatives speculated that the Tylers dug the "well" merely to frustrate Teton's application. The record does include a facsimile of a South Dakota water well completion report that indicates the Tylers' excavation was completed on December 18, 2012—the same day Teton submitted its application for the conditional use permit. The facsimile itself was generated on December 19, and the report was completed by the firm that dug the excavation. Although the excavation produced 12 gallons of water on December 18, the report does not indicate when the excavation began or how long it was in operation before producing the 12 gallons.

GCCC also asserted a number of other deficiencies in Teton's application. GCCC claimed Teton's manure management and operation plan identified an insufficient number of acres for the disposal of manure produced by the CAFO. It further claimed Teton "failed to demonstrate the ability to obtain [sufficient] amounts of water from Grant–Roberts Rural Water System." GCCC also alleged Teton misrepresented: that independent farmers were involved with the CAFO, that the principals of the CAFO operating entity had no stake in the CAFO venture, and that the proposed site is located in a sparsely populated area. Finally, GCCC raised a number of environmental and economic concerns. The Board ultimately determined that the Tylers' excavation was not a "well" within the meaning of the ZOGC setback requirement and approved Teton's application. . . .

GCCC appealed to the circuit court

Nearly three weeks after the circuit court sent its letter of decision to the parties, but prior to the entry of judgment, GCCC submitted an affidavit signed by Tyler explaining the purpose of the excavation was to obtain water for his horse herd. The Board and Teton moved to strike the affidavit from the record. The circuit court granted the motion. . . .

---

animal unit. Finisher swine are 0.4 animal units per head, and nursery swine are 0.1 animal units per head. Thus, 2,000 animal units could consist of 5,000 finisher swine, 20,000 nursery swine, or some combination thereof.

Analysis and Decision

1. whether the board regularly pursued its authority in granting teton's application for a conditional use permit . . .

Private well

GCCC asserts the ZOGC "unambiguously precluded the Board from granting a [conditional use permit]" to Teton because of the presence of a well within 2,640 feet of the proposed CAFO. Section 1304(6) of the ZOGC generally requires any new CAFO to be at least 2,640 feet away from any private well. The ZOGC does not seem to provide a definition for the word *well*. Instead, GCCC directs us to a definition located in South Dakota's statutes on water rights. SDCL 46–1–6(18) defines *well* as "an artificial excavation or opening in the ground, made by means of digging, boring, drilling, jetting, or by any other artificial method, for the purpose of obtaining groundwater." GCCC asserts that "[t]he Board had before it indisputable proof that there was an artificial opening in the ground, made by means of an artificial method, for the purpose of obtaining groundwater[,] . . . within 2,640 feet of the proposed CAFO." Therefore, GCCC concludes, "the Board arbitrarily and willfully disregarded undisputed proof." Rather than dispute the validity of applying this definition to the ZOGC, the Board and Teton instead argue the issue is outside the scope of our review because the Tylers' purpose in excavating was a factual dispute resolved by the Board. The Board asserts "there were evidentiary disputes about whether or not the hole in the ground on the Tylers' property was truly a 'well,' and whether its purpose was to obtain groundwater or merely to frustrate Teton's permit."

We agree that the existence of a well within the setback presented a factual dispute for the Board to resolve. At the hearing, in response to Kathy Tyler's presentation, one of Teton's representatives asserted the Tylers excavated for the sole purpose of frustrating Teton's application. Considering the well completion report offered by Kathy Tyler indicated the excavation had been completed on the same day that Teton submitted its application, the Board could have considered the timing of the excavation — though circumstantial — to support Teton's assertion that it was meant to frustrate the application. According to the hearing's minutes, Teton's engineer also told the Board he "made some calls" and was told a hole is considered a well "when it is grouted and the casing is developed and installed and the stem is down in the well." He told the Board that the Tylers' excavation did not meet any of these requirements at the time Teton submitted its application. Although the parties now dispute the existence of a well within the context of the statutory definition provided by SDCL 46–1–6(18), we see nothing in the ZOGC to suggest the Board was bound by this definition in its decision to approve Teton's application.

Nevertheless, GCCC maintains that "[i]t was undisputed that there was an artificial opening in the ground, made by means of an artificial method, which obtained groundwater[,] . . . within 2,640 feet of the proposed CAFO." While this statement is true, GCCC has materially misstated the statutory definition of the word *well* that it originally invoked. SDCL 46–1–6(18) says "for the purpose of obtaining groundwater" and not "which obtains groundwater."[4] While there

---

4. GCCC asserts that "[t]he phrase 'for the purpose of obtaining groundwater' relates to the opening in the ground." We disagree. The phrase "*for* the purpose of obtaining groundwater," like the phrase

does not seem to be any dispute that the Tylers claimed some amount of water from their excavation, the record clearly reflects a dispute as to their motivation in excavating. Thus, GCCC's claim that "Respondents do not and cannot dispute that a well existed within the setback" is flatly incorrect.

Nor are we persuaded by GCCC's analysis of the underlying purpose behind the ZOGC. GCCC asserts that "the Ordinances do not allow for any exceptions to the well setback requirement" and that "[t]he purpose of the well setback requirement is to prevent pollution to groundwater." These assertions seem to be contradicted by the ZOGC. Section 1304(6) specifically excludes wells owned by the operator of the CAFO from the setback requirement. If GCCC's theory of the purpose behind the ZOGC is correct — i.e., the purpose is to prevent pollution from *entering* groundwater — it would make little sense to be concerned with a well on another property a half mile away, yet not be concerned about polluting groundwater at the center of waste production. Considering this exclusion, the more likely purpose behind the setback requirement seems to be to prevent the disruption of existing water supplies to the neighbors of a proposed CAFO.

We are satisfied that the Board regularly pursued its authority with respect to approving the application despite the Tylers' claim that they dug a well within the setback. While it is undisputed that the Tylers excavated on their property on December 18, 2012, it is apparent from the record that the excavation's status as a well has been in dispute since at least the time of the hearing. Not only was the purpose of the excavation in dispute, Teton's engineer also challenged its status from a mechanical perspective. Because "[c]ertiorari cannot be used to examine evidence for the purpose of determining the correctness of a finding[,]" *Elliott*, 2005 S.D. 92, ¶14, 703 N.W.2d at 367 (quoting *Hines v. Bd. of Adj't of City of Miller*, 2004 S.D. 13, ¶10, 675 N.W.2d 231, 234), we do not decide whether we would have reached the same conclusion as the Board. We decide only that the Board regularly pursued its authority on this issue.

Manure management and operation plan

GCCC asserts Teton's proposed manure management and operation plan did not meet the requirements of the ZOGC "because Teton significantly overstated the amount of land on which it could apply manure." According to GCCC, Teton entered into 16 contracts providing 2,461 acres of land in which to inject manure. GCCC asserts, however, that "[h]alf of the contracts Teton identified include land on which drainage exists" and that "some of the contracts were either signed by an unauthorized person, overstated the actual amount of land provided," or were otherwise incapable of accepting manure. Thus, GCCC concludes, "[t]he Board's failure to ensure Teton's manure plan complied with the Ordinances demonstrates that it failed to regularly pursue its authority[.]"

We are not convinced that the Board failed to regularly pursue its authority on this issue. Although section 1304(10) of the ZOGC requires the application of manure to be set back from certain water sources and structures, an entire property is not rendered unusable by the presence of such setback. Even if the Board was required to accept as true GCCC's assertion that Teton overstated the amount of

---

"*by* means of digging . . . or by any other artificial method," relates to the verb *made*. *See* SDCL 46-1-6(18) (emphasis added). Regardless, there is no distinction material to this dispute between the purpose of an opening in the ground and the purpose of making the opening in the ground.

available land, GCCC offers no estimate of the true available acreage. Without doing so, claiming that Teton overstated the available acres is not synonymous with asserting the true number of available acres was insufficient. Furthermore, section 1304(4) offers little in the way of specific requirements for a manure management and operation plan.[6]

Although GCCC does not attempt to quantify the true available acreage or assert such area was insufficient, it does assert that "Teton's application recognized the inadequacy of its manure plan, admitting that the CAFO would produce 169,226 pounds of phosphorus but that it only had enough land to account for 100,438 pounds of phosphorus." However, GCCC bases this claim on a "phosphorus and acreage assessment" included on page three of Teton's initial nutrient management plan. This assessment does not address the capacity of available acres to absorb manure. Instead, and contrary to GCCC's representations, this assessment reports the total pounds of phosphorus "available for crops" at 169,226 and the total pounds of phosphorus "required by fields" at 100,438.

We are satisfied that the Board regularly pursued its authority with respect to approving the application despite GCCC's claim that Teton's manure management and operation plan failed to comply with the ZOGC. GCCC's claims are far from undisputed and, consequently, are factual determinations properly resolved by the Board . . .

2. WHETHER THE CIRCUIT COURT ERRED IN STRIKING TYLER'S AFFIDAVIT.

GCCC asserts the circuit court erred in its decision to strike Tyler's affidavit from the record. A circuit court that hears an appeal from a board of adjustment's decision has discretion to take additional evidence. *If* upon the hearing *it appears to the court* that testimony is necessary for the proper disposition of the matter, *the court may* take evidence, or appoint a referee to take such evidence as it may direct and report the evidence to the court with the referee's findings of fact and conclusions of law, which constitute a part of the proceedings upon which the determination of the court is made.

---

6. Section 1304(4) of the ZOGC states:

Classes A, B, C, and D Concentrated Animal Feeding Operations must submit a Manure Management and Operation Plan.
    A. Plan must include:
        1. The location and specifics of proposed animal manure facilities.
        2. The operation procedures and maintenance of manure facilities.
        3. Plans and specifications must be prepared or approved by a registered professional engineer, or a Natural Resource Conservation Service (NRCS) engineer. Waste treatment facilities will require inspection by an engineer and as-built plans to be submitted to the County Zoning Officer.
        4. Animal manure shall not be stored longer than two years.
        5. Manure containment structures shall provide for a minimum design volume of three hundred sixty-five (365) days of storage.
        6. Producers shall keep records on manure applications on individual fields which document acceptable manure and nutrient management practices have been followed. These records shall include soils test results for surface two feet of soil, actual and projected crop yields, nutrient analysis of manure, and information about date, rate and method of manure applications for individual fields.
    B. As a condition of the permit, the County Board of Adjustment may require the producer to participate in environmental training programs and become a certified livestock manager.

SDCL 11–2–64 (emphasis added). The operation of this statute — i.e., supplementing the administrative record on appeal — is clearly triggered by the court's determination of need, not by a party's. Even if the court determines there is such need, the statute vests discretion in the circuit court to admit — or not — any offered evidence. . . .

According to GCCC, "[b]ecause the [circuit court] identified Tyler's motivation as an issue that is necessary for the proper disposition of the matter, the [circuit court] should have taken evidence concerning the same [.]" . . .

The circuit court, like this Court, was limited to reviewing whether the Board regularly pursued its authority. SDCL 21–31–8. Although the information contained in the Tyler affidavit *might* have helped resolve the question of the Tylers' motivation in digging the excavation on their property — a question which goes to the merits of the underlying controversy between the parties — the circuit court concluded the affidavit was not necessary to determine whether the Board regularly pursued its authority in regard to GCCC's assertion that a private well was located within the setback required by the ZOGC. Based on our discussion of the same, *see supra*, we cannot conclude that the circuit court's decision was "outside the range of permissible choices[.]"

Notes and Comments

1. *Applying the Substantial Evidence Test.* As you saw earlier in this chapter, in undertaking a review of the evidence in the record, the court determines whether there is "substantial evidence" to support the local government's decision. "Substantial evidence" means "'such relevant evidence as reasonable minds might accept as adequate to support a conclusion' or to put it simply, more than a 'mere scintilla' of evidence." *Hall v. City of Ridgeland*, 37 So. 3d 25, 36 (Miss. 2010). If the evidence is mixed, with some substantial evidence supporting the government's conclusion and some contrary to it, the court will uphold the decision.

Under the substantial evidence test, which is a staple of administrative law, the local factfinder resolves conflicts in the evidence, and the court does not undertake a *de novo* review of that evidence. For example, in *In re Ferrera & Fenn Gravel Pit*, 87 A.3d 483, 487 (Vt. 2013), the court reviewed the evidence supporting a decision that the project would add significantly to the "intensity of what currently exists in this area" and represented a "substantial repeated disturbance." The court rejected appellants claim that the conclusion was "based only on the 'unfounded conjecture and hyperbole' of area residents." There was adequate support in the record, including the testimony of the applicants' own expert who admitted that trucks would measure over seventy decibels "as they go by your house."

2. *The Evidence "in the Record."* The evidence that is reviewed will be found in the administrative record of proceedings. The record in a land use case would include items such as the permit application, the determination of "non-significance" under any State Environmental Policy Act (a subject discussed in Chapter 14), planning commission documents, a transcript of the hearing, and all other materials relied upon by the city council in making its decision.

Generally, the petitioner bears the responsibility of securing and filing the record with the court. *Town of Pittsboro Advisory Plan Comm'n*, 26 N.E.3d 1110, 112

(Ind. Ct. App. 2015) ("bright line rule" that a petitioner "cannot receive consideration of its petition where it has not timely filed the statutorily defined record"). From a practical standpoint, lawyers representing litigants must ensure that the record contains all the evidence that they intend to rely upon. *See Carney's Restaurant, Inc. v. State*, 89 A.D.3d 1250, 1253 (N.Y.A.D. 2011) (petitioners "do not dispute that they failed to submit a plan that was approved by DEC [the Department of Environmental Conservation] but, rather, they allege that their failure to do so was DEC's fault. This contention is not supported by the record, and the affidavit of engineer Thomas Andress, on which petitioners primarily rely as support for this claim, is not part of the administrative record because it was obtained by petitioners subsequent to the hearing."). Thus, the case must be shaped before the administrative hearing is completed, since the record is closed at that point. In addition, once litigation is initiated, the lawyers must again ensure that the record includes all the evidence considered by the local government.

3. *The Neighbors' Motivations.* Modern land use processes afford neighbors opposing projects a considerable opportunity to make their views known. *Guse v. City of New Berlin*, 810 N.W.2d 838, 844 (Wis. Ct. App. 2012) ("we observe that neighbors weigh-in on zoning applications all the time — sometimes objecting at the zoning hearing, sometimes objecting to their elected officials and sometimes both. Nothing out of the ordinary occurred here"). One question that arises is whether the opposition of neighbors — in and of itself — should be sufficient to uphold the denial of a project. In this regard, consider the views of the court of appeal in *Ross v. City of Yorba Linda*, 2 Cal. Rptr. 2d 638, 643 (Ct. App. 1991):

> The city appears to be saying that neighborhood opposition to construction on nearby private property is itself a "rational basis" for a local government body to forbid construction.
>
> This argument, carried to its logical conclusion, would be fundamentally destructive of the basic rights guaranteed by our state and federal Constitutions. If public opinion by itself could justify the denial of constitutional rights, then those rights would be meaningless.

See also Blair Investments v. Roanoke Rapids City Council, 752 S.E.2d 524, 530 (N.C. Ct. App. 2013) ("Respondents allege on appeal that the 'concerns' of local residents constituted substantial, material, and competent evidence. However, respondents neither acknowledge nor attempt to distinguish precedent holding that a board's decision to deny a permit request may not be based on speculative opinions. . . .").

On the other hand, neighbors have intimate knowledge about the characteristics of the area in which they live (not to mention a significant economic investment in their property, if they are owners). *See San Antonio Bd. of Adjustment v. Reilly*, 429 S.W.3d 707 (Tex. Ct. App. 2014) (finding that residents could testify about the architectural, historical and cultural significance of a house, and rejecting the applicant's argument that the board could rely only on expert evidence in deciding this question). Is it possible to separate this knowledge of the area, which can be used to estimate the impacts that a new development will have in that area, from simple political opposition to a new development? *See* Damon Y. Smith, Participatory Planning and Procedural Protections: The Case for Deeper Public Participation in Urban Redevelopment, 29 St. Louis U. Pub. L. Rev. 243,

257 (2009) ("The primary problem with embracing the concept of pure 'resident control' or 'empowerment' is that it is difficult to separate this from 'Not In My Backyard' (NIMBY)-like resident vetoes over neighborhood changes.").

4. *How Much Influence is Too Much?* In *Counceller v. City of Columbus Plan Comm'n,* 42 N.E.3d 146 (Ind. Ct. App. 2015), plaintiff sought to re-subdivide a lot. A local ordinance required that, for a re-subdivision that may have an impact on the existing subdivision, "the applicant shall include the signed consent of 75% of the owners of property in the existing subdivision." The applicant did not receive that consent and argued that the requirement was an "impermissible 'neighborhood veto' ordinance." The court rejected that argument because the ordinance allowed an applicant to seek a waiver of the 75 percent requirement from the planning commission. Do you agree? Does such a requirement violate the applicant's due process rights even if a waiver is possible?

5. *The Rationale for Public Participation.* Unquestionably, the opportunities for members of the public to express their opinions about development proposals have multiplied in recent decades. *See* Douglas A. Jorden and Michele A. Hentrich, Public Participation is on the Rise: A Review of the Changes in the Notice and Hearing Requirements for the Adoption and Amendment of General Plans and Rezonings Nationwide and in Recent Arizona Land Use Legislation, 43 Nat. Resources J. 865, 866 (2003) ("Many states have begun to encourage a broader public role in the planning and zoning process").

What exactly do public participants have at stake? One recent article suggests that unwise developments in urban areas pose the risk of depleting what the article terms "social capital":

> [A] city is only as strong and vital as its neighborhoods. Contemporary urban land use debates once again call our attention to the social costs imposed on intact, socially cohesive communities from land use and development decisions in urban neighborhoods. Much of the discourse of these debates has focused on the physical placement, or displacement, of land uses and the populations who inhabit them. But lurking very close to the surface of debates about physical placement and displacement is a deeper concern about the disruption to, and destruction of, social organization in neighborhoods most impacted by certain land use decisions. Targeted redevelopment efforts in inner-city neighborhoods can, for example, not only physically displace longstanding residents and businesses but also damage or destroy vital social and cultural ties crucial to residents' ability to raise their children, earn a living, and meet other basic social and economic needs.

Sheila R. Foster, The City as an Ecological Space: Social Capital and Urban Land Use, 82 Notre Dame L. Rev. 527, 531-32 (2006). Does this concept of "social capital" give greater legitimacy to increased public participation?

Given the zealousness of some public opponents of development projects, the temptation exists for developers to respond with lawsuits seeking damages. These so-called "SLAPP-suits" — Strategic Lawsuits Against Public Participation — in turn have brought about legislation attempting to protect citizens from such lawsuits. Consider the following case, which construes the Massachusetts SLAPP legislation.

■ PLANTE v. WYLIE

824 N.E.2d 461 (Mass. Ct. App. 2005)

Present: Lenk, Kantrowitz, & Cohen, JJ. Cohen, J.

***

In 1994, the plaintiffs, Edmond H. Plante and Curtis Plante, trustees of Lover's Leap Realty Trust, received approval from the board for a residential subdivision plan on Berlin Road. Two years later, the plaintiffs obtained two septic system permits from the Bolton board of health for a portion of the subdivision that bordered land owned by Roger and Anna Ela. Upon learning, during construction, of a possible problem with their title to the subject property, the plaintiffs attempted to reach an agreement with the Elas regarding ownership, but the boundary issue remained unresolved when Roger Ela died. Thereafter, the Elas' daughter, Nancy Caisse, assisted her mother in negotiations with the plaintiffs.

The conservation trust, a charitable corporation organized . . . for the purpose of assisting and promoting the preservation of Bolton's rural character and natural resources, became involved in the dispute. In November, 1998, the boundary question was discussed at a meeting attended by Edmond Plante (Plante), Caisse, Bonnie Potter (the president of the conservation trust), and Wylie (acting as the conservation trust's attorney), but no agreement was reached. In a letter to Plante dated December 7, 1998, Wylie summarized the meeting, recounting that Plante had asserted that the plaintiffs had a superior claim to the disputed property and had expressed his intention to obtain a court decree, and that Caisse had responded by indicating that she would seek the assistance of the conservation trust in defending her position that the plaintiffs were not entitled to the property or to the expanded development they proposed. In addition to commenting upon the title issue, Wylie also mentioned a "public trail easement" that he asserted had long existed on the property in question. The conservation trust's president, Bonnie Potter, was both referenced in the text of the letter and copied on the letter.

On August 19, 1999, Plante filed a petition for a special permit with the board, seeking expansion of the plaintiffs' original subdivision plan to create a new house lot, referred to as lot 10, and to enlarge the existing lot 8 to accommodate the septic system. It was the plaintiffs' title to lots 8 and 10 that was disputed by the Ela family and the conservation trust. According to the Elas and the conservation trust, the original subdivision plan had identified the disputed area as belonging to "owner unknown" or as belonging to the Elas, and it was not open to the plaintiffs to build upon it. On October 13, 1999, Anna Ela deeded a portion of her property to the conservation trust, intending that it be preserved for conservation use; the conveyance included the boundary area abutting the plaintiffs' proposed subdivision expansion.

When Plante's petition to expand the subdivision was heard by the board, beginning in October, 1999, Wylie appeared in opposition on behalf of the conservation trust and challenged the plaintiffs' ownership of the property proposed for expansion. The board requested that the parties submit evidence regarding the location of the subdivision boundary. Accordingly, in November, 1999, the conservation trust hired its own engineer to investigate the title issue and, in the process, discovered that the conservation trust appeared to own seven and one-half acres of land to which the plaintiffs claimed title, a portion of which the plaintiffs already had developed and sold to third parties.

On December 21, 1999, Wylie met with Plante's attorney, David Philbin, to review the engineer's findings. In January, 2000, with notice to Philbin, Wylie met with the homeowners who had purchased the affected lots from the plaintiffs, and suggested that they contact their own attorneys and title insurance companies.

By letter dated February 4, 2000, Wylie wrote to Philbin to extend a settlement offer, indicating that the conservation trust would release its rights in the lots already developed and sold, in return for the plaintiffs' agreement to release their claims to the disputed lots 8 and 10. Wylie also sought the conservation trust's costs and attorney's fees (as well as those of the affected homeowners) in connection with resolving the title issue. Upon learning that Philbin no longer represented Plante, Wylie sent a similar letter to Plante directly, to which he received no reply. Potter, the conservation trust president, was copied on both of these letters.

On March 6, 2000, Potter learned that heavy equipment and trucks had moved into the disputed area. At Potter's request, Wylie obtained a temporary restraining order against the plaintiffs in the Land Court. On March 13, 2000, the Land Court granted the conservation trust a preliminary injunction prohibiting the further clearing of lots 8 and 10 (the judge noting that fifty to sixty trees already had been cut down on the disputed property). On April 5, 2000, Plante withdrew from the board the plaintiffs' still-pending petition for further development.

A few weeks later, on May 18, 2000, the plaintiffs filed a complaint against Wylie in Superior Court, amending it as of right after Wylie moved to dismiss. Both the original and amended complaints alleged that Wylie interfered with the plaintiffs' exercise of their right to use and enjoy their property; . . . that he engaged in racketeering activity in violation of 18 U.S.C. §1961; and that he committed unfair or deceptive acts or practices. . . . Apparently with the anti-SLAPP statute in mind, the plaintiffs made no allegations concerning Wylie's representation of the conservation trust before the board or in the Land Court, instead limiting their focus to his communications to the plaintiffs regarding the boundary dispute. In particular, although the amended complaint recited earlier background events, the essential factual predicate for the plaintiffs' claims was Wylie's correspondence to the plaintiffs in February, 2000. As the plaintiffs explain in their brief, each of their three causes of action was based upon what they characterize as Wylie's "threat" that the conservation trust would pursue its claim of ownership to land already developed unless the plaintiffs (1) conveyed lots 8 and 10 to the conservation trust, and (2) made payments for legal fees and expenses that, in the plaintiffs' view, were unsubstantiated and unwarranted.

Wylie filed a motion to dismiss the amended complaint, including a special motion to dismiss under G.L. c. 231, §59H. . . .

Discussion. We first consider whether Wylie may avail himself of the anti-SLAPP statute when the statements that form the basis of the plaintiffs' claims were made by him as an attorney on behalf of the conservation trust.

"SLAPP suits have been characterized as 'generally meritless suits brought by large private interests to deter common citizens from exercising their political or legal rights or to punish them for doing so.'" Duracraft Corp. v. Holmes Prod. Corp., 427 Mass. 156, 161, 691 N.E.2d 935 (1998), quoting from Wilcox v. Superior Ct., 27 Cal. App.4th 809, 816-817, 33 Cal. Rptr.2d 446 (1994). Although the anti-SLAPP statute can have broader application, "[t]he typical mischief that the legislation intended to remedy was lawsuits directed at individual citizens of modest means for speaking publicly against development projects." Kobrin v. Gastfriend,

443 Mass. 327, 336, 821 N.E.2d 60 (2005), quoting from Office One, Inc. v. Lopez, 437 Mass. 113, 121-122, 769 N.E.2d 749 (2002).

Unquestionably, a citizens group such as the conservation trust is entitled to invoke the anti-SLAPP statute if a suit is filed against it based solely upon its protected petitioning activities in opposing a development project. The issue remains, however, whether Wylie, as the conservation trust's attorney, may likewise avail himself of the statute. We conclude that he may.

In the recent decision of Kobrin v. Gastfriend, 443 Mass. at 332, 821 N.E.2d 60, the Supreme Judicial Court emphasized that the anti-SLAPP statute is restricted by its language "to those defendants who petition the government on their own behalf. In other words, the statute is designed to protect overtures to the government by parties petitioning in their status as citizens." Thus, the court held that a disinterested paid expert witness in a disciplinary case before the Board of Registration of Medicine was not entitled to the protection of the anti-SLAPP statute because he was not seeking redress for a grievance of his own or otherwise petitioning on his own behalf. Id. at 330, 821 N.E.2d 60.

We think, however, that an attorney's representation of petitioning citizens stands on a very different footing. Indeed, the statute would provide but hollow protection for citizens who wish to exercise their right of petition if statements made by an attorney on their behalf were not covered by the anti-SLAPP statute to the same extent as statements made by them directly. The statute is designed to deter lawsuits filed to intimidate citizens from legitimately petitioning the government for redress of grievances and to provide a mechanism for the prompt dismissal of such lawsuits before the petitioning party has been forced to incur significant costs of defense. . . . Such suits directed against the attorneys who represent petitioning parties are just as likely to exert a chilling effect on petitioning activity as suits directed against the parties themselves, and the costs to attorneys and their clients if such suits cannot promptly be dismissed are just as likely to impede the clients' right to petition, not to mention their right to be represented. For these reasons . . . we conclude that an attorney who is sued for voicing the positions of a petitioning client may bring a special motion to dismiss under the anti-SLAPP statute. . . .

We now turn to the merits of Wylie's special motion to dismiss. . . .

In seeking dismissal under the anti-SLAPP statute, Wylie was required to "make a threshold showing through the pleadings and affidavits that the claims against [him] are 'based on' the petitioning activities alone and have no substantial basis other than or in addition to the petitioning activities." Duracraft Corp. v. Holmes Prod. Corp., 427 Mass. at 167-168, 691 N.E.2d 935, quoting from G.L. c. 231, §59H . . . [A]n overarching consideration in identifying protected petitioning activities is whether they involve the moving "party's exercise of its right of petition under the constitution of the United States or of the commonwealth." Kobrin v. Gastfriend, 443 Mass. at 332, 821 N.E.2d 60, quoting from G.L. c. 231, §59H. When citizens make overtures to the government, such activity may come within the ambit of the statute; there is, however, no statutory requirement that petitioning parties directly commence or initiate proceedings. Id. at 338, 821 N.E.2d 60.

[A]s a general matter, the conservation trust's activities in opposing the plaintiffs' development before the board (and later in the Land Court) are precisely the types of activities that the statute was designed to shield. At issue is whether the statute's protection extends to communications with respect to settlement, the wrinkle being that, although Wylie's settlement letters were sent while the board proceedings were pending, they were communicated to the plaintiffs and not directed to the board.

The specific categories of petitioning activities delineated in §59H provide guidance on this issue. "A party's exercise of its right of petition" is defined in the statute as:

> any written or oral statement made before or submitted to a legislative, executive, or judicial body, or any other governmental proceeding; any written or oral statement made in connection with an issue under consideration or review by a legislative, executive, or judicial body, or any other governmental proceeding; any statement reasonably likely to encourage consideration or review of an issue by a legislative, executive, or judicial body or any other governmental proceeding; any statement reasonably likely to enlist public participation in an effort to effect such consideration; or any other statement falling within constitutional protection of the right to petition government" (emphasis supplied).

G.L. c. 231, §59H, inserted by St. 1994, c. 283, §1.

Of particular relevance here is the category "any written or oral statement made in connection with an issue under consideration or review by a legislative, executive, or judicial body, or any other governmental proceeding." . . . [W]e think that, in keeping with the objectives of the statute, it must be construed to include statements made by one participant in a pending governmental proceeding to another in an effort to settle the controversy. Even though such statements are communicated to other private citizens rather than directly to the government, they are closely and rationally related to the proceedings proposed to be compromised, and they are in furtherance of the objective served by governmental consideration of the issue under review-namely, the resolution of grievances. . . .

Here, the boundary issue was not just an isolated dispute between neighbors; it was an integral part of the issue under consideration by the board, that is, whether the plaintiffs should be permitted to expand their subdivision when there remained substantial questions about the plaintiffs' ownership of the land they were developing. The issue raised by Wylie regarding house lots already built upon and sold directly pertained to the proceedings then before the board, which involved the proposed expansion of the same subdivision. Indeed, the title problem with existing lots was discovered as a result of the board's request that the parties submit evidence on the boundary issue. It was during the conservation trust's ensuing investigation that it became evident that the plaintiffs' title problems . . . also involved previously developed land.

Wylie's February 4, 2000, letter . . . reflected the conservation trust's concern that both the originally filed subdivision plan and the proposed expansion evidenced inconsistencies in the plaintiffs' representations to the planning board regarding their ownership of the land in question. The letter also offered a global settlement whereby the conservation trust would release its rights in the previously sold lots with problematic title, in exchange for the plaintiffs' transfer to the conservation trust of lots 8 and 10, which were the subject of the pending board proceedings, together with the payment of associated fees and expenses. Thus, whether viewed from the perspective of the plaintiff developers, the conservation trust, or the town planning board, the resolution of title issues pertaining to the previously sold lots and those pertaining to the proposed expansion of the development were inextricably intertwined.

Conclusion. For the foregoing reasons, we conclude that Wylie met his initial burden of showing that the plaintiffs' action against him was based on protected petitioning activities alone and had no substantial basis other than or in addition to the petitioning activities. . . . Therefore, to defeat his motion, it was incumbent upon the plaintiffs to show that Wylie's exercise of his right to petition was devoid of any reasonable factual support or any arguable basis in law, and that his acts caused them actual injury. . . . In other circumstances we might be inclined to remand the case for consideration of these issues. Here, however, given the success of Wylie and the conservation trust in the Land Court action, it is manifest from the record that the plaintiffs cannot establish the first of these conjunctive requirements — that Wylie's statements were devoid of any reasonable factual or legal basis . . .

. . . The case is remanded for the entry of new orders allowing the motion and awarding to Wylie his costs and reasonable attorney's fees pursuant to G.L. c. 231, §59H . . .

Notes and Comments

1. *"SLAPP" Suits.* Developers have instituted legal actions against opponents of their projects, seeking damages for delays in the project caused by the opponents, for allegedly defamatory statements made by opponents, or for intentional interference with prospective advantage or contractual relations. *See Sandholm v. Kuecker* 962 N.E.2d 418, 427 (Ill. 2012) ("The paradigm SLAPP suit is 'one filed by developers, unhappy with public protest over a proposed development, filed against leading critics in order to silence criticism of the proposed development.' . . ."). These "SLAPP" suits raise a variety of issues, not the least of which is the potential "chilling effect" on the exercise of First Amendment rights.

For citizens contemplating opposing a project, the specter of paying large damage awards to a developer, or at least of having to bear the expense of defending such litigation, is frightening. *See* Lori Potter & W. Cory Haller, SLAPP 2.0: Second Generation of Issues Related to Strategic Lawsuits Against Public Participation, 45 Envtl. L. Rep. News & Analysis 10136 (2015) ("The significance of the chilling effect of a SLAPP is hard to overstate . . . Frequently a defendant will cease petitioning activities immediately after being named in a SLAPP complaint or after settlement of the case, because the psychological and financial costs of carrying on, even with a successful defense, are so burdensome.").

Predictably, the SLAPP suit was soon followed by yet a further round of litigation: the so-called SLAPP-back suit brought by citizen activists seeking damages for injury to their reputations and wallets caused by the SLAPP suit. A book and a long series of law review articles chronicled the whole situation. The classic treatments are George W. Pring & Penelope Canan, SLAPPs: Getting Sued for Speaking Out (1996) and George W. Pring, SLAPPs: Strategic Lawsuits Against Public Participation, 7 Pace Envtl. L. Rev. 3 (1989). *See also* George W. Pring & Penelope Canan, Strategic Lawsuits Against Public Participation ("SLAPPs"): An Introduction for Bench, Bar and Bystanders, 12 Bridgeport L. Rev. 937 (1992).

2. *The Anti-SLAPP Statutes.* Over half the states have responded to the phenomenon with so-called anti-SLAPP statutes. Carson Hilary Barylak, Reducing Uncertainty in Anti-SLAPP Protection, 71 Ohio St. L.J. 845 (2010). A Texas court of appeal summarized how the anti-SLAPP statute works in that state:

> Appellants filed a motion to dismiss under the TCPA [Texas Citizens Participation Act], which requires a trial court to dismiss a lawsuit that "is based on, relates to, or is in response to" the defendant's exercise of any of their constitutional rights of free speech, petition, or association. [Tex. Civ. Prac. & Rem. Code Ann.] §27.005(b). The moving party must prove by a preponderance of the evidence that they are being sued on this basis. *Id.* The party bringing the action can prevent dismissal by showing that they have established "by clear and specific evidence a prima facie case for each essential element of the claim in question." *Id.* §27.005(c). Once a defendant brings a motion to dismiss under this chapter, all discovery in the lawsuit is suspended. *Id.* §27.003(c).

San Jacinto Title Servs. of Corpus Christi, LLC. v. Kingsley Properties, LP, 452 S.W.3d 343, 346 (Tex. Ct. App. 2013)

You also should note that, in addition to SLAPP statutes, other defenses to lawsuits like the one in *Plante* might be available. *See, e.g., Dlugokecki v. Vieira*, 907 A.2d 1269 (Conn. Ct. App. 2006) (neighbor's statements opposing wetlands permit were absolutely privileged, and thus plaintiff's slander action must be dismissed); *Anderson Dev. Co. v. Tobias*, 116 P.3d 323 (Utah 2005) (so-called "Noerr-Pennington" Doctrine, protecting the right to petition the government, protected citizens' statements to city council even if they misrepresented their ability to raise funds to purchase land).

3. *Applying the SLAPP Statute in* Plante. Was the Court correct in its application of the Massachusetts SLAPP statute? The statute is directed to protecting "exercise of [the] right of petition." How could it apply here when the lawyer involved never made any direct petition to the government? Why would the Court read the statute as broadly as it did?

Did the Court act correctly in ordering the trial court to dismiss the suit, rather than just remanding? Was the plaintiff ever given the opportunity to develop his case in the normal manner of civil litigation?

4. *Construction.* Anti-SLAPP statutes constitute an invitation to defendants to use them, particularly given that many of them authorize an award of attorney's fees to a defendant if the anti-SLAPP motion prevails. The outcomes of such motions often require a close reading of the statute. As the court of appeals put it in *City of Costa Mesa v. D'Alessio Investments*, 154 Cal. Rptr. 3d 698 (Ct. App. 2013), "The first step of the anti-SLAPP analysis requires careful consideration of the statutory language in light of the legal theories of recovery, not a mere cataloging of claims or consideration of general principles of free speech." For example, should the anti-SLAPP suit be a defense to an enforcement action brought by the local government against the defendant, where the defendant alleges a history of prior disagreements with the local government? The Maine Supreme Court said no in *Town of Madawaska v. Cayer*, 103 A.3d 547 (Me. 2014). *See, e.g., Penllyn Greene Associates v. Clouser*, 890 A.2d 424 (Pa. Commw. Ct. 2005) (respondents' representations to real estate agencies, the press, and home buyers were not protected).

5. *Balancing the Interests at Stake.* The critical issues are both substantive and procedural. On a substantive level, the impacts of a SLAPP suit on First Amendment rights are obviously important. At the same time, however, untrue or malicious opposition to a project can cause the project's demise and, with it, significant economic injury. You must consider what is the appropriate balance between the right to comment and oppose a project, on the one hand, and responsibility for those statements, on the other. Which should be weighed more heavily?

In *Equilon Enterprises, L.L.C. v. Consumer Cause, Inc.*, 52 P.3d 685 (Cal. 2002), the California Supreme Court considered the showing that a defendant must make to receive protection from a SLAPP suit. The matter started when a consumer group served a notice of intent to sue for private enforcement of the California Safe Drinking Water and Toxic Enforcement Act, Cal. H. & Safe. Code §25249.7, subd. (d). The notice alleged that oil companies had been polluting the groundwater with discharges of various chemicals. The companies responded by filing a lawsuit for declaratory and injunctive relief seeking, among other relief, an injunction preventing Consumer Cause from filing an action. Defendant Consumer Cause then moved to strike the complaint under the state's anti-SLAPP legislation.

Plaintiff claimed that, to prevail, a defendant must demonstrate that the cause of action "was brought with the intent of chilling the defendant's exercise of constitutional speech or petition rights." 52 P.3d at 688. The court, however, rejected that claim. The court held that under the plain meaning of the statute, it applied to all claims "arising from" protected activity, not just those where a plaintiff sought to "chill" the defendant's rights.

The Rhode Island Supreme Court reached a similar result in *Hometown Properties, Inc. v. Fleming*, 680 A.2d 56 (R.I. 1996) (statements are protected under anti-SLAPP statute unless they amount to a "sham" petition). Is this standard of protection too broad? *Compare Vultaggio v. Yasko*, 572 N.W.2d 450 (Wis. 1998) (neighbor's statements made in a public hearing about a property owner's upkeep of properties were conditionally privileged, rather than absolutely privileged, and in a defamation action the issue of whether the neighbor abused the privilege was a jury question).

6. *Devising an Appropriate Procedural Mechanism.* On the procedural level, the issue is how to implement meaningful protection of First Amendment rights. Bear in mind that development interests are, on the whole, more likely to be able to afford large-scale, discovery-intensive SLAPP litigation than are citizens or citizens groups who are defendants. The solution of many statutes is to allow the defendants to bring an early "special motion" to strike the suit, a motion that requires the plaintiff to substantiate its claims. In the meantime, discovery is stayed. *See Middle-Snake-Tamarac Rivers Watershed Dist. v. Stengrim*, 784 N.W.2d 834, 839 (Minn. 2010) (noting the "unique procedural framework" of the anti-SLAPP statutes).

Plaintiffs argue that this procedure is unfair because it allows a plaintiff no discovery rights before the motion is filed. If you think that some discovery is appropriate, how should it be limited to prevent a crushing burden on individual or citizens group defendants—a burden that in many cases would impel them to a quick settlement requiring them to cease all opposition to the project?

One interesting question is whether a state's anti-SLAPP statute applies in federal litigation. The general rule, of course, is that federal courts sitting in diversity cases apply state substantive law and federal procedural rules. Is the anti-SLAPP statute procedural, and thus inapplicable? Or does it have a substantive component? The case law has not been entirely uniform. *Compare Phoenix Trading, Inc. v. Loops LLC*, 732 F.3d 936 (9th Cir. 2013) (applying the statute) *with Abbas v. Foreign Policy Group, LLC*, 783 F.3d 1328 (D.C. Cir. 2015). Does the procedure violate the plaintiff's right to a jury trial, since the trial court decides factual issues when applying the anti-SLAPP statute? The Washington Supreme Court thought so in *Davis v. Cox*, 351 P.3d 862 (Wash. 2015).

Some states have recognized an additional problem: so-called public interest cases brought by plaintiffs that may be the subject of SLAPP motions brought by defendants. The response has been a so-called "public interest" exception for plaintiffs exempting them from the anti-SLAPP law. *See Save Westwood Village v. Luskin*, 182 Cal. Rptr. 3d 328 (Ct. App. 2014) (plaintiffs' action against regents and donors of funds for a hotel on campus could not use the exception, as the donors' funding of the hotel was protected speech).

The SLAPP suit issue is also discussed in Chapter 16, which addresses the question of siting facilities opposed by neighbors — the so-called NIMBY phenomenon.

F. THE ROLE OF THE FEDERAL COURTS UNDER THE CIVIL RIGHTS ACT

Land use decisions are overwhelmingly the province of local governments in the United States. Thus, judicial review of such actions for the most part occurs in the state courts. Aggrieved landowners, however, often feel that the state courts are not sufficiently attuned to the economic ramifications of local government's land use actions, or to the arbitrariness that they perceive in local government decision making. As a result, they may seek to file litigation in the federal courts, which they perceive as a more favorable forum. After all, federal courts are used to adjudicating constitutional claims, and they hear many cases under the federal Civil Rights Act. The constitutional violations alleged in such suits are discussed in Chapters 7 and 8.

The federal courts, however, have been very careful in responding to these cases. They fear that if every local government unfairness in the land use field becomes a potential civil rights violation for failure to accord procedural due process, or if every reduction in land value caused by a rezoning is a potential substantive due process violation, the federal courts could be inundated with lawsuits over such matters. Keep these judicial concerns about institutional consequences in mind as you read the following case, which is illustrative of litigation brought in federal court challenging a local government land use action.

■ CENERGY-GLENMORE WIND FARM v. TOWN OF GLENMORE
769 F.3d 485 (7th Cir. 2014)

Before TINDER and HAMILTON, Circuit Judges, and KAPALA, District Judge.
HAMILTON, Circuit Judge.

I. Factual and Procedural Background

. . . CEnergy alleges that Prelude, a company whose assets it later purchased, contracted in 2007 with a family in Glenmore to build a wind farm on the family's property. Prelude also obtained a conditional use permit from Glenmore to develop the farm.

Roughly two years later, Prelude entered into a power purchase agreement with the Wisconsin Public Service Corporation (WPS) to sell wind turbine-generated electricity for 20 years at specified rates. The agreement was binding on WPS only if Prelude obtained all necessary permits and satisfied various other requirements by March 1, 2011.

Prelude learned in September 2010 that before construction could begin, it would need to obtain a building permit for each of the seven planned wind turbines. The company tried to submit applications for the permits to the Town Board, Glenmore's legislative body, but the Board refused to accept the applications unless the company provided additional information about the project.

By December 31, 2010, Prelude provided the Board with all requested information and told the Chair of the Board that the building permits would need to be approved by March 1, 2011, for the power purchase agreement with WPS to take effect. Without the power purchase agreement, Prelude told the Chair, the wind farm project would not be feasible because the energy market had changed substantially since the execution of the agreement with WPS. Also in December 2010, CEnergy agreed to purchase Prelude's assets, including the right to develop the wind farm. The sale closed in February 2011, on the eve of the WPS contract deadline.

In the meantime, public sentiment in Glenmore had turned decidedly against the wind farm project, as the Town Board well knew. Angry citizens had gathered at the Board's public meetings in January and February 2011 to oppose the plan. Unbeknownst to CEnergy, the Chair of the Board was receiving "threats to his physical safety should he approve the wind turbine project."

Although CEnergy had asked the Town Board to take up the issue of the building permits at both the January and February meetings, the Board did not do so, ostensibly because the town's attorney needed more time to review the information Prelude had submitted in December 2010. CEnergy contends that the Board members actually avoided taking up the issue "because of threats made to the physical safety of those officials by a mob of citizens opposing the project."

The Town Board "finally allowed CEnergy to complete and submit" applications for the building permits on March 1, 2011, and considered the applications at a meeting on March 7. At that meeting, the Board voted to grant the permits and then adjourned. But citizens in attendance became "accusatory and threatening" toward Board members and other town officials. The Chair reopened the meeting in response to the clamor. After further discussion, the Board voted to rescind the grant of the permits. A little over a week later, the Board held a special meeting and again reversed course, voting to nullify the actions it had taken after adjournment on March 7, thus reinstating the earlier vote in favor of granting the permits. The permits still were not actually issued, however, because the attorney for Glenmore contended that the applications were still missing crucial information.

As it turned out, even the initial vote on March 7 had come too late to save the wind farm project. WPS, perhaps pleased to escape from what had become for it an unprofitable deal, had sent CEnergy a letter on March 4 backing out of the power purchase agreement. As a principal reason, WPS cited CEnergy's failure to obtain the necessary permits by March 1.

After learning that the deal with WPS could not be salvaged, CEnergy filed this suit [under the Civil Rights Act, 42 U.S.C. §1983] claiming that Glenmore deprived it of property without substantive due process of law when the Town Board delayed granting the building permits. In support of this claim, CEnergy alleges in its complaint that it had "vested property rights granted to it in the CUP [conditional use permit] and the requested building permits." The Town Board's decision to take no action on the building permits "at least until after March 1" was meant to thwart the wind farm project, making the decision "an arbitrary and egregious abuse of [the Board's] authority" that "shock[s] the conscience" and cost CEnergy a contract worth more than $7 million in profits. . . .

II. ANALYSIS

. . . We note at the outset . . . that federal courts, as we have explained time and again, are not zoning boards of appeal. . . . State and local land-use decisions are entitled to great deference when constitutional claims are raised in federal court. . . .

On the issue of arbitrariness, we have said that a land-use decision must "shock the conscience" to run afoul of the Constitution. *Bettendorf v. St. Croix County*, 631 F.3d 421, 426 (7th Cir. 2011). We also have suggested that the action must have been "arbitrary and capricious," . . . In yet another formulation, the Supreme Court has explained that a land-use decision must be arbitrary to the point of being "egregious" to implicate substantive due process. *Cuyahoga Falls*, 538 U.S. at 198, 123 S.Ct. 1389. These standards should not be viewed as distinct, at least in the land-use context. . . .

However the standard is formulated, the Glenmore Town Board's decision to delay action on CEnergy's building permit requests could not have been arbitrary in the constitutional sense. As far as the Constitution is concerned, popular opposition to a proposed land development plan is a rational and legitimate reason for a legislature to delay making a decision. See *River Park*, 23 F.3d at 167 (explaining that "the idea in zoning cases is that the due process clause permits municipalities to use political methods to decide").

Even if the Board's treatment of the building permit applications had been arbitrary in the constitutional sense, CEnergy still would have failed to state a substantive due process claim. We have held repeatedly that a plaintiff who ignores potential state law remedies cannot state a substantive due process claim based on a state-created property right. E.g., *Lee v. City of Chicago*, 330 F.3d 456, 467 (7th Cir.2003); *Centres*, 148 F.3d at 704; *Polenz*, 883 F.2d at 558–59. Without this requirement, procedural due process claims based on "random and unauthorized" deprivations of property (which might also be described as "arbitrary") could be brought as substantive due process claims even when a post-deprivation remedy was available . . .

As the district court explained, the standard process in Glenmore for obtaining a building permit is set out in the "Town of Glenmore Zoning Ordinance." Under Section E.2 of that ordinance, permit requests are to be submitted in writing to the "Glenmore Town Zoning Administrator." If the Administrator does not make a decision on the application within 10 days, the application is considered denied, and the applicant then has 30 days to appeal to the "Board of Appeals." The process under the ordinance seemingly does not involve the Town Board at all. Nonetheless, CEnergy made no attempt to proceed under the ordinance, even after the Town Board refused to accept its permit applications in September 2010 and began making excuses for not taking action on the permit requests despite knowing of the deadline CEnergy faced.

Nor did CEnergy take advantage of another potential option under state law: seeking a writ of mandamus to force the town to act on the permit applications. . . .

Confusingly, CEnergy contends elsewhere in its appellate brief that the decision whether to issue the permits was not "subject to legislative or political whims." Yet the company chose to ask a legislative body, the Town Board, to vote on the permit requests rather than proceeding under the zoning ordinance or arguing in state court for mandamus relief on the basis that the Board's consideration of the permit requests was actually an administrative function rather than a legislative one. CEnergy is thus like the unsuccessful plaintiff in *River Park*, which alleged in support of its due process claim that the city council was obliged by state law to approve a subdivision plan but intentionally delayed approval until the subdivision project was no longer feasible. CEnergy also "went along with the political process until it was too late" for another course of action and then "lost the political fight." 23 F.3d at 167. Now CEnergy seeks a judgment in federal court that would cost each resident of Glenmore roughly $6000. The company, however, must live with its strategic choices. No do-over is available through federal litigation. *Id.*

The judgment of the district court is AFFIRMED.

Notes and Comments

1. *Renewed Interest in the Federal Courts.* After the United States Supreme Court decided the *Village of Euclid* and *Nectow* zoning cases, discussed in Chapter 2, for about the next fifty years the Supreme Court almost universally refused to involve itself in issues arising from state land use regulation. As a result, land use law was largely a matter for the state courts. In recent years, however, the Supreme Court has re-entered the field, issuing a large number of decisions involving the Takings Clause (the most important of which you will examine in Chapter 7). With the Court's renewed concern over the constitutional fairness of land use regulation has come increasing pressure for the federal courts to provide remedies under the Civil Rights Act. A Section 1983 cause of action can also be brought in state court. *See, e.g. Loudon House LLC v. Town of Colonie*, 123 A.D.3d 1406 (N.Y. Sup. Ct. App. Div. 2014). But the vast majority of plaintiffs prefer the federal venue.

2. *The Abstention Doctrine.* A common response by municipal defendants is to ask the federal court to abstain if an issue of state law remains to be decided. *See, e.g., Victor Materials Co. v. City of Tehuacana*, 238 F.3d 382, 390 (5th Cir. 2001) (citing four categories of abstention: (1) *Pullman*-type abstention to avoid decision of a federal constitutional question where the case may be disposed of on questions of state law; (2) *Burford*-type abstention, to avoid needless conflict with the administration by a state of its own affairs; (3) abstention to leave to the states the resolution of unsettled questions of state law; and (4) abstention to avoid duplicative litigation). *Compare MLC Automotive v. Town of Pines*, 532 F.3d 269 (4th Cir. 2008) (upholding district

court's *sua sponte* order of abstention in action based on rezoning of property when dealership sought a permit, with the *town* opposing abstention); and *Addiction Specialists, Inc. v. The Township of Hampton*, 411 F.3d 399 (3d Cir. 2005) (abstention proper to challenges to state zoning law) *with Neufeld v. City of Baltimore*, 964 F.2d 347 (4th Cir. 1992) (district court improperly abstained where the case involved local land use issues only peripherally and there were no difficult interpretations of state law involved) and *Town of Nags Head v. Toloczko*, 728 F.3d 391, 396-97 (4th Cir. 2013) (while "[w]e have traditionally viewed questions of state and local land use and zoning law as the paradigm of *Burford* abstention," court would not abstain here where "North Carolina law is clear that the Town has no authority to enforce the public trust doctrine in the first place").

Where the plaintiff has sought monetary damages and the federal court abstains, it will generally retain jurisdiction over the case rather than dismissing it outright. *See Railroad Comm'n of Texas v. Pullman Co.*, 312 U.S. 496 (1941); *Quackenbush v. Allstate Ins. Co.*, 517 U.S. 706, 721 (1996) (federal courts can dismiss based on abstention only where the relief sought by the plaintiff is equitable or otherwise discretionary); *Carroll v. City of Mount Clemens*, 139 F.3d 1072 (6th Cir. 1998) (trial court properly abstained in action alleging that city ordinance which required rooming houses to have separate bathrooms in each unit violated Fair Housing Act, but the case should have been stayed rather than dismissed).

3. *A Cause of Action for Violation of Procedural Due Process.* The cases in which federal relief is sought include those alleging violations of procedural due process. Perhaps the simplest case is where a defendant acts without granting a hearing at all. In this situation, the court will apply settled Supreme Court law on when a hearing is called for before depriving a plaintiff of property. *See, e.g., Weinberg v. Whatcom County*, 241 F.3d 746 (9th Cir. 2001) (question of fact existed as to whether the county had to provide pre-deprivation hearing before issuing a stop work order, but the county did have to hold a hearing before vacating the defendant's approved plats).

The review will otherwise center on whether the local government provided adequate process. *See, e.g., Foxy Lady, Inc. v. City of Atlanta, Georgia*, 347 F.3d 1232 (11th Cir. 2003) (to establish a procedural due process violation under Section 1983, plaintiff must establish (1) the deprivation of a constitutionally protected liberty or property interest, (2) state action, and (3) constitutionally inadequate process); *Wedgewood Ltd. P'ship I v. Township of Liberty, Ohio*, 610 F.3d 340 (6th Cir. 2010) (enactment of zoning instructions violated Wedgewood's procedural due process rights). Most importantly, however, some circuits have held that if a state provides an adequate opportunity for seeking judicial relief in the state courts, no procedural due process violation will lie. *Id.; see also Sunrise Corp. of Myrtle Beach v. City of Myrtle Beach*, 420 F.3d 322 (4th Cir. 2005) (procedural due process claim fails where state court granted plaintiffs the permit they sought). The stringency of these tests is just one example of the federal judiciary's continued resistance to becoming heavily involved in land use cases. *See Sylvia Dev. Corp. v. Calvert County*, 48 F.3d 810, 828 (4th Cir. 1995) ("Resolving the routine land-use disputes that inevitably and constantly arise among developers, local residents, and municipal officials is simply not the business of the federal courts").

4. *A Cause of Action for Violation of Substantive Due Process or Equal Protection.* Another typical cause of action is the allegation that the local body violated the plaintiff's substantive due process rights or denied the plaintiff equal protection. These causes of action are discussed in Chapter 7.

5. *Section 1983 Actions.* Section 1983 of the federal Civil Rights Act of 1871 is the vehicle that plaintiffs use to bring actions in federal court alleging damages for land use decisions, although the act also can be used in the state court. That section provides:

> Every person who, under color of any statute, ordinance, regulation, custom or usage, of any State . . . subjects, or causes to be subjected, any citizen of the United States or other person within the jurisdiction thereof to the deprivation of any rights, privileges or immunities secured by the Constitution and laws, shall be liable to the party injured in an action at law, suit in equity, or other proper proceeding for redress.

Litigation under Section 1983 in the land use context raises a wide variety of technical issues. For example, certain immunities are available to defendants. *See Lake Country Estates, Inc. v. Tahoe Regional Planning Agency*, 440 U.S. 391 (1979) (absolute immunity of state legislators also applies to members of bi-state regional planning agency); *County Concrete Corp. v. Township of Roxbury*, 442 F.3d 159, 173 (3d Cir. 2006) (members of local legislative bodies are entitled to absolute legislative immunity for actions taken in a purely legislative capacity). In contrast, only a qualified good faith immunity may be available in other instances. *See Hussein v. City of Perrysburg*, 617 F.3d 828, 832 (6th Cir. 2010) (defendants entitled to qualified immunity "because state officials are permitted under the Constitution to inform citizens of the officials' view that they are violating state or local law"). The general American rule on attorney's fees is that each party bears its own costs for such fees. Under the Civil Rights Attorney's Fees Award Act, 42 U.S.C. §1988, however, prevailing plaintiffs can recover their attorney's fees. But they have to win. *See National Amusements Inc. v. Borough of Palmyra*, 716 F.3d 57, 64 (3d Cir. 2013) (plaintiffs sought attorney's fees in case where they won interim relief, but "[w]e have never held . . . that a party may recover attorney's fees . . . for interim relief when a district court ultimately dismisses the party's §1983 claims *on their merits.*").

6. *A Very Narrow Door.* Consider the following statement from the First Circuit Court of Appeals in *Snyder v. Gaudet*, 756 F.3d 30, (1st Cir. 2014), which concerns a series of city enforcement actions that ensued after the plaintiff fired an employee who served as a member of the local city council:

> We acknowledge that many citizens looking at the facts of this case would perceive an abuse of government power. Indeed, we have assumed, solely for the purposes of this appeal, that Collura acted in bad faith, and that Gaudet and Powell knowingly contributed to her retaliatory effort. But local governments make countless decisions every day, many of which inevitably disadvantage someone who can credibly claim that a local official acted out of personal hostility. This is especially so in our smaller cities and towns, where many people know their public officials. State and local law often provides recourse for challenging the imposition of fines or the burdens of administrative rulings by local officials that violate state or local law. So, too, the political process may provide a venue for correcting or deterring abuses. And federal courts obviously play an important role in adjudicating claims that such abuses violate federal law. Where, as here, however, municipal officials did not violate any clearly established federal law, federal law provides no basis for making local government officials pay damages.

Do you agree with the court that aggrieved parties have remedies in other venues so that federal jurisdiction is largely unnecessary?

7

Takings

The Takings Clause of the Fifth Amendment provides: "[N]or shall private property be taken for public use, without just compensation." U.S. Const. amend. V The state constitutions contain similar takings provisions. With the possible exception of the First Amendment, takings represents the most potent and frequently-invoked constitutional basis for challenging land use regulations at the federal, state, and local levels. A solid, working understanding of takings doctrine is essential for anyone working in the land use field.

A. INTRODUCTION

1. Eminent Domain v. Inverse Condemnation

It is useful at the outset to distinguish between direct exercises of the eminent domain power and so-called inverse condemnation claims. The notion that the government has the authority to force the sale of private property through the power of eminent domain to secure a site for a post office or a school, or to acquire a right of way for a road, for example, is as old as the Republic and relatively noncontroversial. The power is essential to deal with "hold outs" — property owners who are unwilling to sell to the public, regardless of the price offered, and even if the government needs the land for an important, perhaps vital, public purpose. Interestingly, the power of eminent domain is not expressly conferred on the federal government by the Constitution; instead, it has long been assumed to exist as a matter of practical necessity. As the Supreme Court explained over a century ago, eminent domain "appertains to every independent government. It requires no constitutional recognition; it is an attribute of sovereignty." *Boom Co. v. Patterson*, 98 U.S. 403, 406 (1878).

In a direct condemnation action, the government initiates a lawsuit to condemn the property. If the court decides the condemnation can proceed, the court orders transfer of ownership of the property to the government and orders the government to pay "just compensation" to the prior owner. By contrast, in an inverse condemnation action, government officials typically maintain that they have not taken any property, but private owners affected by a government action disagree, and they (not the government) initiate a lawsuit seeking to establish that a taking has occurred and to obtain payment of just compensation. While these forms of litigation are quite different, each type of suit is brought under the Takings Clause, and the basic legal doctrine governing both types of claims is the same.

2. History

While the courts have recognized the propriety of direct condemnations from early in the nation's history, inverse condemnation actions did not emerge until the latter half of the nineteenth century. In the first such case, *Pumpelly v. Green Bay Co.*, 80 U.S. 166 (1871), the Supreme Court awarded compensation when a state authorized a company to build a dam that flooded private land, observing:

> It would be a very curious and unsatisfactory result, if in construing a provision of constitutional law, always understood to have been adopted for protection and security to the rights of the individual as against the government . . . , it shall be held that if the government refrains from the absolute conversion of real property to the uses of the public it can destroy its value entirely, can inflict irreparable and permanent injury to any extent, can, in effect, subject it to total destruction without making any compensation, because, in the narrowest sense of that word, it is not *taken* for the public use.

Id. at 177-78. Observing that such an interpretation "would pervert the constitutional provision into a restriction upon the rights of the citizen," the Court ruled that the takings claim should be allowed to proceed.

In the early twentieth century, the Supreme Court recognized that regulatory restrictions on the permitted use of private property also can give rise to viable takings claims. In *Pennsylvania Coal Co. v. Mahon*, 260 U.S. 393 (1922), the Court addressed a takings claim arising from the Kohler Act, a Pennsylvania statute that prohibited a mining company from exploiting underground coal seams in a fashion that would cause surface subsidence. Relying on the same kind of analogical reasoning as the *Pumpelly* Court, Justice Oliver Wendell Holmes stated that the Kohler Act had "very nearly the same effect for constitutional purposes as appropriating or destroying [the property]," and that when regulations "go too far" they should be regarded as takings. *Id.* at 414.

For nearly 100 years since that decision, the Supreme Court has struggled with defining the meaning of the phrase "too far." Prior to the *Mahon* decision, the Supreme Court declared that "all property in this country is held under the implied obligation that the owner's use of it shall not be injurious to the community." *Mugler v. Kansas*, 123 U.S. 623, 665 (1887). It is still a vexing question today how to reconcile the "too far" principle of *Mahon* with the principle articulated in *Mugler* that no private property owner can claim an entitlement to injure the community. Generally speaking, the Court has declared that land-use regulation should be deemed to amount to a taking only "under extreme circumstances." *United States v. Riverside Bayview, Homes, Inc.*, 474 U.S. 121 (1985). But what, exactly, qualifies as extreme?

Commentators have argued with some force there is little textual or historical support for the notion that the Takings Clause applies to regulations at all, an argument that is obviously bolstered by the relative novelty of regulatory takings doctrine in historical terms. *See* Douglas T. Kendall & Charles P. Lord, The Takings Project: Using Federal Courts to Attack Community and Environmental Protections, Community Rights Counsel (April 1998) at http://communityrights.org/CombatsJudicialActivism/TP/TPcontents.php (last visited Nov. 11 (2016). As a textual matter, regulations that simply restrict the use of property, even if they diminish the value of the property, are not naturally understood to "take" private property. Furthermore, as a matter of history, the evidence suggests that the drafters of the Bill of Rights did not intend the Takings Clause to apply to regulatory action. *See* John F. Hart, Colonial Land Use Law and Its Significance for Modern Takings Doctrine, 109 Harv. L. Rev. 1252, 1283 (1996); William Michael Treanor, The Original Understanding of the Takings Clause and the Political Process, 95 Colum. L. Rev. 782, 811 (1995). But *see* Eric Claeys, Takings, Regulations, and Natural Property Rights, 88 Cornell L. Rev. 1549, 1561–65 (2003) (presenting a dissenting viewpoint). Significantly, the late Justice Antonin Scalia, a stalwart champion of private property owners, acknowledged the merits of the dominant academic view of the original understanding of the Takings Clause, observing that "early constitutional theorists did not believe the Takings Clause embraced regulations of property at all." *Lucas v. South Carolina Coastal Council*, 505 U.S. 1003, 1028 n.15 (1992).

3. Richard Epstein and Judicial Activism

Despite its debatable foundations, regulatory takings is unquestionably an established, significant part of modern constitutional law. Moreover, over the last 30 years, a relatively conservative Supreme Court has embraced an increasingly expansive reading of the Takings Clause as applied to regulation. A good portion of the credit for this legal innovation properly belongs to Professor Richard Epstein, a prolific libertarian scholar who in 1985 collected his work on the takings issue into a single volume, titled Takings: Private Property and the Power of Eminent Domain (1985). Professor Epstein boldly asserted that the Takings Clause could and should be invoked to support "a level of judicial intervention" in government regulatory affairs "far greater than we have had ever had before." *Id.* at 30-31. He called for a revision of takings doctrine that would render "constitutionally infirm or suspect many of the heralded reforms and institutions of the twentieth century: zoning, rent control, workers' compensation laws, transfer payments, [and] progressive taxation." His novel theory is based on the idea that government should "compensate" property owners whenever regulations diminish the value of private property to any degree. *Id.* at 57. Without denying that government has the power to protect the public from certain harmful land uses, Epstein argues that this power should be cabined to the prevention of traditional, common law nuisances, effectively arguing that most modern land use and environmental regulation should be deemed takings.

Epstein's revolutionary theories came in for serious criticism from scholars representing a variety of ideological positions. *Compare* Joseph L. Sax, Takings,

53 Cornell L. Rev. 279, 280 (1986) ("[T]he book purports to be constitutional theory, but it makes no effort to come to terms with more than a century of constitutional law development. Constitutional decisions (and common law developments) that do not fit the theory are simply discarded as wrong.") *with* Robert W. Bork, The Tempting of America: The Political Seduction of the Law, 230 (1990) ("My difficulty is not that Epstein's constitution would repeal much of the New Deal and the modern regulatory welfare state but rather than these conclusions are not plausibly related to the original understanding of the takings clause."). Nevertheless, Epstein's academic theories have had an enormous influence both on how the takings issue is argued and how takings cases have been decided. Epstein is very far from running the table, so to speak, but he has had a practical influence that most scholars only dream of.

Epstein's 1986 takings book quickly was identified as providing a useful intellectual underpinning for deregulatory efforts by officials in the administration of President Ronald Reagan. As explained by Harvard Law Professor and former U.S. Solicitor General Charles Fried:

> Attorney General [Edwin] Meese and his young advisors — many drawn from the ranks of the then fledgling Federalist Societies and often devotees of the extreme libertarian views of Chicago law professor Richard Epstein — had a specific, aggressive, and it seemed to me, quite radical project in mind: to use the Takings Clause of the Fifth Amendment as a severe brake upon federal and state regulation of business and property.

Order and Law: Arguing the Regan Revolution — A Firsthand Account 183 (1991).
    As Fried further explained:

> The grand plan was to make government pay compensation as for a taking of property every time its regulation impinged too severely on a property right — limiting the possible uses for a parcel of land or restricting or tying up a business in regulatory red tape. If the government labored under so severe an obligation, there would be, to say the least, much less regulation.

The Reagan administration used the takings issue to advance its deregulatory agenda in a variety of ways, including by issuing an Executive Order on Property Rights (E.O. 12630), by filing briefs supportive of property rights arguments and, most importantly, by appointing judges at all levels of the federal court system sympathetic to Epstein's agenda. *See* Kendall & Lord, The Takings Project, *supra* at 20.

In keeping with his agenda to change the law of takings, Epstein called for judges to be "activist" in their disregard of prior precedent and in their development of new law. Richard Epstein, "Needed: Activist Judges for Economic Rights," Wall Street Journal (Nov. 14, 1985). It is fair to say that over the last 30 years a majority of the modern Supreme Court has responded to this challenge by expanding the scope of regulatory takings doctrine. The Supreme Court has not decided every modern takings case in favor of property owners, and the Court sometimes takes (seemingly contradictory) steps in the direction of expansion and steps in the direction of restraint. Yet the overall thrust of the Court's development of takings doctrine has been clear. Epstein's fingerprints are evident not merely in Court citations to his work, but in the reshaping of specific features of legal doctrine, even as the Court as a whole has held back from embracing his thinking *in toto. See Lucas v. South Carolina Coastal Council,* 505 U.S. 1003, 1067-71 (1992) (adopting Epstein's nuisance exception to takings liability); *Nollan v. California Coastal Council,* 483 U.S. 825 (1987) (establishing the "essential nexus" test for development exactions).

The takings project has proceeded in the uneasy shadow of *Lochner v. New York,* 198 U.S. 45 (1905). In that famous case, the Court invoked substantive due process doctrine to strike down a New York State law limiting the maximum number of hours bakers could work. Subsequently, *Lochner* has become a virtual shorthand for judicial overreaching in the review of social or economic regulations. *See Ferguson v. Skrupa,* 372 U.S. 726, 729 (1963) ("There was a time when the Due Process Clause was used by this Court to strike down laws which were thought unreasonable, that is, unwise or incompatible with some particular economic or social philosophy," citing *Lochner*). Dissenters from the takings project, including some members of the Supreme Court itself — *see Dolan v. City of Tigard,* 512 U.S. 374, 405 (Stevens, J. dissenting) (accusing the Court of "resurrecti[ng] . . . a species of substantive due process analysis that it firmly rejected decades ago") — have observed that the takings project shares some of same problematic features as *Lochner*: dubious support in the text and original understanding of the Constitution, and excessive judicial second guessing of policy decisions by the political branches of government. The charge of Lochnerizing is substantiated by Professor Epstein's open acknowledgement that his agenda seeks in part to revive *Lochner* (*see* Richard Epstein, *Takings, supra* at 128), and by the Court's own occasional recognition that an expansive reading of the Takings Clause risks creating the same traps for the judiciary as *Lochner* did. *See Lingle v. Chevron USA, Inc.,* 544 U.S. 528, 545 (2005) ("The reasons for deference to legislative judgments about the need for, and likely effectiveness of, regulatory actions are by now well established, and we think they are no less applicable here."). Time will tell whether the takings project eventually suffers the same eclipse as *Lochner.*

4. *The* Armstrong *Principle*

If there is a single reliable lodestar in modern takings doctrine it is the so-called *Armstrong* principle: "The Fifth Amendment's guarantee that private property shall not be taken for a public use without just compensation was designed to bar Government from forcing some people alone to bear public burdens which, in all fairness and justice, should be borne by the public as a whole." *Armstrong v. United States,* 364 U.S. 40 49 (1960). The phrase appeals to a universal sense of fairness, but in practice obviously can mean either a lot or a little, which no doubt helps explains the popularity of this principle. The *Armstrong* principle highlights the fact that takings doctrine is primarily concerned with the burdensomeness of governmental action (usually — but not always — expressed in economic terms), as opposed to its potential inequity or irrationality, concerns primarily addressed in constitutional-law terms by the Equal Protection Clause and the Due Process Clause, respectively. At the same, the reference to the issue of whether an owner has been "singled out" to bear a particular burden captures the idea that generally applicable regulations are more apt to produce the kind of reciprocity of advantage that should help insulate regulations from takings claims. *See* John Echeverria, The Triumph of

Justice Stevens and the Principle of Generality, 7 Vt. J. Envtl. 22 (2005-06). The *Armstrong* principle points up the practical fact that the compensatory remedy for takings provides a direct means to correct unfairly distributed burdens.

5. The Basic Structure of Takings Cases

By way of introduction to takings litigation, it is useful to focus on the key substantive words of the Takings Clause, all or most of which have practical significance in any takings case: "[N]or shall *private property* be *taken* for *public use,* without *just compensation.*" In other words, the key terms to consider are: (1) property, (2) taking, (3) public use, and (4) just compensation. The essential import of each term is briefly described below.

The Supreme Court has repeatedly said that the Constitution does not create property interests. *Phillips v. Washington Legal Found.*, 524 U.S. 156, 174 n.2 (1998). "Rather, they are created and their dimensions are defined by existing rules or understandings that stem from an independent source, such as state law." *Webb's Fabulous Pharmacies, Inc. v. Beckwith,* 449 U.S. 155, 161 (1980). At the same time, the term "property" appears in the federal Takings Clause and what interests qualify as property within the meaning of that provision necessarily presents a question of federal law. Thus, the most useful and accurate way to think about "property" in the takings context is to recognize that federal law prescribes a "pattern" defining what qualifies as property, but state law (or some federal law other than the Takings Clause) determines whether a claimant holds an interest that matches the federal pattern. *See* Thomas Merrill, The Landscape of Constitutional Property, 86 Virginia L. Rev. 885, 952-54 (2000). Often, determining whether a claimant possesses property is easy; there is usually no doubt that someone who owns land possesses property for takings purposes. On the other hand, in *Eastern Enterprises v. Apfel,* 524 U.S. 498 (1998), a majority of the justices (albeit in separate opinions concurring in and dissenting from the Court's judgment) recognized that a federal law retroactively imposing liability on companies for their workers' health care costs did not affect property within the meaning of the Takings Clause. In some instances, the qualified nature of the interest created by federal or state law will demonstrate that it does not rise to the level of being property. *See Bowen v. Gilliard*, 483 U.S. 587 (1987) (expectation of receiving payments under statute authorizing Federal Aid to Families with Dependent Children did not constitute property, given that statute did not create a legal entitlement to benefits at a particular level). In addition, some federal or state law may represent such a fundamental, longstanding "background principle" limiting private interests in using a particular resource that a takings claimant cannot claim a "property" right to exploit the resource. *See Lucas v. South Carolina Coastal Council,* 505 U.S. 1003, 1027-30 (1992). The nature and scope of different background principles have become recurring issues in takings challenges to land use and environmental regulations post-*Lucas. See* Michael C. Blumm & Lucus Ritchie, Lucas's Unlikely Legacy, The Rise of Background Principles as Categorical Takings Defenses, 29 Harv. Envtl. L. Rev. 321 (2005).

Many cases turn, naturally enough, on the meaning of the term "taking." When the government directly appropriates property—that is, actually "takes" property — by transferring it to public ownership, the fact of a taking is self-evident. But determining whether there has been a taking is more difficult in a case that turns on analogy to traditional takings, as when it is alleged that a regulation amounts to a taking. In its most comprehensive statement on the issue, the Court has said that its regulatory takings precedents share a "common touchstone" — the attempt "to identify regulatory actions that are *functionally equivalent* to the classic taking in which government directly appropriates private property or ousts the owner from his domain." *Lingle v. Chevron U.S.A., Inc.*, 544 U.S. 528, 539 (2005) (emphasis added). Thus, the Court's regulatory takings inquiry generally "focuses directly upon *the severity of the burden* that government imposes upon private property rights." *Id.* (emphasis added). The severity of a regulatory burden is measured along either of two vectors: in the case of a physical taking, based on the extent of the interference with "the owner's right to exclude others from entering and using her property — perhaps the most fundamental of all property interests," *id.*; and in the case of regulatory restrictions on the *use* of property, based on the magnitude of the economic impact of the regulation. *Id.* at 539-40. The specific takings tests the Supreme Court has developed to implement these general principles are discussed in detail below.

[handwritten: general "takings" test]

The third issue is whether a taking is for a "public use." The Supreme Court has long embraced a relatively expansive definition of public use that encompasses any reasonable and lawful public purpose. As the Court explained in *Kelo v. City of New London*, 545 U.S. 469, 483 (2005), "For more than a century, our public use jurisprudence has wisely eschewed rigid formulas and intrusive scrutiny in favor of affording legislatures broad latitude in determining what public needs justify the use of the takings power." The public use question most often arises in the context of direct condemnations (like *Kelo*); if an exercise of eminent domain is not for a "public use," the government cannot proceed with the taking, whether or not it is able and willing to pay just compensation to the affected landowners. At the same time, the public use requirement also applies in an inverse condemnation claim. Thus, a party seeking to recover just compensation for an alleged regulatory taking needs to be able to show that the restriction, even if unfairly burdensome in economic terms, is still lawful and reasonable such that there is taking for "public use." *See Lingle.* 544 U.S. at 543 (explaining that a viable inverse-condemnation action "presupposes that the governed has acted in pursuit of valid purposes").

[handwritten: public use]

The final issue in takings cases is "just compensation." If the government has taken private property for public use but has not paid for it, the government will be liable in a suit under the Takings Clause seeking just compensation. This is the basic form of most inverse condemnation cases. A just compensation award is generally calculated based on the fair market value of the property "taken." When the government pays just compensation on account of a permanent taking it should, at least in theory, receive title to the property it has seized. But the "just compensation" issue also may be pertinent in deciding whether there has been an actionable violation of the Takings Clause at all. The Takings Clause does not make it unconstitutional to take private property for public use; such a taking violates the Constitution only if it is without "just compensation." Thus if a taking of property for public use does not trigger the just compensation requirement — for example, because the government has imposed no compensable injury — no action will lie

[handwritten: just comp? $]

under the Takings Clause. *See Brown v. Legal Found. of Washington,* 538 U.S. 216 (2003) (state's use of interest earned by small or short-term deposits in client trust accounts to finance legal services for the poor did not violate the Fifth Amendment when the accounts would have generated no net funds for the clients in absence of the program).

B. MODERN TAKINGS TESTS

As discussed above, in *Lingle,* the Court stated that all of its various regulatory takings tests are designed to ferret out those government actions that, due to the severity of their impacts, are the "functional equivalent" of traditional takings. In studying each of the takings tests below, consider how well they serve this purpose.

1. Penn Central

■ PENN CENTRAL TRANSPORTATION CO. v. NEW YORK CITY
438 U.S. 104 (1978)

Justice BRENNAN delivered the opinion of the Court.

The question presented is whether a city may, as part of a comprehensive program to preserve historic landmarks and historic districts, place restrictions on the development of individual historic landmarks — in addition to those imposed by applicable zoning ordinances — without effecting a "taking" requiring the payment of "just compensation." Specifically, we must decide whether the application of New York City's Landmarks Preservation Law to the parcel of land occupied by Grand Central Terminal has "taken" its owners' property in violation of the Fifth and Fourteenth Amendments.

I

A

Over the past 50 years, all 50 States and over 500 municipalities have enacted laws to encourage or require the preservation of buildings and areas with historic or aesthetic importance. These nationwide legislative efforts have been precipitated by two concerns. The first is recognition that, in recent years, large numbers of historic structures, landmarks, and areas have been destroyed without adequate consideration of either the values represented therein or the possibility of preserving the destroyed properties for use in economically productive ways. The second is a widely shared belief that structures with special historic, cultural, or architectural significance enhance the quality of life for all. Not only do these buildings and their workmanship represent the lessons of the past and embody precious features of our heritage, they serve as examples of quality for today. "[H]istoric conservation is but one aspect of the much larger problem, basically an environmental one, of enhancing — or perhaps developing for the first time — the quality of life for people."

New York City, responding to similar concerns and acting pursuant to a New York State enabling Act, adopted its Landmarks Preservation Law in 1965 . . . Final designation as a landmark results in restrictions upon the property owner's options concerning use of the landmark site. First, the law imposes a duty upon the owner to keep the exterior features of the building "in good repair" to assure that the law's objectives not be defeated by the landmark's falling into a state of irremediable disrepair. Second, the [NYC Landmarks Preservation] Commission must approve in advance any proposal to alter the exterior architectural features of the landmark or to construct any exterior improvement on the landmark site, thus ensuring that decisions concerning construction on the landmark site are made with due consideration of both the public interest in the maintenance of the structure and the landowner's interest in use of the property. . . .

Although the designation of a landmark and landmark site restricts the owner's control over the parcel, designation also enhances the economic position of the landmark owner in one significant respect. Under New York City's zoning laws, owners of real property who have not developed their property to the full extent permitted by the applicable zoning laws are allowed to transfer development rights to contiguous parcels on the same city block. A 1968 ordinance gave the owners of landmark sites additional opportunities to transfer development rights to other parcels. Subject to a restriction that the floor area of the transferee lot may not be increased by more than 20% above its authorized level, the ordinance permitted transfers from a landmark parcel to property across the street or across a street intersection. In 1969, . . . [t]he class of recipient lots was expanded to include lots "across a street and opposite to another lot or lots which except for the intervention of streets or street intersections f[or]m a series extending to the lot occupied by the landmark building [, provided that] all lots [are] in the same ownership." In addition, the 1969 amendment permits, in highly commercialized areas like midtown Manhattan, the transfer of all unused development rights to a single parcel.

B

This case involves the application of New York City's Landmarks Preservation Law to Grand Central Terminal (Terminal). The Terminal, which is owned by the Penn Central Transportation Co. and its affiliates (Penn Central), is one of New York City's most famous buildings. Opened in 1913, it is regarded not only as providing an ingenious engineering solution to the problems presented by urban railroad stations, but also as a magnificent example of the French beaux-arts style. . . .

On August 2, 1967, following a public hearing, the Commission designated the Terminal a "landmark" and designated the "city tax block" it occupies a "landmark site". . . .

On January 22, 1968, appellant Penn Central, to increase its income, entered into a renewable 50-year lease and sublease agreement with appellant UGP Properties, Inc. (UGP), a wholly owned subsidiary of Union General Properties, Ltd., a United Kingdom corporation. Under the terms of the agreement, UGP was to construct a multistory office building above the Terminal. UGP promised to pay Penn Central $1 million annually during construction and at least $3 million annually thereafter. The rentals would be offset in part by a loss of some $700,000 to

$1 million in net rentals presently received from concessionaires displaced by the new building. Appellants UGP and Penn Central then applied to the Commission for permission to construct an office building atop the Terminal. . . . After four days of hearings at which over 80 witnesses testified, the Commission denied th[e] application. . . .

[A]ppellants filed suit in New York Supreme Court, Trial Term, claiming, *inter alia*, that the application of the Landmarks Preservation Law had "taken" their property without just compensation in violation of the Fifth and Fourteenth Amendments. . . . [The trial court ruled in favor of Penn Central, but the ruling was reversed on appeal within the state court system.] We affirm.

II

The issues presented by appellants are (1) whether the restrictions imposed by New York City's law upon appellants' exploitation of the Terminal site effect a "taking" of appellants' property for a public use within the meaning of the Fifth Amendment, which of course is made applicable to the States through the Fourteenth Amendment, and, (2), if so, whether the transferable development rights afforded appellants constitute "just compensation" within the meaning of the Fifth Amendment. We need only address the question whether a "taking" has occurred.

A

Before considering appellants' specific contentions, it will be useful to review the factors that have shaped the jurisprudence of the Fifth Amendment injunction "nor shall private property be taken for public use, without just compensation." The question of what constitutes a "taking" for purposes of the Fifth Amendment has proved to be a problem of considerable difficulty. While this Court has recognized that the "Fifth Amendment's guarantee . . . [is] designed to bar Government from forcing some people alone to bear public burdens which, in all fairness and justice, should be borne by the public as a whole," *Armstrong v. United States*, this Court, quite simply, has been unable to develop any "set formula" for determining when "justice and fairness" require that economic injuries caused by public action be compensated by the government, rather than remain disproportionately concentrated on a few persons. Indeed, we have frequently observed that whether a particular restriction will be rendered invalid by the government's failure to pay for any losses proximately caused by it depends largely "upon the particular circumstances [in that] case."

In engaging in these essentially ad hoc, factual inquiries, the Court's decisions have identified several factors that have particular significance. The economic impact of the regulation on the claimant and, particularly, the extent to which the regulation has interfered with distinct investment-backed expectations are, of course, relevant considerations. So, too, is the character of the governmental action. A "taking" may more readily be found when the interference with property can be characterized as a physical invasion by government, than when interference arises from some public program adjusting the benefits and burdens of economic life to promote the common good.

"Government hardly could go on if to some extent values incident to property could not be diminished without paying for every such change in the general law," *Pennsylvania Coal Co. v. Mahon*, 260 U.S. 393, 413 (1922), and this Court has accordingly recognized, in a wide variety of contexts, that government may execute laws or programs that adversely affect recognized economic values. Exercises of the taxing power are one obvious example. A second are the decisions in which this Court has dismissed "taking" challenges on the ground that, while the challenged government action caused economic harm, it did not interfere with interests that were sufficiently bound up with the reasonable expectations of the claimant to constitute "property" for Fifth Amendment purposes. *See, e.g., United States v. Willow River Power Co.*, 324 U.S. 499 (1945) (interest in high-water level of river for runoff for tailwaters to maintain power head is not property). . . .

More importantly for the present case, in instances in which a state tribunal reasonably concluded that "the health, safety, morals, or general welfare" would be promoted by prohibiting particular contemplated uses of land, this Court has upheld land-use regulations that destroyed or adversely affected recognized real property interests. Zoning laws are, of course, the classic example, which have been viewed as permissible governmental action even when prohibiting the most beneficial use of the property. . . .

Goldblatt v. Hempstead, [369 U.S. 590 (1962)] is a recent example. There, a 1958 city safety ordinance banned any excavations below the water table and effectively prohibited the claimant from continuing a sand and gravel mining business that had been operated on the particular parcel since 1927. The Court upheld the ordinance against a "taking" challenge, although the ordinance prohibited the present and presumably most beneficial use of the property and had, like the regulations in *Miller* and *Hadacheck*, severely affected a particular owner. The Court assumed that the ordinance did not prevent the owner's reasonable use of the property since the owner made no showing of an adverse effect on the value of the land. Because the restriction served a substantial public purpose, the Court thus held no taking had occurred. It is, of course, implicit in *Goldblatt* that a use restriction on real property may constitute a "taking" if not reasonably necessary to the effectuation of a substantial public purpose, see *Nectow v. Cambridge*, [277 U.S. 183 (1928)] cf. *Moore v. East Cleveland*, 431 U.S. 494, 513–514 (1977) (Stevens, J., concurring), or perhaps if it has an unduly harsh impact upon the owner's use of the property.

Pennsylvania Coal Co. v. Mahon, 260 U.S. 393 (1922), is the leading case for the proposition that a state statute that substantially furthers important public policies may so frustrate distinct investment-backed expectations as to amount to a "taking." There the claimant had sold the surface rights to particular parcels of property, but expressly reserved the right to remove the coal thereunder. A Pennsylvania statute, enacted after the transactions, forbade any mining of coal that caused the subsidence of any house, unless the house was the property of the owner of the underlying coal and was more than 150 feet from the improved property of another. Because the statute made it commercially impracticable to mine the coal, and thus had nearly the same effect as the complete destruction of rights claimant had reserved from the owners of the surface land, the Court held that the statute was invalid as effecting a "taking" without just compensation. . . .

B

In contending that the New York City law has "taken" their property in violation of the Fifth and Fourteenth Amendments, appellants make a series of arguments, which, while tailored to the facts of this case, essentially urge that any substantial restriction imposed pursuant to a landmark law must be accompanied by just compensation if it is to be constitutional. Before considering these, we emphasize what is not in dispute. Because this Court has recognized, in a number of settings, that States and cities may enact land-use restrictions or controls to enhance the quality of life by preserving the character and desirable aesthetic features of a city, appellants do not contest that New York City's objective of preserving structures and areas with special historic, architectural, or cultural significance is an entirely permissible governmental goal. They also do not dispute that the restrictions imposed on its parcel are appropriate means of securing the purposes of the New York City law. Finally, appellants do not challenge any of the specific factual premises of the decision below. They accept for present purposes both that the parcel of land occupied by Grand Central Terminal must, in its present state, be regarded as capable of earning a reasonable return, and that the transferable development rights afforded appellants by virtue of the Terminal's designation as a landmark are valuable, even if not as valuable as the rights to construct above the Terminal. In appellants' view none of these factors derogate from their claim that New York City's law has effected a "taking."

They first observe that the airspace above the Terminal is a valuable property interest. They urge that the Landmarks Law has deprived them of any gainful use of their "air rights" above the Terminal and that, irrespective of the value of the remainder of their parcel, the city has "taken" their right to this superadjacent airspace, thus entitling them to "just compensation" measured by the fair market value of these air rights.

Apart from our own disagreement with appellants' characterization of the effect of the New York City law, the submission that appellants may establish a "taking" simply by showing that they have been denied the ability to exploit a property interest that they heretofore had believed was available for development is quite simply untenable. Were this the rule, this Court would have erred not only in upholding laws restricting the development of air rights, but also in approving those prohibiting both the subjacent and the lateral development of particular parcels. "Taking" jurisprudence does not divide a single parcel into discrete segments and attempt to determine whether rights in a particular segment have been entirely abrogated. In deciding whether a particular governmental action has effected a taking, this Court focuses rather both on the character of the action and on the nature and extent of the interference with rights in the parcel as a whole — here, the city tax block designated as the "landmark site."

Secondly, appellants, focusing on the character and impact of the New York City law, argue that it effects a "taking" because its operation has significantly diminished the value of the Terminal site. Appellants concede that the decisions sustaining other land-use regulations, which, like the New York City law, are reasonably related to the promotion of the general welfare, uniformly reject the proposition that diminution in property value, standing alone, can establish a "taking, and that the "taking" issue in these contexts is resolved by focusing on the uses the regulations permit. Appellants, moreover, also do not dispute that a showing of diminution in property value would not establish a taking if the restriction had been imposed as a result of historic-district legislation, but appellants argue that New York City's regulation of individual landmarks is fundamentally different from zoning or from historic-district legislation because the controls imposed by New York City's law apply only to individuals who own selected properties.

Stated baldly, appellants' position appears to be that the only means of ensuring that selected owners are not singled out to endure financial hardship for no reason is to hold that any restriction imposed on individual landmarks pursuant to the New York City scheme is a "taking" requiring the payment of "just compensation." Agreement with this argument would, of course, invalidate not just New York City's law, but all comparable landmark legislation in the Nation. We find no merit in it.

It is true, as appellants emphasize, that both historic-district legislation and zoning laws regulate all properties within given physical communities whereas landmark laws apply only to selected parcels. But, contrary to appellants' suggestions, landmark laws are not like discriminatory, or "reverse spot," zoning: that is, a land-use decision which arbitrarily singles out a particular parcel for different, less favorable treatment than the neighboring ones. In contrast to discriminatory zoning, which is the antithesis of land-use control as part of some comprehensive plan, the New York City law embodies a comprehensive plan to preserve structures of historic or aesthetic interest wherever they might be found in the city, and as noted, over 400 landmarks and 31 historic districts have been designated pursuant to this plan.

Equally without merit is the related argument that the decision to designate a structure as a landmark "is inevitably arbitrary or at least subjective, because it is basically a matter of taste," thus unavoidably singling out individual landowners for disparate and unfair treatment. The argument has a particularly hollow ring in this case. For appellants not only did not seek judicial review of either the designation or of the denials of the certificates of appropriateness and of no exterior effect, but do not even now suggest that the Commission's decisions concerning the Terminal were in any sense arbitrary or unprincipled. But, in any event, a landmark owner has a right to judicial review of any Commission decision, and, quite simply, there is no basis whatsoever for a conclusion that courts will have any greater difficulty identifying arbitrary or discriminatory action in the context of landmark regulation than in the context of classic zoning or indeed in any other context.

Next, appellants observe that New York City's law differs from zoning laws and historic-district ordinances in that the Landmarks Law does not impose identical or similar restrictions on all structures located in particular physical communities. It follows, they argue, that New York City's law is inherently incapable of producing the fair and equitable distribution of benefits and burdens of governmental action which is characteristic of zoning laws and historic-district legislation and which they maintain is a constitutional requirement if "just compensation" is not to be afforded. It is, of course, true that the Landmarks Law has a more severe impact on some landowners than on others, but that in itself does not mean that the law effects a "taking." Legislation designed to promote the general welfare commonly burdens some more than others. The owners of the . . . gravel and sand mine in *Goldblatt v. Hempstead* were uniquely burdened by the legislation sustained in those cases. Similarly, zoning laws often affect some property owners more severely than others but have not been held to be invalid on that account. For example, the property owner in *Euclid* who wished to use its property for industrial purposes was affected far more severely by the ordinance than its neighbors who wished to use their land for residences". . . .

In any event, appellants' repeated suggestions that they are solely burdened and unbenefited is factually inaccurate. This contention overlooks the fact that the New York City law applies to vast numbers of structures in the city in addition to the Terminal — all the structures contained in the 31 historic districts and over 400 individual landmarks, many of which are close to the Terminal. Unless we are to reject the judgment of the New York City Council that the preservation of landmarks benefits all New York citizens and all structures, both economically and by improving the quality of life in the city as a whole — which we are unwilling to do — we cannot conclude that the owners of the Terminal have in no sense been benefited by the Landmarks Law. . . .

c

Rejection of appellants' broad arguments is not, however, the end of our inquiry, for all we thus far have established is that the New York City law is not rendered invalid by its failure to provide "just compensation" whenever a landmark owner is restricted in the exploitation of property interests, such as air rights, to a greater extent than provided for under applicable zoning laws. We now must consider whether the interference with appellants' property is of such a magnitude that "there must be an exercise of eminent domain and compensation to sustain [it]." That inquiry may be narrowed to the question of the severity of the impact of the law on appellants' parcel, and its resolution in turn requires a careful assessment of the impact of the regulation on the Terminal site.

[T]he New York City law does not interfere in any way with the present uses of the Terminal. Its designation as a landmark not only permits but contemplates that appellants may continue to use the property precisely as it has been used for the past 65 years: as a railroad terminal containing office space and concessions. So the law does not interfere with what must be regarded as Penn Central's primary expectation concerning the use of the parcel. More importantly, on this record, we must regard the New York City law as permitting Penn Central not only to profit from the Terminal but also to obtain a "reasonable return" on its investment.

Appellants, moreover, exaggerate the effect of the law on their ability to make use of the air rights above the Terminal in two respects. First, it simply cannot be maintained, on this record, that appellants have been prohibited from occupying *any* portion of the airspace above the Terminal. While the Commission's actions in denying applications to construct an office building in excess of 50 stories above the Terminal may indicate that it will refuse to issue a certificate of appropriateness for any comparably sized structure, nothing the Commission has said or done suggests an intention to prohibit *any* construction above the Terminal. The Commission's report emphasized that whether any construction would be allowed depended upon whether the proposed addition "would harmonize in scale, material and character with [the Terminal]". . . .

Second, to the extent appellants have been denied the right to build above the Terminal, it is not literally accurate to say that they have been denied *all* use of even those pre-existing air rights. Their ability to use these rights has not been abrogated; they are made transferable to at least eight parcels in the vicinity of the Terminal, one or two of which have been found suitable for the construction of new office buildings. Although appellants and others have argued that New York City's transferable development-rights program is far from ideal, the New York courts here supportably found that, at least in the case of the Terminal, the rights afforded are valuable. While these rights may well not have constituted "just compensation" if a "taking" had occurred, the rights nevertheless undoubtedly mitigate whatever financial burdens the law has imposed on appellants and, for that reason, are to be taken into account in considering the impact of regulation.

On this record, we conclude that the application of New York City's Landmarks Law has not effected a "taking" of appellants' property. The restrictions imposed are substantially related to the promotion of the general welfare and not only permit reasonable beneficial use of the landmark site but also afford appellants opportunities further to enhance not only the Terminal site proper but also other properties.[36]

Affirmed.

Justice REHNQUIST dissented, joined by Chief Justice BURGER and Justice STEVENS.

Of the over one million buildings and structures in the city of New York, appellees have singled out 400 for designation as official landmarks. The owner of a building might initially be pleased that his property has been chosen by a distinguished committee of architects, historians, and city planners for such a singular distinction. But he may well discover, as appellant Penn Central Transportation Co. did here, that the landmark designation imposes upon him a substantial cost, with little or no offsetting benefit except for the honor of the designation. The question in this case is whether the cost associated with the city of New York's desire to preserve a limited number of "landmarks" within its borders must be borne by all of its taxpayers or whether it can instead be imposed entirely on the owners of the individual properties. . . .

[handwritten: who eats up the costs.]

I.

The Fifth Amendment provides in part: "nor shall private property be taken for public use, without just compensation." In a very literal sense, the actions of appellees violated this constitutional prohibition. Before the city of New York declared Grand Central Terminal to be a landmark, Penn Central could have used its "air rights" over the Terminal to build a multistory office building, at an apparent value of several million dollars per year. Today, the Terminal cannot be modified in *any* form, including the erection of additional stories, without the permission of the Landmark Preservation Commission, a permission which appellants, despite good-faith attempts, have so far been unable to obtain. Because the Taking Clause of the Fifth Amendment has not always been read literally, however, the constitutionality of appellees' actions requires a closer scrutiny of this Court's interpretation of the three key words in the Taking Clause — "property," "taken," and "just compensation."

Appellees do not dispute that valuable property rights have been destroyed. . . . While neighboring landowners are free to use their land and "air rights" in any way

36. We emphasize that our holding today is on the present record, which in turn is based on Penn Central's present ability to use the Terminal for its intended purposes and in a gainful fashion. The city conceded at oral argument that if appellants can demonstrate at some point in the future that circumstances have so changed that the Terminal ceases to be "economically viable," appellants may obtain relief. *See* Tr. of Oral Arg. 42–43.

consistent with the broad boundaries of New York zoning, Penn Central, absent the permission of appellees, must forever maintain its property in its present state. The property has been thus subjected to a nonconsensual servitude not borne by any neighboring or similar properties. . . . [But] "not every destruction or injury to property by governmental action has been held to be a 'taking' in the constitutional sense. . . ." [A]n examination of the two exceptions where the destruction of property does *not* constitute a taking demonstrates that a compensable taking has occurred here.

[First, a]s early as 1887, the Court recognized that the government can prevent a property owner from using his property to injure others without having to compensate the owner for the value of the forbidden use. . . . Thus, there is no "taking" where a city prohibits the operation of a brickyard within a residential area, or forbids excavation for sand and gravel below the water line. Nor is it relevant, where the government is merely prohibiting a noxious use of property, that the government would seem to be singling out a particular property owner . . .

The nuisance exception to the taking guarantee is not coterminous with the police power itself. The question is whether the forbidden use is dangerous to the safety, health, or welfare of others. . . .

The prohibition in question . . . was "not a prevention of a misuse or illegal use but the prevention of a legal and essential use, an attribute of its ownership." Appellees are not prohibiting a nuisance. The record is clear that the proposed addition to the Grand Central Terminal would be in full compliance with zoning, height limitations, and other health and safety requirements. Instead, appellees are seeking to preserve what they believe to be an outstanding example of beaux-arts architecture. Penn Central is prevented from further developing its property basically because *too good* a job was done in designing and building it. The city of New York, because of its unadorned admiration for the design, has decided that the owners of the building must preserve it unchanged for the benefit of sightseeing New Yorkers and tourists.

[Second, e]ven where the government prohibits a noninjurious use, the Court has ruled that a taking does not take place if the prohibition applies over a broad cross section of land and thereby "secure[s] an average reciprocity of advantage." It is for this reason that zoning does not constitute a "taking." While zoning at times reduces *individual* property values, the burden is shared relatively evenly and it is reasonable to conclude that on the whole an individual who is harmed by one aspect of the zoning will be benefited by another.

Here, however, a multimillion dollar loss has been imposed on appellants; it is uniquely felt and is not offset by any benefits flowing from the preservation of some 400 other "landmarks" in New York City. Appellees have imposed a substantial cost on less than one one-tenth of one percent of the buildings in New York City for the general benefit of all its people. It is exactly this imposition of general costs on a few individuals at which the "taking" protection is directed. . . .

[Finally, a]ppellees, apparently recognizing that the constraints imposed on a landmark site constitute a taking for Fifth Amendment purposes, do not leave the property owner empty-handed. As the Court notes . . . the property owner may theoretically "transfer" his previous right to develop the landmark property to adjacent properties if they are under his control. Appellees have coined this system "Transfer Development Rights," or TDR's.

Of all the terms used in the Taking Clause, "just compensation" has the strictest meaning. The Fifth Amendment does not allow simply an approximate compensation but requires "a full and perfect equivalent for the property taken". . . .

Appellees contend that, even if they have "taken" appellants' property, TDR's constitute "just compensation." Appellants, of course, argue that TDR's are highly imperfect compensation. Because the lower courts held that there was no "taking," they did not have to reach the question of whether or not just compensation has already been awarded. . . . Because the record on appeal is relatively slim, I would remand to the Court of Appeals for a determination of whether TDR's constitute a "full and perfect equivalent for the property taken."

II

Over 50 years ago, Mr. Justice Holmes, speaking for the Court, warned that the courts were "in danger of forgetting that a strong public desire to improve the public condition is not enough to warrant achieving the desire by a shorter cut than the constitutional way of paying for the change." *Pennsylvania Coal Co. v. Mahon*, 260 U.S., at 416. The Court's opinion in this case demonstrates that the danger thus foreseen has not abated. The city of New York is in a precarious financial state, and some may believe that the costs of landmark preservation will be more easily borne by corporations such as Penn Central than the overburdened individual taxpayers of New York. But these concerns do not allow us to ignore past precedents construing the Eminent Domain Clause to the end that the desire to improve the public condition is, indeed, achieved by a shorter cut than the constitutional way of paying for the change.

Notes and Comments

1. *The Parcel as a Whole Rule.* The *Penn Central* Court held that the company's takings claim had to be evaluated in relation to the "parcel as a whole" — thus giving birth to what now is popularly known as the "parcel as a whole rule." The plaintiffs alleged a taking of the "air rights" atop Grand Central Terminal and claimed they were entitled to compensation for the taking of that specific stick in their bundle of property rights — "irrespective of the value of the remainder of their parcel." The plaintiffs' purpose in making this argument was to make the adverse economic impact of the restriction appear substantial, maximizing their chances of a takings recovery. The government's purpose in arguing for a broader parcel definition was just the opposite, to make the economic impact appear more modest, minimizing the chances of a takings recovery.

The Court ruled in favor of the government, concluding that the relevant parcel consisted not of the air rights alone but "of the city tax block designated as the 'landmark site.'" Defined in this fashion, the relevant parcel included the existing terminal, which was a valuable part of the company's train operations and also contained substantial leasable space. Once the Court defined the parcel in this fashion, it had little difficulty concluding there was no taking, observing that the landmarks law did "not interfere with what must be regarded as Penn Central's primary expectation concerning the use of the parcel," and that the company could still "obtain a 'reasonable return' on its investment."

The parcel issue–or the denominator question, as it is sometimes called–is a recurring question in takings litigation. For example, if a firm owns both the surface estate and the subsurface mineral estate, does the relevant property include both interests or can the owner allege a taking of the restricted mineral estate alone? *See Keystone Bituminous Coal Ass'n v. DeBenedictis*, 480 U.S. 470 (1987) (relevant parcel includes both estates). If the Army Corps of Engineers denies a property owner permission to fill some wetland acres on a portion of a larger real estate tract, is the takings claim evaluated by looking at the restricted wetland acres alone or the entire tract? *See Walcek v. United States*, 303 F.3d 1349 (Fed. Cir. 2002) (entire tract). In *Tahoe-Sierra Pres. Council v. Tahoe Regional Planning Agency*, 535 U.S. 302 (2002), the Court held that the parcel as a whole rule applies in the temporal dimension, meaning that analysis of a takings claim based on a development moratorium should consider the fact that regulatory restrictions will be lifted once the moratorium ends.

Academic commentary on the parcel as a whole rule is voluminous. *See, e.g.,* Daniel L. Siegel, How the History and Purpose of the Regulatory Takings Doctrine Help to Define the Parcel as a Whole Rule, 36 Vt. L. Rev. 693 (2012) (advocating a pro-government viewpoint); John Fee, Unearthing the Denominator in Regulatory Takings Claims, 61 U. Chi. L. Rev. 1535, 1563 (1994) (advocating a pro-developer position).

2. *The Future of the Parcel as a Whole Rule*. The Supreme Court has repeatedly reaffirmed and applied the parcel as a whole rule, but without providing a great deal of guidance on its scope and proper application. *Compare Tahoe Sierra, supra; Concrete Pipe and Products of California, Inc. v. Construction Laborers Pension Trust for Southern California*, 508 U.S. 602 (1993) (applying the parcel rule) *with Hodel v. Irving*, 481 U.S. 704, 716 (1987) (holding that federal legislation effected a taking of "the fundamental right to pass on property to ones' heirs," and ignoring the parcel issue). In the absence of detailed guidance from the high court, most lower courts have applied a multifactor approach in analyzing the nuanced questions that frequently arise in applying the parcel rule. For example, in determining whether a legally subdivided parcel of real estate represents a single parcel or multiple parcels, the U.S. Court of Appeals for the D.C. Circuit, in a leading case, said that it evaluates "several factors to determine the relevant parcel: the degree of contiguity, the dates of acquisition, the extent to which the parcel has been treated as a single unit, and the extent to which the restricted lots benefit the unregulated lot." *District Intown Properties Ltd. P'ship v. District of Columbia*, 198 F.3d 874, 880 (D.C. Cir. 1999).

As this book was going to print, the Supreme Court was preparing to schedule oral argument in *Murr v. State of Wisconsin*, No. 15-214, presenting the question of how to define the relevant parcel in a takings challenge to a "lot merger" provision of a zoning ordinance. This case may produce important new guidance on the proper application of the parcel as a whole rule.

3. *Applying the* Penn Central *Factors*. A first-time reader of *Penn Central* will have understandable difficulty extracting from the Court's opinion a clear, definitive analytic framework for evaluating regulatory takings claims. But within a few years of that decision, the Court distilled down *Penn Central's* discursive description of takings doctrine to a non-exclusive list of three factors — "the economic impact of the regulation, its interference with reasonable investment backed expectations, and the character of the governmental action — that have particular significance." *Kaiser Aetna v. United States*, 444 U.S. 164, 175 (1979). Twenty-five years later, the

Court went so far as to describe this three-part analysis as the "polestar" of its takings jurisprudence. *Tahoe-Sierra Preservation Council v. Tahoe Regional Planning Agency*, 535 U.S. 302, 336 (2002), quoting *Palazzolo v. Rhode Island*, 533 U.S. 606, 633 (2001) (O'Connor, J, concurring). *Penn Central* unquestionably represents the most important test in takings litigation today.

4. *Takings and /or Due Process.* The *Penn Central* decision also launched one of the most confused and confusing subplots in the development of takings doctrine — the notion that a successful takings claim can be based on a showing that a regulation "failed to substantially advance a legitimate state interest." This ostensible takings test hopelessly muddled takings and due process doctrines, making takings law quite chaotic and unpredictable. The problem was not solved until 2005, when in *Lingle v. Chevron U.S.A., Inc.*, 544 U.S. 528, 548 (2005), a unanimous Supreme Court repudiated the test, holding that "the 'substantially advances' formula is not a valid takings test, and indeed . . . that it has no proper place in our takings jurisprudence."

In *Penn Central*, the Court discussed at length the case of *Goldblatt v. Hempstead*, 369 U.S. 590 (1962), in which the Court rejected a takings challenge to a regulation of a sand and gravel operation. Fatefully, the Court stated: "It is, of course, implicit in *Goldblatt* that a use restriction on real property may constitute a "taking" if not reasonably necessary to the effectuation of a substantial public purpose, *see Nectow v. Cambridge*, [277 U.S. 183 (1928)] *cf. Moore v. East Cleveland, 431 U.S. 494, 513–514 (1977)* (Stevens, J., concurring), or perhaps if it has an unduly harsh impact upon the owner's use of the property." This description of the framework for takings analysis is obviously quite different from the three-part analytic framework for which the *Penn Central* case is most famous. It is also plainly drawn from due process precedents, not takings precedents: *Nectow* (discussed in Chapter 2) is obviously a substantive due process case; in *Moore*, Justice Stevens, in a solitary concurring opinion, expressed the view (never apparently repeated by himself or any other justice) that the Court had "fused" the takings and due process inquiries "into a single standard."

In the years following the *Penn Central* decision, the Supreme Court, in addition to deploying the three-factor framework, also derived a separate, two-part test from *Penn Central*. In *Agins v. City of Tiburon*, 447 U.S. 255, 260 (1980), the Court declared that "[t]he application of a general zoning law to particular property effects a taking if the ordinance does not substantially advance legitimate state interests . . . , or denies an owner economically viable use of his land, see *Penn Central*. . . . " In addition to relying on this test to support rejecting the takings claim in *Agins*, the Court also relied on the test in *Keystone Bituminous Coal Ass'n v. De Benedictis*, 480 U.S. 470 (1987), and referenced the test in dicta in several others cases. *See, e.g., Lucas v. South Carolina Coastal Council*, 505 U.S. 1003, 1016 (1992). Lower courts, most notably the U.S. Court of Appeals for the Ninth Circuit, invoked the substantially advance formula to support rulings in favor of takings claimants. *See, e g., Richardson v. City and County of Honolulu*, 124 F.3d 1150 (9th Cir. 1997) (striking down a law establishing a mechanism for converting leasehold interests in condominium units into fee interests as a taking using the substantially advance test).

More than 25 years after the *Penn Central* decision launched the "substantially advance" test, the Court repudiated this takings test *in toto* in *Lingle v. Chevron*. In doing so, the Court reversed a decision by the Ninth Circuit upholding a ruling that a Hawaii gas station rent control law resulted in a taking because it failed to substantially advance a legitimate governmental interest. The Court said there was "no question" that the test was derived from due process precedents, not takings precedents. The Court also observed that the test implied a kind of means-ends analysis, an inquiry which "has some logic in the context of a due process challenge," 544 U.S. at 542, but is not a valid basis for identifying a taking, which turns on the burdensomeness of the government action. Not only is an inquiry into the validity of government action a poor fit in takings doctrine, the Court explained, but it is inconsistent with the premise of a valid takings claim that the government has acted for a "public use," — that is, a "valid public purpose."

Finally, the Court stated that the substantially advances formula was "not only doctrinally untenable," but it also presented "serious practical difficulties" because it "would require courts to scrutinize the efficacy of a vast array of state and federal regulations — a task for which courts are not well suited." With a veiled reference to the *Lochner* era, the Court concluded, "[t]he reasons for deference to legislative judgments about the need for, and likely effectiveness of, regulatory actions are by now well established, and we think they are no less applicable here."

In considering some of the Supreme Court's most recent takings decisions (excerpted below), consider whether the Court has adhered to the principle of judicial restraint articulated in *Lingle*.

A Note on Applying the *Penn Central* Factors

While the *Penn Central* analysis is firmly entrenched, the Court has given little guidance on how the different factors should be defined or how they should be applied together to generate a judicial decision. *See* Thomas Merrill, The Character of the Governmental Action, 36 Vt. L. Rev. 649 (2012); John D. Echeverria, Making Sense of *Penn Central*, 39 Envtl. L. Rep. News & Analysis 10471 (2009). Nonetheless, based on Supreme Court and certain lower court decisions applying *Penn Central*, it is possible to put some meat on the bones of the three factors.

1. *Economic Impact.* The courts have developed several techniques for measuring the adverse economic impact of regulatory restrictions on property for the purpose of takings analysis. First, using the so-called "with-and-without-method," courts commonly compare the market value of the property on the assumption that the regulation does not apply to the property with the current market value of the property subject to the regulatory restriction that is the focus of the takings claim. To determine these figures, counsel for the parties hire expert appraisers who develop market-value estimates by comparing the value of the subject property (with and without the restrictions) compared to other, comparable properties in the area. The Supreme Court has never specifically addressed the quantum of economic impact necessary to establish a taking. However, the Court has stated that the impact must be "extreme," *United States v. Riverside Bayview Homes, Inc.*, 474 U.S. 121, 126 (1985), and lower courts have made the same point with greater specificity. *See, e.g., Rose Acres Farms, Inc. v. United States*, 373 F.3d 1177, 1195 (Fed Cir. 2004) (taking requires "severe economic deprivation"); *Warren Trust Co. v. United States*, 107 Fed. Cl. 533, 568 (2012) (deprivations of value "well in excess of 85%" generally necessary to establish a taking).

There are several interrelated justifications for requiring a seemingly high level of economic impact to justify a finding of takings liability. First, as discussed above, the entire doctrine of regulatory takings is problematic from a historical perspective, arguably making it appropriate to confine this invented judicial doctrine to a narrow sphere. Second, there is the functional argument that an expansive regulatory takings doctrine would severely interfere with the necessary and ordinary operations of government; as the *Mahon* Court put it, "[g]overnment hardly could go on if to some extent values incident to property could not be diminished without paying for every such change in the general law." 260 U.S. 393, 413 (1922). Third, use of a high threshold can be justified to counteract the tendency of the before-and-after methodology to exaggerate the "economic loss" caused by regulation. An appraiser's estimate of the value a property would have if a restriction were lifted from that property alone necessarily misstates the actual net impact of the restriction. Regulations can reduce property values by blocking certain development, but they also can raise value by increasing the scarcity and hence the value of development opportunities and by protecting amenities in the community. To accurately calculate the impact of regulatory restrictions on property value one would have to calculate the value a property would have if the regulation had never been adopted and had never been applied to anyone in the community — a very complex economic calculus that is far beyond the capacity of ordinary litigants.

Another, somewhat less commonly used, method for defining economic impact is to compare the purchase price of the property with its current market value subject to regulations. *See, e.g., Florida Rock Indus., Inc. v. United States*, 791 F.2d 893, 905 (Fed. Cir. 1986) ("[i]n determining . . . economic impact, the owner's opportunity to recoup its investment . . . cannot be ignored"); *Walcek v. United States*, 49 Fed. Cl. 248, 266-67 (2001), *aff'd*, 303 F.3d 1349 (Fed. Cir. 2002). In the unique context of utility/common-carrier rate-setting, courts apply a special test focused on whether the utility is being limited to charging rates that are "so low as to be confiscatory." *Duquesne Light Co. v. Barasch*, 488 U.S. 299, 310 (1989). But, in general, including in the realm of land use regulations, loss of anticipated profits is generally regarded as "a slender reed upon which to rest a takings claim." *Andrus v. Allard*, 444 U.S. 51, 66 (1979).

2. *Investment-Backed Expectations.* The second *Penn Central* factor focuses on whether and to what degree the government action interferes with investment-backed expectations. In *Palazzolo v. Rhode Island*, 535 U.S. 606 (2001), the Court rejected the so-called "notice rule," a bright-line test adopted by many lower courts that called for the automatic rejection of takings claims based on regulations already in place when the complainant purchased the property. Even while the Court explicitly rejected the absolute notice rule in *Palazzolo*, a majority of the justices (one concurring and the others dissenting) recognized that notice of regulatory restrictions in place at the time of purchase should at least be a *factor* in the takings analysis. Most lower courts have adopted the view that advance notice is a relevant consideration in deciding whether to award compensation under the Takings Clause. *See, e.g., Appolo Fuels, Inc. v. United States*, 381 F.3d 1338, 1348 (Fed. Cir. 2004) (*Palazzolo* did not reject the principle that "the regulatory regime in place at the time the claimant acquires the property at issue helps to shape the reasonableness of those expectations").

A second interpretation of the expectations factor focuses on whether adoption of the new regulation was in some sense foreseeable. A leading case breaks this inquiry into several elements, including: (1) whether the plaintiff operated in a "highly regulated industry;" (2) whether the plaintiff was aware of the problem that spawned the regulation at the time it purchased the property; and (3) whether the plaintiff could have "reasonably anticipated" the possibility of such regulation in light of the "regulatory environment" at the time of purchase. *Commonwealth Edison Co. v. United States*, 271 F.3d 1327, 1350 n.22 (Fed. Cir. 2001) (*en banc*).

Finally, in some cases courts focus on the specific purpose of the property purchase and whether that purpose has been frustrated. A classic example of severe interference with such investment expectations is *Lucas v. South Carolina Coastal Council*, 505 U.S. 1003 (1992), in which David Lucas purchased two lots for coastal development and then was met, only a few years later, with a new state law barring construction on his lots. The *Penn Central* case represents a polar opposite example, because the historic landmark regulation had no effect on the company's original motivation for buying the site and building Grand Central Terminal which was to operate a railroad station.

3. *Character.* The final factor is the most elusive. In *Penn Central* itself, the Court provided illustrations of how the character factor might be applied, stating "[a] taking may more readily be found when the interference with property can be characterized as a physical invasion by government [citing *United States v. Causby*, 328 U.S. 256 (1946)], than when interference arises from some public program adjusting the benefits and burdens of economic life to promote the common good." 438 U.S. at 124. *Causby* involved a relatively obvious physical intrusion because the case arose from military aircraft flying at low altitude over the claimants' property; the Court's reference to *Causby* suggested that government actions causing physical invasions of private property should be more apt to be called takings than those imposing legal restrictions on the use of property. However, the Court's subsequent adoption of a special, *per se* takings rule for permanent physical invasions of private property, *see Loretto v. Teleprompter Manhattan CATV Corp.*, 458 U.S. 419 (1982), reduces the significance of this definition of the character factor in *Penn Central* cases.

The character factor also has been interpreted to refer to the relative harmfulness of the regulated activity. *See, e g., Rose Acre Farms, Inc. v. United States*, 559 F.3d 1260 (Fed. Cir. 2009) (stating that "it is appropriate to consider the harm-preventing purpose of a regulation" in the context of evaluating a takings challenge to a regulation designed to control the spread of salmonella poisoning). Another definition considers whether the regulation creates a so-called "reciprocity of advantage" — that is, whether the regulation singles out one or a few owners to bear burdens or whether the regulation applies broadly across the community. *See Keystone v. Bituminous Coal Ass'n v. DeBenedictis*, 480 U.S. 470, 488 (1987). Some courts have asserted that the public importance of the goal of the regulation, considered as part of the character factor, should reduce the risk of takings liability, *see, e.g., Bass Enterprises Prod. Co v. United States*, 381 F.3d 1360 (Fed Cir. 2004), though one might question whether the relative importance of the governmental goal should make the public more rather than less willing to pay! In a very specialized context, the Supreme Court struck down as a taking federal legislation limiting the inheritance rights of Native Americans, observing that the "character of the Government regulation here is extraordinary." *Hodel v. Irving*, 481 U.S. 704, 716 (1987). This enumeration of the ways in which the courts have deployed the character factor is far from exhaustive. *See* John Echeverria, Making Sense of *Penn Central*, 39 Envtl. L. Rep. News & Analysis 10471 (2009).

2. *The* Loretto *Per Se Rule for Permanent Physical Occupations*

■ LORETTO v. TELEPROMPTER MANHATTAN CATV CORP.
458 U.S. 419 (1982)

Justice MARSHALL delivered the opinion of the Court.

This case presents the question whether a minor but permanent physical occupation of an owner's property authorized by government constitutes a "taking" of property for which just compensation is due under the Fifth and Fourteenth Amendments of the Constitution. New York law provides that a landlord must permit a cable television company to install its cable facilities upon his property. In this case, the cable installation occupied portions of appellant's roof and the side of her building. The New York Court of Appeals ruled that this appropriation does not amount to a taking. Because we conclude that such a physical occupation of property is a taking, we reverse.

I

Appellant Jean Loretto purchased a five-story apartment building located at 303 West 105th Street, New York City, in 1971. The previous owner had granted appellees Teleprompter Corp. and Teleprompter Manhattan CATV (collectively Teleprompter) permission to install a cable on the building and the exclusive privilege of furnishing cable television services to the tenants. The New York Court of Appeals described the installation as follows:

> On June 1, 1970 TelePrompter installed a cable slightly less than one-half inch in diameter and of approximately 30 feet in length along the length of the building about 18 inches above the roof top, and directional taps, approximately 4 inches by 4 inches by 4 inches, on the front and rear of the roof. By June 8, 1970 the cable had been extended another 4 to 6 feet and cable had been run from the directional taps to the adjoining building at 305 West 105th Street.

Teleprompter also installed two large silver boxes along the roof cables. The cables are attached by screws or nails penetrating the masonry at approximately two-foot intervals, and other equipment is installed by bolts.

Initially, Teleprompter's roof cables did not service appellant's building. They were part of what could be described as a cable "highway" circumnavigating the city block, with service cables periodically dropped over the front or back of a building in which a tenant desired service. Crucial to such a network is the use of so-called "crossovers" — cable lines extending from one building to another in order to reach a new group of tenants. Two years after appellant purchased the building, Teleprompter connected a "noncrossover" line — *i.e.*, one that provided CATV service to appellant's own tenants — by dropping a line to the first floor down the front of appellant's building.

Prior to 1973, Teleprompter routinely obtained authorization for its installations from property owners along the cable's route, compensating the owners at the standard rate of 5% of the gross revenues that Teleprompter realized from the particular property. To facilitate tenant access to CATV, the State of New York enacted §828 of the Executive Law, effective January 1, 1973. Section 828 provides that a landlord may not "interfere with the installation of cable television facilities upon his property or premises," and may not demand payment from any tenant for permitting CATV, or demand payment from any CATV company "in excess of any amount which the [State Commission on Cable Television] shall, by regulation, determine to be reasonable." The landlord may, however, require the CATV company or the tenant to bear the cost of installation and to indemnify for any damage caused by the installation. Pursuant to §828(1)(b), the State Commission has ruled that a one-time $1 payment is the normal fee to which a landlord is entitled. The Commission ruled that this nominal fee, which the Commission concluded was equivalent to what the landlord would receive if the property were condemned pursuant to New York's Transportation Corporations Law, satisfied constitutional requirements "in the absence of a special showing of greater damages attributable to the taking."

Appellant did not discover the existence of the cable until after she had purchased the building. She brought a class action against Teleprompter in 1976 on behalf of all owners of real property in the State on which Teleprompter has placed CATV components, alleging that Teleprompter's installation was a trespass and, insofar as it relied on §828, a taking without just compensation. . . .

II

A

In *Penn Central,* the Court surveyed some of the general principles governing the Takings Clause. The Court noted that no "set formula" existed to determine, in all cases, whether compensation is constitutionally due for a government restriction of property. Ordinarily, the Court must engage in "essentially ad hoc, factual inquiries." But the inquiry is not standardless. The economic impact of the regulation, especially the degree of interference with investment-backed expectations, is of particular significance. "So, too, is the character of the governmental action. A 'taking' may more readily be found when the interference with property can be characterized as a physical invasion by government, than when interference arises from some public program adjusting the benefits and burdens of economic life to promote the common good."

As *Penn Central* affirms, the Court has often upheld substantial regulation of an owner's use of his own property where deemed necessary to promote the public interest. At the same time, we have long considered a physical intrusion by government to be a property restriction of an unusually serious character for purposes of the Takings Clause. Our cases further establish that when the physical intrusion reaches the extreme form of a permanent physical occupation, a taking has occurred. In such a case, "the character of the government action" not only is an important factor in resolving whether the action works a taking but also is determinative.

When faced with a constitutional challenge to a permanent physical occupation of real property, this Court has invariably found a taking. As early as 1872, in *Pumpelly v. Green Bay Co.*, 80 U.S. 166, this Court held that the defendant's construction, pursuant to state authority, of a dam which permanently flooded plaintiff's property constituted a taking. A unanimous Court stated, without qualification, that "where real estate is actually invaded by superinduced additions of water, earth, sand, or other material, or by having any artificial structure placed on it, so as to effectually destroy or impair its usefulness, it is a taking, within the meaning of the Constitution." Seven years later, the Court reemphasized the importance of a physical occupation by distinguishing a regulation that merely restricted the use of private property. In *Northern Transportation Co. v. Chicago*, 99 U.S. 635 (1879), the Court held that the city's construction of a temporary dam in a river to permit construction of a tunnel was not a taking, even though the plaintiffs were thereby denied access to their premises, because the obstruction only impaired the use of plaintiffs' property. The Court distinguished earlier cases in which permanent flooding of private property was regarded as a taking as involving "a physical invasion of the real estate of the private owner, and a practical ouster of his possession." In this case, by contrast, "[n]o entry was made upon the plaintiffs' lot."

Since these early cases, this Court has consistently distinguished between flooding cases involving a permanent physical occupation, on the one hand, and cases involving a more temporary invasion, or government action outside the owner's property that causes consequential damages within, on the other. A taking has always been found only in the former situation. . . .

More recent cases confirm the distinction between a permanent physical occupation, a physical invasion short of an occupation, and a regulation that merely restricts the use of property. In *United States v. Causby*, 328 U.S. 256 (1946), the Court ruled that frequent flights immediately above a landowner's property constituted a taking, comparing such overflights to the quintessential form of a taking:

> If, by reason of the frequency and altitude of the flights, respondents could not use this land for any purpose, their loss would be complete. It would be as complete as if the United States had entered upon the surface of the land and taken exclusive possession of it.

As the Court further explained,

> We would not doubt that, if the United States erected an elevated railway over respondents' land at the precise altitude where its planes now fly, there would be a partial taking, even though none of the supports of the structure rested on the land. The reason is that there would be an intrusion so immediate and direct as to subtract from the owner's full enjoyment of the property and to limit his exploitation of it.

The Court concluded that the damages to the respondents "were not merely consequential. They were the product of a direct invasion of respondents' domain."

Two wartime takings cases are also instructive. In *United States v. Pewee Coal Co.*, 341 U.S. 114 (1951), the Court unanimously held that the Government's seizure and direction of operation of a coal mine to prevent a national strike of coal miners constituted a taking, though members of the Court differed over which losses suffered during the period of Government control were compensable. The plurality had little difficulty concluding that because there had been an "actual taking of possession and control," the taking was as clear as if the Government held full title and ownership. In *United States v. Central Eureka Mining Co.*, 357 U.S. 155 (1958), by contrast, the Court found no taking where the Government had issued a wartime order requiring nonessential gold mines to cease operations for the purpose of conserving equipment and manpower for use in mines more essential to the war effort. Over dissenting Justice Harlan's complaint that "as a practical matter the Order led to consequences no different from those that would have followed the temporary acquisition of physical possession of these mines by the United States," the Court reasoned that "the Government did not occupy, use, or in any manner take physical possession of the gold mines or of the equipment connected with them."

Although this Court's most recent cases have not addressed the precise issue before us, they have emphasized that physical *invasion* cases are special and have not repudiated the rule that any permanent physical *occupation* is a taking. The cases state or imply that a physical invasion is subject to a balancing process, but they do not suggest that a permanent physical occupation would ever be exempt from the Takings Clause.

Penn Central Transportation Co. v. New York City, as noted above, contains one of the most complete discussions of the Takings Clause. The Court explained that resolving whether public action works a taking is ordinarily an ad hoc inquiry in which several factors are particularly significant — the economic impact of the regulation, the extent to which it interferes with investment-backed expectations, and the character of the governmental action. The opinion does not repudiate the rule that a permanent physical occupation is a government action of such a unique character that it is a taking without regard to other factors that a court might ordinarily examine. . . .

B

The historical rule that a permanent physical occupation of another's property is a taking has more than tradition to commend it. Such an appropriation is perhaps the most serious form of invasion of an owner's property interests. . . . [A]n owner suffers a special kind of injury when a *stranger* directly invades and occupies the owner's property. [P]roperty law has long protected an owner's expectation that he will be relatively undisturbed at least in the possession of his property. To require, as well, that the owner permit another to exercise complete dominion literally adds insult to injury. Furthermore, such an occupation is qualitatively more severe than a regulation of the *use* of property, even a regulation that imposes affirmative duties on the owner, since the owner may have no control over the timing, extent, or nature of the invasion.

The traditional rule also avoids otherwise difficult line-drawing problems. Few would disagree that if the State required landlords to permit third parties to install swimming pools on the landlords' rooftops for the convenience of the tenants, the requirement would be a taking. If the cable installation here occupied as much space, again, few would disagree that the occupation would be a taking. But constitutional protection for the rights of private property cannot be made to depend on the size of the area permanently occupied. Indeed, it is possible that in the future, additional cable installations that more significantly restrict a landlord's use of the roof of his building will be made. Section 828 requires a landlord to permit such multiple installations.

Finally, whether a permanent physical occupation has occurred presents relatively few problems of proof. The placement of a fixed structure on land or real property is an obvious fact that will rarely be subject to dispute. Once the fact of occupation is shown, of course, a court should consider the *extent* of the occupation as one relevant factor in determining the compensation due. For that reason, moreover, there is less need to consider the extent of the occupation in determining whether there is a taking in the first instance.

c

Teleprompter's cable installation on appellant's building constitutes a taking under the traditional test. The installation involved a direct physical attachment of plates, boxes, wires, bolts, and screws to the building, completely occupying space immediately above and upon the roof and along the building's exterior wall. . . .

Appellees raise a series of objections to application of the traditional rule here. Teleprompter notes that the law applies only to buildings used as rental property, and draws the conclusion that the law is simply a permissible regulation of the use of real property. We fail to see, however, why a physical occupation of one type of property but not another type is any less a physical occupation. Insofar as Teleprompter means to suggest that this is not a permanent physical invasion, we must differ. So long as the property remains residential and a CATV company wishes to retain the installation, the landlord must permit it.

Teleprompter also asserts the related argument that the State has effectively granted a tenant the property right to have a CATV installation placed on the roof of his building, as an appurtenance to the tenant's leasehold. The short answer is that §828(1)(a) does not purport to give the *tenant* any enforceable property rights with respect to CATV installation, and the lower courts did not rest their decisions on this ground. Of course, Teleprompter, not appellant's tenants, actually owns the installation. Moreover, the government does not have unlimited power to redefine property rights.

Finally, we do not agree with appellees that application of the physical occupation rule will have dire consequences for the government's power to adjust landlord-tenant relationships. This Court has consistently affirmed that States have broad power to regulate housing conditions in general and the landlord-tenant relationship in particular without paying compensation for all economic injuries that such regulation entails. See, *e.g., Heart of Atlanta Motel, Inc. v. United States,* 379 U.S. 241 (1964) (discrimination in places of public accommodation); *Queenside Hills Realty Co. v. Saxl,* 328 U.S. 80 (1946) (fire regulation); *Bowles v. Willingham,* 321 U.S. 503 (1944) (rent control); *Home Building & Loan Assn. v. Blaisdell,* 290 U.S. 398 (1934) (mortgage moratorium); *Edgar A. Levy Leasing Co. v. Siegel,* 258 U.S. 242 (1922) (emergency housing law); *Block v. Hirsh,* 256 U.S. 135 (1921) (rent control). In none of these cases, however, did the government authorize the permanent occupation of the landlord's property by a third party. Consequently, our holding today in no way alters the analysis governing the State's power to require landlords to comply with building codes and provide utility connections, mailboxes, smoke detectors, fire extinguishers, and the like in the common area of a building. So long as these regulations do not require the landlord to suffer the physical occupation of a portion of his building by a third party, they will be analyzed under the multifactor inquiry generally applicable to nonpossessory governmental activity. *See Penn Central Transportation Co. v. New York City, 438 U.S. 104 (1978).*

III

Our holding today is very narrow. We affirm the traditional rule that a permanent physical occupation of property is a taking. In such a case, the property owner entertains a historically rooted expectation of compensation, and the character of the invasion is qualitatively more intrusive than perhaps any other category of property regulation. We do not, however, question the equally substantial authority upholding a State's broad power to impose appropriate restrictions upon an owner's *use* of his property.

Furthermore, our conclusion that §828 works a taking of a portion of appellant's property does not presuppose that the fee which many landlords had obtained from Teleprompter prior to the law's enactment is a proper measure of the value of the property taken. The issue of the amount of compensation that is due, on which we express no opinion, is a matter for the state courts to consider on remand.

The judgment of the New York Court of Appeals is reversed, and the case is remanded for further proceedings not inconsistent with this opinion.

It is so ordered.

Justice BLACKMUN, with whom Justice BRENNAN and Justice WHITE join, dissenting.

If the Court's decisions construing the Takings Clause state anything clearly, it is that "[t]here is no set formula to determine where regulation ends and taking begins."

In a curiously anachronistic decision, the Court today acknowledges its historical disavowal of set formulae in almost the same breath as it constructs a rigid *per se* takings rule: "a permanent physical occupation authorized by government is a taking without regard to the public interests that it may serve." To sustain its rule against our recent precedents, the Court erects a strained and untenable distinction between "temporary physical invasions," whose constitutionality concededly "is subject to a balancing process," and "permanent physical occupations," which are "taking[s] without regard to other factors that a court might ordinarily examine." *Ante*, at 3174.

In my view, the Court's approach "reduces the constitutional issue to a formalistic quibble" over whether property has been "permanently occupied" or "temporarily invaded." The Court's application of its formula to the facts of this case vividly illustrates that its approach is potentially dangerous as well as misguided. Despite its concession that "States have broad power to regulate . . . the landlord-tenant relationship . . . without paying compensation for all economic injuries that such regulation entails," *ante*, at 3178, the Court uses its rule to undercut a carefully considered legislative judgment concerning landlord-tenant relationships. I therefore respectfully dissent. . . .

Notes and Comments

1. Loretto *on Remand.* On remand from the Supreme Court, the N.Y. Appellate Division refused to award attorneys' fees to Mrs. Loretto on the ground that she had failed to "establish the deprivation of any federal right." *Loretto v. Group W Cable*, 522 N.Y.S.2d 543, 545 (App. Div. 1987). The court said that while Mrs. Loretto established the fact of a "taking," that showing alone "does not amount to the deprivation of a right." After observing that in takings cases "no constitutional violation

occurs until just compensation is denied," the court concluded that Mrs. Loretto had failed to demonstrate a right to compensation and thereby "prove any underlying constitutional violation." The court said Mrs. Loretto's showing of a taking was thus "of purely academic interest." Do you agree that Mrs. Loretto's victory was purely academic?

2. *Does* Loretto *Make Sense?* The opinion for the Court in *Loretto* makes a series of argument based on precedent and logic for a strict *per se* rule of takings liability for permanent physical occupations of private property. But is the Court's *per se* rule defensible? In *Penn Central*, the company apparently suffered millions of dollars in losses due to development restrictions, but was denied recovery; yet in *Loretto*, the Court established that a claimant subject to a physical occupation, no matter how modest, will be entitled to compensation for any losses suffered. Does that make sense? Also, in *Heart of Atlanta Motel, Inc. v. United States*, 379 U.S. 241 (1964), the Court addressed a takings challenge brought by a hotel owner complaining that he was compelled to accept African Americans as guests by the Civil Rights Acts. The Court rejected the claim out of hand. In *Loretto* the Court explicitly indicated that *Heart of Atlanta Motel* remains good law but on what plausible theory is the holding in *Heart of Atlanta Motel* compatible with the principle that a government-compelled physical occupation of private property is *always* a taking? Is a *per se* takings rule defensible even it appears to produce ridiculous results at the margins?

3. *The Inapplicability of the Parcel as a Whole Rule.* One important distinction between traditional regulatory takings cases and takings cases involving permanent physical occupations is that the parcel as a whole rule applies in the former type of case but not in the latter type of case. If an owner possesses a 100-acre tract that includes a 1-acre area of wetlands, and the Army Corps of Engineers denies the owner permission to fill the wetlands, courts will generally decide whether there has been taking by examining the economic impact of the decision on the value of the entire 100 acres. On the other hand, if the Army Corps of Engineers builds a dam and floods 1 acre out of 100, the courts will find a taking of the 1 acre regardless of the fact that the owner can still use the remaining 99 acres. *See Tahoe-Sierra Pres. Council v. Tahoe Regional Planning Agency*, 535 U.S. 302 (2002).

4. *Arkansas Game and Fish Commission.* In its 2012 decision in *Arkansas Game and Fish Comm'n v. United States*, 133 S. Ct. 511 (2011), the Supreme Court addressed the question of what test governs a takings claim based on a *temporary* physical occupation of private property. The Court rejected the position of the U.S. Court of Appeals for the Federal Circuit that a government-caused temporary inundation of land with water cannot give rise to takings liability. At the same time, the Court rejected the position of the petitioners that the *per se* rule of *Loretto* should be extended to temporary physical occupations. Instead, the Court said that temporary occupation takings claims should be evaluated based on a *Penn Central*-like analysis that focuses on the degree to which the occupation was "intended" or "the foreseeable result of authorized government action," the "character of the land at issue," the owner's "reasonable investment-backed expectations" regarding the land's use, and the severity of the interference with the owner's property interest.

As the Court emphasized in *Penn Central*, any type of direct physical intrusion raises special concerns under the Takings Clause. But this does not mean that every government intrusion, no matter how modest or brief, will necessarily be held to be a taking. *See Boise Cascade Corp. v. United States*, 296 F.3d 1339 (Fed. Cir. 2002) (requirement that landowner allow government agents to conduct surveys for presence of endangered wildlife on private property was not a taking). In the case of a temporary physical occupation governed by a *Penn Central*-type analysis, should the parcel as a whole rule come into play–or not?

5. *Appropriations v. Invasions. Loretto* is sometimes said to stand for the single sweeping proposition that "physical takings" of private property should invariably be held to be compensable takings. But a moment's reflection reveals that physical takings need to be divided into at least two subcategories: physical occupations and invasions, and appropriations. With respect to physical occupations, the Supreme Court has determined that different takings tests should apply depending upon whether the physical occupation is permanent or temporary. But does the same distinction apply to direct appropriations — that is, when the government physically seizes possession and control of some property? In a handful of older cases the Supreme Court appeared to rule that direct appropriations constitute takings regardless of the duration of the appropriation. *See, e.g., Kimball Laundry v. United States, 338 U.S. 1 (1949); United States v. General Motors Corp.,* 323 U.S. 373 (1945); *United States v. Petty Motor Co.,* 327 U.S. 372 (1946).

6. *Raisins.* In the 2015 case of *Horne v. Department of Agriculture,* 135 S. Ct. 2419, the Supreme Court ruled that the *per se* rule for physical takings of real property applies as well to personal property, which in that case was raisins. The *Horne* case arose form a complex New Deal-era agricultural program that required raisin growers to turn over a portion of their crops to the government each year as a condition of selling raisins in the commercial marketplace. The Court rejected any distinction between real and personal property for takings purposes in sweeping terms: "The Government has a categorical duty to pay just compensation when it takes your car, just as when it takes your home." However, as with other sweeping *per se* takings rules, it is difficult to know how this rule applies at the margins. In 1996, the Court rejected the argument that a civil forfeiture results in a taking, stating, "The government may not be required to compensate an owner for property which it has already lawfully acquired under the exercise of governmental authority other than the power of eminent domain." *Bennis v. Michigan,* 516 U.S. 442 (1996). Is *Bennis,* which involved forfeiture of an automobile, still good law after *Horne?* Is it a *per se* taking if an animal control officer removes an abused animal from the possession of its abuser?

7. *Trying to Fit into the* Per Se *Rule.* A good deal of takings litigation involves efforts by claimants to try to fit their cases into the highly favorable (for claimants) *per se* physical takings category. Such efforts are fraught with challenges because, as the Court emphasized in *Loretto,* this *per se* rule is very narrow. In *FCC v. Florida Power Corp.,* 480 U.S. 245 (1987), the Court ruled that *Loretto* only applies when the permanent physical occupation is coerced, and therefore it did not apply when a utility voluntarily entered a contract to allow a cable company to attach its cable to the utility's poles. Later, in *Yee v. City of Escondido,* 503 U.S. 519 (1992), the Court rejected an argument that a rent control ordinance triggered the *Loretto* rule. *See also Stearns Co. v. United States,* 396 F.3d 1354 (Fed Cir. 2005) (application of Surface Mining Control & Reclamation Act to mineral property not a physical taking). *But see Casitas Mun. Water Dist. v. United States,* 543 F.3d 1276 (Fed Cir. 2008) (ruling, based on a special set of assumed facts, that government directive requiring that water be diverted through a fish ladder constituted a *per se* physical taking).

3. *The* Lucas *Per Se Rule*

■ LUCAS v. SOUTH CAROLINA COASTAL COUNCIL
505 U.S. 1003 (1992)

Justice SCALIA delivered the opinion of the Court.

In 1986, petitioner David H. Lucas paid $975,000 for two residential lots on the Isle of Palms in Charleston County, South Carolina, on which he intended to build single-family homes. In 1988, however, the South Carolina Legislature enacted the Beachfront Management Act, which had the direct effect of barring petitioner from erecting any permanent habitable structures on his two parcels. A state trial court found that this prohibition rendered Lucas's parcels "valueless." This case requires us to decide whether the Act's dramatic effect on the economic value of Lucas's lots accomplished a taking of private property under the Fifth and Fourteenth Amendments requiring the payment of "just compensation."

I

A

South Carolina's expressed interest in intensively managing development activities in the so-called "coastal zone" dates from 1977 when, in the aftermath of Congress's passage of the federal Coastal Zone Management Act of 1972, the legislature enacted a Coastal Zone Management Act of its own. In its original form, the South Carolina Act required owners of coastal zone land that qualified as a "critical area" to obtain a permit from the newly created South Carolina Coastal Council (Council) (respondent here) prior to committing the land to a "use other than the use the critical area was devoted to on [September 28, 1977]." §48–39–130(A).

In the late 1970's, Lucas and others began extensive residential development of the Isle of Palms, a barrier island situated eastward of the City of Charleston. Toward the close of the development cycle for one residential subdivision known as "Beachwood East," Lucas in 1986 purchased the two lots at issue in this litigation for his own account. No portion of the lots, which were located approximately 300 feet from the beach, qualified as a "critical area" under the 1977 Act; accordingly, at the time Lucas acquired these parcels, he was not legally obliged to obtain a permit from the Council in advance of any development activity. His intention with respect to the lots was to do what the owners of the immediately adjacent parcels had already done: erect single-family residences. . . .

The Beachfront Management Act brought Lucas's plans to an abrupt end. Under that 1988 legislation, the Council was directed to establish a "baseline" connecting the landward-most "point[s] of erosion . . . during the past forty years" in the region of the Isle of Palms that includes Lucas's lots. In action not challenged here, the Council fixed this baseline landward of Lucas's parcels. That was significant, for under the Act construction of occupiable improvements was flatly prohibited seaward of a line drawn 20 feet landward of, and parallel to, the baseline. The Act provided no exceptions.

B

Lucas promptly filed suit in the South Carolina Court of Common Pleas, contending that the Beachfront Management Act's construction bar effected a taking of his property without just compensation. Lucas did not take issue with the validity of the Act as a lawful exercise of South Carolina's police power, but contended that the Act's complete extinguishment of his property's value entitled him to compensation regardless of whether the legislature had acted in furtherance of legitimate police power objectives. Following a bench trial, the court agreed. Among its factual determinations was the finding that "at the time Lucas purchased the two lots, both were zoned for single-family residential construction and . . . there were no restrictions imposed upon such use of the property by either the State of South Carolina, the County of Charleston, or the Town of the Isle of Palms." The trial court further found that the Beachfront Management Act decreed a permanent ban on construction insofar as Lucas's lots were concerned, and that this prohibition "deprive[d] Lucas of any reasonable economic use of the lots, . . . eliminated the unrestricted right of use, and render[ed] them valueless." The court thus concluded that Lucas's properties had been "taken" by operation of the Act, and it ordered respondent to pay "just compensation" in the amount of $1,232,387.50.

The Supreme Court of South Carolina reversed. It found dispositive what it described as Lucas's concession "that the Beachfront Management Act [was] properly and validly designed to preserve . . . South Carolina's beaches." Failing an attack on the validity of the statute as such, the court believed itself bound to accept the "uncontested . . . findings" of the South Carolina Legislature that new construction in the coastal zone — such as petitioner intended — threatened this public resource. The court ruled that when a regulation respecting the use of property is designed "to prevent serious public harm," (citing, *inter alia, Mugler v. Kansas,* 123 U.S. 623 (1887)), no compensation is owing under the Takings Clause regardless of the regulation's effect on the property's value.

II

[The Court initially rejected the argument that the case was not ripe for judicial review. This section of the opinion is omitted.]

III

A

Prior to Justice Holmes's exposition in *Pennsylvania Coal Co. v. Mahon,* 260 U.S. 393 (1922), it was generally thought that the Takings Clause reached only a "direct appropriation" of property, or the functional equivalent of a "practical ouster of [the owner's] possession," Justice Holmes recognized in *Mahon,* however, that if the protection against physical appropriations of private property was to be meaningfully enforced, the government's power to redefine the range of interests included in the ownership of property was necessarily constrained by constitutional limits. If, instead, the uses of private property were subject to unbridled, uncompensated qualification under the police power, "the natural tendency of human nature [would be] to extend the qualification more and more until at last private property disappear[ed]." These considerations gave birth in that case to the oft-cited maxim that, "while property may be regulated to a certain extent, if regulation goes too far it will be recognized as a taking."

Nevertheless, our decision in *Mahon* offered little insight into when, and under what circumstances, a given regulation would be seen as going "too far" for purposes of the Fifth Amendment. In 70-odd years of succeeding "regulatory takings" jurisprudence, we have generally eschewed any "'set formula'" for determining how far is too far, preferring to "engag[e] in . . . essentially ad hoc, factual inquiries." We have, however, described at least two discrete categories of regulatory action as compensable without case-specific inquiry into the public interest advanced in support of the restraint. The first encompasses regulations that compel the property owner to suffer a physical "invasion" of his property. In general (at least with regard to permanent invasions), no matter how minute the intrusion, and no matter how weighty the public purpose behind it, we have required compensation. . . .

The second situation in which we have found categorical treatment appropriate is where regulation denies all economically beneficial or productive use of land. As we have said on numerous occasions, the Fifth Amendment is violated when land-use regulation "does not substantially advance legitimate state interests *or denies an owner economically viable use of his land.*"[7]

We have never set forth the justification for this rule. Perhaps it is simply, as Justice Brennan suggested, that total deprivation of beneficial use is, from the land-owner's point of view, the equivalent of a physical appropriation. Surely, at least, in the extraordinary circumstance when *no* productive or economically beneficial use of land is permitted, it is less realistic to indulge our usual assumption that the legislature is simply "adjusting the benefits and burdens of economic life" in a manner that secures an "average reciprocity of advantage" to everyone concerned. And the *functional* basis for permitting the government, by regulation, to affect property values without compensation — that "Government hardly could go on if to some extent values incident to property could not be diminished without paying for every such change in the general law" — does not apply to the relatively rare situations where the government has deprived a landowner of all economically beneficial uses.

On the other side of the balance, affirmatively supporting a compensation requirement, is the fact that regulations that leave the owner of land without economically beneficial or productive options for its use — typically, as here, by requiring land to be left substantially in its natural state — carry with them a heightened risk that private property is being pressed into some form of public service under the

---

7. Regrettably, the rhetorical force of our "deprivation of all economically feasible use" rule is greater than its precision, since the rule does not make clear the "property interest" against which the loss of value is to be measured. When, for example, a regulation requires a developer to leave 90% of a rural tract in its natural state, it is unclear whether we would analyze the situation as one in which the owner has been deprived of all economically beneficial use of the burdened portion of the tract, or as one in which the owner has suffered a mere diminution in value of the tract as a whole. Unsurprisingly, this uncertainty regarding the composition of the denominator in our "deprivation" fraction has produced inconsistent pronouncements by the Court. The answer to this difficult question may lie in how the owner's reasonable expectations have been shaped by the State's law of property — *i.e.*, whether and to what degree the State's law has accorded legal recognition and protection to the particular interest in land with respect to which the takings claimant alleges a diminution in (or elimination of) value. In any event, we avoid this difficulty in the present case, since the "interest in land" that Lucas has pleaded (a fee simple interest) is an estate with a rich tradition of protection at common law, and since the South Carolina Court of Common Pleas found that the Beachfront Management Act left each of Lucas's beachfront lots without economic value.

guise of mitigating serious public harm. As Justice Brennan explained: "From the government's point of view, the benefits flowing to the public from preservation of open space through regulation may be equally great as from creating a wildlife refuge through formal condemnation or increasing electricity production through a dam project that floods private property." The many statutes on the books, both state and federal, that provide for the use of eminent domain to impose servitudes on private scenic lands preventing developmental uses, or to acquire such lands altogether, suggest the practical equivalence in this setting of negative regulation and appropriation.

We think, in short, that there are good reasons for our frequently expressed belief that when the owner of real property has been called upon to sacrifice *all* economically beneficial uses in the name of the common good, that is, to leave his property economically idle, he has suffered a taking.[8]

B

The trial court found Lucas's two beachfront lots to have been rendered valueless by respondent's enforcement of the coastal-zone construction ban. Under Lucas's theory of the case, which rested upon our "no economically viable use" statements, that finding entitled him to compensation. Lucas believed it unnecessary to take issue with either the purposes behind the Beachfront Management Act, or the means chosen by the South Carolina Legislature to effectuate those purposes. The South Carolina Supreme Court, however, thought otherwise. In its view, the Beachfront Management Act was no ordinary enactment, but involved an exercise of South Carolina's "police powers" to mitigate the harm to the public interest that petitioner's use of his land might occasion. By neglecting to dispute the findings enumerated in the Act or otherwise to challenge the legislature's purposes, petitioner "concede[d] that the beach/dune area of South Carolina's shores is an extremely valuable public resource; that the erection of new construction, *inter alia,* contributes to the erosion and destruction of this public resource; and that discouraging new construction in close proximity to the beach/dune area is necessary to prevent a great public harm." In the court's view, these concessions brought petitioner's challenge within a long line of this Court's cases sustaining against Due Process and Takings Clause challenges the State's use of its "police powers" to enjoin a property owner from activities akin to public nuisances. *See Mugler v. Kansas,* 123 U.S. 623 (1887) (law prohibiting manufacture of alcoholic beverages); *Hadacheck v. Sebastian,* 239 U.S. 394 (1915) (law barring operation of brick mill in residential area); *Miller v. Schoene,* 276 U.S. 272 (1928) (order to destroy diseased cedar trees to prevent infection of nearby orchards); *Goldblatt v. Hempstead,*

---

8. Justice Stevens criticizes the "deprivation of all economically beneficial use" rule as "wholly arbitrary," in that "[the] landowner whose property is diminished in value 95% recovers nothing," while the landowner who suffers a complete elimination of value "recovers the land's full value." This analysis errs in its assumption that the landowner whose deprivation is one step short of complete is not entitled to compensation. Such an owner might not be able to claim the benefit of our categorical formulation, but, as we have acknowledged time and again, "[t]he economic impact of the regulation on the claimant and . . . the extent to which the regulation has interfered with distinct investment-backed expectations" are keenly relevant to takings analysis generally. *Penn Central.* It is true that in at least some cases the landowner with 95% loss will get nothing, while the landowner with total loss will recover in full. But that occasional result is no more strange than the gross disparity between the land-owner whose premises are taken for a highway (who recovers in full) and the landowner whose property is reduced to 5% of its former value by the highway (who recovers nothing). Takings law is full of these "all-or-nothing" situations.

369 U.S. 590 (1962) (law effectively preventing continued operation of quarry in residential area).

It is correct that many of our prior opinions have suggested that "harmful or noxious uses" of property may be proscribed by government regulation without the requirement of compensation. For a number of reasons, however, we think the South Carolina Supreme Court was too quick to conclude that that principle decides the present case. The "harmful or noxious uses" principle was the Court's early attempt to describe in theoretical terms why government may, consistent with the Takings Clause, affect property values by regulation without incurring an obligation to compensate — a reality we nowadays acknowledge explicitly with respect to the full scope of the State's police power. We made this very point in *Penn Central Transportation Co.*, where, in the course of sustaining New York City's landmarks preservation program against a takings challenge, we rejected the petitioner's suggestion that *Mugler* and the cases following it were premised on, and thus limited by, some objective conception of "noxiousness":

> [T]he uses in issue in *Hadacheck, Miller,* and *Goldblatt* were perfectly lawful in themselves. They involved no "blameworthiness, . . . moral wrongdoing or conscious act of dangerous risk-taking which induce[d society] to shift the cost to a pa[rt]icular individual." These cases are better understood as resting not on any supposed "noxious" quality of the prohibited uses but rather on the ground that the restrictions were reasonably related to the implementation of a policy — not unlike historic preservation — expected to produce a widespread public benefit and applicable to all similarly situated property.

"Harmful or noxious use" analysis was, in other words, simply the progenitor of our more contemporary statements that "land-use regulation does not effect a taking if it 'substantially advance[s] legitimate state interests'. . . ."

The transition from our early focus on control of "noxious" uses to our contemporary understanding of the broad realm within which government may regulate without compensation was an easy one, since the distinction between "harm-preventing" and "benefit-conferring" regulation is often in the eye of the beholder. It is quite possible, for example, to describe in *either* fashion the ecological, economic, and esthetic concerns that inspired the South Carolina legislature in the present case. One could say that imposing a servitude on Lucas's land is necessary in order to prevent his use of it from "harming" South Carolina's ecological resources; or, instead, in order to achieve the "benefits" of an ecological preserve. Whether one or the other of the competing characterizations will come to one's lips in a particular case depends primarily upon one's evaluation of the worth of competing uses of real estate. A given restraint will be seen as mitigating "harm" to the adjacent parcels or securing a "benefit" for them, depending upon the observer's evaluation of the relative importance of the use that the restraint favors. Whether Lucas's construction of single-family residences on his parcels should be described as bringing "harm" to South Carolina's adjacent ecological resources thus depends principally upon whether the describer believes that the State's use interest in nurturing those resources is so important that *any* competing adjacent use must yield.

When it is understood that "prevention of harmful use" was merely our early formulation of the police power justification necessary to sustain (without compensation) *any* regulatory diminution in value; and that the distinction between regulation that "prevents harmful use" and that which "confers benefits" is difficult, if not impossible, to discern on an objective, value-free basis; it becomes self-evident that noxious-use logic cannot serve as a touchstone to distinguish regulatory "takings" — which require compensation — from regulatory deprivations that do not require compensation. *A fortiori* the legislature's recitation of a noxious-use justification cannot be the basis for departing from our categorical rule that total regulatory takings must be compensated. If it were, departure would virtually always be allowed. The South Carolina Supreme Court's approach would essentially nullify *Mahon*'s affirmation of limits to the noncompensable exercise of the police power. Our cases provide no support for this: None of them that employed the logic of "harmful use" prevention to sustain a regulation involved an allegation that the regulation wholly eliminated the value of the claimant's land.

Where the State seeks to sustain regulation that deprives land of all economically beneficial use, we think it may resist compensation only if the logically antecedent inquiry into the nature of the owner's estate shows that the proscribed use interests were not part of his title to begin with. This accords, we think, with our "takings" jurisprudence, which has traditionally been guided by the understandings of our citizens regarding the content of, and the State's power over, the "bundle of rights" that they acquire when they obtain title to property. It seems to us that the property owner necessarily expects the uses of his property to be restricted, from time to time, by various measures newly enacted by the State in legitimate exercise of its police powers; "[a]s long recognized, some values are enjoyed under an implied limitation and must yield to the police power." And in the case of personal property, by reason of the State's traditionally high degree of control over commercial dealings, he ought to be aware of the possibility that new regulation might even render his property economically worthless (at least if the property's only economically productive use is sale or manufacture for sale). *See Andrus v. Allard*, 444 U.S. 51, 66-67 (1979) (prohibition on sale of eagle feathers). In the case of land, however, we think the notion pressed by the Council that title is somehow held subject to the "implied limitation" that the State may subsequently eliminate all economically valuable use is inconsistent with the historical compact recorded in the Takings Clause that has become part of our constitutional culture.[15]

Where "permanent physical occupation" of land is concerned, we have refused to allow the government to decree it anew (without compensation), no matter how weighty the asserted "public interests" involved, though we assuredly *would* permit the government to assert a permanent easement that was a pre-existing limitation

---

15. After accusing us of "launch[ing] a missile to kill a mouse," *post*, at 2904, Justice Blackmun expends a good deal of throw-weight of his own upon a noncombatant, arguing that our description of the "understanding" of land ownership that informs the Takings Clause is not supported by early American experience. That is largely true, but entirely irrelevant. The practices of the States *prior* to incorporation of the Takings and Just Compensation Clauses, *see Chicago, B. & Q.R. Co. v. Chicago*, 166 U.S. 226 (1897) — which, as Justice Blackmun acknowledges, occasionally included *outright physical appropriation* of land without compensation, *see post*, at 2915 — were out of accord with *any* plausible interpretation of those provisions. Justice Blackmun is correct that early constitutional theorists did not believe the Takings Clause embraced regulations of property at all, *see post*, at 2915, and n. 23, but even he does not suggest (explicitly, at least) that we renounce the Court's contrary conclusion in *Mahon*. Since the text of the Clause can be read to encompass regulatory as well as physical deprivations (in contrast to the text originally proposed by Madison, *see* Speech Proposing Bill of Rights (June 8, 1789), in 12 J. Madison, The Papers of James Madison 201 (C. Hobson, R. Rutland, W. Rachal, & J. Sisson ed. 1979) ("No person shall be . . . obliged to relinquish his property, where it may be necessary for public use, without a just compensation"), we decline to do so as well.

upon the land owner's title. [See] *Scranton v. Wheeler,* 179 U.S. 141, 163 (1900) (interests of "riparian owner in the submerged lands . . . bordering on a public navigable water" held subject to Government's navigational servitude). We believe similar treatment must be accorded confiscatory regulations, i.e., regulations that prohibit all economically beneficial use of land: Any limitation so severe cannot be newly legislated or decreed (without compensation), but must inhere in the title itself, in the restrictions that background principles of the State's law of property and nuisance already place upon land ownership. A law or decree with such an effect must, in other words, do no more than duplicate the result that could have been achieved in the courts — by adjacent landowners (or other uniquely affected persons) under the State's law of private nuisance, or by the State under its complementary power to abate nuisances that affect the public generally, or otherwise.[16]

On this analysis, the owner of a lake-bed, for example, would not be entitled to compensation when he is denied the requisite permit to engage in a landfilling operation that would have the effect of flooding others' land. Nor the corporate owner of a nuclear generating plant, when it is directed to remove all improvements from its land upon discovery that the plant sits astride an earthquake fault. Such regulatory action may well have the effect of eliminating the land's only economically productive use, but it does not proscribe a productive use that was previously permissible under relevant property and nuisance principles. The use of these properties for what are now expressly prohibited purposes was *always* unlawful, and (subject to other constitutional limitations) it was open to the State at any point to make the implication of those background principles of nuisance and property law explicit. In light of our traditional resort to "existing rules or understandings that stem from an independent source such as state law" to define the range of interests that qualify for protection as "property" under the Fifth and Fourteenth Amendments, this recognition that the Takings Clause does not require compensation when an owner is barred from putting land to a use that is proscribed by those "existing rules or understandings" is surely unexceptional. When, however, a regulation that declares "off-limits" all economically productive or beneficial uses of land goes beyond what the relevant background principles would dictate, compensation must be paid to sustain it.

The "total taking" inquiry we require today will ordinarily entail (as the application of state nuisance law ordinarily entails) analysis of, among other things, the degree of harm to public lands and resources, or adjacent private property, posed by the claimant's proposed activities, see, *e.g.,* Restatement (Second) of Torts §§826, 827, the social value of the claimant's activities and their suitability to the locality in question, see, *e.g., id.,* §§828(a) and (b), 831, and the relative ease with which the alleged harm can be avoided through measures taken by the claimant and the government (or adjacent private landowners) alike, see, *e.g., id.,* §§827(e), 828(c), 830. The fact that a particular use has long been engaged in by similarly situated owners ordinarily imports a lack of any common-law prohibition (though changed circumstances or new knowledge may make what was previously

16. The principal "otherwise" that we have in mind is litigation absolving the State (or private parties) of liability for the destruction of "real and personal property, in cases of actual necessity, to prevent the spreading of a fire" or to forestall other grave threats to the lives and property of others. *Bowditch v. Boston,* 101 U.S. 16, 18-19 (1880); *see United States v. Pacific R., Co.,* 120 U.S. 227, 238-239 (1887).

permissible no longer so, *see id.*, §827, Comment *g.* So also does the fact that other landowners, similarly situated, are permitted to continue the use denied to the claimant.

It seems unlikely that common-law principles would have prevented the erection of any habitable or productive improvements on petitioner's land; they rarely support prohibition of the "essential use" of land. The question, however, is one of state law to be dealt with on remand. We emphasize that to win its case South Carolina must do more than proffer the legislature's declaration that the uses Lucas desires are inconsistent with the public interest, or the conclusory assertion that they violate a common-law maxim such as *sic utere tuo ut alienum non laedas.* As we have said, a "State, by *ipse dixit,* may not transform private property into public property without compensation. . . ." Instead, as it would be required to do if it sought to restrain Lucas in a common-law action for public nuisance, South Carolina must identify background principles of nuisance and property law that prohibit the uses he now intends in the circumstances in which the property is presently found. Only on this showing can the State fairly claim that, in proscribing all such beneficial uses, the Beachfront Management Act is taking nothing.

The judgment is reversed, and the case is remanded for proceedings not inconsistent with this opinion.

So ordered.

Justice KENNEDY concurring in the judgment.

. . . Although we establish a framework for remand . . . , we do not decide the ultimate question whether a temporary taking has occurred in this case. The facts necessary to the determination have not been developed in the record. Among the matters to be considered on remand must be whether petitioner had the intent and capacity to develop the property and failed to do so in the interim period because the State prevented him. Any failure by petitioner to comply with relevant administrative requirements will be part of that analysis.

The South Carolina Court of Common Pleas found that petitioner's real property has been rendered valueless by the State's regulation. The finding appears to presume that the property has no significant market value or resale potential. This is a curious finding, and I share the reservations of some of my colleagues about a finding that a beach-front lot loses all value because of a development restriction. While the Supreme Court of South Carolina on remand need not consider the case subject to this constraint, we must accept the finding as entered below. Accepting the finding as entered, it follows that petitioner is entitled to invoke the line of cases discussing regulations that deprive real property of all economic value.

The finding of no value must be considered under the Takings Clause by reference to the owner's reasonable, investment-backed expectations. The Takings Clause, while conferring substantial protection on property owners, does not eliminate the police power of the State to enact limitations on the use of their property. The rights conferred by the Takings Clause and the police power of the State may coexist without conflict. Property is bought and sold, investments are made, subject to the State's power to regulate. Where a taking is alleged from regulations which deprive the property of all value, the test must be whether the deprivation is contrary to reasonable, investment-backed expectations.

There is an inherent tendency towards circularity in this synthesis, of course; for if the owner's reasonable expectations are shaped by what courts allow as a proper exercise of governmental authority, property tends to become what courts say it is.

Some circularity must be tolerated in these matters, however, as it is in other spheres. The definition, moreover, is not circular in its entirety. The expectations protected by the Constitution are based on objective rules and customs that can be understood as reasonable by all parties involved.

In my view, reasonable expectations must be understood in light of the whole of our legal tradition. The common law of nuisance is too narrow a confine for the exercise of regulatory power in a complex and interdependent society. The State should not be prevented from enacting new regulatory initiatives in response to changing conditions, and courts must consider all reasonable expectations whatever their source. The Takings Clause does not require a static body of state property law; it protects private expectations to ensure private investment. I agree with the Court that nuisance prevention accords with the most common expectations of property owners who face regulation, but I do not believe this can be the sole source of state authority to impose severe restrictions. Coastal property may present such unique concerns for a fragile land system that the State can go further in regulating its development and use than the common law of nuisance might otherwise permit.

The Supreme Court of South Carolina erred, in my view, by reciting the general purposes for which the state regulations were enacted without a determination that they were in accord with the owner's reasonable expectations and therefore sufficient to support a severe restriction on specific parcels of property. The promotion of tourism, for instance, ought not to suffice to deprive specific property of all value without a corresponding duty to compensate. Furthermore, the means, as well as the ends, of regulation must accord with the owner's reasonable expectations. Here, the State did not act until after the property had been zoned for individual lot development and most other parcels had been improved, throwing the whole burden of the regulation on the remaining lots. This too must be measured in the balance.

With these observations, I concur in the judgment of the Court.

[Justice Blackmun filed a lengthy dissent, arguing that the South Carolina Supreme Court's decision should have been upheld based on the Court precedents stating that regulations designed to protect the public from harm do not constitute takings. Justice Stevens filed a second dissenting opinion, contending that the State had not unfairly singled out David Lucas to bear a regulatory burden, given that the coastal law applied along the State's entire ocean coast. Justice Souter filed a "separate statement," essentially arguing that the finding of the trial court that the law had rendered the property "valueless" was so implausible that the Court should have dismissed the petition for certiorari as improvidently granted.]

Notes and Comments

1. *Significance of* Lucas. *Lucas* is an enormously significant case because it is the first Supreme Court ruling of the modern era upholding on the merits a takings challenge to restrictions on land or natural resource use (though, technically, the Court merely reversed the South Carolina Supreme Court's rejection of the takings claim and remanded the case the further proceedings). *Cf. Nollan v. California Coastal Comm'n*, 483 U.S. 825 (1987) (holding that a permit condition requiring owner to dedicate easement to public use was a taking). In prior cases, including most notably *Penn Central*, the Supreme Court had indicated that regulatory takings

claims were theoretically viable, but its decisions typically dealt with issues relating to procedure, *see Williamson County Reg. Planning Comm'n v. Hamilton Bank*, 473 U.S. 172 (1985) (takings claim held to be not "ripe"), or remedy, *First English Evangelical Lutheran Church v. County of Los Angeles*, 482 U.S. 304 (1987) (default remedy for a taking is payment of "just compensation"), without confronting the actual merits of the claims. *Lucas* got to the meat of the issue. *See also City of Monterey v. Del Monte Dunes at Monterey, Ltd.*, 526 U.S. 687 (1999) (upholding takings award).

David Lucas' victory in *Lucas* unquestionably has had a profound impact on the regulation of land in the United States. The prospect of defeat in a takings lawsuit, including having to pay a large just compensation award, has deterred local communities from adopting and enforcing strict regulations limiting development of hazardous or environmentally sensitive areas. At the same time, in part because the *Lucas* decision has had such a powerful deterrent effect, and because the decision arguably has a very narrow scope, there are few reported examples of landowners invoking *Lucas* to support successful takings cases. *See* Carole Nicole Brown & Dwight H. Merriam, On the Twenty-Fifth Anniversary of *Lucas*; Making or Breaking the Takings Claim (forthcoming in Iowa L. Rev.) (documenting the small number of litigation successes under *Lucas*).

The academic literature on *Lucas* is voluminous; some of the most useful and illuminating articles include the following: Richard A. Epstein, *Lucas v. South Carolina Coastal Council*, A Tangled Web of Expectations, 45 Stan. L. Rev. 1369 (1993); Richard J. Lazarus, Putting the Correct 'Spin" on *Lucas,* 45 Stan. L. Rev. 1411 (1993); Joseph L. Sax, Property Rights and the Economy of Nature: Understanding *Lucas v. South Carolina Coastal Council*, 45 Stan. L. Rev. 1433 (1993) 1423 (1993).

2. *Scope of the* Lucas *Per Se* Rule. One basic question about *Lucas* is the scope of this *per se* rule. The trial court in *Lucas* made a finding that the regulation rendered the property "valueless," and Justice Scalia highlighted that finding in his opinion. Does this mean that *Lucas* only applies when a regulation literally eliminates all property value? The Court has sent conflicting signals on this issue. In *Tahoe-Sierra v. Tahoe Reg. Planning Agency*, 535 U.S. 302, 330 (2002), the Court said that *Lucas* requires "the permanent 'obliteration of the value' of a fee simple estate," suggesting that a reduction in property value to zero is required. On the other hand, in *Palazzolo v. Rhode Island*, 533 U.S. 606, 631 (2001), the Court indicated that the government could not escape liability for a *Lucas* taking by showing that the owner was "left with a token interest." In that case, the Court held that one valuable building lot on an 18-acre parcel was more than a token interest.

A related question is whether *Lucas* is ultimately concerned with economic *value* or the ability to develop and otherwise profitably *use* property. Some of the language in *Lucas* suggests that the Court was concerned about the destruction of the economic value of the property. Other language suggests that the Court was principally concerned about the fact that the coastal council had adopted a total ban on building on Lucas's lots. In *Wyer v. Board of Envtl. Prot.*, 747 A.2d 192 (Me. 2002), the Maine Supreme Court confronted a case squarely presenting this question. The Maine coastal dune regulations prohibited plaintiff from developing his lot, and the State denied the owner's application for a variance; but the lot retained significant economic value based on the willingness of abutters to purchase the lot in order to enlarge their own properties. The plaintiff claimed a *Lucas* taking, but the Maine court rejected the claim, reasoning that plaintiff "failed to meet his burden of proof that the denial of the variance rendered the property substantially useless and stripped it of all practical value."

3. *Background Principles.* Though the concept was arguably implicit in prior Court precedent, *Lucas* also is significant for its articulation of the concept of "background principles." As the Court explained, a takings claim based on a regulation destroying all value will fail "if the logically antecedent inquiry into the nature of the owner's estate shows that the proscribed use interests were not part of his title to begin with." 505 U.S. at 1027. Such a limitation cannot be newly decreed by the legislature, but "must inhere in the title itself, in the restrictions that background principles of the State's law of property and nuisance already place upon land ownership."

To a degree not likely anticipated by the late Justice Scalia, the "background principles" concept has supported numerous successful defenses to takings claims in a variety of different contexts. *See* Michael Blum & Lucas Ritchie, *Lucas's* Unlikely Legacy: The Rise of Background Principles as Categorical Takings Defenses, 29 Harv. Envtl. L. Rev. 321 (2005) (offering an encyclopedic survey of post-*Lucas* background principles cases). Thus, the background principles concept has been deployed to defeat takings claims based on: the public trust in tidelands, *see Esplanade Properties, LLC v. City of Seattle*, 307 F.3d 978 (9th Cir. 2002); state nuisance doctrine, *Rith Energy, Inc. v. United States*, 44 Fed. Cl. 366 (1999), *aff'd on other grounds*, 247 F.3d 1355 (Fed. Cir. 2001); and the federal government's sovereign rights in the Exclusive Economic Zone and "the fish and resources therein." *American Pelagic Fishing Co. v United States*, 379 F.3d 1363 (Fed. Cir. 2004).

4. *Justice Kennedy.* As in so many Supreme Court takings cases in the modern era, Justice Kennedy is properly viewed as the swing vote in *Lucas.* Justice Kennedy concurred only in the judgment in *Lucas.* The five-Justice majority included Justice Byron White, who retired shortly after the decision came down, to be replaced by Justice Ruth Bader Ginsburg, a reliable (but by no means automatic) vote for the government in takings cases. As a result, Justice Kennedy's opinion in *Lucas* has particular significance for predicting how the present Court might apply the *Lucas* precedent in the future.

Kennedy articulates several positions that are more favorable to government than the Court's majority opinion. First, he states that even when a regulation is alleged to bar all economic use, the takings claim must be evaluated in light of the reasonableness of the owner's "investment-backed expectations." This position conflicts with the arguable position of the majority (at least in *dictum*) that a lack of reasonable investment-backed expectations is irrelevant in a *Lucas*-type case. Not surprisingly, the lower courts have adopted conflicting positions on this issue post-*Lucas. Compare Good v. United States*, 189 F.3d 1355, 1361 (Fed. Cir. 1999) (stating that "[t]he *Lucas* Court did not hold that the denial of all economically beneficial or productive use of land eliminates the requirement that the landowner have reasonable, investment-backed expectations") *with Palm Beach Isles Assocs. v. United States*, 208 F.3d 137 (Fed. Cir. 2000) (stating that the reasonableness of investment-backed expectations is irrelevant in a *Lucas*-type case). Second, and relatedly, Kennedy opined that nuisance doctrine "is too narrow a confine" to be the exclusive justification for land use regulations, even regulations that eliminate all economically productive use. In particular, he observed, "[c]oastal property may present such unique concerns for a fragile land system that the State can go further in regulating its development and use than the common law of nuisance might otherwise permit." 505 U.S. at 1035.

C. PROCEDURAL ISSUES IN TAKINGS CASES

Apart from dealing with the different substantive standards for determining takings liability, takings litigants also confront various important procedural issues. The *First English* case, excerpted below, includes a landmark ruling that addresses the issue of what relief a successful regulatory takings claimant is entitled to receive. The second excerpted case, *Williamson County,* addresses the hurdles that need to be overcome for a claimant to present a "ripe" takings claim.

■ FIRST ENGLISH EVANGELICAL LUTHERAN
CHURCH v. COUNTY OF LOS ANGELES
482 U.S. 304 (1987)

Chief Justice Rehnquist delivered the opinion of the Court.

In this case the California Court of Appeal held that a landowner who claims that his property has been "taken" by a land-use regulation may not recover damages for the time before it is finally determined that the regulation constitutes a "taking" of his property. We disagree, and conclude that in these circumstances the Fifth and Fourteenth Amendments to the United States Constitution would require compensation for that period.

In 1957, appellant First English Evangelical Lutheran Church purchased a 21–acre parcel of land in a canyon along the banks of the Middle Fork of Mill Creek in the Angeles National Forest. The Middle Fork is the natural drainage channel for a watershed area owned by the National Forest Service. Twelve of the acres owned by the church are flat land, and contained a dining hall, two bunkhouses, a caretaker's lodge, an outdoor chapel, and a footbridge across the creek. The church operated on the site a campground, known as "Lutherglen," as a retreat center and a recreational area for handicapped children.

In July 1977, a forest fire denuded the hills upstream from Lutherglen, destroying approximately 3,860 acres of the watershed area and creating a serious flood hazard. Such flooding occurred on February 9 and 10, 1978, when a storm dropped 11 inches of rain in the watershed. The runoff from the storm overflowed the banks of the Mill Creek, flooding Lutherglen and destroying its buildings.

In response to the flooding of the canyon, appellee County of Los Angeles adopted Interim Ordinance No. 11,855 in January 1979. The ordinance provided that "[a] person shall not construct, reconstruct, place or enlarge any building or structure, any portion of which is, or will be, located within the outer boundary lines of the interim flood protection area located in Mill Creek Canyon. . . ." The ordinance was effective immediately because the county determined that it was "required for the immediate preservation of the public health and safety. . . ." The interim flood protection area described by the ordinance included the flat areas on either side of Mill Creek on which Lutherglen had stood.

The church filed a complaint in the Superior Court of California a little more than a month after the ordinance was adopted. . . . [The church] sought to recover from the Flood Control District in inverse condemnation . . . [based on] loss of use of Lutherglen. The defendants moved to strike the portions of the complaint alleging that the county's ordinance denied all use of Lutherglen, on the view that the

California Supreme Court's decision in *Agins v. Tiburon*, 24 Cal.3d 266 (1979), aff'd on other grounds, 447 U.S. 255 (1980), rendered the allegation "entirely immaterial and irrelevant[, with] no bearing upon any conceivable cause of action herein."

In *Agins v. Tiburon* the California Supreme Court decided that a landowner may not maintain an inverse condemnation suit in the courts of that State based upon a "regulatory" taking. In the court's view, maintenance of such a suit would allow a landowner to force the legislature to exercise its power of eminent domain. Under this decision, then, compensation is not required until the challenged regulation or ordinance has been held excessive in an action for declaratory relief or a writ of mandamus and the government has nevertheless decided to continue the regulation in effect. Based on this decision, the trial court in the present case granted the motion to strike the allegation that the church had been denied all use of Lutherglen. It explained that "a careful re-reading of the *Agins* case persuades the Court that when an ordinance, even a non-zoning ordinance, deprives a person of the total use of his lands, his challenge to the ordinance is by way of declaratory relief or possibly mandamus." Because the appellant alleged a regulatory taking and sought only damages, the allegation that the ordinance denied all use of Lutherglen was deemed irrelevant.

On appeal, the California Court of Appeal . . . affirmed the trial court's decision to strike the allegations concerning appellee's ordinance. The California Supreme Court denied review. . . .

Appellant asks us to hold that the California Supreme Court erred in *Agins v. Tiburon* in determining that the Fifth Amendment, as made applicable to the States through the Fourteenth Amendment, does not require compensation as a remedy for "temporary" regulatory takings — those regulatory takings which are ultimately invalidated by the courts. For the reasons explained below . . . we . . . hold that on these facts the California courts have decided the compensation question inconsistently with the requirements of the Fifth Amendment.

I

[The Court's discussion of whether the case properly presented the remedial issue is omitted.]

II

Consideration of the compensation question must begin with direct reference to the language of the Fifth Amendment, which provides in relevant part that "private property [shall not] be taken for public use, without just compensation." As its language indicates, and as the Court has frequently noted, this provision does not prohibit the taking of private property, but instead places a condition on the exercise of that power. This basic understanding of the Amendment makes clear that it is designed not to limit the governmental interference with property rights *per se*, but rather to secure *compensation* in the event of otherwise proper interference amounting to a taking. Thus, government action that works a taking of property rights necessarily implicates the "constitutional obligation to pay just compensation."

We have recognized that a landowner is entitled to bring an action in inverse condemnation as a result of "'the self-executing character of the constitutional provision with respect to compensation. . . .'" It has been established at least since *Jacobs v. United States*, 290 U.S. 13 (1933), that claims for just compensation are grounded in the Constitution itself:

> The suits were based on the right to recover just compensation for property taken by the United States for public use in the exercise of its power of eminent domain. *That right was guaranteed by the Constitution.* The fact that condemnation proceedings were not instituted and that the right was asserted in suits by the owners did not change the essential nature of the claim. The form of the remedy did not qualify the right. It rested upon the Fifth Amendment. Statutory recognition was not necessary. A promise to pay was not necessary. Such a promise was implied because of the duty to pay imposed by the Amendment. *The suits were thus founded upon the Constitution of the United States. Id., at 16* (Emphasis added.)

Jacobs, moreover, does not stand alone, for the Court has frequently repeated the view that, in the event of a taking, the compensation remedy is required by the Constitution. . . . While the typical taking occurs when the government acts to condemn property in the exercise of its power of eminent domain, the entire doctrine of inverse condemnation is predicated on the proposition that a taking may occur without such formal proceedings.

While the California Supreme Court may not have actually disavowed this general rule in *Agins*, we believe that it has truncated the rule by disallowing damages that occurred prior to the ultimate invalidation of the challenged regulation. The California Supreme Court justified its conclusion at length in the *Agins* opinion, concluding that:

> In combination, the need for preserving a degree of freedom in the land-use planning function, and the inhibiting financial force which inheres in the inverse condemnation remedy, persuade us that on balance mandamus or declaratory relief rather than inverse condemnation is the appropriate relief under the circumstances.

We, of course, are not unmindful of these considerations, but they must be evaluated in the light of the command of the Just Compensation Clause of the Fifth Amendment. The Court has recognized in more than one case that the government may elect to abandon its intrusion or discontinue regulations. Similarly, a governmental body may acquiesce in a judicial declaration that one of its ordinances has effected an unconstitutional taking of property; the landowner has no right under the Just Compensation Clause to insist that a "temporary" taking be deemed a permanent taking. But we have not resolved whether abandonment by the government requires payment of compensation for the period of time during which regulations deny a landowner all use of his land.

In considering this question, we find substantial guidance in cases where the government has only temporarily exercised its right to use private property. In *United States v. Dow*, 357 U.S. 17 26 (1958), though rejecting a claim that the Government may not abandon condemnation proceedings, the Court observed that abandonment "results in an alteration in the property interest taken — from [one of] full ownership to one of temporary use and occupation. . . . In such cases compensation would be measured by the principles normally governing the taking of a right to use property temporarily. Each of the cases cited by the *Dow* Court involved appropriation of private property by the United States for use during World War II. Though the takings were in fact "temporary," there was no question that compensation would be required for the Government's interference with the use of the property; the Court was concerned in each case with determining the proper measure of the monetary relief to which the property holders were entitled.

These cases reflect the fact that "temporary" takings which, as here, deny a landowner all use of his property, are not different in kind from permanent takings, for which the Constitution clearly requires compensation. It is axiomatic that the Fifth Amendment's just compensation provision is "designed to bar Government from forcing some people alone to bear public burdens which, in all fairness and justice, should be borne by the public as a whole." In the present case the interim ordinance was adopted by the County of Los Angeles in January 1979, and became effective immediately. Appellant filed suit within a month after the effective date of the ordinance and yet when the California Supreme Court denied a hearing in the case on October 17, 1985, the merits of appellant's claim had yet to be determined. The United States has been required to pay compensation for leasehold interests of shorter duration than this. The value of a leasehold interest in property for a period of years may be substantial, and the burden on the property owner in extinguishing such an interest for a period of years may be great indeed. Where this burden results from governmental action that amounted to a taking, the Just Compensation Clause of the Fifth Amendment requires that the government pay the landowner for the value of the use of the land during this period. Invalidation of the ordinance or its successor ordinance after this period of time, though converting the taking into a "temporary" one, is not a sufficient remedy to meet the demands of the Just Compensation Clause. . . .

Nothing we say today is intended to abrogate the principle that the decision to exercise the power of eminent domain is a legislative function "'for Congress and Congress alone to determine.'" Once a court determines that a taking has occurred, the government retains the whole range of options already available — amendment of the regulation, withdrawal of the invalidated regulation, or exercise of eminent domain. Thus we do not, as the Solicitor General suggests, "permit a court, at the behest of a private person, to require the . . . Government to exercise the power of eminent domain. . . ." We merely hold that where the government's activities have already worked a taking of all use of property, no subsequent action by the government can relieve it of the duty to provide compensation for the period during which the taking was effective.

We also point out that the allegation of the complaint which we treat as true for purposes of our decision was that the ordinance in question denied appellant all use of its property. We limit our holding to the facts presented, and of course do not deal with the quite different questions that would arise in the case of normal delays in obtaining building permits, changes in zoning ordinances, variances, and the like which are not before us. We realize that even our present holding will undoubtedly lessen to some extent the freedom and flexibility of land-use planners and governing bodies of municipal corporations when enacting land-use regulations. But such consequences necessarily flow from any decision upholding a claim of constitutional right; many of the provisions of the Constitution are designed to limit the flexibility and freedom of governmental authorities, and the Just Compensation Clause of the Fifth Amendment is one of them. As Justice Holmes aptly noted more than 50 years ago, "a strong public desire to improve the public condition is not enough to warrant achieving the desire by a shorter cut than the constitutional way of paying for the change."

Here we must assume that the Los Angeles County ordinance has denied appellant all use of its property for a considerable period of years, and we hold that invalidation of the ordinance without payment of fair value for the use of the property during this period of time would be a constitutionally insufficient remedy. The judgment of the California Court of Appeal is therefore reversed, and the case is remanded for further proceedings not inconsistent with this opinion.

It is so ordered.

Justice STEVENS, with Justices BLACKMUN and O'CONNOR joining in part, dissenting.

One thing is certain. The Court's decision today will generate a great deal of litigation. Most of it, I believe, will be unproductive. But the mere duty to defend the actions that today's decision will spawn will undoubtedly have a significant adverse impact on the land-use regulatory process. The Court has reached out to address an issue not actually presented in this case, and has then answered that self-imposed question in a superficial and, I believe, dangerous way.

Four flaws in the Court's analysis merit special comment. First, the Court unnecessarily and imprudently assumes that appellant's complaint alleges an unconstitutional taking of Lutherglen. Second, the Court distorts our precedents in the area of regulatory takings when it concludes that all ordinances which would constitute takings if allowed to remain in effect permanently, necessarily also constitute takings if they are in effect for only a limited period of time. Third, the Court incorrectly assumes that the California Supreme Court has already decided that it will never allow a state court to grant monetary relief for a temporary regulatory taking, and then uses that conclusion to reverse a judgment which is correct under the Court's own theories. Finally, the Court errs in concluding that it is the Takings Clause, rather than the Due Process Clause, which is the primary constraint on the use of unfair and dilatory procedures in the land-use area.

[Most of this lengthy dissent is omitted.]

[In conclusion, t]he policy implications of today's decision are obvious and, I fear, far reaching. Cautious local officials and land-use planners may avoid taking any action that might later be challenged and thus give rise to a damages action. Much important regulation will never be enacted, even perhaps in the health and safety area. Were this result mandated by the Constitution, these serious implications would have to be ignored. But the loose cannon the Court fires today is not only unattached to the Constitution, but it also takes aim at a long line of precedents in the regulatory takings area. It would be the better part of valor simply to decide the case at hand instead of igniting the kind of litigation explosion that this decision will undoubtedly touch off.

I respectfully dissent.

Notes and Comments

1. *The Run up to* First English. The 1987 decision in *First English* represented the culmination of a lengthy debate in the Supreme Court about the proper remedy for a successful regulatory takings claim. In several prior cases, the Justices had discussed the merits of the issue, but repeatedly perceived some roadblock to reaching

the merits of the question that served to delay its final resolution. *See MacDonald, Sommer & Frates v. Yolo County*, 477 U.S. 340 (1986); *Williamson Cty. Reg. Planning Comm'n v. Hamilton Bank*, 473 U.S. 172 (1985); *San Diego Gas & Electric Co. v. City of San Diego*, 450 U.S. 621 (1981); *Agins v. City of Tiburon*, 447 U.S. 255 (1980). The issue of the appropriate remedy for a taking was also hotly debated in the academy in the run up to *First English. See, e.g.,* Williams, Smith, Siemon, Mandelker, & Babcock, The White River Junction Manifesto, 9 Vt. L. Rev. 193 (1984).

2. *Significance of* First English. The *First English* decision is undoubtedly one of the Supreme Court's most important and consequential takings decisions. Prior to *First English,* local governments could proceed to develop and implement new regulations relatively secure in the understanding that if the regulation turned out to go "too far" in takings terms, they would not suffer any direct financial repercussions (apart from the potentially considerable costs of paying for their legal defense and reimbursing the legal fees of successful plaintiffs, for example pursuant to 42 U.S.C. §1988). After *First English,* communities face the risk that if they guess wrong on the takings liability question in a particular case, they will be required to pay just compensation for the period between the date of adoption of the regulation and the date it is rescinded. Given the sometimes complicated and time-consuming nature of takings litigation, the potential financial burden on a local government from a temporary takings award can be catastrophic. *See* Christopher Serkin, Strategic Land Use Litigation: Pleading Around Municipal Insurance, 43 B.C. Envtl. Aff. L. Rev. 463, 476 n.100 (2016) (describing the $36.8 million takings judgment against the community of Half Moon Bay, California). As Professor Serkin put it, "[i]f the municipality is small enough, and the judgment large enough, regulatory takings liability can even manifest as an existential threat." *Id.* at 476. The threat of takings liability to the municipal treasury, and hence the deterrent effect of potential takings awards, are compounded by the fact that insurance companies generally do not offer municipalities coverage against the risk of regulatory takings liability. Do you see why?

3. *Is Equitable Relief an Option After* First English? One interesting doctrinal puzzle in the aftermath of *First English* is whether litigants have the option to sue for equitable relief based on a taking in lieu of pursuing a claim for financial compensation. *First English* held that takings litigants could not be *precluded* from suing for financial compensation for a temporary taking. But does the *First* English decision — along with other Supreme Court precedent — also establish that compensation is, at least generally speaking, the *exclusive* remedy for a regulatory taking?

First English itself includes language that supports the view that compensation is the exclusive remedy for a taking:

> As its language indicates, and as the Court has frequently noted, this provision does not prohibit the taking of private property, but instead places a condition on the exercise of that power. This basic understanding of the Amendment makes clear that it is designed not to limit the governmental interference with property rights *per se,* but rather to secure *compensation* in the event of otherwise proper interference amounting to a taking.

482 U.S. at 314 (emphasis in original). *See also Lingle v. Chevron USA, Inc.* 544 U.S. 528, 543 (2005) ("[T]he Takings Clause presupposes that the government has acted in pursuit of a valid public purpose. The Clause expressly requires compensation where government takes private property '*for public use.*' It does not bar the government from interfering with property rights, but rather requires compensation 'in

the event of *otherwise proper interference* amounting to a taking,'" citing *First English*) (emphasis is original). In accordance with this understanding, the Supreme Court has repeatedly said that a takings claimant cannot sue for equitable relief, but must instead seek just compensation. *See, e.g., United States v. Riverside Bay View Homes, Inc.,* 474 U.S. 121, 127-28 (1985).

On the other hand, the Supreme Court (and the lower courts) has sometimes allowed takings claimants to proceed with requests for equitable relief. The question is whether some of these outliers simply overlook the established doctrine, whether all or most of the Court cases involving equitable relief can be rationalized as logical exceptions to the general rule, or whether the general understanding that compensation is the default remedy for takings is due for an overhaul. The question is exhaustively explored in Thomas Merrill, Anticipatory Remedies for Takings, 128 Harv. L. Rev. 1630 (2015) (arguing for equitable and other "anticipatory remedies" in takings cases) and John Echeverria, Eschewing Anticipatory Remedies for Takings, 128 Harv. L. Rev.F. 202 (2015) (responding to Merrill).

The language of the Takings Clause implies that if the government has not deprived a property owner of compensation owed for a taking, no relief should be available on any theory. The Supreme Court upheld this understanding of the Takings Clause in *Brown v. Legal Found. of Washington,* 538 U.S. 216 (2003), in which the Court held that a requirement that client funds be placed an IOLTA account to help support legal services for the poor did not violate the Takings Clause where, given the peculiarities of federal banking regulation, the client would not have earned interest on the money in the absence of the requirement.

4. First English *on Remand.* The dissenters in *First English* objected to the Court's assumption that the Los Angeles flood plain regulation designed to protect the plaintiff's campground from the risk of flooding was a compensable taking. 482 U.S. at 328 (asserting that the majority "does not, and could not under our precedents, hold that the allegations sufficiently alleged a taking or that the county's effort to preserve life and property could ever constitute a taking"). On remand the California Court of Appeals rejected the takings claim, concluding that "the uses [the ordinance] did deny could be constitutionally prohibited under the County's power to protect public safety." *First English Evangelical Lutheran Church v. City. of Los Angeles,* 258 Cal. Rptr. 893, 902 (1989).

■ WILLIAMSON COUNTY REGIONAL PLANNING COMMISSION v. HAMILTON BANK OF JOHNSON CITY
473 U.S. 172 (1985)

Justice BLACKMUN delivered the opinion of the Court.

Respondent, the owner of a tract of land it was developing as a residential subdivision, sued petitioners, the Williamson County (Tennessee) Regional Planning Commission and its members and staff, in United States District Court, alleging that petitioners' application of various zoning laws and regulations to respondent's property amounted to a "taking" of that property. At trial, the jury agreed and awarded respondent $350,000 as just compensation for the "taking." Although the jury's verdict was rejected by the District Court, which granted a judgment notwithstanding the verdict to petitioners, the verdict was reinstated on appeal. Petitioners and their *amici* urge this Court to overturn the jury's award on the ground that a temporary regulatory interference with an investor's profit expectation does not constitute a "taking" within the meaning of the Just Compensation Clause of the Fifth Amendment, or, alternatively, on the ground that even if such interference does constitute a taking, the Just Compensation Clause does not require money damages as recompense. Before we reach those contentions, we examine the procedural posture of respondent's claim.

I

A

Under Tennessee law, responsibility for land-use planning is divided between the legislative body of each of the State's counties and regional and municipal "planning commissions." The county legislative body is responsible for zoning ordinances to regulate the uses to which particular land and buildings may be put, and to control the density of population and the location and dimensions of buildings. The planning commissions are responsible for more specific regulations governing the subdivision of land within their region or municipality for residential development. Enforcement of both the zoning ordinances and the subdivision regulations is accomplished in part through a requirement that the planning commission approve the plat of a subdivision before the plat may be recorded.

Pursuant to §13–7–101, the Williamson County "Quarterly Court," which is the county's legislative body, in 1973 adopted a zoning ordinance that allowed "cluster" development of residential areas. Under "cluster" zoning,

> both the size and the width of individual residential lots in . . . [a] development may be reduced, provided . . . that the overall density of the entire tract remains constant — provided, that is, that an area equivalent to the total of the areas thus "saved" from each individual lot is pooled and retained as common open space.

Cluster zoning thus allows housing units to be grouped, or "clustered" together, rather than being evenly spaced on uniform lots.

As required by §13–3–402, respondent's predecessor-in-interest (developer) in 1973 submitted a preliminary plat for the cluster development of its tract, the Temple Hills Country Club Estates (Temple Hills), to the Williamson County Regional Planning Commission for approval. At that time, the county's zoning ordinance and the Commission's subdivision regulations required developers to seek review and approval of subdivision plats in two steps. The developer first was to submit for approval a preliminary plat, or "initial sketch plan" indicating, among other things, the boundaries and acreage of the site, the number of dwelling units and their basic design, the location of existing and proposed roads, structures, lots, utility layouts, and open space, and the contour of the land. Once approved, the preliminary plat served as a basis for the preparation of a final plat. Under the Commission's regulations, however, approval of a preliminary plat "will not constitute acceptance of the final plat." Approval of a preliminary plat lapsed if a final plat was not submitted within one year of the date of the approval, unless the Commission granted an extension of time, or unless the approval of the preliminary plat was renewed. The final plat, which is the official authenticated document that is recorded, was required to conform substantially to the preliminary plat, and, in addition, to include such details as the lines of all streets, lots, boundaries, and building setbacks.

On May 3, 1973, the Commission approved the developer's preliminary plat for Temple. The plat indicated that the development was to include 676 acres, of which 260 acres would be open space, primarily in the form of a golf course. A notation on the plat indicated that the number of "allowable dwelling units for total development" was 736, but lot lines were drawn in for only 469 units. The areas in which the remaining 276 units were to be placed were left blank and bore the notation "this parcel not to be developed until approved by the planning commission." The plat also contained a disclaimer that "parcels with note 'this parcel not to be developed until approved by the planning commission' not a part of this plat and not included in gross area." The density of 736 allowable dwelling units was calculated by multiplying the number of acres (676) by the number of units allowed per acre (1.089). Although the zoning regulations in effect in 1973 required that density be calculated "on the basis of total acreage less fifty percent (50%) of the land lying in the flood plain . . . and less fifty percent (50%) of all land lying on a slope with a grade in excess of twenty-five percent (25%)," no deduction was made from the 676 acres for such land.

Upon approval of the preliminary plat, the developer conveyed to the county a permanent open space easement for the golf course, and began building roads and installing utility lines for the project. The developer spent approximately $3 million building the golf course, and another $500,000 installing sewer and water facilities. Before housing construction was to begin on a particular section, a final plat of that section was submitted for approval. Several sections, containing a total of 212 units, were given final approval by 1979. The preliminary plat, as well, was reapproved four times during that period.

In 1977, the county changed its zoning ordinance to require that calculations of allowable density exclude 10% of the total acreage to account for roads and utilities. In addition, the number of allowable units was changed to one per acre from the 1.089 per acre allowed in 1973. The Commission continued to apply the zoning ordinance and subdivision regulations in effect in 1973 to Temple Hills, however, and reapproved the preliminary plat in 1978. In August 1979, the Commission reversed its position and decided that plats submitted for renewal should be evaluated under the zoning ordinance and subdivision regulations in effect when the renewal was sought. The Commission then renewed the Temple Hills plat under the ordinances and regulations in effect at that time.

In January 1980, the Commission asked the developer to submit a revised preliminary plat before it sought final approval for the remaining sections of the subdivision. The Commission reasoned that this was necessary because the original preliminary plat contained a number of surveying errors, the land available in the subdivision had been decreased inasmuch as the State had condemned part of the land for a parkway, and the areas marked "reserved for future development" had never been platted. A special committee (Temple Hills Committee) was appointed to work with the developer on the revision of the preliminary plat.

The developer submitted a revised preliminary plat for approval in October 1980. Upon review, the Commission's staff and the Temple Hills Committee noted several problems with the revised plat. First, the allowable density under the zoning ordinance and subdivision regulations then in effect was 548 units, rather than the 736 units claimed under the preliminary plat approved in 1973. The difference reflected a decrease in 18.5 acres for the parkway, a decrease of 66 acres for the 10% deduction for roads, and an exclusion of 44 acres for 50% of the land lying on slopes exceeding a 25% grade. Second, two cul-de-sac roads that had become necessary because of the land taken for the parkway exceeded the maximum length allowed for such roads under the subdivision regulations in effect in both 1980 and 1973. Third, approximately 2,000 feet of road would have grades in excess of the maximum allowed by county road regulations. Fourth, the preliminary plat placed units on land that had grades in excess of 25% and thus was considered undevelopable under the zoning ordinance and subdivision regulations. Fifth, the developer had not fulfilled its obligations regarding the construction and maintenance of the main access road. Sixth, there were inadequate fire protection services for the area, as well as inadequate open space for children's recreational activities. Finally, the lots proposed in the preliminary plat had a road frontage that was below the minimum required by the subdivision regulations in effect in 1980.

The Temple Hills Committee recommended that the Commission grant a waiver of the regulations regarding the length of the cul-de-sacs, the maximum grade of the roads, and the minimum frontage requirement. Without addressing the suggestion that those three requirements be waived, the Commission disapproved the plat on two other grounds: first, the plat did not comply with the density requirements of the zoning ordinance or subdivision regulations, because no deduction had been made for the land taken for the parkway, and because there had been no deduction for 10% of the acreage attributable to roads or for 50% of the land having a slope of more than 25%; and second, lots were placed on slopes with a grade greater than 25%.

The developer then appealed to the County Board of Zoning Appeals for an "interpretation of the Residential Cluster zoning [ordinance] as it relates to Temple Hills." On November 11, 1980, the Board determined that the Commission should apply the zoning ordinance and subdivision regulations that were in effect in 1973 in evaluating the density of Temple Hills. It also decided that in measuring which lots had excessive grades, the Commission should define the slope in a manner more favorable to the developer.

On November 26, respondent, Hamilton Bank of Johnson City, acquired through foreclosure the property in the Temple Hills subdivision that had not yet been developed, a total of 257.65 acres. This included many of the parcels that had been left blank in the preliminary plat approved in 1973. In June 1981, respondent submitted two preliminary plats to the Commission — the plat that had been approved in 1973 and subsequently reapproved several times, and a plat indicating respondent's plans for the undeveloped areas, which was similar to the plat submitted by the developer in 1980. The new plat proposed the development of 688 units; the reduction from 736 units represented respondent's concession that 18.5 acres should be removed from the acreage because that land had been taken for the parkway.

On June 18, the Commission disapproved the plat for eight reasons, including the density and grade problems cited in the October 1980 denial, as well as the objections the Temple Hills Committee had raised in 1980 to the length of two cul-de-sacs, the grade of various roads, the lack of fire protection, the disrepair of the main-access road, and the minimum frontage. The Commission declined to follow the decision of the Board of Zoning Appeals that the plat should be evaluated by the 1973 zoning ordinance and subdivision regulations, stating that the Board lacked jurisdiction to hear appeals from the Commission.

B

Respondent then filed this suit in the United States District Court for the Middle District of Tennessee, pursuant to 42 U.S.C. §1983, alleging that the Commission had taken its property without just compensation and asserting that the Commission should be estopped under state law from denying approval of the project. Respondent's expert witnesses testified that the design that would meet each of the Commission's eight objections would allow respondent to build only 67 units, 409 fewer than respondent claims it is entitled to build, and that the development of only 67 sites would result in a net loss of over $1 million. Petitioners' expert witness, on the other hand, testified that the Commission's eight objections could be overcome by a design that would allow development of approximately 300 units.

After a 3-week trial, the jury found that respondent had been denied the "economically viable" use of its property in violation of the Just Compensation Clause, and that the Commission was estopped under state law from requiring respondent to comply with the current zoning ordinance and subdivision regulations rather than those in effect in 1973. The jury awarded damages of $350,000 for the temporary taking of respondent's property. The court entered a permanent injunction requiring the Commission to apply the zoning ordinance and subdivision regulations in effect in 1973 to Temple Hills, and to approve the plat submitted in 1981.

The court then granted judgment notwithstanding the verdict in favor of the Commission on the taking claim, reasoning in part that respondent was unable to derive economic benefit from its property on a temporary basis only, and that such a temporary deprivation, as a matter of law, cannot constitute a taking. In addition, the court modified its permanent injunction to require the Commission merely to apply the zoning ordinance and subdivision regulations in effect in 1973 to the project, rather than requiring approval of the plat, in order to allow the parties to resolve "legitimate technical questions of whether plaintiff meets the requirements of the 1973 regulations," through the applicable state and local appeals procedures.

A divided panel of the United States Court of Appeals for the Sixth Circuit reversed. The court held that application of government regulations affecting an owner's use of property may constitute a taking if the regulation denies the owner all "economically viable" use of the land, and that the evidence supported the jury's finding that the property had no economically feasible use during the time between the Commission's refusal to approve the preliminary plat and the jury's verdict. Rejecting petitioners' argument that respondent never had submitted a plat that complied with the 1973 regulations, and thus never had acquired rights that could be taken, the court held that the jury's estoppel verdict indicates that the jury must have found that respondent had acquired a "vested right" under state law to develop the subdivision according to the plat submitted in 1973. Even if respondent had no vested right under state law to finish the development, the jury was entitled to find that respondent had a reasonable investment-backed expectation that the development could be completed, and that the actions of the Commission interfered with that expectation.

The court rejected the District Court's holding that the taking verdict could not stand as a matter of law. A temporary denial of property could be a taking, and was to be analyzed in the same manner as a permanent taking. Finally, . . . the court determined that damages are required to compensate for a temporary taking.

II

We granted certiorari to address the question whether Federal, State, and Local governments must pay money damages to a landowner whose property allegedly has been "taken" temporarily by the application of government regulations [this issue was resolved two years later in *First English* — eds.] . . . [W]e find that the question is not properly presented, and must be left for another day. For . . . we conclude that respondent's claim is premature.

III

Because respondent has not yet obtained a final decision regarding the application of the zoning ordinance and subdivision regulations to its property, nor utilized the procedures Tennessee provides for obtaining just compensation, respondent's [takings] claim is not ripe.

A

As the Court has made clear in several recent decisions, a claim that the application of government regulations effects a taking of a property interest is not ripe until the government entity charged with implementing the regulations has reached a final decision regarding the application of the regulations to the property at issue. In *Hodel v. Virginia Surface Mining & Reclamation Assn., Inc.*, 452 U.S. 264 (1981), for example, the Court rejected a claim that the Surface Mining Control and Reclamation Act of 1977 effected a taking because:

> There is no indication in the record that appellees have availed themselves of the opportunities provided by the Act to obtain administrative relief by requesting either a variance from the approximate-original-contour requirement of §515(d) or a waiver from the surface mining restrictions in §522(e). If [the property owners] were to seek administrative relief under these procedures, a mutually acceptable solution might well be reached with regard to individual properties, thereby obviating any need to address the constitutional questions. The potential for such administrative solutions confirms the conclusion that the taking issue decided by the District Court simply is not ripe for judicial resolution."

Similarly, in *Agins v. Tiburon* the Court held that a challenge to the application of a zoning ordinance was not ripe because the property owners had not yet submitted a plan for development of their property . . . In *Penn Central Transp. Co. v. New York City*, the Court declined to find that the application of New York City's Landmarks Preservation Law to Grand Central Terminal effected a taking because, although the Landmarks Preservation Commission had disapproved a plan for a 50-story office building above the terminal, the property owners had not sought approval for any other plan, and it therefore was not clear whether the Commission would deny approval for all uses that would enable the plaintiffs to derive economic benefit from the property.

Respondent's claim is in a posture similar to the claims the Court held premature in *Hodel*. Respondent has submitted a plan for developing its property, and thus has passed beyond the *Agins* threshold. But, like the *Hodel* plaintiffs, respondent did not then seek variances that would have allowed it to develop the property according to its proposed plat, notwithstanding the Commission's finding that the plat did not comply with the zoning ordinance and subdivision regulations. It appears that variances could have been granted to resolve at least five of the Commission's eight objections to the plat. The Board of Zoning Appeals had the power to grant certain variances from the zoning ordinance, including the ordinance's density requirements and its restriction on placing units on land with slopes having a grade in excess of 25%. The Commission had the power to grant variances from the subdivision regulations, including the cul-de-sac, road-grade, and frontage requirements. Indeed, the Temple Hills Committee had recommended that the Commission grant variances from those regulations. Nevertheless, respondent did not seek variances from either the Board or the Commission.

Respondent argues that it "did everything possible to resolve the conflict with the commission," and that the Commission's denial of approval for respondent's plat was equivalent to a denial of variances. The record does not support respondent's claim, however. There is no evidence that respondent applied to the Board of Zoning Appeals for variances from the zoning ordinance. As noted, the developer sought a ruling that the ordinance in effect in 1973 should be applied, but neither respondent nor the developer sought a variance from the requirements of either the 1973 or 1980 ordinances. Further, although the subdivision regulations in effect in 1981 required that applications to the Commission for variances be in writing, and that notice of the application be given to owners of adjacent property, the record contains no evidence that respondent ever filed a written request for variances from the cul-de-sac, road-grade, or frontage requirements of the subdivision regulations, or that respondent ever gave the required notice. . . .

As in *Hodel*, *Agins*, and *Penn Central*, then, respondent has not yet obtained a final decision regarding how it will be allowed to develop its property. Our reluctance to examine taking claims until such a final decision has been made is compelled by the very nature of the inquiry required by the Just Compensation Clause. Although "[t]he question of what constitutes a 'taking' for purposes of the Fifth Amendment has proved to be a problem of considerable difficulty," this Court consistently has indicated that among the factors of particular significance in the inquiry are the economic impact of the challenged action and the extent to which it interferes with reasonable investment-backed expectations. Those factors simply cannot be evaluated until the administrative agency has arrived at a final, definitive position regarding how it will apply the regulations at issue to the particular land in question.

Here, for example, the jury's verdict indicates only that it found that respondent would be denied the economically feasible use of its property if it were forced to develop the subdivision in a manner that would meet each of the Commission's eight objections. It is not clear whether the jury would have found that the respondent had been denied all reasonable beneficial use of the property had any of the eight objections been met through the grant of a variance. Indeed, the expert witness who testified regarding the economic impact of the Commission's actions did not itemize the effect of each of the eight objections, so the jury would have been unable to discern how a grant of a variance from any one of the regulations at issue would have affected the profitability of the development. Accordingly, until the Commission determines that no variances will be granted, it is impossible for the jury to find, on this record, whether respondent "will be unable to derive economic benefit" from the land.

Respondent asserts that it should not be required to seek variances from the regulations because its suit is predicated upon 42 U.S.C. §1983, and there is no requirement that a plaintiff exhaust administrative remedies before bringing a §1983 action. The question whether administrative remedies must be exhausted is conceptually distinct, however, from the question whether an administrative action must be final before it is judicially reviewable. While the policies underlying the two concepts often overlap, the finality requirement is concerned with whether the initial decisionmaker has arrived at a definitive position on the issue that inflicts an actual, concrete injury; the exhaustion requirement generally refers to administrative and judicial procedures by which an injured party may seek review of an adverse decision and obtain a remedy if the decision is found to be unlawful or otherwise inappropriate. . . .

B

A second reason the taking claim is not yet ripe is that respondent did not seek compensation through the procedures the State has provided for doing so. The Fifth Amendment does not proscribe the taking of property; it proscribes taking without just compensation. Nor does the Fifth Amendment require that just compensation be paid in advance of, or contemporaneously with, the taking; all that is required is that a "'reasonable, certain and adequate provision for obtaining compensation'" exist at the time of the taking. If the government has provided an adequate process for obtaining compensation, and if resort to that process "yield[s] just compensation," then the property owner "has no claim against the Government" for a taking . . . Thus, we have held that taking claims against the Federal Government are premature until the property owner has availed itself of the process provided by the Tucker Act, 28 U.S.C. §1491. Similarly, if a State provides an adequate procedure for seeking just compensation, the property owner cannot claim a violation of the Just Compensation Clause until it has used the procedure and been denied just compensation.

The recognition that a property owner has not suffered a violation of the Just Compensation Clause until the owner has unsuccessfully attempted to obtain just compensation through the procedures provided by the State for obtaining such compensation is analogous to the Court's holding in *Parratt v. Taylor*, 451 U.S. 527 (1981). There, the Court ruled that a person deprived of property through a random and unauthorized act by a state employee does not state a claim under the Due Process Clause merely by alleging the deprivation of property. In such a situation, the Constitution does not require predeprivation process because it would be impossible or impracticable to provide a meaningful hearing before the deprivation. Instead, the Constitution is satisfied by the provision of meaningful postdeprivation process. Thus, the State's action is not "complete" in the sense of causing a constitutional injury "unless or until the State fails to provide an adequate postde-privation remedy for the property loss." Likewise, because the Constitution does not require pretaking compensation, and is instead satisfied by a reasonable and adequate provision for obtaining compensation after the taking, the State's action here is not "complete" until the State fails to provide adequate compensation for the taking.

Under Tennessee law, a property owner may bring an inverse condemnation action to obtain just compensation for an alleged taking of property under certain circumstances. The statutory scheme for eminent domain proceedings outlines the procedures by which government entities must exercise the right of eminent domain. The State is prohibited from "enter[ing] upon [condemned] land" until these procedures have been utilized and compensation has been paid the owner, but if a government entity does take possession of the land without following the required procedures,

> the owner of such land may petition for a jury of inquest, in which case the same proceedings may be had, as near as may be, as hereinbefore provided; or he may sue for damages in the ordinary way. . . .

The Tennessee state courts have interpreted [Tennessee law] to allow recovery through inverse condemnation where the "taking" is effected by restrictive zoning laws or development regulations. Respondent has not shown that the inverse con-demnation procedure is unavailable or inadequate, and until it has utilized that procedure, its taking claim is premature.

IV

[The Court's discussion of the alternative due process claim is omitted.]

V

We therefore reverse the judgment of the Court of Appeals and remand the case for further proceedings consistent with this opinion.

It is so ordered.

[Justice White dissented from the holding that the issues in this case were not ripe for resolution. Justice Powell took no part in the decision of this case. Justice Brennan, with whom Justice Marshall joined, concurred with the Court's resolution of the ripeness issue. Justice Stevens concurred, reasoning that the takings claim was not ripe and the temporary takings claim did not state a viable claim under the Takings Clause.]

Notes and Comments

1. *The (Relatively) Noncontroversial Finality Ripeness Rule.* One of the rules announced in *Williamson County*, the so-called "finality ripeness" rule, is relatively noncontroversial and has been reaffirmed and enforced by the Supreme Court on numerous occasions. *See, e g., MacDonald Sommer & Frates v. Yolo County*, 477 U.S. 340 (1986) (affirming ruling that takings claim was not ripe where developer submitted one subdivision application, received a notice of rejection from the county, and took

no further steps to determine what intensity of development the county might permit); *Palazzolo v. Rhode Island*, 533 U.S. 606 (2001) (ruling that developer was not required to submit an additional application in order to ripen a takings claim where the agency's interpretation of the regulations barred the claimants from "engaging in *any* filling or development on wetlands"); *Suitum v. Tahoe Regional Planning Agency*, 520 U.S. 725 (1997) (ruling that takings claim was ripe where agency had no discretion to permit development of environmentally sensitive land and the market value of "transferable development right" to which owner was entitled was readily ascertainable). There is also an enormous volume of reported lower court decisions addressing the takings finality issue.

The finality issue poses a considerable litigation hazard for a takings claimant. A developer may feel aggrieved by local regulators, and may wish to promptly file suit to obtain relief and/or to gain greater leverage in ongoing negotiations. But if a takings lawsuit turns out to be unripe (perhaps many years later, when the issue is finally resolved by an appellate court), the developer will have been denied the opportunity to present the merits of her argument and will have wasted significant time, effort, and money.

2. *The Controversial Just Compensation Ripeness Rule.* In contrast to the finality ripeness rule, there is significant controversy about *Williamson County's* second "ripeness" rule — that a takings claim is not ripe in federal court until a litigant has first sought compensation in state court. In 2005, former Chief Justice Rehnquist, joined by three other justices, called for reexamination of this aspect of *Williamson County*. *See San Remo Hotel, LLP v. City & County of San Francisco*, 545 U.S. 323, 348 (2005) (Rehnquist, C.J. concurring) (stating that *Williamson County* "may have been mistaken" in establishing the state litigation requirement and expressing the belief that "the Court should reconsider whether plaintiffs asserting a Fifth Amendment takings claim based on the final decision of a state or local government entity must first seek compensation in state courts."). As of 2016, the issue remains alive and unresolved. *See Arrigoni Enterpises, LLC v. Town of Durham*, 136 S. Ct. 1409 (2016) (Thomas, J., dissenting) (dissenting from denial of a petition for certiorari seeking reconsideration of *Williamson County's* state-litigation requirement). The Pacific Legal Foundation and other private property rights groups have been strong advocates for overturning this aspect of *Williamson County*, so far to no avail.

The continuing controversy is no doubt attributable to the complexity of the issue. The *Williamson County* Court actually describes two slightly different versions of a rule relating to the takings compensation remedy. First, it refers to the rule that a party suing the United States under the Takings Clause is said to have "no claim" so long as he has the opportunity to sue for just compensation in the U.S. Court of Federal Claims pursuant to the Tucker Act. Second, it refers to a rule that a property owner cannot seek just compensation under the Takings Clause from a local government in federal court if there is an opportunity to sue for just compensation in state court. The first version of this rule appears to be based on the idea that, as matter of substantive Fifth Amendment takings doctrine, the default remedy for a taking is financial compensation; so long as the U.S. Court of Federal Claims is available to grant compensatory relief, it is the only forum in which such a claim can be pursued, because it is the only federal court in which Congress has issued a general waiver of sovereign immunity in takings cases. The second version of the ripeness rule appears to be based on the distinct theory that a unit of local government cannot be said to have violated the Takings Clause if the state that created the local government has its own compensation procedures and the property owner has not yet availed herself of those procedures. Under the second version, either the federal or state courts could entertain the claim for just compensation (because local governments enjoy sovereign immunity in neither federal nor state court); thus, the preference for one court over another in litigation involving local governments necessarily has a different basis than the preference for one court or another in suits involving the federal government.

While the basis for the rule in the context of litigation against the federal government appears clear enough (sovereign immunity), it is less clear what the basis for the rule is in the local government context. *Williamson County* suggests that the local government version of the rule is supported by *Parrat v. Taylor*, 451 U.S. 527 (1981), in which the Supreme Court held that a state prisoner cannot challenge prison officials' tortious actions under the Due Process Clause without first pursuing a traditional tort recovery in state court. Under this theory, a unit of local government in a particular state cannot be said to have "taken" anything unless and until the courts of that state have received and rejected a request for just compensation. The local government version of the rule also may be justified on federalism grounds, on the theory that takings litigation against local governments often involves local property and land use issues best handled by the state courts. *See San Remo Hotel, LLP v. City & County of San Francisco*, 545 U.S. 323, 348 (2005) (Rehnquist, C.J., concurring) (laying out this rationale). *See also* Stewart E. Sterk, The Demise of Federal Takings Litigation, 48 Wm. & Mary L. Rev. 251, 292-95 (2006) (defending *Williamson County* on federalism grounds).

The confusion about the substantive legal basis for the just compensation ripeness rule has in turned produced confusion about whether and to what extent the requirement is waivable or can otherwise be disregarded. In *Stop the Beach Renourishment, Inc. v. Florida Dept. of Envtl. Prot.*, 560 U.S. 702, 729 (2010), the Supreme Court, without extensive analysis, held that the compensation requirement is not jurisdictional. *See also Horne v. Department of Agriculture*, 133 S. Ct. 2053, 262 (2013) (describing just compensation requirement as, "not strictly speaking, jurisdictional"). That the just compensation requirement is not jurisdictional has been held by some courts to support the conclusion that a defendant's voluntary removal of a takings claim from state to federal court should be deemed a waiver of the *Williamson County* requirement that claims against local governments be filed in state court. *See Sansotta v. Town of Nags Head*, 724 F.3d 533 (4th Cir. 2013); *Athanasiou v. Town of Westhampton*, 30 F. Supp. 3d 84 (D. Mass. 2014).

3. *Re-litigating the Takings Claim.* While there is debate over the justification for the rule that a property owner suing a local government under the Takings Clause does not have a "ripe" claim in federal court and must instead sue in state court, it is clear that once a litigant pursues a takings claim in state court she cannot subsequently re-litigate the claim in federal court. In *San Remo Hotel, LP v. City and County of San Francisco*, 545 U.S. 323 (2005), the Supreme Court held that, as a result of the Full Faith and Credit Clause, once hotel owners in San Francisco had had an opportunity to litigate their takings challenge to a city hotel room conversion ordinance, they were barred by the doctrine of issue preclusion from re-litigating the claims in federal district court. The Supreme Court ruled that standard issue-preclusion principles applied notwithstanding the fact that the plaintiffs had been compelled to litigate their claims in the first instance in state court by *Williamson County*. Of course, this conclusion makes it harder to characterize *Williamson County* as being about

"ripeness;" *San Remo Hotel* suggests that, generally speaking, it will *never* become possible to file a takings claim against local government in federal court.

4. *Assertion of Jurisdiction Not a Taking.* A takings lawsuit also can be "too early" if it seeks recovery for a taking based on an agency's assertion that a property owner must secure a permit in order to proceed with development. In *United States v. Riverside Bayview Homes*, 474 U.S. 121 (1985), the Court held that the mere assertion of regulatory jurisdiction by a governmental agency cannot constitute a regulatory taking. The Court explained:

> A requirement that a person obtain a permit before engaging in a certain use of his or her property does not itself "take" the property in any sense: after all, the very existence of a permit system implies that permission may be granted, leaving the landowner free to use the property as desired. Moreover, even if the permit is denied, there may be other viable uses available to the owner. Only when a permit is denied and the effect of the denial is to prevent "economically viable" use of the land in question can it be said that a taking has occurred.

Id. at 127.

D. EXACTIONS

The Supreme Court has developed a specialized takings jurisprudence addressing "exactions," which can be broadly defined as conditions attached to development authorizations. The exactions canon was established in two conveniently rhyming cases, *Nollan v. California Coastal Comm'n*, 483 U.S. 825 (1987), and *Dolan v. City of Tigard*, 512 U.S. 374 (1994). Nearly 20 years later, in *Koontz v. St. Johns River Water Management District*, 133 S. Ct. 2586 (2013), the Court expanded and arguably also considerably muddled the takings exactions doctrine.

■ NOLLAN v. CALIFORNIA COASTAL COMMISSION
483 U.S. 825 (1987)

Justice SCALIA delivered the opinion of the Court.

James and Marilyn Nollan appeal from a decision of the California Court of Appeal ruling that the California Coastal Commission could condition its grant of permission to rebuild their house on their transfer to the public of an easement across their beachfront property. The California court rejected their claim that imposition of that condition violates the Takings Clause of the Fifth Amendment, as incorporated against the States by the Fourteenth Amendment. We noted probable jurisdiction.

I

The Nollans own a beachfront lot in Ventura County, California. A quarter-mile north of their property is Faria County Park, an oceanside public park with a public beach and recreation area. Another public beach area, known locally as "the Cove," lies 1,800 feet south of their lot. A concrete seawall approximately eight feet high separates the beach portion of the Nollans' property from the rest of the lot. The historic mean high tide line determines the lot's oceanside boundary.

The Nollans originally leased their property with an option to buy. The building on the lot was a small bungalow, totaling 504 square feet, which for a time they rented to summer vacationers. After years of rental use, however, the building had fallen into disrepair, and could no longer be rented out.

The Nollans' option to purchase was conditioned on their promise to demolish the bungalow and replace it. In order to do so under [California law], they were required to obtain a coastal development permit from the California Coastal Commission. On February 25, 1982, they submitted a permit application to the Commission in which they proposed to demolish the existing structure and replace it with a three-bedroom house in keeping with the rest of the neighborhood.

The Nollans were informed that their application had been placed on the administrative calendar, and that the Commission staff had recommended that the permit be granted subject to the condition that they allow the public an easement to pass across a portion of their property bounded by the mean high tide line on one side, and their seawall on the other side. This would make it easier for the public to get to Faria County Park and the Cove. The Nollans protested imposition of the condition, but the Commission overruled their objections and granted the permit subject to their recordation of a deed restriction granting the easement.

On June 3, 1982, the Nollans filed a petition for writ of administrative mandamus asking the Ventura County Superior Court to invalidate the access condition. They argued that the condition could not be imposed absent evidence that their proposed development would have a direct adverse impact on public access to the beach. The court agreed, and remanded the case to the Commission for a full evidentiary hearing on that issue.

On remand, the Commission held a public hearing, after which it made further factual findings and reaffirmed its imposition of the condition. It found that the new house would increase blockage of the view of the ocean, thus contributing to the development of "a 'wall' of residential structures" that would prevent the public "psychologically . . . from realizing a stretch of coastline exists nearby that they have every right to visit." The new house would also increase private use of the shorefront. These effects of construction of the house, along with other area development, would cumulatively "burden the public's ability to traverse to and along the shorefront." Therefore the Commission could properly require the Nollans to offset that burden by providing additional lateral access to the public beaches in the form of an easement across their property. The Commission also noted that it had similarly conditioned 43 out of 60 coastal development permits along the same tract of land, and that of the 17 not so conditioned, 14 had been approved when the Commission did not have administrative regulations in place allowing imposition of the condition, and the remaining 3 had not involved shorefront property.

The Nollans filed a supplemental petition for a writ of administrative mandamus with the Superior Court, in which they argued that imposition of the access condition violated the Takings Clause of the Fifth Amendment, as incorporated against the States by the Fourteenth Amendment. The Superior Court ruled in their favor on statutory grounds, finding, in part to avoid "issues of constitutionality," that the California Coastal Act of 1976, authorized the Commission to impose public access conditions on coastal development permits for the replacement of an existing single-family home with a new one only where the proposed development would have an adverse impact on public access to the sea. In the court's view, the administrative record did not provide an adequate factual basis for concluding that replacement of the bungalow with the house would create a direct or cumulative burden on public access to the sea. Accordingly, the Superior Court granted the writ of mandamus and directed that the permit condition be struck.

The Commission appealed to the California Court of Appeal. While that appeal was pending, the Nollans satisfied the condition on their option to purchase by tearing down the bungalow and building the new house, and bought the property. They did not notify the Commission that they were taking that action.

The Court of Appeal reversed the Superior Court. It disagreed with the Superior Court's interpretation of the Coastal Act, finding that it required that a coastal permit for the construction of a new house whose floor area, height or bulk was more than 10% larger than that of the house it was replacing be conditioned on a grant of access. It also ruled that the requirement did not violate the Constitution [under California precedent]. . . . It ruled that the Nollans' taking claim also failed because, although the condition diminished the value of the Nollans' lot, it did not deprive them of all reasonable use of their property. Since, in the Court of Appeal's view, there was no statutory or constitutional obstacle to imposition of the access condition, the Superior Court erred in granting the writ of mandamus. The Nollans appealed to this Court, raising only the constitutional question.

II

Had California simply required the Nollans to make an easement across their beachfront available to the public on a permanent basis in order to increase public access to the beach, rather than conditioning their permit to rebuild their house on their agreeing to do so, we have no doubt there would have been a taking. To say that the appropriation of a public easement across a landowner's premises does not constitute the taking of a property interest but rather (as Justice Brennan contends) "a mere restriction on its use," is to use words in a manner that deprives them of all their ordinary meaning. Indeed, one of the principal uses of the eminent domain power is to assure that the government be able to require conveyance of just such interests, so long as it pays for them. Perhaps because the point is so obvious, we have never been confronted with a controversy that required us to rule upon it, but our cases' analysis of the effect of other governmental action leads to the same conclusion. We have repeatedly held that, as to property reserved by its owner for private use, "the right to exclude [others is] 'one of the most essential sticks in the bundle of rights that are commonly characterized as property.'" In *Loretto* we observed that where governmental action results in "[a] permanent physical occupation" of the property, by the government itself or by others, "our cases uniformly have found a taking to the extent of the occupation, without regard to whether the action achieves an important public benefit or has only minimal economic impact on the owner." We think a "permanent physical occupation" has occurred, for purposes of that rule, where individuals are given a permanent and continuous right to pass to and fro, so that the real property may continuously be traversed, even though no particular individual is permitted to station himself permanently upon the premises. . . .

Given, then, that requiring uncompensated conveyance of the easement out-right would violate the Fourteenth Amendment, the question becomes whether requiring it to be conveyed as a condition for issuing a land-use permit alters the outcome. We have long recognized that land-use regulation does not effect a taking if it "substantially advance[s] legitimate state interests" and does not "den[y] an owner economically viable use of his land." Our cases have not elaborated on the standards for determining what constitutes a "legitimate state interest" or what type of connection between the regulation and the state interest satisfies the require-ment that the former "substantially advance" the latter.[3] [The Court repudiated the "substantially advance" theory in *Lingle* in 2005 — eds.] They have made clear, however, that a broad range of governmental purposes and regulations satisfies these requirements. The Commission argues that among these permissible pur-poses are protecting the public's ability to see the beach, assisting the public in overcoming the "psychological barrier" to using the beach created by a developed shorefront, and preventing congestion on the public beaches. We assume, without deciding, that this is so — in which case the Commission unquestionably would be able to deny the Nollans their permit outright if their new house (alone, or by reason of the cumulative impact produced in conjunction with other construction) would substantially impede these purposes, unless the denial would interfere so drastically with the Nollans' use of their property as to constitute a taking.

The Commission argues that a permit condition that serves the same legitimate police-power purpose as a refusal to issue the permit should not be found to be a taking if the refusal to issue the permit would not constitute a taking. We agree. Thus, if the Commission attached to the permit some condition that would have protected the public's ability to see the beach notwithstanding construction of the new house — for example, a height limitation, a width restriction, or a ban on fences — so long as the Commission could have exercised its police power (as we have assumed it could) to forbid construction of the house altogether, imposition of the condition would also be constitutional. Moreover (and here we come closer to the facts of the present case), the condition would be constitutional even if it con-sisted of the requirement that the Nollans provide a viewing spot on their property for passersby with whose sighting of the ocean their new house would interfere. Although such a requirement, constituting a permanent grant of continuous access to the property, would have to be considered a taking if it were not attached to a development permit, the Commission's assumed power to forbid construction of the house in order to protect the public's view of the beach must surely include the power to condition construction upon some concession by the owner, even a con-cession of property rights, that serves the same end. If a prohibition designed to

3. Contrary to Justice Brennan's claim, our opinions do not establish that these standards are the same as those applied to due process or equal protection claims. To the contrary, our verbal formulations in the takings field have generally been quite different. We have required that the regulation "substan-tially advance" the "legitimate state interest" sought to be achieved, not that "the State '*could rationally have decided*' that the measure adopted might achieve the State's objective." Justice Brennan relies prin-cipally on an equal protection case, and two substantive due process cases, in support of the standards he would adopt. But there is no reason to believe (and the language of our cases gives some reason to disbelieve) that so long as the regulation of property is at issue the standards for takings challenges, due process challenges, and equal protection challenges are identical; any more than there is any reason to believe that so long as the regulation of speech is at issue the standards for due process challenges, equal protection challenges, and First Amendment challenges are identical. *Goldblatt v. Hempstead*, 369 U.S. 590 (1962), does appear to assume that the inquiries are the same, but that assumption is inconsis-tent with the formulations of our later cases.

accomplish that purpose would be a legitimate exercise of the police power rather than a taking, it would be strange to conclude that providing the owner an alternative to that prohibition which accomplishes the same purpose is not.

The evident constitutional propriety disappears, however, if the condition substituted for the prohibition utterly fails to further the end advanced as the justification for the prohibition. When that essential nexus is eliminated, the situation becomes the same as if California law forbade shouting fire in a crowded theater, but granted dispensations to those willing to contribute $100 to the state treasury. While a ban on shouting fire can be a core exercise of the State's police power to protect the public safety, and can thus meet even our stringent standards for regulation of speech, adding the unrelated condition alters the purpose to one which, while it may be legitimate, is inadequate to sustain the ban. Therefore, even though, in a sense, requiring a $100 tax contribution in order to shout fire is a lesser restriction on speech than an outright ban, it would not pass constitutional muster. Similarly here, the lack of nexus between the condition and the original purpose of the building restriction converts that purpose to something other than what it was. The purpose then becomes, quite simply, the obtaining of an easement to serve some valid governmental purpose, but without payment of compensation. Whatever may be the outer limits of "legitimate state interests" in the takings and land-use context, this is not one of them. In short, unless the permit condition serves the same governmental purpose as the development ban, the building restriction is not a valid regulation of land use but "an out-and-out plan of extortion."

III

The Commission claims that it concedes as much, and that we may sustain the condition at issue here by finding that it is reasonably related to the public need or burden that the Nollans' new house creates or to which it contributes. We can accept, for purposes of discussion, the Commission's proposed test as to how close a "fit" between the condition and the burden is required, because we find that this case does not meet even the most untailored standards. The Commission's principal contention to the contrary essentially turns on a play on the word "access." The Nollans' new house, the Commission found, will interfere with "visual access" to the beach. That in turn (along with other shorefront development) will interfere with the desire of people who drive past the Nollans' house to use the beach, thus creating a "psychological barrier" to "access." The Nollans' new house will also, by a process not altogether clear from the Commission's opinion but presumably potent enough to more than offset the effects of the psychological barrier, increase the use of the public beaches, thus creating the need for more "access." These burdens on "access" would be alleviated by a requirement that the Nollans provide "lateral access" to the beach.

Rewriting the argument to eliminate the play on words makes clear that there is nothing to it. It is quite impossible to understand how a requirement that people already on the public beaches be able to walk across the Nollans' property reduces any obstacles to viewing the beach created by the new house. It is also impossible to understand how it lowers any "psychological barrier" to using the public beaches, or how it helps to remedy any additional congestion on them caused by construction of the Nollans' new house. We therefore find that the Commission's imposition of the permit condition cannot be treated as an exercise of its land-use power for any of these purposes. Our conclusion on this point is consistent with the approach taken by every other court that has considered the question, with the exception of the California state courts.

Justice Brennan argues that imposition of the access requirement is not irrational. In his version of the Commission's argument, the reason for the requirement is that in its absence, a person looking toward the beach from the road will see a street of residential structures including the Nollans' new home and conclude that there is no public beach nearby. If, however, that person sees people passing and repassing along the dry sand behind the Nollans' home, he will realize that there is a public beach somewhere in the vicinity. The Commission's action, however, was based on the opposite factual finding that the wall of houses completely blocked the view of the beach and that a person looking from the road would not be able to see it at all.

Even if the Commission had made the finding that Justice Brennan proposes, however, it is not certain that it would suffice. We do not share Justice Brennan's confidence that the Commission "should have little difficulty in the future in utilizing its expertise to demonstrate a specific connection between provisions for access and burdens on access," that will avoid the effect of today's decision. We view the Fifth Amendment's Property Clause to be more than a pleading requirement, and compliance with it to be more than an exercise in cleverness and imagination. As indicated earlier, our cases describe the condition for abridgement of property rights through the police power as a "*substantial* advanc[ing]" of a legitimate state interest. We are inclined to be particularly careful about the adjective where the actual conveyance of property is made a condition to the lifting of a land-use restriction, since in that context there is heightened risk that the purpose is avoidance of the compensation requirement, rather than the stated police-power objective.

We are left, then, with the Commission's justification for the access requirement unrelated to land-use regulation:

> Finally, the Commission notes that there are several existing provisions of pass and repass lateral access benefits already given by past Faria Beach Tract applicants as a result of prior coastal permit decisions. The access required as a condition of this permit is part of a comprehensive program to provide continuous public access along Faria Beach as the lots undergo development or redevelopment.

That is simply an expression of the Commission's belief that the public interest will be served by a continuous strip of publicly accessible beach along the coast. The Commission may well be right that it is a good idea, but that does not establish that the Nollans (and other coastal residents) alone can be compelled to contribute to its realization. Rather, California is free to advance its "comprehensive program," if it wishes, by using its power of eminent domain for this "public purpose," but if it wants an easement across the Nollans' property, it must pay for it.

Reversed.

Justice BRENNAN, joined by Justice MARSHALL, dissented.

Appellants in this case sought to construct a new dwelling on their beach lot that would both diminish visual access to the beach and move private development closer to the public tidelands. The Commission reasonably concluded that such "buildout," both individually and cumulatively, threatens public access to the shore. It sought to offset this encroachment by obtaining assurance that the public may walk along the shoreline in order to gain access to the ocean. The Court finds this an illegitimate exercise of the police power, because it maintains that there is no reasonable relationship between the effect of the development and the condition imposed.

The first problem with this conclusion is that the Court imposes a standard of precision for the exercise of a State's police power that has been discredited for the better part of this century. Furthermore, even under the Court's cramped standard, the permit condition imposed in this case directly responds to the specific type of burden on access created by appellants' development. Finally, a review of those factors deemed most significant in takings analysis makes clear that the Commission's action implicates none of the concerns underlying the Takings Clause. The Court has thus struck down the Commission's reasonable effort to respond to intensified development along the California coast, on behalf of landowners who can make no claim that their reasonable expectations have been disrupted. The Court has, in short, given appellants a windfall at the expense of the public. . . .

There can be no dispute that the police power of the States encompasses the authority to impose conditions on private development. It is also by now commonplace that this Court's review of the rationality of a State's exercise of its police power demands only that the State "*could rationally have decided*" that the measure adopted might achieve the State's objective. *Minnesota v. Clover Leaf Creamery Co.*, 449 U.S. 456, 466 (1981) (emphasis in original).[1] In this case, California has employed its police power in order to condition development upon preservation of public access to the ocean and tidelands. The Coastal Commission, if it had so chosen, could have denied the Nollans' request for a development permit, since the property would have remained economically viable without the requested new development. Instead, the State sought to accommodate the Nollans' desire for new development, on the condition that the development not diminish the overall amount of public access to the coastline. Appellants' proposed development would reduce public access by restricting visual access to the beach, by contributing to an increased need for community facilities, and by moving private development

---

1. *See also Williamson v. Lee Optical of Oklahoma, Inc.,* 348 U.S. 483, 487-488 (1955) ("[T]he law need not be in every respect logically consistent with its aims to be constitutional. It is enough that there is an evil at hand for correction, and that it might be thought that the particular legislative measure was a rational way to correct it"); *Day-Brite Lighting, Inc. v. Missouri,* 342 U.S. 421, 423 (1952) ("Our recent decisions make it plain that we do not sit as a super-legislature to weigh the wisdom of legislation nor to decide whether the policy which it expresses offends the public welfare. . . . [S]tate legislatures have constitutional authority to experiment with new techniques; they are entitled to their own standard of the public welfare").

Notwithstanding the suggestion otherwise, our standard for reviewing the threshold question whether an exercise of the police power is legitimate is a uniform one. As we stated over 25 years ago in addressing a takings challenge to government regulation:

The term "police power" connotes the time-tested conceptional limit of public encroachment upon private interests. Except for the substitution of the familiar standard of "reasonableness," this Court has generally refrained from announcing any specific criteria. The classic statement of the rule in *Lawton v. Steele,* 152 U.S. 133, 137 (1894), is still valid today: . . . "[I]t must appear, first, that the interests of the public . . . require [government] interference; and, second, that the means are reasonably necessary for the accomplishment of the purpose, and not unduly oppressive upon individuals." Even this rule is not applied with strict precision, for this Court has often said that "debatable questions as to reasonableness are not for the courts but for the legislature. . . ." *E.g., Sproles v. Binford, 286 U.S. 374, 388 (1932).*

Goldblatt v. Hempstead, 369 U.S. 590, 594-595 (1962).

closer to public beach property. The Commission sought to offset this diminution in access, and thereby preserve the overall balance of access, by requesting a deed restriction that would ensure "lateral" access: the right of the public to pass and repass along the dry sand parallel to the shoreline in order to reach the tidelands and the ocean. In the expert opinion of the Coastal Commission, development conditioned on such a restriction would fairly attend to both public and private interests.

The Court finds fault with this measure because it regards the condition as insufficiently tailored to address the precise type of reduction in access produced by the new development. The Nollans' development blocks visual access, the Court tells us, while the Commission seeks to preserve lateral access along the coastline. Thus, it concludes, the State acted irrationally. Such a narrow conception of rationality, however, has long since been discredited as a judicial arrogation of legislative authority. "To make scientific precision a criterion of constitutional power would be to subject the State to an intolerable supervision hostile to the basic principles of our Government." *Sproles v. Binford,* 286 U.S. 374, 388 (1932). Cf. *Keystone Bituminous Coal Assn. v. DeBenedictis,* 480 U.S. 470, 491, n. 21 (1987) ("The Takings Clause has never been read to require the States or the courts to calculate whether a specific individual has suffered burdens . . . in excess of the benefits received").

[The balance of Justice Brennan's lengthy dissent is omitted.]

[Justice Blackmun also dissented, stating that the did not "understand the Court's opinion in this case to implicate in any way the public-trust doctrine," and disagreeing with "the Court's rigid interpretation of the necessary correlation between a burden created by development and a condition imposed pursuant to the State's police power to mitigate that burden." Justice Stevens filed a dissent reprising his dissent in *First English,* arguing that "because of the Court's remarkable ruling in *First English,* local governments and officials must pay the price for the necessarily vague standards in this area of the law."]

■ DOLAN v. CITY OF TIGARD
512 U.S. 374 (1994)

Chief Justice REHNQUIST delivered the opinion of the Court.

Petitioner challenges the decision of the Oregon Supreme Court which held that the city of Tigard could condition the approval of her building permit on the dedication of a portion of her property for flood control and traffic improvements. We granted certiorari to resolve a question left open by our decision in *Nollan,* of what is the required degree of connection between the exactions imposed by the city and the projected impacts of the proposed development.

I

The State of Oregon enacted a comprehensive land use management program in 1973. The program required all Oregon cities and counties to adopt new comprehensive land use plans that were consistent with the statewide planning goals. The plans are implemented by land use regulations which are part of an integrated hierarchy of legally binding goals, plans, and regulations. Pursuant to the State's requirements, the city of Tigard, a community of some 30,000 residents on the southwest edge of Portland, developed a comprehensive plan and codified it in its Community Development Code (CDC). The CDC requires property owners in the area zoned Central Business District to comply with a 15% open space and landscaping requirement, which limits total site coverage, including all structures and paved parking, to 85% of the parcel. After the completion of a transportation study that identified congestion in the Central Business District as a particular problem, the city adopted a plan for a pedestrian/bicycle pathway intended to encourage alternatives to automobile transportation for short trips. The CDC requires that new developments facilitate this plan by dedicating land for pedestrian pathways where provided for in the pedestrian/bicycle pathway plan.

The city also adopted a Master Drainage Plan (Drainage Plan). The Drainage Plan noted that flooding occurred in several areas along Fanno Creek, including areas near petitioner's property. The Drainage Plan also established that the increase in impervious surfaces associated with continued urbanization would exacerbate these flooding problems. To combat these risks, the Drainage Plan suggested a series of improvements to the Fanno Creek Basin, including channel excavation in the area next to petitioner's property. Other recommendations included ensuring that the floodplain remains free of structures and that it be preserved as greenways to minimize flood damage to structures. The Drainage Plan concluded that the cost of these improvements should be shared based on both direct and indirect benefits, with property owners along the waterways paying more due to the direct benefit that they would receive. . . .

Petitioner Florence Dolan owns a plumbing and electric supply store located on Main Street in the Central Business District of the city. The store covers approximately 9,700 square feet on the eastern side of a 1.67-acre parcel, which includes a gravel parking lot. Fanno Creek flows through the southwestern corner of the lot and along its western boundary. The year-round flow of the creek renders the area within the creek's 100-year floodplain virtually unusable for commercial development. The city's comprehensive plan includes the Fanno Creek floodplain as part of the city's greenway system.

Petitioner applied to the city for a permit to redevelop the site. Her proposed plans called for nearly doubling the size of the store to 17,600 square feet and paving a 39-space parking lot. The existing store, located on the opposite side of the parcel, would be razed in sections as construction progressed on the new building. In the second phase of the project, petitioner proposed to build an additional structure on the northeast side of the site for complementary businesses and to provide more parking. The proposed expansion and intensified use are consistent with the city's zoning scheme in the Central Business District.

The City Planning Commission (Commission) granted petitioner's permit application subject to conditions imposed by the city's CDC. The CDC establishes the following standard for site development review approval:

> Where landfill and/or development is allowed within and adjacent to the 100-year floodplain, the City shall require the dedication of sufficient open land area for greenway adjoining and within the floodplain. This area shall include portions at a suitable elevation for the construction of a pedestrian/bicycle pathway within the floodplain in accordance with the adopted pedestrian/bicycle plan.

Thus, the Commission required that petitioner dedicate the portion of her property lying within the 100-year floodplain for improvement of a storm drainage system along Fanno Creek and that she dedicate an additional 15-foot strip of land adjacent to the floodplain as a pedestrian/bicycle pathway. The dedication required by that condition encompasses approximately 7,000 square feet, or roughly 10% of the property. In accordance with city practice, petitioner could rely on the dedicated property to meet the 15% open space and landscaping requirement mandated by the city's zoning scheme. The city would bear the cost of maintaining a landscaped buffer between the dedicated area and the new store.

The Commission made a series of findings concerning the relationship between the dedicated conditions and the projected impacts of petitioner's project. First, the Commission noted that "[i]t is reasonable to assume that customers and employees of the future uses of this site could utilize a pedestrian/bicycle pathway adjacent to this development for their transportation and recreational needs." The Commission noted that the site plan has provided for bicycle parking in a rack in front of the proposed building and "[i]t is reasonable to expect that some of the users of the bicycle parking provided for by the site plan will use the pathway adjacent to Fanno Creek if it is constructed." In addition, the Commission found that creation of a convenient, safe pedestrian/bicycle pathway system as an alternative means of transportation "could offset some of the traffic demand on [nearby] streets and lessen the increase in traffic congestion."

The Commission went on to note that the required floodplain dedication would be reasonably related to petitioner's request to intensify the use of the site given the increase in the impervious surface. The Commission stated that the "anticipated increased storm water flow from the subject property to an already strained creek and drainage basin can only add to the public need to manage the stream channel and floodplain for drainage purposes." Based on this anticipated increased storm water flow, the Commission concluded that "the requirement of dedication of the floodplain area on the site is related to the applicant's plan to intensify development on the site." The Tigard City Council approved the Commission's final order, subject to one minor modification; the city council reassigned the responsibility for surveying and marking the floodplain area from petitioner to the city's engineering department.

[The Court's description of the administrative and lower court proceedings is omitted.]

II

The Takings Clause of the Fifth Amendment of the United States Constitution, made applicable to the States through the Fourteenth Amendment, provides: "[N]or shall private property be taken for public use, without just compensation." One of the principal purposes of the Takings Clause is "to bar Government from forcing some people alone to bear public burdens which, in all fairness and justice, should be borne by the public as a whole." Without question, had the city simply required petitioner to dedicate a strip of land along Fanno Creek for public use, rather than conditioning the grant of her permit to redevelop her property on such a dedication, a taking would have occurred. Such public access would deprive petitioner of the right to exclude others, "one of the most essential sticks in the bundle of rights that are commonly characterized as property."

On the other side of the ledger, the authority of state and local governments to engage in land use planning has been sustained against constitutional challenge as long ago as our decision in *Village of Euclid v. Ambler Realty Co.*, 272 U.S. 365 (1926). "Government hardly could go on if to some extent values incident to property could not be diminished without paying for every such change in the general law. . . ."

[Ordinary] land use regulations . . . differ in two relevant particulars from the present case. First, they involved essentially legislative determinations classifying entire areas of the city, whereas here the city made an adjudicative decision to condition petitioner's application for a building permit on an individual parcel. Second, the conditions imposed were not simply a limitation on the use petitioner might make of her own parcel, but a requirement that she deed portions of the property to the city. In *Nollan*, we held that governmental authority to exact such a condition was circumscribed by the Fifth and Fourteenth Amendments. Under the well-settled doctrine of "unconstitutional conditions," the government may not require a person to give up a constitutional right — here the right to receive just compensation when property is taken for a public use-in exchange for a discretionary benefit conferred by the government where the benefit sought has little or no relationship to the property. *See Perry v. Sindermann*, 408 U.S. 593 (1972). . . .

Petitioner contends that the city has forced her to choose between the building permit and her right under the Fifth Amendment to just compensation for the public easements. Petitioner does not quarrel with the city's authority to exact some forms of dedication as a condition for the grant of a building permit, but challenges the showing made by the city to justify these exactions. She argues that the city has identified "no special benefits" conferred on her, and has not identified any "special quantifiable burdens" created by her new store that would justify the particular dedications required from her which are not required from the public at large.

III

In evaluating petitioner's claim, we must first determine whether the "essential nexus" exists between the "legitimate state interest" and the permit condition exacted by the city. *Nollan.* If we find that a nexus exists, we must then decide the required degree of connection between the exactions and the projected impact of the proposed development. We were not required to reach this question in *Nollan*, because we concluded that the connection did not meet even the loosest standard. Here, however, we must decide this question.

A

We addressed the essential nexus question in *Nollan* . . . We agreed that the Coastal Commission's concern with protecting visual access to the ocean constituted a legitimate public interest. . . . We resolved, however, that the Coastal Commission's regulatory authority was set completely adrift from its constitutional moorings when it claimed that a nexus existed between visual access to the ocean and a permit condition requiring lateral public access along the Nollans' beachfront lot. . . . No such gimmicks are associated with the permit conditions imposed by the city in this case. Undoubtedly, the prevention of flooding along Fanno Creek and the reduction of traffic congestion in the Central Business District qualify as the type of legitimate public purposes we have upheld. It seems equally obvious that a nexus exists between preventing flooding along Fanno Creek and limiting development within the creek's 100-year floodplain. . . . The same may be said for the city's attempt to reduce traffic congestion by providing for alternative means of transportation.

B

The second part of our analysis requires us to determine whether the degree of the exactions demanded by the city's permit conditions bears the required relationship to the projected impact of petitioner's proposed development. *Nollan*, 483 U.S., at 834, quoting *Penn Central*, 438 U.S. at 127 ("'[A] use restriction may constitute a "taking" if not reasonably necessary to the effectuation of a substantial government purpose'"). Here the Oregon Supreme Court deferred to what it termed the "city's unchallenged factual findings" supporting the dedication conditions and found them to be reasonably related to the impact of the expansion of petitioner's business.

The city required that petitioner dedicate "to the City as Greenway all portions of the site that fall within the existing 100-year floodplain [of Fanno Creek] . . . and all property 15 feet above [the floodplain] boundary." In addition, the city demanded that the retail store be designed so as not to intrude into the greenway area. The city relies on the Commission's rather tentative findings that increased storm water flow from petitioner's property "can only add to the public need to manage the [floodplain] for drainage purposes" to support its conclusion that the "requirement of dedication of the floodplain area on the site is related to the applicant's plan to intensify development on the site."

The city made the following specific findings relevant to the pedestrian/bicycle pathway:

> In addition, the proposed expanded use of this site is anticipated to generate additional vehicular traffic thereby increasing congestion on nearby collector and arterial streets. Creation of a convenient, safe pedestrian/bicycle pathway system as an alternative means of transportation could offset some of the traffic demand on these nearby streets and lessen the increase in traffic congestion.

The question for us is whether these findings are constitutionally sufficient to justify the conditions imposed by the city on petitioner's building permit. Since state courts have been dealing with this question a good deal longer than we have, we turn to representative decisions made by them.

In some States, very generalized statements as to the necessary connection between the required dedication and the proposed development seem to suffice. We think this standard is too lax to adequately protect petitioner's right to just compensation if her property is taken for a public purpose.

Other state courts require a very exacting correspondence, described as the "specifi[c] and uniquely attributable" test. The Supreme Court of Illinois first developed this test in *Pioneer Trust & Savings Bank v. Mount Prospect*, 176 N.E.2d 799, 802 (1961). Under this standard, if the local government cannot demonstrate that its exaction is directly proportional to the specifically created need, the exaction becomes "a veiled exercise of the power of eminent domain and a confiscation of private property behind the defense of police regulations." We do not think the Federal Constitution requires such exacting scrutiny, given the nature of the interests involved.

A number of state courts have taken an intermediate position, requiring the municipality to show a "reasonable relationship" between the required dedication and the impact of the proposed development. Typical is the Supreme Court of Nebraska's opinion in *Simpson v. North Platte*, 292 N.W.2d 297, 301 (1980), where that court stated:

> The distinction, therefore, which must be made between an appropriate exercise of the police power and an improper exercise of eminent domain is whether the requirement has some reasonable relationship or nexus to the use to which the property is being made or is merely being used as an excuse for taking property simply because at that particular moment the landowner is asking the city for some license or permit.

Thus, the court held that a city may not require a property owner to dedicate private property for some future public use as a condition of obtaining a building permit when such future use is not "occasioned by the construction sought to be permitted." . . .

We think the "reasonable relationship" test adopted by a majority of the state courts is closer to the federal constitutional norm than either of those previously discussed. But we do not adopt it as such, partly because the term "reasonable relationship" seems confusingly similar to the term "rational basis" which describes the minimal level of scrutiny under the Equal Protection Clause of the Fourteenth Amendment. We think a term such as "rough proportionality" best encapsulates what we hold to be the requirement of the Fifth Amendment. No precise mathematical calculation is required, but the city must make some sort of individualized determination that the required dedication is related both in nature and extent to the impact of the proposed development.

Justice Stevens' dissent . . . [asserts] that the city's conditional demands for part of petitioner's property are "a species of business regulation that heretofore warranted a strong presumption of constitutional validity." But simply denominating a governmental measure as a "business regulation" does not immunize it from constitutional challenge on the ground that it violates a provision of the Bill of Rights. . . . We see no reason why the Takings Clause of the Fifth Amendment, as much a part of the Bill of Rights as the First Amendment or Fourth Amendment, should be relegated to the status of a poor relation in these comparable circumstances. We turn now to analysis of whether the findings relied upon by the city here, first with respect to the floodplain easement, and second with respect to the pedestrian/bicycle path, satisfied these requirements.

It is axiomatic that increasing the amount of impervious surface will increase the quantity and rate of storm water flow from petitioner's property. Therefore, keeping the floodplain open and free from development would likely confine the pressures on Fanno Creek created by petitioner's development. In fact, because petitioner's property lies within the Central Business District, the CDC already required that petitioner leave 15% of it as open space and the undeveloped floodplain would have nearly satisfied that requirement. But the city demanded more — it not only wanted petitioner not to build in the floodplain, but it also wanted petitioner's property along Fanno Creek for its greenway system. The city has never said why a public greenway, as opposed to a private one, was required in the interest of flood control.

The difference to petitioner, of course, is the loss of her ability to exclude others. As we have noted, this right to exclude others is "one of the most essential sticks in the bundle of rights that are commonly characterized as property." It is difficult to see why recreational visitors trampling along petitioner's floodplain easement are sufficiently related to the city's legitimate interest in reducing flooding problems along Fanno Creek, and the city has not attempted to make any individualized determination to support this part of its request.

The city contends that the recreational easement along the greenway is only ancillary to the city's chief purpose in controlling flood hazards. It further asserts that unlike the residential property at issue in *Nollan*, petitioner's property is commercial in character, and therefore, her right to exclude others is compromised. The city maintains that "[t]here is nothing to suggest that preventing [petitioner] from prohibiting [the easements] will unreasonably impair the value of [her] property as a [retail store]."

Admittedly, petitioner wants to build a bigger store to attract members of the public to her property. She also wants, however, to be able to control the time and manner in which they enter. The recreational easement on the greenway is different in character from the exercise of state-protected rights of free expression and petition that we permitted in *PruneYard*. In *PruneYard*, we held that a major private shopping center that attracted more than 25,000 daily patrons had to provide access to persons exercising their state constitutional rights to distribute pamphlets and ask passers-by to sign their petitions. We based our decision, in part, on the fact that the shopping center "may restrict expressive activity by adopting time, place, and manner regulations that will minimize any interference with its commercial functions." By contrast, the city wants to impose a permanent recreational easement upon petitioner's property that borders Fanno Creek. Petitioner would lose all rights to regulate the time in which the public entered onto the greenway, regardless of any interference it might pose with her retail store. Her right to exclude would not be regulated, it would be eviscerated. . . . We conclude that the findings upon which the city relies do not show the required reasonable relationship between the floodplain easement and the petitioner's proposed new building.

With respect to the pedestrian/bicycle pathway, we have no doubt that the city was correct in finding that the larger retail sales facility proposed by petitioner will increase traffic on the streets of the Central Business District. The city estimates that the proposed development would generate roughly 435 additional trips per day. Dedications for streets, sidewalks, and other public ways are generally reasonable exactions to avoid excessive congestion from a proposed property use. But on the record before us, the city has not met its burden of demonstrating that the additional number of vehicle and bicycle trips generated by petitioner's development reasonably relate to the city's requirement for a dedication of the pedestrian/ bicycle pathway easement. The city simply found that the creation of the pathway "could offset some of the traffic demand . . . and lessen the increase in traffic congestion."

As Justice Peterson of the Supreme Court of Oregon explained in his dissenting opinion, however, "[t]he findings of fact that the bicycle pathway system '*could* offset some of the traffic demand' is a far cry from a finding that the bicycle pathway system *will*, or is *likely to*, offset some of the traffic demand." No precise mathematical calculation is required, but the city must make some effort to quantify its findings in support of the dedication for the pedestrian/bicycle pathway beyond the conclusory statement that it could offset some of the traffic demand generated.

IV

Cities have long engaged in the commendable task of land use planning, made necessary by increasing urbanization, particularly in metropolitan areas such as Portland. The city's goals of reducing flooding hazards and traffic congestion, and providing for public greenways, are laudable, but there are outer limits to how this may be done. "A strong public desire to improve the public condition [will not] warrant achieving the desire by a shorter cut than the constitutional way of paying for the change." *Pennsylvania Coal.*

The judgment of the Supreme Court of Oregon is reversed, and the case is remanded for further proceedings not inconsistent with this opinion.

It is so ordered.

Justice STEVENS, joined by Justices BLACKMUN and GINSBURG, dissented

The record does not tell us the dollar value of petitioner Florence Dolan's interest in excluding the public from the greenway adjacent to her hardware business. The mountain of briefs that the case has generated nevertheless makes it obvious that the pecuniary value of her victory is far less important than the rule of law that this case has been used to establish. It is unquestionably an important case.

Certain propositions are not in dispute. The enlargement of the Tigard unit in Dolan's chain of hardware stores will have an adverse impact on the city's legitimate and substantial interests in controlling drainage in Fanno Creek and minimizing traffic congestion in Tigard's business district. That impact is sufficient to justify an outright denial of her application for approval of the expansion. The city has nevertheless agreed to grant Dolan's application if she will comply with two conditions, each of which admittedly will mitigate the adverse effects of her proposed development. The disputed question is whether the city has violated the Fourteenth Amendment to the Federal Constitution by refusing to allow Dolan's planned construction to proceed unless those conditions are met.

The Court is correct in concluding that the city may not attach arbitrary conditions to a building permit or to a variance even when it can rightfully deny the application outright. I also agree that state court decisions dealing with ordinances that govern municipal development plans provide useful guidance in a case of this kind. Yet the Court's description of the doctrinal underpinnings of its decision, the phrasing of its fledgling test of "rough proportionality," and the application of that test to this case run contrary to the traditional treatment of these cases and break considerable and unpropitious new ground.

[A substantial portion of Justice Steven's dissenting opinion is omitted.]

The Court has made a serious error by abandoning the traditional presumption of constitutionality and imposing a novel burden of proof on a city implementing an admittedly valid comprehensive land use plan. Even more consequential than its incorrect disposition of this case, however, is the Court's resurrection of a species of substantive due process analysis that it firmly rejected decades ago.

The Court begins its constitutional analysis by citing *Chicago, B. & Q.R. Co. v. Chicago,* 166 U.S. 226, 239 (1897), for the proposition that the Takings Clause of the Fifth Amendment is "applicable to the States through the Fourteenth Amendment." That opinion, however, contains no mention of either the Takings Clause or the Fifth Amendment; it held that the protection afforded by the Due Process Clause of the Fourteenth Amendment extends to matters of substance as well as procedure, and that the substance of "the due process of law enjoined by the Fourteenth Amendment requires compensation to be made or adequately secured to the owner of private property taken for public use under the authority of a State." It applied the same kind of substantive due process analysis more frequently identified with a better known case that accorded similar substantive protection to a baker's liberty interest in working 60 hours a week and 10 hours a day. *See Lochner v. New York, 198 U.S. 45 (1905).*

Later cases have interpreted the Fourteenth Amendment's substantive protection against uncompensated deprivations of private property by the States as though it incorporated the text of the Fifth Amendment's Takings Clause. There was nothing problematic about that interpretation in cases enforcing the Fourteenth Amendment against state action that involved the actual physical invasion of private property. Justice Holmes charted a significant new course, however, when he opined that a state law making it "commercially impracticable to mine certain coal" had "very nearly the same effect for constitutional purposes as appropriating or destroying it." The so-called "regulatory takings" doctrine that the Holmes dictum kindled has an obvious kinship with the line of substantive due process cases that *Lochner* exemplified. Besides having similar ancestry, both doctrines are potentially open-ended sources of judicial power to invalidate state economic regulations that Members of this Court view as unwise or unfair.

This case inaugurates an even more recent judicial innovation than the regulatory takings doctrine: the application of the "unconstitutional conditions" label to a mutually beneficial transaction between a property owner and a city. The Court tells us that the city's refusal to grant Dolan a discretionary benefit infringes her right to receive just compensation for the property interests that she has refused to dedicate to the city "where the property sought has little or no relationship to the benefit." Although it is well settled that a government cannot deny a benefit on a basis that infringes constitutionally protected interests—"especially [one's] interest in freedom of speech—the "unconstitutional conditions" doctrine provides an inadequate framework in which to analyze this case.

Dolan has no right to be compensated for a taking unless the city acquires the property interests that she has refused to surrender. Since no taking has yet occurred, there has not been any infringement of her constitutional right to compensation.

Even if Dolan should accept the city's conditions in exchange for the benefit that she seeks, it would not necessarily follow that she had been denied "just compensation" since it would be appropriate to consider the receipt of that benefit in any calculation of "just compensation." Particularly in the absence of any evidence on the point, we should not presume that the discretionary benefit the city has offered is less valuable than the property interests that Dolan can retain or surrender at her option. But even if that discretionary benefit were so trifling that it could not be considered just compensation when it has "little or no relationship" to the property, the Court fails to explain why the same value would suffice when the required nexus is present. In this respect, the Court's reliance on the "unconstitutional conditions" doctrine is assuredly novel, and arguably incoherent. The city's conditions are by no means immune from constitutional scrutiny. The level of scrutiny, however, does not approximate the kind of review that would apply if the city had insisted on a surrender of Dolan's First Amendment rights in exchange for a building permit. One can only hope that the Court's reliance today on First Amendment cases, and its candid disavowal of the term "rational basis" to describe its new standard of review, do not signify a reassertion of the kind of superlegislative power the Court exercised during the *Lochner* era.

The Court has decided to apply its heightened scrutiny to a single strand — the power to exclude — in the bundle of rights that enables a commercial enterprise to flourish in an urban environment. That intangible interest is undoubtedly worthy of constitutional protection — much like the grandmother's interest in deciding which of her relatives may share her home in *Moore v. East Cleveland*, 431 U.S. 494 (1977). Both interests are protected from arbitrary state action by the Due Process Clause of the Fourteenth Amendment. It is, however, a curious irony that Members of the majority in this case would impose an almost insurmountable burden of proof on the property owner in the *Moore* case while saddling the city with a heightened burden in this case.

In its application of what is essentially the doctrine of substantive due process, the Court confuses the past with the present. On November 13, 1922, the village of Euclid, Ohio, adopted a zoning ordinance that effectively confiscated 75 percent of the value of property owned by the Ambler Realty Company. Despite its recognition that such an ordinance "would have been rejected as arbitrary and oppressive" at an earlier date, the Court (over the dissent of Justices Van Devanter, McReynolds, and Butler) upheld the ordinance. Today's majority should heed the words of Justice Sutherland:

> Such regulations are sustained, under the complex conditions of our day, for reasons analogous to those which justify traffic regulations, which, before the advent of automobiles and rapid transit street railways, would have been condemned as fatally arbitrary and unreasonable. And in this there is no inconsistency, for while the meaning of constitutional guaranties never varies, the scope of their application must expand or contract to meet the new and different conditions which are constantly coming within the field of their operation. In a changing world, it is impossible that it should be otherwise.

In our changing world one thing is certain: uncertainty will characterize predictions about the impact of new urban developments on the risks of floods, earthquakes, traffic congestion, or environmental harms. When there is doubt concerning the magnitude of those impacts, the public interest in averting them must outweigh the private interest of the commercial entrepreneur. If the government can demonstrate that the conditions it has imposed in a land use permit are rational, impartial and conducive to fulfilling the aims of a valid land use plan, a strong presumption of validity should attach to those conditions. The burden of demonstrating that those conditions have unreasonably impaired the economic value of the proposed improvement belongs squarely on the shoulders of the party challenging the state action's constitutionality. That allocation of burdens has served us well in the past. The Court has stumbled badly today by reversing it.

I respectfully dissent.

Justice SOUTER also dissented.

Notes and Comments

1. *The Impact of* Nollan *and* Dolan. There has been a robust debate about the significance of the *Nollan* and *Dolan* cases. Both decisions were produced by sharply divided courts, with four justices dissenting in each case. The dissenters quite obviously viewed the rulings as notable departures from prior law. On the other hand, in *Dolan*, Chief Justice Rehnquist addressed the required constitutional "fit" between exactions and development impacts relative to the extensive state law governing exactions. He characterized the "rough proportionality" standard adopted by the Court as being roughly average in terms of stringency as compared to the standards adopted by state courts.

It is difficult to gauge the extent to which *Nollan* and *Dolan* may have affected the behavior of government regulators. One study, based largely on interviews with land use planners in California, concluded that the decisions caused some local governments to avoid imposing exactions they otherwise would have imposed. *See* Anne E. Carlson & Daniel Pollock, Takings on the Ground: How the Supreme Court's Takings Jurisprudence Affects Local Land Use Decisions, 35 U.C. Davis L. Rev. 103, 106-08 (2001). However, the study also concluded that the relatively rigorous analysis mandated by *Nollan* and *Dolan* led some communities to conclude they were underestimating some of the effects of development and to increase the level of their exactions. Interestingly, the authors also concluded that *Nollan* and *Dolan* would likely make it easier for communities to justify exactions to address certain types of impacts (such as increased traffic), and harder to justify exactions to address other types of impacts (such as degradation of the environment).

As a legal matter, the more demanding legal standards in *Nollan* and *Dolan* have unquestionably given developers new grounds for suing local communities and, equally important, for making credible threats of litigation. A 2014 survey of published appellate decisions showed that challenges to exactions under *Dolan* apparently succeeded about half the time, a rate of success that is only modestly lower than the rate of success in lawsuits that rest on a "strict scrutiny" test. *See* John Echeverria, *Koontz*: The Very Worst Takings Decision Ever? 22 N.Y.U. Envtl. L. J. 1, 8 (2014).

2. *Ad Hoc v. Legislative Conditions.* Another hotly debated question is whether *Nollan* and *Dolan* apply only to exactions imposed through a project-specific regulatory review process or whether they apply as well to exactions imposed by legislative mandate. *Nollan* and *Dolan* both apparently involved *ad hoc* exactions (though this, too, is debatable) and so the question is whether *Nollan* and *Dolan* should be applied more broadly. The lower courts are split on the issue, with a majority apparently maintaining that *Nollan* and *Dolan* only apply to *ad hoc* exactions. *See, e.g., Parking Ass'n of Georgia, Inc. v. City of Atlanta*, 450 S.E.2d 200 (Ga. 1994); *Ehrlich v. City of Culver City*, 911 P.2d 429 (Cal. 1996). *But see Town of Flower Mound v. Stafford Estates Ltd. P'ship*, 135 S.W.3d 620 (Tex. 2004); *Home Builders Ass'n of Dayton and Miami Valley v. Beavercreek*, 729 N.E.2d 349 (Ohio 2000). One argument for extending *Nollan* and *Dolan* is that, from a landowner's perspective, it makes no difference whether the exaction is imposed through an *ad hoc* administrative process or as a result of a legislative mandate. In either case, the burden imposed on the landowner by the

exaction is the same. On the other hand, *ad hoc* exactions arguably raise a greater concern than legislative mandates about the potential abuse of government authority to exact property interests in a way that "singles out" particular owners. In addition, legislative judgments are arguably entitled to greater judicial deference than administrative decisions, given that legislative mandates may be based on more deliberate and careful study than administrative decisions.

To date, the Supreme Court has declined to step into this debate, despite several invitations to do so. *See California Bldg. Indus. Ass'n v. City of San Jose,* 136 S. Ct. 928, 929 (2016) (Thomas, J. concurring in the denial of certiorari) (arguing that "property owners and local governments are left uncertain about what legal standard governs legislative ordinances and whether cities can legislatively impose exactions that would not pass muster if done administratively, presenting "compelling reasons for resolving this conflict at the earliest practicable opportunity"). *See also Parking Ass'n of Georgia, Inc. v. Atlanta,* 515 U.S. 1116 (1995) (Thomas, J., dissenting from denial of certiorari).

3. *Exactions Remedies?* Yet another unresolved issue is the appropriate remedy for an exaction that flunks the *Nollan/Dolan* tests. As explained above, the default remedy for a regulatory taking is payment of just compensation. According to the logic of *Nollan* and *Dolan,* an exaction that fails either the "essential nexus" or the "rough proportionality" test represents a taking and, therefore, a landowner subject to such an exaction should be entitled to a monetary recovery, either for a permanent or a temporary taking. But the precedent is not so clear. In *Nollan,* the property owners filed a "petition for a writ of administrative mandamus" in the California Superior Court, and the U.S. Supreme Court resolved the merits of the takings issue without addressing the issue of remedy. In *Dolan,* the property owner appealed the city's permit conditions by filing with the Oregon Land Use Board of Appeals on the ground that the exaction constituted an uncompensated taking; the U.S. Supreme Court again resolved the merits of the takings issue without discussing remedy. Understandably, these precedents have left the lower courts in a state of uncertainty. *See* Scott Woodward, The Remedy for a "*Nollan/Dolan* Unconstitutional Condition Violation," 38 Vt. L. Rev. 701 (2014).

4. Nollan/Dolan *and the Erstwhile "Substantially Advance" Takings Test.* One doctrinal puzzle is how the *Nollan/Dolan* exactions tests relate to the "substantially advance" takings test which the Supreme Court repudiated in *Lingle v. Chevron U.S.A. Inc.,* 544 U.S. 528 (2005). The Court's decisions in both *Nollan* and *Dolan* invoked the "substantially advance formula, raising the question of whether the holding of *Lingle* effectively overrules or at least undermines *Nollan and Dolan.* The Supreme Court anticipated and answered the question in the negative in *Lingle.* While acknowledging that both *Nollan* and *Dolan* quoted the "substantially advance" formula, the Court explained that both cases proceeded on the premise that there would have been a taking if the government had appropriated the easements at issue directly. Further, the specific issue in each case was whether and under what circumstances requiring an owner to turn over an easement will constitute a taking if it is mandated as a condition of the grant of a permit. "That is worlds apart," the Court explained, "from a rule that says a regulation affecting property constitutes a taking on its face solely because it does not substantially advance a legitimate government interest." 544 U.S. at 547-48.

■ KOONTZ v. ST. JOHNS RIVER WATER MANAGEMENT DISTRICT
133 S. Ct. 2586 (2013)

Justice ALITO delivered the opinion of the Court.

Our decisions in *Nollan* and *Dolan* provide important protection against the misuse of the power of land-use regulation. In those cases, we held that a unit of government may not condition the approval of a land-use permit on the owner's relinquishment of a portion of his property unless there is a "nexus" and "rough proportionality" between the government's demand and the effects of the proposed land use. In this case, the St. Johns River Water Management District (District) believes that it circumvented *Nollan* and *Dolan* because of the way in which it structured its handling of a permit application submitted by Coy Koontz Sr., whose estate is represented in this Court by Coy Koontz Jr. The District did not approve his application on the condition that he surrender an interest in his land. Instead, the District, after suggesting that he could obtain approval by signing over such an interest, denied his application because he refused to yield. The Florida Supreme Court blessed this maneuver and thus effectively interred those important decisions. Because we conclude that *Nollan* and *Dolan* cannot be evaded in this way, the Florida Supreme Court's decision must be reversed.

I

A

In 1972, petitioner purchased an undeveloped 14.9-acre tract of land on the south side of Florida State Road 50, a divided four-lane highway east of Orlando. The property is located less than 1,000 feet from that road's intersection with Florida State Road 408, a tolled expressway that is one of Orlando's major thoroughfares.

A drainage ditch runs along the property's western edge, and high-voltage power lines bisect it into northern and southern sections. The combined effect of the ditch, a 100-foot wide area kept clear for the power lines, the highways, and other construction on nearby parcels is to isolate the northern section of petitioner's property from any other undeveloped land. Although largely classified as wetlands by the State, the northern section drains well; the most significant standing water forms in ruts in an unpaved road used to access the power lines. The natural topography of the property's southern section is somewhat more diverse, with a small creek, forested uplands, and wetlands that sometimes have water as much as a foot deep. A wildlife survey found evidence of animals that often frequent developed areas: raccoons, rabbits, several species of bird, and a turtle. The record also indicates that the land may be a suitable habitat for opossums.

The same year that petitioner purchased his property, Florida enacted the Water Resources Act, which divided the State into five water management districts and authorized each district to regulate "construction that connects to, draws water from, drains water into, or is placed in or across the waters in the state." Under the Act, a landowner wishing to undertake such construction must obtain from the relevant district a Management and Storage of Surface Water (MSSW) permit, which may impose "such reasonable conditions" on the permit as are "necessary to assure" that construction will "not be harmful to the water resources of the district."

In 1984, in an effort to protect the State's rapidly diminishing wetlands, the Florida Legislature passed the Warren S. Henderson Wetlands Protection Act, which made it illegal for anyone to "dredge or fill in, on, or over surface waters" without a Wetlands Resource Management (WRM) permit. Under the Henderson Act, permit applicants are required to provide "reasonable assurance" that proposed construction on wetlands is "not contrary to the public interest," as defined by an enumerated list of criteria. Consistent with the Henderson Act, the St. Johns River Water Management District, the district with jurisdiction over petitioner's land, requires that permit applicants wishing to build on wetlands offset the resulting environmental damage by creating, enhancing, or preserving wetlands elsewhere.

Petitioner decided to develop the 3.7-acre northern section of his property, and in 1994 he applied to the District for MSSW and WRM permits. Under his proposal, petitioner would have raised the elevation of the northernmost section of his land to make it suitable for a building, graded the land from the southern edge of the building site down to the elevation of the high-voltage electrical lines, and installed a dry-bed pond for retaining and gradually releasing stormwater runoff from the building and its parking lot. To mitigate the environmental effects of his proposal, petitioner offered to foreclose any possible future development of the approximately 11-acre southern section of his land by deeding to the District a conservation easement on that portion of his property.

The District considered the 11-acre conservation easement to be inadequate, and it informed petitioner that it would approve construction only if he agreed to one of two concessions. First, the District proposed that petitioner reduce the size of his development to 1 acre and deed to the District a conservation easement on the remaining 13.9 acres. . . . In the alternative, the District told petitioner that he could proceed with the development as proposed, building on 3.7 acres and deeding a conservation easement to the government on the remainder of the property, if he also agreed to hire contractors to make improvements to District-owned land several miles away. Specifically, petitioner could pay to replace culverts on one parcel or fill in ditches on another. Either of those projects would have enhanced approximately 50 acres of District-owned wetlands. When the District asks permit applicants to fund offsite mitigation work, its policy is never to require any particular offsite project, and it did not do so here. Instead, the District said that it "would also favorably consider" alternatives to its suggested offsite mitigation projects if petitioner proposed something "equivalent."

Believing the District's demands for mitigation to be excessive in light of the environmental effects that his building proposal would have caused, petitioner filed suit in state court. Among other claims, he argued that he was entitled to relief under Fla. Stat. §373.617(2), which allows owners to recover "monetary damages" if a state agency's action is "an unreasonable exercise of the state's police power constituting a taking without just compensation."

B

[The Florida Circuit Court found a *Nollan/Dolan* violation, and the ruling was affirmed by the Florida District Court of Appeal. The Florida Supreme Court reversed, distinguishing *Nollan* and *Dolan* on the ground that in this case the District had not approved an application on the condition that the applicant accede to the District's demands; instead, the District denied his application after the applicant refused to agree to the conditions proposed by the District. In addition, the Florida Supreme Court majority drew a distinction between a demand for an interest in real property (as in *Nollan* and *Dolan*) and a demand for money.]

II

A

We have said in a variety of contexts that "the government may not deny a benefit to a person because he exercises a constitutional right." In *Perry v. Sindermann,* 408 U.S. 593 (1972), for example, we held that a public college would violate a professor's freedom of speech if it declined to renew his contract because he was an outspoken critic of the college's administration. And in *Memorial Hospital v. Maricopa County,* 415 U.S. 250 (1974), we concluded that a county impermissibly burdened the right to travel by extending healthcare benefits only to those indigent sick who had been residents of the county for at least one year. Those cases reflect an overarching principle, known as the unconstitutional conditions doctrine, that vindicates the Constitution's enumerated rights by preventing the government from coercing people into giving them up.

Nollan and *Dolan* "involve a special application" of this doctrine that protects the Fifth Amendment right to just compensation for property the government takes when owners apply for land-use permits. *Lingle v. Chevron U.S.A. Inc.,* 544 U.S. 528, 547 (2005). Our decisions in those cases reflect two realities of the permitting process. The first is that land-use permit applicants are especially vulnerable to the type of coercion that the unconstitutional conditions doctrine prohibits because the government often has broad discretion to deny a permit that is worth far more than property it would like to take. By conditioning a building permit on the owner's deeding over a public right-of-way, for example, the government can pressure an owner into voluntarily giving up property for which the Fifth Amendment would otherwise require just compensation. So long as the building permit is more valuable than any just compensation the owner could hope to receive for the right-of-way, the owner is likely to accede to the government's demand, no matter how unreasonable. Extortionate demands of this sort frustrate the Fifth Amendment right to just compensation, and the unconstitutional conditions doctrine prohibits them.

A second reality of the permitting process is that many proposed land uses threaten to impose costs on the public that dedications of property can offset. Where a building proposal would substantially increase traffic congestion, for example, officials might condition permit approval on the owner's agreement to deed over the land needed to widen a public road. Respondent argues that a similar rationale justifies the exaction at issue here: petitioner's proposed construction project, it submits, would destroy wetlands on his property, and in order to compensate for this loss, respondent demands that he enhance wetlands elsewhere. Insisting that landowners internalize the negative externalities of their conduct is a hallmark of responsible land-use policy, and we have long sustained such regulations against constitutional attack.

Nollan and *Dolan* accommodate both realities by allowing the government to condition approval of a permit on the dedication of property to the public so long as there is a "nexus" and "rough proportionality" between the property that the government demands and the social costs of the applicant's proposal. Our precedents thus enable permitting authorities to insist that applicants bear the full costs of their proposals while still forbidding the government from engaging in "out-and-out . . . extortion" that would thwart the Fifth Amendment right to just compensation. Under *Nollan* and *Dolan* the government may choose whether and how a permit applicant is required to mitigate the impacts of a proposed development, but it may not leverage its legitimate interest in mitigation to pursue governmental ends that lack an essential nexus and rough proportionality to those impacts.

B

The principles that undergird our decisions in *Nollan* and *Dolan* do not change depending on whether the government *approves* a permit on the condition that the applicant turn over property or *denies* a permit because the applicant refuses to do so. We have often concluded that denials of governmental benefits were impermissible under the unconstitutional conditions doctrine. In so holding, we have recognized that regardless of whether the government ultimately succeeds in pressuring someone into forfeiting a constitutional right, the unconstitutional conditions doctrine forbids burdening the Constitution's enumerated rights by coercively withholding benefits from those who exercise them.

A contrary rule would be especially untenable in this case because it would enable the government to evade the limitations of *Nollan* and *Dolan* simply by phrasing its demands for property as conditions precedent to permit approval. Under the Florida Supreme Court's approach, a government order stating that a permit is "approved if" the owner turns over property would be subject to *Nollan* and *Dolan,* but an identical order that uses the words "denied until" would not. Our unconstitutional conditions cases have long refused to attach significance to the distinction between conditions precedent and conditions subsequent. To do so here would effectively render *Nollan* and *Dolan* a dead letter.

The Florida Supreme Court puzzled over how the government's demand for property can violate the Takings Clause even though "'no property of any kind was ever taken,'" but the unconstitutional conditions doctrine provides a ready answer. Extortionate demands for property in the land-use permitting context run afoul of the Takings Clause not because they take property but because they impermissibly burden the right not to have property taken without just compensation. As in other unconstitutional conditions cases in which someone refuses to cede a constitutional right in the face of coercive pressure, the impermissible denial of a governmental benefit is a constitutionally cognizable injury.

Nor does it make a difference, as respondent suggests, that the government might have been able to deny petitioner's application outright without giving him the option of securing a permit by agreeing to spend money to improve public lands. Virtually all of our unconstitutional conditions cases involve a gratuitous governmental benefit of some kind. Yet we have repeatedly rejected the argument that if the government need not confer a benefit at all, it can withhold the benefit because someone refuses to give up constitutional rights. Even if respondent would have been entirely within its rights in denying the permit for some other reason, that greater authority does not imply a lesser power to condition permit approval on petitioner's forfeiture of his constitutional rights.

That is not to say, however, that there is *no* relevant difference between a consummated taking and the denial of a permit based on an unconstitutionally extortionate demand. Where the permit is denied and the condition is never imposed, nothing has been taken. While the unconstitutional conditions doctrine recognizes that this *burdens* a constitutional right, the Fifth Amendment mandates a particular *remedy*—just compensation—only for takings. In cases where there is an excessive demand but no taking, whether money damages are available is not a question of federal constitutional law but of the cause of action—whether state or federal—on which the landowner relies. Because petitioner brought his claim pursuant to a state law cause of action, the Court has no occasion to discuss what remedies might be available for a *Nollan/Dolan* unconstitutional conditions violation either here or in other cases.

C

. . . [W]e decline to reach respondent's argument that its demands for property were too indefinite to give rise to liability under *Nollan* and *Dolan*. The Florida Supreme Court did not reach the question whether respondent issued a demand of sufficient concreteness to trigger the special protections of *Nollan* and *Dolan*. It relied instead on the Florida District Court of Appeals' characterization of respondent's behavior as a demand for *Nollan/Dolan* purposes. Whether that characterization is correct is beyond the scope of the questions the Court agreed to take up for review. If preserved, the issue remains open on remand for the Florida Supreme Court to address. This Court therefore has no occasion to consider how concrete and specific a demand must be to give rise to liability under *Nollan* and *Dolan*.

Finally, respondent argues that we need not decide whether its demand for offsite improvements satisfied *Nollan* and *Dolan* because it gave petitioner another avenue for obtaining permit approval. Specifically, respondent said that it would have approved a revised permit application that reduced the footprint of petitioner's proposed construction site from 3.7 acres to 1 acre and placed a conservation easement on the remaining 13.9 acres of petitioner's land. Respondent argues that regardless of whether its demands for offsite mitigation satisfied *Nollan* and *Dolan*, we must separately consider each of petitioner's options, one of which did not require any of the offsite work the trial court found objectionable.

Respondent's argument is flawed because the option to which it points—developing only 1 acre of the site and granting a conservation easement on the rest—involves the same issue as the option to build on 3.7 acres and perform offsite mitigation. We agree with respondent that, so long as a permitting authority offers the landowner at least one alternative that would satisfy *Nollan* and *Dolan*, the landowner has not been subjected to an unconstitutional condition. But respondent's suggestion that we should treat its offer to let petitioner build on 1 acre as an alternative to offsite mitigation misapprehends the governmental benefit that petitioner was denied. Petitioner sought to develop 3.7 acres, but respondent in effect told petitioner that it would not allow him to build on 2.7 of those acres unless he agreed to spend money improving public lands. Petitioner claims that he was wrongfully denied a permit to build on those 2.7 acres. For that reason, respondent's offer to approve a less ambitious building project does not obviate the need to determine whether the demand for offsite mitigation satisfied *Nollan* and *Dolan*.

III

We turn to the Florida Supreme Court's alternative holding that petitioner's claim fails because respondent asked him to spend money rather than give up an easement on his land. A predicate for any unconstitutional conditions claim is that the government could not have constitutionally ordered the person asserting the claim to do what it attempted to pressure that person into doing. For that reason, we began our analysis in both *Nollan* and *Dolan* by observing that if the government had directly seized the easements it sought to obtain through the permitting process, it would have committed a *per se* taking. The Florida Supreme Court held that petitioner's claim fails at this first step because the subject of the exaction at issue here was money rather than a more tangible interest in real property. Respondent and the dissent take the same position, citing the concurring and dissenting opinions in *Eastern Enterprises v. Apfel,* 524 U.S. 498 (1998), for the proposition that an obligation to spend money can never provide the basis for a takings claim.

We note as an initial matter that if we accepted this argument it would be very easy for land-use permitting officials to evade the limitations of *Nollan* and *Dolan.* Because the government need only provide a permit applicant with one alternative that satisfies the nexus and rough proportionality standards, a permitting authority wishing to exact an easement could simply give the owner a choice of either surrendering an easement or making a payment equal to the easement's value. Such so-called "in lieu of" fees are utterly commonplace, and they are functionally equivalent to other types of land use exactions. For that reason and those that follow, we reject respondent's argument and hold that so-called "monetary exactions" must satisfy the nexus and rough proportionality requirements of *Nollan* and *Dolan.*

A

In *Eastern Enterprises,* the United States retroactively imposed on a former mining company an obligation to pay for the medical benefits of retired miners and their families. A four-Justice plurality concluded that the statute's imposition of retroactive financial liability was so arbitrary that it violated the Takings Clause. Although Justice Kennedy concurred in the result on due process grounds, he joined four other Justices in dissent in arguing that the Takings Clause does not apply to government-imposed financial obligations that "d[o] not operate upon or alter an identified property interest." Relying on the concurrence and dissent in *Eastern Enterprises,* respondent argues that a requirement that petitioner spend money improving public lands could not give rise to a taking.

Respondent's argument rests on a mistaken premise. Unlike the financial obligation in *Eastern Enterprises,* the demand for money at issue here did "operate upon . . . an identified property interest" by directing the owner of a particular piece of property to make a monetary payment. In this case, unlike *Eastern Enterprises,* the monetary obligation burdened petitioner's ownership of a specific parcel of land. In that sense, this case bears resemblance to our cases holding that the government must pay just compensation when it takes a lien — a right to receive money that is secured by a particular piece of property. The fulcrum this case turns on is the direct link between the government's demand and a specific parcel of real property. Because of that direct link, this case implicates the central concern of *Nollan* and *Dolan:* the risk that the government may use its substantial power and discretion in land-use permitting to pursue governmental ends that lack an essential nexus and rough proportionality to the effects of the proposed new use of the specific property at issue, thereby diminishing without justification the value of the property.

In this case, moreover, petitioner does not ask us to hold that the government can commit a *regulatory* taking by directing someone to spend money. As a result, we need not apply *Penn Central's* "essentially ad hoc, factual inquir[y]," at all, much less extend that "already difficult and uncertain rule" to the "vast category of cases" in which someone believes that a regulation is too costly. Instead, petitioner's claim rests on the more limited proposition that when the government commands the relinquishment of funds linked to a specific, identifiable property interest such as a bank account or parcel of real property, a "*per se* [takings] approach" is the proper mode of analysis under the Court's precedent.

Finally, it bears emphasis that petitioner's claim does not implicate "normative considerations about the wisdom of government decisions." *Eastern Enterprises,* 524 U.S., at 545 (opinion of Kennedy, J.). We are not here concerned with whether it would be "arbitrary or unfair" for respondent to order a landowner to make improvements to public lands that are nearby. Whatever the wisdom of such a policy, it would transfer an interest in property from the landowner to the government. For that reason, any such demand would amount to a *per se* taking similar to the taking of an easement or a lien.

B

Respondent and the dissent argue that if monetary exactions are made subject to scrutiny under *Nollan* and *Dolan,* then there will be no principled way of distinguishing impermissible land-use exactions from property taxes. We think they exaggerate both the extent to which that problem is unique to the land-use permitting context and the practical difficulty of distinguishing between the power to tax and the power to take by eminent domain.

It is beyond dispute that "[t]axes and user fees . . . are not 'takings.'" We said as much in *County of Mobile v. Kimball,* 102 U.S. 691, 703 (1881), and our cases have been clear on that point ever since. This case therefore does not affect the ability of governments to impose property taxes, user fees, and similar laws and regulations that may impose financial burdens on property owners.

At the same time, we have repeatedly found takings where the government, by confiscating financial obligations, achieved a result that could have been obtained by imposing a tax. Most recently, in *Brown v. Legal Foundation of Washington,* 538 U.S. 216 (2003), we were unanimous in concluding that a State Supreme Court's seizure of the interest on client funds held in escrow was a taking despite the unquestionable constitutional propriety of a tax that would have raised exactly the same revenue. Our holding in *Brown* followed from *Phillips v. Washington Legal Foundation,* 524 U.S. 156 (1998), and *Webb's Fabulous Pharmacies, Inc. v. Beckwith,* 449 U.S. 155 (1980), two earlier cases in which we treated confiscations of money as takings despite their functional similarity to a tax. Perhaps most closely analogous to the present case, we have repeatedly held that the government takes property when it seizes liens, and in so ruling we have never considered whether the government could have achieved an economically equivalent result through taxation.

Two facts emerge from those cases. The first is that the need to distinguish taxes from takings is not a creature of our holding today that monetary exactions are subject to scrutiny under *Nollan* and *Dolan*. Rather, the problem is inherent in this Court's long-settled view that property the government could constitutionally demand through its taxing power can also be taken by eminent domain.

Second, our cases show that teasing out the difference between taxes and takings is more difficult in theory than in practice. *Brown* is illustrative. Similar to respondent in this case, the respondents in *Brown* argued that extending the protections of the Takings Clause to a bank account would open a Pandora's Box of constitutional challenges to taxes. But also like respondent here, the *Brown* respondents never claimed that they were exercising their power to levy taxes when they took the petitioners' property. Any such argument would have been implausible under state law; in Washington, taxes are levied by the legislature, not the courts.

The same dynamic is at work in this case because Florida law greatly circumscribes respondent's power to tax. If respondent had argued that its demand for money was a tax, it would have effectively conceded that its denial of petitioner's permit was improper under Florida law. Far from making that concession, respondent has maintained throughout this litigation that it considered petitioner's money to be a substitute for his deeding to the public a conservation easement on a larger parcel of undeveloped land.

This case does not require us to say more. We need not decide at precisely what point a land-use permitting charge denominated by the government as a "tax" becomes "so arbitrary . . . that it was not the exertion of taxation but a confiscation of property." For present purposes, it suffices to say that despite having long recognized that "the power of taxation should not be confused with the power of eminent domain," we have had little trouble distinguishing between the two.

C

Finally, we disagree with the dissent's forecast that our decision will work a revolution in land use law by depriving local governments of the ability to charge reasonable permitting fees. Numerous courts — including courts in many of our Nation's most populous States — have confronted constitutional challenges to monetary exactions over the last two decades and applied the standard from *Nollan* and *Dolan* or something like it. Yet the "significant practical harm" the dissent predicts has not come to pass. That is hardly surprising, for the dissent is correct that state law normally provides an independent check on excessive land use permitting fees.

The dissent criticizes the notion that the Federal Constitution places any meaningful limits on "whether one town is overcharging for sewage, or another is setting the price to sell liquor too high." But only two pages later, it identifies three constraints on land use permitting fees that it says the Federal Constitution imposes and suggests that the additional protections of *Nollan* and *Dolan* are not needed. In any event, the dissent's argument that land use permit applicants need no further protection when the government demands money is really an argument for overruling *Nollan* and *Dolan*. After all, the Due Process Clause protected the Nollans from an unfair allocation of public burdens, and they too could have argued that the government's demand for property amounted to a taking under the *Penn Central* framework. We have repeatedly rejected the dissent's contention that other constitutional doctrines leave no room for the nexus and rough proportionality requirements of *Nollan* and *Dolan*. Mindful of the special vulnerability of land use permit applicants to extortionate demands for money, we do so again today. . . .

We hold that the government's demand for property from a land-use permit applicant must satisfy the requirements of *Nollan* and *Dolan* even when the government denies the permit and even when its demand is for money. The Court expresses no view on the merits of petitioner's claim that respondent's actions here failed to comply with the principles set forth in this opinion and those two cases. The Florida Supreme Court's judgment is reversed, and this case is remanded for further proceedings not inconsistent with this opinion.

It is so ordered.

[Justice Kagan, joined by Justices Ginsburg, Breyer, and Sotomayor, dissented. Justice Kagan agreed with the majority that "the *Nollan–Dolan* standard applies not only when the government approves a development permit conditioned on the owner's conveyance of a property interest (*i.e.,* imposes a condition subsequent), but also when the government denies a permit until the owner meets the condition (*i.e.,* imposes a condition precedent)." The dissenting opinion did not explain the basis for this conclusion or opine on whether the majority's reasoning was persuasive or not. However, the dissenters rejected the majority's conclusion that the *Nollan/Dolan* standard applies to a permit condition requiring the payment of money, reasoning that the precondition for applying *Nollan/Dolan* is that the condition, viewed independently, must constitute a taking, and *Eastern Enterprises* establishes that a government directive to pay money does not constitute a taking of private property. Justice Kagan also contended that the District had not made the kind of "unequivocal demand" necessary to trigger *Nollan/Dolan* and that unless the meaning of a "demand" triggering liability under *Koontz* were tightly cabined, the decision would have a chilling effect on the ability of local officials to hold mutually beneficial negotiations with developers. The dissent closed with the following words:]

> The majority's errors here are consequential. The majority turns a broad array of local land-use regulations into federal constitutional questions. It deprives state and local governments of the flexibility they need to enhance their communities — to ensure environmentally sound and economically productive development. It places courts smack in the middle of the most everyday local government activity. As those consequences play out across the country, I believe the Court will rue today's decision. I respectfully dissent.

Notes and Comments

1. *Consistency with* Nollan, Dolan, *or* Lingle? *Koontz*, like *Nollan* and *Dolan* beforehand, was decided by a sharply divided 5-to-4 Court. The Court did not issue the decision until the final days of the 2013 Term, suggesting it found the case to present considerable challenges. It remains to be seen whether the case represents a modest extension of *Nollan* and *Dolan*, or the harbinger of a more comprehensive overhaul of modern takings doctrine.

At least on a superficial level, the two holdings in *Koontz* have considerable intuitive appeal. Prior to *Koontz*, it was firmly established that the demanding *Nollan/Dolan* tests applied in the situation where the government demanded that property be turned over to the government as a condition of receiving a permit. In *Koontz*, the Court ruled that the same legal standard applies to a government decision *not* to issue a permit because the applicant objects to a proposed exaction. As the Court put it, why should it matter if the exaction is a "condition precedent" or a "condition subsequent?" Similarly, prior to *Koontz* it was established that requiring a developer to surrender an interest in land could trigger *Nollan* and *Dolan*. Yet *Koontz* raised the question why not also when the government requires a developer to turn over money of equal value? As the Court put it, monetary exactions are "functionally equivalent to other types of land use exactions."

On a doctrinal level, however, the rulings in *Koontz* are harder to justify. As the Court explained in *Nollan* and *Dolan*, the "essential nexus" and "rough proportionality" tests were based on the premise that the government could have denied the permits without triggering regulatory takings liability. The power to deny the permits without liability was the foundation for the Court's conclusion that government does not necessarily take property when it grants a permit subject to an exaction even though the exaction, viewed independently, would be a *per se* taking. Given the analytic foundation on which *Nollan* and *Dolan* are built, it is difficult to see how the *Nollan* and *Dolan* standards can apply to a denial of a permit application–regardless of whether the denial is motivated by the government's inability to obtain the owner's consent to the condition. Furthermore, even if the government sought to impose an exaction that would not meet constitutional standards, the denial of the permit does not, in the Court's words, impose a "forfeiture of constitutional rights." The owner retains the option of accepting the permit and suing for just compensation based on the exaction. *See* John Echeverria, The Costs of *Koontz*, 39 Vt. L. Rev. 573, 575-86 (2015). Is this critique persuasive, or does Justice Alito, speaking for the Court, have the better of the argument?

2. *Monetary Exactions.* The ruling that the *Nollan/Dolan* standards apply to monetary exactions appears even harder to rationalize, as Justice Kagan argued in her dissent. The *Nollan* and *Dolan* Courts justified applying a heightened standard of review on the ground that the exactions, if they had been imposed independently and outside of a regulatory process, would have constituted *per se* takings. The problem with extending *Nollan* and *Dolan* to monetary exactions is that in *Eastern Enterprises v. Apfel*, 524 U.S. 498 (1998), the Court established that government mandates to pay money do not affect "property" within the meaning of the Takings Clause and therefore cannot constitute takings. The *Koontz* Court accepted this understanding of the scope of the Takings Clause, but nonetheless ruled that *Nollan/Dolan* apply to a monetary exaction attached to a land use permit, because the exaction is at least being imposed on an owner of real property. Under that reasoning, however, *any* condition attached to a permit relating to the use of real property would be subject to review under *Nollan/Dolan*. The Court also said that the link between the monetary exaction and real property meant that the case "implicate[d] the central concern of *Nollan* and *Dolan*: the risk that the government may use its substantial power and discretion in land-use permitting to pursue governmental ends that lack an essential nexus and rough proportionality to the effects of the proposed new use of the specific property at issue, thereby diminishing without justification the value of the property." 133 S. Ct. at 2600. Does that sound like a revival of the "substantially advance" test repudiated in 2005 in *Lingle*? Or is the *Koontz* Court articulating some new and different standard?

3. Koontz's *Potential Chilling Effect*. The *Koontz* decision may have a chilling effect on the ability of local communities and developers to engage in mutually advantageous negotiations. It is given even after *Koontz* that the government retains broad

authority to regulate the use of land and can deny development permits without fear
of takings liability except in exceptional cases when a restriction destroys all or
substantially all of a property's value. On the other hand, *Koontz* establishes that,
once a community makes a "demand" that a developer accept some exaction, but
the community and the developer fail to agree on the exaction, the demanding
Nollan/Dolan standards will apply to the community's subsequent denial of the
permit application. This naturally has given rise to the concern that well-advised
local officials will decline to engage in any negotiations with developers out of fear of
falling into a takings liability trap. *See* Sean F. Nolon, Bargaining for Development
Post-*Koontz*: How the Supreme Court Invaded Local Government, 67 Fla. L. Rev. 171
(2015)

   4. *The Remedy for a* Koontz *Violation?* It is a mystery what the appropriate remedy
for a *Nollan/Dolan* violation should be, as discussed above. But it is even more mys-
terious what the remedy should be for a *Koontz* unconstitutional condition violation.
In *Koontz*, Justice Alito forthrightly acknowledged that the traditional takings
remedy would not apply:

> Where the permit is denied and the condition is never imposed, nothing has been
> taken. While the unconstitutional conditions doctrine recognizes that this *burdens* a
> constitutional right, the Fifth Amendment mandates a particular *remedy*—just com-
> pensation—only for takings.

133 S. Ct. at 2597. Justice Alito went on to say that whether some type of damages
remedy might be available would depend on the cause of action upon which the
plaintiff relies. Because Mr. Koontz had brought his claim under Florida law, Justice
Alito said the issue of the appropriate remedy had to be resolved under Florida law.
On remand, strangely enough, the Florida courts upheld a just compensation award
to Koontz based on the theory that he had suffered a taking of his land. *See St. Johns
River Water Mgmt. Dist. v. Koontz*, 183 So. 3d 396 (Fla. App. 2014), *review denied*, 2016
WL 688284 (Fl.,Feb. 19, 2016).

   The *Koontz* decision strongly suggests that, at least in litigation against local
governments, 42 U.S.C. §1983 should be available to support awards of actual
damages (as opposed to "just compensation") based on unconstitutional conditions claims. *See* Christopher Kieser, What We Have Here is a Failure to Compensate:
The Case for a Federal Damages Remedy in *Koontz* "Failed Exactions," 40 Wm. &
Mary Envtl. L. & Pol'y Rev. 163 (2015). However, §1983 does not provide a cause of
action against the United States.

E. EMINENT DOMAIN

■ KELO v. CITY OF NEW LONDON
545 U.S. 469 (2005)

   Justice Stevens delivered the opinion of the Court.
   In 2000, the city of New London approved a development plan that, in the
words of the Supreme Court of Connecticut, was "projected to create in excess of
1,000 jobs, to increase tax and other revenues, and to revitalize an economically

distressed city, including its downtown and waterfront areas." In assembling the land needed for this project, the city's development agent has purchased property from willing sellers and proposes to use the power of eminent domain to acquire the remainder of the property from unwilling owners in exchange for just compensation. The question presented is whether the city's proposed disposition of this property qualifies as a "public use" within the meaning of the Takings Clause of the Fifth Amendment to the Constitution.

I

The city of New London (hereinafter City) sits at the junction of the Thames River and the Long Island Sound in southeastern Connecticut. Decades of economic decline led a state agency in 1990 to designate the City a "distressed municipality." In 1996, the Federal Government closed the Naval Undersea Warfare Center, which had been located in the Fort Trumbull area of the City and had employed over 1,500 people. In 1998, the City's unemployment rate was nearly double that of the State, and its population of just under 24,000 residents was at its lowest since 1920.

These conditions prompted state and local officials to target New London, and particularly its Fort Trumbull area, for economic revitalization. To this end, respondent New London Development Corporation (NLDC), a private nonprofit entity established some years earlier to assist the City in planning economic development, was reactivated. In January 1998, the State authorized a $5.35 million bond issue to support the NLDC's planning activities and a $10 million bond issue toward the creation of a Fort Trumbull State Park. In February, the pharmaceutical company Pfizer Inc. announced that it would build a $300 million research facility on a site immediately adjacent to Fort Trumbull; local planners hoped that Pfizer would draw new business to the area, thereby serving as a catalyst to the area's rejuvenation. After receiving initial approval from the city council, the NLDC continued its planning activities and held a series of neighborhood meetings to educate the public about the process. In May, the city council authorized the NLDC to formally submit its plans to the relevant state agencies for review. Upon obtaining state-level approval, the NLDC finalized an integrated development plan focused on 90 acres of the Fort Trumbull area.

The Fort Trumbull area is situated on a peninsula that juts into the Thames River. The area comprises approximately 115 privately owned properties, as well as the 32 acres of land formerly occupied by the naval facility (Trumbull State Park now occupies 18 of those 32 acres). The development plan encompasses seven parcels. Parcel 1 is designated for a waterfront conference hotel at the center of a "small urban village" that will include restaurants and shopping. This parcel will also have marinas for both recreational and commercial uses. A pedestrian "riverwalk" will originate here and continue down the coast, connecting the waterfront areas of the development. Parcel 2 will be the site of approximately 80 new residences organized into an urban neighborhood and linked by public walkway to the remainder of the development, including the state park. This parcel also includes space reserved for a new U.S. Coast Guard Museum. Parcel 3, which is located immediately north of the Pfizer facility, will contain at least 90,000 square feet of research and development office space. Parcel 4A is a 2.4–acre site that will be used either to support the adjacent state park, by providing parking or retail services for visitors, or to support the nearby marina. Parcel 4B will include a renovated marina, as well as the final stretch of the riverwalk. Parcels 5, 6, and 7 will provide land for office and retail space, parking, and water-dependent commercial uses.

The NLDC intended the development plan to capitalize on the arrival of the Pfizer facility and the new commerce it was expected to attract. In addition to creating jobs, generating tax revenue, and helping to "build momentum for the revitalization of downtown New London," the plan was also designed to make the City more attractive and to create leisure and recreational opportunities on the waterfront and in the park.

The city council approved the plan in January 2000, and designated the NLDC as its development agent in charge of implementation. The city council also authorized the NLDC to purchase property or to acquire property by exercising eminent domain in the City's name. The NLDC successfully negotiated the purchase of most of the real estate in the 90-acre area, but its negotiations with petitioners failed. As a consequence, in November 2000, the NLDC initiated the condemnation proceedings that gave rise to this case.

II

Petitioner Susette Kelo has lived in the Fort Trumbull area since 1997. She has made extensive improvements to her house, which she prizes for its water view. Petitioner Wilhelmina Dery was born in her Fort Trumbull house in 1918 and has lived there her entire life. Her husband Charles (also a petitioner) has lived in the house since they married some 60 years ago. In all, the nine petitioners own 15 properties in Fort Trumbull — 4 in parcel 3 of the development plan and 11 in parcel 4A. Ten of the parcels are occupied by the owner or a family member; the other five are held as investment properties. There is no allegation that any of these properties is blighted or otherwise in poor condition; rather, they were condemned only because they happen to be located in the development area.

In December 2000, petitioners brought this action in the New London Superior Court. They claimed, among other things, that the taking of their properties would violate the "public use" restriction in the Fifth Amendment. After a 7-day bench trial, the Superior Court granted a permanent restraining order prohibiting the taking of the properties located in parcel 4A (park or marina support). It, however, denied petitioners relief as to the properties located in parcel 3 (office space). After the Superior Court ruled, both sides took appeals to the Supreme Court of Connecticut. That court held, over a dissent, that all of the City's proposed takings were valid . . .

III

Two polar propositions are perfectly clear. On the one hand, it has long been accepted that the sovereign may not take the property of *A* for the sole purpose of transferring it to another private party *B*, even though *A* is paid just compensation. On the other hand, it is equally clear that a State may transfer property from one private party to another if future "use by the public" is the purpose of the taking; the condemnation of land for a railroad with common-carrier duties is a familiar example. Neither of these propositions, however, determines the disposition of this case.

As for the first proposition, the City would no doubt be forbidden from taking petitioners' land for the purpose of conferring a private benefit on a particular private party. Nor would the City be allowed to take property under the mere pretext of a public purpose, when its actual purpose was to bestow a private benefit. The takings before us, however, would be executed pursuant to a "carefully considered" development plan. The trial judge and all the members of the Supreme Court of Connecticut agreed that there was no evidence of an illegitimate purpose in this case . . .

On the other hand, this is not a case in which the City is planning to open the condemned land — at least not in its entirety — to use by the general public. Nor will the private lessees of the land in any sense be required to operate like common carriers, making their services available to all comers. But although such a projected use would be sufficient to satisfy the public use requirement, this "Court long ago rejected any literal requirement that condemned property be put into use for the general public." Indeed, while many state courts in the mid-19th century endorsed "use by the public" as the proper definition of public use, that narrow view steadily eroded over time. Not only was the "use by the public" test difficult to administer (*e.g.*, what proportion of the public need have access to the property? at what price?), but it proved to be impractical given the diverse and always evolving needs of society. Accordingly, when this Court began applying the Fifth Amendment to the States at the close of the 19th century, it embraced the broader and ·more natural interpretation of public use as "public purpose." See, *e.g., Fallbrook Irrigation Dist. v. Bradley,* 164 U.S. 112 (1896). Thus, in a case upholding a mining company's use of an aerial bucket line to transport ore over property it did not own, Justice Holmes' opinion for the Court stressed "the inadequacy of use by the general public as a universal test." *Strickley v. Highland Boy Gold Mining Co.,* 200 U.S. 527, 531 (1906).[9] We have repeatedly and consistently rejected that narrow test ever since.

The disposition of this case therefore turns on the question whether the City's development plan serves a "public purpose." Without exception, our cases have defined that concept broadly, reflecting our longstanding policy of deference to legislative judgments in this field.

In *Berman v. Parker,* 348 U.S. 26 (1954), this Court upheld a redevelopment plan targeting a blighted area of Washington, D. C., in which most of the housing for the area's 5,000 inhabitants was beyond repair. Under the plan, the area would be condemned and part of it utilized for the construction of streets, schools, and other public facilities. The remainder of the land would be leased or sold to private parties for the purpose of redevelopment, including the construction of low-cost housing.

The owner of a department store located in the area challenged the condemnation, pointing out that his store was not itself blighted and arguing that the creation of a "better balanced, more attractive community" was not a valid public use. Writing for a unanimous Court, Justice Douglas refused to evaluate this claim in isolation, deferring instead to the legislative and agency judgment that the area "must be planned as a whole" for the plan to be successful. The Court explained that "community redevelopment programs need not, by force of the Constitution,

---

9. *See also Clark v. Nash,* 198 U.S. 361 (1905) (upholding a statute that authorized the owner of arid land to widen a ditch on his neighbor's property so as to permit a nearby stream to irrigate his land).

be on a piecemeal basis — lot by lot, building by building." The public use underlying the taking was unequivocally affirmed:

> We do not sit to determine whether a particular housing project is or is not desirable.
> The concept of the public welfare is broad and inclusive. . . . The values it represents
> are spiritual as well as physical, aesthetic as well as monetary. It is within the power of the
> legislature to determine that the community should be beautiful as well as healthy,
> spacious as well as clean, well-balanced as well as carefully patrolled. In the present case,
> the Congress and its authorized agencies have made determinations that take into
> account a wide variety of values. It is not for us to reappraise them. If those who govern
> the District of Columbia decide that the Nation's Capital should be beautiful as well as
> sanitary, there is nothing in the Fifth Amendment that stands in the way.

In *Hawaii Housing Authority v. Midkiff,* 467 U.S. 229 (1984), the Court considered a
Hawaii statute whereby fee title was taken from lessors and transferred to lessees (for
just compensation) in order to reduce the concentration of land ownership. We unanimously upheld the statute and rejected the Ninth Circuit's view that it was "a naked
attempt on the part of the state of Hawaii to take the property of A and transfer it to B
solely for B's private use and benefit." Reaffirming *Berman's* deferential approach to
legislative judgments in this field, we concluded that the State's purpose of eliminating
the "social and economic evils of a land oligopoly" qualified as a valid public use. Our
opinion also rejected the contention that the mere fact that the State immediately
transferred the properties to private individuals upon condemnation somehow diminished the public character of the taking. "[I]t is only the taking's purpose, and not its
mechanics," we explained, that matters in determining public use.

In that same Term we decided another public use case that arose in a purely
economic context. In *Ruckelshaus v. Monsanto Co.,* 467 U.S. 986 (1984), the Court
dealt with provisions of the Federal Insecticide, Fungicide, and Rodenticide Act
under which the Environmental Protection Agency could consider the data (including trade secrets) submitted by a prior pesticide applicant in evaluating a
subsequent application, so long as the second applicant paid just compensation
for the data. We acknowledged that the "most direct beneficiaries" of these provisions were the subsequent applicants, but we nevertheless upheld the statute under
Berman and *Midkiff.* We found sufficient Congress' belief that sparing applicants the
cost of time-consuming research eliminated a significant barrier to entry in the
pesticide market and thereby enhanced competition.

Viewed as a whole, our jurisprudence has recognized that the needs of society
have varied between different parts of the Nation, just as they have evolved over time
in response to changed circumstances. Our earliest cases in particular embodied a
strong theme of federalism, emphasizing the "great respect" that we owe to state
legislatures and state courts in discerning local public needs. For more than a century, our public use jurisprudence has wisely eschewed rigid formulas and intrusive
scrutiny in favor of affording legislatures broad latitude in determining what public
needs justify the use of the takings power.

IV

Those who govern the City were not confronted with the need to remove blight
in the Fort Trumbull area, but their determination that the area was sufficiently

distressed to justify a program of economic rejuvenation is entitled to our deference. The City has carefully formulated an economic development plan that it believes will provide appreciable benefits to the community, including — but by no means limited to — new jobs and increased tax revenue. As with other exercises in urban planning and development, the City is endeavoring to coordinate a variety of commercial, residential, and recreational uses of land, with the hope that they will form a whole greater than the sum of its parts. To effectuate this plan, the City has invoked a state statute that specifically authorizes the use of eminent domain to promote economic development. Given the comprehensive character of the plan, the thorough deliberation that preceded its adoption, and the limited scope of our review, it is appropriate for us, as it was in *Berman,* to resolve the challenges of the individual owners, not on a piecemeal basis, but rather in light of the entire plan. Because that plan unquestionably serves a public purpose, the takings challenged here satisfy the public use requirement of the Fifth Amendment.

To avoid this result, petitioners urge us to adopt a new bright-line rule that economic development does not qualify as a public use. Putting aside the unpersuasive suggestion that the City's plan will provide only purely economic benefits, neither precedent nor logic supports petitioners' proposal. Promoting economic development is a traditional and long-accepted function of government. There is, moreover, no principled way of distinguishing economic development from the other public purposes that we have recognized. In our cases upholding takings that facilitated agriculture and mining, for example, we emphasized the importance of those industries to the welfare of the States in question; in *Berman,* we endorsed the purpose of transforming a blighted area into a "well-balanced" community through redevelopment; in *Midkiff,* we upheld the interest in breaking up a land oligopoly that "created artificial deterrents to the normal functioning of the State's residential land market;" and in *Monsanto,* we accepted Congress' purpose of eliminating a "significant barrier to entry in the pesticide market." It would be incongruous to hold that the City's interest in the economic benefits to be derived from the development of the Fort Trumbull area has less of a public character than any of those other interests. Clearly, there is no basis for exempting economic development from our traditionally broad understanding of public purpose.

Petitioners contend that using eminent domain for economic development impermissibly blurs the boundary between public and private takings. Again, our cases foreclose this objection. Quite simply, the government's pursuit of a public purpose will often benefit individual private parties. For example, in *Midkiff,* the forced transfer of property conferred a direct and significant benefit on those lessees who were previously unable to purchase their homes. In *Monsanto,* we recognized that the "most direct beneficiaries" of the data-sharing provisions were the subsequent pesticide applicants, but benefiting them in this way was necessary to promoting competition in the pesticide market. The owner of the department store in *Berman* objected to "taking from one businessman for the benefit of another businessman," referring to the fact that under the redevelopment plan land would be leased or sold to private developers for redevelopment. Our rejection of that contention has particular relevance to the instant case: "The public end may be as well or better served through an agency of private enterprise than through a department of government — or so the Congress might conclude. We cannot say that public ownership is the sole method of promoting the public purposes of community redevelopment projects."

It is further argued that without a bright-line rule nothing would stop a city from transferring citizen *A*'s property to citizen *B* for the sole reason that citizen *B* will put the property to a more productive use and thus pay more taxes. Such a one-to-one transfer of property, executed outside the confines of an integrated development plan, is not presented in this case. While such an unusual exercise of government power would certainly raise a suspicion that a private purpose was afoot, the hypothetical cases posited by petitioners can be confronted if and when they arise. They do not warrant the crafting of an artificial restriction on the concept of public use.

Alternatively, petitioners maintain that for takings of this kind we should require a "reasonable certainty" that the expected public benefits will actually accrue. Such a rule, however, would represent an even greater departure from our precedent. "When the legislature's purpose is legitimate and its means are not irrational, our cases make clear that empirical debates over the wisdom of takings — no less than debates over the wisdom of other kinds of socioeconomic legislation — are not to be carried out in the federal courts." Indeed, earlier this Term we explained why similar practical concerns (among others) undermined the use of the "substantially advances" formula in our regulatory takings doctrine. *See Lingle v. Chevron U.S.A. Inc., 544 U.S. 528, 544 (2005).* The disadvantages of a heightened form of review are especially pronounced in this type of case. Orderly implementation of a comprehensive redevelopment plan obviously requires that the legal rights of all interested parties be established before new construction can be commenced. A constitutional rule that required postponement of the judicial approval of every condemnation until the likelihood of success of the plan had been assured would unquestionably impose a significant impediment to the successful consummation of many such plans.

Just as we decline to second-guess the City's considered judgments about the efficacy of its development plan, we also decline to second-guess the City's determinations as to what lands it needs to acquire in order to effectuate the project. "It is not for the courts to oversee the choice of the boundary line nor to sit in review on the size of a particular project area. Once the question of the public purpose has been decided, the amount and character of land to be taken for the project and the need for a particular tract to complete the integrated plan rests in the discretion of the legislative branch."

In affirming the City's authority to take petitioners' properties, we do not minimize the hardship that condemnations may entail, notwithstanding the payment of just compensation. We emphasize that nothing in our opinion precludes any State from placing further restrictions on its exercise of the takings power. Indeed, many States already impose "public use" requirements that are stricter than the federal baseline. Some of these requirements have been established as a matter of state constitutional law, while others are expressed in state eminent domain statutes that carefully limit the grounds upon which takings may be exercised. As the submissions of the parties and their *amici* make clear, the necessity and wisdom of using eminent domain to promote economic development are certainly matters of legitimate public debate. This Court's authority, however, extends only to determining whether the City's proposed condemnations are for a "public use" within the meaning of the Fifth Amendment to the Federal Constitution. Because over a century of our case law interpreting that provision dictates an affirmative answer to that question, we may not grant petitioners the relief that they seek.

The judgment of the Supreme Court of Connecticut is affirmed.

It is so ordered.

Justice KENNEDY joined in the Court's opinion and filed a concurring opinion.

I join the opinion for the Court and add these further observations.

This Court has declared that a taking should be upheld as consistent with the Public Use Clause, as long as it is "rationally related to a conceivable public purpose." This deferential standard of review echoes the rational-basis test used to review economic regulation under the Due Process and Equal Protection Clauses. The determination that a rational-basis standard of review is appropriate does not, however, alter the fact that transfers intended to confer benefits on particular, favored private entities, and with only incidental or pretextual public benefits, are forbidden by the Public Use Clause.

A court applying rational-basis review under the Public Use Clause should strike down a taking that, by a clear showing, is intended to favor a particular private party, with only incidental or pretextual public benefits, just as a court applying rational-basis review under the Equal Protection Clause must strike down a government classification that is clearly intended to injure a particular class of private parties, with only incidental or pretextual public justifications. *See Cleburne v. Cleburne Living Center, Inc.*, 473 U.S. 432 (1985). As the trial court in this case was correct to observe: "Where the purpose [of a taking] is economic development and that development is to be carried out by private parties or private parties will be benefited, the court must decide if the stated public purpose — economic advantage to a city sorely in need of it — is only incidental to the benefits that will be confined [sic] on private parties of a development plan."

A court confronted with a plausible accusation of impermissible favoritism to private parties should treat the objection as a serious one and review the record to see if it has merit, though with the presumption that the government's actions were reasonable and intended to serve a public purpose. Here, the trial court conducted a careful and extensive inquiry into "whether, in fact, the development plan is of primary benefit to . . . the developer [*i.e.*, Corcoran Jennison], and private businesses which may eventually locate in the plan area [*e.g.*, Pfizer], and in that regard, only of incidental benefit to the city . . .

The trial court concluded . . . that benefiting Pfizer was not "the primary motivation or effect of this development plan;" instead, "the primary motivation for [respondents] was to take advantage of Pfizer's presence." Likewise, the trial court concluded that "[t]here is nothing in the record to indicate that . . . [respondents] were motivated by a desire to aid [other] particular private entities." Even the dissenting justices on the Connecticut Supreme Court agreed that respondents' development plan was intended to revitalize the local economy, not to serve the interests of Pfizer, Corcoran Jennison, or any other private party. This case, then, survives the meaningful rational-basis review that in my view is required under the Public Use Clause.

Petitioners and their *amici* argue that any taking justified by the promotion of economic development must be treated by the courts as *per se* invalid, or at least presumptively invalid. Petitioners overstate the need for such a rule, however, by making the incorrect assumption that review under *Berman* and *Midkiff* imposes no meaningful judicial limits on the government's power to condemn any property it likes. A broad *per se* rule or a strong presumption of invalidity, furthermore, would prohibit a large number of government takings that have the purpose and expected effect of conferring substantial benefits on the public at large and so do not offend the Public Use Clause.

My agreement with the Court that a presumption of invalidity is not warranted for economic development takings in general, or for the particular takings at issue in this case, does not foreclose the possibility that a more stringent standard of review than that announced in *Berman* and *Midkiff* might be appropriate for a more narrowly drawn category of takings. There may be private transfers in which the risk of undetected impermissible favoritism of private parties is so acute that a presumption (rebuttable or otherwise) of invalidity is warranted under the Public Use Clause. This demanding level of scrutiny, however, is not required simply because the purpose of the taking is economic development.

This is not the occasion for conjecture as to what sort of cases might justify a more demanding standard, but it is appropriate to underscore aspects of the instant case that convince me no departure from *Berman* and *Midkiff* is appropriate here. This taking occurred in the context of a comprehensive development plan meant to address a serious citywide depression, and the projected economic benefits of the project cannot be characterized as *de minimis*. The identities of most of the private beneficiaries were unknown at the time the city formulated its plans. The city complied with elaborate procedural requirements that facilitate review of the record and inquiry into the city's purposes. In sum, while there may be categories of cases in which the transfers are so suspicious, or the procedures employed so prone to abuse, or the purported benefits are so trivial or implausible, that courts should presume an impermissible private purpose, no such circumstances are present in this case.

[Justice O'Connor, joined by Chief Justice Rehnquist, Justice Scalia and Justice Thomas, dissented. Justice O'Connor contended that the Takings Clause, properly read, does not permit the taking of private property, even if accompanied by payment of just compensation, to promote economic development. She asserted that such a use of the eminent domain power went beyond the three permissible uses of the eminent domain under the Court's precedents: to transfer property from private to public ownership; to acquire property when the property will be devoted to actual public use; or to prevent some use of private property that "inflict[s] affirmative harm on society." She concluded her opinion by stating:

> Any property may now be taken for the benefit of another private party, but the fallout from this decision will not be random. The beneficiaries are likely to be those citizens with disproportionate influence and power in the political process, including large corporations and development firms. As for the victims, the government now has license to transfer property from those with fewer resources to those with more. The Founders cannot have intended this perverse result. "[T]hat alone is a *just* government," wrote James Madison, "which *impartially* secures to every man, whatever is his *own*." For the National Gazette, Property (Mar. 27, 1792), reprinted in 14 Papers of James Madison 266 (R. Rutland et al. eds.1983).

545 U.S. at 505. Justice Thomas, while joining in Justice O'Connor's dissent, filed a separate dissent, arguing that, "[t]he most natural reading of the Clause is that it allows the government to take property only if the government owns, or the public

has a legal right to use, the property, as opposed to taking it for any public purpose or necessity whatsoever." *Id.* at 508.]

Notes and Comments

1. *The Holdout Problem.* While not well explained in the *Kelo* decision, if there is a justification for the existence of the eminent domain power it lies in the need for the government to deal with potential holdouts — the risk that individual owners, for idiosyncratic or even irrational reasons, will refuse to sell their properties to the public and thereby defeat important public goals. The problems created by hold-outs, and the necessity for eminent domain to overcome holdouts, are generally accepted in the case of major infrastructure projects, such as interstate highways, gas pipelines, or military bases. The same rationale can (though in particular cases may not) justify the use of eminent domain to support downtown redevelopment projects of the kind at issue in *Kelo.* The holdout rationale for the eminent domain power may or may not outweigh the serious personal and social costs of the use of this power, either as a matter of constitutional doctrine or as a matter of public policy. Moreover, even if there are persuasive arguments for maintaining the eminent domain power (in some or all contexts), legislators and other policy makers have various options for tempering the use of this power. *See* Robert Dreher & John Echeverria, Georgetown Environmental Law & Policy Institute, *Kelo's* Unanswered Questions (2005) at http://www.gelpi.org/gelpi/current_research/documents/GELPIReport_Kelo.pdf (last visited Nov. 11, 2016).

2. *The Political Response to* Kelo. The *Kelo* decision generated a strong political backlash. Politicians lambasted the decision on a bipartisan basis. *See* The *Kelo* Decision: Investigating Takings of Homes and Other Private Property: Hearing Before the S. Comm. on the Judiciary, 109th Cong. (2005); Protecting Property Rights After *Kelo*: Hearing Before the Subcomm. on Commerce, Trade, and Consumer Protection of the H. Comm. on Energy and Commerce, 109th Cong. (2005). Shortly after the *Kelo* decision, the U.S. House of Representatives passed a bill designed to block local governments from using eminent domain for economic development; the legislative effort stalled in the Senate after a furious lobbying battle and the personal intervention of New York City's powerful mayor, Michael Bloomberg. In the years after the *Kelo* decision, virtually every state legislature has debated the merits of the decision and the need for corrective legislation. Over 40 states eventually adopted new legislation limiting the use of eminent domain. These new laws run the gamut from the purely symbolic to the highly restrictive; interestingly, a few states, after initially adopting very restrictive legislation, passed new measures embracing a more nuanced approach. *See* Ilya Somin, The Limits of Backlash, Assessing the Political Response to *Kelo*, 93 Minn. L. Rev. 2100 (2009).

3. *The Legal Response to* Kelo. Justice Stevens pointedly invited the state courts to consider interpreting their state constitutions to impose restrictions on the use of the eminent domain power that went beyond the limits imposed by the U.S. Constitution. In response to this suggestion, several state supreme courts have limited the scope of the eminent domain power or modified the procedures governing its use. *See, e.g., City of Norwood v. Horney,* 853 N.E. 2d 1115 (Ohio 2006); *Board of County Commissioners of Muskogee County v. Lowery,* 1236 P.3d 639 (Okla. 2006). Other state

courts have reaffirmed the traditional, broad view of the eminent domain power. *See Goldstein v. New York State Urban Dev. Corp.*, 921 N.E.2d 164 (N.Y. 2009).

4. *Was* Kelo *Wrongly Decided?* Many critics of *Kelo* have argued that the case was wrongly decided. The late Justice Antonin Scalia, who dissented in *Kelo,* described the decision as "one of the Court's biggest mistakes of political judgment, of estimating how far . . . it could stretch beyond the text of the Constitution without provoking overwhelming public criticism and resistance," and in 2014 predicted that "*Kelo* will not survive." Ilya Somin, The Grasping Hand 238 (2015) (quoting various news accounts of the justice's public speeches). Not surprisingly perhaps, the author of the *Kelo* opinion, Justice Stevens, defended the outcome as a model exercise of judicial restraint. Justice John Paul Stevens, *Kelo,* Popularity, and Substantive Due Process, 63 Alabama L. Rev. 941 (2012). Notwithstanding the controversy, the Supreme Court has not revisited the merits of the *Kelo* decision in the ten years since the case was decided, at least not directly. *Cf. Horne v. Department of Agriculture,* 135 S. Ct. 2419, 2433 (2015) (Thomas, J., dissenting) (implicitly criticizing the expansive understanding of the public use requirement applied by the Court in holding that a federal raisin marketing order resulted in a taking for public use).

On a more technical level, some critics, such as Professor Ilya Somin, have criticized the Kelo decision as being inconsistent with precedent. Both *Berman* and *Midkiff,* discussed at length in the Court's opinion, embrace a highly deferential stance on the exercise of eminent domain. But these cases can be narrowly described as involving the use of the eminent domain power to control uses of private property that are harmful to the public; Justice O'Connor's dissenting opinion, joined by three other justices, adopted this interpretation. The more directly relevant precedents, however, are a series of cases from around the beginning of the last century in which the Court upheld the use of eminent domain to support private mining and irrigation projects, also discussed in the opinion of the Court in *Kelo. See Strickley v. Highland Boy Gold Mining Co.,* 200 U.S. 527, 531 (1906); *Fallbrook Irrigation Dist. v. Bradley,* 164 U.S. 112 (1896).

While these cases explicitly address whether the government was engaged in legitimate takings for "public" use, Professor Somin contends these cases are actually due process cases, not takings cases. He has derived some support for this position from Justice Stevens who agrees they are due process precedents. *See Kelo,* Popularity and Substantive Due Process, at 947-48. Ultimately, however, Justice Stevens offers Professor Somin no help. Since leaving the bench, Justice Stevens has adopted the novel position that the Takings Clause imposes *no* constraints on the use of the eminent domain power, and that the kind of exercise of the eminent domain power at issue in *Kelo* is entirely legitimate under the deferential standard of the Due Process Clause. *Id.* Regardless of whether the Takings Clause or the Due Process Clause is the pertinent constitutional provision, how deferential should the courts be in reviewing exercises of the eminent domain power, to promote economic development or for other purposes?

8

The First Amendment and Other Constitutional Protections

This chapter explores the important and much-litigated issue of how the First Amendment constrains land use regulations affecting speech and religious observance. In addition, this chapter discusses how Congress has expanded upon constitutional protections for religious activity through enactment of the Religious Freedom Restoration Act of 1993 (RFRA) and the Religious Land Use and Institutionalized Persons Act of 2000 (RLUIPA). Finally, this chapter addresses how the Due Process Clause and the Equal Protection Clause control land use regulatory action.

A. INTRODUCTION

1. Some Basic First Amendment Principles

The First Amendment is a powerful legal tool for challenging land use regulation. Such regulation can touch on freedom of expression or freedom of religion in a myriad of contexts, ranging from the zoning of adult entertainment to the application of historic preservation laws to houses of worship. Since the law of the First Amendment is complex, a basic knowledge of First Amendment principles is essential to understanding and analyzing those land use cases that touch on them, as well as to advising clients on constitutional obligations. Accordingly, the introduction to this chapter begins with a brief primer on First Amendment law.

The First Amendment to the United States Constitution declares, "Congress shall make no law respecting an establishment of religion, or prohibiting the free exercise thereof; or abridging the freedom of speech, or of the press; or the right of the people peaceably to assemble, and to petition the Government for a redress of grievances." U.S. Const. amend. I. Few legal concepts are as simple to state yet as complex in interpretation as freedom of speech. The complexity of interpretation in part stems from its evolution over generations. The First Amendment has been applied and interpreted during times of national fear as well as during times of peace, during times of both liberal and conservative political leadership, and during times in which the interpretative philosophies of the judiciary have changed markedly.

The Supreme Court has frequently spoken of the freedom of speech as a matter of both the content of speech and the context in which it is uttered. *Schenck v. United States*, 249 U.S. 47 (1919). Thus, certain speech, based on its content, might receive constitutional protection when uttered in one context but not in another. A book containing passages depicting explicit sex may be protected and beyond regulation. By contrast, screening a toned-down film adaptation of that book may result in a criminal prosecution in some jurisdictions or may be subject to zoning that restricts the location of screenings.

Similarly, speech that is innocuous and inoffensive may nevertheless be prohibited because of the context in which it is being uttered. Demonstrators supporting government-provided health care cannot march down Main Street at the same time that demonstrators opposing government-provided health care are marching up Main Street. The first group may be awarded a permit, and the second asked to march elsewhere, or at a different time. A political poster containing sexual innuendo may be protected in a museum or on a billboard, but it can be excluded from a public school. *See Bethel Sch. Dist. No. 403 v. Fraser*, 478 U.S. 675 (1986) (school may suspend high school student for use of sexually suggestive language in political speech).

In general, regulation tends to be suspect and likely to be invalidated when the target of the regulation is the message of the speaker. *Reed v. Town of Gilbert*, 135 S. Ct. 2218 (2015) (content-based regulation of non-commercial speech is subject to strict scrutiny); *City of Cincinnati v. Discovery Network, Inc.*, 507 U.S. 410 (1993) (news-rack ordinance invalid for lack of a "close fit" between the community's legitimate interest in protecting esthetic values and a selective ban on "commercial handbills"). However, when a regulation of speech seeks to achieve important public health or safety objectives, it may still be sustained. *Turner v. Safley*, 482 U.S. 78 (1987) (security concerns support a bar on most inmate-to-inmate mail correspondence).

2. Categories of Speech and Content-Based Regulation

Speech also may be regulated based upon its content. Freedom of expression litigation has always focused on balancing the interests of the speaker and a free society against significant government interests. Historically, the problem has been that the balancing process can be extremely subjective.

The Supreme Court has taken a middle ground between the subjectivity of balancing and the objectivity of an absolute test, using an approach referred to as "definitional balancing." Melville Nimmer, The Right to Speak from Times to Time, 56 Cal. L. Rev. 935 (1968). Under definitional balancing, for each type of expression the Court has developed a test that is designed to reduce subjectivity and protect the values of free expression, yet permit reasonable regulation to advance important government interests. Of course, critics would charge that freedom of speech has been sacrificed or that its protection has damaged our security and quality of life, and that the developed tests retain a broad subjectivity.

To regulate speech that advocates illegal activities, the Supreme Court has required that the speech must be directed toward producing imminent illegal activity and that the illegal activity is likely to occur. *Brandenburg v. Ohio*, 395 U.S. 444 (1969). Similarly, "fighting words" — speech that is likely to be responded to with violence — are unprotected. *Chaplinsky v. New Hampshire*, 315 U.S. 568 (1942). Defamation (words that inflict injury due to their falsity) is not protected if the speaker has actual knowledge of the falsity or has uttered them with reckless disregard for the truth. *New York Times v. Sullivan*, 376 U.S. 254 (1964). *But cf. Gertz v. Welch*, 418 U.S. 323 (1974) (mere fault such as negligence applies where victim is not a public official or public figure). Pornography may be punishable as obscenity depending on whether (1) the average person, applying contemporary community standards, would find that the work, taken as a whole, appeals to the prurient interest; (2) the work depicts or describes, in a patently offensive way, sexual conduct specifically defined by the applicable state law; and (3) the work, taken as a whole, lacks serious literary, artistic, political, or scientific value. *Miller v. California*, 413 U.S. 15 (1973). Commercial speech, i.e., speech that offers goods or services for sale, applies still another set of tests that are discussed below.

3. Land Use Controls and the First Amendment

Land use controls frequently affect the ability to communicate, and thus pose First Amendment issues. A principal area of conflict is regulation of signs, billboards, and newsracks. How might the First Amendment limit a community's efforts to achieve aesthetic excellence in part through the removal and prohibition of signs and billboards? How can a community deal with the perceived ugliness of proliferating newsracks? Another area of conflict with the First Amendment is in the regulation of adult entertainment. Is regulation of adult movie theaters, book stores, or topless bars a type of illegitimate content-based discrimination?

These are the speech-based questions addressed in this chapter. Chapter 13, discussing discrimination in housing, also raises questions about the First Amendment rights of those who may protest and oppose housing developed for protected minorities. In addition, Chapter 17 will address the subject of aesthetic and architectural controls that can directly or indirectly affect expressive activity.

B. SIGNS AND BILLBOARDS

Signs and billboards present some of the most vexing issues facing property owners and land use regulators. Signs and billboards are viewed by many as presenting serious threats to the aesthetic characteristics of a community; in this sense, regulation of signs and billboards pursues some of the same objectives as other forms of land use regulation discussed elsewhere in this book. In addition, regulations of signs and billboards address other public concerns, such as public safety, economic development, protection of property values, and blight prevention.

The most distinctive feature of signs and billboards, however, is that they are intended to *communicate* some type of message to motorists and other passersby, with the result that government regulation of these structures triggers the protections afforded speech by the First Amendment. Much of what appears on signs and billboards is so-called "commercial speech" — speech designed to serve the economic interests of the "speaker" and meet the economic needs of the listener. Until about 40 years ago, commercial speech was not protected by the First Amendment at all; however, a series of modern U.S. Supreme Court decisions have established that the First Amendment provides a significant measure of protection for commercial speakers, including companies that own or lease billboards to advertise the goods or services they produce. In addition, signs and billboards are sometimes used to communicate political speech — speech dealing with issues of public interest or social concern — which enjoys maximum protection under the First Amendment.

In 2015, the Supreme Court issued a major decision expanding First Amendment limitations on sign regulations.

■ REED v. TOWN OF GILBERT
135 S. Ct. 2218 (2015)

Justice THOMAS delivered the opinion of the Court, in which Chief Justice ROBERTS, and Justices SCALIA, KENNEDY, ALITO, and SOTOMAYOR joined.

The town of Gilbert, Arizona (or Town), has adopted a comprehensive code governing the manner in which people may display outdoor signs. . . . The Sign Code identifies various categories of signs based on the type of information they convey, then subjects each category to different restrictions. One of the categories is "Temporary Directional Signs Relating to a Qualifying Event," loosely defined as signs directing the public to a meeting of a nonprofit group. The Code imposes more stringent restrictions on these signs than it does on signs conveying other messages. We hold that these provisions are content based regulations of speech that cannot survive strict scrutiny.

I

A

The Sign Code prohibits the display of outdoor signs anywhere within the Town without a permit, but it then exempts 23 categories of signs from that requirement. These exemptions include everything from bazaar signs to flying banners. Three categories of exempt signs are particularly relevant here. The first is "Ideological Sign[s]." This category includes any "sign communicating a message or ideas for noncommercial purposes that is not a Construction Sign, Directional Sign, Temporary Directional Sign Relating to a Qualifying Event, Political Sign, Garage Sale Sign, or a sign owned or required by a governmental agency." Of the three categories discussed here, the Code treats ideological signs most favorably, allowing them to be up to 20 square feet in area and to be placed in all "zoning districts" without time limits. The second category is "Political Sign[s]." This includes any "temporary sign designed to influence the outcome of an election called by a public body." The Code treats these signs less favorably than ideological signs. The Code allows the placement of political signs up to 16 square feet on residential property and up to 32 square feet on nonresidential property, undeveloped municipal property, and "rights-of-way." These signs may be displayed up to 60 days before a primary election and up to 15 days following a general election. The third category is "Temporary Directional Signs Relating to a Qualifying Event." This includes any "Temporary Sign intended to direct pedestrians, motorists, and other passersby to a 'qualifying event.'" A "qualifying event" is defined as any "assembly, gathering, activity, or meeting sponsored, arranged, or promoted by a religious, charitable, community service, educational, or other similar non-profit organization." The Code treats temporary directional signs even less favorably than political signs. Temporary directional signs may be no larger than six square feet. They may be placed on private property or on a public right-of-way, but no more than four signs may be placed on a single property at any time. And, they may be displayed no more than 12 hours before the "qualifying event" and no more than 1 hour afterward.

B

Petitioners Good News Community Church (Church) and its pastor, Clyde Reed, wish to advertise the time and location of their Sunday church services. The Church is a small, cash-strapped entity that owns no building, so it holds its services at elementary schools or other locations in or near the Town. In order to inform the public about its services, which are held in a variety of different locations, the Church began placing 15 to 20 temporary signs around the Town, frequently in the public right-of-way abutting the street. . . . This practice caught the attention of the Town's Sign Code compliance manager, who twice cited the Church for violating the Code. . . .

[P]etitioners filed a complaint in the United States District Court for the District of Arizona. . . . [T]he District Court granted summary judgment in favor of the Town. The Court of Appeals . . . affirmed, holding that the Code's sign categories were content neutral. The court concluded that "the distinctions between Temporary Directional Signs, Ideological Signs, and Political Signs . . . are based on objective factors relevant to Gilbert's creation of the specific exemption from the permit requirement and do not otherwise consider the substance of the sign." . . . As the court explained, "Gilbert did not adopt its regulation of speech because it disagreed with the message conveyed" and its "interests in regulat[ing] temporary signs are unrelated to the content of the sign." Accordingly, the court believed that the Code was "content-neutral as that term [has been] defined by the Supreme Court." In light of that determination, it applied a lower level of scrutiny to the Sign Code and concluded that the law did not violate the First Amendment. We granted certiorari, and now reverse.

II

A

The First Amendment, applicable to the States through the Fourteenth Amendment, prohibits the enactment of laws "abridging the freedom of speech." U.S. Const., Amdt. 1. Under that Clause, a government, including a municipal government vested with state authority, "has no power to restrict expression because of its message, its ideas, its subject matter, or its content." *Police Dept. of Chicago v.*

Mosley, 408 U.S. 92, 95 (1972). Content based laws — those that target speech based on its communicative content — are presumptively unconstitutional and may be justified only if the government proves that they are narrowly tailored to serve compelling state interests.

Government regulation of speech is content based if a law applies to particular speech because of the topic discussed or the idea or message expressed. *E.g., Sorrell v. IMS Health, Inc.,* 564 U.S. 552 (2011). . . . This commonsense meaning of the phrase "content based" requires a court to consider whether a regulation of speech "on its face" draws distinctions based on the message a speaker conveys. Some facial distinctions based on a message are obvious, defining regulated speech by particular subject matter, and others are more subtle, defining regulated speech by its function or purpose. Both are distinctions drawn based on the message a speaker conveys, and, therefore, are subject to strict scrutiny.

Our precedents have also recognized a separate and additional category of laws that, though facially content neutral, will be considered content-based regulations of speech: laws that cannot be "'justified without reference to the content of the regulated speech,'" or that were adopted by the government "because of disagreement with the message [the speech] conveys." Those laws, like those that are content based on their face, must also satisfy strict scrutiny.

B

The Town's Sign Code is content based on its face. It defines "Temporary Directional Signs" on the basis of whether a sign conveys the message of directing the public to church or some other "qualifying event." It defines "Political Signs" on the basis of whether a sign's message is "designed to influence the outcome of an election." And it defines "Ideological Signs" on the basis of whether a sign "communicat[es] a message or ideas" that do not fit within the Code's other categories. It then subjects each of these categories to different restrictions. The restrictions in the Sign Code that apply to any given sign thus depend entirely on the communicative content of the sign. If a sign informs its reader of the time and place a book club will discuss John Locke's Two Treatises of Government, that sign will be treated differently from a sign expressing the view that one should vote for one of Locke's followers in an upcoming election, and both signs will be treated differently from a sign expressing an ideological view rooted in Locke's theory of government. More to the point, the Church's signs inviting people to attend its worship services are treated differently from signs conveying other types of ideas. On its face, the Sign Code is a content-based regulation of speech. We thus have no need to consider the government's justifications or purposes for enacting the Code to determine whether it is subject to strict scrutiny.

C

In reaching the contrary conclusion, the Court of Appeals offered several theories to explain why the Town's Sign Code should be deemed content neutral [, including] that the Sign Code was content neutral because the Town "did not adopt its regulation of speech [based on] disagree[ment] with the message conveyed," and its justifications for regulating temporary directional signs were "unrelated to the content of the sign." In its brief to this Court, the United States similarly contends that a sign regulation is content neutral — even if it expressly draws distinctions based on the sign's communicative content — if those distinctions can be "'justified without reference to the content of the regulated speech.'"

But this analysis skips the crucial first step in the content-neutrality analysis: determining whether the law is content neutral on its face. A law that is content based on its face is subject to strict scrutiny regardless of the government's benign motive, content-neutral justification, or lack of "animus toward the ideas contained" in the regulated speech. We have thus made clear that "'[i]llicit legislative intent is not the *sine qua non* of a violation of the First Amendment,'" and a party opposing the government "need adduce 'no evidence of an improper censorial motive.'" Although "a content-based purpose may be sufficient in certain circumstances to show that a regulation is content based, it is not necessary." In other words, an innocuous justification cannot transform a facially content-based law into one that is content neutral.

The Court of Appeals and the United States misunderstand our decision in [*Ward v. Rock Against Racism,* 491 U.S. 781 (1989),] as suggesting that a government's purpose is relevant even when a law is content based on its face. That is incorrect. *Ward* had nothing to say about facially content-based restrictions because it involved a facially content-*neutral* ban on the use, in a city-owned music venue, of sound amplification systems not provided by the city. In that context, we looked to governmental motive, including whether the government had regulated speech "because of disagreement" with its message, and whether the regulation was "'justified without reference to the content of the speech.'" But *Ward*'s framework "applies only if a statute is content neutral." Its rules thus operate "to protect speech," not "to restrict it." The First Amendment requires no less. Innocent motives do not eliminate the danger of censorship presented by a facially content-based statute, as future government officials may one day wield such statutes to suppress disfavored speech. That is why the First Amendment expressly targets the operation of the laws — *i.e.,* the "abridg[ement] of speech" — rather than merely the motives of those who enacted them. U.S. Const., Amdt. 1. "'The vice of content-based legislation . . . is not that it is always used for invidious, thought-control purposes, but that it lends itself to use for those purposes.'" . . .

Finally, the Court of Appeals characterized the Sign Code's distinctions as turning on "'the content-neutral elements of who is speaking through the sign and whether and when an event is occurring.'" That analysis is mistaken on both factual and legal grounds.

To start, the Sign Code's distinctions are not speaker based. The restrictions for political, ideological, and temporary event signs apply equally no matter who sponsors them. If a local business, for example, sought to put up signs advertising the Church's meetings, those signs would be subject to the same limitations as such signs placed by the Church. And if Reed had decided to display signs in support of a particular candidate, he could have made those signs far larger — and kept them up for far longer — than signs inviting people to attend his church services. If the Code's distinctions were truly speaker based, both types of signs would receive the same treatment.

In any case, the fact that a distinction is speaker based does not, as the Court of Appeals seemed to believe, automatically render the distinction content neutral. Because "[s]peech restrictions based on the identity of the speaker are all too often simply a means to control content," we have insisted that "laws favoring some speakers over others demand strict scrutiny when the legislature's speaker preference reflects a content preference." Thus, a law limiting the content of newspapers, but only newspapers, could not evade strict scrutiny simply because it could be characterized as speaker based. Likewise, a content-based law that restricted the political speech of all corporations would not become content neutral just because it singled out corporations as a class of speakers. Characterizing a distinction as speaker based is only the beginning — not the end — of the inquiry.

Nor do the Sign Code's distinctions hinge on "whether and when an event is occurring." The Code does not permit citizens to post signs on any topic whatsoever within a set period leading up to an election, for example. Instead, come election time, it requires Town officials to determine whether a sign is "designed to influence the outcome of an election" (and thus "political") or merely "communicating a message or ideas for noncommercial purposes" (and thus "ideological"). That obvious content-based inquiry does not evade strict scrutiny review simply because an event (*i.e.,* an election) is involved.

And, just as with speaker-based laws, the fact that a distinction is event based does not render it content neutral. The Court of Appeals cited no precedent from this Court supporting its novel theory of an exception from the content-neutrality requirement for event-based laws. As we have explained, a speech regulation is content based if the law applies to particular speech because of the topic discussed or the idea or message expressed. A regulation that targets a sign because it conveys an idea about a specific event is no less content based than a regulation that targets a sign because it conveys some other idea. Here, the Code singles out signs bearing a particular message: the time and location of a specific event. This type of ordinance may seem like a perfectly rational way to regulate signs, but a clear and firm rule governing content neutrality is an essential means of protecting the freedom of speech, even if laws that might seem "entirely reasonable" will sometimes be "struck down because of their content-based nature." *City of Ladue v. Gilleo,* 512 U.S. 43, 60 (1994) (O'Connor, J., concurring).

III

Because the Town's Sign Code imposes content-based restrictions on speech, those provisions can stand only if they survive strict scrutiny, "'which requires the Government to prove that the restriction furthers a compelling interest and is narrowly tailored to achieve that interest.'" [The Court concluded that, "[a]ssuming for the sake of argument that . . . preserving the Town's aesthetic appeal and traffic safety . . . are compelling governmental interests," the Sign Code failed the test because its distinctions between different types of signs were "hopelessly underinclusive."]

IV

Our decision today will not prevent governments from enacting effective sign laws. The Town asserts that an "'absolutist'" content-neutrality rule would render "virtually all distinctions in sign laws . . . subject to strict scrutiny," but that is not the case. Not "all distinctions" are subject to strict scrutiny, only *content-based* ones are. Laws that are *content neutral* are instead subject to lesser scrutiny. The Town has ample content-neutral options available to resolve problems with safety and aesthetics. For example, its current Code regulates many aspects of signs that have nothing to do with a sign's message: size, building materials, lighting, moving parts, and portability. And on public property, the Town may go a long way toward entirely forbidding the posting of signs, so long as it does so in an evenhanded, content-neutral manner. . . . We acknowledge that a city might reasonably view the general regulation of signs as necessary because signs "take up space and may obstruct views, distract motorists, displace alternative uses for land, and pose other problems that legitimately call for regulation." At the same time, the presence of certain signs may be essential, both for vehicles and pedestrians, to guide traffic or to identify hazards and ensure safety. A sign ordinance narrowly tailored to the challenges of protecting the safety of pedestrians, drivers, and passengers — such as warning signs marking hazards on private property, signs directing traffic, or street numbers associated with private houses — well might survive strict scrutiny. The signs at issue in this case, including political and ideological signs and signs for events, are far removed from those purposes. As discussed above, they are facially content based and are neither justified by traditional safety concerns nor narrowly tailored. . . .

We reverse the judgment of the Court of Appeals and remand the case for proceedings consistent with this opinion.

It is so ordered.

Justice Alito, with whom Justice Kennedy and Justice Sotomayor join, concurring.

I join the opinion of the Court but add a few words of further explanation.

As the Court holds, what we have termed "content-based" laws must satisfy strict scrutiny. Content-based laws merit this protection because they present, albeit sometimes in a subtler form, the same dangers as laws that regulate speech based on viewpoint. Limiting speech based on its "topic" or "subject" favors those who do not want to disturb the status quo. Such regulations may interfere with democratic self-government and the search for truth. As the Court shows, the regulations at issue in this case are replete with content-based distinctions, and as a result they must satisfy strict scrutiny. This does not mean, however, that municipalities are powerless to enact and enforce reasonable sign regulations. I will not attempt to provide anything like a comprehensive list, but here are some rules that would not be content based:

Rules regulating the size of signs. These rules may distinguish among signs based on any content-neutral criteria, including any relevant criteria listed below.

Rules regulating the locations in which signs may be placed. These rules may distinguish between free-standing signs and those attached to buildings.

Rules distinguishing between lighted and unlighted signs.

Rules distinguishing between signs with fixed messages and electronic signs with messages that change.

Rules that distinguish between the placement of signs on private and public property.

Rules distinguishing between the placement of signs on commercial and residential property.

Rules distinguishing between on-premises and off-premises signs.

Rules restricting the total number of signs allowed per mile of roadway.

Rules imposing time restrictions on signs advertising a one-time event. Rules of this nature do not discriminate based on topic or subject and are akin to rules restricting the times within which oral speech or music is allowed.

In addition to regulating signs put up by private actors, government entities may also erect their own signs consistent with the principles that allow governmental speech.

They may put up all manner of signs to promote safety, as well as directional signs and signs pointing out historic sites and scenic spots.

Properly understood, today's decision will not prevent cities from regulating signs in a way that fully protects public safety and serves legitimate esthetic objectives.

[Justices GINSBURG, BREYER, and KAGAN concurred in the judgment, agreeing that this particular ordinance violated the First Amendment, but arguing for a more nuanced balancing test for determining whether sign regulation unconstitutionally impinges on speech.]

Notes and Comments

1. Reed's *Resolution of the Conflict in the Lower Courts.* The decision in *Reed* resolved a long-simmering conflict in the lower federal courts. *See* Alan C. Weinstein & Brian J. Connolly, Sign Regulation after *Reed:* Suggestions for Coping with Legal Uncertainty, 47 Urb. Law. 569 (2015). The U.S. Supreme Court had long said that regulation based on the content of the message being conveyed is constitutionally impermissible. *See Police Dep't of Chi. v. Mosley*, 408 U.S. 92, 95 (1972) ("above all else, the First Amendment means that government has no power to restrict expression because of its message, its ideas, its subject matter, or its content"). But some U.S. Supreme Court decisions left uncertain what content-based regulation actually is and how strictly the prohibition against content-based distinctions should be enforced. The U.S. Court of Appeals for the Ninth Circuit ruled in *Reed* that the town's temporary sign regulations were content neutral as applied and therefore constitutional. *Reed v. Town of Gilbert*, 707 F.3d 1057 (9th Cir. 2013). In reaching this conclusion the Ninth Circuit examined the purpose and motivation behind the regulation; it concluded that the ordinance did not violate the First Amendment because the town "did not adopt its regulation of speech because it disagreed with the message conveyed" and the town's regulatory objectives were unrelated to the content of the signs' messages. The Ninth Circuit's approach mirrored the approach followed in several other circuits. *See, e.g., Brown v. Town of Cary*, 706 F.3d 294 (4th Cir. 2013); *Melrose, Inc. v. City of Pittsburg*, 613 F.3d 380 (3d Cir. 2010). By contrast, other circuits had interpreted Supreme Court precedent to support the "absolutist" position that any content-based regulation is inherently suspect and therefore invalid under the First Amendment unless it can withstand strict scrutiny. *See, e.g., Neighborhood Enters., Inc. v. City of St Louis*, 644 F.3d 728 (8th Cir. 2011); *Solantic, LLC v. City of Neptune Beach*, 410 F.3d 1250 (11th Cir. 2005). *Reed*

resolved the conflict in the lower courts in favor of the "absolutist" position. What are the advantages of the absolutist position? What are the disadvantages?

Some commentators have read the *Reed* decision as a major shift in First Amendment jurisprudence. *See* Adam Liptak, Court's Free-Speech Expansion Has Far-Reaching Consequences, NY Times (Aug. 17, 2015) at http://www.nytimes .com/2015/08/18/us/politics/courts-free-speech-expansion-has-far- reaching-con sequences.html (last visited Nov. 11, 2016. Others, without discounting the importance of the decision, have contended that *Reed* can and should be read narrowly. *See* Note, Free Speech Doctrine After *Reed v. Town of Gilbert*, 129 Harv. L. Rev. 1981 (2016).

2. *What Kinds of Regulation Are Permissible After* Reed? The major question after *Reed* is how absolutist will the "absolutist" position turn out to be? While *Reed* appears to establish a relatively clear, bright-line test, the decision raises the obvious concern that rules authorizing various kinds of innocuous signs, or mandating signs designed to protect public health and safety, may be struck down as unconstitutional because they are content-based. Consider rules governing "no trespassing" signs, or "for sale" signs, or signs warning of the presence of hazardous waste sites. Are all rules and regulations authorizing such signs (and not others) presumptively unconstitutional because they are content-based? Those concurring only in the judgment in *Reed* objected that the Court's opinion could invalidate a wide variety of common-sense sign rules that do not implicate the core social and political values served by the First Amendment. Justice Alito joined the majority opinion but in his separate concurring opinion offered a list of types of sign regulations that he believed would be permissible under the majority opinion. Is Justice Alito's list consistent with the Court's opinion (which he joined), or is there reason to doubt whether all of the types of sign regulations he lists are permissible after *Reed*? Apart from his list, are there other common sense sign rules that ought to be permissible under the First Amendment?

The majority sought to soften the blow from its new bright-line test by stating:

> the presence of certain signs may be essential, both for vehicles and pedestrians, to guide traffic or to identify hazards and ensure safety. A sign ordinance narrowly tailored to the challenges of protecting the safety of pedestrians, drivers, and passengers — such as warning signs marking hazards on private property, signs directing traffic, or street numbers associated with private houses — well might survive strict scrutiny.

But the strict scrutiny test is highly demanding. Is it clear that such common sign rules can survive the demanding strict scrutiny test? Or does the majority opinion imply the development of a modified version of strict scrutiny which will not, contrary to the test's usual application, be "fatal in fact?" And, if so, with what possible implications for First Amendment jurisprudence generally?

3. Reed *and Commercial Speech.* While the sign code at issue in *Reed* established a comprehensive permitting scheme for all types of signs, the case focused on the distinction drawn in the code between three types of noncommercial signs, dubbed "political," "ideological," and "temporary event." The Supreme Court has long drawn a distinction for First Amendment purposes between commercial and noncommercial speech, a distinction the Court relied upon in the *Metromedia* billboard case, discussed below. Because *Reed* focused on content-based regulation of noncommercial speech, it implicitly raises the question of whether a different, less demanding standard might apply to content-based regulation of commercial speech. There is a respectable argument that the relatively deferential test

established in *Central Hudson Gas & Elec. Corp. v. Public Serv. Comm'n*, 447 U.S. 557 (1980), still applies in First Amendment challenges to content-based regulation of commercial speech. *See* Note, *Free* Speech Doctrine After *Reed v. Town of Gilbert*, 129 Harv. L. Rev. 1981, 1990 (2016) (arguing that "*Reed* probably does not apply if the challenged regulation addresses only commercial speech").

4. *City of Ladue v. Galileo.* The most recent Supreme Court case to address local sign regulation prior to *Reed* was *City of Ladue v. Gilleo*, 512 U.S. 43 (1994), in which the Court applied a more forgiving standard for how the First Amendment constrains sign regulation. The case was brought by a homeowner prohibited from displaying an anti-war sign in front of her home. The ordinance banned residential signs, subject to certain limited exceptions, such as "residence identification" signs, "for sale" signs, and signs warning of safety hazards. Emphasizing the importance of the home as a platform for expressing personal views on political questions, the Court struck down the ordinance. However, the Court said:

> While signs are a form of expression protected by the Free Speech Clause, they pose distinctive problems that are subject to municipalities' police powers. Unlike oral speech, signs take up space and may obstruct views, distract motorists, displace alternative uses for land, and pose other problems that legitimately call for regulation. It is common ground that governments may regulate the physical characteristics of signs — just as they can, within reasonable bounds and absent censorial purpose, regulate audible expression in its capacity as noise.

Id. at 48. In addition, the Court emphasized that its ruling did not eliminate the city's ability to restrict certain forms of signs:

> Nor do we hold that every kind of sign must be permitted in residential areas. Different considerations might well apply. For example, in the case of signs (whether political or otherwise) displayed by residents for a fee, or in the case of off-site commercial advertisements on residential property. We also are not confronted here with mere regulation short of a ban.

Id. at 58 n.17.

In notable contrast to the reasoning in *Reed*, the *Ladue* Court did not say that the ordinance's inclusion of exemptions for signs conveying particular messages (e.g., "For Sale") necessarily made the ordinance constitutionally suspect. While the Court observed that the ordinance's exemptions created "risks of viewpoint and content discrimination," it nonetheless assumed for the sake of argument that that the various exemptions were "free of impermissible content or viewpoint discrimination" and could therefore be constitutional. Setting aside the exemptions, the Court nonetheless ruled that the city's broad restrictions on residential signs violated the First Amendment because they "almost completely foreclosed a venerable means of communication that is both unique and important." For in-depth analysis of *Ladue, see* Stephanie L. Bunting, Unsightly Politics: Aesthetics, Sign Ordinances, and Homeowners' Speech in *City of Ladue v. Gilleo*, 20 Harv. Envtl. L. Rev. 473 (1996). *See also* Daniel N. McPherson, Municipal Regulation of Political Signs: Balancing First Amendment Rights Against Aesthetic Concerns, 45 Drake L. Rev. 767 (1997). Query how the Supreme Court would analyze a claim similar to that presented in *Ladue* in the aftermath of *Reed?*

A handful of other Supreme Court rulings provide guidance on the constitutionality of sign regulation under the First Amendment. In *Linmark Assocs., Inc. v.*

Township of Willingboro, 431 U.S. 85 (1977), the Court struck down an "anti-block-busting" ordinance that prohibited homeowners from placing "For Sale" or "Sold" signs on their property. Although the Court accepted the importance of the city's goal of maintaining stable, integrated housing, the Court ruled that the First Amendment prevented the township from "achieving its goal by restricting the free flow of truthful information." In *City Council of L.A. v. Taxpayers for Vincent,* 466 U.S. 789 (1984), the Court, recognizing the government's special authority over and responsibility for management of publicly-owned land, upheld a Los Angeles ordinance that prohibited the posting of signs on public property.

"Commercial speech" is speech that offers goods or services for sale. Such speech may be protected where it concerns lawful activity and is not misleading. To regulate commercial speech, the government must demonstrate that the regulation seeks to implement a substantial government interest, the regulation directly advances that interest, and the goal is not attainable by less restrictive alternatives. *Central Hudson Gas & Elec. Corp. v. Public Serv. Comm'n,* 447 U.S. 557 (1980).

By recognizing that commercial expression is protected by the First Amendment, the Court has subjected government regulation of commercial billboards for aesthetic reasons to constitutional scrutiny. For example, can a community adopt a revitalization strategy that calls for controlling the size, design, or placement of commercial signs without violating the First Amendment? Can a new community develop around a plan that includes an aesthetic element excluding commercial signs?

A split Court addressed these issues in the following case. The opinion is a difficult one, so be forewarned.

■ METROMEDIA, INC. v. CITY OF SAN DIEGO
453 U.S. 490 (1981)

Justice WHITE announced the judgment of the Court and delivered an opinion, in which Justices STEWART, MARSHALL, and POWELL joined.

This case involves the validity of an ordinance of the city of San Diego, Cal., imposing substantial prohibitions on the erection of outdoor advertising displays within the city.

I

Stating that its purpose was "to eliminate hazards to pedestrians and motorists brought about by distracting sign displays" and "to preserve and improve the appearance of the City," San Diego enacted an ordinance to prohibit "outdoor advertising display signs. . . ."[1]

1. The general prohibition of the ordinance reads as follows:

B. OFF-PREMISE OUTDOOR ADVERTISING DISPLAY SIGNS PROHIBITED

Only those outdoor advertising display signs, hereinafter referred to as signs in this Division, which are either signs designating the name of the owner or occupant of the premises upon which such signs are placed, or identifying such premises; or signs advertising goods manufactured or produced or services rendered on the premises upon which such signs are placed shall be permitted. The following signs shall be prohibited:

The ordinance provides two kinds of exceptions to the general prohibition: onsite signs and signs falling within 12 specified categories. Onsite signs are defined as those designating the name of the owner or occupant of the premises upon which such signs are placed, or identifying such premises; or signs advertising goods manufactured or produced or services rendered on the premises upon which such signs are placed.

The specific categories exempted from the prohibition include: government signs; signs located at public bus stops; signs manufactured, transported, or stored within the city, if not used for advertising purposes; commemorative historical plaques; religious symbols; signs within shopping malls; for sale and for lease signs; signs on public and commercial vehicles; signs depicting time, temperature, and news; approved temporary, off-premises, subdivision directional signs; and "[t]emporary political campaign signs." Under this scheme, on-site commercial advertising is permitted, but other commercial advertising and noncommercial communications using fixed-structure signs are everywhere forbidden unless permitted by one of the specified exceptions.

Appellants are companies that were engaged in the outdoor advertising business in San Diego at the time the ordinance was passed. Each owns a substantial number of outdoor advertising displays (approximately 500 to 800) within the city. These signs are all located in areas zoned for commercial and industrial purposes, most of them on property leased by the owners to appellants for the purpose of maintaining billboards. Each sign has a remaining useful income-producing life of over 25 years, and each sign has a fair market value of between $2,500 and $25,000. Space on the signs was made available to "all comers" and the copy on each sign changed regularly, usually monthly. . . . Although the purchasers of advertising space on appellants' signs usually seek to convey a commercial message, their billboards have also been used to convey a broad range of noncommercial political and social messages. Appellants brought suit in state court to enjoin enforcement of the ordinance. . . .

III

This Court has often faced the problem of applying the broad principles of the First Amendment to unique forums of expression. *See, e. g., Consolidated Edison Co. v. Public Service Comm'n,* 447 U.S. 530 (1980) (billing envelope inserts); *Carey v. Brown,* 447 U.S. 455 (1980) (picketing in residential areas); *Schaumburg v. Citizens for a Better Env't,* 444 U.S. 620 (1980) (door-to-door and on-street solicitation); *Greer v. Spock,* 424 U.S. 828 (1976) (Army bases); *Erznoznik v. City of Jacksonville,* 422 U.S. 205 (1975) (outdoor movie theaters); *Lehman v. City of Shaker Heights,* 418 U.S. 298 (1974)

---

1. Any sign identifying a use, facility or service which is not located on the premises.

2. Any sign identifying a product which is not produced, sold or manufactured on the premises.

3. Any sign which advertises or otherwise directs attention to a product, service or activity, event, person, institution or business which may or may not be identified by a brand name and which occurs or is generally conducted, sold, manufactured, produced or offered elsewhere than on the premises where such sign is located.

(advertising space within city-owned transit system). Even a cursory reading of these opinions reveals that at times First Amendment values must yield to other societal interests. These cases support the cogency of Justice Jackson's remark in *Kovacs v. Cooper*, 336 U.S. 77, 97 (1949): Each method of communicating ideas is "a law unto itself" and that law must reflect the "differing natures, values, abuses and dangers" of each method. We deal here with the law of billboards.

Billboards are a well-established medium of communication, used to convey a broad range of different kinds of messages. . . . But whatever its communicative function, the billboard remains a "large, immobile, and permanent structure which like other structures is subject to . . . regulation." Moreover, because it is designed to stand out and apart from its surroundings, the billboard creates a unique set of problems for land-use planning and development. . . .

Billboards, then, like other media of communication, combine communicative and noncommunicative aspects. As with other media, the government has legitimate interests in controlling the noncommunicative aspects of the medium, but the First and Fourteenth Amendments foreclose a similar interest in controlling the communicative aspects. Because regulation of the noncommunicative aspects of a medium often impinges to some degree on the communicative aspects, it has been necessary for the courts to reconcile the government's regulatory interests with the individual's right to expression. . . . Performance of this task requires a particularized inquiry into the nature of the conflicting interests at stake here, beginning with a precise appraisal of the character of the ordinance as it affects communication.

As construed by the California Supreme Court, the ordinance restricts the use of certain kinds of outdoor signs. That restriction is defined in two ways: first, by reference to the structural characteristics of the sign; second, by reference to the content, or message, of the sign. Thus, the regulation only applies to a "permanent structure constituting, or used for the display of, a commercial or other advertisement to the public." Within that class, the only permitted signs are those (1) identifying the premises on which the sign is located, or its owner or occupant, or advertising the goods produced or services rendered on such property and (2) those within one of the specified exemptions to the general prohibition, such as temporary political campaign signs. To determine if any billboard is prohibited by the ordinance, one must determine how it is constructed, where it is located, and what message it carries.

Thus, under the ordinance (1) a sign advertising goods or services available on the property where the sign is located is allowed; (2) a sign on a building or other property advertising goods or services produced or offered elsewhere is barred; (3) noncommercial advertising, unless within one of the specific exceptions, is everywhere prohibited. The occupant of property may advertise his own goods or services; he may not advertise the goods or services of others, nor may he display most noncommercial messages. . . .

IV

Appellants' principal submission is that enforcement of the ordinance will eliminate the outdoor advertising business in San Diego and that the First and Fourteenth Amendments prohibit the elimination of this medium of communication. Appellants contend that the city may bar neither all offsite commercial signs nor all noncommercial advertisements and that even if it may bar the former, it may not bar the latter.

[I]n *Central Hudson* we held: "The Constitution . . . accords a lesser protection to commercial speech than to other constitutionally guaranteed expression. The protection available for a particular commercial expression turns on the nature both of the expression and of the governmental interests served by its regulation." We then adopted a four-part test for determining the validity of government restrictions on commercial speech as distinguished from more fully protected speech. (1) The First Amendment protects commercial speech only if that speech concerns lawful activity and is not misleading. A restriction on otherwise protected commercial speech is valid only if it (2) seeks to implement a substantial governmental interest, (3) directly advances that interest, and (4) reaches no further than necessary to accomplish the given objective. Appellants agree that the proper approach to be taken in determining the validity of the restrictions on commercial speech is that which was articulated in *Central Hudson*, but assert that the San Diego ordinance fails that test. We do not agree.

There can be little controversy over the application of the first, second, and fourth criteria. There is no suggestion that the commercial advertising at issue here involves unlawful activity or is misleading. Nor can there be substantial doubt that the twin goals that the ordinance seeks to further — traffic safety and the appearance of the city — are substantial governmental goals. . . . Similarly, we reject appellants' claim that the ordinance is broader than necessary and, therefore, fails the fourth part of the *Central Hudson* test. If the city has a sufficient basis for believing that billboards are traffic hazards and are unattractive, then obviously the most direct and perhaps the only effective approach to solving the problems they create is to prohibit them. The city has gone no further than necessary in seeking to meet its ends. Indeed, it has stopped short of fully accomplishing its ends: It has not prohibited all billboards, but allows onsite advertising and some other specifically exempted signs.

The more serious question, then, concerns the third of the *Central Hudson* criteria: Does the ordinance "directly advance" governmental interests in traffic safety and in the appearance of the city? It is asserted that the record is inadequate to show any connection between billboards and traffic safety. . . . [However, w]e . . . hesitate to disagree with the accumulated, common-sense judgments of local lawmakers and of the many reviewing courts that billboards are real and substantial hazards to traffic safety. There is nothing here to suggest that these judgments are unreasonable. . . .

We reach a similar result with respect to the second asserted justification for the ordinance — advancement of the city's esthetic interests. It is not speculative to recognize that billboards by their very nature, wherever located and however constructed, can be perceived as an "esthetic harm." San Diego, like many States and other municipalities, has chosen to minimize the presence of such structures. Such esthetic judgments are necessarily subjective, defying objective evaluation, and for that reason must be carefully scrutinized to determine if they are only a public rationalization of an impermissible purpose. But there is no claim in this case that San Diego has as an ulterior motive the suppression of speech, and the judgment involved here is not so unusual as to raise suspicions in itself.

It is nevertheless argued that the city denigrates its interest in traffic safety and beauty and defeats its own case by permitting onsite advertising and other specified signs. Appellants question whether the distinction between onsite and offsite advertising on the same property is justifiable in terms of either esthetics or traffic safety. The ordinance permits the occupant of property to use billboards located on that property to advertise goods and services offered at that location; identical billboards, equally distracting and unattractive, that advertise goods or services available elsewhere are prohibited even if permitting the latter would not multiply the number of billboards. Despite the apparent incongruity, this argument has been rejected, at least implicitly, in all of the cases sustaining the distinction between offsite and onsite commercial advertising. . . .

In the first place, whether onsite advertising is permitted or not, the prohibition of offsite advertising is directly related to the stated objectives of traffic safety and esthetics. This is not altered by the fact that the ordinance is under-inclusive because it permits onsite advertising. Second, the city may believe that offsite advertising, with its periodically changing content, presents a more acute problem than does onsite advertising. Third, San Diego has obviously chosen to value one kind of commercial speech — onsite advertising — more than another kind of commercial speech — offsite advertising. The ordinance reflects a decision by the city that the former interest, but not the latter, is stronger than the city's interests in traffic safety and esthetics. The city has decided that in a limited instance — onsite commercial advertising — its interests should yield. We do not reject that judgment. As we see it, the city could reasonably conclude that a commercial enterprise — as well as the interested public — has a stronger interest in identifying its place of business and advertising the products or services available there than it has in using or leasing its available space for the purpose of advertising commercial enterprises located elsewhere. It does not follow from the fact that the city has concluded that some commercial interests outweigh its municipal interests in this context that it must give similar weight to all other commercial advertising. Thus, offsite commercial billboards may be prohibited while onsite commercial billboards are permitted.

The constitutional problem in this area requires resolution of the conflict between the city's land-use interests and the commercial interests of those seeking to purvey goods and services within the city. In light of the above analysis, we cannot conclude that the city has drawn an ordinance broader than is necessary to meet its interests, or that it fails directly to advance substantial government interests. In sum, insofar as it regulates commercial speech the San Diego ordinance meets the constitutional requirements of *Central Hudson*.

V

It does not follow, however, that San Diego's general ban on signs carrying noncommercial advertising is also valid under the First and Fourteenth Amendments. The fact that the city may value commercial messages relating to onsite goods and services more than it values commercial communications relating to offsite goods and services does not justify prohibiting an occupant from displaying its own ideas or those of others.

As indicated above, our recent commercial speech cases have consistently accorded noncommercial speech a greater degree of protection than commercial speech. San Diego effectively inverts this judgment, by affording a greater degree of protection to commercial than to noncommercial speech. There is a broad exception for onsite commercial advertisements, but there is no similar exception for noncommercial speech.

The use of onsite billboards to carry commercial messages related to the commercial use of the premises is freely permitted, but the use of otherwise identical billboards to carry noncommercial messages is generally prohibited. The city does not explain how or why noncommercial billboards located in places where commercial billboards are permitted would be more threatening to safe driving or would detract more from the beauty of the city. Insofar as the city tolerates billboards at all, it cannot choose to limit their content to commercial messages; the city may not conclude that the communication of commercial information concerning goods and services connected with a particular site is of greater value than the communication of noncommercial messages.

Furthermore, the ordinance contains exceptions that permit various kinds of noncommercial signs, whether on property where goods and services are offered or not, that would otherwise be within the general ban. A fixed sign may be used to identify any piece of property and its owner. Any piece of property may carry or display religious symbols, commemorative plaques of recognized historical societies and organizations, signs carrying news items or telling the time or temperature, signs erected in discharge of any governmental function, or temporary political campaign signs. No other noncommercial or ideological signs meeting the structural definition are permitted, regardless of their effect on traffic safety or esthetics.

Although the city may distinguish between the relative value of different categories of commercial speech, the city does not have the same range of choice in the area of noncommercial speech to evaluate the strength of, or distinguish between, various communicative interests. With respect to noncommercial speech, the city may not choose the appropriate subjects for public discourse: . . . Because some noncommercial messages may be conveyed on billboards throughout the commercial and industrial zones, San Diego must similarly allow billboards conveying other noncommercial messages throughout those zones.[20]

Finally, we reject appellees' suggestion that the ordinance may be appropriately characterized as a reasonable "time, place, and manner" restriction. The ordinance does not generally ban billboard advertising as an unacceptable "manner" of communicating information or ideas; rather, it permits various kinds of signs. Signs that are banned are banned everywhere and at all times. We have observed that time, place, and manner restrictions are permissible if "they are justified without reference to the content of the regulated speech, . . . serve a significant governmental interest, and . . . leave open ample alternative channels for communication of the information." Here, it cannot be assumed that "alternative channels" are available, for the parties stipulated to just the opposite: "Many businesses and politicians and other persons rely upon outdoor advertising because other forms of advertising are insufficient, inappropriate and prohibitively expensive." . . . It is apparent as well that the ordinance distinguishes in several ways between permissible and impermissible signs at a particular location by reference to their content. . . .

---

20. Because a total prohibition of outdoor advertising is not before us, we do not indicate whether such a ban would be consistent with the First Amendment. *But see Schad v. Mount Ephraim*, 452 U.S. 61 (1981), on the constitutional problems created by a total prohibition of a particular expressive forum, live entertainment in that case. Despite Justice Stevens' insistence to the contrary, we do not imply that the ordinance is unconstitutional *because* it "does not abridge enough speech." . . .

Justice BRENNAN, with whom Justice BLACKMUN joins, concurring in the judgment.

Believing that "a total prohibition of outdoor advertising is not before us," the plurality does not decide "whether such a ban would be consistent with the First Amendment." Instead, it concludes that San Diego may ban all billboards containing commercial speech messages without violating the First Amendment, thereby sending the signal to municipalities that bifurcated billboard regulations prohibiting commercial messages but allowing noncommercial messages would pass constitutional muster. I write separately because I believe this case in effect presents the total ban question, and because I believe the plurality's bifurcated approach itself raises serious First Amendment problems and relies on a distinction between commercial and noncommercial speech unanticipated by our prior cases. . . .

The characterization of the San Diego regulation as a total ban of a medium of communication has more than semantic implications, for it suggests a First Amendment analysis quite different from the plurality's. Instead of relying on the exceptions to the ban to invalidate the ordinance, I would apply the tests this Court has developed to analyze content-neutral prohibitions of particular media of communication. Most recently, in *Schad v. Mount Ephraim*, 452 U.S. 61 (1981), this Court assessed "the substantiality of the governmental interests asserted" and "whether those interests could be served by means that would be less intrusive on activity protected by the First Amendment," in striking down the borough's total ban on live commercial entertainment. . . . In the case of billboards, I would hold that a city may totally ban them if it can show that a sufficiently substantial governmental interest is directly furthered by the total ban, and that any more narrowly drawn restriction, *i.e.*, anything less than a total ban, would promote less well the achievement of that goal. Applying that test to the instant case, I would invalidate the San Diego ordinance. The city has failed to provide adequate justification for its substantial restriction on protected activity. . . .

Justice STEVENS, dissenting in part.

If enforced as written, the ordinance at issue in this case will eliminate the outdoor advertising business in the city of San Diego. The principal question presented is, therefore, whether a city may prohibit this medium of communication. Instead of answering that question, the plurality focuses its attention on the exceptions from the total ban and, somewhat ironically, concludes that the ordinance is an unconstitutional abridgment of speech because it does not abridge enough speech. . . . .

Although it is possible that some future applications of the San Diego ordinance may violate the First Amendment, I am satisfied that the ordinance survives the challenges that these appellants have standing to raise. Unlike the plurality, I do not believe that this case requires us to decide any question concerning the kind of signs a property owner may display on his own premises. I do, however, believe that it is necessary to confront the important question, reserved by the plurality, whether a city may entirely ban one medium of communication. My affirmative answer to that question leads me to the conclusion that the San Diego ordinance should be upheld; that conclusion is not affected by the content-neutral exceptions that are the principal subject of the debate between the plurality and the Chief Justice.

Chief Justice BURGER, dissenting.

Today the Court takes an extraordinary—even a bizarre—step by severely limiting the power of a city to act on risks it perceives to traffic safety and the environment posed by large, permanent billboards. Those joining the plurality opinion invalidate a city's effort to minimize these traffic hazards and eyesores simply because, in exercising rational legislative judgment, it has chosen to permit a narrow class of signs that serve special needs.

Justice REHNQUIST, dissenting.

I agree substantially with the views expressed in the dissenting opinions of the Chief Justice and Justice Stevens and make only these two additional observations: (1) In a case where city planning commissions and zoning boards must regularly confront constitutional claims of this sort, it is a genuine misfortune to have the Court's treatment of the subject be a virtual Tower of Babel, from which no definitive principles can be clearly drawn; and (2) I regret even more keenly my contribution to this judicial clangor, but find that none of the views expressed in the other opinions written in the case come close enough to mine to warrant the necessary compromise to obtain a Court opinion.

In my view, the aesthetic justification alone is sufficient to sustain a total prohibition of billboards within a community, regardless of whether the particular community is "a historical community such as Williamsburg" or one as unsightly as the older parts of many of our major metropolitan areas. Such areas should not be prevented from taking steps to correct, as best they may, mistakes of their predecessors. Nor do I believe that the limited exceptions contained in the San Diego ordinance are the types which render this statute unconstitutional. The closest one is the exception permitting billboards during political campaigns, but I would treat this as a virtually self-limiting exception which will have an effect on the aesthetics of the city only during the periods immediately prior to a campaign. As such, it seems to me a reasonable outlet, limited as to time, for the free expression which the First and Fourteenth Amendments were designed to protect.

Unlike Justice Brennan, I do not think a city should be put to the task of convincing a local judge that the elimination of billboards would have more than a negligible impact on aesthetics. Nothing in my experience on the bench has led me to believe that a judge is in any better position than a city or county commission to make decisions in an area such as aesthetics. Therefore, little can be gained in the area of constitutional law, and much lost in the process of democratic decision making, by allowing individual judges in city after city to second-guess such legislative or administrative determinations.

Notes and Comments

1. *What Did the Court Rule in* Metromedia*?* The *Metromedia* decision is a deeply baffling decision; as Justice Rehnquist commented, the collection of divergent opinions is "a virtual Tower of Babel." Under the approach of *Marks v. United States*, 430 U.S. 188, 193 (1977), "[w]hen a fragmented Court decides a case and no single rationale explaining the result enjoys the assent of five Justices, the holding of the Court may be viewed as that position taken by those Members who concurred in the judgments on the narrowest grounds." In *Metromedia*, however, it is difficult to discern *any* common ground that forms a "holding" based on the plurality opinion authored by Justice White and the concurring opinion authored by Justice Brennan. Justice White viewed the ordinance as imposing a broad restriction on off-site billboard advertising subject to various exceptions, whereas Justice Brennan

interpreted the ordinance as a total prohibition of outdoor advertising. Justice White concluded, in effect, that the exceptions meant that the ordinance regulated too little speech, whereas Justice Brennan thought it regulated too much speech.

Nonetheless, the decision is probably fairly read as endorsing relatively strict regulatory restrictions on billboards, especially those carrying a commercial message. The four-justice plurality was clear in its reasoning that insofar as the ordinance restricted commercial outdoor advertising, even if selectively, it was constitutional. Justice Stevens agreed with Justice White that the constitutionality of the ordinance was not "undercut by the distinction San Diego has drawn between onsite and offsite commercial signs," and the two other dissenting justices rejected the appellants' First Amendment challenge to the ordnance altogether. Implicitly, a firm majority endorsed regulation of outdoor advertising under the First Amendment.

2. *Commercial v. Non-Commercial Speech.* The ruling in *Metromedia* turns on the distinctive levels of protection afforded commercial versus non-commercial speech under the First Amendment. The application of First Amendment protections to purely commercial speech is a relatively recent development. Prior to the 1970s, purely commercial advertisements of services or goods for sale were considered to be outside the scope of First Amendment protection. However, in *Virginia Pharmacy Bd. v. Virginia Citizens Consumer Council,* 425 U.S. 748 (1976), the Court held that speech proposing no more than a commercial transaction enjoys a substantial degree of First Amendment protection: A State may not completely suppress the dissemination of truthful information about a lawful activity merely because it is fearful of that information's effect upon its disseminators and its recipients. At the same time, *Virginia Pharmacy* did not equate commercial and non-commercial speech for First Amendment purposes; in fact, it expressly indicated that they deserve different levels of protection from the courts. Generally speaking, the Supreme Court has been moving in the direction of granting more protection for commercial speech, a development with potentially important but so far unrealized implications for billboard regulation. *See Sorrrell v. IMS Health,* 564 U.S. 552 (2011).

While *Reed* involved noncommercial speech, and did not specifically address content-based regulation of commercial speech, the Court's elevated concern about content-based regulation and its heavy reliance on the *Sorrell* decision seems to open the door to possible future challenges to content-based regulation of commercial speech. *See* Alan C. Weinstein & Brian J. Connolly, Sign Regulation After *Reed:* Suggestions for Coping with Legal Uncertainty, 47 Urb. Law. 569 (2015).

3. *On-Site Versus Off-Site Regulation. Metromedia* recognized that regulators can draw a sharp distinction between on-site and off-site advertising, at least in the context of commercial advertising. Post-*Metromedia*, lower courts have frequently relied on this distinction in upholding billboard regulation. *See, e.g., RTM Media, LLC v. City of Houston,* 584 F.3d 220 (5th Cir. 2009) (provision of city's sign code prohibiting off-premise commercial signs did not violate free speech in treating commercial signs differently from noncommercial signs; provision was specifically crafted to address the safety and aesthetic concerns associated with billboards, and there was substantial evidence that the vast majority of the area's billboards were commercial and that the code had been effective in reducing signage by approximately half over a 28-year period); *Outdoor Media Group, Inc. v. City of Beaumont,* 506

F.3d 895 (9th Cir. 2007) (recognizing that off-site advertising, with its periodically changing content, presented a more acute safety problem than on-site advertising, but ruling that ordinance violated the First Amendment because it imposed greater restrictions on noncommercial billboards and regulated noncommercial speech based on content).

Reed arguably creates some uncertainty about whether an ordinance distinguishing between on-site and off-site regulation should be considered a form of content regulation subject to strict scrutiny. Applying the "absolutist" approach to content regulation, many sign ordinances that distinguish between on-site and off-site regulation are explicitly, or at least implicitly, content-based. *See* Darrel Menthe, Writing on the Wall: The Impending Demise of Modern Sign Regulation Under the First Amendment and State Constitutions, 18 Geo. Mason. U. Civ. Rts. 1 (2007) (arguing that the on-site/off-site distinction is not only constitutionally unsupportable but is under assault and rapidly collapsing, as courts are increasingly reluctant to engage in the contortions necessary to avoid the obvious conclusion that this distinction is impermissibly based on content).

4. *Time, Place, and Manner Restrictions. Metromedia* (and *Reed*) are generally read not to draw into question the legitimacy of regulations governing the physical and structural aspects of advertising. *See, e.g., Get Outdoors II, LLC v. City of San Diego, California,* 506 F.3d 886 (9th Cir. 2007) (sustaining size and height sign restrictions as a valid time, place, and manner regulation, meeting *Central Hudson*); *KH Outdoor, LLC v. City of Trussville,* 458 F.3d 1261 (11th Cir. 2006) (invalidating sign ordinance favoring commercial over noncommercial speech in allowing temporary political and campaign posters no larger than eight square feet, yet allowing billboards up to 800 square feet limited only to commercial speech); *G.K. Ltd. Travel v. City of Lake Oswego,* 436 F.3d 1064 (9th Cir. 2006) (sustaining sign ordinance regulating type, size, and design of all erected signs and prohibiting pole signs).

5. *Mobile Billboards.* Mobile advertising arguably raises distinctive police power concerns warranting greater intrusion on First Amendment interests. *See Showing Animals Respect & Kindness v. City of West Hollywood,* 83 Cal. Rptr. 3d 134 (Ct. App. 2008) (sustaining ordinance prohibiting mobile billboards as narrowly tailored to achieve significant government interests in aesthetics, safety, and air pollution reduction). *See also Ballen v. City of Redmond,* 466 F.3d 736 (9th Cir. 2006) (invalidating sign ordinance prohibiting portable signs with ten categories of signs exempted; the ordinance was more extensive than necessary under *Central Hudson* and some exemptions were content-based).

6. *Buy My Car!* Can municipalities prohibit the placement of "For Sale" signs on parked or moving vehicles? *See, e.g., Pagan v. Fruchey,* 492 F.3d 766 (6th Cir. 2007) (traffic ordinance prohibiting "For Sale" signs on vehicles parked on a public street, absent evidence of interests in traffic or pedestrian safety or aesthetic concerns, is a content-based, invalid regulation). Would this regulatory strategy be even harder to sustain in light of *Reed?*

7. *Motel Signs.* Can a community bar a motel from advertising weekly rates? *Suburban Lodges of America, Inc. v. City of Columbus Graphics Comm'n,* 761 N.E.2d 1060 (Ohio Ct. App. 2000) (sustaining variance denial from on-premises, freeway-oriented sign ordinance that limited text that may be included). Again, such a restriction would be subject to searching, probably fatal scrutiny following *Reed.*

8. *Protecting Residential Areas.* Can commercial signs be prohibited in residential districts? *City of Rochester Hills v. Schultz,* 592 N.W.2d 69 (Mich. 1999) (furthers the

goal of preserving the residential character of the community). *See also Long Island Bd. of Realtors, Inc. v. Village of Massapequa Park*, 277 F.3d 622 (2d Cir. 2002) (sustaining ordinance limiting size, placement, number, and duration of commercial sign placement on residential property under facial challenge); *Coffery v. Fayette County*, 610 S.E.2d 41 (Ga. 2005) (restricting signs in residential areas to one sign no more than six feet square per lot invalid unless it is the least restrictive means to serve aesthetics and traffic safety).

9. *Vendors, Artisans, Street Performers, and Panhandlers.* How might a town regulate public performances, street musicians, and artisans selling their jewelry, paintings, or objet d'art, or begging by the poor? If newspapers are protected, are tables placed on public sidewalks for distribution of literature similarly protected? *See Hunt v. City of Los Angeles*, 638 F.3d 703 (9th Cir. 2011) (former ordinances regulating vending on boardwalk, which exempted sale of merchandise carrying or making religious, political, philosophical, or ideological messages or statement which was "inextricably intertwined" with the merchandise, was facially void for vagueness); *Berger v. City of Seattle*, 569 F.3d 1029 (9th Cir. 2009) (en banc ruling that rule requiring performers to obtain permits before performing was not sufficiently narrowly tailored to meet standard for a valid time, place, and manner regulation of speech); *Travis v. Park City Mun. Corp.*, 565 F.3d 1252 (10th Cir. 2009) (sustaining city's refusal to allow display and sale of artwork in public park without obtaining permit and complying with relevant city ordinances). *Compare* Robert C. Ellickson, Controlling Chronic Misconduct in City Spaces: Of Panhandlers, Skid Rows, and Public-Space Zoning, 105 Yale L.J. 1165 (1996) *with* Stephen R. Munzer, *Ellickson* on "Chronic Misconduct" in Urban Spaces: Of Panhandlers, Bench Squatters, and Day Laborers, 32 Harv. C.R. C.L. L. Rev. 1 (1997).

10. *Labor Solicitation.* In *Comite de Jornaleros de Redondo Beach v. Redondo Beach, Cal.*, 657 F.3d 936 (9th Cir. 2011), the court overturned an injunction against the city's ban on day laborer solicitation. The ban prohibiting the solicitation of employment from passing motorists was held to be a reasonable time, place, and manner regulation that was content-neutral.

C. ADULT USE ZONING

Must cities permit adult movie theaters in order to comply with the First Amendment? Must cities zone a reasonable number of sites to accommodate adult film exhibitions? The following case is a somewhat dated, but (at least arguably) the most authoritative and comprehensive Supreme Court decision on the subject.

■ CITY OF RENTON v. PLAYTIME THEATRES, INC.
475 U.S. 41 (1986)

Justice REHNQUIST delivered the opinion of the Court, in which Chief Justice BURGER, and Justices WHITE, POWELL, STEVENS, and O'CONNOR joined. Justice BLACKMUN concurred in the result.

This case involves a constitutional challenge to a zoning ordinance, enacted by appellant city of Renton, Washington. . . . Appellees, Playtime Theatres, Inc., and Sea-First Properties, Inc., filed an action in the United States District Court for the Western District of Washington seeking a declaratory judgment that the Renton ordinance violated the First and Fourteenth Amendments and a permanent injunction against its enforcement. The District Court ruled in favor of Renton and denied the permanent injunction, but the Court of Appeals for the Ninth Circuit reversed and remanded for reconsideration. We . . . now reverse the judgment of the Ninth Circuit.

In May 1980, the Mayor of Renton, a city of approximately 32,000 people located just south of Seattle, suggested to the Renton City Council that it consider the advisability of enacting zoning legislation dealing with adult entertainment uses. No such uses existed in the city at that time. Upon the Mayor's suggestion, the City Council referred the matter to the city's Planning and Development Committee. The Committee held public hearings, reviewed the experiences of Seattle and other cities, and received a report from the City Attorney's Office advising as to developments in other cities. . . .

In April 1981, acting on the basis of the Planning and Development Committee's recommendation, the City Council enacted Ordinance No. 3526. The ordinance prohibited any "adult motion picture theater" from locating within 1,000 feet of any residential zone, single- or multiple-family dwelling, church, or park, and within one mile of any school. The term "adult motion picture theater" was defined as "[a]n enclosed building used for presenting motion picture films, video cassettes, cable television, or any other such visual media, distinguished or characteri[zed] by an emphasis on matter depicting, describing or relating to 'specified sexual activities' or 'specified anatomical areas' . . . for observation by patrons therein."

In early 1982, respondents acquired two existing theaters in downtown Renton, with the intention of using them to exhibit feature-length adult films. The theaters were located within the area proscribed by Ordinance No. 3526. At about the same time, respondents filed the previously mentioned lawsuit challenging the ordinance on First and Fourteenth Amendment grounds, and seeking declaratory and injunctive relief. While the federal action was pending, the City Council amended the ordinance in several respects, adding a statement of reasons for its enactment and reducing the minimum distance from any school to 1,000 feet. . . .

The District Court . . . denied respondents' requested permanent injunction, and entered summary judgment in favor of Renton. The court found that the Renton ordinance did not substantially restrict First Amendment interests, that Renton was not required to show specific adverse impact on Renton from the operation of adult theaters but could rely on the experiences of other cities, that the purposes of the ordinance were unrelated to the suppression of speech, and that the restrictions on speech imposed by the ordinance were no greater than necessary to further the governmental interests involved. Relying on *Young v. American Mini Theatres, Inc.*, 427 U.S. 50 (1976) . . . the court held that the Renton ordinance did not violate the First Amendment.

The Court of Appeals for the Ninth Circuit reversed. The Court of Appeals first concluded, contrary to the finding of the District Court, that the Renton ordinance constituted a substantial restriction on First Amendment interests. Then . . . the Court of Appeals held that Renton had improperly relied on the experiences of other cities in lieu of evidence about the effects of adult theaters on Renton, that

Renton had thus failed to establish adequately the existence of a substantial governmental interest in support of its ordinance, and that in any event Renton's asserted interests had not been shown to be unrelated to the suppression of expression. The Court of Appeals remanded the case to the District Court for reconsideration of Renton's asserted interests.

In our view, the resolution of this case is largely dictated by our decision in *Young v. American Mini Theatres, Inc., supra.* There, although five Members of the Court did not agree on a single rationale for the decision, we held that the city of Detroit's zoning ordinance, which prohibited locating an adult theater within 1,000 feet of any two other "regulated uses" or within 500 feet of any residential zone, did not violate the First and Fourteenth Amendments. The Renton ordinance, like the one in *American Mini Theatres,* does not ban adult theaters altogether, but merely provides that such theaters may not be located within 1,000 feet of any residential zone, single- or multiple-family dwelling, church, park, or school. The ordinance is therefore properly analyzed as a form of time, place, and manner regulation.

Describing the ordinance as a time, place, and manner regulation is, of course, only the first step in our inquiry. This Court has long held that regulations enacted for the purpose of restraining speech on the basis of its content presumptively violate the First Amendment. On the other hand, so-called "content-neutral" time, place, and manner regulations are acceptable so long as they are designed to serve a substantial governmental interest and do not unreasonably limit alternative avenues of communication.

At first glance, the Renton ordinance, like the ordinance in *American Mini Theatres,* does not appear to fit neatly into either the "content-based" or the "content-neutral" category. To be sure, the ordinance treats theaters that specialize in adult films differently from other kinds of theaters. Nevertheless, as the District Court concluded, the Renton ordinance is aimed not at the *content* of the films shown at "adult motion picture theatres," but rather at the *secondary effects* of such theaters on the surrounding community. The District Court found that the City Council's "*predominate* concerns" were with the secondary effects of adult theaters, and not with the content of adult films themselves. But the Court of Appeals . . . held that this was not enough to sustain the ordinance. According to the Court of Appeals, if "*a motivating factor*" in enacting the ordinance was to restrict respondents' exercise of First Amendment rights the ordinance would be invalid, apparently no matter how small a part this motivating factor may have played in the City Council's decision.

This view of the law was rejected in *United States v. O'Brien,* 391 U.S. [361,] 382–386 [(1986)]: the very case that the Court of Appeals said it was applying: "It is a familiar principle of constitutional law that this Court will not strike down an otherwise constitutional statute on the basis of an alleged illicit legislative motive." . . .

The District Court's finding as to "predominate" intent, left undisturbed by the Court of Appeals, is more than adequate to establish that the city's pursuit of its zoning interests here was unrelated to the suppression of free expression.

In short, the Renton ordinance is completely consistent with our definition of "content-neutral" speech regulations as those that "are *justified* without reference to the content of the regulated speech." The ordinance does not contravene the fundamental principle that underlies our concern about "content-based" speech regulations: that "government may not grant the use of a forum to people whose views it finds acceptable, but deny use to those wishing to express less favored or more controversial views." . . .

The appropriate inquiry in this case, then, is whether the Renton ordinance is designed to serve a substantial governmental interest and allows for reasonable alternative avenues of communication. It is clear that the ordinance meets such a standard. As a majority of this Court recognized in *American Mini Theatres,* a city's "interest in attempting to preserve the quality of urban life is one that must be accorded high respect." Exactly the same vital governmental interests are at stake here.

The Court of Appeals ruled, however, that because the Renton ordinance was enacted without the benefit of studies specifically relating to "the particular problems or needs of Renton," the city's justifications for the ordinance were "conclusory and speculative." We think the Court of Appeals imposed on the city an unnecessarily rigid burden of proof. The record in this case reveals that Renton relied heavily on the experience of, and studies produced by, the city of Seattle. In Seattle, as in Renton, the adult theater zoning ordinance was aimed at preventing the secondary effects caused by the presence of even one such theater in a given neighborhood. *See Northend Cinema, Inc. v. Seattle,* 90 Wash.2d 709, 585 P.2d 1153 (1978). . . .

We hold that Renton was entitled to rely on the experiences of Seattle and other cities, and in particular on the "detailed findings" summarized in the Washington Supreme Court's *Northend Cinema* opinion, in enacting its adult theater zoning ordinance. The First Amendment does not require a city, before enacting such an ordinance, to conduct new studies or produce evidence independent of that already generated by other cities, so long as whatever evidence the city relies upon is reasonably believed to be relevant to the problem that the city addresses. That was the case here. Nor is our holding affected by the fact that Seattle ultimately chose a different method of adult theater zoning than that chosen by Renton, since Seattle's choice of a different remedy to combat the secondary effects of adult theaters does not call into question either Seattle's identification of those secondary effects or the relevance of Seattle's experience to Renton.

We also find no constitutional defect in the method chosen by Renton to further its substantial interests. Cities may regulate adult theaters by dispersing them, as in Detroit, or by effectively concentrating them, as in Renton. "It is not our function to appraise the wisdom of [the city's] decision to require adult theaters to be separated rather than concentrated in the same areas. . . . [T]he city must be allowed a reasonable opportunity to experiment with solutions to admittedly serious problems." Moreover, the Renton ordinance is "narrowly tailored" to affect only that category of theaters shown to produce the unwanted secondary effects. . . .

Finally, turning to the question whether the Renton ordinance allows for reasonable alternative avenues of communication, we note that the ordinance leaves some 520 acres, or more than five percent of the entire land area of Renton, open to use as adult theater sites. The District Court found, and the Court of Appeals did not dispute the finding, that the 520 acres of land consists of "[a]mple, accessible real estate," including "acreage in all stages of development from raw land to developed, industrial, warehouse, office, and shopping space that is criss-crossed by freeways, highways, and roads." . . .

In sum, we find that the Renton ordinance represents a valid governmental response to the "admittedly serious problems" created by adult theaters. Renton has not used "the power to zone as a pretext for suppressing expression," but rather has sought to make some areas available for adult theaters and their patrons, while at the same time preserving the quality of life in the community at large by preventing those theaters from locating in other areas. This, after all, is the essence of zoning. Here, as in *American Mini Theatres*, the city has enacted a zoning ordinance that meets these goals while also satisfying the dictates of the First Amendment. The judgment of the Court of Appeals is therefore

> *Reversed.*

Justice BRENNAN dissented, with Justice MARSHALL dissenting.

Renton's zoning ordinance selectively imposes limitations on the location of a movie theater based exclusively on the content of the films shown there. The constitutionality of the ordinance is therefore not correctly analyzed under standards applied to content-neutral time, place, and manner restrictions. But even assuming that the ordinance may fairly be characterized as content neutral, it is plainly unconstitutional under the standards established by the decisions of this Court. Although the Court's analysis is limited to cases involving "businesses that purvey sexually explicit materials," and thus does not affect our holdings in cases involving state regulation of other kinds of speech, I dissent.

Notes and Comments

1. *Young v. American Mini Theatres, Inc.* The decision in *City of Renton v. Playtime Theaters, Inc.*, 475 U.S. 41 (1985), built on the Court's prior decision in *Young v. American Mini Theatres, Inc.*, 427 U.S. 50 (1976), the first case in which the Court addressed how the First Amendment and the local zoning power interact. In *Young,* a five-justice majority (though failing to fully coalesce around a single rationale), rejected a First Amendment challenge to a City of Detroit zoning regulation that prohibited adult theaters within 1000 feet of any two other similar "regulated uses." The ordinance at issue in *City of Renton* was comparable in design to the ordinance at issue in *Young,* except that the former sought to *concentrate* adult uses in a small area while the latter sought to *disperse* adult uses throughout the community. As the Court made clear in *City of Renton*, this distinction does not make any particular difference in the analysis of the First Amendment issue.

The *Young* plurality observed that while "the First Amendment will not tolerate the total suppression of erotic materials that have some arguably artistic value," it is nonetheless the case "that society's interest in protecting this type of expression is of a wholly different, and lesser, magnitude than the interest in untrammeled political debate." Based on the premise that "the State may legitimately use the content of these materials as the basis for placing them in a different classification from other motion pictures," it concluded that the ordinance was "justified by the city's interest in preserving the character of its neighborhoods." *Cf. id.* at 76 (Powell, J.) (concurring in the judgment based on the conclusion that there was "no indication that the application of the . . . [o]rdinance to adult theaters has the effect of suppressing production of or, to any significant degree, restricting access to adult movies."). Four justices dissented on the ground that the ordinance established an illegitimate system of "content-based restrictions on the geographic location of motion picture theaters that exhibit nonobscene but sexually oriented films."

2. *Alameda Books.* In *City of Los Angeles v. Alameda Books*, 535 U.S. 425 (2002), the Court's latest decision directly addressing zoning regulation of adult uses under the First Amendment, the Court once again rejected the First Amendment argument. The ordinance at issue in the *Alameda Books* case prohibited theaters or other types of adult establishments from locating within 1000 feet of another such enterprise or within 500 feet of any religious institution, school, or public park. Thus, like the ordinance at issue in *Young,* the ordinance primarily sought to disperse (rather than concentrate) adult uses. The Court followed *Renton* by analyzing the ordinance as a time, place, and manner regulation because it did not ban adult establishments altogether. The Court also followed *Renton* by treating the ordinance as content neutral because it was not aimed at the content of the speech offered by the adult establishments but rather at the "secondary effects" of such establishments on the surrounding community, and therefore was subject to review under a deferential "intermediate scrutiny" standard.

The relatively narrow problem addressed in *Alameda Books* was whether the city could justify an amendment to its ordinance that not only called for dispersal of adult "establishments" but also of distinct "operations" (e.g., retail sale and video booths) that could be physically housed in one establishment. The specific legal issue in the case was whether the city could successfully defend the ordinance on the basis of a study completed prior to the adoption of the amendment that provided empirical support for the conclusion that dispersing adult establishments reduces secondary effects.

The plurality opinion, supported by four justices, concluded that the city's theory that dispersing adult operations would reduce secondary effects "was consistent with" the prior study and therefore met the *Renton* standard that a community must point to evidence that is "'reasonably believed to be relevant' for demonstrating a connection between speech and a substantial, independent government interest." Justice Kennedy concurred in the judgment, expressing concern that the plurality had not been sufficiently attentive to First Amendment interests. Nonetheless, he agreed with the bottom line conclusion that the ordinance was not unconstitutional, reasoning that the ordinance might "cause a substantial reduction in secondary effects while reducing speech very little."

3. *The Court's Message.* The overall message of the Court's adult zoning cases appears to be that government bears a relatively light evidentiary burden to demonstrate that a restriction on adult enterprises, even though they are deserving of First Amendment protection, is justified in order to control secondary effects. *See* Rebecca Shwayri, Case Comment, Sex Meets the City: Lowering a City's Evidentiary Burden on Zoning Ordinances, 55 Fla. L. Rev. 927 (2003) (*Alameda Books*). It is illuminating to contrast and compare the showing required of local governments in this context with the showing required of local governments to justify development "exactions" challenged under the Takings Clause. *See Dolan v. City of Tigard,* 512 U.S. 374 (1994); *Nollan v. California Coastal Comm'n,* 483 U.S. 825 (1987) (both excerpted in Chapter 7). Are the different standards justified by the different values protected by the First Amendment and the Takings Clause, respectively? Do the different standards turn on its head Chief Justice Rehnquist's famous remark, "We see no reason why the Takings Clause of the Fifth Amendment, as much a part of the Bill of Rights as the First Amendment or Fourth Amendment, should be relegated to the status of a poor relation in these comparable circumstances." *Dolan,* 512 U.S. at 392.

4. *Adult Use Zoning After Reed?* There is considerable doctrinal tension between the Supreme Court's recent decision in *Reed v. Town of Gilbert*, 135 S. Ct. 2218 (2015) and the "secondary effects" doctrine developed in the adult cases. Tellingly, concurring justices in *Reed* who rejected the majority's "absolutist" opposition cited *Renton* with approval, but the majority made no reference to the secondary effects doctrine. The *Reed* Court held that strict scrutiny applies to all regulations that are content-based "on their face" — that is, that apply "to particular speech because of the topic discussed or the idea or message expressed." Moreover, the *Reed* Court repudiates the rationale for the secondary effects doctrine: that a regulation the scope of which is defined by content is legitimate if the distinction can be justified by concerns unrelated to the content. *Reed* flatly says that this approach "skips the crucial first step in the content-neutrality analysis: determining whether the law is content neutral on its face. A law that is content based on its face is subject to strict scrutiny regardless of the government's benign motive, content-neutral justification, or lack of animus toward the idea contained in the regulated speech."

Logic aside, lower courts are unlikely to disregard the teachings of *Renton* for regulation of adult land uses. Even when a Supreme Court ruling undermines other Court precedent, the general rule is that the lower courts "are bound to follow them until expressly overruled by the Supreme Court." *Eberhart v. United States*, 546 U.S. 12, 14-15 (2005). Moreover, it is exceedingly hard to read the tea leaves on how individual justices, despite *Reed*'s apparently broad scope, would actually apply its logic in other cases. Justice Thomas, the author of the opinion for the Court in *Reed*, joined Justice O'Connor's plurality opinion in *Alameda Books* upholding the ordinance based on the secondary effects doctrine; on the other hand, Justices Ginsburg and Breyer, who joined in rejecting the absolutist position in *Reed*, joined Justice Souter in dissent in *Alameda Books*. Sex, perhaps, is different.

5. *Licensing of Adult Businesses.* Communities frequently impose licensing obligations on adult businesses, which themselves may raise First Amendment issues. Compare *FW/PBS, Inc. v. City of Dallas*, 493 U.S. 215 (1990) (procedures must avoid undue delay) *with City of Littleton v. Z.J. Gifts D-4, L.L.C.*, 541 U.S. 774 (2004) (opportunity for judicial review of adverse licensing decisions in accordance with state's ordinary review procedures was sufficient to satisfy First Amendment requirements). *See also Blue Moon Entm't, LLC v. Bates City*, 441 F.3d 561 (8th Cir. 2006) (finding application of conditional use permit for adult businesses a prior restraint that may be challenged facially).

6. *Secondary Effects Studies.* Numerous lower court cases focus on the adequacy of secondary effects studies, generally giving local governments wide latitude. *See Big Dipper Entm't, L.L.C. v. City of Warren*, 641 F.3d 715 (6th Cir. 2011) (sustaining city zoning ordinance when city relied on 49 studies and reports discussing negative secondary effects, produced over a span of three decades, even though city did not conduct the studies and studies were from other states or were somewhat dated); *H & A Land Corp. v. City of Kennedale*, 480 F.3d 336 (5th Cir. 2007) (survey drafted by experts, pretested and administered to large national pool of respondents, was not "shoddy" and was sufficient to support secondary effects of adult business ordinance prohibiting adult businesses within 800 feet of churches, schools, residences, day care centers, parks, and other sexually-oriented businesses and certain overlay districts); *PAO Xiong v. City of Moorhead*, 641 F. Supp. 2d 822 (D. Minn. 2009) (ruling that city was not required to disregard studies conducted by other cities even though studies were all between 16 and 30 years old); *Plaza Group Properties, LLC v. Spencer*

County Plan Comm'n, 877 N.E.2d 877 (Ind. Ct. App. 2007) (largely rural county was entitled to rely on studies of effects of adult business in urban areas).

Scholars differ on the legitimacy of the secondary effects theory. *Compare* Bryant Paul, Daniel Linz, & Bradley J. Shafer, Government Regulation of "Adult" Businesses Through Zoning and Anti-Nudity Ordinances: Debunking the Legal Myth of Negative Secondary Effects, 6 Comm. L. & Pol'y 355 (2001) (criticizing secondary effects studies) *with* Richard McCleary & Alan C. Weinstein, Do "Off-Site" Adult Businesses Have Secondary Effects? Legal Doctrine, Social Theory, and Empirical Evidence, 31 Law & Pol'y 217 (2009) (theoretical and empirical study supporting secondary effects with ambient crime doubling after opening of adult business as compared to control area, with victimization risk most acute in night-time hours).

7. *Alternative Means of Communication.* To satisfy the *Renton* requirements, a city must ensure that there are reasonable alternative avenues of communication. In most cases, this requirement means a showing of the physical and legal availability of alternative sites. *See, e.g., Big Dipper Entm't, L.L.C. v. City of Warren*, 641 F.3d 715 (6th Cir. 2011) (reasonable alternative avenues of communication existed since 27 sites remained available for applicant's business and only 2 applications for adult businesses were filed in the city during the preceding 5 years); *Daytona Grand, Inc. v. City of Daytona Beach*, 490 F.3d 860 (11th Cir. 2007) (the number of sites available for adult businesses under the new zoning regime must be greater than or equal to the number of adult businesses in existence at the time the new zoning regime takes effect; twenty-four sites in the district were available for First Amendment purposes, notwithstanding that all of the land in the district was owned by a single private landowner who could be reluctant or unwilling to develop or sell the land). *See also* Ashley C. Phillips, Comment, A Matter of Arithmetic: Using Supply and Demand to Determine the Constitutionality of Adult Entertainment Zoning Ordinances, 51 Emory L. J. 319 (2002).

8. *Regulation of Nude Dancing.* In *Barnes v. Glen Theatre, Inc.*, 501 U.S. 560 (1991), a divided Supreme Court upheld the application of an anti-nudity public indecency statute to prohibit non-obscene nude dancing in commercial establishments. Chief Justice Rehnquist's plurality opinion for three members of the Court ruled that nude bar dancing is not expressive conduct. He determined that the general anti-nudity statute was conduct-based and thus unrelated to the suppression of expression. He was joined by concurring Justice Scalia, who would go further to eliminate all expression-based defenses to general laws. Four dissenting justices found the activity to be protected expression.

In *Erie v. Pap's A.M.*, 529 U.S. 277 (2000), the Court returned to the subject of nude dancing, this time extending the *Barnes* principle to sustain a local public indecency ordinance. The ordinance made it an offence to knowingly appear in a public place in a state of nudity. The law defined "public place" to include places of entertainment, taverns, restaurants and clubs, thereby reaching nude dancing. A four-justice plurality found nude dancing to be expressive behavior, but the city's interest in the restriction was found to be unrelated to the suppression of expression. The plurality also employed the secondary effects doctrine in finding that the law was directed to the effects of such establishments rather than at the erotic message of the dance. Justice Scalia, joined by Justice Thomas, repeated his *Barnes* argument that general laws not targeted at speech are not subject to First Amendment judicial review.

9. *Adult Entertainment and Alcoholic Beverages.* Pursuant to the authority recognized in the Twenty-First Amendment, states may exclude nude dancing in establishments serving liquor. *Newport v. Iacobucci,* 479 U.S. 92 (1986); *New York State Liquor Auth. v. Bellanca,* 452 U.S. 714 (1981); *California v. LaRue,* 409 U.S. 109 (1972). In communities where the states have not elected to exercise suppressive liquor control authority, may local communities nevertheless regulate liquor consumption in places of adult entertainment based on secondary effects studies? *See Legend Night Club v. Miller,* 637 F.3d 291 (4th Cir. 2011) (Maryland statute that effectively prohibited night club owners from selling alcoholic beverages and providing for revocation of liquor licenses for all establishments that presented entertainment involving nudity or simulated sexual behavior was overly broad); *181 South Inc. v. Fischer,* 454 F.3d 228 (3d Cir. 2006) (New Jersey statute prohibiting lewdness or immoral activity on liquor-licensed premises sustained under First Amendment); *Artistic Entm't, Inc. v. City of Warner Robins,* 223 F.3d 1306 (11th Cir. 2000) (endorsing such ordinances yet finding a prior restraint when an ordinance did not include procedural protections from bureaucratic delay).

D. CHURCH AND WORSHIP REGULATION

The first words of the First Amendment read as follows: "Congress shall make no law respecting establishment of religion, or prohibiting the free exercising thereof." These two clauses are conventionally referred to as the "Establishment Clause" and the "Free Exercise Clause," respectively. While these clauses, by their terms, speak only to federal government action, specifically congressional action, the Supreme Court has long recognized that both constitutional provisions apply to state and local governments via incorporation into the Due Process Clause of Fourteenth Amendment. *See Everson v. Board of Educ.,* 330 U.S. 1 (1947) (the Establishment Clause); *Cantwell v. Connecticut,* 310 U.S. 296 (1940) (the Free Exercise Clause).

While the Establishment Clause and the Free Exercise Clause are each important guarantees of religious liberty, they are complementary as well as in tension with one another. For example, the Establishment Clause clearly bars the government from establishing a state religion, and this prohibition can be viewed as furthering the goals of the Free Exercise Clause by providing space in society for a multiplicity of religious viewpoints. On the other hand, efforts to "protect" the exercise of religious freedoms can be viewed as going so far in the direction of endorsing particular religions that they may be viewed as falling afoul of the Establishment Clause. For a comprehensive discussion of these complexities, see Erwin Chemerinsky, Constitutional Law 1973-75 (4th ed. 2013).

An important element of this topic is congressional legislation effectively creating new statutory rights to exercise religion that go beyond the protections afforded by the Free Exercise Clause as authoritatively interpreted by the U.S. Supreme Court. The two major statutory enactments are the Religious Freedom Restoration Act (RFRA) of 1993, 42 U.S.C. §2000bb, and the Religious Land Use and Institutionalized Persons (RLUIPA) Act of 2000, 42 U.S.C. §2001c-1. Because these measures (especially the second one) have important practical implications for state and local land use regulation, they are discussed in some detail below.

For convenience, the discussion of religion in the land use context can be divided between the Establishment Clause and the Free Exercise Clause. As will become apparent, the Free Exercise Clause (and its statutory supplements, in particular RLUIPA) has given rise to many more legal issues in the land use context than the Establishment Clause.

1. The Establishment Clause

Understanding the Supreme Court's Establishment Clause jurisprudence presents a challenge of mind-numbing complexity that goes beyond the scope of this land use text. As discussed, it is broadly accepted that the Establishment Clause prohibits the federal government (or state governments) from establishing an official state religion. It also bars explicit governmental policy favoring one religion over another. But beyond that, there is a great deal of uncertainty, including about what test or tests should be applied to resolve Establishment Clause claims.

The classical test, articulated in *Lemon v. Kurtzman*, 403 U.S. 602 (1971), requires that government action (1) have a secular purpose, (2) not have a principal or primary effect that either advances or inhibits religion, and (3) not foster "an excessive government entanglement with religion." But the Court has frequently questioned the value of the *Lemon* test. *See, e g., Van Orden v. Perry*, 545 U.S. 677, 686 (2005) (observing that "[m]any of our recent cases simply have not applied the *Lemon* test . . . [and o]thers have applied it only after concluding that the challenged practice was invalid under a different Establishment Clause test," and stating that the *Lemon* test was "not useful" for resolving the case). In its most recent Establishment Clause case, the Court resolved a challenge to a town's practice of opening town board meetings with a prayer by reference to historical traditions without mentioning the *Lemon* test. *See Town of Greece v. Galloway*, 134 S. Ct. 1811 (2014). Additional complexity is created by the fact that the modern Court has gradually moved the line defining when government involvement in the religious sphere goes too far for Establishment Clause purposes. *Compare Aguilar v. Felton*, 473 U.S. 402 (1985) (holding that the Establishment Clause barred the New York City Board of Education from sending public school teachers into parochial schools to provide remedial education to disadvantaged children) *with Agostini v. Felton*, 521 U.S. 203 (1997) (overruling *Aguilar* in light of subsequent changes in the Supreme Court's Establishment Clause jurisprudence).

Establishment Clause issues relating to land use have most frequently arisen in the context of cases challenging various kinds of expressive displays or monuments in public buildings or on public land. The cases are numerous and varied with outcomes often turning on subtle factual nuances. *See, e.g, McCreary County v. ACLU of Kentucky*, 545 U.S. 844 (2005) (ruling that display of Ten Commandments in courthouse violated the Establishment Clause in light of "manifest purpose" to emphasize and celebrate religious message); *Allegheny County v. Greater Pittsburgh ACLU*, 492 U.S. 573 (1989) (ruling that placement of holiday creche display on courthouse steps violated the Establishment Clause, but placement of Chanukah menorah outside city-county building, along with Christmas tree and "a sign saluting liberty," did not); *Lynch v. Donnelly*, 465 U.S. 668 (1984) (ruling that city's inclusion of nativity scene in municipal Christmas display did not violate the Establishment Clause); *Stone v. Graham*, 449 U.S. 39 (1980) (display of Ten

Commandments in public classroom served predominantly religious purpose and
therefore violated the Establishment Clause).

The following is a relatively recent case in which a divided Supreme Court
struggled with an Establishment Clause challenge to a Ten Commandments monument installed on the grounds of the State Capitol in Texas.

■ VAN ORDEN v. PERRY
545 U.S. 677 (2005)

Chief Justice Rehnquist announced the judgment of the Court and delivered an
opinion, in which Justice Scalia, Justice Kennedy and Justice Thomas joined.

The question here is whether the Establishment Clause of the First Amendment allows the display of a monument inscribed with the Ten Commandments on
the Texas State Capitol grounds. We hold that it does.

The 22 acres surrounding the Texas State Capitol contain 17 monuments and
21 historical markers commemorating the "people, ideals, and events that compose
Texan identity." The monolith challenged here stands 6-feet high and 3 1/2-feet
wide. It is located to the north of the Capitol building, between the Capitol and the
Supreme Court building. Its primary content is the text of the Ten Commandments.
An eagle grasping the American flag, an eye inside of a pyramid, and two small
tablets with what appears to be an ancient script are carved above the text of the Ten
Commandments. Below the text are two Stars of David and the superimposed Greek
letters Chi and Rho, which represent Christ. The bottom of the monument bears the
inscription "PRESENTED TO THE PEOPLE AND YOUTH OF TEXAS BY THE
FRATERNAL ORDER OF EAGLES OF TEXAS 1961."

The legislative record surrounding the State's acceptance of the monument
from the Eagles — a national social, civic, and patriotic organization — is limited to
legislative journal entries. After the monument was accepted, the State selected a
site for the monument based on the recommendation of the state organization
responsible for maintaining the Capitol grounds. The Eagles paid the cost of erecting the monument, the dedication of which was presided over by two state
legislators.

Petitioner Thomas Van Orden is a native Texan and a resident of Austin. . . .
Van Orden testified that, since 1995, he has encountered the Ten Commandments
monument during his frequent visits to the Capitol grounds. His visits are typically
for the purpose of using the law library in the Supreme Court building, which is
located just northwest of the Capitol building.

Forty years after the monument's erection and six years after Van Orden began
to encounter the monument frequently, he sued numerous state officials in their
official capacities . . . , seeking both a declaration that the monument's placement
violates the Establishment Clause and an injunction requiring its removal. After a
bench trial, the District Court held that the monument did not contravene the
Establishment Clause. It found that the State had a valid secular purpose in recognizing and commending the Eagles for their efforts to reduce juvenile delinquency.
The District Court also determined that a reasonable observer, mindful of the history, purpose, and context, would not conclude that this passive monument conveyed the message that the State was seeking to endorse religion. The Court of

Appeals affirmed the District Court's holdings with respect to the monument's purpose and effect. We granted certiorari, and now affirm.

Our cases, Janus like, point in two directions in applying the Establishment Clause. One face looks toward the strong role played by religion and religious traditions throughout our Nation's history. . . . The other face looks toward the principle that governmental intervention in religious matters can itself endanger religious freedom.

This case, like all Establishment Clause challenges, presents us with the difficulty of respecting both faces. Our institutions presuppose a Supreme Being, yet these institutions must not press religious observances upon their citizens. One face looks to the past in acknowledgment of our Nation's heritage, while the other looks to the present in demanding a separation between church and state. Reconciling these two faces requires that we neither abdicate our responsibility to maintain a division between church and state nor evince hostility to religion by disabling the government from in some ways recognizing our religious heritage. . . .

In this case we are faced with a display of the Ten Commandments on government property outside the Texas State Capitol. Such acknowledgments of the role played by the Ten Commandments in our Nation's heritage are common throughout America. We need only look within our own Courtroom. Since 1935, Moses has stood, holding two tablets that reveal portions of the Ten Commandments written in Hebrew, among other lawgivers in the south frieze. Representations of the Ten Commandments adorn the metal gates lining the north and south sides of the Courtroom as well as the doors leading into the Courtroom. Moses also sits on the exterior east facade of the building holding the Ten Commandments tablets. . . . Similar acknowledgments can be seen throughout a visitor's tour of our Nation's Capital. . . .

Of course, the Ten Commandments are religious — they were so viewed at their inception and so remain. The monument, therefore, has religious significance. According to Judeo-Christian belief, the Ten Commandments were given to Moses by God on Mt. Sinai. But Moses was a lawgiver as well as a religious leader. And the Ten Commandments have an undeniable historical meaning, as the foregoing examples demonstrate. Simply having religious content or promoting a message consistent with a religious doctrine does not run afoul of the Establishment Clause.

There are, of course, limits to the display of religious messages or symbols. For example, we held unconstitutional a Kentucky statute requiring the posting of the Ten Commandments in every public schoolroom. *Stone v. Graham*, 449 U.S. 39 (per curiam). In the classroom context, we found that the Kentucky statute had an improper and plainly religious purpose. As evidenced by Stone's almost exclusive reliance upon two of our school prayer cases, it stands as an example of the fact that we have "been particularly vigilant in monitoring compliance with the Establishment Clause in elementary and secondary schools." Neither *Stone* itself nor subsequent opinions have indicated that *Stone's* holding would extend to a legislative chamber, or to capitol grounds.

The placement of the Ten Commandments monument on the Texas State Capitol grounds is a far more passive use of those texts than was the case in *Stone*, where the text confronted elementary school students every day. Indeed, Van Orden, the petitioner here, apparently walked by the monument for a number of years before bringing this lawsuit. . . . Texas has treated its Capitol grounds monuments as representing the several strands in the State's political and legal history. The inclusion of the Ten Commandments monument in this group has a dual significance, partaking of both religion and government. We cannot say that Texas' display of this monument violates the Establishment Clause of the First Amendment.

The judgment of the Court of Appeals is affirmed.

It is so ordered.

Justice SCALIA, concurring.

I join the opinion of THE CHIEF JUSTICE because I think it accurately reflects our current Establishment Clause jurisprudence — or at least the Establishment Clause jurisprudence we currently apply some of the time. I would prefer to reach the same result by adopting an Establishment Clause jurisprudence that is in accord with our Nation's past and present practices, and that can be consistently applied — the central relevant feature of which is that there is nothing unconstitutional in a State's favoring religion generally, honoring God through public prayer and acknowledgment, or, in a nonproselytizing manner, venerating the Ten Commandments.

Justice THOMAS, concurring.

The Court holds that the Ten Commandments monument found on the Texas State Capitol grounds does not violate the Establishment Clause. Rather than trying to suggest meaninglessness where there is meaning, the Chief Justice rightly recognizes that the monument has "religious significance." He properly recognizes the role of religion in this Nation's history and the permissibility of government displays acknowledging that history. For those reasons, I join the Chief Justice's opinion in full.

This case would be easy if the Court were willing to abandon the inconsistent guideposts it has adopted for addressing Establishment Clause challenges, and return to the original meaning of the Clause. I have previously suggested that the Clause's text and history "resis[t] incorporation" against the States. *See* Elk Grove Unified School Dist. v. Newdow, 542 U.S. 1, 45-46 (2004) (opinion concurring in judgment). If the Establishment Clause does not restrain the States, then it has no application here, where only state action is at issue.

Even if the Clause is incorporated, or if the Free Exercise Clause limits the power of States to establish religions . . . , our task would be far simpler if we returned to the original meaning of the word "establishment" than it is under the various approaches this Court now uses. The Framers understood an establishment "necessarily [to] involve actual legal coercion." "In other words, establishment at the founding involved, for example, mandatory observance or mandatory payment of taxes supporting ministers." And "government practices that have nothing to do with creating or maintaining . . . coercive state establishments" simply do not "implicate the possible liberty interest of being free from coercive state establishments. . . ."

Justice BREYER, concurring in the judgment.

. . . If the relation between government and religion is one of separation, but not of mutual hostility and suspicion, one will inevitably find difficult borderline cases. And in such cases, I see no test-related substitute for the exercise of legal judgment. That judgment is not a personal judgment. Rather, as in all constitutional cases, it must reflect and remain faithful to the underlying purposes of the Clauses, and it must take account of context and consequences measured in light of those purposes. While the Court's prior tests provide useful guideposts — and might well lead to the same result the Court reaches today, no exact formula can dictate a resolution to such fact-intensive cases.

The case before us is a borderline case. It concerns a large granite monument bearing the text of the Ten Commandments located on the grounds of the Texas State Capitol. On the one hand, the Commandments' text undeniably has a religious message, invoking, indeed emphasizing, the Deity. On the other hand, focusing on the text of the Commandments alone cannot conclusively resolve this case. Rather, to determine the message that the text here conveys, we must examine how the text is used. And that inquiry requires us to consider the context of the display.

In certain contexts, a display of the tablets of the Ten Commandments can convey not simply a religious message but also a secular moral message (about proper standards of social conduct). And in certain contexts, a display of the tablets can also convey a historical message (about a historic relation between those standards and the law) — a fact that helps to explain the display of those tablets in dozens of courthouses throughout the Nation, including the Supreme Court of the United States.

Here the tablets have been used as part of a display that communicates not simply a religious message, but a secular message as well. The circumstances surrounding the display's placement on the capitol grounds and its physical setting suggest that the State itself intended the latter, nonreligious aspects of the tablets' message to predominate. And the monument's 40-year history on the Texas state grounds indicates that that has been its effect.

The group that donated the monument, the Fraternal Order of Eagles, a private civic (and primarily secular) organization, while interested in the religious aspect of the Ten Commandments, sought to highlight the Commandments' role in shaping civic morality as part of that organization's efforts to combat juvenile delinquency. The Eagles' consultation with a committee composed of members of several faiths in order to find a nonsectarian text underscores the group's ethics-based motives. The tablets, as displayed on the monument, prominently acknowledge that the Eagles donated the display, a factor which, though not sufficient, thereby further distances the State itself from the religious aspect of the Commandments' message.

The physical setting of the monument, moreover, suggests little or nothing of the sacred. The monument sits in a large park containing 17 monuments and 21 historical markers, all designed to illustrate the "ideals" of those who settled in Texas and of those who have lived there since that time. The setting does not readily lend itself to meditation or any other religious activity. But it does provide a context of history and moral ideals. It (together with the display's inscription about its origin) communicates to visitors that the State sought to reflect moral principles, illustrating a relation between ethics and law that the State's citizens, historically speaking, have endorsed. That is to say, the context suggests that the State intended the display's moral message — an illustrative message reflecting the historical "ideals" of Texans — to predominate.

If these factors provide a strong, but not conclusive, indication that the Commandments' text on this monument conveys a predominantly secular message, a further factor is determinative here. As far as I can tell, 40 years passed in which the presence of this monument, legally speaking, went unchallenged (until the single legal objection raised by petitioner). And I am not aware of any evidence suggesting that this was due to a climate of intimidation. Hence, those 40 years suggest more strongly than can any set of formulaic tests that few individuals, whatever their system of beliefs, are likely to have understood the monument as amounting, in any significantly detrimental way, to a government effort to favor a particular religious sect, primarily to promote religion over nonreligion, to "engage in" any "religious practic[e]," to "compel" any "religious practic[e]," or to "work deterrence" of any "religious belief." Those 40 years suggest that the public visiting the capitol grounds has considered the religious aspect of the tablets' message as part of what is a broader moral and historical message reflective of a cultural heritage.

This case, moreover, is distinguishable from instances where the Court has found Ten Commandments displays impermissible. The display is not on the grounds of a public school, where, given the impressionability of the young, government must exercise particular care in separating church and state. This case also differs from *McCreary County*, where the short (and stormy) history of the courthouse Commandments' displays demonstrates the substantially religious objectives of those who mounted them, and the effect of this readily apparent objective upon those who view them. That history there indicates a governmental effort substantially to promote religion, not simply an effort primarily to reflect, historically, the secular impact of a religiously inspired document. And, in today's world, in a Nation of so many different religious and comparable nonreligious fundamental beliefs, a more contemporary state effort to focus attention upon a religious text is certainly likely to prove divisive in a way that this longstanding, pre-existing monument has not. . . .

[I]n reaching the conclusion that the Texas display falls on the permissible side of the constitutional line, I rely less upon a literal application of any particular test than upon consideration of the basic purposes of the First Amendment's Religion Clauses themselves. This display has stood apparently uncontested for nearly two generations. That experience helps us understand that as a practical matter of degree this display is unlikely to prove divisive. And this matter of degree is, I believe, critical in a borderline case such as this one.

At the same time, to reach a contrary conclusion here, based primarily on the religious nature of the tablets' text would, I fear, lead the law to exhibit a hostility toward religion that has no place in our Establishment Clause traditions. Such a holding might well encourage disputes concerning the removal of longstanding depictions of the Ten Commandments from public buildings across the Nation. And it could thereby create the very kind of religiously based divisiveness that the Establishment Clause seeks to avoid. . . .

I concur in the judgment of the Court.

[Justices STEVENS, O'CONNOR, GINSBURG, and SOUTER dissented, arguing that the display of the monument on the capitol grounds violated the First Amendment.]

2. Free Exercise Clause

The Free Exercise Clause represents the second branch of the protection afforded religion by the First Amendment. The basic idea animating the Free Exercise Clause is that government generally has no business controlling individuals' choices about religious faith and observance. The idea is simple enough to state in the abstract. The interesting and complex cases arise from the conflict between individuals' choices with respect to religion and the government's efforts to pursue other, non-religious objectives in a fashion that incidentally affects the exercise of religion. The study of how this conflict plays out in the land use context unavoidably begins with the important non-land use case discussed below.

A Note on *Emloyment Division, Department of Human Resources of Oregon v. Smith* and the **Religious Freedom Restoration Act**

1. The *Smith* Decision. In the landmark case of *Department of Human Resources of Oregon v. Smith*, 494 U.S. 872 (1990), the U.S. Supreme Court addressed the question of whether Oregon's Employment Division violated the Free Exercise Clause by denying unemployment benefits to Native Americans who had been fired from their jobs for ingesting peyote. Oregon criminal law prohibited the knowing or intentional possession of a "controlled substance," such as peyote, and Oregon employment law denied unemployment benefits to employees fired for "misconduct." The Native Americans contended that they could not be denied unemployment benefits in accord with the Free Exercise Clause because they ingested the peyote for sacramental purposes at a church service.

By a 6 to 3 vote, the Supreme Court, overruling a decision by the Oregon Supreme Court, rejected the Free Exercise Clause claim. Writing for the Court, Justice Antonin Scalia asserted that the Native Americans challenging Oregon law sought to carry the meaning of "prohibiting the free exercise [of religion]" too far. He reasoned that so long as the prohibition on a religious practice is not "the object" of the government action, but merely "the incidental effect of a generally applicable and otherwise valid provision, the First Amendment has not been offended."

Justice O'Connor concurred in the judgment. She objected to the majority's creation of a "categorical" exception for generally applicable laws to the usual rule that impairments of religious rights can only be justified by "a compelling state interest and by means narrowly tailored to achieve that interest." While she thought the question was a "close one," she concluded that Oregon's enforcement of its law met this high standard. Three other justices dissented, arguing that enforcement of the Oregon law did not meet the compelling state interest test.

Many observers saw *Smith* as a dramatic departure from prior precedent. Historically, the Court had applied strict scrutiny in legal challenges to government actions that constrain religious practices, requiring a compelling state interest and no less restrictive alternative to serve that interest *See, e.g., Thomas v. Review Bd.*, 450 U.S. 707 (1981) (state may not deny unemployment compensation for refusal to work on military armaments due to religious convictions); *Sherbert v. Verner*, 374 U.S. 398 (1963) (violative of Free Exercise Clause for state to deny unemployment compensation to one discharged for conscientious refusal to work on the Sabbath). Whatever the merits of that debate, after 1990, *Smith* represents the law of the land, at least in constitutional law terms.

While the term "land use" was not mentioned in *Smith* (environmental protection, by contrast, was), the implications of this decision for regulation of the siting of churches and other religious institutions are straightforward and profound. Under

Smith, religious groups are entitled to no special consideration in the application of land use laws, and are not entitled to any exemption from general laws applicable to other landowners. Of course, religious organizations are still entitled to protection under the First Amendment from laws that target them for special treatment because of religion, and they can invoke the Due Process Clause and/or the Equal Protection Clause to challenge arbitrary or unequal treatment. But planners and local land use regulators, in drafting their plans and regulations, are not required to build in special accommodations for religious groups simply because they are religious groups. If a municipality is entitled to reject a proposed building because it would be too large for the neighborhood, it would not matter whether or not the applicant was a church. If a proposed land use change would generate an unacceptable level of traffic, the application can be denied on that basis without regard to whether the drivers were church goers or not.

The *Smith* decision was severely criticized by some religious organizations and others who believed that, in the land use arena and in other fields, local governments unduly interfered with the construction of churches, temples, mosques, and other religious institutions. The Court's traditional strict scrutiny test offered religious institutions a strong lever in negotiating with local communities for regulatory approvals and, if necessary, a basis for suing to compel communities to grant such approvals. The *Smith* decision, its critics contended, left religious institutions too vulnerable to burdensome regulation in all but the most egregious cases of overt religious discrimination. The *Smith* decision was the subject of much controversy and the focus of numerous congressional hearings. *See* Religious Freedom Restoration Act of 1991, Hearings on H.R. 2797 before the Subcommittee on Civil and Constitutional Rights of the House Committee on the Judiciary, 102d Cong., 2d Sess. (1993); The Religious Freedom Restoration Act, Hearing on S. 2969 before the Senate Committee on the Judiciary, 102d Cong., 2d Sess. (1993); Religious Freedom Restoration Act of 1990, Hearing on H.R. 5377 before the Subcommittee on Civil and Constitutional Rights of the House Committee on the Judiciary, 101st Cong., 2d Sess. (1991). The debate led to the enactment of the Religious Freedom Restoration Act of 1993, P.L. 103-141, discussed below.

2. *The Religious Freedom Restoration Act (RFRA)* In response to *Smith*, Congress passed RFRA for the explicit purpose of overturning the Court's ruling and restoring the strict scrutiny test that, according to the dissenters in *Smith* and some others, represented the law prior to *Smith*. The act states that "laws 'neutral' toward religion may burden religious exercise as surely as laws intended to interfere with religious exercise," and that "government should not substantially burden religious exercise without compelling justifications." Despite the fact that "the compelling interest test as set forth in Federal court rulings is a workable test for striking sensible balances between religious liberty and competing prior governmental interests," Congress complained, the *Smith* decision "virtually eliminated the requirement that the government justify burdens on religious exercise imposed by laws neutral toward religion." Accordingly, Congress adopted RFRA "to restore the compelling interest test as set forth in *Sherbert v. Verner,* 374 U.S. 398 (1963) and *Wisconsin v. Yoder,* 406 U.S. 205 (1972), and to guarantee its application in all cases where free exercise of religion is substantially burdened."

To carry out this new statutory policy, enforceable in court by any person whose religious exercise is burdened in violation of the act, Congress declared: "Government shall not substantially burden a person's exercise of religion, even if the burden results from a rule of general applicability," subject to the exception that the government may impose such a burden "if it demonstrates that application of the burden to the person (1) is in furtherance of a compelling governmental interest and (2) is the least restrictive means of furthering that compelling government interest." For the purpose of the act, government was defined to include every branch and official at every level of government, federal, state, or local.

While RFRA did not explicitly refer to land use regulation, it plainly applied to local land use regulators. Thus, to return to the example cited above, whereas a local government might well be able to impose a limitation on building size against land owners generally, it could do so in the case of a church only if it could show that the limitation served a compelling interest and was the least restrictive means to accomplish the government's objective. Likewise, whereas a restriction to control traffic levels in the community might ordinarily be enforceable, it could be enforced against religious institutions only if the government could show a compelling interest and that it was employing the least restrictive means.

Then, in 1997, in *City of Boerne v. Flores*, 521 U.S. 507 (1997), the Supreme Court declared RFRA unconstitutional as applied to state and local governments. Significantly, the *Boerne* case arose from a city's decision to deny a church a building permit. The case presents a complex question about the scope of Congress's legislative power under the Fourteenth Amendment that is tangential to the subject of this text, but the case nicely illustrates the kind of local regulation of church building Congress sought to address in RFRA.

■ CITY OF BOERNE v. FLORES,
521 U.S. 507 (1997)

Justice KENNEDY delivered the opinion of the Court.

A decision by local zoning authorities to deny a church a building permit was challenged under the Religious Freedom Restoration Act of 1993. The case calls into question the authority of Congress to enact RFRA. We conclude the statute exceeds Congress' power.

I

Situated on a hill in the city of Boerne, Texas, some 28 miles northwest of San Antonio, is St. Peter Catholic Church. Built in 1923, the church's structure replicates the mission style of the region's earlier history. The church seats about 230 worshippers, a number too small for its growing parish. Some 40 to 60 parishioners cannot be accommodated at some Sunday masses. In order to meet the needs of the congregation the Archbishop of San Antonio gave permission to the parish to plan alterations to enlarge the building.

A few months later, the Boerne City Council passed an ordinance authorizing the city's Historic Landmark Commission to prepare a preservation plan with proposed historic landmarks and districts. Under the ordinance, the commission must preapprove construction affecting historic landmarks or buildings in a historic district.

Soon afterwards, the Archbishop applied for a building permit so construction to enlarge the church could proceed. City authorities, relying on the ordinance and

D. Church and Worship Regulation

429

the designation of a historic district (which, they argued, included the church), denied the application. The Archbishop brought this suit challenging the permit denial. . . .

The Archbishop relied upon RFRA as one basis for relief from the refusal to issue the permit. The District Court concluded that by enacting RFRA Congress exceeded the scope of its enforcement power under §5 of the Fourteenth Amendment. The court certified its order for interlocutory appeal and the Fifth Circuit reversed, finding RFRA to be constitutional. We granted certiorari, and now reverse.

III

A

Under our Constitution, the Federal Government is one of enumerated powers. The judicial authority to determine the constitutionality of laws, in cases and controversies, is based on the premise that the "powers of the legislature are defined and limited; and that those limits may not be mistaken, or forgotten, the constitution is written."

Congress relied on its Fourteenth Amendment enforcement power in enacting the most far-reaching and substantial of RFRA's provisions, those which impose its requirements on the States. The Fourteenth Amendment provides, in relevant part:

Section 1. . . . No State shall make or enforce any law which shall abridge the privileges or immunities of citizens of the United States; nor shall any State deprive any person of life, liberty, or property, without due process of law, nor deny to any person within its jurisdiction the equal protection of the laws. . . .

Section 5. The Congress shall have power to enforce, by appropriate legislation, the provisions of this article.

The parties disagree over whether RFRA is a proper exercise of Congress' §5 power "to enforce" by "appropriate legislation" the constitutional guarantee that no State shall deprive any person of "life, liberty, or property, without due process of law" nor deny any person "equal protection of the laws."

In defense of the Act, respondent the Archbishop contends, with support from the United States, that RFRA is permissible enforcement legislation. Congress, it is said, is only protecting by legislation one of the liberties guaranteed by the Fourteenth Amendment's Due Process Clause, the free exercise of religion, beyond what is necessary under *Smith*. It is said the congressional decision to dispense with proof of deliberate or overt discrimination and instead concentrate on a law's effects accords with the settled understanding that §5 includes the power to enact legislation designed to prevent, as well as remedy, constitutional violations. It is further contended that Congress' §5 power is not limited to remedial or preventive legislation.

All must acknowledge that §5 is "a positive grant of legislative power" to Congress. In *Ex parte Virginia*, 100 U.S. 339, 345-346 (1879), we explained the scope of Congress' §5 power in the following broad terms: "Whatever legislation is appropriate, that is, adapted to carry out the objects the amendments have in view, whatever tends to enforce submission to the prohibitions they contain, and to secure to all persons the enjoyment of perfect equality of civil rights and the equal protection of the laws against State denial or invasion, if not prohibited, is brought within the domain of congressional power. Legislation which deters or remedies constitutional violations can fall within the sweep of Congress' enforcement power even if in the process it prohibits conduct which is not itself unconstitutional and intrudes into "'legislative spheres of autonomy previously reserved to the States.'" For example, the Court upheld a suspension of literacy tests and similar voting requirements under Congress' parallel power to enforce the provisions of the Fifteenth Amendment, *see* U.S. Const., Amdt. 15, §2, as a measure to combat racial discrimination in voting, despite the facial constitutionality of the tests under *Lassiter v. Northampton County Bd. of Elections*, 360 U.S. 45 (1959). We have also concluded that other measures protecting voting rights are within Congress' power to enforce the Fourteenth and Fifteenth Amendments, despite the burdens those measures placed on the States.

It is also true, however, that "[a]s broad as the congressional enforcement power is, it is not unlimited." In assessing the breadth of §5 enforcement power, we begin with its text. Congress has been given the power "to enforce" the "provisions of this article." We agree with respondent, of course, that Congress can enact legislation under §5 enforcing the constitutional right to the free exercise of religion. The "provisions of this article," to which §5 refers, include the Due Process Clause of the Fourteenth Amendment. Congress' power to enforce the Free Exercise Clause follows from our holding in *Cantwell v. Connecticut*, 310 U.S. 296, 303 (1940), that the "fundamental concept of liberty embodied in [the Fourteenth Amendment's Due Process Clause] embraces the liberties guaranteed by the First Amendment."

Congress' power under §5, however, extends only to "enforc[ing]" the provisions of the Fourteenth Amendment. The Court has described this power as "remedial." The design of the Amendment and the text of §5 are inconsistent with the suggestion that Congress has the power to decree the substance of the Fourteenth Amendment's restrictions on the States. Legislation which alters the meaning of the Free Exercise Clause cannot be said to be enforcing the Clause. Congress does not enforce a constitutional right by changing what the right is. It has been given the power "to enforce," not the power to determine what constitutes a constitutional violation. Were it not so, what Congress would be enforcing would no longer be, in any meaningful sense, the "provisions of [the Fourteenth Amendment]."

While the line between measures that remedy or prevent unconstitutional actions and measures that make a substantive change in the governing law is not easy to discern, and Congress must have wide latitude in determining where it lies, the distinction exists and must be observed. There must be a congruence and proportionality between the injury to be prevented or remedied and the means adopted to that end. Lacking such a connection, legislation may become substantive in operation and effect. History and our case law support drawing the distinction, one apparent from the text of the Amendment. . . .

The Fourteenth Amendment's history confirms the remedial, rather than substantive, nature of the Enforcement Clause. . . . The remedial and preventive nature of Congress' enforcement power, and the limitation inherent in the power, were confirmed in our earliest cases on the Fourteenth Amendment. . . .

If Congress could define its own powers by altering the Fourteenth Amendment's meaning, no longer would the Constitution be "superior paramount law, unchangeable by ordinary means." It would be "on a level with ordinary legislative acts, and, like other acts, . . . alterable when the legislature shall please to alter it." *Marbury v. Madison*, 2 L. Ed. 60. Under this approach, it is difficult to conceive of a principle that would limit congressional power. Shifting legislative majorities could change the Constitution and effectively circumvent the difficult and detailed amendment process contained in Article V.

We now turn to consider whether RFRA can be considered enforcement legislation under §5 of the Fourteenth Amendment.

B

Respondent contends that RFRA is a proper exercise of Congress' remedial or preventive power. The Act, it is said, is a reasonable means of protecting the free exercise of religion as defined by *Smith*. It prevents and remedies laws which are enacted with the unconstitutional object of targeting religious beliefs and practices. To avoid the difficulty of proving such violations, it is said, Congress can simply invalidate any law which imposes a substantial burden on a religious practice unless it is justified by a compelling interest and is the least restrictive means of accomplishing that interest. If Congress can prohibit laws with discriminatory effects in order to prevent racial discrimination in violation of the Equal Protection Clause, then it can do the same, respondent argues, to promote religious liberty.

While preventive rules are sometimes appropriate remedial measures, there must be a congruence between the means used and the ends to be achieved. The appropriateness of remedial measures must be considered in light of the evil presented. Strong measures appropriate to address one harm may be an unwarranted response to another, lesser one.

A comparison between RFRA and the Voting Rights Act is instructive. In contrast to the record which confronted Congress and the Judiciary in the voting rights cases, RFRA's legislative record lacks examples of modern instances of generally applicable laws passed because of religious bigotry. The history of persecution in this country detailed in the hearings mentions no episodes occurring in the past 40 years. The absence of more recent episodes stems from the fact that, as one witness testified, "deliberate persecution is not the usual problem in this country." "[L]aws directly targeting religious practices have become increasingly rare." Rather, the emphasis of the hearings was on laws of general applicability which place incidental burdens on religion. Much of the discussion centered upon anecdotal evidence of autopsies performed on Jewish individuals and Hmong immigrants in violation of their religious beliefs, and on zoning regulations and historic preservation laws (like the one at issue here), which, as an incident of their normal operation, have adverse effects on churches and synagogues. It is difficult to maintain that they are examples of legislation enacted or enforced due to animus or hostility to the burdened religious practices or that they indicate some widespread pattern of religious discrimination in this country. Congress' concern was with the incidental burdens imposed, not the object or purpose of the legislation. This lack of support in the legislative record, however, is not RFRA's most serious shortcoming. Judicial deference, in most cases, is based not on the state of the legislative record Congress compiles but "on due regard for the decision of the body constitutionally appointed to decide." As a general matter, it is for Congress to determine the method by which it will reach a decision.

Regardless of the state of the legislative record, RFRA cannot be considered remedial, preventive legislation, if those terms are to have any meaning. RFRA is so out of proportion to a supposed remedial or preventive object that it cannot be understood as responsive to, or designed to prevent, unconstitutional behavior. It appears, instead, to attempt a substantive change in constitutional protections. Preventive measures prohibiting certain types of laws may be appropriate when there is reason to believe that many of the laws affected by the congressional enactment have a significant likelihood of being unconstitutional. Remedial legislation under §5 "should be adapted to the mischief and wrong which the [Fourteenth] [A]mendment was intended to provide against."

RFRA is not so confined. Sweeping coverage ensures its intrusion at every level of government, displacing laws and prohibiting official actions of almost every description and regardless of subject matter. RFRA's restrictions apply to every agency and official of the Federal, State, and local Governments. RFRA applies to all federal and state law, statutory or otherwise, whether adopted before or after its enactment. RFRA has no termination date or termination mechanism. Any law is subject to challenge at any time by any individual who alleges a substantial burden on his or her free exercise of religion. . . .

The stringent test RFRA demands of state laws reflects a lack of proportionality or congruence between the means adopted and the legitimate end to be achieved. If an objector can show a substantial burden on his free exercise, the State must demonstrate a compelling governmental interest and show that the law is the least restrictive means of furthering its interest. Claims that a law substantially burdens someone's exercise of religion will often be difficult to contest. Requiring a State to demonstrate a compelling interest and show that it has adopted the least restrictive means of achieving that interest is the most demanding test known to constitutional law. If "'compelling interest' really means what it says . . . , many laws will not meet the test. . . . [The test] would open the prospect of constitutionally required religious exemptions from civic obligations of almost every conceivable kind." Laws valid under *Smith* would fall under RFRA without regard to whether they had the object of stifling or punishing free exercise. We make these observations not to reargue the position of the majority in *Smith* but to illustrate the substantive alteration of its holding attempted by RFRA. Even assuming RFRA would be interpreted in effect to mandate some lesser test, say, one equivalent to intermediate scrutiny, the statute nevertheless would require searching judicial scrutiny of state law with the attendant likelihood of invalidation. This is a considerable congressional intrusion into the States' traditional prerogatives and general authority to regulate for the health and welfare of their citizens.

The substantial costs RFRA exacts, both in practical terms of imposing a heavy litigation burden on the States and in terms of curtailing their traditional general regulatory power, far exceed any pattern or practice of unconstitutional conduct under the Free Exercise Clause as interpreted in *Smith*. Simply put, RFRA is not designed to identify and counteract state laws likely to be unconstitutional because of their treatment of religion. In most cases, the state laws to which RFRA applies are not ones which will have been motivated by religious bigotry. If a state law disproportionately burdened a particular class of religious observers, this circumstance might be evidence of an impermissible legislative motive. RFRA's substantial-burden test, however, is not even a discriminatory effects or disparate-impact test. It is a reality of the modern regulatory state that numerous state laws, such as the zoning regulations at issue here, impose a substantial burden on a large class of individuals. When the exercise of religion has been burdened in an incidental way by a law of general application, it does not follow that the persons affected have been burdened any more than other citizens, let alone burdened because of their religious beliefs. In addition, the Act imposes in every case a least restrictive means requirement — a requirement that was not used in the pre-*Smith* jurisprudence RFRA purported to codify — which also indicates that the legislation is broader than is appropriate if the goal is to prevent and remedy constitutional violations. . . .

Our national experience teaches that the Constitution is preserved best when each part of the Government respects both the Constitution and the proper actions and determinations of the other branches. When the Court has interpreted the Constitution, it has acted within the province of the Judicial Branch, which embraces the duty to say what the law is. When the political branches of the Government act against the background of a judicial interpretation of the Constitution already issued, it must be understood that in later cases and controversies the Court will treat its precedents with the respect due them under settled principles, including *stare decisis,* and contrary expectations must be disappointed. RFRA was designed to control cases and controversies, such as the one before us; but as the provisions of the federal statute here invoked are beyond congressional authority, it is this Court's precedent, not RFRA, which must control.

It is for Congress in the first instance to "determin[e] whether and what legislation is needed to secure the guarantees of the Fourteenth Amendment," and its conclusions are entitled to much deference. Congress' discretion is not unlimited, however, and the courts retain the power, as they have since *Marbury v. Madison,* to determine if Congress has exceeded its authority under the Constitution. Broad as the power of Congress is under the Enforcement Clause of the Fourteenth Amendment, RFRA contradicts vital principles necessary to maintain separation of powers and the federal balance. The judgment of the Court of Appeals sustaining the Act's constitutionality is reversed.

It is so ordered.

Justice STEVENS, concurring.

In my opinion, the Religious Freedom Restoration Act of 1993 (RFRA) is a "law respecting an establishment of religion" that violates the First Amendment to the Constitution.

If the historic landmark on the hill in Boerne happened to be a museum or an art gallery owned by an atheist, it would not be eligible for an exemption from the city ordinances that forbid an enlargement of the structure. Because the landmark is owned by the Catholic Church, it is claimed that RFRA gives its owner a federal statutory entitlement to an exemption from a generally applicable, neutral civil law. Whether the Church would actually prevail under the statute or not, the statute has provided the Church with a legal weapon that no atheist or agnostic can obtain. This governmental preference for religion, as opposed to irreligion, is forbidden by the First Amendment.

Justice SCALIA with whom Justice STEVENS joined, concurred in part. Justices O'CONNOR, BREYER, and SOUTER dissented.

Notes and Comment

1. *RFRA and the Federal Government.* The Court in *Boerne* held that RFRA was unconstitutional as applied to the states and their subdivisions based on §5 of the Fourteenth Amendment. The Court has never expressly addressed the constitutionality of RFRA as applied to the federal government, and some of the logic of *Boerne* suggests that the Court's holding should not apply to it. In *Gonzales v. O'Centro Espirita Beneficente Unia Do*, 546 U.S. 418 (2006), the Court upheld a RFRA claim by a religion against the federal government, applying a robust reading of the statute without questioning the act's constitutionality. *See also Burwell v. Hobby Lobby*, 134 S. Ct. 2751 (2014) (holding, by a 5-to-4 vote, that RFRA creates an exemption from the contraceptive mandate under the Affordable Care Act (ACA) requiring employers to cover certain contraceptives for their female employees). With RFRA confined to the federal government as a result of *Boerne*, the act likely will have minimal effects on land use law and policy — except in the context of federal land management. *See, e.g, Navajo Nation v. U.S. Forest Serv.*, 535 F.3d 1058 (9th Cir. 2008) (en banc ruling that Forest Service did not violate RFRA in authorizing the use of recycled wastewater to make artificial snow for a commercial ski resort located on a mountain considered sacred by tribes).

2. *RFRA and the Establishment Clause.* Justice Stevens' concurring opinion in *Boerne* raises the fascinating question of whether Congress's efforts to bolster rights under the Free Exercise Clause may go so far as to create an Establishment Clause problem. In *Cutter v. Wilkinson*, 544 U.S. 709 (2005), the Supreme Court rejected a facial challenge under the Establishment Clause to §3 of RLUIPA, addressing burdens on religious exercise by "institutionalized persons." The Court ruled that statutory efforts to lessen governmental burdens on religion do not necessarily run afoul of the Establishment Clause, stating, "[t]his Court has long recognized that the government may . . . accommodate religious practices . . . without violating the Establishment Clause." The Court stressed that there is "play in the joints" between the Free Exercise Clause and the Establishment Clause, permitting the government "to accommodate religion beyond free exercise requirements, without offending the Establishment Clause." However, the *Cutter* Court stressed that it was presented with only a facial claim and that it might reach a different result in an as applied Establishment Clause case, depending on the facts of the case.

3. *State RFRAs.* A number of states filled the gap in coverage created by the *Boerne* decision by adopting state-level religious freedom restoration acts. According to the National Conference of State Legislatures, 21 states have enacted state RFRAs. *See* http://www.ncsl.org/research/civil-and-criminal-justice/state-rfra-statutes.aspx (last visited July 18, 2016). These laws generally are intended to parallel the federal RFRA, but are not necessarily identical to the federal law. *See, e.g.,* Ariz. Rev. Stat. §41-1493.01; Conn. Gen. Stats. §52-571b; La. Rev. Stat. §13:5231 *et seq.*

4. *Texas.* The Texas Religious Freedom Restoration Act (TRFRA), Tex. Civ. Prac. & Rem. Code §110.003(a)-(b), provides that "a government agency may not substantially burden a person's free exercise of religion [unless it] demonstrates that the application of the burden to the person . . . is in furtherance of a compelling governmental interest [and] is the least restrictive means of furthering that interest." A pastor, Richard Wayne Barr, began a religious halfway house in the City of Sinton, Texas, to offer housing, biblical instruction, and counseling to low-level

offenders released from prison on probation or parole. In response, the city council adopted an ordinance, providing that: "A correctional or rehabilitation facility may not be located in the City of Sinton within 1000 feet of a residential area, a primary or secondary school, property designated as a public park or public recreation area by any governmental authority, or a church, synagogue, or other place of worship." In *Barr v. City of Sinton*, 295 S.W.3d 287 (Tex. 2009), reversing the Texas Court of Appeals, the Texas Supreme Court ruled that TRFA's strict scrutiny applies to local zoning regulations. Furthermore, the court ruled that the ordinance was invalid under TRFA because it imposed a substantial burden on Barr's ministry, and the city failed to demonstrate either that the ordinance served a compelling governmental interest or that it employed the least restrictive means to accomplish its goal.

5. *Other State RFRA Litigation.* State RFRA legislation is a common subject of litigation, in both federal and state courts across the country. *See, e.g., World Outreach Conference Ctr. v. City of Chicago*, 591 F.3d 531 (7th Cir. 2009) (ruling that a local land use regulation imposed a substantial burden under the Illinois RFRA); *St. John's United Church of Christ v. City of Chicago*, 502 F.3d 616 (7th Cir. 2007) (amendment to Illinois Religious Freedom Restoration Act (IRFRA) did not violate religious cemetery's rights under Free Exercise Clause); *Warner v. City of Boca Raton*, 420 F.3d 1308 (11th Cir. 2005) (sustaining ordinance restricting vertical grave decorations against challenges pursuant to the Florida RFRA).

6. *Academic Commentary.* The State RFRA's have been the focus of substantial academic commentary. *See, e.g.,* Steven D. Ginsberg and Natalie J. Carlos, Zoning in Florida Under the Religious Freedom Restoration Acts: What City Officials Should Watch Out For in Defending Their Ordinances Against Freedom of Religion Claims, 12 St. Thomas L. Rev. 157 (1999); James A. Hanson, Law Summary—Missouri's Religious Freedom Restoration Act: A New Approach to the Cause of Conscience, 69 Mo. L. Rev. 853 (2004); Douglas Laycock, State RFRAs and Land Use Regulation, 32 U.C. Davis L. Rev. 755 (1999).

7. *Strict Scrutiny Under State Constitutions.* Some states have interpreted their state constitutional free exercise provisions to require strict scrutiny of local regulation affecting religion. *City Chapel Evangelical Free, Inc. v. City of South Bend*, 744 N.E.2d 443 (Ind. 2001) (city condemnation of church building subject to defense based upon burden on religious liberty).

A Note on the Religious Land Use and Institutionalized Persons Act

In 2000, in the aftermath of the decision in *Boerne*, Congress enacted the Religious Land Use and Institutionalized Persons Act (RLUIPA). *See* 42 U.S.C. §2000cc. This second act has a much narrower focus than RFRA, and deals only with "land use as a religious exercise" and the religious practices of "institutionalized persons." It omits any direct reference to the *Smith* decision and does not seek (at least explicitly) to implement any particular reading of the Free Exercise Clause. The act establishes a "general rule" that:

> No government shall impose or implement a land use regulation in a manner that imposes a substantial burden on the religious exercise of a person, including a religious assembly or institution, unless the government demonstrates that imposition of the burden on that person, assembly or institution (A) is in furtherance of a compelling

governmental interest; and (B) is the least restrictive means of furthering that compelling governmental interest.

42 U.S.C. §2000cc(a)(1)(A)-(B).

The act carefully defines the types of regulations to which the land use provision applies. The "general rule" applies to the "burden" resulting from a land use rule of general applicability when the burden is imposed by a program or activity that receives federal financial assistance. It also applies in the situation where the substantial burden "affects, or removal of that substantial burden would affect, commerce with foreign nations, among the several States, or with Indian tribes, even if the burden results from a rule of general applicability." Finally, the general rule applies when the land use regulatory process that permits "the government to make . . . individualized assessments of the proposed uses for the property involved." These provisions were carefully crafted to avoid some of the Court's statements in *Boerne* about what constitutes permissible remedial legislation under the Fourteenth Amendment and the identified constitutional defects with RFRA. Do you see how?

RLUIPA also includes a number of other targeted provisions designed to protect religion from land use regulators. Under the heading of "equal terms," RLUIPA states that "[n]o government shall impose or implement a land use regulation in a manner that treats a religious assembly or institution on less than equal terms with a nonreligious assembly or institution." Under the heading of "nondiscrimination" the act states that "[n]o government shall impose or implement a land use regulation that discriminates against any assembly or institution on the basis of religion or religious denomination." In addition, the act provides that, "[n]o government shall impose or implement a land use regulation that (A) totally excludes religious assemblies from a jurisdiction; or (B) unreasonably limits religious assemblies, institutions, or structures within a jurisdiction."

The last noteworthy provision of RLUIPA in the context of land use regulation reads as follows:

> A government may avoid the preemptive force of any provision of this Act by changing the policy or practice that results in a substantial burden on religious exercise, by retaining the policy or practice and exempting the substantially burdened religious exercise, by providing exemptions from the policy or practice for applications that substantially burden religious exercise, or by any other means that eliminates the substantial burden.

42 U.S.C. §2000cc(3)(e). RLUIPA has generated a great deal of litigation in the lower federal courts. Two important decisions illustrating divergent approaches to interpretation of the act are excerpted below.

■ CIVIL LIBERTIES FOR URBAN BELIEVERS v. CITY OF CHICAGO
342 F.3d 752 (7th Cir. 2003)

BAUER, Circuit Judge

Appellants, an association of Chicago-area churches and five individual member churches thereof, appeal from the district court's entry of summary judgment in favor of Appellee, the City of Chicago, on Appellants' claims challenging the Chicago Zoning Ordinance ("CZO"), under the federal Religious Land Use and Institutionalized Persons Act ("RLUIPA") and the United States Constitution. For the reasons set forth below, we affirm the decision of the district court.

The CZO broadly divides the city into R, B, C, and M zones for residential, business, commercial, and manufacturing uses, respectively. Each zone, in turn, is subdivided into numbered districts and subdistricts. A majority of Chicago land available for development is zoned R. . . . Churches are permitted uses as of right in all R zones, but are termed Variations in the Nature of Special Uses ("Special Use") in all B zones as well as C1, C2, C3, and C5 districts. All Special Uses, whether of a religious or nonreligious nature, require approval by the Zoning Board of Appeals ("ZBA") following a public hearing. Special Use approval is expressly conditioned upon the design, location, and operation of the proposed use consistent with the protection of public health, safety, and welfare, and the proposed use must not substantially injure the value of neighboring property. Factoring such expenses as application, title search, and legal fees, as well as appraisal and neighbor notification costs, the aggregate cost of obtaining Special Use approval approaches $5000. Before a church may locate in a C4 district or an M zone, the Chicago City Council must vote in favor of a Map Amendment, effectively rezoning the targeted parcel. Development for church use of land consisting of two or more acres (necessary for congregations exceeding roughly 500 members) requires approval by City Council vote of a Planned Development.

Civil Liberties for Urban Believers ("CLUB") is an unincorporated association of 40 to 50 Chicago-area religious or not-for-profit Illinois corporations ranging in size from 15 to 15,000 congregants. Five of these individual member churches joined CLUB as plaintiffs in an action challenging the validity of the CZO. The district court summarized as follows the encounters of the five individual plaintiff churches with Chicago's zoning framework as alleged in Appellants' complaint:

> Christ Center began meeting in a high school auditorium in 1990, but soon experienced difficulties at this location due to various school functions that interrupted weekly worship. As a result, Christ Center began searching for a building to purchase. The church was unsuccessful in locating an appropriate building in any R districts. In the summer of 1992, Christ Center located a suitable building at 1139-43 West Madison in Chicago. The building was located in a C district and Christ Center promptly applied for a special use permit. After completing the application process, Christ Center reached out to gain the support of neighbors and Alderman Theodore Mazola. Most neighbors favored a taxpaying entity in the neighborhood rather than a church and Alderman Mazola stated that he would support the church's special use permit on any street but Madison. The Zoning Board eventually convened a special hearing on September 18, 1992. On October 18, 1992, the special use permit was denied. Christ Center subsequently found a second building in an M district at 123 South Morgan. The owner of the building also agreed to provide financing. However, the Chicago Department of Planning and Development informed Christ Center that it would oppose any rezoning application because the particular area was designated to become an entertainment area and the presence of a church would inhibit such development. Christ Center subsequently choose not to file an application for rezoning. In the fall of 1993, Christ Center obtained property at 4445 South King Drive, successfully obtained a special use permit and now operates a church at this location. Christ Center now claims that it paid substantial sums in attorneys fees, appraisal fees, zoning application charges, title

charges and other expenses attempting to find suitable property. [Other complaint summaries are omitted.] . . .

In February 2000, in response to Appellants' remaining constitutional challenges to the CZO's designation of churches vis-à-vis various nonreligious assembly uses in B, C, and M zones, the City Council amended the CZO to require clubs, lodges, meeting halls, recreation buildings, and community centers to obtain Special Use approval in order to locate within any B and C zones and a Map Amendment in order to locate within any M zone. The amendments also (i) exempt churches from the requirement that a Special Use applicant affirmatively demonstrate that the proposed use "is necessary for the public convenience at that location" and (ii) provide that a Special Use permit shall automatically issue in the event that the ZBA fails to render a decision within 120 days of the date of application. Several months thereafter, Congress reacted to the Supreme Court's decision in *City of Boerne* with the enactment of RLUIPA and Appellants subsequently amended their complaint once more to include claims against Chicago pursuant to RLUIPA. . . .

In granting summary judgment in favor of Chicago, the district court determined that the February 2000 amendments to the CZO removed "any potential substantial burden" on religious exercise. . . .

Appellants argue that the CZO violates RLUIPA's substantial burden provision, which requires land-use regulations that substantially burden religious exercise to be the least restrictive means of advancing a compelling government interest, as well as its nondiscrimination provision, which prohibits land-use regulations that either disfavor religious uses relative to nonreligious uses or unreasonably exclude religious uses from a particular jurisdiction.

In order to prevail on a claim under the substantial burden provision, a plaintiff must first demonstrate that the regulation at issue actually imposes a substantial burden on religious exercise. RLUIPA defines "religious exercise" to encompass "any exercise of religion, whether or not compelled by, or central to, a system of religious belief," including "[t]he use, building, or conversion of real property for the purpose of religious exercise." This definition reveals Congress's intent to expand the concept of religious exercise contemplated both in decisions discussing the precursory RFRA . . . and in traditional First Amendment jurisprudence . . .

Although the text of the statute contains no similar express definition of the term "substantial burden," RLUIPA's legislative history indicates that it is to be interpreted by reference to RFRA and First Amendment jurisprudence. ("The term 'substantial burden' as used in this Act is not intended to be given any broader interpretation than the Supreme Court's articulation of the concept of substantial burden on religious exercise."). Chicago cites a decision of this Court which held that, within the meaning of RFRA, a substantial burden on religious exercise "is one that forces adherents of a religion to refrain from religiously motivated conduct, inhibits or constrains conduct or expression that manifests a central tenet of a person's religious beliefs, or compels conduct or expression that is contrary to those beliefs." Substituting RLUIPA's broader definition of religious exercise, which need not be "compelled by or central to" a particular religion, . . . the meaning of "substantial burden on religious exercise" could be read to include the effect of any regulation that "inhibits or constrains the use, building, or conversion of real property for the purpose of religious exercise." Such a construction might lend support to Appellant's contention that the CZO, insofar as it contributes to other existing constraints upon the use of specific parcels as churches, substantially burdens religious exercise. However, this cannot be the correct construction of "substantial burden on religious exercise" under RLUIPA. Application of the substantial burden provision to a regulation inhibiting or constraining *any* religious exercise, including the use of property for religious purposes, would render meaningless the word "substantial," because the slightest obstacle to religious exercise incidental to the regulation of land use — however minor the burden it were to impose — could then constitute a burden sufficient to trigger RLUIPA's requirement that the regulation advance a compelling governmental interest by the least restrictive means. We therefore hold that, in the context of RLUIPA's broad definition of religious exercise, a land-use regulation that imposes a substantial burden on religious exercise is one that necessarily bears direct, primary, and fundamental responsibility for rendering religious exercise — including the use of real property for the purpose thereof within the regulated jurisdiction generally — effectively impracticable.

Appellants contend that the scarcity of affordable land available for development in R zones, along with the costs, procedural requirements, and inherent political aspects of the Special Use, Map Amendment, and Planned Development approval processes, impose precisely such a substantial burden. However, we find that these conditions — which are incidental to any high-density urban land use — do not amount to a substantial burden on religious exercise. While they may contribute to the ordinary difficulties associated with location (by any person or entity, religious or nonreligious) in a large city, they do not render impracticable the use of real property in Chicago for religious exercise, much less discourage churches from locating or attempting to locate in Chicago. . . . Significantly, each of the five individual plaintiff churches has successfully located within Chicago's city limits. That they expended considerable time and money so to do does not entitle them to relief under RLUIPA's substantial burden provision. . . . Otherwise, compliance with RLUIPA would require municipal governments not merely to treat religious land uses on an equal footing with nonreligious land uses, but rather to favor them in the form of an outright exemption from land-use regulations. Unfortunately for Appellants, no such free pass for religious land uses masquerades among the legitimate protections RLUIPA affords to religious exercise.

Though the substantial burden and nondiscrimination provisions are operatively independent of one another, RLUIPA's governmental discretion provision, upon which the district court relied in order to find that the February 2000 CZO amendments corrected any violation of the substantial burden provision, appears not to reflect this distinction. That subsection provides, in part, that "a government may avoid the preemptive force of *any provision* of [RLUIPA] by changing the policy or practice *that results in a substantial burden* on religious exercise" (emphasis added). Rather than remove any substantial burden on religious exercise, however, the February 2000 amendments simply place churches on an equal footing with nonreligious assembly uses, thereby correcting any potential violation of the nondiscrimination provision. Despite subsection 2000cc-3(e)'s reference to removal of a "substantial burden," we read it to afford a government the discretion to take corrective action to eliminate a nondiscrimination provision violation, whether or not it was the result of a substantial burden on religious exercise. Thus do we find that, under RLUIPA's governmental discretion provision, the February 2000 amendments to the CZO render RLUIPA's nondiscrimination provision inapplicable to this case.

Insofar as Appellants cannot demonstrate on these facts that the CZO substantially burdens religious exercise, and because the February 2000 Amendments to the CZO bring it into compliance with RLUIPA's nondiscrimination provision, Appellants fail to make a sufficient showing on essential elements of their RLUIPA claims. Chicago is therefore entitled to summary judgment on those claims.

Having found RLUIPA inapplicable to the facts of this case, we need not address the issue of RLUIPA's constitutionality, raised by the parties as well as the United States of America, as Intervenor, and various Amici Curiae. . . .

■ GURU NANAK SIKH SOCIETY OF YUBA CITY v. COUNTY OF SUTTER
456 F.3d 978 (9th Cir. 2006)

BEA, Circuit Judge:

We must decide whether a local government's denial of a religious group's application for a conditional use permit to construct a temple on a parcel of land zoned "agricultural" constituted a "substantial burden" under RLUIPA. . . . We find that the County imposed a substantial burden on Guru Nanak Sikh Society of Yuba City's ("Guru Nanak's") religious exercise under RLUIPA because the stated reasons and history behind the denial at issue, and a previous denial of Guru Nanak's application to build a temple on a parcel of land zoned "residential," to a significantly great extent lessened the possibility of Guru Nanak constructing a temple in the future. We also decide that the County did not assert, much less prove, compelling interests for its action; last, we find the relevant portion of RLUIPA is a permissible exercise of Congress's remedial power under Section Five of the Fourteenth Amendment.

Guru Nanak is a non-profit organization dedicated to fostering the teachings and practices of the Sikh religion. In 2001, Guru Nanak attempted to obtain a conditional use permit (CUP) for the construction of a Sikh temple — a gurudwara — on its 1.89-acre property on Grove Road in Yuba City ("the Grove Road property"). The proposed use included about 5,000 square feet dedicated to an assembly area and related activities. The proposed temple site would have held religious ceremonies for no more than seventy-five people at a time. The Grove Road property was in an area designated for low-density residential use (R-1), intended mainly for large lot single family residences; churches and temples are only conditionally permitted in R-1 districts, through issuance of a CUP.

The Sutter County Planning Division, part of the County Community Services Department, issued a report recommending that the Planning Commission grant a CUP for the Grove Road property. The report stated that while the permit presented potential conflicts with established residences in the area, the conflicts could be minimized by specifically recommended conditions that would be consistent with the General Plan of Sutter County. However, at a public meeting, the Planning Commission voted unanimously to deny the CUP. The denial was based on citizens' voiced fears that the resulting noise and traffic would interfere with the existing neighborhood. Following the Commission's denial, Guru Nanak began searching for a different parcel of property for the proposed temple.

In 2002, Guru Nanak acquired the property at issue in this case, a 28.79-acre parcel located on George Washington Boulevard in an unincorporated area of the County, to build a temple there. The site is zoned "AG" (general agricultural district) in the Sutter County Zoning Code. As in R-1 districts, churches and temples are only conditionally permitted in AG districts, through issuance of a CUP. The parcel includes a walnut orchard and an existing 2,300 square foot single family residence, which Guru Nanak proposed to convert into a Sikh temple by increasing the size of the building by approximately 500 square feet. All of the surrounding properties have identical zoning designations and have orchards. The nearest residence to the property is at least 200 feet north of the parcel's northern boundary. The residence to be converted into the temple is located 105 feet south of that northern boundary.

Another Sikh temple already exists on a ten-acre parcel of land zoned "agricultural" located next to Bogue Road, less than a mile southeast from the proposed temple's parcel. Within Yuba City's sphere of influence, the Bogue Road Sikh temple is surrounded by land zoned "agricultural."

Guru Nanak filed an application for a CUP to build a temple limited to approximately 2,850 square feet on the proposed site. The proposed use of the property was for a Sikh temple, assembly hall, worship services, and weddings. As with the Grove Road property, the proposed facility was intended to accommodate religious services of no more than seventy-five people at a time. Various county and state departments reviewed Guru Nanak's application and added a variety of conditions regarding the environmental impact of the proposed use including a twenty-five foot "no development" buffer along the north side of the property, a requirement that ceremonies remain indoors, and required landscaping.

Guru Nanak had to accept these conditions to receive the Planning Division's recommendation to the Planning Commission. The Planning Division issued a "mitigated negative declaration" (i.e. that the proposed temple would not create a significant environment impact) because "although the proposed [temple] could have a significant impact on the environment[,] . . . the recommended mitigation measures would reduce the possible impacts to a less-than-significant level." The Planning Division cited the temple's maximum attendance of 75 people, minor building conversion, and stipulated mitigation measures as reasons for finding a less-than-significant impact on the environment.

The Planning Commission held a public meeting to consider Guru Nanak's permit application. A member of Guru Nanak testified that while its previous application was for a 1.9-acre lot in a residential area, the subject application pertained to a 28.8-acre lot that did not border anyone's front or back yard. He also stated that Guru Nanak would accept all the Planning Division's proposed conditions on the land's use. Various potential neighbors spoke against the proposed temple, complaining mainly that the temple would increase traffic and noise, interfere with the agricultural use of their land, and lower property values. The Commission approved the application 4-3, subject to the conditions required by the Planning Division and stipulated to by Guru Nanak, with the commissioners echoing the reasoning voiced by both sides.

Several neighbors filed timely appeals to the Sutter County Board of Supervisors. The Planning Division filed another report in response to the appeals, addressing the specific complaints of the concerned neighbors and continuing to recommend approval of Guru Nanak's CUP application. Subject to revised mitigation conditions including an expanded one-hundred foot setback, the Planning Division found that the proposed temple's effect on neighbors' pesticide spraying, nearby traffic, and noise levels would be minimal. . . .

The four-member Board of Supervisors unanimously reversed the Planning Commission's approval and denied Guru Nanak's application. Supervisor Kroon flatly rejected the project based on the "right to farm": the property had been agricultural and should remain so. He argued that long-time farmers should not be affected by someone who wishes to change the use of the property. Supervisor Nelson stated that he was concerned that Guru Nanak's proposed use "was too far away from the city" and would not promote orderly growth. He commented that such development is detrimental to the surrounding agricultural uses and that Guru Nanak should locate its church nearer to his and other existing churches. Supervisors Munger and Silva agreed that the proposed temple site's separation from existing infrastructure, termed "leapfrog development," was a poor idea and denied the application on that ground.

The Sutter County General Plan is a long-term guide for physical development of land within the County. The Plan empowers the County's Community Services Department to ensure that "new development adjacent to agricultural areas be designed to minimize conflicts with adjacent agricultural uses." The Plan disfavors development not contiguous to areas currently designated for urban or suburban uses—leapfrog development—because it "has the potential to create land use conflicts and, in most instances, make [s] the provision of services more difficult."

The Sutter County Zoning Code designates twenty-two types of districts. Within each of these districts, the Code categorizes uses as "permitted" as a matter of right, uses that require a "zoning clearance," or uses that require a use permit. Zoning clearance uses need only the review and approval of the Community Services Director. Conditional use permit uses require a more comprehensive review through the Sutter County Planning Commission, and require a public hearing. A church must apply for a CUP to locate within any district available to it. Six of the twenty-two types of districts are made available to churches through the Zoning Code: general agricultural (AG); food processing, agricultural and recreation combining (FPARC); one-family residence (R-1), two-family residence (R-2), neighborhood apartment (R-3), and general apartment (R-4).

The district court granted summary judgment for Guru Nanak because it concluded the County substantially burdened Guru Nanak's religious exercise, and that the County did not proffer evidence of compelling interests to justify such burden. The district court reasoned that "[t]o meet the 'substantial burden' standard, the governmental conduct being challenged must actually inhibit religious activity in a concrete way, and cause more than a mere inconvenience." Applying its definition of the substantial burden standard to the facts, the district court held that "the denial of the use permit, particularly when coupled with the denial of [Guru Nanak's] previous application, actually inhibits [Guru Nanak's] religious exercise." . . .

This court reviews de novo the district court's order granting summary judgment. In reviewing the district court decision, "we must determine, viewing the evidence in the light most favorable to the nonmoving party, 'whether there are any genuine issues of material fact and whether the district court correctly applied the relevant substantive law.'"

We decide that the County made an individualized assessment of Guru Nanak's CUP, thereby making RLUIPA applicable, and that the County's denial of Guru

Nanak's CUP application constituted a substantial burden, as that phrase is defined by RLUIPA.

RLUIPA is Congress's latest effort to protect the free exercise of religion guaranteed by the First Amendment from governmental regulation. . . . Before we apply the terms of RLUIPA, of course, we first must determine if RLUIPA even applies, by examining whether the actions of the County are "individualized assessments of the proposed uses for the property involved." The County argues that its denial of Guru Nanak's second CUP application falls outside the legislative scope of RLUIPA because its use permit process is a neutral law of general applicability. However, the plain meaning of §2000cc(2)(c) belies this contention. RLUIPA applies when the government may take into account the particular details of an applicant's proposed use of land when deciding to permit or deny that use.

The Sutter County Zoning Code does not permit churches as a matter of right in any of the six types of zoned areas available for church construction. Rather, an entity intending to build a church must first apply for a CUP and be approved by the County. The Zoning Code states, "The County realizes that certain uses . . . may have the potential to negatively impact adjoining properties and uses. Such uses therefore require a more comprehensive review and approval procedure in order to evaluate and mitigate any potentially detrimental impacts." The Zoning Code also outlines how the Sutter County Planning Commission, which has original jurisdiction over such use applications, should determine whether to approve or reject an application:

> The Planning Commission may approve or conditionally approve a use permit if it finds that the establishment, maintenance, or operation of the use or building applied for will or will not, under the circumstances of the particular case, be detrimental to the health, safety, and general welfare of persons residing or working in the neighborhood of such proposed use, or be detrimental or injurious to property and improvement in the neighborhood or to the general welfare of the County. Additionally, the Commission shall find that the use or activity approved by the use permit is consistent with the General Plan [of Sutter County].

The County Board of Supervisors reviews the Planning Commission's conditional use decisions "de novo and all applications, papers, maps, exhibits and staff recommendations made or presented to the Planning Commission may be considered." The Sutter County Zoning Code directs the Planning Commission and the Board of Supervisors to "implement [its] system of land use regulations [by making] individualized assessments of the proposed uses of the land involved."

By its own terms, it appears that RLUIPA does not apply directly to land use regulations, such as the Zoning Code here, which typically are written in general and neutral terms. However, when the Zoning Code is applied to grant or deny a certain use to a particular parcel of land, that application is an "implementation" under 42 U.S.C. §2000cc(2)(c). That is to say, land use regulations through zoning codes necessarily involve case-by-case evaluations of the propriety of proposed activity against extant land use regulations. RLUIPA therefore governs the actions of the County in this case.

We next turn to the issue whether the County's denial of Guru Nanak's CUP application substantially burdened its religious exercise within the meaning of RLUIPA. . . . Guru Nanak bears the burden to prove the County's denial of its application imposed a substantial burden on its religious exercise. . . . [I]nterpreting

RLUIPA, this court has held: "[F]or a land use regulation to impose a 'substantial burden,' it must be 'oppressive' to a 'significantly great' extent. That is, a 'substantial burden' on 'religious exercise' must impose a significantly great restriction or onus upon such exercise." . . . We need not and do not decide that failing to provide a religious institution with a land use entitlement for a new facility for worship necessarily constitutes a substantial burden pursuant to RLUIPA. At the same time, we do decide the County imposed a substantial burden here based on two considerations: (1) that the County's broad reasons given for its tandem denials could easily apply to all future applications by Guru Nanak; and (2) that Guru Nanak readily agreed to every mitigation measure suggested by the Planning Division, but the County, without explanation, found such cooperation insufficient.

The Zoning Code permits churches in six types of districts. Churches must apply for a CUP within any or all of the six available districts. Each of the district classifications available to churches is intended to provide an area for a distinct form of development. The CUP application process is intended to ensure that a religious group's proposed property use conforms with the type of development that the particular district contemplates.

Guru Nanak initially applied for a CUP to construct a Sikh temple on a 1.89-acre property in an R-1 (One Family Residence) District. The Sutter County Community Services Department had recommended approval of the proposed use because mitigation measures, agreed to by Guru Nanak, would have minimized conflicts with surrounding land. Nevertheless, the County Planning Commission unanimously rejected the application, citing neighbors' complaints regarding increased noise and traffic.

Guru Nanak predictably responded to these voiced complaints by attempting to locate its temple on property far from residents who would be bothered by noise and traffic. The County's stated reasons for denying Guru Nanak's first application implied to Guru Nanak that it should not attempt to locate its temple in higher density districts (two-family residence, neighborhood apartment, general apartment, and the combining district) where nearby neighbors would be similarly bothered.[15]

Accordingly, Guru Nanak proposed a smaller temple, with the same seventy-five person capacity, on a much larger parcel of agricultural land.[16] The agricultural parcel left much more space between the temple and adjacent properties; that space mitigated the temple's noise and traffic impact on surrounding persons. Both the Community Services Department and the Planning Commission approved this second application because the parcel's size, along with additional setback and

15. Although one could argue that higher density districts—such as apartment and combining districts—are likely still available for Guru Nanak's temple because apartment dwellers are probably more noise tolerant than neighbors in a low density residential district, the County's land use law does not allow such a distinction. The Sutter County General Plan states that "[n]ot all land uses are equally affected by noise"; however, "residences of all types" are grouped together as being noise sensitive. The Sutter County Zoning code characterizes apartments districts as residential under the General Plan, and permits "one-family dwellings . . . when occupied or used by . . . persons employed on the premises" as of right in combining. Therefore, neighbors located in either two-family residence, apartment, or combining districts would be equally justified under the General Plan to complain about the noise created by a nearby proposed temple as neighbors located in low density residential districts. A Guru Nanak CUP application for a temple in any of these districts could be denied for the exact same broad reasons as its first CUP application.

16. During the public hearing at which the Sutter County Planning Commission approved Guru Nanak's second application, Commissioner Griffin commented, "We turned . . . down [Guru Nanak's first application] because the noise impact on the neighbors was going to be severe. And more or less told them that they needed to find more acreage to set up their facility, and they did that."

use conditions, adequately addressed the noise, traffic, and other complaints related to the temple's possible impact on surrounding agricultural uses.

The County Board of Supervisors' denial of Guru Nanak's second application frustrated Guru Nanak's attempt to comply both with the reasons given for the County's first denial and the Planning Division's various requirements for Guru Nanak to locate a temple on land zoned "agricultural." The Board's primary reason for denying Guru Nanak's second application was that the temple would contribute to "leapfrog development." Although the Zoning Code conditionally permits churches and other non-agricultural activities within agricultural districts, the County could use its concern with leapfrog development effectively to deny churches access to all such land; a great majority of agriculturally zoned land near Yuba City is separated from existing urban development. Moreover, many other churches already exist on agriculturally zoned land, including another Sikh temple located on Bogue Road less than a mile away from the proposed temple. The Bogue Road Sikh temple's parcel of land, like Guru Nanak's land, is surrounded by other agricultural parcels of land, to the extent such parcels are within Yuba City's sphere of influence. Hence, the County inconsistently applied its concern with leapfrog development to Guru Nanak. At the very least, such inconsistent decision-making establishes that any future CUP applications for a temple on land zoned "agricultural" would be fraught with uncertainty.

In denying the second CUP application, the Board of Supervisors disregarded, without explanation, the Planning Division's finding that Guru Nanak's acceptance of various mitigation conditions would make the proposed temple have a less-than-significant impact on surrounding land uses. We "cannot view [the denial of the second CUP application] 'in isolation'; [rather, it] 'must be viewed in the context of [Guru Nanak's permit process] history.'" . . . Similarly, during both of its CUP application processes, Guru Nanak agreed to every mitigation condition the Planning Division found necessary to recommend the land entitlements. Regarding the second application in particular, Guru Nanak agreed to a host of conditions proposed specifically to allay the County's concerns with leapfrog development — including a one-hundred foot setback to allow for pesticide spraying, and that all its religious ceremonies be held indoors and limited to seventy-five people. Nevertheless, in denying the second application, the Board of Supervisors neither related why any of such mitigation conditions were inadequate nor suggested additional conditions that would render satisfactory Guru Nanak's application. . . .

The County effectively concedes that it has no compelling interest, much less that the restrictions are narrowly tailored to accomplish such interest. The County presents no such argument in its briefs. Because the County "shall bear the burden of persuasion," to prove narrowly tailored, compelling interests, we hold that the district court properly invalidated the County's denial of Guru Nanak's CUP application. . . .

Notes and Comments

1. *Are* Civil Liberties for Urban Believers (CLUB) *and* Guru Nanak Sikh Society *Consistent?* Did the Seventh Circuit in *CLUB* apply a more deferential standard than the Ninth Circuit in *Guru Nanak Sikh Society?* Which decision is more consistent with the text of RLUIPA and the act's basic purpose? While both the Seventh and the

Ninth Circuits claim to apply the substantial burden provision, is the burden more substantial in *Guru Nanak Sikh Society*? Can the differences between the decisions be explained by reference to the distinction between a legislative policy and a site-specific administrative decision? Would the county have fared better in *Guru Nanak Sikh Society* if it had been protecting agricultural land and barring urbanized traffic in a farm district with narrow roads, tractors, and trucks? Was that course foreclosed by the county's prior approval of church and residential development in the district?

2. *Divergent Judicial Opinions.* The lower courts are split on how to read RLUIPA. *Compare Bethel World Outreach Ministries v. Montgomery County Council*, 706 F.3d 548 (4th Cir. 2013) (plaintiff does not have to show that County "targeted" it in order to succeed on substantial burden claim) *with Andon, LLC v. City of Newport News, Virginia*, 813 F.3d 510, 515 (4th Cir. 2016) (rejecting substantial burden and distinguishing *Bethel World* on the ground that, in *Andon*, "the plaintiffs here never had a reasonable expectation that the property could be used as a church"). *See also Chabad Lubavitch of Litchfield County, Inc. v. Litchfield Historic Dist. Comm'n*, 768 F.3d 183 (2d Cir. 2014) (remanding to District Court to determine whether substantial burden exists by applying various factors); *Petra Presbyterian Church v. Village of Northbrook*, 489 F.3d 846 (7th Cir. 2007) (zoning excluding churches from industrial districts did not substantially burden exercise of religious rights under RLUIPA); *Grace United Methodist Church v. City of Cheyenne*, 451 F.3d 643 (10th Cir. 2006) (denial of permit to allow church operation of day care center, where the denial was based on an ordinance restricting day care to 12 children, did not violate RLUIPA as it was a neutral policy of general applicability); *City of Woodinville v. Northshore United Church of Christ*, 211 P.3d 406 (Wash. 2009) (city violated RLUIPA when its moratorium on all land use permit applications placed a substantial burden on the church by preventing use of church property as a temporary encampment for the homeless).

3. *Scholarly Commentary on RLUIPA.* There is voluminous scholarly commentary on RLUIPA, both attacking and defending its constitutionality and policy wisdom. *See, e.g.,* Zachary Bray, RLUIPA and the Limits of Religious Institutionalism, 2016 Utah L. Rev. 41 (rejecting an "institutional interpretation" of RLUIPA that would suggest religious institutions play a distinctive role in developing the framework for religious liberty); John Infranca, Institutional Free Exercise and Religious Land Use, 34 Cardozo L. Rev. 1693 (2013) (the concept of institutional free exercise and the treatment of institutions in other land use contexts clarifies land use protections for religious institutions); Marci Hamilton, The Constitutional Limitations on Congress's Power Over Local Land Use: Why the Religious Land Use and Institutionalized Persons Act is Unconstitutional, 2 Alb. Gov't L. Rev. 366 (2009) (criticizing RLUIPA on public policy grounds and questioning the act's constitutionality); Patricia E. Salkin & Amy Lavine, The Genesis of RLUIPA and Federalism: Evaluating the Creation of a Federal Statutory Right and Its Impact on Local Government, 40 Urb. Law. 195 (2008) (questioning need for RLUIPA, discussing the range of judicial interpretations, and observing that the law undermines traditional local land regulation autonomy).

4. *Is RLUIPA Constitutional?* As discussed above, in *Cutter v. Wilkinson*, 544 U.S. 709 (2005), the Supreme Court rejected a facial challenge to RLUIPA under the Establishment Clause, but left the door open to potential as applied challenges. Is RLUIPA distinguishable from RFRA and *Boerne*? Did Congress once again attempt

to substantively define the Free Exercise Clause, but in a less obvious way? In *Elsinore Christian Ctr. v. City of Lake Elsinore*, 291 F. Supp. 2d 1083 (C.D. Cal. 2003), the court ruled that RLUIPA exceeded the enforcement powers of the Fourteenth Amendment, but the Ninth Circuit reversed the ruling in an unpublished opinion, citing *Guru Nanak. Elsinore Christian Ctr. v. City of Lake Elsinore*, 197 Fed. Appx. 718 (9th Cir. 2006). *See also Freedom Baptist Church of Delaware County v. Township of Middletown*, 204 F. Supp. 2d 857 (E.D. Pa. 2002) (holding that RLUIPA was within the Section Five power). For academic commentary on the constitutional issues, *see* Ira C. Lupu & Robert W. Tuttle, The Forms and Limits of Religious Accommodation: The Case of RLUIPA, 32 Cardozo L. Rev. 1907 (2011) (arguing that RLUIPA is unconstitutional); Frank T. Santoro, Section Five of the Fourteenth Amendment and the Religious Land Use and Institutionalized Persons Act, 24 Whittier L. Rev. 493 (2002) (tentatively supporting congressional authority).

5. *Appropriate Relief?* In *Sossamon v. Texas*, 563 U.S. 277 (2011), the Supreme Court held that the RLUIPA provision authorizing "appropriate relief" in successful suits against states did not "clearly and unequivocally" abrogate states' sovereign immunity from suit for money damages, meaning that awards of such relief were barred by sovereign immunity. The Court overruled various circuit court rulings to the contrary. *See, e.g., Smith v. Allen*, 502 F.3d 1255 (11th Cir. 2007).

6. *RLUIPA and Eminent Domain.* Municipalities might use condemnation to exclude religious uses. Does RLUIPA reach the exercise of eminent domain? Is explicit condemnation a form of land use regulation covered by RLUIPA? *See Tree of Life Christian Schools v. City of Arlington*, 823 F.3d 365, 373 (6th Cir. 2016) ("we observe that the government could ensure commercial use of the property at issue without violating the federal statute. Using eminent domain, Upper Arlington could force TOL Christian Schools to sell the land to the government, and sell the land to a buyer that the government thinks offers superior economic benefits."); *St. John's United Church of Christ v. City of Chicago*, 502 F.3d 616 (7th Cir. 2007) (city's plan to condemn and relocate cemetery was not "land use regulation" within meaning of RLUIPA); *Cottonwood Christian Ctr. v. Cypress Redevelopment Agency*, 218 F. Supp. 2d 1203 (C.D. Cal. 2000) (applying RLUIPA "strict scrutiny" standard and enjoining the city from carrying out eminent domain proceedings on a site which the city wanted for redevelopment but on which the church wanted to build a facility). *See also* Kenneth G. Leonczyk, Jr., RLUIPA and Eminent Domain: How a Plain Reading of a Flawed Statute Creates an Absurd Result, 13 Tex. Rev. L. & Pol. Tex. 311 (2009) (arguing that RLUIPA does not cover eminent domain but should be amended to require protection from condemnation); Christopher Serkin & Nelson Tebbe, Condemning Religion: RLUIPA and the Politics of Eminent Domain, 85 Notre Dame L. Rev. 1 (2009) (arguing that RLUIPA should not apply to condemnation).

7. *Megachurches.* The very large church with restaurants, a mall of shops, recreation, and parking for thousands presents a special set of issues. Does RLUIPA apply to such land uses? Do all facets of such land uses qualify as churches? Do they receive too much deference or not enough? *See, e.g.,* Jennifer S. Evans-Cowley & Kenneth Pearlman, Six Flags Over Jesus: RLUIPA, Megachurches, and Zoning, 21 Tul. Envtl. L. J. 203 (2008) (offering recommendations for regulating the harmful impacts on megachurches); Yusuf Z. Malik, Comment, The Religious Land Use and Institutionalized Persons Act: A Perspective on the Unreasonable Limitations Provision, 78 Tenn. L. Rev. 531 (2011) (arguing that RLUIPA's drafters did not anticipate the growth nor the protection of megachurches and their attendant secular amenities,

including multipurpose facilities, and that RLUIPA fails to address secular land use by religious institutions).

In addition to the substantial burden standard, RLUIPA also includes a provision prohibiting regulation that discriminates against religion or religious institutions. The next case addresses this provision of RLUIPA.

■ CENTRO FAMILIAR CRISTIANO BUENAS NUEVAS v. CITY OF YUMA
651 F.3d 1163 (9th Cir. 2011)

KLEINFELD, Circuit Judge

We address the "equal terms" provision of the Religious Land Use and Institutionalized Persons Act (RLUIPA) [42 U.S.C. §§2000cc].

I. FACTS

Centro Familiar Cristiano Buenas Nuevas, founded in 1998, is a Christian congregation of around 250 members, associated with the Arizona Southern Baptist Convention. The church sued for a declaratory judgment, injunction, and damages, when the City of Yuma prevented it from conducting church services in a building it had bought for that purpose.

The parties agreed to consolidate the preliminary injunction hearing with trial on the merits, and stipulated to many of the facts. No facts are at issue on appeal. We describe the facts in accord with the trial judge's findings of fact. This is a sort of reverse urban blight case, with the twist that instead of bars and nightclubs being treated as blighting their more genteel environs, the church is treated as blighting the bar and night-club district.

The City of Yuma, through the 1990s, tried to revive its Old Town Main Street area as a tourist district. The city decided to salt Main Street with a "mixture of commercial, cultural, governmental, and residential uses that will help to ensure a lively pedestrian-oriented district." The three-block Main Street area included a large, vacant building that had been a J.C. Penney department store from 1952 to 1976, then declined into factory and warehouse space for garment manufacturers, then a temporary facility for a bakery in 1998, and then a vacant hulk. The church bought the building in 2007.

The church had been looking for space because the half of a former movie theater it had been renting was inadequate. It bought the old J.C. Penney store because it was cheap, and because the municipality did not impose parking requirements on Main Street. The old vacant store, with a big public parking lot in back, was in foreclosure, and had to be purchased fast in order to get the distress sale price. The city told the church that it would need a conditional use permit to hold church services there, but the owner of the building was not willing to hold off on selling while the permit was sought, so the church had to buy knowing that the permit might be denied.

Some owners of neighboring properties objected to a permit on various grounds. A major concern was that a church would prevent issuance of liquor licenses, because state law prohibited new bars, nightclubs, or liquor stores within

300 feet of a church. The Community Planning Staff of the City of Yuma prepared a report for the City Planning and Zoning Commission recommending denial of a conditional use permit. The report noted positive features of granting the permit, such as "rehabilitation of a deteriorated and long-vacant building in the Old Town District." But, the staff concluded, use of the building as a church would be inconsistent with a "24/7 downtown neighborhood involving retail, residential, office and entertainment." The liquor license problem was the "pivotal factor." The city wanted the three-block Main Street to be an entertainment district, and the state prohibition on liquor licenses for bars, nightclubs, and liquor stores within 300 feet of it would blight a whole block for purposes of an entertainment district. The Commission accordingly denied the conditional use permit.

Had Centro Familiar been a secular organization rather than a church, it would not have needed the conditional use permit. The Yuma City Code requires religious organizations, (and schools, which also have the effect of preventing issuance of liquor licenses within 300 feet) to obtain a conditional use permit (CUP) to operate in the Old Town District, but "Membership organizations (except religious organizations)" may operate in Old Town without a permit. Many uses, not just membership organizations and entertainment venues, may operate without a conditional use permit. Auditoriums, performing art centers, and physical fitness facilities; museums, art galleries, and botanical and zoological gardens; single-and multiple-family dwellings; and even jails and prisons may operate in Old Town and on Main Street as of right.

Centro Familiar sued for a declaratory judgment invalidating the City Code provision subjecting churches but not secular membership organizations to conditional use permits, an injunction to require issuance of the permit, and damages for the financial consequences to the church of the denial. The district court concluded that the different treatment of churches did not violate RLUIPA or other provisions of law, and entered judgment for the city.

Two subsequent events have changed the circumstances of the case. First, while this appeal was pending, the church lost the property to foreclosure. Second, Arizona passed a state version of RLUIPA, a state statute very similar to the federal statute. [Ariz. Rev. Stat. §41-1493.03 (2010)] Arizona also changed the statutory ban on liquor licenses within 300 feet of a church, allowing for waiver. We withdrew this case from submission so that counsel could address the effect of the changed law. Counsel for the church filed a letter brief addressing the foreclosure, and both sides filed subsequent supplemental briefs on the effect of the new statutes.

II. Analysis

Centro Familiar argues that RLUIPA is not a mere restatement of the Free Exercise Clause, that requiring a conditional use permit for churches but not other organizations violates RLUIPA, and that even if RLUIPA were a mere codification of the Free Exercise Clause, the City Code would violate that as well. The United States has filed an amicus curiae brief in support of the church, though not agreeing with it on all points.

A. MOOTNESS

The claims for declaratory judgment and injunction are moot. The church no longer owns the old J.C. Penney store building, so the city could not be required to issue a conditional use permit for the building to the church. Nor could the church be entitled to a declaration that a code provision and statute violate federal law, because they no longer affect the church. The dispute does not fall within the "capable of repetition, yet evading review" exception, both because the statute now allows for waiver of the liquor license restriction, and because there is no reason to suppose that any similar subsequent denial would be unreviewable.

The damages claim, though, is not moot. The complaint seeks compensatory damages "for the Church's monetary expenses incurred as a result of the City's" permit denial. The letter brief claims that the permit denial forced the church to pay for two facilities for two years, one check for the J.C. Penney building that it could not use, and another for a facility in which to hold services, and the church lost the property because it could not afford to pay for two facilities in order to use one. . . .

B.   RLUIPA

The facts are not at issue. We review the legal conclusions of the district court de novo.

RLUIPA has two separate provisions limiting government regulation of land use. One prohibits governments from implementing land use regulations that impose "a substantial burden" on religious exercise unless the government demonstrates that they further a "compelling governmental interest" by the "least restrictive means." That "substantial burden" provision is not at issue here.

The second RLUIPA land use provision prohibits a government from imposing a land use restriction on a religious assembly "on less than equal terms" with a nonreligious assembly. This "equal terms" provision is the one before us. We have not had occasion to construe it. . . .

The statutory text of the equal terms provision says: "No government shall impose or implement a land use regulation in a manner that treats a religious assembly or institution on less than equal terms with a nonreligious assembly or institution."

42 U.S.C. §2000cc(b)(1). Most of the elements of the prohibition are not at issue: (1) there must be an imposition or implementation of a land-use regulation, (2) by a government, (3) on a religious assembly or institution. The challenge here is to an imposition by the ordinance itself, not to implementation of a facially nondiscriminatory ordinance, so we need not construe the "implement" term. What is at issue is the fourth element, that the imposition be "on less than equal terms with a nonreligious assembly or institution."

The Old Town District portion of the Yuma City Code says that "religious organizations" are permitted only upon the granting of a conditional use permit, but numerous other uses are permitted as of right, and do not need a conditional use permit. The uses permitted as of right include several uses that would seem to put a damper on entertainment, such as "correction centers," or create a dead block uninteresting to tourists and locals seeking "lively" entertainment, such as "multiple-family dwellings." Speaking to membership organizations specifically, the ordinance allows as of right, without a conditional use permit, "membership organizations (except religious organizations)." It is hard to see how an express exclusion of "religious organizations" from uses permitted as of right by other "membership organizations" could be other than "less than equal terms" for religious organizations.

The statute imposes the burden of persuasion on the government, not the religious institution, once the religious institution establishes a prima facie case:

> If a plaintiff produces prima facie evidence to support a claim alleging a violation of the Free Exercise Clause or a violation of section 2000cc of this title, the government shall bear the burden of persuasion on any element of the claim, except that the plaintiff shall bear the burden of persuasion on whether the law (including a regulation) or government practice that is challenged by the claim substantially burdens the plaintiff's exercise of religion.

It is undisputed that Centro Familiar is a religious institution, and the express distinction drawn by the ordinance establishes a prima facie case for unequal treatment.

The statute does not provide for "strict scrutiny" of a "compelling governmental interest" to see if the government can excuse the equal terms violation.[37] The Constitutional phrases, "substantial burden," "compelling governmental interest," and "least restrictive means," are all included in the "substantial burden" provision, not the "equal terms" provision. The statutory burden of proof provision speaks to all parts of the statute, and also the Free Exercise Clause of the Constitution. It does not impose new language into any provisions of the statute. The equal terms provision does not use language from the Free Exercise Clause, or otherwise support the conclusion that Congress meant merely to meaninglessly say "the Constitution applies to land use provisions."

Congress expressly provided for broad construction "in favor of a broad protection of religious exercise, to the maximum extent permitted by the terms of this chapter." Both because the language of the equal terms provision does not allow for it, and because it would violate the "broad construction" provision, we cannot accept the notion that a "compelling governmental interest" is an exception to the equal terms provision, or that the church has the burden of proving a "substantial burden" under the equal terms provision.

That is not to say that anything allowable for any institution has to be allowed for a church under the equal terms provision. The Third Circuit gave the example that when a town allows a ten-member book club, it would also have to permit a 1000-member church.[42] This is not the case, but the reason why is not the "substantial burden" and "compelling government interest" test. That test is for the "substantial burden" subsection, not the "equal terms" subsection. The reason is that a 1000-member church is not equal, for land-use purposes, to a ten-member book club.

Under the equal terms provision, analysis should focus on what "equal" means in the context. Equality is always with respect to a characteristic that may or may not be material. For example, one can legitimately treat a tall person differently from a short person for the purposes of picking a basketball team, but not for the purposes of picking a jury. Likewise, a ten-member book club is equal to a ten-member church for purposes of parking burdens on a street, but unequal to a 1000-member church. Equality, "except when used of mathematical or scientific relations, signifies not equivalence or identity, but proper relation to relevant concerns." Thus, an

37. We recognize that the Eleventh Circuit does read the "strict scrutiny" provisions from the substantial burden subsection into the separate equal terms subsection, but we do not agree. *See Midrash Sephardi, Inc. v. Town of Surfside*, 366 F.3d 1214, 1232 (11th Cir. 2004) ("a violation of §(b)'s equal treatment provision, consistent with the analysis employed in *Lukumi*, must undergo strict scrutiny").
42. *Lighthouse Inst. for Evangelism, Inc. v. City of Long Branch*, 510 F.3d 253, 268 (3d Cir. 2007).

ordinance that allowed membership organizations below some size would not have to allow churches substantially above that size, if parking were a relevant concern.

The city may be able to justify some distinctions drawn with respect to churches, if it can demonstrate that the less-than-equal-terms are on account of a legitimate regulatory purpose, not the fact that the institution is religious in nature. In this respect, our analysis is about the same as the Third Circuit's: we look to see if the church is "similarly situated as to the regulatory purpose." The Seventh Circuit, en banc, has refined this test to avoid inappropriate subjectivity by requiring equality with respect to "accepted zoning criteria," such as parking, vehicular traffic, and generation of tax revenue. That refinement is appropriate where necessary to prevent evasion of the statutory requirement, though it makes no practical difference in this case.

The city violates the equal terms provision only when a church is treated on a less than equal basis with a secular comparator, similarly situated with respect to an accepted zoning criteria. The burden is not on the church to show a similarly situated secular assembly, but on the city to show that the treatment received by the church should not be deemed unequal, where it appears to be unequal on the face of the ordinance.

In this case, no "accepted zoning criteria" justifies the exception of religious organizations in the "as of right" ordinance provision, "Membership organizations (except religious organizations)." The City Code does not address vehicular traffic or parking needs, as a neutral restriction on the size of membership organizations might. It does not address generation of tax revenue, since it allows all sorts of non-taxpayers to operate as of right, such as the United States Postal Service, museums, and zoos. The church exception does not address the "street of fun" criterion, since the city allows jails and prisons to operate on the three-block Old Town Main Street.

The only criterion that may justify the exception for churches is the damper they put on liquor licenses for bars and nightclubs. Schools, which also invoke the damper, are also required to have conditional use permits before they operate. However, there are three reasons that, taken together, explain why the 300-foot restriction on liquor licenses does not vitiate the inequality.

First, the language of the City Code says "religious organizations," not "uses which would impair issuance of liquor licenses." The ordinance gives no indication that schools and churches are being treated similarly for the same reason. The limitation on educational institutions is in a separate section, not the one establishing the unequal treatment of religious groups. The provision creating the inequality says that "Membership organizations (except religious organizations)" may operate as of right. It does not say "membership organizations, except religious and educational organizations."

Second, the ordinance's exception is too broad to be explained away by the liquor license restriction. It excludes not only churches, but also religious organizations that are not churches. Religious organizations that are not "churches" do not cause the 300-foot restriction on liquor licenses to operate, but are nevertheless required to obtain a conditional use permit. The Arizona statute defines a "church" as "a building which is erected or converted for use as a church, where services are regularly convened, which is used primarily for religious worship and schooling and which a reasonable person would conclude is a church by reason of design, signs or architectural or other features." To be considered a church under the Arizona statute, a building must appear to be a church because of its architecture, and the group occupying it must regularly convene services there. The Yuma City Code's definition of "religious organizations" covers more than just visibly identifiable churches in which services are regularly held. "Religious organizations" include "religious organizations operated for worship, religious training or study, government or administration of an organized religion, or for promotion of religious activities."

An advertising agency is allowed in Old Town as of right, but not if it promotes religion. The heads of a fraternal lodge or a merchants' association could have a permanent meeting room in Old Town, but the heads of a religious group could not, even though this would not bring into effect the 300-foot restriction on liquor licenses for bars if the meeting room is not in a church. An office building could administer a restaurant chain, but could not host a chapel, even though the office building is not a church. The exclusion of religious organizations is too broad for the liquor license statute to explain it away, because it excludes religious uses other than churches.

The exclusion of "educational services" from use as of right similarly indicates that the ordinance was not written with the liquor license restriction in mind. Only schools serving kindergarten through twelfth grade throw a wet blanket on liquor licenses, but the City Code also excludes colleges, universities, professional schools, and libraries. And the exception disallowing religious organizations from operating as of right pertains regardless of whether the statute allows waiver of the liquor license restriction, as it did not when this case arose, but does now.

Third, many of the uses permitted as of right would have the same practical effect as a church of blighting a potential block of bars and nightclubs. An apartment building taking up the whole block may be developed as of right, and so may a post office or prison. Prisons have bars, but not the kind promoting "entertainment."

Thus the ordinance before us expressly treats religious organizations on a less than equal basis. In order to excuse facial treatment of a church on "less than equal terms," the land-use regulation must be reasonably well adapted to "accepted zoning criteria," even though "strict scrutiny" in a Constitutional sense is not required. The Yuma City Code's exclusion of religious organizations is not reasonably well adapted to the zoning criteria it is purported to serve. And it therefore violates the equal terms provision of RLUIPA.

Because Yuma requires religious assemblies to obtain a conditional use permit, and does not require similarly situated secular membership assemblies to do the same, it violates RLUIPA's equal terms provision. Because it does, we need not reach Centro Familiar's argument that the ordinance violates the Free Exercise Clause.

III. Conclusion

Because the Yuma City Code violates the equal terms provision, we reverse. On remand, the district court shall proceed as appropriate to adjudicate Centro Familiar's claim to damages.

Notes and Comments

1. *Equal Treatment.* The Equal Terms Provision of RLUIPA plainly implements the same principle of equal treatment as the Equal Protection Clause of the Fourteenth Amendment. The *Centro Familiar* court makes clear that the Equal Terms

Provision is less demanding than RLUIPA's Substantial Burden test. But how does RLUIPA's Equal Terms Provision compare with the Equal Protection Clause?

2. *Other Lower Court Litigation.* RLUIPA's Equal Terms Provision has been the subject of extensive lower court litigation. *See, e.g., Roman Catholic Bishop of Springfield v. City of Springfield*, 724 F.2d 78 (1st Cir. 2013) (city ordinance requiring application to alter or demolish exterior architectural features of a closed parish building did not violate Equal Terms Provision); *Elijah Group, Inc. v. City of Leon Valley*, 643 F.3d 419 (5th Cir. 2011) (city ordinance held to violate Equal Terms Provision of RLUIPA because it provided that churches were not allowed in certain business zones, but allowed many nonreligious, nonretail buildings, such as private clubs or lodges, pursuant to special use permits); *International Church of Foursquare Gospel v. City of San Leandro*, 673 F.3d 1059 (9th Cir. 2011) (denial of rezoning application and a conditional use permit to build new church facilities on industrially-zoned land violated the Equal Terms Provision); *Bey v. City of Tampa Code Enforcement*, 607 Fed. Appx. 892, 899 (11th Cir. 2015) (rejecting claim because complaint "did not identify any particular nonreligious assembly or institution or allege with specificity how . . . application [of the city's code] resulted in her religious assembly being treated on less than equal terms.").

3. *Academic Literature.* The literature on the Equal Terms Provision is prolific. *See, e.g.,* Daniel P. Lennington, Thou Shalt Not Zone: The Overbroad Applications and Trouble Implications of RLUIPA's Land Use Provisions, 29 Seattle U. L. Rev. 805 (2006) (arguing that act is too broad and vague, with the result that courts have split on the level of scrutiny, burden, and results; the author argues for application of the equal protection purposefulness standard of the race cases as a legislative amendment).

E. DUE PROCESS CLAUSE CHALLENGES

The Due Process Clauses of the Fifth and Fourteenth Amendments prohibit deprivations "of like, liberty, or property, without due process of law." Due Process Clause challenges to land use restrictions confront substantial obstacles, as illustrated in different ways by the following two cases:

■ RRI REALTY CORP. v. INCORPORATED VILLAGE OF SOUTHAMPTON
870 F.2d 911 (2d Cir. 1989)

NEWMAN, Circuit Judge

This appeal concerns primarily the issue of whether an applicant for a building permit, subsequently ordered to be issued by a state court, had a sufficiently clear entitlement to the permit to constitute a property interest protected by the Due Process Clause. The issue arises on an appeal by the Village of Southampton, New York, and various Village officials, from a judgment of the District Court for the Eastern District of New York . . . , after a jury trial, awarding RRI Realty Corp. ("RRI") $2.7 million in damages and attorney's fees pursuant to 42 U.S.C.

§§1983, 1988 (1982). RRI claimed that the Village officials, acting in their official capacity, had wrongfully denied RRI's application for a building permit, thereby depriving RRI of its property without due process of law. . . .

We conclude that the record was insufficient to support a finding of such a clear entitlement to the permit as to establish a property interest protected by the Fourteenth Amendment. Accordingly, we reverse the judgment of the District Court. . . .

BACKGROUND

In 1979, RRI purchased a 63-room mansion and surrounding oceanfront property in the Village of Southampton. After planning extensive renovations for the mansion, RRI held discussions with the Village Building Inspector, Eugene Romano, regarding procedures for acquiring the requisite building permit. Although the plans were somewhat inchoate, it was clear that several features of the proposed design exceeded height restrictions in the local zoning code. Romano issued a limited building permit to RRI, covering only minor structural renovations; he advised RRI not to apply for successive building permits as plans changed but to make one omnibus building permit application when its plans became final. RRI also applied for, and received, a height variance from the Zoning Board of Appeals ("ZBA") in anticipation of future construction.

Construction began in early 1981. By the spring of 1983, renovation had proceeded far enough to permit RRI to complete the final design plans for the residence. Under local law, RRI had to submit these plans to the Village's Architectural Review Board ("ARB") for approval before the Building Inspector could issue a permit. *See* Southampton, N.Y., Code §116.32 (1984) (hereinafter "Code"). The ARB approved RRI's final overall design in May 1983. The Building Inspector then instructed RRI to submit an application to his office for a comprehensive building permit. Romano also told RRI to apply to the ZBA for another variance-this one covering the portion of the proposed structure that would exceed the height limitations of the previous variance.

With RRI's application pending before the ZBA, RRI and the Building Inspector devised a plan to divide the building permit application into three stages. Stage one represented the structural work covered by the initial building permit already issued by Romano. Stage two — the permit for which is the subject of this litigation — represented the balance of the construction that was in conformity with the zoning law and the initial variance. Stage three included that part of the structure for which a new height variance was required.

RRI submitted an application to the Building Inspector for a stage-two building permit in February 1984 along with final plans, which covered the entire project but were marked to indicate the three stages of construction. In early April, RRI, apparently at the Building Inspector's request, submitted a new set of plans that did not include any stage-three alterations. These altered plans showed a house missing most of its roof, parts of one side, and an entire new wing. On April 11, the Building Inspector referred these revised plans and the permit application to the ARB for its final consideration. Apparently, under the Code, the ARB had to approve these more detailed designs even though it had approved plans for the overall project in 1983.

In early May 1984, the Building Inspector notified RRI, as he had throughout the spring, that a permit was about to be issued. However, no permit was forthcoming. The ARB decided to take no action on the building permit application. No one informed RRI of this decision. At about this time, the RRI project became a target of community rumor and a controversial matter in Village politics. Prominent Southampton residents attacked the project for attracting undesirable elements and promoting improper behavior. Reacting to this pressure, the Acting Mayor, a member of the Village Board of Trustees, ordered the Building Inspector to issue a stop-work order on May 17 because RRI lacked a building permit for all of the post-stage-one construction. The ZBA also denied RRI's application for its stage-three variance.

On June 1, 1984, RRI commenced an Article 78 proceeding in New York Supreme Court, Suffolk County, against the Building Inspector and the ARB to compel issuance of a stage-two building permit and to cancel the stop-work order. The court granted summary judgment for RRI. . . . The court ordered issuance of a permit for what was "concededly legal work."

RRI received its building permit in August 1986 and commenced this action for damages caused by the delay in the issuance of the stage two permit and for attorney's fees and costs. The jury found in favor of RRI, awarding it $1.9 million in damages. The judgment also includes $762,970.36 for attorney's fees and costs.

DISCUSSION

The gravamen of the complaint is that RRI had a property interest in the stage-two permit, that Village officials arbitrarily and capriciously deprived RRI of its property interest in this permit, and that this violation of substantive due process was an official Village policy for which the municipality is liable for damages under section 1983. *See Monell v. Department of Social Services,* 436 U.S. 658 (1978); *see also City of St. Louis v. Praprotnik,* 485 U.S. 112 (1988). In the view we take of the case, it becomes necessary to consider only the threshold issue of whether the evidence sufficed to create a jury issue as to whether RRI had a property interest in the stage-two permit.

I. DEVELOPMENT OF THE LEGAL STANDARD

Federal courts have followed a somewhat uneven course in explicating the rationale for and the extent to which the substantive component of the Due Process Clause of the Fourteenth Amendment protects landowners in disputes with local agencies empowered to limit the permissible uses of their property. Though appellate courts frequently invoke Justice Marshall's observation that the role of the Supreme Court (and presumably of every other federal court as well) "should not be to sit as a zoning board of appeals," *Village of Belle Terre v. Boraas,* 416 U.S. 1, 13 (1974) (Marshall, J., dissenting), their willingness to entertain a claim that a local land use regulator has acted arbitrarily or capriciously sometimes leads them to require trial courts to make an inquiry similar to the sort of determination that zoning boards of appeal routinely make.

The initial effort to subject local land use decisions to constitutional scrutiny involved challenges to new zoning restrictions imposed upon property owners. The Supreme Court's first consideration of such a challenge, though occurring in an era when substantive due process was often a formidable protection against governmental regulation, met with a significant rebuff. *Village of Euclid v. Ambler Realty Co.,* 272

U.S. 365 (1926). The Supreme Court ruled that zoning regulations will survive substantive due process challenge unless they are "clearly arbitrary and unreasonable, having no substantial relation to the public health, safety, morals, or general welfare." *Id.* at 395, 47 S. Ct. at 121. With the decline of substantive due process as a protection against economic regulation, zoning regulation continued easily to survive constitutional challenge. *See Goldblatt v. Town of Hempstead,* 369 U.S. 590 (1962). Pertinent to the later development of the case law concerning land use regulation is the fact that in the early zoning cases, there was no dispute as to whether the plaintiff had a property interest within the meaning of the Fourteenth Amendment; his property interest was in the land he owned, land that the local regulating body sought to restrict as to use. . . .

The analytical framework applicable to constitutional challenges to land regulation was affected by the Supreme Court's 1972 decisions in *Board of Regents v. Roth,* 408 U.S. 564 (1972), and *Perry v. Sindermann,* 408 U.S. 593 (1972). Though concerned with an interest in employment, rather than land, and the protection of procedural, rather than substantive, due process, both decisions were potentially pertinent to land regulation in their announcement that a property interest, within the meaning of the Fourteenth Amendment, includes not only what is owned but also, in some limited circumstances, what is sought. This expanded concept of property, however, requires more than "an abstract need or desire" or "a unilateral expectation" of what is sought. *Board of Regents v. Roth,* 408 U.S. at 577. Instead, there must be "a legitimate claim of entitlement." *Id; see Perry v. Sindermann,* 408 U.S. at 601.

After 1972, some courts considering constitutional challenges to land regulation began their inquiry by citing *Roth* and asking whether the plaintiff had a "clear entitlement" to the approval he was seeking from the land use regulating body. *See Creative Environments, Inc. v. Estabrook,* 680 F.2d 822, 831 (1st Cir.) (request for approval of subdivision plan; property interest assumed); *United Land Corporation of America v. Clarke,* 613 F.2d 497, 501 (4th Cir. 1980) (request for approval of soil erosion permit; no protectable interest "in the permit" because of discretionary authority in administrator). This same approach is reflected in *Scott v. Greenville County,* 716 F.2d 1409 (4th Cir. 1983), one of the few decisions rejecting dismissal on summary judgment of a claim that a denial of approval for land use was arbitrary and capricious and hence a denial of substantive due process. In a thoughtful opinion by Chief Judge Winter, the Court inquired whether an applicant for a building permit had a "'protectible property interest in the permit' sufficient to trigger federal due process guarantees." *Id.* at 1418 (citing *United Land Corporation of America v. Clarke, supra,* 613 F.2d at 501). Chief Judge Winter concluded that the applicant had a clear entitlement to the permit under state law. In *Scott,* the applicant was not the owner of the property, although his option to purchase it would seem to have given him an interest that itself could have been considered "property" under the Due Process Clause. Chief Judge Winter characterized the interest in the applied for permit as a "'species of property,'" *id.* at 1421 (quoting *Logan v. Zimmerman Brush Co.,* 455 U.S. 422, 429 (1982)), though he noted that it is not in the same category as property that is protected by the Fourteenth Amendment's incorporation of the "takings" clause of the Fifth Amendment, *id.* & n. 20.

Many post-1972 land regulation decisions, however, have not pursued the *Roth* analysis in land regulation cases. Instead of inquiring as to the plaintiff's degree of entitlement to what he sought, these decisions have implicitly assumed that the pertinent property interest is the property the plaintiff owns and simply examined whether the action of local regulators in denying an application for the proposed use of the land was arbitrary and capricious. This has occurred both in decisions rejecting substantive due process challenges, and in the few decisions upholding such claims, at least against a motion for summary judgment or for dismissal for failure to state a claim.

Bello is a clear example of a court focusing exclusively on whether the local land use regulator acted arbitrarily and capriciously without inquiry as to whether the protected property interest is in the land the plaintiff owns and is seeking to use or in the permit he requires for his intended use; the Court extracted from prior cases, including those concerned with denial of equal protection, like *Arlington Heights v. Metropolitan Development Corp.*, 429 U.S. 252 (1977), a general rule that "the deliberate and arbitrary abuse of government power violates an individual's right to substantive due process." *Bello v. Walker, supra,* 840 F.2d at 1129. *See Shelton v. City of College Station,* 780 F.2d 475, 479 (5th Cir. 1986) (in banc) (declining to determine whether property interest was in the right to seek a zoning variance or in the right to use the plaintiff's property. . . .

In this Circuit, our post-*Roth* cases considering a landowner's claim of a due process violation in the denial of an application for regulated use of his land have been significantly influenced by the *Roth* "entitlement" analysis. In *Yale Auto Parts, Inc. v. Johnson,* 758 F.2d 54 (2d Cir. 1985), the landowner had been denied a permit to use his property for an automobile junkyard business. Expressly invoking *Roth,* Judge Mansfield focused initially on whether the landowner had "a legitimate claim of entitlement" to the license he sought and formulated the test for this inquiry to be that "absent the alleged denial of due process, there is either a certainty or a very strong likelihood that the application would have been granted." *Id.* at 59. Finding that the licensing authorities had discretion in the issuance of the requested permit, the Court affirmed dismissal of the claim for lack of a protected property interest *in the permit,* even though the Court acknowledged that the allegations of the complaint alleged "egregious misconduct" by the defendants in the denial of the permit, *id.* at 59.

We have adhered to the property interest analysis of *Yale Auto Parts* both in finding a claimed interest in a land use application insufficient to constitute Fourteenth Amendment property, *Dean Tarry Corp. v. Friedlander,* 826 F.2d 210 (2d Cir.1987) (approval sought for municipal development plan), and in finding such an interest sufficient, at least for purposes of surviving summary judgment, *Sullivan v. Town of Salem,* 805 F.2d 81 (2d Cir. 1986) (application for certificates of occupancy). Our latest decision in this area, though citing the entitlement test of *Roth* and our application of that test in *Yale Auto Parts* to the permit being sought, appears to have found the requisite property interest to be an aspect of the rights enjoyed by the plaintiff as owner of his property. *Brady v. Town of Colchester,* 863 F.2d 205 (2d Cir. 1988). *Brady* is an unusual case, however, in that the owner was obliged by the local authorities to seek a permit for commercial use of his property, whereas his position was that his property was already zoned for commercial use, that no permit was required, and that the local decision obliging him to seek a permit was wholly unjustified.

It is not readily apparent why land regulation cases that involve applications to local regulators have applied the *Roth* entitlement test to inquire whether an entitlement exists in what has been applied for-whether a zoning variance, a business license, or a building permit-instead of simply recognizing the owner's indisputable property interest in the land he owns and asking whether local government has exceeded the limits of substantive due process in regulating the plaintiff's use of his property by denying the application arbitrarily and capriciously. As Justice Stevens has observed, "the opportunity to apply for [a zoning amendment] is an aspect of property ownership protected by the Due Process Clause of the Fourteenth Amendment." *City of Eastlake v. Forest City Enterprises, Inc.,* 426 U.S. 668, 683 (1976) (Stevens, J., with whom Brennan, J., joins, dissenting). Indeed, the entitlement inquiry will not often aid the analysis in this context. When a local regulator's discretionary decision to deny an application is not arbitrary or capricious, the plaintiff will usually be deemed not to have a sufficient entitlement to constitute a protected property interest. On occasion, however, as *Yale Auto Parts* demonstrates, the plaintiff may be deemed *not* to have a protected property interest in the requested permit, even in a case where the denial of the permit *is* arbitrary. The fact that the permit could have been denied on non-arbitrary grounds defeats the federal due process claim. Focusing on the authority of the local regulator thereby permits the threshold rejection of some federal due process claims, without awaiting exploration of whether the regulator acted so arbitrarily as to offend substantive due process in the particular case. In any event, *Yale Auto Parts* and its progeny have committed this Circuit to the "entitlement" inquiry in land use regulation cases.

If federal courts are not to become zoning boards of appeals (and not to substitute for state courts in their state law review of local land-use regulatory decisions), the entitlement test of *Yale Auto Parts*—"certainty or a very strong likelihood" of issuance—must be applied with considerable rigor. Application of the test must focus primarily on the degree of discretion enjoyed by the issuing authority, not the estimated probability that the authority will act favorably in a particular case. *See Walentas v. Lipper,* 862 F.2d 414, 419 (2d Cir. 1988); *RR Village Ass'n, Inc. v. Denver Sewer Corp.,* 826 F.2d 1197, 1201-02 (2d Cir. 1987); *Sullivan v. Town of Salem, supra,* 805 F.2d at 85. *Yale Auto Parts* rejected the claim of a property interest in the permit being sought because of the discretion of the local regulating body. Even if in a particular case, objective observers would estimate that the probability of issuance was extremely high, the opportunity of the local agency to deny issuance suffices to defeat the existence of a federally protected property interest. The "strong likelihood" aspect of *Yale Auto Parts* comes into play only when the discretion of the issuing agency is so narrowly circumscribed that approval of a proper application is virtually assured; an entitlement does not arise simply because it is likely that broad discretion will be favorably exercised. Since the entitlement analysis focuses on the degree of official discretion and not on the probability of its favorable exercise, the question of whether an applicant has a property interest will normally be a matter of law for the court.

II. APPLICATION OF THE LEGAL STANDARD

In the instant case, RRI argues that absent the alleged denial of due process, there was a "certainty or a very strong likelihood" that Village officials would have granted RRI's application. RRI points to the ARB's approval of RRI's initial overall design and to the fact that stage-two construction was in full compliance with the zoning law. Moreover, there is correspondence between the Building Inspector and RRI, as well as discussions between Romano, the Board of Trustees, and the ARB to support RRI's assertion that approval of the application could be expected. Finally, RRI argues that since the ARB's time limits within which to act on the application had expired, it forfeited any discretion it may have had and was required to approve the permit.

Our reading of *Yale Auto Parts* and its progeny leads us to reject RRI's analysis. Even though there is evidence of officials' statements that approval of the application was probably forthcoming, the fact remains that the ARB had discretion to deny RRI's application for a stage-two permit. The Village Code confers wide discretion on the ARB in reviewing the final design plans:

> The [ARB] is charged with the duty of exercising sound judgment and of rejecting plans which, in its opinion, are not of harmonious character because of proposed style, materials, mass, line, color. . . . Code, *supra*, §116-33.B. . . .

[Judge GARTH, dissenting, accepted the Second Circuit's "clear entitlement" theory, but disagreed with the majority's application of that standard to the facts of this case.] "Contrary to the majority. ., I would hold that RRI had a legitimate claim of entitlement to the issuance of its building permit — a claim constituting a property interest sufficient to invoke constitutional protection."

■ UNITED ARTISTS v. TOWNSHIP OF WARRINGTON
316 F.3d 392 (3d Cir. 2003)

ALITO, Circuit Judge. . . .

I.

A.

The dispute underlying this case arises out of a development race between United Artists' proposed multiplex and a competing multiplex theater development proposed by Regal Cinema and developer Bruce Goodman. The record shows that the two companies were competing to obtain approval of their plans by the Township because the market could support only one of the theaters. Goodman agreed to pay the Township an annual "impact fee" of $100,000, but United Artists refused the Township's repeated requests for such a payment. United Artists asserts that, because of Goodman's promise to pay this fee, the Township allowed his project to "sail through the land development process," while United Artists' proposal was repeatedly stalled.

The Board of Supervisors' review process consisted of two phases, preliminary approval and final approval. In January 1996, United Artists submitted a preliminary plan for its theater to the Township Planning Commission, an independent body of local officials that makes recommendations regarding land-use plans to the Board of Supervisors. Along with the preliminary plan, United Artists submitted a traffic impact study, which led the Township to require, as a precondition to the issuance of an occupancy permit, the installation of a separate left-turn lane into the theater. United Artists failed to acquire the property necessary to make this improvement and expressed its intention to request a waiver of the condition or to sue for relief. United Artists claims that its failure to construct the road improvement was a mere pretext for the Township's refusal to support its theater proposal and that this refusal was actually motivated by the Township's desire to obtain an impact fee from Goodman and Regency Cinema.

After granting preliminary approval of United Artists' proposal, the Township attempted to change the terms of that approval by requiring United Artists to obtain an easement for the road improvement and to complete the installation of signals before construction could begin, rather than before the time of occupancy, as was originally provided in the preliminary approval. . . .

In the meantime, the Board granted preliminary approval of the Goodman proposal on February 4, 1997 — one month after the initial application was submitted — and final approval was granted on May 21, 1997. By contrast, United Artists did not receive preliminary approval until March 18, 1997, 14 months after submitting its initial application. The Board then tabled its vote on United Artists' application for final approval on three occasions, each time asking if United Artists would pay an impact fee. The Board granted final approval of the United Artists proposal on September 16, 1997. The Goodman/Regal Cinema multiplex was completed in 1999; United Artists never built a theater in Warrington.

B.

United Artists' complaint in this case asserted procedural and substantive due process claims under 42 U.S.C. §1983, as well as supplementary state law claims. As defendants, the complaint named the Township and the members of the Board of Supervisors — Gerald Anderson, Joseph Lavin, Douglas Skinner, Wayne Bullock, and Katherine Watson ("Supervisors") — in both their official and individual capacities. Asserting the defense of qualified immunity, the Supervisors moved for summary judgment, and in December 1999, the District Court denied the Supervisors' motion with respect to the substantive due process, claim, while granting that motion with respect to the procedural due process claim. . . .

[O]ur task is "'to determine first whether the plaintiff has alleged a deprivation of a constitutional right at all,' before reaching the question of whether the right was clearly established at the time." *Johnson v. Newburgh Enlarged School District*, 239 F.3d 246, 251 (2d Cir. 2001) (quoting *Lewis*, 523 U.S. at 841 n. 5, 118 S. Ct. 1708). . . . To answer this question, we must determine the appropriate legal standard to apply to substantive due process claims. . . .

III.

B.

In *County of Sacramento v. Lewis*, 523 U.S. 833, 118 S. Ct. 1708, 140 L. Ed.2d 1043 (1998), the Supreme Court explained the standard that applies when a plaintiff alleges that an action taken by an executive branch official violated substantive due process. The Court observed that "the core of the concept" of due process is "protection against arbitrary action" and that "only the most egregious official conduct can be said to be 'arbitrary in the constitutional sense.'" *Id.* at 845-46 (citation omitted). After noting its long history of speaking of "the cognizable level of executive abuse of power as that which shocks the conscience," *id.* at 846 (citing *Rochin v. California*, 342 U.S. 165 (1952)), the Court continued:

> Most recently, in *Collins v. Harker Heights*, [503 U.S. 115, 128 (1992)], we said again that the substantive component of the Due Process Clause is violated by executive action *only when it* "can properly be characterized as arbitrary, or conscience shocking, in a constitutional sense."

Lewis, 523 U.S. at 847 (emphasis added). At the same time, however, the *Lewis* Court acknowledged that "the measure of what is conscience-shocking is no calibrated yard stick," *Lewis*, 523 U.S. at 847, and that "[d]eliberate indifference that shocks in one environment may not be so patently egregious in another." *Id.* at 850. . . .

Despite *Lewis* and the post-*Lewis* Third Circuit cases . . . United Artists maintains that this case is not governed by the "shocks the conscience" standard, but by the less demanding "improper motive" test that originated with *Bello v. Walker*, 840 F.2d 1124 (3d Cir. 1988), and was subsequently applied by our court in a line of land-use cases. In these cases, we held that a municipal land use decision violates substantive due process if it was made for any reason "unrelated to the merits," *Herr v. Pequea Township*, 274 F.3d 109, 111 (3d Cir. 2001) (citing cases), or with any "improper motive." *See, e.g., Woodwind Estates, Ltd. v. Gretkowski*, 205 F.3d 118 (3d Cir. 2000).

These cases, however, cannot be reconciled with *Lewis's* explanation of substantive due process analysis. Instead of demanding conscience-shocking conduct, the *Bello* line of cases endorses a much less demanding "improper motive" test for governmental behavior. Although the District Court opined that there are "few differences between the [shocks the conscience] standard and the improper motive standard," we must respectfully disagree. . . . The "shocks the conscience" standard encompasses "only the most egregious official conduct." *Lewis*, 523 U.S. at 846. In ordinary parlance, the term "improper" sweeps much more broadly, and neither *Bello* nor the cases that it spawned ever suggested that conduct could be "improper" only if it shocked the conscience. We thus agree with the Supervisors that the *Bello* line of cases is in direct conflict with *Lewis*. . . .

Since *Lewis*, our court has applied the "shocks the conscience" standard in a variety of contexts. . . . There is no reason why land use cases should be treated differently. We thus hold that, in light of *Lewis*, *Bello* and its progeny are no longer good law.

We note that our holding today brings our Court into line with several other Courts of Appeals that have ruled on substantive due process claims in land-use disputes. *See, e.g., Chesterfield Development Corp. v. City of Chesterfield*, 963 F.2d 1102, 1104-05 (8th Cir. 1992) (holding that allegations that the city arbitrarily applied a zoning ordinance were insufficient to state a substantive due process claim, and stating in dicta that the "decision would be the same even if the City had knowingly enforced the invalid zoning ordinance in bad faith. . . . A bad-faith violation of state law remains only a violation of state law."); *PFZ Properties, Inc. v. Rodriguez*, 928 F.2d 28, 32 (1st Cir. 1991) ("Even assuming that ARPE engaged in delaying tactics and refused to issue permits for the Vacia Talega project based on considerations outside the scope of its jurisdiction under Puerto Rico law, such practices, without more, do not rise to the level of violations of the federal constitution under a substantive due process label.").

E. Due Process Clause Challenges

Application of the "shocks the conscience" standard in this context also prevents us from being cast in the role of a "zoning board of appeals." *Creative Environments, Inc. v. Estabrook*, 680 F.2d 822, 833 (1st Cir. 1982) (quoting *Village of Belle Terre v. Boraas*, 416 U.S. 1, 13 (1974) (Marshall, J., dissenting)) . . . The First Circuit in *Estabrook* observed that every appeal by a disappointed developer from an adverse ruling of the local planning board involves some claim of abuse of legal authority, but "[i]t is not enough simply to give these state law claims constitutional labels such as 'due process' or 'equal protection' in order to raise a substantial federal question under section 1983." *Estabrook*, 680 F.2d at 833. Land-use decisions are matters of local concern, and such disputes should not be transformed into substantive due process claims based only on allegations that government officials acted with "improper" motives. . . .

We vacate the District Court's denial of the Supervisors' summary judgment motion and remand the case for further proceedings to determine whether United Artists can survive the Supervisors' summary judgment motion. . . .

COWEN, Circuit Judge, dissenting. . . .

[T]ossing every substantive Due Process egg into the nebulous and highly subjective "shocks the conscious" basket is unwise. It leaves the door ajar for intentional and flagrant abuses of authority by those who hold the sacred trust of local public office to go unchecked. "Shocks the conscience" is a useful standard in high speed police misconduct cases which tend to stir our emotions and yield immediate reaction. But it is less appropriate, and does not translate well, to the more mundane world of local land use decisions, where lifeless property interests (as opposed to bodily invasions) are involved. In this regard, it appears rather difficult to analogize the intentional and illegal denial of a building permit to the forced pumping of the human stomach, the infamous fact pattern that begat "shocks the conscience" as a term of constitutional significance. *See Rochin v. California*, 842 U.S. 166, 172-73 (1952). It is the jurisprudential equivalent of a square peg in a round hole. . . .

III.

Even if "shocks the conscience" is the language we must employ to the exclusion of any other (which it is not), the alleged behavior in this case resolutely shocks the conscience. Public officials, sworn to uphold the law, deliberately extracted money, knowing that it was improper for them to do so. In contemporary America, under compelling norms of basic human decency, it would be shocking that such officials improperly and illegally obtained money in matters that come before them. There is little if any distinction between the taking of money for the purposes alleged in this case, and money taken to line the officials' individual pockets. For all of the foregoing reasons, I must dissent.

A Note on the Standard of Liability for Violation of Substantive Due Process Clause

Considerable uncertainty reigns regarding the appropriate liability test to be applied in substantive due process challenges to land use regulations. The decision by future Supreme Court Justice Samuel Alito in the *United Artists* case, excepted above, articulates one standard that is quite deferential to local authorities and that apparently follows Supreme Court precedent, such as it is.

In the seminal case of *Euclid v. Ambler Realty*, 272 U.S. 365, 395 (1926), the Supreme Court upheld a zoning ordinance against a substantive due process challenge, stating that the ordinance should be upheld unless it is "clearly arbitrary and unreasonable, having no substantial relation to the public health, safety, morals, or general welfare." Two years later, in *Nectow v. City of Cambridge*, 277 U.S. 183 (1928), the Court struck down a city's decision to zone a particular area for residential rather than industrial use. While purporting to apply the standard articulated in *Euclid*, the Court's ruling was hardly deferential; to justify the result in *Nectow*, the Court simply relied on a special master's finding that the public interest "will not be promoted" by the challenged zoning classification. The Court then issued no further guidance on how the Due Process Clause should apply in the land use field for another 40 years. In this intervening period, the Court underwent a constitutional revolution, virtually abandoning the Due Process Clause as a check on social and economic legislation. *See Williamson v. Lee Optical*, 348 U.S. 483, 488 (1955) ("The day is gone when this court uses the Due Process Clause of the Fourteenth Amendment to strike down state laws, regulatory of business and industrial conditions, because they may be unwise, improvident, or out of harmony with a particular school of thought."). In sum, *Euclid* (and *Nectow*) no doubt remain important precedents; however, so much has changed in constitutional doctrine over the last 90 years that these old chestnuts have only so much value today regarding application of the Due Process Clause.

The modern Supreme Court continues to shy away from the Due Process Clause as a basis for invalidating economic regulation, as opposed, for example, to social legislation. *See Lawrence v. Texas*, 539 U.S. 588 (2003) (invalidating anti-sodomy laws under the Due Process Clause). But the Court has continued to suggest that the substantive due process doctrine remains available to strike down genuinely egregious government regulation. The basic notion appears to be that the Due Process Clause imposes a constraint on truly "arbitrary" government action. *See* Richard H. Fallon, Jr., Some Confusions About Due Process, Judicial Review, and Constitutional Remedies, 93 Colum. L. Rev. 309, 310 (1993) (observing that the Due Process Clause imposes a "general duty on government officials to behave 'rationally' in their selection of both ends and means"). Under this overarching inquiry into arbitrariness, the Court has articulated different criteria for identifying "what is fatally arbitrary . . . depending on whether it is legislation or a specific act of a governmental officer that is at issue." *City of Sacramento v. Lewis*, 523 U.S. 833, 846 (1998). Executive branch action is said to violate due process if it "shocks the conscience." *Rochin v. California*, 342 U.S. 165, 172 (1952). Legislation violates due process if it lacks any rational basis. *Williamson v. Lee Optical*, 348 U.S. 483, 488 (1955) ("[I]t is enough that there is an evil at hand for correction, and that it might be thought that the particular legislative measure was a rational way to correct it."). *See generally* Kames R. Bimbauer & Toni Massaro, Outrgaeous and Irrational, 100 Minn. L. Rev. 281 (2015) (describing these two types of due process challenges in depth). Some commentators have suggested that the "shocks the conscience" standard should only apply in situations where government actors lack time for deliberation, such as police officers in pursuit of a fleeing suspect, and should not apply when there is time for deliberation, such as in making a land use regulatory decision. *See* Clifford B. Levine & L. Jason Blake, United Artists: Reviewing the

Conscience Shocking Test Under Section 1983, 1 Seton Hall Cir. Rev. 101 (2005). Judge Cowen, in dissent in *United Artists,* obviously shares this perspective.

In recent years, the Supreme Court has not explored in detail how these due process standards should apply in the land use context. However, in *City of Cuyahoga Falls v. Buckeye Cmty. Hope Found.,* 538 U.S. 188 (2003), the Court rejected a claim that a city's failure to award a developer a permit to build low income housing violated due process. The *Cuyahoga* Court did not explicitly reiterate the "shocks the conscience test," but it cited *City of Sacramento v. Lewis,* and observed that "in our evaluations of "abusive executive action," we have held that "only the most egregious official conduct can be said to be "arbitrary in the constitutional sense." *Id.* at 199. In addition, the Court's 2005 decision in *Lingle v. Chevron USA, Inc.,* 544 U.S. 528 (2005), speaks indirectly, yet loudly, to the issue of the standard of review in substantive due process cases, as discussed below.

With this limited guidance, the federal appeals courts apply widely varying standards in due process challenges to land use regulations. The U.S. Court of Appeals for the First Circuit, in line with the Third Circuit, applies a highly deferential "shocks the conscience" test. *See Collins v. Nuzzo,* 244 F.3d 246, 250-51 (1st Cir. 2001) (rejecting a due process challenge to a city's denial of a permit to operate a used car lot, stating that a due process violation can be made out only in a "truly horrendous situation" where the government action is "shocking or violative of universal standards of decency;" and stating, "This unforgiving standard guards against "insinuat[ing] the oversight and discretion of federal judges into areas traditionally reserved for state and local tribunals."). *See also Pagan v. Calderon,* 448 F.3d 16, 32 (1st Cir. 2006) ("[I]n order to shock the conscience, conduct must at the very least be extreme and egregious, or, put another way, truly outrageous, uncivilized, and intolerable."). The Second Circuit has followed the same approach. *See Ferran v. Town of Nassau,* 41 F.3d 363, 369 (2d Cir. 2006) (plaintiffs "must show that the Town's alleged acts against their land were 'arbitrary,' 'conscience-shocking,' or 'oppressive in the constitutional sense,' not merely 'incorrect or ill-advised.' ...").

Other federal courts, such as the Sixth Circuit, apply a less demanding standard. *See Paterek v. Village of Armada,* 801 F.3d 630 (6th Cir. 2015) (reversing a district court dismissal on summary judgment of a due process challenge to conditions added to a land use permit and a certificate of occupancy on the ground that there were material issues as to whether the government action was "arbitrary and capricious"). *See also Centres, Inc. v. Town of Brookfield,* 148 F.3d 699, 704 (7th Cir. 1998) (applying an "arbitrary and unreasonable" test); *Dodd v. Hood River City,* 59 F.3d 852, 864 (9th Cir. 1995) (in putting property into a forest use zone, the county did not act arbitrarily or without a rational basis for its decision, and its decision was "at least debatable").

Given the diverse approaches followed in the various federal circuits, it is impossible to state a "general rule" for determining how liability is established in substantive due process challenges to land use regulations.

Notes and Comments

1. *Land Use Due Process Litigation in the Federal Courts.* After the Supreme Court decided the *Village of Euclid* and *Nectow* cases, discussed in Chapter 2, both of which

involved substantive due process challenges to zoning regulation, the Supreme Court retreated from the land use arena for the next 40 years. After the Court finally emerged from its land use slumber, it initially issued only a handful of decisions, consistently rejecting due process challenges to land use regulations. *See Goldblatt v. Hempstead*, 369 U.S. 590 (1962) (rejecting due process challenge to municipal regulation of sand and gravel operation); *Village of Belle Terre v. Boraas*, 416 U.S. 1 (1974) (rejecting due process challenge to municipal ordinance limiting number of unrelated individuals who may live in a dwelling). As a result, for much of the twentieth century, it was largely left to the state courts to provide content to substantive due process doctrine in the land use context. Starting in the 1980s, the Supreme Court fully reengaged with land use, issuing a substantial number of decisions involving the Takings Clause (the most important of which are excerpted in Chapter 7). But the Court has continued largely to ignore due process challenges to land use rules; when it has addressed due process claims in recent years, the Court has continued to provide litigants scant encouragement that due process claims will prevail. *See City of Cuyahoga Falls v. Buckeye Cmty. Hope*, 538 U.S. 188 (2003).

The Supreme Court's lack of interest in expanding substantive due process doctrine in the land use context flows from a confluence of discordant philosophies on the Court. On the one hand, some members of the Court subscribe to the widely held view, at least in the post-*Lochner* era, that substantive due process should rarely be used to invalidate social or economic legislation. *See, e.g., Eastern Enters. v. Apfel*, 524 U.S. 498 (1988) (Breyer, J,. dissenting) (agreeing that the Due Process Clause provided the appropriate basis for judging the constitutionality of federal coal worker legislation, but rejecting the challenge on the merits). On the other hand, other justices have adopted the position that the substantive branch of due process only protects "fundamental rights," leading to the conclusion that substantive due process doctrine is unavailable for the purpose of challenging most regulations, including land use regulations. *See City of Cuyahoga Falls v. Buckeye Cmty. Hope*, 538 U.S. 188, 200-01 (2003) (Scalia, concurring, joined by Thomas, J.). Thus, for different reasons, the liberal and conservative wings of the modern Court have joined forces to discourage due process challenges.

Whatever the explanation for the Supreme Court's lack of interest, the Court's non-engagement on substantive due process in the land use context has meant that the lower federal courts (and the state courts) have been left to muddle through on their own, with predictably divergent outcomes.

2. *The Predicate Property Issue.* An important threshold issue that has divided the lower courts is what constitutes a protected "property" interest sufficient to trigger application of the Due Process Clause. One view, exemplified by the Second Circuit *RRI Realty Corp.* case, excepted above, is that a litigant cannot assert a substantive due process claim based on a denial of a permit or some other land use authorization unless the claimant has a clear entitlement to receive the authorization. The Second Circuit has consistently adhered to this view. *See Clubside, Inc. v. Valentin*, 468 F.3d 144, 153 (2d Cir. 2006) ("This Circuit applies a 'clear entitlement' analysis to determine whether a landowner has a constitutionally cognizable property interest in the benefit sought."). Some other circuits have adopted the same position. *See, e.g., Hyde Park Co. v. Santa Fe City Council*, 226 F.3d 1207 (10th Cir. 2000) (plaintiff had no protectable property interest in having the city council approve a subdivision plat for its property). The other, apparently less popular, view is that a claimant's ownership of real estate satisfies the need for some identifiable property interest for the

purpose of the Due Process Clause; under this view, a landowner can challenge the denial of a land use permit under the Due Process Clause regardless of whether she has an entitlement to a permit. *See, e.g., DeBlasio v. Zoning Bd. of Adjustment for Twp. of West Amwell,* 53 F.3d 592 (3d Cir. 1995); *Burrell v. City of Kankakee,* 815 F.2d 1127, 1129 (7th Cir. 1987).

The "entitlement" theory in land use cases derives from the "new property" theory developed in the context of procedural due process challenges to denials of government benefits. *See Perry v. Sindermann,* 408 U.S. 593 (1972); *Board of Regents v. Roth,* 408 U.S. 564 (1972). *See generally* Charles Reich, The New Property, 73 Yale L. J. 733 (1964). These landmark decisions *expanded* the scope of property for due process purposes beyond traditional common law property interests, such as ownership rights in land. *See Roth,* 408 U.S. at 571-72 ("The Court has . . . made clear that the property interests protected by procedural due process extend well beyond actual ownership of real estate, chattels, or money."). As a result, some commentators have questioned whether it is logical to apply new property theory to *limit* the ability of claimants holding real property to pursue substantive due process challenges. *See* Daniel R. Mandelker, Entitlement to Substantive Due Process: Old Versus New Property in Land Use Regulation, 3 Wash. U. J. L. & Pol'y 61 (2000) (arguing that the entitlement rule is "problematic and courts should abolish it"); Peter Byrne, Due Process Land Use Claims After *Lingle,* 34 Ecol. L. Q. 471, 476 (2007) (observing that "the entitlement requirement is surely inconsistent with *Euclid* and *Nectow,* which welcomed facial and as applied due process challenges to discretionary land use decisions"). Federal courts embracing the entitlement theory are likely motivated by a desire to limit their involvement in local land use matters, as captured by the memorable declaration that the role of a federal court "should not be to sit as a zoning board of appeals." *RRI Realty Corp. v. Incorporated Village of Southampton,* 870 F.2d 911, 914 (2d Cir. 1989) (quoting *Village of Belle Terre v. Boraas,* 416 U.S. 1, 13 (1974) (Marshall, J., dissenting)).

3. Agins *and Ersatz Takings Doctrine.* For many years, figuring out how to apply the Due Process Clause in the land use context was made more complicated by the Supreme Court's conflation of due process and takings doctrine, a problem which was not finally resolved until the Court's landmark decision in *Lingle v. Chevron USA, Inc.,* 544 U.S. 528 (2005). In *Agins v. City of Tiburon,* 447 U.S. 255, 260 (1980), the Court declared that "application of a general zoning law to particular property effects a taking if the ordinance does not substantially advance legitimate state interests." The only authority the Court cited for this ostensible takings test was *Nectow v. Cambridge,* 277 U.S. 183 (1928), an important land use case to be sure, but one decided under the Due Process Clause, not the Takings Clause. Insofar as this test focuses on the legitimacy of the government's ends, and the reasonableness of the means selected to achieve those ends, it sounds in due process, not takings. Thus, *Agins* launched a confusing 25-year period during which claimants could assert what amounts to a due process claim dressed up with a takings label. (The Supreme Court foreshadowed its misstep in *Agins* in its earlier decision in *Penn Central Transp. Co. v. City of New York,* 438 U.S. 104, 127 (1978), by stating in *dictum* that it was "implicit in *Goldblatt* [*v. Hempstead,* 369 U.S. 590 (1962)] that a use restriction on real property may constitute a 'taking' if not reasonably necessary to the effectuation of a substantial public purpose."). *See also* Brad Karkkainen, The Police Power Revisited: Phantom Incorporation and the Roots of the Takings

"Muddle," 90 Minn. L. Rev. 826 (2006) (providing an in-depth description and analysis of the Supreme Court's conflation of takings and due process doctrines).

This error might have had little doctrinal or practical significance except for the fact that the *Agins* Court stated that a law should be regarded as a taking if it "does not *substantially* advance legitimate state interests." That formulation is distinctly at odds with the highly deferential standard of review in substantive due process cases in the post-*Lochner* era, suggesting that a plaintiff asserting a due process claim in the guise of a takings claim would have a much greater chance of success than a plaintiff asserting a straightforward due process claim. In the wake of *Agins*, it is hardly surprising that sophisticated property rights advocates eschewed due process claims in favor of *Agins* "substantially advance" takings claims. *See, e.g.*, RS Radford, Why Rent Control Is a Regulatory Taking, 6 Fordham Envtl. L. J. 755 (1995). In addition, the Supreme Court issued a long series of opinions reciting the *Agins* "substantially advance" test, lending credibility to the idea that the takings standard was less deferential than the due process standard. *See Monterey v. Del Monte Dunes at Monterey, Ltd.*, 526 U.S. 687, 704 (1999). At the same time, given its inherent implausibility, some litigants and courts essentially ignored the *Agins ersatz* takings test. However, the validity and proper application of this ostensible takings test was extensively litigated in the U.S. Court of Appeals for the Ninth Circuit, and that court eventually affirmed specific takings claims based on the substantially advance theory. *See e.g., Richardson v. City & Cnty. of Honolulu*, 124 F.3d 1150 (9th Cir. 1997) (ruling that rent control ordinance was a taking because it failed to substantially advance a legitimate state interest).

4. The Lingle *Correction.* In *Lingle v. Chevron USA Inc.*, a unanimous Supreme Court essentially confessed error and repudiated the substantially advance takings test. The Court stated that there was "no question" that this ostensible takings test had been derived from due process precedents. 544 U.S. at 540. The Court also observed that the test "has some logic in the context of a due process challenge," but it "is not a valid method of discerning whether private property has been 'taken' for purposes of the Fifth Amendment." *Id.* at 542. Lastly, the Court observed that the substantially advances formula "can be read to demand heightened means-ends review of virtually any regulation of private property." This type of review "would require courts to scrutinize the efficacy of a vast array of state and federal regulations — a task for which courts are not well suited," and "it would empower — and might often require — courts to substitute their predictive judgments for those of elected legislatures and expert agencies." *Id.* at 544.

Lingle plainly interred the substantially advance takings test, thereby clarifying both the scope and the boundaries of takings doctrine. But it can also be read to confirm that land use regulations are potentially subject to challenge under the Due Process Clause. While the *Lingle* Court rejected the notion that a means-ends inquiry can properly fit into takings doctrine, it did not question that it is possible to bring a direct claim of this type under the Due Process Clause. Indeed, Justice Anthony Kennedy, in a concurring opinion, observed that the Court's opinion "does not foreclose the possibility that a regulation might be so arbitrary or irrational as to violate due process," and that [t]he failure of a regulation to accomplish a stated or obvious objective would be relevant to that inquiry." *Id.* at 548-49. Not surprisingly, some lower courts have cited *Lingle* as affirmative support for the viability of substantive due process challenges to land use regulations. *See, e.g., A Helping Hand LLC v. Baltimore Cnty.*, 515 F3d 356, 369 n.6 (4th Cir. 2008); *Crown Point Dev., Inc. v. City of Sun Valley*, 506 F.3d 851 (9th Cir. 2007).

The Supreme Court's repudiation of the heightened standard of review apparently called for by the *Agins* "substantially advance" test supports the conclusion that a similar heightened standard of review would be inappropriate in substantive due process cases as well. Justice Sandra Day O'Connor clearly had more than takings doctrine in mind when she said: "The reasons for deference to legislative judgments about the need for, and likely effectiveness of, regulatory actions are by now well established, and we think they are no less applicable here." *Lingle*, 544 U.S. at 545. *See also* Peter Byrne, Due Process Land Use Claims After *Lingle*, 34 Ecol. L. Q. 471, 472 (2007) ("How likely is it that landowners will be able to prevail against local governments on substantive due process claims challenging land use decisions? In federal court, the answer will—and should—be virtually never.").

5. *The* Graham *deflection.* In *Graham v. Connor*, 490 U.S. 386 (1989), the Supreme Court rejected an argument that a claim that law enforcement officials used excessive force could be based on the Due Process Clause rather than the Fourth Amendment, stating: "Because the Fourth Amendment provides an explicit textual source of constitutional protection against this sort of physically intrusive governmental conduct, that Amendment, not the more generalized notion of 'substantive due process,' must be the guide for analyzing these claims." Thus, *Graham*, in the land use context no less than in any other realm, provides defendants an argument for deflecting a claim under the Due Process Clause.

6. *Due Process in the State Courts.* Given the hostility of many federal courts to due process challenges to local land use regulations, it is hardly surprising that the state courts have played an outsize role in the development of due process doctrine in the land use context. In comparison with the federal courts interpreting the federal constitution, the state courts are often more welcoming of substantive due process claims under their state constitutions. Nonetheless, the burden on a plaintiff to demonstrate a substantive due process violation is heavy. The Washington Supreme Court, for example, has articulated the test as follows: (1) whether the regulation is aimed at achieving a legitimate public purpose; (2) whether it uses means reasonably necessary to achieve that purpose; and (3) whether it is unduly oppressive on the landowner. *Presbytery of Seattle v. King County*, 787 P.2d 907, 912 (Wash. 1990). Given the stringency of the test, most of the decisions reject such claims. *See, e.g., Mettler Walloon, LLC v. Melrose Twp.*, 761 N.W.2d 293, 311-312 (Mich. Ct. App. 2008) (although there was a conflict of interest in voting on the project after the city attorney erroneously advised there was no conflict, that action did not violate substantive due process because "[t]hat advice was incorrect, but it was not irrational."); *Smith Inv. Co. v. Sandy City*, 958 P.2d 245 (Utah Ct. App. 1998) (down-zoning debatably promoted permissible city goals, including reducing oversupply of space zoned for retail and solving traffic problems, and thus did not violate substantive due process).

F. EQUAL PROTECTION CHALLENGES

The Equal Protection Clause of the Fourteenth Amendment—"No State shall . . . deny to any person within its jurisdiction the equal protection of the laws" — provides an alternative constitutional ground for challenging land use regulations. The Fourteenth Amendment, added to the Constitution following the Civil War, applies only to the states (and their subdivisions). However, apparently recognizing how odd it would be to have a constitutional principle of equal treatment that applies only to the states and not to the federal government, the Supreme Court in *Bolling v. Sharpe*, 347 U.S. 497 (1954), held that the Equal Protection Clause applies to the federal government through the Due Process Clause of the Fifth Amendment. Thus, the Equal Protection Clause — like the Takings Clause, the Due Process Clause, and the First Amendment — applies to official decision-making at all levels of government in the United States.

Legal challenges to alleged government discrimination related to housing have frequently been brought under the Equal Protection Clause. The application of equal protection doctrine in the housing context is discussed in detail in Chapter 13. This section focuses on the application of the Equal Protection Clause in so-called "class of one" cases, a recent and important innovation in equal protection doctrine with important land use implications.

■ VILLAGE OF WILLOWBROOK v. OLECH
528 U.S. 562 (2000)

Per Curiam

Respondent Grace Olech and her late husband Thaddeus asked petitioner Village of Willowbrook (Village) to connect their property to the municipal water supply. The Village at first conditioned the connection on the Olechs granting the Village a 33-foot easement. The Olechs objected, claiming that the Village only required a 15-foot easement from other property owners seeking access to the water supply. After a 3-month delay, the Village relented and agreed to provide water service with only a 15-foot easement.

Olech sued the Village, claiming that the Village's demand of an additional 18-foot easement violated the Equal Protection Clause of the Fourteenth Amendment. Olech asserted that the 33-foot easement demand was "irrational and wholly arbitrary"; that the Village's demand was actually motivated by ill will resulting from the Olechs' previous filing of an unrelated, successful lawsuit against the Village; and that the Village acted either with the intent to deprive Olech of her rights or in reckless disregard of her rights. App. 10, 12.

The District Court dismissed the lawsuit pursuant to Federal Rule of Civil Procedure 12(b)(6) for failure to state a cognizable claim under the Equal Protection Clause. Relying on Circuit precedent, the Court of Appeals for the Seventh Circuit reversed, holding that a plaintiff can allege an equal protection violation by asserting that state action was motivated solely by a "'spiteful effort to "get" him for reasons wholly unrelated to any legitimate state objective.'" 160 F.3d 386, 387 (1998) (quoting *Esmail v. Macrane*, 53 F.3d 176, 180 (C.A.7 1995)). It determined that Olech's complaint sufficiently alleged such a claim. 160 F.3d, at 388. We granted certiorari to determine whether the Equal Protection Clause gives rise to a cause of action on behalf of a "class of one" where the plaintiff did not allege membership in a class or group. 527 U.S. 1067 (1999).

Our cases have recognized successful equal protection claims brought by a "class of one," where the plaintiff alleges that she has been intentionally treated differently from others similarly situated and that there is no rational basis for the difference in treatment. See *Sioux City Bridge Co. v. Dakota County*, 260 U.S. 441 (1923); *Allegheny Pittsburgh Coal Co. v. Commission of Webster Cty.*, 488 U.S. 336 (1989). In so doing, we have explained that "'[t]he purpose of the equal protection clause of the Fourteenth Amendment is to secure every person within the State's jurisdiction against intentional and arbitrary discrimination, whether occasioned by express terms of a statute or by its improper execution through duly constituted agents.'" *Sioux City Bridge Co., supra,* at 445 (quoting *Sunday Lake Iron Co. v. Township of Wakefield*, 247 U.S. 350, 352 (1918)).

That reasoning is applicable to this case. Olech's complaint can fairly be construed as alleging that the Village intentionally demanded a 33-foot easement as a condition of connecting her property to the municipal water supply where the Village required only a 15-foot easement from other similarly situated property owners. See *Conley v. Gibson*, 355 U.S. 41, 45-46 (1957). The complaint also alleged that the Village's demand was "irrational and wholly arbitrary" and that the Village ultimately connected her property after receiving a clearly adequate 15-foot easement. These allegations, quite apart from the Village's subjective motivation, are sufficient to state a claim for relief under traditional equal protection analysis. We therefore affirm the judgment of the Court of Appeals, but do not reach the alternative theory of "subjective ill will" relied on by that court.

It is so ordered.

Justice BREYER, concurring in the result.

The Solicitor General and the village of Willowbrook have expressed concern lest we interpret the Equal Protection Clause in this case in a way that would transform many ordinary violations of city or state law into violations of the Constitution. It might be thought that a rule that looks only to an intentional difference in treatment and a lack of a rational basis for that different treatment would work such a transformation. Zoning decisions, for example, will often, perhaps almost always, treat one landowner differently from another, and one might claim that, when a city's zoning authority takes an action that fails to conform to a city zoning regulation, it lacks a "rational basis" for its action (at least if the regulation in question is reasonably clear).

This case, however, does not directly raise the question whether the simple and common instance of a faulty zoning decision would violate the Equal Protection Clause. That is because the Court of Appeals found that in this case respondent had alleged an extra factor as well — a factor that the Court of Appeals called "vindictive action," "illegitimate animus," or "ill will." 160 F.3d 386, 388 (C.A.7 1998). And, in that respect, the court said this case resembled *Esmail v. Macrane*, 53 F.3d 176 (C.A.7 1995), because the *Esmail* plaintiff had alleged that the municipality's differential treatment "was the result not of prosecutorial discretion honestly (even if ineptly-even if arbitrarily) exercised but of an illegitimate desire to 'get' him." 160 F.3d, at 388.

In my view, the presence of that added factor in this case is sufficient to minimize any concern about transforming run-of-the-mill zoning cases into cases of constitutional right. For this reason, along with the others mentioned by the Court, I concur in the result.

Notes and Comments

1. *Equal Protection in General.* To understand the application of the Equal Protection Clause in the land use context, it is useful to step back and consider the Supreme Court's equal protection jurisprudence as whole. While it is generally recognized that the Fourteenth Amendment was adopted to address the plight of the former slaves, the Supreme Court has interpreted this provision to establish a general prohibition against unjustified disparate treatment. Because laws routinely involve line drawing, the Court has found distinguishing between justified and unjustified disparate treatment a problem of considerable difficulty. Moreover, state and local governments, in the land use field as elsewhere, adopt many laws that treat different persons differently, creating the specter that the Equal Protection Clause, applied expansively, could turn many local disputes into federal constitutional issues, potentially forcing federal courts to resolve disputes that could and arguably should be resolved by state courts under state law. These concerns go a long way toward explaining the general (but not completely consistent) effort by the Supreme Court and lower federal courts to limit the reach of the Equal Protection Clause.

2. *Equal Protection Rules.* The Supreme Court has established some relatively clear and stable rules governing claims under the Equal Protection Clause. The Court has (more or less) consistently applied what is called a "deferential rational basis" standard in reviewing legal classifications not involving a "suspect" classification or affecting a "fundamental right." Generally speaking, the rational basis standard requires that, to survive a constitutional challenge, the government need only show that the action furthers a "legitimate" (not an "important" or "compelling") governmental interest or purpose and that the classification bears some sort of "rational" relationship to the governmental goal. *See Royster Guano v. Virginia,* 253 U.S. 412 (1920). To defend a piece of legislation under the rational basis standard, the court need not point to the actual legislative purpose; it is sufficient if some "conceivable" legislative purpose is legitimate. *FCC v. Beach Commc'ns, Inc.,* 508 U.S. 307 (1993). In addition, laws will not be struck down under the rational basis test even if they are significantly "underinclusive," *see Railway Express Agency v. New York,* 336 U.S. 106 (1949), or significantly "overinclusive." *See NYC Transit Auth. v. Beazer,* 440 U.S. 568 (1979). While rational basis equal protection cases are notoriously hard to win, the Supreme Court has upheld such claims on a few occasions in recent decades, giving rise to debate about whether these cases simply demonstrate that rational basis review is not completely toothless or whether these particular cases reflect a special "rational basis with bite" standard applicable in special circumstances. *See* Erwin Chemerinsky, Constitutional Law 718 (4th ed. 2013)

Laws classifying persons based on race, national origin and (generally) alien status are said to be subject to "strict scrutiny," meaning that they will be upheld only if they are "necessary" to achieve a "compelling" governmental purpose. Likewise, classifications affecting a fundamental right, including the right to procreate, voting, access to the judicial process, and interstate travel are reviewed under the strict scrutiny standard. Intermediate scrutiny is used to review discrimination based on gender and against nonmarital children; under this test, a law will be upheld it is substantially related to an important governmental purpose. In the land use field, outside the context of allegedly discriminatory restrictions on access to housing, these higher levels of scrutiny are not likely to have much relevance.

3. Olech's *Ambiguity.* In *Olech,* the Court issued a brief, *per curiam* decision, and there was no dissenting opinion, suggesting that the case presented neither a novel nor an important issue. But, in fact, the case has given rise to significant controversy and uncertainty. *See* William D. Araiza, Irrationality and Animus in Class-of-One Equal Protection Cases, 34 Ecology L. Q. 493 (2007). The central issue in the post-*Olech* debate has been whether a plaintiff asserting a class-of-one claim must demonstrate, in addition to some irrational classification, that the defendant was motivated by ill-will or "animus" toward the plaintiff. The District Court in *Olech* granted the village's motion to dismiss, ruling that the plaintiff had not articulated a sufficient level of animus to support a viable claim. The Seventh Circuit, in an opinion by Judge Richard Posner, reversed, stating that the complaint was sufficient because it alleged "a totally illegitimate animus toward the plaintiff by the defendant." The Supreme Court, however, ruled that the allegation that the demand for a 33-foot easement was "irrational and wholly arbitrary" — "quite apart from the Village's subjective motivation" — was sufficient to state a claim.

In his concurring opinion, Justice Breyer expressed concern that "a rule that looks only to an intentional difference in treatment and a lack of a rational basis for that different treatment" risked converting "many ordinary violations of city or state law into violations of the Constitution." He thought that the case did not "directly raise the question" whether such barebones allegations would be sufficient to state a claim, because the appeals court had read the complaint to include an allegation of personal animus. Because he thought that "added factor" was sufficient to cabin the scope of a class-of-one equal protection lawsuit, he concurred in the result.

4. Olech *in the Lower Courts.* In the aftermath of *Olech,* the lower federal courts have generally worked hard to cabin class-of-one equal protection claims. As explained by the Tenth Circuit:

> In the wake of *Olech,* the lower courts have struggled to define the contours of class-of-one cases. All have recognized that, unless carefully circumscribed, the concept of a class-of-one equal protection claim could effectively provide a federal cause of action for review of almost every executive and administrative decision made by state actors. It is always possible for persons aggrieved by government action to allege, and almost always possible to produce evidence, that they were treated differently from others, with regard to everything from zoning to licensing to speeding to tax evaluation. It would become the task of federal courts and juries, then, to inquire into the grounds for differential treatment and to decide whether those grounds were sufficiently reasonable to satisfy equal protection review. This would constitute the federal courts as general-purpose second-guessers of the reasonableness of broad areas of state and local decision making: a role that is both ill-suited to the federal courts and offensive to state and local autonomy in our federal system.

Jennings v. City of Stillwater, 383 F.3d 1199, 1210–11 (10th Cir. 2004). *See also Loesel v. City of Frankenmuth,* 692 F.3d 452 (6th Cir. 2012) (expressing the same concern). As Professor Williams Araiza has explained, even if deferential rational basis review will ordinarily cause a claim to fail on the merits, the ease with which an *Olech* claim can be pled allows plaintiffs to draft complaints that will easily survive motions to dismiss. *See* Araiza, Irrationality and Animus in Class-of-One Equal Protection Cases, 34 Ecology L. Q. at 513-14.

One basic question following *Olech* has been whether the lower courts should follow what the Court said (that an allegation of animus was unnecessary to state a viable claim) or what the Court actually did, at least according to Justice Breyer's telling (affirm the sufficiency of a complaint that, in fact, included an allegation of animus). Not surprisingly, given that each of these alternative readings of *Olech* is plausible, the lower courts have split on this issue. Some have concluded that animus is required, *see, e.g., Najas Realty, LLC v. Seekonk Water Dist.*, 821 F.3d 134 (1st Cir. 2016) (affirming dismissal of class-of-one lawsuit because plaintiffs "fail[ed] to state a plausible claim that bad faith or malice were the driving factors behind" government officials' rejection of development proposal), while others have concluded that it is not. *See, e g., Nevel v. Vill. of Schaumberg*, 297 F.3d 673, 680 (7th Cir. 2002).

5. *Comparators.* Some courts seeking to cabin *Olech* claims have stressed the requirement that an equal protection claimant show that she is comparable to someone else who received different treatment. For example, in *Fortress Bible Church v. Feiner*, 694 F.3d 208 (2d Cir. 2012), the Second Circuit stated that "a class-of-one claim requires a claimant to show an extremely high degree of similarity between itself and its comparators." *Id.* at 222. To prevail on a class-of-one claim, the court said, the plaintiff must show that "(i) no rational person could regard the circumstances of the plaintiff to differ from those of a comparator to a degree that would justify the differential treatment on the basis of a legitimate government policy; and (ii) the similarity in circumstances and difference in treatment are sufficient to exclude the possibility that the defendants acted on the basis of a mistake." *Id. See also Ruston v. Town Bd. for Skaneateles*, 610 F.3d 55, 59–60 (2d Cir. 2010).

6. *Other Approaches.* Other courts have adopted still other approaches for limiting class-of-one cases. For example, in *Loesel v. City of Frankenmuth*, 692 F.3d 452 (6th Cir. 2012), the Sixth Circuit stated: "Class-of-one claims are generally viewed skeptically because such claims have the potential to turn into an exercise in which juries are second-guessing the legislative process." *Id.* at 461. Based on this premise, the court declared:

> That is why a plaintiff must overcome a "heavy burden" to prevail based on the class-of-one theory. . . . The [plaintiffs] must show that they were treated differently than those similarly situated in all material respects. In addition, they must show that the adverse treatment they experienced was so unrelated to the achievement of any combination of legitimate purposes that the court can only conclude that the government's actions were irrational. This showing is made either by negativing every conceivable reason for the government's actions or by demonstrating that the actions were motivated by animus or ill-will.

Id. at 462.

7. *The Supreme Court's* Engquist *Decision.* Since *Olech* was decided in 2000, the Supreme Court has not revisited the class-of-one theory in the land use context. However, the Court subsequently issued a major class-of-one decision, *Engquist v. Oregon Dep't of Agric.*, 553 U.S. 591 (2008), ruling that the class-of-one theory is not available to government workers challenging public employment decisions. The Court stressed the traditional common law approach of treating public workers as "at will" employees as well as the broad discretion built into public employment decision-making.

Enguist is susceptible to at least two alternatives readings: as walling off public employment decisions from class-of-one challenges or, more broadly, as walling off decisions that involve so much discretion that courts cannot properly review them.

The latter reading would permit litigants to raise *Engquist* as a bar to equal protection challenges to discretionary land use decisions. Lower courts have adopted varying readings of *Engquist* in land use cases. *Compare Fortress Bible Church v. Feiner,* 694 F.3d 208 (2d Cir. 2012) (ruling that *Engquist* did not bar class-of-one challenge to town officials' rejection of discretionary land use approvals) *with Catcove Corp. v. Patrick Heaney,* 685 F. Supp. 2d 328, 333 (E.D.N.Y. 2010) (ruling that *Enquist* barred class-of-one challenge to town's refusal to approve proposed zoning changes; "zoning is a classic example of a 'state action' that involves 'discretionary decision making.'").

7. *Other than Class-of-One Cases.* If the class-of-one theory is not available, the Equal Protection Clause still remains available as a basis for challenging garden variety land use regulations. Such cases (at least in the absence of alleged discrimination based on a suspect classification, such as race, discussed in Chapter 13) are governed by the traditional, highly deferential standards that apply in equal protection cases generally.

For example, in *Pennell v. City of San Jose,* 485 U.S. 1 (1988), the Supreme Court considered — and rejected — an equal protection challenge by a group of landlords to a city rent control ordinance that required officials to consider the "hardship to a tenant" of a rent increase in administering a rent control law. The plaintiffs contended that the law violated equal protection because it treated landlords differently depending upon whether they had tenants who qualified for hardship treatment. Applying the "rationally related to a legitimate state interest" test, the Court did not break a sweat in determining that the claim failed:

> In light of our conclusion . . . that the Ordinance's tenant hardship provisions are designed to serve the legitimate purpose of protecting tenants, we can hardly conclude that it is irrational for the Ordinance to treat certain landlords differently on the basis of whether or not they have hardship tenants. The Ordinance distinguishes between landlords because doing so furthers the purpose of ensuring that individual tenants do not suffer "unreasonable" hardship; it would be inconsistent to state that hardship is a legitimate factor to be considered but then hold that appellees could not tailor the Ordinance so that only legitimate hardship cases are redressed.

Id. at 14. In response to the landlords' argument that they were not the "cause" of the community's housing problems which the ordinance sought to address, the Court said, "this is beside the point — if a landlord does have a hardship tenant, regardless of the reason why, it is rational for [city officials] to take that fact into consideration when establishing a rent that is 'reasonable under the circumstances.'" *Id.* at 15.

9

■

Regional, State, and Federal Land Use Regulation

A. INTRODUCTION

1. The Quiet (and Very Slow) Revolution

In a well-known book published in 1972, the authors posited that a fundamental change in land use controls was occurring in the United States. Their thesis was as follows:

> This country is in the midst of a revolution in the way we regulate the use of our land. It is a peaceful revolution, conducted entirely within the law. It is a quiet revolution, and its supporters include both conservatives and liberals. . . .
>
> The *ancien regime* being overthrown is the feudal system under which the entire pattern of land development has been controlled by thousands of individual local governments, each seeking to maximize its tax base and minimize its social problems, and caring less what happens to all the others.
>
> The tools of the revolution are new laws taking a wide variety of forms but each sharing a common theme — the need to provide some degree of state or regional participation in the major decisions that affect the use of our increasingly limited supply of land.

Fred Bosselman & David Callies, Council on Envtl. Quality, The Quiet Revolution in Land Use Control 1 (1971).

Now, many decades later, it is apparent that the fundamental change in the governmental level of regulatory control detected in the early 1970s has proceeded more slowly than anticipated. In the vast majority of states, local control of land use continues as the dominant force shaping this country's landscape. With a few well-recognized exceptions that are discussed herein, local zoning and growth management has been resistant to attempts at moving the locus of land use power to the state or regional level. In addition, unlike other areas of law that have been substantially "federalized," the field of land use regulation has largely resisted federal preemption or interference.

The student of land use controls must recognize the roots of this deep-seated resistance to change in the level of government that regulates land use. One powerful reason is the pervasive conviction that, because land use decisions have an important impact on living conditions in local communities, those elected representatives who are closest to the community should decide them. Furthermore, because local government operates much of the infrastructure that services new development, local governments have a legitimate claim to authority over decisions about developments that will contribute to and use that infrastructure.

But other potent political forces — forces at odds with each other on many land use issues — also tend to reinforce local control of land use. Local elected officials resist the loss of power that state control or oversight of land use regulation would bring. Land use authority is the most important power remaining at the local government level, particularly in states where state legislation or voter initiative has circumscribed the power to raise property taxes. City councilors tenaciously defend this last bastion of their authority. In some states, county legislators bemoan the loss of this power as their counties have seen considerable incorporation of cities in areas they once controlled, thus removing them from land use regulation.

The development community is, in general, also satisfied with the local control. Many developers believe that their ability to influence land use decisions is maximized at the local level and would be diminished if those decisions were removed to the regional or state level.

Finally, the "third parties" in many land use disputes, citizens' groups and their members, who are often the dominant force in local planning and zoning programs, care deeply about protecting the character of their neighborhoods and the financial investment in their homes. These grassroots citizen groups have substantial electoral clout in local elections. They worry about a diminution in their influence if state or regional regulation should replace the current system.

2. The Critiques of Local Regulation

These various political forces coalesce into a tremendous resistance to proposals that local government should not have the final word on land use decisions. There are, however, strong arguments that complete local autonomy over land use decisions is both illogical and inefficient. The cumulative impacts of land use decisions by cities and counties are not self-contained; instead, those impacts can ripple throughout the region in which the local jurisdiction is situated. For example, the location of a large shopping center in a city will have economic and environmental spillover effects; neighboring jurisdictions may well bear the traffic impacts of such a center, while the region will feel the air quality effects of increased automobile emissions. At the same time, however, the local jurisdiction in which the shopping center is located will likely garner the revenue from any sales taxes accruing to local cities, and the construction of a large shopping center in one city will likely mean that other developers will be uninterested in locating a competing facility anywhere close to this one.

Also, the exercise of land use control by local communities, all acting independently and in their own self-interest, has produced a regional landscape of low-density, automobile-dependent sprawl, a pattern of development that, in the view of critics, may well prove unsustainable into the future. Regional transportation planning may be needed to encourage transit-oriented development that will support greener and more sustainable urban core areas. Under our present arrangement, local urban planning may work to undermine the benefits of major investments in regional transit planning such as light rail or bus rapid transit development. Watershed, environmental, wildlife habitat, energy, and economic issues affected by the built environment also often transcend local jurisdictional boundaries. Many believe, for these and other reasons, that we need a more integrated and holistic regional approach to the development of our built environment.

The state and federal governments are already involved in some decisions about how an area develops. They build and maintain the principal transportation arteries in metropolitan regions, and their agencies regulate many development decisions for environmental protection purposes. This regional pattern of low-density sprawl that results from this hodgepodge jurisdictional arrangement is thought by many to impose enormous social, economic, resource, energy, and environmental costs on our society and has generated the beginnings of a movement for sustainable development in this country. Smart growth, new urbanism, and sustainable development planning concepts related to these issues are discussed in Chapter 11.

3. Regional and State Oversight

These types of problems have led to experimentation with state and regional review of certain types of land use decision making. In a few instances, this experimentation has taken the form of direct state intervention into the land use decision-making process. Hawaii began the movement in 1961 when it adopted a top-down system of statewide land use regulation that greatly limits the local role in such decisions. This system is unique to Hawaii, which because of its size, history, and politics, is perhaps best suited to a transfer of land use power to the state level. More typical is the bottom-up land use approach adopted in Oregon. Under this system, local governments bear the responsibility of preparing comprehensive land use plans. Those plans, however, must be consistent with a series of goals set at the state level, goals that emphasize protection of forests and farmlands, as well as the securing of affordable housing through increased residential densities inside urban growth boundaries.

An Oregon state agency has the authority to review all local plans for consistency with the statewide goals, and once the local government receives the state's "acknowledgment" that its plan adequately reflects these goals, its development decisions must then be consistent with the plan. Thereafter, a variety of parties are authorized to appeal the local government's decisions to a state land use appeals board, which has authority to review the local agency's determinations of consistency. All of these procedures occur with considerable emphasis on public participation. Also mandated are regional councils with binding regional plans and regional growth boundaries.

While the Oregon system is based on comprehensive statewide planning, in Vermont regional commissions review major development proposals against a series of statutory criteria that relate to infrastructure capacity, environmental degradation, and other impacts. These regulatory decisions are also guided by land use plans developed by state-supported regional planning commissions and by local communities.

Other states have chosen to form regional bodies that review local land use decisions for specific areas or for certain projects with significant impacts on natural resources. State regulation of development in coastal areas is a prominent example of this approach This regulatory mechanism was championed by the American Law Institute's Model Land Development Code, completed in 1975, which stressed the need to regulate projects with impacts that were not contained within local jurisdictional boundaries. *See* Model Land Development Code Art. 7, §7-301(1) (Am. Law Inst. 1976). Other states have formed regional bodies to protect specific areas of environmental significance, such as the Chesapeake Bay region, the San Francisco Bay region, and the Adirondack Mountains. This regional approach is illustrated in this chapter by *330 Concord St. Neighborhood Ass'n v. Campsen*, 424 S.E.2d 538 (Ct. App. 1992), a South Carolina case focusing on regulation of the coastal zone in that state.

4. Intergovernmental Disputes and State Preemption

The efforts of states to alter the traditional model of local government control over land use are important for they may be the precursor of fundamental change in how land use is controlled. As the chapter's title implies, however, there are other forms of intergovernmental limitations on local government's discretion over land use. One important area might be termed "boundary" limitations: the extent to which a neighboring city, a special purpose district, or a state agency must respect city or county zoning in implementing a project in that local jurisdiction. The competing policy concerns are obvious. The jurisdiction in which the development will be located has a strong interest in ensuring even-handed implementation of its planning, zoning, and other land use controls. A specific development not called for in the local plan can wreak havoc with a well-considered land use scheme.

At the same time, the agency seeking to site a facility in a city or county's jurisdiction may well face local opposition. Certain types of governmental projects produce benefits that are spread throughout the region but impose specific costs on the locality where the project will be sited. For example, every regional area needs at least one facility to serve as a jail, but local opposition to the siting of that jail may be intense. If local governments can use their land use powers to resist the siting of such facilities, and state or regional agencies cannot override that power, the implementation of important public tasks can be stymied.

Resolution of these challenges is most appropriately the subject of legislation, but the statutes in many instances are silent. Thus, the matter is often left to the courts by default, and they have used a variety of approaches to resolve it. Most recently, courts are rejecting traditional immunity doctrines and applying more analytical approaches to this issue. This is what happened in *City of Everett v. Snohomish County*, a principal case in this chapter. Courts addressing these issues are often making essentially legislative judgments about governmental immunity questions.

A variation on this form of intergovernmental conflict can occur when one local jurisdiction seeks to annex land outside of its current boundaries. Such action, of course, has important land use implications, as you will see from a principal case included in this chapter, *City of Albuquerque v. State Municipal Boundary Commission*. Disputes over annexations also center on the provision of necessary municipal services.

Another form of intergovernmental conflict arises out of the considerable environmental legislation adopted by states over the last 40 years. This legislation typically gives a state agency permitting authority over specific types of industrial and business developments, and that permitting authority often requires the state agency to consider factors related to land use before granting the permit. For example, a state regulatory board may have authority over mining activities and may be mandated to consider, among other factors, whether the location of a mine is likely to endanger groundwater or to discharge pollutants that might impact adjoining land uses.

This type of legislation often does not expressly deprive local governments of their traditional land use authority over such facilities. Nonetheless, the overlap in regulatory authority invites claims by applicants that state law preempts local regulation of such developments. In recent years, courts have increasingly grappled with such claims.

5. The Federal Role

Finally, in addition to some state and regional limitations on local government's land use powers, there is a federal role in land use decision making. In the 1970s, Congress seriously considered enacting national land use legislation, and from time to time commentators again float such proposals. In general, Congress has refused to directly intervene in local land use planning and zoning, leaving it to the states and local governments to devise the institutional arrangements that best suit their needs. This refusal, however, does not mean that the federal government exercises no preempting influence on land use. There are a number of federal regulatory statutes relating to, among other activities, religious uses, strip mining, cellular communications, manufactured housing, railroads, persons with disabilities, sex offenders, natural gas storage facilities, and application of biosolids to agricultural land. There is also an array of federal environmental laws that have a direct impact on local planning and development. These statutes are discussed later in this chapter and in Chapter 11.

Also, as owner and custodian of one-third of the nation's land, Congress and the federal land management agencies, such as the Bureau of Land Management and the Forest Service, make land use decisions that significantly affect not only the federal lands but also adjoining jurisdictions. The federal influence is particularly great in the western United States, where federal, state, and private land is often intermingled in the trademark "checkerboard" pattern that has existed since the states first entered the Union.

One of the most important developments of the last 35 years has been the passage of federal legislation requiring the principal federal land management agencies, the Bureau of Land Management, in the Department of the Interior, and the Forest Service, in the Department of Agriculture, to create land use plans for federal lands. These planning efforts, undertaken pursuant to the Forest and Rangeland Renewable Resources Planning Act and the National Forest Management Act, both codified at 16 U.S.C. §1600-1687, and the Federal Land Policy and Management Act, 43 U.S.C. §1701-85, for the first time have systematically attempted to inventory federal lands and plan for their future.

Even on nonfederal lands, however, the federal government exercises a powerful influence on local land use through its participation in transportation decisions and funding of state and local transportation projects. Most importantly, the interstate transportation system is largely a federally funded undertaking, and the location of freeway extensions, to take one example, can result in pressures to develop adjacent land. And historically, funding actions on urban freeways have had a mammoth impact on our cities. Joseph F.C. DiMento & Cliff Ellis, Changing Lanes: Visions and Histories of Urban Freeways (2013). More recently, the federal government has initiated some major programs for transit funding grants linked to smart growth and new urbanist development projects.

6. State and Regional Regulation in the Future

If new controls are adopted, they likely will reflect knowledge of the models addressed in this chapter, some of which themselves have been rethought. It may be worth noting that the state and regional reforms of local planning and zoning in Vermont, Oregon, and Florida, which are discussed herein, have all generally failed to significantly curtail low-density automobile-dependent regional sprawl within their boundaries. Their effects on growth and urban and rural form have been significant but not as great as advocates had sought and opponents had feared.

B. DIRECT STATE OVERSIGHT OF LOCAL REGULATION

State oversight of city or county land use regulation could take several forms. For example, the state could simply transfer authority over some (all?) land use decisions from the local government to the state level. Alternatively, the system could allow for selected appeals to a state (regional?) body from decisions that have significant effects outside of the local jurisdiction or that have important environmental effects.

The first two cases in this chapter illustrate the systems in place in Vermont and Oregon, and the notes following discuss in detail how other states have constructed a system of state oversight of local regulation. As you read the cases and the notes, you should begin to make judgments about which of these systems is preferable from the standpoints of planning, politics, and law.

■ FOLAND v. JACKSON COUNTY
897 P.2d 801 (1991)

Van Hoomissen, Justice.

Statutory Framework

The underlying dispute in this case can best be understood within the statutory framework in which it arises. The Legislative Assembly has created a broad program for comprehensive land use planning coordination. *See generally* ORS Ch. 197

(Comprehensive Land Use Planning Coordination). To supervise that program, the Legislative Assembly created the Land Conservation and Development Commission (LCDC) and gave that agency certain duties and powers. ORS 197.030 *et seq.* One of LCDC's duties is to adopt state-wide land use planning "goals" (the goals) that LCDC considers necessary to carry out, *inter alia*, the statutory program of land use planning coordination. ORS 197.225; ORS 197.040(1)(c); ORS 197.015(8).

Cities and counties of Oregon generally are required to conduct all land use planning in accordance with the goals adopted by LCDC. ORS 197.175(1). To serve that purpose, the statutes directed each city and county to prepare and adopt a "comprehensive plan" for land use decisions. ORS 197.175(2)(a). A comprehensive plan must comply with the goals. ORS 197.250.

The statutes also provide for LCDC "acknowledgment" of a comprehensive plan's compliance with the goals. ORS 197.251(1), in part, reads: "Upon the request of a local government, [LCDC] shall by order grant, deny or continue acknowledgment of compliance with the goals." The acknowledgment process allows persons to submit written comments and objections to the plan, requires LCDC to prepare a report concerning acknowledgment, and allows an opportunity for the city or county and persons who submitted comments at the earlier stage to submit written exceptions to the report. ORS 197.251(2). The incentive for a city or county to seek acknowledgment is that once LCDC grants acknowledgment, the city or county no longer is technically required to make land use decisions in compliance with the goals; rather, it is required only to make land use decisions in compliance with the acknowledged plan and other acknowledged ordinances adopted by the city or county. ORS 197.175(2)(d); ORS 197.015(11); *compare* ORS 197.175(2)(c) (if comprehensive plan is not acknowledged then city or county must make land use decisions in compliance with the goals). . . .

One of a city's or county's duties in regard to its comprehensive plan is to review that plan and, if necessary, amend and revise it to comply with the goals. ORS 197.250 (compliance required); ORS 197.255 (review required); ORS 197.175(2)(a) (amend and revise). Various procedures, including notice to LCDC, must be followed before an acknowledged plan may be amended. ORS 197.610 *et seq.* LCDC is also required to review periodically acknowledged plans to ensure their continuing compliance with the goals. ORS 197.640(1). LCDC may require a city or county to amend its acknowledged plan. ORS 197.647(4)(b).

If a plan previously has been acknowledged, then an amendment to that plan is also acknowledged by operation of law if no notice of intent to appeal is filed within 21 days from the date on which the city or county mails notice of the amendment to persons who are entitled to such notice. ORS 197.625(1); ORS 197.830(8); *see also* ORS 197.615(2)(a) (identifying persons entitled to notice of adoption of amendment). During the 21 day period, any person who participated either orally or in writing in the proceeding leading to the adoption of the amendment may challenge that decision through an appeal to LUBA. ORS 197.620; ORS 197.830. Filing of an appeal delays acknowledgment of an amendment unless and until LUBA or the appellate courts affirm the decision. ORS 197.625.

Notes and Comments

1. *The Need for State Intervention.* Consider first whether there is any need for state intervention in local land use decisions. What rationales might support such intervention? Factors that you may wish to evaluate include: (1) the need to direct growth into specific areas of a state; (2) the arbitrariness of local government boundaries; (3) the possibility that specific projects may cause environmental degradation; (4) the need for large public investments to support new developments; (5) the possibility that all the benefits of a new project will accrue to one local jurisdiction while another local jurisdiction, which receives no benefits, is significantly burdened; (6) local government's possible lack of the expertise needed to regulate large developments; (7) the likely local opposition to the siting of critically needed energy facilities and distribution systems; (8) the cumulative impact of local self-interested low-density zoning and growth management programs as a significant cause of automobile-dependent regional sprawl; and (9) the social, economic, resource, energy, environmental, and security problems associated with low-density, automobile-dependent regional sprawl. *See* Lynn Fisher & Nicholas Marantz, Can State Law Combat Exclusionary Zoning? Evidence from Massachusetts, 52 Urb. Stud. 1071 (2015) (empirical study of Massachusetts Gen. Law Ch. 40B, which provides for appealing zoning decisions based on exclusionary local zoning policies). The study lends credence to the notion that state regulation of local land use can help remove barriers to development of lower income housing, suggesting that Chapter 40B has been more successful with respect to rental development than condominium development.

2. *The Oregon System.* As illustrated in *Foland*, Oregon's State Land Use Act has several key features. The principal requirement is that all local governments must prepare land use plans that are consistent with goals established by a state agency, the Land Conservation and Development Commission (LCDC). The LCDC, whose members are appointed by the governor and confirmed by the state senate, has promulgated 19 goals. Until a plan is "acknowledged" by the LCDC, decisions by local governments on development projects must be consistent with the state goals. *See, generally,* Steven R. Schell, NIMBYs, Stakeholders, and Legitimate Expectations — A View of 40 Years of Changes in Oregon's Land Use Regulation, 46 Urb. Law. 97 (2014).

Once the LCDC reviews and acknowledges that the local plan sufficiently takes the statewide goals into account, the city or county is no longer required to make decisions in compliance with those goals. Instead, only compliance with the acknowledged local plan is then mandated; an acknowledgment essentially operates as an affirmation that the statewide policies are being carried out through the local plan. As *Foland* indicates, later amendments to local plans are deemed acknowledged by operation of law unless a notice of intent to appeal is filed with the LCDC.

The Oregon system attempts to integrate state and other public agency actions into the implementation process by requiring state agencies and special districts to carry out the local plans. Cities and counties also are required to undertake a periodic review process to ensure that their plans continue to comply with the statewide planning goals.

The Oregon system includes an enforcement mechanism. Citizens who believe that a local decision is inconsistent with a city or county plan may file an administrative appeal with a special state administrative appeals board, the Land Use Board of Appeals (LUBA). Also given authority to file an appeal is the state Department of Land Conservation and Development, which acts as staff to the LCDC. Judicial review of LUBA decisions may be sought directly in the state court of appeals, bypassing the trial courts.

3. *The Influence of Measure 37.* The Oregon planning system was affected by a new law that allowed for zoning damage lawsuits. This law, known as Measure 37, required that just compensation be paid to private owners when a land use regulation that was enacted after the owner acquired title reduced the fair market value of the land. In lieu of paying just compensation, the measure allowed the state and local governments to waive the regulation and allow the property owners to develop the land free from the restriction.

In 2006, the Oregon Supreme Court upheld the constitutionality of Measure 37, but in 2007 advocates of urban planning succeeded in a special election in which Oregon voters approved Ballot Measure 49, essentially repealing Measure 37. *See* John D. Echeverria & Thekla Hansen-Young, The Track Record on Takings Legislation: Lessons from Democracy's Laboratories, 28 Stan. Envtl. L.J. 439 (2009). The Oregon Department of Land Conservation and Development reported in 2011 that the effect of the earlier measure 37 "cannot be overstated . . . [T]he measure gave property owners the ability to collect monetary compensation unless government acted within 10 days of the filing of a claim, and the total amount of claims exceeded $17 billion." Or. Dep't of Land Conservation and Dev., Ballot Measures 37 (2004) and 49 (2007): Outcomes and Effects (Jan. 2011) at 3.

The controversy over urban planning in Oregon continues. *See* David Boulanger, The Battle Over Property Rights in Oregon: Measures 37 and 49 and the Need for Sustainable Land Use Planning, 45 Willamette L. Rev. 313 (2008); Keith Aoki, All the King's Horses and All the King's Men: Hurdles to Putting the Fragmented Metropolis Back Together Again? Statewide Land Use Planning, Portland Metro and Oregon Measure 37, 21 J. L. & Pol. 397 (2005); Edward Sullivan & Ronald Eber, The Long and Winding Road: Farmland Protection in Oregan, 18 San Joaquin Agric. L. Rev. (2009).

4. *"Amendments," "Refinements," and Public Accountability.* Under the Oregon law, an amendment to a plan previously "acknowledged" will be acknowledged by operation of law if no one appeals. Will local governments respond to political pressures by adopting small amendments to plans while citizens, having been active in the original acknowledgment process, now turn their attention elsewhere?

The issue arose in a part of the *Foland* case not reproduced. As part of an amendment to its plan, the City adopted a map that included a "refinement clause." This clause stated in essence that the mapping was a "generalized representation" of soils inventory, and that "[m]ore precise soils resource mapping" would be used to interpret the location of some sites. When the City later used the refinement clause to approve a development, citizens challenged it. They found, however, that because the refinement clause had been "acknowledged" by operation of law, they could not attack the City's action, which was taken under that acknowledged "refinement clause."

Is the refinement clause an acceptable method of using more precise information about soils as it becomes available? Might the clause insulate from judicial review actions that are, in reality, changes in the local jurisdiction's plan? As noted above, the Oregon law does call for periodic review of a county's plan for continuing compliance with the state's goals. Is that periodic review sufficient to prevent de facto, piecemeal amendments to the local plan through the use of the refinement clause? *See City of W. Linn v. Land Conservation & Dev. Comm'n*, 201 Or. App. 419 (2005) (upholding LCDC decision accepting economist's opinion as to population growth in connection with decision to expand regional urban growth boundary).

5. *Consistency with Goals.* Because the Oregon system depends on the implementation of statewide goals through local plans, the rigor with which LCDC and the courts insist upon compliance with those goals is extremely important. The case law indicates that the courts have generally required strict adherence to the goals. *See, e.g., Hildenbrand v. City of Adair Vill.*, 217 Or. App. 623 (2008) (holding that for purposes of Goal 14, a statewide planning goal requiring a change of urban growth boundary to be based on demonstrated need for additional land, a city, to justify the quantity of land proposed for addition to the city's urban boundary, was required to project the likely development under the city's high-density residential zoning designation, rather than assume that all development would occur under the lowest density permitted by the zoning designation); *Department of Land Conservation & Dev. v. Yamhill Cty.*, 183 Or. App. 556 (2002) (Land Use Board of Appeals erred in allowing county to take an "exception" — essentially, a variance — to Goal 3 and thereby rezone land from exclusive farm use to allow construction of a single-family dwelling); *Port of St. Helens v. Land Conservation & Dev. Comm'n*, 165 Or. App. 487 (2000) (commission's order requiring the county to delete certain provisions of its plan pertaining to mining did not violate Goal 9, which concerns economic development).

A Note on the Florida System

Florida has had a long and winding history with state planning influence. Changes in the law have reflected changes in state political leadership and significant economic cycles in the state.

The Florida System I. As noted in the introduction to this chapter, §7-301 of the Model Land Development Code (Am. Law Inst. 1976) called for a "State Land Planning Agency" to review "developments of regional impact." These developments were those "which, because of the nature or magnitude of the development or the nature or magnitude of its effect on the surrounding environment," were likely to present issues "of state or regional significance." *Id.* In general, DRIs are large housing or commercial developments, and large public infrastructure projects such as highways, airports, and landfills.

Florida was the leading state to adopt a system implementing the principal features of the Model Code, although several other states, including Massachusetts, Georgia, Colorado, and Washington, to some extent also incorporated aspects of the DRI model into their land use system. The Florida Environmental Land and Water Management Act of 1972 provided for state oversight of two types of developments: (1) areas of "critical state concern" and (2) developments with regional impacts. Areas of critical state concern are those designated by the Legislature, such as the Florida Keys. *See* the Florida Keys Area Protection Act, Fla. Stat. §380.0552(1) (2006); *Askew v. Cross Key Waterways*, 372 So. 2d 913, 925 (Fla. 1978) (finding that the statute, which then allowed the governor and cabinet, acting as the "Administration Commission," to designate critical areas, was an unconstitutional delegation of legislative power). Regulation of areas of "critical concern" will be discussed below in this chapter.

A "development of regional impact" is defined as a project with a "substantial effect upon the health, safety, or welfare of citizens of more than one county." Fla. Stat. §380.06(1) (2006); *see, e.g., Battaglia Properties, Ltd. v. Florida Land & Water Adjudicatory Comm'n*, 629 So. 2d 161, 162 (Fla. Dist. Ct. App. 1993) (the magnitude of development sought on a vacant tract of land about 120 acres in size rendered it a DRI).

Whenever a local government issues a development order for a DRI or for a project in a critical area, the owner, the developer, an "appropriate regional planning agency," or the state land planning agency can appeal the order to the Florida Land and Water Adjudicatory Commission. Citizens, however, lack standing to appeal. *Friends of the Everglades, Inc. v. Board of Cty. Comm'rs.*, 456 So. 2d 904, 909 (Fla. Dist. Ct. App. 1984). The Commission is made up of the governor of the state and members of his or her cabinet, and hearings before the Commission are *de novo*. The state bears the burden of proof that an adverse impact will result if the permit is granted, but the burden then shifts to the applicant to prove that the proposed curative measures are adequate. *Graham v. Estuary Props., Inc.*, 399 So. 2d 1374, 1379 (Fla. 1981), *cert. denied*, 454 U.S. 1083 (1981).

1993 amendments to the Act provided for the gradual phasing out of the DRI review. Most significantly, if a project is located within a municipality whose land use plan and regulations have been found consistent with statewide goals, the project is exempt from DRI review.

Effective in 2015, a new development otherwise subject to DRI review shall be approved by a local government pursuant to a comprehensive plan amendment; this is done within the state coordinated review process. Fla. Stat. Ann. §163.3184(4) (West 2012). Also, in areas that meet the criteria of Dense Urban Land Areas, projects are exempt from DRI review.

For a discussion of legislation in other states, such as Georgia and Connecticut, implementing the DRI concept, *see* Marya Morris, Regulating Regional Impacts: Toward Model Legislation, 47 Land Use L. & Zoning Dig. 3 (Aug. 1995). However, the Model Act was not widely adopted. Stuart Meck, Highlights of the American Planning Association's Growing Smart Project: New Tools for Planning and Management of Development, 25 Zoning & Plan. L. Rep. 49 (2002).

The Florida System II. The Florida DRI approach resulted in a great deal of controversy as it was implemented throughout the 1970s and early 1980s. In mid-1985, Florida adopted new legislation that is much closer to the Oregon model.

Under this law, known as the Local Government Comprehensive Planning and Land Development Regulation Act, Fla. Stat. Ann. §§163.3161–163.3217 (West 2006 & Supp. 2012), each local government must adopt a comprehensive plan, which must contain specific types of goals, objectives, and policies. Fla. Admin. Code. Ann. r. §9J-5.005 (2001) (regulations regarding the content of the plans adopted by the Florida Department of Community Affairs). The plans must also provide that adequate public facilities are available when a development is approved. Fla. Stat. Ann. §163.3180 (West 1990) ("concurrency"). *See Clay v. Monroe Cty.*, 849 So. 2d 363 (Fla. Dist. Ct. App. 2003) (upholding denial of permits for development of residences on key due to concurrency problem with highway service).

The Act provides for state review of the local plans. The local government must transmit its draft plan or any proposed plan amendment to the Department of

Community Affairs, which has 30 days to decide whether to conduct a review (although under certain circumstances a review is mandatory). The Department's review will take the form of an "Objections, Recommendations, and Comments Report." After receiving the report, the local government has 60 days to review it and adopt the actual plan or amendment.

After the local government takes action, the Department reviews the actual plan or amendment, and at conclusion of the review it publishes a "Notice of Intent" finding the plan either in compliance or not in compliance with the Act. Fla. Stat. Ann. §163.3184(4) (West 2006). Administrative hearings then follow. *See Florida Wildlife Fed'n v. Collier Cty.*, 819 So. 2d 200 (Fla. Dist. Ct. App. 2002) (administrative hearing on whether local plan properly mapped Natural Resource Protection Areas designed to protect indigenous fauna and flora, especially the highly endangered Florida panther); *St. Joe Paper Co. v. Dep't of Cmty. Affairs*, 657 So. 2d 27 (Fla. Dist. Ct. App. 1995) (citizens group should not have been allowed to intervene in administrative hearing process resulting in a final order by the Administration Commission). To be in compliance, the plan or amendment must meet certain criteria, including consistency with the now-codified State Comprehensive Plan, regional plans, and other state-imposed criteria. *See 1000 Friends of Fla., Inc. v. State Dep't of Cmty. Affairs*, 824 So. 2d 989 (Fla. Dist. Ct. App. 2002) (upholding Department's determination that city's amendments to the intergovernmental coordination element of its general plan were valid).

If the plan or amendment is not in compliance, the Department does not have the authority to render it ineffective or to adopt a substitute plan. Rather, enforcement depends upon financial sanctions, which the government and cabinet, acting as the "Administration Commission," may levy against the noncomplying local government. Fla. Stat. Ann. §163.3184(11) (West 2006); *see Florida League of Cities, Inc. v. Admin. Comm'n*, 586 So. 2d 397 (Fla. Dist. Ct. App. 1991) (upholding sanctions policy for late submittal of plans). Once the plan is adopted and is in compliance, all actions taken by government agencies with regard to development orders must be consistent with the plan. Fla. Stat. Ann. §163.3194(1)(a) (West 1990). Early compliance was considerable: as of 1992, more than 70 percent of Florida's municipalities had plans in compliance with state goals. Furthermore, local governments must adopt development regulations that implement and are consistent with the plan.

Even More Changes. Statutory provisions concerning the requirement and contents of comprehensive plans adopted by the Florida Dept. of Community Affairs have been repealed with the passage of the Community Planning Act of 2011. Fla. Admin. Code Ann. R. 9J-5.001-9J5.026 (repealed 2011); *see* Linda Loomis Shelley & Karen Brodeen, Home Rule Redux: The Community Planning Act of 2011, 85 Fla. G. J. (2011).

The changes were intended to greatly reduce state oversight and afford broader discretion to local governing bodies. Also, through a separate bill, the state planning department, the Department of Community Affairs, was eliminated as a separate state agency, and its growth management functions were transferred to a newly created Department of Economic Opportunity. Florida's Community Planning Act of 2011 established streamlined review procedures for plan amendments and fewer substantive review and approval criteria applicable to local comprehensive plans. The changes eliminated the concurrency requirement for transportation, schools, and parks and recreational facilities, and prohibited any local initiative or referendum (a curtailment of local control) with respect to any development order or plan amendment.

Which process has more to commend it from the standpoint of effective and reasonable land use control: the DRI process (Florida System I) or the comprehensive plan process (Florida System II)? In this regard, you may be interested in knowing that more than 90 percent of the development in Florida prior to 1993 did not even go through the DRI process, leading those whose projects did go through the appeals process to complain of unequal treatment. *See* John M. DeGrove, Planning and Growth Management in the States 9–10 (1992); *Leon Cty. v. State Dep't of Cmty. Affairs*, 666 So. 2d 1003 (Fla. Dist. Ct. App. 1996) (pipeline and petroleum storage facility were not subject to DRI review). With respect to the review of local plans, the Department of Community Affairs initially found about half of the local plans to be "not in compliance." Planning and Growth Management, supra, at 15. The Florida state urban planning system was controversial with local cities, property rights advocates, and development interests. *See* Brian Goldberg, New Reactions to Old Growth: Land Use Law Reform in Florida, 34 Colum. J. Envtl. L. 191 (2009).

In 2011, Florida legislation authorized local governments to identify "Adaptation Action Areas" to address sea-level rise and related issues in local comprehensive plans. A second Florida law, enacted in 2015, also identifies sea-level rise as a concern; it mandates that local governments begin to address it and other causes of flood-related risks through their comprehensive planning process. David L. Markell, Sea-Level Rise and Changing Times for Florida Local Governments, 42 Colum. J. of Envtl. L. (forthcoming 2016).

Florida's response to the Quiet Revolution has moved in cycles, and the most recent changes reflect concern with an economic downturn and an anti-government orientation. "The current retreat from meaningful state or regional authority to address those impacts is particularly worrisome, as Florida most certainly will continue to grow in the future. The state now has reduced its role to *ad hoc* protection of yet undefined 'important state and regional resources and facilities,' with minimal administrative resources devoted to the task." Nancy Stroud, A History and New Turns in Florida's Growth Management Reform, 45 J. Marshall L. Rev. 397, 415 (2012).

In contrast to the Oregon planning system and the Florida "critical area" approach, under the Vermont Land Use and Development Act, agencies employ a set of criteria to review development applications. The following case exemplifies this approach.

■ **IN RE KISIEL**
772 A.2d 35 (2000)

DOOLEY, J.

Landowners Mark and Pauline Kisiel appeal the Environmental Board's decision denying their application for an Act 250 permit to subdivide and develop a 158-acre tract of land into five residential lots in the Town of Waitsfield. . . .

The property in question is located at the end of Bowen Road, an unmaintained class 4 town highway, in the Town of Waitsfield on the western side of the Northfield Range. At the time landowners submitted their application for the five-unit subdivision, the Town's zoning ordinance permitted minimum five-acre residential lots on the subject parcel, which is situated within the Town's Forest Reserve District — defined as land in the Northfield Range with an elevation in excess of 1500 feet.[1] The elevation of the project tract ranges from 1500 to 2000 feet, with the proposed construction occurring between 1500 and 1700 feet. To provide vehicular access to the project tract, landowners proposed improving 2400 feet of Bowen Road.

In February 1996, the Waitsfield Planning Commission granted subdivision approval for the proposed project. The Commission noted that its decision to grant a permit followed public discussions of the proposal on four occasions, a site visit, two public hearings, and deliberations by the Commission on four separate dates in late 1995 and early 1996. The subdivision permit contained more than twenty specific conditions, several of which concerned the proposed improvements to Bowen Road. The permit required landowners to pay for the upgrade and maintenance of the road. . . .

In January 1997, the Waitsfield Selectboard approved landowners' request to improve Bowen Road by granting them a Permit for Work in the Public Right of Way. Once again, the permit contained several conditions that reflected the Town's concern with preserving the historic uses of the roadway. The permit required landowners (1) to provide a public trail easement that would allow access to the municipal forest for various recreational uses, (2) to provide easements for logging and natural resources management, and (3) to construct a public parking lot that would facilitate public access to the forest through their property. The permit also stated that the improvements to the road would not "require the Town to upgrade Bowen Road's town highway classification." *See* 19 V.S.A. §708(b) ("A class 4 highway need not be reclassified to class 3 merely because there exists within a town one or more class 3 highways with characteristics similar to the class 4 highway.").

In November 1997, the District No. 5 Environmental Commission issued a land-use permit authorizing the subdivision under Act 250, 10 V.S.A. §§6001-6108. Notwithstanding the earlier permits granted by the Town, the Town appealed the Commission's decision to the Board, which received extensive prefiled testimony, conducted a site visit, and held an evidentiary hearing. In June 1998, the Board issued its decision, ruling that the application complied with several of the criteria contained in 10 V.S.A. §6086(a), but failed to comply with others, including criterion (10), which requires "conformance with any duly adopted local or regional plan." *Id.* §6086(a)(10). The Board found, in this regard, that the proposal to upgrade Bowen Road was not in compliance with the plan's goal of maintaining the "status" of class 4 roads, and further found that the proposal was inconsistent with the goal of precluding development on "steep" slopes. In response to a subsequent motion to alter, the Board amended several of its findings, but otherwise reaffirmed its decision denying the application. This appeal followed.

We have decided a number of cases involving the compliance of a development proposal with criterion 10 of Act 250, which requires that the proposed development be "in conformance with any duly adopted local or regional plan." 10 V.S.A.

---

1. There was testimony that, after granting landowners a permit to proceed with their development, the Town enacted interim zoning that prohibited residential development above 1700 feet and restricted such development between 1500 and 1700 feet to a conditional use.

§6086(a)(10). Before we examine the specifics of the plan provisions before us, we find it instructive to review two of those decisions, which we find central to the resolution of this case.

The first is *In re Green Peak Estates*, 154 Vt. 363, 577 A.2d 676 (1990), in which we upheld a decision of the Environmental Board that the second and third phases of a subdivision development were not in conformance with either the town or regional plan. The facts of *Green Peak Estates* have some similarities to the facts of this case because the developer was attempting to develop residential lots in a higher-elevation undeveloped area. Unlike this case, however, the town had no subdivision regulations, and the planning commission opposed the development as inconsistent with the town plan. Moreover, the regional plan specifically provided that "[o]n slopes greater than 20%, residential development should not be permitted." *Id.* at 368, 577 A.2d at 679. The Board found that this specific provision of the regional plan was consistent with the more general provisions of the town plan that established an objective of keeping the "rugged and poorly accessible mountain and forest areas free from development." *Id.* Because at least half of the proposed subdivision was to be located on a slope exceeding 20 percent, the Board found that the development did not conform with the regional plan. We affirmed, holding that "the Board's commonsense interpretation of the plan's policy on this point is consistent with the overall approach to use of the region's intermediate uplands." *Id.* at 369, 577 A.2d at 679.

The second decision is *In re Molgano*, 163 Vt. 25, 653 A.2d 772 (1994), in which the Board also found a development proposal was not in conformance with a town and regional plan. This time, however, we reversed the Board's decision because of two critical elements not present in *Green Peak Estates*. First, the town had adopted specific zoning ordinances consistent with the town plan and had issued a zoning permit to the developer under these ordinances. Second, the language of the town plan on which the Board relied was "broad," "nonregulatory," and "at best, ambiguous" with respect to the issues before the Board. *Id.* at 29-30, 653 A.2d at 775.

Regarding the first difference, we found error in the Board's holding that the zoning ordinances and decisions were irrelevant to criterion 10 review, noting that implementation of a town plan is done through zoning ordinances so that the ordinances control the plan. We concluded:

> Because the Board's interpretation would effectively give nonregulatory abstractions in the Town Plan the legal force of zoning laws, we agree with Molgano that the Board erred as a matter of law in concluding that the Town's zoning bylaws were not germane to the meaning of the Town Plan.

Id. at 31, 653 A.2d at 775.

As suggested in the above quote, we also found error in the Board's holding with respect to the second difference. In discussing language from the regional plan, which we found to be "broad and vague," we distinguished *Green Peak Estates* as involving "a specific policy against [the] type of development" at issue. *Id.* at 31, 653 A.2d at 776 . . . (language of regional plan should be enforced under criterion 10 when it is "clear and unqualified, and creates no ambiguity").

The case can be resolved based on the distinctions between *Molgano* and *Green Peak Estates*. We first turn to the specific plan provisions, and the claims of the parties with respect to them, starting with the Board's holding that the development was not in conformance with the plan's provisions concerning developments on steep slopes. The Board found that the project was not in compliance with Objective 2.a of Goals 1.1 and 1.2 found in section IV of the town plan. The latter goals relate to the preservation and responsible use of the Town's natural features and resources. The Objective in question provides as follows:

> Objective 2. To protect Waitsfield's fragile resources and sensitive natural areas and reduce environmental hazards and prevent the loss of life and property from flooding. a. Prevent the creation of parcels which will result in development on *steep slopes*, critical wetlands and floodplain; and consider amending the Waitsfield Zoning Bylaws to create standards to prevent such development. (Emphasis added.)

In challenging the Board's conclusion that their project failed to comply with Objective 2.a, landowners rely primarily on subsection 1.2 of section III of the Town plan dealing with "fragile features" of the environment. This section cautions that "steep slopes and hillsides" are generally unsuitable for development because of problems relating to sewage disposal and soil erosion, as well as the potential impact on scenic landscape and wildlife habitat. Although the section does not specifically define "steep" slopes, it characterizes certain gradients as follows:

> Generally, slopes with a gradient of 0.6 percent are considered slights; 6-15 percent, moderate; 15-25 percent, severe; and greater than 25 percent, extreme. Consideration of soils conditions and erosion control are extremely important prior to development, with the steepest slopes being unsuitable for development. Resource Map 2 shows those areas which are characterized by severe and extreme slopes.

Landowners emphasize that, with the exception of a portion of one driveway, their project would be confined to slopes ranging between 5-20 percent, and therefore below what the plan characterized as "extreme." The Board rejected this argument below, indicating that construction on gradients characterized as "severe" (15 to 25 percent) was sufficient to establish noncompliance with the Objective to prevent development on steep slopes.

There is no doubt that the Town could limit or preclude development on steep slopes for sound reasons of soil conservation, sewage disposal, view preservation, and the like. This is, of course, the holding of *Green Peak Estates*. But, unlike the regional plan in *Green Peak Estates*, the Waitsfield town plan does not specifically define a "steep" slope; nor does the Town's zoning ordinance provide any specific standards. The parties are thus left to debate the Town's intent, with landowners claiming that the Town intended to apply the prohibition only to "extreme" slopes with grades over 25 percent, and the Town asserting that the prohibition includes slopes characterized as "severe," i.e., having grades between 15 and 25 percent. The Board's decision did not elaborate on the basis of its ruling, and nothing in the plan — or the zoning ordinance — provides contextual guidance on this point.

As we explained in *Molgano*, 163 Vt. at 30, 653 A.2d at 775, zoning bylaws are designed to implement the town plan, and may provide meaning where the plan is ambiguous. Conversely, in the absence of pertinent zoning bylaws, the Board may not "give nonregulatory abstractions in the Town Plan the legal force of zoning laws." *Id.* at 31, 653 A.2d at 775. This is precisely what the Board did here. The town plan sets forth an abstract policy against development on steep slopes, but provides no specific standards to enforce the policy. Indeed, the plan itself acknowledges this deficiency; it expressly recommends within the steep-slope section that the Town "consider amending the Waitsfield Zoning Bylaws to create standards to prevent such development." Nothing in the record, however, indicates that the Town has enacted such standards.[2] Absent some objective measure to guide enforcement of the steep-slope prohibition, there was no basis for the Board to conclude that the project was not in compliance with this policy. Cf. *Green Peak Estates*, 154 Vt. at 368, 577 A.2d at 679 (enforcing specific standard prohibiting development on slopes in excess of 20 percent). Thus, we agree with landowners that the Board erred in concluding that the project was not in compliance with Objective 2.a of the town plan relating to steep slopes.

The Board's second determination that the development does not conform to the town plan concerns the Town's goal of maintaining the "status" of class 4 roads. One of the goals listed in the town plan, Goal 5.2, is: "The improvement and expansion of alternative, non-automobile transportation modes." Among the objectives designed to achieve this goal is Objective 4: "To provide alternatives to the heavy reliance on individual automobiles." Subpart g of this objective provides as follows: "Maintain the current *status* of all class four Town Highways to promote their use for walking, bicycling and horseback riding." (Emphasis added.) The inventory and analysis section of the town plan (section III) that precedes the stated goals and objectives includes the following paragraphs on roads and residential development within the Forest Reserve District:

> The forest reserve district includes the least accessible areas of town. Few roads provide access, most of those being unmaintained class 4 roads (such as . . . Bowen Road . . .). However, proposals to *upgrade* these roads to *class 3 status* have been made in recent years, and the subdivision of large parcels for residential development has resulted in the construction of private roads. Should these trends continue the current character of the forest reserve district could be significantly altered. Road improvements would likely result in increased pressure to subdivide large parcels for year-round residences, and could lead to the fragmentation of existing habitat. . . .
>
> Because of the geographic conditions throughout this district, road improvements are expensive and difficult to maintain. This is exacerbated by the distance from other Town roads and services. Further, emergency vehicle access is difficult on steep, narrow roads, and the potential for conflict between automobile traffic and logging operations exist in this area. Existing class 4 roads, and certain private logging roads, also provide exceptional recreation opportunities, including hiking, biking, horseback riding and hunting access to remote areas. This experience could be diminished through increased automobile access.
>
> . . . In order to limit the adverse impacts of additional residential development in this district, the *upgrade of roads* and subdivision of large forest parcels *should be discouraged.* If residential development does occur, careful site selection and screening of new homes should occur, and landowners should be encouraged to restrict further subdivision of large parcels.

(Emphasis added.)

---

2. Apparently, as noted above, the interim zoning enacted subsequent to landowners' permit application prohibited residential development above 1700 feet and restricted such development above 1500 feet. There was no evidence that the ordinance addressed steep-slope standards.

Another part of the inventory and analysis section of the plan concerning transportation includes the following language:

> Class 4 roads provide excellent walking opportunities, especially in the Northfield Range where such class 4 roads as the Bowen Road . . . offer access to largely undeveloped mountains. . . .
>
> In addition to class 4 roads, many miles of private logging roads and trails are available to the public through the generosity of landowners. However, many of these private roads are at risk of being posted and access prohibited as landowner-user conflicts arise. . . .
>
> In the future the Town may explore the potential for formalizing many of these informal trails through the dedication of permanent easements. The continuing subdivision of land poses both a risk to this informal network *and an opportunity to encourage path easements as a condition to subdivision approval.*

(Emphasis added.) This language supports Objective 3.j (Goal 6.2) of the plan to "secure permanent access to traditional hiking trails in Town, including trail access to the Scrag Municipal Forest from both the north and the south."

In its decision, the Board focused on the word "status" in Objective 4.g, concluding that it was not synonymous with the word "classification." According to the Board, improving a previously unmaintained class 4 highway to the extent that it could handle vehicular traffic would violate the plan's stated objective of "maintain[ing] the current status of all class four Town Highways to promote their use for walking, bicycling and horseback riding."

Landowners argue that the Board has erroneously defined the word status to mean the condition of the road rather than its legal classification. They note that the word "status," when used in connection with highways, often describes legal or statutory standing. . . . Other language in the plan supports this argument. As indicated above, a related section refers to "proposals to *upgrade* these roads *to class 3 status*," thereby suggesting that the word "status" in Objective 4.g means classification.

We recognize that the Board is required to follow ordinary rules of statutory construction in construing the plan, and that we must accord great deference to the Board's decision. *In re MBL Assocs.*, 166 Vt. at 607, 693 A.2d at 700-01. Nevertheless, we conclude that the landowners' position must prevail over the Board's interpretation of the plan in this instance for a number of reasons.

First, although the Board relied upon the most specific and concrete expression of the plan's policy on class 4 roads, other expressions of the policy contained in the plan are far less specific or definitive. As with the policy on steep slopes, there is little specificity on how the class-4-road policy should be enforced and, indeed, the enforcement language is quite tentative. We conclude that the meaning of the plan is ambiguous.[3] This conclusion is underscored by the candid admission of counsel for the Town that differences in meaning urged by it and landowners are "subtle." In contrast to the town plan in *Green Peak Estates*, which provided that certain development should not be permitted, here the plan provides that the upgrade of roads "should be discouraged." Thus, we are concerned that in addition to attempting to

---

3. The dissent finds the plan language "concrete and precise," 171 Vt. at—, 772 A.2d at 145, primarily by rephrasing the terminology to say that the plan restricts upgrading the "condition" of the road rather than its "status." We agree that if the drafters of the plan had used the word "condition," it would be precise. They chose instead to use the ambiguous word "status," causing the disagreement.

construe and apply an ambiguous plan, the Board has also given "nonregulatory abstractions in the Town Plan the legal force of zoning laws," action that we criticized in *Molgano,* 163 Vt. at 31, 653 A.2d at 775.

Second, and more important, the central teaching of *Molgano* is that where there is ambiguity in the wording of a plan, the Board must look to the interpretation of the plan by the municipal bodies responsible for its implementation and enforcement. When we look at what the Town of Waitsfield has done, and what is has not done, with respect to the development before us, we conclude that this evidence strongly supports landowners' position.

As described above, both the Waitsfield Planning Commission and the Waitsfield Board of Selectmen reviewed this development proposal. Both approved of landowners' plans to improve Bowen Road without upgrading its classification to class 3. Both resolved the conflict between use of the road by automobiles and by hikers, bikers, snowmobilers or horseback riders by requiring landowners to construct a public trail along the road for nonautomobile uses. Both used the permit decisions before them to secure "trail access to the Scrag Municipal Forest," a specific objective of the town plan. In making the many discretionary decisions involved in its evaluation of landowners' subdivision proposal, and in the formulation of the twenty specific conditions it imposed, the planning commission was required to "refer to the goals, objectives, and policies . . . established by the Town plan in making discretionary decisions." Waitsfield Subdivision Regulations §3.1. The selectboard, acting pursuant to its power to control the maintenance of roads, see 19 V.S.A. §303, faced precisely the same decision as the Board — whether to allow landowners to improve Bowen Road for automobile travel to their development — and issued the permit to allow the development. These municipal actions are directly contrary to the plan interpretation accepted by the Board.

We also find that what the Town chose not to do supports landowners' interpretation of the plan. For all practical purposes, the interpretation adopted by the Board would ban further residential development within the Forest Reserve District by the intentional continuation of bad and impassable roads, even though the provisions of the town plan plainly contemplate limited development, and the zoning ordinance in place at the time of landowners' application allowed residential developments as a permitted use.[5] *See Molgano,* 163 Vt. at 33, 653 A.2d at 776-77 ("where . . . a developer diligently pursues a proposal through the local and state permitting processes before seeking an Act 250 permit, conformance under §6086(a)(10) is to be measured with regard to zoning laws in effect at the time of a proper zoning permit application"). The Town's implementation scheme to allow residential development in the district, but to regulate it through the subdivision and road improvement permit process, is blocked by the Board's determination that no development can occur, a determination based on the Town's own plan.

The purpose of Act 250 "is not to supersede local regulation" of land development. *See In re Trono Constr. Co.,* 146 Vt. 591, 593, 508 A.2d 695, 696 (1986). Although Act 250 gives to the Board, and this Court on appeal from the Board's decisions, the power to override a town's implementation of its own plan, this power should be exercised only when the local construction of the town plan is plainly

---

5. We do not agree that the plan bans subdivisions but not single family homes, as the dissent surmises. Whether landowners constructed one home or more, the Board's interpretation of the plan would prevent them from reaching their property by automobile.

erroneous. No other policy will maintain local control of land use planning and promote fairness and consistency in state and local regulatory review. We must give deference to the determination of the Board, but the Board in turn must give deference to the determinations of local bodies in applying the plan.

We recognize that we are endorsing the primacy of local determinations as to the meaning of town plans in a case in which the Town is arguing that its implementation of its plan should be ignored. For whatever reasons, the Town is attempting, through Act 250, to undo its own regulatory decisions, without attempting to reopen them in the Town processes. The only explanation in the record lies in the testimony of the chairman of the planning commission that (1) the Town has now adopted an interim zoning ordinance prohibiting residential development on land at an altitude above 1700 feet and requiring conditional use approval for development of land lying between 1500 and 1700 feet, and (2) the Town has more information as a result of the Act 250 process in the way of "environmental impact and scientific knowledge," specifically on the water issues and the visual impact.

The Town is certainly entitled to insist that the Board thoroughly review all the relevant criteria of Act 250 with respect to the development proposal. It is not entitled, however, to use Act 250 to retroactively apply its new zoning regime to a development to which it is not applicable. . . .

We hold that when the language of the Waitsfield town plan is reviewed in light of its application by the regulatory bodies responsible for its implementation within the Town, it cannot be construed to prohibit the improvement of Bowen Road as part of landowners' development proposal. Thus, we conclude that the Board erred in holding that the proposal violated criterion 10.

Reversed and remanded.

AMESTOY, C.J., dissenting. . . .

I do not agree with the majority's conclusion that the Board erred in determining that the road improvements necessary for vehicular access to a proposed five-lot subdivision in the Town's Forest Reserve District would violate the town plan's stated objective of "[m]aintain[ing] the current status of all class four Town Highways to promote their use for walking, bicycling and horseback riding." As the record makes clear, the Board's decision was consistent with the plan, the zoning ordinance, and traditional usage within the Forest Reserve District, which together evinced a clear policy of allowing *limited* residential development and seasonal homes, but discouraging multi-unit subdevelopments of the kind at issue here. Therefore, I would affirm the decision of the Board denying landowners' application for an Act 250 permit.

I.

This case was tried and appealed as a straightforward issue of textual interpretation. In connection with their proposed subdivision project, landowners planned to upgrade approximately 2400 feet of Bowen Road, an unmaintained class four road, through substantial widening and drainage improvements. The issue before the Board was whether the proposed upgrade was consistent with the town plan, one objective of which was to "[m]aintain the current status of all class four Town Highways to promote their use for walking, bicycling, and horseback riding." Landowners argued that "maintain the current status" does not mean "maintain the current physical condition," but rather maintain the class four "legal classification." In support of their contention, landowners cited several cases and statutes which appear to employ the term "status" as the functional equivalent of legal classification, and two other sections of the town plan which arguably provided contextual support for their position.

The Town argued, and the Board found, that the meaning and purpose of the restriction was to restrict the physical improvement of class four roads. Reading the plan as a whole made plain that the goal of the restriction was not merely to maintain Bowen Road's "legal" status, but to preserve the character of the Forest Reserve District. The plan cautioned that improving the few unmaintained roads in the district could significantly alter its unspoiled character by creating pressure for substantial development, and that existing recreational opportunities such as horseback riding, hiking, bicycling, and hunting "could be diminished through increased automobile access." The majority argues, however, that regardless of the Board's conclusion, the restriction on upgrades of class four roads constitutes little more than a "nonregulatory abstraction" of the kind criticized in *In re Molgano*, 163 Vt. 25, 31, 653 A.2d 772, 775 (1994). The argument was not advanced by landowners at trial or in their appellate briefs. The reason is clear. The provision restricting upgrades on class four roads is concrete and precise. The Town's objective is to *maintain* the existing condition of class four roads, particularly in the Forest Reserve District, in order to limit vehicular access and development, and to preserve existing recreational opportunities and open space. There is nothing abstract about this policy and objective. . . .

Notes and Comments

1. *The Vermont System's Structure.* The Vermont Land Use and Development Act, commonly referred to as Act 250, is an example of direct state intervention into land use decision making, although its genesis and continuing acceptability derive from its dependence on local and regional planning and citizen involvement. Unlike the Florida DRI law, which requires state review only when an appeal is filed on a specific project, Act 250 requires certain applicants to apply directly to one of nine state-created "District Environmental Commissions," V.S.A. tit. 10 §6026 (1997). The three-member commissions have power to issue permits for all covered developments, defined in 10 V.S.A. §6001(3)(A).

The applicant, the affected municipality, its planning commission, the regional planning commission, and affected state agencies are parties to the hearing, and citizens may petition to be included. 10 V.S.A. §6085(c). The District Commission may deny, issue with conditions, or simply issue a permit. Any appeals from the commissions' decisions were originally heard by a nine-member Vermont Environmental Board. In 2004 a new entity, the Natural Resources Board, was formed from two existing boards, and now a Land Use Panel of the Board oversees compliance with the Act. Appeals from the District Commissions are heard by an Environmental Court, the "Environmental Division" of Vermont's Superior Court. Decisions of the court may be appealed to the Vermont Supreme Court. A subchapter was added in 2013 to provide a mechanism to allocate the costs of mitigating the impacts of land use projects to the transportation system "in a manner that is equitable and that supports the planning goals of the Act." 24 V.S.A. §4302. (Added 2013, No. 145 (Adj. Sess.), §2).

2. *The Scope of the Vermont Law.* A large number of development applications are subject to Act 250 approval. They include: (1) all housing projects of ten or more lots, or fewer in towns without permanent zoning and subdivision regulations; (2) commercial or industrial projects involving more than one acre in towns without land use regulations, or more than ten acres in towns with land use regulations; (3) all state or municipal projects involving ten or more acres; and (4) other specifically noted projects such as communication towers. Agricultural uses and others are specifically exempted. 10 V.S.A. §60013(D). The state environmental agency reviews all applications for permits and makes recommendations on them to the District Environmental Commission.

The criteria set forth in Act 250 that govern permit applications cover a variety of concerns, ranging from traffic to effects on schools to fiscal impacts. *See* V.S.A. tit. 10 §6086(a) (1997 and Supp. 2003). As a result, many of the judicial decisions under Act 250 turn on whether substantial evidence supports a finding by the District Commission that a project meets these criteria and whether the Commission's findings support its overall conclusions. *See, e.g., In re Munson Earth Moving Corp.,* 737 A.2d 906, 911 (Vt. 1999) (ruling that "findings do not lead logically to its conclusion that appellant's subdivision would endanger the public investment in government facilities"); and *In re Wal Mart Stores, Inc.,* 702 A.2d 397 (1997) (ruling that substantial evidence supported findings on issues of market impact as well as impact on educational and other government services).

Act 250 allocates the burden of proof somewhat strangely. Permit applicants bear the burden of showing that the project will not cause undue air pollution, water pollution, soil erosion, or strain on water supplies. In contrast, project opponents bear the burden of demonstrating that a project would unreasonably burden roads and other public services, or would unduly impact natural, aesthetic, or historic sites. Vt. Stat. Ann. tit. 10 §§6086(a), 6088(b) (1997 and Supp. 2003). Appeals from the district environmental commissions to the Environmental Court are heard de novo. *See* 10 V.S.A. §8504.

3. *The* Kisiel *Decision.* The *Kisiel* case involves one of Act 250's key criteria: "conformance with any duly adopted local or regional plan." Any proposed project must conform with duly adopted local and regional plans. This criterion requires the court to consider how it will approach the plan and what deference, if any, it will give to the local government's interpretation of its own plan. How did the *Kisiel* court resolve that issue? What about the fact that the local government seems to have changed its position toward the development in question — should this change affect the board's review? The court's review?

The court apparently adopted an interpretation of the plan's restriction on road upgrades that the landowners did not advance. Is that an appropriate position for the court to take?

Finally, the Court finds that the plan is vague about development allowed on steep slopes. Do local governments generally have a tendency to adopt vague policies in plans in the hope that they will retain more discretion over development decisions? Does Act 250 create an incentive in the opposite direction to adopt clear and definitive policies.

4. *Jurisdiction, Open Questions, and Malpractice.* Act 250 does not apply to every development. The word "development" in the Act is defined in part as "the

construction of improvements on a tract or tracts of land, owned or controlled by a person, involving more than 10 acres of land within a radius of five miles" 10 V.S.A. §6001(3). In *Committee to Save the Bishop's House, Inc. v. Medical Ctr. Hosp. of Vermont,* 400 A.2d 1015 (Vt. 1979), a hospital was going to demolish a historic house on a 1.44-acre lot. It proposed to build a parking lot. The hospital itself had two "units." One consisted of 26.7 acres, and a second (which included the lot with the house in question) of 5.9 acres. The two units were separated by a distance of one-half mile at their nearest point. Does the demolition come within Act 250? Is there any additional information you would need to answer the question? *See also In re Vermont Verde Antique Int'l, Inc.,* 811 A.2d 181 (Vt. 2002) (invalidating rule that allowed district coordinators to issue jurisdictional orders *sua sponte*).

Since it is not always clear when a project is subject to regulatory requirements, or whether certain kinds of transactions are prohibited, a lawyer representing clients should undertake careful research. Failure to do so can bring unfortunate consequences. *See Roberts v. Chimileski,* 820 A.2d 995 (Vt. 2003). In that case, the plaintiff brought a malpractice action after he was prosecuted for making an illegal subdivision. He claimed that his lawyer failed to disclose the "inherent risk" of whether the development scheme conformed to Act 250. The court upheld a decision for the defendant that malpractice had not been proven. A dissent argued that "[i]t requires no extensive discussion to establish that the unsettled scope of the term 'controlled' [in the Act] obligated defendants to advise their clients about the risky nature of their scheme, or m.o., to circumvent the Act. . . ." (Morse, J., dissenting).

5. *Interpreting the Vermont Act.* In a recent decision, *In re Waterfront Park Act 250 Amendment,* 2016 VT 39 (Vt. Apr. 15, 2016), the Vermont Supreme Court interpreted Act 250 Rule 34(E), which establishes a framework for determining whether a party may seek to amend an Act 250 permit. The city applied for an amendment to a permit to allow for hosting festivals and public events in a city park. The city argued for an amended permit without any express conditions regarding the timing, duration, and frequency of events and sound levels. The city's view was that the City Parks and Recreation Commission should regulate these matters. A neighbor to the park challenged the application, seeking to remove conditions in the original permit governing the timing and frequency of events at the park and the maximum allowable sound levels. She appealed the Environmental Court's ruling on the threshold question of whether the city was entitled to request the permit amendment under Rule 34(E).

The Vermont Supreme Court agreed with the Environmental Court's conclusion that the city was entitled to grant the amended application, reasoning that the factors supporting flexibility in this case outweighed those calling for finality:

> The Park has been a dynamic resource to the City, and its increased use has been and will continue to be important to the City's cultural, recreational and social life, and its prosperity. While neighbor's reliance on the prior permit limitations carries some weight, in this case it is outweighed by other factors so that it is not unreasonable to consider proposed amendments to the permit.

2016 VT 39, ¶29, _____ A.3d _____, 2016 WL 1538830, at *7 (2016).

In the following case, the Vermont Supreme Court addressed the amending and conditioning of permits under Act 250.

■ IN RE TREETOP DEVELOPMENT COMPANY ACT 250 DEVELOPMENT
2016 VT 20 (Vt. Feb. 12, 2016)

This appeal is the latest chapter in an ongoing dispute between the Treetop at Stratton Condominium Association, Inc. (Association) and the Stratton Corporation, Treetop Development Company, LLC, Treetop Three Development Company, LLC, and Intrawest Stratton Development Corporation (collectively, Stratton) over an improperly constructed stormwater management system. The pending matter follows the Association's appeal of the District 2 Environmental Commission's (Commission) refusal to impose additional conditions on Stratton's Act 250 permit, which the Environmental Division of the Superior Court determined to be invalid and unenforceable. For the reasons stated herein, we affirm.

On November 18, 2002, the District 2 Environmental Commission issued Act 250 Permit # 2W1142 to Stratton for the construction of twenty-five three-unit townhouses (the Treetop Project) in the Town of Stratton, Vermont. Included in the Act 250 permit was approval for the development and construction of the infrastructure required for the occupancy, use, and management of the Treetop Project and associated infrastructure, including a stormwater management system.

A Stratton Corporation affiliate, the Treetop Development Company, LLC, completed construction of the Treetop Project in 2006, at which point all seventy-five townhouses were sold and conveyed to third-party owners. Each individual owner acquired an undivided percentage interest in the Treetop Project's common areas and facilities, including the stormwater management systems, which were managed and administered by the Association.

In response to problems with the stormwater management system, the Association filed suit against Stratton in 2009 seeking damages and remediation for various construction defects in the Treetop Project, including those involving the stormwater management system. The parties ultimately reached a settlement agreement, which, relevant to this appeal, required Stratton to apply for and obtain corrective permit amendments and pay for any work necessary to bring the stormwater management aspects of the Treetop Project into compliance with its Act 250 permit. On August 13, 2012, Stratton filed an application with the Commission to amend its Act 250 permit to reflect deviations from the original permit, specifically "to authorize changes in the original as-built plans to the permit plans submitted." These changes included repairs and modifications to the stormwater management system necessary to fix leaks and seepage and to bring the system into compliance with the terms of General Permit 3–9010.

In its Findings of Fact and Conclusions of Law, the Commission expressed its concern over Stratton's "failure to build its stormwater system in compliance with its prior permits." The Commission conceded that "[w]hile Stratton's plan is not the only way to [correct significant stormwater problems], it is the plan on the table[,] ... [and it] has been approved by the Agency of Natural Resources and is implementable immediately." Emphasizing the importance that "the water quality and safety issues be resolved satisfactorily as soon as possible," the Commission concluded that "issuing a permit with conditions is the most effective way to achieve this outcome." The Commission provided that it would add "protections in the permit to ensure that solutions proposed by Stratton are effective in addressing the problems," and that it would "retain jurisdiction over these matters." In its conclusion, the Commission found that the Treetop Project would be in compliance with Act 250 criteria if it was "completed and maintained as represented in the application and other representations of the Applicants, and in accordance with the findings and conclusions of this decision and the conditions [herein]."

Following a decision by the Commission on October 21, 2013 to approve Act 250 Permit # 2W1142–D (amended permit) with conditions, both Stratton and the Association moved to alter and amend the amended permit. After making minor changes, the Commission issued a Memorandum of Decision on November 15, 2013, granting the amended permit. The amended permit included several conditions, including conditions that required Stratton to repair the stormwater retention pond pursuant to approved plans on or before September 1, 2014, and to provide weekly reports on the progress of the repairs until completion. By that time of year, however, the weather made further site work impossible. Relevant to this appeal, permit Condition 14 provided:

> The Commission reserves the right to review erosion, the ability of the land to hold water, stormwater management and revegetation issues outlined in these proceedings *and to evaluate and impose additional conditions as needed.*

(Emphasis added.) Importantly, neither party appealed the amended permit, which became final and binding on December 15, 2013.

In January 2014, the Association provided the Commission with information about the status of the stormwater management system, including a letter from Stratton's engineer, plans for remediation dated December 13, 2013, and the Association's response to those filings. Shortly thereafter, on February 7, 2014, the Commission issued a Notice of Reconvened Hearing on the amended permit. The notice was issued pursuant to the authority the Commission reserved unto itself under Condition 14 and indicated the Commission's intent to discuss whether additional conditions were necessary to address problems with the stormwater management system. Following hearings, the Commission issued a Memorandum of Decision on May 16, 2014 "declin[ing] to impose additional permit conditions with respect to [the amended permit]," and affirming the "adequacy of the conditions of the permit, which was not appealed." The Commission also noted that, "given there is an active enforcement action [underway] by both [the Agency of Natural Resources] and the [Natural Resources Board], we are assured that there will be oversight regarding compliance with the relevant state requirements, including conditions of [the amended permit], which were not appealed."

The Association timely appealed the Commission's May 16, 2014 Memorandum of Decision declining to impose further conditions on Stratton to the Environmental Division of the Superior Court. Stratton then moved to dismiss the appeal, alleging that the questions raised on appeal were either collateral attacks on the unappealed amended permit or outside the scope of the Environmental Division's de novo review. On November 14, 2014 the Environmental Division dismissed the appeal, finding, relevant to the matter now before this Court, that:

> [t]he sole purpose of Condition 14 is to ensure compliance with the initial Permit and Permit Amendment. This authority does not belong to the Commission. Rather, it rests with the Natural Resources Board's authority to ensure compliance with an Act 250

Permit and its conditions through its enforcement powers . . . [T]he Association cannot use Condition 14 to privately enforce the Permit or Permit Amendment.

Treetop Dev. Co. Act 250 Application, No. 77–6–14 Vtec, slip op., at 3 (Envtl. Div. Vt. Sup. Ct. Nov. 14, 2014) . . . In response, the Environmental Division noted that "[i]t would be irrational to read the Commission's decision on the [amended permit] as granting an Act 250 permit despite insufficient findings of compliance with Act 250," and that "a district commission simply cannot use a permit condition to reserve the authority to reopen a final and binding Act 250 permit sua sponte in order to enforce the permit or impose conditions." Id. The Environmental Division further provided that "[t]he injustice alleged by the Association stems from its free, calculated, and deliberate choice not to take an appeal" from the amended permit. Id . . .

The Association alleges that the Environmental Division erred in granting Stratton's motion to dismiss the appeal because Condition 14 is a valid and enforceable permit condition reserving jurisdiction over the stormwater system at the Treetop Project and allowing the Commission to amend or add conditions as necessary to bring the system into compliance with Act 250. The Association also asserts that it based its decision not to appeal the amended permit on the Commission's reservation of authority to impose further conditions in order to ensure the stormwater management system's compliance with Act 250, and that Stratton's motion to dismiss is a collateral attack on Condition 14. Stratton, on the other hand, contends that under the Association's view, Condition 14 amounts to a key that can be used to re-open the door to amend the permit at any time and impose additional conditions, preventing finality. Both Stratton and the NRB argue that Condition 14 is an unenforceable condition subsequent and that the Association's appeal is a collateral attack on the amended permit We find that condition 14 is invalid . . .

Act 250, codified at 10 V.S.A. §§6001 through 6093, was enacted "to protect Vermont's lands and environment by requiring statewide review of 'large-scale changes in land utilization.'" In re Audet, 2004 VT 30, ¶13, 176 Vt. 617, 850 A.2d 1000 (mem.) (quoting Comm. to Save Bishop's House, Inc. v. Med. Ctr. Hosp. of Vt., Inc., 137 Vt. 142, 151, 400 A.2d 1015, 1020 (1979)). To that end, it falls to the nine District Environmental Commissions to consider Act 250 permit applications and amendments in the context of the ten statutory criteria listed in 10 V.S.A. §6086(a). The Commissions may approve or deny any such applications, although approval requires that the Commissions make affirmative findings under all ten statutory criteria before issuing a permit. . . . "It follows, therefore, that findings of fact and conclusions of law on only some criteria — but not all — are not equivalent to a permit.". Any changes to the permit or the conditions therein must be made pursuant to the formal permit amendment procedure outlined in the Act 250 Rules. Appeals of the Commission's decision, including decisions approving or denying a permit or the conditions therein, must be filed within thirty days of the date of the decision. 10 V.S.A. §8504(a).

In order to ensure continued compliance with the statutory criteria, the Commission is entitled to grant conditional approval by imposing reasonable conditions on a project. See id. §6086(c); Act 250 Rule 32(A) . . . Permissible conditions include those with prospective application that are intended to alleviate adverse impacts that either are or would otherwise be caused or created by a project, or those necessary to ensure that the development is completed as approved, such as those requiring permittees to take specific action when triggered by certain events, incorporating a schedule of actions necessary for continued compliance with Act 250 criteria, and requiring future compliance related filings, including affidavits of compliance with respect to certain permit conditions. For example, this includes conditions limiting development to areas of land subject to Act 250 jurisdiction, establishing hours of operation, directing the placement of specific machinery, and requiring reclamation following completion of a project.

The power to enforce compliance with Act 250 permits and the underlying conditions is vested exclusively in the NRB and the Agency of Natural Resources (ANR), and not with the Commission . . . It therefore falls to the NRB, and not the Commission, to determine whether violations of Act 250, or permits issued thereunder, exist and to exercise the discretion granted under 10 V.S.A. §6027(g) to initiate enforcement actions.

By its terms, Condition 14 reserves continuing jurisdiction over the stormwater system at the Treetop Project, creating for the Commission a mechanism to continuously amend the permit as necessary to redress future Act 250 violations or failures under the terms of the approved project by adding additional conditions. Not only does this exceed the Commission's authority, which is limited to considering permit applications in the context of the ten statutory criteria and either approving or denying the application, and amending permits under the procedure outlined in In re Stowe Club Highlands, 166 Vt. 33, 37, 687 A.2d 102, 105 (1996), but it prevents finality, an integral part of the land use permitting process. Furthermore, unlike a condition with prospective application intended to alleviate adverse impacts, Condition 14 allows the Commission to circumvent the requirement that projects which have been permitted satisfy the statutory criteria and prospectively expropriate the NRB's enforcement authority, effectively creating a de facto mechanism of internal enforcement for the Commission. This reservation of extra-statutory authority renders the Commission's permit approval illusory, simultaneously approving stormwater system remediation under a set of parameters and reserving the authority to alter these parameters at any time, including when necessary to correct violations of Act 250. Such an open-ended condition, effectively endowing the Commission with the prospective extra-statutory authority to re-open the amended permit and perpetually act, is an invalid condition subsequent.

Although the permit itself was unappealed, and is therefore final and binding on the parties, this does not make Condition 14 enforceable. In our discussions of the failure to appeal zoning permits, this Court has consistently held that the parties are bound by the terms of the permit, even where the municipal body's actions in granting the permit exceeded their authority.

This result does not leave the Association without possible recourse relative to Stratton's alleged violations of the amended permit and Act 250, generally. As indicated above, both NRB and ANR have undertaken enforcement actions against Stratton pursuant to their authority in 10 V.S.A. §§6027(g) and 8004. The agencies have indicated that "there will be oversight regarding compliance with the relevant state requirements, including conditions of [the amended permit], which were not appealed." The NRB and ANR are empowered to enforce Act 250 and the amended permit and the Association, as an interested party, may participate, and in fact is participating, in those proceedings by the rights vested under 10 V.S.A. §8020. The Association remains free to raise any concerns it might have about Stratton's compliance with the permit conditions and may request that the NRB or ANR enforce or investigate possible violations under 10 V.S.A. §8005(a)(2).

Affirmed.

Notes and Comments

1. *The Conditions.* Why does the Vermont Supreme Court conclude that Condition 14 was unenforceable? Are you convinced?

2. *Pros and Cons.* What are the strengths and weaknesses that you see in the institutional structure of the Oregon system in comparison to the Vermont and Florida systems? In evaluating such systems, you must consider them from several perspectives.

a. *Politics.* From a political standpoint, does the system strike the appropriate balance between local control and state oversight, such that it is likely to stand the test of time? The politics of such a balance can be delicate. In Vermont, for example, the legislature at one point had enacted legislation requiring local land use decisions to conform to 32 statewide goals. The result was revolt; some 200 local jurisdictions voted on town meeting day not to participate in the planning needed to implement that system.

b. *Implementation.* You must also consider the systems from the standpoint of implementation. Which type of system is likely to be more effective in attaining its goals? For example, under the Vermont system the District Environmental Commissions apply a set of criteria, such as whether a project will cause "undue" or "unreasonable" effects. Vt. Stat. Ann. tit. 10 §6086(a) (2016) (board or district commission shall find that the subdivision or development will not result in undue water or air pollution, will not cause an unreasonable burden on an existing water supply, will not place an unreasonable burden on the local government's ability to provide municipal or governmental services, etc.). Is this the best type of system to implement effective state oversight of projects?

c. *Planning.* From a planning standpoint, which state has arranged its processes in the most fair and effective manner? Consider that Oregon's creation of an administrative appeal board, the Land Use Board of Appeals (LUBA), whose decisions are subject to review directly in the state court of appeals, results in a planning and legal dynamic that is quite different from the norm. One obvious benefit is that LUBA's decisions are more likely to be based on planning expertise than those issued by the courts, and LUBA has the ability to fashion a consistent body of precedent that will do much to shape interpretations of Oregon planning law. Do you see any problems with this institutional arrangement?

An important practical factor is that the Land Conservation and Development Commission, the state agency that oversees the planning process in Oregon, has had a staff that aids the commission. The staff is an important player in the plan acknowledgment process, providing both expertise and critical recommendations to the LCDC.

Another aspect of the "planning" issue involves matching the state's role with the kind of institutional planning efforts it will undertake. For example, in larger states, precise mapping of uses for the entire state could be extraordinarily difficult. The state may be better suited to focusing on certain policy goals and seeking to ensure that state agencies support those goals throughout the state. *See* Fred

Bosselman, A Role for State Planning: Intergenerational Equity and Adaptive Management, 12 U. Fla. J. L. & Pub. Pol'y 311 (2001) (suggesting that state planning should focus on "intergenerational equity" — broadly, giving adequate attention to the needs of future generations — and "adaptive management" — a process "in which the objectives and strategies of the plan are under continuous review" to take into account changes in technology, ecological knowledge, etc.).

A Note on the Hawaii System

Hawaii early on turned to a system of direct state land use regulation with a central planning structure. In 1961, the Legislature passed Act 187, the Hawaii Land Use Law, which resulted in the classification of all lands in the state into four categories: urban, agriculture, low-density rural, and conservation. The Act is implemented through a Land Use Commission whose nine members are appointed by the governor. The commission regulates development on urban, agricultural, and low-density rural land. *See Ka Pa'Akai O Ka'Aina v. Land Use Comm'n,* 7 P.3d 1068 (Haw. 2000) (Commission's findings and conclusions do not indicate that it fulfilled its obligation to preserve and protect customary and traditional rights of native Hawaiians). In 2005, Act 183 was passed. It provided for policies and procedures for identifying agricultural land. Haw. Rev. Stat. §205-41 (2008). Act 233, which followed in 2008, attempted to fulfill a state constitutional mandate to conserve and protect important agricultural lands. It created incentives, including tax credits and expedited regulatory processing, to encourage landowners to designate their lands as important agricultural land.

The role of local government is restricted in Hawaii. Only about 4 percent of the state's land is classified as urban, and the counties control development only in this category, with the state controlling the rest. For example, the Hawaii Department of Land and Natural Resources grants permits for land uses in conservation districts. David L. Callies, It All Began in Hawaii, 45 J. Marshall L. Rev. 317 (2012); David L. Callies, Land-Use Planning in the Fiftieth State, in State and Regional Comprehensive Planning 127 (Peter A. Buchsbaum & Larry J. Smith eds. 1993).

In 1978, the Hawaii legislature adopted a statewide land use plan. It identified goals, objectives, and priorities for the state and a basis for coordinating state and county planning activities. There are 12 state "functional plans," which are to implement and conform to the state plan. *See Lum Yip Kee, Ltd. v. City and County of Honolulu,* 767 P.2d 815 (Haw. 1989). Counties are to adopt plans that must "take into consideration" the policies, guidelines, and objectives of the state plan, and local zoning and subdivision ordinances generally must conform to these county plans.

Profesor David Callies concludes that the quiet revolution has "run its course" in Hawaii:

> First, it is worth observing that Hawai'i's system of broadly deciding what land should be developed and what should not has been effective in preserving open land, whether in agriculture or in conservation uses, as well as preventing sprawl beyond existing areas for development, throughout the state, and in particular on O'ahu, the locus of the City and County of Honolulu, and the home of eighty percent of the state's permanent residents.

He also suggests that comprehensive plans and planning are "endangered" in the state, citing several political and economic challenges to implementation of the law. *See* Callies, 45 J. Marshall L. Rev. at 345.

C. REGIONAL CRITICAL AREA CONTROLS

In addition to some efforts to implement statewide land use management, a few states have implemented controls at the regional level. These efforts, sometimes known as "critical area legislation," often stem from concerns over environmental protection. They are targeted either at areas thought generically to be of particular environmental concern (such as areas along the coast) or at other specific areas whose resources are deemed to be of statewide if not national significance (such as the New Jersey Pinelands, the Chesapeake Bay, the San Francisco Bay, and the Adirondack Mountains). The following case exemplifies this type of system.

■ 330 CONCORD STREET v. CAMPSEN
424 S.E.2d 538 (Ct. App. 1992)

CURETON, Judge:

This case involves a permit to build a restaurant partly within the critical zone of the waters of the Cooper River in Charleston Harbor. George Campsen sought a permit to construct a restaurant as part of a joint project with the proposed South Carolina Marine Science Museum and the National Park Service Fort Sumter Tour Boat Facility. The South Carolina Coastal Council approved the permit application. An appeal was taken to the circuit court by 330 Concord Street Neighborhood Association and the League of Women Voters of Charleston County. . . .

George Campsen has been a concessionaire with the National Park Service for the Fort Sumter tour boats since the 1960's. The Park Service has been looking for a new landing facility for the tour boats. A proposal was conceived by the National Park Service, the City of Charleston, and Mr. Campsen to construct an aquatic science museum, tour boat facility, and a restaurant at a site on the Cooper River in Charleston County. The restaurant would be privately owned by Mr. Campsen. The tour boat facility would be owned by the National Park Service and the aquatic science museum would be owned by the City of Charleston. The plans envisioned a common parking area and public promenade. All the buildings as planned encroached upon the critical zone in some degree. Permits were issued by the Coastal Council for the aquarium and tour boat facility. These permits are not in issue.

As originally conceived, the restaurant was 31,000 square feet. This concept was downsized to 19,950 square feet and the building was moved landward. Under the revised plan, approximately 3200 square feet are within the mudflat area. Of this amount 1400 square feet is above mean high water in an area covered by concrete rubble and 1800 square feet is below mean high water. The environmental impact is the effect on primary productivity from shading caused by the restaurant. Shading would affect organisms that use sunlight for photosynthesis.

The parties agree the restaurant is a "nonwater dependent structure" as defined by Coastal Council regulations. *See* 23A S.C. Code Ann. Regs. 30-1(C)(10) (1983). Under council's regulations, a "nonwater dependent structure" is prohibited from being constructed in critical areas "unless there is no significant environmental impact, an overriding public need can be demonstrated and no feasible alternatives exist." *Id.* at 30-12(M).

Coastal Council issued a permit for the restaurant after finding the project satisfied the three criteria under the regulation. . . .

I.

The first criterion is "no significant environmental impact." Both sides presented expert witnesses in the field of biology. These witnesses examined the site and analyzed the effect of shading upon the productivity of the estuarine system. They disagreed about the significance of the environmental impact.

The appellants also assert the Coastal Council failed to follow its precedent. The appellants introduced evidence of a prior administrative decision of Coastal Council which denied a permit for an already built packing plant that shaded less area in the mudflats than would be covered by the Campsen restaurant. Coastal Council denied the permit finding there was a significant environmental impact from the shading and "the possible cumulative effects of this type of development could be devastating to the coast line of South Carolina." Appellants assert Coastal Council ignored this precedent and did not consider the cumulative effects of similar development when considering the restaurant permit.

Under the substantial evidence test, the possibility of drawing two inconsistent conclusions from the evidence does not prevent the agency's decision from being supported by substantial evidence. *Lark v. BiLo Inc.*, 276 S.C. 130, 136, 276 S.E.2d 304, 307 (1981). An administrative agency is generally not bound by the principle of *stare decisis* but it cannot act arbitrarily in failing to follow established precedent. *Courtesy Motors Inc., v. Ford Motor Co.*, 9 Va. App. 102, 384 S.E.2d 118 (1989). Given the conflicting expert opinions, we find the conclusion of the agency on the issue of environmental impact is supported by substantial evidence. As to the precedential effect of the prior administrative decision, we have examined the record in this case and the order from the prior case. While they both deal with mudflat areas, there appear to be distinguishing factors between the cases. Most notably, nothing in the prior case suggests any of the public benefits involved in this case. We do not find Council acted arbitrarily in failing to follow its prior decision.

II.

The second criterion is whether "an overriding public need can be demonstrated." Both the Coastal Council and the circuit court found the record established the public need for the restaurant at the proposed site. The term "overriding public need" is not defined in Coastal Council's statutes and regulations.

In finding "public need," the Coastal Council and the circuit court outlined the testimony of various witnesses at the hearing. Only the respondents presented evidence on this point. The witnesses stated the restaurant was an integral part of the three phase development consisting of the aquatic science museum, tour boat facility, and restaurant. The plans had been coordinated to have a common use parking facility and public promenade between the buildings. Although the museum and tour boat facility would still be built if the permit for the restaurant was denied, the witnesses stated the restaurant would provide a needed food service to the public. No other restaurant was within walking distance and the witnesses testified their expectation was people would spend several hours visiting the museum and taking the boat tour. The presence of the three facilities in one location was considered an advantage to tourism. Several witnesses also testified the restaurant would provide jobs for people living in a nearby economically depressed area. Development of this area in this manner was consistent with the City of Charleston's tourism management plan.

Appellants assert the Council and court improperly evaluated "public need" by equating it with "public want" and "public support." In other words, they contend public need is not established simply because the public may want or generally support a project. . . .

In considering whether there is substantial evidence of an overriding public need, we find persuasive prior case authority which holds evidence of a purely economic benefit is insufficient as a matter of law to establish an overriding public interest. *S.C. Wildlife Fed'n v. S.C. Coastal Council*, 296 S.C. 187, 371 S.E.2d 521 (1988). The council viewed the restaurant in conjunction with the museum and tour boat facility on this issue. There was no challenge by the appellants to the "public need" for the aquatic science museum and the tour boat facility. Considered in this context, we find substantial evidence to support the finding of the agency and the circuit court that "public need" had been established. The museum and tour boat facility will provide educational and recreational benefits to the public as well as an economic benefit to the community. Unlike the *S.C. Wildlife Federation* case, there is evidence of more than a purely economic benefit.

III.

The third criterion is "no feasible alternatives exist." In reviewing the evidence, the Coastal Council and the circuit court found the criterion had been met.

The respondents presented the testimony of the restaurant architect, restaurant consultant, and a real estate appraiser. Their testimony related to alternative floor plans for the restaurant, the need for service access, problems with setback restrictions, the value of offstreet parking in the city and the potential loss of parking spaces by further moving the restaurant, and the economic viability of a smaller restaurant. The appellants cross-examined these witnesses but did not offer evidence on this matter. Based upon the evidence, the agency and circuit court found the criterion was met.

Appellants' main argument is the evidence presented by the respondents was opinion testimony which lacked a proper factual foundation and, thus, had no probative value. They assert the restaurant plan is an effort to put too much private commercial space into too small an area and there is no reason why the restaurant cannot be further downsized and removed entirely from the critical area. We have reviewed the testimony of the witnesses and cannot say as a matter of law the testimony has no probative value. Given our standard of review, we find no error since the conclusion reached by Coastal Council based upon the record before it is one a reasonable mind might have reached.

AFFIRMED.

Notes and Comments

1. *Questions Arising from* Campsen. Under a more demanding standard of review, could the court have reached the conclusion it did in Campsen? Are you convinced by the court's "public need" analysis? Does the court give a free pass to the respondents, meeting the "no feasible alternative" criterion? What changes might have satisfied both sides in the case?

2. *Regional Controls for Areas of Special Concern.* In light of the reasons set out above for moving toward regional controls on land use, when might a regional system of regulation be more appropriate than a statewide system? *See* Richard Briffault, The Local Government Boundary Problem in Metropolitan Areas, 48 Stan. L. Rev. 1115 (1996) (discussing the various problems associated with local government boundaries). With the rise of the environmental movement in the late 1960s, concerns related to protecting specific regional resources and special areas led to state legislation designed to protect and manage those resources. Because the resources at stake spanned numerous local jurisdictions, regulation on a regional basis was thought the only realistic solution.

Two of the earliest initiatives established regulatory systems managing land uses in the San Francisco Bay region and the Adirondack Mountains, and these efforts provided the models for later legislation that proceeded along the same lines. The California Coastal Commission and the New Jersey Pinelands Commission also are examples of agencies with regional regulatory powers over development in special areas. Proposals for the adoption of special area regional controls continue today. *See* Clair Wischusen, Who Is Regulating the Regulators: A Proposal for State Oversight of Natural Resource Zoning Regulations in Pennsylvania, 27 Temp. J. Sci. Tech. & Envtl. L. 315 (2008); John Costonis, Two Years and Counting: Land Use and Louisiana's Post-Katrina Recovery, 68 La. L. Rev. 349 (2008).

3. *Justifying a Regional Approach Context.* This official description of the New Jersey Pinelands National Reserve and the Pinelands Area offers a justification for a regional approach:

In the center of America's most populous region lies over a million acres of forests, farms, and scenic towns — the New Jersey Pinelands.

The Pinelands is a patchwork of pine oak forests, tea-colored streams ad rivers, spacious farms, crossroad hamlets, and small towns stretched across southern New Jersey. In the country's early years it had been a place where fortunes were made from lumber, iron and glass. But the early industries died out, and as the state's major roads bypassed the area, the "Pine Barrens" gradually became known as a remote part of New Jersey abounding in local legends like the "Jersey Devil."

By the end of the 1960's, as the full weight of postwar urban sprawl came to bear on other parts of New Jersey, the path of Pinelands history forked again. Would the Pinelands become the locale of grandiose development projects, such as a jetport and a city of a quarter million, or would the region's value come to be based on its open spaces, natural features, and traditional lifestyles, which uncontrolled development would damage or obliterate?

It took years of study and debate before the choice was made. But gradually the realization set in that the Pinelands was an environmental asset of national and international importance, deserving safeguards to divert the flow of growth from metropolitan Philadelphia, northern New Jersey, and New York. Nearby Atlantic City's casino gambling boom crystallized awareness of the need for Pinelands development controls.

Pinelands Commission, State of New Jersey, *CMP Summary* at http://www.nj.gov/pinelands/cmp/summary/ (last visited Sept. 21, 2016).

4. *The Model Act and "Critical Area" Regulation.* Another important impetus for change was the American Law Institute's Model Land Development Code adopted in 1975. Section 7-201 of the Model Act called for regulation of "areas of critical state concern."

As noted above in this chapter, in addition to regulating developments of regional impact, Florida also followed the Model Act's scheme by implementing state regulation of developments in "areas of critical state concern." *See* Fla. Stat. Ann. §§380.05, 380.07(2); *Askew v. Cross Key Waterways*, 372 So. 2d 913 (Fla. 1978) (describing the process leading to the designation of the Florida Keys as an area of critical state concern); *see also* Thomas G. Pelham, Regulating Areas of Critical State Concern: Florida and the Model Code, 18 Urn. L. Ann. 3 (1980). Under the Florida scheme, four areas have been designated. They are Big Cypress Area of Critical State Concern, Green Swamp Area, City of Key West and the Florida Keys Areas, and Apalachicola Bay Area.

Likewise, the Chesapeake Bay is protected under the Chesapeake Bay Critical Area Protection Program. *See* Timothy Henderson and James Doyle, Ever Expanding Reach of the Critical Area Commission, 41 Md. Bar. J. 38 (2008). *See generally* Thomas A. Borden, Using Regional Planning to Protect Public Trust Resources, 237 N. J. Law (2005).

5. *Regional and Coastal Zone Regulation: The Federal Influence.* The federal government has strongly encouraged states to regulate development in coastal areas. The Coastal Zone Management Act (CZMA), 16 U.S.C. §§1451-1466, authorizes the National Oceanic and Atmospheric Administration in the Department of Commerce to award grants for the preparation of coastal zone management plans. The planning requirements are stringent. *See* 15 C.F.R. Part 923 (2016). For example, a state must establish a planning process for energy facilities to be located within the coastal zone that may "significantly affect" that zone. 16 U.S.C. §1455(d)(2). After a state's plan is completed, it must be approved by the Secretary of Commerce. *See American Petroleum Inst. v. Knecht*, 456 F. Supp. 889 (C.D. Cal. 1978), *aff'd*, 609 F.2d 1306 (9th Cir. 1979) (California plan complied with CZMA requirements relating to energy facility siting). After certification, every applicant for a federal license or permit seeking to conduct an activity affecting the coastal zone must certify that the proposed activity comports with the state's program. *See* Steven R. Schell, Living with the Legacy of the 1970's: Federal/State Coordination in the Coastal Zone, 14 Envtl. L. 751 (1984).

6. *The Contours of Regional and Critical Area Regulation.* Regional and critical area land use regulatory systems raise the following issues:

a. *Designating the Regulated Area.* Critical area regulation must begin by defining the area that is subject to regulation. This identification can occur either in a statute that specifically sets forth the precise boundaries of the agency's jurisdiction or through the agency's subsequent administrative implementation of a general statutory definition. The agency usually will prepare a map that outlines with particularity its jurisdictional limits.

b. *The Administering Body.* Any regional system requires the establishment of a regulatory body. In some instances, that body is a statewide commission, such as the South Carolina Coastal Council in the principal case just read. The Adirondack Park Agency consists of three state cabinet-level officials and eight members appointed by the governor with the advice and consent of the state Senate, while the San Francisco Bay Conservation and Development Commission has 27 members, almost half of whom are representatives of local governments.

The California Coastal Commission operated for almost thirty years under a structure in which a majority of its members were appointed by legislative officials and all members were removable at will. However, in *Marine Forests Soc'y v. California Coastal Comm'n*, 104 Cal. App. 4th 1232 (2002), a California court of appeal found that this arrangement violated the separation of powers doctrine because the members could be appointed or removed at will. Do you see any practical problems if members are removable at will? Would it bother you if, during a heated controversy over an issue, the governor fired his appointees and replaced them before a vote on the issue?

Then, in *Marine Forests Soc'y v. California Coastal Comm'n*, 36 Cal. 4th 1 (2005), the California Supreme Court held that a revised statutory scheme did not violate the California Constitution. Under the revised scheme, the legislature still appointed two-thirds of the commission to a term that had been extended to four years but had no at-will removal power. The governor maintained at-will appointment powers of one-third of the members. The California Supreme Court found that the California Constitution did not preclude the legislature from enacting a provision that allowed it to appoint a member or members of an executive commission or board.

Behavior of Coastal Commission members and absence of transparency in commission procedures have again become a focus of considerable recent controversy. A commission executive director beloved to environmentalists was removed of his duties allegedly for being insufficiently flexible to developmental goals, and the commission has been criticized for its *ex parte* communications. *See* Dan Weikel & Kim Christensen, "How A Ban on Ex Parte Communications by the Coastal Commission Could Change the Balance Of Power," Los Angeles Times (May 14, 2016).

c. *Planning.* How should the agency go about its task of regulating? The typical pattern of regional regulation requires the agency to prepare a comprehensive land use plan for the area in question. Thus, New York legislation required the Adirondack Park Agency to create a "land use and development plan" for the entire area of the park, including private lands, as well as another plan for state lands only. N.Y. Exec. Law §805. In the New Jersey Pinelands, protection is to occur through implementation of the New Jersey Pinelands Comprehensive Management Plan. N.J. Stat. Ann. §13:18A-8. Depending on the significance of the resource and the politics of the situation, approval of the plan by the state legislature may be required. In the Adirondacks, for example, the New York State Legislature ratified the Park Agency's plan for regulating development on private lands.

d. *Regulatory Controls.* The principal implementation method used is usually a permitting system employing restrictions and site-specific conditions. Transfer of development rights schemes also are used in these programs.

e. *The Local Role.* Any system of regional controls must determine the relationship between the local governments in the jurisdictional area, which traditionally have power over land use, and the state or regional body that now also has regulatory authority. Under the Lake Tahoe arrangement, any political subdivision within the region may adopt higher standards than the regional agency, but the regional agency's standards act as a regulatory floor. Cal. Gov't Code §66801, art. VI(a). Another possibility is that the local governments may be required to revise their own plans and ordinances to conform to the regional planning effort. *See* N.J. Admin. Code tit. 7 §7:50-3.11 (1996) (counties must conform master plans and ordinances to Pinelands Comprehensive Master Plan).

The regulatory system for the region or the critical area may not make every land use decision subject to regional or statewide control. For example, the North Carolina Coastal Area Management Act authorizes the Division of Coastal Resources to grant permits for "major" developments, while "minor" developments remain exclusively within the province of local government. N.C. Gen. Stat. §113A-118(d)(1) (2003); *see also* N.Y. Exec. Law §810 (McKinney 1996) (local governments may be given authority to regulate "Class B regional projects" in the Adirondack Park if their land use programs are approved by the park agency, but "Class A regional projects" must be approved by the Park Agency). Another method is the straightforward "double-veto" system: a project must obtain approval from both the local government and the regional body.

7. *Critical Areas and Takings.* Where the regional agency is charged with protecting a "critical area" or an environmentally sensitive area, it may find itself denying development proposals outright. In such instances, the question of whether the regulatory action constitutes a taking may arise. For example, in *Candlestick Properties, Inc. v. S.F. Bay Conservation and Dev. Comm'n*, 11 Cal. App. 3d 557 (1970), the plaintiff was denied permission to fill in part of San Francisco Bay. The court rejected a contention that the denial constituted a taking, even though the parcel was submerged at high tide and, according to the owners, could not be used unless it was filled. Is this holding still good law after *Lucas v. South Carolina Coastal Council*, a principal case discussed in Chapter 7?

D. THE NEW REGIONALISM: SPRAWL

In recent years, the topics of regional sprawl, smart growth, and sustainable development have received increasing attention in the general media and in the professional planning literature both in this country and throughout the world. A low-density pattern of isolated, automobile-dependent development now characterizes not just newer outlying suburbs but also many older suburbs and even much of the built environment in many of larger older cities. The myriad problems and costs associated with automobile-dependent development are enormous and growing. This energy consumptive pattern of development is increasingly seen as undesirable, unaffordable, and probably unsustainable. We discussed planning issues related to sprawl, smart growth, new urbanism, and sustainable development in Chapter 4, and we will return to some of those issues later in Chapter 11.

Improved transit is often viewed as critical in addressing sustainable development issues, such as household transit and energy costs, infrastructure costs, disabling congestion, economic development, environmental protection, and climate change. Studies show that building type and transit location can reduce resource and energy consumption by as much as 70 percent. That saving would translate into a substantial increase in household disposable income. *See* Jonathan Rose Companies, Location Efficiency and Housing Type: Boiling It Down to BTUs (EPA Smart Growth Report) (2011); Cambridge Systemics, Inc., Moving Cooler: An Analysis of Transportation Strategies for Reducing Green House Gas Emissions (2009).

The following article discusses the need for regional land use planning to support regional transportation planning and transit-oriented development in our metropolitan areas. The topic of transportation planning and redevelopment is also discussed in Chapter 15.

■ **EDWARD H. ZIEGLER, SUSTAINABLE URBAN DEVELOPMENT AND THE NEXT AMERICAN LANDSCAPE: SOME THOUGHTS ON TRANSPORTATION, REGIONALISM, AND URBAN PLANNING LAW REFORM IN THE 21ST CENTURY**
43 URB. LAW. 91 (2011)

There is growing awareness of the importance of coordinated urban planning policy at the metropolitan level in creating less automobile-dependent and prosperous urban core areas. Movement toward a more metropolitan governing arrangement through regional plans for housing, energy, transit, as well as economic and environmental policies and public and private infrastructure development is increasingly advocated as an antidote to the problems of automobile-dependent regional sprawl. This type of increased regional focus is the transitional challenge for urban planning policy and practice in this country in the twenty-first century. What follows are some thoughts on the reform of local urban planning policy in the United States toward a more holistic, integrated, and regional framework for managing growth.

I.

Without substantial reform (that includes a focus on metropolitan planning), local planning and zoning programs are likely to continue as a significant cause of unsustainable automobile-dependent regional sprawl and are unlikely to provide sustainable and affordable private options in regard to jobs, housing, energy, transit, and infrastructure.

Local zoning and growth management operate in the United States largely to expand our low density pattern of regional sprawl. Excluded development simply locates (sprawls) further out away from an urban core area. Sprawl, in this respect, is the product of the very visible hand of local government urban planning policy. Cities that tout their green development initiatives should be at least honest enough to count their "zoning policy" responsibility for their "exclusion-driven GHG [green house gas] emissions" (as a result of the automobile driving of workers in the city who must find housing elsewhere, and from their own city residents who need to drive elsewhere to find jobs) as well as for their "indirect land conversion GHG emissions" (that result from the enormous costs and amounts of energy associated with "excluded" new land development away from the urban core). The truth of the matter is that cities are great at talking the "green talk," but are often quite lousy at walking the "green walk" in local urban planning policy.

II.

Without substantial reform (that includes a focus on metropolitan planning), the higher density housing expected in our metropolitan areas in the years ahead will likely be built on scattered and isolated buffer sites, without mixed uses, and will continue to be largely, if not completely, automobile dependent.

Local low density zoning and exclusionary growth management programs are becoming increasingly dysfunctional in view of the changing market demographics and demand for attractive and affordable multi-unit housing in the United States. That is, of course, no guarantee of their immediate demise. Under existing low density zoning regimes, these higher density developments are likely to be poorly planned and relegated to isolated and residual buffer zones. By default, they are likely to be designed under existing zoning regimes with densities that are still completely automobile dependent. They are unlikely to be planned and developed as green communities within a regional growth management framework. In short, the higher densities expected in this country in the years ahead will not alone result in more sustainable urban areas in our metropolitan regions. Unless planned and designed otherwise, our communities and regions are likely to remain automobile-dependent places, where, like Los Angeles (the highest density urbanized area in the United States), Americans will live their lives in poorly planned and automobile-dependent environments. Los Angeles is fast becoming like traffic plagued Jakarta and everywhere else in America is fast becoming like Los Angeles. If this continues to occur, life in America will surely be poorer and planned largely around high fuel costs and traffic congestion.

III.

Without substantial reform (that includes a focus on metropolitan planning), we are probably wildly optimistic about the extent and benefits of light rail transit-oriented development (TOD) in our metropolitan areas in this country, as TOD will likely be severely limited in both scope and density and will likely provide few opportunities for automobile-free living arrangements, particularly for the less affluent.

In the United States, regionally important TOD areas are nearly always under local zoning control and more compact and intensive development is often prohibited or substantially scaled back when opposed by neighbors, which it often is. TOD that consists, for example, of a park-and-ride lot, a pod shopping plaza, or a Taco Bell, and a nearby two- or three-story apartment or office building is not an alternative sustainable development vision but merely an expensive attempt at traffic mediation. TOD areas are truly Smart Growth when neighborhood density and mixed uses allow many residents to live, work, shop, and play without owning an automobile or without having to use public transit on a daily basis. TOD sites, also, are too often just that — undersized, individual sites — when what is needed is space for whole neighborhoods and communities. Under European transit models, a TOD area might include a one-mile or more radius around a transit stop and have blended densities of twenty-five to one hundred units per acre. Densities in Europe often are related and commensurate to the purpose and policy of public infrastructure and transit investment. That is still a novel idea in America. Both the Bay Area Rapid Transit (BART) rail transit system in San Francisco and the Washington D.C. Metro rail system, each constructed over thirty years ago, are still anticipating the development of European style densities at many TOD sites in nearby station areas.

Given the expected low density and limited scope of these projects, we are probably wildly optimistic about the potential benefits of planned TOD in this country. Growth management plans with respect to areas selected for TOD, or for other intensive urban core area development, will likely require regionally coordinated designation of both "growth" and "no growth" areas. These plans, of course, would need to be regionally integrated and coordinated with major public transit and infrastructure investment decisions. None of this seems possible, however, without some new regional governing arrangement.

IV.

Without substantial reform (including a focus on metropolitan planning), this country is unlikely to be rich enough in the future to afford two world class transit systems — a public light rail/bus transit system and a private-automobile transit and infrastructure system.

Many metropolitan areas in the United States have regional transportation planning for light rail or high speed bus service. However, so called TOD at station stops, or key transit nodes, and along key corridors is often not occurring in this country at true transit-friendly densities. This is due, in part, to local low-density, NIMBY-dominated zoning schemes and to the profusion of alternative development sites within a region allowed in the absence of regional TOD urban building plans. TOD densities today seldom actually justify the enormous financial infrastructure investment in fixed rail public transit, nor do they make possible neighborhoods where many households can live, work, shop, and play without daily use of an automobile. Population density controls transit efficiency and affordability. European-like metropolitan rail networks make sense only when supported by adequate regional core area densities.

Without sufficient, supporting TOD density, the United States may very well go broke attempting to finance both roads and light rails in the years ahead. In light rail friendly Portland, Oregon, for example, road improvement spending has declined, residential density is about half that of Los Angeles, transit ridership is less than expected, and the number one issue for citizens is traffic congestion. In a compact city like Barcelona, Spain, that city's world class fixed rail transit network can efficiently and affordably serve about 2 million people in the metropolitan area. In a sprawling metro area like Denver, a similar transit system serving 2 million people might have to cover an area about 20 times larger than the area served by the Barcelona transit system. One thing seems certain; we are not rich enough now, and surely will not be rich enough in the future, to finance two costly and efficient transit networks (both private auto and public transit) in our expanding metropolitan areas. Regional transit planning is, in all likelihood, unaffordable and unsustainable without regional urban planning. This may ultimately prove to be a hard lesson for us to learn.

V. Towards a Conclusion

We are passing along to the next generation an infrastructure of bridges, highways, tunnels, viaducts, rail lines, port facilities, levies, and transmission grids that are all badly in need of replacement and repair. Higher oil prices will make all of us poorer through rising prices for gasoline, food, commodities, building materials, pharmaceuticals, computers, and nearly all consumer products and services. Rising prices, moreover, will slow job creation, decrease investment, dampen consumer spending, and act as a drain on economic growth. Already we spend about six billion person hours stuck in traffic each year (that's about a full working year for 3 million people and an estimated sixty billion dollar loss in economic productivity) and we are likely to be adding over one-hundred million more vehicles to further congest our nation's roads by midcentury.

Higher densities that are likely to occur in this country's metropolitan areas in the years ahead hold the potential for addressing many of our sustainable development problems, but only if this new development embodies a green design policy that provides transit-friendly and automobile-free lifestyle options. Urban planning policies need to be crafted to support regional transit planning with new growth in designated urban core areas within a region at densities that allow many residents the choice of attractive automobile-free living arrangements.

Notes and Comments

1. *The New Regionalism I: Problematic Issues of Local Control.* The author of the above article argues for regional urban planning to support regional transportation planning. Do you think this is necessary? Is this problem a significant cause of the housing/jobs mismatch that congests our nation's roads?

A number of states enacted legislation authorizing the preparation of regional plans by regional planning commissions in the post–World War II era. With few exceptions, however, these laws did not require that the plans be implemented, nor did they give regional planning agencies actual authority over land use decisions. Moreover, the regional regulatory programs discussed earlier were generally not created for the purpose of curtailing sprawl. Even in Oregon, regional plans and urban growth boundaries were intended to preserve farmland from premature development, and sprawl largely continued over the years within the growth boundaries, as those boundaries were expanded from time to time to accommodate new growth. Growth boundaries are discussed later herein and in Chapter 11.

Areas of regional planning concern include climate change, transportation, infrastructure, utilities and public services, economic development and job creation, housing, waste management and recycling, heating and cooling networks, watershed management, waste water treatment, food security, public health, wildlife, open space, forest protection, air and water pollution, active recreational opportunities, public finance, energy costs, green building standards, and alternative energy development, along with more intangible concerns related to design, aesthetics, and creating integrated mixed-use and pedestrian-friendly neighborhoods.

2. *The New Regionalism II: The Increasing Focus on Metropolitan Areas.* Most Americans live, work, shop, and play scattered about a metropolitan landscape far from any downtown urban core. Urban core areas in large cities today contain only about 10 percent of a region's jobs, although in the last decade there has been a small shift of employment to cities. In the United States, the top 100 metropolitan areas are home to 65 percent of the nation's population (including 85 percent of the nation's immigrants and 77 percent of the nation's minorities), and those 100 regions generate two-thirds of the nation's jobs and three-quarters of the nation's economic GDP. Those largest 100 metropolitan areas also contain over 9000 local governments, and one-third of these metropolitan areas span state jurisdictional boundaries. Nearly all the growth in the years ahead in this country (perhaps 200 million additional people in the next 60 years) will be located in just 20 mega regions of the United States. Two out of three people in this country will live in these 20 mega regions by 2040.

There is an increasing interest in the potential of metropolitan planning to support public and private transportation and infrastructure investment decisions, environmental protection, resource management, energy consumption, affordable housing, and economic development. Recent reports by the Brookings Institution, the Urban Land Institute, Smart Growth America, the American Planning Association, America 2050, and other organizations highlight the need for fashioning new regional frameworks for planning and development of our built environment. China, following a number of European nations, has now embraced an explicit regional urban planning policy. *See generally* Edward Ziegler, The Case for Megapolitan Growth Management in the 21st Century: Regional Urban Planning and Sustainable Development in the United States, 41 Urb. Law. 147 (2009); Peter Pollock, A Comment on Making Sustainable Land Use Planning Work, 80 U. Colo. L. Rev. 999 (2009); Nancy Perkins, Livability, Regional Equity, and Capability: Closing in on Sustainable Land Use, 37 U. Balt. L. Rev. 157 (2008).

The absence of metropolitan governing arrangements that can address regional planning problems is a quintessential development dilemma.

3. *The New Regionalism III: Toward a New Federal, State, and Local Synthesis.* There are recent national policy changes that may point toward the eventual emergence of a new federal, state, and local metropolitan smart growth policy. At the federal level, the "Federal Interagency Partnership for Sustainable Communities" creates for the first time a national green urban policy for metropolitan areas in this country. The program brings together the coordinated expertise of four major federal agencies, the United States Departments of Transportation, Energy, Housing, and Environmental Protection, in an attempt to move federal policy toward greater national funding and support for public transit and non-automobile mobility in urban areas, including regional rail transit systems and enhanced metropolitan planning. The program provides funding for coordination of regional transportation plans and urban planning for transit friendly development.

There also are state initiatives including The Sustainable Communities and Climate Protection Act of 2008 in California, which conditions federal and state transportation funds on the adoption of regional urban development plans for higher density and more transit-friendly development strategies. Regional planning commissions are responsible for reviewing and crafting metropolitan-wide plans that promote state and regional GHG-emission goals. The law is discussed in Chapter 11.

E. JURISDICTIONAL CONFLICTS AND ADJUSTMENTS: ANNEXATION, PREEMPTION, AND ACCOMMODATION

■ CITY OF ALBUQUERQUE v. STATE OF NEW MEXICO MUNICIPAL BOUNDARY COMMISSION
131 N.M. 665 (2002)

OPINION

PICKARD, Judge.

West Tijeras Canyon Ltd. filed an annexation petition with the Municipal Boundary Commission, seeking to have its property annexed to the City of Albuquerque. The Commission determined that the annexation met the requirements of NMSA 1978, §3-7-15(A) (1965) and ordered the property annexed to the City. . . . We hold that the Commission was required to not only consider, but give substantial deference to, the City's opposition to the annexation petition. We therefore affirm the district court's decision reversing the Commission's order.

FACTS AND PROCEEDINGS

The Municipal Boundary Commission is an independent administrative board vested with the authority to hear petitions for annexation. *See* NMSA 1978, §3-7-11 (1995). The Commission may hear petitions from either municipalities seeking to annex new territory or from landowners hoping to stretch the boundaries of a municipality to include their property. The Commission's decision-making process is governed by Section 3-7-15(A), which provides that:

> At the public hearing held for the purpose of determining if the territory proposed to be annexed to the municipality shall be annexed to the municipality, the municipal boundary commission shall determine if the territory proposed to be annexed:
>
> (1) is contiguous to the municipality; and
> (2) may be provided with municipal services by the municipality to which the territory is proposed to be annexed.

If the Commission finds that the two requirements of Section 3-7-15(A) are met, then under Section 3-7-15(B) it must approve the annexation.

West Tijeras owns a 165 acre parcel of land in Bernalillo Country. The property lies south of Interstate 40, sharing its borders with the Four Hills neighborhood in

Albuquerque on the west and the Canon de Carnue Land Grant to the east. In 1998, West Tijeras approached the Albuquerque City Council, asking the City to annex the property and change the property's "Country A-1" zoning designation to allow for denser development. The Council voted to deny annexation. About six months later, West Tijeras presented a petition to the Commission seeking to have 101 acres of the property annexed into the City. West Tijeras's main purpose in seeking annexation is to gain access to City water and sewer services. If the property remains county land, West Tijeras can only develop using water wells and septic tanks.

At the Commission's hearing on the petition, the City maintained its opposition to the annexation. The Commission examined the two statutory requirements set out in Section 3-7-15(A). The first requirement, contiguity, was not at issue. A difference of opinion arose, however, as to whether the second requirement was met. The Commission Chairman indicated that West Tijeras need only show that the City was capable of providing services to the area, stating that "the criteria is not whether the City will or wants to . . . it's whether they can. . . ." The City, however, argued that the second requirement would not be met as long as the City was opposed to providing services to the property. Rejecting this interpretation, the Commission voted unanimously in favor of the annexation. . . .

[The district court overturned the annexation. West Tijeras and the Commission jointly appealed.]

DISCUSSION

Appellants argue that the Commission's initial interpretation of the statute was correct, and therefore the Commission was required to approve the annexation once West Tijeras demonstrated that the City was able to provide services to the area. Appellees, on the other hand, assert that the Commission erred in substituting the word "can" for "may," and argue that the annexation can only be approved with the City's consent. This is a case of first impression. It appears that the Commission has never before been asked to approve the annexation of territory to a municipality over the objection of that municipality. We must now determine the implications of the legislature's use of the world "may" within this statute.

. . . "When appropriate, we will rely on rules of grammar to aid our construction of the plain language of a statute." *Wilson v. Denver*, 1998-NMSC-016, ¶ 16, 125 N.M. 308, 961 P.2d 153. Appellants cite to numerous dictionaries, including Black's Law Dictionary, to support their argument that the two words are sometimes used interchangeably. On the other hand, NMSA 1978, §12-2A-4(B) (1997) instructs us that "'[m]ay' confers a power, authority, privilege or right." In contrast, "can" connotes ability. *See, e.g., William Strunk Jr. & E. B. White, The Elements of Style* (4th ed. 2000) ("*Can.* Means 'am (is, are) able.' Not to be used as a substitute for *may.*"). In the context of the annexation statutes and the statutes relating to municipal planning, the word "may" in Section 3-7-15(A) cannot reasonably be interpreted as "can" in the manner Appellants suggest.

We acknowledge that our Supreme Court indicated in *Mutz* that the statutory test could be satisfied "if the municipality demonstrates the ability to provide services to the territory to be annexed." *Mutz*, 101 N.M. at 701, 688 P.2d at 19. In *Mutz*, however, it was the municipality, not landowners, petitioning for annexation. The municipality's willingness to provide services was not at issue. The *Mutz* Court, in explaining the difference in meaning between "may" and "must," recognized that "may," as used in this particular statute, is permissive. *Id.* We are confident that the legislature intended that the Commission find something more than mere physical ability when the legislature directed the Commission to insure that services "may be provided" rather than "can be provided."

Nonetheless, we do not read the statute as requiring landowners to seek a municipality's consent to annexation when presenting an annexation petition to the Commission. The legislature provided two options for landowners who wish to see their property annexed to a municipality. The most commonly exercised option is the "petition method," which is set out in NMSA 1978, §§3-7-17 and 17.1 (1998). Using that method, if landowners holding a majority of the acres in the territory proposed to be annexed are in favor of annexation, they can petition directly to the governing body of the municipality. The municipality may then "express its consent or rejection" by ordinance. *See* §§3-7-17(A)(4);-17.1(B)(2). This was the approach first taken by West Tijeras in seeking to have its property annexed. The alternative option is the "boundary commission method," which is governed by NMSA 1978, §§3-7-11 through 16 (1965, as amended through 1995). Once again, approval is required from landowners holding a majority of the acres in the territory proposed. Unlike the petition method, however, the statutes governing the boundary commission method provide no mechanism through which a municipality can express its consent.

If the legislature had intended to require municipal consent under the boundary commission method, it would have included a consent provision in the governing statutes, just as it did in the petition method statutes. Moreover, if municipal consent was required under the boundary commission method, then there would be no meaningful difference between the two options available to landowners. If a municipality was withholding its consent to annexation, there would be no reason for landowners to approach the Commission. Since we presume that the legislature does not intend to enact useless statutes, . . . we do not think this is a correct interpretation of Section 3-7-15.

The City argues that the legislature could not have intended to give landowners the power to force a municipality to annex property despite the municipality's objection, or to allow the Commission to override the City's planning decisions. The Commission, however, does have that power. The state legislature has the power to create and to destroy municipal corporations, and to enlarge or diminish their boundaries, with or without consent of either the municipalities or the affected residents. . . . The legislature delegated its authority to determine municipal boundaries to the Commission. *See* §3-7-11(A). When it did so, it provided a defined set of guidelines for the Commission to follow under Section 3-7-15. The Commission, therefore, has the authority to annex property over the objections of the municipality involved.

In sum, we cannot adopt either party's position wholesale. In our opinion, the City could not unilaterally defeat West Tijeras's petition by withholding its consent to the annexation, but the Commission could not annex property over the City's objection upon a mere showing that the City is capable of providing services to the area. We are still left, then, with some ambiguity as to the meaning of the statutory language. The ambiguity arises, in part, from the use of passive voice in the statutory language. The statute instructs the Commission to determine "if the territory proposed to be annexed . . . may be provided with municipal services by the municipality to which the territory is proposed to be annexed." *Id.* While may is permissive, it is not clear whose permission is required in this context.

THE COMMISSION SHOULD HAVE DEFERRED TO THE CITY'S OPPOSITION TO THE ANNEXATION

. . . The statutes governing annexation, when read together, demonstrate an overall intent to assure that residents who are annexed into a municipality receive services from that municipality. . . .

In keeping with the legislature's intent to assure that residents within an annexed territory have access to municipal services, we think that when the legislature directed the Commission to determine that services "may be provided," it wanted to assure that residents would have the right to demand such services if the territory was annexed. . . .

When a municipality petitions the Commission, there is again no question that the municipality is willing to annex the territory, so the Commission's task is to insure that the provision of services is physically possible. . . . When landowners present annexation petitions, the Commission must make further inquiries and consider the municipality's position regarding annexation. As part of that inquiry the Commission should have not only considered the City's opposition to the annexation, but should have given the City's position considerable deference.

The City's objection to the annexation relates directly to the statutory requirement that services "may be provided" to the area proposed to be annexed. Much of the City's time and resources are directed toward planning and growth management efforts. In doing so, City officials have evaluated how best to provide service to existing territory and where it would be best able to expand services to meet anticipated population growth. Appellants' arguments that the City is capable of providing services to the area disregards the City's right to determine where and how those services should be provided. As one example, West Tijeras presented testimony that the City could provide social services to residents if the land is developed. The City, however, is already concerned that it is not providing sufficient services to seniors living in the nearby area. Annexation would also impact the City's provision of police, fire, and emergency services; schools; social services; street maintenance; refuse pickup; and many other services. Annexation of the West Tijeras land would put an additional burden on the City and undermine its efforts to provide an adequate level of services to those areas already within its municipal boundaries.

The City presented evidence that annexation of the West Tijeras property conflicted with a number of its established policies. The annexation conflicts with the Albuquerque Bernalillo County Comprehensive Plan, which designated the land as Rural Area. The Comprehensive Plan states that Rural Areas "shall generally retain their rural character with development consisting primarily of ranches, farms and single-family homes on large lots." Annexation of the West Tijeras property conflicts with the City's infill policy, Resolution 70, which expresses a strong preference that development occur within existing infrastructure so that the City's resources are not directed toward extending its infrastructure to new areas. These policies reflect the City's considered evaluation of how best to provide services to current and future residents. Based on these policies, the City expressed its opinion that it did not want to extend its service area to include the West Tijeras property. The Commission should have deferred to the City's opinion as to the wisdom of extending its services to the area.

Appellants contend the City's planning policies are not relevant to the Commission's inquiry, because the City can control the level of development in the area through its zoning power. Annexation alone, however, will obligate the City to provide some services to the area, including police and fire services. Roads may need to be built to provide access for emergency services. School services may have to be provided if families with children move into the area. In addition, municipal zoning authority is not unlimited, so the City may not be able to accomplish by zoning what it wishes to accomplish.

THE COMMISSION'S DECISIONS MUST BE REASONABLE

Appellants also contend it would be unfair to consider the City's opposition to annexation when the Commission is required to disregard the concerns of residents who oppose annexation. . . .

. . . [W]hen the provision of services is at issue, the Commission must apply a reasonableness standard rather than rely solely on a technical determination that it is physically possible to extend municipal services to the proposed area. As one City official explained during the hearing on this annexation, "You can make anything feasible if you spend enough money." Yet the City could reasonably argue that the provision of services would be so expensive or burdensome as to be prohibitive. Thus, even when looking at whether the provision of services is physically possible, the decision must be made within reason. Similarly, when the City argues that annexation would be inconsistent with its planning decisions regarding the provision of services to the area, it is unreasonable for the Commission to find that services may be provided to the area. The Commission should only exercise its authority to annex property over a municipality's objections based on a finding that those objections are unreasonable under the circumstances. Because we think it is clear that the City was raising reasonable concerns based on well-established policies, we hold that it was unreasonable for the Commission to approve the annexation.

We recognize that many residents who have been subject to forced annexation have felt that the statutory scheme unfairly denies them the opportunity to object on reasonable grounds because those grounds fall outside the two statutory requirements. To the extent that the residents' objections relate to the two statutory requirements, the Commission should hear and consider those objections. The statute as written, however, leaves no room for consideration of other matters. For that reason, the district court was incorrect when it held that the Commission was required to make an overall determination that the annexation was reasonable and that the Commission could not order the territory annexed over the objections of "the people." In this case in particular, the residents who spoke in opposition to the annexation lived outside the annexation territory, so their objections were beyond the scope of the Commission's inquiry.

Notes and Comments

1. *Questions.* Municipalities become larger when they annex new territories. Why would a city want to annex land? Why would a city object to an annexation

petition? Should a city have to affirmatively agree to an annexation before it can be approved? In *City of Albuquerque*, the opinion indicates that the proposed annexation would be inconsistent with the city's growth policies. How are local services and local growth policies related? *See West v. City of Princeton*, 901 N.E.2d 1141 (Ind. Ct. App. 2009) (rejecting claim that city's only goal for annexation was revenue generation); *Board of Trs. v. Town of Clarkstown*, 292 A.D.2d 450 (App. Div. 2002) (holding that village annexation of five acres of undeveloped land was justified by village need for development of affordable multi-unit housing).

Did the court in *City of Albuquerque* read the applicable statute correctly? Where does it include the condition of "reasonableness" that the court finds? In an omitted part of the opinion, the court noted that an alternative method of annexation required the commission "to determine if the benefits of the government . . . are or can be available within a reasonable time to the territory proposed to be annexed." Will this support the "reasonableness" requirement? Note that this language was not applicable to the annexation methods at issue in this case.

2. *More Questions.* The court declares that the commission "should have deferred to the City's opinion about the wisdom of extending its services to the area." Why? What reasons for deference are present? More broadly, what is the court's holding in this case?

3. *Annexation: Authority and Process.* Annexation decisions are handled in many different ways. In some instances, a commission of local officials makes the decision. Other arrangements are possible. *See, e.g., McNamara v. Office of Strategic & Long Range Planning*, 628 N.W.2d 620 (Minn. Ct. App. 2001) (administrative law judge, employed by a state agency, had the power to hold hearings and issue a decision on annexation petitions). Some jurisdictions provide for annexation agreements. *City of Springfield v. Judith Jones Dietsch Tr.*, 746 N.E.2d 1272, 1276 (Ill. Ct. App. 2001) ("Preannexation agreements serve to further important governmental purposes, such as the encouragement of expanding urban areas uniformly, economically, efficiently, and fairly.").

The procedure under which an annexation can occur, however, is up to the state legislature. That body, often guided by state constitutional provisions, has the power to establish the conditions under which municipalities can grow. The subject is covered more generally in courses on Local Government Law.

4. *Annexation: Zoning and Services.* As the discussion of the city's policies in *City of Albuquerque* indicates, annexation decisions have important land use effects. Depending on which jurisdiction annexes land, the property either can be more intensively developed or allowed less intense uses. Annexation is thus highly political and can lead to zoning litigation. *See, e.g., Shumaker Enter. v. City of Austin*, 325 S.W.3d 812 (Tex. Ct. App. 2010) (owner of annexed land had no vested right not to comply with new city zoning and permit requirement); *Crumbaker v. Hunt Midwest Mining, Inc.*, 69 P.3d 601 (Kan. 2003) (holding that when county property is annexed to city, the property retains its county zoning classification and any accompanying land use restrictions until the annexing city changes the zoning); *Esling v. Krambeck*, 663 N.W. 2d 671 (S.D. 2003) (holding that city annexing county property had authority to rezone annexed area, in spite of county enacted six-year moratorium on rezonings in the area). Would the same principal apply to development agreements entered into by a county? *See also Cape v. City of Beaverton*, 68 P.3d 261 (Or. Ct. App. 2003) (holding that city annexation of territory was a final "land use decision" that was subject to jurisdiction of Land Use Board of Appeals even though

city had an intergovernmental agreement with county under which property annexed to city would remain under county's comprehensive plan and zoning ordinance, until city adopted its own plan and zoning designations for the territory).

At the same time, however, annexation involves questions of efficiency. The most important issue is often what services will be provided to the territory being annexed. Statutes may require the body considering the annexation question to examine a variety of services. *See, e.g., Prestige v. City of Petal,* 841 So. 2d 1048 (Miss. 2003) (holding that the twelve indicia of reasonableness of annexations are independent tests viewed together to determine reasonableness; however, the ultimate determination must be whether the annexation is reasonable under all the circumstances); and *Brahm v. Beavercreek Twp. Bd. of Trustees,* 757 N.E.2d 857 (Ohio Ct. App. 2001) (County Board of Commissioners acted arbitrarily in concluding that one service factor — superior snow and ice removal services — outweighed the other evidence on services); *Par, of Acadia v. Town of Duson,* 909 So. 2d 642 (La. Ct. App. 2005) (holding annexation of five acres unreasonable because no direct access from town existed and no services would be provided).

5. *Annexation Agreements: Infrastructure, Services, and Zoning.* Annexation agreements are not uncommon, particularly where consent of an area's owners is required or simply desired by a city. The agreements often may involve city obligations in the future related to services, infrastructure, or land use controls in the annexed area. Courts have disagreed about the legality and enforceability of such agreements. A number of court decisions have upheld the validity of such agreements where the agreement is either authorized by statute or the court finds that the agreement did not totally abdicate the city's legislative authority in regard to the development of the land.

In *Geraines B.V. v. City of Greenwood Village,* 583 F. Supp. 830 (D. Colo. 1984) a federal district court upheld an annexation agreement between a city and commercial landowners whereby the city promised to share road improvement costs, obtain the owners' approval before including the land in a special assessment district, and remove certain development restrictions in exchange for the owners' consent to annexation. The city later sought to repudiate the agreement on the ground that it constituted the illegal bargaining away of its police power. Finding that the agreement was not ultra vires, the court upheld the agreement ruling that illegal abdication of the police power only occurs when a city "completely surrenders its powers to rezone property for an indefinite period of time." The court also ruled that, under the circumstances here, the city's repudiation of the agreement would violate the U.S. Constitution's "Contract's Clause."

6. *Annexation and City Services?* Because cities supply services, can they agree to do so only on condition that the landowner seeks annexation to the city? The cases are split. *Compare Sloan v. City of Conway,* 555 S.E.2d 684, 688 (N.C. Ct. App. 2001) (finding such a condition valid "as a means of broadening City's tax base") *with Verry v. City of Belle Fourche,* 598 N.W.2d 544 (S.D. 1999) (contra).

7. *Surprising "Non-Cities."* You may be surprised to learn that not every large, urbanized area in the United States has been incorporated into a municipality. For example, Reston, Virginia (pop. 56,407) and Silver Springs, Md. (pop. 76,540) are not cities. Nor is a large part of the so-called Las Vegas, Nevada "strip," which is known as Paradise, Nevada. Residents of these areas rely on county governments for services. Haya El Nasser, Some Big Places Find Paradise in *Not* Being Real Cities, U.S.A. Today, at 1A (June 25, 2003).

F. GOVERNMENTAL IMMUNITY FROM ZONING

Another set of limitations on local governmental land use powers arises from the relationship of local governments to adjacent governmental entities, to special districts, or to state agencies. Surprisingly often, state legislatures have not clearly delineated the split of authority between the respective governmental authorities. In many instances, a dispute is nonetheless settled amicably; for example, local governments and school districts rarely find themselves at odds for long periods of time. In some cases, however, the courts must devise a solution.

In the following case, the court rejects the past legal framework for resolving such disputes.

■ CITY OF EVERETT v. SNOHOMISH COUNTY
112 Wash. 2d 433 (1989)

OPINION

ANDERSEN, Justice.

This "sibling rivalry" case involves a zoning dispute between a county and city. Snohomish County claims its zoning authority is paramount and the City of Everett claims it is not. It is the City's argument that the statutes empowering the City to dispose of its sewage sludge and solid waste, together with the City's general eminent domain power, establish its authority to locate a disposal facility in the County even though it does not comply with the County's zoning regulations.

The City of Everett owns and operates a sewage treatment plant on Smith Island in the estuary of the Snohomish River. At this facility the City discharges treated domestic, commercial and industrial wastes into the Snohomish River. It does so subject to effluent limitations and monitoring and reporting requirements imposed by a state permit.

In September 1985, the United States Environmental Protection Agency (EPA) found that the City had violated the permit requirements by allowing the accumulation of sewage sludge or solid wastes in the facility's treatment lagoons, thereby reducing that facility's treatment capacity. The EPA ordered the City to submit a plan and schedule for removal and disposal of the excess sludge. In its effort to comply with the EPA order, the City formulated a sludge management program which entailed removal of the sludge to a 952-acre site on nearby Ebey Island. This site, on another island in the Snohomish River, lies outside the City and within unincorporated Snohomish County.

The City then acquired an option to purchase the Ebey Island property and applied to the Snohomish Health District for a sludge utilization permit. The health district agreed to issue this permit on condition that the City first obtain a zoning code conditional use permit from the County. The City applied for a permit, but a Snohomish County hearing examiner denied the application. In so doing, the examiner found that the sludge exhibited high levels of heavy metals and that the property was characterized by low soil pH, flooding and a high water table. It was the examiner's conclusion that the City's proposed use of the site was incompatible with the use of surrounding property for agricultural purposes. The Snohomish County Council upheld the decision.

The City thereupon brought this action against Snohomish County. The City moved for summary judgment in its favor on the siting dispute and the Superior Court granted it. The County petitioned this court for direct review. We granted review and address the critical issue in the case.

ISSUE

Are the land use activities of an intruding subunit of government (the City) immune from the zoning regulations of the host subunit of government (the County)?

DECISION

Legislative intent determines whether the intruding subunit of government (the City) is immune from the zoning regulations of the host subunit (the County). In reviewing the statutes empowering the pertinent activities of both subunits of government in this case, it is apparent that the intent of the Legislature is that the City be required to comply with the County's zoning regulations in establishing a sewage sludge and solid waste disposal site in the County. The problem presented in this case is but illustrative of the broader problem of an almost unlimited range of potential controversies that can develop when push comes to shove between various subunits of government. Where all else fails, it is incumbent upon the courts to determine which subunit of government, if any, has the paramount authority in a given situation. A review of the numerous cases on the subject nationwide suggests that the most vexing of such problems are those involving the siting of unpopular but essential facilities such as sewage treatment, sewage sludge and solid waste disposal, penal and certain health care institutions. It is very clear, particularly in the case of sewage and solid waste disposal facilities, that while everyone contributes to the problem, no one wants to be part of the solution. Since this case involves a zoning dispute, it is appropriate to note one preliminary matter. This is, that while it has sometimes been declared to be a general rule that zoning regulations or restrictions of a subunit of government do not apply to the State, its agencies and subunits of government, unless the Legislature has manifested a contrary intent, this court has declined to adopt any such blanket rule of governmental immunity from local zoning ordinances.

In past years, in deciding controversies involving zoning conflicts between subunits of government, particularly before the present day profusion of municipal corporations and state and local agencies, courts tended to resort to four traditional "tests."

One such test is the *superior sovereignty test*. Under this test, where one governmental unit seeks immunity from the zoning restrictions of another governmental unit, the unit which is higher in the governmental hierarchy will be held to prevail. The difficulty with this test is that "superior authority" in the political hierarchy does not necessarily imply superior ability in allocating land uses.

A second of these traditional tests is the *governmental-proprietary test*. Using this test, a subunit of government will be deemed immune from conflicting zoning regulations when it performs governmental functions, but will be subject to such regulations when it acts in a proprietary capacity. A review of the cases applying this test, however, demonstrates that different courts often reach entirely different conclusions on similar facts.

A third test used is the *eminent domain test*. Under the eminent domain test, any governmental unit with condemnation authority may be considered automatically immune from zoning restrictions. This test, however, is susceptible to being used as a bludgeon to allow an intruding subunit of government to locate an offensive facility, such as a sewage treatment plant, anywhere in a host subunit's area that it wants to, even, for example, in a single family residential neighborhood. Nor is there anything in the constitutional requirement that eminent domain powers be exercised only when there is a finding that property is being taken for a "public use" that offers protection in such cases. This, in turn, is in disregard of the State's expressed concern for planned environments.

Yet a fourth test is the *balancing of interests test*, which has been favored by some commentators and courts dissatisfied with the other tests noted. This more recent test calls for taking into consideration the nature of the governmental unit seeking immunity, the land use involved and its effects as well as the public interest served by such use. Attractive as this particular test appears to some who find the other tests unsatisfactory, it is an approach which has now been rejected by some courts which consider it to be discredited. The Supreme Court of Pennsylvania, for example, calls the test too uncertain, pointing to the inevitable litigation that results from the knowledge that the next court might "balance" differently from the last. *Department of General Servs. v. Ogontz Area Neighbors Ass'n*, 505 Pa. 614, 483 A.2d 448 (1984). The Supreme Court of Georgia in turn, finds this balancing test to be "too nebulous and judicially unmanageable." *Macon Ass'n for Retarded Citizens v. e County Planning & Zoning Comm'n*, 252 Ga. 484, 490, 314 S.E.2d 218 (1984).

Considerable dissatisfaction with all four of these traditional tests and combinations thereof has been evinced by numerous courts and commentators for a variety of reasons, including the reasons noted in connection with the preceding enumeration of the tests. They have been variously described as simplistic abstractions, unhelpful epithets, ritualistic, enigmatic and as leading to the proliferation of inconsistent results.

As one court cogently explains, "[t]he question of what governmental units or instrumentalities are immune from municipal land use regulations, and to what extent, is not one properly susceptible of absolute or ritualistic answer. Courts have, however, frequently resolved such conflicts in perhaps too simplistic terms and by the use of labels rather than through reasoned adjudication of the critical question of which governmental interest should prevail in the particular relationship or factual situation." *Rutgers v. Piluso*, 60 N.J. 142, 150, 286 A.2d 697 (1972).

The crux of the matter, as we see it, and the real determinant in cases such as this, is *legislative intent*. As one court has aptly summarized in the context of a sibling rivalry zoning dispute, [the] common thread running through these cases, although not clearly stated in some, is an attempt to determine the intent of the Legislature when deciding whether a governmental unit is subject to a municipal zoning ordinance. We hold today that the legislative intent, where it can be discerned, is the test for determining whether a governmental unit is immune from the provisions of local zoning ordinances. *Dearden v. Detroit*, 403 Mich. 257, 264, 269 N.W.2d 139 (1978).

We agree with this statement of the law and so hold in this case. This succinct statement of principle fully accords with the views this court has previously expressed in analogous cases. While it is true that the analysis of statutory law to discern legislative intent is often difficult, particularly where the legislative design is complex, it is nevertheless a judicial function which courts are both capable of and experienced at performing. By the same measure, the Legislature is also the body empowered to prescribe by statute the extent to which state facilities should be subject to local land use controls, as well as to confer authority upon subunits of government and to establish priorities between them.

So it is here that the Legislature, in empowering cities to acquire property within and without their corporate limits and to acquire, construct and operate sewage and solid waste disposal systems, did not provide detailed standards to guide them in selecting sites to dispose of their sewage sludge and solid wastes. Nor did the Legislature purport to preempt the field of zoning regulations or otherwise oust the counties from their zoning authority. Thus, as we perceive the intent of the Legislature through a careful examination of the statutory authority extended by the Legislature to both the City and the County in the matters before us, the City was obliged to comply with the County's zoning code. Accordingly, we conclude that the trial court erred in ruling to the contrary.

Reversed and remanded.

CALLOW, C.J., and UTTER, BRACHTENBACH, DOLLIVER, DORE, PEARSON, DURHAM and SMITH, JJ., concur.

Notes and Comments

1. *Intergovernmental Zoning Conflicts.* The Washington Supreme Court in *City of Everett* rejects all three of the traditional tests for governmental immunity from zoning: (1) the superior sovereign test; (2) the governmental-proprietary test; and (3) the eminent domain test. The court also rejects the more recent "balancing of interests" test adopted by some state courts. The court adopts what might be called an "exclusive intent based test" for immunity. The intergovernmental dispute can be horizontal between local "sibling rivals," as in *City of Everett*, or it can be a vertical dispute between a local government and a state agency. Which of these tests do you believe is best suited to resolve these types of conflicts?

One important factor is whether the test provides realistic guidance to state and local decision makers in determining that future projects are or are not subject to local controls. Do the traditional tests or the "balancing of interests" test provide guidance of this type? Under the latter type of test, is a court equipped to determine the weight of the "public interest" behind a particular land use proposed by the state? The *City of Everett* court rejects the "balancing of interests" test as unmanageable and as too unpredictable, noting its description by one court as "an invitation to litigation." Under this "balancing" analysis, however, court decisions often seemed to create a presumption of zoning applicability with the burden on the governmental entity involved to show attempted good faith compliance with applicable zoning and its unreasonableness as applied. *See, e.g., Brown v. Kansas Forestry, Fish, & Game Comm'n,* 576 P.2d 230 (Kan. App. 1978); *Rutgers, State Univ. v. Piluso,* 286 A.2d 697 (N.J. 1972); *Brownfield v. State,* 407 N.E.2d 1365 (Ohio 1980).

Interestingly, state courts using the new "exclusive intent" approach described in *City of Everett* often seem to, in effect, rule that where statutory intent is unclear, zoning is applicable unless unreasonable as applied to the governmental entity involved. This part of the Washington court's opinion on the potential unreasonableness of the county's zoning is omitted in the *City of Everett* opinion above. *See, e.g., Kee v. Pennsylvania Tpk. Comm'n*, 743 A.2d 546 (Pa. Commw. Ct. 1999) (holding state expansion of service plaza is subject to local zoning); and *City of Malibu v. Santa Monica Mts. Conservancy*, 119 Cal. Rptr. 777 (Ct. App. 2002) (applying intent test to find no zoning immunity). How different, really, are the two tests?

The "exclusive intent" approach may be more predictable as a straightforward doctrine that, absent a clear grant of statutory immunity, reasonable zoning restrictions apply unless the government entity involved can clearly show by either statutory construction or frustration of purpose a legislative intent to grant immunity from zoning. An opposite presumption, of course, also would provide that predictability. *See Davidson Cty. v. City of High Point*, 354 S.E.2d 280 (N.C. App. 1987) (expansion of sewerage treatment plant held immune from local zoning where statute does not directly address the issue). *See generally* Gary Taylor & Mark Wyckoff, Intergovernmental Zoning Conflicts Over Public Facilities Siting: A Model Framework for Standard State Acts, 41 Urb. Law. 653 (2009).

Obviously, in any case the state can legitimately argue that it cannot allow local, parochial land use controls to stymie its project. What governmental interests may be damaged if state projects are automatically exempt from local regulation? What about the effective implementation of the local master or general plan? Which presumption do you favor in these types of cases — local control or preemptive siting authority?

2. *Zoning Immunity for Public Utilities.* Zoning immunity doctrines similar to those discussed above are applied by state courts to public utilities. Again the question is one of statutory intent and construction. Usually, an entity claiming immunity has the burden of showing statutory intent and recent state court decisions reflect a presumption of zoning applicability in the absence of some clear statutory grant of immunity. *See, e.g., Native Vill. of Eklutna v. Alaska R.R. Corp.*, 87 P.3d 41, 323 (Alaska 2004) (no clear statutory immunity for railroads); *Trustees of Wash. Twp. v. Davis*, 767 N.E.2d 261 Ohio 2002) (while statute exempts a "public utility" or railroad from local zoning or land use regulation, an AM radio station constructing a transmission tower was not a public utility). *But see Crown Commc'n N.Y., Inc. v. DOT*, 4 N.Y.3d 159 (2005) (installation of private antennae on state-owned telecommunication towers is exempt from local zoning).

In New York, the opinion in *Matter of County of Monroe v. City of Rochester*, 72 N.Y. 2d 338 (1988), established for the state a "balance of public interests" approach wherein, unless statutorily exempt, an encroaching government is presumed to be subject to host community zoning. In deciding, whether to actually subject the encroaching government to its zoning, several factors are to be weighed. These are:

1. The nature and scope of the instrumentality seeking immunity;
2. The encroaching government's legislative grant of authority;
3. The kind of function or land use involved;
4. The effect local land use regulation would have on the enterprise concerned;
5. Alternative locations for the facility in less restrictive zoning areas;
6. The impact upon legitimate local interests;
7. Alternative methods of providing the proposed improvement;
8. The extent of the public interest to be served by the improvements; and
9. Intergovernmental participation in the project development process and an opportunity to be heard.

State of New York James A. Coon Local Government Technical Series, Governmental Immunity from Zoning, at 1. Is this a workable framework? Another important question is which entity actually makes the determination of immunity.

3. *The City as Landowner Within Its Boundaries.* Is a city subject to its own zoning ordinances? Unless the zoning ordinance expressly provides otherwise, the answer has usually been no as a result of application of various traditional immunity doctrines. *See, e.g., Alves v. Bd. of Educ. for City of Guntersville,* 922 So. 2d 129 (Ala. Civ. App. 2005) (holding that city was immune from own zoning ordinance where building would store equipment for governmental function). There is an emerging line of cases holding that immunity must be expressly found within the terms of the ordinance itself. *See, e.g., Clark v. Town of Estes Park,* 686 P.2d. 777, 779 (Colo. 1984). *See generally* 4 Edward H. Ziegler, Rathkopf's the Law of Zoning and Planning ch. 76 at 76.2 (4th ed. 2005 & Supp. 2016).

4. *The City as Landowner Outside Its Boundaries.* When a city owns property outside of its jurisdiction and wants to construct a municipal project on that property, will the project be subject to the land use controls of the jurisdiction in which the property is located (providing that those controls exist)? In *City of Everett,* the answer was that this is a statutory immunity question, but the statute is often silent on the issue. The outcome will depend on the test applied.

For example, in *County of Will v. City of Naperville,* 589 N.E.2d 1090 (Ill. Ct. App. 1992), the city wanted to build a fire station outside of its own limits but within the jurisdiction of the county. The city relied on a state statute that apparently gave it authority over city-owned property outside the city limits, but the court held that the county's land use authority controlled. In contrast, in *City of Washington v. Warren County, Missouri,* 899 S.W.2d 863 (Mo. 1995), the Missouri Supreme Court concluded that, under the "power of eminent domain test" mentioned in *Brown,* the city was not subject to the county's zoning ordinance in constructing an addition to airport property that the city owned and operated.

5. *Zoning and Municipal Jurisdiction.* In general, a city's police power does not extend outside its boundaries, and its land use regulatory authority is likewise limited. The power to zone is coextensive with the boundaries of local jurisdiction. *See, e.g., Manorhaven v. Ventura Yacht Servs., Inc.,* 166 A.D.2d 685, 685 (Sup. Ct. App. Div. 1990) ("[a]s a general rule, the jurisdiction of an incorporated village is confined to its territorial limits"). This limitation, however, can raise problems when a neighboring jurisdiction approves a land use near the boundary that has effects on the adjacent jurisdiction. *See, e.g., City of Walnut Creek v. Cty. of Contra Costa,* 162 Cal. Rptr. 224 (Ct. App. 1980) (city sued to overturn the county's approval of an apartment complex located on county land adjacent to the city); *Town of Bedford v. Village of Mount Kisco,* 306 N.E.2d 155 (1973) (town sued adjoining village for adopting an ordinance rezoning an area from single family dwellings to permit six-story multiple dwellings).

What happens if the actual homes and most of a subdivision lie outside the municipal jurisdiction, but part of the subdivision plan marked "[r]eserved for a road" is within that jurisdiction? *See Town of N. Yarmouth v. Moulton,* 710 A.2d 252 (Me. 1998) (town had jurisdiction over entire subdivision); *Hamilton Hills Grp., LLC v. Hamilton Twp. Zoning Hearing Bd.,* 4 A.3d 788 (Pa. Commw. Ct. 2010) (holding city could limit its zoning consideration as to open space requirements to that part of development only within its own jurisdiction even though land to be developed was located in several jurisdictions).

6. *Extraterritorial Effects and the Presumption of Validity.* The use of extraterritorial planning and zoning usually takes place where the land outside of the municipality has not been annexed and is undeveloped. The disputes among adjacent local governments, however, also occur when two cities that are urbanized disagree over a particular project, or where a particular project — although located entirely within the jurisdictional boundaries of the local governmental entity approving it — has regional impacts.

One way to approach such disputes is to alter the way in which the court undertakes judicial review of such actions. For instance, in *Associated Home Builders v. City of Livermore*, 557 P.2d 473 (Cal. 1976), the California Supreme Court devised a test for determining whether a local zoning enactment served the "regional welfare." *See also Lusardi v. Curtis Point Property Owners Ass'n*, 430 A.2d 881 (N.J. 1981) (single-family zoning for beachfront property was invalid in part because it ignored the statewide policy that favored the recreational use of beachfront property); *Save A Valuable Env't v. City of Bothell*, 576 P.2d 401 (Wash. 1978) (where zoning ordinance will have a serious environmental effect outside the enacting city's jurisdictional boundaries, the zoning must serve the welfare of the entire affected community).

Another response is application of reviews under environmental impact laws, covered in Chapter 14. In some jurisdictions, local governments are required to circulate environmental impact reports on projects with trans-jurisdictional impacts to neighboring municipalities. The latter can emphasize the negative external effects of approval of the project. While many of these laws do not have substantive effects, the procedures can highlight approaches to mitigation and accommodation that may avoid litigation.

7. *Extraterritorial Planning and Zoning.* In some situations, where the area outside the city has not been annexed to a municipality, states attempt to deal with these "border" problems by enacting statutes authorizing the limited, extraterritorial exercise of land use authority. Many states allow municipalities to "pre-plan" for areas outside of their current regulatory jurisdictions. *See, e.g.*, N.Y. Gen. Mun. Law §237; Marygold Shire Melli & Robert S. Devoy, Extraterritorial Planning and Urban Growth, 55 Wis. L. Rev. (1959). But planning in and of itself has no regulatory effect. Accordingly, numerous states provide for extraterritorial zoning, and about half of these statutes also authorize municipal regulation of subdivisions outside the municipality's jurisdiction.

8. *Constitutional Questions.* The exercise of extraterritorial zoning or subdivision powers raises some constitutional questions. For example, do residents of an area have a constitutional right to vote when their land is located outside of a local jurisdiction's boundaries but is subject to that jurisdiction's extraterritorial zoning power? In *Holt Civic Club v. City of Tuscaloosa, Alabama*, 439 U.S. 60 (1978), a statute authorized the city to exercise its police jurisdiction (but not its land use power) over areas beyond the city's boundaries. The Supreme Court held that this arrangement did not violate the constitutional voting rights of those citizens who were subject to the police jurisdiction but who, because of their location outside the city limits, were not allowed to vote in the municipal elections. *See also Macon Cty. v. Town of Highlands*, 654 S.E.2d 17 (N.C. Ct. App. 2007) (holding that determination of means for providing proportional representation, based on population, for residents of area to be regulated by town pursuant to exercise of its extraterritorial jurisdiction, was a matter left to discretion of town).

9. *Cooperative Agreements.* Yet another approach to the problem of extraterritorial impacts is to authorize municipalities to reach agreements to carry out land use regulation jointly. *See* N.Y. Gen. Mun. Law §119-u ("each city, town or village is hereby authorized to enter into, amend, cancel and terminate agreements with any other municipality or municipalities to undertake all or a portion of such [land use] powers, functions and duties"). Does a city have the power to reach such an agreement without express statutory authority? *See Alameda County Land Use Ass'n v. City of Hayward*, 45 Cal. Rptr. 2d 752 (Ct. App. 1995) (memorandum of understanding between cities and counties, under which each city agreed that individual general plan amendments would be ineffective in their jurisdiction unless like amendments were made in all other cities, was an invalid divestment of local power). *Compare Dateline Builders, Inc. v. City of Santa Rosa*, 194 Cal. Rptr. 258 (Ct. App. 1983) (city could refuse to extend its utility service to an area outside its city limits where it had entered into an agreement with the county to implement a joint general plan for the county area in question).

Should a city be able to reach an agreement with a *landowner* outside the city's jurisdiction in order to resolve a dispute about land use on that property? *See People v. City of Batavia*, 414 N.E.2d 916, 920 (Ill. Ct. App. 1980) ("there is no independent power to enter into restrictive covenants to regulate use of land beyond the city's borders").

An interesting variation of the agreement theme is found in *Board of County Comm'rs v. City & County of Denver*, 40 P.3d 25 (Colo. Ct. App. 2001). In order to solve disputes over annexation when it was attempting to construct Denver International Airport, the City of Denver entered into an "intergovernmental agreement" with a city. Under that agreement, the city and other "third party beneficiary" cities were entitled to payments as liquidated damages if the airport exceeded certain noise levels. When just that situation occurred, Denver resisted the payments. The court upheld the contract and the damages.

A Note on State Law Preemption of Local Regulation

As state environmental and other kinds of regulation have greatly expanded in recent years, so have claims that state law preempts certain local government regulations of private facilities. Preemption claims have centered on, among other things, landfills and solid waste disposal facilities, wetlands, harbor development, public utilities, billboards, hazardous waste sites, mining activities, group homes, and airports.

1. *Express Preemption.* Preemption can be either express or implied. A state statute expressly precluding local regulation or authorizing a state agency to preempt local action generally will settle the question. *See, e.g., Hawthorne v. Village of Olympia Fields*, 790 N.E.2d 475 (Ill. Ct. App. 2002) (holding local zoning prohibition on child care in residential area is expressly preempted by state law); *In re Hartz/Damascus Bakery, Inc.*, 960 A.2d 747 (Super. Ct. App. Div. 2008) (Meadowlands Commission has exclusive jurisdiction over all development in Meadowlands). *But see Borough of Avalon v. New Jersey Dep't of Envtl Prot.*, 959 A.2d 1215 (Super. Ct. App. Div. 2008) (holding that state agency "public access" rule applicable to cities on tidal waterways was invalid preemption of basic municipal power).

2. *Implied Preemption.* In the absence of language expressly preempting local regulation, the outcome of the implied preemption analysis will turn on a careful reading of the state statutory language and a consideration of the legislative intent. *See, e.g., Ramsey Cty. Farm Bureau v. Ramsey Cty.*, 755 N.W.2d 920 (N.D. 2008) (preemption of local regulation of certain aspects of animal feeding operations); *American Transmission Co., LLC v. Dane Cty.*, 772 N.W.2d 731 (Wis. Ct. App. 2009) (preemption of local controls on soil erosion and wetlands from high voltage transmission lines); *Tosi v. City of Fresno*, 74 Cal. Rptr. 3d 727 (Ct. App. 2008) (preemption of local regulation of sale of scrap metal); *Granville Farms, Inc. v. City of Granville*, 612 S.E.2d 156 (N.C. App. 2005) (preemption of local regulation of land application of biosolids); *City of Northglenn v. Ibarra*, 62 P.3d 151 (Colo. 2003) (preemption applied to city ordinance prohibiting unrelated registered sex offenders from living together in single-family home as applied to adjudicated delinquent children in foster care homes supervised by state agency).

For recent court decisions applying statutory construction and implied preemption analysis to allow local regulation, *see Huntley & Huntley, Inc. v. Borough Council of Borough of Oakmont*, 964 A.2d 855 (Pa. 2009) (allowing local control of location and configuration of oil and gas drilling); *Md. Reclamation Associates, Inc. v. Harford Cty.*, 994 A.2d 842 (Md. 2010) (allowing local zoning of rubble landfills); *Smith v. Town of Pittston*, 820 A.2d 1200 (Me. 2003) (holding town ordinance prohibiting the spreading of sewer sludge on land was not preempted by the state regulation).

3. *Dual Authority.* Finally, some statutory schemes attempt to accommodate both state and local regulation. *See, e.g., Rodgers v. Conservation Comm'n of Barnstable*, 853 N.E.2d 199 (Mass. Ct. App. 2006) (allowing local permit denial to prevent harm to recreational shellfishing despite state wetlands regulation); *Big Creek Lumber Co. v. County of Santa Cruz*, 136 P.3d 821 (Cal. 2006) (holding county restrictions on location of timber operations is not preempted by state Forest Practice Act); *Town of Concord v. Duwe*, 4 N.Y.3d 870 (2005) (allowing local regulation of solid waste management); *Blagbrough Family Trust v. Town of Wilton*, 893 A.2d 679 (N.H. 2006) (allowing local wetland setback regulations); *Peter Garrett Gunsmith, Inc. v. City of Dayton*, 98 S.W.3d 517 (Ky. Ct. App. 2002) (state law prohibiting local regulation of guns did not prohibit local zoning restrictions on the location of gun shops). *See generally* 3 Edward H. Ziegler, Rathkopf's The Law of Zoning and Planning, ch. 48 (4th ed. 2005 and Supp. 2016) (comprehensive listing and discussion of state preemption cases).

4. *Constitutionally Created Entities.* A special case involves the interplay between entities with constitutionally created powers and local governments. The University of California has entered into memoranda of understanding with local governments when there have been potential conflicts over the exempt status of a campus and the assertion of local land use power by a city. More special is the relationship between joint powers authorities and the University, with both asserting eminent domain powers.

G. THE FEDERAL INFLUENCE OVER LAND USE

As this book has stressed, land use regulation largely remains within the province of local governments. While some regional and state controls over land use have been enacted, the federal government (except with respect to the federal lands, such as national forests) has mostly left the matter to state law. Congress to date has rejected almost all incursions of federal law into the bulk of local government's land use authority. But the sheer size and variety of functions performed by the federal government mean that actions by Congress and the President have important effects on land use. Sometimes the federal government acts as a land manager over the one-third of the nation's lands within its ownership. At other times it performs functions — building highways, funding sewage systems, locating military bases and other federal facilities, and so forth — that markedly affect local land use. The notes that follow provide an overview of the federal influence in the field of land use regulation.

A Note on Federal Law Affecting Land Use

1. *The Federal Constitutional Framework for Local Controls.* It should be recalled that all the federal constitutional claims discussed elsewhere in this book set a bottom-line framework for state and local regulation of land use and development. Obviously, regulation that a court finds violates these (or similar state) constitutional standards is invalid and unenforceable under the Supremacy Clause of the United States Constitution. These federal standards include substantive and procedural due process, equal protection, regulatory takings, and First Amendment issues (free speech and expression — signs, billboards, leaflets, newsracks, and adult uses, and religious Free Exercise claims, as well as Establishment Clause claims related to public religious displays). The principal constitutional constraints are discussed at length in Chapter 8.

Occasionally other types of federal constitutional claims arise. *See Island Silver & Spice v. Islamorada, Village of Islands*, 475 F. Supp. 2d 1281 (S.D. Fla. 2007) (holding that zoning discrimination against national big-box retail chain with more than 20,000 square feet of floor space in favor of local stores violated Dormant Commerce Clause of the U.S. Constitution). And for an early Supreme Court case, see *Minnesota v. Clover Leaf Creamery Co.*, 449 U.S. 456 (1981) (no violation of equal protection or commerce clauses when state statute banned retail sale of milk in plastic nonreturnable, nonrefillable containers, but permitted such sale in other nonreturnable, nonrefillable containers).

2. *Federal Preempting Controls and Regulation.* A number of federal preempting statutes are important in the field of land use regulation and generate significant litigation related to the validly of local regulation. These federal statutes are discussed below.

a. *The Religious Land Use and Institutionalized Persons Act of 2000*, at 42 U.S.C.A. §2000cc, directly preempts local controls on religious land uses that violate that law's provisions related to discrimination against or substantially burdening religious exercise related to the use of land. This statute is discussed at length in Chapter 8. *See generally* 2 Edward H. Ziegler, Rathkopf's The Law of Zoning and Planning, ch. 29 at 29.18 (4th ed. 2005 and Supp. 2016).

b. *The Federal Fair Housing Amendments' Act of 1988*, at 42 U.S.C.A §3601, extends the antidiscrimination provisions of federal civil rights statutes to the disabled and is made to apply to local government zoning programs and establishes an affirmative obligation on governments and private housing providers to make reasonable accommodations in regard to rules, policies, and practices. Litigation under this statute affecting zoning controls is discussed in Chapter 13. *See generally* 2 Edward H. Ziegler, Rathkopf's The Law of Zoning and Planning, ch. 25 at 25.11 (4th ed. 2005 and Supp. 2016).

c. *The National Manufactured Housing Construction and Safety Act of 1974*, at 42 U.S.C.A. §5400, establishes a code of building design and safety requirements for new manufactured housing and mobile homes, and expressly preempts inconsistent state and local construction standards. In effect, local communities can no longer exclude manufactured housing based on health and safety building and design standards. Local zoning controls (including exclusion), however, are unaffected by this law. We cover this in part below in *Shanzenbach v. Town of Opal, Wyo.*, 706 F.3d 1269 (10th Cir. 2013). *See generally* Edward H. Ziegler, Rathkopf's The Law of Zoning and Planning, ch. 28 at 28.30 (4th ed. 2005 and Supp. 2016).

d. *Federal Broadcasting Statutes and The Telecommunications Act of 1996*, at 47 U.S.C.A. §332(c)(7) (West 2016), preempt certain local controls on amateur home radio towers and satellite dishes (they can be locally regulated but not banned) and establish a number of preempting standards for local control of wireless cellular towers and facilities, which, again, can be locally regulated but not banned. The statute prohibits local discrimination between providers, requires that service be allowed in all areas, and preempts local regulation related to the effects of nonionizing electromagnetic radiation. Also, local permit decisions must be in writing, supported by substantial evidence, and be made within a reasonable time. All of these federal statutory issues have been much litigated in the federal courts, which have jurisdiction to hear claims arising under this act and also to order the issuance of permits. Local permit denials of cellular towers based on aesthetics have been frequently, but not always, overturned in federal court. *T-Mobile Ne. LLC v. Loudoun Cty. Bd. of Supervisors.*, 748 F.3d 185 (4th Cir. 2014). *See generally* Edward H. Ziegler, Rathkopf's The Law of Zoning and Planning, ch. 79 at 79.18 (4th ed. and Supp. 2016).

e. *Federal Statutes on Aviation Safety and Noise.* Federal statutes have been held to preempt local regulation of aircraft flights, as well as aircraft safety or noise, including both large and small aircraft and large and small airports. Municipal proprietors generally are allowed to impose flight and noise controls on their own airport operations. The statutes also are held not to preempt local zoning that restricts airport location or that governs nearby land use and development. *See generally* Edward H. Ziegler, Rathkopf's The Law of Zoning and Planning, ch. 85 at 85.4 (4th ed. and Supp. 2016).

f. *Miscellaneous Federally Regulated Activities.* There are often preemption issues arising from local regulation of activities that also are regulated by federal agencies. These cases may present either express or implied preemption claims. While federal agencies are generally immune from state or local land use controls (unless federal law provides otherwise), these regulatory preemption cases are decided on the basis of established federal preemption case law that looks to statutory intent and construction, and impact on the federal regulatory scheme. *See Johnson v. American Towers, LLC*, 781 F.3d 693 (4th Cir. 2015) (finding state statute calling for blocking of certain contraband cellular phones within prison facilities to be preempted by the federal prohibition on blocking wireless signals). The court stated:

> [It] would be impossible for the Defendants to simultaneously comply with federal prohibitions on blocking wireless signals and a putative state-law duty to block wireless

signals to and from certain cell phones inside the prison. This is the very definition of conflict preemption. Compliance with both a putative common-law duty and federal law would be a "physical impossibility" and therefore the former is preempted by the Communications Act.

Id. at 709.

See *Weaver's Cove Energy, LLC v. Rhode Island Coastal Res. Mgmt. Council,* 583 F. Supp. 2d 259 (D. R.I. 2008) (holding that the federal 2005 Natural Gas Act preempted state or local regulation of location and siting of liquefied natural gas terminal storage facility). *Compare Norfolk Southern Ry Co. v. City of Alexandria,* 608 F.3d 150 (4th Cir. 2010) (federal law preempted local haul ordinance involving truck deloading of railcars), *with Florida E. Coast Ry. Co. v. City of W. Palm Beach,* 266 F.3d 1324 (11th Cir. 2001) (city's regulation of activities under a railroad's lease was not preempted because it was not "regulation of rail transportation").

The area of manufactured housing provides a good example of the application of preemption principles (and also raises issues about regulation for aesthetics purposes addressed more fully in Chapter 17).

■ SCHANZENBACH v. TOWN OF OPAL, WYOMING
706 F.3d 1269 (10th Cir. 2013)

HARTZ, Circuit Judge.

Plaintiff Roger Schanzenbach owned several properties in the Wyoming town of Opal. Intending to install mobile manufactured homes on these properties, he applied for permits with town authorities. The town council issued several building permits to Schanzenbach but shortly thereafter enacted an ordinance that included a provision banning the installation of any manufactured home that was older than 10 years at the time of the relevant permit application (the 10-Year Rule). When the permits were about to lapse and Schanzenbach requested an extension, the town council denied his request. It also rejected his applications for new permits because the proposed houses were more than 10 years old.

Schanzenbach brought an action against Opal and its town council in the United States District Court for the District of Wyoming. He asserted a claim that the 10-Year Rule was preempted by the National Manufactured Housing Construction and Safety Standards Act of 1974 (the Manufactured Housing Act) as well as a variety of constitutional claims. The district court awarded summary judgment to the defendants. Schanzenbach's appeal raises claims based on preemption, equal protection, and substantive due process. We affirm the district court's grant of summary judgment on these claims. The 10-Year Rule was not preempted . . .

I. BACKGROUND

Schanzenbach owned several lots in Opal, a town of less than 200 people. In November 2008 he applied for building permits to install four manufactured homes, one on each of four consecutive lots. All four homes were more than 10 years old at the time. On January 21, 2009, the town council approved the permits. Each permit stated that it "shall expire by limitations and become null and void if construction or work authorized is not commenced within forty-five (45) days" of the estimated completion date of December 31, 2009 (that is, by February 14, 2010).

In the following weeks the town council began considering Ordinance 2009-001, entitled "An Ordinance Regulating Construction and Standards for Buildings Placed in the Town of Opal." . . . The ordinance was approved on March 23, 2009, and became effective on that date. It contains the 10-Year Rule, which restricts the age of houses brought into Opal. Under the ordinance, "Any building moved into the town to be placed on any lot shall be no more than ten (10) years of age at the time of application. Proof of construction or manufacture date must be provided at time of application." *Id.*

Although Schanzenbach apparently spent about $27,000 between March and November of 2009 in preparing for construction on his lots in Opal, in late November he wrote the town council a letter explaining that the start of construction would be delayed until the following Spring, after the required commencement date of February 14, 2010. Schanzenbach requested a two-year extension on the four building permits, but the town council denied the extension on December 8. Defendant Jeremy Summers, the mayor of Opal, wrote Schanzenbach a letter the following August stating that the reason for the denial was that the manufactured homes did not meet the requirements of the 10-Year Rule. Schanzenbach submitted applications for new building permits in September 2010, but Mayor Summers rejected them for noncompliance with the 10-Year Rule. . . .

II. DISCUSSION

Because Schanzenbach is appealing from a grant of summary judgment, we review the district court's decision de novo, "applying the same standards that the district court should have applied."

A. PREEMPTION OF THE 10-YEAR RULE

Schanzenbach argues that the district court erred in granting summary judgment to Defendants on his claim that the 10-Year Rule is invalid under the Constitution's Supremacy Clause because it is preempted by the Manufactured Housing Act. *See* U.S. CONST. art. VI, cl. 2 ("This Constitution, and the Laws of the United States which shall be made in Pursuance thereof . . . shall be the supreme Law of the Land; and the Judges in every State shall be bound thereby, any Thing in the Constitution or Laws of any State to the Contrary notwithstanding."). The court held that the 10-Year Rule is not preempted because it regulates the aesthetics of manufactured homes rather than their construction or safety . . .

The Supreme Court has recently provided a useful summary of preemption doctrine:

> There is no doubt that Congress may withdraw specified powers from the States by enacting a statute containing an express preemption provision. State law must also give way to federal law in at least two other circumstances. First, the States are precluded from regulating conduct in a field that Congress, acting within its proper authority, has determined must be regulated by its exclusive governance. The intent to displace state law altogether can be inferred from a framework of regulation so pervasive that Congress left no room for the States to supplement it or where there is a federal interest so dominant that the federal system will be assumed to preclude enforcement of state laws

on the same subject. Second, state laws are preempted when they conflict with federal law. This includes cases where compliance with both federal and state regulations is a physical impossibility and those instances where the challenged state law stands as an obstacle to the accomplishment and execution of the full purposes and objectives of Congress. In preemption analysis, courts should assume that the historic police powers of the States are not superseded unless that was the clear and manifest purpose of Congress. *Arizona v. United States*, 132 S. Ct. 2492 (2012). . . .

An examination of the Manufactured Housing Act shows that its core concern is the creation of uniform standards for construction and safety of manufactured housing in the United States, with the resulting reduction in the costs of such homes. The Act recites the following purposes:

> (1) to protect the quality, *durability, safety,* and affordability of manufactured homes; (2) to facilitate the availability of affordable manufactured homes and to increase home ownership for all Americans; (3) to provide for the establishment of practical, *uniform,* and, to the extent possible, performance-based Federal *construction standards* for manufactured homes; (4) to encourage innovative and cost-effective construction techniques for manufactured homes; (5) to protect residents of manufactured homes with respect to personal injuries and the amount of insurance costs and property damages in manufactured housing, consistent with the other purposes of this section; (6) to establish a balanced consensus process for the development, revision, and interpretation of Federal *construction and safety* standards for manufactured homes and related regulations for the enforcement of such standards; (7) to ensure *uniform* and effective enforcement of Federal *construction and safety* standards for manufactured homes; and (8) to ensure that the public interest in, and need for, affordable manufactured housing is duly considered in all determinations relating to the Federal standards and their enforcement.

42 U.S.C. §5401(b) (*emphases added*). The Act instructs the Secretary of Housing and Urban Development (HUD) to promulgate regulations establishing appropriate Federal manufactured home construction and safety standards. *Id.* at §5403(a)(1); *see id.* at §5402(11) (defining Secretary).

The HUD standards govern many different facets of a manufactured home's design and construction. They prescribe requirements to assure the adequacy of architectural planning considerations which assist in determining a safe and healthful environment, 24 C.F.R. §3280.101 (2012), such as minimum window areas to assure adequate light and ventilation, *see id.* at §3280.103(a), ceiling heights, *see id.* at §3280.104, and room dimensions, see id. §3280.109. They impose fire-safety requirements, *see id.* at §§3280.201-.209; set standards for building materials, *see id.* at §3280.304; and regulate a home's thermal protection, *see id.* at §§3280.501-.511, its plumbing systems, *see id.* at §§3280.601-.612, its heating and cooling systems, *see id.* at §§3280.701-715, and its electrical systems, *see id.* at §§3280.801.816.

In furtherance of the Act's purpose of providing uniform construction standards, the Act explicitly preempts conflicting local standards in §5403(d), entitled Supremacy of Federal standards. It states:

Whenever a Federal manufactured home construction and safety standard established under this chapter is in effect, *no State or political subdivision of a State shall have any authority either to establish, or to continue in effect, with respect to any manufactured home covered, any standard regarding the construction or safety applicable to the same aspect of performance of such manufactured home which is not identical to the*

Federal manufactured home construction and safety standard. Federal preemption under *this subsection shall be broadly and liberally construed* to ensure that disparate State or local requirements or standards do not affect the uniformity and comprehensiveness of the standards promulgated under this section nor the Federal superintendence of the manufactured housing industry as established by this chapter. Subject to section 5404 of this title, there is reserved to each State the right to establish standards for the stabilizing and support systems of manufactured homes sited within that State, and for the foundations on which manufactured homes sited within that State are installed, and the right to enforce compliance with such standards, except that such standards shall be consistent with the purposes of this chapter and shall be consistent with the design of the manufacturer.

42 U.S.C. §5403(d) (2012) (*emphasis added*).

HUD, under the Secretary's statutory authority to issue, amend, and revoke such rules and regulations as he deems necessary to implement the Act, *id.* at §5424, has promulgated regulations that further address the preemptive effect of the HUD standards. In relevant part they provide:

> (a) No State manufactured home standard regarding manufactured home *construction and safety* which covers aspects of the manufactured home governed by the Federal standards shall be established or continue in effect with respect to manufactured homes subject to the Federal standards and these regulations unless it is identical to the Federal standards. . . . (d) No State or locality may establish or enforce *any rule or regulation or take any action that stands as an obstacle to the accomplishment and execution of the full purposes and objectives of Congress.* The test of whether a State rule or action is valid or must give way *is whether the State rule can be enforced or the action taken without impairing the Federal superintendence of the manufactured home industry* as established by the Act.

24 C.F.R. §3282.11 (2016) (*emphases added*).

That the preemptive effect of the Manufactured Housing Act is limited to local laws governing the construction and safety of manufactured homes is sufficiently clear that Schanzenbach does not argue otherwise. His only gloss on the preemptive effect of the Act is that he contends that construction and safety encompass durability, a proposition that we can concede for purposes of this appeal.

Although this court has not yet had occasion to decide whether a local law governed construction or safety within the preemptive scope of the Act and its regulations, the Fifth and Eleventh Circuits have done so. We find their guidance helpful. Two Eleventh Circuit decisions provide useful bookends. In *Scurlock v. City of Lynn Haven*, 858 F.2d 1521, 1523–25 (11th Cir.1988), the Eleventh Circuit held that a local ordinance was preempted because it required manufactured homes to adhere to local building and electrical codes that were more stringent than the safety standards imposed by the Act and its regulations. In *Georgia Manufactured Housing Ass'n, Inc. v. Spalding County*, 148 F.3d 1304, 1306 (11th Cir.1998), by contrast, the court denied a claim that the Manufactured Housing Act preempted a local ordinance requiring manufactured homes to have roofs that rose by at least 4 inches for every 12 inches of horizontal run. It held that the ordinance was not preempted because, unlike the measure in Scurlock, the pitched-roof requirement had no purported basis in consumer protection, but instead was simply a straightforward declaration that the County does not want low-pitched roofs in its residential areas. *Id.* at 1310. The court explained that the construction and safety standards preempted by the Act are those standards that protect consumers from various potential hazards associated with manufactured housing, whereas a zoning requirement related to aesthetics is not preempted because the goals and effects of such a standard have nothing to do with consumer protection, but instead seek to control the aesthetic quality of a municipality's neighborhoods. *Id.* . . .

The Fifth Circuit has adopted a similar view. In *Texas Manufactured Housing Ass'n, Inc. v. City of Nederland*, 101 F.3d 1095, 1098 (5th Cir.1996), the court confronted a Manufactured Housing Act preemption challenge to a local ordinance that prohibit[ed] the placement of trailer coaches on any lot within city limits except in a duly authorized trailer park. *Id.* (internal quotation marks omitted). It held that the ordinance regulated merely the placement and permitting of trailer coaches for the purpose of protecting property values; it did not expressly link its provisions in any way to local safety and construction standards. *Id.* at 1100. It therefore was not preempted by the Act. *See id.*

Opal's 10-Year Rule is far more similar to the ordinances in Georgia Manufactured and Texas Manufactured than to the ordinance in Scurlock. Unlike the ordinance in Scurlock, the 10-Year Rule does not purport to supplant any specific standard imposed by the Act or its regulations—at least, not any standard that Schanzenbach has identified. Rather, the rule simply embodies the town council's judgment that the aesthetics and property values of its neighborhoods would be protected by preventing the installation of homes older than 10 years. It is not a rule that regulates the construction or safety of manufactured homes, 42 U.S.C. §5403(d) (2012), nor does it stand[] as an obstacle to any provision or purpose of the Act, 24 C.F.R. §3282.11(d) (2016).

Schanzenbach argues that the 10-Year Rule relates to the durability of manufactured homes. We disagree. The durability of the home is irrelevant under the ordinance. The rule does not, for example, prohibit all manufactured housing that is not durable enough to last more than 10 years. No matter how durable the home, its age may bar it from being moved into town. And a home less than 10 years old when moved into town is entitled to remain no matter how undurable it may be. Schanzenbach urges us to examine the 10-Year Rule in light of the surrounding provisions of Ordinance 2009-001. He points out that the ordinance contains numerous requirements that clearly govern construction and safety—for example, it prescribes minimum structural, plumbing, and electrical standards—and that Defendants have conceded that these provisions are preempted by the Act. But not all the provisions of Ordinance 2009-001 concern construction or safety: for example, one is essentially the same as the pitched-roof requirement in Georgia Manufactured. In any event, the only provision challenged by Schanzenbach is the 10-Year Rule. He has offered no argument that the ordinance must be stricken in its entirety (including the 10-Year Rule) because some provisions are preempted. We therefore affirm the district court's grant of summary judgment on the claim that Opal's 10-Year Rule is preempted by federal law.

Notes and Comments

1. *The Holding of* Schanzenbach. Could a durable ugly manufactured home be sited under the Town of Opal ordinance? Did the court correctly apply the precedents from the other circuits?

2. *Future Developments?* Could Greenwich, Connecticut, and Beverly Hills, California, soon see manufactured homes if challenges to denial of development permits are brought under the Manufactured Housing Act?

A Note on Federal and Indian Lands

1. *Land Use Planning on Federal Lands.* Lands owned by the federal government constitute one-third of the nation's land, although those lands are largely distributed in the western part of the country. How the United States government uses this property is of significant concern to private property owners who live nearby, as well as to municipalities and other local government entities. In the western part of the United States, the importance of the use of federal lands is further complicated by the pattern of intermixed federal, state, and private landownership — the famous "checkerboard" pattern common in that part of the country. *See* U.S. Public Land Law Review Commission, One-Third of Our Nation's Land: A Report to the President and to the Congress (1970).

A variety of federal laws affect land use on federal properties. Students usually examine these laws in a separate course on public land law or natural resources law, or sometimes in the environmental law course. Since 1970, however, Congress has passed several new laws that emphasize the completion of land use plans for federal lands. The most important of these new laws are the Forest and Rangeland Renewable Resources Planning Act (RPA) and the National Forest Management Act ("NFMA"), both codified at 16 U.S.C. §§1600-1687and the Federal Land Policy and Management Act (FLPMA), 43 U.S.C. §§1701-1785). (Another federal law that has significant effects on federal land uses is the Endangered Species Act, which is discussed below in Chapter 14 of this casebook.) *See* Federico Cheever, Four Failed Forest Standards: What We Can Learn from the History of the National Forest Management Act's Substantive Timber Management Provisions, 77 Ore L. Rev. 960 (1998).

2. *RPA and NFMA.* Enacted in 1974, the RPA requires the U.S. Forest Service to develop long-range land use plans for the national forest lands. Every ten years, the Forest Service is to prepare an assessment of the renewable resources throughout the national forests, and every five years the Service is to prepare a program proposing long-range planning objectives for the Service's activities. This information provides the backdrop for the NFMA, which requires the Forest Service to prepare forest-by-forest plans. Management decisions must then conform to those plans; permits, contracts, and other vehicles authorizing use of the National Forest lands must "be consistent with" the "land and resource management plans." 16 U.S.C. §1604(i) (2000). *See, e.g., Native Ecosystems Council v. Dombeck*, 304 F.3d 886 (9th Cir. 2002) (Forest Service did not violate NFMA when it amended its management plan to allow more roads to remain open after a timber sale); *Native Ecosystems Council v. Weldon*, 697 F.3d 1043 (9th Cir. 2012) (Forest Service did not violate NFMA with its wildfire fuel thinning program as part of its forest management plan because it took the requisite "hard look" at the impact on local wildlife populations).

3. *FLPMA.* FLPMA's land use planning provisions are not as extensive as those under the RPA and NFMA. Under FLPMA, the Bureau of Land Management (BLM) is required to develop land use plans for the public lands under the agency's jurisdiction. 43 U.S.C. §1712(c) (1986). Section 1712 mandates that BLM utilize

"multiple use, sustained yield" management principles and "give priority to the designation and protection of areas of critical environmental concern." *See, e.g., Public Lands Council v. Babbitt*, 529 U.S. 728, 738 (2000) ("FLPMA strengthened the Department's existing authority to remove or add land from grazing use, allowing such modification pursuant to a land use plan"); *Natural Res. Def. Council, Inc. v. Hodel*, 624 F. Supp. 1045, 1059 (D. Nev. 1985) (finding that BLM land use planning was to deal with "broader issues [such as] long-term resource conflicts, long-term range trends, [and] planning of range improvements"), *aff'd*, 819 F.2d 927 (9th Cir. 1987).

Once the plans are prepared, the agency is required to manage the public lands "in accordance with land use plans developed . . . under section 1712." 43 U.S.C. §1732(a). *See Norton v. Southern Utah Wilderness Alliance*, 542 U.S. 55 (2004) (holding that plan commitment to monitor off-road vehicles in designated areas did not create a legally binding commitment to monitor under provision of FLPMA requiring BLM to act in accordance with its land use plans). *See generally* Roger Flynn, Daybreak on the Land: The Coming of Age of the Federal Land Policy and Management Act, 29 Vt. L. Rev. 815 (2005) (overview of FLPMA, its implications for land use management particularly in the West, and its burgeoning role in litigation over land use decisions in the West); Jan. G. Laitos & Thomas A. Carr, The Transformation on Public Lands, 26 Ecol. L.Q. 140 (1999) (arguing that recreational rather than commodity development is now the predominant federal land use). For a good historical perspective and thoughts on the future, *see* Martin Nie & Emily Schembra, The Important Role of Standards in National Forest Planning, Law, and Management, 44 Envtl. L. Rep. News & Analysis 10281 (2014).

4. *Local Land Use Controls on Federal Lands.* The "Property Clause" of the United States Constitution gives Congress plenary power to make rules and regulations respecting the federal lands. In *Kleppe v. New Mexico*, 426 U.S. 529, 543 (1976), the Court stated that "[a]bsent consent or cession, the state undoubtedly retains jurisdiction over federal lands within its territory, but Congress equally surely retains the power to enact legislation respecting those lands pursuant to the Property Clause." Thus, the question becomes whether Congress has preempted local control in the situation in question.

In *Ventura County v. Gulf Oil Co.*, 601 F.2d 1080 (9th Cir. 1979), *summarily aff'd without opinion*, 445 U.S. 947 (1980), the Ninth Circuit Court of Appeals rebuffed a county's attempt to require that a lessee of federal land obtain an "open space use permit" for its oil exploration and extraction activities.

Eight years later, the Supreme Court considered a somewhat similar situation in *California Coastal Comm'n v. Granite Rock Co.*, 480 U.S. 572 (1987). The Granite Rock Company had a "location claim" under the Mining Act to mine limestone in a national forest and had secured all necessary federal approvals to begin mining. The California Coastal Commission, however, contended that Granite Rock was subject to the state's regulatory jurisdiction and was required to secure a permit from it. Like Gulf Oil Company in *Ventura*, Granite Rock claimed that federal law preempted the state and local regulation.

In a not so obvious outcome after *Ventura*, a five-member majority of the Court held that federal law did not preempt the state permit requirement on its face, although conditions actually placed on the project by the Coastal Commission might result in preemption. The Court found that state land use planning was preempted, but it distinguished such planning from state "environmental regulation," which was not. Interestingly, the majority did not even cite *Ventura*; the case was mentioned only in passing in Justice Scalia's dissent. Are "land use regulation" and "environmental regulation" distinct classes of regulation or do they overlap to a significant degree?

5. *The Sagebrush Rebellion.* In the last 40 years, the federal government's paradigm for control of federal lands has changed from one of disposal and consumption to one more oriented toward preservation and environmental protection, with a concomitant increase in regulation and bureaucracy. In reaction to this change, some Western local governments began to argue not only that the federal government was mismanaging the federal lands, but also that local government has significant legal rights to control land uses on federal lands. The part of this movement led by governmental entities and public officials has been denominated the "Sagebrush Rebellion" or sometimes the "County Supremacy" movement, while action by private citizens seeking increased economic uses of the public lands has been pushed under the rubric of the "Wise Use" movement.

From a legal standpoint, the courts have rejected the local governments' claims of increased rights to control land uses on federal lands. In *Boundary Backpackers v. Boundary County*, 913 P.2d 1141 (1996), the Idaho Supreme Court considered a county land use plan that, among other provisions, purported to require the federal government to give notice to the county before taking actions "that would affect the economic stability, custom, or culture" of the county. The plan also prohibited any further designations of wilderness areas in the county and stated that federally managed lands "that are difficult to manage or which lie in isolated tracts shall be targeted for disposal." The Idaho Supreme Court found that federal land use statutes preempted these provisions and struck them down.

6. *Land Use Regulation and Indian Lands.* An interesting if complicated aspect of the federal influence on land use regulation is the question of whether federal law precludes local governments from regulating land use on Indian reservations. The general rule is that there is no state or local regulatory authority over Indian conduct or Indian property in Indian Country. *See* Cohen's Handbook of Federal Indian Law §6.03(1)(a) (Nell Jessup Newton et al. eds., 2012 ed.). Federal law and inherent tribal sovereignty also limit states or local governments from regulating nonmembers of tribes within Indian Country in order to protect tribal self-government. *Id.* §6.03(2)(a). As a result of the federal government's nineteenth-century efforts to break up Indian tribal ownership, parcels of land within Indian reservations may be owned by nonmembers, and states and local governments may claim regulatory authority over these fee lands.

The upshot is that local governments will generally lack authority to regulate land use within Indian Country in the absence of federal authorization or some compelling state interest that supports regulation of nonmembers and outweighs the federal and tribal interests in tribal self-government.

Only the Indian tribe has authority to control the use of land on a reservation when that land is owned by the tribe itself or its members. In recent years, Indian tribes have exercised their prerogatives by authorizing large or environmentally significant land use projects on Indian land. *See, e.g.,* Judy Pasternak & Eric Bailey, A Game of Casino Hardball: Corruption Charges Fly in a Tribal Dispute Over Land Use and Lots of Income, L.A. Times, at A1 (Nov. 5, 2002) (describing various casinos proposed on tribal land in California, and noting that tribal casinos brought in $12 billion in revenue during 2001).

If Indian land is owned in fee by a corporation, a more contextual analysis is called for by federal law, and the outcome may turn on whether the corporation is controlled by tribal members or not. With respect to land owned by nonmembers of the tribe, a majority of the Supreme Court could not agree on an opinion in *Brendale v. Confederated Tribes & Bands of Yakima Indian Nation*, 492 U.S. 408 (1989), leaving open the possibility that local government zoning authority over nonmember-owned land may be consistent with federal law in some circumstances. Four judges essentially concluded that tribes lack authority to zone reservation land owned in fee by nonmembers, while three others would have held that tribes have authority to regulate all fee land within the reservation. Justice Stevens, joined by Justice O'Connor, concurred with the three justices but believed that the tribe's zoning authority depends on the extent to which the nonmember's acquisition of land has deprived the tribe of the ability "to establish the essential character of the region" and to establish "a coherent scheme of land use." *Id.* at 446. *See also Gobin v. Snohomish County*, 304 F.3d 909 (9th Cir. 2002).

In this case, the tribe approved a tribal member's residential subdivision on tribal land. The county, however, also claimed jurisdiction because the subdivision, which would be sold to members of the public, was larger than the county would have approved. The court held that the county had no jurisdiction over the subdivision, rejecting the claim that Congress authorized state land use regulation when it made the lands freely encumberable. The court also refused to apply the "exceptional circumstances" exception, which allows state regulation notwithstanding express congressional intent, rejecting the argument that the county's environmental interests met the test for the exception

7. *The Federal Government and Transportation Policy.* Federal law has shaped the interstate freeway system, which has been federally funded and designed. The effect of the freeway system on local land use has long been recognized. *See, e.g.,* Bruce Katz, The Federal Role in Curbing Sprawl, 67 Annals of Am. Acad. Of Pol. And Sci. (2000) ("Federal and state transportation policies generally support the expansion of road capacity at the fringe of metropolitan areas and beyond, enabling people and businesses to live miles from urban centers but still benefit from metropolitan life."). Critics have charged that federal transportation policy has resulted in urban sprawl and over-reliance on the automobile as a means of transportation.

Federal transportation law is a complex subject that defies short description. Planning has been at the core of the law. Both the Federal Highway Administration and the Federal Transit Administration have required large urban areas to undertake a transportation planning process in order to qualify for federal funds.

In 1991, Congress passed the Interstate Surface Transportation Efficiency Act, Public L. No. 102-240, 105 Stat. 1914 (1991). Known as "ISTEA" (pronounced "ice-tea"), the law aimed to profoundly change transportation planning, and thus, if implemented as intended, would have important effects on land use. A recent article summarized the changes it brought as follows:

> Since their creation in 1975, MPOs have been required to plan for alternative transportation modes, as well as encourage public participation in the transportation planning process. Under ISTEA, however, this focus broadened to include better integration of modes, increased public involvement, adherence to clean air standards, and development of congestion management strategies. . . . The legislation shifted the focus of planning away from increasing capacity through new highway construction, to

solving congestion by expanding travel options. ISTEA required that all modes of transportation — highways, mass transit, bikeways, and pedestrian ways — as well as airports, seaports, and intermodal facilities, be considered as an integrated system.

ISTEA also charged metropolitan and state transportation agencies with improving coordination of their planning efforts. The act stressed roadway connectivity within and outside the boundaries of urbanized areas, as well as analysis of the impacts of transportation policy decisions on land use. Long-range transportation plans and programs were to be consistent with land development plans. State and metropolitan planning agencies were also obligated to consider the overall social, economic, energy and environmental effects of their transportation decisions.

Underlying all of these planning considerations was the mandate that long-range transportation plans be financially constrained and balanced against future revenue sources.

ISTEA expired at the end of 1997 and was replaced by the Transportation Equity Act (TEA-21), Pub. L. No. 102-240, 105 Stat. 1914 (1998). Technical corrections were made in the TEA 21 Restoration Act. In 2015, President Obama signed the Fixing America's Surface Transit (FAST) Act, P.L. No. 114-90. Controversy continues to surround federal transit funding plans for various transit options, including light rail and high-speed inter-regional rail plans. Notice, as discussed earlier herein, regional transit planning is not now supported by regional urban planning.

8. *National Land Use Legislation?* Unlike other areas of law that are substantially influenced by federal legislation, land use authority remains principally a local activity (with some regional and state inroads as detailed in this chapter). Not that long ago, however, it seemed likely that federal legislation would play a much stronger role in the development of land use law. In the early 1970s, several bills mandating increased state and local efforts in the land use field received serious consideration in Congress, and President Nixon even indicated some support for them. The Land Use Policy and Planning Assistance Act of 1973, S. 268, 93rd Cong., 1st Sess. (1973)), which passed the Senate, would have offered states certain monetary incentives to plan and mandated increased coordination between federal activities and those plans. The bills, however, were defeated in 1974 and 1975, and efforts at congressional action in this area have not received serious consideration since then. As a result, any efforts to make land use more "national" have been informal. Edward J. Sullivan & Carrie Richter, Out of the Chaos: Towards a National System of Land-Use Procedures, 34 Urb. Law. 449, 450 (2002) (noting there is "no national system of land-use planning or regulation" but there have been "three major efforts to systematize the procedures connected with land-use planning and regulation").

9. *Treaties and Land Use.* Finally, although land use questions rarely rise to the level of impacting international law, the increasing number of international trade agreements may eventually affect local discretion in the land use field. The North American Free Trade Act (NAFTA), for example, contains a provision requiring governments to compensate property owners if a government either expropriates property or takes measures "tantamount to . . . appropriation." *See* Vicki Been, NAFTA's Investment Protections and the Division of Authority for Land Use and Environmental Controls, 20 Pace Envtl. L. Rev. 19, 20 (2002) ("pending NAFTA regulatory takings claims have the potential to upset many aspects of land use and environmental law"). And bilateral treaties or agreements can have immense impacts on local land use patterns. If the Keystone pipeline had been approved

by the United States, adding another phase of a major project to bring synthetic crude oil (syncrude) and diluted bitumen (dilbit) from Canadian tar sands oil across the Canadian border, the effect on local control of properties traversed or impacted by the pipeline could have been significant.

Among the concerns raised: Would eminent domain actions preclude local control over affected properties? Would there be preemption of attempts to use traditional police powers to address setbacks, environmental impact analysis, and application of noise regulations? Would local wetlands regulations still be applicable? How would local and state water quality standards be applied?

A Final Thought: The quiet revolution had some effects (and in certain states, significant effects), but in general there has been no substantial move to state regulation of land use. However, the major forces that led to the movement for supra-municipal regulatory influence have in most states remained active. Decision-making is still fiscalized in many counties or regions. Negative externalities continue to be exported. Regional fair share of needed land uses has not been reached in most states. Locally unwanted land uses remain unwanted and not sited. And environmental challenges that cross jurisdictions remain intractable.

10

Alternative Methods for Land Use Decision Making

A. INTRODUCTION

1. Models of Land Use Regulation

This chapter examines alternative means of making land use decisions: using the initiative and referendum, employing private land use instruments such as covenants, negotiating agreements between developers and local jurisdictions, utilizing alternative dispute resolution mechanisms such as mediation to reach decisions, and the most radical alternative, deregulating the current system.

From the student's perspective, analysis of these alternatives serves an important practical purpose. Many of the alternative decision-making mechanisms examined in this chapter are increasingly being used, and the practitioner must adapt to them. The types of skills needed to represent clients professionally and successfully using these mechanisms can be quite different from those needed to participate in the traditional land use regulatory process. For example, a lawyer preparing a set of covenants, negotiating a development agreement, or participating in a mediation session performs quite different functions from one representing a client in a public hearing.

Looking at these alternative mechanisms, however, also serves a broader purpose. In an article entitled New Models for Local Land Use Decisions, 79 Nw. U.L. Rev. 1155 (1984-1985), Professor Carol Rose employed the concept of models as a vehicle for examining the operation of the land use regulatory system. She began by characterizing the function of land use controls as follows:

> [O]ne quite fruitfully can . . . envision[] the whole field of local land use processes as a
> series of variations on a theme of dispute resolution. Since the beginning of modern

land use regulation, courts, legislators, administrative bodies, and academic commentators have struggled to define procedures appropriate for controversies that arise over local governmental control of land use. To a very considerable degree, their efforts can be grouped and classified as alternative patterns or models for resolving disputes.

Id. at 1155.

As used in this context, a model generalizes the features found in decision-making processes, thus facilitating both critical examination of those processes and comparisons with alternative ways of making decisions. Thinking in terms of models lends perspective to the study of land use regulation by aiding students in reaching conclusions about the strengths and weaknesses of the current system, an important pedagogical goal of the class, and in identifying the skills needed to practice in each model. That type of perspective is particularly important as land use regulation evolves in the twenty-first century, for the law may be in the midst of a long-term shift toward a new model that emphasizes bargaining as a central means of making important land use decisions.

In short, the examination of alternative mechanisms in this chapter serves a practice-oriented function by requiring students to identify the kinds of skills needed to use those mechanisms. At the same time, it enables the student to see the broader operation of land use regulation.

2. The Legislative and Adjudicative Models

Students using this casebook are already familiar with the features of two models of dispute resolution employed in the land use field: legislation and adjudication. At its inception in the 1920s, modern land use regulation embraced the idea that local jurisdictions act in a legislative capacity, in the same sense as state legislatures, when they adopt most land use regulations. But do local bodies truly act legislatively when they make land use decisions? This issue was addressed in a principal case included in Chapter 6, the *Albuquerque Commons Partnership* decision. The case raises the issue of whether a second model, adjudication, was a better lens through which to view much of local land use regulation. The adjudicative model sees the local body as acting more like a court than as a legislature. It is applying standards — perhaps, most significantly, the policies found in the general plan — to determine how specific parcels of land may be used in particular situations.

The first alternative means of making land use decisions that is studied in this chapter, use of the initiative and referendum, is a variant on the legislative model of land use regulation. If land use decisions are legislative in nature, then citizens should be able to use both the initiative and referendum power — both legislative powers — to enact land use laws and to repeal legislative decisions previously made by local elected officials. As in other legislative processes, however, use of the initiative and referendum means that the voices of individual landowners will not be heard to the same extent that they will be if, for example, the adjudicative model is used. Furthermore, the initiative bypasses the planning procedures carried out at the local level. In *Griswold v. City of Homer*, 186 P.3d 558 (Alaska 2008), the court considers whether the existence of these procedures renders the initiative unavailable to local electors.

Perhaps the most troublesome question about initiatives and referenda is their effect on orderly land use planning, the concept that underlies the "consistency doctrine" explored earlier in Chapter 5. What will become of the use of expertise in planning, as envisioned in the Standard Planning Enabling Act and embodied in the requirement that planning commissions must pass upon planning and zoning decisions, if the electorate zones or plans through initiatives? Will citizens employ their powers of direct democracy to block needed projects? Will the devices be used arbitrarily? These questions lie at the heart of the debate over initiatives and referenda.

3. Private Law: Covenants, Conditions, and Controversy

The assumption of this casebook, as reflected in the development of land use law over most of the last century, is that land use is generally governed by a public law system. The local government decides uses of land and is largely responsible for the governance of land use. Cities and counties likewise provide trash disposal, water, sewage treatment, road maintenance, and all the other services commonly associated with municipal government.

This model of governance and the provision of services is not preordained, however, and in some areas of the country another model is supplanting it: private government. The phenomenon can be seen in new "gated" developments whose streets, unlike those of traditional developments, are not open to the public. Services within those gates are provided by contractual arrangement, and homeowners associations rather than popularly elected officials administer the system. In such areas, private law using covenants has largely supplanted public regulation and administration.

In this chapter you will examine the workings of such private systems, starting with a reading of some actual "covenants, conditions, and restrictions." But you will also examine the social consequences of using such systems, for their use has touched off a raging debate. Are private communities the logical successor to the kinds of closed communities that have been with us since the Middle Ages and simply an alternative, more economically efficient means of meeting the needs and desires of homeowners? Or do such communities pose a direct threat to both the vitality of local government and the American tradition of community involvement?

4. The Bargaining Model: Development Agreements and Mediation

Another model of land use decision making, related to the private law model, is bargaining. One of the most important developments in the last 30 years of land use regulation has been the ascendancy of this model through the widespread use of development agreements and negotiations between developers and municipalities to determine the conditions under which annexations and developments will take place. Development agreements are the direct descendants of contract zoning, which is defined as a "process by which a local government enters into an agreement with a developer whereby the government extracts a performance or promise from a developer in exchange for [the government's] agreement to rezone the property." *McLean Hosp. Corp. v. Town of Belmont*, 778 N.E.2d 1016, 1020 (Mass. Ct. App. 2002) (*quoting* 3 Rathkopf, Zoning & Planning §44.11 (Zeigler rev. ed. 2001)). However, if the local government can arrange the agreement so that it is not in the form of a contract, courts have generally allowed it. That situation raises a key question: If the practical result of bargaining allowed by the contract zoning cases is the same as if the parties *had* entered into a contract, why not allow localities to formalize the agreement in such a document?

Two major obstacles stood in the way of using contract more broadly. One was the influential idea underlying Euclidian zoning that the government establishes the ground rules for development through the adoption of a zoning and land use scheme, and development follows that scheme. Negotiating land uses is at least partially inconsistent with this scheme, for the outcome of negotiations may depend more upon the bargaining skills of the parties and the relative strengths of their bargaining positions than upon the agreement's adherence to planning standards established by the municipality. Second, a feeling has long existed, often articulated under the rubric that a city cannot "bargain away its police power," that bargaining in the land use context poses some vague but unacceptable risks to the public interest. For example, should a current legislative body be able to "tie the hands" of future elected officials for as long as 30 years?

Strong countervailing considerations have pushed the two concerns to the side but have not entirely obliterated them. These considerations include the perceived need for governments to impose precise conditions that will tailor the design of a development and the realization that mixed land use developments bring benefits that Euclidian zoning cannot. But a third consideration is perhaps even more important: the desire of localities to shift the costs of new public infrastructure to developers. Bargaining can serve all three purposes. Moreover, if "all property is unique," as the property law maxim has it, then prospective, Euclidian-type regulation cannot foresee all the problems that might arise at the individual development stage. Bargaining is well-suited to deal with site-specific problems.

A shift to a new model seldom can occur without the need to resolve a host of anticipated (and often unanticipated) issues that arise. If bargaining will take place, who will be authorized to undertake it? How will the system ensure that deals do not violate the public interest? If conditions underlying a previously reached agreement change at some later time, will the local government have the right to break the contract because a larger public interest is involved? What remedies will be provided for breach of contract? These types of issues are explored in *Sprenger, Grubb & Associates v. City of Hailey*, 903 P.2d 741 (Idaho 1995), set forth in this chapter.

There are other important questions about bargaining. The agreement reached in each set of negotiations is unique. One landowner may negotiate a much better deal than another landowner, perhaps in the amount or types of exactions required of the landowners, even though their lands are similarly situated. Are we prepared to accept these unequal results because of the value we place on the bargaining process as a whole to achieve important societal goals? Additionally, while a key component of the current regulatory process is the public's right to participate in the decision making, public participation is not easily integrated into the bargaining process between a developer and a local jurisdiction. Another case in this chapter, *Toll Bros., Inc. v. Board of Chosen Freeholders*, explores the limits of using contracts in the land use context.

The use of mediation is a variant on the bargaining model. In mediation, a third party facilitates parties' efforts to reach an agreement to settle a dispute. In this sense, mediation is closely related to the bargaining model; both assume that the "give and take" of negotiation will produce a mutually agreeable outcome. A third-party mediator facilitates that "give and take." But with both development agreements and mediation, the ultimate choice about whether to enter into an agreement lies with the parties. In contrast, if another form of alternative dispute resolution, arbitration, is used, the actual decision is ceded to a neutral third party. For this reason, arbitration in the land use context has not proved popular.

Mediation raises many of the same problems as negotiation concerning the consistency of its procedures with the accepted and legally required norms of public decision making. For example, mediation poses a potential conflict with state open-meeting laws, as the desire for frank exchanges of views can clash with the public's right to know. Despite these types of issues, however, the use of mediation seems to be slowly on the rise. Developers increasingly recognize that resolving problems through the normal regulatory process often results in long delays and high costs, while localities see bargaining as a means of gaining greater control over the details of projects.

5. The Market Model: Deregulation

A final model of land use regulation is the market model. In the land use context, this model would radically change the current land use system through deregulation. The goal here is both increased efficiency in the provision of land uses and greatly lessened government interference in the operation of the development market.

With the exception of Houston, Texas, which continues to be the only major United States city refusing to zone, current land use regulation has largely rejected the use of this model. Students, however, should not quickly dismiss it as an impractical academic pipe-dream. Regulation in other sectors of the economy, such as telecommunications and electric utilities, was long thought to be permanently embedded in law, but these sectors have been at least partly deregulated in the past decades. Moreover, discomfort with the inefficiencies of the present regulatory system, which the student has already seen in the discussions in this casebook on issues such as permit streamlining and the vested rights rules, continues to grow. Complete deregulation is not likely, but experiments with it in various states are distinct possibilities.

B. POPULAR DECISION MAKING: INITIATIVES AND REFERENDA

The last three decades saw an explosion of the use of popular decision-making devices in the land use field. Unhappy with the performance of local government officials, citizens circulated initiative petitions designed generally to control growth in some fashion. In addition, they second-guessed the decisions of local officials by utilizing the referendum process to pass on those decisions. In *Griswold v. City of Homer*, the court considers whether land use decisions made by initiative are consistent with the underlying state law on land use.

■ GRISWOLD v. CITY OF HOMER

186 P.3d 558 (Alaska 2008)

OPINION
EASTAUGH, Justice.
***

II. FACTS AND PROCEEDINGS

When Fred Meyer, Inc. publicly announced plans in late 2002 to build a 95,000-square-foot store in Homer, the city began an extensive review of its existing zoning code to determine whether it needed to alter floor area limits for retail and wholesale stores. For two years, beginning in March 2003, the question was considered by a special task force, by the Homer Advisory Planning Commission, and by the Homer City Council in more than a dozen hearings. After analyzing issues including traffic impact, the ideal rate of development, landscaping, maintaining the local character of Homer, and protecting groundwater, the planning commission made a series of recommendations to the city council regarding the appropriate floor area for retail and wholesale stores.

While those hearings were still being conducted, Homer voters in March 2004 filed with the city clerk an initiative petition that proposed a "footprint area" of 66,000 square feet for retail and wholesale business buildings in the Central Business District, General Commercial 1 District, and General Commercial 2 District. On April 12, 2004, the city council passed Ordinance 04-11(A), which set building floor area limits of 35,000 square feet in the Central Business District, 20,000 to 45,000 square feet in the General Commercial 1 District, and 45,000 square feet in the General Commercial 2 District. On the same day, in response to the initiative petition, the city council scheduled an election on the initiative for June 15, 2004. The voters approved the initiative at the June 15 election; the initiative became effective on June 21, 2004 as Ordinance 04-18.

Stating that a change in the zoning code sections was "required to properly convey the will of the voters," and that an ordinance was "necessary to implement the will of the voters," in February 2005 the city council enacted Ordinance 05-02, adopting a maximum floor area of 66,000 square feet for retail and wholesale business buildings in the three affected zoning districts. Ordinance 05-02 amended Ordinance 04-11(A) to reflect the text of the initiative. Ordinance 05-02 also effectively defined "footprint area" as "floor area," meaning "the total area occupied by a building, taken on a horizontal plane at the main grade level, exclusive of steps and any accessory buildings."

Frank Griswold challenged the initiative in the superior court, claiming among other things that the initiative process could not be used to amend the zoning code. . . .

III. Discussion

***

B. The Initiative Was an Invalid Exercise of the City's Legislative Authority Because It Bypassed the Homer Advisory Planning Commission.

Griswold argues that the zoning initiative is invalid for several reasons. He contends, among other things, that the zoning authority delegated to the City of Homer requires it to pass only zoning ordinances that are consistent with the city's comprehensive plan. The city . . . responds that the voters' constitutional right to enact initiatives should be broadly construed to permit the voters to amend zoning laws. The city contends that because the city council has the power to enact zoning ordinances, the voters must have the same power.

The power to initiate cannot exceed the power to legislate. To decide whether Homer voters could invoke the initiative process to amend the City of Homer zoning code we must determine the extent of the city council's zoning power and the explicit and implicit limitations on that power. The city's zoning power flows from two sources: Alaska statutes providing for planning, platting, and land use regulation by local governments, and Kenai Peninsula Borough ordinances delegating zoning powers to cities within the borough.

We first review the statutory sources of that power. Alaska Statute 29.40.010 requires first and second class boroughs to provide for "planning, platting, and land use regulation on an areawide basis." If a city within a borough consents by ordinance, the borough assembly may delegate any of its land use regulation powers to the city. Alaska Statute 29.40.020(a) provides that the borough "shall establish a planning commission" and AS 29.40.020(b) provides that the planning commission "shall prepare and submit a proposed comprehensive plan in accordance with AS 29.40.030. . . ." Section .030 describes "a comprehensive plan" as "a compilation of policy statements, goals, standards, and maps for guiding the physical, social, and economic development, both private and public, of the first or second class borough."

These statutes require "areawide" planning and creation of a comprehensive plan "for the systematic and organized development" of the community, and they implicitly recognize the importance of the planning commission and the comprehensive plan to the process of regulating land use.

A planning commission has statutory responsibilities beyond drafting the comprehensive plan. Per AS 29.40.020(b)(2), the commission must also "review, recommend, and administer measures necessary to implement the comprehensive plan, including measures provided under AS 29.40.040." Because "zoning regulations" are one of the "measures provided under AS 29.40.040," subsection .020(b)(2) requires the planning commission to "review, recommend, and administer" zoning regulations "necessary to implement the comprehensive plan." The assembly by ordinance "shall adopt or amend" land use provisions "[i]n accordance with a comprehensive plan" and "in order to implement the comprehensive plan."

The statutes therefore expressly require that the planning commission have an active role in creating a comprehensive plan for "systematic and organized" local development, reviewing and recommending zoning regulations, and adopting measures "necessary to implement the comprehensive plan." The statutes implicitly recognize that the planning commission plays an important part in the formation and amendment of local land use regulations by providing assistance to the borough (or city) to ensure that development proceeds in a "systematic and organized" manner.

[The court then discussed the city's power under the Alaska statutory system, in which cities are delegated powers from boroughs].

The City of Homer created the Homer Advisory Planning Commission . . . The city charged the commission with holding hearings and preparing recommendations for the city council when a zoning amendment is proposed. In addition, the commission may propose amendments to the zoning code.

The relevant state statutes are clear. A borough or a city, having the power possessed by the City of Homer, cannot pass or amend a zoning ordinance without involving its planning commission in reviewing that ordinance. This review includes considering whether a proposed ordinance is consistent with the comprehensive plan. A borough assembly or city council may eventually choose not to follow the recommendations of the planning commission, but the statutes preclude bypassing the planning commission altogether. . . .

It is for this reason that zoning by initiative is invalid. The Homer City Council does not have the power to pass piecemeal zoning amendments without at least giving the Homer Advisory Planning Commission opportunity to review the proposals and make recommendations. Therefore, voters, who have no obligation to consider the views of the planning commission or be informed by its expertise, cannot use the initiative process to eliminate the planning commission's role in "areawide" land use planning and regulation, and thus potentially undermine the comprehensive plan for "systematic and organized" local development. . . .

The city also contends that initiatives are not "governed by all the procedures ordinarily applicable to the enactment of city council ordinances." The city seems to argue that because notice and a hearing are required for a city council ordinance but not an initiative, it is acceptable for initiatives to bypass certain procedural requirements. But as seen above, the participation of the city's planning commission in the zoning process required by the legislature and the borough is more than just a mere procedural requirement.

The facts in this case illustrate how the initiative process limits or even eliminates the intended role of a planning commission. The planning commission spent many months considering appropriate floor area limits for business buildings in the affected zoning districts. The city council charged the commission with "develop[ing] standards for addressing large retail and wholesale development" and "recommend[ing] a size cap for large retail and wholesale development." To that end, the commission, city council, and a task force conducted more than a dozen hearings. The commission reviewed recommendations from the Large Structure Impact Task Force and the Chamber of Commerce Legislative Committee; researched necessary improvements to lighting, landscaping, stormwater drainage, and parking; and developed standards for traffic and economic impact analyses. The commission explicitly applied the standards found in the Homer Comprehensive Plan in its decision-making process. And before the initiative election, the city council considered the planning commission's recommendations and amended the zoning code, adopting different floor area limitations for the subject zoning districts. The voters then approved the initiative and adopted a single, and greater, limitation for all three districts before the commission completed its findings.

Given the public hearings that were being conducted and the opportunity for public debate, it is logical to ask whether the voters had, in effect, the same access as the council to the recommendations of the planning commission, and thus whether the initiative process did not actually bypass the planning commission. The council was required to consider the commission's recommendations, even if it ultimately rejected them. The council acts as a collegial and public body; it is a matter of public record whether it addresses the commission's recommendations and attempts to reconcile proposed amendments with the comprehensive plan and state and borough ordinances. That is not at all the process an initiative election follows. Just as the council cannot choose to completely ignore the recommendations in adopting a zoning amendment, the voters cannot pass an initiative in which the commission's recommendations play no formal, or perhaps even informal, role at all.

The commission does more than simply give notice of hearings and allow the public to be heard on the subject of zoning ordinances. If a zoning amendment is proposed, the commission's role is to analyze the impact of the proposed changes in light of the city's development goals as stated in the comprehensive plan, and to suggest other changes that should accompany the proposed zoning amendment.

Even if a city council chooses to disregard the recommendations of the city planning commission, its decision has been informed by the planning commission's consideration of the potential social and regulatory costs and benefits of the proposed amendment. The city's planning commission's role is not merely "procedural," but is substantive. Homer voters therefore could not bypass the commission by using the initiative power.

We REVERSE the superior court's grant of summary judgment and REMAND for entry of judgment for Griswold.

CARPENETI, Justice, dissenting.
***

[The majority's] approach not only ignores the fact that initiative elections stand apart from the traditional legislative process, but also weakens voters' ability to participate directly in the affairs of the city in which they live. In Brooks v. Wright we stated that the constitutional framers "chose to include the initiative process as a law-making tool with full knowledge of the risks inherent to direct democracy." [971 P.2d 1025, 1029 (Alaska 1999)]. . . .

[T]he court bases its decision to prohibit zoning by initiative on the concern that allowing zoning by initiative would undermine comprehensive zoning. But zoning ordinances, whether they are enacted by the voters or by the city council, are subject to post-enactment review. We explained in Brooks that "[c]oncerned parties can . . . bring a post-election substantive challenge to what they may believe is an ill-advised law."

Notes and Comments

1. *The Terminology of Direct Democracy.* In considering the use of direct democratic devices to make land use decisions, you must first get the terminology straight. An initiative is proposed legislation drafted by individual citizens that is included in a petition and then circulated among voters. When a certain number of signatures of registered voters (a number mandated by state law) is gathered, the initiative is then

placed on the ballot for the voters to consider at the next election. Alternatively, in some local jurisdictions the local elected officials can simply adopt the initiative outright, obviating the need for an election.

In contrast, a referendum occurs after the local elected body, such as a city council, has adopted legislation. Voters then circulate a petition to repeal the new legislation. Once again, if the required number of signatures among registered voters is secured, the local elected body then faces the choice of either rescinding the legislation voluntarily or submitting it to a vote. *See, e.g.*, Eugene McQuillan, The Law of Municipal Corporations §§16.47.69 (3d ed. 2011); *Grant County Concerned Citizens v. Grant County Bd. of Comm'rs*, 794 N.W.2d 462, 466 (S.D. 2011) (the initiative is the power "to propose bills and laws and to enact or reject them at the polls," while the referendum is the right of the people "to have submitted for their approval or rejection any act . . . passed by the legislature" which would generally become law without action by the electorate).

The "political wars" fought over local initiatives and referenda are fierce. Kenneth A. Stahl, The Artifice of Local Growth Politics: At-Large Elections, Ballot-Box Zoning, and Judicial Review, 94 Marq. L. Rev. 1, 3 (2010) (describing the "local political process" as one "that both developers and neighborhood groups perceive as illegitimate," a situation leading to use of initiatives and referenda). Most recently, the initiative power has been used in attempts to enact reforms of state redevelopment powers and to require compensation for some types of land use regulation. At the same time, developers can take advantage of the initiative process to circulate initiatives that would approve developments while bypassing local procedures, such as the preparation of an environmental impact statement on the proposal. *See Tuolumne Jobs & Small Business Alliance v. Superior Court*, 330 P.3d 912, 59 Cal. 4th 1029 (2014) (Wal-Mart initiative petition that proposed to streamline approval for the construction and operation of a Wal-Mart "Supercenter" did not require the preparation of an environmental impact report by the city council before the council adopted the initiative rather than submitting it to the voters).

2. *The* Eastlake *Decision.* In *City of Eastlake v. Forest City Enterprises, Inc.*, 426 U.S. 668 (1976), the U.S. Supreme Court considered the constitutionality of a city charter provision requiring that proposed land use changes must be ratified by 55 percent of the votes cast at an election. The Court stated that the issue was whether the provision violated the due process rights of a landowner. The Court then upheld the provision.

The opinion first found that the provision was not an unconstitutional delegation of legislative power. It stated, "In establishing legislative bodies, the people can reserve to themselves power to deal directly with matters which might otherwise be assigned to the Legislature." 426 U.S. at 672. The Court then turned to the allegation that the provision violated federal constitutional guarantees because the voters were given no standards to guide their decision. The Court also rejected this argument, finding that "here, rather than dealing with a delegation of power, we deal with a power reserved by the people to themselves." *Id.* at 675.

How broad was the holding in *Eastlake?* Some have cited the case for the general proposition that use of the referendum power and, by inference, use of the initiative power do not violate due process. Others have suggested that the actual holding is much narrower. *See* Robert H. Freilich & Derek B. Guemmer, Removing Artificial

Barriers to Public Participation in Land-Use Policy: Effective Zoning and Planning by Initiative and Referenda, 21 Urb. Law. 511, 513 (1976).

3. *The* City of Cuyahoga Falls *Decision.* In a 2003 decision involving yet another Ohio referendum, the Supreme Court tangentially returned to the subject of direct democracy. In *City of Cuyahoga Falls, Ohio v. Buckeye Cmty. Hope Found.*, 538 U.S. 188, 123 S. Ct. 1389 (2003), the City of Cuyahoga Falls approved the site plan for a low-income housing complex. The citizens overturned the approval in a referendum, and the project developers brought suit. In *Buckeye Cmty. Hope Found. v. City of Cuyahoga Falls*, 607 N.E.2d 181 (Ohio 1998), the Ohio Supreme Court held that a referendum was unavailable because the approval of the site plan was an administrative rather than a legislative act.

The U.S. Supreme Court held this claim could not withstand scrutiny. The Court first found that the refusal to issue permits while the referendum was pending "in no sense constituted egregious or arbitrary government conduct." 538 U.S. at 198. The Court then went on to state:

> As a matter of federal constitutional law, we have rejected the distinction that respondents ask us to draw, and that the Ohio Supreme Court drew as a matter of state law, between legislative and administrative referendums. In *Eastlake v. Forest City Enterprises, Inc.*, 426 U.S., at 672, 675, we made clear that because all power stems from the people. . . . The people retain the power to govern through referendum "'with respect to any matter, legislative or administrative, within the realm of local affairs." *Id.*, at 674, n.9. Cf. *James v. Valtierra*, 402 U.S., at 137. Though the "substantive result" of a referendum may be invalid if it is "arbitrary and capricious," *Eastlake v. Forest City Enterprises, supra*, at 676, respondents do not challenge the referendum itself. The subjection of the site-plan ordinance to the City's referendum process, regardless of whether that ordinance reflected an administrative or legislative decision, did not constitute *per se* arbitrary government conduct in violation of due process.

Id. at 199. Is the Court saying that, as a matter of constitutional law, even administrative matters are subject to referendum if state law allows? Or is it simply affirming that the submission of an administrative matter to voters cannot, as a matter of law, rise to the level of "egregiousness" that would support a due process violation?

4. *Legislative v. Administrative.* Most states hold that administrative matters are not subject to the initiative process. What exactly *is* an "administrative matter"? In recent years numerous decisions have grappled with that issue, with many concluding that the matter addressed by the initiative was administrative, and thus outside the initiative power.

In *Vagneur v. City of Aspen*, 295 P.3d 493 (Colo. 2013), proponents submitted two initiatives that would have re-designed the planned highway entrance to Aspen, Colorado. The initiatives were complex, but in part it dealt with the conveyance of city-owned property. The court recognized that deciding whether an ordinance was legislative or administrative was "a difficult question to answer." The court continued: "The distinction can become particularly challenging at the municipal level because the governing body of a municipality often wields both legislative and executive powers and frequently acts in an administrative as well as a legislative capacity by the passage of resolutions and ordinances." 295 P.3d at 504. In this case, the court found that the decision was administrative and was heavily influenced by the fact that the city had previously engaged in a lengthy planning process with state and federal agencies. The dissent disagreed, finding that changes in use of open space or sales of open space were legislative.

How about this test: "[A]n act exceeds the scope of the initiative power if it compels or bars action by elected officials that would seriously hamper governmental functions." *Friends of Congress Square Park v. City of Portland*, 91 A.3d 601, 607 (Me. 2014). *See also Phillips v. City of Whitefish*, 375 Mont. 456, 330 P.3d 442, 451 (2014) (setting out four factors to be weighed in determining whether an act is administrative and observing that "an act of a governing body is not likely to be either solely legislative or solely administrative, underscoring that these cases are not black and white.").

5. *Legislative v. Adjudicative Again.* It is hornbook law that the initiative and referendum are available only to enact or repeal legislation. As a consequence, legal issues concerning the use of the initiative or referendum are closely related to the materials, discussed in this casebook in Chapter 6, on whether a land use decision is deemed legislative or adjudicative (or administrative) in nature.

If a state holds that that small-tract rezonings are quasi-judicial in nature, that holding will also limit the rights of citizens to enact initiatives or pass referenda relating to decisions of this type. *See, e.g., Fritz v. City of Kingman*, 957 P.2d 337, 338 (Ariz. 1998) ("In multiple decisions over a lengthy period, this court has consistently held that zoning decisions are legislative acts subject to referendum."). *Compare Krejci v. City of Saratoga Springs*, 2013 UT 74, 322 P.3d 662 (Utah 2013) (site-specific rezoning was legislative and thus subject to referendum) *with In Re Arnold*, 443 S.W.3d 269, 277 (Tex. Ct. App. 2014) (original zoning is subject to referendum, but individual amendments are not).

6. *Criticism I: Abrogation of Process.* In general, commentators have strongly criticized the use of initiatives and referenda in the land use field. *See, e.g.,* Marcilynn A. Burke, The Emperor's New Clothes: Exposing the Failures of Regulating Land Use Through the Ballot Box, 84 Notre Dame L. Rev. 1453, 1461 (2009) ("[T]he use of ballot initiatives to adopt land use regulation produces a planning failure. Successful land use planning requires technical expertise and long-term vision to advance the public interest, while protecting the rights of disadvantaged social groups. Ballot initiatives by their nature are limited in scope and interest-group centric."). *Compare* Daniel P. Selmi, Reconsidering the Use of Direct Democracy in Making Land Use Decisions, 18 UCLA J. Envtl. L. & Land Use 293 (2002) (arguing that the objections to the use of direct democracy in the land use field are overstated).

One objection to the use of initiatives, adopted by the majority in *Griswold*, is that they are inconsistent with the procedural rights found in state land use law. Such rights include the right to a public hearing before enactments like zoning ordinances may be passed. Because initiatives are circulated directly to the people, these processes are bypassed. The standard response to the objection that direct democracy abrogates important procedures is that the political dialogue taking place during the electoral process more than compensates for other public participation rights that cannot be exercised during the initiative process. Is the public dialogue during an election a sufficient replacement for the public hearings that would otherwise take place? What about the "expertise," such as scrutiny by the planning commission and the staff, that is unavailable during an election?

These same objections, of course, cannot be made with respect to referenda. (Do you see why?) As a result, should courts favor the use of referenda to make land use decisions over the use of the initiative power?

7. *Criticism II: Interference with Planning.* Another objection to the use of initiatives and referenda is that they are inconsistent with the principle that land use regulation must be based upon proper planning. *See, e.g., 1000 Friends of Washington v. McFarland,* 149 P.3d 616, 625 (Wash. 2007) ("By both explicit goal and structure, the GMA [Growth Management Act] seeks coordinated planning ... [A]llowing referenda is structurally inconsistent with this mandate. ..."); *Nordmarken v. City of Richfield,* 641 N.W.2d 343, 349 (Minn. Ct. App. 2002) ("referendum would necessarily proceed without an overriding concept of current and future development and land use needs of the community and of neighboring communities and without benefit of the expertise of land use professionals"); Malia McPherson, From the Well Up: A California County Confronts Fracking at the Polls, Geo. Envtl. L. Rev. Online 1 (Dec. 14, 2015) (noting that issues settled by a successful initiative "are particularly difficult to overturn later" and this is "especially the case for local level initiatives focused on community concerns such as land use ...").

This objection assumes that the "rational planning model," discussed in Chapter 5 of this casebook, actually prevails when most land use decisions are made. Do you agree? Or does the political component of such decisions made at the local government level far outweigh any planning expertise that goes into them? Consider the Florida court of appeal's conclusion in *Citizens for Responsible Growth v. City of St. Pete Beach,* 940 So. 2d 1144, 1151 (Fla. Ct. App. 2006): "[T]he citizens of the City ... are entitled to express their views on how their City Commission should handle land use problems, despite a pervasive statutory framework implementing a statewide policy on growth and redevelopment." Does this statement explain *why* they are so entitled?

The objection that use of the initiative power conflicts with proper planning would not seem to have as much force for rezonings by initiative or referenda in jurisdictions that have adopted a "consistency" requirement of the type discussed in Chapter 5. *See Sustainable Growth Initiative Committee v. Jumpers, LLC,* 128 P.3d 452, 462 (Nev. 2006) (genuine issue of fact existed as to whether initiative capping growth at 2 percent per year is consistent with the master plan).

8. *Criticism III: Complexity.* In *Mouty v. The Sandy City Recorder,* 122 P.3d 521 (Utah. 2005), the court considered a referendum on a rezoning. It noted that "we have been hesitant to hold that an unqualified referendum right extends to municipal considerations involving necessarily complex issues, as the resolution of such matters may be best left to the mechanisms generally employed by municipal governments." *Id.* at 530. Why are land use matters "complex"? The court also seemed to infer, in interpreting a state statute, that direct democracy was not suited to the "highly involved undertaking" of "a development of a comprehensive zoning scheme or the annexation of property." In contrast, a zoning amendment to a single piece of property "is not of the same character." *Id.* Does the court have it backwards? Aren't there more dangers using direct democracy for single pieces of property than for widespread rezonings?

C. THE PRIVATE LAND USE MODEL: COVENANTS, CONDITIONS, AND RESTRICTIONS

Before the advent of zoning, and before *Village of Euclid v. Ambler Realty,* reprinted in Chapter 2, the common law had methods for implementing land use restrictions. Covenants and easements, for example, could be used to restrict land-owners' abilities to use property. The common law doctrine of nuisance was available to adjust conflicting land uses on adjacent properties.

Covenants provide a means of regulating land that is separate from the public regulatory system. *See, e.g., Mannweiler v. LaFlamme*, 700 A.2d 57 (Conn. Ct. App. 1997) (although city approved applicant's request to subdivide property and construct two houses, the property was still subject to a covenant and restriction allowing only one private residence for the use of one family, although certain defenses might be available). They remain very important in the modern land use practice because of the increasing trend toward "privatization" of some developments.

A Note on the Common Law and Land Use

Public legislative mechanisms for regulating land use are largely a twentieth-century development. The common law, however, had devices for adjusting and restricting the rights to use land. These devices, while largely supplanted by zoning and public regulation, nonetheless continue to play an important role in "filling gaps." Most importantly, the common law mechanism of covenants is increasingly used to restrict land use in private developments. One estimate is that homeowner associations established through covenants govern over half of the new housing in the country's 50 largest metropolitan areas. Eran Ben-Joseph, *Land Use and Design Innovations in Private Communities*, Land Lines (Oct. 2004) at 8.

1. *Nuisance.* The common law cause of action for nuisance resolves competing land uses. Nuisances are divided into two categories: (1) private nuisance, which is a substantial and unreasonable inference with the use and enjoyment of land, and (2) public nuisance, which is the interference with a right common to the general public. The difference between the two is largely one of degree. Traditionally, however, a private individual could not sue for public nuisance unless the plaintiff had suffered harm of a "different kind" from that suffered by the public generally. *See, e.g., In re Lead Paint Litig.*, 924 A.2d 424, 497 (N.J. 2007).

Courts have labeled some activities as "nuisances per se," or nuisances under all circumstances. *Woodsmall v. Lost Creek Twp. Conservation Club, Inc.*, 933 N.E.2d 899, 903 (Ind. Ct. App. 2010) ("A nuisance may be a nuisance per se, something which cannot be lawfully conducted or maintained (such as a house of prostitution or an obstruction encroaching upon a public highway)."). In most cases, however, whether an activity is a nuisance depends upon the circumstances under which it is undertaken. *Burch v. Nedpower Mount Storm, LLC*, 647 S.E.2d 879, 893 (W. Va. 2007) (wind power generating facility not a nuisance per se). Thus, courts will label an activity as a nuisance only after examining the specific circumstances of the property's use in that case and the effect of the particular use on neighboring properties.

The central issue in determining whether an activity on land is a nuisance is deciding whether the activity constitutes "a substantial and unreasonable interference" with the use or enjoyment of land. *Crosstex North Texas Pipeline, L.P. v. Gardiner*, ___ S.W. 3d ___ (Tex. 2016). The interference must offend persons of "ordinary sensibilities" in a particular locality. *Blue Ink, Ltd. v. Two Farms, Inc.*, 218 Md. App. 77, 96 A.3d 810, 823 (2014). This determination requires a balancing, and under nuisance law that balancing weighs the utility of the defendant's conduct against the harm that the plaintiff has suffered. Restatement (Second) of Torts §826 (1989). The Restatement sets forth a variety of factors that are pertinent to determining the "gravity of harm" to the plaintiff: (1) the extent of the harm; (2) the character of the harm; (3) the social value that the law attaches to the type of use or enjoyment invaded; (4) the suitability of the particular use or enjoyment invaded to the character of the locality; and (5) the burden on the person harmed of avoiding the harm. Restatement (Second) of Torts, §827 (1989). At the same time, the court examines the defendant's actions, and the Restatement sets forth a number of factors that are relevant to this examination: (1) the social value that the law attaches to the primary purpose of the conduct; (2) the suitability of the conduct to the character of the locality; (3) whether it is practical to prevent or avoid the invasion, if the activity is maintained; and (4) whether it is impractical to maintain the activity if it is required to bear the cost of compensating for the invasion. Restatement (Second) §828 (1989). *See Wilson v. Southern California Edison Co.*, 184 Cal. Rptr. 3d 26, 234 Cal. App. 4th 123, 161-62 (2015) (citing both 827 and 828).

As far as remedies are concerned, courts often have enjoined conduct and ordered defendants to pay damages. *See, e.g., McVicars v. Christensen*, 156 Idaho 58, 320 P.2d 948, 951 (2014) ("Remedies for nuisance can include abatement, injunction, and damages."). In balancing the rights of the parties, some courts have placed significance on whether the defendant's activities pre-date those of the plaintiff, that is, whether the plaintiff has "come to the nuisance." *See Amaral v. Cuppels*, 831 N.E.2d 915, 920 (Mass. Ct. App. 2005) ("coming to the nuisance" is a factor that weighs heavily in whether the court grants relief). For example, in one famous case, *Spur Indus., Inc. v. Del E. Webb Dev. Co.*, 494 P.2d 700 (Ariz. 1972), the court agreed to enjoin the defendant's agricultural operation, which caused a nuisance to a retirement community located nearby. However, because the plaintiff retirement community had "come to the nuisance," the court ordered that the plaintiff compensate the defendant. *Id.* at 708 ("It does not seem harsh to require a developer, who has taken advantage of the lesser land values in a rural area . . . to indemnify those who are forced to leave as a result.").

Courts also have the power to grant injunctive relief as well. Here, however, the courts will engage in the well-established process of "balancing the equities" in deciding whether such equitable relief is appropriate. *See Boomer v. Atlantic Cement Co.*, 257 N.E.2d 870 (N.Y. 1970).

2. *Easements.* You are undoubtedly familiar with the concept of easements from your real property class. An easement "'creates a nonpossessory right to enter and use land in the possession of another and obligates the possessor not to interfere with the uses authorized by the easement.' . . ." *Martin v. Simmons Properties, LLC.*, 467 Mass. 1, 2 N.E.3d 885, 892 (2014). Easements are divided into two categories: affirmative and negative. An affirmative easement is a nonpossessory right to use land that belongs to another, while a negative easement — a view easement is an example — is a restriction that the owner places on her own land to benefit another person or other land. *Patterson v. Paul*, 448 Mass. 658, 863 N.E.2d 527, 533 (2007). "Ordinarily, four elements must be established to show a reciprocal negative easement: (1) a common grantor, (2) a designation of land subject to restrictions, (3) a general plan or scheme of restrictions, and (4) covenants running with the land in accordance with such plan or scheme." *Gambrell v. Schriver*, 440 S.E.2d 393, 395 (S.C. Ct. App. 1994).

Easements can be express or implied. *See, e.g., Woods v. Shannon,* 378 Mont. 365, 344 P.3d 413, 416 (2015) ("The easement at issue in this case is . . . an express easement, not an easement implied by necessity."). They can also be prescriptive, arising through the adverse use of another person's land. *Brannock v. The Lotus Fund,* 367 P.3d 888 (N.M. App. (2015) (evidence established prescriptive easement over a road). Various technical rules of property law govern easements (and, to a greater extent covenants, as is discussed below). *See* Susan F. French, Toward a Modern Law of Servitudes: Reweaving the Ancient Strands, 55 S. Cal. L. Rev. 1261 (1982) ("The law of easements, real covenants and equitable servitudes is the most complex and archaic body of American property law remaining in the twentieth century."). For example, an easement may be "appurtenant" to the land, a term meaning that the easement benefits land that the holder of the easement owns. *Nature Conservancy of Wisconsin, Inc. v. Altnau,* 756 N.W.2d 641, 645 (Wis. Ct. App. 2008) ("A benefit is appurtenant if the right to enjoy that benefit is tied to the ownership of a particular parcel of land. A benefit is in gross if it is not appurtenant."). This benefited land is known as the "dominant estate." In contrast, an easement "in gross" is not attached to land but is for the personal benefit of the person who holds it. *Wetlands Am. Trust, Inc. v. White Cloud Nine Ventures L.P.,* 291 Va.153, 782 S.E.2d 131, 137 n.5 (2016).

Historically, the courts at common law limited negative easements to four categories: light, air, drainage of an artificial stream, and lateral support. Thus, from a land use perspective, negative easements are less important than affirmative easements.

3. *Covenants and Servitudes.* The third principal type of common law device for affecting land use originates in contract law. Parties could contract to restrict other uses of land, and this restriction would be enforceable either through a covenant that would "run with the land" or an equitable "servitude."

The key point to remember is that individuals who are not parties to the original contracts can enforce the terms of that contract through property law. Typically, such restrictions are recorded as part of deeds conveying property. Subsequent owners are thus charged with constructive notice of the restriction. *See, e.g., Martellini v. Little Angels Day Care,* 847 A.2d 838, 842 (2004) (operators of family day care facility were on constructive notice of covenant restricting use of property to "single family private residence purposes."). The grantees acquire by implication an equitable right, referred to as an implied reciprocal negative easement or an equitable servitude, to enforce the restrictions. *Country Cmty. Timberlake Village, L.P. v. HMW Special Utility Dist. of Harris,* 438 S.W.3d 661, 668 (Tex. App. 2014). Like easements, covenants can be affirmative (e.g., requiring an owner to contribute to a share of the neighborhood's maintenance expenses) or negative (e.g., requiring an owner to refrain from using the property for certain kinds of businesses). Some courts recognize a third category, restrictive covenants (e.g., grantee agrees to refrain from using her property in a particular manner). *Terry Weisheit Rental v. David Grace, LLC,* 12 N.E.3d 930, 937 (Ind. App. 2014) (discussing all three types). Historically, courts were inclined to disallow the running of affirmative covenants, but the modern trend is decidedly to the contrary.

A restrictive covenant is a real covenant that runs with the land of the dominant and servient estates only if: (1) the subject of the covenant touches and concerns the land, (2) there is privity of estate between the party enforcing the contract and the party against whom the covenant is being enforced, and (3) the original covenanting parties intended the benefits and burdens of the covenant to run with the land. *See, e.g., Jeremiah 29:11, Inc. v. Seifort*, 161 P.3d 750, 753 (Kan. 2007); *Smalley v. Stowe Mountain Club, LLC*, 25 A.3d 539, 543 (Vt. 2011) ("it is readily apparent that — construed in context — the 200-foot restriction, like the other residential covenants, was intended to run with the land"). For example, in *1515-1519 Lakeview Boulevard Condo. Ass'n v. Apartment Sales Corp.*, 43 P.3d 1233 (Wash. 2002), the City of Seattle approved a condominium on condition that the owners record a covenant releasing the city from potential liability for landslide damages. (The city thought this alternative was better than a denial of the project, which would likely bring a takings claim.) When, almost inevitably, the development slid, the court had to consider whether the covenant "ran with the land" and thus bound future property owners.

The "touch and concern" requirement is perhaps the most difficult requirement to explain. As one commentator put it, the requirement is one "that can be explored and felt better than it can be defined." William B. Stoebuck, Running Covenants: An Analytical Primer, 52 Wash. L. Rev. 861, 869 (1977); *Schodowski, v. Tellico Village Property Owners Ass'n*, ____ S.E.3d ____ (Tenn. Ct. App. 2016) (noting uncertainty over the "touch and concern" requirement). One court, citing this article, noted that a covenant meeting this requirement "can be one that calls for either doing physical things to the land such as building a wall, or refraining from doing physical things to the land such as a promise ' . . . not to build a structure, or not to build multifamily dwellings.' . . ." *Cypress Gardens Ltd. v. Platt*, 952 P.2d 467, 470 (N.M. Ct. App. 1997); *see also Gambrell v. Nivens*, 275 S.W.3d 429, 438 (Tenn. Ct. App. 2008) ("building restrictions embodied in a covenant between owners in fee satisfy" the "touch and concern" requirement).

Both covenants and easements are employed in many modern developments, and considerable legal skills are required to craft them. For example, both condominiums and increasing numbers of large-scale private developments, which have individual homes and "common areas" all owners can use, are subject to "Covenants, Conditions and Restrictions" (CC&Rs) that are recorded and run with the land. *See Westwood Homeowners Ass'n, Inc. v. Lane County*, 864 P.2d 350, 355 (Or. 1993) ("Each lot within Westwood PUD is, therefore, both the dominant and the servient estate or tenement with respect to the CC&Rs involved; the benefits and burdens of mutual promises attach to the ownership of each lot."). Injunctive relief is a remedy for violation of a covenant. *Cullen v. Tarini*, 15 A.3d 968, 982-83 (R.I. 2011) (upholding injunction and refusing to "balance the equities" where defendants "knowingly and admittedly" violated the covenant).

The following materials will introduce you to some of the issues involved in this type of private land use control. First, read carefully the excerpt from a large set of CC&Rs. As you do so, note the important restrictions on land ownership as well as the rights and obligations that they impose. The restrictions operate in a manner that is far different from public regulation. Then you will read a case in which restrictions of this type resulted in litigation.

■ JO ANNE P. STUBBLEFIELD, DECLARATION OF COVENANTS, CONDITIONS, AND RESTRICTIONS FOR BEACHSIDE

SPO 12 ALI-ABA 475 (2008)

ARTICLE I CREATION OF COMMUNITY . . .

1.2. BINDING EFFECT.

This Declaration governs the property described in Exhibit "A," and any other property submitted to this Declaration in the future. This Declaration shall run with the title to such property and shall bind anyone having any right, title, or interest in any portion of such property, their heirs, successors, successors-in-title, and assigns.

Declarant, the Association, and their respective legal representatives, heirs, successors, and assigns may enforce this Declaration. This Declaration shall be effective for a minimum of 25 years from the date it is Recorded. After 25 years, this Declaration shall be extended automatically for successive 10 year periods unless at least 75% of the then Owners sign a document stating that the Declaration is terminated and that document is Recorded within the year before any extension. In such case, this Declaration shall expire on the date specified in the termination document. . . .

ARTICLE III USE AND CONDUCT

3.1. RESTRICTIONS ON USE, OCCUPANCY, AND ALIENATION.

The restrictions set forth in this Section may be amended only in accordance with Article XX.

(a) *Residential and Related Uses.* Residential Lots shall be used primarily for residential and related purposes. No business shall be conducted in, on, or from any Residential Lot, except that an Owner or another resident of the Lot may conduct business activities on such Lot if the business activity:

(i) is not apparent or detectable by sight, sound, or smell from outside of a permitted structure;

(ii) complies with applicable zoning requirements;

(iii) does not involve regular visitation of the Lot by clients, customers, suppliers, or other business invitees, or door-to-door solicitation within the Community; and

(iv) is consistent with the residential character of the Community and does not constitute a nuisance, or a hazardous or offensive use, or threaten the security or safety of others within the Community, as determined in the Board's sole discretion. . . .

3.5. PROTECTION OF OWNERS AND OTHERS.

Except as may be set forth in this Declaration (either initially or by amendment) or in the initial Use Restrictions set forth in Exhibit "C," the Association's actions with respect to Use Restrictions and rules must comply with the following:

(a) *Similar Treatment.* Similarly situated Owners must be treated similarly; however, the Use Restrictions and rules may vary by Neighborhood.

(b) *Displays.* Owners' rights to display religious and holiday signs, symbols, and decorations on their Lots of the kinds normally displayed in single-family residential neighborhoods shall not be abridged, except that the Association may adopt time, place, and manner restrictions with respect to such displays.

The Association shall not regulate the content of political signs; however, it may regulate the time, place, and manner of posting such signs (including design criteria). . . .

ARTICLE IV ARCHITECTURE AND LANDSCAPING

4.1. GENERAL.

Except for work done by or on behalf of Declarant or any Declarant Affiliate, no structure or thing shall be placed, erected, or installed upon any Lot, and no improvements or other work (including staking, clearing, excavation, grading and other site work, exterior alterations, or planting or removal of landscaping) shall take place within Beachside, except in compliance with this Article and the Design Guidelines.

Any Owner may remodel, paint, or redecorate the interior of any structure on his or her Lot without approval. However, modifications to the interior of screened porches, patios, and any other portions of a Lot visible from outside a structure are subject to approval.

Each dwelling shall be designed by and built in accordance with the plans and specifications of a licensed architect acceptable to Declarant, unless Declarant, in its sole discretion, or its designee otherwise approves. . . .

4.3. GUIDELINES AND PROCEDURES.

(a) *Design Guidelines.* Declarant shall prepare Design Guidelines for the Community, which may contain general provisions applicable to all of Beachside as well as specific provisions which vary from Neighborhood to Neighborhood and according to property use or product type. Among other things, the Design Guidelines shall restrict the use of specified plant species and require the review and approval of all plant species in accordance with the Development Order.

4.4. NO WAIVER OF FUTURE APPROVALS.

Each Owner acknowledges that the people reviewing applications under this Article will change from time to time and that opinions on aesthetic matters, as well as interpretation and application of the Design Guidelines, may vary accordingly. In addition, each Owner acknowledges that it may not always be possible to identify objectionable features until work is completed, at which time, it may or may not be unreasonable to require that such objectionable features be changed. However, the Reviewer may refuse to approve similar proposals in the future. Approval of applications or plans shall not constitute a waiver of the right to withhold approval of similar applications, plans, or other matters subsequently or additionally submitted for approval.

4.5. VARIANCES.

The Reviewer may authorize variances from compliance with the Design Guidelines and any procedures when circumstances such as topography, natural obstructions, hardship, or aesthetic or environmental considerations require, but only in accordance with duly adopted rules and regulations. No variance shall (a) be effective unless in writing; (b) be contrary to this Declaration; or (c) prevent the Reviewer from denying a variance in other circumstances. A variance requires Declarant's written consent for so long as Declarant or any Declarant Affiliate owns any portion of the Community or has the unilateral right to annex property, and, thereafter, requires the Board's written consent. . . .

ARTICLE VII ASSOCIATION POWERS AND RESPONSIBILITIES . . .

7.4. COMPLIANCE AND ENFORCEMENT.

(a) The Board may impose sanctions for Governing Document violations, which sanctions include those listed below and any others described elsewhere in the Governing Documents. The Board may establish a range of penalties for different violations, with violations of the Declaration, unsafe conduct, and harassment or intentionally malicious conduct treated more severely than other violations. The following sanctions require prior notice and an opportunity for a hearing in accordance with the By-Laws:

(i) imposing reasonable monetary fines, not to exceed the limit established for individual violations under Florida law (or per day limitations in the case of a continuing violation), which shall constitute a lien upon the violator's Lot (fines may be imposed within a graduated range). There is no limit on the aggregate amount of any fine for a continuing violation;

(ii) suspending an Owner's right to vote (except that no notice or hearing is required if the Owner is more than 90 days delinquent in paying any Regular Assessment);

(iii) suspending any Person's right to use Common Area amenities (except that no notice or hearing is required if the Owner is more than 30 days delinquent in paying any assessment or other charge owed the Association); provided, nothing shall authorize the Board to impair an Owner or occupant's access to his or her Lot;

(iv) suspending any services the Association provides (except that no notice or hearing is required if the Owner is more than 30 days delinquent in paying any assessment or other charge owed to the Association);

(v) exercising self-help or taking action to abate any violation of the Governing Documents occurring on a Lot in a non-emergency situation (including removing personal property that violates the Governing Documents); and

(vi) levying Benefited Assessments to cover costs the Association incurs to bring a Lot into compliance with the Governing Documents. . . .

7.15. INCIDENTAL TAKE PERMIT — U.S. FISH AND WILDLIFE SERVICE.

Beachside is subject to that certain "Incidental Take Permit for Beachside and Camp Creek," issued by the U.S. Fish and Wildlife Service under the Endangered Species Act, and which incorporates that certain Habitat Conservation Plan dated June, 1999 (collectively, the "Incidental Take Permit"). Each Owner and the Association by taking title to a Lot or any other portion of Beachside, acknowledges the obligation to comply with the terms and conditions of the Incidental Take Permit. The Association's costs incurred in complying with the Incidental Take Permit, including actions taken as minimization or mitigation measures, shall be Common

Expenses and shall be included in the Association's annual budget and assessed against all Owners as provided in Article VIII.

ARTICLE IV DISPUTE RESOLUTION

14.1. AGREEMENT TO ENCOURAGE RESOLUTION OF DISPUTES WITHOUT LITIGATION.

(a) Declarant, the Association and its officers, directors, and committee members, all Persons subject to this Declaration, and any Person not otherwise subject to this Declaration who agrees to submit to this Article (collectively, "Bound Parties"), agree to attempt to resolve disputes involving Beachside without the emotional and financial costs of litigation. Accordingly, each Bound Party agrees not to, directly or indirectly, file a law suit for a Claim described in subsection (b), without first submitting the Claim to the alternative dispute resolution procedures described in Section 14.2.

14.2. DISPUTE RESOLUTION PROCEDURES.

(a) *Notice.* The Bound Party asserting a Claim ("Claimant") against another Bound Party ("Respondent") shall give written notice ("Notice") by mail or personal delivery to each Respondent, and to the Board, stating plainly and concisely:

(i) the nature of the Claim, including the Persons involved and Respondent's role in the Claim;

(ii) the legal basis of the Claim (*i.e.*, the specific authority out of which the Claim arises);

(iii) the Claimant's proposed resolution or remedy; and

(iv) the Claimant's desire to meet with the Respondent to discuss in good faith ways to resolve the Claim.

(b) *Negotiation.* The Claimant and Respondent shall make every reasonable effort to meet in person and confer for the purpose of resolving the Claim by good faith negotiation. If requested in writing, accompanied by a copy of the Notice, the Board may appoint a representative to assist the parties in negotiating a resolution of the Claim.

(c) *Mediation.* If the Bound Parties have not resolved the Claim through negotiation within 30 days of the date of the Notice (or within such other agreed upon period), the Claimant shall have 30 additional days to submit the Claim to mediation with an entity designated by the Association (if the Association is not a party to the Claim) or to an independent agency providing dispute resolution services in the Ocean County area. Each Bound Party shall present the mediator with a written summary of the Claim.

If the Claimant does not submit the Claim to mediation within such time, or does not appear for and participate in good faith in the mediation when scheduled, the Claimant shall be deemed to have waived the Claim, and the Respondent shall be relieved of any and all liability to the Claimant (but not third parties) on account of such Claim.

If the Bound Parties do not settle the Claim within 30 days after submitting the matter to mediation, or within such time as determined reasonable by the mediator, the mediator shall issue a notice of termination of the mediation proceedings indicating that the Parties are at an impasse and the date that mediation was terminated. Except as provided in Section 14.2(e), the Claimant shall thereafter be entitled to file suit or to initiate administrative proceedings on the Claim, as appropriate.

Each Bound Party shall bear its own costs of the mediation, including attorneys' fees, and each Party shall share equally all fees charged by the mediator.

(d) *Settlement.* Any settlement of the Claim through negotiation or mediation shall be documented in writing and signed by the Bound Parties. If any Bound Party thereafter fails to abide by the terms of such agreement, then any other Bound Party may file suit or initiate administrative proceedings to enforce such agreement without the need to again comply with the procedures set forth in this Section. In such event, the Bound Party taking action to enforce the agreement shall, upon prevailing, be entitled to recover from the non-complying Bound Party (or each one in equal proportions) all costs incurred in enforcing such agreement, including, without limitation, attorneys' fees and court costs.

■ TURUDIC v. STEPHENS
31 P.3d 465 (Or. Ct. App. 2001)

HASELTON, P.J. . . .

Plaintiffs Andy and Luisa Turudic are the owners of two American mountain lions, more commonly known as cougars. In 1993, plaintiffs decided to move from Missouri to Oregon, in part because Oregon law, subject to certain statutory restrictions and local ordinances, permits the keeping of exotic animals such as cougars.

Plaintiffs purchased property in Susan Estates, a small subdivision in rural Yamhill County, in an area zoned "very low density, 5 acre minimum." There are no zoning restrictions on the type of animals that can be kept on a particular piece of property.

Before moving to Susan Estates, in researching the property, plaintiffs obtained copies for two sets of CCRs. The first set, entitled "Declaration of Covenants and Restrictions of Susan Estates" (original CCRs), was adopted at the time of the original development in 1981. The second set, entitled "First Amendment to Declaration of Covenants and Restrictions" (amended CCRs), was adopted in 1987 as a comprehensive revision to the original CCRs. The parties agree that the amended CCRs apply to plaintiffs' property and the issues regarding both plaintiffs' cougars and the holding pen. . . .

Plaintiffs began building their home in late spring 1994. Construction of the cougar holding pen, which meets or exceeds state standards for animal care and public safety and has been approved by the Oregon Department of Fish and Wildlife, began in mid-September and was completed on October 13, 1994. Plaintiffs did not obtain the approval of the Susan Estates Homeowners' Association board before undertaking or completing either their home or the cougar pen project.

At 3:00 in the morning on October 19, 1994, plaintiffs, without notice to their neighbors, moved the cougars into the holding pen. Two days later plaintiffs first became aware of their neighbors' concerns about the cougars when a deputy sheriff contacted them in response to a neighbor's complaint.

On November 8, 1994, a majority of the members of the Susan Estates home-owners' association met to discuss the cougar issue. Plaintiffs were not invited. At that meeting, the members agreed that the cougars were a nuisance and should be removed from plaintiffs' property. They also resolved to disapprove any "cougar-cage outbuildings." Consequently, on November 30, 1994, counsel for the Association wrote to plaintiffs, expressing concerns both about the cougars and about plaintiffs' failure to seek Board approval for both their house and the cougar pen.

Plaintiffs responded by offering to build a secondary safety fence around the existing cougar pen, and by submitting house plans to the Board. Plaintiffs did not submit plans for the cougar pen. On February 22, 1995, a representative for the Association wrote to plaintiffs, stating that plaintiffs' house plans had been approved but that the cougar pen was rejected under the "nuisance provisions" of the CCRs. . . .

In March 1995, plaintiffs brought this action. Plaintiffs sought a declaratory judgment that neither the pen nor the cougars could be prohibited under the amended CCRs and that, in all events, the Association was precluded from enforcing the CCRs because of the doctrine of laches. Plaintiffs further argued that the Association breached its obligations when it failed to follow the annual meeting provisions of the amended CCRs, failed to enforce the nuisance provisions as to other lot owners, and acted unreasonably and capriciously in denying approval for the cougar pen. . . .

Defendants counterclaimed, alleging that the cougars were a nuisance under both the CCRs and common law. . . .

The trial court subsequently issued a detailed letter opinion addressing the remaining cougar- and holding pen-related issues. That opinion rested on three determinations that are central to this appeal. *First*, plaintiffs' maintenance of the cougars was not a nuisance under either the common law or the amended CCRs. *Second*, nevertheless, plaintiffs' maintenance of the cougars was not a permitted "residential use" under the CCRs. *Third*, construction of the cougar pen without the Board's prior approval violated the amended CCRs.[8] Consequently, given its determination that the maintenance of the cougars was not a nuisance but that plaintiffs had otherwise violated the amended CCRs, the court entered a judgment rejecting plaintiffs' claims for declaratory relief and breach of contract, and rejecting defendants' nuisance-related counterclaims, but directing that both the cougars and the holding facility be removed from plaintiffs' property. . . .

We begin with the cougars. The amended CCRs, which all parties agree apply to plaintiffs' property, authorize the Board to regulate "the use . . . of the Property in such a manner as to preserve and enhance lot and structure values, farming, and to maintain the natural vegetation and topography." Amended CCRs, Art. IV, sec.2. Limitations on "use" are set forth in Article V, section 1, which provides, in pertinent part:

> (b) *Use of the property*. Property may be reasonably and normally used for agricultural farming, tree farming or residential use only.
> (c) *Nuisances*. No nuisance shall be permitted to exist or operate upon any Property so as to be detrimental to any other Property in the vicinity thereof or to its occupants.

---

8. The court also determined that enforcement of the CCRs was not barred by laches both because the delay was insufficient and because plaintiffs had "unclean hands" by virtue of failing to warn their neighbors about the cougars and then surreptitiously moving the animals onto the property.

> The decision of the Association as to what is a nuisance is presumptively correct. No normal or reasonable use of the Property, as described in subparagraph (b) above, shall be a nuisance.

Here, as noted, the trial court concluded that the cougars were not a nuisance under either the amended CCRs or common law.

Defendants do not challenge those determinations on appeal. Thus, for purpose of this appeal, we necessarily assume that plaintiffs' keeping of the cougars is *not* a nuisance under either the common law or the CCRs.

Given that posture, the issue narrows to whether keeping the cougars is a permissible "residential use" within the meaning of Article V, subsection 1(b). In construing the "residential use" provision of the amended CCRs, we follow the methodology prescribed in *Yogman v. Parrott,* 325 Or. 358, 361-66, 937 P.2d 1019 (1997). Under *Yogman,* "[t]o interpret a contractual provision, including a restrictive covenant, the court follows three steps." 325 Or. at 361, 937 P.2d 1019. First, the court must examine "the text of the disputed provision, in the context of the document as a whole. . . . If the provision is clear, the analysis ends." *Id.* If, however, the provision, when so viewed, remains ambiguous, the court must look to "extrinsic evidence of the contracting parties' intent" to resolve the ambiguity. *Id.* at 363, 937 P.2d 1019. Finally, if that analysis is not dispositive, the court must look to relevant maxims of construction, including the maxim that restrictive covenants should be "'construed most strictly against the covenant.'" *Id.* at 364-65, 937 P.2d 1019 (quoting *Scott Co. v. Roman Catholic Archbishop,* 83 Or. 97, 105, 163 P. 88 (1917); *see also Swanson v. Warner,* 125 Or. App. 524, 526, 865 P.2d 493 (1993).

We begin, then, with the text and context of the "residential use" provision. Article V, subsection 1(b) of the amended CCRs describes, and limits, permitted uses of property within the subdivision:

> *Use of the Property.* Property may be *reasonably and normally* used for agricultural farming, tree farming or *residential use only.*

(Emphasis added.)

"Residential," as commonly understood, means "of, relating to, or connected with residence or residences." *Webster's Third New Int'l Dictionary,* 1931 (unabridged ed. 1993). "Residence," in turn, means "the place where one actually lives or has his home. . . ." *Id.* Thus, a "residential use" is one that involves activities generally associated with a personal dwelling.

Plaintiff assert — and we agree — that keeping family pets is a "residential activity." *See Aldridge v. Saxey,* 242 Or. 238, 249, 409 P.2d 184 (1965) (concluding that covenant precluding the use of property for nonresidential purposes did not preclude the landowners from keeping 16 German Shepherds and 5 smaller dogs on their property). Plaintiffs further offered uncontradicted testimony that they keep and care for the cougars as pets and not for any commercial purpose, such as breeding or exhibiting the animals for pay. Andy Turudic described the role that the cougars play in plaintiffs' lives:

> [They] are an integral part of our family life. We have a very strong bond with our animals. . . . They give me and my wife both immense pleasure.

Thus, although the cougars may be more exotic than goldfish or hamsters, they are, nevertheless, indisputably family pets. Given that the cougars are family pets, and that their presence does not present a nuisance, the maintenance of the cougars constitutes a "residential use" within the meaning of the amended CCRs.

Defendants argue, however, that the amended CCRs permit only "reasonable" and "normal" residential uses — and assert that the keeping of cougars is neither. Defendants' argument fails for several reasons. First, as a textual matter, subsection 1(b) does not refer to "reasonable and normal. . . . residential use." Rather, it states that the property may be "*reasonably and normally* used for [farming] or residential use only." (Emphasis added.) Thus, defendants' argument transforms adverbs into adjectives — a transformation that is particularly significant with respect to "normally" and "normal." It is one thing to say that property shall "normally" — *i.e.*, typically or usually — be used for farming and residential purposes. It is quite another to say that property can only be used for "normal" — *i.e.*, presumably ordinary or decidedly nonexotic — uses. Here, plaintiffs "normally" use their property for residential uses.

Second, to the extent that defendants claim contextual support for their "reasonable and normal" use argument, they point to the language of the nuisance provision, subsection 1(c). That reliance is, however, unavailing. Subsection 1(c) refers to "normal *or* reasonable" use — that is, it is phrased in the disjunctive, not defendants' putative conjunctive. . . . Thus, any use described in subsection 1(b) that is *either* "reasonable" *or* "normal" is not a nuisance under subsection 1(c); a use that is not "normal," but is nevertheless "reasonable," must be permitted. Moreover, as noted, the trial court explicitly determined that the use here was not a "nuisance" under subsection 1(c). Logically, in so holding, the court necessarily determined that the use was either "normal" or "reasonable," or both. As noted, defendants do not contest that determination. . . .

Third, to the extent that the phrase "may be reasonably and normally used.for residential use only" remains ambiguous after resort to context, including subsection 1(c), the covenant is to be "construed most strictly against the covenant." *Yogman*, 325 Or. at 364-65, 937 P.2d 1019. Here, that canon assumes special significance because of the conduct of the Association, which seeks to enforce the covenant. As noted, plaintiffs have undertaken considerable efforts to eliminate potential risks associated with keeping the cougars. Those efforts have been highly successful — so successful that the trial court found that any risk from the cougars did not rise to the level of a common-law nuisance. "[T]he potential for actual injury to a person is so remote that the fear of the neighbors cannot be said to be objectively reasonable." Nevertheless, marginal risks remain — *e.g.*, the risk of a trespassing child thrusting his or her hand into the cage or of a stranger releasing the cougars — and plaintiffs offered to undertake additional measures that would have eliminated even that potential. But the Association refuses to approve those reasonable measures. . . .

In effect, the Association contends that plaintiffs' maintenance of the cougars is not "reasonable" because of the Association's own refusal to approve reasonable safety measures. The self-serving circularity is patent. Such a construction of subsection 1(b) cannot be squared with the "construed most strictly against the covenant" canon.

We thus conclude that the keeping of the cougars in their holding pen is a permitted residential use under Article V, subsection 1(b) of the amended CCRs.

That conclusion, however, necessarily depends on the premise that the cougars' holding pen lawfully exists, and will continue to exist, on plaintiffs' property. Consequently, we turn to the trial court's determination that the cougar pen must be removed from the property. . . .

We agree that, at least in the abstract, the amended CCRs give the Board the authority to either approve or disapprove construction of structures such as the cougar pen. In particular, the amended CCRs provide:

> No . . . building, fence or other structure shall be erected, placed or altered on any lot or parcel until the proposed building plans, plot plans showing the proposed location of such building or structures . . . have been approved in writing by the Board, its successors or assigns. Refusal or approval of plans or location may be based by the Board upon any reason, including purely aesthetic conditions, which, in the sole discretion of the Board, shall be deemed sufficient.

Amended CCRs, Art. V, sec. 1(e)(2).

That broad authority to approve or disapprove a structure for "any reason" is balanced, however, by Article IV, section 8 of the amended CCRs, which requires that, "In all matters relating to their duties as the Board of the Association, the Board must act reasonably and not capriciously." It is in light of those contractual rights and obligations that we assess the Board's actions here.

In its February 22, 1995, letter, the Board notified plaintiffs that structural approval for their cougar pen had been denied and that the cougar pen had to be removed. The letter further stated:

> [N]o further construction of cages for housing cougars or any other felid shall be constructed. *This action is predicated on the basis of the nuisance provisions of the Susan Estates Covenants and Restrictions.* (Emphasis added.)

No alternative explanation was given, and the evidence at trial did not show any additional bases for the Board's decision to deny approval of the plans. For example, there was no evidence that the Board denied approval because the cougar pen violated any "aesthetic" or design requirements of the CCRs or because the cougars or their holding pen might adversely affect property values. Thus, the sole basis of the Board's denial of approval was its belief that maintenance of the cougars was a nuisance.

The trial court concluded that that denial was sufficient basis for enjoining plaintiffs to remove the cougar pan. We respectfully disagree for two related reasons. First, . . . defendants do not dispute on appeal [that] the cougars here are not a nuisance under the CCRs. Thus, while the Board may deny approval of a structure for any reasonable and not capricious reason, the sole basis for disapproval here was legally erroneous — and, indeed, objectively unreasonable: "[T]he fear of the neighbors cannot be said to be objectively reasonable." Denial on such a basis is unreasonable and capricious.

Second, in a related sense, the Board's disapproval was, in purpose and effect, a collateral preclusion of a lawful permitted use under the CCRs. That is, the Board's disapproval was not, actually, of the structure *qua* structure but of the structure's function. The disapproval of the holding pen here is analogous to a homeowners' association refusing to approve plans for a home that includes a billiard room because the association's members disapprove of billiards. Here, the keeping of pets, including exotic pets, in safe facilities is a permitted "residential use." *See* 176 Or. App. at 185-88, 31 P.3d at 470-71. Consequently, so long as the structure for holding such pets does not violate some other (*e.g.*, design-related) requirement of the CCRs, the preapproval process cannot be employed as a subterfuge to preclude that permitted use. Such a denial is unreasonable and capricious. . . .

Notes and Comments

1. *The Beachside CC&Rs.* Were you surprised by the stringency of the restrictions that the *Beachside* CC&Rs place on use of the property? Do you think most homeowners, who are certainly on constructive notice of these provisions, are actually aware of them before they purchase the property?

2. *The Breadth of CC&Rs.* The breadth of CC&Rs is illustrated by the myriad disputes that have arisen between owners in the same development, or between owners and the homeowners association. For example, there was the case of the walkway painted pink (*Captain's Walk Homeowners Ass'n v. Penney*, 794 N.Y.S.2d 82 (App. Div. 2005)); the case of the unscreened recreational vehicle (*Schwartz v. Banbury Woods Homeowners Ass'n, Inc.*, 675 S.E.2d 382 (N.C. Ct. App. 2009)); the case of the "three cats" ("Boo-Boo, Dockers, and Tulip") (*Nahrstedt v. Lakeside Village Condo. Ass'n*, 878 P.2d 1275 (Cal. 1994)); the case of the "smoking ban" at the club (*Laganella v. Boca Grove Golf and Tennis Club, Inc.*, 690 So. 2d 705 (Fla. Dist. Ct. App. 1997)); the case of the illegal "shed" (*Glisson v. IRHA of Loganville, Inc.*, 656 S.E.2d 924 (Ga. Ct. App. 2008)); the case of the "skate ramp" (*Lake Pointe Townhomes Homeowners' Ass'n v. Bruce*, 900 N.E.2d 636 (Ohio Ct. App. 2008)); and the case of the backyard swing set (*Saguaro Highlands Cmty. Ass'n v. Biltis*, 229 P.3d 1036 (Ariz. Ct. App. 2010)).

Newspapers regularly chronicle these types of disputes. *See, e.g.,* Marc Lacey, An Election Year Flap: Homeowner's Fight Involves Flat Tied to Tea Party, Pittsburgh Post-Gazette, Sept. 5, 2010, at A12 (homeowner flew "Don't Tread on Me" flag from his roof, but homeowners association ordered him to remove "the debris" from his roof); Ian Hamilton, Frisco Man's F-150 Garaged after Stonebriar HOA dispute, The Dallas Morning News (Oct. 6, 2015) (HOA outlawed pickup trucks from parking in driveway but allowed "luxury" vehicles such as Cadillac Escalades and Lincoln Mark LTs); Katy McLaughlin, Neighbor Disputes Turn Wealthy Areas into War Zones, The Wall Street Journal (July 28, 1916) (litigation over whether trimming of hedge was required by HOA rules). *See* Paula A. Franzese, Does It Take a Village? Privatization, Patterns of Community Restrictiveness and the Demise of Community, 47 Vill. L. Rev. 553, 555-56 (2002) (covenants regulate the permissibility and style of one's screen and storm doors, the ratio of grass, trees, and shrubs allowed on one's property, the mounting of basketball hoops, the retrieval of dog droppings, the posting of for-sale signs, the trimming of bushes, and the color of window curtains (citing cases)).

Pet provisions are the most frequently litigated lifestyle restriction. Rebecca J. Huss, No Pets Allowed: Housing Issues and Companion Animals, 11 Animal L. 69 (2004). For example, in *Eldorado Cmty. Improvement Ass'n, Inc. v. Billings,* 374 P.3d 737 (N.M. Ct. App. 2016), the court resolved a dispute over whether hens qualified as pets under the CC&Rs. The court concluded: "We are not persuaded that in permitting pet chickens 'the sky will fall.' Such a Chicken Little-esque view of possible results and calamity is not convincing."

3. *Technical Requirements.* As you know from your property law course and from the Note above, compliance with the law of covenants is quite technical and requires attention to detail by the lawyer and close research of the property law in a particular state. For example, in *Citizens for Covenant Compliance v. Anderson,* 906 P.2d 1314 (Cal. 1995), defendants sought to plant and harvest grapes, operate a winery, and keep llamas on their property. The neighbors brought suit, claiming that the CC&Rs for the subdivision limited the activities on defendants' property. Defendants raised a technical defense: since the CC&Rs were recorded *before* any of the properties they purport to govern were sold, defendants claimed that they were not bound because the restrictions were not mentioned in any deed or other document when the property was sold.

After saluting the properties of wine ("In vino veritas"), Justice Arabian proceeded to wade through the thickets of covenant law to conclude that subsequent purchasers were bound. 906 P.2d at 1316. The court's ruling had a practical bent to it: the rule simplifies the enforcement of CC&Rs by necessitating the recording of only one document containing them.

4. *Enforcement.* When a dispute between owners or between the association and an owner turns nasty, the enforcement provisions of the CC&Rs become important. What restrictions are placed on the ability of the homeowners' association to enforce the Beachside CC&Rs set out above? What restrictions are placed on owners who wish to contest decisions or raise issues? Are those restrictions reasonable?

The association's enforcement "arsenal" normally consists of the power to fine as well as the power to seek injunctive relief. *See, e.g., Liebler v. Point Loma Tennis Club,* 47 Cal. Rptr. 2d 783 (Cal. App. 1995) (association had power to impose fines against an owner who violated a rule that prohibited nonresident owners from using the common area recreational facilities); *Taylor v. McCollom,* 958 P.2d 207, 213 (Or. Ct. App. 1998) (refusing injunctive relief for a violation of a covenant protecting plaintiff's view where the cost to defendants of tearing off and lowering their roof would be "very substantial," and defendants did not willfully violate the covenant).

If a court is reviewing a decision by a community association, the case may well turn on the test that the court applies. Many courts apply a "business judgment" test modeled on corporate law. Thus, in *Reiner v. Ehrlich,* 212 Md. App. 142, 66 A.3d 1132 (2013), an intermediate Maryland appellate court found that the business judgment test precluded review of a homeowners' association decision about materials that asphalt could not be used in re-roofing a unit. *See* Paula A. Franzese, Common Interest Communities: Standards of Review and Review of Standards, 3 Wash. U. J. L. & Pol'y 663 (2000) (arguing for a "multi-factored reasonableness test anchored in whether the restriction or board decision at issue is rationally related to the association's purposes or imposes burdens that are disproportionate to any benefits").

If the association in its discretion refuses to enforce, at least some sets of covenants allow enforcement by individual property owners. *See, e.g., Williams v. Southern Trace Prop. Owners Ass'n,* 981 So. 2d 196 (La. Ct. App. 2008). Of course, not everyone has standing to enforce the restrictions in a covenant. In *McCrann v. Pinehurst, LLC,* 737 S.E.2d 771 (N.C. App. 2013), the court found that landowners who owned property adjacent to the property restricted by a covenant did not have standing to sue over waiver of the covenants.

5. *Amendments.* Land use circumstances can change, and governments adapt to such changes by amending their plans, zoning ordinances, etc. Are private land use instruments capable of the same kind of flexibility? For example, could a development that is subject to CC&Rs amend them to decide that no property can be rented out? That only individuals 55 or older are allowed to live there? Because they are contractual in nature, the ability to amend largely depends upon the language in the covenants. Thus, for example, in *Wilson v. Playa de Serrano*, 123 P.3d 1148 (Az. Ct. App. 2006), an Arizona court rejected the association's attempt to amend its bylaws to require that townhouses must be occupied by persons 55 years of age or older. "Although the declaration [of covenants, conditions, and restrictions] does allocate certain powers to the association and its board, these powers are largely limited to constructing, managing, and maintaining the common areas." *Id.* at 1150.

More generally, in a recent article, The Rule of Reason in Property Law, 46 U.C. Davis L. Rev. 1369, 1416 (2013), Professor Joseph William Singer argues that modern covenants law tends to subject covenants to "general judgments of reasonableness." Thus, he notes: "Recent legal changes have made each owner's land use rights contingent on retroactive covenants and rules imposed by a majority of neighbors in the association, and it limits the powers of homeowners associations by requiring them to exercise their powers reasonably." *Id.* at 1417. *See also* Herbert Hovenkamp, Fractured Markets and Legal Institutions, 100 Iowa L. Rev. 617, 1644 (2015) (noting that some subdivisions try to alleviate "excessive stability" in CC&Rs by permitting non-unanimous voting to change an existing restriction, a development which in turn has prompted some courts to intervene and protect minority rights in the democratic voting system).

6. *The Airbnb "Problem."* What about amending the CC&Rs to prohibit short-term rentals of the "Airbnb" type? In *Adams v. Kimberley One Townhouse Owner's Ass'n, Inc.*, 352 P.3d 491 (Idaho 2015), the homeowners' association received complaints about short-term renters. The association responded by proposing an amendment that prohibited rentals for fewer than six months, and the amendment passed. The owner of the offending unit sued, but the Idaho Supreme Court unanimously upheld the amendment. *See also Estates at Desert Ridge Trails v. Vazquez*, 300 P.3d 736 (N.M. Ct. App. 2013) (terms "residential purpose" and "single family" in CC&Rs did not bar short term rentals). *Compare Wilkinson v. Chiwawa Cmty. Ass'n*, 327 P.3d 614 (Wash. 2014) (rejecting a restriction on short-term rental activity.)

Absent an amendment, the validity of short-term rentals will depend on the wording of the CC&Rs. Numerous disputes over the issue have broken out. *See, e.g,* Kelly Smith, Minnetonka Lawsuit Shows Struggle for Homeowners' Association in Airbnb Era, Minneapolis Star Tribune (June 9, 2016) (homeowners' association started enforcement after resident advertised on Airbnb, and resident responded by suing the homeowners' association); Deirdre Fernandes, Condo Boards Slap Hefty Fines on Neighbors for Airbnb Rentals, The Boston Globe (July 7, 2015).

7. *Defenses.* What rights and defenses are available to an owner when he or she believes that a homeowners' association has acted arbitrarily? The place to start, as always, is with the provisions of the covenants and restrictions themselves. In the case of the *Beachside* CC&Rs, what rights does an owner have to contest an arbitrary decision? Does the homeowners' association have to provide direct proof of the adoption of a height limit before that limit can be enforced? In *Clear Lake Riviera*

Cmty. Ass'n v. Cramer, 105 Cal. Rptr. 3d 815 (Cal. Ct. App. 2010), the court enforced a height limit, explaining: "It is a permissible inference from this evidence that the guideline had been properly adopted, since the application of the guideline likely would have encountered resistance had it not been properly adopted. Further support for proper adoption is found in the height guideline's long history of enforcement . . ." *Id.* at 821. Are you convinced by this reasoning?

The case law does recognize some ability to resist when the association's application of the rules has not been evenhanded. For example, what if the homeowners' association has acquiesced in prior violations of a provision, but now seeks to enforce that provision against an owner not involved in the previous violations? *See Ridgewood Homeowners' Ass'n v. Mignacca,* 813 A.2d 965 (R.I. 2003) (no waiver where "no evidence was presented that these infractions were brought to the attention of the association or its board as a whole, or that the association considered and declined to enforce the covenant"). A related possibility is the defense of laches. Additionally, courts sometimes will grant relief from covenants where there has been a "change in the circumstances and the neighborhood materially affecting the lands." *Marco Island Civic Ass'n, Inc. v. Mazzini,* 881 So. 2d 99, 101 (Fla. Ct. App. 2004) (rejecting argument that covenant restricting property to single-family residence of no more than two stories should no longer be followed). *See also Dumbarton Improvement Ass'n v. Druid Ridge Cemetery Co.,* 434 Md. 37, 73 A.3d 224 (2013) (rejecting "changed circumstances" defense and finding that original 1913 deed was still in effect requiring that 200 acres be maintained as a cemetery).

The covenants also often provide that the enforcing party may be able to recover its attorney's fees as well. *See Raman Chandler Properties, L.C. v. Caldwell's Creek Homeowners' Ass'n,* 178 S.W.3d 384 (Tex. Ct. App. 2005) (awarding fees in a dispute over an access easement). Thus, a homeowners' association may sue to enforce the CC&Rs and, if successful, recover fees from one of its members.

Do these holdings give too much weight to the property rights created by the covenant? If you think so, what rule should the court adopt? Should the court give more deference to the day-to-day interpretation of that use covenant by the affected landowners?

Covenants, easements, and the like are conceptually different from the types of public regulation of land use that we have spent our time on in this casebook. Most significantly, they allow parties to decide contractually how they wish to restrict their uses of land. As such, proponents argue that private land use arrangements promote freedom of individual choice in land use matters and are consistent with the market system. The growth in such developments has been rapid. As of 2015, the umbrella trade group representing "association-governed communities" estimated that by the end of 2016, there will be between 342,000 and 344,000 associations (up from 10,000 in 1970). About 68 million residents are governed by these associations. *See* https://www.caionline.org/AboutCommunityAssociations/Pages/StatisticalInformation.aspx (last visited Nov. 11, 2016). But as more and more developments become "privatized," critics have claimed that so-called private or "gated" communities have significant negative effects on society. Consider the following contrasting viewpoints.

■ SHERRYL D. CASHIN, PRIVATIZED COMMUNITIES AND THE "SECESSION OF THE SUCCESSFUL": DEMOCRACY AND FAIRNESS BEHIND THE GATE

28 Fordham Urb. L.J. 1675 (2001)

INTRODUCTION

In the twentieth century we became a nation of homeowners . . . Among this vast majority of American property owners is a significant and growing subset who live in common interest developments ("CIDs") . . . CIDs typically require owners who buy units in the development to pay monthly or annual fees to a residential association that manages common areas, provides desired services, and enforces rules or covenants that apply to all who live in the development. CIDs include planned unit developments of single-family homes, condominiums, and cooperative apartments. . . .

Among the services that homeowners associations typically provide, in exchange for mandatory fees paid by CID residents, are trash and snow removal, road maintenance, and recreational facilities. These private contractual arrangements for the provision of formerly "public" services have put the nation on a course toward civic secession. The wedge begins with the creation of a large class of property owners the members of which increasingly feel that they are paying twice — in the form of property taxes and residential association fees for privately administered services. This attitude threatens to predominate in the twenty-first century because in areas of rapid growth, most new residential developments now take the form of a CID.

I. SECESSION OF THE SUCCESSFUL — HOW CIDS ATTENUATE THE SOCIAL CONTRACT

A. Property Owner Consciousness

. . . A governance mechanism constructed primarily to protect and preserve private property rights does not build a sense of community. Instead, it cultivates an attitude that is a driving force animating property rights. . . .

The CID structure . . . doubly undermines the notion of citizenship and participation in a larger polity. First, participation in the CID is premised upon property ownership rather than the concept of one person, one vote, which demarcates a reduced, privatized sphere of fealty for the CID resident. Second, the civic or public realm within the CID is impoverished because the sole rationale for the homeowners association is protecting private property, and direct engagement with the CID community is not required to do this.

B. Homogeneity

Although homogeneity is not intrinsic to the CID concept, in practice CIDs tend to be highly homogeneous by income and race. Economic and racial selection is fueled by the practices of real estate developers and other actors in the real estate industry. Developers tend to tailor new planned developments to particular income brackets, and the real estate industry is notorious for racial steering that contributes to a high degree of racial segregation, particularly of African Americans. Because CIDs are becoming the norm in high-growth, developing areas, the widespread use of exclusionary zoning in such areas also contributes to the homogeneity of CIDs. . . .

As a result of this homogeneity, the possibility for cooperation between CID and non-CID communities is lessened. Homogeneity also decreases the potential for empathy with racial and economic groups that are not represented in the CID because of a lack of direct daily experience with such groups. Finally, where homogeneity is achieved, protecting it often becomes a primary rationale, which in turn may encourage CID residents to support exclusionary policies that limit certain opportunities for non-CID residents. . . .

II. CIVIC SECESSION AND THE POLITICAL ECONOMY

CIDs create a risk that, as more and more citizens separate themselves into homogenous private communities, their ties to the larger polity will become attenuated and they will increasingly resist governmental efforts to address problems that they do not perceive as "theirs." . . .

B. Structured Inequality

. . . To the extent that CIDs cultivate reduced empathy for persons or problems beyond the CID border, the most potent long-term impact of CIDs (and socioeconomic residential segregation) will be a reduced tax base for addressing the problems of the poor. Even at the federal level, where all U.S. taxpayers must participate, there is a risk of increasing resistance on the part of the CID class, and others geographically removed from the poor, to expending federal funds for redistributive aims.

Bringing CIDs or gates to poor or minority communities will not equalize the situation and, in some cases, it may even make matters worse. As noted, even affluent blacks are harmed by racial isolation. Organizing a racially isolated community through the creation of a CID is not likely to overcome the systematic disinvestment by whites and commercial actors that tends to accompany racial isolation, particularly of African Americans. In addition, empirical research on the impact of gating existing low-income communities suggests that such strategies had little impact. . . .

■ ROBERT H. NELSON, PRO-CHOICE LIVING ARRANGEMENTS REALITY CHECK
Forbes, June 14, 1999, 222

[An] episode of TV's X-Files featured a neighborhood association that threatens to kill a resident for having a burned-out lightbulb in the yard. The plot was over the top, as usual — but it reflects a growing, real-life fear about the power of residential neighborhood associations. Today 15% of Americans belong to condominium, cooperative or homeowner associations and one-third of new housing is being built under such private governance. . . .

As more Americans privatize their communities, I predict, the associations will want to control their social environments as well — ultimately trying to create whole neighborhoods of people of the same age, profession, sexual orientation, religion or even ethnic origin. How far will they be allowed to go?

The very idea of an exclusive community makes some civil libertarians cringe. What's next, they'd ask, racial covenants? These were rightly banned by the Supreme Court in 1948.

But while ruling out the kind of bigotry that once poisoned housing all across the country, we ought to be able to tolerate a lot more experimentation in voluntary homeowner groups than we do now. Freedom from racial discrimination is a basic American right — but so is freedom of association. . . .

Former Labor Secretary Robert Reich not long ago called the spread of private communities a "secession of the successful" from full participation in American life. But in a nation built on the strength and individuality of local communities, when was it decided — and by whom — that it is bad for people of the same background and interests to live together? Reich's thinking exemplifies the sour grapes attitude of the governing elite, worried it will have less control over other people's lives. . . .

Editorialists of all stripes complain that a sense of community is lost from American life. . . .

Private communities can help fill this void. To do so, they will have to be given greater legal powers to control their social environments and to insist that residents conform. . . .

To be clear: I am taking here about private residential communities, not municipalities. Public government should never favor a particular class of resident. People should never be made to leave their homes by any entity, public or private. And there are some forms of exclusion — based on physical handicap, for example — that must remain unacceptable in any context. But it would be a big mistake to reflexively ban all kinds of discrimination.

It is time to give community associations discretion, within reason, to choose members. Given the diversity of culture in this country, I am confident that few Americans would be unable to find a group of like-minded neighbors. In a society where people fear for their children's safety even at school, it is clear that a key institution for forming and defending ethical values — the local community — is in desperate shape. We must allow Americans the freedom to constitute their neighborhoods according to deeply felt personal bonds.

Given their spectacular growth, private regulation through covenants unquestionably has a large appeal. The following article suggests that even public communities have found ways to implement the kind of restrictions found in covenants.

■ HANNAH WISEMAN, PUBLIC COMMUNITIES, PRIVATE RULES
98 Geo. L.J. 697 (2010)

Although private covenanted communities in suburbs are quickly becoming the norm in housing, many individuals in existing, public neighborhoods want rules that are similar to private covenants: they demand similar means by which to structure their communities. Traditional zoning, however, fails to dictate desired community characteristics such as architectural style, and public neighborhoods cannot, practically, impose complex sets of private covenants on existing property owners. Several scholars have accordingly suggested that public communities should be able to form their own private homeowners' associations and covenants. Under this scenario, the private model would be transferred to the public realm.

The use of private covenants and associations to govern existing public neighborhoods has not taken hold, however. Instead, public communities have found other creative ways to implement covenant-type or "private" rules, which are like covenants because of their detailed restrictions on and requirements for property uses. And they have implemented these rules through the public process, forming, in addition to the private rule-bound subdivision, two types of public rule-bound communities. These communities have largely failed to capture the attention of the legal literature. First, in a growing number of old neighborhoods, communities are developing private-type rule-sets to preserve existing character. These rules often apply in addition to the base rules in the city-wide zoning code and are thus typically described as an "overlay." In "overlay communities," the city allows communities to write, as part of the overlay, sublocal rules that apply only to their neighborhood and are more detailed than the local government code. These rules are ultimately approved by the city government and incorporated into the city-wide zoning code, and they often aim for some of the following: to protect historic, cultural, environmental, commercial, or even industrial community resources; to require certain types of design for newly constructed or modified buildings; or to preserve building scale (sometimes in an effort to combat gentrification). As Richard Briffault explains, these types of regimes "impose rules tailored to the concerns of particular neighborhoods."

The second public type of rule-bound community is a hybrid: it uses both the private covenants that define suburban subdivisions and an overlay to the municipal zoning code to create a unique urban or inner-suburban ethos. This community is more traditionally referred to as an urban planned unit development, but this Article will call it a "hybrid community" to highlight its unique rule characteristics. Through hybrid communities, cities — in projects often initiated and led by a city redevelopment agency or a similar organization — work with a developer (or serve as the developer themselves) to raze and rebuild or substantially modify entire downtown blocks or old industrial properties in order to construct new urban environments. Once it has selected a site and a developer has committed to the project, the city outlines a vision for the community with the help of a long public input process. The city often includes affordable housing, "green housing" for the eco-conscious dweller, stores and businesses that are within easy walking distance of residences, a network of sidewalks and bike paths, and parks and other open space as part of this vision. The city government then writes and votes on overlay rules, which incorporate this vision and dictate the design of the development and uses permitted within it. The developer of the project constructs the community in accordance with the public overlay and passes ownership of the built area to a property owners' association, which in turn implements private covenants for the development. The covenants in a hybrid community are similar to the covenants in a suburban private covenanted subdivision, but they are often influenced by the unique urbanized vision of the public overlay.

Notes and Comments

1. *Cost Minimization and Social Capital.* One article identifies two principal arguments in favor of the "privatization" of land uses like that described in the excerpts above: (1) private production is assumed to be less costly due to the salutary impact

of market incentives on efficiency; and (2) privatization will enhance the level of "social capital" — i.e., the "features of social organization such as networks, norms, and social trust that facilitate coordination and cooperation for mutual benefit" — among members of a community. Dell Champlin, The Privatization of Community: Implications for Urban Policy, 32 J. of Econ. Issues 595 (1998). There is a strong argument that privatization should be preferred for economic efficiency reasons. *See* Clayton P. Gillette, Courts, Covenants, and Communities, 61 U. Chi. L. Rev. 1375, 1390 (1994).

Do you agree with these arguments? Are there other benefits of privatization that you see? What about allowing individuals to maximize their sense of security in an era in which public institutions are sometimes perceived as unable to prevent crime?

2. *Segregation.* Some have criticized gated communities as symbols of segregation. Consider the following excerpt:

> Meanwhile, critics have seized on gated communities as symbols of social segregation. Evan McKenzie, author of "Privatopia: Homeowner Associations and the Rise of Residential Private Government," thinks gates cause social and economic segregation the same way race-restricted covenants did in an earlier era. People who live in gated communities are saying that they don't support public services that support a community.

Lois M. Baron, The Great Gate Debate, 21 Builder Magazine, Mar. 1, 1998, at 92. Do you agree? If so, is the remedy to deny approval of gated communities? Interestingly, one article examined the case law and concluded that courts have generally ruled against gated communities in disputes with nonresidents of those communities over such issues as access. Ron Levi, Gated Communities in Law's Gaze: Material Forms and the Production of a Social Body in Legal Adjudication, 34 Law & Soc. Inquiry 635, 661 (2009).

What about the freedom of association that Professor Nelson advocates in his article? Since gated communities control access to the area, could they charge individuals for the right to enter the area? *See also* Laura T. Rahe, The Right to Exclude: Preserving the Autonomy of the Homeowners' Association, 34 Urb. Law. 521 (2002) (supporting the rights of homeowners' associations to exclude).

3. *Rights and the Appropriate Model.* One aspect of the debate is what exactly is the role of homeowners' associations in the governance of gated communities. There are a number of possible models: (1) the Corporate Model, because the powers, duties, and liabilities of the directors of organizations in the for-profit and nonprofit sectors are much the same; (2) the Trust Model, because the homeowners association performs duties that are analogous to that of a trustee; and (3) the Municipal Model, because the homeowners association performs many of the same duties as a local government. *See* Wayne S. Hyatt & Jo Anne P. Stubblefield, The Identity Crisis of Community Associations: In Search of the Appropriate Analogy, 27 Real Prop., Prob., & Trust J. 589, 622-641 (1993) (examining these and several other models). Which of these models, if any, seems to fit the homeowners association best?

How the law views the homeowners' associations (i.e., what "model" is appropriate) has important ramifications. For example, one author has suggested that, for constitutional purposes, courts should view residential associations as "state actors" under the state action doctrine. David J. Kennedy, Residential Associations as State

Actors: Regulating the Impact of Gated Communities on Nonmembers, 105 Yale L.J. 761 (1995). Which model does this view reflect?

In *Committee for a Better Twin Rivers v. Twin Rivers Homeowners' Ass'n*, 929 A.2d 1060 (N.J. 2007), the plaintiffs lived in a private, non-gated planned unit development covering approximately one square mile with a population of approximately 10,000 residents. They alleged that the Association "had effectively replaced the role of the municipality in the lives of its residents, and therefore the Association's internal rules and regulations should be subject to the free speech and free association clauses of the New Jersey Constitution." *Id.* at 1064. Among other allegations, they challenged a policy limiting signs to one per lawn and one per window. The New Jersey Supreme Court found no constitutional violation. *See also Watchtower Bible v. Sagardia de Jesus*, 634 F.3d 3 (1st Cir. 2011) (upholding the constitutionality of Puerto Rico's "Controlled Access Law," which allows neighborhoods to control vehicular and public access to neighborhoods while the streets remain public).

4. *Other Rights*. Homeowners' associations use an altered form of voting. Instead of "one person, one vote," voting is predicated on unit homeownership. Further, the manner of voting can be idiosyncratic, as democratic norms do not necessarily govern the boards that lead homeowners' associations. Is legislation needed here? Or, as the authors of a recent article suggested, would the institution of an auction work better in these circumstances? Abraham Bell & Gideon Parchomovsky, Governing Communities by Auction, 81 U. Chi. L. Rev. 1, 3 (2014) ("[W]ell-designed auctions can provide common-interest communities with a better decision-making mechanisms. An auction's main advantage over voting lies in its ability to reflect the intensity of participants' preferences. At the same time, auctions avoid many of the strategic manipulations and much of the minority oppression to which votes are prey.").

Are there constitutional rights that limit the rules that homeowners' associations can adopt? What about the Second Amendment's right to bear arms? Could a homeowners' association adopt a rule that bars residents from keeping weapons? Christopher J. Wahl, Comment, Keeping Heller out of the Home: Homeowners' Associations and the Right to Keep and Bear Arms, 15 U. Pa. J. Const. L. 1003 (2013).

5. *The "Freedom of Contract" Myth?* The restrictions imposed by homeowners' associations rest on a contractual model. By buying a unit subject to CC&Rs, owners voluntarily contract to be bound by the covenants that run with the land and the other rules imposed by a homeowners' association pursuant to those covenants. But is that assumption about individuals freely contracting simply a myth? One article argues:

> Courts unrealistically presume that purchasing property within a CIC [Common-Interest Community] is in itself an adequate manifestation of assent to be bound to CIC governing provisions. General deference to parties' substantive choices in contracting is proper. But freedom of contract is an inadequate justification for covenant enforcement in the context of privately governed communities. Such covenants do not necessarily represent voluntary owner assent to obligation and do not necessarily reflect neighborhood preferences. The covenants are perpetual, non-negotiable contracts of adhesion, bundled with one of the most personal, expensive, and complicated purchases an individual will ever make — the purchase of a home. As servitudes, CIC covenants enjoy duration and specific enforceability that go beyond typical contract rights . . .

Andrea J. Boyack, Common Interest Community Covenants and the Freedom of Contract Myth, 22 J.L. & Pol'y 767, 770 (2014). Do you agree? If so what is the appropriate legal response? The author argues for a multi-pronged approach including legislation of constitutional protections for members of CICs and requiring "bona fide, deliberate assent" before holding owners bound to CIC obligations." *Id.* at 772. Do those remedies constitute excessive interference with the right to contract? *See also* Ryan McCarl, When Homeowners Associations Go Too Far: Political Responses to Unpopular Rules in Common Interest Communities, 43 Real Est. L.J. 453 (2015) (discussing when legislatures are likely to intervene in disputes arising from actions by homeowners' associations).

6. *Privatization and Taxes.* Homeowners' associations, through the assessment of dues, provide benefits (street maintenance, street lighting, recreation facilities, and so forth) that municipalities normally provide and pay for through the assessment of property taxes. *See* Susan F. French, Making Common Interest Communities Work: The Next Step, 37 Urb. Law. 359 (2005) (by approving such projects "local government can escape the liability to maintain trees and parks or to provide other services that the homeowners can be made to provide for themselves"). *See Pheasant Run Condo. Homes Ass'n v. City of Brookfield,* 331 Wis. 2d 730, 795 N.W.2d 492 (App. 2011) (city allowed to treat private roads differently from public roads). Other differences in service exist. *See* Karen Gantt, Natural Disasters and Private Road Residents: When "And I'm a Taxpayer" Isn't Enough, 42 Real Est. L.J. 434 (Spring 2014) ("Condominium owners and others are also discovering that in the event of natural disasters they will not receive state or federal assistance like single family homeowners.").

The assumption has been that developers simply choose to build privatized developments. However, local laws increasingly compel developers — either directly or indirectly — to choose this form of development. Paula A. Franzese and Steven Siegel, Trust and Community: The Common Interest Community as Metaphor and Paradox, 72 Mo. L. Rev. 1111, 1112 (2007) (local laws now virtually compel them, largely as means of "load-shedding municipal functions and services"). Should local laws be neutral on this issue?

Residents may deduct such property taxes from their federal income taxes, thus receiving a tax benefit. Dues paid by those in homeowners associations, however, are not deductible. Does fairness require that those dues be made deductible?

7. *Privatization and the Environment.* Some recent disputes have concerned conflicts between regulations of homeowners associations and actions by individuals intending to benefit the environment. For example, some disputes have involved homeowners' attempts to use solar devices. *See* Sammy Roth, Homeowners Associations Make it Hard to go Solar, The Desert Sun (May 18, 2015) (stating that some homeowners' associations require members to pay application fees and deposits as large as $3000 to install solar equipment, while others make it difficult to install solar at all. A number of states now limit the ability of homeowners' associations to restrict the installation of solar-energy systems. *See Tesoro Del Valle Master Homeowners Ass'n v. Griffin,* 133 Cal. Rptr. 3d 167 (Ct. App. 2011) (upholding jury verdict finding that design guidelines of homeowner's association did not violate California Solar Rights Act, which prohibits restrictions that effectively prohibit the installation of a solar energy system).

D. BARGAINING: DEVELOPMENT AGREEMENTS

Another alternative method for land use decision making is bargaining. While bargaining has informally taken place in land use processes for decades, the principal modern vehicle using it is the development agreement. In *Bollech v. Charles County, Maryland*, 166 F. Supp. 2d 443 (D. Md. 2001), *aff'd* 69 Fed. Appx. 178 (4th Cir. 2003), the court adopted the following definition of the term:

> Development agreements are defined as agreements between a municipality and a developer under which site conditions may be imposed but the right to develop in compliance therewith is vested at least for a certain period of time.

166 F. Supp. 2d at 453 (internal quotations omitted). To begin looking at these agreements, whose use is rapidly expanding, we examine excerpts from Florida statutes authorizing local jurisdictions and developers to enter into such agreements.

■ FLORIDA STATUTES ANNOTATED
§§163.3223-163.3235 (2016)

163.3223. APPLICABILITY

Any local government may, by ordinance, establish procedures and requirements, as provided in §§163.3220-163.3243, to consider and enter into a development agreement with any person having a legal or equitable interest in real property located within its jurisdiction.

163.3225. PUBLIC HEARINGS

(1) Before entering into, amending, or revoking a development agreement, a local government shall conduct at least two public hearings. At the option of the governing body, one of the public hearings may be held by the local planning agency. . . .

(2) . . .

(b) The notice shall specify the location of the land subject to the development agreement, the development uses proposed on the property, the proposed population densities, and the proposed building intensities and height and shall specify a place where a copy of the proposed agreement can be obtained.

163.3227. REQUIREMENTS OF A DEVELOPMENT AGREEMENT

(1) A development agreement shall include the following:

(a) A legal description of the land subject to the agreement, and the names of its legal and equitable owners;

(b) The duration of the agreement;

(c) The development uses permitted on the land, including population densities, and building intensities and height;

(d) A description of public facilities that will service the development, including who shall provide such facilities; the date any new facilities, if needed, will be constructed; and a schedule to assure public facilities are available concurrent with the impacts of the development;

(e) A description of any reservation or dedication of land for public purposes;

(f) A description of all local development permits approved or needed to be approved for the development of the land;

(g) A finding that the development permitted or proposed is consistent with the local government's comprehensive plan and land development regulations;

(h) A description of any conditions, terms, restrictions, or other requirements determined to be necessary by the local government for the public health, safety, or welfare of its citizens; and

(i) A statement indicating that the failure of the agreement to address a particular permit, condition, term, or restriction shall not relieve the developer of the necessity of complying with the law governing said permitting requirements, conditions, term, or restriction.

(2) A development agreement may provide that the entire development or any phase thereof be commenced or completed within a specific period of time.

163.3229. DURATION OF A DEVELOPMENT AGREEMENT AND RELATIONSHIP TO LOCAL COMPREHENSIVE PLAN

The duration of a development agreement shall not exceed 30 years, unless it is extended by mutual consent of the governing body and the developer, subject to a public hearing in accordance with §163.3225. No development agreement shall be effective or be implemented by a local government unless the local government's comprehensive plan and plan amendments implementing or related to the agreement are in compliance with §163.3184 [setting forth the process for adoption of comprehensive plans or plan amendments].

163.3231. CONSISTENCY WITH THE COMPREHENSIVE PLAN AND LAND DEVELOPMENT REGULATIONS

A development agreement and authorized development shall be consistent with the local government's comprehensive plan and land development regulations.

163.3233. LOCAL LAWS AND POLICIES GOVERNING A DEVELOPMENT AGREEMENT

(1) The local government's laws and policies governing the development of the land at the time of the execution of the development agreement shall govern the development of the land for the duration of the development agreement.

(2) A local government may apply subsequently adopted laws and policies to a development that is subject to a development agreement only if the local government has held a public hearing and determined:

(a) They are not in conflict with the laws and policies governing the development agreement and do not prevent development of the land uses, intensities, or densities in the development agreement;

(b) They are essential to the public health, safety, or welfare, and expressly state that they shall apply to a development that is subject to a development agreement;

(c) They are specifically anticipated and provided for in the development agreement;

(d) The local government demonstrates that substantial changes have occurred in pertinent conditions existing at the time of approval of the development agreement; or

(e) The development agreement is based on substantially inaccurate information supplied by the developer. . . .

163.3235. PERIODIC REVIEW OF A DEVELOPMENT AGREEMENT

A local government shall review land subject to a development agreement at least once every 12 months to determine if there has been demonstrated good faith compliance with the terms of the development agreement. If the local government finds, on the basis of substantial competent evidence, that there has been a failure to comply with the terms of the development agreement, the agreement may be revoked or modified by the local government.

Notes and Comments

1. *The Benefits of Bargaining.* Development agreements offer significant benefits both to local jurisdictions and to developers. One recent article has flatly concluded that the "negotiated approach . . . is now the de facto dominant land use regime in contemporary land use law." Alejandro Esteban Comacho, Mustering the Missing Voices: A Collaborative Model for Fostering Equality, Community Involvement and Adaptive Planning in Land Use Decisions, 24 Stan. Envtl. L.J. 269, 270 (2005).

From the developer's perspective, the agreement provides certainty that the regulatory conditions for a project will not change as the project is implemented. From the local jurisdiction's viewpoint, the development agreement offers an attractive vehicle for funding infrastructure and other improvements in an era in which public funding has been curtailed. *See* Barry R. Knight & Susan P. Schoettle, Current Issues Related to Vested Rights and Development Agreements, 25 Urb. Law. 779, 788 (1993) ("[T]he developer obtains vested rights and a degree of certainty regarding the land development regulations applicable to his project while the local government receives assistance in the provision of public facilities and infrastructure and may achieve long-range planning goals such as open space conservation, water and air quality protection, environmental mitigation, and affordable housing.").

2. *Bargaining as a Function of Local Government.* Bargaining of the kind necessary to forge a development agreement differs significantly from other land use decision-making processes. In one article on the subject, a local member of the board of supervisors observed in commenting on a completed development agreement: "We wanted something developed there . . . but we wanted something beneficial to the city. It's no different from two large corporations getting together. We're just a municipal corporation." William Fulton, Building and Bargaining in California, Cal. Law. 37, 41 (Dec. 1984). Notice how that view of the local government's function in approaching a development agreement differs from the traditional view of local government regulating in the public interest.

An article by one of the casebook's authors has argued that the use of development agreements is transforming the land use process by challenging a series of underlying "norms" of the traditional land use system. For example, one of the underlying precepts of land use regulation is that governments must treat similarly situated applicants in the same fashion. The article argues that bargaining may undermine the norm:

> Adhering to the equal protection norm is difficult in the context of bargaining, as the variety of factors that play a role in negotiations can easily lead to disparate outcomes among similarly situated landowners. Perhaps most importantly, negotiating parties will not necessarily reach agreement at a single point. Instead, negotiation theory postulates a "bargaining zone" within which both parties will be satisfied, and the interplay of various factors determines where the parties will end up in that zone. For example, parties may differ in the bargaining resources that they bring to the table. If one developer has more information available than another in an otherwise comparable situation, the first developer is likely to have bargaining power superior to that of the second. Negotiating skills and styles also affect the outcome of negotiations, as do the parties' background situations, decision biases, personality differences, and emotions.
>
> These variables in the bargaining process render it likely that negotiated outcomes will differ on otherwise similar developments. . . .

Daniel P. Selmi, The Contract Transformation in Land Use Regulation, 63 Stan. L. Rev. 591, 628-29 (2011).

3. *Bargaining and Planning.* In earlier chapters, you have learned about the emphasis in many jurisdictions on the need for comprehensive planning to precede development. Is the notion of "bargaining" to reach an agreement inconsistent with the notion of comprehensive land use planning? Will the bargaining outcomes simply drive changes in the municipality's plans?

One expert has suggested that local politicians may be more eager to engage in bargaining for development agreements than in long-range planning because long-range, comprehensive planning, which necessarily involves somewhat abstract policies and objectives, "appears a less than useful exercise to many political leaders who win or lose elections by what they can achieve in two-year terms." Douglas R. Porter, The Relation of Development Agreements to Plans and Planning, in Development Agreements: Practice, Policy, and Prospects 149 (Douglas R. Porter & Lindell L. Marsh eds., 1989).

4. *Bargaining and Third Parties.* Earlier chapters of this casebook have noted the rise of third-party influence in land use decisions and examined the role that neighbors and citizens groups play in the process. Does the public's right to participate in any later public hearing at which the agreement is ratified provide sufficient participation for third parties? Presumably, third parties retain the right to challenge the adoption of the development agreement. *See Morra v. Grand County*, 230 P.3d 1022 (Utah 2010) (citizens had standing to challenge ordinance approving an amended development agreement).

5. *Bargaining and Democracy.* In *216 Sutter Bay Associates v. County of Sutter*, 68 Cal. Rptr. 2d 492 (Ct. App. 1997), the board of supervisors passed a general plan amendment allowing for large-scale development in the southern part of the county. Opponents then collected enough signatures to place a referendum on the general plan amendment on the ballot. In the meantime, elections had resulted in a new board majority opposing the plan amendment, and the new board members would take office on January 4, 1993.

In December 1992, the old board approved 18 development agreements based on the pro-growth general amendment. Then, "[f]or good measure, the old Board approved another development agreement on the morning of January 4, just hours before leaving office." 68 Cal. Rptr. 2d at 495. After the new board took office, it enacted a moratorium and repealed the development agreements, actions which the court upheld. Was the old board's use of the development agreement concept appropriate?

The political situation was somewhat similar in *Nicolet Minerals Co. v. Town of Nashville*, 641 N.W.2d 497 (Wis. Ct. App. 2002). Here, a local government reached agreement with a mining company granting it the required approvals. Public sentiment opposed the agreement, and the incumbent members of the board were then defeated. When the new board tried to rescind the agreement, the court upheld it.

Are these idiosyncratic situations, or do they illustrate any dangers that development agreements may pose? Is legislation to address these situations needed? If so, what should it say?

6. *Community Benefit Agreements.* A typical development agreement is negotiated between a municipality and a developer. It can be argued, however, that these negotiations — which may take place outside the public eye — do not capture the full spectrum of interests affected. Consider, for example, the large development proposed for the Atlantic Yards in Brooklyn. Citizens who live nearby can be greatly affected by such a large development. *See* Alejandro E. Camacho, Community Benefits Agreements: A Symptom, Not the Antidote, of Bilateral Land Use Regulation, 78 Brook. L. Rev. 355 (2013) (noting that bilateral development agreements limit participation opportunities for other affected parties).

One potential solution is a community benefit agreement. Such an agreement has been defined as "a legally binding contract (or set of related contracts), setting forth a range of community benefits regarding a development project, and resulting from substantial community involvement." Julian Gross, Community Benefits Agreements: Definitions, Values, and Legal Enforceability, 17 J. Affordable Housing & Community Dev. L. 35, 37 (2007/2008). The agreement is likely to result in a wide variety of benefits to the local community at large, such as job training and low-income housing. One article summarized the potential benefits as follows:

> (1) ensuring that the benefits of development projects inure to low-income citizens affected by the development, as well as to developers; (2) engaging community groups and encouraging civic participation in the development process; (3) holding developers responsible for adverse environmental impacts of development; and (4) allowing the land use approval process to be less contentious as potential opposition to a project is placated with negotiations over community benefits in exchange for project support.

Aaron McKean, Local Government Legislation: Community Benefits, Land Banks, and Politically Engaged Community Economic Development, 24 J. Affordable Housing & Community Dev. L. 133, 138 (2015).

While carrying out a community development agreement will make the development more expensive for the project proponent, it may result in increased support for the project, perhaps even avoiding litigation. Professor Comacho also suggests that the community benefit agreement would help "reorient[] the governmental authority to serve as mediator rather than negotiator of the land use conflict." *Id.* at 357. Do you think this reorientation would be a favorable development? Are multi-party negotiations for community benefits agreements feasible or too unwieldy to work well?

7. *Issues.* Negotiating development agreements requires a close reading of the statutes, like the Florida statutes set forth above, that authorize the local jurisdiction to enter into the agreement. Interestingly, although development agreements have been used extensively in some states, there are relatively few appellate opinions discussing them, and some key legal questions regarding their use remain unanswered. In particular, consider the following issues:

a. *Authority.* The statutes that you just read authorize local jurisdictions to enter into development agreements, although at least one court has upheld a local jurisdiction's ability to enter into an agreement without such authority. *See Giger v. City of Omaha*, 442 N.W.2d 182 (Neb. 1989). However, given the significant legal concerns that they raise, and their departure from traditional land use processes, entering into such agreements without explicit statutory authority is problematic.

In *Santa Margarita Area Residents Together v. San Luis Obispo County*, 100 Cal. Rptr. 2d 740 (Ct. App. 2000), the county and a developer signed a development agreement, following mediation, which froze zoning in return for the developer's commitment to submit a specific plan. The agreement specifically envisaged a second development agreement pertaining to actual construction. The court rejected plaintiff's contention that the agreement did not approve an "actual development project," reasoning that it "establishes the scope of the Project and precise parameters for future construction as well as procedure to process Project approvals." *Id.* at 745. The agreement had the effect of avoiding any initiative that might affect the property. Is that a valid use of the development agreement power?

b. *Vested Rights.* Agreements can give developers vested rights. *City of Golden v. Parker*, 138 P.3d 285, 294 (Colo. 2006) (finding that factors for a vested right were met where the right originated in a contract with a developer). From the developer's standpoint, perhaps the key issue is whether the local jurisdiction can later impose additional conditions on the project. At what point would those new conditions interfere with the vested rights guaranteed by the agreement? What do the Florida statutes say about this issue?

c. *Duration.* The duration of the agreement is another key issue. One thought to keep in mind is the possibility that the longer the term of the contract, the greater the chance that a court will find that the local government has "contracted away" the police power.

d. *Amendments.* In some instances the land that is the subject of the development agreement will later be annexed to a city (perhaps a newly formed city) that is not a party to the original agreement. Can the agreement itself bind the annexing city to its terms (particularly the promise not to impose conditions on the development not spelled out in the development agreement) if that city is not a signatory to the agreement? *See Home Builders Ass'n of Central Arizona v. City of Maricopa*, 158 P.3d 869 (Ariz. Ct. App. 2007) (city formed after county had entered in to a development agreement was bound by its provisions).

e. *Enforcement.* Who can enforce the agreements? Hawaii allows enforcement by any parties or by successors in interests. Haw. Rev. Stat. §46-127(a). Florida authorizes "any party or aggrieved or adversely affected person" to seek injunctive relief or challenge compliance with the development agreement statutes. Fla. Stat. Ann. §163.3243. In *Kansas City Hispanic Ass'n Contractors Enterprise, Inc. v. City of*

Kansas City, 279 S.W.3d 551 (Mo. Ct. App. 2009), the court ruled that a contractors association could not enforce a development agreement under a third-party beneficiary theory.

The negotiation and implementation of a development agreement involves a unique combination of private, common law contractual principles and public law governance principles, such as adherence to limitations on land use authority found in state law. The following case illustrates some of these problems.

■ SPRENGER, GRUBB & ASSOCIATES, INC. v. CITY OF HAILEY
903 P.2d 741 (Idaho 1995)

SILAK, Justice.

I. NATURE OF THE CASE

This appeal concerns a decision by the Hailey City Council to change the zoning classification of certain land owned by appellant Sprenger, Grubb & Associates (SGA) from "Business" to "Limited Business." SGA appealed to the district court, and the district court upheld the City Council's action. SGA again appeals. . . .

III. FACTS & PROCEDURAL BACKGROUND

In 1973, the City of Hailey and McCulloch Properties, Inc. (MPI), the predecessor to SGA, entered into a development agreement which provided for the annexation of 654 acres of MPI's property into the City and the development of a "master planned residential-recreational neighborhood." The property, today known as Woodside Subdivision (Woodside), consisted of certain areas specifically designated as residential areas, and other areas designated for business development. The subject of this appeal is 12.6 acres within Woodside, which had been classified as a Business District from 1973 until 1993, when the Hailey City Council adopted Hailey City Ordinance No. 623, rezoning the 12.6 acres to a Limited Business District. The 12.6 acres is completely surrounded by property zoned and developed as General Residential and is one and a half miles south of Hailey's downtown business area.

The MPI-Hailey development agreement set forth certain fees and obligations for MPI, ranging from cash contributions, to building a recreation center and a sewage treatment facility. Hailey has acknowledged that MPI fulfilled its obligations under the development agreement. Hailey's obligations under the agreement included the annexation and zoning of the Woodside property, along with other action to aid in the development of Woodside. Paragraph 9 of the development agreement provided that the agreement "shall inure to the benefit of and be binding upon HAILEY and upon MPI and upon its successors and assigns."

Since 1973, Hailey has grown and developed, including substantial development in various portions of Woodside. In 1977, MPI sold its interest in Woodside to SGA. SGA supported various favorable rezoning changes throughout Woodside from 1978 to 1989. In June 1991, the Hailey City Council annexed other properties located next to Hailey's downtown business area, and these properties were also classified as "Business District."

In 1990, Hailey's Mayor R. Keith Roark supported "downzoning" the 12.6 acres in Woodside based upon the property's distance from the "downtown business core." In July, 1990, the Hailey City Council amended its comprehensive plan, defining the existing business core as a discrete area demarcated by certain city streets within Hailey. The ordinance further prescribed that expansions of the Business and Limited Business Districts were to occur around the "existing core," as defined. The Hailey Planning and Zoning Commission (Zoning Commission) was requested to "downzone" the property in question from Business District to General Residential District in 1990 and again in 1992, and the Zoning Commission denied both requests. Later in 1992, Mayor Roark directed the City Planning and Zoning Administrator to request the Zoning Commission to rezone the 12.6 acres from Business to Limited Business District. Again, the Zoning Commission denied the request. The Zoning Commission decided that the existing Business District classification conformed to the City's comprehensive plan, and that the proposed zone change to Limited Business did not conform to the comprehensive plan.

The City Planning and Zoning Administrator appealed the Zoning Commission's decision to disallow the rezoning request. This appeal was heard by the Hailey City Council in July 1993, in conjunction with a public hearing. The public comment at the hearing was overwhelmingly in favor of rezoning the 12.6 acres in Woodside. At the hearing, SGA requested Mayor Roark to recuse himself from being the presiding officer on the basis of his alleged lack of impartiality. Mayor Roark denied that request. However, Mayor Roark did not vote at the July 1993 hearing because three City Council members were present, and it would be unnecessary for him to cast a tie-breaking vote.

At the conclusion of the hearing, the three attending Hailey City Council members unanimously voted to reverse the Zoning Commission's decision, and thus, to rezone (or downzone) the 12.6 acres in Woodside to Limited Business. Subsequently, in August 1993, the City Council issued its written Findings of Fact and Conclusions of Law, relative to its prior verbal decision rendered after the hearing. In its conclusions of law, the City Council concluded among other things that "the existence of a large retail commercial property outside the Hailey Business Core, as defined in the Hailey Comprehensive Plan, is not in accordance with the current Hailey Comprehensive Plan, adopted in 1983." . . . The district court upheld the City Council's action, and SGA again appeals. . . .

V. ANALYSIS

A. DEVELOPMENT AGREEMENT

SGA argues that the development agreement between the City and MPI was a binding contract, wherein the City agreed to a regulatory freeze, or to zone consistent with MPI's development plan. SGA contends the rezoning is a breach of the development agreement.

We have reviewed the provisions of the development agreement which SGA cites in support of its argument, and do not believe the development agreement created the claimed regulatory freeze. Paragraph 4(a) of the development agreement says generally that Hailey shall "take all other action as may be required by MPI to develop the annexed real property in accordance with the terms and provisions of the MPI Master Plan and this agreement." Paragraph 8, under the heading "Interpretation of Agreement" provides that "[i]t is understood that the development of the annexed real property in accordance with the terms of this Agreement and exhibits attached hereto shall be in substantial compliance with the MPI Master Plan. . . ." At most, these provisions seem to indicate the City's general agreement that the development will move forward in "substantial compliance" with the MPI Master Plan. At issue, therefore, is whether the City's rezoning action is *not* in substantial compliance with the MPI Master Plan.

We have reviewed the MPI Master Plan, which was attached as Exhibit A to the development agreement. The primary features of the planned 650 acre development included approximately 418 acres for residential lots, 22 acres of neighborhood parks, an 18-acre school site, and a 9-acre tennis club/recreation facility. About 32% of the gross area was to be open space, parks, greenbelts, and recreation areas. (Master Plan p. 5)

However, the MPI Master Plan also speaks of "[a]dequate commercial areas to serve the daily needs of the project's inhabitants." (MPI Master Plan p. 6) It mentions "[n]eighborhood convenience shopping locations designed to serve local residents within 'walking distance' to minimize needless vehicle traffic." (Master Plan p. 6) The "central commercial area" was located so as to "minimize pedestrians crossing a major street when walking from shop to shop." (Master Plan p. 7)

We conclude that the MPI Master Plan did envision a comparatively small commercial area for some "convenience shopping locations" for the "project's inhabitants." However, the MPI Master Plan did not foretell a major retail shopping center, such as a "K-Mart" or "Shopko." We believe that the Woodside development may proceed in "substantial compliance" with the MPI Master Plan despite Hailey's rezoning of the central commercial area to a Limited Business zone. Permitted uses within the Limited Business zone include: motels, boarding houses, professional offices, hospitals, medical clinics, daycare facilities, personal service establishments, churches, schools, and recreation facilities. (Hailey Ordinance No. 532, Section 4.5.2) Moreover, the Limited Business zone allows other "conditional uses" upon receipt of a conditional use permit, which include: convenience stores, service stations, pharmacies and medical supply stores, indoor restaurants, electrical and plumbing contractors, and garden supply nurseries. (Hailey Ordinance No. 532, Section 4.5.3) With such uses allowed in Woodside's central commercial area, we believe the development may proceed in substantial compliance with the MPI Master Plan. We do not find in either the development agreement or the MPI Master Plan any explicit language amounting to a "regulatory freeze" or an agreement for permanent zoning. Hence, we reject SGA's contention that Hailey breached the development agreement.

Having found no breach of a "regulatory freeze" or permanent zoning obligation in the development agreement, we need not decide whether such a provision could even be enforced against a City Council exercising its police powers many years later. *See Idaho Falls v. Grimmett,* 63 Idaho 90, 97, 117 P.2d 461, 464 (1941) (police power of a municipality cannot be bartered away even by express contract).

_____

Is a development agreement a binding contract, or is it just another form of land use regulation? Consider the following case:

■TOLL BROS., INC. v. BOARD OF CHOSEN FREEHOLDERS OF THE COUNTY OF BURLINGTON

194 N.J. 223, 944 A.2d 1 (N.J. 2008)

LONG, J.

[The Court first set forth a lengthy summary of the background of a development agreement, the subsequent changes to the project, and the developer's request to be relieved of its contractual obligation in the agreement to pay more than its pro rata share of improvements.]

II

Toll Brothers argues that the MLUL [Municipal Land Use Law] prohibits exactions from a developer that are not necessitated by its project; that irrelevant or disproportionate conditions cannot be imposed as a basis for approval; that that rule is equally applicable to a developer's agreement, which is nothing more than an implementing tool with no independent enforceability; and that, in light of the reduction of its project by 870,000 square feet, it is entitled to apply to the County Planning Board for a concomitant reduction in its share of the road improvements based on changed circumstances. According to Toll Brothers, it only agreed to the conditions when its original plan for 1.2 million square feet of development was still in effect, and it immediately sought relief from the conditions when its position materially changed. Finally, it argues that the County always knew that any imposed conditions were subject to change if the scope of the project was materially altered and, therefore, the County could not reasonably have relied on the conditions or the developer's agreement in dealing with other applicants.

The County's argument, in essence, is that the developer's agreement is a binding contract, separate from the conditions of approval; that unlike the conditions of approval, the developer's agreement is not subject to the constraints in the MLUL or to a changed circumstances analysis; that even if changed circumstances can be advanced, only complete abandonment of a project warrants relief; that Toll Brothers cannot establish that traffic conditions generated by its present plans do not require the improvements; and that Toll Brothers continually represented its willingness to complete the road improvements, as a result of which the County changed its position vis-à-vis later developers to its detriment. For all those reasons, the County argues that Toll Brothers is barred from relief. . . .

[I]t is beyond dispute that under the MLUL, a planning body may not condition site plan approval on a developer paying for improvements that are unconnected to its development, or if connected, paying an amount that is disproportionate to the benefits conferred on the developer. . . .

A "developer's agreement" is a contract between a developer and a public authority that details the manner in which the conditions of approval will be fulfilled. Although not mentioned in the MLUL except in connection with general development plans under *N.J.S.A.* 40:55D-45.2(1), "the practice of entering into developer's agreements on developments not covered by the statute has become common and has been recognized by some courts." . . .

The principal benefit of the developer's agreement is its ability to foster cooperation between public and private entities and to insure a common understanding and predictability within the development process. Such agreements provide obvious advantages for both contracting parties. For developers, they offer an opportunity to negotiate with municipalities, which, in turn, is thought to lower the costs of development and to allow developers to plan well in advance of final approval. Shelby D. Green, *Development Agreements: Bargained-For Zoning That Is Neither Illegal Contract Nor Conditional Zoning*, 33 *Cap. U.L. Rev.* 383, 394 (2004). In a word, such agreements smooth the development process and presumably limit strife over the nuts and bolts of the actual construction of the off-tract improvements.

By its very nature, a developer's agreement is not, as the County contends, an independent contractual source of obligation. Indeed, as the developer's agreement in this case expressly declares, its purpose is to help carry out the conditions imposed by the Board: "It is the desire of the County and the Applicant to enter into this agreement in order to *more clearly define the responsibilities and obligations of the Applicant in completing the improvements required by the Planning Board* in connection with the above referenced development." (Emphasis added.)

That language is emblematic of the fact that a developer's agreement is an ancillary instrument, tethered to the conditions of approval, and exists solely as a tool for the implementation of the resolution establishing the conditions. Accordingly, if the resolution establishing the conditions remains in effect, the developer's agreement can be enforced. However, if the resolution changes, the developer's agreement enjoys no independent status and must be renegotiated. In essence, the continued vitality of the resolution is an implied condition in the developer's agreement, the failure of which will nullify that agreement because it eliminates the possibility that the fundamental purpose for which the developer's agreement was created will be attained. *Edwards v. Leopoldi*, 20 *N.J.Super.* 43, 89 *A.2d* 264 (App. Div.), *certif. denied*, 10 *N.J.* 347, 91 *A.2d* 671 (1952).

To suggest, as the County does, that the developer's agreement should somehow bar Toll Brothers from making the changed circumstances application that the MLUL recognizes misconceives the relationship between the conditions and the developer's agreement; it is the developer's agreement that is dependent on the conditions and not vice versa. Likewise, although the County correctly asserts that a contract generally is not subject to a changed circumstances analysis, that argument misses the point. It is the resolution that the MLUL subjects to modification based on changed circumstances. Depending on the outcome, the developer's agreement stands or falls. In short, we do not view the ancillary developer's agreement as a bar to Toll Brothers' application for modification of the resolution setting the conditions of approval.

If we were to conclude otherwise and bar Toll Brothers from returning to the Board for modification, the effect would be to approve public entities and developers entering into "voluntary" agreements in violation of the specific provisions of the MLUL. Such an approach cannot be countenanced.

Although we have not previously confronted the issue of the greater than pro-rata exactions in developer's agreements head on, in *Swanson v. Planning Board of Hopewell*, 149 *N.J.* 59, 692 *A.2d* 966 (1997), which we dismissed on timeliness grounds, Justice Stein, joined by Justices Handler and O'Hern, laid the groundwork for our analysis of the issue. Noting that the policies underlying *N.J.S.A.* 40:55D-42 require developers "to contribute to the cost of off-site improvements to only those improvements the need for which arose as a direct consequence of the particular subdivision or development under review," Justice Stein stated that municipalities making zoning decisions "subject to influence by a payment from a developer substantially in excess of any amount that lawfully could have been imposed is fundamentally incompatible with the principles underlying the MLUL." *Id.* at 64-65, 66, 692 A.2d 966. "[A] developer's voluntary contribution to defray the cost of a municipal obligation, should not be permitted to influence or affect municipal zoning decisions." *Id.* at 66, 692 A.2d 966. He went on: "Our case law has been extremely sensitive to the threat presented by unlawful exactions imposed by a municipality on developers whether the developers are reluctant or enthusiastic participants in the transaction" and warned that "municipal officials must be scrupulously careful to avoid the imposition of conditions of approvals of development applications that, even though acceptable to the applicants, could not be imposed without their consent." *Id.* at 67, 68, 692 A.2d 966.

Authorizing off-tract improvements beyond a developer's pro-rata share through the guise of "volunteerism" is problematic from many perspectives. At heart, it fails to provide an adequate safeguard against municipal duress to procure otherwise unlawful exactions because the line between true volunteerism and compulsion is a fragile one. *Nunziato v. Edgewater Planning Bd.*, 225 *N.J.Super.* 124, 133-34, 541 A.2d 1105 (App. Div. 1988) ("Without legislated standards the possibilities for abuse in such negotiations between an applicant and a regulatory body, no matter how worthy the cause, are unlimited."); *Marlboro Twp. v. Holmdel Planning Bd.*, 279 *N.J.Super.* 638, 653 A.2d 1183 (App. Div.), *certif. denied*, 141 *N.J.*98, 660 A.2d 1196 (1995) (admonishing illegal exactions as potential trade-offs for approval) . . .

Indeed, it is hard to explain why a private developer would offer more than its fair share contribution without a *quid pro quo*. In addition to the problem of compulsion, so-called voluntary contributions are not much different than a pay-to-play system, where developers are rewarded for their "philanthropic" gifts. Allowing such a scheme not only impacts the developers willing to pay, but threatens the livelihood of those unable or unwilling to submit to the illicit exaction toll . . .

Most importantly, even if materially disproportional contractual exactions could be categorized as purely voluntary, they would be unenforceable insofar as they plainly violate the nexus and proportionality requirements in the MLUL that serve as the Legislature's check on a municipality's limited planning power. The exercise of that power must conform with the MLUL even if embodied in a contract; a developer and a municipality cannot do by contract what the statute prohibits. *Houston Petrol. Co. v. Auto. Prods. Credit Ass'n, Inc.*, 9 *N.J.* 122, 129, 87 A.2d 319 (1952) ("A municipality cannot act as an individual does. It must proceed in conformity with the statutes, or in the absence of statute agreeably to the common law, by ordinance or resolution or emotion. . . . Especially this is so where real property is concerned. . . ." (quoting *Anschelewitz v. Belmar*, 2 *N.J.* 178, 183, 65 A.2d 825 (1949))); *Twp. of Hopewell v. Gruchowski*, 29 *N.J.Super.* 605, 610, 103 A.2d 177 (Law Div. 1954) ("The township may not do by indirection that which it cannot do by direction."). In short, the County cannot look to the developer's agreement to insulate it from a changed circumstances application. If the MLUL would bar the County from imposing full responsibility for the relocation of the Centerton Road/Creek Road intersection on Toll Brothers, the developer's agreement can have no contrary effect.

Notes and Comments

1. *Terms.* As the *Sprenger* case demonstrates, from the parties' perspective the actual terms of the agreement are critical. Another example is found in *River's Edge Investments, LLC v. City of Bend*, 265 P.3d 786 (Or. Ct. App. 2010). There a developer alleged that the city had breached a development agreement by imposing certain "system development charges" when the developer constructed a convention facility. The court had to construe two "competing contract provisions" that dealt specifically with fees. One of them declared: "When building permit applications are filed for all or any portion of the Proposed Development, the applicant shall pay and the City shall collect the System Development Charges . . . in effect at the time of each application." The court rejected the developer's assertion that the provision merely spoke to "timing" and held it required payment of the fees.

Compare Country Meadows West P'ship v. Village of Germantown, 614 N.W.2d 498 (Wis. Ct. App. 2000) (village exceeded the scope of the parties' subdivision agreements when it imposed fees for parks, libraries, storm and sewage treatment systems, fire and police protection facilities, and emergency medical facilities that were not set forth in the agreements) *with First State Bank v. Town of Omro*, 366 Wis. 2d 219, 873 N.W.2d 247 (Ct. App. 2015) (development agreement did not preclude the town from levying a special assessment on lots for road completion where the developer had defaulted on the agreement and the subdivision's roads remained unfinished ten years later).

The *Sprenger* case continued on. The city thereafter voted to amend the city's zoning to redesignate the property in question from "B" to "GR"—general residential. In *Sprenger, Grubb & Associates*, 936 P.2d 343 (Idaho 1999), the Idaho Supreme Court invalidated the action because the general plan did not meet the statutory requirements. *See* discussion of planning and consistency in Chapter 5.

2. *Project Size.* Would you expect large, multi-year and multi-phased developments or small developments to be the subject of the most development agreements? Given the certainty that such agreements provide to developers, one might expect that only the first category of projects would employ development agreements as a vehicle for approval, since these types of long-term developments are more in need of protection against later regulatory changes. Some early empirical evidence, however, indicates that such agreements are often used for smaller projects as well. *See* Richard Cowart, Experience, Motivations, and Issues, in Development Agreements: Practice, Policy and Prospects 26 (Douglas R. Porter & Lindell L. Marsh eds. 1989) (survey collecting over 100 development agreements in California and reviewing a sample of 40 projects in detail "showed a wide variety of types of projects, size of projects, and provisions in the agreements").

3. *"Contracting Away the Police Power."* In Chapter 2 of this casebook, you learned that one of the principal concerns with contract zoning was the objection that such zoning "contracted away" the city's police power. The same objection can be raised with respect to development agreements. There are now a few related decisions on this issue. *See Morgran Co., Inc. v. Orange County*, 818 So. 2d 640, 643 (Fla. Dist. Ct. App. 2002) ("The problem in this case lies with Orange County's obligation to 'support' Morgran's request for rezoning, as part of that development agreement. If the Board . . . has already contracted to 'support' Morgran's request for rezoning, it has invalidly contracted away its discretionary power. . . ."); *P.C.B. Partnership v. City of Largo*, 549 So. 2d 738 (Fla. Dist. Ct. App. 1989) (overturning an agreement

entered into prior to the state's development agreement statute on the grounds that the local government had contracted away its police powers).

4. *Contractual Complexity.* As cities and developers have become more acquainted with development agreements, those agreements have grown more complex and lengthier. Negotiating a comprehensive agreement can take a significant period of time, and the skills required—both legal and non-legal—are considerable. For a sample of a full development agreement, see Theodore C. Taub, Redevelopment, Development Agreements, and Protecting the Public In the Public-Private Partnership, Am. L. Inst.-Am. Bar Assn. Land Use Institute (August 25-27, 2005) (Westlaw citation SL005 ALI-ABA 773), App. A.

5. *Breach.* Although development agreements are contracts, they have significant public policy ramifications associated with them. If a party breaches a contract, what should the remedy be? In *City of Hollywood v. Diamond Parking, Inc.*, 950 So. 2d 472 (Fla. Ct. App. 2007), the court of appeal reversed a trial court judgment of $1 million against the city for breach of contract. The appeal turned on whether the developer had obtained a financial commitment within one year, as the contract required.

The municipality fared quite differently in *Mammoth Lakes Land Acquisition v. Town of Mammoth Lakes*, 120 Cal. Rptr. 3d 797 (Ct. App. 2011). After signing a development agreement, the town "changed its priorities and no longer wanted the hotel/condominium project." *Id.* at 802. The court of appeal affirmed a jury verdict for $30 million in damages. The developer also received over $2.3 million in attorney's fees. The court of appeal rejected a variety of defenses offered by the town, including that the town had "retracted" any repudiation of the contract and that the developer had not exhausted its administrative remedies. *See also Leon County v. G.J. Gluesenkampf, Jr.*, 873 So. 2d 460 (Fla. Ct. App. 2004) (a party's contractual obligation is discharged when the party's performance of the contract is prevented by governmental order).

Can you think of any mechanism for a city (or a developer, for that matter) to protect itself from a large damage award if the agreement is breached? Could the agreement preclude a damage award?

6. *Arbitration.* Like many commercial contracts, a development agreement can contain an arbitration clause. These provisions raise a number of questions. First, what disputes are actually subject to arbitration? In *Naumes, Inc. v. City of Chelan*, 339 P.3d 504 (Wash. Ct. App. 2014), a dispute arose over a proposed modification of a site plan after a development agreement was signed, and the developer argued that the dispute was subject to arbitration. The court held it was not, and that the developer had to pursue the normal administrative appeal process.

More broadly, can the city subject itself to binding arbitration concerning disputes? Or has it literally "contracted away" the police power through such mechanisms, if the end result of the arbitration is an outcome that the city's elected officials disagree with?

7. Nollan, Dolan, *and* Toll. Do the Supreme Court's *Nollan* and *Dolan* decisions, which you read in Chapter 7, constrain the types of exactions that a local government can negotiate with a developer? Or does the fact that the agreement is "voluntary" free the parties from the constitutional constraints that would otherwise apply if the exactions were imposed as conditions on a development approval? Most development agreements have proceeded on the assumption that

Nollan and *Dolan* are not binding, and to date no case law has developed on the point. Would you expect any? Who would have the incentive to challenge such provisions?

One article suggests, "[a] respectable case can be made for the proposition that development agreements quite simply constitute a novel packaging of regulatory requirements, one that implicates very little contract doctrine." Judith Welch Wegner, Moving Toward the Bargaining Table: Contract Zoning, Development Agreements, and the Theoretical Foundations of Government Land Use Deals, 65 N.C. L. Rev. 957, 1000 (1987). If a development agreement is less like a contract and more like traditional regulation, the constitutional restrictions in *Nollan* and *Dolan* cannot be dismissed so easily. Furthermore, is it really accurate to conclude, as suggested above, that the development agreement does not guarantee the right to develop? *See* James D. Brown, Biophilic Laws: Planning for Cities with Nature, 34 Va. Envtl. L.J. 52, 61-62 (2016) (suggesting that cities "need to give careful consideration to the requirement of takings jurisprudence for a rational nexus" in crafting development agreements).

An additional problem, after the Supreme Court's decision in *Koontz v. St. Johns River Water Mgmt. Dist.*, 133 S. Ct. 2856 (2013), is whether pre-contract negotiations might be used as evidence in a later takings claim. *See* discussion of *Koontz* in Chapter 7.

8. *A Premium on Negotiating.* In *The Guidiville Rancheria of California v. United States*, 5 F. Supp. 3d 1142 (N.D. Cal. 2013), a city signed a development agreement with Upstream Point Molate, LLC, granting the company the right to negotiate for development of a casino on Indian land. The company was required to make, and did make, payments to secure this right. After a series of events, and a settlement of an earlier lawsuit, the city refused to approve the project because of adverse environmental impacts identified in environmental impact report. The court rejected a suit for breach of contract. It found:

> The terms of the LDA [Land Development Agreement] itself gave the City discretion to approve, or disapprove, the Casino Project and any Alternative Project. While Upstream argues that the LDA is "sales contract" not an "options agreement," the plain terms of the LDA state that the transfer of the property to Upstream is "on and subject to the terms, covenants and conditions set forth herein." (LDA §1.1(a).) One of those conditions was CEQA review and approval, with ultimate approval authority vested in the City. The payments made by Upstream to the City were categorized in the LDA as "Non-refundable Consideration," earned by the City in exchange for Upstream's right to continue working to get the Casino Project approved, not for any particular outcome. (LDA §1.2.) None of those funds were recoverable by Upstream in the event the Casino Project was disapproved by the City or any other party, "or if the [Casino] Project otherwise bec[a]me[ ] legally or economically infeasible." (LDA §2.2.)

Id. at 1151-52.

The court later awarded the city $1,927,317.50 in attorneys' fees based upon the contract. *The Guidiville Rancheria of California v. United States*, 2015 WL 4934408 (N.D. Cal. 2015). As this book was going to press, that matter was being appealed.

What went wrong here? If you represented the developer, how would you avoid this outcome?

E. DISPUTE RESOLUTION: MEDIATION

The increasingly controversial nature of land use has led to an explosion of litigation over many highly controversial decisions. This litigation has overwhelmingly addressed the procedural regularity of the approval process, not the underlying concerns of the plaintiff. Moreover, like other forms of litigation, land use litigation has caused delays in project implementation even if it is ultimately unsuccessful.

This model of opposition has caused commentators to suggest that alternative means of resolving the disputes would result in better outcomes for all parties. The following materials discuss the primary method suggested: mediation.

The attractiveness of mediation in this context is obvious. It can lead to a mutually agreeable compromise or settlement, which will save the costs and attendant delay of litigation. Given these benefits, although mediation is growing, why isn't it used more widely in land use disputes? Keep this fundamental question in mind as you review the following materials.

■ SEAN NOLON, ONA FERGUSON, AND PAT FIELD, THE MUTUAL GAINS APPROACH TO RESOLVING LAND USE DISPUTES
In *Land in Conflict: Managing and Resolving Land Use Disputes (2013)*

POWER AND RIGHTS CANNOT RESOLVE COMPLEX DISPUTES

When a community is faced with disputes on land use, the interactions between stakeholders provide valuable lessons to help us understand how disputes are managed. A decision-making system is "a coordinated set of processes or mechanisms that interact with each other to prevent, manage, and/or resolve disputes" (Bordone 2008, 2). The processes of land use decision-making systems can vary in efficiency, effectiveness, and satisfaction. According to the field of dispute system design, there are three principal approaches to resolving disputes (Ury, Brett, and Goldberg 1988; Costantino and Sickles Merchant 1996).

- Rely on power. Use one's leverage to force or coerce someone to act.
- Adjudicate rights. Rely on an arbiter to decide who is right. Set up adjudicatory processes to determine who has legally enforceable rights and who does not.
- Reconcile interests. Try to satisfy needs, concerns, and fears of everyone involved. These approaches help us analyze the limitations of the systems used to resolve land use disputes. Most land use systems are designed to adjudicate rights, not reconcile interests. Power- and rights-based systems are less likely to produce durable outcomes because results can be overturned when the power balance changes. In local communities, the power balance is always shifting with new elections and court challenges. While power and rights approaches may allow for quick decisions, the results of those decisions are not likely to last or satisfy many of the people involved, and they might be challenged through administrative and judicial appeals. These approaches often destroy relationships among the involved parties by creating winners and losers and by fostering mistrust and hostility.

Projects and decisions that require long-term implementation depend on the support of a wide range of stakeholders beyond the current elected officials to ensure their sustainability over time. These are the decisions that are appropriate for processes that reconcile interests.

The vast majority of land use decisions are easy to make. Does a landowner's request to build an addition fit within the zoning ordinance? Does the request for an area variance meet the requirements of the statute? Is the lighting proper? Is there enough off-street parking? From a systems perspective, most decisions are appropriately and efficiently handled by adjudicating rights. The standard, required process is a rights based, adjudicatory process.

However, with some significant and complex decisions, parties have many interests that are not likely to be addressed in a rights-based approach. In addition, the questions raised in complicated decisions present many interconnected issues. These "polycentric" disputes make it difficult, if not impossible, for a board or a judge to find common ground. For example, can public access to a waterfront be enhanced while ensuring a successful, private development? Can new uses support or enhance adjacent, current land uses? Can new development contribute to the tax base for an entire community? These are questions that are better answered by the most-affected stakeholders through interest-based processes. If the board assumes the rights- based process is appropriate in more complex decisions, it will likely miss an opportunity to reconcile numerous, important community interests.

Communities have a choice when it comes to process: they can continue using the rights-based, required process for all types of decisions, which may deter people from participating, create deep divides among segments of the community, and overlook opportunities for creative problem solving; or they can use a different process appropriate for the nature of the decision being made.

■ EDITH M. NETTER, USING MEDIATION TO RESOLVE LAND USE DISPUTES
15 Zoning & Plan. L. Rep. 25, 27-28 (April 1992)

WHEN AND WHY SHOULD MEDIATION BE USED? . . .

Any case can be mediated if the parties have something to gain from settling instead of going to trial and if each has something it can offer the other side. The attorneys or their clients also must believe that negotiations will not be successful without the assistance of a third party. Since many attorneys are (or consider themselves to be) skilled negotiators, why use a mediator? Circumstances where mediation is useful include where:

1. there is a history of failed negotiations between the attorneys or their clients;
2. the attorney is having difficulty convincing his or her client that the case is not as "good" as the client makes it out to be;
3. the outcome of the case is uncertain and it makes sense, therefore, to retain control.

Mediation also can be used before a permit is issued or a zoning ordinance or plan is created. It should be considered where negotiation already is being used and is deemed appropriate from legal and policy vantage points. The following example illustrates how mediation can be beneficial where a developer submits an application for a controversial development approval. In this example, the neighbors vehemently oppose the proposed project, which includes twenty-five residential buildings. They say they will agree not to oppose a project with ten or fewer buildings. A mediation process is commenced at the suggestion of the city planner. The mediator, brought in by the planner because he foresees considerable controversy over the proposed project, involves the developer, the neighbors, and the planner in a negotiation process. The developer then agrees to revise the plan so that it now provides for a mixed-use project (mostly residential with some commercial), which includes ten buildings and a new site design. The developer is satisfied with the result because the commercial uses would provide a higher return on his investment than would the residential uses alone. The neighbors have agreed not to oppose the project because it is less dense, there is more green space, and the site design reflects the characteristics of the community. The developer then submits the revised plan for special permit approval. The public hearings are held, the neighbors do not oppose and the project is approved with some modifications.

The period before an application is submitted is one stage in the development review process where mediation can occur. Another could be after the permit application is made. Whereas a mediation that occurs before an application is submitted may lead to a developer revising an application, the parties to a post-application mediation process must understand that the decision-making entity still has the authority to approve, deny, or modify the plans. In both instances, mediation is being used to supplement the public hearing process instead of as an alternative to litigation. Regardless of the point at which mediation occurs (so long as it is before a decision is made), it offers the following advantages:

- Positions have not hardened. At this juncture it is easier to engage in joint problem-solving.
- Improved communications and creative problem-solving. Often public hearings do not offer opportunities for meaningful dialogue. More often than not, the parties are showcasing their positions for the benefit of the media.
- Cost savings. If parties are invested in the process that leads to settlement and they feel the decision is satisfactory, they will not bring a lawsuit.
- Improved community relationships. If parties are satisfied with an outcome, they are more likely to work cooperatively in the future.
- Less political fallout. Where a project or policy is controversial, a mediated outcome will mean board members are still responsible for the decision, but there has been a process, in addition to the public hearing, which has carefully taken into account divergent points of view.

The disadvantages of using mediation include that the decision-makers may not accept the recommendation that arises out of the mediation process or that they may accept the recommendation because they want consensus, not because it promotes the public interest as reflected in the underlying regulatory scheme.

In the pre-permit setting, mediation should be considered for those land use disputes that allow discretion on the part of decision-makers. A good example of a discretionary or flexible permitting process is a planned unit development (PUD). Typically involving some combination of a zone change, special permit and site plan review, PUDs are designed to allow decision-makers a great deal of flexibility when they make decisions. There is room, therefore, to negotiate so long as the negotiations remain within the confines of the permit standards. Other types of permits, such as variances, do not allow for discretion. A decision on a variance concerns whether or not a project meets a statutory standard of hardship. Either the standard is or is not met, so negotiation should not be considered. On the other hand, there are many instances where land use decision-making involves considerable discretion and therefore, provides opportunities for negotiation.

Special permits also may be appropriate for mediation. For example, a special permit standard stating that developments shall be "in harmony with the neighborhood" can be interpreted in different ways. . . . Considerable leeway is left for negotiation, if a commission chooses to do so. Another example is a garden-variety rezoning, such as a change from residential to commercial. Here planning commissions, when rendering advice to local legislative bodies, such as city councils, generally have a great deal of discretion. In this context, the use of a mediator to resolve disputes between various factions in the community may not only be appropriate but beneficial as well.

Notes and Comments

1. *Role Conflicts.* What role does a mediator play? Is the mediator strictly neutral? Or does she assess positions, give opinions, and otherwise take actions in an attempt to move the parties? *See* Lela P. Love, The Top Ten Reasons Why Mediators Should Not Evaluate, 24 Fla. St. U. L. Rev. 937, 938 (1997) (arguing that an "evaluative" mediator — one who "gives advice, makes assessments, states opinions . . . including opinions on the likely court outcome, proposes a fair or workable resolution to an issue or the dispute, or presses the parties to accept a particular resolution" — plays a role that is inconsistent with the role of a mediator). On the other hand, shouldn't a mediator be able to suggest a "workable resolution," as long as the parties trust the mediator's impartiality?

A Florida law, the Florida Land Use and Environmental Dispute Resolution Act, enables the appointment of a "special magistrate." The magistrate's "first responsibility" is "to facilitate a resolution of the conflict between the owner and the governmental entities" by acting as a "facilitator or mediator." If an acceptable solution is not reached, however, the magistrate is to "determine whether the action by the governmental entity . . . is unreasonable or unfairly burdens the real property." Fla. Stat. Ann. §70.51(a). Is this combination of roles workable?

2. *Mediation v. Litigation.* Lawyers representing clients in a land use dispute often will not consider the possibility of using mediation to settle the dispute. One article catalogued a series of reasons why settling a land use case is difficult, among them: (1) unlike civil actions amenable to settlement by payment of a sum of money, land use cases do not typically present an unlimited array of obvious compromise solutions; (2) because municipal officials are politically accountable, they may choose to avoid the political consequences of settling with a developer;

(3) zoning law inhibits the municipality's power to offer a settlement that changes the land use restrictions on the plaintiff's property; and (4) neighbors might challenge any such settlement. Stewart E. Sterk, Structural Obstacles to Settlement of Land Use Disputes, 91 B.U. L. Rev. 227, 229 (2011).

Still, the use of mediation in such disputes appears to be on the rise. One article, based on research conducted between 2003 and 2006, identified 27 land use dispute resolution programs. Twenty were state level programs, often authorized by state statutes, while seven are local or community based programs. The issues addressed by the programs fall into four categories: (1) disputes over site-specific issues; (2) disputes occurring during the process of comprehensive planning and growth management; (3) disputes from conflicts between agencies and levels of government; and (4) disputes that focus on natural resources and conservation. The programs differ in who is allowed to participate in the mediation process. Matthew McKinney, Patrick Field, and Sarah Bates, Responding to Streams of Land Use Disputes: A Systems Approach, 60 Plan. & Envtl. L. No. 4 (April 2008) 3-4. *See also* Jonathan M. Davidson & Susan L. Trevarthen, Land Use Mediation: Another Smart Growth Alternative, 33 Urb. Law. 705 (2001) (discussing numerous examples of mediated land use disputes); Jon Murray, Denver Moves Ahead with Aerotropolis Planning While Mediation Underway, The Denver Post (Jan. 5, 2015). And a few cities have enacted mediation programs for land use disputes. *See* http://www.encinitasca.gov/index.aspx?page=475 (last visited Nov. 11, 2016) ("With actions on December 9, 2015 and January 13, 2016, the Encinitas City Council approved a voluntary mediation program for general dispute cases and land use/development cases for a one-year period.").

3. *Choosing Mediation.* Consider also the following comparison of a case settled by mediation with another case that is being litigated. Both cases occurred in Oregon:

Bott's Marsh

The Bott's Marsh case is a dispute over the development of a wetland area.... A developer proposed filling a wetland area large enough to allow for the development of a marina, motel-boatel, restaurant, shops and parking facilities. There has been much opposition, which so far has resulted in one trip to the Oregon Supreme Court....

Results: Time spent to date on obtaining permits has been seven years and five months. Costs to DSL in attorneys fees alone has been $12,665, and costs to the developer for attorney and consulting fees is estimated to be approximately $250,000.

Hedges Creek Marsh

This case involves the proposed development by Zidell Resources of a 140-acre parcel, including 48 acres of freshwater wetlands, into a residential and light industrial area. Tualitin's Wetlands Protection Ordinance required that before Zidell could get the city's approval of the proposed development, it had to work out all conflicts with the applicable state agencies and interest groups.... This process began in early 1988 with unassisted negotiations between the various interested parties and progressed into mediated negotiations. By March 1990 the parties had reached a final agreement on all outstanding issues....

Results: Time spent to date has been two years and six months. The costs of mediation were $3,000, half paid by DSL and half by Zidell. Attorneys fees, consulting fees and staff time costs for Zidell were approximately $14,000.

Lucinda D. Moyano, A Tale of Two Wetlands, 52 Or. St. Bar Bull. 39 (1992). Does this summary validate the position taken in the excerpt from the book Land In Conflict?

4. *Advantages and Disadvantages.* The Netter article lists the following benefits of using mediation: (1) ease of problem solving because parties' positions have not hardened; (2) opportunities for meaningful dialogue among parties; (3) cost savings over litigation as an alternative; (4) improved relations among the parties in the future; (5) less political fallout.

Critics list a number of possible disadvantages to mediation: (1) there is no certainty that the process will result in a settlement; (2) the outcome of the dispute does not have to be "principled," i.e., based on law; (3) an imbalance of negotiation skills could be reflected in the solution; (4) no one is accountable for the result of a mediation, and city council members may somehow "abrogate their responsibility" by agreeing to a mediated settlement. Barbara McAdoo & Larry Bakken, Mediation in Public Interest Law, 22 Urb. Law. 179, 189-190 (1990).

Which of these benefits and disadvantages, if any, do you find convincing?

5. *The Timing of Mediation I.* Mediation can be a lengthy process. Consider the following summary of what must be accomplished:

Once the venue is established, there are several procedures commonly followed in neutral-assisted negotiations. The stakeholders must be determined, some pre-assessment of their issues done, a method of bringing them into the negotiations identified, the parties convened at a properly-called first meeting, the role of the neutral and the agenda clarified, a process for the negotiation agreed upon along with ground rules for proceeding, a timetable for resolution established, and a variety of matters decided, such as whether the meetings are open to the public, whether the negotiations are confidential, and whether the participants are restricted in their contacts with the press.

There is much more . . .

One of the principal objectives of this type of settlement is to build trust among the disputants so that they can be candid about what it is that they really want to achieve and then work productively to accomplish these objectives. This takes time and is achieved at the first few meetings when stakeholders meet each other through discussions about the procedures, by learning the critical issues in need of resolution, and by determining the facts related to them. Gradually, stakeholders move from discussing their positions . . . to revealing what they truly want to achieve. Once interests are revealed, the neutral can lead parties through a discussion of options or alternatives to the initial development proposal.

John R. Nolon and Jessica A. Bacher, Changing Times — Changing Practice: New Roles for Lawyers in Resolving Complex Land Use and Environmental Disputes, 27 Pace Envtl. L. Rev. 7, 24-25 (Special Ed. 2009-2010). Does the sheer length and possible complexity of this process deter lawyers from using it?

6. *The Timing of Mediation II.* Is mediation as valuable after the governmental approval (perhaps after a court has ordered it) as it is before the governmental approval? Consider the following position taken by a chief lawyer for the City of New York:

[W]hen a final decision in a land use case is challenged in court, the back and forth and inevitable compromises resulting from the public process have already taken place. For a court then to direct the parties to see if, through an alternative dispute resolution process, they could somehow resolve factual disputes already decided — or compromise still more of their differences — ignores the compromises that have already occurred and will make compromises in future disputes difficult to reach. Insisting on ADR in these cases will encourage litigation — after all, the neighborhood advocacy group will know they may gain still more by suing — and will discourage would-be developers from compromising during the public process, since they will know they may have to make still further concessions when the suit is commenced and the matter is sent to ADR.

Michael A. Cardozo, The Use of ADR Involving Local Governments: The Perspective of the New York City Corporation Counsel, 34 Fordham Urb. L.J. 979, 803 (2007). Do you agree?

7. *Mediation Issues.* Consider the following issues raised by mediation:

a. *Choosing the Mediator.* Would a court have the power to impose mediation unilaterally? If the court strongly suggested mediation, what would be the downside of rejecting the offer? Would you be willing to accept a mediator who was not an attorney? Under the Florida law mentioned above that calls for for mediation, the special magistrate is frequently an attorney specializing in land use or government law. Mark S. Bentley, Understanding the Florida Land Use and Environmental Dispute Resolution Act, 37 Stetson L. Rev. 381, 403-04 (2008).

b. *Timing.* What if the timetable for the use of a mediator is inconsistent with the timetable for either completing a judicial proceeding or initiating judicial review? Can the parties just stipulate to tolling those deadlines, or is a court order necessary?

c. *Delay in Mediation.* If you represent a project proponent, how will you ensure that the negotiation does not drag out for a lengthy period of time? Under this scenario your client is hurt financially, because it must pay the carrying costs on its investment in land while the return on that investment is delayed. *See* Pa. Stat. Ann. tit. 53, §10908.1 (if a municipality offers mediation, it shall "assure that, in each case, the mediating parties, assisted by the mediator as appropriate, develop terms and conditions for . . . completing mediation, including time limits for such completion.").

d. *The Role of Third Parties.* Should third parties, such as neighbors who object to a proposal, be given a formal role in a mediation? Consider that any party who is not a signatory to any mediated settlement retains the right to initiate litigation against a project. *See Thomas v. Lima Twp. Bd. of Trustees*, 1996 WL 243804 (Ohio Ct. App. 1996) (unpublished court of appeal decision in which opponents sought to intervene in litigation after board reached a settlement with project applicants through mediation).

e. *Admissions.* Can facts that come out in an unsuccessful mediation be used later in litigation? *See Medeiros v. Hawaii County Planning Comm'n*, 797 P.2d 59, 64 (Haw. Ct. App. 1990) (president of community association wrote a letter to the Planning Commission "pointing out that, during mediation, Applicants revealed there will be hydrogen sulfide emission from the wells, contrary to their statement in the application").

In *Wilmington Hospitality v. New Castle County*, 788 A.2d 536 (Del. Ch. Ct. 2001), *appeal refused, Wilmington Hospitality v. Republic Bank*, 781 A.2d 697 (Del. 2001), a developer sought court enforcement of a purported agreement arrived at in a dispute resolution process. The court held that the mediation was confidential, and the plaintiff could not rely on discussions in that process to prove an agreement.

8. *Open Meeting Laws and Mediation.* The techniques used by mediators can include caucusing with individual parties and shuttling from "room to room" to seek an acceptable resolution. The parties must decide which tradeoffs to accept,

and which to reject, at that moment. The model of land use regulation reflected in most state laws, however, is one of open decision making in a public forum. Can the two be reconciled? Should so-called public meetings laws, which generally require that meetings of a quorum of public officials must be held publicly, apply to mediations?

The issue arose in *Sovereign v. Dunn*, 498 N.W.2d 62 (Minn. Ct. App. 1993), in which two of the five members of the city council of the City of Lake Elmo attended a series of nonpublic mediation sessions in an attempt to resolve a border dispute with a neighboring city. The court held that the meetings did not constitute a "committee, subcommittee, board, department or commission" under the act because the group was not capable of exercising the decision-making powers of a governmental body (a capacity presumed where a quorum exists), and there was no delegation of power from the governing body. *Id.* at 67.

What would be wrong with requiring all mediation discussions to be open to the public?

9. *Settlement Parameters.* Any settlement among the parties cannot violate the substantive law of either the state or the local jurisdiction. For example, in *Ad-Ex, Inc. v. City of Chicago*, 617 N.E.2d 333 (Ill. App. Ct. 1993) the court refused to accept a settlement in which the city agreed to waive a set-back requirement for signs. *Compare Summit Twp. Taxpayers Assoc. v. Summit Twp. Bd. of Supervisors*, 411 A.2d 1263 (Pa. Commw. Ct. 1980) (settlement upheld even though it required the grant of a variance).

F. MARKET-BASED SYSTEMS: DEREGULATION

As your study of land use controls has revealed, the ability to make use of privately held land is heavily regulated in the United States. By this point you should have a good understanding of the tools by which such regulation is undertaken and the goals of the regulatory system. You should also have some sense of the costs that regulation imposes, both on landowners and, ultimately, on homebuyers.

Are these costs worthwhile? Or could a system with much less government intervention accomplish the goals sought while, at the same time, reducing the costs of land development? Consider the costs of the land use system outlined in these remarks by the Chairman of the Council on Economic Advisers, an economist. Then consider the option chosen by Houston, Texas, as explained by its Director of Planning and Development in the brief memorandum that follows.

■ REMARKS BY JASON FURMAN, CHAIRMAN, COUNCIL ON ECONOMIC ADVISERS, BARRIERS TO SHARED GROWTH: THE CASE OF LAND USE REGULATION AND ECONOMIC RENTS
The Urban Institute (Nov. 20, 2015)

. . . In today's remarks, I will focus on how excessive or unnecessary land use or zoning regulations have consequences that go beyond the housing market to impede mobility and thus contribute to rising inequality and declining productivity growth.

While land use regulations sometimes serve reasonable and legitimate purposes, they can also give extranormal returns to entrenched interests at the expense of everyone else. As such, land use regulations are an example of a broader range of situations that may give rise to economic rents. By this I do not mean the check you write to your landlord every month, but a situation in which any factor of production — in this case, land — is paid more than is needed to put it in production. . . .

ZONING GIVES RISE TO RENTS BY RESTRICTING SUPPLY

Zoning restrictions — be they in the form of minimum lot sizes, off-street parking requirements, height limits, prohibitions on multifamily housing, or lengthy permitting processes — are supply constraints. Basic economic theory predicts — and many empirical studies confirm — that housing markets in which supply cannot keep up with demand will see housing prices rise. Mayer and Somerville (2000) conclude that land use regulation and levels of new housing construction are inversely correlated, with the ability of housing supply to expand to meet greater demand being much lower in the most heavily regulated metro areas. Quigley and Raphael (2005) show that new construction is not as prevalent in areas characterized by growth restrictions. Glaeser and Ward (2009) found that an increase of one acre in a Greater Boston town's average minimum lot size is associated with about 40 percent fewer new permits.

Land use restrictions themselves are endogenous and at least partly the result of active rent seeking behavior by homeowners. In his 2001 book *The Homevoter Hypothesis*, William Fischel asserts that homeowners propose and vote for zoning policies to mitigate housing marketspecific risks faced in their investment portfolios. Homeowners whose homes have the highest property values are both most invested and most likely to support stringent zoning policies (Fennell, 2002). This behavior fits the definition of rent-seeking, as it suggests people are trying to raise the value of their properties at the expense of greater building. The homeowners are not acting out of some nefarious intent — they are trying to safeguard an asset, but the net effect can be to choke off housing supply and mobility.

Moreover, this rent seeking behavior is often framed as serving some meritorious purpose, complicating the community's ability to determine whether a particular proposed regulation is merited or misguided. With high house prices and further hedges against property value depreciation in local regulations, some individuals are priced out of the market entirely, and homes in highly zoned areas also become even more attractive to wealthy buyers. Thus, in addition to constraining supply, zoning shifts demand outward, exerting further upward pressure on prices and thus also, economic rents (Quigley and Raphael, 2004). Supply Restrictions Reduce Affordability Restricted supply leads to higher prices and less affordability. We see the association in the relationship between land use regulations and affordability in several dozen U.S. metro areas . . . [T]his could both reflect land use restrictions leading to higher prices or higher prices leading people to seek more land use restrictions or other factors. This house price appreciation experienced especially in those cities towards the right of the figure presents affordability challenges for nearly all, but they can hit the poorest Americans the hardest.

As the figure makes clear, the affordability challenge is not evenly distributed across the country. There is considerable variation across the United States in zoning policies and associated markup of prices above construction costs, both geographically and in different types of construction. As a result of zoning as well as differences in labor markets, housing demand, and natural supply constraints resulting from land itself, economic rents and thus housing affordability vary substantially across the country's states and metro areas. Moreover, this dispersion appears to have grown over time. Gyourko et al. (2013) shows how the real home price distribution has widened over the last several decades, coinciding with increased variation in land use restrictions as some communities have added them and others have not. . . .

ZONING IMPACTS LABOR MARKETS, PRODUCTIVITY, AND INEQUALITY

The topics I have covered so far are not just issues for housing markets — these issues directly affect the broader economy. Zoning can reinforce divergence across labor markets by impeding market forces that would otherwise help reduce income inequality and boost productivity. High productivity cities — like Boston and San Francisco — have higher-income jobs relative to low productivity cities. Normally, these higher wages would encourage workers to move to these high-productivity cities — a dynamic that brings more resources to productive areas of the country, allows workers in low-productivity areas to earn more, improves job matches and competes away any above-market wages (another type of economic rents) in the high productivity cities. But when zoning restricts the supply of housing and renders housing more expensive — even relative to the higher wages in the high productivity cities — then workers are less able to move, particularly those who are low income to begin with and who would benefit most from moving. As a result, existing income inequality across cities remains entrenched and may even be exacerbated, while productivity does not grow as fast it normally would. This last result — from a paper out this past year by Chang-Tai Hsieh and Enrico Moretti — frames excessively restrictive zoning policies as hindrances to productivity growth. . . .

OTHER CONSEQUENCES OF LAND USE RESTRICTIONS

I have described what I see to be the consequences of zoning regulation for housing markets, affordability, labor productivity, and inequality. But the consequences of zoning are much broader and include:

- Greater environmental damage: when strict zoning policies cap a city's density, they ensure that the city's residents must on average occupy more land than they otherwise would and travel greater distances to and from work as well, both of which increase carbon production, all else equal (Glaeser, 2011).
- Worsening of house price bubbles: tighter land use regulations may exacerbate house price bubbles. Gyourko, Glaeser, and Saiz (2008) demonstrate that cities with more restrictive zoning and thus a more inelastic housing supply have historically been more likely to experience house price bubbles and that these episodes of elevated prices tend to last longer.
- Reduced public good provision: zoning that restricts multi-use may also prevent the expansion of public goods provision. New retail, commercial,

or industrial tenants may bring not only increased tax revenue but also may necessitate public or private investment in infrastructure to facilitate the flow of goods and people from their locations. . . .

■ MEMORANDUM FROM DIRECTOR, PLANNING AND DEVELOPMENT, CITY OF HOUSTON

http://www.houstontx.gov/planning/Forms/devregs/2016_no_zoning_letter.pdf
(last visited Nov. 11, 2016)

To: Whom It May Concern
From: Director Patrick Walsh, P.E. Planning & Development Department
Effective Date: January 1, 2016

The City of Houston does not have a zoning ordinance. This is the city of Houston's no zoning letter applicable to any property inside the city of Houston. This does not address any separately filed restrictions that may be applicable to the property. You may use this letter to present to your lender. This letter will be updated on January 1, 2017. All applicable development regulations and subdivisions laws can be obtained through a review of the City Code of Ordinances, which is located on the City of Houston Internet site accessed through www.houstonplanning.com or www.houstontx.gov/planning.

Notes and Comments

1. *Zoning and Economic Impacts.* A substantial body of academic articles and books strongly suggests that zoning and other similar land use regulations should be abolished. *See, e.g.,* Bernard H. Siegan, Land Use Without Zoning (1972); Douglas Kmiec, Deregulating Land Use: An Alternative Free Enterprise Development System, 130 U. Pa. L. Rev. 28 (1981); Jan Z. Krasnowiecki, Abolish Zoning, 31 Syracuse L. Rev. 719 (1980). A particularly important article is Robert C. Ellickson, Alternatives to Zoning: Covenants, Nuisance Rules, and Fines As Land Use Controls, 40 U. Chi. L. Rev. 681 (1973). Professor Ellickson believes that a mechanism for internalizing land use externalities is needed but advocates use of private deed restrictions and enforcement of nuisance laws.

The remarks of Dr. Furman, the Chairman of the Council on Economic Advisers, update those criticisms in light of the high cost of housing as of 2016. Criticism of zoning is increasing and has been the subject of articles in the national media. *See, e.g.,* David Brooks, Where America Is Working, The N.Y. Times (June 3, 2016) (discussing "opportunity cities" that "are less regulated, so it's easier to start a business"). Dr. Furman argues that zoning has unacceptably high costs and other impacts, citing an array of academic articles. If zoning is too economically burdensome, is there a lesser form of regulation that would be better?

2. *Zoning and Exclusion.* One stream of criticism of zoning argues, as does Dr. Furman, that land use controls are tools to promote the exclusion of the

poor and minorities. *See, e.g.,* Michael C. Lens & Paavo Monkkonen, Do Strict Land Use Regulations Make Metropolitan Areas More Segregated by Income?, 82 J. Am. Plan. Assn. vol. 1 (2016) (concluding that density restrictions drive urban income segregation of the rich, but not the poor); J. Peter Byrne, Are Suburbs Unconstitutional?, 85 Geo. L.J. 2265 (1997). Others, advocating the need for increasing housing opportunities, also strongly criticize land use controls. *See, e.g.,* United States President's Commission on Housing, The Report of the President's Commission on Housing 202 (1982) (recommending reconsideration of the decision in *Village of Euclid v. Ambler Realty,* read in Chapter 2 of this casebook, which sustained the constitutionality of zoning). A 2009 article accuses land use regulation of undermining African-American enterprise. Stephen Clowney, Invisible Businessman: Undermining Black Enterprise with Land Use Rules, 2009 U. Ill. L. Rev. 1061, 1064 ("[Z]oning . . . has sharply limited the formation and expansion of entrepreneurship in black neighborhoods.").

3. *Houston as a Free Market Exemplar.* As the memorandum from Houston's Director of Planning and Development indicates, Houston is a city—the only large city in the United States—without zoning. On several occasions in the past, the citizens of Houston voted whether to adopt zoning, most recently in November 1993. The ballot measure was defeated 52 to 48 percent after a vigorous campaign. Julie Mason, Haves, Have-Nots Joined Same Side to Defeat Zoning, Houston Chronicle Nov. 4, 1993, at 25. Many articles cite the Houston experience as evidence that zoning is unnecessary. *See* Bernard H. Siegan, Non-Zoning Is the Best Zoning, 31 Cal. W.L. Rev. 127, 130 (1994). The criticism aligns itself with the economist's stress on markets bringing increased economic efficiency.

While Houston does not regulate uses, it does regulate parking, setbacks, density, lot size, and other metrics commonly found in zoning ordinances. Ryan Holeywell, Forget What You've Heard, Houston Really Does Have Zoning (Sort of) at http://urbanedge.blogs.rice.edu/2015/09/08/forget-what-youve-heard-houston-really-does-have-zoning-sort-of/#.V7DUCk0rLIU (last visited Nov. 11, 2017). Further, many areas are subject to restrictions established by covenants.

4. *The Houston High-Rise Controversy.* The lack of zoning does not mean that land use conflicts are absent from Houston. In 2007, a developer proposed a 23-story tower in a neighborhood of million dollar homes. The development plan included either 187 condominiums or 236 apartments, a restaurant, a boutique grocery store, and parking for 450 vehicles. The mayor stated that zoning would not happen on his "watch" and proposed a city ordinance that would allow the rejection of development for traffic reasons. *See* Kris Hudson, Lack of Zoning Laws a Challenge in Houston, The Chicago Tribune 31 (Nov. 18, 2007).

Ultimately, as might be expected, the issue went to court, with the neighbors seeking to enjoin the development as a prospective nuisance and also seeking damages. The court's description of the homeowners' reaction to the land use proposal vividly captures the depth of the dispute:

> In 2007, Developer devised plans to build a 23-story mixed-use building, which would include 226 apartments, a spa, retail, restaurant and office space, and a multi-level parking garage. Developer filed its plans with the City. Knowing the project would be a departure in scale from surrounding properties, Developer anticipated opposition from area residents and advised the neighborhood associations about the plans.

The opposition was vehement, with residents fearing negative effects on their established neighborhoods, including impacts on traffic, aesthetics, privacy, and market values of their homes. Residents mobilized into a group called "Stop Ashby Highrise," erected signs in the area, sent numerous letters to Developer's principals and city officials, and signed petitions, all imploring Developer not build the project. The two Houston mayors who served consecutively during relevant times also opposed the project. The residents and Developer attempted, unsuccessfully, to negotiate a compromise with respect to the size and nature of the project. Otherwise, the parties have remained entrenched in their positions for years, with Developer determined to build and area residents determined to stop the project.

1717 Bisssonnet, LLC v. Loughhead, ____ S.W.3d ____ (June 30, 2016) at http://www.search.txcourts.gov/SearchMedia.aspx?MediaVersionID=c2c8e1e2-e8bd-4001-a024-ba6ac5f35197&coa=coa14&DT=Opinion&MediaID=d005b6c2-9c41-4561-ae6f-1be5389ba49b (last visited Nov. 11, 2016).

The trial court refused injunctive relief but, aided by a jury determination, awarded the plaintiffs $1.6 million in damages. The court of appeal reversed the damage award, finding that Texas did not award damages for prospective nuisances. It affirmed the denial of injunctive relief.

5. *Not Houston?* One article has suggested that Houston is not a good example of a free market in land use. Jane E. Larson, Free Markets Deep in the Heart of Texas, 84 Geo. L.J. 179 (1995). The late Professor Larson noted that, although Houston has no planning agency or zoning ordinance, it has adopted other land use regulations such as controls on lot sizes, business placement, and setback requirements. Her article asserts that a "better example" of an unregulated market exists in the unincorporated Texas counties ("colonias") that border Mexico, where there are no zoning laws and, until recently, no subdivision or infrastructure requirements. She found that "average housing conditions fall below minimum standards of human habitability that apply in other communities," endangering the health and safety of residents and those of surrounding communities. *Id.* at 185. Professor Larson also wondered "why the kind of empirical evidence presented in this article has been so rare in the land use debate." *Id.* at 228.

Two articles have debated, based on studies of land use before zoning in New Haven, Connecticut, whether zoning was needed to avoid conflicts in land uses. *Compare* Andrew J. Cappell, Note, A Walk Along Willard: Patterns of Land Use Coordination in Pre-Zoning New Haven, 101 Yale L.J. 617, 637 (1991) ("the introduction of zoning into New Haven was not necessitated by actual conditions of local land use, but rather was the work of certain elites"); with Steven Clowney, Note, A Walk Along Willard: A Revised Look at Land Use Coordination in Pre-Zoning New Haven, 115 Yale L.J. 116, 172 (2005) (initial study ignores many of the complexities of land use regulation in pre-zoning New Haven).

6. *The Persistence of Zoning.* In other areas of the economy, such as the airline, telecommunications, and electric industries, academic criticism of a regulatory regime has brought about extensive deregulation. Despite the academic criticism of zoning, however, there have been very few political attempts to repeal all zoning. *See* Eric H. Steele, Participation and Rules — The Functions of Zoning, 1986 Am. B. Found. Res. J. 709, 713 (1987) (noting that resistance to changing the basic nature of zoning "springs from a widespread, if unarticulated, perception that the institution is serving some vital social function").

Professor William Fischel, an economist and student of zoning, has discussed what he terms a "model" of zoning adopted by economists, which sees zoning as an unacceptable restraint on development. He then asks why rational economic actors would not change it. His answer is that homeownership places most people's major asset in a "single basket." The difficulty in changing zoning operates as an alternative to an insurance policy against actions that would devalue existing homes. William A. Fischel, The Evolution of Zoning Since the 1980s: The Persistence of Localism, in Daniel H. Cole and Elinor Ostrom (eds.), Property in Land and Other Resources 288 (2012). Do you agree?

Does the resistance to changing the present system validate the criticism of zoning? See Bradley C. Karkkainen, Zoning: A Reply to the Critics, 10 J. Land Use & Envtl. L. 45, 47 (1994) (arguing that "many of the critiques, despite the broad claims of their authors, should not be taken as general indictments of zoning, but rather as indicators of particular dysfunctions that must be addressed if zoning is to work effectively"). Should the solution be some experimentation, rather than the "all or nothing" suggestions that have dominated so far? See Nicolle Stelle Garnett, Review, Save the Cities, Stop the Suburbs?, 116 Yale L.J. 598, 629 (2006) (suggesting the possibility of incremental deregulation of land use in poor areas as a means of encouraging needed "busyness" in those areas).

PART FOUR

EVOLVING ISSUES IN LAND USE REGULATION

11

Confronting New Land Use Challenges: Smart Growth, Climate Change, Health, and Vulnerable Populations

A. INTRODUCTION

In the twenty-first century, land use management in the United States confronts a series of novel challenges. As described in previous chapters, early land use regulation, epitomized by Euclidean zoning, largely focused on separating potentially conflicting uses, and in particular on maintaining the peace and tranquility of residential neighborhoods. These early regulatory efforts were in large part a response to the perceived adverse effects of intensive industrial development on neighboring communities. Today, land use planning and regulatory tools are being used to achieve other, arguably more ambitious goals, including promoting smart growth and sustainability, mitigating and adapting to climate change, resolving health care problems, and meeting the needs of the homeless. At the same time, contemporary land use planning and regulation are still generally being utilized to achieve their traditional function of separating different land uses, sometimes in conflict with more modern land use objectives.

Government and regulation are both part of the problem as well as potential solutions to modern land use problems. Throughout this casebook we have seen the contributions, not necessarily inevitable but real, of planning, zoning, and related regulatory controls to spatial outcomes that do a disservice to particular groups. The adverse effects can be racial, socio-economic, familial, and health- or poverty-related. Land use regulation can also affect, both negatively as well as positively, the environment and even the sustainability of the planet. The overarching goal, more or less universally embraced, is to develop new and better land use tools that will help address these adverse effects and not compound them.

The chapter opens with a section on smart growth and sustainability, emphasizing the historical links between the growth management efforts that were launched in the 1970s and the modern smart growth and sustainability movements. The chapter then turns to the most pressing environmental challenge of the modern era, climate change. This material explores how the present reality and the future threat of climate affect land use and describes initiatives in the land use arena to respond to climate change.

Next we explore the relationship between land use and public health, discussing both why land use policies are thought to have contributed to public health problems and how land use laws and policies are being reformed to promote more healthful development patterns. The chapter also discusses how land use law and policy serve — and do not serve — those in need of support and rehabilitation of many kinds: physical, mental, and behavioral, as well as the land use aspects of the production and distribution of federally controlled substances for either medical or recreational goals, most notably marijuana. Finally, we consider those who lack access to safe and affordable housing, including the homeless and the mentally ill.

A key theme of this chapter is that the land use system affects all of these areas and all of these different populations. A burgeoning literature describes and dissects the secondary effects of the land use system addressed in this chapter. And local governments have begun to address these effects through changes in their land use regulations. In short, the topics addressed in this chapter are on the cutting edge of land use regulation.

B. FROM GROWTH CONTROL TO SMART GROWTH

A Note on the Management of Growth

The Burgeoning Concerns over Growth. The terms "sustainability" and "smart growth" could not be found in earlier generations of land use casebooks. But some of the goals now being pursued under the banners of "sustainability" and "smart growth" were originally pursued in the name of "growth control" or "growth management." In fact, specific tools and approaches developed to advance "growth control" have now been incorporated by the sustainability and smart growth movements.

To quickly recap the relevant history, around 1970, traditional Euclidian zoning came to be widely viewed as inadequate for addressing the major problems associated with development. In particular, critics contended that traditional zoning was ineffective in controlling the location of growth, the rate of growth, the amount of growth, and the quality of new development.

These critiques were in part a reflection of the problems created by the rapid expansion of American metropolitan regions, and especially the explosion of suburban development, in the decades following World War II. Between 1945 and 1967, the population of the United States increased from about 139 million people to over 200 million people, with the greatest growth in the South and the West. In some places growth proceeded in a continuous, seemingly inexorable manner; in other areas, new "boomtowns" appeared.

This extensive development led to widespread concerns about loss of open space, conversion of agricultural lands, burdens on local infrastructure, and decline in small town "community character." The rapid rate of growth, often featuring poorly planned developments, led to a "first wave" of criticism of "urban sprawl." Other by-products of this development boom became evident: increased traffic congestion and air pollution, decay of inner cities, and loss of a sense of place. With recognition of these new environmental and aesthetic concerns came an equally powerful economic worry: that new developments were not paying their own way with respect to the public facilities that they required. As a result, cities and towns increasingly found it difficult to fund the local services needed by new developments.

Growth Control. In response to this explosive growth and its perceived adverse effects, some communities took the novel step of adopting explicit growth management regulations. Some of these efforts were carried out within the framework of traditional zoning. For example, some communities adopted very low density zoning with the goal to protect the character of an area, farmland, and open space. Another more innovative approach to growth control was the adoption of temporary moratoria: short-term "freezes" on development designed to facilitate a planning process to determine whether new permanent land use controls should be instituted. Development moratoria frequently provoked bitter opposition, not least because they were sometimes adopted in response to specific development proposals that conformed to the existing zoning and other regulatory standards. Some states adopted legislation restricting the authority of local governments to adopt moratoria.

Moratoria also gave rise to constitutional "takings" objections, which were ultimately largely put to rest by the Supreme Court's 2002 decision in *Tahoe-Sierra Property Owners Ass'n v. Tahoe Regional Planning Agency*, 535 U.S. 302 (2002). In that decision the Court rejected the argument that a complete ban on development of limited duration necessarily resulted in a taking, while leaving open the possibility that, depending on the particular facts and circumstances, a moratorium of long duration might cause a taking.

Regulating for the long-term, some cities and towns adopted so-called rate-of-growth controls, absolute caps on the number of building permits that can be issued in a particular year. These types of controls raised, among other issues, questions about how a limited number of building authorizations should be allocated among competing applicants. Other rate-of-growth systems tied new development approvals to public or private improvements in infrastructure and services, such as roads, sewage systems, schools, and so forth. These controls, coupled with zoning use, density restrictions, and site plan review, attempted to better govern the rate, location, amount, and quality of growth and development.

Another approach to manage growth was to create urban growth boundaries, separating the areas near the established urban core where growth would be encouraged from those areas, outside the boundaries, where agriculture, natural resource production, and open space would take precedence. The premise of this approach was that an urban growth limit should be set, and new development should mostly be required to proceed within the growth boundary. *See* Douglas R. Porter, State Growth Management: The Intergovernmental Experiment, 13 Pace L. Rev. 481, 497 (1993).

These legal innovations predictably led to litigation involving questions about the statutory authority of local governments and the limits of the police power. In the landmark decision *Golden v. Planning Bd. of the Town of Ramapo*, 285 N.E.2d

(N.Y. 1972), which you read in Chapter 3, the New York Court of Appeals upheld the famous Ramapo ordinance, a regulatory scheme that tied residential building to the completion of infrastructure and capital improvement benchmarks over an 18-year cycle. In another major decision, *Construction Indus. Ass'n v. City of Petaluma*, 522 F.2d 897 (9th Cir. 1975), the United States Court of Appeals for the Ninth Circuit rejected various constitutional challenges to Petaluma's yearly cap on the number of building permits that it would issue.

These decisions set the pattern for judicial decisions upholding a variety of growth control mechanisms over the next four decades. Because the courts in each of these major cases upheld the growth control devices at issue, other local jurisdictions patterned their own ordinances after those adopted by the Town of Ramapo and the City of Petaluma. Thus, these decisions had nationwide effects on land use practices.

The apotheosis of the growth control movement is probably the Oregon statewide land use program, launched in 1973. Guided by 19 statutory planning goals and the Land Conservation and Development Commission, Oregon municipalities establish and periodically revise urban growth boundaries designed to concentrate most development in and adjacent to already urbanized areas while preserving the state's farmland and forestland. While it has been a regular target of political controversy and has been tweaked in numerous ways over the last 50 years, the Oregon program remains in place today. (The distinctive Oregon approach to land use is discussed in greater detail in Chapter 9.)

From Growth Control to Smart Growth. While traditional growth control measures still exist in some places, growth control has gradually been overtaken by new paradigms, a development captured by the terms "smart growth" and "sustainable development." To some extent these new labels simply represent old wine in new bottles. But they also represent a significant change in the goals of land use regulation as well as the means used to achieve these goals. Rhetorically, at least, they seek to replace a largely negative agenda with a more positive one.

There are many explanations for this change in direction. Partly it reflects fatigue and frustration resulting from the contentious political battles over growth control measures. In part, it also reflects the rise of the property rights movement starting in 1980s and the increased threat that communities would suffer monetary liability if they institute strong land use controls.

However, the shift also reflected disillusion caused by the unintended adverse consequences of growth control measures. Large lot zoning was seen as failing to change the low-density and automobile-dependent pattern of development prevalent since World War II. Indeed, large lot zoning sometimes contributes to sprawl development, by forcing new development to "leap frog" over communities subject to growth controls into rural areas even further from centers of employment and commercial activity.

Other criticisms emerged, centering around the charge that such ordinances unduly hamper the supply of new housing and have a particularly deleterious effect on the underprivileged. Critics also weighed in with economic arguments that growth controls were a prime contributor to the skyrocketing housing prices found in many parts of the country and that they unduly inhibit job creation and economic development. Finally, growth control was criticized for not helping to repair the homogeneity of much modern development. *See* Andes Duany et al., Suburban Nation: The Rise of Sprawl and the Decline of the American Dream

143 (2000) (observing that Portland's growth boundary sanctioned "twenty years of bad growth" and "contains within it thousands of acres of the most mundane sprawl").

The smart growth reform movement emerged as a response to the perceived limitations of the growth control movement. Rather than focusing on limiting development in rural areas, the smart growth agenda affirmatively seeks to promote growth in compact urban centers. *See* Smart Growth America's homepage at https://smartgrowthamerica.org/ (last visited Oct. 7, 2016). In addition, smart growth advocates champion compact, transit-oriented, walkable, bicycle-friendly land use, including neighborhood schools, complete streets, and mixed-use development with a range of housing choices. The American Planning Association, Smart Growth America, and other groups have advocated changes in traditional land use regulations designed to promote smart growth. In dramatic contradiction to the original goals of zoning, smart growth advocates seek to promote a multiplicity of urban land uses, with the goal of enlivening the urban experience.

The focus of the growth debate today has also shifted to the notion of promoting sustainable growth and development. Critics suggest that the land use system must address sustainability issues related to low-density regional sprawl, such as infrastructure costs and maintenance, economic development, resource and energy conservation, green development, social equity, economic stability, global competition, health, and climate change.

The Future. The debate about forms of growth in this country will inevitably continue. Demographers now tell us that during the next 40 years, the population of the United States may grow by 100 million people. If some forms of urban planning have been part of the problem in the past, the search today is to find ways to utilize planning to address the challenge of building a sustainable future.

An important aspect of the "sustainable development" concept has been the change from a development system that effectively encourages sprawl to one that seeks "in-fill" development of existing, often-urbanized areas. The piece below from the Congress for the New Urbanism gives a flavor of the goals and purposes of sustainable development. Note the emphasis on mixed uses and transit. The second excerpt seeks to offer a robust working definition of "smart growth."

■ CONGRESS FOR THE NEW URBANISM, THE CHARTER OF THE NEW URBANISM
https://www.cnu.org/who-we-are/charter-new-urbanism
(last visited Oct. 7, 2016).

We advocate the restructuring of public policy and development practices to support the following principles: neighborhoods should be diverse in use and population; communities should be designed for the pedestrian and transit as well as the car; cities and towns should be shaped by physically defined and universally accessible public spaces and community institutions; urban places should be framed by architecture and landscape design that celebrate local history, climate, ecology, and building practice. . . .

The Region: Metropolis, City, and Town

The metropolitan region is a fundamental economic unit of the contemporary world. Governmental cooperation, public policy, physical planning, and economic strategies must reflect this new reality.

Development patterns should not blur or eradicate the edges of the metropolis. Infill development within existing urban areas conserves environmental resources, economic investment, and social fabric, while reclaiming marginal and abandoned areas. Metropolitan regions should develop strategies to encourage such infill development over peripheral expansion.

Where appropriate, new development contiguous to urban boundaries should be organized as neighborhoods and districts, and be integrated with the existing urban pattern. Noncontiguous development should be organized as towns and villages with their own urban edges, and planned for a jobs/housing balance, not as bedroom suburbs.

Affordable housing should be distributed throughout the region to match job opportunities and to avoid concentrations of poverty.

The physical organization of the region should be supported by a framework of transportation alternatives. Transit, pedestrian, and bicycle systems should maximize access and mobility throughout the region while reducing dependence upon the automobile.

Revenues and resources can be shared more cooperatively among the municipalities and centers within regions to avoid destructive competition.

The Neighborhood, the District, and the Corridor

Neighborhoods should be compact, pedestrian friendly, and mixed-use. Districts generally emphasize a special single use, and should follow the principles of neighborhood design when possible. Corridors are regional connectors of neighborhoods and districts; they range from boulevards and rail lines to rivers and parkways.

Many activities of daily living should occur within walking distance, allowing independence to those who do not drive especially the elderly and the young. Interconnected networks of streets should be designed to encourage walking, reduce the number and length of automobile trips, and conserve energy.

Within neighborhoods, a broad range of housing types and price levels can bring people of diverse ages, races, and incomes into daily interaction, strengthening the personal and civic bonds essential to an authentic community.

Transit corridors, when properly planned and coordinated, can help organize metropolitan structure and revitalize urban centers. In contrast, highway corridors should not displace investment from existing centers.

Appropriate building densities and land uses should be within walking distance of transit stops, permitting public transit to become a viable alternative to the automobile.

Concentrations of civic, institutional, and commercial activity should be embedded in neighborhoods and districts, not isolated in remote, single-use complexes. Schools should be sized and located to enable children to walk or bicycle to them.

The economic health and harmonious evolution of neighborhoods, districts, and corridors can be improved through graphic urban design codes that serve as predictable guides for change.

A range of parks, from tot-lots and village greens to ball fields and community gardens, should be distributed within neighborhoods. Conservation areas and open lands should be used to define and connect different neighborhoods and districts.

THE BLOCK, THE STREET, AND THE BUILDING

In the contemporary metropolis, development must adequately accommodate automobiles. It should do so in ways that respect the pedestrian and the form of public space.

Streets and squares should be safe, comfortable, and interesting to the pedestrian. Properly configured, they encourage walking and enable neighbors to know each other and protect their communities.

Civic buildings and public gathering places require important sites to reinforce community identity and the culture of democracy. They deserve distinctive form, because their role is different from that of other buildings and places that constitute the fabric of the city.

All buildings should provide their inhabitants with a clear sense of location, weather and time. Natural methods of heating and cooling can be more resource-efficient than mechanical systems.

Preservation and renewal of historic buildings, districts, and landscapes affirm the continuity and evolution of urban society.

■ BRIAN W. OHM, REFORMING LAND PLANNING LEGISLATION AT THE DAWN OF THE 21ST CENTURY: THE EMERGING INFLUENCE OF SMART GROWTH AND LIVABLE COMMUNITIES
32 Urb. Law. 181, 190-191 (2000)

Smart growth has no precise definition. An exhibition on smart growth at the National Building Museum in Washington, D.C., describes smart growth as a reaction to the pattern of development in the United States since World War II. According to a commentator for the Urban Land Institute, smart growth is not anti-growth. Rather it focuses on how growth occurs. It is an evolving approach to development that balances economic development with environmental protection and a better quality of life. While smart growth avoids the use of the term "growth management," these descriptions of smart growth sound similar to definitions of growth management and the recognized purposes of growth management. Nonetheless, smart growth is a recognition that the existing growth management programs have not solved the issues of sprawl nor promoted sustainable land patterns. The current problems associated with growth and change are similar to the problems communities have faced for decades. While states have passed a variety of laws to address the issues, according to one commentator, success is in the eye of the beholder. Progress has been made on some issues, such as environmental protection. Other issues, such as the concentration of poverty within older cities, have magnified. . . .

The general principles articulated by the Smart Growth Network help define the objectives of smart growth: (1) mix land uses; (2) take advantage of compact building design; (3) create housing opportunities and choices; (4) create walkable communities; (5) foster distinctive, attractive communities with a strong sense of place; (6) preserve open space, farmland, natural beauty, and critical environmental areas; (7) strengthen and direct development toward existing communities; (8) provide a variety of transportation choices; (9) make development decisions predictable, fair, and cost-effective; and (10) encourage community and stakeholder collaboration in development decisions. A common theme behind many of these principles involves increasing the density of development. This poses a major challenge given that the exodus from the cities following the Second World War was a rebellion against density. People want to live in a small community with access to a big city.

Notes and Comments

1. *The Theory and Reality of Smart Growth, Sustainable Development, and New Urbanism.* Does the Congress for the New Urbanism manifesto attempt too much? Most studies find that higher density, mixed-use, and transit-friendly neighborhoods that provide households with good pedestrian and transit-friendly choices in living arrangements can significantly reduce the costs of transportation, energy, infrastructure, and public services. They also can provide a variety of other significant benefits. *See* Reid Ewing & Shima Hamidi, Longitudinal Analysis of Transit's Land Use Multiplier in Portland, 80 J. Am. Planning Ass'n 123, 133 (2014); Kyle Mott, Redevelopment Reimagined: A Proposal to Revive California's Redevelopment Agencies to Attain the Greenhouse Gas Reduction Targets of Senate Bill 375, 17 Chap. L. Rev. 233 (2013); William Hudnut, Changing Metropolitan America: Planning for a Sustainable Future, Urb. Land Inst. (2008).

A fast growing segment of today's real estate market in the United States seems to support smaller scale, mixed-use, and transit-friendly development. Much of the recent urban planning literature focuses on implementing this new urbanist vision. *See* Audres Duany, The Smart Growth Manual (2010); Robert Steuteville, New Urbanism Best Practices Guide (4th ed. 2009); Gerald Fisher, The Comprehensive Plan as an Indispensable Compass for Navigating Mixed-Use Zoning Decisions Through the Precepts of the Due Process, Takings, and Equal Protection Clauses, 40 Urb. Law. 831 (2008); Richard Geller, The Legality of Form Based Zoning Codes, 26 J. Land Use & Envtl. L. 35 (2010). Hence, the newly coined term, "new urbanism," that substantially overlaps with "smart growth."

General economic conditions and housing markets help drive growth and development in this country. In some areas of the country urban sprawl is an economically rational response to very high housing prices in inner cities, such as San Francisco, New York, and Los Angeles. The high costs of urban housing, a major turnaround in the last two decades, is a factor behind more 18- to 34-year-old people living at their family homes than in any previous time. Richard Fry, For First Time in Modern Era, Living With Parents Edges Out Other Living Arrangements for 18 to 34-Year Olds, Pew Res. Center (May 24, 2016), http://www.pewsocialtrends.org/2016/05/24/for-first-time-in-modern-era-living-with-parents-edges-out-other-living-arrangements-for-18-to-34-year-olds (last visited Oct. 6, 2016).

2. *Political Will and New Planning Challenges.* In recent years there has been an undeniable decline of public faith in the efficacy of strong government planning. This is reflected in the adoption of "takings" legislation in some states, such as Arizona and Florida (and briefly in Oregon, where voters approved a ballot measure

that essentially repudiated a prior ballot measure adopting a taking measure), as described in Chapter 9. It is also reflected in the stripping of local governments of eminent domain redevelopment powers in the aftermath of the Supreme Court's *Kelo* decision (a principal case in Chapter 7).

Yet many proponents of new urbanism, smart growth, and sustainable development view strong urban planning, land use regulation, and eminent domain as potentially critical tools for creating a more sustainable society. Whatever might be their actual costs and benefits, smart growth, new urbanism, and sustainable development planning proposals typically require an active and integrated urban planning framework (perhaps even one regional in scope) for implementation. *See* Timothy Polmateer, How Localism's Rationales Limit New Urbanism's Success and What New Regionalism Can Do About It, 41 Fordham Urb. L.J. 1085 (2014); Edward Ziegler, Sustainable Urban Development and the Next American Landscape: Some Thoughts on Transportation, Regionalism, and Urban Planning Law Reform in the 21st Century, 43 Urb. Law. 91 (2011); Arthur Nelson, The Mass Market for Suburban Low-Density Development is Over, 44 Urb. Law. 811 (2012.

3. *Comprehensive Plans and the New World of Land Use.* New planning concepts and ideas related to promoting smart growth, new urbanism, and sustainable development have worked a transformation in the goals and policies related to growth and land development in some communities. Comprehensive plans (addressed in Chapter 5) and zoning now sometimes embrace policies and concerns related to smart growth and sustainable development. The long list of issues addressed in the plans include: open space, landmark trees, wildlife habitat, air pollution, light pollution, watershed protection, animal migration corridors, native wildflowers, weed eradication, landscaping, fences, view orientation, stone building surfaces, historic preservation, building design and colors, roof slant and front porch preferences, lawn ornaments, solar orientation, flags and signs, neighborhood gardens, weekend markets and festivals, home food production, home occupations, parking preferences, and recycling. They also include a variety of global warming prevention strategies as well as community art, policies regarding displaced persons, and "saving the rainforests" programs. In short, comprehensive plans are now sometimes vehicles for fostering urban arrangements that fall within several different patterns, all of which can be described as aimed at sustainability.

Professor Michael Lewyn, however, has raised important questions about how land use plans, the traditional holy grail of local land use management, can be adapted to the smart growth era. *See* Michael Lewyn, The (Somewhat) False Hope of Comprehensive Planning, 37 U. Haw. L. Rev. 39 (2015) (contending that a municipal comprehensive plan is neither necessary nor sufficient for "smart" growth, and, in fact can be used just as easily to promote sprawl as smart growth). *See also* Michael Lewyn, Plans Are Not Enough, 42 Real Est. L.J. 240 (2013) (providing additional detail about how comprehensive plans can be counterproductive in achieving "smart growth").

4. *Skepticism.* Some are skeptical of the political viability of the sustainable development platform. In Steve Calandrillo et al., Making "Smart Growth" Smarter, 83 Geo. Wash. L. Rev. 829 (2015), the authors hone in on the breadth of the change required by smart growth principles:

> Though it would clearly take a complicated revamping of many areas of American law
> (not to mention cultural expectations), it is rarely—if ever—suggested that the

United States reexamine its individualistic conception of private property rights. The historic and legal ways that private property rights are construed in the United States, namely, the robust "bundle of rights" provided to persons who own property and the accompanying sense of entitlement both pose significant impediments to sustainable, coordinated land use management.

C. CLIMATE CHANGE: THE ULTIMATE CHALLENGE TO SUSTAINABILITY

Scientists and leading policy makers regard climate change as the primary obstacle to achieving the goal of sustainable development over the long term. Land use decisions can have an important influence on the pace of climate change, and the effects of climate change have important implications for settlement patterns and other land use choices. As you read the following short primer on climate change, notice the land use implications of present and future climate change.

■ JOHN T. ABATZOGLOU ET AL., A PRIMER ON GLOBAL CLIMATE CHANGE SCIENCE, IN DIMENTO AND DOUGHMAN (EDS.), CLIMATE CHANGE: WHAT IT MEANS FOR US, OUR CHILDREN, AND OUR GRANDCHILDREN
(2d ed. MIT Press 2014)

The earth's climate system includes a series of checks and balances that, in the past, have worked together to maintain a stable climate. However, mounting evidence suggests that this balancing act has been tested over the last century and a half. Multiple indicators — including increasing air and ocean temperatures, increasing sea level, and retreating glaciers and sea ice — all point to a warming planet.

EARTH'S CLIMATE SYSTEM

The earth's climate system can be thought of as an elaborate balancing act of energy, water, and chemistry through the atmosphere, oceans, ice masses, biosphere, and land surface. These internal components of the climate system influence the fate of energy emitted by the sun and received by the earth. Solar energy, or solar *radiation*, serves as the impetus of energy in the earth's climate system. Roughly 30 percent of the solar radiation directed toward the earth is reflected back to space by bright, reflective surfaces, including snow cover, sand, and clouds. This is the same phenomenon that keeps a white car much cooler than a black car on a hot day.

Just as the sun emits energy, so does each object whose temperature is above absolute zero, including the Earth's surface. Absolute zero is the temperature at which, in theory, particles have no energy (Merall 2013). Emitted energy, or *radiation,* from both the sun and the earth travels in the form of waves that are similar to the waves moving across the surface of a pond. However, the energy emitted by the sun and earth is quite different. Each emits radiation at distinctly different *wavelengths* (the distance between adjacent crests in the wave) and temperatures. While the hot sun emits energy at short wavelengths (referred to as *shortwave radiation, including visible light)*, the much cooler earth emits radiation at longer wavelengths (referred to as *longwave,* or *thermal, radiation*).

For the earth to maintain a stable temperature, there must be a balance between the amount of radiation absorbed by the earth and the amount of energy emitted from the earth back to space. According to simple energy-balance calculations, the average temperature of the earth's surface in the absence of an atmosphere should be -18°C (0°F). Fortunately, the earth has an atmosphere that traps much of the thermal radiation emitted by the earth's surface, but allows most of the solar radiation to pass through. This acts somewhat like a one-way mirror seen in interrogation rooms on crime dramas. Certain trace gases in the earth's atmosphere, called *greenhouse gases,* selectively absorb longer wavelengths of energy emitted by the earth, heating the surrounding atmosphere. This energy is ultimately reflected back to the earth's surface. As a result, the earth's surface has a more difficult time cooling off, and the earth's surface and its lower atmosphere warm significantly.

Greenhouse gases are a natural component of the earth's atmosphere, with water vapor accounting for much of the greenhouse effect. The warming effect of water vapor can be observed during winter nights when the earth's surface has an extended period of time to cool off. A cloudy winter night is typically warmer than a clear winter night. Clouds and water vapor trap the heat radiating from the surface and keep surface temperatures from dropping as much as they would on a clear night. Overall, the natural greenhouse effect allows the average surface temperature

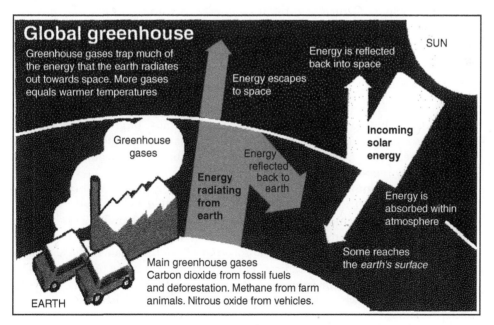

Figure 2.1
Fundamental Dynamics of the Greenhouse Effect.

of the earth to warm from a frigid -18°C (0°F) to a more comfortable 15°C (59°F). Thus, the chemical makeup of the atmosphere is crucial in establishing a climate that is hospitable to life (See Figure 2.1)

Our description of energy balance thus far applies to the earth as a whole. At local scales, the energy balance equation changes. To understand this, consider that solar radiation is much more intense near the equator than near the poles as a result of the curvature of the earth's surface and tilt of the earth's axis. The amount of solar radiation received in the tropics is much larger than that received at the poles. However, the rate at which earth emits energy (radiation) to space does not differ as dramatically from the equator to the poles. As a result, there is a net loss of energy near the poles and a net gain of energy in the tropics. Therefore, the ocean and atmosphere transport excess heat from the tropics to the heat-deficient polar regions via winds and ocean currents. If this transfer did not occur, there would be a rapid cooling of the poles and a dramatic warming of the tropics. Because our atmosphere and oceans redistribute this energy imbalance, much of our earth is livable. The atmosphere responds to unequal heating of the earth's surface by generating atmospheric motion. . . .

The land surface and the biosphere both affect and are affected by atmospheric temperature and humidity, and can alter the amount of solar radiation reflected back to space. Vegetation also plays a key role in the *carbon cycle*, which is the exchange of carbon among atmosphere, ocean, and land (biosphere included). Plants are active participants in the carbon cycle as they absorb CO_2 through photosynthesis and expel CO_2 through respiration. It is currently thought that plants take up more carbon from the atmosphere than they emit, and are therefore net *sinks* of atmospheric carbon (Le Quere et al. 2009). By contrast, changes in land use — such as deforestation and subsequent burning of forest material — release stored carbon into the atmosphere and are net *sources* of carbon to the atmosphere. In particularly productive ecosystems such as tropical rainforests, deforestation not only provides a source of atmospheric carbon, but also removes a net sink that would otherwise take up atmospheric carbon to build woody biomass through photosynthesis.

THE IMPORTANCE OF GREENHOUSE GASES TO CLIMATE

. . . The composition of the earth's atmosphere governs the climate of the planet and establishes conditions vital for life. The ability of greenhouse gases to warm the surface of the planet depends on four main factors: their efficiency in absorbing heat energy, their concentration and distribution in the atmosphere, and how long they remain in the atmosphere.

Although the atmosphere is primarily composed of nitrogen and oxygen, these gases do not interact with the thermal radiation emitted by the earth. However, greenhouse gases including carbon dioxide (CO_2), methane (CH_t), nitrous oxide (N_2O), halocarbons, ozone (O_3), and water vapor (H_2O) are very effective at absorbing thermal radiation. The absorption of energy by air molecules heats the atmosphere, which then reradiates energy back to the surface of the earth. This process prevents the earth from cooling. Another important property of greenhouses gases is that while they are effective at absorbing thermal radiation, they are essentially transparent to solar radiation. Hence, the overall influence of greenhouse gases is to warm the planet to approximately 33°C (59°F), which is remarkable given their seemingly small concentrations in the makeup of the atmosphere. . . .

EFFICIENCY OF GREENHOUSE GASES IN ABSORBING HEAT

Scientists estimate the heat-trapping efficiency of different greenhouse gases using an index called *global warming potential* (GWP). This represents the ratio of energy trapped by the earth-atmosphere system for a given mass of a particular gas in comparison with the ability of the same mass of CO_2 to trap energy over a specified period of time. The GWP of CO_2 is defined as 1. By comparison, methane has a GWP of 21, meaning that a given mass of methane can heat the planet twenty-one times as much as the same mass of CO_2. Other greenhouse gases have even larger GWPs. Nitrous oxide and halocarbons have GWPs of 300 and over 5,000, respectively. So although carbon dioxide is notorious for its role in global warming, other, less well-known greenhouse gases also play potent roles in the global warming process.

QUANTITIES OF GREENHOUSE GASES

Scientists can quantify the composition of the atmosphere prior to the historical record by examining other physical records that provide a stand-in for direct measurements. Bubbles of air embedded within ice cores extracted from the Greenland and Antarctic ice sheets reveal a substantial amount of information on past changes in climate. The cores tell us that from about 800,000 years ago until the beginning of the Industrial Revolution in the late 1700s, CO_2 varied from about 180 parts per million (ppm) during glacial periods to about 280 ppm during interglacial periods (Liithi et al. 2008). During interglacial periods, such as the one we are in today, levels of atmospheric CO_2 have previously been relatively constant, maintained through a balance of carbon exchanges between the atmosphere, biosphere, and oceans. *Anthropogenic*, or human-made, carbon emissions have resulted in an imbalance in the carbon cycle and an accumulation of carbon in the atmosphere. Atmospheric CO_2 levels at Mauna Loa, Hawaii, reached as high as 400 ppm in May 2013 (Mohan 2013). The rate of increase of atmospheric CO_2 since 2000 has a higher average than the rate of increase for each decade going back to the 1960s (Tans and Keeling 2013). The question is: how will these high levels of CO_2 affect our climate?

INDUSTRY AND GREENHOUSE GASES

Atmospheric concentrations of greenhouse gases have largely been balanced by the carbon cycle over the life history of the planet. Carbon cycles through the atmosphere via photosynthesis and respiration by land and sea flora, via air-sea exchanges (*fluxes*), and via "slow-turnover" geologic processes. While important for the evolution of the atmosphere, the relatively slow pace of the geologic carbon cycle (millions of years) is important only in controlling long-term variations in levels of atmospheric carbon dioxide.

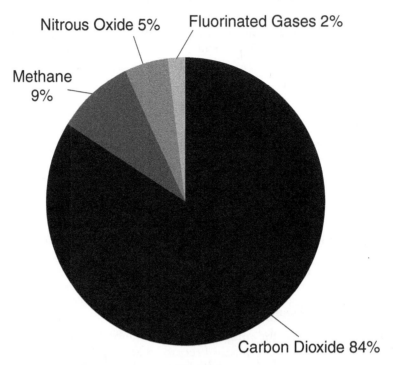

Figure 2.2
United States Emissions of Greenhouse Gases by Type in 2011.

Source: US Environmental Protection Agency (2013a). Inventory of U.S. Greenhouse Gas Emissions and Sinks 1990-2011.

The Industrial Revolution marked a turning point in the balance of energy in the earth's climate system. The rise of industry and technology resulted in an increase in the burning of wood and coal that serve as *sources* of carbon into the atmosphere. At the same time, changes in land use, including deforestation, worsened this imbalance by removing a potential sink for carbon. Carbon sources and sinks refer to parts of the carbon cycle that transfer carbon into and out of the atmosphere, respectively. Today, human activity is responsible for releasing approximately 9 billion metric tons of carbon per year into the atmosphere, with the ocean and land absorbing approximately half of that carbon (Le Quere et al. 2009). The accumulation of atmospheric carbon is analogous to a rising pool of water in a bathtub with a drain that is partially closed. The drain represents the sinks for atmospheric carbon in the oceans and the land, whereas the output of the faucet represents carbon in the atmosphere from sources such as fossil fuel burning and land-use change. If water comes out of the faucet faster than the drain can remove it, the water level in the bathtub will rise. Similarly, if sources of carbon outweigh the sinks, the amount of carbon in the atmosphere will continue to rise.

Electricity generated by the burning of fossil fuels accounted for more than a third of manmade carbon dioxide released in 2011 in the United States (EPA

2013b). In contrast, other energy sources — including nuclear, solar, wind, hydro-electric, and geothermal energy sources — emit minimal, if any, greenhouse gases. Using biomass to generate electricity can also reduce net greenhouse gas emissions. Forest trimmings, orchard prunings, livestock manure, cheese-processing waste, restaurant waste, gases from wastewater treatment plants, and gas from landfills are all forms of biomass. Biomass generally removes carbon dioxide from the air when growing and emits methane, which is a more potent greenhouse gas than carbon dioxide, when it decays. When managed sustainably, displacing the use of fossil fuels with full combusted or anaerobically digested biomass to generate electricity can reduce net greenhouse gas emissions.

The transportation sector is the second biggest source of carbon dioxide emissions in the United States. Every gallon of gasoline consumed releases about 2.5 kilograms (5.5 pounds) of carbon into the atmosphere. Fuel economies of many automobiles have improved dramatically over the past few decades because of technological improvements, but the carbon dioxide emitted from vehicles in the United States is still approximately equal to that emitted from all sources in India (even though the population of India is nearly four times that of the United States).

In addition to CO2 emissions, more than half of today's methane emissions are attributable to human activities, such as burning biomass, cultivating rice, creating landfills, and managing livestock (Solomon et al. 2007, chapter 7.4.1). Although much lower in atmospheric concentrations compared to CO2, methane is the second most important greenhouse gas due to its strong GWP. Atmospheric concentrations of methane have increased by more than 150 percent since the beginning of the Industrial Revolution as a direct result of human activities (EPA 2013a, Introduction, 5). Methane releases from agricultural and natural sources are expected to increase in a warming planet, regardless of human activity. Studies argue that warming may melt huge expanses of high-latitude permafrost and release large reserves of methane that have been locked away in deep soils (Zimov, Schuur, and Chapin 2006) and beneath the oceans (Pearce 2007).

What can land use law contribute to the necessary mitigation and adaptation responses to climate change? In the last 15 years we have learned that the contribution can be significant. Legislation linking land use, sustainability, and climate change includes traditional planning law, such as that on the comprehensive or master plan discussed in Chapter 5, as well as innovative new laws that link climate change directly to land use. The courts have also been presented with the challenge of resolving climate change land use disputes. Consider the following policies included in a local general plan.

■ BROWARD COUNTY, FLORIDA, COMPREHENSIVE PLAN: CLIMATE CHANGE ELEMENT (2016)

http://www.broward.org/Planning/FormsPublications/Documents/Climate-Change-Element.pdf (last visited Sept. 18, 2016)

Goal 19.0. Achieve a sustainable, climate resilient community by: promoting energy efficiency and greenhouse gas reduction strategies; protecting and adapting public infrastructure, services, natural systems and resources from climate change impacts; and continuing to coordinate and communicate locally and regionally to monitor and address the changing needs and conditions of the community.

GREENHOUSE GAS EMISSIONS REDUCTION, RENEWABLE ENERGY PRODUCTION, AND DISTRIBUTION

Objective 19.1. Mitigate the causes of climate change while providing for cleaner energy solutions and a more energy efficient way of life for visitors and residents. . . .

Policy 19.1.4. Broward County should plan for and facilitate the development of infrastructure that provides public access to alternative fuels and electric vehicle charging stations by 2015. Actions should include:

a) Planning for deployment and optimal distribution of a regional system;
b) Negotiating inter-local agreements with County, State, municipal and private entities to share existing and proposed infrastructure; and
c) Developing expedited permitting processes for private installation of alternative fuel and electric vehicle charging infrastructure.

MITIGATION, PROTECTION, AND ADAPTATION WITHIN THE TRANSPORTATION SYSTEM

Objective 19.2. Advance transportation and land-use choices that: reduce fossil fuel use and vehicle miles travelled; improve the mobility of people, goods and services; provide a diverse, efficient and equitable choice of transportation options; and increase the County's resiliency to the impacts of climate change.

Policy 19.2.2. Broward County shall continue to support and coordinate with local municipalities to further mixed land uses which promotes functional, walkable mixed-use development designs and projects by providing flexibility in development review for these projects, revising the zoning and land development codes to support such projects, and promoting the adoption of specific goals in local Comprehensive Plans to support and establish sustainable development patterns, especially in areas at reduced risk to sea level rise, as defined by the Priority Planning Areas for Sea Level Rise Map in the Broward County Land Use Plan. . . .

MITIGATION, PROTECTION, AND ADAPTATION WITHIN THE BUILT ENVIRONMENT

Objective 19.3. Improve the climate resiliency and energy-efficiency of new and existing buildings and public infrastructure, and develop adaptation strategies for areas vulnerable to climate change-related impacts. . . .

Policy 19.3.2. Broward County, in conjunction with its municipalities, should work cooperatively to review and re-evaluate current zoning codes, regulations and policies according to sustainable community development practices, such as those outlined in the criteria recommended by the United States Green Building Council's Leadership in Energy and Environmental Design for Neighborhood Development (LEED-ND) certification, or by application of a national rating system for local governments, such as the STAR Community Index™ (STAR). . . .

Policy 19.3.13. Broward County shall, in coordination with its local municipalities, designate Adaptation Action Areas (AAA), per Florida State Law, in order to:

(f) Identify areas that are vulnerable to the impacts of rising sea level;
(g) Identify and implement adaptation policies to increase community resilience;
(h) Enhance the funding potential of infrastructure adaptation projects.

The Broward County Commission, the Broward County Planning Council or a municipality may apply for Adaptation Action Area of Regional Significance designation [under Florida state planning law], if the problem(s) and proposed solution(s) of the proposed area demonstrate regional significance ...

SOCIAL CONSIDERATIONS, PUBLIC HEALTH, AND EDUCATION

Policy 19.8.3. Broward County shall seek to strengthen the local economy by promoting green economic growth and green-collar work training programs in order to: create resiliency; reduce reliance on fossil-fuel-based economies; provide a positive focus for economic development; advance the use of sustainable materials, technologies and services; and encourage local jobs in sustainable businesses which offer a living wage and make it possible for local climate change goals to be met.

Policy 19.8.4. Broward County should review codes and regulations to enable and encourage eco-industrial development and business practices in line with the concept of the circular economy. Specifically, business models and land development patterns should be encouraged which promote by-product exchanges (so that one company's waste stream is another's source of raw materials) as to more efficiently use resources (materials, water, energy) throughout society.

RIGHT TO HEALTHY AND SAFE ENVIRONMENT

Policy 19.8.5. Broward County shall consider the public health consequences of climate change, such as extreme temperatures and vector-borne diseases, and take steps to build capacity to respond to or prevent those consequences. Specifically, the County should:

.... Consider possible public health impacts of climate change in existing planning, programs, policies, and regulations ...
Create a community-wide public health climate change adaptation plan.

RESOURCE MANAGEMENT (WASTE, MATERIALS ECONOMY, LOCAL FOOD)

Policy 19.8.7. Broward County shall continue to pursue the source reduction, reuse, recycling, and recovery model of waste management, consistent with the Solid Waste Element of the Broward County Comprehensive Plan, in order to meet the State of Florida goal of recycling seventy-five percent of municipal solid waste (including net waste combusted) by 2030, work towards the zero waste by 2030 goal established in the Broward County Climate Change Action Plan, and continue to provide the environmental and social benefits of lowering greenhouse gas emissions, producing alternative energy, and reducing toxins in our land and water.

Policy 19.8.8. Broward County should develop, in conjunction with local municipalities and businesses, a sustainable and energy-efficient materials economy through cooperative materials management systems and infrastructure, in order to maximize the recovery and reuse of waste, water, wastewater, and other materials in ways that capture their economic value, conserve embedded energy, and minimize net life-cycle emissions of greenhouse gases and other pollutants.

Policy 19.8.9. Broward County, in conjunction with its municipalities, should create programs and policies which encourage and support composting, community garden networks and local food production, in order to meet the multiple goals of reduced emissions and energy consumption, while increasing the resiliency and long term food security of the community.

Green Infrastructure, Pedestrian Access, and Community Connectivity

Policy 19.8.11. Broward County, in conjunction with its municipalities, shall, when possible, increase bicycle and pedestrian connections between residential areas and public/civic areas, such as schools, libraries and parks, and enhance street networks for greater connectivity and multimodal use in order to:

a) reduce motor vehicle traffic;
b) reduce greenhouse gas emissions; and
c) increase neighborhood health and safety.

Policy 19.8.12. Broward County and its municipalities should encourage urban canopy placement and enhancement that contributes to quality walking environments.

Other local jurisdictions have adopted similar plans. *See, e.g.,* King County Washington Comprehensive Plan (2013) (incorporating GHG emission reduction strategies) http://www.kingcounty.gov//media/depts/permitting-environmental-review/dper/documents/growth-management/comprehensive-plan-2012/Complete SearchableDocument_131114.ashx?la=en (last visited Sept. 18, 2016); and City of Portland Oregon Climate Action Plan (2015) https://www.portlandoregon.gov/bps/66993 (last visited Sept. 18, 2016).

While we more fully address the concept of environmental impact assessment in Chapter 14, the excerpt from the following case suggests the importance of environmental impact assessment as a strategy to address climate change. The project at issue involved major improvements to a refinery that required a number of land use approvals, including a conditional use permit.

■ COMMUNITIES FOR A BETTER ENVIRONMENT v. THE CITY OF RICHMOND
108 Cal. Rptr. 3d 478 (Ct. App. 2010)

Ruvolo, P.J.

A. Improper Deferral of Greenhouse Gas Mitigation Measures

Respondents complained that the final EIR [environmental impact report] provided only a perfunctory list of possible measures to mitigate the Project's

significant contribution to greenhouse gas emissions and improperly deferred identification of these measures until *after* the CEQA [the California Environmental
Quality Act] process. . . .

It should first be pointed out that the formulation of greenhouse gas mitigation
measures was delayed due to the City's reluctance to make a finding early in the EIR
process that the greenhouse gas emissions generated by the Project would create a
significant effect on the environment. The draft EIR concluded that "[w]hen
considering the maximum potential emissions" created by the Project, it could
result in a "net increase in CO2 emissions of approximately 898,000 metric tons"
per year. However, the draft EIR explicitly declined to state conclusions about the
extent of any impacts or potential mitigation.

After numerous objections to the City's treatment of the greenhouse gas issue,
the final EIR acknowledged the environmental significance of greenhouse gas emissions and the effect of those emissions on global warming, but still avoided labeling
the Project's contribution to climate change as a significant effect on the environment. Instead, the Final EIR stated that making a significance determination for
greenhouse gas impacts of the Project would be too speculative.

After issuance of the final EIR in January 2008, there was an outpouring of
public comment arguing that the EIR had failed to provide a convincing and
complete explanation as to why the increase of greenhouse gas emissions caused
by the Project would not have a significant impact on the environment. Those
commenting, including California's Attorney General, submitted numerous scientific reports and studies regarding the relationship between climate change and
greenhouse gas emissions and the expected impacts on the environment.

The proposition that climate-change impacts are significant environmental
impacts requiring analysis under CEQA was bolstered by several ongoing developments. First, the Legislature enacted the Global Warming Solutions Act of 2006,
which implements deep reductions in greenhouse gas emissions after recognizing
that [g]lobal warming poses a serious threat to the economic well-being, public
health, natural resources, and the environment of California. . . . (Health & Saf.
Code, §38501, subd. (a).) Through this enactment, the Legislature has expressly
acknowledged that greenhouse gases have a significant environmental effect. Also,
in January 2008, a white paper was issued by the California Air Pollution Control
Officers Association . . . Among other topics, the paper discusses different
approaches for making a determination whether a project's greenhouse gas emissions would be significant or less-than-significant.

Based on the foregoing, the City belatedly issued a finding in a newly published
volume of the EIR issued in May 2008, that it now believes that the Proposed Project's estimated new emissions of 898,000 metric tons per year of GHGs [greenhouse
gases] prior to mitigation would most likely be a significant effect on the environment. Having recognized and acknowledged that incremental increases in greenhouses gases would result in significant adverse impacts to global warming, the EIR
was now legally required to describe, evaluate and ultimately adopt feasible mitigation measures which would mitigate or avoid those impacts. (§21002.1, subd. (b);
see also, Guidelines, §§15126.4, subd. (a)(1), 15091.) As amici point out, [t]he
quantity of emissions the EIR aims to mitigate is far from trivial. Mitigating the
898,000 tons of greenhouse gas emissions the [P]roject would generate is equivalent
to taking 160,000 cars off the road.

In response to this significance finding, the EIR puts forth some proposed mitigation measures to ensure that the Project's operation shall result in no net increase in GHG emissions over the Proposed Project baseline. The centerpiece of the mitigation plan is Mitigation Measure 4.3-5(e), which was ultimately adopted by the City Council in approving the Project. Mitigation Measure 4.3-5(e) states: "No later than one (1) year after approval of this Conditional Use Permit, Chevron shall submit to the City, for approval by the City Council, a plan for achieving complete reduction of GHG emissions up to the maximum estimated Renewal Project GHG emissions increase over the baseline (898,000 metric tons per year. . . .)"

First, the mitigation plan requires Chevron, within one year of Project approval, to hire and fully fund a qualified independent expert to complete an inventory of greenhouse gas emissions and to identify potential emissions reduction opportunities. In preparing the mitigation plan, Chevron shall consider implementation of measures that achieve GHG reductions including, *but not limited to*, the following measures: (Italics added.) Mitigation Measure 4.3-5(e) then lists a handful of candidate mitigation measures. Among the mitigation measures proposed are "Add/ improve heat exchangers" and "initiate carbon sequestration, capture and export." Another mitigation measure proposes "Replac[ing] stationary, non-emergency diesel internal combustion engines," while another proposes "Reduc[ing] mobile emission sources through 'transportation smart' development such as Greenprint." Mitigation Measure 4.3-5(e) outlines the priority by which measures should be implemented, with first priority given to on-site mitigation at the Refinery before mitigation measures are to take place elsewhere.

In the writ proceeding below, respondents argued that the City failed in not submitting a plan to mitigate greenhouse gas emissions during the environmental review process, but instead proceeding by preparing a menu of potential mitigation measures, with the specific measures to be selected by Chevron and approved by the City Council a year after Project approval. . . .

[W]e agree with the trial court that the City's decision to approve the Project, after giving the City Council final approval over a mitigation plan that Chevron formulates a year later outside the EIR process, does not satisfy CEQA's requirements. We emphasize once again that the time to analyze the impacts of the Project and to formulate mitigation measures to minimize or avoid those impacts was during the EIR process, *before* the Project was brought to the Planning Commission and City Council for final approval. Because the City belatedly acknowledged at the very end of the EIR process that the Project's greenhouse gas emissions would constitute a significant impact on the environment, the City was obviously unable to gather sufficient information during the EIR process itself to develop specific mitigation measures. The solution was not to defer the specification and adoption of mitigation measures until a year after Project approval; but, rather, to defer approval of the Project until proposed mitigation measures were fully developed, clearly defined, and made available to the public and interested agencies for review and comment.

Notes and Comments

1. *Local Planning.* The Broward County Plan includes novel policies and objectives related to global warming. How will these additions to the plan change the county's "usual" practice in reviewing land use applications? Are they easily

implemented? Will there be opposition to their implementation? Are you surprised by the extent of the proposals? *See, generally,* Design for Health, Addressing Climate Change with Comprehensive Planning and Ordinances, http://designfor-health.net/wp-content/uploads/2012/02/BCBS_ISClimateChange_072908.pdf (last visited Oct. 6, 2016). Consideration of climate change through comprehensive planning returns us to questions addressed in Chapter 5 about the efficacy of planning. Without a strong consistency requirement, will the attempt to affect climate change mitigation through planning be effective? Even in a strong consistency jurisdiction, are the phrases used in these plans subject to a wide range of interpretations that will ultimately make them less than action-forcing?

The *City of Richmond* case illustrates the connection between land use approvals and mitigation measures for global warming. The California environmental impact reporting law requires that a local government fully analyze measures that would mitigate global warming, and other jurisdictions without such requirements can be expected to adopt similar measures. Is the land use system an appropriate vehicle for addressing potential impacts on climate change? Or is this is an example of an area, discussed in Chapter 9, where a regional or statewide approach is needed?

2. *More Directly Linking Land Use and Sustainable Development.* The California Sustainable Communities and Climate Protection Act of 2008 (Sustainable Communities Act, SB 375, Chapter 728, Statutes of 2008) supports California's climate action goals to reduce greenhouse gas (GHG) emissions through coordinated transportation and land use planning. SB 375 is a complex law that links levels of government to land use, transportation, and sustainability goals. It directs the California Air Resources Board to set regional targets for GHG emissions. Metropolitan planning organizations (MPOs) are supposed to collaborate with the Board to establish the emissions targets for the regions. Each MPO is required to include a "Sustainable Communities Strategy" in the regional transportation plan demonstrating how the region will meet its GHG emission targets. If the strategy does not meet the target, the region must propose an "alternative planning strategy" that would meet the targets if it were implemented. Decisions allocating state transportation funds must then be consistent with the Sustainable Communities Strategy.

The law affects land use development in several ways. For development projects that are consistent with the regional Sustainable Communities Strategy, the state's environmental impact analysis—illustrated in the *City of Richmond* excerpt—is streamlined. The law also changes the housing element required for local general plans by linking it to the common land use assumptions for regional housing and transportation planning.

The complex law is ripe for litigation. *Cleveland Nat'l Forest Found. v. San Diego Ass'n of Governments,* 231 Cal. App. 4th 1056 (2014), petition for review granted in part, is a much followed leading case. The California Court of Appeal held that a regional planning agency implementing SB 375 abused its discretion by omitting from its environmental analysis a discussion of the transportation plan's consistency with the state climate policy of continual GHG emissions reductions through 2050. An executive order signed by then-Governor Arnold Schwarzenegger set the 2050 date. Further, the court found that the agency inadequately addressed mitigation of the transportation plan's GHG emissions impacts.

For a case where plaintiffs challenged what they called the draconian characteristics of a Sustainable Community plan, *see Bay Area Citizens v. Association of Bay*

Area Governments, 204 Cal. Rptr. 3d 224 (Ct. App. 2016). The court upheld the plan, concluding that the relevant agencies correctly declined to count statewide emissions reductions in developing their regional plan because doing so would have been improper "double counting" of reductions.

3. *Overcoming Local Opposition.* Some progressive steps on climate change mitigation confront opposition by local interests. Challenges to the use of renewables under local land use law are an example. Neighbors sometimes oppose distributed renewable energy generators, such as wind turbines, as undesirable land use nuisances. In Troy A. Rule, Renewable Energy and the Neighbors, 2010 Utah L.Rev. 1223, the author outlines the problem:

> In spite of state and federal policies aimed at promoting distributed renewable energy, local land use regulations continue to deter many landowners from installing small wind turbines and solar panels. . . . A handful of communities have voluntarily adopted provisions that accommodate these green LULUs . . . but most have proven reluctant to do so. Existing state and federal attempts to address communities' reluctance have been either overaggressive or not strong enough to overcome local resistance.

4. *Common Law Nuisance.* Perhaps the most famous of the actions brought on common law theories was *Kivalina v. ExxonMobil Corp.,* 696 F.3d 849 (9th Cir. 2012). The complaint filed by the native Inupiat village of Kivalina alleged that defendant energy and electric producers' actions releasing carbon dioxide were linked to climate change effects on the village. The village is on the tip of a barrier reef about 70 miles above the Arctic Circle in Alaska; its present population is around 400 people. The village faces relocation because of melting ice; the ice historically acted as a wave barrier. Without this barrier, the village is starting to fall into the ocean.

In *Bell v. Cheswick,* 734 F.3d 188 (3d Cir. 2013), the plaintiffs were a class made up of at least 1500 individuals who own or inhabit residential property within one mile of GenOn's Cheswick Generating Station, a 570-megawatt coal-fired electrical generation facility in Spring Dale, Pennsylvania (the "Plant"). Complaining of ash and contaminants settling on their property, the class brought suit against GenOn under several state law tort theories. The court of appeal held that state common law tort actions were not preempted. The court explained:

> [A]pplication of the source State's law does not disturb the balance among federal, source-state, and affected-state interests. Because the Act specifically allows source States to impose stricter standards, the imposition of source-state law does not disrupt the regulatory partnership established by the permit system. Second, the restriction of suits to those brought under source-state nuisance law prevents a source from being subject to an indeterminate number of potential regulations. Although [source-state] nuisance law may impose separate standards and thus create some tension with the permit system, a source only is required to look to a single additional authority, whose rules should be relatively predictable. Moreover, States can be expected to take into account their own nuisance laws in setting permit requirements.

In light of your knowledge of difficulties in establishing elements of a tort action, despite *Bell,* is it good lawyering to add common law causes of action to climate change lawsuits? Some think not. *See* Keith Goldberg, No Future for Climate Change Torts, Attys Say, Law 360 (May 23, 2013) http://www.law360.com/articles/444225/no-future-for-climate-change-torts-attys-say (last visited Oct. 7, 2016) ("[A]ttorneys say the pursuit of climate change tort litigation is approaching a dead end, leaving legislation and regulation as the only viable outlets to tackle the issue."). Others are more positive. *See* Amelia Thorpe, Tort-Based Climate Change Litigation and the Political Question Doctrine, 24 J. Land Use & Envtl. L. 79, 79–105 (Fall 2008).

5. *The Public Trust Doctrine.* Another civil law approach is through the public trust doctrine, an ancient doctrine holding that certain resources (particularly the seashore) are subject to protection for certain uses. Some argue the doctrine should apply to the atmosphere. According to one commentator:

> Civil litigation is an effective legal mechanism to expand the public trust doctrine's scope by way of the judiciary. Once a state judiciary can determine the applicability of the public trust doctrine to the Earth's atmosphere, it can affirm its government's fiduciary responsibility to regulate the substances in the atmosphere. This will protect Earth's habitability, and will be an appropriate way to sufficiently address climate change, at least at the state level. By utilizing civil litigation as a legal mechanism to coerce governments into regulating excessive anthropogenic GHG emissions, and ultimately in addressing and combating the harmful effects of climate change, the Earth's atmosphere can be protected for generations to come.

Kassandra Castillo, Climate Change & the Public Trust Doctrine: An Analysis of Atmospheric Trust Litigation, 6 San Diego J. Climate & Energy L. 221, 246 (2014-2015). For an opposing view *see* Andrew Ballentine, Full of Hot Air; Why the Atmospheric Trust Litigation Theory Is an Unworkable Attempt to Expand the Public Trust Doctrine Beyond its Common Law Foundations, 12 Dartmouth L.J. 98 (2014).

Is application to climate change and the atmosphere an appropriate use of the once very limited doctrine? Does it have the potential of jeopardizing the successful use of the doctrine in more mainline cases?

An exhaustive list of climate litigation under various legal challenges is provided by The Sabin Center for Climate Change Law at Columbia University. *See* http://www.arnoldporter.com//media/files/climatechange-chemicallegislation/climatechangelitigationchart.pdf (last visited Oct. 7, 2016).

6. *Choose Your Theory.* Is reliance on deficiencies in environmental impact assessments a superior strategy? Does your answer depend on whether the cause of action is based upon a state or federal environmental impact assessment challenge? How will a court address whether reasonable alternatives to the proposed actions are addressed? We cover environmental impact assessment again in Chapter 14.

7. *Uber and Climate Change.* Is the explosive use of Uber and other shared riding services a transportation innovation that mitigates or exacerbates climate change? *Compare* Stephen R. Miller, Uber-ing the Last Mile Home: New Approaches to Public Transit in Low Density Suburbs, Land Use Prof Blog (Aug. 30, 2016) http://law-professors.typepad.com/land_use/2016/08/uber-ing-the-last-mile-home-new-approaches-to-public-transit-in-low-density-suburbs.html (last visited Oct. 7, 2016) with attempts to regulate Uber because of its alleged contributions to congestion and emissions. Sarah Berger, New York City Uber Study Finds Traffic Congestion Could Get Worse, International Bus. Times (Jan. 14, 2016).

A Note on Land Use Law and Adapting
to Sea Level Rise

The Ongoing Effects of Climate Change. Adaptation to climate change is essential whatever the success of even the most aggressive and successful mitigation attempts. The effects of climate change on coastal cities are already being experienced. Streets are being inundated by sea water intrusion, and housing foundations are being destroyed. Commercial zones are more regularly flooded, while erosion of both private and public beaches is ongoing.

Almost two million housing units are located within one meter of high tide along American coastlines. Vulnerable areas exist in New York City, Long Island, the New Jersey shore, Norfolk, Virginia, Charleston, South Carolina, and several coastal cities in Florida, New Orleans, as well as the California coast. *See* Jessica A. Bacher & Jeffrey P. LeJavaa, Shifting Sands and Burden Shifting: Local Land Use Responses to Sea Level Rise in Light of Regulatory Takings Concerns, 35 No. 8 Zoning and Plan. L. Rep. 1 (2012). The impacts of sea level rise are critical in some areas. *See, for example,* the dramatic descriptions and mixed political response in Miami. Elizabeth Colbert, The Siege of Miami, The New Yorker (Dec. 21, 2015) available at http:// www.newyorker.com/magazine/2015/12/21/the-siege-of-miami   (last   visited Oct. 6, 2016).

Local Government Regulations. Some municipalities have begun to address sea level rise by utilizing land use controls. Tools include environmental impact assessment requirements, more specific requirements such as comprehensive plan elements dedicated to sea level rise, development standards for building and related activities near the coast, and consistency requirements linking development permission to the plan and zone obligations. Generally, the measures do not preclude all residential or commercial development in coastal zones. Instead, they mandate requirements to limit potential damage from storm surges and sea level rise. *See* Jessica A. Bacher & Jeffrey P. LeJava, Shifting Sands and Burden Shifting: Local Land Use Responses to Sea Level Rise in Light of Regulatory Takings Concerns, 35 No. 8 Zoning and Plan. L. Rep. 1 (2012).

State-level Responses to Sea Level Rise. Coastal states have responded in various ways to the threat of sea level rise. Some specific laws and regulations require policymakers or planners to consider sea-level rise when creating policy for land use planning or development, as in Massachusetts and Rhode Island. Others require consideration of sea level rise when reviewing certain permit applications, as in Florida and Maryland. However, most states take a less formal approach, in that there are no statutory or regulatory requirements to account for sea level rise, though authorities may consider sea level rise in practice. *See generally* OLR Research Report 2012-R-0418, Sea-Level Rise Adaptation Policy in Various States, https:// www.cga.ct.gov/2012/rpt/2012-R-0418.htm (last visited Oct. 6, 2016). Pursuant to California's Global Warming Solutions Act of 2006 (AB 32), the state California Coastal Commission has promulgated a set of interpretive guidelines which, though not legally binding, provide an overview of the best available science on sea level rise and recommended methodologies to be used in local coastal planning and regulatory actions by local authorities. California Coastal Commission, Sea Level Rise Policy Guidance: Interpretive Guidelines for Addressing Sea Level Rise in Local Coastal Programs and Coastal Development Permits (2015).

Rolling Coastal Management Statutes. A number of states rely on "rolling easements" to prevent inappropriate development along coastline that is vulnerable to sea level rise. These states include Texas, Maine, Massachusetts, North Carolina, South Carolina, Rhode Island, and Oregon. Rolling easements allow publicly-owned tidelands to migrate inland as a result of sea level rise or other natural forces at the expense of existing structures. Rhode Island adopted a cutting-edge "rolling" approach to coastal management after the state legislature recognized that unregulated development of shoreline properties was impacting public trust lands. In 1971, the Rhode Island legislature created the Coastal Resources Management Council, giving it broad discretion to preserve all of Rhode Island's coastal resources. As a result, the Council adopted the Coastal Resources Management Program (CRMP), a complex administrative regime that allows the Council to balance public interests with economic uses of the coastline.

The CRMP identifies six different water types: conservation areas, low-intensity use, high-intensity boating, multipurpose waters, commercial and recreational harbors, and industrial waterfronts. The state has also designated ten categories of coastal features: tidal waters; beaches and dunes; undeveloped barriers; moderately-developed barriers; developed barriers; coastal wetlands; headlands, bluffs and cliffs; rocky shores; manmade shores; and areas of historic/archaeological significance. The CRMP then places limitations or requirements on different activities based on the water "type" and coastal "features," a sort of "sea level rise" zoning for coastal lands which governs the construction of residential structures, docks and piers, beach nourishment, and construction of commercial and industrial buildings. This regime allows the local permitting authorities in the state to use their site plan review. *See* Jessica Grannis, et al., Coastal Management in the Face of Rising Seas: Legal Strategies for Connecticut, 5 Sea Grant L. & Pol'y 59 (2012).

Similarly, the Texas Open Beaches Act relies on the public trust doctrine to provide for dynamic public easements that move with the coastal vegetation lines. The state's embrace of this doctrine has allowed the state to address sea level rise in three ways. First, along Gulf-facing beaches, as a result of the Open Beaches Act structures on the beach can be removed as the dune vegetation line moves inland as a result of sea level rise. Second, the state's Dune Protection Act protects critical dunes and prevents construction too close to established protection lines. Finally, this statutory authority has allowed some counties to adopt strong setback rules that prevent development from up to 350 feet from dune protection lines. *See generally* Richard McLaughlin, Rolling Easements as a Response to Sea Level Rise in Coastal Texas: Current Status of the Law After *Severance v. Patterson*, 26 J. Land Use & Envtl. L. 365 (2011).

However, a challenge to Texas' rolling easements doctrine raises important questions and will likely subject the state to litigation for decades. In *Severance v. Patterson*, 370 S.W.3d 705 (Tex. Sup. Ct. 2012), the Texas Supreme Court ruled that rolling easements exist if they were created by the slow process of erosion. They do not, however, exist if created by a sudden, rapid change known as "avulsion," such as when the shoreline moves following a major storm surge brought on by a hurricane. How will future court decisions distinguish between natural erosion and rapid "avulsions"? Will other state courts interpreting the dimensions of rolling easements reach a similar conclusion?

Rolling Easements as Takings. Although the Texas Supreme Court did not address the question in *Severance*, the implementation of a "living shoreline" approach begs another important question: With what takings framework should restrictions based on these land use controls be addressed? Can a potential defendant in a takings lawsuit based on these types of rolling restrictions avoid application of the Lucas *per se* takings test by pointing out that the regulation permits use of the property until rising seas make that dangerous and impractical? In environmental impact analysis of projects planned within vulnerable zones should alternatives need to include the same development in less vulnerable areas of the municipality? Does your answer depend on the availability of transfer of development rights within the jurisdiction?

Consider the following ordinance:

■ COLLIER COUNTY, FLORIDA, LAND DEVELOPMENT CODE

3.02.00 — FLOODPLAIN PROTECTION

3.02.03 — APPLICABILITY

This section shall apply to all areas of special flood hazard in the unincorporated area of the County, and identified by the Federal Insurance Administration in its flood insurance rate map (FIRM), dated November 17, 2005, and any revisions thereto.

3.02.06 — GENERAL STANDARDS FOR FLOOD HAZARD REDUCTION

In all areas of special flood hazards, the following provisions are required:

A. All new construction and substantial improvements shall be anchored to prevent flotation, collapse, or lateral movement of the structure.

B. New construction and substantial improvements in the A Zones may be built on unconstrained, but compacted, fill, if in compliance with the Collier County Building Code Ordinance. No significant water is permitted to flow from the subject premises onto abutting properties or into adjoining waters which are not County-approved drainage system(s).

C. Residential Construction — new construction or substantial improvement of any residential structure shall have the lowest floor elevated to or above the base flood elevation.

D. Non-residential Construction — new construction and substantial improvements of non-residential structures shall have the lowest floor (including basement) elevated to or above the base flood level or, together with the attendant utility and sanitary facilities, be designed so that, below the base flood level, the structure is essentially waterproofed with walls substantially impermeable to the passage of water and with structural components having the capability of resisting hydrostatic and hydrodynamic loads and effects of buoyancy. Floodproofing is prohibited in the velocity (V) zones. The property owners shall provide a certification by a registered professional engineer or registered professional architect that the design standards of this section are satisfied. . . .

3.02.08 — REGULATIONS WITHIN THE FLOODWAYS

A. When floodways are designated within areas of special flood hazard, additional criteria shall be met. Since the floodway is an extremely hazardous area due to the velocity of flood waters, which carry debris, potential projectiles, and erosion potential, the following provision shall apply:

1. Encroachments, including fill, new construction, substantial improvements and other developments, are prohibited, unless the property owner provides a certification by a professional registered engineer demonstrating that such encroachments shall not result in a significant increase in flood levels during occurrence of the base flood discharge . . .

3.02.10 — STANDARDS FOR SUBDIVISION PLATS

A. All subdivision plats shall be consistent with the need to minimize flood damage.

B. All subdivision plats shall have public utilities and facilities, such as sewer, gas, electrical, and water systems, located and constructed to minimize flood damage.

C. All subdivision plats shall have adequate drainage provided to reduce exposure to flood hazards.

D. Base flood elevation data shall be shown on the Master Subdivision Plan.

E. All final plats presented for approval shall clearly indicate the finished elevation of the roads and the average finished elevation of the lots or home site . . .

3.03.03 — PRIORITY FOR LOCATION OF STRUCTURES, DEVELOPMENT, OR SITE ALTERATIONS

A. Any proposed structure or site alteration on a shoreline shall be located within the boundaries of the subject parcel with the most impacted coastal habitats existing on the subject parcel receiving the highest priority for siting of the proposed structure or site alteration. The following categories of impacts, 1 through 7, shall be used to determine the priority for location of development or site alteration:

1. Areas presently developed.
2. Disturbed uplands.
3. Disturbed freshwater wetlands.
4. Disturbed brackish water and marine wetlands.
5. Viable unaltered uplands.
6. Viable unaltered freshwater wetlands.
7. Viable unaltered brackish water and marine wetlands.

B. If "1. Areas presently developed" exists on the subject parcel, it shall be the preferred site for the proposed structure or site alteration. If "1" is not present, and "2. Disturbed uplands" exists on the subject parcel, "2" shall be the preferred site for development or site alteration. This siting process shall continue in the same manner through "7," until a specific area is identified as an appropriate location for the proposed structure or site alteration on the subject parcel.

C. In the event that the proposed development or site alteration requires a larger area than is available in the highest category of impacted habitat, then any adjoining land in the next highest category of impacted habitat shall, in addition, be allocated for location of the proposed development or site alteration. Where there is a mixture of categories of impacted habitat, and it is not possible to follow the priorities noted above, the proposed development or site alteration shall be planned to maximize the use of land for development in the highest ranked categories and to minimize the use of land in the lowest ranked categories. The burden of proof shall be on the applicant to establish that a higher ranked category of impacted habitat is not feasible for siting the proposed development or site alteration.

3.03.05 — SEA LEVEL RISE

An analysis shall be required demonstrating the impact of a six (6) inch rise in sea level for development projects on a shoreline. This requirement shall be met by inclusion of this analysis in an environmental impact statement (EIS). This requirement shall be waived when an EIS is not required. This analysis shall demonstrate that the development will remain fully functional for its intended use after a 6 inch rise in sea level. In the event that the applicant cannot meet this requirement, a list shall be provided by the applicant of the changes necessary in order for the development to meet the standard. . . .

D. PUBLIC HEALTH AND VULNERABLE POPULATIONS

1. Obesity

In the twentieth century, automobile-dependent regional sprawl was largely perceived as "a quality-of-life" issue. Specific concerns included: absence of human scale and walkability in an extended built environment, lack of sense of place or of charming public spaces, unappealing garage-door architecture and extensive parking lot landscapes, traffic congestion, loss of places friendly to children and the elderly, and loss of nearby open space and wildlife habitat. While all of these problems are still associated with sprawl, today the focus has shifted to examining the relationship between sprawl and public health, and how sprawl affects housing, energy, transportation, and infrastructure costs.

Beyond overall macro effects on sustainability and health, land use law has affected, sometimes quite deleteriously, the well-being of selected populations. Many of them have been marginalized or ignored; at worst, they have been consciously discriminated against. This section covers law related to these subpopulations.

In 2012 Dr. Richard J. Jackson, a professor at the University of California, Los Angeles, predicted that the generation of Americans born since 1980 may be the first to live shorter lives than their parents. A committee of the America Heart Association suggested that there were ways to counter the harmful health behaviors of Americans that are linked to poor health. Almost 35 percent of adults in the United States are obese, and the prevalence of diabetes had grown to 7.2 percent in 2013. Some of the changes necessary to reverse these trends were readily obvious, such as cessation of smoking.

Two others were not as widely appreciated and link directly to land use patterns: being physically active and following certain dietary guidelines. For example, the committee recommended that individuals "[g]et regular physical exercise, at least 150 minutes a week of moderate physical activity or 75 minutes a week of vigorous activity, or a combination of the two." They should also drink "at most 36 ounces of sugar-sweetened drinks (less than 450 calories, or the equivalent in other sweets) a week . . ." Donald M. Lloyd Jones, et al., Defining and Setting National Goals for Cardiovascular Health and Disease Reduction, Circulation (Feb. 2, 2010), http://circ .ahajournals.org/content/121/4/586 (last visited Sept. 18, 2016). *See* Jane E. Brody, Rediscovering the Kitchen for Heart Health, The New York Times, (Aug. 2, 2016), http://well.blogs.nytimes.com/2016/08/01/rediscovering-the-kitchen-and-other-tips-for-heart-health/?_r=0 (last visited Sept. 18, 2016) (discussing these recommendations).

Numerous studies demonstrate that when neighborhoods are designed to encourage walking and cycling, people engage in those activities more frequently. *See* Ding Ding & Klaus Gebel, Built Environment, Physical Activity, and Obesity: What Have We Learned from Reviewing the Literature? Vol. 18 Issue 1, Health & Place, at 100 (Jan. 2012); *see also* Harvard School of Public Health, Environmental Barriers to Activity, How Our Surroundings Can Help or Hinder Active Lifestyles, https://www.hsph.harvard.edu/obesity-prevention-source/obesity-causes/physical-activity-environment/#references (last visited Oct. 7, 2016). Higher density is associated with more frequent walking and cycling because physical proximity to shops and stores provides citizens a choice about whether to walk, bike, or drive to these destinations. By contrast, less dense cities tend to foster a more car-centered existence.

The new emphasis on promoting health through better land use decisions calls for a reinterpretation of the original purposes of land use regulation. Those purposes were addressed to harms that development would pose. The language of the Standard Zoning Enabling Act and the first municipal zoning laws invoked harm-prevention:

Section 1. Grant of Power.

For the purpose of promoting health, safety, morals, or the general welfare of the community, the legislative body of cities and incorporated villages is hereby empowered to regulate and restrict the height, number of stories and size of buildings and other structures, the percentage of lot that may be occupied, the size of yards, courts, and other open spaces, the density of population and the location and use of buildings, structures and land of trade, industry, residence or other purposes. . . .

Section 3. Purposes in View

Such regulations shall be made in accordance with a comprehensive plan and designed to lessen congestion in the streets; to secure safety from fire, panic, and other dangers; to promote health and the general welfare; to provide adequate light and air; to prevent the overcrowding of land; to avoid undue concentration of population; to facilitate the adequate provision of transportation, water, sewerage, schools, parks, and other public requirements . . .

The solution of Euclidian zoning was to separate land uses. Today, a new set of harms has arisen, and the health outcomes targeted by the new sustainability are serious. Ironically, the solution is partly to combine some of the same uses that Euclidian zoning sought to separate.

Another strategy to promote good health through land use management is to promote community access to healthy food. Some communities have used land use regulation to provide space for urban gardens and other in-close agriculture uses, and for food distribution facilities. *See* Emily M. Broad Leib, All (Food) Politics Is Local: Increasing Food Access Through Local Government Action, 7 Harv. L. & Pol'y Rev. 321, 322 (2013) ("Many recent local actions focus explicitly on increasing healthy-food access, including amending zoning codes to increase urban agriculture, creating new mobile vending outlets, and enhancing transportation routes to healthy-food retailers."). Other communities have focused on decreasing the supply of unhealthy foods, as illustrated by the model zoning ordinance set out below.

■ NATIONAL POLICY AND LEGAL ANALYSIS NETWORK, FINDINGS FOR MODEL HEALTHY FOOD ZONE ORDINANCE (2012)

http://www.changelabsolutions.org/publications/model-ord-healthy-food-zone (last visited Sept. 18, 2016).

The [Municipality] does ordain as follows:

SECTION I. FINDINGS.

The [Municipality] hereby finds and declares as follows:

WHEREAS, Childhood obesity is one of the most urgent public health challenges facing the nation and the State of [insert state of municipality], with 16.3 percent of children and adolescents ages 2 to 19 obese, and 31.9 percent obese or overweight;

WHEREAS, Overweight children are at greater risk for numerous adverse health consequences, including type 2 diabetes, heart disease, stroke, high blood pressure, high cholesterol, certain cancers, asthma, low self-esteem, depression, and other debilitating diseases;

WHEREAS, Childhood obesity is estimated to cost $14 billion annually in health expenses;

. . .

WHEREAS, Studies have shown strong evidence of an association between frequent eating of fast food, excess energy intake, weight gain, overweight, and obesity [footnotes omitted]

In adolescents, those who ate fast food and other away-from-home foods regularly consumed 600-800 extra calories per week and were more likely to have higher body mass indexes; [footnotes omitted] Greater availability of fast food restaurants is associated with higher individual-level weight status and higher state-level obesity prevalence; [footnotes omitted]

WHEREAS, On a typical day, nearly one-third of U.S. children ages 4 to 19 eat fast food every day;

. . .

WHEREAS, More than one-third of middle and high schools nationwide are located within a half-mile of at least one fast food outlet or convenience store; [footnotes omitted]

WHEREAS, Two-thirds of urban secondary schools have at least one fast food restaurant within walking distance; . . .

NOW THEREFORE, BE IT RESOLVED . . .

The [Municipality] does ordain as follows:

. . . .

NOW THEREFORE, it is the intent of the [*City/City Council*], in enacting this ordinance to promote children's health by regulating the distance between schools [*and other locations frequented by children*] and fast food restaurants [*and mobile vendors*] serving low-nutrient, energy-dense foods.

Section II.

[Article / Section] of the [Municipality] Municipal Code is hereby amended to read as follows:

SEC. ONE. PURPOSE.

The purposes of this [article / chapter] are to promote the health of children by regulating the location and operation of Fast Food Restaurants near schools [*and other locations frequented by children*] and to support efforts of the school district(s) to create healthy food environments for students.

SEC. TWO. DEFINITIONS.

The following words and phrases, whenever used in this [*article / chapter*], shall have the meanings defined in this section unless the context clearly requires otherwise:

"Fast Food Restaurant" means a retail food establishment where food and beverages are: (1) prepared in advance of customer orders or are able to be quickly prepared for consumption on or off the premises; (2) are ordered and served over counters or at drive-through windows; and (3) paid for before being consumed.

SEC. THREE. PROHIBITING FAST FOOD RESTAURANTS NEAR SCHOOLS.

Option One (for communities that do not require a use permit for Fast Food Restaurants):

(a) No Fast Food Restaurant may be located within [*insert appropriate distance for community*] feet of the nearest property line of any public, charter, or private kindergarten, elementary, middle, junior high or high school, or a licensed child-care facility or preschool [*list additional facilities if appropriate, such as playgrounds, youth centers, recreational facilities, arcades, parks, libraries, or residentially zoned parcels*]

Option Two:

(a) A Fast Food Restaurant is allowed only as a conditional use in the following zones: commercial; [*add other zoning districts*] subject to the following regulations:

(1) In any district where a Fast Food Restaurant is permitted or a conditional use, the Fast Food Restaurant may not be located within

[*insert appropriate distance for community*] feet of the nearest property line of any public or private kindergarten, elementary, middle, junior high, or high school, or a licensed child-care facility or preschool [*list additional facilities if appropriate, such as playgrounds, youth centers, recreational facilities, arcades, parks, libraries, or residentially zoned parcels*].

SEC. FOUR. CONTINUATION OF PREEXISTING LIMITED SERVICE/FAST FOOD RESTAURANTS.

(a) Fast Food Restaurants lawfully existing or having an approved [*building*] permit to operate prior to _____ [*insert the effective date of the legislation*] may continue to operate under the following conditions:

  (1)   The restaurant operates in accordance with all applicable federal, state, and local laws;

  (2)   The restaurant does not seek a modification to its permit that would allow any intensification of use;

  (3)   The restaurant operates continuously in the same location, without substantial increase in intensity of operation or square footage;

Another approach is to assess the impacts of land use decisions on health. The use of health impact assessments is growing. Sometimes health impact assessments are integrated into environmental impact statements or reports (discussed in Chapter 14), while in other instances they are produced as freestanding documents. They tend to focus on zoning changes, density restrictions, housing types, and walking and transit related improvements. For example, a health impact assessment prepared for the City of Baltimore assessed proposed changes in the city's zoning code. Johns Hopkins University, Center for Child & Community Health Research, Transform Baltimore Health Impact Assessment (2010), http://www.hiaguide.org/hia/transform-baltimore-health-impact-assessment (last visited Oct. 7, 2016).

In an Oregon city, a health impact assessment of transportation policies addressed the creation of "20 minute neighborhoods." These neighborhoods are defined as "those in which a significant number of regular trips can be made in 20 minutes without using an automobile." City of Eugene, Oregon, A Community Climate and Energy Action Plan for Eugene (2010), https://www.eugene-or.gov/Archive/ViewFile/Item/80 (last visited Oct. 6, 2016). Other health impact assessments are described in Patricia Salkin & Pamela Ko, The Effective Use of Health Impact Assessment (HIA) in Land-Use Decision Making, Zoning Practice (Oct. 2011), http://www.pewtrusts.org/en//media/assets/external-sites/health-impact-project/salkin201_effectiveuseofhiainlanduse.pdf (last visited Oct. 6, 2016). Professors Salkin and Ko note that assessments reflect concerns of health professionals that certain types of development do not enable physical activity. They cite numerous examples of health risks created by poorly planned development: the absence of sidewalks, dangerous intersections, poorly lighted areas, and the absence of access to farmers' markets, to name a few.

Protections of public health and safety can also be implemented by making changes to the already-built environment. Features in this environment that encourage activity include:

Recreational resources, such as walking trails, bicycling trails, parks, gardens and open spaces.

Land use characteristics, such as the density of residential and employment areas, location and density of fast food restaurants, the land use mix, and the number and proximity of stores, businesses, or workplaces.

Neighborhood characteristics, such as sidewalks and streetlights.

As can be seen in the following excerpts from a table compiled by the National Center for Chronic Disease Prevention and Health Promotion, a part of the federal Centers for Disease Control, actions to promote health at the local level are possible. The table includes those recommendations linked directly to land use and development control. Note also that such actions can be controversial, and some are subject to challenge on the basis of constitutional infringements.

■ LAURA KETTEL KHAN, PhD, ET AL., RECOMMENDED COMMUNITY STRATEGIES AND MEASUREMENTS TO PREVENT OBESITY IN THE UNITED STATES

(2009) https://www.cdc.gov/mmwr/preview/mmwrhtml/rr5807a1.htm
(last visited Oct. 7, 2016)

TABLE. Summary of recommended community strategies and measurements to prevent obesity in the United States

Strategy 3 **Communities should improve geographic availability of supermarkets in underserved areas.**
The number of full-service grocery stores and supermarkets per 10,000 residents located within the three largest underserved census tracts within a local jurisdiction.
Communities should provide incentives to food retailers to locate in and/or offer healthier food and beverage choices in underserved areas.

Strategy 5 **Communities should improve availability of mechanisms for purchasing foods from farms.**
The total annual number of farmer-days at farmers' markets per 10,000 residents within a local jurisdiction.

Strategy 9 **Communities should limit advertisements of less healthy foods and beverages.**
A policy exists that limits advertising and promotion of less healthy foods and beverages within local government facilities in a local jurisdiction or on public school campuses during the school day within the largest school district in a local jurisdiction.

Strategies to Create Safe Communities That Support Physical Activity

Strategy 16 **Communities should improve access to outdoor recreational facilities.**
The percentage of residential parcels within a local jurisdiction that are located within a half-mile network distance of at least one outdoor public recreational facility.

Strategy 17   **Communities should enhance infrastructure supporting bicycling.**
Total miles of designated shared-use paths and bike lanes relative to the total street miles (excluding limited access highways) that are maintained by a local jurisdiction.

Strategy 18   **Communities should enhance infrastructure supporting walking.**
Total miles of paved sidewalks relative to the total street miles (excluding limited access highways) that are maintained by a local jurisdiction.

Strategy 19   **Communities should support locating schools within easy walking distance of residential areas.**
The largest school district in the local jurisdiction has a policy that supports locating new schools, and/or repairing or expanding existing schools, within easy walking or biking distance of residential areas.

Strategy 20   **Communities should improve access to public transportation.**
The percentage of residential and commercial parcels in a local jurisdiction that are located either within a quarter-mile network distance of at least one bus stop or within a half-mile network distance of at least one train stop (including commuter and passenger trains, light rail, subways, and street cars).

Strategy 21   **Communities should zone for mixed use development.**
Percentage of zoned land area (in acres) within a local jurisdiction that is zoned for mixed use that specifically combines residential land use with one or more commercial, institutional, or other public land uses.

Strategy 22   **Communities should enhance personal safety in areas where persons are or could be physically active.**
The number of vacant or abandoned buildings (residential and commercial) relative to the total number of buildings located within a local jurisdiction.

Strategy 23   **Communities should enhance traffic safety in areas where persons are or could be physically active.**
Local government has a policy for designing and operating streets with safe access for all users which includes at least one element suggested by the national complete streets coalition (http://www.completestreets.org)

Notes and Comments

1. *Evaluating the Suggested Strategies.* Notice how each of these materials suggests the use of land use tools to implement a health-improvement strategy. Is the Model Healthy Food Zone Ordinance a logical extension of the types of land use controls that have been in effect since the *Village of Euclid* decision? Or is it land regulation on an issue better left to individual choice? Does your opinion depend on whether a measure addresses obesity in children or adults?

What about the measures in the list compiled by the National Center for Chronic Disease Prevention and Health Promotion? Can these be implemented in an already-built environment? Do you see them as qualitatively different from the regulation suggested in the Model Health Food Zone Ordinance? Finally, is a

Health Impact Assessment simply a logical extension of environmental impact assessment? Or is it government overreach? More importantly, will health impact assessment be useful if carried out?

Which of these measures raise potential constitutional issues?

2. *The Relation to Historical Land Use Tools.* Historically, tools have existed, including many described in earlier chapters, for achieving healthier lifestyles through land use controls. The limited use of these tools has arguably allowed for the evolution of communities where walking and biking are rare, and obstacles exist to mixing moderate exercise with undertaking one's daily activities. *See, e.g.,* Patricia Salkin & Amy Lavine, Land Use Law and Active Living: Opportunities for States to Assume a Leadership Role in Promoting and Incentivizing Local Options, 5 Rutgers J. L. & Pub. Pol'y 317 (2008) (discussing various land use tools that can be used to foster smart growth and "active living" policies); Sarah B. Schindler, Of Backyard Chickens and Front Yard Gardens: The Conflict Between Local Governments and Locavores, 87 Tul. L. Rev. 231 (2012) (discussing conflict between local zoning ordinances and local production of food); Patricia Salkin & Amy Lavine, Regional Foodsheds: Are Our Local Zoning and Land Use Regulations Healthy?, 22 Fordham Envtl. L. Rev. 599 (2011) (discussing planning for "regional foodsheds").

3. *More Land Use Examples.* In July 2008, the Los Angeles City Council passed a moratorium on opening or expanding fast food establishments in South Los Angeles. An evaluation conducted by The RAND Corporation found that South Los Angeles residents have, on average, a significantly higher body mass index than residents in Los Angeles County overall. However, the study found that the density of fast food chain restaurants in South Los Angeles was *lower* than in other parts of the county. Accordingly, the study suggested that the ban on fast food outlets was unlikely to be sufficient to reduce obesity. RAND Corp., South Los Angeles Ban on Fast Food Chains Misses the Mark (2009) http://www.rand.org/pubs/research_briefs/RB9489/index1.html (last visited Sept. 18, 2016).

The San Francisco City Council established the San Francisco Geary Boulevard "Formula Retail Eating and Drinking Subdistrict," which bars large fast food restaurants from the district. The intent of the ordinance was to "prevent further proliferation of fast-food restaurant uses" and for other reasons, but with no direct connection to obesity or health set forth. S.F. Municipal Code §781.4. A San Francisco Executive Directive, "Healthy and Sustainable Food for San Francisco" (2009), directs the executive branch departments to promote regional agriculture and economic opportunities that encourage access to healthier foods, including through the zoning code. *See* http://www.sfgov3.org/Modules/ShowDocument.aspx?documentid=74 (last visited Sept. 18, 2016).

See also Kathryn A. Peters, Creating A Sustainable Urban Agriculture Revolution, 25 J. Envtl. L. & Litig. 203 (2010); Sidney F. Ansbacher & Michael T. Olexa, Florida Nuisance Law and Urban Agriculture, Fla. B.J. (Jan. 2015); Chelsea Smialek, Take a Walk Through the Cities' Gardens: Comparing Detroit's New Urban Agriculture Zoning Ordinance to Others of Its Kind, 91 U. Det. Mercy L. Rev. 345 (2014); Kathrin Specht et al., Urban Agriculture of the Future: An Overview of Sustainability Aspects of Food Production in and on Buildings, 31 Agric. Human Values 33 (2014), http://link.springer.com/article/10.1007/s10460-013-9448-4 (last visited Oct. 7, 2016); Yolanda Gonzalez et al., A Case Study: Advancing Public Health through Gardens for Healthy Communities (GHC) in New York City: The Role of Anti-obesity Objectives in Urban Agriculture Policy, in Elizabeth Hodges et al., (eds.) Sewing Seeds in the City 107 (2016), http://link.springer.com/chapter/ 10.1007/978-94-017-7456-7_9 (last visited Oct.7, 2016).

4. *Environmental Justice Implications.* Does urban food policy have any implications for environmental justice, a subject discussed in Chapter 16? For other treatments including an explicit link to environmental justice, *see* Lauren M. Rossena & Keshia M. Pollack, Making the Connection Between Zoning and Health Disparities, 5(3) Envtl. Just. 119, 124 (2012) ("When applied effectively and creatively, zoning can be used to address dozens of public health priorities simultaneously . . . However, the efficacy of zoning as a policy intervention to reduce health disparities is largely unknown.").

2. Sober Homes

Expert opinion on treatment of certain groups of disabled people now favors small-scale residential facilities instead of large, centralized institutions. According to the new viewpoint, the health of the patient or client (sometimes called the "customer") can be best promoted in settings that feel like a home and offer the support of other similarly situated people.

This new approach to health care has direct implications for land use and development control law. What legal obligations do local governments have to support residential developments that serve disabled or marginalized persons? What can communities lawfully do to mitigate any negative impacts associated with the proliferation of this type of treatment facility? Other chapters of this book address related topics, including Chapter 6 (discussing third-party participation in land use decisions), Chapter 13 (focusing on fair housing), and Chapter 16 (discussing Locally Unwanted Land Uses (LULUs)). Here we examine the question of whether the health care needs of certain populations can and should override local regulations that may stymie their recovery. The focus is on the relationships among federal, state, and local governments in meeting the residential treatment needs of one special population, recovering alcoholics or drug users.

The National Association for Recovery Residences lists about 2000 sober homes in its national registry. The growth in the number of these homes, and their real or perceived impacts on neighborhood life, have led to serious conflicts at the local level. Consider this excerpt, typical of recent newspaper articles illustrating this type of conflict. The case excerpt that follows addresses how the Fair Housing Act applies to regulation of sober homes.

■ DENISE G. CALLAHAN, WEST CHESTER PUTS MORATORIUM ON REHAB CENTERS

Butler County Journal-News (Apr. 18, 2016)
http://www.journal-news.com/news/news/local/west-chester-puts-moratorium-on-rehab-centers/nq7KY/ (last visited Sept. 19, 2016)

West Chester Twp. trustees placed an eight-month moratorium on any new drug addiction rehabilitation centers even as they acknowledged the need for them.

The issue arose after a Mason doctor presented a plan to turn a vacant nursing home into a rehab center that residents say would be too close to a day care, ball fields and Lakota students.

"We do need facilities like this," Trustee George Lang said. "So this is not about regulating these businesses out of the township. It is, in my opinion, about looking at the potential secondary effects that may be detrimental to neighboring property owners and looking for ways to mitigate the negative impact."

According to the coroner's office, 189 people died from drug overdoses last year, and 149, or 79 percent, were heroin-related.

A number of neighbors came out last week to oppose a plan — some the same who protested a similar proposal in 2013 — by Professional Psychiatric Services (PPS) to turn the vacant West Chester Nursing and Rehabilitation Center on Ohio 42 into a mental health and addiction center. The site is across from Pisgah Youth Organization ball fields, and a daycare center sits next door.

Karen Werling, owner of Hickory Dickory Tots daycare, said 3,000 Lakota school students are in the immediate area, and many of them are walkers to and from school who would be exposed *ed: sic* drug addicts and to people visiting them in the proposed inpatient rehab.

Werling said rehab centers are necessary, ". . . just not in the middle of our community where we are serving so many young children," she said. "Birds of a feather can sometimes flock together, so not only do you have the inpatient people, but you have all the people coming in to visit with those people."

PPS hasn't applied for zoning yet, but the Mason-based company, owned by Dr. Muhamed Aziz, outlined its services in a letter to the township development department. Sherry Harbin, business and operations manager for PPS, noted 60 percent of the services would be outpatient, research and pharmacy, and 40 percent would be residential services for mental health and substance abuse.

Harbin would not comment on the moratorium, but neighbor Matt Campbell, who is a Pisgah Youth Organization coach, supports the PPS plan. He said Aziz has helped several people he knows.

"Addiction and mental health are largely ignored in the United States, and some communities try to prevent progress on this issue by fear mongering a topic they do not understand . . . ," Campbell said. "The fact of the matter is most of the people are everyday students, teachers, coaches, parents, and they are right here in our community."

The Mental Health and Addiction Recovery Services Board is about to unveil a full-scale plan to ramp up — to the tune of $3.5 million — its addiction services.

Executive Director Scott Rasmus said he isn't certain if they would need to add more providers, like PPS, but they definitely want services that are "convenient" to all Butler County residents. There are other addiction services in West Chester, like the recently expanded Beckett Springs Hospital of West Chester Twp., but Rasmus said they need to tackle the issue.

"We respect their concern, but also we need to look at providing additional services that would work within the communities that are in Butler County," he said. "I'm not quite sure with the business plan, if the expansions we're looking for need to be additional facilities beyond the existing provider set."

Scott Gehring, executive director of Sojourner Recovery Services, which manages nine facilities in the county, said all of their recovery services are in neighborhoods, and they coexist just fine.

"When you're in social services, you come to expect the NIMBYs, the not in my backyard," he said. "But we have established great relationships with all of our neighbors."

Gehring did commend the township trustees for "doing their due diligence" and said he thinks they'll find recovery services are a "positive for the community."

All three trustees backed the moratorium, which will last until Dec. 31.

"It gives us more time to study on . . . the effects of it," Trustee Lee Wong said. "And we will decide what is good for the public."

■ TSOMBANIDIS v. WEST HAVEN FIRE DEPARTMENT
352 F.3d 565 (2d Cir. 2003)

Beverly Tsombanidis, owner of a residence located at 421 Platt Avenue, in West Haven, Connecticut, also known as "Oxford House-Jones Hill" ("OH-JH"); eight "John Does," current or future residents of OH-JH; and Oxford House, Inc. ("OHI") brought this action against the First Fire District for the City of West Haven ("Fire District") and the City of West Haven ("City") under the Fair Housing Act of 1968, as amended by the Fair Housing Amendments Act of 1988, 42 U.S.C. §3601, *et seq.* ("FHAA") and Title II of the Americans with Disabilities Act, 42 U.S.C. §§12131-12165 ("ADA").OHI oversees more than 900 independent Oxford Houses operating both in the United States and abroad that provide homes for recovering alcoholics and drug addicts. Oxford Houses operate on the premise that people recovering from drug and alcohol addictions will remain sober if they live in a supportive environment.

The day-to-day affairs of Oxford Houses are governed democratically by the residents of each house without the presence of a medical or therapeutic professional. OHI has found that residents are more likely to succeed if houses are (1) located in single-family residential neighborhoods away from readily available drugs and alcohol; (2) close to sites for regular Alcoholics Anonymous and Narcotics Anonymous meetings; (3) near commercial areas substantial enough to provide easy access to basic necessities; (4) near a range of employment opportunities accessible by public transportation; and (5) large enough for a minimum of six people to live, yet small enough that bedrooms are shared by residents.

In 1997, Tsombanidis purchased a two-story house in a residential area of detached single-family houses in West Haven, Connecticut. She bought the property to start OH-JH and, in July 1997, entered into a lease with four persons recovering from alcohol and drug addictions. Within days after the original residents moved into OH-JH, neighbors began to question Tsombanidis about the house. After learning of its purpose, neighbors expressed their concerns and it became apparent throughout the fall of 1997 that there was significant community opposition to OH-JH locating in the neighborhood. An anonymous caller to the City complained that OH-JH was operating as an illegal boarding house. Soon thereafter a group of local residents visited Mayor H. Richard Borer complaining about the recovery facility, and a petition signed by eighty-four people was presented to the City Council "protesting the use of the property located at 421 Platt Avenue in a residential neighborhood . . . as a rooming house for people in rehabilitation . . . in violation of numerous planning and zoning codes."

[After receiving a complaint about OH-JH, the City informed Tsombanidis that OH-JH was violating the zoning regulations and ordered Tsombanidis to make certain repairs and evict the tenants. Tsombanidis made the repairs but refused to evict her tenants. The Inspector for the Fire District, Richard Spreyer, then became involved after he informed Tsombanidis that she was in violation of the Fire Code because OH-JH had six unrelated individuals living in the same home. OHI responded to Spreyer by contending that his application of the Fire Code to OH-JH violated the FHAA and the ADA. After consulting with city and state officials, Spreyer determined that OH-JH was still in violation of the Fire Code.]

Plaintiffs brought the present case against the Fire District and the City alleging that both governmental entities violated the FHAA and ADA by intentionally discriminating against plaintiffs, implementing policies that disparately impacted plaintiffs, and failing to make reasonable accommodations. Both defendants moved for summary judgment. The district court held that there was sufficient evidence to go forward on plaintiffs' claim of intentional discrimination against the City but not against the Fire District. . . . The court held that both disparate impact claims could proceed to trial but held that the reasonable accommodation claims were not ripe because plaintiffs had not yet utilized the appropriate administrative proceedings to obtain an accommodation.

In response to the court's ruling that the reasonable accommodation claims were not ripe, Tsombanidis applied to the City of West Haven Zoning Board of Appeals for a special-use exception to continue to use the property as OH-JH. The Zoning Board held a public hearing and subsequently denied the application. Only two months before trial, Tsombanidis requested that the State Fire Marshal exempt her from the fire code. At the subsequent bench trial, John Blaschik, a new Deputy State Fire Marshal, testified that one of the then seven residents of OH-JH could be considered a member of a single family, and the other six could be considered outsiders, making OH-JH a single-family dwelling under the fire code. Spreyer promptly informed Tsombanidis that he would follow this interpretation and that she should disregard the previous notices . . .

With respect to the City, the court held that: (1) the City intentionally discriminated against OH-JH; (2) the zoning and maintenance regulations disparately impacted the residents; and (3) the City failed to reasonably accommodate the residents' handicap after plaintiffs had sought a variance through proper governmental procedures. . . . The court awarded plaintiffs compensatory damages and attorney's fees. . . . The City appeals the intentional discrimination claim, the reasonable accommodation claim and the damages award. It does not contest the disparate impact claim.

II. DISCUSSION

A. STATUTORY FRAMEWORK

Both the FHAA and the ADA prohibit governmental entities from implementing or enforcing housing policies in a discriminatory manner against persons with disabilities. The FHAA makes it unlawful "[t]o discriminate in the sale or rental, or to otherwise make unavailable or deny, a dwelling to any buyer or renter because of a handicap." 42 U.S.C. §3604(f)(1). Similarly, the ADA states "no qualified individual with a disability shall, by reason of such disability, be excluded from participation in or be denied the benefits of the services, programs, or activities of a public entity, or be subject to discrimination by any such entity." 42 U.S.C. §12132. Both statutes require "that covered entities make reasonable accommodations in order to provide qualified individuals with an equal opportunity to receive benefits from or to participate in programs run by such entities." [Citation omitted] To establish discrimination under either the FHAA or the ADA, plaintiffs have three available theories: (1) intentional discrimination (disparate treatment); (2) disparate impact; and (3) failure to make a reasonable accommodation.

Both statutes apply to municipal zoning decisions.

2. Reasonable Accommodation Analysis

Plaintiffs also assert that the Fire District's refusal to treat OH-JH as a one-family dwelling qualifies as a failure to reasonably accommodate the John Doe plaintiffs' handicap as required by the FHAA and the ADA. Plaintiffs contest both the district court's original ripeness decision as well as the holding that the reasonable accommodation provisions were not violated. We affirm both rulings.

[The FHAA and the ADA] "require that changes be made to such traditional rules or practices if necessary to permit a person with handicaps an equal opportunity to use and enjoy a dwelling." [Citation omitted] "Plaintiffs must show that, but for the accommodation, they likely will be denied an equal opportunity to enjoy the housing of their choice." [Citation omitted] A defendant must incur reasonable costs and take modest, affirmative steps to accommodate the handicapped as long as the accommodations sought do not pose an undue hardship or a substantial burden. [Citation omitted]

. . . Appellees never sought an accommodation. In fact, OHI's March 24, 1998 letter notified Inspector Spreyer that Oxford House was not seeking an accommodation in this regard and that its position was that the code was facially invalid under the Federal Fair Housing Act as it was being applied to Oxford House-Jones Hill.

To prevail on a reasonable accommodation claim, plaintiffs must first provide the governmental entity an opportunity to accommodate them through the entity's established procedures used to adjust the neutral policy in question. [Citation omitted] Furthermore, requiring OH-JH to utilize facially neutral procedures to request an accommodation from the fire code is not by itself a failure to reasonably accommodate plaintiffs' handicaps. A governmental entity must know what a plaintiff seeks prior to incurring liability for failing to affirmatively grant a reasonable accommodation. . . . [A] plaintiff must first use the procedures available to notify the governmental entity that it seeks an exception or variance from the facially neutral laws when pursuing a reasonable accommodation claim. Here, OH-JH specifically stated in its original letter it was not seeking an accommodation.

We also affirm the district court's decision that the accommodation plaintiffs ultimately sought was provided two months after it was requested. Plaintiffs did not seek an exception to the fire code until August 2001. During the trial, the Deputy State Fire Marshal testified that under his interpretation of the fire code, seven individuals could live together and still be considered a single-family residence. The next day and before the close of the trial, local Inspector Spreyer informed plaintiffs that all abatement procedures against OH-JH would end. Thus, the accommodation plaintiffs sought — being classified a single-family residence — was granted.

C. CLAIMS AGAINST THE CITY

As stated above, the district court found the City in violation of the FHAA and ADA on all three available theories. Since the City did not contest the disparate impact holding, we do not review the merits of that claim and only address the intentional discrimination and reasonable accommodation claims along with the damages award.

1. Intentional Discrimination

. . . To establish intentional discrimination, plaintiffs must prove that a motivating factor behind the City's refusal to classify OH-JH as a single-family household was the residents' status as recovering drug addicts and alcoholics. [Citation omitted] Factors to be considered in evaluating a claim of intentional discrimination include: "(1) the discriminatory impact of the governmental decision; (2) the decision's historical background; (3) the specific sequence of events leading up to the challenged decision; (4) departures from the normal procedural sequences; and (5) departures from normal substantive criteria." *Tsombanidis I,* 129 F. Supp. 2d at 152 (citing *Village of Arlington Heights,* 429 U.S. at 266-68, 97 S. Ct. 555). These factors are not exclusive or mandatory but merely a framework within which a court conducts its analysis.

The district court's finding of intentional discrimination was not clearly erroneous. Among other things, the district court noted the history of hostility of neighborhood residents to OH-JH and their pressure on the Mayor and other city officials. Evidence supports the court's finding that this hostility motivated the City in initiating and continuing its enforcement efforts. . . . There was also evidence the City rarely took enforcement action against boarding houses in residential neighborhoods. Furthermore, the City failed to acknowledge multiple letters sent by OHI thoroughly explaining OH-JH's policies and procedures and its argument that the residents had a right to be treated as a single-family residence. The court also cited the reaction of Michael McCurry, one of two Property Maintenance Code Officials for the City. McCurry expressed his personal dissatisfaction with OH-JH and ordered Tsombanidis to evict the residents without any authority in the City Code. Finally, there was record support for the court's finding of bias in the denial of OH-JH's request for a special use exception by the Zoning Board of Appeals. We therefore affirm the district court's conclusion that the city intentionally discriminated.

2. Reasonable Accommodation

We also affirm the district court's finding that plaintiffs requested a reasonable accommodation and the City failed to grant it. The City is not required to grant an exception for a group of people to live as a single family, but it cannot deny the variance request based solely on plaintiffs' handicap where the requested accommodation is reasonable. The district court found that these plaintiffs operated much like a family. Additionally, there is evidence that these particular plaintiffs needed to live in group homes located in single-family areas. *See Tsombanidis II,* 180 F. Supp. 2d at 293. The City concedes that, from a municipal services standpoint, it would bear minimal financial cost from the proposed accommodation. While legitimate concerns of residential zoning laws include the integrity of the City's housing scheme and problems associated with large numbers of unrelated transient persons living together, such as traffic congestion and noise, . . . the City points to no evidence that those concerns were present here. The district court's finding was therefore not clearly erroneous. . . .

[P]laintiffs were required to use proper local procedures to request a reasonable accommodation from a governmental entity before bringing an action under the FHAA or ADA in this regard. Plaintiffs used the appropriate channels to seek a variance in the zoning regulations and to cure their ripeness problem. Thus, we agree with the district court that the proceeding before the Zoning Board was the type ordinarily necessary to secure the final result in an FHAA enforcement action brought under a reasonable accommodation theory. Thus, we affirm its inclusion of this award.

Notes and Comments

1 *Regulation of Sober Homes.* The court in *Tsombanidis* notes that West Haven enforces its Zoning Regulations, Property Maintenance Code, and State Building Code primarily by responding to complaints. Do you understand how this strategy is legally questionable with regard to sober homes? Based on *Tsombanidis*, what types of zoning rules do you think can properly be applied to sober homes?

2. *The Impacts of Sober Homes.* What leverage do neighbors have to control the asserted negative impacts of sober homes? Are the impacts real or based, as we have seen in other chapters, on nonscientific risk assessments or even outright bias?

3. *Fair Housing Provisions.* In addressing challenges to the siting of sober homes, local governments must comply with the Fair Housing Act, examined in detail in Chapter 13. Thus, sober homes are legally protected in ways that some other group homes are not from local zoning and other land use restrictions. In some states, sober homes are protected regardless of whether they are for-profit or not-for-profit, and even if they are designed to accommodate a fairly large number of persons.

4. *State Law Protections.* State law provisions also may provide protections. Consider these provisions from the California Health and Safety Code:

11834.20. The Legislature hereby declares that it is the policy of this state that each county and city shall permit and encourage the development of sufficient numbers and types of alcoholism or drug abuse recovery or treatment facilities as are commensurate with local need.

11834.23.

(b) For the purpose of all local ordinances, an alcoholism or drug abuse recovery or treatment facility that serves six or fewer persons shall not be included within the definition of a boarding house, rooming house, institution or home for the care of minors, the aged, or persons with mental health disorders, foster care home, guest home, rest home, community residence, or other similar term that implies that the alcoholism or drug abuse recovery or treatment home is a business run for profit or differs in any other way from a single-family residence.

(c) This section shall not be construed to forbid a city, county, or other local public entity from placing restrictions on building heights, setback, lot dimensions, or placement of signs of an alcoholism or drug abuse recovery or treatment facility that serves six or fewer persons as long as the restrictions are identical to those applied to other single-family residences.

(d) This section shall not be construed to forbid the application to an alcoholism or drug abuse recovery or treatment facility of any local ordinance that deals with health and safety, building standards, environmental impact standards, or any other matter within the jurisdiction of a local public entity. However, the ordinance shall not distinguish alcoholism or drug abuse recovery or treatment facilities that serve six or fewer persons from other single-family dwellings or distinguish residents of alcoholism or drug abuse recovery or treatment facilities from persons who reside in other single-family dwellings.

(e) No conditional use permit, zoning variance, or other zoning clearance shall be required of an alcoholism or drug abuse recovery or treatment facility that serves six or fewer persons that is not required of a single-family residence in the same zone.

Does the reasonable accommodation requirement preclude the application of parking standards to residential treatment homes that may have several adults as opposed to a single nuclear family? How can a municipality balance the interests of neighbors and the needs of the sober home customer?

Some states are approaching the challenges by enacting or considering legislation creating voluntary certificate programs for the home. Massachusetts and Florida are examples. *See* Florida H.B. 21, ch. 2015-100, http://laws.flrules.org/2015/100 (last visited Oct. 7, 2016), and Massachusetts Bill H.1828: An Act relative to ensuring the safety of sober houses, https://malegislature.gov/Bills/188/House/H1828 (last visited Oct. 7, 2016)

5. *Consideration of "Secondary Effects"?* Is there a role for analysis of so-called "secondary effects" (i.e. effects that the principal land use, a sober home, would have in the neighborhood) in the consideration of sober home regulations? *See* T. Peter Pierce, Regulating Sober Living Homes and the Challenges of Implementing ADA and FHA (2016), https://www.cacities.org/Resources-Documents/Member-Engagement/Professional-Departments/City-Attorneys/Library/2016/Spring-2016/5-2016-Spring-Regulating-Sober-Living-Homes-and-th.aspx (last visited Oct. 7, 2016) (describing approaches to regulating larger sober homes consistently with the federal Fair Housing Act and the Americans with Disabilities Act); Matthew M. Gorman et al., Alcoholism, Drug Addiction and the Right to Fair Housing: How the Fair Housing Act Applies to Sober Living Homes, 33 Pub. L.J. 13 (2010).

3. *The Homeless*

The difficult problem of combatting homelessness is evident throughout the United States, and it has significant land use implications. The National Alliance to End Homelessness, citing "Point in Time" counts conducted on a single night in January as required by the Department of Housing and Urban Development, has put forth a "snapshot" of the situation on that night:

- In January 2015, 564,708 people were homeless on a given night in the United States.
- Of that number, 206,286 were people in families, and
- 358,422 were individuals.
- About 15 percent of the homeless population — 83,170 — are considered "chronically homeless" individuals.
- About 2 percent — 13,105 — are considered "chronically homeless" people in families.
- About 8 percent of homeless people — 47,725 — are veterans.

See http://www.endhomelessness.org/pages/snapshot_of_homelessness (last visited Sept. 19, 2016).

The lack of affordable housing is a significant hardship for low-income households and can prevent them from meeting their other basic needs, such as nutrition, or saving for their future.

Homelessness is linked to other conditions. Mental health problems make it difficult or even undesirable for some people to settle into a permanent home. Temporary economic difficulties can lead to a downward spiral, with the newly homeless not knowing where to go for assistance. Discrimination on several bases may close out affordable options to people.

Local and (in some cases) state governments engage in many lawmaking activities that contribute to the challenge of homelessness. They also have used their authority to design solutions, or at least to mitigate this national problem.

The links between homelessness and health and sustainability are many and multidirectional. The homeless tend to lack access to health care and facilities. They tend to be unhealthy. Some of the conditions in which they attempt to survive are public health concerns. When the number of homeless is great, their conditions influence the attractiveness of a region and aspects of the region's own sustainability.

A battery of laws that effectively criminalize homelessness is sweeping the nation, embraced by places like Orlando, Florida; Santa Cruz, California; and Manchester, New Hampshire. According to a survey of 187 major American cities by the National Law Center on Homelessness and Poverty, by the end of 2014, 100 cities had made it a crime to sit on a sidewalk — a 43 percent increase over 2011. The number of cities that banned sleeping in cars jumped to 81 from 37 during that same period. Other cities have outlawed panhandling and authorized the removal of tent camps. Adam Nagourney, "Aloha and Welcome to Paradise, Unless You're Homeless," N.Y. Times (June 3, 2016). *See also* Eric S. Tars et al., Can I Get Some Remedy?: Criminalization of Homelessness and the Obligation to Provide an Effective Remedy, 45 Colum. Hum. Rts. L. Rev. 738 (2014); Farida Ali, Limiting the Poor's Right to Public Space: Criminalizing Homelessness in California, 21 Geo. J. on Poverty L. & Pol'y 197 (2014).

Local land use laws direct where the homeless can or cannot stay. Municipalities can remove opportunities for temporary shelter and sleeping in cars, in campgrounds, on streets, in parks, and even in religious ministry sites.

When housing providers seek permission to use a site as a home or shelter for the homeless, they must navigate the local land use system. Consider the opposition raised in the following case.

■ PHILLIPS SUPPLY CO. v. CINCINNATI BOARD OF ZONING APPEALS

17 N.E.3d 1 (Ohio. App. 2014)

Sylvia S. Hendon, Judge.

This is the second appeal that has come before this court involving the relocation of a homeless shelter from the Cincinnati neighborhood of Over–the–Rhine to the city's Queensgate area. The crux of this appeal is the propriety of the city's issuance of building permits for two specific parcels of land in Queensgate that are to be used for the relocation of the homeless shelter and the placement of related social services.

Plaintiffs-appellants Phillips Supply Company, U.S. Bank, N.A., Trustee of the Charles Phillips Irrevocable Trust u/a/d June 1, 1964, and Dalton Street Properties, Ltd. ("Phillips Supply"), are neighboring business and property owners to the proposed relocation site, who are opposed to the homeless shelter's relocation. Phillips Supply has appealed from the trial court's entry affirming the decision of the Cincinnati Zoning Board of Appeals ("ZBA") that upheld the city's issuance of the building permits. Because the trial court did not abuse its discretion in upholding the decision of the ZBA, we affirm the judgment of that court.

FACTUAL BACKGROUND

Defendant-appellee City Gospel Mission sought to relocate a homeless shelter from Over–the–Rhine to a new facility on the property located at 1805 Dalton Avenue in Queensgate. On an adjacent property at 1211 York Street, they sought to place related services, including the Exodus Program, the Lord's Gym, the Lord's Pantry, Jobs Plus Employment Network, and City Gospel Mission offices. Because Queensgate is zoned as MG, manufacturing general, the city had passed a notwithstanding ordinance that approved the operation of a special assistance shelter on the Dalton Avenue property. Absent this ordinance, the operation of a homeless shelter was not a permitted use in an MG district under the zoning code. Phillips Supply opposed the relocation of the homeless shelter, and it filed suit challenging the city's issuance of the notwithstanding ordinance. The ordinance was upheld by the trial court and affirmed by this court in *State ex rel. Phillips Supply Co. v. City of Cincinnati*, 2012-Ohio-6096, 985 N.E.2d 257 (1st Dist.).

After the notwithstanding ordinance was upheld, the city issued building permits for the renovation of the Dalton Avenue property and the construction of a new building on the York Street property. Phillips Supply appealed the issuance of these permits to the ZBA. It argued that the permit for the Dalton Avenue property should not have been issued because the proposed structure's principal use under the zoning code was "religious assembly," which is prohibited in an MG district. And it argued that the permit for the York Street property should not have been issued because that building's proposed use was "community service facility," another prohibited use in an MG district. The ZBA held a hearing concerning the proposed uses for the two properties, and whether those uses complied with the zoning code.

Extensive testimony about City Gospel Mission, the homeless shelter, and the related social services that would occupy the York Street property was presented at the hearing, much of which was offered by Roger Howell, the president of City Gospel Mission. City Gospel Mission's purpose is to promote the cause of the Christian religion through social-service-based programs. The organization has operated a homeless shelter since 1924. Testimony indicated that the Dalton Avenue property will contain a chapel that takes up approximately 4.4 percent of the property's square footage, and that the property will offer a daily 45–minute chapel service, although no persons residing in the shelter are required to attend that service. When not being used for religious services, the chapel will serve a multi-purpose use.

With respect to the social-service programs to be located in the York Street property, the evidence indicated that the Exodus program is a transitional-housing program for men with life-addictive issues. It is a 365-day program that includes spiritual activities. The Lord's Gym is a physical-fitness program for men to help them grow physically as well as spiritually. Similarly, the Lord's Pantry provides a meal to its patrons while also offering prayer and evangelism. The Jobs Plus Employment Network offers a job-readiness training program and assists its participants in finding employment. The agency is guided by Biblical principles, and incorporates those principles into its programs. The York Street property will also contain City Gospel Mission's administrative offices.

In its decision, the ZBA determined that the proposed use of the Dalton Avenue property, where the homeless shelter was to be placed, was a "special assistance shelter," and that such a use was permitted by the notwithstanding ordinance. It further determined that the York Street property should be classified as a mixed-use facility, and it considered the individual uses for each proposed tenant of the property. It classified the use of the Exodus Program as "transitional housing," the use of the Lord's Gym as "indoor or small-scale recreation and entertainment," the use of the Lord's Pantry as "eating and drinking establishment/restaurants, limited," the use of the Jobs Plus Employment Network as "personal/instructional service," and the use of City Gospel Mission's offices as "office." Each of these individual uses was permitted in an MG district. The ZBA stated in its decision that the fact that the proposed tenants of these two buildings were religiously-oriented organizations and that various programs occurring in these facilities had a faith-based element did not transform the principal use of the facilities into "religious assembly." Because all proposed uses for the two properties were permitted by either the zoning code or the notwithstanding ordinance, the ZBA upheld the issuance of the permits. . . .

DALTON AVENUE PROPERTY

Phillips Supply first contends that the trial court erred by classifying the principal use of the Dalton Avenue property as "special assistance shelter" and not "religious assembly."

Cincinnati Municipal Code 1401–01–S11 defines a special assistance shelter as "a facility for the short-term housing of individuals who are homeless and who may require special services." Religious assembly is defined as "an establishment for religious worship and other religious ceremonies, including religious education, rectories and parsonages, offices, social services, columbaria and community programs." *See* Cincinnati Municipal Code 1401–01–R7. When determining that the Dalton Avenue property's principal use was special assistance shelter, the ZBA stated that:

The facility will provide temporary emergency shelter and associated social services to men who are homeless. . . . The evidence of a daily 45–minute religious service in the Shelter's multipurpose space does not convert the Dalton Property into "an establishment for religious worship and other religious ceremonies," and does not support a categorization of the principal use of the Dalton Property as Religious Assembly. [City Gospel Mission] and [the Foundation of Compassionate American Samaritans] are self-acknowledged religiously-oriented organizations that aim to meet the mental, physical, economic, educational, and social, as well as the spiritual needs of the Shelter guests. The fact that these organizations count religion as one of the inspirations or motivations for operating their social service programs on the Properties does not convert the uses into Religious Assembly uses.

The record is replete with evidence that City Gospel Mission is a religiously-focused organization. Motivated by this religious focus, the organization has, and will continue to, operate a homeless shelter. The purpose of the homeless shelter is to improve all aspects of its residents' lives to help them become more productive members of society. The programming has both spiritual and secular elements, but, as recognized by the ZBA, City Gospel Mission's religious motivation and the small spiritual portion of its programming do not convert its primary use into religious assembly. This is a zoning case. Generally, zoning laws may regulate the use of the land, not the identity of the users. . . .

The ZBA considered the fact that there will be a religious element to the homeless shelter when determining the principal use of the building for zoning purposes. The services to be offered by the homeless shelter clearly fall within the zoning code's definition of special assistance shelter. The trial court's entry upholding the decision of the ZBA classifying the Dalton Avenue property as a special assistance shelter was in no manner arbitrary, unreasonable or unconscionable.

YORK STREET PROPERTY

Phillips Supply also challenges the classification of the York Street property. Under the Cincinnati Zoning Code, a district's zoning designation, in this case MG, identifies "the principal land uses" permitted in that district. *See* Cincinnati Municipal Code 1400–07. Phillips Supply argues that in determining whether a land use is permitted in a particular district, a single principal use must be identified for each building. Thus, it argues that the ZBA erred by finding multiple principal uses of the York Street property, each of which were permitted in an MG district. Rather, it contends that the ZBA should have identified only one principal use for the York Street property, and that the single principal use should have been religious assembly, a use not permitted in an MG district.

1. Multiple Principal Uses

Although this court has never explicitly held that a property may have more than one principal use, we have issued two recent decisions that have implicitly concluded that it is permissible for a property to have multiple principal uses.

In *CityLink Center v. City of Cincinnati*, Citylink, a not-for-profit corporation that had been organized to assist in serving the low-income population of Cincinnati, sought to develop its campus in an area of Cincinnati that had been zoned MG. *CityLink Center*, 1st Dist. Hamilton Nos. C–061037, C–061054 and C061064, 2007-Ohio-5873, 2007 WL 3225547, at ¶ 2. Its proposed tenants were Jobs Plus, Crossroads Health Center, The Lord's Gym, and City Gospel Mission. *Id.* at ¶ 3. This court affirmed the trial court's judgment ordering the issuance of a zoning certificate of compliance to Citylink because the proposed uses for each individual tenant were all permitted in an MG district. *Id.* at ¶ 20. . . .

We hold that a building, such as the York Street property, may have more than one principal use. Whether a building has individual principal uses for each tenant, or whether a building with multiple tenants must be viewed as having one integrated use, must be determined on a case-by-case basis. In this case, the trial court did not abuse its discretion by treating the York Street property as a mixed-use facility with individual principal uses for each tenant and failing to assign the entire property the principal use of religious assembly.

The ZBA classified the use of the Exodus Program as "transitional housing." Cincinnati Municipal Code 1401–01–T defines transitional housing as "housing designed to assist persons in obtaining skills necessary for independent living in permanent housing, including homes for adjustment and halfway houses." The ZBA specifically stated that Phillips Supply had not met its burden of establishing that the Exodus Program should be categorized as having the use of religious assembly because "the incorporation of a faith-based element into the program's required 12–step addiction recovery process does not change the principal use."

The ZBA classified the Lord's Gym as having the principal use of "indoor or small-scale recreation and entertainment." This use is defined in Cincinnati Municipal Code 1401–01–R2 as "the provision of recreation or entertainment to paying participants or spectator . . . [including] small, generally indoor facilities, although some facilities may be outdoors, including: fitness centers, gymnasiums . . . ." The ZBA's decision further stated that the presence of bible study in addition to the fitness training activities did not warrant the classification of the gym as having the use of religious assembly.

The Lord's Pantry was classified as having the use of "eating and drinking establishment/restaurants, limited." Cincinnati Municipal Code 1401–01–E1 defines this use as "[r]estaurants providing food and beverage services to patrons who order and pay before eating. . . . Table service is not provided." The ZBA again specifically noted that the Lord's Pantry did not have the use of religious assembly merely because mentors were available to provide life coaching and prayer.

The Jobs Plus Employment Network was classified by the ZBA as having the principal use of personal instruction service, which is defined in Cincinnati Municipal Code 1401–01–P10 as the provision of instructional services including, as relevant to this case, tutoring and vocational and trade schools. In determining the principal use for this tenant, the ZBA stated that "the evidence that the Bible or religious motivation informs the Jobs Plus training does not establish that the principal use should be Religious Assembly where training and placement are the predominant activity."

Last, the ZBA's decision determined that the principal use of City Gospel Mission's offices was "office." This use is defined by Cincinnati Municipal Code 1401–01–O as "a facility for a firm or organization that primarily provides professional, executive, management or administrative services."

The record indicates that each proposed tenant for the York Street property had its own purpose and position aligned with the social-service campus's overall goal of improving the lives of its participants. Each program does have a spiritual aspect. But, as noted by the ZBA, the spiritual element is a minor part of the programs' overall business aim. The tenants were not part of a larger, collective religious entity, and it was not error for the trial court to fail to assign either each individual tenant, or the overall building, the principal use of religious assembly. . . .

Phillips Supply's assignment of error is overruled, and the judgment of the trial court is affirmed.

———————————

Some land use initiatives aim to counter the negative impact on affordable housing created by certain applications of land use law. One broad approach is through articulation of homeless rights. Several jurisdictions have passed or are considering homeless rights legislation: California, Connecticut, Delaware, Maryland, Minnesota, Missouri, Oregon, Puerto Rico, Rhode Island, Tennessee, Vermont, and Wisconsin. Here is an excerpt from recently enacted legislation in Illinois. Consider how it can affect local governments' land use authority.

■ ILLINOIS BILL OF RIGHTS FOR THE HOMELESS ACT
777 ILCS 45 (1913)

Sec. 5. Legislative intent. It is the long-standing policy of this State that no person should suffer unnecessarily from cold or hunger, be deprived of shelter or the basic rights incident to shelter, or be subject to unfair discrimination based on his or her homeless status. At the present time, many persons have been rendered homeless as a result of economic hardship, a severe shortage of safe and affordable housing, and a shrinking social safety net. It is the intent of this Act to lessen the adverse effects and conditions caused by the lack of residence or a home. . . .

Sec. 10. Bill of Rights.

(a) No person's rights, privileges, or access to public services may be denied or abridged solely because he or she is homeless. Such a person shall be granted the same rights and privileges as any other citizen of this State. A person experiencing homelessness has the following rights:

(1) the right to use and move freely in public spaces, including but not limited to public sidewalks, public parks, public transportation, and public buildings, in the same manner as any other person and without discrimination on the basis of his or her housing status;

(2) the right to equal treatment by all State and municipal agencies, without discrimination on the basis of housing status;

(3) the right not to face discrimination while maintaining employment due to his or her lack of permanent mailing address, or his or her mailing address being that of a shelter or social service provider;

(4) the right to emergency medical care free from discrimination based on his or her housing status;

(5) the right to vote, register to vote, and receive documentation necessary to prove identity . . .

(7) the right to a reasonable expectation of privacy in his or her personal property to the same extent as personal property in a permanent residence.

(b) As used in this Act, "housing status" means the status of having or not having a fixed or regular residence, including the status of living on the streets, in a shelter, or in a temporary residence.

Notes and Comments

1. *Zoning Issues.* While attempts to regulate homelessness sometimes raise novel legal questions, many of the attempts implicate traditional land use issues. The *Phillips Supply* case presents a good example of the intersection of the problem of homelessness with conventional land use regulation. The issues raised should be

familiar to you from Chapter 2. Did the court correctly apply the local zoning ordinance?

The *Phillips Supply* case involved the second lawsuit brought by the neighboring company against the proposed homeless shelter. Did the company have legitimate concerns? Or is this an example of land use litigation being used for improper purposes? What about the plaintiff in *Steffensen-WC, LLC v. Volunteers of America of Utah*, 369 P.3d 483 (Utah Ct. App. 2016), who brought suit after the applicants had sought a conditional use permit for a homeless shelter for young adults, but before any decision had been reached. Plaintiff claimed that that shelter would constitute an anticipatory nuisance. The court easily rejected the argument.

Other cases have involved similar issues. In *Esplanade Ridge Civic Ass'n v. City of New Orleans*, 136 So. 3d 166. (La. Ct. App. 2014), a civic association sought review of a decision by a board of zoning adjustments granting variances to allow construction of a permanent housing facility consisting of 40 individual apartments. The plan for half of the units was to offer on-site supportive services for formerly homeless individuals with disabilities. The court of appeals upheld the issuance of the variances, observing that the RM-3 Residential District was designated to "provide for a variety of dwelling types of medium-high density while protecting the character of the surrounding area by limiting uses and signs." The court refused to classify the property as a residential care center: "[W]e find that this proposed structure most closely resembles an apartment building, or as stated in the RM-3 district, a 'multiple family dwelling' than a 'residential care center.' . . ."

But in *Salt & Light Co., Inc. v. Willingboro Twp. Zoning Bd. of Adjustment*, 32 A.3d 225 (N.J. App. Div. 2011), the court found that the zoning board did not abuse its discretion in denying a use variance for construction of a duplex to provide transitional housing for two homeless families in a neighborhood zoned exclusively for single-family residences. The court thought that the public benefit to be derived from the proposed duplex was outweighed by the detrimental effect upon the integrity of the zoning plan.

2. *The Illinois Bill of Rights and Land Use.* What are the land use implications of the Illinois Bill of Rights for the Homeless? What effect do you think this legislation will have in the world in which the homeless live? The Bill of Rights includes a provision allowing individuals to sue for damages for lost property. The law's principal legislative champion stated: "Unfortunately, in the business we're in, you have to legislate common sense . . . This is a taxpayer, publicly-owned building and regardless of someone's housing status, they're entitled to be in this building just like you or I are. Unfortunately, discrimination happens every day." Illinois Is 2nd State to Pass Homeless Bill of Rights, http://streetwise.org/2013/11/illinois-is-2nd-state-to-pass-homeless-bill-of-rights/ (last visited Sept. 19, 2016).

3. *Preemption?* One solution to local opposition to facilities that would aid the homeless is to preempt local government regulation. This general topic of state preemption of local land use regulation is discussed in the materials on siting in Chapter 16. Do you think preemption is called for in this context?

New York opted for such a solution, at least where a county was the driving force in the effort to aid the homeless. In *Westhab, Inc. v. Village of Elmsford*, 574 N.Y.S.2d 888 (Sup. Ct. 1991), a county contractor was rehabilitating a motel used to house homeless persons. The contractor sought an injunction to prohibit the Village from bringing an action to enforce the Village's building regulations. In response, the Village filed affidavits from the chiefs of its fire and police departments explaining that their departments bore a heavy burden in responding to calls regarding the homeless at the shelter. The court applied a balancing of interests test—discussed in the *City of Everett* case in Chapter 9—to support the conclusion that the county was exempt from the Village regulations.

4. *Encampments and Automobiles.* About a third of cities in the United States impose citywide bans on camping in public, and 18 percent of cities ban sleeping in public. *See* National Law Center on Homeless & Poverty, No Safe Place: The Criminalization of Homelessness in U.S. Cities 7 (2014), https://www.nlchp.org/documents/No_Safe_Place (last visited Sept. 19, 2016). These bans criminalize activity for which the homeless have no meaningful choice.

In *Desertrain v. City of Los Angeles,* 754 F.3d 1147 (9th Cir. 2014), homeless individuals filed a Civil Rights Act action against the city and its police officers challenging the constitutionality of an ordinance prohibiting the use of a vehicle as living quarters. The court of appeals held that the district court abused its discretion by refusing to consider the merits of the claim that the ordinance was void for vagueness.

5. *The Department of Justice "Statement of Interest."* In *Bell v. City of Boise,* 993 F. Supp. 2d 1237 (D. Idaho 2014), *rev'd,* 709 F.3d 890 (9th Cir. 2013), plaintiffs challenged the City of Boise's Camping and Sleeping Ordinances. They sought various forms of relief, including a declaration that present and threatened future enforcement of the ordinances violated plaintiffs' rights to be free from cruel and unusual punishment under the Eighth Amendment and the Idaho Constitution.

Interestingly, the United States Department of Justice filed a "Statement of Interest" in the case. It informed the court:

> The parties disagree about the appropriate framework for analyzing Plaintiffs' claims. Plaintiffs encourage the court to follow *Jones v. City of Los Angeles,* 444 F.3d 1118 (9th Cir. 2006) (vacated after settlement, 505 F.3d 1006 (9th Cir. 2007)), which held that enforcement of anti-camping ordinances may violate the Eighth Amendment on nights where there is inadequate shelter space available for all of a city's homeless individuals. Pls. Mem. at 5. Defendants, on the other hand, assert that Plaintiffs' reliance on Jones is "heavily misplaced, factually unsupported, and immaterial to this case." Defs. Resp. at 7.
>
> Because the summary judgment briefing in this case makes clear that there is a significant dispute between the parties on the applicability of *Jones* and conflicting lower court case law in this area, the United States files this Statement of Interest to make clear that the *Jones* framework is the appropriate legal framework for analyzing Plaintiffs' Eighth Amendment claims. Under the *Jones* framework, the Court should consider whether conforming one's conduct to the ordinance is possible for people who are homeless. If sufficient shelter space is unavailable because a) there are inadequate beds for the entire population, or b) there are restrictions on those beds that disqualify certain groups of homeless individuals (e.g., because of disability access or exceeding maximum stay requirements), then it would be impossible for some homeless individuals to comply with these ordinances. As set forth below, in those circumstances enforcement of the ordinances amounts to the criminalization of homelessness, in violation of the Eighth Amendment.

Statement of Interest of the United States, https://www.justice.gov/crt/file/761211/download (last visited Sept. 19, 2016). *See* Recent Court Filing, 129 Harv. L. Rev. 1476 (2016) (discussing the Statement of Interest).

There have been a number of other, similar challenges. In *Allen v. City of Sacramento*, 183 Cal. Rptr. 3d 654 (Ct. App. 2015), the California Court of Appeal held that a camping ordinance did not result in cruel and unusual punishment and did not violate residents' right to travel. However, it also held that alleged discrimination against homeless persons in enforcement of the camping ordinance violated equal protection.

6. *Sleeping on Public Property.* Is allowing the homeless to sleep on public property a sensible and humane approach? *See Cobine v. City of Eureka*, No. C 16-02239 JSW, 2016 WL 1730084, at *1 (N.D. Cal. May 2, 2016) (temporarily restraining the City of Eureka's plan to evict homeless people living at a homeless encampment on City property that existed since 2002). *See also* the complaint brought against the Mayor of Portland, Oregon in *Building Owners and Managers of Oregon v. Portland Mayor* (Or. Cir. Ct. Apr. 20, 2016), alleging: "Although the Mayor purported to base his Camping Policy on a shortage of affordable housing in the City, the policy is an irrational response that does nothing to create affordable housing and runs contrary to the recommendations of civic groups on how to alleviate the City's housing affordability issues."). *See* http://www.portlandmercury.com/blogtown/2016/04/20/17928662/the-citys-getting-sued-over-its-new-homeless-camping-policies (last visited Oct. 7, 2016).

7. *Ministries for the Homeless.* There is a complex interplay between religious use, municipal land use law, and the homeless. In *Harbor Missionary Church Corp. v. City of San Buenaventura*, 642 Fed. Appx. 726 (9th Cir. 2016), a church brought an action against a city and city officials under the Religious Land Use and Institutionalized Persons Act (RLUIPA) and the First Amendment after the city denied a conditional use permit to continue the church's homeless ministry. The court of appeal held that the denial of the permit substantially burdened the Church's exercise of religion under RLUIPA. Chapter 8 discusses RLUIPA in detail.

8. *Panhandling, Solicitation, and Assembly.* Many local governments ban panhandling and begging, activities that provide necessary sustaining revenue to some and to others negatively affect the quality of urban street life. These orders can raise significant constitutional issues. *See Kelly v. City of Parkersburg*, 978 F. Supp. 2d 624 (S.D. W.Va. 2013) (challenge to ordinance restricting the right to solicit charitable donations on an intersection, claiming the ordinance violated the First Amendment right to free speech and the Fourteenth Amendment right to due process and equal protection). In *Speet v. Schuette*, 726 F.3d 867 (6th Cir. 2013), the court invalidated a Michigan statute that criminalized begging in a public place. It ruled that begging, or the soliciting of alms, is a form of solicitation that the First Amendment protects.

There are numerous other recent cases. *See Comite de Jornaleros de Redondo Beach v. City of Redondo Beach*, 657 F.3d 936 (9th Cir. 2011) (ruling that municipal ordinance that barred individuals from "stand[ing] on a street or highway and solicit[ing], or attempt[ing] to solicit, employment, business, or contributions from an occupant of any motor vehicle" was a facially unconstitutional restriction on speech; it was not narrowly tailored and regulated significantly more speech than necessary, and less restrictive measures existed to achieve traffic and safety goals); *State v. Boehler*, 228 Ariz. 33, 262 P.3d 637 (Ct. App. 2011) (invalidating provision banning panhandlers and other solicitors from orally asking passersby for cash after dark because the ordinance was not narrowly drawn to achieve its purpose and violated the First Amendment's protection of freedom of speech); *Browne v. City of Grand Junction, Colorado*, 27 F. Supp. 3d 1161 (D. Colo. 2014) (striking down ordinance that completely banned panhandling and soliciting from vehicle occupants on any federal or state highways traversing the city; ordinance was a content-based restriction on protected speech in public streets and highways, quintessential public forums); and *Reynolds v. Middleton*, 779 F.3d 222 (4th Cir. 2015) (ordinance prohibiting solicitation within county roadways not narrowly tailored to serve county's significant governmental interests).

9. *Effect of Movement from Transition to Permanent Housing.* Some of the leading thinking on homelessness suggests that the most effective approach to the problem is permanent housing with provision of supportive services to the new residents. But such a change in policy may have unintended consequences. *See* Doug Smith, Is the Shift to Permanent Housing Making L.A.'s Homelessness Problem Even Worse? L.A. Times (Aug.15, 2016), observing:

> [T]he shift toward permanent housing has had a cost: As money has been directed away from programs that combine services with shorter-term housing, the region's homelessness problem has gotten worse. The county's overall homeless population was roughly unchanged from 2015 to 2016. But the "unsheltered population"—those literally living on the street—increased by about 1,400, according to the Los Angeles Homeless Services Authority's annual count.

10. *Balancing Clean and Safe Streets with Privacy Rights.* Difficult choices arise when local governments are pressed by certain constituencies to take strong action to remove unattractive and perhaps even unhealthy belongings of the homeless. Los Angeles, with the country's second largest homeless population, has faced challenges to its approaches. In *Lavan v. City of Los Angeles*, 797 F. Supp. 2d 1005 (C.D. Cal. 2011), *appeal denied*, 693 F.3d 1022 (9th Cir. 2012), the court held that the city's immediate destruction of property it had collected turned what could have been a lawful seizure into an unlawful one. The court ruled that the city had a valid reason for seizing abandoned property of homeless people, but not for immediately destroying it.

11. *Sex Offenders.* The plight of the homeless as a group may evoke sympathy even if you think that they cause certain negative secondary effects. Note, however, that convicted sex offenders also face laws imposing serious barriers to locating housing, making them especially vulnerable to the risk of homelessness. For example, in *In re Taylor*, 343 P.3d 867 (Cal. 2015), a convicted sex offender challenged a residency restriction, adopted pursuant to a state ballot initiative, making it illegal for registered sex offenders "to reside within 2000 feet of any public or private school, or park where children regularly gather." The California Supreme Court ruled the provision unconstitutional, noting:

> Blanket enforcement of the residency restrictions against these parolees has severely restricted their ability to find housing in compliance with the statute, greatly increased the incidence of homelessness among them, and hindered their access to medical treatment, psychological counseling, and other rehabilitative social services available to all parolees.

Id. at 869.

In *Ryals v. City of Englewood*, 364 P.3d 900 (Colo. 2016), the Colorado Supreme Court considered whether a city ordinance that effectively barred certain sex offenders from residing within the city was preempted. Because the court found there was no conflict between state law on the subject and the local regulation, it rejected the preemption claim. A dissenting judge thought that the ordinance would materially impede the state's comprehensive scheme for sex offenders.

Complications can arise when the sex offenders are housed by a religious entity. In *Martin v. Houston*, ____ F. Supp. 3d ____, 2016 WL 4010026 (M.D. Ala. 2016), the court considered whether an ordinance that barred multiple unrelated adult sex offenders from residing in the same home qualified as a zoning law subject to the strictures of RLUIPA. The court ruled:

> The allegations. . . . indicate that Martin carries out his ministry in furtherance of his Christian beliefs, and that the Act effectively forced him to cease this ministry. If not for Houston's threat to bring an enforcement action against him, Martin would have continued to carry out what he believes is his religious duty by providing a Christian housing environment to adult sex offenders. These allegations are sufficient to plausibly allege that the Act imposes a substantial burden on Martin's exercise of religion within the meaning of RLUIPA . . .

Does this group of plaintiffs fall into a different category than the homeless, even though restrictions can, said the court, cause some of them to become homeless?

12. *A Final Word on Homelessness and Land Use Law.* As an evolving area of land use control, providing shelter for the homeless is a fertile area for innovative legal argument and policy change. As an attorney working with local officials, what strategies would you suggest for mitigating problems of the homeless in a large U.S. city? Consider both the needs and rights of the homeless themselves and those of existing residents who wish to maintain a high quality of urban life. How effective might be litigation to force governments to make available public lands for homeless populations? *See* Gale Holland, U.S. Settles Suit over Misuse of West L.A. Veterans Campus, L.A. Times (Jan. 27, 2015). The federal government had been using a veterans' health campus for, among other non-veterans uses, a UCLA baseball stadium, a TV studio and parking, while veterans were forced to sleep on the streets. *See also* National Law Center on Homelessness and Poverty, This Land Is Your Land: How Surplus Federal Property Can Prevent and End Homelessness (2013), https://www.nlchp.org/documents/This_Land_Is_Your_Land (last visited Oct.7, 2016).

4. Users of Medical (and Recreational) Marijuana

A relatively new and rapidly developing issue at the intersection of public health and land use is regulation of the cultivation, processing, and distribution of marijuana. While the federal government still theoretically bans commerce in marijuana, some states have moved in the direction of legalizing marijuana sales, initially for medical purposes, and subsequently for recreational purposes. Because the facilities involved in the marijuana business raise some of the same public concerns as other commercial land uses, as well as some new ones, the move toward legalization of marijuana at the state level has inevitably become, in part, a land use issue.

A Note on Land Use and Marijuana

The Context. Under federal law, marijuana is considered a Schedule I Controlled Substance, which means that, pursuant to 21 U.S.C. §856, it is illegal to profit from any sort of marijuana-related activity. This prohibition includes selling or leasing any property that may be used to cultivate, distribute, process, or sell marijuana. Furthermore, in 2005, the U.S. Supreme Court ruled 6-to-3 that the Commerce Clause of the U.S. Constitution permits Congress to prohibit the wholly intrastate possession and use of marijuana. *Gonzales v. Raich*, 545 U.S. 1 (2005). The case arose out of California's 1996 passage of Proposition 215, which legalized the use of medical marijuana. The Court's ruling threatened to derail the decisions of California and 14 other states that at the time had legalized the distribution of medical marijuana.

However, in 2013, the U.S. Department of Justice (DOJ) released a memorandum announcing that the DOJ will not prioritize the enforcement of federal marijuana laws in states with their own robust marijuana regulations. U.S. Dept. of Justice, Office of the Deputy Attorney General, Memorandum for All United States Attorneys: Guidance Regarding Marijuana Enforcement (2013), http://www.justice .gov/iso/opa/resources/3052013829132756857467.pdf (last visited Oct. 26, 2016). Pursuant to this memorandum (known as the "Cole Memorandum II"), the federal government began to take a more hands-off approach to marijuana. The Cole Memorandum II "has been widely interpreted to signal that the federal government will not enforce its stricter marijuana laws against those complying with [state] laws so long as the new state regulatory regimes effectively prevent the harms the DOJ has identified as federal priorities." Erwin Chemerinsky et al., Cooperative Federalism and Marijuana Regulation (Mar. 19, 2014), UC Irvine School of Law Research Paper No. 2014-25, http://ssrn.com/abstract=2411707 (last visited Oct. 26, 2016).

In the wake of this action, state and local government greatly expanded their legal and policy activity relating to marijuana. Consequently, a wide range of issues has emerged in land use law, as local and state governments have taken varying positions on the methods by which to regulate the cultivation, sale, distribution, and use of marijuana.

The Classes of Marijuana Regulation. With a number of states legalizing the recreational use of marijuana, the public perception of marijuana is undeniably shifting. The way that the law treats marijuana, however, will inevitably continue to be shaped by the vestiges of regulations enacted in response to previous public preferences. For instance, many states and localities that currently permit medical marijuana have established regulations in place to govern medical marijuana businesses. The prospect of branching out into the regulation of recreational marijuana forces lawmakers to determine whether they can reinterpret their existing regulations to apply to such recreational use, or whether they need to craft a new set of laws applicable to the recreational businesses. The lawmakers may do a bit of both, but either way, they will be making a policy statement.

Thus, not all marijuana land use law is the same. It can be divided, perhaps most logically, into laws concerning "medical marijuana" and laws concerning "recreational marijuana." Some land use regulations, like signage and distance ordinances, will often apply similarly to both medical and recreational businesses. But drawing the distinction between medical and recreational use of marijuana helps draw attention to the different policies that arguably should govern land use regulation of each use. For example, it may be obvious why most local governments are in accordance with keeping marijuana-related businesses out of residential areas. However, it may not be as obvious why a medical marijuana processing facility can be located in certain districts where recreational marijuana dispensaries are excluded.

In addressing these materials, consider where and why it might make sense for state and local governments to treat medical and recreational marijuana-related facilities similarly, and where it might make sense to treat them differently. If a state government prohibits municipalities from banning medical marijuana facilities, what are the limits on the zoning techniques (or permit requirements) a city can use to restrict the location of those facilities? Should it matter in this context whether marijuana cultivation activities are for medical or recreational purposes?

We first cover land use laws concerning medical marijuana, which frequently served as models for subsequently enacted land use laws concerning recreational marijuana.

■ TER BEEK v. CITY OF WYOMING
846 N.W.2d 531 (Mich. 2014)

McCormack, J.

The Michigan Medical Marihuana Act (MMMA), MCL 333.26421 *et seq.*, enacted pursuant to a voter initiative in November 2008, affords certain protections under state law for the medical use of marijuana in the state of Michigan. Among them is §4(a) of the MMMA, which immunizes registered qualifying patients from "penalty in any manner" for specified MMMA-compliant medical marijuana use. MCL 333.26424(a). At issue here is the relationship between this immunity, the federal prohibition of marijuana under the controlled substances act (CSA), 21 USC 801 *et seq.*, and a local zoning ordinance adopted by the city of Wyoming which prohibits and subjects to civil sanction any land "[u]ses that are contrary to federal law." City of Wyoming Code of Ordinances, §90–66. . . .

I. Factual and Procedural Background

In 2010, approximately two years after the MMMA went into effect, defendant, the city of Wyoming (the City), adopted an ordinance (the Ordinance) amending the zoning chapter of the Wyoming city code to add the following provision:

Uses not expressly permitted under this article are prohibited in all districts. Uses that are contrary to federal law, state law or local ordinance are prohibited.

City of Wyoming Code of Ordinances, §90–66. Under the city code, violations of the Ordinance constitute municipal civil infractions punishable by "civil sanctions, including, without limitation, fines, damages, expenses and costs," City of Wyoming Code of Ordinances, §1–27(a) to (b), and are also subject to injunctive relief, City of Wyoming Code of Ordinances, §1–27(g).

Plaintiff, John Ter Beek, lives in the City and is a qualifying patient under the MMMA who possesses a state-issued registry identification card. Upon the City's adoption of the Ordinance, Ter Beek filed the instant lawsuit in circuit court. Ter Beek alleges that he wishes to grow, possess, and use medical marijuana in his home in accordance with the MMMA. The Ordinance, however, by its incorporation of the CSA's federal prohibition of marijuana, prohibits and penalizes such conduct. This, Ter Beek contends, impermissibly contravenes §4(a) of the MMMA, which provides that registered qualifying patients "shall not be subject to arrest, prosecution, or penalty in any manner . . . for the medical use of marihuana in accordance with" the MMMA. Accordingly, Ter Beek seeks a declaratory judgment that the Ordinance is preempted by the MMM and a corresponding injunction prohibiting the City from enforcing the Ordinance against him for the medical use of marijuana in compliance with the MMMA. . . .

III. ANALYSIS

A. KEY PROVISIONS OF THE MMMA, THE CSA, AND THE ORDINANCE

. . . §4(a) of the MMMA provides, in relevant part:

A qualifying patient who has been issued and possesses a registry identification card shall not be subject to arrest, prosecution, or penalty in any manner, or denied any right or privilege, including but not limited to civil penalty or disciplinary action by a business or occupational or professional licensing board or bureau, for the medical use of marihuana in accordance with this act. . . . [MCL 333.26424(a).]

The MMMA defines "medical use" as "the acquisition, possession, cultivation, manufacture, use, internal possession, delivery, transfer, or transportation of marihuana or paraphernalia relating to the administration of marihuana to treat or alleviate a registered qualifying patient's debilitating medical condition or symptoms associated with the debilitating medical condition." MCL 333.26423(f). . . .

The CSA, meanwhile, contains no such immunity. Rather, it makes it "unlawful for any person knowingly or intentionally . . . to manufacture, distribute, or dispense, or possess with intent to manufacture, distribute, or dispense, a controlled substance." 21 USC §841(a)(1). The CSA classifies marijuana as a Schedule I controlled substance, 21 USC §812(c)(c)(10), and thus largely prohibits its manufacture, distribution, or possession.

The parties do not dispute that the Ordinance, by prohibiting all "[u]ses that are contrary to federal law," incorporates the CSA's prohibition of marijuana and makes certain violations of that prohibition both punishable by civil sanctions and subject to injunctive relief. Thus, an individual whose medical use of marijuana falls within the scope of §4(a)'s immunity from "penalty in any manner" may nonetheless be subject to punishment under the Ordinance for that use.

[The court first holds that the federal CSA does not preempt §4(a) of the state MMMA.]

C. THE ORDINANCE IS PREEMPTED BY §4(A) OF THE MMMA

[W]e turn next to whether the Ordinance, as applied to Ter Beek, is preempted by §4(a). We agree with the Court of Appeals that it is. The required analysis on this point is not complex.

Under the Michigan Constitution, the City's "power to adopt resolutions and ordinances relating to its municipal concerns" is "subject to the constitution and the law." Const. 1963, art. 7, §22. As this Court has previously noted, "[w]hile prescribing broad powers, this provision specifically provides that ordinances are subject to the laws of this state, i.e., statutes." *AFSCME v. Detroit*, 468 Mich. 388, 410, 662 N.W.2d 695 (2003). The City, therefore, "is precluded from enacting an ordinance if . . . the ordinance is in direct conflict with the state statutory scheme, or . . . if the state statutory scheme preempts the ordinance by occupying the field of regulation which the municipality seeks to enter, to the exclusion of the ordinance, even where there is no direct conflict between the two schemes of regulation." *People v. Llewellyn*, 401 Mich. 314, 322, 257 N.W.2d 902 (1977) (footnotes omitted). A direct conflict exists when "the ordinance permits what the statute prohibits or the ordinance prohibits what the statute permits." *Id.* at 322 n. 4, 257 N.W.2d 902. Here, the Ordinance directly conflicts with the MMMA by permitting what the MMMA expressly prohibits — the imposition of a "penalty in any manner" on a registered qualifying patient whose medical use of marijuana falls within the scope of §4(a)'s immunity.

The City disputes this characterization of the Ordinance, noting that while it permits the imposition of civil sanctions, it does not require them; instead, a violation of the Ordinance can be enforced through equitable relief such as a civil injunction. We agree with the Court of Appeals, however, that enjoining a registered qualifying patient from engaging in MMMA-compliant conduct unambiguously falls within the scope of penalties prohibited by §4(a). For §4(a) makes clear that individuals who satisfy the statutorily specified criteria "shall not be subject to . . . penalty in any manner," a prohibition which expressly includes "civil penalt[ies]." As the Court of Appeals noted, the MMMA does not define "penalty," but that term is commonly understood to mean a "punishment imposed or incurred for a violation of law or rule . . . something forfeited." *Random House Webster's College Dictionary* (2000). . . . Under the Ordinance, individuals are subject to civil punishment for engaging in the medical use of marijuana in accordance with the MMMA; by the plain terms of §4(a), the manner of that punishment — be it requiring the payment of a monetary sanction, or denying the ability to engage in MMMA-compliant conduct — is not material to the MMMA's immunity from it. . . .

Nor do we agree with the City that our decision in *Michigan v. McQueen*, 493 Mich. 135, 828 N.W.2d 644 (2013), mandates a different outcome. In *McQueen*, this Court held that, because the defendants' business, a medical marijuana dispensary, was not being operated in accordance with the MMMA, it was properly enjoined as a public nuisance under MCL 600.3801. *McQueen*, 493 Mich. at 140, 828 N.W.2d 644. The City contends that, because the growth and cultivation of marijuana is a violation of the Ordinance, and violations of zoning ordinances constitute nuisances per se under the Michigan Zoning Enabling Act (MZEA), MCL 125.3407, *McQueen* permits the City's regulation through injunction. *McQueen*, however, affirmed the injunction of the defendants' business not simply because it was a nuisance, but because it was a nuisance that fell outside the scope of conduct permitted under the MMMA. *McQueen* does not, as the City contends, authorize a municipality to enjoin a registered qualifying patient from engaging in medical use of marijuana in compliance with the MMMA, simply by characterizing that conduct as a zoning violation.

Furthermore, contrary to the City's suggestion, the fact that the Ordinance is a local zoning regulation enacted pursuant to the MZEA does not save it from preemption. The City stresses that the MZEA affords local municipalities a broad grant of authority to use their zoning powers to advance local interests, such as "public health, safety, and welfare." MCL 125.3201. The MMMA, however, provides in no uncertain terms that "[t]he medical use of marihuana is allowed under state law to the extent that it is carried out in accordance with" the MMMA, MCL 333.26427(a), and that "[a]ll other acts and parts of acts inconsistent with [the MMMA] do not apply to the medical use of marihuana," MCL 333.26427(e). The City contends that the MMMA does not express a sufficiently clear intent to supersede the MZEA, but we see no ambiguity in the MMMA's plain language to this effect. . . .

Lastly, the City stresses that the MMMA does not create an absolute right to grow and distribute marijuana. Correct. . . . Ter Beek, however, does not seek to assert any such general or absolute right. Nor does our conclusion recognize one. The Ordinance directly conflicts with the MMMA not because it generally pertains to marijuana, but because it permits registered qualifying patients, such as Ter Beek, to be penalized by the City for engaging in MMMA-compliant medical marijuana use. Section 4(a) of the MMMA expressly prohibits this. As such, the MMMA pre-empts the Ordinance to the extent of this conflict.

A Note on the New Legalization of Marijuana

Medical Marijuana and State Regulation. As of August 2016, medical marijuana is legal in 25 states and the District of Columbia. *See* http://medicalmarijuana.procon .org/view.resource.php?resourceID=000881&print=true (last visited Oct. 7, 2016). Many of the states that have legalized medical marijuana have authorized its personal consumption as well as its sale and cultivation for personal use. Generally state legislatures are responsible for outlining how medical marijuana businesses must operate and, in some cases, where those businesses may operate (such as not within specified distances from a school). Most zoning decisions, however, are made at the local level. States make determinations on the amount of marijuana that can be grown and sold, and the standards that facilities must meet, such as building and fire. Local governments will address how marijuana-related businesses fit within their municipality's zoning structure by making determinations such as whether indoor marijuana cultivation fits within an "agriculture" designation.

The state legislature tasks a number of state agencies with promulgating and enforcing regulations with respect to the various areas of the medical marijuana industry. Some agencies regulate who can work in marijuana facilities; others regulate how marijuana businesses must store their products and dispose of their waste. In California, for example, the Medical Marijuana Regulation and Safety Act created 17 different kinds of medical marijuana operational license types. The agencies that issue these licenses range from the Department of Public Health, to the Departments of Fish and Wildlife, to the State Water Resources Control Board. Some legislatures have created new, highly-specific agencies like Alaska's "Marijuana Control Board," which serves as a regulatory and quasi-judicial agency for the control of the cultivation, manufacture, and sale of marijuana in the state.

Local Regulations. Regulations at the local level can be just as complex as those at the state level, if not more. This is because local regulations must attempt not only to reflect the will of the immediate community but also conform to state requirements. In an effort to make the overall implementation of regulations less complex, some states have elected a more localist approach, which allows municipalities to determine the stringency of certain requirements applied to medical marijuana businesses.

In California, for example, even though the state requires many different kinds of licenses, those licenses are useless for a business if that business cannot meet the requirements of the local government. The state licenses are sufficient to allow an entrepreneur to do business only where a local government has declined to address medical marijuana businesses in its regulations. Bestowing this control on municipalities reduces the burden on state governments because some localities will have stricter requirements than the state (making the review process for state licenses easier), while some cities may ban medical marijuana businesses entirely (eliminating the need for the state to review some applications). At the local level, permits may be tied to criteria like the status of the future owner of a medical marijuana business (e.g., as a "Qualified Patient" who can legally purchase marijuana), or the capacity of the business to maintain a reasonable level of security.

The Change in Regulatory Focus. Much of the earlier litigation concerning marijuana almost exclusively involved criminal rather than civil law. In any event, the result of such a turbulent legal environment was that, for many years, the large-scale cultivation of marijuana, its delivery, and its sale by dispensaries generally took place in a somewhat clandestine fashion.

Now that the medical marijuana industry operates much more openly, the legal challenges facing the industry generally involve the types of land use issues similar to those facing bars, liquor stores, adult entertainment clubs, or casinos. The current disputes focus on such issues as the reasonableness of requirements imposed on a medical marijuana business for obtaining a conditional use permit, as opposed to such issues as to whether the police had reasonable cause for searching the premises of a medical marijuana business.

Still, the zoning of medical marijuana businesses, particularly dispensaries, brings with it accessibility concerns that do not apply to the kinds of adult businesses mentioned above—or even to recreational marijuana, for that matter. Although medical marijuana dispensaries are often confronted with the same kind of ethics-based opposition that liquor stores and adult establishments face, these dispensaries serve medical patients, not the general public. And whether patients have access to medical marijuana—i.e., whether a patient has to drive across town (or to another county even) to purchase his or her medicine—is an ethical consideration that gets thrown into the legal and policy mix. States have come to different conclusions on how to best balance these interests.

Preemption. Arizona, Delaware, and Massachusetts have denied local governments the authority to completely ban retail marijuana dispensaries for medical patients. Arizona's medical marijuana act, for instance, permits local governments only to limit dispensaries to certain zoning districts. Massachusetts addressed the accessibility issue, not through legislation, but rather through a statement by Martha M. Coakley, the State Attorney General from 2007 to 2015, which unequivocally ruled that local governments could not ban dispensaries.

Other states have taken very different approaches. In *City of Riverside v. Inland Empire Patients Health and Wellness Ctr., Inc.*, 300 P.3d 494 (Cal. 2013), the California Supreme Court addressed the state's Compassionate Use Act (CUA) and Medical Marijuana Program Act (MMPA), both of which decriminalized the sale and possession of marijuana used for medical purposes. The court held that these laws did not expressly nor impliedly preempt localities from using their land use authority to ban medical marijuana dispensaries as nuisances. In making its decision, the court drew a firm line giving municipalities ultimate control over whether the medical marijuana industry can exist within their borders. Prior to the decision, the California Courts of Appeal were divided on the preemption issue. *Riverside* emphasized that neither the CUA nor the MMPA granted a "'right' of convenient access to marijuana for medicinal use. . . ." *Id.* at 424.

In *Cannabis Action Coal. v. City of Kent*, 351 P.3d 151 (Wash. 2015), the Supreme Court of Washington came to a conclusion similar to that of the court in *Riverside*. In this case, an interest group and various individuals sued the City of Kent seeking to have the city's zoning ordinance prohibiting medical marijuana collective gardens declared preempted and invalid under the state's Medical Use of Cannabis Act. The court found that "because collective gardens are defined to include 'producing' and 'processing' medical marijuana, the statutory context strongly confirms that a city's power [to regulate medical marijuana activity] . . . includes noncommercial collective gardens." 351 P.3d at 157. The legislature aided the court in coming to its conclusion by repealing the conflicting statutes in favor of new language.

Thus, the situations in which state laws preempt local ordinances define how the land use law develops in each state. In Massachusetts, for example, the decision to preempt local governments from completely banning medical marijuana facilities did not prevent local governments from challenging the location of marijuana facilities or imposing strict requirements on those facilities seeking to obtain permits. Were some municipalities in Massachusetts *forced* to make zoning decisions that they may have otherwise opted out of? Does this state of affairs offer a valuable example of how states can function as laboratories for medical marijuana governance?

Permitted Uses. Preemption is not the only matter of concern in the area of medical marijuana zoning. In *City of Corona v. Naulls*, 83 Cal. Rptr. 3d 1 (Ct. App. 2008), for example, an appellate court upheld a city's order to close a medical marijuana dispensary because medical marijuana dispensaries were not among the permitted uses enumerated in the city's zoning code. The court reasoned that, "where a particular use of land is not expressly enumerated in a city's municipal code as constituting a permissible use, it follows that such use is impermissible." (Recall the discussion of permitted uses in Chapter 2). *See also Conejo Wellness Ctr., Inc. v. City of Agoura Hills*, 154 Cal. Rptr. 3d 850 (Ct. App. 2013) and *City of Monterey v. Carrnshimba*, 156 Cal. Rptr. 3d 1 (Ct. App. 2013), both denying medical marijuana dispensaries' assertions of vested rights as lawful nonconforming uses on the grounds that the cities' zoning codes did not specifically list medical marijuana dispensaries as permissible or lawful uses).

These decisions raise a series of questions. Do they seem to put the burden on the locality to make an affirmative effort to address the permissibility of medical marijuana businesses? Is there a rationale for creating a specific categorization for marijuana businesses that then further divides into "medical" and "recreational"? How would one categorize the aspects of the industry that occur prior to sale, such as cultivation, testing, and manufacturing? Would it make any sense for a local government to distinguish between whether those businesses were "medical" or "recreational"?

Below is a sampling of ordinances amending local land use regulations. Consider whether these ordinances seem sufficiently specific.

■ PHOENIX, ARIZONA ORDINANCE G-6151

*https://www.phoenix.gov/lawsite/Documents/g6151%20TA.8.15%
20a.%204.20.16%20e.%205.20.16.pdf (last visited Oct. 7, 2016).*

ANCILLARY SERVICES SUCH AS COUNSELING, OR VOCATIONAL TRAINING.

SECTION 2. That Chapter 6, Section 603.A (Suburban A-1 District -Ranch or Farm Residence), is amended to read:

122. Nonprofit medical marijuana dispensary facility, subject to the following conditions and limitations; failure to comply with the below regulations and requirements . . .

a. 4) A survey sealed by a registrant of the State of Arizona shall be submitted to show compliance with the distance requirements listed below . . .

f. Shall not be located within 500 feet of a residentially zoned districts:

S-1, S-2, RE-43, RE-35, R1-18, R1-14, R1-10, R1-8, R1-6, R-2, R-3, R3-A, R-4, R-4A, R-5, and PAD-1 through PAD-15. This distance shall be measured from the exterior walls of the building or portion thereof in which the dispensary business is conducted or proposed to be conducted to the zoning boundary line of the residentially zoned district.

g. Shall not be located within 1,320 feet of a preschool, kindergarten, elementary, secondary or high school, public park, public community center, dependent care facility, homeless shelter, or youth community center. This distance shall be measured from the exterior walls of the building or portion thereof in which the dispensary business is conducted to the property line of the protected use.

h. Shall not be located within 1,320 feet of a place of worship. This distance shall be measured from the exterior walls of the building or portion thereof in which the dispensary business is conducted to the property line of the place of worship. . . .

k. THERE SHALL BE NO EMISSION OF DUST, FUMES, VAPORS OR ODORS INTO THE ENVIRONMENT FROM THE PREMISES.

■ BUTTE COUNTY, CALIFORNIA, CODE OF ORDINANCES CHAPTER 34A — MEDICAL MARIJUANA CULTIVATION REGULATION

*https://www.municode.com/library/ca/butte_county/codes/
code_of_ordinances?nodeId=CH34AMEMACURE (last visited Oct. 7, 2016).*

34A-8. Setbacks; Other Restrictions.

(a) Each detached structure or outdoor area constituting the single cultivation area in which the marijuana is cultivated shall be set back from the boundaries of the premises as follows:

(1) If the premises is one-half (0.5) of an acre in size or less, each detached structure shall be set back at least fifteen (15) feet from all boundaries of the

premises, unless the Director of the Department of Development Services or his or her designee reduces or waives this requirement based upon a finding of unusual hardship for that particular parcel to comply with such setback requirements.

(2) If the premises is greater than one-half (0.5) of an acre in size but less than five (5) acres in size, each detached structure or outdoor area constituting the single cultivation area shall be set back at least fifty (50) feet from all boundaries of the premises, unless the Director of the Department of Development Services or his or her designee reduces or waives this requirement based upon a finding of unusual hardship for that particular parcel to comply with such setback requirements. Such cultivation area shall be measured from the outer edge of the marijuana plant canopy and not the stalk. Owners of parcels adjacent to such premises shall be notified in writing of any exercise of such discretion under this section.

(3) If the premises is equal to or greater than five (5) acres in size but less than ten (10) acres in size, each detached structure or outdoor area constituting the single cultivation area shall be set back at least seventy-five (75) feet from all boundaries of the premises, unless the Director of the Department of Development Services or his or her designee reduces or waives this requirement based upon a finding of unusual hardship for that particular parcel to comply with such setback requirements. Owners of parcels adjacent to such premises shall be notified in writing of any exercise of such discretion under this section.

(4) If the premises is equal to or greater than ten (10) acres in size, each detached structure or outdoor area shall be set back at least one hundred fifty (150) feet from all boundaries of the premises, unless the Director of the Department of Development Services or his or her designee reduces or waives this requirement based upon a finding of unusual hardship for that particular parcel to comply with such setback requirements. Owners of parcels adjacent to such premises shall be notified in writing of any exercise of such discretion under this section.

A Note on Regulation of Recreational Marijuana

The New Legalization. As noted above, recreational marijuana regulation is often discussed against the backdrop of medical marijuana precedent. Still, given that the laws concerning medical marijuana are constantly being developed and refined, many of the laws and regulations addressing recreational marijuana are experimental by design. These varying approaches to regulating recreational marijuana are somewhat of an ode to federalism, as states (and the localities within them) try out the best methods for policing the recreational use, sale, cultivation, and distribution of the plant and its subsequent products. Fortunately, all of the states that have legalized the recreational use of marijuana have also had the benefit of experimenting with the legalization of medical marijuana for more than a decade.

As of November, 2016, eight states and one territory had legalized recreational marijuana. Colorado and Washington became the first states to legalize recreational marijuana in 2012. Alaska, Oregon, and the District of Columbia followed suit in 2014. California, Nevada, Maine, and Massachusetts followed in 2016. Some states implement regulatory schemes for the taxation and regulation of recreational marijuana production and sale. In contrast, the District of Columbia has only legalized the recreational *use* of marijuana; the distribution, sale, and commercial cultivation or manufacturing of recreational marijuana is still illegal.

Different Issues. Recreational marijuana can pose very different questions for state legislatures regarding how much control they should cede to the municipalities, and what local land use authority should exist. Patient accessibility, for example, is not an issue that states need to consider with recreational marijuana, which may weigh in favor of greater local control. On the flip side, greater state control may be warranted because recreational marijuana dispensaries, unlike medical marijuana dispensaries (which are accessible only to patients), are open to the public. In spite of these differences, there is still an observable level of consistency — at least at the state level — between the medical and recreational marijuana laws adopted by the states. In fact, states that have legalized recreational marijuana have used the occasion to craft laws that, for the most part, treat medical and recreational marijuana facilities the same, unless stated otherwise.

Washington is an example of a state that has, despite retaining state authority to issue licenses through the State Liquor and Cannabis Board, given localities significant control over recreational (and medical) marijuana businesses. Cities, towns, and counties in Washington State can reduce the 1000 foot buffer zone mandated by state law to 100 feet around all entities listed in the statute, except elementary and secondary schools, and public playgrounds.

The two ordinances below both reduce the buffer zones in certain circumstances.

■ CITY OF SHELTON, WASHINGTON, MUNICIPAL CODE
CHAPTER 20.72 MEDICAL AND RECREATIONAL MARIJUANA
http://www.codepublishing.com/WA/Shelton/html/Shelton20/Shelton2072.html
(last visited Oct. 7, 2016).

20.72.020 State-licensed marijuana producers, processors, retailers, and researchers — Where permitted.

A. State-licensed marijuana retail businesses may be located in the general commercial (GC) zoning district, and are prohibited in all other zoning districts.

B. State-licensed marijuana producers, processors, and researchers may be located in the industrial (I) zoning district and in those commercial-industrial (CI) zoning districts that are immediately adjacent to an industrial (I) zoning district, and are prohibited from all other zoning districts.

C. Buffer Zones.

1. Any lot line of property having a state-licensed marijuana producer, processor, retailer, or researcher must be one thousand feet or more from any lot line of property on which any of the following uses, as defined in WAC [Washington Administrative Code] 314-55-010, is located: elementary school; secondary school; or playground.

2. Any lot line of property having a state-licensed marijuana producer, processor, or researcher must be five hundred feet or more from any lot line of property on which any of the following uses, as defined in WAC 314-55-010, is established and operating on the date a complete application is accepted by the Washington State Liquor and Cannabis Board: child care center; game arcade admitting minors; library; public park; public transit center; or recreation center or facility.

■ CITY OF SEATTLE, WASHINGTON, MUNICIPAL CODE

https://www.municode.com/library/wa/seattle/codes/
*municipal_code?nodeId=TIT23LAUSCO_SUBTITLE_IIILAUSRE_*
CH23.42GEUSPR_23.42.058MA (last visited Oct. 7, 2016).

23.42.058

C. Major marijuana activity is allowed in all other zones if the activity and site meet the following requirements:

1. The person operating the major marijuana activity must have a current license issued by the State of Washington pursuant to Title 69 RCW [Revised Code of Washington] authorizing the person to produce, process or sell, at the proposed site, marijuana, marijuana-infused products, useable marijuana, or marijuana concentrates, or to research or test any of those products at the proposed site for quality assurance pursuant to Title 69 RCW;

2. Any lot line of property having a major marijuana activity must be 1,000 feet or more from any lot line of property on which any of the following uses as defined in WAC 314-55-010 is located: elementary school; secondary school; or playground;

3. Any lot line of property having a major marijuana activity that includes the retail sale of marijuana products must be 500 feet or more from any lot line of property on which any of the following uses as defined in WAC 314-55-010 is established and operating; child care center; game arcade; library; public park: public transit center; or recreation center or facility;

4. Any lot line of property having a major marijuana activity that does not include the retail sale of marijuana products must be 250 feet or more from any lot line of property on which any of the following uses as defined in WAC 314-55-010 is established and operating: child care center: game arcade; library; public park; public transit center: or recreation center or facility;

5. Any lot line of property having a major marijuana activity that includes the retail sale of marijuana products must be 350 feet or more from any lot line of other property containing major marijuana activity that includes the retail sale of marijuana products . . .

Oregon and Colorado have also given a significant level of control to the localities. Consider, for instance, how much authority the following Colorado regulation provides municipalities by allowing medical and recreational marijuana to be sold on the same premises:

■ 1 COLO. CODE REGS. §212-2.304
MEDICAL MARIJUANA BUSINESS AND RETAIL MARIJUANA ESTABLISHMENT-SHARED LICENSE PREMISES AND OPERATIONAL SEPARATION

1. A Medical Marijuana Center that prohibits patients under the age of 21 years to be on the Licensed Premises may also hold a Retail Marijuana Store license and operate a dual retail business operation on the same Licensed Premises if the relevant local jurisdiction permits a dual operation at the same location and the two are commonly owned.

2. A Medical Marijuana Center that authorizes medical marijuana patients under the age of 21 years to be on the premises is prohibited from sharing its Licensed Premises with a Retail Marijuana Establishment. Even when the two are commonly owned, the two shall maintain distinctly separate Licensed Premises; including, but not limited to, separate sales and storage areas, separate entrances and exits, separate inventories, separate point-of-sale operations, and separate record-keeping.

3. An Optional Premises Cultivation Operation and a Retail Marijuana Cultivation Facility may share a single Licensed Premises in order to operate a dual cultivation business operation if the relevant local jurisdiction permits a dual operation at the same location and the two are commonly owned.

The Colorado regulation expressly prohibits co-located medical and recreational retail marijuana establishments from sharing marijuana. The ceding of some authority by the state to the localities, combined with regulatory detail about how both medical and recreational marijuana businesses must operate, creates a complex mix of laws and regulations for land use attorneys to navigate.

A Hillsboro, Oregon ordinance includes detailed provisions on the scope of activities involved in regulation of recreational marijuana:

■ HILLSBORO, OREGON, MUNICIPAL CODE
12.40.218 RECREATIONAL MARIJUANA FACILITIES
http://qcode.us/codes/hillsboro/view.php?topic=12-12_40-12_40_218&highlightWords=marijuana (last visited Oct. 7, 2016).

A. Characteristics. Five types of recreational marijuana facilities are defined in Section 12.01.500. For purposes of this Code, recreational marijuana facilities must be licensed by the Oregon Liquor Control Commission. A facility not licensed by the Oregon Liquor Control Commission is not permitted in any zone.

B. Approval Process. Where permitted, recreational marijuana facilities are subject to approval under Section 12.80.040 Development Review. Applications for Development Review approval shall include detailed responses to the applicable standards listed in this section.

C. Standards for Recreational Marijuana Production, Processing, Testing Laboratories, and Wholesale Sales Facilities.

1. Facility Construction Requirements. Recreational marijuana production, processing, testing laboratories, and wholesale sales facilities shall take place consistent with the Use Tables in Subchapter 12.25 and only within buildings compliant with the following standards:

a. In the I-G General Industrial zone, either in existing buildings constructed and occupied as of May 16, 2016 or in new buildings; both subject to compliance with paragraph c below;

b. In the I-P Industrial Park zone, the SC-BP Station Community Business Park zone, and the SCI Station Community Industrial zone: either in existing buildings as of May 16, 2016, or in new buildings of either tilt-up concrete or concrete masonry unit (CMU) construction; both subject to compliance with paragraph c below.

c. In the case of production facilities, views from the exterior of the building into the production area are prohibited. Views of interior lighting in the production area from the exterior of the building are also prohibited.

2. Public Access Prohibited. Access to an industrial facility shall be limited to employees, personnel, and guests over the age of 21, authorized by the facility operator.

3. Security Measures Required.

a. Landscaping shall be continuously maintained to provide clear lines of sight from public rights-of-way to all building entrances.

b. Exterior lighting shall be provided and continuously maintained consistent with Subsection 12.50.240.C.

c. Any security bars installed on doors or windows visible from the public right-of-way shall be installed interior to the door or window, in a manner that they are not visible from the public right-of-way.

4. Odor Mitigation Measures Required. Production and processing facilities shall install and maintain enhanced ventilation systems designed to prevent detection of marijuana odor from adjacent properties or the public right-of-way. Such systems shall include the following features:

a. Installation of activated carbon filters on all exhaust outlets to the building exterior;

b. Location of exhaust outlets a minimum of 10 feet from the property line and 10 feet above finished grade; and

c. Maintenance of negative air pressure within the facility; or

d. An alternative odor control system approved by the Building Official based on a report by a mechanical engineer licensed in the State of Oregon, demonstrating that the alternative system will control odor equally or better than the required activated carbon filtration system.

5. Waste Security Measures Required.

a. Prior to disposal, marijuana waste shall be rendered unusable by either grinding and mixing (at a ratio of at least 1:1) with other compostable materials or yard waste, or by mixing with non-compostable solid waste such as paper, cardboard, plastic, soils, or other approved materials.

b. Marijuana waste shall be temporarily stored in an indoor container until it is rendered unusable.

c. Any facility generating marijuana waste shall use the services of a solid waste franchisee or self-haul such materials to a properly licensed and approved solid waste disposal or recycling facility.

d. An alternative waste security system approved by the Sustainability Program Manager, demonstrating that the alternative system will render marijuana waste unusable equally or better than the required grinding, mixing, and disposal system.

6. Proximity Restrictions. A recreational marijuana production, processing, testing laboratory or wholesale sales facility shall not be located within 100 feet of any single family residential, multi-family residential, mixed use, urban center or institutional zone. For purposes of this paragraph, the distance specified is measured from the closest points between property lines of the affected properties. In the circumstance where a proximity restriction distance bisects a property, that property's eligibility as a location for a facility shall be determined as specified in Section 12.40.194.C.7.

Notes and Comments

1. *The* Ter Beek *Decision.* The Michigan Supreme Court concluded that the local ban conflicted with the state law on the subject, proclaiming the analysis "not complex." Are you convinced? Did the court afford sufficient deference to the local government's land use authority?

2. *The Role of Science.* Do you see a science-backed justification for government bans on medical versus recreational marijuana? How strict will the courts be in reviewing the science behind the bans? Are marijuana bans paternalism in the guise of scientifically established understandings? *See* R. George Wright, Legal Paternalism and the Eclipse of Principle, Indiana University Robert H. McKinney School of Law Research Paper No. 2016-27, http://papers.ssrn.com/sol3/papers.cfm?abstract_id=2797819 (last visited Oct. 7, 2016) (arguing that in the future, disputes over the appropriate scope of legal paternalism will increasingly focus on detailed, contextualized matters).

3. *The Coming Complexity.* As states develop their jurisprudence with respect to recreational marijuana, they must not only consider the interactions between their laws, but also how their laws will affect medical marijuana. Many of the land use problems that will continue to surface as a result of this complexity will not be particularly unique to marijuana-related facilities, but they will certainly shape the development of the legal landscape with respect to marijuana business. For example: Do you anticipate that the application of the secondary effects rationale for highly restricting adult uses (analyzed in Chapter 8) will limit access to recreational marijuana in states where it is legal? Will local governments be able to treat signage for recreational marijuana differently than for other retail establishments?

The marijuana land use arena is ripe for litigation and for legal commentary. Among the growing literature: Robert A. Mikos, Marijuana Localism, 65 Case W. Res. L. Rev. 719 (2015); Scott B. Well, Reefer Madness Redux: The Marijuana Laws in Flux, Orange County Law., at 30, (Aug. 2016); Lisa L. Mead & Adam J. Costa, Zoning for Medical Marijuana: Approaches & Considerations, Boston B.J., at 26 (Spring 2016); Robert T. Hoban & Raushanah A. Patterson, Sprung from Night into the Sun: An Examination of Colorado's Marijuana Regulatory Framework Since Legalization, 8 Ky. J. Equine, Agric. & Nat. Resources L. 225 (2016); John Jennings, Current Topics in Colorado's Regulatory Landscape, 92 Denv. U.L. Rev. Online 183 (2015); Florence Shu-Acquaye, The Role of States in Shaping the Legal Debate on Medical Marijuana, 42 Mitchell Hamline L. Rev. 697 (2016); Erwin Chemerinsky, et al., Cooperative Federalism and Marijuana Regulation, 62 UCLA L. Rev. 74 (2015); and Sarah Swan, Home Rules, 64 Duke L.J. 823 (2015).

4. *Geography and Land Size.* San Bernardino County in California is geographically larger than each of the nine smallest states. Under §19.06.026 of the San Bernardino County Development Code and §5.05 of the County Municipal Code, medical marijuana dispensaries are expressly prohibited in the county. Should arguments about accessibility to medical marijuana or, conversely, about whether medical marijuana businesses constitute nuisances, be couched in geographic terms (i.e., in terms of the size of the local jurisdiction)? The court in *Kirby v. County of Fresno,* 195 Cal. Rptr. 3d 815 (Cal. Ct. App. 2015) (upholding County's ban on marijuana dispensaries, cultivation and storage of medical marijuana) did not think this was necessary. How different is the issue of medical marijuana zoning

from other land use issues that walk such a polarizing line? Can you think of any others?

5. Environmental Impacts. The increasing cultivation of marijuana has not been without its opposition on environmental grounds. *See, e.g.,* Laura Seaman, Marijuana's Environmental Impacts, Stanford Woods Institute for the Environment (July 2015), https://woods.stanford.edu/news-events/news/marijuanas-environmental-impacts (last visited Oct. 7, 2016), and Jennifer K. Carah et al., High Time for Conservation: Adding the Environment to the Debate on Marijuana Liberalization, BioScience (2015), http://bioscience.oxfordjournals.org/content/early/2015/06/19/biosci.biv083.full (last visited Oct. 7, 2016) ("Marijuana cultivation can have significant negative collateral effects on the environment that are often unknown or overlooked."). *But see* The Environmental Benefits of A Legal Marijuana Industry, Leaf Science (Nov. 2013), http://www.leafscience.com/2013/11/17/environmental-benefits-legal-marijuana-industry (last visited Oct. 7, 2016) ("The marijuana industry has a lot of room for environmental innovation, but progress on a wide scale can't be made until cannabis is fully legal.").

12

Securing a Sufficient Housing Supply

A. INTRODUCTION

1. Housing and Land Use Regulation

Meeting the need for housing has long been an implicit goal of land use regulation. Initially, zoning was conceived as a way of protecting housing districts from polluting industries and other nuisance-like activities. Quickly, however, zoning came to be used to separate different classes of housing occupants. In New York City, the Fifth Avenue gentry championed zoning as a means to exclude the commercial loft and its laborers. The more affluent of suburbia utilized zoning to distance their communities from the noise, smell, and pollution of the factory. In the process, they also distanced themselves from the sight of workers and the poor.

Zoning codes and subdivision regulations spoke in neutral tones of environmental concerns, health, safety, and the adequacy of facilities. Implicit in these rules, however, was the assumption that the poor could successfully compete in the marketplace for shelter. Indeed, theorists assumed that the poor would always be provided for, as those better off economically moved to bigger and newer housing, leaving existing housing for the less affluent.

This model of "filtration" continues to dominate housing policy today, despite a lack of scientific support for the validity of the model. In recent decades, urban renewal programs have depleted some of America's housing stock, and abandonment of dilapidated housing is a problem in some shrinking cities and suburbs. Arguably well-intentioned housing code enforcement and increasingly expensive mandates to upgrade housing for health, fire, or earthquake safety have also helped reduce housing supply. Some previously affordable housing has been converted or "gentrified" through rehabilitation to provide homes for the affluent. Similarly, affordable multi-family housing in some instances has been converted to condominiums, a process facilitated by the federal tax advantages of homeownership. The increasing presence of the homeless is a reminder that housing policies have been unsuccessful, and that land use planning for too long has failed to accommodate the rising need for shelter. *See* Most Cities in Mayors' Survey Report Increase in Homelessness; Half Cite Foreclosures as Factor, 37 [Current Developments] Housing Dev. Rptr. (Thomson-West) 41 (Jan. 19, 2009) (23 cities reported that in 2008, between 0.15 and 1.74 percent of their population were living on the streets, in emergency shelters, or in transitional housing; in addition, between 0.01 and 0.79 percent were living in permanent supporting housing for formerly homeless persons).

2. The Suburbs and the Cities

As suburbs developed without adequate housing for the poor, the poor became increasingly concentrated in central cities. At the same time, retail stores, restaurants, and industries relocated to the suburbs and beyond, leaving the poor in a deteriorating metropolis with limited access to the new job markets. Decisions regarding the deployment of transit also have contributed to the current condition; today, a good part of the transit systems is designed to bring suburban dwellers to downtown financial and service-oriented jobs. In the last decade, the picture has become somewhat more complex, with the poor and particularly the non-white poor migrating to older, close-in suburbs. James A. Kushner, Affordable Housing as Infrastructure in the Time of Global Warming, 43 Urb. Law. 179 (2011); James A. Kushner, Urban Neighborhood Regeneration and the Phases of Community Evolution After World War II in the United States, 41 Ind. L. Rev. 575 (2008).

Overall, the result has been destabilized cities with little economic development. The legal and planning literature is replete with expressions of concern about this situation. Zoning has generated a pattern of land use that is frequently compared to a doughnut or a bagel, with the more affluent in the suburbs surrounding a central core of the poor, ethnic minorities, and those dependent on expensive public services including public safety, education, transit, health care, and welfare. This pattern of suburban land use typically contains numerous tracts of single-family, detached homes on lots ranging from one-quarter to three or four acres. The development pattern in the suburbs also features the virtual absence of government-subsidized housing and, frequently, little multi-family housing. The imposition of expensive exactions, development conditions, and impact fees contributes to rendering these suburban homes inaccessible to low income individuals.

The aftermath of the real estate meltdown and foreclosure crisis of the past decade has brought a huge supply of suburban homes that have been vacated or abandoned, along with condominiums in and around cities. Unfortunately, foreclosure and job loss have eliminated home equity and wealth of many in the middle class and the near-affluent. Credit is tight but burgeoning vacancy rates should produce a supply of affordable housing. In addition, the automobile-only access to many suburban neighborhoods renders those communities inaccessible to those on limited budgets who are increasingly carless or unable to afford gasoline, and public transit fails to serve most such communities.

The lack of decent, safe, and sanitary affordable housing is seemingly intractable and worsening. Joint Center for Housing Subsidies, The State of the Nation's Housing 6-16, 27-31 (2008) (describing unraveling markets, escalating household growth, and a weak economy). According to a report of the National Housing Conference based on 1999 American Housing Survey data, more than 13 million households are paying in excess of 50 percent of their income for housing or are living in substandard conditions. One in Seven Households Has Critical Housing Need, Report Says, [Current Developments] Hous. & Dev. Rep. (West) 776 (2002). An inadequate supply of affordable rental housing in the suburbs aggravates inflationary rent increases and can discourage potential employers and investors from locating in the region.

The lack of adequate, affordable housing has other adverse consequences, including heightened racial and economic segregation, long and costly commutes to employment centers often distant from central city housing markets, and exposure to a higher incidence of housing discrimination. "The problem of housing affordability can be seen by looking at the high percentage of low income households who pay a disproportionate share of their incomes (more than 30% by some measures; more than 50% by others) for housing. Of the 20 million lowest income households, over 24 percent pay between 30 percent and 50 percent of their incomes for housing and/or live in inadequate housing. Most of the 7.2 million of the lowest income households pay more than half of their incomes for housing." Paulette J. Williams, The Continuing Crisis in Affordable Housing: Systemic Issues Requiring Systemic Solutions, 31 Fordham Urb. L. J. 413 ns. 39-65 and accompanying text (2004), citing Harv. Joint Ctr. for Hous. Studies, The State of the Nation's Housing: 2002, at 3 (stating that the rise in home prices represents a serious challenge for the nation's lowest income households), at http://www.jchs.harvard .edu/publications/markets/Son2002.pdf (last visited Nov. 11, 2016).

A central focus of state efforts to breach the exclusionary wall of the suburbs, indeed simply to develop affordable housing, has been the availability of financing. In the past, the federal government was the primary source of affordable housing subsidies, but starting with the Nixon administration the federal government reduced its support for housing. With today's agenda of budget-balancing and deficits, communities must look elsewhere to fund low income housing. *See* Florence Wagman Roisman, National Ingratitude: The Egregious Deficiencies of the United States' Housing Programs for Veterans and the "Public Scandal" of Veterans' Homelessness, 38 Ind. L. Rev. 103 (2005); Kristin A. Siegesmund, The Looming Subsidized Housing Crisis, 27 Ind. L. Rev. 1123 (2000) (arguing that the ability of subsidized landlords to exit program participation is exacerbating the housing crisis); Housing Boom Hasn't Eased Low-Income Families' Affordability Problem, Joint Center Report Says, 33 [current developments] Hous. & Dev. Rep. (Thomson-West) 392 (2005) (reporting that shrinking affordable housing stock increasing pressure on low-income families).

3. The Assault on the Zoning Citadel

The Supreme Court's decision in *Village of Euclid v. Ambler Realty Co.*, 272 U.S. 365 (1926) (reprinted in Chapter 2), established a model of judicial deference toward zoning that, some have strongly argued, has been responsible for

12 ■ Securing a Sufficient Housing Supply

institutionalizing a form of economic segregation. Zoning classifications and cost-inflating development criteria, ranging from large lots to expensive infrastructure conditions, have greatly limited housing choices available to many individuals. At the same time, the zoning decisions of local governmental bodies have enjoyed a presumption of regularity, and considerable deference from the courts. Typically immune from judicial invalidation, zoning constitutes a citadel—an institution largely impervious to plaintiffs' attacks. *See, e.g.,* Daniel R. Mandelker, Reversing the Presumption of Constitutionality in Land Use Litigation: Is Legislative Action Necessary?, 30 J. Urb. & Contemp. L. 5 (1986). In some housing cases, however, that citadel proved vulnerable. In 1965, in *National Land & Inv. Co. v. Kohn,* 215 A.2d 597 (Pa. 1965), the Pennsylvania Supreme Court broke with the pattern of general judicial endorsement of local zoning and invalidated a large-lot, suburban zoning scheme that precluded apartment development.

While a few other state courts have followed the lead of Pennsylvania, New Jersey went beyond the prohibitory nature of the Pennsylvania principle. In the landmark decision *Southern Burlington County NAACP v. Township of Mount Laurel,* 336 A.2d 713 (N.J.), *appeal dismissed,* 423 U.S. 808 (1975) (reprinted below), the New Jersey Supreme Court held that states must regulate for the general welfare of all the state's citizens. Individual communities are obligated, the court ruled, to regulate land use in such a way as to make it realistically possible to house all economic segments of the community. Thus, each community had an obligation to affirmatively plan housing for its "fair share" of regional housing needs.

New Jersey's struggle to implement the *Mount Laurel* doctrine has been a long and difficult one. Prodded by increasingly aggressive decisions from the New Jersey Supreme Court, the New Jersey legislature enacted a law creating an administrative process designed to facilitate compliance with *Mount Laurel.* While that initiative appears to have generated the construction of more affordable housing in the suburbs, it has become mired in political controversy in recent years.

Litigation involving exclusionary zoning has involved many groups representing a wide array of interests and has resulted in judicial recognition in the state courts of third-party rights in the development process. Standing to litigate has been granted to developers (even to raise the rights of future occupants), taxpayers, civil rights advocates, housing advocates, and homebuilder organizations. *See Southern Burlington County NAACP v. Township of Mount Laurel,* 456 A.2d 390 (N.J. 1983) (*Mount Laurel II*) (reprinted below) (any individual or group interested in securing low income housing has standing to challenge exclusionary zoning).

Although a few states have altered housing and zoning policy by judicial decision, numerous reforms have come from the state legislatures and local governments. California requires local plans to contain housing elements that plan for affordable housing. Cal. Gov't Code §65302(c), 65580-65589 (West 2016). A number of other jurisdictions have followed this approach in establishing obligations to plan for affordable housing.

4. Inclusionary Zoning

The term "inclusionary zoning" is simply the opposite of exclusionary zoning. Inclusionary zoning encompasses more than just zoning techniques; it includes such mechanisms as (1) zoning for "least cost" housing by allowing smaller homes to be built on smaller lots with a minimum of amenities consistent with minimum housing code standards; (2) mandatory inclusion requirements, whereby developers must set aside a percentage of project units in a development for affordable housing; (3) the use of density bonuses, whereby developments with a percentage of affordable housing are allotted permission to exceed standard density limits; (4) rent "skewing," whereby rents on unsubsidized units are increased to permit reduction of rents on a percentage of the units; and (5) housing "linkage." *See Mount Laurel II* (reprinted below).

"Housing linkage" is the term used to describe impact fees imposed on a development so as to produce affordable housing. The fees are imposed on the type of development that attracts low income workers, either as employees who build the development or as permanent residents who will work in businesses that occupy the development. The fees also reflect the fact that as available land in the local jurisdiction is used up through development, the cost of acquisition for affordable housing development is likely to become higher, discouraging the development of affordable housing.

5. Political Reality and Ethical Obligations

The tension between the need to ensure access to decent housing, the evolving tests for applying the Takings Clause of the Fifth Amendment, and the leaner, deficit-conscious national and state budgets makes the issues in this chapter among the most controversial of our times. The result is an area of law in a dynamic state of flux.

As described above, one of the most important developments in recent land use planning law has been the emergence of a principle, reflected widely in some statutes, that localities have an obligation to plan for affordable housing. This obligation, however, presents a difficulty that we have seen before in other aspects of land use law: the legal obligation may fundamentally conflict with political reality. In various subtle (or less than subtle) ways, local officials may either refuse to plan or balk at implementing those plans. Is there a fundamental flaw in the theory of mandatory planning for affordable housing, in that the theory seeks to override local "politics"? Compare the experience of compliance with civil rights nondiscrimination laws. Even if the political obstacles can be overcome, will constitutional challenges to inclusionary housing mandates derail these policies?

Ultimately, the provision of affordable housing raises fundamental ethical issues that transcend land use. What is the moral obligation of a community toward the poor and the dependent? Should there be an ethical obligation to avoid public policy that adversely affects the poor? Is there a further ethical obligation to study the benefits and adverse impacts or dangers to the community that result from current planning policies and practices towards workers and the poor? The questions are serious and deserve your thought.

B. JUDICIAL INVALIDATION

In the first successful challenge to exclusionary zoning, the Pennsylvania Supreme Court invalidated a scheme providing for a minimum lot size of four acres in a suburban community located in the path of urban development. *National Land & Inv. Co. v. Kohn*, 215 A.2d 597 (Pa. 1965). The court ruled that the zoning restrictions violated substantive due process because the community had failed to exercise its police powers in a manner that served the general welfare. According to the Pennsylvania court, communities must plan for the future and not simply wall it out.

The court rejected the municipality's offered justification of traffic congestion, because the current street system was adequate to accommodate more density. Concerns over sewage also would not support the zoning scheme, the court ruled, since the community had the capacity to develop adequate sewage treatment, and there was no evidence of impending pollution from smaller homesites. The court also rejected the municipality's contention that large lots were useful in retaining the rural character of the community or the setting for the fine old homes in the community, particularly as no market existed for homes on such large lots. *National Land* qualified the community's right to regulate and also established an affirmative obligation to not engage in exclusionary zoning.

Ten years later, the following landmark case defined this obligation in more expansive terms.

■ SOUTHERN BURLINGTON COUNTY N.A.A.C.P. v. TOWNSHIP OF MOUNT LAUREL
336 A.2d 713 (N.J.), appeal dismissed, 423 U.S. 808 (1975)

HALL, J.

This case attacks the system of land use regulation by defendant Township of Mount Laurel on the ground that low and moderate income families are thereby unlawfully excluded from the municipality. . . . There is not the slightest doubt that New Jersey has been, and continues to be, faced with a desperate need for housing, especially of decent living accommodations economically suitable for low and moderate income families. . . .

Plaintiffs represent the minority group poor (black and Hispanic) seeking such quarters. But they are not the only category of persons barred from so many municipalities by reason of restrictive land use regulations. We have reference to young and elderly couples, single persons and large, growing families not in the poverty class, but who still cannot afford the only kinds of housing realistically permitted in most places — relatively high-priced, single-family detached dwellings on sizeable lots and, in some municipalities, expensive apartments. We will, therefore, consider the case from the wider viewpoint that the effect of Mount Laurel's land use regulation has been to prevent various categories of persons from living in the township because of the limited extent of their income and resources. In this connection, we accept the representation of the municipality's counsel at oral argument that the regulatory scheme was not adopted with any desire or intent to exclude prospective residents on the obviously illegal bases of race, origin or believed social incompatibility. . . .

Mount Laurel is a flat, sprawling township, 22 square miles, or about 14,000 acres, in area, on the west central edge of Burlington County. It is roughly triangular in shape, with its base, approximately eight miles long, extending in a northeasterly-southwesterly direction roughly parallel with and a few miles east of the Delaware River. Part of its southerly side abuts Cherry Hill in Camden County. That section of the township is about seven miles from the boundary line of the city of Camden and not more than 10 miles from the Benjamin Franklin Bridge crossing the river to Philadelphia. . . .

The growth of the township has been spurred by the construction or improvement of main highways through or near it. The New Jersey Turnpike, and now route I-295, a freeway paralleling the turnpike, traverse the municipality near its base, with the main Camden-Philadelphia turnpike interchange at the corner nearest Camden. State route 73 runs at right angles to the turnpike at the interchange and route 38 slices through the northeasterly section. Routes 70 and U.S. 130 are not far away. This highway network gives the township a most strategic location from the standpoint of transport of goods and people by truck and private car. There is no other means of transportation. . . .

Under the present ordinance, 29.2% of all the land in the township, or 4121 acres, is zoned for industry. This amounts to 2800 more acres than were so zoned by the 1954 ordinance. The industrial districts comprise most of the land on both sides of the turnpike and routes I-295, 73 and 38. Only industry meeting specified performance standards is permitted. The effect is to limit the use substantially to light manufacturing, research, distribution of goods, offices and the like. Some non-industrial uses, such as agriculture, farm dwellings, motels, a harness racetrack, and certain retail sales and service establishments, are permitted in this zone. At the time of trial no more than 100 acres, mostly in the southwesterly corner along route 73 adjacent to the turnpike and I-295 interchanges, were actually occupied by industrial uses. They had been constructed in recent years, mostly in several industrial parks, and involved tax ratables of about 16 million dollars. The rest of the land so zoned has remained undeveloped. If it were fully utilized, the testimony was that about 43,500 industrial jobs would be created, but it appeared clear that, as happens in the case of so many municipalities, much more land has been so zoned than the reasonable potential for industrial movement or expansion warrants. At the same time, however, the land cannot be used for residential development under the general ordinance. . . .

The general ordinance requirements, while not as restrictive as those in many similar municipalities, nonetheless realistically allow only homes within the financial reach of persons of at least middle income. The R-1 zone requires a minimum lot area of 9375 square feet, a minimum lot width of 75 feet at the building line, and a minimum dwelling floor area of 1100 square feet if a one-story building and 1300 square feet if one and one-half stories or higher. Originally this zone comprised about 2500 acres. Most of the subdivisions have been constructed within it so that only a few hundred acres remain (the testimony was at variance as to the exact amount). The R-2 zone, comprising a single district of 141 acres in the northeasterly corner, has been completely developed. While it only required a minimum floor area of 900 square feet for a one-story dwelling, the minimum lot size was 11,000 square feet; otherwise the requisites were the same as in the R-1 zone. . . .

The record thoroughly substantiates the findings of the trial court that over the years Mount Laurel "has acted affirmatively to control development and to attract a selective type of growth" and that "through its zoning ordinances has exhibited economic discrimination in that the poor have been deprived of adequate housing and the opportunity to secure the construction of subsidized housing, and has used federal, state, county and local finances and resources solely for the betterment of middle and upper-income persons." . . .

This pattern of land use regulation has been adopted for the same purpose in developing municipality after developing municipality. Almost every one acts solely in its own selfish and parochial interest and in effect builds a wall around itself to keep out those people or entities not adding favorably to the tax base. . . .

We conclude that every such municipality must, by its land use regulations, presumptively make realistically possible an appropriate variety and choice of housing. More specifically, presumptively it cannot foreclose the opportunity of the classes of people mentioned for low and moderate income housing and in its regulations must affirmatively afford that opportunity, at least to the extent of the municipality's fair share of the present and prospective regional need therefor. These obligations must be met unless the particular municipality can sustain the heavy burden of demonstrating peculiar circumstances which dictate that it should not be required so to do.

We reach this conclusion under state law and so do not find it necessary to consider federal constitutional grounds urged by plaintiffs. . . . It is elementary theory that all police power enactments, no matter at what level of government, must conform to the basic state constitutional requirements of substantive due process and equal protection of the laws. These are inherent in Art. I, par. 1 of our Constitution, the requirements of which may be more demanding than those of the federal Constitution. . . .

The warning implicates the matter of *whose* general welfare must be served or not violated in the field of land use regulation. Frequently the decisions in this state, including those just cited, have spoken only in terms of the interest of the enacting municipality, so that it has been thought, at least in some quarters, that such was the only welfare requiring consideration. It is, of course, true that many cases have dealt only with regulations having little, if any, outside impact where the local decision is ordinarily entitled to prevail. However, it is fundamental and not to be forgotten that the zoning power is a police power of the state and the local authority is acting only as a delegate of that power and is restricted in the same manner as is the state. So, when regulation does have a substantial external impact, the welfare of the state's citizens beyond the borders of the particular municipality cannot be disregarded and must be recognized and served. . . .

It is plain beyond dispute that proper provision for adequate housing of all categories of people is certainly an absolute essential in promotion of the general welfare required in all local land use regulation. Further the universal and constant need for such housing is so important and of such broad public interest that the general welfare which developing municipalities like Mount Laurel must consider extends beyond their boundaries and cannot be parochially confined to the claimed good of the particular municipality. It has to follow that, broadly speaking, the presumptive obligation arises for each such municipality affirmatively to plan and provide, by its land use regulations, the reasonable opportunity for an appropriate variety and choice of housing, including, of course, low and moderate cost housing, to meet the needs, desires and resources of all categories of people who may desire to live within its boundaries. Negatively, it may not adopt regulations or policies which thwart or preclude that opportunity. . . .

Mount Laurel's zoning ordinance is . . . so restrictive in its minimum lot area, lot frontage and building size requirements, earlier detailed, as to preclude single-family housing for even moderate income families. Required lot area of at least 9375 square feet in one remaining regular residential zone and 20,000 square feet (almost half an acre) in the other, with required frontage of 75 and 100 feet, respectively, cannot be called small lots and amounts to low density zoning, very definitely increasing the cost of purchasing and improving land and so affecting the cost of housing. As to building size, the township's general requirements of a minimum dwelling floor area of 1100 square feet for all one-story houses and 1300 square feet for all of one and one-half stories or higher is without regard to required minimum lot size or frontage or the number of occupants. . . .

Again it is evident these requirements increase the size and so the cost of housing. The conclusion is irresistible that Mount Laurel permits only such middle and upper income housing as it believes will have sufficient taxable value to come close to paying its own governmental way. . . . Without further elaboration at this point, our opinion is that Mount Laurel's zoning ordinance is presumptively contrary to the general welfare and outside the intended scope of the zoning power in the particulars mentioned. A facial showing of invalidity is thus established, shifting to the municipality the burden of establishing valid superseding reasons for its action and non-action. We now examine the reasons it advances.

The township's principal reason in support of its zoning plan and ordinance housing provisions, advanced especially strongly at oral argument, is the fiscal one previously adverted to, i.e., that by reason of New Jersey's tax structure which substantially finances municipal governmental and educational costs from taxes on local real property, every municipality may, by the exercise of the zoning power, allow only such uses and to such extent as will be beneficial to the local tax rate. In other words, the position is that any municipality may zone extensively to seek and encourage the "good" tax ratables of industry and commerce and limit the permissible types of housing to those having the fewest school children or to those providing sufficient value to attain or approach paying their own taxwise. . . .

We have no hesitancy in now saying, and do so emphatically, that, considering the basic importance of the opportunity for appropriate housing for all classes of our citizenry, no municipality may exclude or limit categories of housing for that reason or purpose. . . .

The propriety of zoning ordinance limitations on housing for ecological or environmental reasons seems also to be suggested by Mount Laurel in support of the one-half acre minimum lot size in that very considerable portion of the township still available for residential development. It is said that the area is without sewer or water utilities and that the soil is such that this plot size is required for safe individual lot sewage disposal and water supply. The short answer is that, this being flat land and readily amendable to such utility installations, the township could require them as improvements by developers or install them under the special assessment or other appropriate statutory procedure. The present environmental situation of the area is, therefore, no sufficient excuse in itself for limiting housing therein to single-family dwelling on large lots. . . .

The composition of the applicable "region" will necessarily vary from situation to situation and probably no hard and fast rule will serve to furnish the answer in every case. Confinement to or within a certain county appears not to be realistic, but restriction within the boundaries of the state seem practical and advisable. (This is not to say that a developing municipality can ignore a demand for housing within its boundaries on the part of people who commute to work in another state.) Here we have already defined the region at present as "those portions of Camden, Burlington and Gloucester Counties within a semicircle having a radius of 20 miles or so from the heart of Camden City." The concept of "fair share" is coming into more general use and, through the expertise of the municipal planning adviser, the county planning boards and the state planning agency, a reasonable figure for Mount Laurel can be determined, which can then be translated to the allocation of sufficient land therefor on the zoning map. . . .

We are not at all sure what the trial judge had in mind as ultimate action with reference to the approval of a plan for affirmative public action concerning the satisfaction of indicated housing needs and the entry of a final order requiring implementation thereof. Courts do not build housing nor do municipalities. . . . The municipal function is initially to provide the opportunity through appropriate land use regulations and we have spelled out what Mount Laurel must do in that regard. It is not appropriate at this time, particularly in view of the advanced view of zoning law as applied to housing laid down by this opinion, to deal with the matter of the further extent of judicial power in the field or to exercise any such power. The municipality should first have full opportunity to itself act without judicial supervision. . . . Should Mount Laurel not perform as we expect, further judicial action may be sought by supplemental pleading in this cause. . . .

Notes and Comments

1. *Defining the Doctrine.* How would you define the *Mount Laurel* doctrine? What is the source of power upon which the *Mount Laurel* doctrine is based? What are the specific remedial obligations with which communities must comply? How would you have written the opinion, defined the principle, and structured the relief? Or would you have dissented, and why? For the history of the *Mount Laurel* litigation, *see* David Kirp et al., Our Town: Race, Housing and the Soul of Suburbia (1995) (critical of the practical benefits from the doctrine). For a positive review of the *Mount Laurel* experience, *see* Charles M. Haar, Suburbs Under Siege: Race, Space, and Audacious Judges (1996). *See also* Peter W. Salsich, Jr., Toward a Policy of Heterogeneity: Overcoming a Long History of Socioeconomic Segregation in Housing, 42 Wake Forest L. Rev. 459 (2007) (advocating federal legislation to aid state development of affordable housing and the availability of federal preemption of exclusionary zoning).

2. *The "Developing" City.* What is the meaning of "developing" in *Mount Laurel*? Would a redevelopment plan within a developed city that failed to provide for low income housing violate the *Mount Laurel* doctrine? *See Asian Americans for Equality v. Koch*, 527 N.E.2d 265 (N.Y. 1988) (fair share requirements inapplicable to each individual community, neighborhood, redevelopment, or conversion plan).

3. *Exclusionary Per Se.* In addition to the *Mount Laurel* fair share doctrine, New Jersey permits judicial invalidation of certain land use devices deemed exclusionary and invalid *per se.* In *Home Builders League v. Township of Berlin*, 405 A.2d 381 (N.J. 1979), the New Jersey Supreme Court overturned an ordinance establishing a minimum floor area that applied regardless of the number of occupants living in the home and that was unrelated to any other factor, such as frontage or lot size. The court reasoned that *Mount Laurel* requires regulations to promote the general welfare, and requirements for minimum floor area that inflate costs — leading to economic segregation — but serve no identifiable public purpose are necessarily

invalid. The court observed that minimum floor area requirements do not preclude overcrowding, which could be regulated by a limit on the number of occupants in relation to floor space.

4. *The Traditional and Deferential Zoning Doctrine.* Although a number of jurisdictions have adopted the *Mount Laurel* doctrine, or at least the exclusionary zoning principle of *National Land,* many have refused to adopt the model of heightened judicial scrutiny of local housing patterns. In *Associated Home Builders v. City of Livermore,* 557 P.2d 473 (Cal. 1976), the California Supreme Court sustained an initiative-created moratorium on development until adequate facilities were available. The challengers urged the court to follow the Pennsylvania and New Jersey exclusionary zoning decisions and invalidate the measure. The court refused to do so:

> Not only do those decisions rest, for the most part, upon principles of state law inapplicable in California, but, unlike the present case, all involve ordinances which impede the ability of low or moderate income persons to immigrate to a community but permit largely unimpeded entry by wealthier persons.

Id. at 486-87. The California Supreme Court expressly refused to adopt the New Jersey jurisprudence. Footnote 23 of the *Livermore* decision, which followed at that point, states:

> The most recent of these decisions, [*Mount Laurel*] invalidated a township zoning ordinance which discriminated against low and moderate cost housing. The court based its decision upon an extensive trial record which convinced the court that deference to local legislative bodies would impede measures it found essential to the regional welfare. In [*National Land*] the Pennsylvania Supreme Court, striking down a four-acre minimum lot requirement, independently determined that the zoning ordinance would not promote the general welfare; as we explain in text, California courts do not claim the authority to invalidate ordinances that they believe undesirable so long as it is fairly debatable that the ordinance is reasonably related to the public welfare. . . .

Id. at 487 n.23.

5. *Non-Housing Exclusionary Zoning.* Is exclusionary zoning limited to affordable housing? In *County of Beaver v. Borough of Beaver Zoning Hearing Bd.,* 656 A.2d 157 (Pa. Commw. Ct. 1995), the borough adopted a zoning ordinance excluding jails and prison uses. The court invalidated the ordinance as exclusionary. It reasoned that the total exclusion of any particular use shifts the burden to the borough to justify the exclusion by showing that the use excluded would injure the public's health, safety, welfare, or morals. *See also Omnipoint Communications, Enters., L.P. v. Zoning Hearing Bd. of Easttown Twp.,* 189 F. Supp. 2d 258 (E.D. Pa. 2002) (wireless telephone facilities); *Kyser v. Kasson Twp.,* 786 N.W.2d 543 (Mich. 2010) (gravel mining); *Township of Exeter v. Zoning Hearing Bd. of Exeter Twp.,* 962 A.2d 653 (Pa. 2009) (ordinance prohibiting signs exceeding a size of 25-square-feet constituted a de facto exclusion of billboards, as a 25-square-foot sign could not function effectively).

6. *Surrick.* The Pennsylvania Supreme Court's decision in *Surrick v. Zoning Hearing Bd.,* 382 A.2d 105 (Pa. 1977), is important to exclusionary zoning law. The court's approach does not depend entirely on fair share allocations or calculations. Instead the court asks three questions:

Is the community in the path of urbanization?
Is the community one that is still developing rather than substantially developed?
Is the impact of the challenged policy partially or totally exclusionary?

Upper Providence Township, a suburb of Philadelphia, is bisected by a major route into the city. With a population over 9200, the township of 3800 acres had but 43 acres, or 1.14 percent, zoned B-Business district, the only classification allowing apartments. The B district, however, was substantially developed, containing the community's commercial uses. Surrick, a developer, sought to develop apartments on a 16.25 acre parcel of which the developer owned four acres and held a contract for sale on the remainder contingent on obtaining zoning for the project. The tract was zoned A-1, allowing single-family dwellings on one acre tracts, but was located just above the intersection where the existing B-Business district was located.

Following a denial by the board of supervisors of the requested zone change for the land subject to the contingent contract, the developer modified the proposal to include the entire tract. After the building inspector denied building permits, the developer unsuccessfully sought a variance.

Applying what it characterized alternatively as a substantive due process theory and a fair share test, the court looked to a multitude of factors, including:

Whether the community is a logical area for development and population growth, that is, whether it is in the path of urbanization because of its proximity to a large metropolis and the community's projected population growth;

The community's current level of development, such as the percentage of undeveloped land and the percentage available for multi-family dwellings; that is, whether the community is already highly developed;

Whether the challenged zoning scheme effects an exclusionary result;

Whether the scheme evidences a primary purpose to exclude or to zone out the natural growth of population, although proof of intent is not of critical importance.

The court did not accept the general claim of the township that the project would overburden municipal services. *See also* Katrin C. Rowan, Comment, Anti-Exclusionary Zoning in Pennsylvania: A Weapon for Developers, A Loss for Low-Income Pennsylvanians, 80 Temp. L. Rev. 1271 (2007) (arguing that state's anti-exclusionary zoning policies are generating low-density, predominantly single-family homes but little affordable housing).

7. *Per Se Rules v. Burden Shifts.* Under *Surrick,* the exclusionary character of the land use policy is not per se invalid. Instead, the burden shifts to the government to justify the policy by important concerns. *Fernley v. Board of Supervisors,* 502 A.2d 585, 587 (Pa. 1985). Which is preferable: the New Jersey "fair share" concept or the Pennsylvania test for exclusionary zoning? Under which scheme does the court provide greater deference to local planning? Does the Pennsylvania rule, which requires the plaintiff to prove the lack of adequate housing in the entire region, impose a greater litigation burden on the plaintiff? *See also C & M Developers, Inc. v. Bedminster Twp. Zoning Hearing Bd.,* 820 A.2d 143 (Pa. 2002) (while two-acre minimum lot size need not be supported by an extraordinary justification, one-acre minimum lot size was not reasonably or substantially related to interest in preserving agricultural lands and activities).

8. *Other State Approaches.* Other states have adopted a variety of approaches to the review of zoning ordinances alleged to be exclusionary. As you read about them, ask yourself: what are the favorable features of each approach? The downsides? Which are more likely to result in land use policies that avoid exclusionary practices?

a. *New York.* New York presents a sort of compromise between the approaches of Pennsylvania and New Jersey. It allows a cause of action wherever a community's land use controls fail to accommodate a fair share of regional need. *Berenson v. Town of New Castle*, 341 N.E.2d 236 (N.Y. 1975). The New York approach differs from New Jersey's in that the challenger must offer proof of regional need and the inadequacy of existing land use controls in the challenged community.

b. *Michigan.* For a time, Michigan applied its own version of the Pennsylvania burden-shifting approach to exclusionary zoning. Under this "preferred use" doctrine, exclusion of certain disfavored uses, such as affordable housing, would shift the burden to the locality to justify its planning policy. *Simmons v. City of Royal Oaks*, 196 N.W.2d 811 (Mich. Ct. App. 1972). The Michigan Supreme Court, however, eventually eliminated the burden-shifting rule, and thus traditional scrutiny and the presumption of legislative validity apply. *Kropf v. City of Sterling Heights*, 215 N.W.2d 179 (Mich. 1974).

In *English v. Augusta Township*, 514 N.W.2d 172 (Mich. Ct. App. 1994), a Michigan appellate court found that when a township excluded mobile homes by zoning only one particular parcel that had no chance of development for such use, that zoning constituted illegal exclusionary zoning. The court's theory was that the total exclusion of a legitimate use violates equal protection. The record in *English* also disclosed a pattern of affordable housing exclusion. *But compare Countrywalk Condominiums, Inc. v. City of Orchard Lake Village*, 561 N.W.2d 405 (Mich. Ct. App. 1997) (per curiam) (exclusion of multiple dwellings from the city did not violate equal protection, where the evidence disclosed that the small city was already congested and that multiple dwellings would impact already overburdened roads, thus compromising safety).

c. *New Hampshire.* Without adopting the mathematical fair share analysis of *Mount Laurel* or the same articulated, affirmative obligation that New Jersey imposes on local governments to utilize inclusionary zoning techniques, New Hampshire more closely followed Pennsylvania and New York in invalidating a community's restrictions on apartment development. *Britton v. Town of Chester*, 595 A.2d 492 (N.H. 1991). By limiting apartments to parcels of at least 20 acres and to certain districts, as well as restricting development on steep slope and wetlands areas, the town's regulations left only 1.73 percent of the town's available land for apartments. Although the percentage was not determinative and may have been sufficient to meet the community's affordable housing needs, the challenger prevailed when the de minimis percentage was considered along with the fact that the town planning board was authorized to approve projects without any objective criteria. The decision was based on the statutory enabling requirement that ordinances must promote the general welfare of the "community," which includes the welfare of the entire region.

9. *Site-Specific Relief.* Some courts in various jurisdictions are awarding so-called site-specific relief to successful challengers of exclusionary zoning. *See, e.g., Britton v. Town of Chester*, 595 A.2d 492 (N.H. 1991), discussed in Note 8 above. Site-specific relief typically involves mandating the issuance of a building permit, thus avoiding the uncertainty of remanding the matter to the local legislative and administrative

processes, where agencies may have been recalcitrant, engaged in excessive delay, or failed to act in good faith.

C. STATUTORY HOUSING MANDATES

While numerous challenges to exclusionary zoning have been brought in the courts, in some jurisdictions reform has been pursued through the legislative process. The most aggressive approach was taken by New York, which created a powerful agency to develop affordable housing and override local zoning and land use controls. Fiscal difficulties, which were exacerbated by the collapse of federal subsidies and community opposition to subsidized housing in the suburbs, ultimately destroyed the agency, as opponents succeeded in repealing the agency's preemptive powers. Eleanor L. Brilliant, The Urban Development Corporation: Private Interests and Public Authority (1975); Housing for All Under Law: New Directions in Housing, Land Use and Planning Law 505-508 (Richard P. Fishman ed. 1978) (report of the American Bar Association Advisory Commission on Housing and Urban Growth).

New Jersey, with its establishment of the Council on Affordable Housing under the state's Fair Housing Act, has a hybrid approach. It encourages voluntary compliance with agency-calculated affordable housing goals but also authorizes enforcement through litigation. As discussed below, the New Jersey Supreme Court has expressed dissatisfaction with the progress of legislatively-authorized process, shifting more of the authority for implementing the State's *Mount Laurel* precedents to the courts.

The two remaining formats for legislative reform have been the establishment of affordable housing goals as a statewide mandatory planning obligation, and the creation of an administrative review process to replace litigation. California's general approach to exclusionary zoning and the need for affordable housing is found in statutory provisions mandating that general plans contain a housing element. This element must plan for the housing needs of all economic segments of the population. Cal. Gov't Code §§65302(c), 65580-65589.8 (West 2016). While most growth management schemes have been endorsed by both state and federal courts under traditional *Euclid* zoning deference, the following case suggests that California's housing laws can change the normal outcome.

■ BUILDING INDUSTRY ASSOCIATION OF SAN DIEGO
v. CITY OF OCEANSIDE
33 Cal. Rptr. 2d 137 (Ct. App. 1994)

HUFFMAN, Acting Presiding Justice. . . .

Prop. A, alternatively referred to as Chapter 32A [and] adopted by the Oceanside electorate in April 1987, adopts a "Residential Development Control System" (RDCS) which, with what may be significant exceptions, adopts a maximum number of dwelling units to be constructed each year, called annual allotments. The allotments are 1000 for 1987 and 800 for each year thereafter until December 31, 1999, with power granted to the City Council to modify the annual allotment by an amount no greater than 10 percent more or less for any given year and a requirement the annual allotment for a next succeeding year be adjusted higher or lower in order to redress any excess or deficit in the preceding year. Excepted from the RDCS are the following:

(a) Projects of not more than four residential dwellings, limited to only one such project per developer per calendar year.
(b) Fourplexes or less numbered multiple dwellings on a single existing lot.
(c) Single family residential units on a single existing lot.
(d) Rehabilitation or remodeling of an existing dwelling, or conversion of apartments to condominiums, so long as no additional dwelling units are created.
(e) Units within the legally designated redevelopment project area.
(f) Those specific Units which are formally dedicated for occupancy by low income persons or senior citizens pursuant to the provisions of applicable federal, state, or local laws or programs provided these types of units are spread equitably throughout the city and not concentrated in one neighborhood. . . . This section does not exempt low-income or senior citizen projects built with density bonuses or other development considerations under any program.
(g) Single family dwelling unit projects with lots an average of which are 10,000 square feet or better, which can achieve a minimum of 70% or better, of the maximum awardable points using the Residential Development Evaluation System are exempt. . . .

Under Prop. A, projects are reviewed by a "Residential Development Evaluation Board" (the Board) made up of members of the City's planning commission, who evaluate proposed projects for their impact upon public facilities and services (the "A" criteria) and site and architectural quality (the "B" criteria). A project which does not receive a score of 51 percent on the "A" criteria and 70 percent on the "B" criteria is eliminated from consideration for an annual allocation. The Board's recommendations are forwarded to the City Council, which makes the annual allocations. . . .

Since 1979, the City's general plan had a public facilities and management element (PFME), which stated as its objective "[t]o influence the timing of development and to direct it to those locations within the City that avoid or minimize any adverse fiscal, economic, social or environmental impacts." The PFME divided the City into four areas and gave priority to development in those areas where adequate services were available. The PFME stated a policy of avoiding "direct controls on the number or location of new housing units built. . . ." Neither the [interim growth management element] IGME nor the PFME gave the City the power to regulate the rate, timing or sequencing of development.

The PFME used the method of planning for growth by encouraging assessment districts and impact fees. The PFME was adopted by the City in light of a compound annual growth rate of 6.3 percent since 1970. An environmental impact report (EIR) for the PFME states that development was expected to continue in the range of 900 to 2000 housing units per year through 1995, a range of 2.9 to 7 percent compound annual growth through 1995. The EIR for the PFME points out that that measure rejected the use of a point system, such as would later be used in Prop. A, with the explanation that "[p]oint systems usually are flawed by the potential for a high score for one service to offset a low score for another" and on the theory that "the problem of adding apples and oranges and then considering only the total is difficult to avoid." The EIR also rejected a "periodic comparative evaluation" system, such as Prop. A would later adopt.

In 1986, the year before Prop. A was adopted, the city council adopted a new land use element (LUE) of the general plan, setting forth the city's long-term goals, objectives, and policies for development. The LUE calls for but does not establish a timing mechanism to regulate residential development. At the time the LUE was adopted, the City recognized the PFME had not solved all the City's growth-related problems. However, no official City action had been taken to invalidate the PFME.

In the 1970s, the City's growth rate had reached 8.94 percent per year. While the City's population grew by 89.4 percent from 1970 to 1980, the County's population increased by 37.1 percent. The growth rate as of 1987 was 5 percent annual population increase, equivalent to 60 percent growth if sustained for a decade. The City's expert witness, Dr. Myers, a professor of urban and regional planning, testified that a 1 percent growth rate is normal, and 2 percent per year or 25 percent per decade is a healthy growth rate. In his opinion, at 40 percent growth per decade, it is difficult to "keep up" with a city's growing population. "[W]ith rapid growth the needs escalate . . . and you are always playing catch up."

Conflicting evidence was presented about the City's ability to accommodate growth. The trial court heard evidence that there were severe deficiencies in facilities and services, such as the road system, fire, paramedic and police facilities and response times, schools, libraries, parks and recreation facilities. There were drainage and sewer problems. . . .

Under [Government Code] section 65860, county or city zoning ordinances must be consistent with the entity's general plan, such that "[t]he various land uses authorized by the ordinance are compatible with the objectives, policies, general land uses, and programs specified in such a plan." "Only the general plan in effect at the time the ordinance is adopted is relevant in determining inconsistency."

Moreover, "[a] city may not adopt ordinances and regulations which conflict with the state Planning and Zoning Law." . . .

At the time Prop. A was adopted, the general plan had in effect the PFME, which contained a statement of a number of major policies to be served by the plan. In particular, the PFME stated a policy to "[a]void direct controls on the number or location of new housing units to be built, but provide financial incentives for projects where services can be provided to new and old residents at least cost." . . .

In light of the clear statement in *Lesher*, that a zoning ordinance that conflicts with a general plan is invalid at the time it is passed, and in light of the factual findings that Prop. A adversely affected the availability of low income housing, the only possible finding is that Prop. A does conflict with the City's general plan, specifically the PFME, regarding the imposition of direct controls on the number or location of new housing units to be built. This restriction on land uses is not compatible with the then-existing general plan.

Although the trial court reasoned that the City had the power to adopt a more restrictive type of growth control than that represented by the PFME, it could not do so without validly amending the existing general plan. . . .

Finally, the housing element of Oceanside's general plan states as a policy:

Adequate provision for the housing needs of all economic segments of the community is an issue of the highest priority in Oceanside to meet the low income household assistance goals and to protect, encourage and, where feasible, provide low and moderate income housing opportunities within the intent of State policy to address local needs. . . .

Prop. A does not promote this policy and accordingly must be deemed inconsistent with it. Although we are sympathetic to the goals stated in Prop. A of promoting the quality of life for the citizens of the City, we are bound to find the ordinance invalid under those standards.

[Plaintiffs] BIA and Del Oro next assert that Prop. A conflicts with three particular sections in the State Planning and Zoning Law. The text of the sections on which BIA and Del Oro rely is in relevant part, in the version in effect at the adoption of Prop. A in 1987, as follows:

Section 65008, subdivision (e):

No city, county, or city and county shall, in the enactment or administration of ordinances pursuant to this title, prohibit or discriminate against a residential development or emergency shelter because the development or shelter is intended for occupancy by persons and families of low and moderate income, as defined in Section 50093 of the Health and Safety Code, or persons and families of middle income.

Section 65913.1:

[A] city . . . shall designate and zone sufficient vacant land for residential use with appropriate standards . . . to meet housing needs as identified in the general plan . . . "appropriate standards" shall mean densities and requirements . . . which contribute significantly to the economic feasibility of producing housing at the lowest possible cost given economic and environmental factors, the public health and safety, and the need to facilitate the development of housing for persons and families of low and moderate income. . . .

Section 65915:

(a) When a developer of housing agrees to construct at least (1) 25 percent of the total units of a housing development for persons and families of low or moderate income, . . . or (2) 10 percent of the total units . . . for lower income households, . . . a city, . . . shall either (1) grant a density bonus or (2) provide other incentives of equivalent financial value. . . .

(c) . . . "density bonus" means a density increase of at least 25 percent over the otherwise maximum allowable residential density under the applicable zoning ordinance and land use element of the general plan. . . .

The trial court made key findings that since Prop. A took effect in 1988, affordable housing in the City had dramatically declined. Only 415 total low income and senior citizen units had been excepted from the effect of Prop. A in the period between 1987 and 1990, and they were all in the senior category (plus an additional 28 units in the similar fourplex category). Based on those figures, the trial court made an estimate that some 20,000 persons would be denied affordable housing based on the effect of Prop. A. The trial court expressly found that the exception allowing higher priced units on 10,000 square foot lots was not justified by an asserted imbalance in the current housing stock, such that higher end units were needed in the City. . . . [T]he trial court's overall conclusion on the degree of the City's compliance with its obligations to provide low and moderate income regional share units was that its 1986-1991 compliance was not enough, as the court had to go on to the 1991-1996 period to make a complete analysis, and the City could not show it would meet the regional share for low/moderate income units for that period.

[T]he court further ruled that the evidence showed developers were discouraged from proposing housing that qualified for density bonuses, due to the exclusion of density bonus units from the low income and senior exception. This exclusion, it held, conflicted with the state density bonus law. However, it declined to invalidate the ordinance on that ground, using the theory that section 65915 had not been shown to have been triggered by a developer's specific proposal of a density bonus project.

The three cited Government Code sections, taken together, clearly show an important state policy to promote the construction of low income housing and to remove impediments to the same. Prop. A is such an impediment, and cannot survive such a conflict. Although the City has made efforts to implement a policy to mitigate the harshness of the exemption of density bonus projects from the exception in Prop. A for low income or senior citizen housing, those efforts do not change the text of the initiative measure. . . .

Similarly, when the trial court made its finding that Prop. A did not offend against the provisions of section 65008, subdivision (c), prohibiting discrimination against low income housing, because Prop. A was neutral as to the intended occupants of any development, it disregarded its own factual findings that affordable housing had taken a dramatic decline since the effective date of Prop. A. Prop. A acts to favor the development of larger units on larger lots, with more design and other amenities, through the exemption for 10,000 square foot lots. The City admitted as much, while asserting that such an exemption was needed in order to remedy an imbalance in the current housing supply. The trial court was not persuaded by that argument in Phase I, and we are not persuaded by it at all. . . .

Notes and Comments

1. *Litigating Housing Issues.* In California, the absence of a housing element renders a general plan invalid and presumably forecloses local land use permit approvals. What happens if a community adopts a housing element that is vague or fails to call for development in accordance with affordable housing goals? Planning objectives may be meaningless unless courts are willing to engage in enforcement or an administrative agency with the authority to sanction local government is established.

One problem with the use of litigation as a means of enforcing housing obligations is that few developers are willing to underwrite litigation against a community. Successful developers are profit-motivated, and they are not likely to favor shouldering the expense of costly housing litigation. Neighborhood groups or homeowner associations, even if supportive of affordable housing, generally will not have the resources to hire competent, experienced lawyers to pursue what can become intractable litigation. For example, the opinion in *Building Industry Ass'n v. City of Oceanside*, reprinted above, was the second full opinion of the court of appeals in the case, a vivid demonstration that the litigation was prolix.

2. *The Focus of Judicial Review.* In *Hernandez v. City of Encinitas*, 33 Cal. Rptr. 2d 875 (Ct. App. 1994), a different California Court of Appeals panel rejected a

housing element challenge based on a claim that the city's land use devices impeded affordable housing development. The devices included referenda on zone changes, increasing density or converting non-residentially zoned property for residential use, and imposing maximum densities. The plaintiff also claimed that the city would not implement the goals in its plan. The court in *Hernandez* adopted a deferential standard of review, examining the record for "substantial compliance" with the statutory obligations. Using that standard, it sustained a housing element that facially could satisfy affordable housing need projections by adequate sites zoned for least cost housing. The court also ruled that the use of block grants and federal subsidies adequately addressed the need to conserve the existing affordable housing stock.

This deferential approach to judicial review of housing elements was repeated in *Fonseca v. City of Gilroy*, 56 Cal. Rptr. 3d 374 (Ct. App. 2007), where the court of appeals sustained a general plan housing element, finding that elements were not required to contain a site-specific analysis and that the element complied with the law's "adequate site" requirement. The city's element provided an aggregate inventory of vacant sites and sites potentially available for development; the court did not require an analysis of immediately available sites, nor a showing of feasibility of development on individual sites. The court emphasized that the general plan and its elements were legislative enactments entitled to a presumption of validity. The court said that it would "not review the merits of the housing element at issue or assess the wisdom of the municipality's determination of policy," nor would it judge "whether the programs adopted by the locality are adequate to meet their stated objectives." The court also ruled that the city had not violated the state least-cost zoning law requiring adequate zoning for the least costly housing. Cal. Gov't Code §65913.1(a) (West 2016). Was the *Fonseca* court's deference consistent with the scrutiny of the *Oceanside* court? Were the outcomes affected by *Oceanside* being a developer challenge, while *Fonseca* was a more traditional citizen-initiated case?

California has passed legislation that reverses the traditional presumption of validity afforded legislation and abrogates the effect of *Euclid* where local laws restrict housing development. Cal. Evid. Code §669.5 (West 2016) Is this evidence code provision inconsistent with *Fonseca?* Should the court in *Oceanside* have additionally found the growth measure inconsistent with the statute? Cal. Gov't Code §65589.5(d)(1) (West 2016) requires the community to make findings whenever it rejects affordable housing development or conditions its approval when housing element goals are unmet. Cal. Gov't Code §65584.09(c) (West 2016) requires zoning or rezoning for sites to accommodate the community's fair share of regional housing in the housing element. Cal Gov't Code 65008(b)(1)(D) (West 2016) bars communities from prohibiting or discriminating against multifamily housing projects.. Cal. Gov't Code §65863 (West 2016) prohibits local governments from reducing residential densities below density used by the state to determine housing element compliance unless such downzoning is supported by written findings that reductions are consistent with the general plan and the housing element and that the community can continue to adequately accommodate its share of regional housing need.

3. *The New Jersey Fair Housing Act.* Following *Mount Laurel I*, supra, and *Mount Laurel II*, infra, the New Jersey Legislature passed the New Jersey Fair Housing Act (N.J. Stat. Ann. §§52:27D-301 to 52:27D-329 (West 2016)) to implement the judicially mandated principles. The law established a state commission, called the

Council on Affordable Housing, to set the "fair share" levels mandated by the New Jersey Supreme Court, to issue guidelines, and to review local implementing plans. Although judicial review was preserved, the initial law temporarily suspended the availability of site-specific relief, or a "builder's remedy."

Under the law, communities meeting the obligations of *Mount Laurel* enjoyed a ten-year exemption from further review. N.J. Stat. Ann. §52:27D-307 (West 2016). Controversial provisions authorize limited residency preferences, allowing up to 50 percent of a community's fair share of affordable housing obligation, as allocated by the Council on Affordable Housing, to be set aside for residents and those who work in the community. In addition, the law authorizes Regional Contribution Contracts, which allow communities to transfer up to 50 percent of their obligations to other communities. The law was upheld in *Hills Dev. Co. v. Township of Bernards*, 510 A.2d 621 (N.J. 1986).

In recent years, the work of the Council on Affordable Housing (COAH) has become mired in legal and political controversy. In the 1980s and 1990s, the COAH successfully issued a series of "substantive rules" that included housing allocation formulas and calculations of municipal affordable housing obligations. *See In re Six Month Extension of N.J.A.C. 5:91-1 et seq.*, 855 A.2d 582 (N.J. Super. 2004) (describing these early rulemakings). An additional round of rulemaking led to a judicial challenge by housing advocates resulting in a Supreme Court decision largely striking down the new rule as inadequate under the *Mt. Laurel* precedents. *See In re New Jersey Council on Affordable Housing*, 914 A2d 348 (N.J. 2007). The New Jersey Supreme Court subsequently struck down a modified version of the new rules. *In re Adoption of N.J.A.C. 5:96 & 5:97*, 74 A.3d 893 (N.J. 2013). Most recently, frustrated by the lack of agency action, the New Jersey Supreme Court issued an order dissolving the exhaustion-of-administrative remedies requirement of the Fair Housing Act, allowing builders to go directly to court to test municipalities' compliance with the *Mount Laurel* precedents. *In re Adoption of N.J.A.C. 5:96 and 5:97 ex rel. New Jersey Council on Affordable Housing*, 110 A.3d 31 (N.J. 2015). Meanwhile the Governor issued an executive order attempting to dissolve the COAH. That action prompted a lawsuit from the Fair Share Housing Center, culminating in a 2013 Supreme Court decision holding that the Governor lacked the legal authority to abolish the Council. *In re* Plan for Abolition of Council on Affordable Housing, 70 A.3d 559 (2013).

4. *Growth Management and Housing.* Oregon's legislative growth management scheme, discussed in Chapter 11, calls for each community to establish an urban growth boundary adequate to accommodate projected growth, and to prohibit most forms of urban development outside the boundary. Where a local land use decision is not in conformity with the plan, or where it is alleged that conditions required a plan amendment and the extension of the urban growth boundary, the local decision may be appealed to the Land Use Board of Appeal (LUBA), which is empowered to override local land use control rulings. In *Shelter Resources, Inc. v. City of Cannon Beach*, 879 P.2d 1313 (Or. Ct. App. 1994), the court affirmed a finding by the LUBA that a small city was exempt from obligations to plan for affordable housing. The exemption was based on a statute which required that cities under 2500 in population were only obligated to accommodate "government subsidized housing."

How effective is the legislative scheme? Should the statute be expanded? Should it reach all housing with rents or prices defined as affordable or as a percentage of median income? Should the law specifically apply to housing financed by income tax credits? Would housing financed by a housing trust fund or with revenue from a local redevelopment tax increment qualify as "government subsidized" housing? *See* Robert L. Liberty, Abolishing Exclusionary Zoning: A Natural Policy Alliance for Environmentalists and Affordable Housing Advocates, 30 B.C. Envtl. Aff. L. Rev. 581 (2003) (Oregon). Should the law establish an obligation of the community to include a percentage of affordable housing within each project, neighborhood, or district? Does the law suffer from failure to include a fair share requirement?

5. *Other Alternatives.* Massachusetts pioneered an alternative to judicial review or legislative fiat by establishing an administrative mechanism permitting developers to appeal the denials of affordable housing permits to a state agency with power to override local land use controls. Mass. Gen. Laws ch. 40B §§20-23 (West 2016); *Boothroyd v. Zoning Bd. of Appeals of Amherst,* 868 N.E.2d 83 (Mass. 2007) (zoning board may bypass local zoning bylaw and issue a comprehensive permit for affordable housing even after town achieved a 10 percent minimum threshold, as the town could consider regional need); *Mahoney v. Board of Appeals,* 316 N.E.2d 606 (Mass. 1974), *appeal dismissed,* 420 U.S. 903 (1975) (state agency must remand to allow the local jurisdiction to apply subdivision standards rather than the agency issuing site-specific relief in exclusionary zoning cases); Sharon Perlman Krefetz, The Impact and Evolution of the Massachusetts Comprehensive Permit and Zoning Appeals Act: Thirty Years of Experience with a State Legislative Effort to Overcome Exclusionary Zoning, 22 W. New Eng. 381 (2001) (success but insufficient affordable housing, requiring additional subsidies and state regulation); Jonathan Witten, Adult Supervision Required: The Commonwealth of Massachusetts's Reckless Adventures with Affordable Housing and the Anti-Snob Zoning Act, 35 B.C. Envtl. Aff. L. Rev. 217 (2008) (arguing that a system that requires no planning is myopic and regressive, and that the Massachusetts model to generate affordable housing should be repealed and replaced with a comprehensive planning obligation).

Connecticut provides a variation on Massachusetts, calling for judicial review of denials of affordable housing proposals. *Avalonbay Communities, Inc. v. Zoning Comm'n of the Town of Stratford,* 21 A.3d 926 (Conn. Ct. App. 2011) (evidence was insufficient to support commission's denial of applications based on safety concerns over emergency vehicle response through parkway underpass and width of adjacent public street; an adequate secondary emergency route and perceived concerns regarding environmental issues did not outweigh the need for affordable housing in the town, so as to preclude granting applications); *Wisniowsky v. Planning Comm'n,* 655 A.2d 1146 (Conn. Ct. App. 1995) (granting authority to place multi-family affordable housing in a district zoned for lots of at least an acre, and finding that the proposed project need not be consistent with zoning or the comprehensive plan). *See also* Conn. Gen. Stat. Ann. §8-19(b) (West 2016) (authorizing communities to exempt from subdivision regulations a landowner's first subdivision of property, provided the lot created is for affordable housing to be built by municipality or non-profit). *See* Robert D. Carroll, Note, Connecticut Retrenches: A Proposal to Save the Affordable Housing Appeals Procedure, 110 Yale L. J. 1247 (2001) (critical of legislative amendment limiting appeals).

Finally, Washington's growth management law establishes a statutory mandate for local governments to provide for affordable housing for all segments of the community and calls for a fair share type of obligation. However, the law lacks an implementation mechanism to ensure local performance. Henry W. McGee, Jr., Equity and Efficacy in Washington State's GMA Affordable Housing Goal,

3 Wash. U. J. L. & Poly. 539 (2000), *published in* Evolving Voices in Land Use Law Ch. 8 (Washington U. J. L. & Poly. 2000).

6. *Other States.* The Illinois Affordable Housing Planning and Appeals Act (IAHPA), 310 Ill. Comp. Stat. 67/1-60 (West 2016), mandates planning for affordable housing. If a community's housing stock includes less than 10 percent affordable housing, the community must prepare and adopt an affordable housing plan. 310 Ill. Comp. Stat. 67/25 (West 2016). The law is administered by the Illinois Housing Development Agency, which was not provided administration funding. Developers thwarted in attempts to develop affordable housing in a jurisdiction lacking a certified plan may appeal to a state housing appeals board.. 310 Ill. Comp. Stat. 67/30 (West 2016). Communities under 1000 population are exempt. *See* Charles Hoch, How Plan Mandates Work: Affordable Housing in Illinois, 73 J. Am. Planning Ass'n 86 (2007) (finding local opposition to compliance in many communities). *See also* N.C. Gen. Stat. §41A-5(a)(4) (2009) (state fair housing act prohibits land use discrimination against development containing affordable housing); Edward Goetz, Karen Chapple & Barbara Lukerman, The Minnesota Land Use Planning Act and the Promotion of Low- and Moderate-Income Housing in Suburbia, 22 L. & Inequality 31 (2004) (Minnesota mandatory plan housing element); Michael J. Stewart, Growth and Its Implications: An Evaluation of Tennessee's Growth Management Plan, 67 Tenn. L. Rev. 983, 991-92 (2000) (Tennessee's new growth management legislation mandates a local plan that ensures affordable housing); Sam Stonefield, Affordable Housing in Suburbia: The Importance but Limited Power and Effectiveness of the State Override Tool, 22 W. New Eng. L. Rev. 323 (2001) (discussing Connecticut, Massachusetts, Rhode Island, and New Jersey).

D. INCLUSIONARY ZONING

After years of struggle to shape relief that would enforce its housing standards and the failure of judicial orders to generate affordable housing in exclusionary zoning cases, the New Jersey Supreme Court decided the following case. In it, the court returned to the question of whether simply announcing a local obligation principle was adequate or whether modifying the zoning ordinance will generate affordable housing.

■ SOUTHERN BURLINGTON COUNTY N.A.A.C.P. v. TOWNSHIP OF MOUNT LAUREL
456 A.2d 390 (N.J. 1983)

WILENTZ, C.J. . . .

This Court is more firmly committed to the original *Mount Laurel* doctrine than ever, and we are determined, within appropriate judicial bounds, to make it work. The obligation is to provide a realistic opportunity for housing, not litigation. We have learned from experience, however, that unless a strong judicial hand is used, *Mount Laurel* will not result in housing, but in paper, process, witnesses, trials and appeals. We intend by this decision to strengthen it, clarify it, and make it easier for public officials, including judges, to apply it. . . .

We note that there has been some legislative initiative in this field. We look forward to more. The new Municipal Land Use Law explicitly recognizes the obligation of municipalities to zone with regional consequences in mind. It also recognizes the work of the Division of State and Regional Planning, in the Department of Community Affairs (DCA) in creating the State Development Guide Plan (1980) (SDGP), which plays an important part in our decisions today. Our deference to these legislative and executive initiatives can be regarded as a clear signal of our readiness to defer further to more substantial actions.

In *Oakwood v. Madison*, this Court held that it was sufficient in *Mount Laurel* litigation for courts to look to the "*substance*" of challenged zoning ordinances and to the existence of "*bona fide* efforts" by municipalities to meet their obligations. . . . Unfortunately, experience has taught us that this formulation is too vague to provide adequate guidance for either trial courts or municipalities. . . .

Therefore, proof of a municipality's bona fide attempt to provide a realistic opportunity to construct its fair share of lower income housing shall no longer suffice. Satisfaction of the *Mount Laurel* obligation shall be determined solely on an objective basis: if the municipality has *in fact* provided a realistic opportunity for the construction of its fair share of low and moderate income housing, it has met the *Mount Laurel* obligation to satisfy the constitutional requirement; if it has not, then it has failed to satisfy it. Further, whether the opportunity is "realistic" will depend on whether there is in fact a likelihood — to the extent economic conditions allow — that the lower income housing will actually be constructed. Plaintiff's case will ordinarily include proof of the municipality's fair share of the regional need and defendant's proof of its satisfaction. Good or bad faith, at least on this issue, will be irrelevant. The numberless approach encouraged in *Madison*, where neither plaintiffs nor defendants are required to prove a fair share number, is no longer acceptable. . . .

In order to meet their *Mount Laurel* obligations, municipalities, at the very least, must remove all municipally created barriers to the construction of their fair share of lower income housing. Thus, to the extent necessary to meet their prospective fair share and provide for their indigenous poor (and, in some cases, a portion of the region's poor), municipalities must remove zoning and subdivision restrictions and exactions that are not necessary to protect health and safety. . . .

Once a municipality has revised its land use regulations and taken other steps affirmatively to provide a realistic opportunity for the construction of its fair share of lower income housing, the *Mount Laurel* doctrine requires it to do no more. For instance, a municipality having thus complied, the fact that its land use regulations contain restrictive provisions incompatible with lower income housing, such as bedroom restrictions, large lot zoning, prohibition against mobile homes, and the like, does not render those provisions invalid under *Mount Laurel*. . . .

Satisfaction of the *Mount Laurel* doctrine cannot depend on the inclination of developers to help the poor. It has to depend on affirmative inducements to make the opportunity real.

It is equally unrealistic, even where the land is owned by a developer eager to build, simply to rezone that land to permit the construction of lower income housing if the construction of other housing is permitted on the same land and the latter is more profitable than lower income housing. . . .

Therefore, unless removal of restrictive barriers will, without more, afford a realistic opportunity for the construction of the municipality's fair share of the region's lower income housing need, affirmative measures will be required.

There are two basic types of affirmative measures that a municipality can use to make the opportunity for lower income housing realistic: (1) encouraging or requiring the use of available state or federal housing subsidies, and (2) providing incentives for or requiring private developers to set aside a portion of their developments for lower income housing. Which, if either, of these devices will be necessary in any particular municipality to assure compliance with the constitutional mandate will be initially up to the municipality itself. Where necessary, the trial court overseeing compliance may require their use. We note again that least-cost housing will not ordinarily satisfy a municipality's fair share obligation to provide low and moderate income housing unless and until it has attempted the inclusionary devices outlined below or otherwise has proven the futility of the attempt. . . .

The implication of the observation that lower income housing cannot be built without subsidies is that if the *Mount Laurel* principle requires municipalities to provide a realistic opportunity for such housing through their land use regulations but leaves them free to prevent subsidies through non-action, that obligation is a charade. *Mount Laurel* was never intended to produce the perfect model of a just zoning ordinance; it was intended to provide a realistic opportunity for the construction of lower income housing. . . .

In evaluating the obligation that the municipality might be required to undertake to make a federal or state subsidy available to a lower income housing developer, the fact that some financial detriment may be incurred is not dispositive. Satisfaction of the *Mount Laurel* obligation imposes many financial obligations on municipalities, some of which are potentially substantial. By contrast, a tax abatement for a low or moderate income housing project will have only a minimal effect on the public fisc. Thus viewed, the asserted fiscal reasons justifying the failure to provide a tax abatement may be nothing more than a red herring. The direct and immediate financial impact of a tax abatement agreement between the municipality and the developer may be unimportant when compared with increases in municipal and school district costs caused by the advent of lower income housing. The trial court in a *Mount Laurel* case, therefore, shall have the power to require a municipality to cooperate in good faith with a developer's attempt to obtain a subsidy and to require that a tax abatement be granted for that purpose pursuant to applicable New Jersey statutes where the abatement does not conflict with other municipal interests of greater importance.

B. INCLUSIONARY ZONING DEVICES

There are several inclusionary zoning techniques that municipalities must use if they cannot otherwise assure the construction of their fair share of lower income housing. . . . [W]e in no way intend our list to be exhaustive. . . .

(i) Incentive Zoning

Incentive zoning is usually accomplished either through a sliding scale density bonus that increases the permitted density as the amount of lower income housing provided is increased, or through a set bonus for participation in a lower income housing program. *See* Fox & Davis, 3 *Hasting Const. L.Q.* 1015, 1060-62 (1977).

Incentive zoning leaves a developer free to build only upper income housing if it so chooses. Fox and Davis, in their survey of municipalities using inclusionary devices, found that while developers sometimes profited through density bonuses, they were usually reluctant to cooperate with incentive zoning programs; and that therefore those municipalities that relied exclusively on such programs were not very successful in actually providing lower income housing. *Id.* at 1067.

Sole reliance on "incentive" techniques (or, indeed, reliance exclusively on any one affirmative device) may prove in a particular case to be insufficient to achieve compliance with the constitutional mandate.

(ii) Mandatory Set-Asides

A more effective inclusionary device that municipalities must use if they cannot otherwise meet their fair share obligations is the mandatory set-aside. According to the Department of Community Affairs, as of 1976 there were six municipalities in New Jersey with mandatory set-aside programs, which varied from a requirement that 5 percent of developments in a certain zone be composed of low and moderate income units (Cherry Hill, Camden County) to a requirement that between 15 and 25 percent of all PUDs be reserved for low and moderate income housing (East Windsor, Mercer County).

In addition to the mechanisms we have just described, municipalities and trial courts must consider such other affirmative devices as zoning substantial areas for mobile homes and for other types of low cost housing and establishing maximum square footage zones, *i.e.*, zones where developers cannot build units with *more* than a certain footage or build anything other than lower income housing or housing that includes a specified portion of lower income housing. In some cases, a realistic opportunity to provide the municipality's fair share may require over-zoning, *i.e.*, zoning to allow for *more* than the fair share if it is likely, as it usually is, that not all of the property made available for lower income housing will actually result in such housing.

Although several of the defendants concede that simply removing restrictions and exactions is unlikely to result in the construction of lower income housing, they maintain that requiring the municipality to use affirmative measures is beyond the scope of the courts' authority. We disagree . . . If it is plain, and it is, that unless we require the use of affirmative measures the constitutional guarantee that protects poor people from municipal exclusion will exist "only on paper," then the only "appropriate remedy" is the use of affirmative measures. . . .

3. ZONING FOR MOBILE HOMES

As the cost of ordinary housing skyrockets for purchasers and renters, mobile homes become increasingly important as a source of low cost housing. The evidence clearly supports a finding that mobile homes are significantly less expensive than site-built housing. . . . Therefore, subject to the qualifications noted hereafter, we rule that municipalities that cannot otherwise meet their fair share obligations must provide zoning for low-cost mobile homes as an affirmative device in their zoning ordinances. . . .

Lest we be misunderstood, we do *not* hold that every municipality must allow the use of mobile homes as an affirmative device to meet its *Mount Laurel* obligation, or that any ordinance that totally excludes mobile homes is *per se* invalid. Insofar as the *Mount Laurel* doctrine is concerned, whether mobile homes must be permitted as an affirmative device will depend upon the overall effectiveness of the municipality's attempts to comply. . . .

4. Providing "Least Cost" Housing

There may be municipalities where special conditions such as extremely high land costs make it impossible for the fair share obligation to be met even after all excessive restrictions and exactions, i.e., those not essential for safety and health, have been removed and all affirmative measures have been attempted. In such cases, *and only in such cases*, the *Mount Laurel* obligation can be met by supplementing whatever lower income housing can be built with enough "least cost" housing to satisfy the fair share. . . . Least cost housing means the least expensive housing that builders can provide after removal by a municipality of *all* excessive restrictions and exactions and after thorough use by a municipality of all affirmative devices that might lower costs. Presumably, such housing, though unaffordable by those in the lower income brackets, will be inexpensive enough to provide shelter for families who could not afford housing in the conventional suburban housing market. At the very minimum, provision of least cost housing will make certain that municipalities in "growth" areas of this state do not "grow" only for the well-to-do. . . .

1. Builder's Remedy

It is within the power of trial courts to adjust the timing of builder's remedies so as to cushion the impact of these developments on municipalities where that impact would otherwise cause a sudden and radical transformation of the municipality. . . .

To facilitate this revision, the trial court may appoint a special master to assist municipal officials in developing constitutional zoning and land use regulations. . . .

These impartial experts use their skills to help the parties formulate a remedy that will comply with the trial court's order and supply information that the parties may not have available to them. . . .

Notes and Comments

1. Mt. Laurel *and Judicial Activism.* Was the New Jersey Supreme Court acting within the traditional role of courts, or was the court too activist? The late Professor Haar believed not. Charles M. Haar, Suburbs Under Siege: Race, Space, and Audacious Judges (1996). He concluded that *Mount Laurel* is a model that other jurisdictions should replicate in seeking better planned communities. Nevertheless, the New Jersey Supreme Court remains at the forefront among the state courts in using the judicial power to advance an inclusionary housing policy.

2. *Density Bonuses.* California provides a density bonus of up to 35 percent for developments that include affordable housing. Cal. Gov't Code §65915 (West 2016) (*see* the discussion in *Building Industry Ass'n v. City of Oceanside* (reprinted supra)). The value of density bonuses, however, may be lost if expensive parking obligations are imposed on the additional units. *See also* Cal. Gov't Code §65589.5 (West 2016)

(limiting the approval of any projects below the maximum allowable density because of the adverse effect on affordable housing).

In *Wollmer v. City of Berkeley*, 102 Cal. Rptr. 3d 19 (Ct. App. 2009), the court held that nothing in the Density Bonus Law suggests that a municipality must enact an ordinance any time it wishes to provide more of a density bonus than is required by state law. Furthermore, when an applicant seeks a density bonus for a housing development that includes a required percentage of affordable housing, Cal. Gov't Code §65915 requires that the city not only grant the density bonus but provide additional incentives or concessions where needed.

Density bonuses were also taken up by the court in *Friends of Lagoon Valley v. City of Vacaville*, 65 Cal. Rptr. 3d 251 (Ct. App. 2007). The court held that a city was not precluded from awarding developers a density bonus above the maximum bonus required by state housing law. Furthermore, state law does not require perfect conformity between a proposed development project and the city's applicable general plan; rather, a proposed subdivision map must be in agreement or harmony with the applicable plan. Finally, in *Sequoyah Hills Homeowners Ass'n. v. City of Oakland*, 29 Cal. Rptr. 2d 182 (Ct. App. 1993), the court held that Section 65589.5 makes it reasonable for an environmental impact report not to consider an alternative project that reduces density.

3. *More Incentives.* California Health and Safety Code §33334.2 (West 2016) provides that 20 percent of "tax increment" redevelopment revenue, that is, the higher tax increment produced when a redevelopment project is implemented, must be set aside for increasing, improving, and preserving the community's supply of low and moderate income housing. The percentage can be increased to 25 percent if a court determines that the redevelopment agency has misrepresented the need for affordable housing or other relevant facts. *Id.* §33334.2(c). In recent years, California has virtually abolished redevelopment, making use of such financing problematic. Similarly, Va. Code Ann. §15.2-2305 (2012) provides incentives for providing affordable housing. It authorizes an increase of up to 30 percent of density in areas subject to an affordable housing ordinance.

———————

Inclusionary housing mandates have generated various constitutional challenges. An important, recent decision from the California Supreme Court rejecting one such challenge follows:

■ CALIFORNIA BUILDING INDUSTRY ASSOCIATION V. CITY OF SAN JOSE
61 Cal. 4th 435 (2015)

JUSTICE CANTIL-SAKAUYE
Health and Safety Code section 50003, subdivision (a), currently provides:

The Legislature finds and declares that . . . there exists within the urban and rural areas of the state a serious shortage of decent, safe, and sanitary housing which persons and families of low or moderate income . . . can afford. This situation creates an absolute present and future shortage of supply in relation to demand . . . and also creates inflation in the cost of housing, by reason of its scarcity, which tends to decrease the relative affordability of the state's housing supply for all its residents.

This statutory language was first enacted by the Legislature *over 35 years ago,* in the late 1970s. It will come as no surprise to anyone familiar with California's current housing market that the significant problems arising from a scarcity of affordable housing have not been solved over the past three decades. Rather, these problems have become more severe and have reached what might be described as epic proportions in many of the state's localities. All parties in this proceeding agree that the lack of affordable housing is a very significant problem in this state.

As one means of addressing the lack of a sufficient number of housing units that are affordable to low and moderate income households, more than 170 California municipalities have adopted what are commonly referred to as "inclusionary zoning" or "inclusionary housing" programs. As a 2013 publication of the United States Department of Housing and Urban Development explains, inclusionary zoning or housing programs "require or encourage developers to set aside a certain percentage of housing units in new or rehabilitated projects for low- and moderate-income residents. This integration of affordable units into market-rate projects creates opportunities for households with diverse socioeconomic backgrounds to live in the same developments and have access to [the] same types of community services and amenities. . . ."

In 2010, after considerable study and outreach to all segments of the community, the City of San Jose (hereafter sometimes referred to as the city or San Jose) enacted an inclusionary housing ordinance that, among other features, requires all new residential development projects of 20 or more units to sell at least 15 percent of the for-sale units at a price that is affordable to low or moderate income households.

Very shortly after the ordinance was enacted and before it took effect, plaintiff California Building Industry Association (CBIA) filed this lawsuit in superior court, maintaining that the ordinance was invalid on its face on the ground that the city, in enacting the ordinance, failed to provide a sufficient evidentiary basis "to demonstrate a reasonable relationship between any adverse public impacts or needs for additional subsidized housing units in the City ostensibly caused by or reasonably attributed to the development of new residential developments of 20 units or more and the new affordable housing exactions and conditions imposed on residential development by the Ordinance." The complaint maintained that under the "controlling state and federal constitutional standards governing such exactions and conditions of development approval" the conditions imposed by the city's inclusionary housing ordinance would be valid only if the city produced evidence demonstrating that the requirements were reasonably related to the adverse impact on the city's affordable housing problem *that was caused by or attributable to the proposed new developments that are subject to the ordinance's requirements,* and that the materials relied on by the city in enacting the ordinance did not demonstrate such a relationship. Although the complaint did not explicitly spell out the specific nature of its constitutional claim, CBIA has subsequently clarified that its challenge rests on "the unconstitutional conditions doctrine, as applied to development exactions" under the takings clauses (or, as they are sometimes denominated, the just compensation clauses) of the United States and California Constitutions. CBIA's challenge is based on the premise that the conditions imposed by the San Jose ordinance constitute "exactions" for purposes of that doctrine. The superior court agreed with CBIA's contention and issued a judgment enjoining the city from enforcing the challenged ordinance.

The Court of Appeal reversed the superior court judgment . . . For the reasons discussed below, we conclude that the Court of Appeal decision in the present case should be upheld . . .

I. STATUTORY BACKGROUND

We begin with a brief summary of the California statutes that form the background to the San Jose ordinance challenged in this case.

Nearly 50 years ago, the California Legislature enacted a broad measure requiring all counties and cities in California to "adopt a comprehensive, long-term general plan for the physical development of the county or city." Each municipality's general plan is to contain a variety of mandatory and optional elements, including a mandatory housing element consisting of standards and plans for housing sites in the municipality that "shall endeavor to make adequate provision for the housing needs of all economic segments of the community."

A little more than a decade later, in 1980, declaring (1) that "[t]he availability of housing is of vital statewide importance," (2) that "the early attainment of decent housing and a suitable living environment for every Californian . . . is a priority of the highest order," (3) that "[t]he early attainment of this goal requires the cooperative participation of government and the private sector in an effort to expand housing opportunities and accommodate the housing needs of Californians of all economic levels," and (4) that "*[l]ocal and state governments have a responsibility to use the powers vested in them to facilitate the improvement and development of housing to make adequate provision for the housing needs of all economic segments of the community*" the Legislature enacted a separate, comprehensive statutory scheme that substantially strengthened the requirements of the housing element component of local general plans. The 1980 legislation — commonly referred to as the "Housing Element Law — sets forth in considerable detail a municipality's obligations to analyze and quantify the locality's existing and projected housing needs for all income levels, including the locality's share of the regional housing need as determined by the applicable regional "'[c]ouncil of governments'" and to adopt and to submit to the California Department of Housing and Community Development a multiyear schedule of actions the local government is undertaking to meet these needs. In particular, the legislation requires a municipality, "[i]n order to make adequate provision for the housing needs of all economic segments of the community, . . . [to] [i]dentify actions that will be taken to make sites available during the planning period . . . with appropriate zoning and development standards and with services and facilities to accommodate that portion of the city's or county's share of the regional housing need for each income level" and to "[a]ssist in the development of adequate housing to meet the needs of extremely low, very low, low-, and moderate-income households."

In addition to adopting the Housing Element Law, the Legislature has enacted a variety of other statutes to facilitate and encourage the provision of affordable housing, for example, prohibiting local zoning and other restrictions that preclude the construction of affordable housing units, and requiring local governments to provide incentives, such as density bonuses, to developers who voluntarily include affordable housing in their proposed development projects. Furthermore, with respect to two geographic categories — redevelopment areas and the coastal zone — the Legislature has enacted statutes explicitly directing that new residential development within such areas include affordable housing units.

Although to date the California Legislature has not adopted a statewide statute that requires every municipality to adopt a mandatory inclusionary housing ordinance if needed to meet the municipality's obligations under the Housing Element Law, in recent decades more than 170 California cities and counties have adopted such inclusionary housing ordinances in an effort to meet such obligations. The provisions and legislative history of the affordable housing statutes make it clear that the California Legislature is unquestionably aware of these numerous local mandatory inclusionary housing ordinances and that the existing state legislation is neither inconsistent with nor intended to preempt these local measures.

II. BACKGROUND AND DESCRIPTION OF CHALLENGED SAN JOSE INCLUSIONARY HOUSING ORDINANCE

. . . We summarize the principal provisions of the lengthy ordinance, which runs 57 pages.

The ordinance begins with a list of findings and declarations, detailing the steady increase in the cost of housing in San Jose generally and the substantial need for affordable housing for extremely low, very low, lower, and moderate income households to meet the city's regional housing needs allocation as determined by ABAG. The findings note that "[r]equiring affordable units within each development is consistent with the community's housing element goals of protecting the public welfare by fostering an adequate supply of housing for persons at all economic levels and maintaining both economic diversity and geographically dispersed affordable housing." The findings further observe that requiring builders of new market rate housing to provide some housing affordable to low and moderate income families "is also reasonably related to the impacts of their projects, because: 1. Rising land prices have been a key factor in preventing development of new affordable housing. New market-rate housing uses available land and drives up the price of remaining land. New development without affordable units reduces the amount of land development opportunities available for the construction of affordable housing. 2. New residents of market-rate housing place demands on services provided by both public and private sectors, creating a demand for new employees. Some of these public and private sector employees needed to meet the needs of the new residents earn incomes only adequate to pay for affordable housing. Because affordable housing is in short supply in the city, such employees may be forced to live in less than adequate housing within the city, pay a disproportionate share of their incomes to live in adequate housing in the city, or commute ever increasing distances to their jobs from housing located outside the city. These circumstances harm the city's ability to attain employment and housing goals articulated in the city's general plan and place strains on the city's ability to accept and service new market-rate housing development."

The next section, setting forth the purposes of the ordinance, explains that a principal purpose is to enhance the public welfare by establishing policies requiring the development of housing affordable to low and moderate income households in order to meet the city's regional share of housing needs and implement the goals and objectives of the city's general plan and housing element. A further purpose is to provide for the residential integration of low and moderate income households with households of market rate neighborhoods and to disperse inclusionary units throughout the city where new residential development occurs. In addition, the ordinance is intended to alleviate the impacts that would result from the use of available residential land solely for the benefit of households that are able to afford market rate housing and to mitigate the service burden imposed by households in new market rate residential developments by making additional affordable housing available for service employees. Finally, the ordinance provides residential developers with a menu of options from which to select alternatives to the construction of inclusionary units on the same site as market rate residential developments.

The substantive provisions of the ordinance follow. The requirements contained in the ordinance apply to all residential developments within the city that create 20 or more new, additional, or modified dwelling units. With regard to such developments, the ordinance's basic inclusionary housing requirement specifies that 15 percent of the proposed on-site for-sale units in the development shall be made available at an "affordable housing cost" to households earning no more than 120 percent of the area median income for Santa Clara County adjusted for household size. The ordinance generally defines affordable housing cost by reference to the definition set forth in Health and Safety Code section 50052.5 (S.J.M.C. §5.08.105), which in turn defines affordable housing cost as 30 percent of the area median income of the relevant income group (i.e. extremely low, very low, lower and moderate income).

As an alternative to providing the required number of for-sale inclusionary units on the same site as the market rate units, the ordinance affords a developer a number of compliance options. At the same time, as an apparent incentive to encourage developers to choose to provide on-site inclusionary units, the ordinance provides that when a developer chooses one of the alternative compliance options, the inclusionary housing requirement increases to no less than 20 percent of the total units in the residential development, as contrasted with the no less than 15 percent requirement that applies to on-site inclusionary units. The alternative compliance options include: (1) constructing off-site affordable for-sale units, (2) paying an in lieu fee based on the median sales price of a housing unit affordable to a moderate income family, (3) dedicating land equal in value to the applicable in lieu fee, or (4) acquiring and rehabilitating a comparable number of inclusionary units that are affordable to low or very low income households.

As additional incentives to encourage developers to comply with the ordinance by providing affordable units on site, the ordinance permits a developer who provides all of the required affordable units on the same site as the market rate units to apply for and obtain a variety of economically beneficial incentives, including (1) a density bonus . . . (2) reduction in the number of parking spaces otherwise required by the San Jose Municipal Code, (3) a reduction in minimum set-back requirements, and (4) financial subsidies and assistance from the city in the sale of the affordable units.

The ordinance also addresses the characteristics of the affordable units to be constructed on site. The ordinance requires that such units have the same quality of exterior design and comparable square footage and bedroom count as market rate units, but permits some different "unit types" of affordable units (for example, in developments with detached single-family market rate units, the affordable units may be attached single-family units or may be placed on smaller lots than the market rate units), and also allows the affordable units to have different, but functionally equivalent, interior finishes, features, and amenities, compared with the market rate units.

The ordinance additionally contains a number of provisions intended to ensure that the number of affordable housing units required by the ordinance is not lost upon resale of an affordable unit. To this end, the ordinance requires that the guidelines to be adopted by city officials to implement the ordinance "shall include standard documents . . . to ensure the continued affordability of the inclusionary units approved for each residential development." Such documents may include, but are not limited to, "inclusionary housing agreements, regulatory agreements, promissory notes, deeds of trust, resale restrictions, rights of first refusal, options to purchase, and/or other documents," and shall be recorded against the residential development, all inclusionary units, and any site subject to the provisions of the ordinance. The ordinance further provides that such documents shall include "subordinate shared appreciation documents permitting the city to recapture at resale the difference between the market rate value of the inclusionary unit and the affordable housing cost, plus a share of appreciation realized from an unrestricted sale in such amounts as deemed necessary by the city to replace the inclusionary unit." The ordinance specifies that all inclusionary units "shall remain affordable to the targeted income group for no less than the time periods set forth in California Health and Safety Code Sections 33413(c)(1) and (2)" (S.J.M.C. §5.08.600 B.), and that "all promissory note repayments, shared appreciation payments, or other payments collected under this section" shall be deposited in the City of San Jose affordable housing fee fund, from which funds may be expended exclusively to provide housing affordable to extremely low, very low, lower and moderate income households.

The ordinance further contains a waiver provision, declaring that the ordinance's requirements may be "waived, adjusted, or reduced" by the city "if an applicant shows, based on substantial evidence, that there is no reasonable relationship between the impact of a proposed residential development and the requirements of this chapter, or that applying the requirements of this chapter would take property in violation of the United States or California Constitutions." This section goes on to provide that "[t]he waiver, adjustment or reduction may be approved only to the extent necessary to avoid an unconstitutional result, after adoption of written findings, based on substantial evidence, supporting the determinations required by this section."

Finally, although the ordinance was adopted in January 2010, the city council, in recognition of the significant disruption in the local housing market that had accompanied the nationwide recession, provided that the ordinance would not become operative until the earlier of (1) six months following the first 12–month consecutive period in which 2,500 residential building permits had been issued by the city, with a minimum of 1,250 permits issued for dwelling units outside the San Jose redevelopment area, or (2) January 1, 2013. . . .

IV. Does the San Jose inclusionary housing ordinance, in requiring new residential developments to sell some of the proposed new units at an affordable housing price, impose an "exaction" on developers' property under the takings clauses of the federal and California Constitutions, so as to bring into play the unconstitutional conditions doctrine?

We begin with the well-established principle that under the California Constitution a municipality has broad authority, under its general police power, to regulate the development and use of real property within its jurisdiction to promote the public welfare. The variety and range of permissible land use regulations are extensive and familiar, including, for example, restrictions on the types of activities for which such property may be used (commercial or residential, or specific types of commercial ventures or specific types of residential developments — single family, multiunit), limitations on the density and size of permissible residential development (permissible lot size, number of units per lot, minimum or maximum square footage of units, number of bedrooms), required set-backs, aesthetic restrictions and requirements, and price controls (for example, rent control). As a general matter, so long as a land use restriction or regulation bears a reasonable relationship to the public welfare, the restriction or regulation is constitutionally permissible. (See, e.g., ...; *Euclid v. Ambler Realty Co.*, 272 U.S. 365 (1926)

We review challenges to the exercise of such power deferentially. "In deciding whether a challenged [land use] ordinance reasonably relates to the public welfare, the courts recognize that such ordinances are presumed to be constitutional, and come before the court with every intendment in their favor." Accordingly, a party challenging the facial validity of a legislative land use measure ordinarily bears the burden of demonstrating that the measure lacks a reasonable relationship to the public welfare. Nonetheless . . . , although land use regulations are generally entitled to deference, "judicial deference is not judicial abdication. The ordinance must have a *real and substantial* relation to the public welfare. There must be a reasonable basis in fact, not in fancy, to support the legislative determination. Although in many cases it will be 'fairly debatable' that the ordinance reasonably relates to the regional welfare, it cannot be assumed that a land use ordinance can *never* be invalidated as an enactment in excess of the police power."

In the present case, however, CBIA contends that this traditional standard of judicial review is not applicable and that the conditions that the ordinance imposes upon a proposed new development are valid only if those conditions bear a reasonable relationship to the amount of the city's need for affordable housing that is attributable to the proposed development itself, rather than that the ordinance's conditions bear a reasonable relationship to the public welfare of the city and region as a whole. It also contends that the city, rather than the party challenging the ordinance, bears the burden of proof regarding the validity of the ordinance.

As already noted, although the precise nature and source of CBIA's constitutional claim was somewhat opaque in earlier stages of this litigation, in its briefing in this court CBIA has clarified that its facial constitutional challenge rests upon the takings clauses of the United States and California Constitutions and, more specifically, on the claim "that the Ordinance violates the unconstitutional conditions doctrine, as applied to development exactions." As we shall explain, however, there can be no valid unconstitutional-conditions takings claim without a government exaction of property, and the ordinance in the present case does not effect an exaction. Rather, the ordinance is an example of a municipality's permissible regulation of the use of land under its broad police power.

As a general matter, the unconstitutional conditions doctrine imposes special restrictions upon the government's otherwise broad authority to condition the grant of a privilege or benefit when a proposed condition requires the individual to give up or refrain from exercising a constitutional right. In the takings context, the special limitations imposed by the unconstitutional conditions doctrine upon which CBIA relies derive from the United States Supreme Court's decisions in *Nollan v. California Coastal Commission*, 483 U.S. 825 (1987) and *Dolan v. City of Tigard*, 512 U.S. 374 (1994). . . .

In the present case, contrary to CBIA's contention, the San Jose inclusionary housing ordinance does not violate the unconstitutional conditions doctrine because there is no exaction — the ordinance does not require a developer to give up a property interest for which the government would have been required to pay just compensation under the takings clause outside of the permit process. As summarized above, the principal requirement that the challenged ordinance imposes upon a developer is that the developer sell 15 percent of its on-site for-sale units at an affordable housing price. This condition does not require the developer to dedicate any portion of its property to the public or to pay any money to the public. Instead, like many other land use regulations, this condition simply places a restriction on the way the developer may use its property by limiting the price for which the developer may offer some of its units for sale. Contrary to CBIA's contention, such a requirement does not constitute an exaction for purposes of the *Nollan/Dolan* line of decisions and does not trigger application of the unconstitutional conditions doctrine.

Rather than being an exaction, the ordinance falls within what we have already described as municipalities' general broad discretion to regulate the use of real property to serve the legitimate interests of the general public and the community at large. For example, municipalities may designate certain areas of a city where only residential units may be built and other areas where only commercial projects are permitted. If a municipality finds that it is in the public interest, it may specify where certain types of retail establishments may be operated and other areas where they may not. If a municipality concludes that the city already has a sufficient number of a specific type of business in a particular neighborhood — for example, adult entertainment businesses — it may prohibit other property owners from using their property in that area for such businesses. Similarly, if a municipality determines that a particular neighborhood or the community in general is in special need of a specific type of residential development or business establishment — such as a multiunit residential project or a retail shopping center — it may adopt land use regulations to serve such a need. In addition, of course, a municipality may impose land use limitations on the height of buildings, set-back requirements, density limits (lot size and number of units per lot), bedroom requirements and a variety of other use restrictions.

As a general matter, so long as a land use regulation does not constitute a physical taking or deprive a property owner of all viable economic use of the property, such a restriction does not violate the takings clause insofar as it governs a property owner's future use of his or her property, except in the unusual circumstance in which the use restriction is properly found to go "too far" and to constitute a "regulatory taking" under the ad hoc, multi-factored test discussed by the United States Supreme Court in *Penn Central Transp. Co. v. New York City*, 438 U.S. 104 (1978). Where a restriction on the use of property would not constitute a taking of property without just compensation if imposed outside of the permit process, a permit condition imposing such a use restriction does not require a permit applicant to give up the constitutional right to just compensation in order to obtain the permit and thus does not constitute "an exaction" so as to bring into play the unconstitutional conditions doctrine.

As noted, the legislative history of the ordinance in question establishes that the City of San Jose found there was a significant and increasing need for affordable housing in the city to meet the city's regional share of housing needs under the California Housing Element Law and that the public interest would best be served if new affordable housing were integrated into economically diverse development projects, and that it enacted the challenged ordinance in order to further these objectives. The objectives of increasing the amount of affordable housing in the city to comply with the Housing Element Law and of locating such housing in economically diverse developments are unquestionably constitutionally permissible purposes. CBIA does not argue otherwise.

There are a variety of conditions or restrictions that a municipality could impose on new residential development in an effort to increase the community's stock of affordable housing and promote economically diverse residential developments. For example, a municipality might attempt to achieve these objectives by requiring all new residential developments to include a specified percentage of studio, one-bedroom, or small-square-footage units, on the theory that smaller units are more likely to be affordable to low or moderate income households than larger units. Although such use restrictions might well reduce the value of undeveloped property or lessen the profits a developer could obtain in the absence of such requirements, CBIA cites no authority, and we are aware of none, suggesting that such use restrictions would constitute a taking of property outside the permit process or that a permit condition that imposes such use restrictions on a proposed development would constitute an exaction under the takings clause that would be subject to the *Nollan/Dolan* test.

Here, the challenged ordinance seeks to increase the city's stock of affordable housing and promote economically diverse residential projects by placing controls on the sales price of a portion of a developer's on-site for-sale units rather than by placing restrictions on the size or other features of a portion of the for-sale units. But the fact that the ordinance imposes price controls rather than other use restrictions in order to accomplish its legitimate purposes does not render such price controls an exaction or support application of a constitutionally based judicial standard of review that is more demanding than that applied to other land use regulations. The governing federal and state authorities plainly establish that price controls, like other forms of regulation, are, as a general matter, a constitutionally permissible means to achieve a municipality's legitimate public purposes. . . .

A municipality's authority to impose price controls on developers is, of course, unquestionably subject to constitutional limits. . . . [In particular,] such controls would be unconstitutional if they are found to be confiscatory, that is, if they deny a property owner a fair and reasonable return on its property. In this case, however, the ordinance has not yet been applied to any proposed development, and there is no indication that application of price controls on 15 percent of a development's on-sale units, along with the availability of economically advantageous density bonuses, exemptions from on-site parking requirements, and financial subsidies, would produce a confiscatory result . . .

[S]everal high court cases indicate that other takings analyses also apply to price controls. These latter cases indicate that price controls may be impermissible if found to constitute a "regulatory taking" under the ad hoc, multifactored test set forth in *Penn Central, supra.* Here, however, CBIA has expressly disclaimed any reliance on the *Penn Central* doctrine.

As we have explained, an ordinance that places nonconfiscatory price controls on the sale of residential units and does not amount to a regulatory taking would not constitute a taking of property without just compensation even if the price controls were applied to a property owner who had not sought a land use permit. Accordingly, the inclusionary housing ordinance's imposition of such price controls as a condition of a development permit does not constitute the imposition of an exaction for purposes of the unconstitutional conditions doctrine under the takings clause. . . .

VII. CONCLUSION

As noted at the outset of this opinion, for many decades California statutes and judicial decisions have recognized the critical need for more affordable housing in this state. Over the years, a variety of means have been advanced and undertaken to address this challenging need. We emphasize that the legal question before our court in this case is not the wisdom or efficacy of the particular tool or method that the City of San Jose has adopted, but simply whether, as the Court of Appeal held, the San Jose ordinance is subject to the ordinary standard of judicial review to which legislative land use regulations have traditionally been subjected.

For the reasons discussed above, the judgment of the Court of Appeal is affirmed.

Notes and Comments

1. *Takings or Due Process?* One mystery raised but not resolved by the decision in *City of San Jose* is the constitutional basis for the deferential "reasonable relationship" standard that applies to inclusionary housing requirements in California following this decision. The opinion in *City of San Jose* notes, unhelpfully, that the standard might be based on "due process or takings principles." 61 Cal. 4th at 473 n.18. In a thoughtful concurring opinion, Justice Werdergar contends that, in light of the U.S. Supreme Court's 2005 decision in *Lingle v. Chevron U.S.A., Inc.*, the reasonable relationship test "is best understood to state a due process standard, not a takings." *Id.* at 486. *Lingle* and its significance for modern takings doctrine are discussed in detail in Chapter 7.

2. *Inclusionary Rent Control. City of San Jose* dealt with an inclusionary housing ordinance that required developments above a certain size to *sell* a percentage of the units at affordable prices. Inclusionary housing ordinances addressing rental units potentially raise different issues. In *Palmer/Sixth Street Properties, L.P. v. City of Los Angeles*, 96 Cal. Rptr. 3d 875 (Ct. App. 2009), the California Court of Appeals held

that an affordable housing ordinance applicable to developers' mixed use rental project conflicted with and was preempted by the vacancy decontrol provisions of the Costa-Hawkins Rental Housing Act. The ordinance denied developers the right to establish the initial rental rates for the affordable housing units that were required to be built under the ordinance and preserved at their regulated rent levels for 30 years or the life of the unit. Additionally, the ordinance's in lieu fee option, which provided an alternative to the affordable housing requirements, was inextricably intertwined with the affordable housing requirements because the fee amount was based solely on the number of affordable housing units that a developer must provide.

In *City of San Jose*, the court observed that the city ordinance included a provision applicable to rental units but it explicitly provided that it "shall be operative [only] at such time as current appellate case law in *Palmer/Sixth Street Properties, L.P. v. City of Los Angeles* . . . is overturned, disapproved, or depublished by a court of competent jurisdiction or modified by the state legislature to authorize control of rents of inclusionary units." 61 Cal. 4th at 450 n.6. So far as we know, the city is still waiting. *See also Apartment Ass'n of South Central Wis., Inc. v. City of Madison*, 722 N.W.2d 614 (Wis. Ct. App. 2006) (ruling that a state statute preempted an inclusionary ordinance requiring developers of more than 10 units to set rents on 15 percent of rental units to assure affordability to those at 60 percent of median income).

3. *Keeping Affordable Housing Affordable.* One challenge in providing affordable housing is that over time the housing can increase in value and become unaffordable. One technique to maintain housing affordability is through the execution of affordable housing covenants. *See* Me. Rev. Stat. Ann. tit. 33, §§121-126 (West 1999) (jurisdiction may limit the resale price, place a cap on equity accumulation, or limit purchasers or renters to an economic class of consumers based on income). Are these terms easy to implement? *See also ML Plainsboro Ltd. P'ship v. Township of Plainsboro*, 719 A.2d 1285 (N.J. Super. Ct. App. Div. 1998) (holding that the planning board may not dictate in perpetuity who may use, buy, own, or rent property, and applying the principle to development of a corporate campus restricting occupancy to a single-user owner). *See also* James J. Kelly, Jr., Homes Affordable for Good: Covenants and Ground Leases as Long-Term Resale-Restriction Devices, 29 St. Louis U. Pub. L. Rev. 9 (2009) (advocating perpetual preemptive options in covenants and leases); Benjamin Powell & Edward Stringham. "The Economics of Inclusionary Zoning Reclaimed": How Effective Are Price Controls? 33 Fla. St. U. L. Rev. 471 (2005) (arguing that long-term controls on inclusionary units to maintain them as affordable housing, like rent control, is ineffective); Amy J. Schmitz, Promoting the Promise Manufactured Homes Provide for Affordable Housing, 13 J. Affordable Housing & Commun. Dev. L. 384 (2004); Matthew Towey, The Land Trust Without Land: The Unusual Structure of the Chicago Community Land Trust, 18 J. Affordable Housing & Commun. Dev. L. 335 (2009) (discussing utilization of deed restrictions to retain affordable housing). The ordinance at issue in the *City of San Jose* case addressed the "continued affordability" issue. 61 Cal. 4th at 451-52.

4. *Land Trusts.* Another strategy for providing affordable housing is a community land trust. With a land trust, a government agency or a nonprofit organization acquires the land or home and sells the house, retaining the land. John Emmeus Davis, More Than Money: What Is Shared in Equity Homeownership?, 19 J. Affordable Housing & Commun. Dev. L. 259 (2010) (describing such programs as

community land trusts, limited equity cooperatives, and price-restricted houses and condominiums with affordability covenants lasting longer than 30 years); James J. Kelly, Jr., Maryland's Affordable Housing Land Trust Act, 19 J. Affordable Housing & Commun. Dev. L. 345 (2010) (discussing how existing models of resale restrictions used by community land trust and inclusionary zoning programs can be adapted to meet the affordable housing land trust approach); Ryan Sherriff, Shared Equity Homeownership State Policy Review, 19 J. Affordable Housing & Commun. Dev. L. 279 (2010) (describing land trusts and other government-assisted programs); Montgomery County, Md., Revises Inclusionary Zoning Law to Expand, Preserve Inventory, 32 Hous. & Dev. Rep. (West) 818 (Dec. 20, 2004) (describing amendment to inclusionary ordinance to extend price control period from 20 to 99 years on rental units and 30 years on homeownership housing).

When property is held in a land trust, the buyer is able to make a smaller down payment, because the purchase price and the loan amount do not reflect the land value. Typically the buyer's monthly cost is 25 percent less than for market buyers. In exchange, the buyer has a reduced opportunity for equity appreciation, as the home must be sold to a buyer within eligibility for affordable housing. According to one study, 80 community land trusts experienced a foreclosure rate 30 times lower than the unfettered real estate market in 2007. Julie Farrell Curtin & Lance Bocarsly, Community Land Trusts: A Growing Trend in Affordable Home Ownership, 17 J. Affordable Housing & Commun. Dev. L. 367 (2008); *see also* Community Land Trusts Found to Have Low Foreclosure Rates, 38 [Current Developments] Hous. & Dev. Rep. (West) 688 (2010) (citing prepurchase counseling, requiring permission for refinancing, close monitoring. and reporting to a lender as reducing risk of default). *See also* Dawn Jourdan, Shannon Van Zandt, & Nicole Adair, Meeting Their Fair Share: A Proposal for the Creation of Regional Land Banks to Meet the Affordable Housing Needs in the Rural Areas of Texas, 19 J. Affordable Housing & Commun. Dev. L. 147 (2010) (endorsing the use of vacant and abandoned properties to establish regional land banks for affordable housing as a means of assisting small rural towns in obtaining affordable housing); Stuart Pratt, Comment, A Proposal for Land Bank Legislation in North Carolina, 89 N.C. Law Rev. 568 (2011) (advocating enabling legislation that provides broad flexibility for local land banks to operate and that prioritizes the redevelopment of abandoned and vacant property into affordable housing to stabilize neighborhoods).

E. GOVERNMENT SUBSIDY PROGRAMS AND HOUSING LINKAGE

A Note on the History of Federal Involvement in Housing

Starting in the 1930s, the federal government has played a large and evolving role in providing low- and moderate-income housing. All told, the federal government is responsible for creating millions of units of affordable housing across the country. This effort certainly has not solved America's housing crisis, but it has succeeded in alleviating a problem that would have been far worse in its absence.

As the federal housing strategy has evolved, a number of individual federal programs developed in years past have largely or completely disappeared. In the early 1970s, President Richard Nixon, expressing concerns about the cost, efficacy and equity of the existing housing programs, declared a moratorium on activity under most of these programs. Following that dramatic step, the federal housing programs were relaunched in scaled-down form; they have since become more market-oriented, and more decision-making authority has been delegated by the federal government to local officials. *See* Congressional Research Service, Overview of Federal Housing Assistance Programs and Policy (2014); James A. Kushner et al., Housing and Community Development ch. 3 (4th ed. 2011).

1. *National Housing Goal.* The Housing Act of 1949 (P.L. 81-171) declared a national goal of "a decent home and suitable living environment for every American family," an objective still reflected in the U.S. Code today. *See* 42 U.S. C. §1441. While congressional concern at the time was based in part on an acute shortage of housing, it also reflected the widespread perception that America's housing stock was unsafe and dilapidated. In his State of the Union Address in 1949, President Harry Truman observed that "five million families are still living in slums and firetraps. Three million families share their homes with others." Today, while the concern about the poor quality of some housing has hardly disappeared, the primary policy focus is on affordability. The most important elements of the federal government's effort to address housing needs are described below.

2. *Public Housing.* The original and perhaps best-known federal housing program is public housing, launched by the U.S. Housing Act of 1937 (P.L. 75-412). Public housing developments are owned and operated by local public housing authorities, but they are subsidized and regulated by the federal government. Local housing authorities, with assistance from the federal government, sold bonds and constructed the housing. The federal government has provided continuing support for the authorities' operations. Federal rules mandate that public housing units can only be rented to low-income families (those with income at or below 80 percent of the area median income), and that 40 percent of the units that become available in any given year must be allocated to extremely low-income families (those with income at or below 30 percent of the area median income). Public housing authorities generally have long waiting lists of families seeking the opportunity to rent a unit.

Unfortunately, a great deal of public housing was poorly planned and designed, and projects were often marked by very high density, a lack of amenities, and poor construction. Public housing, by design, attracted poor tenants, generating insufficient rents to pay the escalating costs of maintenance, management, and security — placing ever increasing pressure on the federal government to provide subsidies. The projects were also stigmatized, for their sites were in the heart of the poorest neighborhoods. High crime, poor schools, and few jobs were available to the residents as the projects marked areas of the city where investment by private developers and entrepreneurs evaporated.

In recent decades, both Republican and Democratic administrations have deemphasized public housing as a tool for providing affordable housing. The 1998 Public Housing Reform Act (P.L. 105-276) prohibited local public housing authorities from increasing the total number of public housing units. At the same time, critics of public housing advocated privatization of existing projects, selling the units to tenants. In addition, in a number of celebrated cases, failed public housing project were demolished. Despite having fallen out of fashion as a matter of public policy, public housing supported by the federal government continues to provide homes for roughly 1.2 million families, making public housing the nation's second largest direct housing assistance program.

3. *Section 8.* The largest direct housing assistance program — the so-called Section 8 program — is of more recent vintage, and currently provides housing for roughly 2 million families. Section 8 is a form of tenant-based rental assistance funded by the federal government and administered by local public housing authorities with payments made directly to private landlords. Generally speaking, the Section 8 program makes up the difference between what a low-income tenant can afford to pay and the actual market rent of the unit. While the origins of this approach can be traced back to the 1960s, the Section 8 program was launched by the Housing Act of 1974 (P.L. 93-383), the first comprehensive piece of federal housing legislation adopted in the wake of the Nixon moratorium.

At its best, the Section 8 program has provided access to private sector housing for low-income tenants previously relegated to public or subsidized projects or substandard private sector housing. At its worst, the program may provide a subsidy to marginal landlords operating substandard housing. Barry G. Jacobs et al., Guide to Federal Housing Programs 23-25 (1982); Robert C. Ellickson, The False Promise of the Mixed-Income Housing Project, 57 UCLA L. Rev. 983 (2010) (advocating vouchers to provide greater efficiency and fairness); Adam Zeidel, Affordable Housing: The Case for Demand-Side Subsidies in Superstar Cities, 42 Urb. Law. 135 (2010) (arguing for demand-side subsidies in growing cities without room to grow).

While the Section 8 program was originally intended to be used in new construction and substantial rehabilitation projects, this use of funds was found to be an expensive way of providing housing. Accordingly, in 1983, Congress limited new Section 8 contracts to existing properties. In the same legislation, Congress authorized an experiment (since made permanent) to permit the use of Section 8 funding to supply vouchers. Under the voucher program, eligible families live in the housing of their choice. In addition, vouchers are nationally portable; once a family has secured a voucher it can use it in any part of the country where a voucher program exists.

4. *Low Income Tax Credit Housing.* Arguably the most significant generator of affordable housing today is the low income tax credit established by the Tax Reform Act of 1986 (P.L. 99-514). Frequently utilizing the below-market lending capacity of state housing finance agencies or city-issued bonds, investor-developers agree to maintain affordable rents and, in return, receive substantial federal income tax credits to shelter project and other ordinary income. *See* James E. Wallace, Financing Affordable Housing in the United States, 6 Hous. Pol'y Debate 785, 795, tbl. 3 (1995) (summarizing housing production under the program). The federal government allocates the federal tax credits to housing financing agencies, which in turn award the credits to developers who agree to provide the affordable housing. The developers sell the credits to wealthy investors and use the proceeds to help finance the project construction. By vesting major decision-making authority in state agencies, the tax credit program represents a major step in the devolution of federal housing policy.

The Low Income Tax Credit Housing program has been criticized for its lack of civil rights standards and a pattern of racially segregated site selection. *See* Myron

Orfield, Racial Integration and Community Revitalization: Applying the Fair Housing Act to the Low Income Housing Tax Credit, 58 Vand. L. Rev. 1747 (2005) (arguing that lack of site selection review violates Title VIII); Florence Wagman Roisman, Mandates Unsatisfied: The Low Income Housing Tax Credit Program and the Civil Rights Laws, 52 U. Miani L. Rev. 1011 (1998).

5. *HOME.* The HOME program is a housing block grant patterned after the Community Development Block Grant program that provides funds to local governments to support affordable housing initiatives, including tenant-based rental assistance or home purchasing. The program is designed to provide flexibility to allow local officials to use funds where they are needed most. Duane A. Martin, The President and the Cities: Clinton's Urban Aid Agenda, 26 Urb. Law. 99 (1994). *See also* The American Dream Down Payment Act, 42 U.S.C. §12705 (2006) (provides low-income families up to $10,000 down payment assistance); Living Equitably: Grandparents Aiding Children and Youth Act of 2003, 12 U.S.C. §1701q note (2006) (assisting expansion of intergenerational housing).

6. *More Tax Subsidies.* Ironically, the largest and most generous U.S. housing subsidy is targeted at those who need it least. State and federal income tax laws subsidize home owners an average of $2802 per year, as of 1990, by permitting the deduction of mortgage interest and property taxes. Donald A. Krueckeberg, The Lessons of John Locke or Hernando de Soto: What If Your Dreams Come True?, 15 Hous. Pol'y Debate 1, 15 (2004) (citing Joseph Gyourko & Todd Sinai, The Spatial Distribution of Housing-Related Tax Benefits in the United States 1 (Brookings Inst. Discussion Paper 2001)). The subsidy to the wealthy and those with second homes is even more extraordinary. At the same time, the average renter pays a premium of $1815 per year (*Id.* at 14-16) in the form of tax benefits to the landlord and foregone tax revenues in which the tenant does not share. For a general discussion, see Roberta F. Mann, On the Road Again: How Tax Policy Drives Transportation Choice, 24 Va. Tax. Rev. 587, 647-648 (2005) (arguing homeownership tax deductions encourage overinvestment, inflating housing prices); Thomas Benton Bare, III, Recharacterizing the Debate: A Critique of Environmental Democracy and an Alternative Approach to the Urban Sprawl Dilemma, 21 Va. Envtl. L. 455, 463-464 (2003) (arguing that homeownership tax subsidies stimulate sprawl and class segregation).

7. *State programs.* State housing and finance agencies have proliferated since the 1970s. But with the exception of New York's Mitchell-Lama program, the states have failed to appropriate substantial funds to subsidize housing. Instead, they have simply used bond-issuing power to reduce interest rates and have required the use of federal or other subsidies to reduce rents to affordable levels. *See, e.g., Utah Housing Fin. Agency v. Smart,* 561 P.2d 1052 (Utah 1977) (sustaining constitutionality of state program).

8. *Some Questions.* Does the nature of the housing market suggest strategies to solve the affordable housing problem? If the accurate economic model for housing is one of "reverse filtration," shouldn't the logical response be to subsidize housing for the affluent so as to encourage moving out? In fact, during any single year, there is a larger subsidy to the better-off in the form of tax sheltering, through the deductibility of mortgage interest and property taxes, than the total cost of housing subsidies for the poor from the institution of the New Deal programs under President Roosevelt to recent times. Hearings Before the Task Force on Human Resources

and Block Grants of the House Budget Comm., 97th Cong., 1st Sess. 9 (1981) (testimony of Cushing Dolbeare).

The following excerpt looks at the latest congressional housing program targeted at those of low income, the federal housing trust funds.

■ JAMES A. KUSHNER ET AL., HOUSING AND COMMUNITY DEVELOPMENT LAW
302 (4th ed. 2011)

NATIONAL HOUSING TRUST FUND LEGISLATION

Following years of advocacy, Congress in 2008 tacked onto the Housing and Economic Recovery Act [HERA] of 2008 two new housing development programs, the National Housing Trust Fund ("NHTF"), and the Capital Magnet Fund ("CMF"), HERA, §1131, Pub. L. No. 110-289, 122 Stat. 2654 (2008), adding §§1337-1339 to the Federal Housing Enterprises Financial Safety and Soundness Act of 1992, 12 U.S.C. §1301 *et seq.* The National Housing Trust Fund is a HUD-managed fund designed to provide funds for production, preservation, and rehabilitation of both rental housing and housing for homeownership for Very Low-Income ("VLI") households (50% or less of area median income) and Extremely Low-Income ("ELI") households (30% or less of area median income). The Capital Magnet Fund is a Treasury Secretary-managed fund designed to provide a competitive grant program to encourage private investment in affordable housing, as well as related economic development and community service activities.

After a three-year phase-in period, during which any funds appropriated to the NHTF were to be used to reimburse FHA for its costs in refinancing mortgages to prevent foreclosures, NHTF funds will be allocated as grants to states for redistribution to state housing finance agencies, state housing and community development entities and other "qualified instrumentalities." Seventy-five percent of the funds are to be earmarked for housing benefiting ELI households and the remaining 25% for VLI households.

Notes and Comments

1. *Funding Questions.* How should the NHTF and CMF be funded? Should their funding be subject to the annual appropriation process, or should a funding mechanism be established that operates outside the regular appropriations process? The congressional plan outlined in HERA called for Fannie Mae and Freddie Mac to allocate "an amount equal to 4.2 basis points (0.042 percent) for each dollar of the unpaid principal balance of [each agency's] total new business purchases;" 65 percent of that amount was to be set aside for the Housing Trust Fund and 35 percent for the Capital Magnet Fund. HERA, §1131, adding §§1337(a)(1)(A)-(B), 1137(a)(2)(A)-(B). These provisions were expected to provide approximately $600 million per year.

2. *Beyond Conservatorship.* However, when the two agencies went into conservatorship, that funding source was shelved indefinitely. Advocates of these programs, with support from the Obama administration, then sought appropriations from

Congress. After considerable delay, both of these programs are just getting off the ground as this book is going to press. *See* Community Development and Financial Institutions Fund, U.S. Department of Treasury at https://www.cdfifund.gov/programs-training/Programs/cmf/Pages/default.aspx (last visited Nov. 11, 2016) and Housing Trust Fund, U.S. Department of Housing & Urban Development at https://www.hudexchange.info/programs/htf/ (last visited Nov. 11, 2016).

The decline of the federal role in subsidizing low-income housing, together with the relatively passive role of state governments, underscores the importance of inclusionary programs such as housing linkage. *See* Tim Iglesias and Rochelle E. Lento (eds.), The Legal Guide to Affordable Housing Development (2005). The following case considers the constitutionality of one such program. *Commercial Builders of Northern California v. City of Sacramento* reviews housing impact fees, known in the literature as linkage, that fund local housing trusts to assist the development of affordable housing through developer exactions.

■ COMMERCIAL BUILDERS OF NORTHERN CALIFORNIA v. CITY OF SACRAMENTO
941 F.2d 872 (9th Cir. 1991)

In 1987, the City and County of Sacramento commissioned a consulting firm, Keyser-Marston Associates, to study the need for low-income housing, the effect of nonresidential development on the demand for such housing, and the appropriateness of exacting fees in conjunction with such development to pay for such housing. Keyser-Marston submitted its report, estimating the percentage of new workers in the developments that would qualify as low-income workers and would require housing. As instructed, it also calculated fees for development based on a yearly subsidy of $12,000 per qualified household that would be connected to the development. This figure represented the difference between $42,000, the minimum cost of building a two-bedroom apartment, and $30,000, the maximum rental income expected from a low-income household. Also as instructed, however, in the interest of erring on the side of conservatism in exacting the fees, it reduced its final calculations by about one-half.

Based upon this study, the City of Sacramento enacted the Housing Trust Fund Ordinance on March 7, 1989. The Ordinance lists several city-wide findings, including the finding that nonresidential development is "a major factor in attracting new employees to the region" and that the influx of new employees "create[s] a need for additional housing in the City." Pursuant to these findings, the Ordinance imposes a fee in connection with the issuance of permits for nonresidential development of the type that will generate jobs. The fees, calculated using the Keyser-Marston formula, are to be paid into a fund to assist in the financing of low-income housing. The city projects that the fund will raise about $3.6 million annually, nine percent of the projected annual cost of $42 million for the needed housing. Additional money will come from other sources, such as debt funding and general revenues.

Commercial Builders does not argue that the city lacks a legitimate interest in expanding low-income housing. Rather, it contends that this Ordinance constitutes an impermissible means to advance that interest, because it places a burden of paying for low-income housing on nonresidential development without a sufficient showing that nonresidential development contributes to the need for low-income housing in proportion to that burden. . . .

The appellants contend that . . . the Ordinance . . . must be struck down because the Supreme Court has now articulated a more stringent standard under which courts must analyze the imposition of conditions upon development. The appellants point out that in *Nollan v. California Coastal Comm'n*, 483 U.S. 825 (1987), the Court held that such conditions must not only be ones that the government might "rationally have decided" to employ for a given legitimate public purpose; they must also substantially advance such a purpose. They argue that under the standard articulated in *Nollan*, an ordinance that imposes an exaction on developers can be upheld only if it can be shown that the development in question is directly responsible for the social ill that the exaction is designed to alleviate. . . .

We agree with the City that *Nollan* does not stand for the proposition that an exaction ordinance will be upheld only where it can be shown that the development is directly responsible for the social ill in question. Rather, *Nollan* holds that where there is no evidence of a nexus between the development and the problem that the exaction seeks to address, the exaction cannot be upheld. Where, as here, the Ordinance was implemented only after a detailed study revealed a substantial connection between development and the problem to be addressed, the Ordinance does not suffer from the infirmities that the Supreme Court disapproved in *Nollan*. We find that the nexus between the fee provision here at issue, designed to further the city's legitimate interest in housing, and the burdens caused by commercial development is sufficient to pass constitutional muster.

The appellants also place some significance on the fact that this Ordinance is a fee provision. They contend that the fee represents a transfer of property, i.e., the money paid over to the city. *See Webb's Fabulous Pharmacies, Inc. v. Beckwith*, 449 U.S. 155 (1980) (treating a purely financial exaction as a taking). In this respect, they argue, it more closely resembles a physical taking of property, which automatically falls within the purview of the Fifth Amendment, than a land use regulation, which is subject to a reasonableness analysis. Under appellants' theory, however, compensation would be required for every fee; therefore, every fee would be unconstitutional. We see no valid basis for such a rule. . . .

Finally, the appellants contend that, regardless of the standard to be applied in assessing the validity of the Ordinance, they have raised an issue of material fact in their attack on the conclusions of the Keyser-Marston study. This attack came in the form of an affidavit from their planner, David Wade, suggesting that commercial development may be a less decisive factor in worker migration than the Keyser-Marston study indicates. Wade concluded that, in addition to employment opportunity, the availability of low-income housing is itself partly responsible for any influx of low-income employees to Sacramento. Wade also opined that it is at least as true that employers follow the work force as the converse. This affidavit, appellants argue, sufficiently calls into question the city's findings concerning the nexus between its Ordinance and the social ill it sought to cure to preclude summary judgment.

The appellants' argument lacks merit. Even viewing the Wade affidavit in the light most favorable to the developers, it does not rebut the Keyser-Marston conclusion that commercial development is related to an increase in the need for low-income housing. The Ordinance accounts for what the developers characterize as the indirectness of the connection between the creation of new jobs and the need for low-income housing by charging only a small percentage of what the Keyser-Marston study calculated to be the cost of meeting new low-income housing requirements. As we have already noted, nothing in *Nollan* or any other authority cited by the appellants requires the nexus to be more direct than that achieved through the legislative process that the city here employed. . . .

BEEZER, Circuit Judge, dissenting: I respectfully dissent.

As Justice Scalia warned in *Nollan*, a state can leverage its police power to the point where a regulation of land use becomes an "out-and-out plan of extortion." Sacramento's ordinance is a transparent attempt to force commercial developers to underwrite social policy. Apparently, legislators find it politically more palatable to exact payments from developers than to tax their constituents. The Takings Clause prohibits singling out developers to bear this burden. . . .

When the governmental exaction solves a problem actually created by the development (for example, requiring the developer to provide needed infrastructure), it is not coincidence that the exaction results in a benefit to the development as well as the community. . . . Sacramento would have developers pay not just for public improvements necessitated by development, but for private subsidies with little or no causal connection to development. Not surprisingly, under a scheme requiring no connection, no benefit accrues to the development in return. . . .

Sacramento has commissioned a study that demonstrates at best a tenuous and theoretical connection between commercial development and housing needs. But the Takings Clause requires a cause-and-effect relationship between the two. In my view, Sacramento has not shown such a relationship. Even the study relied on by the city to support the ordinance states that its "nexus analysis does not make the case that building construction is responsible for growth."

The ordinance is nothing more than a convenient way to fund a system of transfer payments. Although Sacramento attempts to justify the ordinance as an exercise of its police power, the city actually is exercising its taxing power — free of the encumbrances generally thought to limit the exercise of that power. . . .

The new workers attracted by the new jobs associated with the new development surely will increase the demand for all manner of goods and services. If Sacramento has shown a sufficient causal connection in this case, we can be expected next to uphold exactions imposed on developers to subsidize small business retailers, child-care programs, food services and health-care delivery systems.

Notes and Comments

1. *Linkage after* Koontz. The constitutionality of linkage programs, upheld in *Commercial Builders*, is sure to be tested in light of the Supreme Court's 2013 decision in *Koontz v. St. John's River Water Mgmt. Dist.*, 133 S. Ct. 2586 (2013). In that case, the Supreme Court, splitting 5-to-4, ruled that so-called "monetary exactions" must satisfy the "essential nexus" and "rough proportionality" tests in order to survive a challenge under the Takings Clause. *See Nollan v. California Coastal Comm'n, 483 U.S. 825 (1987)*, and *Dolan v. City of Tigard*, 512 U.S. 374 (1994). In those decisions, the Court held that a government requirement that a property convey an interest in land (such as an easement) to the government as a condition of obtaining a permit to develop property called for special scrutiny under the Takings Clause. Specifically, such an exaction will be upheld only if there is an "essential nexus" between

the exaction and the government's regulatory objectives and if the burden imposed by the exaction is "roughly proportional" to the projected impacts of the regulated development.

In *Koontz*, the Court addressed the question of whether the *Nollan/Dolan* tests apply when the condition does not require the conveyance of an interest in tangible property but rather the payment or expenditure of money. The Court ruled that *Nollan/Dolan* do apply, contending that permit fees are "functionally equivalent to other types of land use exactions." In dissent, Justice Kagan, speaking for herself and three other justices, disputed this conclusion, pointing out that prior Court precedent had drawn a sharp distinction for takings purposes between government directives to citizens to turn over interests in land and orders to turn over money (such as taxes).

It is debatable how the Ninth Circuit would rule it if were asked to reconsider the holding in *Commercial Builders* in light of *Koontz*. On the one hand, the Ninth Circuit appeared to rest its decision on the fact that the linkage fee involved an obligation to pay money rather an order to turn over tangible property, a distinction that arguably is no longer valid after *Koontz*. On the other hand, the Ninth Circuit also ruled that the government justification for the linkage fee was sufficient to meet the *Nollan* test, suggesting that the Ninth Circuit would continue to rule the same way even if a linkage fee were unambiguously subject to the *Nollan* test after *Koontz*. (The Court in *Commercial Builders* did not address whether the *Dolan* "rough pro-portionality" test could be satisfied, because the Supreme Court had not yet issued that decision). A further issue is whether a linkage fee would be exempt from *Nollan/Dolan* if it were imposed not as the result of a case-specific permitting action, but through enforcement of general legislation. The Ninth Circuit, like some but not all other federal appeals courts, has ruled that *Nollan* and *Dolan* do not apply to legislative exactions. *See McClung v. City of Sumner*, 548 F.3d 1219, 1225 (9th Cir. 2008).

2. *Developers or the Public?* Setting aside the takings questions, as a matter of public policy, how should the burden of linkage programs be allocated? The New Jersey Supreme Court has approved of linkage and encouraged the Council on Affordable Housing to issue regulations adopting this approach for implementing the *Mount Laurel* principle. *Holmdel Builders Ass'n v. Township of Holmdel*, 583 A.2d 277 (N.J. 1990). *See* John J. Ammann, Affordable Housing: New Opportunities and Challenges for Housing Trust Funds, 8 J. Affordable Housing & Commun. Dev. L. 198 (1999); Peter W. Salsich, Jr., Affordable Housing: Can NIMBYism be Trans-formed into OKIM-BYism?, 19 St. Louis U. Pub. L. Rev. 453 (2000) (endorsing inclusion through linkage). *See also* Virginia County Dedicates One Cent of Real Estate Levy to Housing Preservation, Production, 33 [current developments] Hous. & Dev. Rep. (Thomson-West) 329 (2005) (Fairfax County partially funding afford-able housing through earmarking one percent of property taxation revenues). Washington State imposes a $10 document recordation surcharge to provide funds for the state and local housing trust funds. Wash. Rev. Stat. §36.22.178 (West Supp. 2011). *See also* Kristin E. Larsen, Housing Opportunities in Florida: The State Housing Trust Fund, 23 J. Land Use & Envtl. L. J. 161 (2007) (endorsing Florida's block grant trust fund as the largest and most effective in the nation).

3. *Preemption in Colorado.* In *Town of Telluride v. Lot Thirty-Four Venture, L.L.C.*, 3 P.3d 30 (Colo. 2000), the Colorado Supreme Court invalidated an ordinance that imposed an affordable housing mitigation mandate. The ordinance required

property owners to create affordable housing for 40 percent of the employees to be generated from the development. To assure that units remained affordable, the scheme limited the growth of the rental rate below the market rate. The court ruled that this scheme was a form of rent control and therefore preempted by state legislation. It did so even though the ordinance authorized alternatives, such as the actual construction of employee housing, recording deed restrictions on existing units, paying an in-lieu fee for up to 15 percent of the obligation, or conveying land to meet the in-lieu partial option. *See also* Nadia I. El Mallakh, Comment, Does the Costa-Hawkins Act Prohibit Local Inclusionary Zone Programs?, 89 Cal. L. Rev. 1847 (2001) (preemption of rent control may preclude some forms of inclusionary zoning).

The following excerpt looks to changing architecture, transportation, zoning for mixed use, and densification to solve the problem of affordable housing:

■ JAMES A. KUSHNER, AFFORDABLE HOUSING AS INFRASTRUCTURE IN THE TIME OF GLOBAL WARMING
42/43 Urb. Law. 179, 201-214, 221 (2010-2011). . . .

America finds itself nearing the end of the cheap-oil age having invested its national wealth in a living arrangement — suburban sprawl — that has no future.

It may appear surprising, but the most important predicate for affordable housing is the development of efficient transport that can link homes with jobs, medical services, shopping, and other important destinations. The central proposal is to expand public transit to establish a universal convenient and attractive service and to encourage making the choice of public transit over private automobile while the automobile remains a viable mode of circulation. Efficient comfortable transit will generate the demand and supply necessary to allow people to live with access to work but with most trips within walkable neighborhoods. The higher density housing around transit stops and nodes will generate a supply of far more affordable housing than has traditionally been developed in low density suburbs. No longer can a homeseeker find a better house in the outer suburbs for less money because the cost of commuting now exceeds the higher cost of housing in close-in urban areas. The housing bust and foreclosure crisis has also spread urban blight to the suburbs.

Transportation systems, in order to be efficient, must operate within dedicated transit corridors — lanes or fixed rails upon which only transit travels. Although user preference is for fixed rail systems, bus systems cost 5% of fixed rail, light rail, and subways (or heavy rail). Thus, a comprehensive bus rapid transit (BRT) system is possible for less than the price of a rail system serving only a portion of the community. By dedicating lanes for the BRT, providing for pre-boarding fare collection (or even better — eliminating fares), utilizing buses that stop every three blocks with doors that open like subway doors, bus travel is rendered fast and convenient. In Curitiba, Brazil, and Utrecht, Netherlands, BRT has proven fast and friendly. In Curitiba, the buses are privatized with the city simply setting fares and compensating the bus company for miles traveled rather than a percentage of fares so the company is willing to operate less traveled routes and the city need not invest in buses. In

Utrecht, the Numbers 11 and 12 buses go from the Central Station, through an office park and to the University mostly on a dedicated busway both excluding automobiles and designed not to cross intersections thus making BRT as comfortable and convenient as train, subway, or light rail service.

Comprehensive public transport is a precondition for pedestrianizing the city and surrounding suburban transit villages. The elimination of autos from towns will generate a great deal of land currently dedicated to streets, parking lots, automobile sales, and services that can be rededicated to transit corridors, parks, parkways, and sites for housing, commerce, and job locations. . . .

Where parking is provided, it should be no closer than the closest transit stop. Although automobiles and their infrastructure are clearly an element of transportation, it is necessary to recognize that the general American practice of bundling parking and housing by imposing parking ratios upon developers as a condition of project approval adds dearly to the consumer's rent or purchase price. Housing becomes dramatically more affordable by eliminating parking and automobile infrastructure. . . .

Making communities more desirable for the pedestrian can be aided by reducing the area of streets for automobile traffic in commercial and residential areas to dedicate bikeways, green trails, and widening sidewalks for outdoor dining and cafes. Urbanized streets should have speed limits reduced to fifteen miles per hour to attract pedestrians and encourage a shift to public transport. Downtown Portland's traffic moves at this speed making pedestrians more comfortable. Communities should reduce available parking incrementally each year. Vienna, Austria reduces its central city parking by approximately 10% annually, while transit use increases and congestion declines. In addition, pedestrianization and an attractive town center can be encouraged by closing selected streets incrementally each year, expanding pedestrian streets and green space. Freiburg, Germany is rapidly pedestrianizing its town core and each year traffic is removed from a growing pedestrian village. In Vancouver, British Columbia, streets are being closed to be replaced with bike and walkways and public gardens, called green streets. . . .

Establishing a transit-served, higher density village that can accommodate adequate affordable housing will require discontinuing automobile-based development in favor of car-free development. Ordinances might permit only new development that is car-free; traffic-free, or traffic-reduced. Car-free housing is housing that prohibits automobile ownership by residents. Although this might include a temporary hardship exception for residents who require a car for work, there is an increasing demand for such communities, which enjoy gardens and green space instead of garages, parking lots and driveways. In Amsterdam, when notices of a proposed development for the WGL Water Works project were publicized, more than 7000 families and individuals indicated a desire to live in such a community. In Los Angeles, for example, 553,423 households (15% of all and 30% of the poor) own no automobile and rely on public transport and walkable neighborhoods.

Traffic-free developments are those that contain no surface automobile infrastructure but accommodate automobiles in perimeter garages as in the Vauban in Freiburg, Germany, or where parking and automobile infrastructure are below ground such as at the former Reim Airport in Munich or Uno City on the eastern shore of the Danube River in Vienna, Austria. Traffic-reduced projects are those that might accommodate home deliveries with narrow driveways with no parking, such as the Vauban in Freiburg or Slateford Green in Edinburgh, Scotland.

Transit orientation will become the dominant community design model in the United States as gasoline becomes increasingly expensive and the public recognizes the contribution that pollution and green house gas production makes to climate change. Development will reflect higher density and local design preference featuring mixed-use, walkable neighborhoods that will allow most trips to be made on foot and the journey to work accomplished by walking, biking, or by transit.

In experimenting with this new form of development, several problems have emerged. First, lenders, local government, and its planners are skeptical of future trends towards European lifestyles and are afraid of reduced parking opportunity. Thus, local governments typically impose standard parking ratios calling for two or more parking spaces per unit. Underground parking is expensive and the buildings must charge very high rents reflecting the parking infrastructure. As a result, tenants are typically automobile users and little additional transit use results from TOD. Large institutional lenders are also more comfortable with large scale subdivisions, expensive high-rise residential and office development, or traditional suburban-type commercial malls.

Second, by contrast, the creation of transit-served walkable communities has met with success and has generated significant private investment, particularly in apartment and loft renovations. This secondary development has the effect of gentrifying the neighborhood as rents and property sales prices escalate to reflect the new markets and result in the displacement of lower income neighborhood residents.

Mixed use development and transit-oriented apartments with parking are typically more expensive than transit users can afford so rather than supporting transit, higher levels of traffic congestion are generated. Should the neighborhood be attractive, a side effect can be secondary displacement as developers are motivated to buy up housing and potential lofts to develop housing for the affluent thereby raising property values and rents. Even commercial buildings are gentrified as major retail chains are attracted. Office developers may find the real estate values too expensive for economically sound development and respond by dispersing jobs to the outer suburbs thereby generating sprawl when the strategy was to reduce it and create infill transit-oriented development. A study by Reconnecting America, The National Housing Trust, and The Association of Retired Persons (AARP) warns that due to the expiration of federal subsidy contracts, thousands of people living in affordable housing near public transit face higher rents.

Controls will be required to protect the existing supply of affordable housing. Developments must include affordable housing using subsidies and ordinances; rents must be stabilized, and a sufficient supply of TOD neighborhoods must be available to prevent market distortion and inflation. Zoning must be utilized to prevent the development of excessively large spaces designed for the affluent and automobile infrastructure because that will inflate rents and retain the automobile culture along with its concomitant pollution and congestion. As cities and suburbs are transformed to transit villages, restrictive covenants or rent control regimens may be required to ensure against exploitation, displacement, and inflation until supply catches up to demand.

Transit-oriented development can encourage sprawl in the absence of regional planning and adequate smart growth controls. For example, TOD can exacerbate job sprawl. Only 21% of employees live within 3 miles of a central business district (CBD) and 45% work more than 10 miles from CBD. Job sprawl occurs when residential and office development demand inflates transit-oriented site values sending industrial and other developers further out to find more affordable land. Specific zoning should reduce land costs if an adequate supply of land is provided for projected need of various uses. . . .

Inclusionary zoning ordinances, including affordable housing impact fees, require a minimum of affordable housing to be included in developments, and offer density bonuses for developers that include affordable housing. Density bonuses are creative in the sense of generating something for nothing but in theory defy planning as population and density should be proportional to infrastructure. Density bonuses tend to generate more development and that can generate more needs than planned infrastructure capacity, e.g., water, sewers, schools, or traffic congestion. Densification without significant transit improvements can intensify traffic congestion. Nevertheless, a study of inclusionary zoning in San Francisco, Washington, D.C., and suburban Boston reported that there are great variations of mandatory and voluntary programs, but that density bonus programs exempting small projects appear to generate the most affordable housing.

Developer exactions may be characterized as takings. Imposing all costs of affordable housing on developers appears unfair and places an excessive burden on the developer because it is convenient and the developer is dependent on permit issuance. The result may be a few affordable units balanced by the inflation of rents of remaining market rate units thereby excluding most of the less affluent not lucky enough to obtain one of the precious affordable units. Like public transportation, subsidies for affordable housing should be borne by all. Nevertheless, new development should, and may be required to, finance affordable housing to the extent that the need for it is generated by that project.

Another negative secondary effect of bonus densities is that generous density bonuses can displace existing affordable housing by rewarding demolition or conversion leading to displacement of a substantial population of low income tenants in order to create a very few affordable units and generate greater density, higher rents, and more generous profit. The result can be a loss of affordable housing stock and significant displacement of people exacerbating an already tight supply and inflating area rents. A Los Angeles trial court has prohibited the use of density bonuses exceeding the allowable zoning density authorized by state law. Descriptions of the ruling are sparse but it might be limiting density bonuses to the explicit amounts authorized to be granted above zoning limits. A California court of appeals ruling has endorsed awarding density bonus units above the zoning and ordinance target. A prohibition on exceeding zoning density caps would be preempted by the state bonus density authorization. Los Angeles may have been awarding developers additional density in exchange for concessions.

Inclusionary zoning and fair share programs can act as exclusionary zoning: the efforts of fair share have not proven fair. An example is the development of racially isolated projects such as in Mount Laurel, New Jersey. In addition, just as affordable housing calls for a minimum quota for inclusion based on the regional need, such as 5 to 15% of neighborhood housing, there must be a ceiling quota for affordable housing. The problem of neighborhoods containing too many low income households is not simply the inability to sustain neighborhood shops and attract office and business investment, but the result of tipping, where the more affluent cease to be attracted to the neighborhood and commence to migrate to more affluent communities. It has long been understood that neighborhoods that attain a percentage of racial and ethnic minority group members have a tendency to discourage majority group members from moving in and encourage resident majority group members to migrate to other apparently stable communities. This tipping point, however, has never been quantified. Most experts would acknowledge that some neighborhoods, such as where housing subsidies are prevalent will resist turnover due to the attraction of the subsidies and that some majority-dominated neighborhoods might tip on the entry of a single or a few minority households. The question of whether the less affluent carry a tipping point has been researched and indicates that there exists a 15 to 20% threshold after which a neighborhood begins to shift to predominantly lower income households. . . .

A critical component of developing an adequate supply of affordable housing will be to decrease the size of living units. This should be part of an overall strategy to tax the overconsumption of housing. A tax on mansions, second homes, and excessively large dwellings should encourage the development of smaller dwelling units, discourage the waste of energy and materials used to construct large units, and generate revenues that can be used to subsidize housing and green retrofitting. Building codes should limit house and dwelling unit sizes and allow for variances in situations presenting a hardship. American consumption patterns of the affluent have generated an increase in the average house size and the change in a materialist culture often requires that a household contain one or more offices, exercise studio, entertainment center, master suite, and children's suites yielding a McMansion. House sizes should range in size to fit households with small 400 square foot units, 800 square foot two bedroom units, and 1200 square foot three-bedroom units. Communities should tax buildings or dwellings that exceed 400 square feet per occupant. The tax should be based on the model of a "gas guzzler" tax but be part of an annual real property tax scheme that would also establish incentives for the consumption of smaller, higher density units and discourage over-consumption.

Sustainable, affordable, as well as market rate housing calls for the mandatory use of green building codes. These prove to add no expense when the general practice is to use the green building systems and materials and tend to increase construction costs by 5% when contractors are not routinely using the materials and systems. State of the art mechanical, heating and cooling systems, insulation and to the extent feasible, power generation, organic roof, incentives for reuse of older buildings and incentives for multi-family higher density can maximize heating and cooling efficiency. Codes should also include reuse of water from rain for use by toilets and should retain surface water to return to the water table. Communities should also establish regular code review to assure prompt updates as technology improves. Significantly lower utility costs will make apartments more affordable and will more than compensate for any potential increase in construction costs.

Public utilities at the direction of public utility commissions should price energy progressively so that excessive use is charged at a higher rate and conservation rewarded with lower rates. Those buildings that are low density should be designed for central atriums, covered porches and natural ventilation so as to reduce the need for air conditioning. Portland is looking to greening at the neighborhood rather than the structure level, through an eco-district policy that will include the entire neighborhood and develop improvements such as centralized heating plants that will pipe hot water underground to multiple buildings, eliminating the need for chillers and boilers in individual buildings, and provide for rainwater reuse, with rainwater or greywater use in toilets or reuse within the neighborhood.

The United States Leadership in Energy and Environmental Design ("LEED"), established by the United States Green Building Council, provides the most commonly used way of determining whether a building is more or less "green" or "sustainable." Green building awards, however, mask the fact that the average green building generates the need to increase automobile use for commuters and those traveling to the building by 137%, suggesting that sustainability ratings should include the reduction of automobile use and the increase in more sustainable forms of transport. LEED awards better buildings with reduced energy use, better passive and sometimes active solar technology, recycled materials, and lowered water use have nevertheless been criticized for making limited improvements and carbon emissions reductions when the technology exists for far more significantly green materials and systems that can provide facades and roofs as solar generators and carbon sinks. Only about 1000 buildings have been certified since 2000. Despite the fact that some developers cherry-pick low-effort and low-cost LEED point strategies, e.g., installing bamboo flooring and bike racks, and that the cost of certification is relatively high (nearly $100,000), many developers are using the LEED checklist to build greener buildings without pursuing the costly certification, making the program somewhat successful. Unfortunately, one quarter of new buildings receiving LEED certification fail to save as much energy as their designs predicted and most do not track energy consumption once in use. LEED certification has also been criticized for not addressing affordable housing and that cost factors have ruled out energy efficiency for those of lower income and as developers fail to develop affordable housing, those in need travel further and aggravate sprawl.

Rather than emphasize new green architecture, development controls should require building reuse. Half the solid waste dumped into landfills in the United States is the result of building demolition. Taxes on demolition and landfill dumping and other incentives for rehabilitation and building reuse will dramatically cut carbon emissions as well as solid waste. One incentive to encourage compliance with green codes and retrofitting existing structures with sustainable materials and systems will be the taxation of non-green development. This tax might be implemented over time with an increasing amount and can be further encouraged through a program of tax credits, deductions, loans, or grants and below market loans for those on limited income. In addition to incentives for the reuse of older constructed buildings, codes should call for energy retrofit and provide incentives and utility-financed upgrades. Based on the gas guzzler tax model, the tax should focus on energy use, green systems such as heating, cooling, electricity, power source, and building materials such as insulation and windows. Utilities such as electric, water, and gas should be priced progressively so that excessive use is charged at a higher rate with rates increasing over time. Meters could inform the ratepayer of the costs and rates. . . .

The central path to the essential infrastructure of adequate affordable housing includes universal public transport integrated with land use encouraging transit-oriented development and car-free, European urban settlements in both cities and suburbs. Global warming, climate change, and the arrival of peak oil, at a time when the world's fossil fuel demand is reaching insatiable levels, coupled with the increasingly recognized failure of the twentieth century American urban model, requires a new more sustainable regeneration of neighborhoods and urban community design — one that generates improved access, opportunity, and quality of life. The inclusion of all workers, the poor, and the working poor into the fabric of our communities, by offering an adequate supply of affordable housing, constitutes a critical element of truly smart growth.

Notes and Comments

1. *Encouraging Transit-Oriented Development.* Should cities shift to transit-oriented development? If public transport can be extended to residential communities, how can such communities be protected from gentrification and expulsion by increasing rents? Massachusetts has established a voluntary program to reward municipalities that establish zoning districts encouraging affordable housing near public transportation and existing city and town centers or other desirable areas. Mass. Gen. Laws Ann. Ch. 40R §§1-14 (West. 2016). Cities and towns can qualify for up to $600,000 for adopting a district and $3000 for each building permit issued. Mass. Gen. Laws Ann. Ch. 40R §9 (West. 2016). *See* Robert Preer, Housing Deal Gets Popular: Towns Just Hope State Ponies Up Aid, Boston Globe (Sept. 2, 2007) at http://www.boston.com/news/local/articles/2007/09/02/housing_deal_gets_popular?mode=PF.

PART FIVE

THE USE OF LAND USE CONTROLS TO EFFECTUATE GOVERNMENT POLICY OBJECTIVES

13

Housing and Discrimination

A. INTRODUCTION

1. Zoning, Housing, and Discrimination

In one sense, zoning, as an institution, is all about discrimination. Some forms of zoning discrimination are generally regarded as benign or even advantageous. Zoning regulations may severely restrict development on dangerously steep slopes or in environmentally sensitive areas, but impose lesser restrictions on development elsewhere. A traditional function of zoning is to foster aggregation of compatible uses and to separate incompatible uses. In the past, however, zoning also has been used to accomplish the separation of people on the basis of both economic class and race. *See Buchanan v. Warley*, 245 U.S. 60 (1917) (invalidating racial zoning that restricted blocks according to permissible race of occupants). It is the latter type of discrimination that is the focus of this chapter.

America's suburbs were developed and first marketed with the approval of, and financial subsidies from, the federal government. Except for very upscale neighborhoods, subdivision sales were financially dependent on government-insured home loans administered by the Federal Housing Administration and the Veterans Administration. Those programs, however, originally were available only for subdivisions that were subject to racially restrictive covenants excluding all but single race occupants. Federal Housing Administration, Underwriting Manual ¶ 935 (1938) (¶ 980 contained a model racial restrictive covenant). *See* Robert C. Weaver, The Negro Ghetto 152-53, 217-222 (1948) (FHA practice of approving segregated subdivisions); James A. Kushner, Apartheid in America 16-22 (1980), reprinted as James A. Kushner, Apartheid in America: An Historical and Legal Analysis of Contemporary Racial Residential Segregation in the United States, 22 How. L.J.

547, 563-569 (1979) (hereinafter cited as Apartheid). *See also* Deborah Kenn, Institutionalized Legal Racism: Housing Segregation and Beyond, 11 B. U. Pub. Int. L. (2001); John Kimble, Insuring Inequality: The Role of the Federal Housing Administration in the Urban Ghettoization of African Americans, 32 Law & Soc. Inquiry 399 (2007) (describing extensive FHA role in community racial segregation).

Although civil rights laws today prohibit racial and certain other forms of discrimination, housing bias appears to be institutional. In 1979, a national study funded by the U.S. Department of Housing and Urban Development disclosed that two million acts of housing discrimination were perpetrated annually. Ronald E. Wienk et al., U.S. Dept. of Hous. & Urban Dev., Measuring Racial Discrimination in American Housing Markets (1979). In addition to racial discrimination, property owners and government officials may discriminate against the disabled, religious minorities, families with children, the homeless, and on the basis of sexual orientation.

2. Equal Protection in the Land Use Context

The chapter begins with an examination of how the Equal Protection Clause of the Fourteenth Amendment applies in the land use context. In *Washington v. Davis,* 426 U.S. 229 (1976), the Court restricted the use of the Equal Protection Clause as a tool for challenging racial discrimination by requiring a plaintiff to establish that the defendant's action was intentionally designed to discriminate on the basis of race or for some other improper motive. The first case that you will read, *Village of Arlington Heights v. Metro. Hous. Dev. Corp.,* 429 U.S. 252 (1977) (*Arlington I*), addresses how litigants can prove the intent required by *Washington* in the context of zoning. If discriminatory intent can be established, the government policy can be successfully defended against an Equal Protection Clause challenge only in rare, compelling circumstances.

If the discrimination at issue is not based on race or some other suspect classification, the Supreme Court has ruled that the government action should be upheld so long as it is rationally related to a legitimate public purpose. Applying this deferential test, the Court endorsed traditional family zoning in *Village of Belle Terre v. Boraas,* 416 U.S. 1 (1974). On the other hand, while still applying a deferential standard, the Court in *Moore v. City of East Cleveland,* 431 U.S. 494 (1977), struck down a regulation that prohibited members of an extended biological family from living together under one roof. Finally, in *City of Cleburne v. Cleburne Living Ctr., Inc.,* 473 U.S. 432 (1985), the Court, again applying a deferential standard, struck down a regulation of housing for the disabled on the ground that it was irrational. All three of these important cases are excerpted below.

3. Title VIII

The federal Fair Housing Act, passed in 1968 and popularly referred to as "Title VIII" (42 U.S.C. §§3601-3631 (2006)), has become the most effective remedy against discrimination in housing. Most notably, Title VIII allows a violation to be based on a practice or policy that carries a discriminatory impact. *See Inclusive Cmtys. v. Texas*

Dept. of Hous. and Cmty. Affairs, 135 S. Ct. 2507 (2015). In 1988, the statute was expanded to extend protection to the disabled and to families with children.

B. THE FOURTEENTH AMENDMENT

The fundamental source of constitutional equality doctrine is the Fourteenth Amendment. Minorities subjected to unequal treatment through government land use decisions commonly invoke this constitutional provision to seek relief. The principal question that the invocation of this amendment poses is: What does a plaintiff have to prove in order to prevail under equal protection theory?

The Court commonly enforces constitutional protections based on the effects of government actions, such as in the case of the Takings Clause or the Commerce Clause. Initially, the Court appeared to adopt a similar approach in applying the Equal Protection Clause. *See Palmer v. Thompson*, 403 U.S. 217, 224-25 (1971).

However, the Supreme Court subsequently established that a plaintiff must show intent to prove a violation of the Equal Protection Clause. The following case, *Arlington Heights*, builds on the model of intentional discrimination and describes how a prima facie case of discrimination can be assembled using circumstantial evidence.

■ VILLAGE OF ARLINGTON HEIGHTS v. METROPOLITAN HOUSING DEVELOPMENT CORP.
429 U.S. 252 (1977)

Justice POWELL delivered the opinion of the Court. . . .

Arlington Heights is a suburb of Chicago, located about 26 miles northwest of the downtown Loop area. Most of the land in Arlington Heights is zoned for detached single-family homes, and this is in fact the prevailing land use. The Village experienced substantial growth during the 1960s, but, like other communities in northwest Cook County, its population of racial minority groups remained quite low. According to the 1970 census, only 27 of the Village's 64,000 residents were black.

The Clerics of St. Viator, a religious order (Order), own an 80-acre parcel just east of the center of Arlington Heights. Part of the site is occupied by the Viatorian high school, and part by the Order's three-story novitiate building, which houses dormitories and a Montessori school. Much of the site, however, remains vacant. Since 1959, when the Village first adopted a zoning ordinance, all the land surrounding the Viatorian property has been zoned R-3, a single-family specification with relatively small minimum lot-size requirements. On three sides of the Viatorian land there are single-family homes just across a street; to the east the Viatorian property directly adjoins the backyards of other single-family homes.

The Order decided in 1970 to devote some of its land to low- and moderate-income housing. Investigation revealed that the most expeditious way to build such housing was to work through a nonprofit developer experienced in the use of federal housing subsidies under §236 of the National Housing Act. MHDC is such a developer. . . .

After some negotiation, MHDC and the Order entered into a 99-year lease and an accompanying agreement of sale covering a 15-acre site in the southeast corner of the Viatorian property. MHDC became the lessee immediately, but the sale agreement was contingent upon MHDC's securing zoning clearances from the Village and §236 housing assistance from the Federal Government. If MHDC proved unsuccessful in securing either, both the lease and the contract of sale would lapse. The agreement established a bargain purchase price of $300,000, low enough to comply with federal limitations governing land-acquisition costs for §236 housing.

MHDC engaged an architect and proceeded with the project, to be known as Lincoln Green. The plans called for 20 two-story buildings with a total of 190 units, each unit having its own private entrance from the outside. One hundred of the units would have a single bedroom, thought likely to attract elderly citizens. The remainder would have two, three, or four bedrooms. A large portion of the site would remain open, with shrubs and trees to screen the homes abutting the property to the east.

The planned development did not conform to the Village's zoning ordinance and could not be built unless Arlington Heights rezoned the parcel to R-5, its multiple-family housing classification. Accordingly, MHDC filed with the Village Plan Commission a petition for rezoning, accompanied by supporting materials describing the development and specifying that it would be subsidized under §236. The materials made clear that one requirement under §236 is an affirmative marketing plan designed to assure that a subsidized development is racially integrated. MHDC also submitted studies demonstrating the need for housing of this type and analyzing the probable impact of the development. To prepare for the hearings before the Plan Commission and to assure compliance with the Village building code, fire regulations, and related requirements, MHDC consulted with the Village staff for preliminary review of the development. The parties have stipulated that every change recommended during such consultations was incorporated into the plans.

During the spring of 1971, the Plan Commission considered the proposal at a series of three public meetings, which drew large crowds. Although many of those attending were quite vocal and demonstrative in opposition to Lincoln Green, a number of individuals and representatives of community groups spoke in support of rezoning. Some of the comments, both from opponents and supporters, addressed what was referred to as the "social issue" — the desirability or undesirability of introducing at this location in Arlington Heights low- and moderate-income housing, housing that would probably be racially integrated.

Many of the opponents, however, focused on the zoning aspects of the petition, stressing two arguments. First, the area always had been zoned single-family, and the neighboring citizens had built or purchased there in reliance on that classification. Rezoning threatened to cause a measurable drop in property value for neighboring sites. Second, the Village's apartment policy, adopted by the Village Board in 1962 and amended in 1970, called for R-5 zoning primarily to serve as a buffer between single-family development and land uses thought incompatible, such as commercial or manufacturing districts. Lincoln Green did not meet this requirement, as it adjoined no commercial or manufacturing district.

At the close of the third meeting, the Plan Commission adopted a motion to recommend to the Village's Board of Trustees that it deny the request. The motion stated: "While the need for low and moderate income housing may exist in Arlington Heights or its environs, the Plan Commission would be derelict in recommending it at the proposed location." Two members voted against the motion and submitted a minority report, stressing that in their view the change to accommodate Lincoln Green represented "good zoning." The Village Board met on September 28, 1971, to consider MHDC's request and the recommendation of the Plan Commission. After a public hearing, the Board denied the rezoning by a 6-1 vote. . . .

Our decision last Term in *Washington v. Davis*, 426 U.S. 229 (1976), made it clear that official action will not be held unconstitutional solely because it results in a racially disproportionate impact. "Disproportionate impact is not irrelevant, but it is not the sole touchstone of an invidious racial discrimination." Proof of racially discriminatory intent or purpose is required to show a violation of the Equal Protection Clause. Although some contrary indications may be drawn from some of our cases, the holding in *Davis* reaffirmed a principle well established in a variety of contexts.

Davis does not require a plaintiff to prove that the challenged action rested solely on racially discriminatory purposes. Rarely can it be said that a legislature or administrative body operating under a broad mandate made a decision motivated solely by a single concern, or even that a particular purpose was the "dominant" or "primary" one. In fact, it is because legislators and administrators are properly concerned with balancing numerous competing considerations that courts refrain from reviewing the merits of their decisions, absent a showing of arbitrariness or irrationality. But racial discrimination is not just another competing consideration. When there is a proof that a discriminatory purpose has been a motivating factor in the decision, this judicial deference is no longer justified.

Determining whether invidious discriminatory purpose was a motivating factor demands a sensitive inquiry into such circumstantial and direct evidence of intent as may be available. The impact of the official action — whether it "bears more heavily on one race than another," may provide an important starting point. Sometimes a clear pattern, unexplainable on grounds other than race, emerges from the effect of the state action even when the governing legislation appears neutral on its face. The evidentiary inquiry is then relatively easy. . . .

The historical background of the decision is one evidentiary source, particularly if it reveals a series of official actions taken for invidious purposes. The specific sequence of events leading up to the challenged decision also may shed some light on the decision maker's purposes. For example, if the property involved here always had been zoned R-5 but suddenly was changed to R-3 when the town learned of MHDC's plans to erect integrated housing,[16] we would have a far different case. Departures from the normal procedural sequence also might afford evidence that improper purposes are playing a role. Substantive departures too may be relevant, particularly if the factors usually considered important by the decision maker

16. *See, e.g., Progress Development Corp. v. Mitchell*, 286 F. 2d 222 (7th Cir. 1961) (park board allegedly condemned plaintiffs' land for a park upon learning that the homes plaintiffs were erecting there would be sold under a marketing plan designed to assure integration); *Kennedy Park Homes Assn. v. City of Lackawanna*, 436 F. 2d 108 (2d Cir. 1970) (town declared moratorium on new subdivisions and rezoned area for parkland shortly after learning of plaintiffs' plans to build low-income housing). . . .

strongly favor a decision contrary to the one reached.[17] The legislative or administrative history may be highly relevant, especially where there are contemporary statements by members of the decision making body, minutes of its meetings, or reports. In some extraordinary instances the members might be called to the stand at trial to testify concerning the purpose of the official action, although even then such testimony frequently will be barred by privilege.

The foregoing summary identifies, without purporting to be exhaustive, subjects of proper inquiry in determining whether racially discriminatory intent existed. With these in mind, we now address the case before us.

This case was tried in the District Court and reviewed in the Court of Appeals before our decision in *Washington v. Davis, supra.* The respondents proceeded on the erroneous theory that the Village's refusal to rezone carried a racially discriminatory effect and was, without more, unconstitutional. But both courts below understood that at least part of their function was to examine the purpose underlying the decision. In making its findings on this issue, the District Court noted that some of the opponents of Lincoln Green who spoke at the various hearings might have been motivated by opposition to minority groups. The court held, however, that the evidence "does not warrant the conclusion that this motivated the defendants."

On appeal the Court of Appeals focused primarily on respondents' claim that the Village's buffer policy had not been consistently applied and was being invoked with a strictness here that could only demonstrate some other underlying motive. The court concluded that the buffer policy, though not always applied with perfect consistency, had on several occasions formed the basis for the Board's decision to deny other rezoning proposals. "The evidence does not necessitate a finding that Arlington Heights administered this policy in a discriminatory manner." The Court of Appeals therefore approved the District Court's findings concerning the Village's purposes in denying rezoning to MHDC.

We also have reviewed the evidence. The impact of the Village's decision does arguably bear more heavily on racial minorities. Minorities constitute 18% of the Chicago area population, and 40% of the income groups said to be eligible for Lincoln Green. But there is little about the sequence of events leading up to the decision that would spark suspicion. The area around the Viatorian property has been zoned R-3 since 1959, the year when Arlington Heights first adopted a zoning map. Single-family homes surround the 80-acre site, and the Village is undeniably committed to single-family homes as its dominant residential land use. The rezoning request progressed according to the usual procedures. The Plan Commission even scheduled two additional hearings, at least in part to accommodate MHDC and permit it to supplement its presentation with answers to questions generated at the first hearing.

The statements by the Plan Commission and Village Board members, as reflected in the official minutes, focused almost exclusively on the zoning aspects of the MHDC petition, and the zoning factors on which they relied are not novel

17. *See Dailey v. City of Lawton,* 425 F. 2d 1037 (10th Cir. 1970). The plaintiffs in *Dailey* planned to build low-income housing on the site of a former school that they had purchased. The city refused to rezone the land from PF, its public facilities classification, to R-4, high-density residential. All the surrounding area was zoned R-4, and both the present and the former planning director for the city testified that there was no reason "from a zoning standpoint" why the land should not be classified R-4. Based on this and other evidence, the Court of Appeals ruled that "the record sustains the [District Court's] holding of racial motivation and of arbitrary and unreasonable action."

criteria in the Village's rezoning decisions. There is no reason to doubt that there has been reliance by some neighboring property owners on the maintenance of single-family zoning in the vicinity. The Village originally adopted its buffer policy long before MHDC entered the picture and has applied the policy too consistently for us to infer discriminatory purpose from its application in this case. Finally, MHDC called one member of the Village Board to the stand at trial. Nothing in her testimony supports an inference of invidious purpose.

In sum, the evidence does not warrant overturning the concurrent findings of both courts below. Respondents simply failed to carry their burden of proving that discriminatory purpose was a motivating factor in the Village's decision.[21]

Notes and Comments

1. *Practice and Discriminatory Impact.* What was the practice that was alleged to carry a discriminatory impact? Would the failure to consistently adhere to a land use policy establish a case? What percentage of inconsistency would reveal that application of the policy was pretextual? What if the city has a number of objections to a project proposal, including inadequate parking, overcrowded schools, and the likely influx of African Americans? Would *Arlington Heights* provide a remedy for the disappointed developer? Would race be a motivating factor, if not necessarily *the* motivating factor?

2. *Justifying Discrimination.* Had the prima facie case been established in *Arlington Heights*, the village would have had to defend its policy, practice, or action as necessary to serve a compelling state interest. In addition, under such strict scrutiny the defendant must prove the difficult proposition that the state's interest could not be served by less discriminatory alternatives. *Johnson v. California*, 543 U.S. 499 (2005); *Attorney Gen. of N.Y. v. Soto-Lopez*, 476 U.S. 898 (1986).

3. *The State Action Limitation.* The Fourteenth Amendment is limited to state action. *The Civil Rights Cases*, 109 U.S. 3 (1883). The Court, however, has established some exceptions to the rule that the Fourteenth Amendment reaches only government discrimination, such as where a private defendant: (1) has acted together with a state official or a state agency (*Lugar v. Edmundson Oil Co.*, 457 U.S. 922 (1982) (participation by courts in prejudgment attachment)); (2) has a partnership arrangement with a government entity (*Burton v. Wilmington Parking Auth.*, 365 U.S. 715 (1961) (rental to segregated restaurant in public parking garage)); (3) is carrying out a governmental function, one that traditionally has been carried out exclusively by states or local governments (*Marsh v. Alabama*, 326 U.S. 501 (1946) (company town)); or (4) is intertwined with public officials in the enforcement of governmental policy (*Brentwood Acad. v. Tenn. Secondary Sch. Athletic Ass'n*, 531 U.S. 288 (2001) (state athletic association composed of public and private school officials imposed and enforced athletic standards)).

---

21. Proof that the decision by the Village was motivated in part by a racially discriminatory purpose would not necessarily have required invalidation of the challenged decision. Such proof would, however, have shifted to the Village the burden of establishing that the same decision would have resulted even had the impermissible purpose not been considered. If this were established, the complaining party in a case of this kind no longer fairly could attribute the injury complained of to improper consideration of a discriminatory purpose. In such circumstances, there would be no justification for judicial interference with the challenged decision. But in this case respondents failed to make the required threshold showing.

Most land development regulations directly involve the state government or a unit of local government. What forms might a privatized land use regulatory scheme take? Could the use of development agreements, contracts, and private covenants immunize development from the Fourteenth Amendment? *Compare Pitt v. Pine Valley Golf Club*, 695 F. Supp. 788 (D.N.J. 1988) (a private golf club membership restriction was state action as it operated as a zoning ordinance under a public function theory) *with Linn Valley Lakes Property Owners Ass'n v. Brockway*, 824 P.2d 948 (Kan. 1992) (enforcement of private restrictive covenant prohibiting placement of signs on property was not improper state action).

4. *The Referendum and Discrimination.* Could a zoning process that includes a mandatory referendum for zone changes violate equal protection? In *City of Cuyahoga Falls v. Buckeye Cmty. Found.*, 538 U.S. 188 (2003), the Court rejected a challenge to a vote pursuant to a referendum that repealed a zoning authorization for a low-income housing project. The city charter established the referendum process, and the process was not created for a discriminatory purpose. Based on the premise that the Fourteenth Amendment requires involvement of public officials in the challenged government action, the Court ruled that the alleged discriminatory animus of some voters could not support a claim of discrimination by the city.

5. *Segregation and Professional Responsibility.* You should consider the role of attorneys in creating housing segregation. Lawyers' arguments and judges' decisions have helped perpetuate segregation and discrimination in housing. Robert Drinan, Untying the White Noose, 94 Yale L. J. 435, 441-443 (1984). The late Father Drinan would have imposed a canon that lawyers should not engage in any transaction directly or indirectly involving racial discrimination.

Should attorneys, like city planners, have ethical obligations not to advocate programs or projects that are discriminatory, produce segregated neighborhoods, or have adverse consequences for the poor? Would recognition of such an obligation conflict with the principle that everyone is entitled to counsel, not simply when charged with a crime but to support or represent all interests?

6. *Municipal Services Discrimination.* In *Hawkins v. Town of Shaw*, 437 F.2d 1286 (5th Cir. 1971), *aff'd en banc per curiam*, 461 F.2d 1171 (5th Cir. 1972), the Fifth Circuit encountered a stark disparity between the white community of Shaw in the Mississippi Delta and the African-American neighborhoods on the "other side of the tracks." Street paving, sewers, mercury vapor street lighting, and surface water drainage were almost nonexistent in the black community while nearly universal in the white neighborhoods. The city advanced pretextual explanations for the disparity. The Fifth Circuit found a violation of the Equal Protection Clause, but under a theory of disparate effects later rejected by *Arlington Heights*.

How does *Arlington Heights* affect the *Hawkins* form of litigation strategy? Would it be possible to challenge municipal services under the Fair Housing Act, thereby applying an effects test for the *prima facie* case rather than requiring proof of intent?

The Second Circuit has ruled that a disparity in the conditions of New York City's urban parks did not prove discrimination, on the theory that it is not the results but the inputs that must be equal. The court found that lower use levels, higher maintenance costs, and vandalism in minority area parks explained condition disparities. The court accepted the city's argument that greater services and programs were provided in the white affluent areas based on a formula reflecting the past level of use. *Beal v. Lindsay*, 468 F.2d 287 (2d Cir. 1972).

Funding based on levels of use exacerbates discrimination as facilities in poor repair generate lower use statistics and a reduced budget, while heavily used facilities receive increased funding. Consider whether any Title VI (prohibiting discrimination in federally assisted programs) or Title VIII (Fair Housing Act) strategies could be used? Would New York's park funding scheme withstand an "impacts" scrutiny? *See also* Jon Izak Monger, Note, Thirsting for Equal Protection: The Legal Implications of Municipal Water Access in *Kennedy v. City of Zanesville* and the Need for Federal Oversight of Governments Practicing Unlawful Race Discrimination, 59 Cath. U. L. Rev. 587 (2010) (describing litigation successfully challenging denial of water to a black community and advocating for greater federal oversight of infrastructure bias).

C. NONTRADITIONAL LIVING ARRANGEMENTS

Limiting the occupancy of homes based on the relationships among the occupants raises the specter of zoning that interferes with fundamental notions of privacy, personal autonomy, and freedom of association. Limiting the occupancy of homes based on the characteristics on the occupants (other than race or other suspect classifications, which call for strict scrutiny) raises concerns about arbitrary and irrational treatment. The following cases address communal living arrangements and help define some of the constitutional limits on the deferential judicial review model endorsed in *Village of Euclid v. Ambler Realty*.

■ VILLAGE OF BELLE TERRE v. BORAAS
416 U.S. 1 (1974)

Justice DOUGLAS delivered the opinion of the Court.

Belle Terre is a village on Long Island's north shore of about 220 homes inhabited by 700 people. Its total land area is less than one square mile. It has restricted land use to one-family dwellings excluding lodging houses, boarding houses, fraternity houses, or multiple-dwelling houses. The word "family" as used in the ordinance means, "[o]ne or more persons related by blood, adoption, or marriage, living and cooking together as a single housekeeping unit, exclusive of household servants. A number of persons but not exceeding two (2) living and cooking together as a single housekeeping unit though not related by blood, adoption, or marriage shall be deemed to constitute a family."

Appellees the Dickmans are owners of a house in the village and leased it in December 1971 for a term of 18 months to Michael Truman. Later Bruce Boraas became a colessee. Then Anne Parish moved into the house along with three others. These six are students at nearby State University at Stony Brook and none is related to the other by blood, adoption, or marriage. When the village served the Dickmans with an "Order to Remedy Violations" of the ordinance, the owners plus three tenants thereupon brought this action under 42 U.S.C. §1983 for an injunction and a judgment declaring the ordinance unconstitutional. . . .

The present ordinance is challenged on several grounds: that it interferes with a person's right to travel; that it interferes with the right to migrate to and settle within a State; that it bars people who are uncongenial to the present residents; that it expresses the social preferences of the residents for groups that will be congenial to them; that social homogeneity is not a legitimate interest of government; that the restriction of those whom the neighbors do not like trenches on the newcomers' rights of privacy; that it is of no rightful concern to villagers whether the residents are married or unmarried; that the ordinance is antithetical to the Nation's experience, ideology, and self-perception as an open, egalitarian, and integrated society.

We find none of these reasons in the record before us. It is not aimed at transients. It involves no procedural disparity inflicted on some but not on others. . . . It involves no "fundamental" right guaranteed by the Constitution. . . . We deal with economic and social legislation where legislatures have historically drawn lines which we respect against the charge of violation of the Equal Protection Clause if the law be "'reasonable, not arbitrary'" and bears "a rational relationship to a [permissible] state objective." It is said, however, that if two unmarried people can constitute a "family," there is no reason why three or four may not. But every line drawn by a legislature leaves some out that might well have been included. That exercise of discretion, however, is a legislative, not a judicial, function.

It is said that the Belle Terre ordinance reeks with an animosity to unmarried couples who live together. There is no evidence to support it; and the provision of the ordinance bringing within the definition of a "family" two unmarried people belies the charge. The ordinance places no ban on other forms of association, for a "family" may, so far as the ordinance is concerned, entertain whomever it likes. The regimes of boarding houses, fraternity houses, and the like present urban problems. More people occupy a given space; more cars rather continuously pass by; more cars are parked; noise travels with crowds.

A quiet place where yards are wide, people few, and motor vehicles restricted are legitimate guidelines in a land-use project addressed to family needs. This goal is a permissible one within *Berman v. Parker*. The police power is not confined to elimination of filth, stench, and unhealthy places. It is ample to lay out zones where family values, youth values, and the blessings of quiet seclusion and clean air make the area a sanctuary for people. . . .

Justice MARSHALL, dissenting. . . .

The instant ordinance discriminates on the basis of . . . a personal lifestyle choice as to household companions. It permits any number of persons related by blood or marriage, be it two or twenty, to live in a single household, but it limits to two the number of unrelated persons bound by profession, love, friendship, religious or political affiliation, or mere economics who can occupy a single home. Belle Terre imposes upon those who deviate from the community norm in their choice of living companions significantly greater restrictions than are applied to residential groups who are related by blood or marriage, and compose the established order within the community. The village has, in effect, acted to fence out those individuals whose choice of lifestyle differs from that of its current residents. . . .

The ordinance imposes no restriction whatsoever on the number of persons who may live in a house, as long as they are related by marital or sanguinary bonds —

presumably no matter how distant their relationship. Nor does the ordinance restrict the number of income earners who may contribute to rent in such a household, or the number of automobiles that may be maintained by its occupants. In that sense the ordinance is underinclusive. On the other hand, the statute restricts the number of unrelated persons who may live in a home to no more than two. It would therefore prevent three unrelated people from occupying a dwelling even if among them they had but one income and no vehicles. While an extended family of a dozen or more might live in a small bungalow, three elderly and retired persons could not occupy the large manor house next door. Thus the statute is also grossly over-inclusive to accomplish its intended purposes. . . .

A few years after the *Boraas* decision, the Supreme Court ruled that a very similar — though arguably distinguishable — local government restriction on group living was unconstitutional.

■ MOORE v. CITY OF EAST CLEVELAND
431 U.S. 494 (1977)

Justice POWELL announced the judgment of the Court, and delivered an opinion joined by three other justices

East Cleveland's housing ordinance, like many throughout the country, limits occupancy of a dwelling unit to members of a single family. But the ordinance contains an unusual and complicated definitional section that recognizes as a "family" only a few categories of related individuals. Because her family, living together in her home, fits none of those categories, appellant stands convicted of a criminal offense. The question in this case is whether the ordinance violates the Due Process Clause of the Fourteenth Amendment.[3]

I

Appellant, Mrs. Inez Moore, lives in her East Cleveland home together with her son, Dale Moore Sr., and her two grandsons, Dale, Jr., and John Moore, Jr. The two boys are first cousins rather than brothers; we are told that John came to live with his grandmother and with the elder and younger Dale Moores after his mother's death.

In early 1973, Mrs. Moore received a notice of violation from the city, stating that John was an "illegal occupant" and directing her to comply with the ordinance. When she failed to remove him from her home, the city filed a criminal charge. Mrs. Moore moved to dismiss, claiming that the ordinance was constitutionally invalid on its face. Her motion was overruled, and upon conviction she was sentenced to five days in jail and a $25 fine. The Ohio Court of Appeals affirmed after giving full consideration to her constitutional claims, and the Ohio Supreme Court denied review.

---

3. Appellant also claims that the ordinance contravenes the Equal Protection Clause, but it is not necessary for us to reach that contention.

II

The city argues that our decision in *Village of Belle Terre v. Boraas*, 416 U.S. 1 (1974), requires us to sustain the ordinance attacked here. Belle Terre, like East Cleveland, imposed limits on the types of groups that could occupy a single dwelling unit. Applying the constitutional standard announced in this Court's leading land-use case, *Euclid v. Ambler Realty Co.*, 272 U.S. 365 (1926), we sustained the Belle Terre ordinance on the ground that it bore a rational relationship to permissible state objectives.

But one overriding factor sets this case apart from *Belle Terre*. The ordinance there affected only unrelated individuals. It expressly allowed all who were related by "blood, adoption, or marriage" to live together, and in sustaining the ordinance we were careful to note that it promoted "family needs" and "family values." East Cleveland, in contrast, has chosen to regulate the occupancy of its housing by slicing deeply into the family itself. This is no mere incidental result of the ordinance. On its face it selects certain categories of relatives who may live together and declares that others may not. In particular, it makes a crime of a grandmother's choice to live with her grandson in circumstances like those presented here.

When a city undertakes such intrusive regulation of the family, neither *Belle Terre* nor *Euclid* governs; the usual judicial deference to the legislature is inappropriate. "This Court has long recognized that freedom of personal choice in matters of marriage and family life is one of the liberties protected by the Due Process Clause of the Fourteenth Amendment." A host of cases . . . have consistently acknowledged a "private realm of family life which the state cannot enter." Of course, the family is not beyond regulation. But when the government intrudes on choices concerning family living arrangements, this Court must examine carefully the importance of the governmental interests advanced and the extent to which they are served by the challenged regulation.

When thus examined, this ordinance cannot survive. The city seeks to justify it as a means of preventing overcrowding, minimizing traffic and parking congestion, and avoiding an undue financial burden on East Cleveland's school system. Although these are legitimate goals, the ordinance before us serves them marginally, at best.[7] For example, the ordinance permits any family consisting only of husband, wife, and unmarried children to live together, even if the family contains a half dozen licensed drivers, each with his or her own car. At the same time it forbids an adult brother and sister to share a household, even if both faithfully use public transportation. The ordinance would permit a grandmother to live with a single dependent son and children, even if his school-age children number a dozen, yet it forces Mrs. Moore to find another dwelling for her grandson John, simply because of the presence of his uncle and cousin in the same household. We need not labor the point. Section 1341.08 has but a tenuous relation to alleviation of the conditions mentioned by the city. . . .

Reversed.

Justice BRENNAN concurring, joined by Justice MARSHALL.

---

7. It is significant that East Cleveland has another ordinance specifically addressed to the problem of overcrowding. Section 1351.03 limits population density directly, tying the maximum permissible occupancy of a dwelling to the habitable floor area. Even if John Jr. and his father both remain in Mrs. Moore's household, the family stays well within these limits.

I join the plurality's opinion. I agree that the Constitution is not powerless to prevent East Cleveland from prosecuting as a criminal and jailing a 63-year-old grandmother for refusing to expel from her home her now 10-year-old grandson who has lived with her and been brought up by her since his mother's death when he was less than a year old. I do not question that a municipality may constitutionally zone to alleviate noise and traffic congestion and to prevent overcrowded and unsafe living conditions, in short to enact reasonable land-use restrictions in furtherance of the legitimate objectives East Cleveland claims for its ordinance. But the zoning power is not a license for local communities to enact senseless and arbitrary restrictions which cut deeply into private areas of protected family life. East Cleveland may not constitutionally define "family" as essentially confined to parents and the parents' own children. The plurality's opinion conclusively demonstrates that classifying family patterns in this eccentric way is not a rational means of achieving the ends East Cleveland claims for its ordinance, and further that the ordinance unconstitutionally abridges the "freedom of personal choice in matters of . . . family life (that) is one of the liberties protected by the Due Process Clause of the Fourteenth Amendment." I write only to underscore the cultural myopia of the arbitrary boundary drawn by the East Cleveland ordinance in the light of the tradition of the American home that has been a feature of our society since our beginning as a Nation the "tradition" in the plurality's words, "of uncles, aunts, cousins, and especially grandparents sharing a household along with parents and children . . . ." The line drawn by this ordinance displays a depressing insensitivity toward the economic and emotional needs of a very large part of our society.

Chief Justice Burger, dissenting.

It is unnecessary for me to reach the difficult constitutional issue this case presents. Appellant's deliberate refusal to use a plainly adequate administrative remedy provided by the city should foreclose her from pressing in this Court any constitutional objections to the city's zoning ordinance. Considerations of federalism and comity, as well as the finite capacity of federal courts, support this position. In courts, as in hospitals, two bodies cannot occupy the same space at the same time; when any case comes here which could have been disposed of long ago at the local level, it takes the place that might well have been given to some other case in which there was no alternative remedy.

Justice Stewart dissenting, joined by Justice Rehnquist.

In *Village of Belle Terre v. Boraas,* the Court considered a New York village ordinance that restricted land use within the village to single-family dwellings. That ordinance defined "family" to include all persons related by blood, adoption, or marriage who lived and cooked together as a single-housekeeping unit; it forbade occupancy by any group of three or more persons who were not so related. We held that the ordinance was a valid effort by the village government to promote the general community welfare, and that it did not violate the Fourteenth Amendment or infringe any other rights or freedoms protected by the Constitution.

The present case brings before us a similar ordinance of East Cleveland, Ohio, one that also limits the occupancy of any dwelling unit to a single family, but that defines "family" to include only certain combinations of blood relatives. The question presented, as I view it, is whether the decision in *Belle Terre* is controlling, or whether the Constitution compels a different result because East Cleveland's definition of "family" is more restrictive than that before us in the *Belle Terre* case. . . .

In my view, the appellant's claim that the ordinance in question invades constitutionally protected rights of association and privacy is in large part answered by the *Belle Terre* decision. The argument was made there that a municipality could not zone its land exclusively for single-family occupancy because to do so would interfere with protected rights of privacy or association. We rejected this contention, and held that the ordinance at issue "involve(d) no 'fundamental' right guaranteed by the Constitution, such as . . . the right of association . . . or any rights of privacy."

The *Belle Terre* decision thus disposes of the appellant's contentions to the extent they focus not on her blood relationships with her sons and grandsons but on more general notions about the "privacy of the home." Her suggestion that every person has a constitutional right permanently to share his residence with whomever he pleases, and that such choices are "beyond the province of legitimate governmental intrusion," amounts to the same argument that was made and found unpersuasive in *Belle Terre.*

To be sure, the ordinance involved in *Belle Terre* did not prevent blood relatives from occupying the same dwelling, and the Court's decision in that case does not, therefore, foreclose the appellant's arguments based specifically on the ties of kinship present in this case. Nonetheless, I would hold . . . that the existence of those ties does not elevate either the appellant's claim of associational freedom or her claim of privacy to a level invoking constitutional protection.

Justice WHITE, dissenting.

The Fourteenth Amendment forbids any State to "deprive any person of life, liberty, or property, without due process of law," or to "deny to any person within its jurisdiction the equal protection of the laws." Both provisions are invoked in this case in an attempt to invalidate a city zoning ordinance.

I

[Justice White argued for rejecting the Due Process claim, stating,] that the Court has ample precedent for the creation of new constitutional rights should not lead it to repeat the process at will. The Judiciary, including this Court is the most vulnerable and comes nearest to illegitimacy when it deals with judge-made constitutional law having little or no cognizable roots in the language or even the design of the Constitution. Realizing that the present construction of the Due Process Clause represents a major judicial gloss on its terms, as well as on the anticipation of the Framers, and that much of the underpinning for the broad, substantive application of the Clause disappeared in the conflict between the Executive and the Judiciary in the 1930's and 1940's, the Court should be extremely reluctant to breathe still further substantive content into the Due Process Clause so as to strike down legislation adopted by a State or city to promote its welfare. Whenever the Judiciary does so, it unavoidably pre-empts for itself another part of the governance of the country without express constitutional authority. . . .

Mrs. Moore's interest in having the offspring of more than one dependent son live with her qualifies as a liberty protected by the Due Process Clause; but, because of the nature of that particular interest, the demands of the Clause are satisfied once the Court is assured that the challenged proscription is the product of a duly enacted or promulgated statute, ordinance, or regulation and that it is not wholly lacking in purpose or utility. That under this ordinance any number of unmarried children may reside with their mother and that this number might be as destructive of neighborhood values as one or more additional grandchildren is just another argument that children and grandchildren may not constitutionally be distinguished by a local zoning ordinance.

That argument remains unpersuasive to me. Here the head of the household may house himself or herself and spouse, their parents, and any number of their unmarried children. A fourth generation may be represented by only one set of grandchildren and then only if born to a dependent child. The ordinance challenged by appellant prevents her from living with both sets of grandchildren only in East Cleveland, an area with a radius of three miles and a population of 40,000. The ordinance thus denies appellant the opportunity to live with all her grandchildren in this particular suburb; she is free to do so in other parts of the Cleveland metropolitan area. If there is power to maintain the character of a single-family neighborhood, as there surely is, some limit must be placed on the reach of the "family." Had it been our task to legislate, we might have approached the problem in a different manner than did the drafters of this ordinance; but I have no trouble in concluding that the normal goals of zoning regulation are present here and that the ordinance serves these goals by limiting, in identifiable circumstances, the number of people who can occupy a single household. The ordinance does not violate the Due Process Clause . . . .

IV

For very similar reasons, the equal protection claim must fail, since it is not to be judged by the strict scrutiny standard employed when a fundamental interest or suspect classification is involved. . . . Rather, it is the generally applicable standard . . . :

> The constitutional safeguard (of the Equal Protection Clause) is offended only if the classification rests on grounds wholly irrelevant to the achievement of the State's objective. State legislatures are presumed to have acted within their constitutional power despite the fact that, in practice, their laws result in some inequality. A statutory discrimination will not be set aside if any state of facts reasonably may be conceived to justify it. . . .

On this basis, as already indicated, I have no trouble in discerning a rational justification for an ordinance that permits the head of a household to house one, but not two, dependent sons and their children.

Notes and Comments

1. Belle Terre *and* Moore. Is the outcome in *Belle Terre* consistent with the outcome in *Moore?* The *Moore* Court distinguished the East Cleveland ordinance from the ordinance at issues in *Boraas* on the ground that the latter did not prevent biologically related individuals from living together. As Justice Powell put it, East

Cleveland "has chosen to regulate the occupancy of its housing by slicing deeply into the family itself." In addition, the claim in *Boraas* was brought under the Equal Protection Clause, whereas in *Moore* the Court addressed the constitutional challenge under the Due Process Clause, largely ignoring the plaintiff's separate equal protection claim. Yet, in substance, the Court's analysis is remarkably similar in the two cases, except for the outcome.

In *Borass*, the dissenters objected that the ordinance represented an irrational solution to the asserted problem of noise and congestion in a residential neighborhood, pointing out that a family of unrelated persons might possess only one vehicle, while members of a biological family might have multiple vehicles. Justice Douglas, writing for the Court, brushed off this concern by observing that "boarding houses, fraternity houses, and the like present urban problems, and asserting that it is a permissible goal of government to seek to establish [a] quiet place where yards are wide, people few, and motor vehicles restricted."

On the other hand, in *Moore*, Justice Powell embraced the logic of the *Boraas* dissenters, observing that the limitation on family composition served the city's goals of "preventing overcrowding, minimizing traffic and parking congestion, and avoiding an undue financial burden" in only a marginal way, if at all. Using the same kind of hypothetical used by Justice Marshall in his *Boraas* dissent, Justice Powell observed, that "[t]he ordinance permits any family consisting only of husband, wife, and unmarried children to live together, even if the family contains a half dozen licensed drivers, each with his or her own car. At the same time it forbids an adult brother and sister to share a household, even if both faithfully use public transportation." Not surprisingly, Justice Marshall (and Justice Brennan) joined Justice Powell's opinion in *Boraas*.

2. *The Court's Change in Direction.* Between the decision in *Borass* and the decision in *Moore*, Justice John Paul Stevens replaced Justice William Douglas. Justice Stevens' appointment to the Court may help explain the change in Court thinking on group housing; after all, the plaintiff prevailed in *Moore* by a narrow 5-to-4 margin. Also potentially significant was the loss of Justice Douglas' distinctive environmentalist perspective from the Court; he clearly saw the *Boraas* case through the frame of neighborhood preservation: "The police power is . . . ample to lay out zones where family values, youth values, and the blessings of quiet seclusion and clean air make the area a sanctuary for people." On the other hand, even though the *Moore* case did not involve any claims of overt racial discrimination, the Court's decision is plainly more oriented in the direction of protecting individual civil rights.

3. *State Constitutional Law.* Some state courts have refused to follow *Belle Terre* and have recognized a broader right of privacy under state constitutions to protect against the regulation of occupancy based on blood or marriage relationships. *See, e.g., City of Santa Barbara v. Adamson*, 610 P.2d 436 (Cal. 1980); *Charter Twp. of Delta v. Dinolfo*, 351 N.W.2d 831 (Mich. 1984); *State v. Baker*, 405 A.2d 368 (N.J. 1979); *McMinn v. Town of Oyster Bay*, 488 N.E.2d 1240 (N.Y. 1985). *See also* Note, Katia Brener, *Belle Terre* and Single-Family Home Ordinances: Judicial Perceptions of Local Government and the Presumption of Validity, 74 N.Y.U. L. Rev. 447 (1999) (endorsing a perceived trend of state courts to reject the traditional deferential model).

A decade later, the Supreme Court revisited the issue of group homes in the following case:

■ CITY OF CLEBURNE, TEXAS v. CLEBURNE LIVING CENTER, INC.

473 U.S. 432 (1985)

Justice WHITE delivered the opinion of the Court.

A Texas city denied a special use permit for the operation of a group home for the mentally retarded, acting pursuant to a municipal zoning ordinance requiring permits for such homes. The Court of Appeals for the Fifth Circuit held that mental retardation is a "quasi-suspect" classification and that the ordinance violated the Equal Protection Clause because it did not substantially further an important governmental purpose. We hold that a lesser standard of scrutiny is appropriate, but conclude that under that standard the ordinance is invalid as applied in this case.

In July 1980, respondent Jan Hannah purchased a building at 201 Featherston Street in the city of Cleburne, Texas, with the intention of leasing it to Cleburne Living Center, Inc. (CLC), for the operation of a group home for the mentally retarded. It was anticipated that the home would house 13 retarded men and women, who would be under the constant supervision of CLC staff members. The house had four bedrooms and two baths, with a half bath to be added. CLC planned to comply with all applicable state and federal regulations.

The city informed CLC that a special use permit would be required for the operation of a group home at the site, and CLC accordingly submitted a permit application. In response to a subsequent inquiry from CLC, the city explained that under the zoning regulations applicable to the site, a special use permit, renewable annually, was required for the construction of "[h]ospitals for the insane or feeble-minded, or alcoholic [sic] or drug addicts, or penal or correctional institutions." The city had determined that the proposed group home should be classified as a "hospital for the feeble-minded." After holding a public hearing on CLC's application, the City Council voted 3 to 1 to deny a special use permit. . . .

The Equal Protection Clause of the Fourteenth Amendment commands that no State shall "deny to any person within its jurisdiction the equal protection of the laws," which is essentially a direction that all persons similarly situated should be treated alike. Section 5 of the Amendment empowers Congress to enforce this mandate, but absent controlling congressional direction, the courts have themselves devised standards for determining the validity of state legislation or other official action that is challenged as denying equal protection. The general rule is that legislation is presumed to be valid and will be sustained if the classification drawn by the statute is rationally related to a legitimate state interest. . . . The general rule gives way, however, when a statute classifies by race, alienage, or national origin. These factors are so seldom relevant to the achievement of any legitimate state interest that laws grounded in such considerations are deemed to reflect prejudice and antipathy — a view that those in the burdened class are not as worthy or deserving as others. For these reasons and because such discrimination is unlikely to be soon rectified by legislative means, these laws are subjected to strict scrutiny and will be sustained only if they are suitably tailored to serve a compelling state interest. . . . Legislative classifications based on gender also call for a heightened standard of review. . . .

Against this background, we conclude for several reasons that the Court of Appeals erred in holding mental retardation a quasi-suspect classification calling for a more exacting standard of judicial review than is normally accorded economic and social legislation. First, it is undeniable, and it is not argued otherwise here, that those who are mentally retarded have a reduced ability to cope with and function in the everyday world. Nor are they all cut from the same pattern: as the testimony in this record indicates, they range from those whose disability is not immediately evident to those who must be constantly cared for. They are thus different, immutably so, in relevant respects, and the States' interest in dealing with and providing for them is plainly a legitimate one. How this large and diversified group is to be treated under the law is a difficult and often a technical matter, very much a task for legislators guided by qualified professionals and not by the perhaps ill-informed opinions of the judiciary. Heightened scrutiny inevitably involves substantive judgments about legislative decisions, and we doubt that the predicate for such judicial oversight is present where the classification deals with mental retardation.

Second, the distinctive legislative response, both national and state, to the plight of those who are mentally retarded demonstrates not only that they have unique problems, but also that the lawmakers have been addressing their difficulties in a manner that belies a continuing antipathy or prejudice and a corresponding need for more intrusive oversight by the judiciary. . . .

Third, the legislative response, which could hardly have occurred and survived without public support, negates any claim that the mentally retarded are politically powerless in the sense that they have no ability to attract the attention of the lawmakers. . . .

Fourth, if the large and amorphous class of the mentally retarded were deemed quasi-suspect for the reasons given by the Court of Appeals, it would be difficult to find a principled way to distinguish a variety of other groups who have perhaps immutable disabilities setting them off from others, who cannot themselves mandate the desired legislative responses, and who can claim some degree of prejudice from at least part of the public at large. One need mention in this respect only the aging, the disabled, the mentally ill, and the infirm. We are reluctant to set out on that course, and we decline to do so. . . .

Our refusal to recognize the retarded as a quasi-suspect class does not leave them entirely unprotected from invidious discrimination. To withstand equal protection review, legislation that distinguishes between the mentally retarded and others must be rationally related to a legitimate governmental purpose. This standard, we believe, affords government the latitude necessary both to pursue policies designed to assist the retarded in realizing their full potential, and to freely and efficiently engage in activities that burden the retarded in what is essentially an incidental manner. The State may not rely on a classification whose relationship to an asserted goal is so attenuated as to render the distinction arbitrary or irrational. Furthermore, some objectives — such as "a bare . . . desire to harm a politically unpopular group. . . ." — are not legitimate state interests. Beyond that, the mentally retarded, like others, have and retain their substantive constitutional rights in addition to the right to be treated equally by the law.

We turn to the issue of the validity of the zoning ordinance insofar as it requires a special use permit for homes for the mentally retarded. We inquire first whether requiring a special use permit for the Featherston home in the circumstances here deprives respondents of the equal protection of the laws. If it does, there will be no occasion to decide whether the special use permit provision is facially invalid where the mentally retarded are involved, or to put it another way, whether the city may never insist on a special use permit for a home for the mentally retarded in an R-3 zone. . . .

The constitutional issue is clearly posed. The city does not require a special use permit in an R-3 zone for apartment houses, multiple dwellings, boarding and lodging houses, fraternity or sorority houses, dormitories, apartment hotels, hospitals, sanitariums, nursing homes for convalescents or the aged (other than for the insane or feebleminded or alcoholics or drug addicts), private clubs or fraternal orders, and other specified uses. It does, however, insist on a special permit for the Featherston home, and it does so, as the District Court found, because it would be a facility for the mentally retarded. May the city require the permit for this facility when other care and multiple-dwelling facilities are freely permitted?

It is true, as already pointed out, that the mentally retarded as a group are indeed different from others not sharing their misfortune, and in this respect they may be different from those who would occupy other facilities that would be permitted in an R-3 zone without a special permit. But this difference is largely irrelevant unless the Featherston home and those who would occupy it would threaten legitimate interests of the city in a way that other permitted uses such as boarding houses and hospitals would not. Because in our view the record does not reveal any rational basis for believing that the Featherston home would pose any special threat to the city's legitimate interests, we affirm the judgment below insofar as it holds the ordinance invalid as applied in this case.

The District Court found that the City Council's insistence on the permit rested on several factors. First, the Council was concerned with the negative attitude of the majority of property owners located within 200 feet of the Featherston facility, as well as with the fears of elderly residents of the neighborhood. But mere negative attitudes, or fear, unsubstantiated by factors which are properly cognizable in a zoning proceeding, are not permissible bases for treating a home for the mentally retarded differently from apartment houses, multiple dwellings, and the like. . . .

Second, the Council had two objections to the location of the facility. It was concerned that the facility was across the street from a junior high school, and it feared that the students might harass the occupants of the Featherston home. But the school itself is attended by about 30 mentally retarded students, and denying a permit based on such vague, undifferentiated fears is again permitting some portion of the community to validate what would otherwise be an equal protection violation. The other objection to the home's location was that it was located on "a five hundred year flood plain." This concern with the possibility of a flood, however, can hardly be based on a distinction between the Featherston home and, for example, nursing homes, homes for convalescents or the aged, or sanitariums or hospitals, any of which could be located on the Featherston site without obtaining a special use permit. The same may be said of another concern of the Council — doubts about the legal responsibility for actions which the mentally retarded might take. If there is no concern about legal responsibility with respect to other uses that would be permitted in the area, such as boarding and fraternity houses, it is difficult to believe that the groups of mildly or moderately mentally retarded individuals who would live at 201 Featherston would present any different or special hazard.

Fourth, the Council was concerned with the size of the home and the number of people that would occupy it. The District Court found, and the Court of Appeals repeated, that "[i]f the potential residents of the Featherston Street home were not mentally retarded, but the home was the same in all other respects, its use would be permitted under the city's zoning ordinance." Given this finding, there would be no restrictions on the number of people who could occupy this home as a boarding house, nursing home, family dwelling, fraternity house, or dormitory. The question is whether it is rational to treat the mentally retarded differently. It is true that they suffer disability not shared by others; but why this difference warrants a density regulation that others need not observe is not at all apparent. At least this record does not clarify how, in this connection, the characteristics of the intended occupants of the Featherston home rationally justify denying to those occupants what would be permitted to groups occupying the same site for different purposes. . . .

In the courts below the city also urged that the ordinance is aimed at avoiding concentration of population and at lessening congestion of the streets. These concerns obviously fail to explain why apartment houses, fraternity and sorority houses, hospitals and the like, may freely locate in the area without a permit. So, too, the expressed worry about fire hazards, the serenity of the neighborhood, and the avoidance of danger to other residents fail rationally to justify singling out a home such as 201 Featherston for the special use permit, yet imposing no such restrictions on the many other uses freely permitted in the neighborhood.

The short of it is that requiring the permit in this case appears to us to rest on an irrational prejudice against the mentally retarded, including those who would occupy the Featherston facility and who would live under the closely supervised and highly regulated conditions expressly provided for by state and federal law. . . .

Notes and Comments

1. Cleburne *Consensus.* Unlike *Boraas* and *Moore,* the conclusion in *Cleburne* that the city engaged in unconstitutional discrimination was essentially unanimous. Justice Marshall, joined by Justices Brennan and Blackmun, concurred in the judgment, arguing that discrimination against mentally disabled persons should be subject to strict scrutiny, and dissented on the narrow ground that the Court should have granted more sweeping relief.

2. *Heightened Scrutiny in Disguise?* It has long been debated whether the Court in *Cleburne,* despite ostensibly applying the traditional rational basis test, was in fact engaging in more rigorous scrutiny. Applying the rational basis test, can one justify the outcome in *Cleburne? See* 473 U.S. at 456, (Marshall, J. dissenting) ("Cleburne's ordinance surely would be valid under the traditional rational-basis test applicable to economic and commercial regulation."). *See also* James A. Kushner, Substantive Equal Protection: The Rehnquist Court and the Fourth Tier of Judicial Review, 53 Mo. L. Rev. 423 (1988) (arguing that *Cleburne* is one of a number of equal protection rulings applying scrutiny greater than rational basis and less than intermediate scrutiny); Laura C. Bornstein, Student Article, Contextualizing *Cleburne,* 41 Golden Gate U.L. Rev. 91 (2010) (arguing that *Cleburne* was incorrect in ruling that mental retardation is not a suspect or quasi-suspect classification under the Equal Protection Clause).

3. *Interpreting* Cleburne. What is the scope of the holding of *Cleburne?* Could group homes be restricted to commercial and multi-family districts but excluded from single-family home districts? Could homeowners enforce a restrictive covenant prohibiting group home use? *See Bannum, Inc. v. City of Fort Lauderdale,* 157 F.3d 819 (11th Cir. 1998) (no denial of equal protection to refuse a special use permit for a

custodial facility for a supervised residential program serving former convicts, distinguishing *Cleburne* on the basis of public safety concerns). *See generally* Richard B. Saphire, Equal Protection, Rational Basis Review, and the Impact of *Cleburne Living Center, Inc.*, 88 Ky. L. J. 591 (1999-2000).

4. Cleburne, Euclid, *and Housing Distinctions.* Is *Cleburne* consistent with *Village of Euclid v. Ambler Realty Co.*, 272 U.S. 365 (1926) (reprinted in Chapter 2), the case that established deference to zoning? Does the distinction between single-family and low density, multi-family housing survive the scrutiny of *Cleburne?* Did the city offer a rational explanation for separating group homes from other commercial or high-density housing? Would the case have been decided differently if group homes were treated the same as multi-family housing?

5. *Halfway Houses.* In *Community Resources for Justice, Inc. v. City of Manchester*, 917 A.2d 707 (N.H. 2007), a private organization that operates halfway houses sought review of a Zoning Board of Adjustment's (ZBA's) decision denying an application for a permit to build a transitional halfway house for prisoners. Under the city zoning, a correctional facility was not a permitted use. The Superior Court reversed the ZBA decision denying the permit. On appeal, the New Hampshire Supreme Court reversed the lower court and remanded for further proceedings.

The Supreme Court rejected the plaintiff's claim that the city's ban on correctional facilities violated its substantive due process rights under the New Hampshire Constitution. Applying the rational basis test, the court ruled that the ordinance bore a reasonable relationship to several legitimate interests, including "concerns that the prisoners to be housed at a residential transition facility could either pose some threat to the surrounding community, engage in recidivism, exacerbate the city's perceived burden in accommodating a disproportionate share of social services, or affect surrounding property values."

The Supreme Court also clarified the standards governing the plaintiff's state equal protection claim. First, reasoning that the right to sue and enjoy property "is an important substantive right," the Court ruled that an intermediate scrutiny test applies to equal protection challenges to zoning ordinances impairing rights in property. Second, the Court held that intermediate scrutiny requires that challenged legislation be substantially related to an important governmental objective, that the burden to demonstrate that challenged legislation meets this test rests with the governmental defendant, and that in defending against such cases the government may not rely upon justifications that are hypothesized or invented post hoc in response to litigation, nor upon overbroad generalizations. The Supreme Court then remanded the case to the Superior Court. The Superior Court ruled that the city zoning ordinance violated equal protection, and the Supreme Court upheld that ruling on appeal. 949 A.2d 681 (N.H. 2008).

What would be the result if a special use permit was required for group homes in a detached single-family district? Would a requirement that group homes be located 1500 feet from other group homes be valid under *Cleburne?* What if the dispersal policy was designed to avoid segregation of the disabled and to achieve integration?

6. *Title VIII and Disability Discrimination.* As noted in the introduction to this chapter, the Fair Housing Act was amended in 1988 to extend Title VIII to reach discrimination based on handicap. Fair Housing Amendments Act of 1988, Pub. L. No. 100-430, 102 Stat. 1619, *codified at* 42 U.S.C. §§3601-3619, 3631 (2006). As a

result, most challenges to group home regulation and land use practices touching on or affecting disabilities are now reviewed under the statutory standard.

D. FEDERAL STATUTORY LIMITATIONS

In addition to the rights available under the Constitution, Congress has passed an array of civil rights legislation affecting land use planning and development. Congress has broad authority under §5 of the Fourteenth Amendment to pass civil rights legislation. *Katzenbach v. Morgan*, 384 U.S. 641, 648-60 (1966). Thus, Congress has the ability to enact legislation that creates rights building on those afforded by the Constitution.

1. The Fair Housing Act

Title VII of the Civil Rights Act of 1968 (P.L. 90-284) — popularly known as the Fair Housing Act — is the most important piece of federal legislation addressing discrimination in housing. The act reaches discrimination based on race, color, national origin, religion, sex, familial status, and handicap. In addition to authorizing enforcement actions by the federal government, the act grants any person who has been injured by a discriminatory housing practice the right to sue for relief in federal or state court. 42 U.S.C. §3613.

They key substantive provisions of the act are set out below:

Section 803. [42 U.S.C. §3603] . . .

(b) Nothing in section 804 of this title (other than subsection (c)) shall apply to —

(1) any single-family house sold or rented by an owner: Provided, That such private individual owner does not own more than three such single-family houses at any one time: Provided further, That in the case of the sale of any such single-family house by a private individual owner not residing in such house at the time of such sale or who was not the most recent resident of such house prior to such sale, the exemption granted by this subsection shall apply only with respect to one such sale within any twenty-four month period: Provided further, That such bona fide private individual owner does not own any interest in, nor is there owned or reserved on his behalf, under any express or voluntary agreement, title to or any right to all or a portion of the proceeds from the sale or rental of, more than three such single-family houses at any one time: Provided further, That after December 31, 1969, the sale or rental of any such single-family house shall be excepted from the application of this subchapter only if such house is sold or rented (A) without the use in any manner of the sales or rental facilities or the sales or rental services of any real estate broker, agent, or salesman, or of such facilities or services of any person in the business of selling or renting dwellings, or of any

employee or agent of any such broker, agent, salesman, or person and (B) without the publication, posting or mailing, after notice, of any advertisement or written notice in violation of section 804(c) of this title; but nothing in this proviso shall prohibit the use of attorneys, escrow agents, abstractors, title companies, and other such professional assistance as necessary to perfect or transfer the title, or (2) rooms or units in dwellings containing living quarters occupied or intended to be occupied by no more than four families living independently of each other, if the owner actually maintains and occupies one of such living quarters as his residence.

Section 804. [42 U.S.C. §3604]

As made applicable by section 803 of this title and except as exempted by sections 803(b) and 807 of this title, it shall be unlawful—

(a) To refuse to sell or rent after the making of a bona fide offer, or to refuse to negotiate for the sale or rental of, or otherwise make unavailable or deny, a dwelling to any person because of race, color, religion, sex, familial status, or national origin.

(b) To discriminate against any person in the terms, conditions, or privileges of sale or rental of a dwelling, or in the provision of services or facilities in connection therewith, because of race, color, religion, sex, familial status, or national origin.

(c) To make, print, or publish, or cause to be made, printed, or published any notice, statement, or advertisement, with respect to the sale or rental of a dwelling that indicates any preference, limitation, or discrimination based on race, color, religion, sex, handicap, familial status, or national origin, or an intention to make any such preference, limitation, or discrimination.

(d) To represent to any person because of race, color, religion, sex, handicap, familial status, or national origin that any dwelling is not available for inspection, sale, or rental when such dwelling is in fact so available.

(e) For profit, to induce or attempt to induce any person to sell or rent any dwelling by representations regarding the entry or prospective entry into the neighborhood of a person or persons of a particular race, color, religion, sex, handicap, familial status, or national origin.

(f)(1) To discriminate in the sale or rental, or to otherwise make unavailable or deny, a dwelling to any buyer or renter because of a handicap of—

> (A) that buyer or renter,
>
> (B) a person residing in or intending to reside in that dwelling after it is so sold, rented, or made available; or
>
> (C) any person associated with that buyer or renter

(2) To discriminate against any person in the terms, conditions, or privileges of sale or rental of a dwelling, or in the provision of services or facilities in connection with such dwelling, because of a handicap of—

(A) that person; or

(B) a person residing in or intending to reside in that dwelling after it is so sold, rented, or made available; or

(C) any person associated with that person.

(3) For purposes of this subsection, discrimination includes—

(A) a refusal to permit, at the expense of the handicapped person, reasonable modifications of existing premises occupied or to be occupied by such person if such modifications may be necessary to afford such person full enjoyment of the premises, except that, in the case of a rental, the landlord may where it is reasonable to do so condition permission for a modification on the renter agreeing to restore the interior of the premises to the condition that existed before the modification, reasonable wear and tear excepted.

(B) a refusal to make reasonable accommodations in rules, policies, practices, or services, when such accommodations may be necessary to afford such person equal opportunity to use and enjoy a dwelling; or

(C) in connection with the design and construction of covered multifamily dwellings for first occupancy after the date that is 30 months after the date of enactment of the Fair Housing Amendments Act of 1988, a failure to design and construct those dwelling in such a manner that—

(i) the public use and common use portions of such dwellings are readily accessible to and usable by handicapped persons;

(ii) all the doors designed to allow passage into and within all premises within such dwellings are sufficiently wide to allow passage by handicapped persons in wheelchairs; and

(iii) all premises within such dwellings contain the following features of adaptive design:

(I) an accessible route into and through the dwelling;

(II) light switches, electrical outlets, thermostats, and other environmental controls in accessible locations;

(III) reinforcements in bathroom walls to allow later installation of grab bars; and

(IV) usable kitchens and bathrooms such that an individual in a wheelchair can maneuver about the space . . .

(8) Nothing in this title shall be construed to invalidate or limit any law of a State or political subdivision of a State, or other jurisdiction in which this title shall be effective, that requires dwellings to be designed and constructed in a manner that affords handicapped persons greater access than is required by this title. (9) Nothing in this subsection requires that a dwelling be made available to an individual whose tenancy would constitute a direct threat to the health or safety of other individuals or whose tenancy would result in substantial physical damage to the property of others.

Section 805. [42 U.S.C. §3605]

(a) In General. — It shall be unlawful for any person or other entity whose business includes engaging in residential real estate-related transactions to discriminate against any person in making available such a transaction, or in the terms or conditions of such a transaction, because of race, color, religion, sex, handicap, familial status, or national origin. . . .

Section 807. [42 U.S.C. §3607]

(a) Nothing in this subchapter shall prohibit a religious organization, association, or society, or any nonprofit institution or organization operated, supervised or controlled by or in conjunction with a religious organization, association, or society, from limiting the sale, rental or occupancy of dwellings which it owns or operates for other than a commercial purpose to persons of the same religion, or from giving preference to such persons, unless membership in such religion is restricted on account of race, color, or national origin. Nor shall anything in this subchapter prohibit a private club not in fact open to the public, which as an incident to its primary purpose or purposes provides lodgings which it owns or operates for other than a commercial purpose, from limiting the rental or occupancy of such lodgings to its members or from giving preference to its members.

Notes and Comments

1. *History.* The Fair Housing Act, enacted in 1968, is a product of its era. In response to widespread riots and other social unrest, President Lyndon Johnson appointed the so-called Kerner Commission (officially named the National Advisory Commission on Civil Disorders). The Commission famously concluded: "Our nation is moving toward two societies, one black, one white — separate and unequal." Report of the National Commission on Civil Disorders 91 (1968). More specifically, the Commission "found that that both open and covert racial discrimination prevented black families from obtaining better housing and moving to integrated housing." *Texas Dep't of Housing and Cmty. Affairs v. The Inclusive Cmtys. Project, Inc.,* 135 S. Ct. 2507, 2516 (2015). "To reverse '[t]his deepening racial division,'" the Commission recommended adoption of "a comprehensive and enforceable open-occupancy law making it an offense to discriminate in the sale or rental of any housing. . . ." *Id.,* quoting Report at 293. Stirred into action by the assassination of Dr. Martin Luther King, Jr. in April 1968, Congress accepted the recommendation of the Kerner Commission and enacted the Fair Housing Act. *See* History of Fair Housing Act, U.S. Department of Housing and Urban Development at http://portal.hud.gov/hudportal/HUD?src=/program_offices/fair_housing_equal_opp/aboutfheo/history (last visited Nov. 12, 2016).

In its original form, the act addressed housing discrimination based on color, religion, sex, or national origin. As a result of the Fair Housing Act Amendments of 1988 (Pub. L. 100–430), persons with disabilities and families with children were also granted protection under the act.

2. *Legislative Distinctions.* Because the Fair Housing Act provides legislative protections beyond what the Constitution requires, Congress was free to temper its enforcement of its overarching anti-discrimination goal in light of competing social and political considerations. This explains why it was permissible (and perhaps arguably appropriate) for Congress to provide different levels of protection against discrimination for persons in different classes and under different facts and circumstances. What concerns was Congress trying to address by exempting owners of single-family homes from many of the act's prohibitions? What explains the so-called "rooming house" exception? Why did Congress determine that the prohibition on discrimination in advertising should apply to both single-family houses and rooming houses? What unique considerations related to housing for handicapped persons explain the special provisions in the act for those with handicaps? What is the justification for the act's different rules for handicapped persons depending on whether the rules apply to existing buildings or to new construction?

3. *Obama Administration Rule.* In July 2015, the Department of Housing and Urban Development announced the promulgation of a new rule designed to bolster efforts under the Fair Housing Act to reduce racial segregation in residential neighborhoods. While the act includes various familiar provisions outlawing various forms of discrimination, the act also includes several provisions authorizing federal agencies and U.S. Department of Housing and Urban Development (HUD) in particular to administer their programs to advance the goals of the act. 42 U.S.C. §3608. In the past, HUD exercised this authority by requiring local governments participating in HUD programs to conduct periodic assessments of impediments to the achievement of fair housing goals. Under the new rule, localities are required to establish specific fair housing goals and priorities and to submit them to HUD for review and approval. *See* 80 Fed. Reg. 42272 (July 16, 2015). The rule is designed to encourage the development of affordable housing in relatively affluent communities with low minority representation. The initiative generated considerable controversy. *See* Julie Hirschfeld & Binyamin Appelbaum, Obama Unveils Stricter Rules Against Segregation, The New York Times (July 8, 2015) (quoting a housing specialist with the American Enterprise Institute describing the new rule as "just the latest attempt by H.U.D. to social-engineer the American people").

———————

At the end of the 2015 Term, the U.S. Supreme Court issued a major Federal Housing Act decision, deciding by a narrow 5-to-4 vote that a showing that a government policy produces a "disparate impact" is sufficient to establish liability under the act.

■ TEXAS DEPARTMENT OF HOUSING AND COMMUNITY AFFAIRS v. THE INCLUSIVE COMMUNITIES PROJECT, INC.
135 S. Ct. 2507 (2015)

Justice KENNEDY delivered the opinion of the Court.

The underlying dispute in this case concerns where housing for low-income persons should be constructed in Dallas, Texas — that is, whether the housing should be built in the inner city or in the suburbs. This dispute comes to the Court on a disparate-impact theory of liability. In contrast to a disparate-treatment case, where a "plaintiff must establish that the defendant had a discriminatory intent or motive," a plaintiff bringing a disparate-impact claim challenges practices that have a "disproportionately adverse effect on minorities" and are otherwise unjustified by a legitimate rationale. The question presented for the Court's determination is whether disparate-impact claims are cognizable under the Fair Housing Act. . . .

I

A

Before turning to the question presented, it is necessary to discuss a different federal statute that gives rise to this dispute. The Federal Government provides low-income housing tax credits that are distributed to developers through designated state agencies. Congress has directed States to develop plans identifying selection criteria for distributing the credits. Those plans must include certain criteria, such as public housing waiting lists, as well as certain preferences, including that low-income housing units "contribut[e] to a concerted community revitalization plan" and be built in census tracts populated predominantly by low-income residents. Federal law thus favors the distribution of these tax credits for the development of housing units in low-income areas.

In the State of Texas these federal credits are distributed by the Texas Department of Housing and Community Affairs. Under Texas law, a developer's application for the tax credits is scored under a point system that gives priority to statutory criteria, such as the financial feasibility of the development project and the income level of tenants. The Texas Attorney General has interpreted state law to permit the consideration of additional criteria, such as whether the housing units will be built in a neighborhood with good schools. Those criteria cannot be awarded more points than statutorily mandated criteria.

The Inclusive Communities Project, Inc. (ICP), is a Texas-based nonprofit corporation that assists low-income families in obtaining affordable housing. In 2008, the ICP brought this suit against the Department and its officers in the United States District Court for the Northern District of Texas. As relevant here, it brought a disparate-impact claim under §§804(a) and 805(a) of the FHA. The ICP alleged the Department has caused continued segregated housing patterns by its disproportionate allocation of the tax credits, granting too many credits for housing in predominantly black inner-city areas and too few in predominantly white suburban neighborhoods. The ICP contended that the Department must modify its selection criteria in order to encourage the construction of low-income housing in suburban communities.

The District Court concluded that the ICP had established a prima facie case of disparate impact. It relied on two pieces of statistical evidence. First, it found "from 1999–2008, [the Department] approved tax credits for 49.7% of proposed non-elderly units in 0% to 9.9% Caucasian areas, but only approved 37.4% of proposed non-elderly units in 90% to 100% Caucasian areas." Second, it found "92.29% of [low-income housing tax credit] units in the city of Dallas were located in census tracts with less than 50% Caucasian residents."

The District Court then placed the burden on the Department to rebut the ICP's prima facie showing of disparate impact. After assuming the Department's proffered interests were legitimate, the District Court held that a defendant — here the Department — must prove "that there are no other less discriminatory alternatives to advancing their proffered interests." Because, in its view, the Department "failed to meet [its] burden of proving that there are no less discriminatory alternatives," the District Court ruled for the ICP.

The District Court's remedial order required the addition of new selection criteria for the tax credits. For instance, it awarded points for units built in neighborhoods with good schools and disqualified sites that are located adjacent to or near hazardous conditions, such as high crime areas or landfills. The remedial order contained no explicit racial targets or quotas.

While the Department's appeal was pending, the Secretary of Housing and Urban Development (HUD) issued a regulation interpreting the FHA to encompass disparate-impact liability. . . .

The Court of Appeals for the Fifth Circuit held, consistent with its precedent, that disparate-impact claims are cognizable under the FHA. On the merits, however, the Court of Appeals reversed and remanded. Relying on HUD's regulation, the Court of Appeals held that it was improper for the District Court to have placed the burden on the Department to prove there were no less discriminatory alternatives for allocating low-income housing tax credits. In a concurring opinion, Judge Jones stated that on remand the District Court should reexamine whether the ICP had made out a prima facie case of disparate impact. She suggested the District Court incorrectly relied on bare statistical evidence without engaging in any analysis about causation. She further observed that, if the federal law providing for the distribution of low-income housing tax credits ties the Department's hands to such an extent that it lacks a meaningful choice, then there is no disparate-impact liability. . . .

II

The issue here is whether, under a proper interpretation of the FHA, housing decisions with a disparate impact are prohibited. Before turning to the FHA, however, it is necessary to consider two other antidiscrimination statutes that preceded it.

The first relevant statute is §703(a) of Title VII of the Civil Rights Act of 1964. The Court addressed the concept of disparate impact under this statute in *Griggs v. Duke Power Co.*, 401 U.S. 424 (1971). There, the employer had a policy requiring its manual laborers to possess a high school diploma and to obtain satisfactory scores on two intelligence tests. The Court of Appeals held the employer had not adopted these job requirements for a racially discriminatory purpose, and the plaintiffs did not challenge that holding in this Court. Instead, the plaintiffs argued §703(a)(2) covers the discriminatory effect of a practice as well as the motivation behind the practice. Section 703(a), as amended, provides as follows:

> It shall be an unlawful employer practice for an employer —
>
> (1) to fail or refuse to hire or to discharge any individual, or otherwise to discriminate against any individual with respect to his compensation, terms, conditions, or privileges of employment, because of such individual's race, color, religion, sex, or national origin; or

> (2) to limit, segregate, or classify his employees or applicants for employment in any way which would deprive or tend to deprive any individual of employment opportunities or otherwise adversely affect his status as an employee, because of such individual's race, color, religion, sex, or national origin.

The Court did not quote or cite the full statute, but rather relied solely on §703(a)(2).

In interpreting §703(a)(2), the Court reasoned that disparate-impact liability furthered the purpose and design of the statute. The Court explained that, in §703(a)(2), Congress "proscribe[d] not only overt discrimination but also practices that are fair in form, but discriminatory in operation." For that reason, as the Court noted, "Congress directed the thrust of [§703(a)(2)] to the consequences of employment practices, not simply the motivation." In light of the statute's goal of achieving "equality of employment opportunities and remov[ing] barriers that have operated in the past" to favor some races over others, the Court held §703(a)(2) of Title VII must be interpreted to allow disparate-impact claims.

The Court put important limits on its holding: namely, not all employment practices causing a disparate impact impose liability under §703(a)(2). In this respect, the Court held that "business necessity" constitutes a defense to disparate-impact claims. This rule provides, for example, that in a disparate-impact case, §703(a)(2) does not prohibit hiring criteria with a "manifest relationship" to job performance. . . .

The second relevant statute that bears on the proper interpretation of the FHA is the Age Discrimination in Employment Act of 1967. Section 4(a) of the ADEA provides:

> It shall be unlawful for an employer—
>
> (1) to fail or refuse to hire or to discharge any individual or otherwise discriminate against any individual with respect to his compensation, terms, conditions, or privileges of employment, because of such individual's age;
>
> (2) to limit, segregate, or classify his employees in any way which would deprive or tend to deprive any individual of employment opportunities or otherwise adversely affect his status as an employee, because of such individual's age; or
>
> (3) to reduce the wage rate of any employee in order to comply with this chapter.

The Court first addressed whether this provision allows disparate-impact claims in *Smith v. City of Jackson*, 544 U.S. 228 (2005). There, a group of older employees challenged their employer's decision to give proportionately greater raises to employees with less than five years of experience.

Explaining that *Griggs* "represented the better reading of [Title VII's] statutory text," a plurality of the Court concluded that the same reasoning pertained to §4(a)(2) of the ADEA. The *Smith* plurality emphasized that both §703(a)(2) of Title VII and §4(a)(2) of the ADEA contain language "prohibit[ing] such actions that 'deprive any individual of employment opportunities or *otherwise adversely affect* his status as an employee, because of such individual's' race or age." As the plurality observed, the text of these provisions "focuses on the *effects* of the action on the employee rather than the motivation for the action of the employer" and therefore compels recognition of disparate-impact liability. In a separate opinion, Justice Scalia found the ADEA's text ambiguous and thus deferred under *Chevron* to an

Equal Employment Opportunity Commission regulation interpreting the ADEA to impose disparate-impact liability . . . .

Together, *Griggs* holds and the plurality in *Smith* instructs that antidiscrimination laws must be construed to encompass disparate-impact claims when their text refers to the consequences of actions and not just to the mindset of actors, and where that interpretation is consistent with statutory purpose.

Turning to the FHA, the ICP relies on two provisions. Section 804(a) provides that it shall be unlawful:

"To refuse to sell or rent after the making of a bona fide offer, or to refuse to negotiate for the sale or rental of, or otherwise make unavailable or deny, a dwelling to any person because of race, color, religion, sex, familial status, or national origin."

Here, the phrase "otherwise make unavailable" is of central importance to the analysis that follows.

Section 805(a), in turn, provides:

> It shall be unlawful for any person or other entity whose business includes engaging in real estate-related transactions to discriminate against any person in making available such a transaction, or in the terms or conditions of such a transaction, because of race, color, religion, sex, handicap, familial status, or national origin.

Applied here, the logic of *Griggs* and *Smith* provides strong support for the conclusion that the FHA encompasses disparate-impact claims. Congress' use of the phrase "otherwise make unavailable" refers to the consequences of an action rather than the actor's intent. This results-oriented language counsels in favor of recognizing disparate-impact liability. . . .

In addition, it is of crucial importance that the existence of disparate-impact liability is supported by amendments to the FHA that Congress enacted in 1988. By that time, all nine Courts of Appeals to have addressed the question had concluded the Fair Housing Act encompassed disparate-impact claims.

When it amended the FHA, Congress was aware of this unanimous precedent. And with that understanding, it made a considered judgment to retain the relevant statutory text. Indeed, Congress rejected a proposed amendment that would have eliminated disparate-impact liability for certain zoning decisions.

Against this background understanding in the legal and regulatory system, Congress' decision in 1988 to amend the FHA while still adhering to the operative language in §§804(a) and 805(a) is convincing support for the conclusion that Congress accepted and ratified the unanimous holdings of the Courts of Appeals finding disparate-impact liability. . . .

Recognition of disparate-impact claims is consistent with the FHA's central purpose. The FHA . . . was enacted to eradicate discriminatory practices within a sector of our Nation's economy.

These unlawful practices include zoning laws and other housing restrictions that function unfairly to exclude minorities from certain neighborhoods without any sufficient justification. Suits targeting such practices reside at the heartland of disparate-impact liability. The availability of disparate-impact liability, furthermore, has allowed private developers to vindicate the FHA's objectives and to protect their property rights by stopping municipalities from enforcing arbitrary and, in practice, discriminatory ordinances barring the construction of certain types of housing units. Recognition of disparate-impact liability under the FHA also plays a role in uncovering discriminatory intent: It permits plaintiffs to counteract unconscious prejudices and disguised animus that escape easy classification as disparate treatment. In this way disparate-impact liability may prevent segregated housing patterns that might otherwise result from covert and illicit stereotyping.

But disparate-impact liability has always been properly limited in key respects that avoid the serious constitutional questions that might arise under the FHA, for instance, if such liability were imposed based solely on a showing of a statistical disparity. Disparate-impact liability mandates the "removal of artificial, arbitrary, and unnecessary barriers," not the displacement of valid governmental policies. The FHA is not an instrument to force housing authorities to reorder their priorities. Rather, the FHA aims to ensure that those priorities can be achieved without arbitrarily creating discriminatory effects or perpetuating segregation.

Unlike the heartland of disparate-impact suits targeting artificial barriers to housing, the underlying dispute in this case involves a novel theory of liability. This case, on remand, may be seen simply as an attempt to second-guess which of two reasonable approaches a housing authority should follow in the sound exercise of its discretion in allocating tax credits for low-income housing.

An important and appropriate means of ensuring that disparate-impact liability is properly limited is to give housing authorities and private developers leeway to state and explain the valid interest served by their policies. This step of the analysis is analogous to the business necessity standard under Title VII and provides a defense against disparate-impact liability [in employment case]. As the Court explained in *Ricci* [*v. DeStefano*, 557 U.S. 557 (2009)], an entity "could be liable for disparate-impact discrimination only if the [challenged practices] were not job related and consistent with business necessity." Just as an employer may maintain a workplace requirement that causes a disparate impact if that requirement is a "reasonable measure[ment] of job performance," so too must housing authorities and private developers be allowed to maintain a policy if they can prove it is necessary to achieve a valid interest. To be sure, the Title VII framework may not transfer exactly to the fair-housing context, but the comparison suffices for present purposes.

It would be paradoxical to construe the FHA to impose onerous costs on actors who encourage revitalizing dilapidated housing in our Nation's cities merely because some other priority might seem preferable. Entrepreneurs must be given latitude to consider market factors. Zoning officials, moreover, must often make decisions based on a mix of factors, both objective (such as cost and traffic patterns) and, at least to some extent, subjective (such as preserving historic architecture). These factors contribute to a community's quality of life and are legitimate concerns for housing authorities. The FHA does not decree a particular vision of urban development; and it does not put housing authorities and private developers in a double bind of liability, subject to suit whether they choose to rejuvenate a city core or to promote new low-income housing in suburban communities. As HUD itself recognized in its recent rulemaking, disparate-impact liability "does not mandate that affordable housing be located in neighborhoods with any particular characteristic."

In a similar vein, a disparate-impact claim that relies on a statistical disparity must fail if the plaintiff cannot point to a defendant's policy or policies causing that disparity. A robust causality requirement ensures that "[r]acial imbalance . . . does not, without more, establish a prima facie case of disparate impact" and thus protects defendants from being held liable for racial disparities they did not create. Without adequate safeguards at the prima facie stage, disparate-impact liability might cause race to be used and considered in a pervasive way and "would almost inexorably lead" governmental or private entities to use "numerical quotas," and serious constitutional questions then could arise.

The litigation at issue here provides an example. From the standpoint of determining advantage or disadvantage to racial minorities, it seems difficult to say as a general matter that a decision to build low-income housing in a blighted inner-city neighborhood instead of a suburb is discriminatory, or vice versa. If those sorts of judgments are subject to challenge without adequate safeguards, then there is a danger that potential defendants may adopt racial quotas — a circumstance that itself raises serious constitutional concerns.

Courts must therefore examine with care whether a plaintiff has made out a prima facie case of disparate impact and prompt resolution of these cases is important. A plaintiff who fails to allege facts at the pleading stage or produce statistical evidence demonstrating a causal connection cannot make out a prima facie case of disparate impact. For instance, a plaintiff challenging the decision of a private developer to construct a new building in one location rather than another will not easily be able to show this is a policy causing a disparate impact because such a one-time decision may not be a policy at all. It may also be difficult to establish causation because of the multiple factors that go into investment decisions about where to construct or renovate housing units. And as Judge Jones observed below, if the ICP cannot show a causal connection between the Department's policy and a disparate impact — for instance, because federal law substantially limits the Department's discretion — that should result in dismissal of this case.

The FHA imposes a command with respect to disparate-impact liability. Here, that command goes to a state entity. In other cases, the command will go to a private person or entity. Governmental or private policies are not contrary to the disparate-impact requirement unless they are "artificial, arbitrary, and unnecessary barriers." Difficult questions might arise if disparate-impact liability under the FHA caused race to be used and considered in a pervasive and explicit manner to justify governmental or private actions that, in fact, tend to perpetuate race-based considerations rather than move beyond them. Courts should avoid interpreting disparate-impact liability to be so expansive as to inject racial considerations into every housing decision.

The limitations on disparate-impact liability discussed here are also necessary to protect potential defendants against abusive disparate-impact claims. If the specter of disparate-impact litigation causes private developers to no longer construct or renovate housing units for low-income individuals, then the FHA would have undermined its own purpose as well as the free-market system. And as to governmental entities, they must not be prevented from achieving legitimate objectives, such as ensuring compliance with health and safety codes. The Department's *amici*, in addition to the well-stated principal dissenting opinion in this case, call attention to the decision by the Court of Appeals for the Eighth Circuit in *Gallagher v. Magner*, 619 F.3d 823 (2nd Cir. 2010). Although the Court is reluctant to approve or disapprove a case that is not pending, it should be noted that *Magner* was decided without the cautionary standards announced in this opinion and, in all events, the case was settled by the parties before an ultimate determination of disparate-impact liability.

Were standards for proceeding with disparate-impact suits not to incorporate at least the safeguards discussed here, then disparate-impact liability might displace valid governmental and private priorities, rather than solely "remov[ing] . . . artificial, arbitrary, and unnecessary barriers." And that, in turn, would set our Nation back in its quest to reduce the salience of race in our social and economic system.

It must be noted further that, even when courts do find liability under a disparate-impact theory, their remedial orders must be consistent with the Constitution. Remedial orders in disparate-impact cases should concentrate on the elimination of the offending practice that "arbitrar[ily] . . . operate[s] invidiously to discriminate on the basis of rac[e]." If additional measures are adopted, courts should strive to design them to eliminate racial disparities through race-neutral means. Remedial orders that impose racial targets or quotas might raise more difficult constitutional questions.

While the automatic or pervasive injection of race into public and private transactions covered by the FHA has special dangers, it is also true that race may be considered in certain circumstances and in a proper fashion. Just as this Court has not "question[ed] an employer's affirmative efforts to ensure that all groups have a fair opportunity to apply for promotions and to participate in the [promotion] process," it likewise does not impugn housing authorities' race-neutral efforts to encourage revitalization of communities that have long suffered the harsh consequences of segregated housing patterns. When setting their larger goals, local housing authorities may choose to foster diversity and combat racial isolation with race-neutral tools, and mere awareness of race in attempting to solve the problems facing inner cities does not doom that endeavor at the outset.

The Court holds that disparate-impact claims are cognizable under the Fair Housing Act upon considering its results-oriented language, the Court's interpretation of similar language in Title VII and the ADEA, Congress' ratification of disparate-impact claims in 1988 against the backdrop of the unanimous view of nine Courts of Appeals, and the statutory purpose. . . .

The judgment of the Court of Appeals for the Fifth Circuit is affirmed, and the case is remanded for further proceedings consistent with this opinion.
It is so ordered.

[The Chief Justice and Justices Alito, Scalia and Thomas dissented, contending that Congress did not create disparate-impact liability under the Fair Housing Act. Justice Alito wrote the principal dissent, joined by the other three dissenters. Justice Thomas also filed a dissent.]

Notes and Comments

1. *The New HUD Regulations.* The *Inclusive Communities* Court observed that during the course of the litigation the U.S. Department of Housing and Urban Development adopted new regulations, described above, establishing a new "burden-shifting" framework for implementing the Fair Housing Act. 78 Fed. Reg. 11460 (2013), codified at 24 C.F.R. §100.500 (2016). HUD said in its explanation of the new rule that all of the federal courts of appeals had adopted the disparate-impact test of liability. However, the agency observed that the lower federal courts had taken different positions on the issue of which party bears the burden of proof, assuming a defendant has demonstrated that its policy serves a legitimate

public purpose, on the issue of whether an alternative approach would serve the public purpose with less discriminatory effect. Exercising its rulemaking and interpretive authority, HUD adopted the rule to establish nationwide consistency on this issue.

Under the rule, a plaintiff first must make a *prima facie* showing of disparate impact; in other words, the plaintiff "has the burden of proving that a challenged practice caused or predictably will cause a discriminatory effect." 24 C.F.R. §100.500(c)(1) (2014). After a plaintiff has made a *prima facie* case of disparate impact, the burden shifts to the defendant to "prov[e] that the challenged practice is necessary to achieve one or more substantial, legitimate, nondiscriminatory interests." 24 C.F.R. §100.500(c)(2). Finally, if a defendant has satisfied its burden at step two, a plaintiff may "prevail upon proving that the substantial, legitimate, nondiscriminatory interests supporting the challenged practice could be served by another practice that has a less discriminatory effect."24 C.F.R. §100.500(c)(3).

The Supreme Court in *Inclusive Communities* did not comment one way or the other on the validity of the new HUD rule. Before the case reached the Supreme Court, the U.S. Court of Appeals for the Fifth Circuit, while agreeing with the District Court's application of the disparate impact liability test, reversed and vacated on the ground that the District Court's analysis was not consistent with the new HUD rule. *See Inclusive Communities Project, Inc. v. Texas Dep't of Hous. and Cmty. Affairs*, 747 F.3d 275, 282-83 (5th Cir. 2014). On remand, following the Supreme Court decision, the Fifth Circuit remanded the case to the District Court "for further proceedings consistent with our opinion and the opinion of the Supreme Court." *Inclusive Communities Project, Inc. v. Texas Dep't of Hous. and Cmty. Affairs*, 795 F.3d 509 (5th Cir. 2015). Understandably, the District Court interpreted this instruction to mean that it should apply the HUD burden-shifting rule previously embraced by the Fifth Circuit (but not directly addressed by the Supreme Court). *See Inclusive Communitis Project, Inc. v. Texas Dep't of Hous. and Cmty. Affairs*, 2015 WL 5916220 (N.D. Oct. 8, 2015). When this book went to press, the District Court had not yet resolved the merits of the *Inclusive Communities* case.

The validity of the new HUD rule apparently has been addressed by only one court, and that court upheld the rule. *See Property Cas. Insurers Ass'n of Am. v. Donovan*, 66 F. Supp. 3d 1018 (N.D. Ill. 2014) (ruling that HUD's adoption of burden-shifting framework for evaluating disparate impact claims under the Federal Housing Act was reasonable and entitled to deference under *Chevron U.S.A., Inc. v. Natural Resources Defense Council, Inc.*, 467 U.S. 837 (1984)).

2. *"No One Wants to Live in a Rat's Nest."* This was the provocative opening line of Justice Samuel Alito's principal dissent in *Inclusive Communities.* It was a reference to the case of *Gallagher v. Magner*, 619 F.3d 823 (8th Cir. 2010), in which the Eighth Circuit reversed the dismissal of a suit seeking to use the Fair Housing Act to challenge St. Paul, Minnesota's efforts to combat "rodent infestation" and other violations of the city code. The court ruled that the city's "aggressive enforcement of the Housing Code" could give rise to liability because there was evidence that forcing landlords to respond to "rodent infestation, missing dead-bolt locks, inadequate sanitation facilities, inadequate heat, inoperable smoke detectors, [and] broken or missing doors" could increase landlord costs and result in forced sales of properties and tenant evictions. Because minorities were disproportionally represented in "the bottom bracket for household adjusted medium income," the Eighth Circuit concluded that the city's code enforcement efforts had a "disparate impact." The

Supreme Court granted the city's petition for certiorari, *see* 132 S. Ct. 548, but the case was subsequently settled and the petition for certiorari was dismissed. *See* 132 S. Ct. 1302.

Justice Alito's purpose in highlighting the *Magner* case was to support his argument that adopting the disparate-impact theory would expose defendants to wide-ranging litigation that could produce perverse results. As he put it, "[t]he upshot [in *Magner*] was that even St. Paul's good faith attempt to ensure minimally acceptable housing for its poorest residents could not ward off a disparate-impact lawsuit. Today, the Court embraces the same theory that drove the decision in *Magner*. This is a serious mistake." More significantly, Justice Kennedy, speaking for the Court, strongly suggested that *Magner* was incorrectly decided. In interpreting the Fair Housing Act, he said, "governmental entities . . . must not be prevented from achieving legitimate objectives, such as ensuring compliance with health and safety codes." Referring to the *Magner* case specifically, Justice Kennedy declared, "[a]lthough the Court is reluctant to approve or disapprove a case that is not pending, it should be noted *that Magner* was decided without the cautionary standards announced in this opinion and, in all events, the case was settled by the parties before an ultimate determination of disparate-impact liability."

Did *Inclusive Communities* raise the same concerns as the *Magner* case? What did the Supreme Court mean when it referred to *Inclusive Communities* as involving "a novel theory of liability"? The Court also stated that the case "may be seen simply to be an attempt to second guess which of two reasonable approaches a housing authority should follow in the sound exercise of its discretion in allocating tax credits for low-income housing." In what sense can a government decision that has a disproportionate effect on minorities be considered "reasonable"? Does the answer depend in part on whether one understands the purpose of the Fair Housing Act to be promoting racial integration or improving the housing conditions of minorities? Does *Inclusive Communities* sanction policies that perpetuate segregation so long as they directly promote improved minority housing? *See* 135 S. Ct. at 2523 ("The FHA does not decree a particular vision of urban development, and it does not put housing authorities and private developers in a double bind of liability, subject to suit whether they choose to rejuvenate a city core or to promote new low-income housing in suburban communities.").

3. *The "Heartland" of Disparate Impact Litigation.* Justice Kennedy distinguished *Inclusive Communities*, which he regarded as involving a "novel" theory of liability, from other cases that challenge "zoning laws and other housing restrictions that function unfairly to exclude minorities from certain neighborhoods without any sufficient justification." He said, "[s]uits targeting such practices reside at the heartland of disparate-impact liability," citing the following examples: *Town of Huntington v. Huntington Branch, NAACP*, 488 U.S. 15, 16–18 (1988) (*per curiam* decision upholding invalidation under disparate impact theory of zoning law that preventing construction of multi-family rental housing in any portion of a suburban community other than its "urban renewal area," where 52 percent of the residents were minorities); *United States v. City of Black Jack*, 508 F.2d 1179 (8th Cir. 1974) (invalidating ordinance prohibiting construction of any new multi-family dwellings in any portion of the community); *Greater New Orleans Fair Housing Action Ctr. v. St. Bernard Parish*, 641 F. Supp. 2d 563, 569, 577–78 (E.D. La. 2009) (invalidating post-Hurricane Katrina ordinance restricting the rental of housing

units to "blood relatives" in an area of the city that was 88.3 percent white and 7.6 percent black).

Other decisions applying the disparate-impact test indicate that Fair Housing Act challenges to local land use restrictions are not necessarily slam dunks. *See Reinhart v. Lincoln Cty.*, 482 F.3d 1225 (10th Cir. 2007) (rejecting a claim that a new comprehensive land use plan and amended land use regulations had a discriminatory impact based on increasing lot size in rural areas and providing only limited locations for high-density development; developers did not establish amount by which dwelling prices would exceed prices under old regulations, that old prices would have qualified as "affordable," that regulations reduced size of purchaser market for dwellings, and that reduction was disproportionately high for protected group); *Hallmark Developers, Inc. v. Fulton Cty., Ga.*, 466 F.3d 1276 (11th Cir. 2006) (rejecting disparate impact claim that denial of rezoning for project to include mixed use and affordable housing violated Title VIII for lack of disparate effect on minorities as compared to whites); *Affordable Hous. Dev. Corp. v. City of Fresno*, 433 F.3d 1182 (9th Cir. 2006) (affirming a jury verdict rejecting a Title VIII claim based on city's refusal to approve bond issue for low-income housing tax credit affordable housing where community opposition was based on nondiscriminatory concerns about the impact of a large rental project on neighborhood property values and a dispute over the need for the project).

4. Inclusive Communities' *Limitations.* Understandably, the headlines about *Inclusive Communities* highlighted the Court's ruling upholding the use of a disparate-impact test of liability and rejecting the arguments by the four dissenting justices that only a showing of a discriminatory motive should suffice to establish liability under the Fair Housing Act. *See, e.g.*, Adam Liptak, Justices Back Broad Interpretation of Housing Law, The New York Times (June 25, 2015). At the same time, Justice Kennedy's opinion places important limitations on the scope of Federal Housing Act litigation, likely cutting back on the kinds of cases that can successfully be brought under the act in the future as compared to the pre-*Inclusive Communities* situation. To some, these new limitations are a very welcome development. *See* Elizabeth L. McKeen, et al., Robust Causality and Cautionary Standards: Why the *Inclusive* Communities Decision, Despite Upholding Disparate-Impact Liability, Establishes New Protections for Defendant – Part 1, 132 Banking L. J. 553 (2015) ("On closer inspection, *Inclusive Communities* limits disparate-impact liability, equipping defendants with valuable new protections from meritless — and costly — disparate-impact claims. In fact, under the heightened *Inclusive Communities* pleading standard, earlier disparate-impact cases that survived dismissal would today likely be doomed at the outset."). *See also* Roger Clegg, Silver Linings Playbook: "Disparate Impact" and the Fair Housing Act, 2015 Cato. Sup. Ct. Rev. 165, 166 (discussing the "silver linings" of *Inclusive Communities*).

5. *Justice Kennedy's Concerns.* Justice Kennedy's opinion identifies several concerns he had about an expansive disparate-impact theory. First, he alludes to the potential for Federal Housing Act litigation to prevent governments "from achieving legitimate objectives, such as ensuring compliance with health and safety codes." Second, he expresses concern that "the specter of disparate-impact litigation" might cause developers to "no longer construct or renovate housing units for low-income individuals," with the result that "the FHA would . . . undermine its own purpose as well as the free-market system." Third, he refers to "the serious constitutional questions that might arise under the FHA . . . if such liability were

imposed based solely on a showing of statistical disparity." His concern is that a focus on statistics alone at the liability stage could give rise to defensive use of quotas, thereby "perpetuat[ing] race-based considerations rather than mov[ing] beyond them."

Finally, he points to the potential for "double bind" liability if the pursuit of some other legal mandate might subject the government to liability under the Federal Housing Act. In this connection, Justice Kennedy pointed approvingly to Judge Edith Judge's expression of concern that in this case the Department of Housing might be held liable under the Federal Housing Act for complying with the federal policy to make targeted use of investment tax credits in low-income areas. *See Inclusive Communities Project, Inc. v. Texas Dep't of Hous. and Cmyy. Affairs*, 745 F.3d 275, 283-84 (5th Cir. 2014) (Jones, J., specially concurring).

To address these concerns, Justice Kennedy lays out two limitations on Federal Housing Act litigation. First, he states that a defendant should be able to defeat disparate-impact claims by demonstrating that the government action leading to the claims serves some other "valid" government interest or policy. He asserts that "housing authorities and private developers [must] be allowed to maintain a policy if they can prove it is necessary to achieve a valid interest." Thus, "[a]n important and appropriate means of ensuring that disparate-impact liability is properly limited is to give housing authorities and private developers leeway to state and explain the valid interest served by their policies." As examples of valid policies that could at least potentially defeat Federal Housing Act claims, he cites enforcement of public health and safety regulation and encouragement of revitalization of dilapidated housing in urban areas.

Second, Justice Kennedy rules out disparate-impact claims that rely on evidence of a statistical disparity alone. Instead, he says, a "robust causality requirement" must be enforced. By this he means that "a disparate-impact claim that relies on a statistical disparity should fail if the plaintiff cannot point to the defendant's policy or policies causing that disparity."

6. Inclusive Communities *on Remand?* While the Supreme Court affirmed the Fifth Circuit's application of a disparate-impact test, it remanded the case for further proceedings, including to address whether plaintiffs can satisfy the new limitations laid down by the Court. Inevitably, the ultimate outcome on remand will be widely seen as a signal about how to read this new Supreme Court precedent. The Court has given the lower courts a challenging task. First, they will have to determine whether the federal policies governing the allocation of investment tax credits represent a "valid" governmental interest that should preclude liability. Second, as the Court explicitly stated, "if the [plaintiffs] cannot show a causal connection between the Department's policy and a disparate impact — for instance, because federal law substantially limits the Department's discretion — that should result in dismissal of this case."

7. Arlington Heights *on Remand.* The extent to which the Fair Housing Act expands upon the rights conferred by the Equal Protection Clause as interpreted in *Arlington Heights* is demonstrated by the remand proceedings in *Arlington Heights* itself. The Supreme Court's 1997 decision reversed the Seventh Circuit's ruling that the village's refusal to rezone property to permit the construction of low-cost housing violated the Equal Protection Clause. On remand, the Seventh Circuit took up the question of whether the village's action violated the Fair Housing Act, a claim the plaintiffs had pled but not previously pursued. *See Metropolitan*

Hous. Dev. Corp. v. Village of Arlington Heights, 558 F.2d 1283 (7th Cir. 1977). Adopting the view (subsequently endorsed in *Inclusive Communities*) that disparate impact is sufficient to establish a Fair Housing Act violation, the Seventh Circuit ruled that the plaintiffs could proceed with their Fair Housing Act claim, notwithstanding their loss on the equal protection issue in the Supreme Court.

Following a remand to the District Court the parties entered into a settlement calling for a modified project to be built on an alternate site, one that was outside of the Village of Arlington Heights but which the Village would annex. *Metropolitan Hous. Dev. Corp. v. Village of Arlington Heights*, 469 F. Supp. 836 (N.D. Ill. 1979), *aff'd*, 616 F.2d 1006 (7th Cir. 1980) (consent decree approved). In sum, as a result of the Fair Housing Act, low-cost housing got built in a suburban community that would not have been built if the plaintiffs had been compelled to rely on the Equal Protection Clause alone.

8. *Inclusionary Zoning and Discrimination.* As discussed in Chapter 12, New Jersey imposes an obligation on cities to accept their "fair share" of regional housing needs. However, the state has enacted legislation that allows communities to avoid this obligation by paying another community to build up to half of the community's obligation under a regional contribution agreement. Do such regional contribution agreements violate Title VIII? What if a predominantly white suburb pays Newark to build additional affordable housing? *See* Patrick Field et al., Trading the Poor: Intermunicipal Housing Negotiation in New Jersey, 2 Harv. Negot. L. Rev.1 (1997) (challenging the practice of purchasing compliance from a poorer community through regional cooperation agreements).

New Jersey also authorizes communities to set aside a portion of *Mount Laurel* affordable housing for existing town residents. Do residency preferences in a white suburb near a predominantly minority city violate the federal Fair Housing Act? In *In re Township of Warren*, 622 A.2d 1257 (N.J. 1993), the New Jersey Supreme Court overturned a regulation allowing 50 percent of a community's fair share affordable housing allocation to be set aside for households whose members reside or work in the municipality. The court found that the set-aside conflicts with the allocation formula, which does not count existing lower income residents. The court indicated that some type of modified residency preference might be valid, but also expressed concern about possible conflict with the Federal Housing Act due to such a preference's discriminatory effect. *See also United States v. Housing Auth. of the City of Chickasaw*, 504 F. Supp. 716 (S.D. Ala. 1980) (city residency requirement for admission to public housing violated the Federal Housing Act where the City of Chickasaw was 98.8 percent white and was a suburb of Mobile, a city with a substantial minority population).

———————————

The federal Fair Housing Act prohibits the panoply of discriminatory practices found in traditional fair housing cases. However, by extending the protections of Title VIII to the disabled, the act imposes an affirmative obligation on governments and private housing providers to make reasonable accommodations in rules, policies, and practices necessary to afford the disabled equal opportunity in housing. The following case explores the meaning of reasonable accommodation.

■ ADVOCACY CENTER FOR PERSONS WITH DISABILITIES, INC. v. WOODLANDS ESTATES ASSOCIATION INC.

192 F. Supp. 2d 1344 (M.D. Fla. 2002)

Plaintiff, Advocacy Center for Persons with Disabilities, Incorporated (Plaintiff Advocacy Center), is Florida's Protection and Advocacy system, which has standing to sue on its own behalf and on behalf of it[s] constituents. *See* 42 U.S.C. §15043(a)(2)(A)(i) (authorizing an Advocacy and Protection system to pursue legal, administrative, and other appropriate remedies or approaches on behalf of the developmentally disabled). The individual Plaintiffs are developmentally disabled and reside in a group home which is owned by the Upper Pinellas Association for Retarded Citizens (UPARC), located at 110 Arbor Lane, Oldsmar, Pinellas County, Florida. Defendant Woodlands Estates Association, Incorporated (Defendant) is a homeowners' association for East Lake Woodlands Unit One, where the Plaintiffs' group home is located. The property on which the home is located is governed by the Declarations of Covenant and Restrictions for East Lake Woodlands Unit One (the Declarations).

On December 18, 2000, Defendant sent a letter to UPARC, requesting that it take no action in moving Plaintiffs into the home. According to the letter, Defendant claimed that UPARC's proposed use of the home was in violation of Section 2.01, and may potentially violate Section 2.25, of the Declarations. Specifically, Section 2.01 states that:

> The Lots and Buildings shall be used for residential purposes only. . . . No buildings at any time situate[d] on any Lot or Building Plot shall be used for any business, commercial, amusement, hospital, sanitarium, school, clubhouse, religious, charitable, philanthropic, or manufacturing purposes, or as a professional office. . . .

Section 2.25 provides that "no illegal, noxious, or offensive activity, nor shall anything be permitted or done thereon which is or may become a nuisance or a source of embarrassment, discomfort or annoyance to the neighborhood or Development." On January 18, 2001, Defendant filed a complaint against UPARC in the Sixth Judicial Circuit Court in Pinellas County, Florida to enforce the Declarations. Plaintiffs then filed a complaint with this Court, asking for declaratory and injunctive relief on the grounds that Defendant violated the Fair Housing Act, Title 42, United States Code, Section 3601, *et seq.* . . .

The Fair Housing Act, enacted as Title VIII of the Civil Rights Act of 1968, was originally enacted to prohibit discrimination in housing practices on the basis of race, color, religion, or national origin. . . . In 1988, Congress extended coverage to disabled persons. . . . In extending the FHAA to disabled persons, Congress intended to prohibit practices that "restrict the choices" of disabled persons to live where they wish or that "discourage or obstruct [those] choices in a community neighborhood or development." . . .

The FHAA defines "handicap" as "a physical or mental impairment which substantially limits one or more of such person's major life activities." Plaintiffs are developmentally-disabled individuals, and this impairment substantially limits some of their major life activities. . . . First, the Plaintiffs receive assistance in daily living from UPARC, an organization that provides services and supports for developmentally-disabled persons. Second, Thomas Buckley, UPARC's executive director, stated, in his deposition, that Plaintiffs are "mentally retarded" and have "substantial limitations in functioning." . . .

Section 3604(f)(3) of the FHAA provides, in part, that it shall be unlawful:

> 1. To discriminate in the sale or rental, or to otherwise make unavailable or deny, a dwelling to any buyer or renter because of a handicap of . . .
> (B) a person residing in or intending to reside in that dwelling after it is sold . . . or made available. . . .
> 2. To discriminate against any person in the terms, conditions, or privileges of sale or rental of a dwelling . . . because of a handicap of . . .
> (B) a person residing in or intending to reside in that dwelling after it is sold . . . or made available. . . .
> 3. For purposes of this subsection, discrimination includes . . .
> (B) a refusal to make reasonable accommodations in rules, policies, [or] practices . . . when such accommodations may be necessary to afford such person equal opportunity to use and enjoy a dwelling.

42 U.S.C. §3604(f). Plaintiffs who allege a violation of Section 3604(f) may proceed under any and all of three theories: disparate treatment, disparate impact, and failure to make reasonable accommodations. Plaintiffs have alleged their claim under the theory that Defendant failed to make a reasonable accommodation for Plaintiffs in it[s] attempt to enforce the restrictions under Section 2.01 of the Declarations.

The FHAA requires accommodations for disabled persons, if the accommodations are reasonable and necessary, to afford disabled persons equal opportunity to use and enjoy housing. . . . An entity must reasonably accommodate a qualified individual with a disability by making changes in rules, policies, practices, or services, when necessary. . . .

The determination of whether an accommodation is reasonable is highly fact-specific and determined on a case-by-case basis. . . . For example, an accommodation is reasonable if it does not impose "undue financial and administrative burdens" or "changes, adjustments, or modifications to existing programs that would be substantial, or that would constitute fundamental alterations in the nature of the program." . . .

In determining whether a requested accommodation is necessary, "[t]he overall focus should be on 'whether waiver of the rule would be so at odds with the purposes behind the rule that it would be a fundamental and unreasonable change.'" . . . Courts generally balance the burdens imposed on the defendant by the contemplated accommodation against the benefits to the plaintiff. . . .

Although the Eleventh Circuit has not addressed what constitutes a "reasonable accommodation" under the FHAA, several federal courts have. In *Trovato v. City of Manchester, New Hampshire*, the United States District Court for the District of New Hampshire found that the defendant city violated the FHAA when it failed to allow a zoning variance for plaintiffs who suffered from muscular dystrophy. 992 F. Supp. 493 (D.N.H. 1997). The plaintiffs requested the city to allow them to build accessible parking in the front of the home because of the difficulty that they had walking. The court held that the reasonable accommodation requirement of the FHAA clearly applied to zoning ordinances; thus, the city's failure to reasonably accommodate plaintiffs violated the FHAA. *See U.S. v. Village of Marshall, Wisconsin*, 787 F. Supp. 872 (W.D. Wis. 1991) (holding that a Wisconsin statute that established spacing restrictions for proposed community-based residential facilities constituted "rules, policies, practices, or services" under FHAA; thus, the defendant's failure to grant an exception to the statute constituted a failure to make a "reasonable accommodation" under the FHAA).

Conversely, the Fourth Circuit, in *Bryant Woods Inn, Inc. v. Howard County* Maryland, found that the defendant county did not violate the FHAA's requirement to provide reasonable accommodations when it failed to allow a zoning variance for the expansion of a group home. 124 F.3d 597 (4th Cir. 1997). The court reasoned that the expansion would defeat the purpose of the zoning ordinance, resulting in traffic congestion and parking problems; therefore, the accommodation was not reasonable in light of the large burden on the county and the small benefit to the plaintiffs.

Also, in *Groner v. Golden Gate Apartments*, the Sixth Circuit found that the defendant landlord did not violate the FHAA when it failed to renew the lease of a schizophrenic plaintiff. 250 F.3d 1039 (6th Cir. 2001). Because the defendant frequently received complaints from other tenants about the plaintiff's behavior, the court found that renewing his lease was not a reasonable accommodation under the FHAA. However, the Sixth Circuit did find a violation of the reasonable accommodation requirement when the defendant city failed to amend a zoning ordinance to allow a twelve-person elderly adult foster home to operate in a single-family residence district. *Smith & Lee Associates, Inc. v. City of Taylor, Michigan*, 102 F.3d 781 (6th Cir. 1996). . . .

In the instant case, the Court finds that Defendant did not reasonably accommodate Plaintiffs, in violation of the FHAA, when it failed to waive the enforcement of its deed restrictions contained in the Declarations. . . . [T]here is no evidence on the record to show that failing to enforce Section 2.01 of the Declarations would impose an undue financial burden on the Defendant or undermine the basic purpose of the restriction, namely to maintain the residential nature of the neighborhood. . . .

Notes and Comments

1. *Legitimate Enforcement Action?* Was the Association's filing of a lawsuit in state court, together with pretrial attempts to enforce restrictive covenants or equitable servitudes, reasonable and appropriate? Is enforcement of a single-family zoning ordinance by government officials distinguishable from enforcement of covenants by a homeowners' association?

2. *Reasonable Accommodation.* What is a reasonable accommodation? *See Sanghvi v. City of Claremont*, 328 F.3d 532 (9th Cir. 2003) (city refusal to provide sewer connection for an Alzheimer's facility without annexation of the property did not violate reasonable accommodation provision, where granting the connection would have served the economic interests of the facility's owners but not a therapeutic concern of the Alzheimer's patients); *Regional Econ. Cmty. Action Program, Inc. v. City*

of Middletown, 294 F.3d 35 (2d Cir. 2002) (denial of special use permit for two halfway houses based on asserted adverse neighborhood effects did not support reasonable accommodation claim because a proper reasonable accommodation claim must assert that government officials refused to modify or waive a traditional rule or practice); *Lapid-Laurel, L.L.C. v. Zoning Bd. of Adjustment of the Twp. of Scotch Plains*, 284 F.3d 442 (3d Cir. 2002) (rejecting an accommodation claim based on a township's denial of a permit to build a 95-bed facility for the elderly where the developer failed to show that the size of the proposed building was necessary to afford handicapped elderly persons equal opportunity to reside in a residential neighborhood); *Dadian v. Village of Wilmette*, 269 F.3d 831 (7th Cir. 2001) (upholding jury determination that village violated accommodation provision by denying disabled couple permission to build an attached front garage that would have eased access to their home). *Cf. Howard v. City of Beavercreek*, 276 F.3d 802 (6th Cir. 2002) (even if granting a property owner suffering from post-traumatic stress a variance to build a privacy fence could be regarded as a reasonable accommodation, owner was not entitled to relief under the Federal Housing Act because variance denial did not exclude the owner from the neighborhood or home of his choice).

3. *The FHA Exemption for Maximum Occupancy Limits.* The Fair Housing Act includes an exemption from the act for a "restriction[n] regarding the maximum number of occupants permitted to occupy a dwelling." 42 U.S.C. §3607(b)(1). In *City of Edmonds v. Oxford House, Inc.*, 514 U.S. 725 (1995), the Supreme Court addressed whether a city could claim the benefit of this exemption based on a zoning ordinance provision defining "family" in single-family districts as a group of persons, without regard to number, related by genetics, adoption or marriage, or a group of five or fewer unrelated persons. A property owner opened a home for 10-12 adults recovering from alcoholism and drug addiction in a single-family district under the city zoning code. The home was plainly contrary to the zoning ordinance restriction on who can occupy a family home in this district. When the city sued to enforce the zoning code, the owner counter-charged that the city had failed to a make a "reasonable accommodation" permitting maintenance of the home, as required by the Federal Housing Act. The city's first line of defense under the Federal Housing Act was that its definition of family constituted a restriction on the maximum number of occupants within the meaning of the act, relieving the city of the obligation to respond to the failure to accommodate complaint.

The Court rejected the city's position, ruling that the exemption only applies to a traditional housing code provision linking occupancy or the number of occupants to a per person square footage minimum. Under this interpretation of the act, the city's family definition was not an occupancy restriction and therefore the city was not exempt from the act. Justice Thomas, joined by Justices Scalia and Kennedy, dissented, arguing that the city's family definition was within the scope of the act's exemption.

Is *Edmonds* consistent in result with *Belle Terre?* After *Edmonds*, may the Village of Belle Terre enforce its family definition so as to exclude an *Edmonds*-type of group home (ten to twelve adult recovering alcoholics or addicts)?

The *Edmonds* Court did not reach the question of whether, given that the city could no longer claim an exemption from the act, the city's refusal to allow the group home violated the act's accommodation provision. There is no reported subsequent history following the Court's decision. How do you think the lower courts would have resolved the merits of the Federal Housing Act claim on remand?

4. *Group Home Dispersal.* St. Paul, Minnesota, imposed a policy of dispersal of group homes to avoid concentrations on particular streets or in particular neighborhoods. Does the denial of a permit under that policy violate the Federal Housing Act? In *Familystyle of St. Paul, Inc. v. City of St. Paul,* 923 F.2d 91 (8th Cir. 1991), the Eighth Circuit ruled that the city policy did not violate the Federal Housing Act, reasoning that the state policy of deinstitutionalization and placement of the mentally ill in the least restrictive environment possible justified the city's policy of integration. *See also Harding v. City of Toledo,* 433 F. Supp. 2d 867 (N.D. Ohio 2006) (sustaining 500-foot standard for dispersal of group homes against Federal Housing Act, Americans with Disabilities Act and constitutional challenges, the court distinguishing cases involving greater distance requirements, finding 500 feet presumptively valid).

In marked contrast to the Eighth Circuit ruling in *Familystyle,* the Sixth Circuit in *Larkin v. Michigan Dep't of Social Servs.,* 89 F.3d 285 (6th Cir. 1996), ruled that a state dispersal statute violated the Fair Housing Act:

> [T]he challenged portions of [the Michigan Adult Foster Care Licensing] act are facially discriminatory. The spacing requirement prohibits MDSS from licensing any new [Adult Foster Care] facility if it is within 1500 feet of an existing AFC facility. The notice requirements require MDSS to notify the municipality of the proposed facility, and the local authorities to then notify all residents within 1500 feet of the proposed facility. By their very terms, these statutes apply only to AFC facilities which will house the disabled, and not to other living arrangements. As we have previously noted, statutes that single out for regulation group homes for the handicapped are facially discriminatory.

The Sixth Circuit rejected the argument that the dispersal policy was justified by the goal of integrating the disabled into the community. It stated that "integration is not a sufficient justification for maintaining permanent quotas under the FHA ..., especially where, as here, the burden of the quota falls on the disadvantaged minority," and in any event there had been no showing of "how the special needs of the disabled warrant intervention to ensure that they are integrated."

5. *Familial and Age Bias.* The Fair Housing Amendments Act of 1988 extended the Federal Housing Act to prohibit discrimination against families with children. However, §3607(b)(2) exempts senior citizen housing to be occupied solely by persons over age 62 or intended to be occupied by at least one person over the age of 55. Would a proposed group home for foster children or juvenile delinquents enjoy Federal Housing Act protection? *Keys Youth Servs., Inc. v. City of Olathe,* 248 F.3d 1267 (10th Cir. 2001) (ruling that denial of a special use permit for a youth group home was not within the Federal Housing Act, because a group home is not within "familial status" coverage). *See also* Michael J. Davis & Karen L. Gaus, Protecting Group Homes for the Non-Handicapped: Zoning in the Post-*Edmonds* Era, 46 Kan. L. Rev. 777 (1998). Would zoning amendments restricting the opportunity for residential development constitute familial bias? *Easthampton Ctr. v. Township of Easthampton,* 155 F. Supp. 2d 102 (D.N.J. 2001) (no).

Some states have authorized senior citizen zoning. *See, e.g., Taxpayers Ass'n v. Weymouth Twp.* 364 A.2d 1016 (N.J. 1976) (sustaining zoning requiring the head of household or spouse be 52 years of age or older). Can New Jersey enforce its statute after the amendments to the Federal Housing Act? What if the community has an adequate supply of housing for families with children? What if decent housing is in short supply?

The Federal Housing Act was amended by the Housing for Older Persons Act of 1995 (P. L. 104-76). The law formerly contained a requirement, found in the senior citizen exemption from the provision outlawing familial bias, that housing projects for those aged 55 or older must provide "significant facilities and services especially designed to meet the physical or social needs of older persons." The 1995 amendments eliminated that requirement. *See* 42 U.S.C. §3607.

To be eligible for the senior citizen exemption, at least 80 percent of the occupied units must be occupied by at least one person age 55 or older, and the policy must be published and adhered to. In addition, a housing provider is immune from damages for violation of the familial bias provisions if the provider (1) in good faith has stated in writing that the facility complies with the exemption requirements, and (2) has no actual knowledge that the facility is or will not be eligible. *See* Robert G. Schwemm & Michael Allen, For the Rest of Their Lives: Seniors and the Fair Housing Act, 90 Iowa L. Rev. 121 (2004); John Nelson, Comment, The Perpetuation of Segregation: The Senior Citizen Housing Exemption in the 1988 Amendments to the Fair Housing Act, 26 T. Jefferson L. Rev. 103 (2003).

———————————

The sweeping protections of Title VIII of the Federal Housing Act create an interesting — and controversial — tension with the First Amendment. The Federal Housing Act makes it unlawful to "coerce, intimidate, threaten, or interfere with" any person's exercise of his or her rights protected under the act. 42 U.S.C. §3617. Another provision makes it a crime to use "force or threat of force" to interfere with or intimidate a person attempting to exercise their rights under the act. 42 U.S.C. §3631. These provisions raise the question of whether expressions of community opposition to certain types of housing might trigger civil or even criminal liability. For example, could neighborhood opposition to proposed housing for the handicapped violate §3617? What if the form of the opposition was picketing and chanting adjacent to a group home? What if the opposition organized a protest in front of city hall, with members of the protest group speaking in opposition to a use permit? What if they filed a lawsuit challenging the proposed project on environmental grounds? How should the tension with the First Amendment freedoms of expression and petition be resolved? *See* David E. Bernstein, Defending the First Amendment from Antidiscrimination Laws, 82 N.C. L. Rev. 223 (2003); Michael P. Seng, Hate Speech and Enforcement of the Fair Housing Laws, 29 J. Marshall L. Rev. 409 (1996); Mary C. Lee, Note, The Conflict Between "Fair Housing" and Free Speech, 4 Wm. & Mary Bill Rts. J. 1223 (1996) (valuing expression over interference with civil rights).

The U.S. Department of Housing and Urban Development has issued guidelines for administrative investigation and processing of Federal Housing Act complaints that may implicate the First Amendment. *See* Substantive and Procedural Limitations on Filing and Investigative Fair Housing Act Complaints That May Implicate the First Amendment (issued May 26, 2015) at http://portal.hud.gov/hudportal/documents/huddoc?id=5-26-2015notice.pdf (last visited Nov. 12, 2016). The guidelines reflect a political compromise designed to enforce the rights created by the Federal Housing Act while avoiding impairment of freedom of speech and the right to petition. Generally, the guidelines limit HUD review of complaints concerning §3617 to cases involving force, physical harm, or the clear threat of force or physical harm. The guidelines specifically exempt peaceful demonstrations, distribution of literature, holding meetings, communicating with the government, and participating in public hearings. The guidelines permit the filing of complaints based on the filing of lawsuits only with the written consent of HUD headquarters. The guidelines also outlaw subpoenas directed to obtaining membership lists, fund-raising information, or financial data of organizations that may be engaged in protected speech activities. In sum, the guidelines explicitly err on the side of First Amendment protection, and in doing so, they arguably risk failure to protect the victims of harassment and interference.

In *White v. Lee*, 227 F.3d 1214 (9th Cir. 2000), a local nonprofit housing developer, Resources for Community Development (RCD), applied for a land use permit from Berkeley's Zoning Adjustment Board. RCD sought to convert a motel to a multi-family housing unit for homeless persons. The plaintiffs lived close to the Bel Air Motel and were opposed to its proposed conversion. They expressed their opposition in a variety of ways. They wrote to the Berkeley City Council, spoke out before the Zoning Adjustment Board and at other public meetings, and published a newsletter with articles critical of the project. The plaintiffs discussed their opposition to the project with the local press and also attempted to persuade merchants to oppose the Bel Air project.

A housing rights advocacy group filed an administrative complaint with the U.S. Department of Housing and Urban Development. The complaint alleged that three neighbors in Berkeley opposed the conversion of a motel into a multi-family housing unit because they believed that the project would bring people into the neighborhood who were mentally disabled or disabled through substance abuse. The HUD office initiated an eight-month investigation into the neighbors' activities and beliefs. The HUD officials in San Francisco recommended finding that the neighbors had violated the Fair Housing Act, but officials in Washington ultimately concluded that no violation had occurred and that the neighbors had engaged solely in activities protected by the First Amendment.

The three neighbors then filed a civil rights action alleging a violation of their First Amendment rights. In response, the officials argued that the Fair Housing Act required them to investigate whether the neighbors had filed a lawsuit in state court with an unlawful discriminatory motive. At the very least, they argued, they were entitled to qualified immunity. The Ninth Circuit ruled that the investigation into the plaintiffs' activities violated their First Amendment rights and that the defendant officials were not entitled to immunity. The court appeared to interpret the dividing line between constitutional and unconstitutional application of the Title VIII interference provision to be acts involving violence. *Contra Walker v. City of Lakewood*, 272 F.3d 1114 (9th Cir. 2001) (rejecting any requirement for violence to make out a §3617 interference claim).

The *White v. Lee* decision presents the conflict between free speech and the right to engage in a range of behavior that may be undertaken intentionally or unintentionally as part of an effort to exclude from housing the group or members of a minority group protected under the civil rights laws. How far can protestors go in opposing housing for the disabled or housing that might be occupied by persons of minority ethnic membership? Should speech be absolute or limited as in the case of hostile environmental sexual harassment? Should the same limits apply to housing or land use discrimination? Is the home equivalent to the environment of the workplace, or is it entitled to even more protection? What if the protest comes in the form of a march to say "leave our neighborhood"? What if it is in the form of a civilized protest over parking and traffic before the planning commission? What if the protest takes the form of an environmental lawsuit?

2. Other Federal Statutes Addressing Housing Discrimination

While the Fair Housing Act is unquestionably the principal federal statute addressing housing discrimination, there are numerous other federal statutes that come into play in this area.

a. Section 1982

Originally adopted as part of the post-Civil War Civil Rights Act of 1866, 42 U.S.C. §1982 provides: "All citizens of the United States shall have the same right, in every State and Territory, as is enjoyed by white citizens thereof to inherit, purchase, lease, sell, hold, and convey real and personal property." For many years this provision was essentially a dead letter. However, in *Jones v. Alfred H. Mayer Co.*, 392 U.S. 409 (1968), the Supreme Court held that this provision bars all racial discrimination, whether public or private, affecting either the sale or rental of property. Discrimination involving property is a "badge or incident of slavery," the Court ruled. Thus, Congress could reach purely private transactions exercising its power under Thirteenth Amendment powers. The irony in the timing of the Court's decision is that Congress enacted the Fair Housing Act, providing a private remedy against public as well as private housing remedy, in the same year.

However, §1982 has a different scope than the Fair Housing Act, with the result that some forms of discrimination reachable under the Fair Housing Act will not support a §1982 claim, and some forms of housing discrimination can be reached under §1982 but not the Fair Housing Act. The Fair Housing Act addresses discrimination based on various criteria, including race, color, national origin, religion, sex, familial status and handicap; §1982 only reaches racial discrimination. In addition, the Fair Housing Act prohibits discrimination in advertising, but §1982 does not address advertising. On the other hand, the Fair Housing Act includes several exemptions; §1982 has no exemptions. Thus, the owner of a rooming house could not be held liable under the Fair Housing Act for refusing to rent to African-Americans; a claim based on such discrimination would lie under §1982.

Furthermore, as affirmed by the Supreme Court in 2015, in *Inclusive Communities*, a showing of disparate impact is sufficient to establish a violation of the Fair Housing Act. But a showing of discriminatory motive is probably necessary to establish a violation of §1982. *See General Bldg. Contractors Ass'n, Inc. v. Pa.*, 458 U.S. 375 (1982) (holding that 42 U.S.C. §1981, "like the Equal Protection Clause, can be violated only by purposeful discrimination"). *See also City of Memphis v. Greene*, 451 U.S. 100, 120-21 (1981) (declining to reach the question whether §1982 reaches purposeful discrimination).

b. Section 1983

Section 1983 of the Civil Rights Act, 42 U.S.C. §1983 (2006), is the primary vehicle for bringing equal protection, due process, takings, and any other constitutional or federal statutory claims against states and local governments in the land use context. This provision requires state action, *West v. Atkins*, 487 U.S. 42 (1988), and certain public officials enjoy absolute immunity. *Bogan v. Scott-Harris*, 523 U.S. 44 (1998) (local legislators, including a mayor exercising legislative powers such as recommending enactment and approving a budget ordinance, are immune); *Tenny v. Brandhove*, 341 U.S. 367 (1951) (state legislators). State and local administrative officers enjoy qualified immunity. *Scheuer v. Rhodes*, 416 U.S. 232 (1974). Qualified immunity requires that the plaintiff must prove bad faith, typically by demonstrating the violation of a clearly established legal right. *Davis v. Scherer*, 468 U.S. 183 (1984).

c. Section 1985

Section 1985 of the Civil Rights Act, 42 U.S.C. §1985 (2006), covers private conspiracies involving race discrimination under the Thirteenth Amendment. It also reaches conspiracies based on other classifications where state action is present.

d. Title VI

Title VI of the 1964 Civil Rights Act, 42 U.S.C. §2000d (2006), provides a remedy for discrimination on the basis of race, national origin, or religion in programs receiving federal financial assistance, and programs and projects administered or funded by a federal agency. Pursuant to the Civil Rights Restoration Act of 1987, Pub. L. No. 100-259, §6, 102 Stat. 28, 31 (1988), the entire institution receiving federal assistance is subject to Title VI and other civil rights standards. Title VI requires that a plaintiff prove intent in order to recover damages, but the plaintiff must only prove discriminatory impact in order to obtain injunctive relief. *Guardians Ass'n v. Civil Service Comm'n*, 463 U.S. 582 (1983).

e. Other Laws

The Equal Credit Opportunity Act, 15 U.S.C. §1691 (2016), prohibits bias in lending, reinforcing the restrictions on discrimination in lending established by the Fair Housing Act. *See* 42 U.S.C. §3605 (2016). The Federal Home Mortgage Disclosure Act, 12 U.S.C. §§2801-2810 (2016), requires major lenders to disclose the race of applicants and borrowers as well as loan performance by census tract or neighborhood. This disclosure allows analysis of minority lender participation. Under the Federal Community Reinvestment Act, federal lending regulators are required to consider a lender's record in meeting the entire community's lending needs when reviewing requested approvals for mergers and branch operations' expansion. 12 U.S.C. §§2901-2908 (2006).

14

Environmental Protection

A. INTRODUCTION

1. The Intersection of Land Use and Environmental Law

This chapter highlights a development that has been responsible for much of the complexity found in modern land use regulation: the integration of environmental protection into land use decisions. If you had taken a course in land use controls before 1970, this chapter would not have existed in your casebook. At that time little environmental legislation existed, and the sparse body of environmental law was largely separated from the well-established system of land use controls implemented by local governments.

The rise of modern environmental regulation generally dates from 1969, when Congress passed the National Environmental Policy Act, the law that requires federal agencies to prepare environmental impact statements on actions that may have a significant effect on the environment. A deluge of new federal statutes then followed over the next five years, including the Clean Air Act Amendments of 1970, the Federal Water Pollution Control Act Amendments of 1972 (later renamed the Clean Water Act), the Endangered Species Act of 1973, the Resource Conservation and Recovery Act, and the Coastal Zone Management Act. Later, during the waning days of the administration of President Jimmy Carter in 1980, Congress enacted the Comprehensive Environmental Response, Compensation, and Liability Act, known as "CERCLA" or more commonly as the "Superfund," which imposes liability for the cleanup of hazardous waste sites. Each of these landmark laws implicates how land is and can be used.

2. The Impact on Applicants for Land Use Approvals

The predominant regulatory method employed by environmental laws is the issuance of permits by either the federal government or by states whose regulatory programs have received federal approval. The changes wrought by the laws, however, were much more profound than just adding a new permit or two. In particular, states have also established substantive regulatory requirements aimed at protecting the environment.

These requirements take several forms. First, in many instances states attempted to integrate environmental protection into the traditional tools of land use control. For example, local general plans may be required to include provisions that are designed to protect open space and other natural resources, such as agriculture. Second, some states enacted legislation to protect so-called critical areas, regions of a state that are environmentally sensitive, by establishing regional or state agencies with permit power over developments in these areas. Regions such as the Chesapeake and San Francisco Bays were the subject of legislation that removed the final authority for development approvals from its usual location at the local governmental level and elevated it to regional or state agencies. Third, states passed environmental legislation directed toward specific environmental problems, such as hazardous waste disposal, and these problems often had a land use component to them. More recently state and federal climate change law may require implementation by local land use controls, as we saw in Chapter 11.

This barrage of legislation has fundamentally affected the regulatory requirements that applicants seeking large-scale land use approvals must meet. Major industrial developments, for example, now must secure more than local land use permits; they must also obtain state environmental permits and, in all likelihood, federal permits as well. The lawyer representing a company seeking to site a new industrial facility could well need a general plan amendment, a zone change, and a site approval from a local government; a "prevention of significant deterioration" or "nonattainment" area permit from the state pursuant to the Clean Air Act; a discharge permit issued by a state agency under the Clean Water Act; and a wetlands permit issued by the federal Army Corps of Engineers. A residential developer in a rural area may find that, in addition to local regulatory requirements intended to protect open space, federal requirements protecting endangered species also apply. Indeed, as the student will see in *Tanglewood East Homeowners v. Charles-Thomas, Inc.*, a case included in this chapter, it is even possible for a residential developer to run afoul of CERCLA, the federal hazardous waste cleanup legislation.

3. Land Use Tools for Environmental Protection

In this chapter, you will see environmental protection requirements implemented through traditional land use controls. In *State of New Hampshire v. Rattee*, the case on agricultural protection that is included in this chapter, the local jurisdiction utilized an easement for the purpose of agricultural protection. You will examine how regional and state critical-area programs implement planning mechanisms to protect sensitive resources.

Students also will see how the federal government's regulatory mechanisms for protecting wetlands and endangered species can profoundly affect the ability to develop land. Two of the cases chosen on these subjects, *United States v. Bailey* and *Babbitt v. Sweet Home Chapter of Communities for a Greater Oregon*, respectively illustrate the sweep of the permitting power of the Corps of Engineers over wetlands and the prohibitions in the Endangered Species Act.

This chapter offers the student a chance to integrate and build upon materials covered earlier in the course. For example, the basic planning mechanisms and regulatory tools, such as zoning and subdivision controls, have been adapted to serve new environmental protection goals. Here we also cover the law relevant to hydraulic fracturing, or fracking, an activity that implicates many areas of environmental and land use control. The chapter also relates directly to the material in Chapter 7 on the takings issue, for regulations under environmental protection law can greatly restrict the landowner's ability to use the property.

4. Currency and Controversy

If you pick up today's newspaper or check news with an Internet source, the chances are good that you will see some reference to an environmental dispute of the type examined in this chapter. The material is controversial. Part of the controversy is philosophical, with development interests and environmentalists simply at odds over the "right" amount of environmental protection. In other respects, however, the controversy stems from complaints about the costs that the system can impose upon individual landowners.

One problem is that no correlation necessarily exists between the costs imposed by regulation and the ability of the individuals upon whom they fall to bear them. The extent of the costs depends solely on the resource that is found on the landowner's property. If it turns out that one person owns property upon which an endangered species is located, or that vast parts of the property are covered by wetlands, the law may restrict development on a large part of the property, with potentially serious economic results for the owner. Furthermore, under our approach to hazardous waste sites, the complexity of trying to clean them up can delay development for years, and CERCLA generally imposes liability on all "deep pockets" associated with the site. Thus, the current landowner may be liable for the entire cost of cleanup even though it was not directly responsible for the contamination.

Partly as a result of these costs, and partly because of disputes over the need for these regulatory requirements in the first instance, debate continues over possible changes to the requirements. At the same time, albeit at a much lower level of political attention, it is becoming clear that some of these environmental protection mechanisms are not attaining their goals. In particular, scientists have argued that to be successful, any attempt to protect endangered species must pay greater attention to the habitat that the species depend on for survival and must manage the species on an ecosystem basis. The Endangered Species Act, with its focus on preventing individual actions that affect species on particular properties, is not well-designed to carry out systematic ecosystem protection, although habitat planning is now more common. And, as we saw in Chapter 11, growing concern over "sustainable development" is a feature of both domestic and international law, for example, with a focus on global warming.

The debate over the future of environmental law suggests the need to look at alternative ways of attaining environmental protection goals. To mention a few: creative use of regulated markets, "transferable rights or credits," tax systems, set asides, and mitigation banking.

B. WETLANDS

We begin with the controversial subject of wetlands regulation. The importance of this area of environmental regulation to land use is suggested by two factors. First, the range of acreage that fulfills the definition of a "wetland" is large. Second, Section 404 of the federal Clean Water Act vests considerable power in the United States Army Corps of Engineers and the federal Environmental Protection Agency to deny approval to developments that propose to fill wetlands.

■ UNITED STATES v. BAILEY
571 F.3d 791 (8th Cir. 2009)

Before WOLLMAN, HANSEN, and BYE, Circuit Judges.

WOLLMAN, Circuit Judge.

Gary Bailey constructed a road on a parcel of wetlands in Lake of the Woods County (County), Minnesota, without obtaining a permit under Section 404 of the Clean Water Act (Act). The United States Army Corps of Engineers (Corps) ordered Bailey to restore the land to its previolation condition. Bailey refused, and the United States brought an action under Section 309(b) of the Act to enforce the restoration order and to enjoin Bailey from discharging further pollutants into the wetland. . . .

Bailey appeals, contending that the district court erred in concluding that the Corps has jurisdiction over his property, in granting summary judgment in favor of the United States, and in entering an injunction to enforce the restoration order. He also argues that the restoration order is arbitrary and capricious. We affirm.

I. FACTUAL BACKGROUND

Bailey owns a parcel of land along the western shore of the Lake of the Woods (Lake), which is located in northern Minnesota. At issue in this lawsuit is a thirteen-acre site that consists of approximately twelve acres of wetland, as defined by the Corps.

In the early 1990s, Bailey considered developing the site and received a general permit from the Corps to excavate a harbor. The permit, however, excluded fills for commercial development or residential housing. In 1993, the Corps advised Bailey that the intended harbor was located on wetland and informed him that he would need additional permits to place dredged or fill material on the site. In 1994, after Bailey and a Corps official visited the site, the Corps suggested that Bailey hire a consultant "to help you delineate this highly diverse site and prepare the required application that was previously provided to you." The harbor project was eventually abandoned.

Bailey decided to plat the site for residential development and sell the lakeside property. The development was named Sunny Beach and consisted of fourteen lots, each having approximately 100 feet of lakefront. In 1998, Bailey hired Mark LaValla to build a road through the site to provide access to the lots. Bailey did not seek any permits from the Corps before LaValla began constructing the road.

LaValla cleared a roadway sixty-six feet wide and about a quarter of a mile long, running parallel to the Lake's shoreline. LaValla dug ditches on either side of the road and used the excavated material to build up the road. Before the road was complete, on June 11, 1998, employees of the local Soil and Water Conservation District visited the site and told LaValla that the road construction was not properly permitted and that he should stop construction, which he did. . . .

On June 17, 1998, Bailey filed a Local-State-Federal Project Notification Form with the County wherein he proposed building an access road for logging on the site. Bailey believed that his application would be accepted, and he alleges that an official from the Soil and Water Conservation District told him that the Corps would approve the permit and that he should finish the road. Without waiting for a decision on his application, Bailey instructed LaValla to finish work on the access road. LaValla completed the road, topping the roadbed with 2000 square yards of gravel.

The Corps received a copy of Bailey's notification form on August 17, 1998, and treated it as an after-the-fact application for a permit under Section 404 of the Act. On September 17, 1998, after the road was complete, the Corps notified Bailey in writing that the work was done in violation of the Act, that his permit was incomplete, that no additional work should be done on the road without a permit, and that if his permit was ultimately denied, he would be required to restore the land to its previous condition.

Bailey intended to dedicate the road to the County so that the road would become public and be maintained by the County. Accordingly, the road had to be built to meet the County's road specifications. . . . LaValla completed the work on the road that summer.

While the road was being completed, Bailey was also preparing to plat the site. In October 1998, shortly after he received the notice of violation from the Corps, Bailey filed an application with the County to plat fourteen residential lots on the site. The County's environmental services director recommended the approval of the Sunny Beach plat, and the County's board of commissioners approved the plat on December 22, 1998. Upon approval of the plat, the road became a public road, although the County disputes the nature and extent of its property rights.

On June 12, 2001, the Corps denied Bailey's Section 404 permit application. On October 22, 2001, after a period of public notice and comment, the Corps ordered Bailey to restore the property at his own expense. The restoration order required Bailey to (1) remove the dredged and fill material used in construction of the road; (2) fill in the ditches with native, loamy soils; (3) seed the restored area with a specified seed mixture; and (4) control certain weed species for three years following restoration. Bailey refused to comply with the restoration order, and the United States brought this enforcement action. . . .

II. Issues on Appeal

Bailey raises the following arguments on appeal: (1) that the district court erred in applying Justice Kennedy's opinion in *Rapanos v. United States*, 547 U.S. 715, 126

S. Ct. 2208, 165 L.Ed.2d 159 (2006), to determine whether the Corps had jurisdiction over the site and that even if Justice Kennedy's opinion controls, the Corps has failed to show that the wetland has a significant nexus to or is adjacent to the Lake of the Woods; (2) that the Corps' denial of the after-the-fact permit and its restoration order are arbitrary and capricious; and (3) that the district court abused its discretion when it approved the restoration plan.

A. SUMMARY JUDGMENT AND THE CORPS' JURISDICTION UNDER THE ACT

Congress enacted the Clean Water Act in 1972 "to restore and maintain the chemical, physical, and biological integrity of the Nation's waters." 33 U.S.C. §1251. The Act prohibits the discharge of any pollutant from any point source into navigable waters of the United States without a proper permit from the Secretary of the Army (through the Corps) or from the EPA. §§1311, 1342, 1344. The Corps and the EPA share responsibility for implementing and enforcing the Act's permit scheme for the discharge of pollutants into navigable waters, and the extent of the Corps' jurisdiction has been hotly contested in cases around the country. . . . Bailey challenges the Corps' assertion of jurisdiction over the site, arguing that the land onto which he discharged the pollutants did not constitute "navigable waters" under the Act.

The Act defines navigable waters as "the waters of the United States, including the territorial seas." §1362(7). The regulations promulgated by the Corps define navigable waters as "navigable-in-fact" or "traditionally navigable" waters and the wetlands adjacent to such waters. 33 C.F.R. §328.3(a).

1. The Supreme Court's Opinions in *Rapanos v. United States*

In *Rapanos v. United States*, the Supreme Court addressed how the term "navigable waters" should be construed under the Act and the extent to which the term includes wetlands. All members of the Court agreed that "navigable waters" encompassed something more than traditional navigable-in-fact waters. 547 U.S. at 730-31, 126 S.Ct. 2208 (plurality opinion); 767, 126 S. Ct. 2208 (Kennedy, J., concurring); 788, 126 S. Ct. 2208 (Stevens, J., dissenting). There was no majority opinion, with five justices concluding that remand was necessary for consideration of whether the wetlands at issue in *Rapanos* were "navigable waters" covered by the Act and whether the EPA and the Corps had impermissibly extended their regulatory jurisdiction under the Act. Justice Scalia wrote the plurality opinion, joined by three other justices; Justice Kennedy wrote a concurring opinion; and Justice Stevens wrote the dissenting opinion, joined by three other justices.

The plurality opinion limits federal authority over "navigable waters" to "those wetlands with a continuous surface connection to bodies that are 'waters of the United States' in their own right, so that there is no clear demarcation between 'waters' and wetlands, are 'adjacent to' such waters and covered by the Act." *Id.* at 742, 126 S. Ct. 2208. The plurality test requires two findings:

> First, that the adjacent channel contains a "wate[r] of the United States," (*i.e.*, a relatively permanent body of water connected to traditional interstate navigable waters); and second, that the wetland has a continuous surface connection with that water, making it difficult to determine where the "water" ends and the "wetland" begins.

Id.

In his concurring opinion, Justice Kennedy rejected these two requirements as "unduly dismissive of the interests asserted by the United States in these cases" and recognized that the rationale for the Act's regulation of wetlands is the functions that wetlands perform in relation to the integrity of other waters — "functions such as pollutant trapping, flood control, and runoff storage." *Id.* at 777, 779, 126 S. Ct. 2208. Accordingly, Justice Kennedy determined that the government's jurisdiction under the Act extends to wetlands that "possess a significant nexus to waters that are or were navigable in fact or that could reasonably be so made." *Id.* at 759, 126 S. Ct. 2208 (internal quotations omitted). "[W]etlands possess the requisite nexus, and thus come within the statutory phrase 'navigable waters,' if the wetlands, either alone or in combination with similarly situated lands in the region, significantly affect the chemical, physical, and biological integrity of the covered waters more readily understood as 'navigable.'" *Id.* at 780, 126 S. Ct. 2208. A wetland would not satisfy Justice Kennedy's test if its effect on water quality were speculative or insubstantial. *Id.* Justice Kennedy also concluded that if the wetland is adjacent to navigable-in-fact waters, then the Corps "may rely on adjacency to establish its jurisdiction." *Id.* at 782, 126 S. Ct. 2208.

The dissenters determined that to the extent the Act requires a significant nexus, the requirement "is categorically satisfied as to wetlands adjacent to navigable waters or their tributaries." *Id.* at 807, 126 S. Ct. 2208. The dissent specifically noted that all four dissenters would uphold the Corps' jurisdiction in cases that satisfy either the plurality's test or Justice Kennedy's. *Id.* at 810 n. 14, 126 S. Ct. 2208. . . .

2. The Circuit Courts' Application of *Rapanos v. United States*

When a majority of the Supreme Court agrees only on the outcome of a case and not on the grounds for that outcome, "the holding of the Court may be viewed as that position taken by those Members who concurred in the judgments on the narrowest grounds." *Marks v. United States*, 430 U.S. 188, 193, 97 S. Ct. 990, 51 L.Ed.2d 260 (1977) (internal quotations omitted). . . . Because there is little overlap between the plurality's and Justice Kennedy's opinions, it is difficult to determine which holding is the narrowest.

Of those circuit courts that have considered *Rapanos*, most have concluded that Justice Kennedy's opinion constitutes the narrowest holding . . .

The First Circuit has concluded that the *Marks* rule is unworkable as applied to *Rapanos* and has instead followed the dissent's instruction to find jurisdiction if either the plurality's test or Justice Kennedy's test is met. *United States v. Johnson*, 467 F.3d 56, 66 (1st Cir. 2006). . . .

[W]e join the First Circuit in holding that the Corps has jurisdiction over wetlands that satisfy either the plurality or Justice Kennedy's test.

3. Justice Kennedy's Jurisdictional Test Is Met in This Case Because the Wetland Is Adjacent to Lake of the Woods

Justice Kennedy's opinion holds that when a wetland is adjacent to the navigable-in-fact waters, then a significant nexus exists as a matter of law. *Rapanos*, 547 U.S. at 780, 126 S. Ct. 2208 . . . If the wetland is adjacent to non-navigable tributaries of navigable-in-fact waters, then the Corps must show that the wetland "significantly affect[s] the chemical, physical, and biological integrity" of the navigable-in-fact waters. *Rapanos*, 547 U.S. at 780, 126 S. Ct. 2208.

Justice Kennedy found the Corps' definition of adjacent to be reasonable when applied to wetland adjacent to navigable-in-fact waters, 547 U.S. at 774, 126 S. Ct. 2208, and the Corps defines "adjacent" to mean "bordering, contiguous, or neighboring." 33 C.F.R. §328.3(c) . . .

Bailey argues that the Corps has failed to meet its burden on summary judgment to show that the wetland at issue is adjacent to the Lake. Specifically, Bailey argues that the Corps has not shown that the fifteen-foot corridor closest to the Lake has wetland hydrology because it did not sample the soil saturation. Without wetland hydrology, the corridor cannot be deemed a wetland. Bailey also contends that a genuine issue of material fact exists as to whether the 100-foot corridor closest to the Lake is wetland because Gary Lockner, the County's environmental services director, testified in a related proceeding that it is not. . . . To determine whether these corridors constitute wetlands, we review the definition of wetlands and explain the Corps' evaluation of the site.

The Corps defines wetlands as "those areas that are inundated or saturated by surface or ground water at a frequency and duration sufficient to support, and that under normal circumstances do support, a prevalence of vegetation typically adapted for life in saturated soil conditions." 33 C.F.R. §328.3(b). The Corps conducts wetland delineations to determine the presence and extent of wetland, using the criteria set forth in the 1987 Corps of Engineers Wetlands Delineation Manual (1987 Manual) and Corps' guidance interpreting the 1987 Manual.

In general, the 1987 Manual defines land as wetland when, under normal conditions: (1) the land is dominated by hydrophytic vegetation (plants that have the ability to grow, effectively compete, reproduce and/or persist in anaerobic soil conditions caused by inundated or saturated soil conditions); (2) the land has wetland hydrology (inundated or saturated to the surface for at least five percent of the growing season in most years); and (3) the land consists of hydric soils (soils formed under conditions of saturation, flooding, or ponding long enough during the growing season to develop anaerobic conditions in the upper part of the soil). The Corps uses defined field indicators to determine whether the land is wetland by investigating the plants, water, and soil.

To determine whether an area is dominated by hydrophytic vegetation, the Corps establishes at least one sample point within each plant community and surveys the herbaceous vegetation within a five-foot radius and the woody vegetation within a thirty-foot radius. The Corps consults a list of plant species published by the United States Fish and Wildlife Services, which assigns an indicator status to individual plant species reflecting their probability of occurrence in wetlands. Hydrophytic vegetation is present if greater than fifty percent of the dominant plant species are obligate wetland plants, facultative wetland plants, or facultative plants (excluding facultative negative).[4]

To determine whether the land has wetland hydrology, the Corps requires either one primary indicator, such as direct observation of soil saturation within twelve inches of the surface, or two secondary indicators, such as the FAC-neutral test and local soil survey data. The FAC-neutral test uses vegetation as a secondary

---

4. Obligate wetland plants are those that occur almost always in wetlands under natural conditions (greater than 99 percent probability), but which may also occur rarely in nonwetlands. Facultative wetland plants occur usually in wetlands (greater than 67 percent probability), but also occur in nonwetlands. Facultative plants occur in both wetlands and nonwetlands.

indicator of hydrology. If obligate wetland plants and facultative wetland plants outnumber facultative upland plants and obligate upland plants, then the sample meets the FAC-neutral test and tests positive as a secondary indicator of hydrology. The rationale is that obligate wetland plants and facultative wetland plants occur in wetlands 67 to 99 percent of the time. Facultative plants, which occur in both wetlands and nonwetlands, are considered neutral.

An interdisciplinary team consisting of Steve Eggers, a senior ecologist with the Corps; Rod Heschke, a soil scientist with the United States Department of Agriculture; and Kelly Urbanek, a senior project manager and biologist with the Corps, conducted field investigations to delineate the wetland at the site. Consistent with the 1987 Manual, they established at least one sample point where a change in soils, hydrology, vegetation, or topography occurred, which resulted in a survey of forty-six sample points along established transects. They sampled vegetation, saturation levels, and soil types, concluding that the wetland encompassed the entire site except for approximately 1.31 acres.

According to the expert report prepared by Eggers and Heschke, there is no upland border along the site's shoreline. Thirteen of the forty-six sample points were within 15 to 101 feet of the cut bank of the shoreline. All thirteen of these sample points were dominated by hydrophytes and had hydric soils. Eleven of the thirteen had saturated soils within twelve inches of the surface, a primary indicator of wetland hydrology. The twelfth met two secondary indicators of wetland hydrology, the FAC-neutral test and the local soil survey data. The thirteenth sample point lacked sufficient indicators of wetland hydrology. Eggers and Heschke concluded that the area surrounding the thirteenth point is drained by a preexisting ditch and does not constitute a wetland.

Although the Corps did not sample the soil saturation, a primary indicator of wetland hydrology, within the fifteen-foot corridor of land closest to the Lake, two secondary indicators — the FAC-neutral test and local soil survey data — were met. Eggers found that the FAC-neutral test was met in the fifteen-foot corridor based on his observation of the vegetation closest to the lakeshore. Eggers established three sample points at the fifteen-foot mark, and he surveyed the herbaceous vegetation within the five-foot radius of the sample points and the saplings and shrubs within the thirty-foot radius. Eggers observed no changes in vegetation between the Lake and the sample points at the fifteen-foot mark that would have necessitated further sampling and determined that the land closest to the Lake tests positive under the FAC-neutral test. The other secondary indicator was local soil survey data, which Heschke reviewed. Heschke concluded that the soils within fifteen feet of the Lake are hydric based on his observations of the site, the National Cooperative Soil Survey, and the prevalence of the hydric soils in the surrounding area. The Corps thus presented sufficient evidence to allow a fact-finder to conclude that the fifteen-foot corridor closest to the Lake's shoreline consisted of wetland hydrology.

Bailey failed to rebut the Corps' evidence . . .

Bailey also contends that the 100-foot corridor closest to the Lake is not wetland, but he has again failed to submit evidence sufficient to create a genuine issue of material fact . . .

The Corps has submitted competent and extensive evidence in this case to show that the site is situated in a wetland adjacent to navigable-in-fact waters, whereas

Bailey has failed to present contrary evidence sufficient to create a genuine issue of material fact that the land closest to the Lake is not wetland.

[The Court then went on to uphold the Restoration Order and the District Court's permanent injunction to enforce that Order.]

Notes and Comments

1. *The Scope and Importance of Wetlands.* For years, wetlands were routinely filled — with little thought given to the consequences. Prior to the 1960s, wetlands "were considered disease-ridden wastelands and were failed and drained at an alarming rate." Lori A. Sutter et al., Science and Policy of U.S. Wetlands, 29 Tul. Envtl. L.J. 31, 32 (2015). By the late 1990s, however, the filling of wetlands became subject to extensive regulation by a variety of federal, state, and local agencies.

It has been estimated that there were originally 221 million acres of wetlands in the continental United States. A 2009 report found that between 2004 and 2009, the net wetland loss was estimated to be 62,300 acres, bringing the nation's total wetland acreage to just over 100 million acres in the continental United States, excluding Alaska and Hawaii. *See* U.S. Fish and Wildlife Service, Status and Trends of Wetlands in the Conterminous United States: 2004 to 2009 (2011) http://www.fws.gov/wetlands/Status-And-Trends-2009/index.html (last visited Nov. 5, 2016).

Wetlands play an important ecological role:

> Wetlands are prized for many reasons, including their aesthetic value. But wetlands also provide important ecosystem services to plant, animal, and human communities. Wetlands serve as natural wastewater treatment facilities, filtering out pollutants and improving water quality. They absorb the impact of floods and stabilize runoff by retaining water and releasing it gradually. Wetlands similarly temper catastrophic climatic events.
>
> Wetlands are "nurseries of life" that serve as home to millions of plants and animals that rely on them for food, habitat, and breeding grounds. Although they cover less than five percent of the land surface, wetlands host thirty-one percent of all plant species in the lower forty-eight states. They are among the most fertile and biologically productive ecosystems in the world, rivaling tropical rainforests and coral reefs in the number and diversity of species they support. More than one-third of threatened or endangered species live only in wetlands, and many species are dependent on wetlands to reproduce.

Mark Squillace, From "Navigable Waters" to "Constitutional Waters": The Future of Federal Wetlands Regulation, 40 U. Mich. J.L. Reform 799, 805 (2007).

2. *Wetlands Within the CWA Framework.* The Supreme Court decision in *Rapanos*, while technical, is extremely important from a practical perspective. If a development is subject to CWA regulation, its permit may be denied, or it may be required to undertake extensive mitigation. Equally important, the regulatory process itself is lengthy. Furthermore, as the *Bailey* case illustrates, a developer who acts without a permit is subject to an enforcement action that can result in an injunction requiring restoration of the wetland. A criminal prosecution is also possible. *See United States v. Lucas*, 516 F.3d 316 (5th Cir. 2008) (prosecution for conspiracy to violate the Clean Water Act).

What is the difference between the position taken by the four-person plurality in *Rapanos* and the dissent in that case? Is Justice Kennedy's position, which includes a "significant nexus" requirement, sufficiently grounded in the statutory language of the CWA? More broadly, is a court the appropriate entity to decide questions like this one? *See* Dwight H. Merriam, Up the Creek Without a Paddle: The U.S. Supreme Court Decides Little in Deciding *Rapanos* and *Carabell*, 48 Planning & Envtl. L. 3, 10-11 (Aug. 2006) (transcript of oral argument in *Rapanos* shows that "the judicial branch is not the best place to resolve complex issues of physical hydrology, habitat preservation, and the public's interest in sustainable development."); Michael Farrell, A Wetland Functions Approach to Applying the Opinions from the *Rapanos* Decision, 19 U. Denv. Water L. Rev. 61 (2015).

The *Rapanos* decision brought confusion. *Compare United States v. Robison*, 505 F.3d 1208 (11th Cir. 2007) (applying Justice Kennedy's concurring test) *with United States v. Donovan*, 661 F.3d 174 (3d Cir. 2011) (applying Justice Kennedy's test or Justice Scalia's test). The U.S. Army Corps of Engineers issued a guidance interpreting its jurisdiction under the CWA after *Rapanos*. The guidance instructs the agency's personnel to assert jurisdiction whenever either the Kennedy test or the test of the four-justice plurality is met. *See* EPA/Corps, Clean Water Act Jurisdiction Following the U.S. Supreme Court's Decision in *Rapanos v. United States & Carabell v. United States* (Dec. 2, 2008). *See also Precon Dev. Corp., Inc. v. U.S. Army Corps of Engineers*, 633 F.3d 278 (6th Cir. 2011) (acknowledging the guidance but finding insufficient evidence of a "significant nexus" between 448 acres of similarly situated wetlands and the Northwest River).

Then, in 2015, EPA and the Corps of Engineers adopted a comprehensive rule defining the "waters of the United States." 4 C.F.R. §110.1(1) (2015). Among other features, the rule protects tributaries that show physical features of flowing water and sets boundaries for covering nearby waters. *See generally* U.S. EPA, Fact Sheet, Clean Water Rule (2015) at https://www.epa.gov/sites/production/files/2015-05/documents/fact_sheet_summary_final_1.pdf (last visited Sept. 21, 2016); Erin Ryan, Federalism, Regulatory Architecture, and the Clean Water Rule: Seeking Consensus on the Waters of the United States, 46 Envtl. L. 277, 299-308 (2016) (summarizing the rule). The new EPA rule was enormously controversial and was met with a deluge of litigation. Ultimately, the U.S. Court of Appeals for the Sixth Circuit issued a stay on the rule's enforcement pending the outcome of the litigation, which was undecided when this edition went to press. *In Re E.P.A.*, 803 F.3d 804 (6th Cir. 2015).

3. *"Ripping" and "Sidecasting."* Another important jurisdictional issue involves the kinds of activities that subject a party to the Act's regulatory provisions. The Clean Water Act prohibits the "discharge of any pollutant" into the nation's waters, which include wetlands (subject to the *Rapanos* case). A discharge is "any addition of any pollutant" from a point source. 33 U.S.C. §1362(12). A pollutant, in turn, is defined to include rock and sand. What if a farmer, in order to put in new crops, engages in "deep ripping" — dragging four- to seven-foot metal prongs through the soil, thereby puncturing the protective clay layer which prevents surface water from penetrating deeply into the soil?

In *Borden Ranch P'ship v. U.S. Army Corps of Engineers* 261 F.3d 810 (9th Cir. 2001), the court held that this activity was subject to the Corps' jurisdiction. The activity also did not fall into the "farming exception," which exempts discharges from "normal farming . . . and ranching activities, such as plowing." 33 U.S.C. §1344(f)(1)(A). That section was subject to yet another exception where the discharge was used to bring the area of the navigable water into a use to which it was not previously subject. *Id.*§1344(f)(2). With Justice Kennedy recusing himself, a divided Supreme Court split 4 to 4, thereby affirming the judgment. *Borden Ranch P'ship v. U.S. Army Corps of Engineers*, 537 U.S. 99, 123 S. Ct. 599 (2002).

A related practice is "sidecasting." As the court explained in *United States v. Cundiff*, 555 F.3d 200, 213-14 (6th Cir. 2009):

> Sidecasting involves the addition of dredged or excavated dirt from a removal site (here, the ditches the Cundiffs dug), to some disposal site (here, the Cundiffs' own wetlands). Sidecasting's purpose is to fill wetlands to dry them out. Although it is plausible to read "addition" as covering only completely foreign materials, that reading is foreclosed because "pollutant" is *defined* in the Act to specifically include "dredged spoil"—the Cundiffs would read that term out of the Act. Further, the Act is not concerned with mere "material," but instead with the addition of "pollutants"— material can be benign in one spot and seriously disruptive to the surrounding ecological system in another.

Under decisions like this one, the CWA's wetlands provisions have important implications for the development industry. *See Benham v. Ozark Materials River Rock, LLC,* 2013 WL 5372316 (N.D. Okla. 2013) ("The actions complained of by Benham involve more than incidental fallback. Specifically, he alleges that Ozark is engaged in 'sidecasting' and other regulated dredging and filling of wetlands without a permit, all in violation of §404.").

4. *Finality.* Given the reach of the Clean Water Act to regulate land use developments and the potential cost of compliance, a determination by EPA or the U.S. Army Corps of Engineers that an area falls within the agencies' jurisdiction is important. One question was whether a party is entitled to immediately seek judicial review of that determination or must await the full regulatory outcome at a much later date. The federal circuits split on that question. In 2016, the U.S. Supreme Court put the question to rest. The Court found that a peat mining company was entitled to seek review of a jurisdictional determination that the property contained "waters of the United States and thus were subject to the permitting requirements of the Clean Water Act." *United States Army Corps of Engineers v. Hawkes Co., Inc.,* __ U.S. __, 136 S. Ct. 1807 (2016).

5. *The Federal Regulatory Agencies.* One of the reasons for the controversy surrounding wetlands regulation lies in the number of federal agencies with a role in it. The principal federal agency in charge is the U.S. Army Corps of Engineers, which issues a permit under §404 of the Clean Water Act, 33 U.S.C. §1344. The U.S. Environmental Protection Agency also plays a big role. The EPA (in conjunction with the Corps) not only develops guidelines that must be satisfied before a permit may be issued (*see* 40 C.F.R. §§230 *et seq.*), the agency also may "veto" the issuance of a permit by the Corps. Furthermore, the U.S. Fish and Wildlife Service (part of the Department of the Interior) and the National Marine Fisheries Service (part of the Department of Commerce) must be allowed to comment on applications for §404 permits.

6. *Permit Standards: Public Interest and Alternatives.* From the applicant's standpoint the focus of the process is on the standards used to determine whether to

grant the §404 permit. The U.S. Army Corps of Engineers uses a "public interest" review to make this determination. Under this standard, the U.S. Army Corps of Engineers weighs a wide variety of diverse factors, from environmental to economic considerations. The evaluation also examines the existence of alternative locations and methods to accomplish the project's objectives. The specific weight given each factor "is determined by its importance and relevance to the particular proposal." 33 C.F.R. §320.4(a).

Is a plaintiff likely to prevail in challenging a determination by the U.S. Army Corps of Engineers under the public interest standard? Consider the court of appeal's conclusion in *Town of Norfolk v. Army Corps of Engineers*, 968 F.2d 1438, 1454 (1st Cir. 1992) ("Under the 'public interest' review, the Corps conducts a general balancing of a number of economic and environmental factors and its ultimate determinations are entitled to substantial deference."). How predictable is this standard for landowners attempting to determine whether they can fill wetlands on their property? In *Hoosier Envtl. Council v. United States Army Corps of Engineers*, 723 F.3d 1053, 1063 (7th Cir. 2013), Judge Posner all but wrote off the standard, terming it "overly ambitious" and stating that it "should perhaps be considered aspirational." He termed it "unrealistic" that the Corps could "analyze each of these [public interest] factors in depth, attach a weight to each, and by adding up all the weights determine whether to approve a project."

The U.S. Army Corps of Engineers also uses the so-called Section 404 Guidelines, developed jointly with EPA, in making its permit determinations. A critical part of the Guidelines places the burden on the applicant to show that there is no practical alternative to the proposed activity that would have a less adverse impact on the aquatic environment. 40 C.F.R. §230.10(a). Thus, the Guidelines are in part a land use planning mechanism, with a federal agency making the final determination whether alternative potential sites are "available."

What factors should be considered in the determination of the availability of alternatives? How important is the project's purpose, and is that purpose easy for an agency to determine? In *National Wildlife Ass'n v. Whistler*, 27 F.3d 1341 (3d Cir. 1994), plaintiff proposed a housing project on a bluff outside the Corps' jurisdiction, but it needed a Section 404 permit to give boats access to the Missouri River. The U.S. Army Corps of Engineers limited its alternatives analysis to the boat access area, excluding the housing development and allowing the developer to avoid the presumption against permit issuance for a nonwater-dependent use. The court upheld this decision.

In *Hillsdale Envtl. Loss Prevention, Inc. v. U.S. Army Corps of Engineers*, 702 F.3d 1156 (10th Cir. 2012), the Corps used the permit applicant's "criteria" to determine whether there was a practicable alternative for site selection of a BNSF freight rail terminal. BNSF required the site to be "close to existing rail tracks and highways, large enough to handle the projected volume of freight, and within 30 miles of BNSF's existing intermodal facility at the Argentine Yard."

7. *Permit Standards: Mitigation.* Finally, an important aspect of the permit process is mitigation of wetlands impacts, and the Corps and EPA have adopted regulations to implement mitigation. Compensatory Mitigation for Losses of Aquatic Resources, 73 Fed. Reg. 19,594-601 (April 10, 2008) ("compensatory mitigation is a critical tool in helping the federal government to meet the longstanding national goal of 'no net loss' of wetland acreage and function").

The Code reads:

§332.3 General compensatory mitigation requirements.

(a) *General considerations.*

(1) The fundamental objective of compensatory mitigation is to offset environmental losses resulting from unavoidable impacts to waters of the United States authorized by DA permits. The district engineer must determine the compensatory mitigation to be required in a DA permit, based on what is practicable and capable of compensating for the aquatic resource functions that will be lost as a result of the permitted activity. When evaluating compensatory mitigation options, the district engineer will consider what would be environmentally preferable. In making this determination, the district engineer must assess the likelihood for ecological success and sustainability, the location of the compensation site relative to the impact site and their significance within the watershed, and the costs of the compensatory mitigation project. In many cases, the environmentally preferable compensatory mitigation may be provided through mitigation banks or in-lieu fee programs because they usually involve consolidating compensatory mitigation projects where ecologically appropriate, consolidating resources, providing financial planning and scientific expertise (which often is not practical for permittee-responsible compensatory mitigation projects), reducing temporal losses of functions, and reducing uncertainty over project success. Compensatory mitigation requirements must be commensurate with the amount and type of impact that is associated with a particular DA permit. Permit applicants are responsible for proposing an appropriate compensatory mitigation option to offset unavoidable impacts.

(2) Compensatory mitigation may be performed using the methods of restoration, enhancement, establishment, and in certain circumstances preservation. Restoration should generally be the first option considered because the likelihood of success is greater and the impacts to potentially ecologically important uplands are reduced compared to establishment, and the potential gains in terms of aquatic resource functions are greater, compared to enhancement and preservation.

See, e.g., Kentuckians for the Commonwealth v. U.S. Army Corps of Engineers, 746 F.3d 698, 712 (6th Cir. 2014) (Corps did not act arbitrarily and capriciously in approving mitigation plan); Albert C. Lin, 2015 Utah L. Rev. 45, 48 (2015) (compensatory mitigation has failed to achieve the "no net loss of wetlands" goal).

8. *State and Local Wetlands Protection.* In addition to the federal role in regulating wetlands, large numbers of states also have substantial programs regulating development that might affect wetlands. At least 15 states, primarily located in the northeastern part of the country, have freshwater wetlands protection statutes. *See, e.g., ZRB, LLC v. N.J. Dep't of Envtl. Protection,* 959 A.2d 866 (N.J. Super. App. Div. 2008) (upholding denial of permit under the New Jersey Freshwater Wetlands Protection Act on the basis that wetlands were of "exceptional resource value" because they were the habitat for the barred owl, a threatened species under New Jersey law). Some states have passed comprehensive legislation establishing state regulatory bodies whose principal (or even sole) concern is with wetlands. Other states regulate through their coastal zone regulatory schemes (discussed in Chapter 9), which limit wetlands covered to specified parts of the state. Some local governments (over 2000 by one estimate) have also used their land use authority to adopt zoning ordinances or conservation ordinances intended to protect wetlands. *See Frances Erica Lane, Inc. v. Board of Zoning Appeals of Town of Stratford,* 88 A.3d 580 (Conn. 2014). A local zoning board denied a permit to develop a wetland. The court upheld the denial of

the variance permit which sought to obtain an exception from the setback requirement in order to build a road over a wetland. The local wetlands commission had granted the permit to build the road.

9. *Other CWA Provisions Affecting Land Use.* Other provisions of the Clean Water Act are increasingly affecting the development of land. If a developer engages in a "construction activity" that disturbs more than five acres of land, then it must receive a Storm Water General Permit and have a Storm Water Pollution Prevention Plan. *See* 40 C.F.R. §122.26. EPA also issues permits for wastewater treatment plants. *See Crutchfield v. County of Hanover*, 325 F.3d 211 (4th Cir. 2003). Finally, for polluted bodies of water, EPA must issue so-called "total maximum daily loads" (TMDLs) of pollutants. These can significantly limit land uses adjacent to the body of water. *See Barnum Timber Co. v. U.S. E.P.A.*, 633 F.3d 894 (9th Cir. 2011) (landowner undertaking timber harvesting operations had standing to challenge designation of river as an "impaired water body," a designation that would require the establishment of TMDLs).

C. ENDANGERED SPECIES

The centerpiece of regulatory efforts to preserve endangered species, the Endangered Species Act (ESA), has long been controversial. When first passed in 1973, the Act moved easily through Congress, but by 1978 it was the subject of a major Supreme Court case. Now, as you will see, efforts to implement it in a creative fashion that will lessen its economic impacts are leading to cutting-edge "habitat conservation planning." This type of planning will have significant effects on the land use practices of local governments that are located within the planning area.

■ BABBITT v. SWEET HOME CHAPTER OF COMMUNITIES FOR A GREATER OREGON
514 U.S. 687 (1995)

Justice STEVENS delivered the opinion of the Court.

The Endangered Species Act of 1973, 87 Stat. 884, 16 U.S.C. §1531 (1988 ed. and Supp. V) (ESA or Act), contains a variety of protections designed to save from extinction species that the Secretary of the Interior designates as endangered or threatened. Section 9 of the Act makes it unlawful for any person to "take" any endangered or threatened species. The Secretary has promulgated a regulation that defines the statute's prohibition on takings to include "significant habitat modification or degradation where it actually kills or injures wildlife." This case presents the question whether the Secretary exceeded his authority under the Act by promulgating that regulation.

I

Section 9(a)(1) of the Endangered Species Act provides the following protection for endangered species:

Except as provided in sections 1535(g)(2) and 1539 of this title, with respect to any endangered species of fish or wildlife listed pursuant to section 1533 of this title it is unlawful for any person subject to the jurisdiction of the United States to. . . .

(B) take any such species within the United States or the territorial sea of the United States[.]

16 U.S.C. §1538(a)(1).

Section 3(19) of the Act defines the statutory term "take": "The term 'take' means to harass, harm, pursue, hunt, shoot, wound, kill, trap, capture, or collect, or to attempt to engage in any such conduct." 16 U.S.C. §1532(19). The Act does not further define the terms it uses to define "take." The Interior Department regulations that implement the statute, however, define the statutory term "harm":

> *Harm* in the definition of "take" in the Act means an act which actually kills or injures wildlife. Such act may include significant habitat modification or degradation where it actually kills or injures wildlife by significantly impairing essential behavioral patterns, including breeding, feeding, or sheltering.

50 CFR §17.3 (1994).

This regulation has been in place since 1975.

A limitation on the §9 "take" prohibition appears in §10(a)(1)(B) of the Act, which Congress added by amendment in 1982. That section authorizes the Secretary to grant a permit for any taking otherwise prohibited by §9(a)(1)(B) "if such taking is incidental to, and not the purpose of, the carrying out of an otherwise lawful activity." 16 U.S.C. §1539(a)(1)(B).

In addition to the prohibition on takings, the Act provides several other protections for endangered species. Section 4, 16 U.S.C. §1533, commands the Secretary to identify species of fish or wildlife that are in danger of extinction and to publish from time to time lists of all species he determines to be endangered or threatened. Section 5, 16 U.S.C. §1534, authorizes the Secretary, in cooperation with the States, *see* 16 U.S.C. §1535, to acquire land to aid in preserving such species. Section 7 requires federal agencies to ensure that none of their activities, including the granting of licenses and permits, will jeopardize the continued existence of endangered species "or result in the destruction or adverse modification of habitat of such species which is determined by the Secretary . . . to be critical." 16 U.S.C. §1536(a)(2).

Respondents in this action are small landowners, logging companies, and families dependent on the forest products industries in the Pacific Northwest and in the Southeast, and organizations that represent their interests. They brought this declaratory judgment action . . . to challenge the statutory validity of the Secretary's regulation defining "harm," particularly the inclusion of habitat modification and degradation in the definition. Respondents challenged the regulation on its face. . . .

II

Because this case was decided on motions for summary judgment, we may appropriately make certain factual assumptions in order to frame the legal issue.

First, we assume respondents have no desire to harm either the red-cockaded wood-pecker or the spotted owl; they merely wish to continue logging activities that would be entirely proper if not prohibited by the ESA. On the other hand, we must assume *arguendo* that those activities will have the effect, even though unintended, of det-rimentally changing the natural habitat of both listed species and that, as a conse-quence, members of those species will be killed or injured. Under respondents' view of the law, the Secretary's only means of forestalling that grave result — even when the actor knows it is certain to occur — is to use his §5 authority to purchase the lands on which the survival of the species depends. The Secretary, on the other hand, submits that the §9 prohibition on takings, which Congress defined to include "harm," places on respondents a duty to avoid harm that habitat alteration will cause the birds unless respondents first obtain a permit pursuant to §10.

The text of the Act provides three reasons for concluding that the Secretary's interpretation is reasonable. First, an ordinary understanding of the word "harm" supports it. The dictionary definition of the verb form of "harm" is "to cause hurt or damage to: injure," Webster's Third New International Dictionary 1034 (1966). In the context of the ESA, that definition naturally encompasses habitat modification that results in actual injury or death to members of an endangered or threatened species.

Respondents argue that the Secretary should have limited the purview of "harm" to direct applications of force against protected species, but the dictionary definition does not include the word "directly" or suggest in any way that only direct or willful action that leads to injury constitutes "harm." Moreover, unless the stat-utory term "harm" encompasses indirect as well as direct injuries, the word has no meaning that does not duplicate the meaning of other words that §3 uses to define "take." . . .

Second, the broad purpose of the ESA supports the Secretary's decision to extend protection against activities that cause the precise harms Congress enacted the statute to avoid.

Third, the fact that Congress in 1982 authorized the Secretary to issue permits for takings that §9(a)(1)(B) would otherwise prohibit, "if such taking is incidental to, and not the purpose of, the carrying out of an otherwise lawful activity," 16 U.S.C. §1539(a)(1)(B), strongly suggests that Congress understood §9(a)(1)(B) to pro-hibit indirect as well as deliberate takings. The permit process requires the applicant to prepare a "conservation plan" that specifies how he intends to "minimize and mitigate" the "impact" of his activity on endangered and threatened species, 16 U.S.C. §1539(a)(2)(A), making clear that Congress had in mind foreseeable rather than merely accidental effects on listed species. No one could seriously request an "incidental" take permit to avert §9 liability for direct, deliberate action against a member of an endangered or threatened species, but respondents would read "harm" so narrowly that the permit procedure would have little more than that absurd purpose. "When Congress acts to amend a statute, we presume it intends its amendment to have real and substantial effect." *Stone v. INS*, 514 U.S. 386, 387 (1995). Congress' addition of the §10 permit provision supports the Secretary's conclusion that activities not intended to harm an endangered species, such as habitat modification, may constitute unlawful takings under the ESA unless the Secretary permits them.

The Court of Appeals made three errors in asserting that "harm" must refer to a direct application of force because the words around it do. First, the court's premise was flawed. Several of the words that accompany "harm" in the §3 definition of "take," especially "harass," "pursue," "wound," and "kill," refer to actions or effects that do not require direct applications of force. Second, to the extent the court read a requirement of intent or purpose into the words used to define "take," it ignored §9's express provision that a "knowing" action is enough to violate the Act. Third, the court employed *noscitur a sociis* to give "harm" essentially the same function as other words in the definition, thereby denying it independent meaning. The canon, to the contrary, counsels that a word "gathers meaning from the words around it." *Jarecki v. G.D. Searle & Co.*, 367 U.S. 303, 307 (1961). The statutory context of "harm" suggests that Congress meant that term to serve a particular function in the ESA, consistent with but distinct from the functions of the other verbs used to define "take." The Secretary's interpretation of "harm" to include indirectly injuring endangered animals through habitat modification permissibly interprets "harm" to have "a character of its own not to be submerged by its association." *Russell Motor Car Co. v. United States*, 261 U.S. 514, 519 (1923). . . .

The judgment of the Court of Appeals is reversed.

It is so ordered.

Notes and Comments

1. *Preserving Species.* The first case under the Endangered Species Act to reach the Supreme Court was *Tennessee Valley Authority v. Hill,* 437 U.S. 153 (1978). Then-Chief Justice Warren Berger's opinion noted:

> It may seem curious to some that the survival of a relatively small number of three-inch fish among all the countless millions of species extant would require the permanent halting of a virtually completed dam for which Congress has expended more than $100 million. . . . We conclude, however, that the explicit provisions of the Endangered Species Act require precisely that result.

Id. at 172-173. Why put such an emphasis on preserving species? Professor Oliver A. Houck suggests that the Endangered Species Act operates as a surrogate for the health of ecosystems, which American laws have not yet attempted to protect in a broader manner. Oliver A. Houck, Why Do We Protect Endangered Species, and What Does That Say About Whether Restrictions on Private Property to Protect Them Constitute "Takings"?, 80 Iowa L. Rev. 297, 301 (1995); *see also* Robert L. Hirschman, Predictions and Prescriptions for the Endangered Species Act, 34 Envtl. L. 451, 452 (2004) ("Environmentalists often deploy the canary in a coal mine rationale to defend the ESA's unrelenting concern for the survival of all species: Extinction of any one life form is an indication of a weakening in the fabric of nature that might ultimately cause harm to us."). Is that a convincing justification for the stringent protections required by the ESA?

2. *The ESA and Land Use.* In the four decades since its passage, the Endangered Species Act has produced a series of high-profile confrontations, usually regarding proposed federal projects. These have ranged from the above noted dispute over the construction of the Tellico Dam in Tennessee (pitting the famous "snail darter" against an already completed dam) to the headlines over protection of the spotted owl in the old-growth forests of the Northwest and the alleged loss of jobs that

protection of the owl caused in the timber industry. Most recently, *see* N.Y. Times Editorial Board, The Salmon's Swim for Survival, N.Y. Times (July 4, 2016) (addressing salmon habitat restoration in the conflict among the hydroelectric industry's development patterns, Indian fishing treaties, and species preservation).

Over the last two decades, however, the ESA's effect on more traditional land use activities, such as subdivision approvals, has become more apparent. *See* Brian Seasholes, The Hidden Costs of Environmental Regulations, O.C. Register (June 25, 2016), http://www.ocregister.com/articles/critical-720548-habitat-housing.html (last visited Nov. 5, 2016) ("The huge economic costs of designating critical habitat have a couple significant effects for individuals and families. The complex process can make the home-buying process much more expensive by making the building process much longer, by driving up the costs of the land and housing and by reducing the number of homes available. Trying to build housing near critical habitats becomes more difficult and more expensive, especially for lower income families."). *See also Greater Yellowstone Coalition v. Flowers*, 359 F.3d 1257 (10th Cir. 2004) (challenge to permit for housing development and golf course near nesting territory of the bald eagle); *Defenders of Wildlife v. Flowers*, 44 F.3d 1066 (9th Cir. 2005) (upholding decision that developments would not affect pygmy owl). *See also Friends of Endangered Species v. Jantzen*, 760 F.2d 976 (9th Cir. 1985) (effect of Mission Blue butterfly on 2235 unit residential development); *Home Builders Ass'n of Northern California v. U.S. Fish and Wildlife Service*, 616 F.3d 983 (9th Cir. 2010) (rejecting challenge to designation of about 850,000 acres of land as critical habitat for various endangered or threatened species found in vernal pools).

Furthermore, the backlog on listing species is very large. Associated Press, Hundreds of Endangered Species Get Federal Protection, Wash. Post (Sept. 10, 2011) (federal judge approved settlements requiring the government to consider protection under the ESA for more than 700 animal and plant species). *See also* Michael Wines, Endangered or Not, But at Least No Longer Waiting, N.Y. Times (March 6, 2013).

3. *The Effects of the ESA.* There is a large debate over the ESA's effect. One study found the effects less than burdensome. Stephen M. Meyer, The Economic Impact of the Endangered Species Act on the Housing and Real Estate Markets, 6 N.Y.U. Envtl. L.J. 450, 474 (1998) (concluding that the ESA "has not had a burdensome impact on real estate industry performance or new single family home construction rates"). Yet a more recent empirical study of home building permit issuances in 400 California cities suggests that critical habitat [CH] designation under the ESA does reduce the number of home building permits to a significant degree: "[T]he proposal of the median-sized CH results in a 23.5 percent decrease in the supply of housing permits in the short run and a 37.0 percent decrease in the long run. The results indicate the proposal of CH acts as a signal that all development in that [municipal area] will be more costly." Jeffrey Zabel and Robert Paterson, The Effects of Critical Habitat Designation on Housing Supply: An Analysis of California Housing Construction Activity, 46 J. Reg. Sci. 67 (2006)

4. Sweet Home *and the Reach of the ESA.* The reach of the act as well as its potential to affect land use are apparent from the *Sweet Home* case. A study by the General Accounting Office found that more than 50 percent of all listed species depend exclusively upon nonfederal land for survival. Additionally, 90 percent of all listed species and candidate species rely to a significant degree on nonfederal habitat. U.S. General Accounting Office, Endangered Species Act: Information on Species

Protection, Nonfederal Lands, GAO/RCED 95-16 (Dec. 1994). *See also* Craig Groves, et al, Owning up to Our Responsibilities: Who Owns Lands Important for Biodiversity, in Stein et al., Precious Heritage: The Status of Biodiversity in the United States (Oxford University Press 2000) 278-79: "Based on an analysis of the data presented . . . Federal lands support at least one example of about three-fifths (59%) of federal listed species, and a similar percentage of imperiled species."

Could the administration of a president who opposes the extensive sweep of the ESA repeal the broad regulatory definition of "harm" that includes significant habitation modification or degradation?

5. *The ESA Process.* The *Sweet Home* case outlines some parts of the process under the ESA. That process begins with the listing by the Secretary of the Interior of species as endangered or threatened. 16 U.S.C. §1533 (2012). *See, e.g., Defenders of Wildlife v. Jewell,* 815 F.3d 1 (D.C. Cir. 2016) (upholding decision not to list dunes sagebrush lizard as endangered). At the same time, the Secretary must designate "critical habitat" for the species, i.e., the specific geographical areas on which are found physical or biological features essential to the conservation of the species. 16 U.S.C. §1532(5)(A)(i). Federal agencies then cannot take action that adversely modify critical habitat. 16 U.S.C. §1532(5)(C); *see* U.S. Fish & Wildlife Service, Critical Habitat: What Is It? (2016), https://www.fws.gov/endangered/esa-library/pdf/critical_habitat.pdf (last visited Sept. 22, 2016). In 2016, the U.S. Fish and Wildlife Service adopted new regulations that tightened the definition of an "adverse modification."

The key provisions protecting the listed species are found in Sections 7 and 9 of the Act. Section 7 requires that federal agencies "insure" that their actions are not likely to jeopardize protected species or their habitats. 16 U.S.C. §1536(a)(2). If protected species are found in the area of the proposed action, the agency must prepare a "biological assessment" analyzing whether the action is likely to affect the species and its "critical habitat." If such an effect is likely, the agency must formally consult with the U.S. Fish and Wildlife Service or the National Marine Fisheries Service.

Section 9 prohibits "any person or agency" from "taking" any endangered species of fish or wildlife. 16 U.S.C. §1538(a)(1)(B)-(C). As you saw in *Sweet Home,* habitat modification is included within the meaning of "harm," and thereby within "take." The U.S. Fish and Wildlife Service must specify whether action will result in an "incidental take" of protected species. 16 U.S.C. §1536(b)(4). If so, the agency can issue a permit under Section 10 of the Act allowing an "incidental take" of the species. The Service issues an "Incidental Take Statement" specifying the impact of the taking on the species, those measures necessary to minimize the impact, and terms and conditions to implement those measures. Any "Incidental Take Statement" must specify the take that is allowed. *See Union Neighbors United, Inc. v. Jewell,* 831 F.3d 564 (D.C. Cir. 2016) (reviewing permit allowing incidental take of endangered Indiana bats for a project that would install 100 industrial wind turbines). A numerical limit is often used. *See, e.g., Fund for Animals v. Rice,* 85 F.3d 535 (11th Cir. 1996) (landfill may take 52 snakes during construction and 2 snakes per year thereafter); *Mt. Graham Red Squirrel v. Madigan,* 954 F.2d 1441 (9th Cir. 1992) (telescope construction may take six red squirrels per year).

The Incidental Take Statement, "if followed, exempts the action agency from the prohibition on takings found in Section 9 of the ESA." *National Wildlife Fed'n v. National Marine Fisheries Serv.,* 481 F.3d 1224, 1230 (9th Cir. 2007).

6. *Planning to Protect Species.* In considering the effect of the Endangered Species Act on land use, it is important to think about the structure of the act's regulatory mechanism. Its focus is on preventing actions by private parties and the government that might jeopardize protected species or their habitats. Thus, it proceeds on a project-by-project basis, looking narrowly at the effect that a specific action may have on a specific endangered species.

This reactive approach invites confrontations with developers when proposals, some close to final approval, are delayed or rejected because of impacts on endangered species. At the same time, the approach is insufficient to ensure that the principal goal of the act, the survival of endangered species, is met. Species survival depends largely on whether the species has sufficient habitat in which to thrive, but the ESA's case-by-case regulatory mechanism does not necessarily provide for the kind of comprehensive planning needed for multiple species.

The problems with the present approach have led to efforts at comprehensive habitat protection. To qualify for an "incidental take" under §10 of the ESA, the landowner must submit a "conservation plan" whose purpose is to "minimize and mitigate" the impact on the species. These types of plans could preserve species while, at the same time, giving clear signals to developers about areas in which development can occur without running afoul of the ESA.

Here is a brief explanation of how these plans, known as "Habitat Conservation Plans," work:

■ U.S. FISH & WILDLIFE SERVICE, HABITAT CONSERVATION PLANS UNDER THE ENDANGERED SPECIES ACT

http://www.fws.gov/endangered/esa-library/pdf/hcp.pdf (last visited Nov. 12, 2016)

WHAT NEEDS TO BE IN HCPs?

Section 10 of the Act and its implementing regulations define the contents of HCPs. They include:

- an assessment of impacts likely to result from the proposed taking of one or more federally listed species.
- measures that the permit applicant will undertake to monitor, minimize, and mitigate for such impacts, the funding available to implement such measures, and the procedures to deal with unforeseen or extraordinary circumstances.
- alternative actions to the taking that the applicant analyzed, and the reasons why the applicant did not adopt such alternatives.
- additional measures that the Fish and Wildlife Service may require. . . .

WHAT ARE NO SURPRISES ASSURANCES?

The FWS provides "No Surprises" assurances to non-Federal landowners through the section 10(a)(1)(B) process. Essentially, State and private landowners are assured that if "unforeseen circumstances" arise, the FWS will not require the commitment of additional land, water, or financial compensation or additional restrictions on the use of land, water, or other natural resources beyond the level otherwise agreed to in the HCP without the consent of the permitholder. The government will honor these assurances as long as permitholders are implementing the terms and conditions of the HCPs, permits, and other associated documents in good faith. In effect, the government and permit-holders pledge to honor their conservation commitments.

WHAT IS THE PROCESS FOR GETTING AN INCIDENTAL TAKE PERMIT?

The applicant decides whether to seek an incidental take permit. While FWS staff members provide detailed guidance and technical assistance throughout the process, the applicant develops an HCP and applies for a permit. The components of a completed permit application are a standard application form, an HCP, an Implementation Agreement (if applicable), the application fee, and a draft National Environmental Policy Act (NEPA) analysis. A NEPA analysis may result in a categorical exclusion, an environmental assessment, or an environmental impact statement. While processing the permit application, the FWS prepares the incidental take permit and a biological opinion under section 7 of the Act and finalizes the NEPA analysis documents. Consequently, incidental take permits have a number of associated documents.

WHAT KINDS OF ACTIONS ARE CONSIDERED MITIGATION?

Mitigation measures are actions that reduce or address potential adverse effects of a proposed activity on species included in an HCP. They should address specific conservation needs of the species and be manageable and enforceable. Mitigation measures may take many forms, including, but not limited to, payment into an established conservation fund or bank; preservation (via acquisition or conservation easement) of existing habitat; enhancement or restoration of degraded or a former habitat; establishment of buffer areas around existing habitats; modifications of land use practices, and restrictions on access. Which type of mitigation measure used for a specific HCP is determined on a case by case basis, and is based upon the needs of the species and type of impacts anticipated.

The following excerpt is from a regional habitat conservation plan approved by the federal government.

■ HAYS COUNTY (TEXAS) REGIONAL HABITAT CONSERVATION PLAN
(Approved May 13, 2011)

The Hays County Regional Habitat Conservation Plan ("RHCP") was developed by the Hays County Commissioners' Court with the assistance of the Citizens' Advisory Committee, Biological Advisory Team, County staff, and a team of environmental, legal, and economic consultants. The RHCP was developed in connection with the County's application for an Endangered Species Act (ESA) Section

10(a)(1)(B) incidental take permit authorizing the take of two federally endangered songbirds, the golden-cheeked warbler and the black-capped vireo. The ESA requires that an applicant for an incidental take permit prepare a habitat conservation plan that describes, among other things, how the impacts caused by take authorized by the permit will be minimized and mitigated to the maximum extent practicable. Pursuant to ESA Section 10(a)(1)(B), the RHCP describes a locally controlled approach for compliance with the ESA. The County's permit would authorize incidental "take" of the golden-cheeked warbler and black-capped vireo, and the RHCP describes the mitigation provided for the impacts of such take. The RHCP is also designed to benefit a host of other wildlife species, water resources, and people. The conservation program of the RHCP is based on a phased conservation banking approach with a goal of assembling between 10,000 and 15,000 acres of preserve land over the 30-year duration of the RHCP. The RHCP will help the County serve the needs of its growing population and will promote responsible economic development, good public infrastructure, and open space preservation (including habitat protection for endangered species).

1.0 Purpose and Need for the Hays County RHCP

☐ The population of Hays County is expected to increase 150% to 300% over the next 30 years, making it one of the fastest growing populations in Texas. . . . Population growth will drive new private land development and public infrastructure projects in the county.

☐ Projected development and infrastructure projects could cause the loss of approximately 22,000 acres of potential habitat for the federally endangered golden-cheeked warbler in Hays County over the next 30 years. Similarly, the county could lose approximately 3,300 acres of potential black-capped vireo habitat. . . .

☐ The ESA prohibits the "taking" of federally endangered or threatened species without authorization. Take includes activities that result in significant habitat modification or degradation resulting in actual death or injury of listed species by significantly impairing essential behavioral patterns, including breeding, feeding, or sheltering . . .

☐ The RHCP will allow the County and other public and private entities to obtain ESA incidental take authorization in a more efficient, streamlined, and timely manner. . . . Processing individual incidental take authorizations (i.e., authorization where a RHCP is not available) typically take 1 to 2 years. Under the RHCP, incidental take authorization could be obtained within a matter of weeks and potentially at less cost than obtaining individual incidental take authorization.

2.0 Benefits to Hays County and the Community

☐ The RHCP will benefit the golden-cheeked warbler and black-capped vireo in Hays County by . . . :
  • Creating a preserve system within Hays County that effectively mitigates for incidental take of the golden-cheeked warbler and black-capped vireo

and coordinates and consolidates mitigation requirements from projects scattered across the county into larger, more biologically significant preserve blocks. The RHCP preserve system will protect sufficient acres of warbler and vireo habitat to generate enough mitigation credits to balance the anticipated level of participation in the RHCP. The County's goal is to protect and manage between 10,000 and 15,000 acres for endangered species in Hays County in perpetuity.

- Encouraging compliance with the ESA by providing an efficient means of authorization. By implementing the RHCP and providing an efficient and reliable mechanism for ESA compliance, the County is hopeful that there will be an increase in ESA compliance across Hays County, resulting in more conservation actions for these species.
- Providing for perpetual management and monitoring of preserve lands to maintain, enhance, or create quality habitat for the golden-cheeked warbler and black-capped vireo.
- Contributing to the recovery of the warbler and vireo by protecting large areas of habitat for these species in Hays County and helping to promote connectivity among other existing endangered species preserves in the region. . . .

☐ Implementing the RHCP will benefit Hays County in the following ways:
- The RHCP will provide a streamlined process for ESA compliance for County sponsored projects, such as the construction or improvement of roads, bridges, and other County infrastructure. The RHCP was initiated in response to a need for ESA compliance during the planning and construction of Winters Mill Parkway near Wimberley. With the passage of the 2008 Road Bond program and the general obligation of the County to provide services to its growing population, other County projects are likely to require permitting through the ESA in the coming years. The RHCP will reduce the time and potentially the cost associated with obtaining incidental take authorization for future County projects by streamlining tasks such as assessing impacts and providing appropriate mitigation . . .

☐ Private landowners, business entities, organizations, and other municipalities may also benefit by implementation of the RHCP . . . , including:
- The RHCP provides a locally created solution to endangered species issues that incorporates stakeholder concerns and gives long-term ESA permitting assurances to the County and RHCP participants.
- The RHCP offers a new, voluntary option for ESA compliance that would be available to private landowners, businesses, and other entities in Hays County. This new compliance option would reduce the time and cost associated with obtaining incidental take authorization under the ESA, particularly with respect to developing individual HCPs, waiting for applications to be processed by the USFWS, and obtaining appropriate mitigation for project impacts. . . .

3.0 BASIC ELEMENTS OF THE RHCP

☐ The "permit area" for the RHCP includes all of Hays County, and the County's Permit will have a term of 30 years (i.e., 2010 through 2039). . . .

☐ The RHCP and Permit will cover incidental take of the endangered golden-cheeked warbler and endangered black-capped vireo (the warbler and vireo are the "covered species" in the RHCP). The RHCP may also benefit 56 other potentially rare or sensitive species in Hays County and will provide funding to study one or more of these species . . .

☐ Activities that could cause take of the covered species and that would be covered by the Permit include construction, operation, and maintenance of public projects and infrastructure and residential, commercial, and industrial development . . .

☐ The RHCP will cover up to 9,000 acres of acres of habitat loss for the warbler and up to 1,300 acres of habitat loss for the vireo resulting from participating projects over 30 years. The 10,300 acres of take authorization will be sufficient to provide ESA compliance for the amount of anticipated participation in the RHCP . . .

☐ To mitigate for take of the covered species authorized by the Permit, Hays County will create a preserve system and operate a "phased" conservation bank. . . . Under the phased conservation bank approach, habitat protection would always occur in advance of authorized impacts through the RHCP.

- The preserve system will be assembled on a phased basis as needed to create mitigation credits for the conservation bank and as potential preserve parcels become available from willing partners.
- The County will preserve between 10,000 and 15,000 acres by the end of the 30-year permit duration, in order to utilize the full amount of take authorization sought in the RHCP . . . ; however, there is no pre-determined preserve system size, location, or configuration.
- Habitat for the covered species protected within the preserve system will create mitigation credits for the conservation bank.
- Banking mitigation credits allows an equivalent amount of take authorization to be accessed. Therefore, mitigation will always be provided before an equivalent amount of take . . .

Notes and Comments

1. *Species by Species Protection.* From an environmental standpoint, HCPs are an improvement over the normal course of regulation under the Endangered Species Act. They approach the problem of preservation from the perspective of what the species needs to survive, rather than from the impact of a specific development or action on that species. Academic commentators have argued that the overall goal must be protection of biodiversity in general. A. Dan Tarlock, Biodiversity Conservation in the United States: A Case Study in Incompleteness and Indirection, 32 Envtl. L. Rep. 10529 (2002) ("The ESA is a backwards approach to biodiversity because it only indirectly addresses the major cause of biodiversity loss, habitat destruction, and does not concern itself with other causes such as the invasion of exotic species and air and water pollution.").

2. *Preparing an HCP.* Preparing an HCP is complex. For the larger HCPs, a multitude of federal, state, and governmental agencies are involved, and the process

usually must recognize a variety of different landowners. The Balcones Canyonlands Conservation Plan, which encompasses all of Travis County, Texas (including the City of Austin), provides for five preserve areas ranging in aggregate size from 29,159 acres to a probable maximum of 35,300 acres. The legal skills required for negotiating such agreements and the technical backup required to represent a client properly are different from those needed in the typical local land use dispute. *See generally* Timothy Beatley, Habitat Conservation Planning (Univ. of Texas Press, 2014).

Despite these complexities, however, a surprising number of HCPs have already been completed. What benefits do developers see in supporting HCPs? What about the attitude of local governments towards them? *See* William H. Simon, Wisconsin Law Review Symposium Afterward, 2010 Wis. L. Rev. 727, 729 (2010) (noting that land developers found an interest in collaborating with environmentalists to create Habitat Conservation Plans, but only after the Endangered Species Act precluded them from developing in the absence of such plans.) Consider also the resistance of state legislatures and local governments, covered in Chapter 9 of this casebook, to statewide or regional planning. Has that resistance been circumvented through the "back door" of habitat conservation planning as a means of complying with the Endangered Species Act?

3. *"No Surprises."* HCPs usually cover areas that are relatively undeveloped. Will landowners enter into an HCP, which may require them to pay large amounts of money to implement its provisions, if the possibility exists that, over the life of the plan (perhaps 30 years), circumstances may change and the federal government may seek additional mitigation or dollar contributions from them? This concern led the U.S. Fish and Wildlife Service (USFWS) and the National Marine Fisheries Service (NMFS) to promulgate a "No Surprises" policy, mentioned in the excerpt above. *See* 50 C.F.R. §222.307; *Bear Valley Mut. Water Co. v. Jewell*, 790 F.3d 927 (9th Cir. 2015) (rejecting as speculative a challenge that a change in critical habitat for the threatened Santa Ana sucker fish violated the "no surprises" rule).

Is this "no surprises" policy consistent with the provisions against "taking" of species found in Sections 7 and 9 of the ESA?

4. *Applying Economic Incentives.* A repeated criticism of the existing law of endangered species protection — and one often made of environmental regulation in general — is that it overemphasizes regulatory mandates by the government. Critics argue that the system would work much better if it relied less on this type of "command and control" regulation and more on the use of economic incentives.

For example, under the current regulatory system for endangered species, it has been suggested that a landowner who wishes to develop his or her property but discovers an endangered species on it sees only economic disaster in that discovery. Any landowner inclined toward lawbreaking might even be tempted to destroy the species rather than report it. *See* Kim Murphy, Taking Aim at the Endangered Species Act, Wash. Post (January 25, 2011) A03 (""'Shoot, shovel and shut up" is a joke in Montana,' said Rep. Denny Rehberg, referring to a long-standing reference among landowners across the West — perhaps partly in jest — about the best way to deal with a federally protected endangered species . . ."); Jonathan Remy Nash, Trading Species: A New Direction for Habitat Trading Programs, 32 Col. J. Envtl. L. 1, 10 (2007) ("counter-intuitively, the Act creates incentives to destroy habitat rather than to preserve it.").

Critics say what is needed is a system with economic incentives built in that will reward landowners for preserving the species rather than penalizing them by preventing development of their property. Others have suggested that "mitigation banks," like those used under wetlands law, be created for endangered species. *See* Jamison E. Colburn, Trading Spaces: Habitat Mitigation "Banking" Under Fish & Wildlife Service Guidelines, 20 Nat. Resources & Env't 33 (Summer 2000. For an additional perspective *see* John Davidson, The New Public Lands: Competing Models for Protecting Public Conservation Values on Privately Owned Lands, 39 Envtl. L. Rep. News & Analysis 10368 (2009):

> The emergence of new hybrid categories of public interest lands represents an opportunity to advance the public interest. In recent decades, the U.S. government has acquired partial property interests over large acreages, meaning these properties must now be managed in accordance with governing statutes and regulations. Critics of this new model argue that the hybrid of public/private ownership is inefficient and too many resources are required to monitor and enforce applicable regulations. To address these concerns, land trusts and other private conservation organizations that hold the new public lands are implementing a private system capable of protecting these hybrid interests across time. Land trusts are now voluntarily accepting a regime of strict accreditation standards to guarantee that each easement held is backed by endowed funds sufficient to support enforcement, and that there is in place a fully informed and regulated monitoring process.

5. *Success?* A considerable number of HCPs have now been prepared, but the success of the program is, as yet, not clear. One in-depth study is Alejandro E. Camacho, Elizabeth Taylor & Melissa Kelly, Lessons From Area-Wide Multi-Agency Habitat Conservation Plans in California, 46 Envtl. L. Rep. 10222 (2016) (concluding that "regulators and applicants must clearly engage stakeholders about the underlying trade offs among plan scale, depth, duration, cost, certainty and efficacy" to promote better planning). The debate over the efficacy and effects of the Endangered Species Act continues. *Compare* Damien M. Schiff, The Endangered Species Act at 40: A Tale of Radicalization, Politicization, Bureaucratization, and Senescence, 37 SPG Environs Envtl. L. & Pol'y J. 105 (2014) (Act "imposes significant burdens on the actors — among them large corporations, small farmers, individual homeowners, state and local governments — who fall within its ambit") John Buse, A Different Perspective on the Endangered Species Act at 40: Responding to Damien M. Schiff, 38 Fall Environs Envtl. L & Pol'y J. 145 (2014) ("We need not destroy the ESA to save it."). *See also* Daniel J. Rohlf, The Endangered Species Act at Forty: The Good, the Bad, and the Ugly, 20 Animal L. 251 (2014).

In the meantime, a property owners group has challenged the constitutionality of the act, claiming that regulation of prairie dogs as a threatened species is beyond Congressional powers under the Commerce Clause and the Necessary and Proper Clause. *People for the Ethical Treatment of Property Owners v. U.S. Fish & Wildlife Service*, 57 F. Supp. 3d 1337 (D. Utah 2014). The case is now on appeal to the Tenth Circuit Court of Appeals. *See also Markle Interests, L.L.C. v. United States Fish and Wildlife Serv.*, 827 F.3d 452, 477 (5th Cir. 2016) (rejecting landowners challenge to critical habitat designation and Commerce Clause challenge, noting that "every other circuit that has addressed similar challenges has also upheld the ESA as a valid exercise of Congress's Commerce Clause power").

D. HAZARDOUS WASTE CLEANUP AND LAND USE

Initially, you may find it hard to see how the cleanup of hazardous waste from contaminated property, pursuant to federal and state hazardous waste cleanup laws, is directly related to land use. Three practical aspects of hazardous waste cleanup will help to illuminate the connection. First, you must consider the economics of cleaning up hazardous waste. As parties have implemented the federal Comprehensive Environmental Response, Compensation, and Liability Act (CERCLA), 42 U.S.C. §§9601-9675 (2012), the high cost of cleaning up sites has become all too clear. Moreover, attaining the last percentage of cleanup, so that a site is left in pristine condition rather than with low, background levels of contaminants remaining on it, increases the costs astronomically. This increment of expense has led to the much debated question of exactly "how clean is clean" under CERCLA.

Second, the practical difficulties of carrying out the cleanup are often substantial. For example, the technology for cleanup is not only expensive, in some instances it may not even exist, particularly if the contamination has spread to the groundwater table.

Third, as you will soon see, CERCLA generally operates by spreading liability — for the most part, through the imposition of joint and several liability — among all responsible parties, including the owner of the site. The potential for liability under federal and state law merely because of ownership of a site is enough to discourage many prospective purchasers. As a result, rather than re-using existing, contaminated industrial sites that must be cleaned up — areas known as "brownfields" — companies seek to locate on new, undeveloped areas — known as "greenfields" — that have no potential liability attached to them.

Thus, hazardous waste cleanup laws indirectly drive future land uses on many properties. Initially, though, you need a feel for the breadth of CERCLA liability and how that liability affects land use. The following case will provide that understanding.

■ TANGLEWOOD EAST HOMEOWNERS v. CHARLES-THOMAS, INC.
849 F.2d 1568 (5th Cir. 1988)

Before POLITZ and JOHNSON, Circuit Judges, and BOYLE, District Judge. POLITZ, Circuit Judge: . . .

BACKGROUND

. . . Appellant, First Federal Savings & Loan Association of Conroe, is a lending institution. The other defendants against whom appellees have complained are residential developers, construction companies, and real estate agents and agencies. All participated in the development of the Tanglewood East Subdivision in Montgomery County, Texas. The complainants-appellees are owners of property in that subdivision. The subdivision was built on the site upon which the United Creosoting Company operated a wood-treatment facility from 1946 to 1972. During that quarter century substantial amounts of highly-toxic waste accumulated on the property. In 1973 certain of the defendants acquired the property, filled in and graded the creosote pools, and began residential development.

In 1980, Tanglewood homeowners and residents complained to Texas authorities about toxic problems and all development ceased. In 1983 the Environmental Protection Agency placed the site on its National Priorities List for cleaning under the Comprehensive Environmental Response, Compensation and Liability Act (CERCLA), commonly known as the "Superfund Act," 42 U.S.C. §§9601, *et seq.* The cleanup, expected to cost millions of dollars, will require the demolition of six homes and the construction of bunkers to contain the hazardous materials.

The purchasers of the subdivision lots invoked CERCLA . . . and sought damages, response and cleaning costs, and injunctive relief. . . .

ANALYSIS

A. CERCLA . . .

Under 42 U.S.C. §9607(a) (1988), CERCLA provides a private cause of action where a release or threatened release of a hazardous substance causes response costs to be incurred. The persons covered are:

1. the owner and operator of . . . a facility,
2. any person who at the time of disposal of any hazardous substance owned or operated any facility at which such hazardous substances were disposed of,
3. any person who by contract, agreement, or otherwise arranged for disposal or treatment, or arranged with a transporter for transport for disposal or treatment, of hazardous substances owned or possessed by such person . . . , and
4. any person who accepts or accepted any hazardous substances for transport to disposal or treatment facilities. . . .

1. PRESENT OWNERS

Appellant maintains that under §9607(a)(1), the only owner and operator who discharged hazardous materials was the United Creosoting Company, who abandoned the site in 1972. We find nothing in the wording of §9607(a) to exclude present owners of properties previously contaminated. . . . Section 9607(a)(2) expressly applies to past owners and operators who contaminate their surroundings; it is therefore manifest that §9607(a)(1) applies to current owners of adulterated sites. . . .

"Facility" is defined in §9601(9) to include:

(A) any building, structure, installation, equipment, pipe or pipeline (including any pipe into a sewer or publicly owned treatment works), well, pit, pond, lagoon impoundment, ditch, landfill, storage container, motor vehicle, rolling stock, or aircraft, or (B) *any site or area where a hazardous substance has been deposited, stored, disposed of, or placed, or otherwise come to be located;* but does not include any consumer product in consumer use or any vessel. (Emphasis added.)

The statute leaves no room for doubt; the Tanglewood East development is a covered facility. . . .

2. Past Owners

Section 9607(a)(2) applies to persons who owned or operated a facility at the time of the disposal of the toxins. Appellant contends that the only person who qualifies under that section is United Creosoting Company. We do not so read the statute. Referring to 42 U.S.C. §6903(3), we find "disposal" defined to include:

the discharge, deposit, injection, dumping spilling, leaking, or placing of any solid waste or hazardous waste into or on any land or water so that such solid waste or hazardous waste or any constituent thereof may enter the environment or be emitted into the air or discharged into any waters, including ground waters.

We recognize merit in appellees' argument that this definition of disposal does not limit disposal to a one-time occurrence — there may be other disposals when hazardous materials are moved, dispersed, or released during landfill excavations and fillings.

3. Post Arrangers and Transporters

Appellant next argues that defendants neither arranged for nor transported any hazardous material for disposal or treatment under §9607(a)(3) and (4). This argument rests on the narrow interpretation of disposal, which we reject, and a like interpretation of "treatment" which is defined by §6903(34) as:

any method, technique, or process, including neutralization, designed to change the physical, chemical, or biological character or composition of any hazardous waste so as to neutralize such waste or so as to render such waste nonhazardous, safer for transport, amenable for recovery, amenable for storage, or reduced in volume. *Such term includes any activity* or processing *designed to change the physical form* or chemical composition *of hazardous waste* so as to render it nonhazardous. (Emphasis added.)

Appellees argue that the activity of filling and grading the creosote pools constituted treatment to render the waste non-hazardous, and that those involved in that activity are covered persons under §9607(a)(3). Furthermore, since disposal may be merely the "placing of any . . . hazardous waste into or on any land. . . ." §6903(3), those who move the waste about the site may fall within the terms of the provision. Under these readings of the terms "disposal" and "treatment," relevant evidence under the complaint may establish that some of the defendants were arrangers for, or transporters of, the toxic materials. . . .

In light of the foregoing, we are satisfied that the complaint may not be dismissed for failure to state a claim upon which relief under CERCLA may be granted. . . .

C. REMEDIES UNDER CERCLA

Section 9607(a)(4) provides that covered persons shall be liable for all costs of removal or

remedial action incurred by the United States Government or a State or an Indian Tribe not inconsistent with the national contingency plan; any other necessary costs of response incurred by any other person consistent with the national contingency plan. . . .

. . . Appellees have alleged that their costs are consistent with the national contingency plan. It remains for them to prove such. The issue of consistency cannot be resolved on the pleadings alone, but must await development of relevant evidence. . . .

The judgment of the district court is AFFIRMED.

Notes and Comments

1. *The Range of CERCLA Defendants.* The *Tanglewood* litigation may have introduced you to a whole new legal world that has generated a deluge of litigation: liability under the Comprehensive Environmental Response, Compensation, and Liability Act, otherwise known as "CERCLA." The reach of CERCLA and its state counterparts (almost every state has some version of a mini-CERCLA) is substantial. CERCLA "is a 'sweeping' federal remedial statute enacted . . . to ensure that '*every-one* who is potentially responsible for hazardous-waste contamination may be forced to contribute to the costs of cleanup.' . . ." *U.S. v. General Battery Corp.*, 423 F.3d 294, 297-98 (3d Cir. 2005) [quotation citations omitted]. There is, for example, much litigation over whether a product manufacturer or seller has "arranged for disposal" under the Act. *See, e.g., Vine Street LLC v. Borg Warner Corp.*, 776 F.3d 312 (5th Cir. 2015) (property owner unsuccessfully tried to have the designer and seller of dry cleaning equipment declared an "arranger" and thus subject to liability under CERCLA); *Pakootas v. Teck Cominco Metals, Ltd.*, 830 F.3d 975 (9th Cir. 2016) (operator of smelter did not arrange for disposal of hazardous substances under CERCLA).

Consider carefully how this statute applies in the *Tanglewood* factual context. It is relatively easy to see why the subdivision site in *Tanglewood* is a "facility," although this location is not the type of operation that you might ordinarily associate with the word "facility." Which of the four liability categories would apply to the developer of the property? That developer certainly did not send waste for disposal on the property; it was simply trying to build homes. What about the operator of the bulldozer: would that person be liable? Note also that, while the homeowners are plaintiffs in this case, they would also be liable for cleanup costs. For further examples of CERCLA liability, *see Kaiser Aluminum & Chem. Corp. v. Catellus Dev. Corp.*, 976 F.2d 976 (9th Cir. 1992) (excavator of property found liable as "disposer" under CERCLA); *Niagara Mohawk Power Corp. v. Chevron U.S.A. Inc.*, 596 F.3d 112, 118 (2d Cir. 2010) ("At the center of this [CERCLA] dispute is a contaminated site . . . that over the last 100 years has played host to various industrial activities . . .").

The *Tanglewood* case is an example of private litigation brought under §107 of CERCLA seeking recovery of cleanup costs. Under CERCLA, the federal Environmental Protection Agency can take action to address cleanup of a site, and the agency has a number of arrows in its enforcement quiver. It can use money from the so-called Superfund to clean up property and then file suit against various responsible parties under §107 of CERCLA seeking reimbursement of its expenditures. It may also issue a §106 administrative order to parties requiring them to clean up, with violation of the order subject to a penalty equal to three times the cleanup costs, or it can seek injunctive relief in federal court.

2. *The Scope of CERCLA Liability.* Once you see the range of possible defendants in a CERCLA case, you must consider the scope of liability. Cleaning up hazardous

waste sites is a costly business, and the costs skyrocket if the waste has migrated into the groundwater below a site.

What is each defendant liable for? Most courts have found that joint and several liability applies unless the harm from the waste is found divisible. *See O'Neil v. Picillo,* 883 F.2d 176 (1st Cir. 1989), *cert. denied,* 493 U.S. 1071 (1990) (small party defendants are jointly and severally liable); *In re Bell Petroleum Services, Inc.,* 3 F.3d 889 (5th Cir. 1993) (joint and several liability improper if defendant meets burden of proving that a reasonable basis for apportioning environmental liability exists). Is the standard strict liability, or must fault be proven? *See Environmental Transp. Systems, Inc. v. Ensco, Inc.,* 763 F. Supp. 384 (C.D. Ill. 1991), *aff'd,* 969 F.2d 503 (7th Cir. 1992) (contractor held strictly liable for release of PCBs resulting from an accident involving the subcontractor's truck). In *Burlington Northern and Santa Fe Ry. Co. v. U.S.,* 556 U.S. 599 (2009), the Supreme Court held that "apportionment is proper when 'there is a reasonable basis for determining the contribution of each cause to a single harm.' . . ." (citing Restatement (Second) of Torts §433A(1)(b).)

Finally, you should also know that the number of sites subject to CERCLA liability has turned out to be much larger than was originally thought. Under CERCLA, the federal government may only clean up sites listed on the National Priorities List (NPL). Even if a site is not currently listed on the NPL, however, the possibility exists that EPA might list the site at some time in the future. Equally important, because CERCLA provides private causes of action, as illustrated by the *Tanglewood* case, even less-contaminated sites are subject to CERCLA.

This is just a short sketch of what is a very complex law. For more information, *see* Susan Cooke, The Law of Hazardous Waste Management: Cleanup, Liability and Litigation (1995); Donald L. Stever, The Law of Chemical Regulation and Hazardous Waste (1986). *See also* Martha L. Judy & Katherine N. Probst, Superfund at 30, 11 Vt. J. Envtl. L. 191 (2009).

3. *Twists and Turns in the Supreme Court.* From the parties' standpoint, the key issue under CERCLA is who pays. From a land use standpoint, however, the central issue is whether the property will be cleaned up, and to what degree. Both issues conjoined in two Supreme Court cases. In *Cooper Indus., Inc. v. Aviall Services, Inc.,* 543 U.S. 157 (2004), a party cleaned up the site voluntarily before anyone had sued it under CERCLA. After the cleanup the party sought contribution from other potentially responsible parties under Section 113 of CERLA. However, the court held that contribution was unavailable where the party seeking it had not been sued.

Critics bemoaned the fact that, under the logic of *Aviall,* parties would not voluntarily clean up contaminated sites for reuse if there was no possibility of contribution. *See, e.g.,* Charles F. Helsten, Heather K. Lloyd and Harvey M. Sheldon, The Effect of *Aviall* on the Vitality of Brownfields Programs, Am. Bar Assn. Envtl. Transactions and Brownfields Committee Newsletter (Vol. 7, No. 2) (Mar. 2005) ("prior to this decision, parties often initiated quick private remedial actions and presumed that once those remedial actions were completed . . . they could then simply pursue a private contribution claim under Section 13(f)(3)(B) against liable parties."). However, in *United States v. Atlantic Research Corp.,* 51 U.S. 128 (2007), the Court found that a party who had voluntarily cleaned up a site could seek contribution via a different route: Section 107 of CERCLA.

4. *State Property Transfer Laws and Superliens.* CERCLA is a liability statute that does not directly affect property transfers; instead, it principally imposes liability for cleanup costs. Some states take a different approach to solving hazardous waste

contamination problems, focusing on property transfers. They have enacted legislation requiring that sellers provide notice of property contamination prior to the transfer. The notice required can vary; some statutes require notice to state authorities or potential purchasers, while others mandate notice in the deed or other transfer instrument. On disclosure statutes generally, *see* David B. Farer, Transaction-Triggered Environmental Laws and Transfer Notice Laws, SU035-ALI-CLE 1087 (2013) (listing state transaction-triggered environmental laws); Sarah L. Inderbitzin, Taking the Burden Off the Buyer: A Survey of Hazardous Waste Disclosure Statutes, 1 Envtl. Law. 513 (1995).

The most far-reaching state legislation is New Jersey's Industrial Site Recovery Act ("ISRA," formerly known as the Environmental Cleanup Responsibility Act, or "ECRA"), N.J. Stat. Ann. §13:1K-6 to -14 (2012). ISRA applies when an industrial establishment either closes or transfers ownership or operations, requiring the seller to notify the state of its intentions. Before the sale can occur, the transferor must take steps to ensure that hazardous wastes at the site have been cleaned up or the state has approved a cleanup plan. *See Federal Pac. Elec. Co. v. New Jersey Dept. of Envtl. Protection*, 334 N.J. Super. 323 (A.D. 2000) (overturning remedial action workplan designed to comply with ISRA); *Champion Laboratories, Inc. v. Metex Corp.*, 2005 WL 1606921 (D.N.J. 2005) (describing how site purchase triggered ISRA). Most significantly, a buyer may void the sale and recover damages if the seller fails to comply with ISRA's requirements. N.J. Stat. Ann §13:1K. In 2009, the Site Remediation Reform Act, N.J.S.A. 58:10C-1 *et seq.*, allowed for delegation of oversight to private parties. *See* Tom Rath, Deregulation By Any Other Name: New Jersey's Site Remediation Reform Act in Federal Context, 63 Admin. L. Rev. 323 (2011).

5. *Risk-Based Cleanup.* An important component of the cleanup is defining the cleanup levels required. Many of the state programs require "risk-based" cleanup; in other words, they attempt to define cleanup standards by evaluating the actual risks to human health posed by the site. *See generally* Heidi Gorovitz Robinson, Legislative Innovation in State Brownfields Redevelopment Programs, 16 J. Envtl. L. & Litig. 1, 10 (2001) (discussing state approaches using risk-based standards).

Other programs emphasize that the intended use of the property must be considered in determining the cleanup level required. If a site will be reused for industry, it does not require cleanup to a level that would be required for, say, a proposed residential use. These types of cleanup standards would allow for the use of engineering controls, which are measures designed to contain contamination on the site rather than to fully remediate it, such as putting a "cap" over contaminated soil. They would also utilize institutional or "managerial" controls on sites, such as warning signs and fences, notice requirements in deeds, leases, or property transfer documents, as well as land use controls.

A Note on Brownfields and Greenfields

1. *Brownfields and Greenfields.* Hazardous waste laws have particularly important effects on the ability of urban areas to redevelop and re-use industrial sites that are presently abandoned. If a party desires to purchase a piece of property that is contaminated with hazardous wastes, that party risks becoming subject to CERCLA liability. Many of the properties that are contaminated were previously used for

industrial purposes and are located in urban areas. The infrastructure for their reuse for business or commercial purposes is already in place, and their locations are often attractive from a transportation standpoint. Nonetheless, if you were contemplating buying or leasing such property, how attractive would it have to be before you would act, given your knowledge of the potential liability under CERCLA?

If you concluded that you would shy away from owning or otherwise dealing with land subject to CERCLA liability, your conclusion is the same as that of many business persons who have been properly advised by their counsel about the potential liability under CERCLA. *See* National Governors Ass'n, New Mission for Brownfields 13 (2000) (the "specter of liability" is an impediment to investigating and remediating soil and groundwater contamination). The problem is not just the expensive liability attached to cleaning up hazardous waste (including the possibility that the buyer may underestimate the dollars required); it also includes the delays in getting federal and state agencies to approve the method of cleanup.

Thus, many businesses have avoided what have become known as "brownfields." CERCLA has defined the term to mean "real property, the expansion, redevelopment, or reuse of which may be complicated by the presence or potential presence of a hazardous substance, pollutant, or contaminant." 42 U.S.C. §9601(39)(A). Users of the term are often referring to abandoned, inactive, or underutilized industrial sites located primarily in urban areas. Instead of utilizing brownfields, companies have opened new businesses in "greenfields," which are "suburban and exurban locations that developers have been thought to prefer for new construction." Joel B. Eisen, Brownfields Development: From Individual Sites to Smart Growth, 39 Envtl. L. Rep. News & Analysis 10285 (2009). Greenfields are located on the outskirts of a built-up area and have not been previously used for urban or industrial activities.

The land use implications of these decisions are significant. EPA estimates that there are more than 450,000 brownfields in the United States. EPA, Brownfields and Land Revitalization: Basic Information, http://www.epa.gov/brownfields/basic_info.htm (last visited Nov. 5, 2016). The existence of brownfields makes redevelopment of urban areas much more difficult. Cities receive less property tax revenue from brownfields sites, and inner-city neighborhoods fail to benefit from the jobs that the location of industry on these sites might provide. As blighted industrial or commercial areas remain vacant, the cycle of deterioration in those areas continues. At the same time, if businesses exhibit a preference for locating in "greenfields," which are suburban areas, they create impacts on the transportation system as well as secondary environmental impacts such as increased air pollution. Finally, the use of greenfields exacerbates urban sprawl.

2. *Solving the Brownfields Dilemma.* As CERCLA's inability to ensure expeditious site cleanup became more and more obvious, individuals began to realize that the key to cleanups was to encourage voluntary actions on the part of site owners. EPA has joined in this effort to encourage voluntary action through its Brownfields Program. A principal thrust of this movement, however, has come from states, many located in the Northeast and Midwest, that have enacted legislation to promote voluntary cleanups and implemented policies designed with this goal in mind.

These state programs sometimes do not use the nomenclature "brownfield." *See* the Alabama Land Recycling and Economic Redevelopment Act, Ala. Code 1975 §22-30-E-1, *et seq.*; and Pennsylvania's Land Recycling and Environmental Remediation Standards Act, 35 Pa. Stat. §6026.101 *et seq.* (2012). *See, more generally,* David A.

Dana, State Brownfields Programs as Laboratories of Democracy?,14 N.Y.U. Envtl. L.J. 86 (2005) (noting that "a new regime has arisen: state voluntary cleanup programs or, as they are often labeled, brownfields programs.").

A key component of this effort is changes in the level of cleanup required. The voluntary cleanup programs emphasize the need for more certainty in establishing cleanup standards, so that lenders and investors can determine in advance whether a brownfields development economically "pencils out." Other important components of the effort include (1) providing certainty that, once a state has "signed off" on a brownfields cleanup, the federal or state governments will not later decide to bring an action against the new landowner; (2) establishing a fast-track process for rapid government approval of cleanups; (3) providing financial incentives to spur interest in brownfields redevelopment; and (4) reducing the possibility that lenders may be held liable for lending on contaminated property.

3. *The Small Business Liability Relief and Brownfields Revitalization Act.* This law was passed by Congress and signed into law in January 2002. Pub. L. No. 107-118, 115 Stat. 2355 (2002) (codified as amended in scattered sections of 42 U.S.C. §§9601-9628). The law has several important provisions. First, it clarifies that bona fide prospective purchasers of property are exempt from CERCLA liability, even if they have knowledge of contamination, if they meet certain requirements, including exercising "appropriate care" of the hazardous wastes. The act also protects contiguous property owners who had no knowledge or reason to know their property would be contaminated, and it contains provisions for settlements for low volume or low toxicity waste contributors to CERCLA sites. It clarified that existing "innocent landowners" may avoid liability if they have conducted due diligence and have no knowledge or reason to know of the contamination. Finally, the law also provides for conditional expedited settlements with persons who can demonstrate an inability or limited ability to pay response costs. *See* Charles S. Warren and Toni L. Finger, Courts Shed Light on the Application of CERCLA's Bona Fide Prospective Purchaser Defense, 41 Envtl. L. Rep. News & Analysis 10790 (Sept. 2011).

The Fourth Circuit, interpreting the scope of "appropriate care" under CERCLA's "Bona Fide Prospective Purchaser Defense" (BFPP), held that the current owner of a portion of a former fertilizer facility failed to establish a BFPP defense for liability exemption. The Court affirmed the District Court's holding that the owner was a PRP [Potentially Responsible Party] through its failure to establish a number of the eight criteria for the BFPP defense, including the exercise of appropriate care. *PCS Nitrogen v. Ashley II*, 714 F.3d 161 (4th Cir. 2013). *See* Nicholas Orlando, Appropriate Care Under the Brownfield Amendments: A Better Standard of Care After the Fourth Circuit's Holding in *PCS Nitrogen v. Ashley II*, 5 Seattle J. Envtl. L. 25 (2015) (concluding that the opinion reflects "a poor policy choice in light of the stated goals of the Brownfield Amendments" and suggesting that the standard of care should be re-defined to "impose[] less stringent duties on the prospective purchaser than due care").

Finally, the second part of the act (Title II, called "Brownfields Revitalization and Environmental Restoration") includes various funding mechanisms for brownfields revitalization.

The literature on the brownfields issue is voluminous. Major sources include Michael B. Gerrard, ed., Brownfields Law and Practice: The Cleanup and

Redevelopment of Contaminated Land (1999 and Supp. 2016); Brownfields: A Comprehensive Guide to Redeveloping Contaminated Property (Todd S. Davis and Kevin D. Margolis eds. (2d ed. 2002); Joel B. Eisen, Finality in Brownfields Remediation and Reuse, 41 Sw. L. Rev. 773 (2012); and William R. Weissman and J. Michael Sowinski, Jr., Revitalizing the Brownfields Revitalization and Environmental Restoration Act: Harmonizing the Liability Defense Language to Achieve Brownfields Restoration, 33 Va. Envtl. L.J. 257 (2015).

As you can see from the discussion of CERCLA above, a critical question is the extent of the cleanup that will be required for any property in question. Often, so-called "institutional controls," a term that includes land use measures, are used. In the following excerpt EPA explains their use.

■ OFFICE OF SOLID WASTE AND EMERGENCY RESPONSE, U.S. EPA, A CITIZEN'S GUIDE TO UNDERSTANDING INSTITUTIONAL CONTROLS AT SUPERFUND, BROWNFIELDS, FEDERAL FACILITIES, UNDERGROUND STORAGE TANK, AND RESOURCE CONSERVATION AND RECOVERY ACT CLEANUPS
(Feb. 2005)

WHAT ARE INSTITUTIONAL CONTROLS?

ICs are generally administrative and legal tools that do not involve construction or physically changing the site. ICs are generally divided into four categories:

1. **Government Controls** — include local laws or permits (e.g., county zoning, building permits, and Base Master Plans at military facilities);
2. **Proprietary Controls** — include property use restrictions based on private property law (e.g., easements and covenants);
3. **Enforcement Tools** — include documents that require individuals or companies to conduct or prohibit specific actions (e.g., environmental cleanup consent decrees, unilateral orders, or permits); and,
4. **Informational Devices** — include deed notices or public advisories that alert and educate people about a site.

In many site cleanups, ICs help reduce the possibility that people will come in contact with contamination and may also protect expensive cleanup equipment from damage. The use of ICs is not a way "around" treatment, but rather part of a balanced, practical approach to site cleanup that relies on both engineered and non-engineered remedies.

WHEN ARE ICs USED?

ICs are normally used when waste is left onsite and when there is a limit to the activities that can safely take place at the site (i.e., the site cannot support unlimited use and unrestricted exposure) and/or when cleanup equipment remains onsite. ICs are often used throughout a site cleanup, including when:

- contamination is first discovered (i.e., to protect people from coming in contact with potentially harmful materials while the contamination is being investigated)
- cleanup work is ongoing (in some cases it may take many years to complete cleanup)
- some amount of contamination remains onsite as part of cleanup remedy.

ICs can play an important role when a cleanup is conducted and when it is too difficult or too costly to remove all contamination from a site. ICs are rarely used alone to deal with contamination at a site. Typically, ICs are part of a larger cleanup solution and serve as a non-engineered layer of protection. ICs are designed to keep people from using the site in a way that is not safe and/or from doing things that could damage the cleanup equipment, thus, potentially jeopardizing protection of people and the environment. For example, an IC may be necessary at a former landfill to notify the community and guard against excavators digging through a clay barrier that is meant to stop rain water from entering the landfill.

Most cleanups will need to use a combination of engineered remedies and ICs. ICs provide an additional level of safety and help to make sure the remedy remains securely in place. Also, it is important to understand that a cleanup is not finished until all necessary action has been taken to protect people and the environment from contamination at the site.

WHY CAN'T ALL THE CONTAMINATION BE REMOVED?

Removing all traces of contamination from a site is often not possible or practicable because of the types and location of contamination. However, the presence of some residual contamination does not mean that a site can't be used safely.

Use of a site with residual contamination is considered safe if exposure to contamination is prevented. ICs can help a site be reused. A common example of a site reuse is when a surface barrier layer is installed over contaminated soil and the area is used for athletic fields, a golf course, or a park because ICs are in place to prevent disturbance of the barrier layer.

Are ICs Reliable? All ICs have strengths and weaknesses. With this understanding, it is important to choose the best combination of ICs that will be protective of human health and the environment. One key challenge is that ICs are often implemented, monitored, and enforced by various levels of federal, state, tribal, or local governments. Therefore, it is critical to make sure there are enough IC safeguards and overlaps so no significant risk to human health or the environment or damage to the remedy occur.

EPA guidance encourages the use of ICs in "layers" and/or in "series" to enhance overall protectiveness. Layering ICs means using more than one IC at the same time, all with the same goal (e.g., a consent decree, deed notice, and covenant stopping the use of drinking water wells). Using ICs in series uses different ICs over time when site circumstances or IC processes change. For example, restrictions can gradually be reduced as progress is made toward cleanup goals. Used in such overlapping ways ICs can be more securely relied upon to provide an important measure of safety. Thus, usually more than one kind of IC is put in place at a single site.

────────────

Here is an example of an environmental covenant designed to control land use:

■ THIS PROPERTY IS SUBJECT TO AN ENVIRONMENTAL COVENANT HELD BY THE COLORADO DEPARTMENT OF PUBLIC HEALTH AND ENVIRONMENT PURSUANT TO SECTION 25-15-321, C.R.S.

ENVIRONMENTAL COVENANT

ASARCO Incorporated ("Asarco") grants an Environmental Covenant ("Covenant") this 4th day of October, 2004 to the Hazardous Materials and Waste Management Division of the Colorado Department of Public Health and the Environment ("the Department") pursuant to §25-15-321 of the Colorado Hazardous Waste Act, §25-15-101, *et seq.* The Department's address is 4300 Cherry Creek Drive South, Denver, Colorado 80246-1530.

WHEREAS, Asarco is the owner of certain property commonly referred to as The Globe Plant, located at 495 E. 51st Ave., Denver, Colorado 80216, more particularly described in Attachment A, attached hereto and incorporated herein by reference as though fully set forth (hereinafter referred to as "the Property"); and WHEREAS, pursuant to the Consent Decree lodged in the United States District Court for the District of Colorado on October 6, 2004 pursuant to United States of America and State of Colorado v. Asarco, Inc. Civil Action No. 04-RB-2070, the Property is the subject of enforcement and remedial action pursuant to the Comprehensive Environmental Response, Compensation and Liability Act, 42 U.S.C. §§9601, *et seq.* ("CERCLA"); and

WHEREAS, the purpose of this Covenant is to ensure protection of human health and the environment by restricting uses that are not compatible with soil remediation levels at the Globe Plant; and

WHEREAS, Asarco desires to subject the Property to certain covenants and restrictions as provided in Article 15 of Title 25, Colorado Revised Statutes, which covenants and restrictions shall burden the Property and bind Asarco, its heirs, successors, assigns, and any grantees of the Property, their heirs, successors, assigns and grantees, and any users of the Property, for the benefit of the Department.

NOW, THEREFORE, Asarco hereby grants this Environmental Covenant to the Department, and declares that the Property as described in Attachment A shall hereinafter be bound by, held, sold, and conveyed subject to the following requirements set forth in paragraph 1 below, which shall run with the Property in perpetuity and be binding on Asarco and all parties having any right, title or interest in the Property, or any part thereof, their heirs, successors and assigns, and any persons using the land. As used in this Environmental Covenant, the term "Owner" means the record owner of the Property and, if any, any other person or entity otherwise legally authorized to make decisions regarding the transfer for the Property or placement of encumbrances on the Property, other than by the exercise of eminent domain, and any heirs, successors and assigns thereof.

1. ENVIRONMENTAL PROTECTION COVENANT — USE RESTRICTIONS:

a. The use of the property for residential purposes or to raise crops or livestock is prohibited;

b. The use of the property for child or animal day care facilities, including child or animal day camps and educational facilities, is prohibited;

c. Except for remediation purposes, any use or extraction of any groundwater, including the unconfined, alluvial aquifer, is prohibited;

d. Any excavation into the cover of the Former Neutralization Pond or construction of structures on the Former Neutralization Pond is prohibited;

e. Any excavation, grading, construction, drilling, digging, or any other activity that may damage the integrity of the soil cap at the Plant Site Operable Unit ("Cap") is prohibited without the submission and approval by the Department of a plan for the management and disposition of disturbed and contaminated materials. Any damage to the integrity of the Cap will be followed by repair of the Cap so that the repaired Cap consists of at least 12 inches of borrow soils meeting specifications approved by the Department and a vegetative cover or two inches of asphalt or other durable cover;

f. Except as permitted in paragraph e, any activity that will impair the effectiveness of the remedy is prohibited, including any activity that will interfere with groundwater extraction and remediation. . . .

3. MODIFICATIONS

This Covenant runs with the land and is perpetual, unless modified or terminated pursuant to this paragraph. Owner or its successors and assigns may request that the Department approve a modification or termination of the Covenant. The request shall contain information showing that the proposed modification or termination shall, if implemented, ensure protection of human health and the environment.

Notes and Comments

1. *The CERCLA Presumption and Future Land Use.* The underlying issue in determining the level of cleanup is whether the cost and bureaucratic difficulty of cleaning a site up to background levels is preferable to flexibility in cleanup that may result in a lesser cleanup coupled with land use restrictions. To date, Congress has inclined toward the former. The state voluntary cleanup statutes, in contrast, are much more flexible on cleanup levels. As one author put it, the state statutes "envision voluntary cleanups that trade increased health risks to the affected community for the prospect of new jobs and higher tax revenues." Joel B. Eisen, "Brownfields of Dreams"? Challenges and Limits of Voluntary Cleanup Programs and Incentives, 96 U. Ill. L. Rev. 883, 887 (1996). Another author put the policy issue as follows: "[S]hould institutional controls be used only as a last resort when cleanup is

impossible, or should they be used more broadly to maximize reuse of contaminated property?" Susan C. Borinsky, The Use of Institutional Controls in Superfund and Similar Laws, 7 Fordham Envtl. L.J. 1 (1995). What do you think?

In Seth Schofield, In Search of the Institution in Institutional Controls: The Failure of the Small Business Liability Relief and Brownfields Revitalization Act of 2002 and the Need for Legislation, 12 N.Y.U. Envtl. L.J. 946 (2005), the author criticizes the federal law as insufficient:

> [T]he tools used to restrict future land use, known as institutional controls (ICs), currently fail to achieve the preference for permanence espoused in section 121.8. The consequence of this strategy is that, until Congress provides EPA with adequate legal tools to restrict land use in perpetuity and to memorialize and monitor those sites, the current use-restricted cleanup paradigm merely proliferates the human health and environmental risks of contaminated properties. This proliferation also comes with the risk of economic liability for current and future generations.

2. *Deciding on Future Uses.* Do you see how the future land use planned for the contaminated property affects the determination of the residual risk that would remain after various types of cleanups at the site have been completed? How should this future land use be decided? Is it simply a matter for the local government, or do the state and federal governments also play a role?

3. *Implementing the Land Use Restriction.* Assuming you decide that more limited cleanup is appropriate in some instances, what kinds of land use controls should be instituted to ensure that the public health is protected? Relying solely on local land use regulations, such as zoning, is impractical for a number of reasons, including the fact that such restrictions are subject to change. How can the state or federal government ensure that the local government will actually implement the restriction on certain land uses?

The obvious solution is a deed restriction, like the covenant you just read, an easement that runs with the land, or some other similar property instrument. How should the law ensure that these restrictions are implemented? *See* U.S. EPA, Institutional Controls: A Guide to Planning, Implementing, Maintaining, and Enforcing Institutional Controls at Contaminated Sites (Dec. 2012) (recommending "full-cycle planning (i.e., planning, implementing, maintaining, enforcing, modifying if necessary and terminating) . . . to ensure the long-term durability, reliability, and effectiveness of ICs [Institutional Controls].")).

Land use controls are increasingly used in cleanups. One report stated that, for fiscal years 2001 through 2003, 83 percent of CERCLA "Superfund" cleanups used them. Amy Jiron et al., Notes from the Field: Land Use Controls Tracking; A Status Report 5 (2006). *See also* Amy L. Edwards (ed.), Implementing Institutional Controls at Brownfields and Other Contaminated Sites (2012).

4. *But Will It Work?* The various states have put significant efforts into redeveloping brownfields. One article, however, suggested that these efforts miss the broader picture. Heidi Gorovitz Robertson, One Piece of the Puzzle: Why State Brownfields Programs Can't Lure Businesses to the Urban Cores Without Finding the Missing Pieces, 51 Rutgers L. Rev. 1075 (1999). This analysis remains relevant many years later. One problem is that lenders "feel squeamish" about the possibility of becoming liable if they undertake brownfields funding. *Id.* at 1088. Another large

problem is that non-environmental factors, such as building size and configuration, construction costs, access to interstate highways, and the ability to attract a suitable workforce, "appear as important to companies making relocation decisions as the environmental status of prospective sites." *Id.* at 1121. In other words, while governments are focused on brownfields issues, businesses may have larger concerns.

E. PROTECTION OF AGRICULTURE AND OPEN SPACE

The next subject addressed in this chapter is the preservation of agriculture and open space. The principal case included below demonstrates how a traditional land use tool is used to protect agriculture and preserve open space.

■ IN RE RATTEE
761 A.2d 1076 (N.H. 2000)

Brock, C.J.

This is a consolidated appeal from decisions of the New Hampshire Agricultural Lands Preservation Committee (ALPC) and the Superior Court (*Brennan,* J.) denying the request of Steven Rattee to construct a home on land subject to an agricultural preservation restriction (APR). We affirm in part and vacate in part.

. . . In May 1996, Rattee purchased at a foreclosure sale 185 acres of land on the east and west sides of Mountain Road in Concord for $216,000 and approximately $28,000 in back taxes. The deed granted to him stated that the land was subject to the terms of an APR and stated where the APR was recorded in the Merrimack County Registry of Deeds. In 1982, Rattee's predecessor in title, Horace Blood, had granted by deed the APR on approximately 103 acres of the property to the State of New Hampshire (grantee), acting through the ALPC and the commissioner of the department of agriculture (commissioner). The State paid approximately $406,000 to acquire the APR.

The APR states, in pertinent part:

> The Grantor, his heirs, . . . successors and assigns, . . . covenant and agree that they are restrained from constructing on, . . . or otherwise improving the Site for uses that result in rendering the Site no longer suitable for agricultural use. . . . Such restraint . . . shall include prohibition of:
>
> 1. Construction or placement of building or structures except those to be used for agricultural purposes or for dwellings to be used for family living by the landowner, his immediate family or employees. Construction or placement of (a) dwellings to be used for family living . . . shall be subject to the prior approval of the Grantee. Approval for such construction or placement shall be granted only when it will not defeat or derogate from the intent of this restriction. Any building or structure and the land upon which it is situated shall not be sold or otherwise severed from the Site unless the Grantee releases such dwelling, permanent structure or land from the restriction pursuant to RSA 36-D:7 (Supp.) . . .

The foregoing restriction is intended to conform to and have the benefit of RSA 36-D (Supp.) and RSA 477:45-47 (Supp.).

In 1987, the prior owners constructed on land subject to the APR a small house that remains. Also included in the 185 acres purchased by the petitioner is an adjacent 3.3 acre "farmstead site," which is exempt from the APR and upon which stood a house. According to Rattee, in 1996 he arranged for that house to be burned down as a fire department exercise because it was in very poor condition.

In the fall of 1996, Rattee excavated a field on land subject to the APR to construct a new 5500 square foot home and a 1500 foot driveway that would destroy two acres. He applied for a building permit from the City of Concord, but did not seek building or placement approval from the ALPC. Shortly thereafter, the State advised Rattee that he was in violation of the APR. Rattee asserted that the APR did not apply because the house was going to be his home, and thus was subject to an exception for "dwellings used for family living by the landowner." RSA 36-D:1, II (current version at RSA 432:18, II). . . .

On appeal, Rattee argues that: (1) the State, acting through the ALPC, lacked authority to acquire the right to require prior approval for the construction of owner residences on APR sites; (2) the APR did not effectively convey to the State the right to determine the location of owner residences on the site; (3) the ALPC acted unreasonably in disapproving Rattee's application; and (4) the ALPC and the trial court improperly ruled that sections of the APR site on either side of Mountain Road cannot be sold separately without the ALPC's approval.

With respect to the first argument, we do not agree that the State lacked authority to purchase or acquire more rights than are contained in the statutory definition of an APR, specifically the right to regulate construction of owner residences on APR sites. The provision requiring prior approval for construction or placement of owner residences was part of a voluntary conveyance of property rights to the State. Even if we assume that the prior approval provision exceeds the authority given to the State by RSA chapter 36-D, no rule of law bars the State from purchasing such a right.

We also reject the argument that the APR did not convey to the State the right to determine the location of owner housing on the site. Rattee contends that the statement in the APR that it "is intended to conform to and have the benefit of RSA 36-D" restricts the rights conveyed to those enumerated in RSA chapter 36-D. Therefore, while the APR language requiring prior approval may be clear, Rattee argues that it is rendered ambiguous by the statement that the APR is intended to conform to RSA chapter 36-D, which does not have a prior approval provision. The State counters that the prior approval provision is a "necessary, appropriate and reasonable means for accomplishing the public policy objective of preserving good quality agricultural land for future agricultural production." . . .

The stated purpose of RSA chapter 36-D is to "recognize the importance of preserving the limited land suitable for agricultural production, to safeguard the public health and welfare by encouraging the maximum use of food and fiber producing capabilities of the state's agriculturally suitable land and to ensure the protection of agricultural land facing conversion to non-agricultural uses." Laws 1979, 301:1. Thus, while the APR statute and deed both reserve the right to construct "dwellings to be used for family living," requiring prior approval for such construction is consistent with the statutory purpose. Prior approval ensures that family dwellings will be constructed in a manner that minimizes their impact on agricultural production and prevents potential abuse of the family dwelling exception. Therefore, we conclude that the prior approval provision in the APR conforms to, and indeed strengthens, RSA chapter 36-D. *Cf. Bennett*, 576 N.E.2d at 1368 (APR prior approval provision enforceable, even if the condition of approval did not fall within the statutory definition of APR, because it was consistent with the public policy expressed in the Massachusetts APR statute).

We disagree with Rattee that this conclusion is unreasonable due to the statutory language preserving for the landowner all customary rights of ownership, including the right to carry out all regular agricultural practices not prohibited by the statutory definition of an APR. *See* RSA 36-D:7 (current version at RSA 432:24, 1). We interpret this language in accordance with the statutory purpose of RSA chapter 36-D. While the statute may reserve certain rights for the landowner, it is reasonable for the APR to include a prior approval provision to ensure that the exercise of the family dwelling exception does not defeat the statutory purpose of "preserving the limited land suitable for agricultural production." Laws 1979, 301:1. For the same reason, we disagree that the statement that the APR "is intended to conform to and have the benefit of RSA 36-D" restricts the rights conveyed in the APR to those enumerated in RSA chapter 36-D.

Because we conclude that the prior approval provision conforms to RSA chapter 36-D, we reject the argument that the APR is ambiguous. Accordingly, we interpret the intended meaning of the prior approval provision from the language of the deed and need not consider extrinsic evidence. . . .

Rattee next argues that the ALPC's conclusion that "construction of a house would damage agricultural use of the land was unsupported by any evidence." We disagree. Because both the statute and the deed carve out of their prohibitions on construction an exception for "dwellings used for family living by the landowner," RSA 36-D:1, II, we agree with Rattee that the existence of the small house does not preclude him from constructing another residence. The APR provides, however, that the ALPC shall grant approval for construction "only when it will not defeat or derogate from the intent of [the] restriction." The statutory purpose of an APR is "to recognize the importance of preserving the limited land suitable for agricultural production . . . and to ensure the protection of agricultural land facing conversion to non-agricultural uses." Laws 1979, 301:1. In his application to the ALPC, Rattee proposed constructing a 5500 square foot home. The proposed home and accompanying 1500 foot driveway would remove two acres of productive soil from cultivation. Given the availability of the adjacent 3.3 acre farmstead site that is exempt from the APR, we agree with the ALPC that the proposed construction "is far from the least disruptive alternative available to . . . [Rattee]." Thus, we conclude that sufficient evidence in the record supports the ALPC's decision to deny this particular application, and that the decision is reasonable in light of the standard for approval stated in the APR. *See Petition of Hoyt*, 143 N.H. at 534, 727 A.2d at 1002. We also note that the ALPC's decision was "without prejudice . . . to [Rattee's] submission of a subsequent application containing a construction proposal which is consistent with the purpose of the [APR]."

Rattee next argues that the ALPC's decision was unreasonable because the ALPC improperly and without statutory authority considered several factors not relevant to its decision, including how much time the petitioner would devote to farming. Even if we assume that the ALPC improperly considered these factors, any error was harmless because Rattee did not meet his burden of showing that the alleged error resulted in material prejudice. . . .

We need not decide the fourth issue on appeal. Rattee argues that the ALPC and the trial court improperly ruled that sections of the APR site on either side of Mountain Road cannot be subdivided or sold separately without the ALPC's approval. In his brief, Rattee states that "the question of separate sale or subdivision of [his] land is not directly material to the central question in this case." He also notes that at trial the State argued that the issue was not before the trial court. Rattee argued to the trial court that the separate sale issue was significant because if he could sell the land on the west side of Mountain Road, which includes the existing small house, then the ALPC could not tell him that he could use that house instead of constructing a new one on the east side of Mountain Road. We interpret these statements to mean that the separate sale issue was relevant only if the existing house precludes the construction of an additional house. Because we conclude that it does not, the separate sale issue was not relevant and need not have been reached by the ALPC or the trial court. Accordingly, we vacate the decisions of the ALPC and the trial court to the extent they concluded that the land covered by the APR cannot be sold separately, subdivided, or otherwise severed without obtaining a release.

Affirmed in part; vacated in part.

Notes and Comments

1. *The* Rattee *Holding.* How can the state purchase "more rights" than are contained in the statutory definition of an agricultural preservation restriction? Isn't the state restricted to its statutory authority, even if the conveyance is "voluntary"? Even if this restriction existed, however, would Rattee have standing to raise this issue?

Why wasn't Rattee's proposed house consistent with the purpose of the statute? After all, it would only use two of the 185 acres. If the plan was not consistent, what are the parameters of the Commission's ability to reject the landowner's plans?

In another case, a conservation easement stated: "[I]t is the purpose of this Easement to foster responsible conservation practices while permitting Grantor to engage in certain recreational uses on the Property." The owners proposed to use the roads on the property for wagon rides, horse-drawn sleigh rides, hiking, snowshoeing, skiing, fishing, and ice skating, all made available to "paying guests." Would those uses violate the conservation easement? *See Windham Land Trust v. Jeffords,* 967 A.2d 690 (Me. 2009).

2. *The Need for Open Space and Agricultural Preservation.* In the early 1970s, a theme in the land use literature was the need to preserve "open space" against rapidly encroaching urbanization. In the years that followed, preservation of open space through traditional means such as low-density zoning became commonplace. In addition, cities and counties used their powers to mandate exactions as conditions of development approval as a means of acquiring certain lands for parks and other types of open space.

Somewhat later, others argued that agricultural land was being rapidly converted to urban uses and that government must take action to preserve agricultural land. A 1997 report by the American Farmland Trust, entitled Farming on the Edge, concluded that 79 percent of the nation's fruit crop, 69 percent of its vegetables, and 52 percent of its dairy products are produced on land vulnerable to development. The 2002 update, at http://www.farmlandinfo.org/farming-edge-sprawling-development-threatens-americas-best-farmland (last visited Nov. 5, 2016), reported the figures: "86 percent of U.S. fruits and vegetables, and 63 percent of our dairy products, are produced in urban-influenced areas," a significant increase in the threat to both categories of agricultural products from the previous report.

The need for preserving agricultural land, however, is not universally accepted. The National Association of Home Builders responded to the earlier American Farmland Trust report by asserting that "the conversion of some agricultural land into developable land is simply a fact of life, given the nation's growing population." Economists in particular argue that increases in per-acre agricultural productivity are such that no loss of agricultural production has occurred as prime agricultural land has been urbanized.

Nonetheless, many states determined to take action to preserve farmland, using a variety of legal mechanisms described below. This legislative effort was supported by other nonfarm interests, principally environmentalists, who saw any increases in agricultural preservation as gains both in their battles to prevent leapfrog urbanization of land outside the urban core and to preserve additional open space. While the rationales for open space preservation and agricultural protection are not necessarily the same, the efforts to preserve agriculture and open space have much in common, particularly since agriculture can be seen as a type of open space use. *See, e.g.,* Report of the Subcommittee on Innovative Growth Management Measures: Preservation of Agricultural Land and Open Space, 23 Urb. Law. 821 (1991) ("Agricultural land is the open space in some areas of the country."). *See* Ved Nanda, Agriculture and the Polluter Pays Principle, 54 Am. J. Comp. L. 317 (2006) ("the polluter in agricultural activities rarely pays because subsidies and farm price or income support still constitute the core of U.S. agrienvironmental policy.").

Are there any reasons for preserving agriculture other than to ensure the production of food? For example, one recurring theme in the literature of American democracy is the famous Jeffersonian ideal of the family farm. Should land use regulation be mobilized toward the goal of preserving the family farm?

3. *Methods of Preservation.* All of the following techniques have been used by both public and private entities to preserve lands:

(a) *Open Space Zoning.* Perhaps the most effective method of preservation is to employ the standard zoning ordinance as a means to preserve agricultural land or other types of open space. *See, e.g., Naser v. Town of Deering Zoning Bd. of Adjustment,* 950 A.2d 157, 159 (N.H. 2008) (zoning ordinance "regulates open space developments and permits an applicant to increase density by decreasing lot sizes provided a requisite amount of open space is preserved on the property"); *In re Cutler Group, Inc.,* 880 A.2d 39 (Pa. Commw. Ct. 2005) (appeal from denial of "Open Space Design Option" under zoning ordinance). A city might enact low-density or large-lot zoning techniques. It is also possible to adopt a zoning ordinance that makes agricultural use the exclusive use in an area. Legal tools for "promoting a comprehensive and holistic approach to agricultural natural resource conservation, land use planning, and land management, which incorporates watershed-based land use controls and regulation of the effects of agricultural land use on other critical natural resources, specifically water" are:

> local comprehensive planning; agricultural districts; agricultural protection zoning; cluster zoning; transfer of development rights (TDR) programs; growth management laws; farmland loss mitigation policies; state and local right-to-farm laws; farm viability programs; tax relief credit; and abatement programs, payment for ecosystem services (PES) provided by environmentally friendly farming practices and standardized certification of related farm products.

Lara Dumond Guercio, Local and Watershed Land Use Controls: A Turning Point for Agriculture and Water Quality, 62 Planning & Envtl. Law No. 2 (2010). *See also* Barton H. Thompson, Jr., EcoFarming: A Realistic Vision for the Future of Agriculture?, 1 UCI L.1167 (2011).

Landowners subject to such rezonings may resist them as arbitrary and capricious. *See, e.g., Dunes West Golf Club, LLC v. Town of Mount Pleasant,* 737 S.E. 2d 601 (S.C. 2013) (upholding denial of rezoning of golf course on basis of town's conservation creation open space zoning district ordinance). Alternatively, citizen groups may claim that the size of the parcel allowed is insufficient to ensure preservation of agriculture. *See Thompson v. Land Conservation and Dev. Comm'n,* 204 P.3d 808 (Or. Ct. App. 2009) (finding that evidence supported the Commission's conclusion that a 40-acre minimum parcel size was sufficient to maintain "existing commercial agricultural enterprises" in the area).

(b) *Conservation Easements.* Landowners can use property law to voluntarily restrict other types of uses on their property, thus ensuring that agricultural use of the property will continue. A technique whose use has steadily increased over the last 20 years is the so-called conservation easement. Landowners are often willing to donate conservation easements on their properties because there are tax advantages in doing so. Under the Internal Revenue Code, a contribution of a "qualified real property interest to a qualified organization exclusively for conservation purposes" is deductible. 26 C.F.R. §1.170A-14(a) (2012). A "perpetual conservation restriction" — including a "restrictive covenant" — is a "qualified real property interest." *Id.* §1.170A-14(b)(2). *See* Shea B. Airey, Conservation Easements in Private Practice, 44 Real Prop. Tr. & Est. L.J. 745 (2010) (discussing the different tax incentives for conservation easements). The easements may be held by public agencies, by private individuals or associations, or by land trusts. *See* Land Trust Alliance, 2010 National Land Trust Census Report (reporting that, as of 2010, 8,833,368 acres were held under easement by state and local land trusts, a figure much larger than the 2,326,064 acres held in 2000).

If you were representing a group that agrees to take title to a conservation easement, what legal problems might you foresee that the group should consider before it actually receives title? For example, how might you ensure that the group's rights would be enforceable in the event of a dispute in the future? And what about possible tort liability, since your client will now be an owner of a property interest?

See, e.g., Stitzel v. State of Maryland, 6 A.3d 935 (Md. Ct. Sp. App. 2010) (where easement stated that land could not be subdivided without approval of Agricultural Land Preservation Foundation, the Foundation had standing to set aside a purported conveyance).

What about the imposition of a condition, attached to approval of a site plan for a single family home, that a landowner dedicate a conservation restriction on environmentally sensitive portions of the property? Is that condition subject to the constitutional safeguards of the *Nollan* and *Dolan* decisions, discussed in Chapter 4? The New York Court of Appeals held that it was not an exaction because there was no "dedication of property" involved. *Smith v. Town of Mendon,* 822 N.E.2d 1214, 1219 (N.Y. 2004). The court found it important that the landowners could still apply for permission to conduct activities within the areas covered by the restriction, and the landowners still retained the "right to exclude others." Do you agree with that conclusion? The dissent argued that the majority was "simply wrong" in concluding that the Town was not requiring a dedication, because the conservation easement was a nonpossessory interest in real property. *Id.* at 1225 (Read, J., dissenting).

(c) *Agricultural Preservation Easements.* The "agricultural preservation easement" at issue in *Rattee* is a variation on this theme. Instead of situating ownership of the easement in a private party, the state purchases the easement. The easement restricts future land uses on the property or gives the state the right of approval over those uses. This type of restriction can lead to interpretive difficulties. In *Twomey v. Comm'r of Food & Agric.,* 759 N.E.2d 691 (Mass. 2001), the state purchased an "agricultural preservation restriction" from a farm owner. As the court noted, this was a conservation servitude, or easement in gross, that gave the commissioner authority over future building on the property. The court, however, held that the easement's provisions were inconsistent with the commissioner's adoption of an "irrebuttable presumption" that approval of any dwelling on the farm would defeat the purpose of farmland preservation.

While the court overturned his actions, the commissioner's reasoning was interesting. The commissioner was concerned about urbanization of "once rural areas." He reasoned that any new building would make the property unaffordable for farmers to acquire, thus defeating the purpose of the act. The court referred to this as a "loophole" in the act; because there was no requirement in the restriction that the property be used as a farm, it could be occupied for purely residential purposes. *Id.* at 694. *See also Long Green Valley Ass'n. v. Bellevale Farms, Inc.,* 68 A.3d 843 (Md. 2013) (because agricultural preservation easement did not create a charitable trust, it could not be enforced by association and its members). And in *Lewis and Clark County v. Hampton,* 333 P.3d 205 (Mont. 2014), the county planning commission agreed to revoke an agricultural covenant, provided that the landowner met 13 conditions of approval that would mitigate the impacts of development. The court held that the covenant was properly revoked. *See, generally,* Rachel Armstrong, On Infertile Ground: Growing a Local Food System Through Agricultural Conservation Easements, 19 Drake J. Agric. L. 149 (2014).

(d) *Property Tax Incentives.* A key reason why urbanization can force an end to agricultural uses on adjacent land is the effect of that urbanization on property taxes. As nearby land develops, the agricultural property may become more valuable as the market envisions residential rather than agricultural uses for it, and the property tax on it may increase markedly. Since the financial return of the agricultural operations has not changed, that increase can put severe financial pressure on those operations.

One response is to allow land in agricultural uses to be assessed at agricultural use value for property tax purposes. Many states have adopted provisions that allow for some tax relief of this sort, usually either through a differential assessment or a form of deferred taxation. For example, the Metropolitan Agricultural Preserves Act, Minn. Stat. Ann. §§473H.02 *et seq.* (2012), which applies only to certain counties within the state, authorizes differential assessments for lands that meet the definition of an "agricultural preserve." Minn. Stat. Ann. §§473H.10 provides that ad valorem taxes will be assessed according to the agricultural preserve rate.

(e) *Right to Farm Laws.* One typical pattern of agricultural land conversion occurs when a residential development is built next to an agricultural use. The new homeowners may start to complain about the externalities from the agricultural operations, and those complaints may lead to litigation alleging that the agricultural operations constitute a nuisance, or to local legislation curbing the scope of the agricultural operations.

A common response to this situation is state "right to farm" legislation. *See, e.g.,* Kan. Stat. Ann. §§2-3201 *et seq.* (2012); Fla. Stat. Ann. §823.14. (2012). In general, "right to farm" statutes attempt to protect agricultural operations that were in place prior to the time that the residential use existed. A principal method of achieving this goal used in the statutes is to codify the so-called "coming to the nuisance" defense, which prevents nuisance recovery by plaintiffs who knew of the existing agricultural land use, and its nuisance-like conditions, at the time they bought their property. Other state statutes prohibit local governments from enacting laws to restrict agricultural operations.

The "right to farm" laws now regularly generate a considerable amount of litigation. *See Shore v. Maple Lane Farms, LLC,* 411 S.W.3d 405 (Tenn. 2013) (holding outdoor concerts with amplified music on farm did not have a connection to producing farm products and thus did not fall within Tennessee Right to Farm law); *Village of Lafayette v. Brown,* 27 N.E.3d 687 (Ill. Ct. App. 2015) (state Farm Nuisance Suit Act preempted local ordinance declaring commercial farming with the Village boundaries was a nuisance); *Tinicum Twp. v. Nowicki,* 99 A.3d 586 (Pa. Commw. Ct. 2014) (mulching operation, which took place at different location where trees were felled, was not protected by Pennsylvania Right to Farm Act). In *Hale v. State,* 314 P.3d 345 (Or. App. 2013), plaintiffs sought to have the Right to Farm and Right to Forest Act declared unconstitutional for depriving them of a remedy for injuries they suffered, but the court found the claim was not yet justiciable because it was based on hypothetical events. The New Jersey version of the "right to farm" legislation gives county agricultural development boards primary jurisdiction over disputes under the act. *See also Gilbert v. Synagro Ctr., LLC,* 131 A.3d 1 (Pa. 2015) (wherein *inter alia* the appeals court found that the trial court properly held that biosolids application falls within the Right to Farm Act's definition of "normal agricultural operation," which bars appellees' nuisance claims); *Parker v. Obert's Legacy Dairy, LLC,* 988 N.E.2d 319 (Ind. Ct. App. 2013)

(Right to Farm Act precluded suits for odors and other discomforts from a concentrated feeding operation).

4. *The Debate over Conservation Easements.* Of the methods described above, the use of conservation easements has become increasingly common and has generated vigorous debate. *See* Nancy McLaughlin and Jeff Pidot, Conservation Easement Enabling Statutes: Perspectives on Reform, 2013 Utah L. 811 (presenting an exchange of ideas between the two authors with different backgrounds but a shared commitment to, and understanding of, the importance of land conservation); Christopher Serkin, Entrenching Environmentalism: Private Conservation Easements Over Public Land, 77 U. Chi. L. Rev. 341 (2010). Among other claims, critics argue that easements are difficult to accurately value, that the protected lands are chosen by happenstance rather than by environmental value, and that easements are ineffectively enforced. *See* Anna Vinson, Re-Allocating the Conservation Landscape: Conservation Easements and Regulation Working in Concert, 18 Fordham Envtl. L. Rev. 273, 278-81 (2007) (summarizing the criticism).

There is also a debate over whether such easements should be treated as restricted or unrestricted charitable gifts, i.e., over how easily they may be modified or terminated. The issue is debated in the following three articles: C. Timothy Lindstrom, *Hicks v. Dowd*: The End of Perpetuity, 8 Wyo. L. Rev. 62 (2008); Nancy A. McLaughlin & W. William Weeks, In Defense of Conservation Easements: A Response to the End of Perpetuity, 9 Wyo. L. Rev. 1 (2009); C. Timothy Lindstrom, Conservation Easements, Common Sense, and the Charitable Trust Doctrine, 9 Wyo. L. Rev. 397 (2009). Still others have suggested that, from a tax perspective, "the revenue loss from the charitable deductions for easement donations might well be far more than the public benefit provided." Daniel Halperin, Incentives for Conservation Easements: The Charitable Deduction or a Better Way, 74 Law & Contemp. Probs. 29, 32 (2011).

Some argue that it is bad public policy to tie up lands in perpetuity, when both the science and needs of future generations may change. Jessica Owley, Changing Property in a Changing World: A Call for the End of Perpetual Conservation Easements, 30 Stan. Envtl. L.J. 121, 122 (2011) ("conservation easements are perpetual (often private) arrangements, usually lacking flexibility, making them inappropriate tools for environmental protection in the context of climate change and evolving understandings of conservation biology"); Julia D. Mahoney, The Illusion of Perpetuity and the Preservation of Privately Held Lands, 44 Nat. Resources J. 573, 584 (2004) ("Enhanced understanding of ecological processes, along with technological developments, evolving cultural values, and physical changes in the natural world itself, will compel later generations to revisit many of the preservation choices made today."). On the subject of conservation easements generally, *see* Symposium, Conservation Easements: New Perspectives in an Evolving World, 74 Law & Contemp. Probs. 1 (2011); Roger Colinvaus, Conservation Easements: Design Flaws, Enforcement Challenges and Reform, 33 Utah Envtl. L. Rev. 69 (2013) (part of symposium on Perpetual Conservation Easements in the 21st Century).

5. *The Need for and Scope of Farm Protection.* Some of the legislation intended to preserve farms has the effect of at least partially exempting farms from land use regulation. *See* 53 Pa. Stat. Ann. §10603(h) (2012) ("Zoning ordinances may not

restrict agricultural operations or changes to or expansions of agricultural operations in geographic areas where agriculture has traditionally been present unless the agricultural operation will have a direct adverse effect on the public health and safety."); *Premium Farms v. County of Holt*, 640 N.W.2d 633 (Neb. 2002) (county retained authority, under state statute exempting farm building from regulations, to require a conditional use permit for a confined livestock operation housing over 1000 "animal units"); Keith H. Hirokawa, Sustainable Habitat Restoration: Fish, Farms, and Ecosystem Services, 23 Ford. Envtl. L. Rev. 1, 8 (2012) ("farms have been given special treatment or even immunization from the reach of environmental law, and agricultural regulations are seldom intended to minimize the environmental impacts of farming practices."); Nadia S. Adawi, State Preemption of Local Control Over Intensive Livestock Operations, 44 Envtl. L. Rep. News & Analysis 10506 (2014) (discussing state preemption of local control over intensive livestock operations at the local level).

In recent years, however, the environmental externalities from farming have generated considerable controversy. For example, large industrialized pig farming operations have caused water pollution. Does this pollution argue for increased regulation of farms, rather than for deregulation? *See, e.g.,* J.B. Ruhl, Farms, Their Environmental Harms, and Environmental Law, 27 Ecol. L.Q. 263 (2000) (documenting the environmental harms caused by farms and arguing for increased regulation of them). Others suggest the right to farm laws simply extend too much protection to farms. Terence J. Centner, 33 B.C. Envtl. Aff. L. Rev. 87, 88 (2006).

6. *"Ag-Gag" Laws.* Another hot topic is the so-called "ag-gag" law, which criminalize activities of whistleblowers who are investigating and filming industrial farms. *See* Malorie Sneed & Jessica Brockway, 2015 State Legislative Review, 22 Animal L. 437, 438 (2016) ("In 2014, four state legislatures attempted to pass ag-gag bills. The Idaho, Indiana, and Tennessee legislatures succeeded in their efforts. The Idaho law was soon ruled unconstitutional, and among five other states that attempted to pass similar legislation in 2015, two were successful."). *See also* Vanessa Zboreak, "Yes, in Your Backyard!" Model Legislative Efforts to Prevent Communities from Excluding CAFOs, 5 Wake Forest J.L. & Pol'y 147 (2015).

7. *The Romanticism of Wineries.* Are the romantic and beautiful landscapes of wineries an indication of environmental harmony? Wineries use considerable water and displace other agricultural land uses.

The Ohio Supreme Court has clarified how the "agricultural exemption" contained in Ohio zoning law applies to wineries. The court agreed with appellant Myrddin Winery in ruling that Ohio law does not grant a township or county zoning authority over buildings or structures used for the "vinting" and selling of wine if they are on property used for viticulture — i.e., the growing of grapes. The decision clarifies Ohio's agricultural zoning exemption that establishes limits on local zoning authority over agricultural land uses. But what is an agricultural land use? The decision in *Terry v. Sperry*, 956 N.E.2d 276 (Ohio 2011) provides some clarity: the township or county has no zoning authority over buildings used for making and selling wine on property where wine grapes are growing.

8. *Looking Forward.* The relationships among environmental protection, agricultural protection, and sustainability (Chapter 11) are the focus of emerging trends in the law. There is an evolving "food law" sensibility that reflects concerns with healthy products, local production, a sustainable lifestyle, and animal protection

and rights. Food law courses, blogs, and teaching materials are appearing as the "field" begins to define its identity and parameters.

F. ENVIRONMENTAL IMPACT REPORTING LAWS

In 1969, Congress passed the National Environmental Policy Act (NEPA), 42 U.S.C. §4321-4370d (2000), a law that was to have a profound effect on major actions by the federal government. NEPA requires that federal agencies prepare an Environmental Impact Statement (EIS) on all major federal actions that may have a significant effect on the human environment. Among other topics, the EIS examines the significant environmental effects of a project, alternatives to that project, the effects of those alternatives, and significant effects that cannot be avoided if the project is approved. Most importantly, members of the public may bring suit to enjoin an action's implementation on the ground that the action does not comply with NEPA.

NEPA only applies to federal projects and thus has no effect on day-to-day land use decisions made at the local level. However, a number of states have also passed some form of the EIS requirement. In some of those states, the EIS process plays a significant part in the approval of land use projects. Practitioners of land use law in states with extensive law in this area must become experts on their state's "little NEPA." For an exhaustive treatment across the states, *see* 1 Rathkopf's, The Law of Zoning and Planning §9:1 State Environmental Impact Review (4th ed.).

■ LANZCE G. DOUGLASS, INC. v. CITY OF SPOKANE VALLEY
225 P.3d 448 (Wash. Ct. App. 2010)

SWEENEY, J.

FACTS

Lanzce G. Douglass, Inc., Lanzce G. Douglass Investments, LLC, and Lanzce G. Douglass (Douglass) applied to the City of Spokane Valley (City) for approval of a preliminary plat to divide 17 acres into 81 single-family lots and for approval of a preliminary planned unit development (PUD) overlay for the Ponderosa area of Spokane County (County). Douglass applied a month later to the County for preliminary plat approval to subdivide an adjacent 28 acres of property into a 100-lot development called Ponderosa Ridge. Both properties are zoned low density residential, which allows six dwellings per acre. The Ponderosa Neighborhood Association (Neighborhood Association) has resisted further development in the area.

The Ponderosa area is about three square miles of land on the east side of Browne's Mountain. The area is covered with grasses, shrubs, and scattered pine trees. And the area has suffered numerous wildfires over the years, including a significant firestorm in October 1991. The firestorm in 1991 destroyed 14 homes and threatened an additional 105 homes near the site where these projects were proposed.

The County therefore began to require that development projects in the Ponderosa area address the need for access by fire-fighting vehicles and egress by residents during wildfires. For example, the County required one developer to set aside $500 per lot to construct an additional access road. The County also denied two other applications for preliminary plats in the early 1990s because of concerns over evacuation.

Spokane County Fire District 8 opposed a project called Mica View Estates in 2001 because the roads serving the Ponderosa area could not safely handle a major evacuation or access by emergency vehicles. The County then installed a gated and locked railroad crossing north of Mica View Estates that provided emergency access into and out of the area. This was a temporary alternative to the construction of a new public access road in the Ponderosa area. And so the County approved the Mica View Estates project in 2003, but it also required that the developer set aside $500 per lot for a new railroad crossing when needed.

Douglass submitted a traffic impact analysis for both of its projects. Those studies included evaluations of the existing roads and specifically how those roads would handle evacuation in a wildfire emergency. One of two access sites into and out of the Ponderosa area is the intersection of Dishman-Mica and Schafer roads. It is controlled by a traffic signal. And there were problems at this intersection during the 1991 firestorm. Congestion at the intersection inhibited evacuation of residents and made it difficult for emergency personnel to enter the area.

Douglass's traffic impact analysis assumed that all of the then-existing 1,281 homes in the Ponderosa area would be notified of an emergency at the same time and all would be evacuated in 30 minutes. And it concluded that residential development will actually "become itself a fire break to the overall Ponderosa neighborhood." Administrative Record (AR) at 4102. The analysis then concluded that the intersections in the study area would continue to function at acceptable levels even with the traffic from Douglass's proposed projects. The traffic impact study was revised in January 2005. The revised study noted that "[p]er the City of Spokane Valley, Firestorm and emergency access has not been included in this study." AR at 474. . . .

Douglass submitted a revised site plan to the City for the Ponderosa PUD in March of 2007. And it completed the environmental checklist required by the State Environmental Policy Act (SEPA), ch. 43.21C RCW. The City issued a mitigated determination of nonsignificance. The mitigated determination of nonsignificance meant that Douglass did not have to prepare an environmental impact statement. The Neighborhood Association appealed the City's decision to approve the project. And the same hearing examiner who approved the Ponderosa Ridge project held a public hearing.

As part of the process, the hearing examiner conducted a statistical analysis. He concluded from this analysis that even under ideal conditions and using emergency personnel at the intersections, nearly 20 percent of the traffic from the existing houses and none of the traffic from the current project (or the Ponderosa Ridge project and others) could be evacuated from the area in 30 minutes.

He made appropriate findings of fact and he concluded that the City's mitigated determination of nonsignificance was clearly erroneous because the project is reasonably likely to have more than a moderate adverse effect on the environment.

The hearing examiner then reversed the mitigated determination of nonsignificance "based on the lack of adequate community egress from the Ponderosa area in the event of a firestorm event that would require evacuation of the area." Clerk's Papers (CP) at 88 (conclusion of law 43). And he ordered the City planning division to issue a determination of significance. That determination would require an environmental impact study . . . .

DECISION UNDER REVIEW

The City concluded that the Ponderosa PUD would not have a probable significant adverse impact on the environment. The only mitigation required by the City was that the developer protect any archaeological resources discovered during construction. The hearing examiner concluded, however, that the project "will add a significant volume of traffic to the already inadequate community egress from the Ponderosa area in the event of a wildfire or other emergency." CP at 87 (conclusion of law 27). And this conclusion then led to his further conclusions that the project is therefore "reasonably likely to have more than a moderate adverse effect on the quality of the environment"; and that the mitigated determination of nonsignificance was therefore clearly erroneous. CP at 87 (conclusion of law 27). The hearing examiner's analytical approach here is sound.

THIRTY MINUTE EVACUATION REQUIREMENT . . .

The hearing examiner concluded that:

[t]he ability to evacuate the Ponderosa area in approximately 30 minutes during a wildfire event, such as the 1991 firestorm, is critical to public safety, considering the large number of homes and approved lots in the area, location of the community in an urban/wildland interface with a high wildfire hazard, the rate at which wildfire can spread in the area, and the lack of definitive evidence in the record that alternative strategies such as sheltering in place, or going to a place of safety, would be effective or have been planned for by emergency authorities.

CP at 85 (conclusion of law 18). . . .

The hearing examiner summarizes evidence here. . . . [H]e finds that the planning division did not consider the evacuation concerns of Fire District 1 or the county sheriff and did not have an opportunity to review the underlying data of the fire evacuation analysis or other evidence presented by the Neighborhood Association at the hearing. And, necessarily, preparation of an environmental impact statement would give the City the opportunity to do that. His legal conclusion (based on this finding) is that the project is reasonably likely to have more than a moderate adverse effect on the environment.

Approval of the plat here has not been denied. Instead, the examiner considered the inadequacy of the mitigated determination of nonsignificance given the evidence before him. And he determined that an environmental impact statement was necessary to address whether appropriate provisions have been made in the plat for public health and safety. RCW 58.17.110(1) . . .

Douglass also argues that the record does not support the finding that the area cannot be evacuated in 30 minutes because it is based solely on the opinion of

Thomas Cova, the Neighborhood Association's expert. We do not read the record that way.

Mr. Cova testified that there are no national, regional, or local requirements for evacuation within 30 minutes. But an article written by Mr. Cova for the August 2005 *Natural Hazards Review* entitled "Public Safety in the Urban-Wildland Interface: Should Fire-Prone Communities Have a Maximum Occupancy?" concluded that "if a community has a high fire hazard (or greater), then the minimum evacuation time should be at most 30 min[utes]." AR at 2858-67, 2863. The Ponderosa area has a high fire risk.

[T]he record also shows that Spokane County Fire District 8 established fire district requirements for the proposed Ponderosa PUD in July 2004. Those requirements included an evacuation study:

> Final approval of plat shall be contingent on the completion of an evacuation study that will be conducted by Fire District 8 and other applicable agencies. The study will determine the ability to safely evacuate residents using the existing egress routes . . . .
>
> Traffic study should cover the need for an evacuation and the capability of the road system exiting the Ponderosa development to handle approximately 5000-6000 vehicles in a set period of time.

AR at 5228; *see* also CP at 48 (finding of fact 225).

Todd Whipple is Douglass's traffic engineer. He prepared a fire evacuation analysis with the assistance of a Fire District 8 lieutenant. He based his model on a worst-case scenario — all of the then-existing 1,281 homes in the Ponderosa area trying to evacuate within the same 30 minutes. Mr. Whipple concluded that the intersection at Dishman-Mica/Schafer would be congested during an evacuation given these conditions. Even so, he went on to conclude that traffic control at the intersections would allow for adequate evacuation, because actual notice of evacuation would be door-to-door (staggering the number of vehicles on the road at one time).

The hearing examiner evaluated Mr. Whipple's conclusions using statistics and appropriate computer software. He used the same statistics and computer software that Mr. Whipple used. And he concluded that Mr. Whipple's analysis assumed ideal conditions: "that delay will not result from such potential human and firestorm factors as stalled vehicles, traffic accidents, lost visibility due to smoke, fallen trees, etc." CP at 64 (finding of fact 349). The hearing examiner found that the addition of the vehicles from the Ponderosa development and the contiguous Ponderosa Ridge project would be significantly higher through the two egress intersections than reflected in Douglass's evacuation analysis. The hearing examiner also noted that the evacuation analysis intentionally did not study lane or corridor capacity. That is important because falling trees or stalled vehicles could block a lane and affect traffic flow. The hearing examiner concluded that even under ideal traffic flow rates and with emergency personnel controlling the intersections, 20 percent of the current traffic and none of the additional traffic from the Ponderosa PUD could be evacuated in 30 minutes . . .

When viewed in the light most favorable to the Neighborhood Association, the evidence supports the hearing examiner's finding that vehicles from the Ponderosa project cannot evacuate the Ponderosa area within 30 minutes in the event of a wildfire emergency . . .

REVERSAL OF THE MITIGATED DETERMINATION OF
NONSIGNIFICANCE . . .

Douglass filed an environmental checklist. The City planning division reviewed it. The transportation section of the checklist merely refers to the access from this project and the Ponderosa Ridge project. Concerns about public services including fire protection are not addressed. The planning division nonetheless concluded that the project would not have a probable significant adverse impact on the environment, if mitigated to protect archaeological resources.

We review a threshold determination that an environmental impact statement is not required by the clearly erroneous standard. *Norway Hill Pres. & Prot. Ass'n v. King County Council*, 87 Wash.2d 267, 275, 552 P.2d 674 (1976); *Boehm v. City of Vancouver*, 111 Wash. App. 711, 718, 47 P.3d 137 (2002) . . .

The hearing examiner concluded that a "significant volume" of traffic from the project area "cannot be evacuated from the area in 30 minutes through the two Dishman-Mica exits." CP at 85 (conclusion of law 19). The fire evacuation analysis failed to consider the additional traffic generated by the Ponderosa development and other projects that had been approved in the Ponderosa area. And he concluded that "[s]uch additional trips are relevant in determining the cumulative impact on community egress during an evacuation, and the ability of project traffic to timely evacuate." CP at 85 (conclusion of law 19).

Douglass contends the hearing examiner's decision effectively requires it to alleviate preexisting regional problems and it is not legally required to do that . . .

Douglass's plat has not been conditioned on improving a preexisting deficiency. The hearing examiner here reversed the mitigated determination of nonsignificance and remanded for preparation of an environmental impact statement to address emergency evacuation. Yes, the hearing examiner refers to evacuation of the entire Ponderosa area and considers evidence that even the current population is inadequately served by the two egress roads. But his decision is not based on preexisting deficiencies. It focuses instead on the cumulative effect of the traffic from the Ponderosa development. An environmental impact statement analyzes the "direct, indirect, and cumulative impacts" of a proposed project. WAC 197-11-060(4)(e).

SEPA requires that decision makers consider more than the narrow, limited environmental impact of the current proposal. *Cheney v. City of Mountlake Terrace*, 87 Wash.2d 338, 344, 552 P.2d 184 (1976). And so the hearing examiner properly considered the impact of adding traffic from the Ponderosa PUD to the current egress roads. He concluded that an environmental impact statement was necessary to address what are probable significant adverse effects of the proposed project on the ability to safely evacuate the area. WAC 197-11-360(1); RCW 43.21C.031; SVMC 21.20.100,.110. That is an appropriate consideration and an appropriate conclusion.

An environmental impact statement must be prepared whenever significant adverse impacts on the environment are probable, not just when they are inevitable. *King County*, 122 Wash.2d at 663, 860 P.2d 1024. *King County* notes that government approval of a land use proposal may "acquire virtually unstoppable administrative inertia." *Id.* at 664, 860 P.2d 1024. Postponement of environmental review allows project momentum to build, carrying the project forward even if adverse environmental effects are discovered later. *Id.* (quoting William H. Rodgers, Jr., *The Washington Environmental Policy Act*, 60 Wash. L. Rev. 33, 54(1984)).

Douglass suggests that the approval of several other development projects in the Ponderosa area, including Ponderosa Ridge, requires approval of this project without addressing the probable adverse environmental impacts of the cumulative impact. But at some point, population growth in an area will overwhelm the roads. The evidence supports the hearing examiner's findings that the City failed to adequately evaluate emergency evacuation (*see* CP at 85-86 (conclusions of law 18-25)), and those findings support the hearings examiner's conclusions that an environmental impact statement is necessary. *Univ. Place*, 144 Wash.2d at 652, 30 P.3d 453; *Hilltop Terrace*, 126 Wash.2d at 34, 891 P.2d 29.

Kulik, C.J., and Brown, J., concur.

Notes and Comments

1. *Projects and "Threshold Determinations."* State environmental policy acts (SEPAs) typically apply to discretionary decisions or actions taken by state or local agencies. *See, e.g., Sierra Club v. Office of Planning, State of Hawaii*, 126 P.3d 1098 (Haw. 2006) (petition to reclassify land from agricultural to urban was an "action" triggering the environmental review process); *Parchester Village Neighborhood Council v. City of Richmond*, 105 Cal. Rptr. 3d 305 (Cal. Ct. App. 2010) (city's entering into a municipal services agreement for a proposed casino to be built by an Indian tribe was not a "project"). If the project "may" have a significant effect on the environment, the agency must examine the environmental consequences of the project in an environmental impact statement. Since most local land use decisions, such as subdivision approvals, rezonings, and the like, are discretionary in nature, they are subject to the state's SEPA. If the agency's decision is ministerial, then no EIS is needed because information in the EIS could not affect the agency's decision whether to approve the project.

To make the "threshold determination" of whether an action may have a significant effect on the environment, and thus whether an EIS is required, the local agency first prepares an "initial study." In this study, the agency examines a variety of potential impacts to determine whether they *may* be significant. If the agency decides that there is no potential for a significant effect, it prepares a written determination to that end, sometimes called a "negative declaration."

Plaintiffs may challenge a municipality's compliance with the SEPA. *See, e.g., Save the Pine Bush, Inc. v. Common Council of the City of Albany*, 918 N.E.2d 917 (N.Y. 2009) (organization had standing to challenge compliance when it was alleged that its members used the area for recreation). The courts require that agencies take a close look at the possible effects before reaching their conclusion about whether an EIS is needed. In New York, for example, the public agency must identify the relevant areas of environmental concern, take a "hard look" at them, and make a "reasoned evaluation" of the basis for any determination not to prepare an EIS. *H.O.M.E.S. v. New York State Urban Dev. Corp.*, 418 N.Y.S.2d 827 (Sup. Ct. App. Div. 1979). California requires preparation of an impact report whenever there is a "fair argument" based on substantial evidence of a significant impact—even if there is substantial evidence to the contrary. *Compare In re Prevention of Significant Deterioration Permit (PSD Air Quality Permit Application of Hyperion Energy Center*, 826 N.W.2d 649

(N.D. 2013) (preparation of EIS was optional and failure to prepare one was not an abuse of discretion).

2. *No Evasions Allowed. Laurel Heights Improvement Ass'n v. Regents of the Univ. of California*, 764 P.2d 278 (1988) gives a valuable summary of the California Environmental Quality Act (CEQA), a pioneer state environmental impact law. Here, the court addressed an argument by the University of California Regents about uncertainty of future use of a controversial building project:

> An implicit premise of the Regents' position is that their task will be more difficult if they must consider the environmental effects of less-than-definite future plans. This premise is flawed. We find no authority that exempts an agency from complying with the law, environmental or otherwise, merely because the agency's task may be difficult. If CEQA is unduly burdensome, the solution lies with the Legislature, not with this court.

3. *Dissecting* Lanzce G. Douglass. When is an environmental impact statement required under the Washington SEPA? Is the "evacuation" issue really a potential environmental impact? Is the project "causing" the environmental impact? Or would an extraneous force — a wildfire — be the cause?

Here, the developer challenged the requirement of an EIS. Normally, such litigation under SEPAs is brought by plaintiffs seeking to overturn a decision not to prepare an EIS. By way of comparison, in *Arvin Enterprises, Inc. v. South Valley Area Planning Comm'n*, 125 Cal. Rptr. 2d 140 (Ct. App. 2002), the court required an environmental impact report where a developer had 21 houses in various stages of approval in one geographic area. Is the difference here that in *Arvin*, the developer seemed to "piecemeal" a larger development, and thus disguise its full impact? *See also Chinese Staff and Workers' Ass'n v. Burden*, 932 N.Y.S.2d 1 (App. Div. 2011) (upholding, over a dissent, a negative declaration on a rezoning affecting a 128-block area in Brooklyn).

When plaintiffs — usually development interests — have tried to challenge the decision to prepare an EIS before the document is actually completed, courts generally find that the action is not ripe. *See, most recently, Ranco Sand and Stone Corp. v. Vecchio*, 49 N.E.2d 1165 (N.Y. 2016) (decision to prepare EIS on application to rezone property from residential to heavy industrial was not ripe for judicial review).

4. *Preparation and Content of the EIS.* Once a draft EIS is prepared, the agency will then circulate the draft for public comment. Both other public agencies with interests in the project and private citizens may submit comments on the discussion in the EIS. The agency considering the project usually must prepare written responses to those comments.

The EIS must examine the environmental impacts of the project, alternatives to the project, and mitigation measures that would reduce the project's impacts. In states with EIS requirements, the tests used by courts to examine the adequacy of the discussion in the EIS are relatively uniform. The court does not examine the document for accuracy; instead, it determines whether the EIS was sufficient for informed decision making. The test most widely used is called the "rule of reason." *See, e.g., Orange County v. North Carolina Dep't of Transp.*, 265 S.E.2d 890, 912 (N.C. Ct. App. 1980).

The SEPA case law reveals a wide variety of issues regarding the "adequacy" of the EIS. Plaintiffs may argue that:

1. The EIS omitted an analysis of existing environmental conditions as the "baseline" for examining the environmental impacts of a light rail project. *Neighbors for Smart Rail v. Exposition Metro Line Constr. Auth.*, 304 P.3d 499 (2013).

2. The discussion of the environmental effects that the project will generate was insufficient. *See e.g., Glaser v. City of Seattle*, 162 P.3d 1134 (Wash. Ct. App. 2007) (EIS described adaptive management plan in sufficient detail to evaluate the project's impacts).

3. The EIS did not discuss a sufficient number of alternatives, or the discussion of the included alternatives was insufficient. *Uptown Holdings, LLC v. City of New York*, 98 N.Y.S.2d 657 (App. Div. 2010) (discussion of four alternatives in an EIS for an urban renewal project was a reasonable range of alternatives); *Clean Wisconsin, Inc. v. Public Serv. Comm'n of Wisconsin*, 700 N.W.2d 768 (Wis. 2005) (EIS adequately considered alternatives to coal-fired power plants).

4. The EIS did not sufficiently analyze the cumulative impacts of the project or improperly "segmented" the project so that the project's impacts seem smaller than the overall environmental impacts that will actually occur. *See, e.g., Cathcart-Maltby-Clearview Cmty. Council v. Snohomish County*, 634 P.2d 853, 859 (Wash. 1981) (EIS did not have to discuss buildout over 25 years).

5. *Decision Making Under SEPAs.* Once the EIS is completed, the public agency then must use the document in making its decision whether to approve the underlying project. In reaching its decision, the agency's obligation is to consider the environmental effects as disclosed in the EIS and to balance those impacts against the benefits of the project in determining whether to approve it. *Town of Henrietta v. Department of Envtl. Conservation*, 430 N.Y.S.2d 440, 446 (Sup. Ct. App. Div. 1980) ("SEQRA must also be recognized as not a mere disclosure statement but rather as an aid in an agency's decision-making process to evaluate and balance the competing factors."). As part of the analysis, the SEPA may require the agency to consider whether mitigation measures or alternatives would reduce the impacts from the project. *See City of Marina v. Bd. of Trustees of the California State Univ.*, 138 P.3d 692 (Cal. 2006) (university improperly failed to consider mitigation measures for new campus); *Town of Canton v. Commissioner of the Massachusetts Highway Dep't*, 919 N.E.2d 1278, 1280-82 (Mass. 2010) ("before any agency may take action on a project, it is required to make substantive findings certifying that all feasible measures have been taken to avoid or minimize environmental impacts, if any, of a project.").

Professor Michael Gerrard has opined that "the greatest effect of EISs is on the people who write them, not the people who read them." Michael B. Gerrard, The Effect of NEPA Outside the Courtroom, 39 Envtl. L. Rep. News & Analysis 10615 (2009). He suggests that projects are designed to avoid certain permit requirements (such as a dredge and fill permit) or to avoid one or two adverse impacts that would trigger an EIS.

6. *SEPAs and Land Use.* In states that have enacted SEPAs, those laws are very important to the land use process for a number of reasons. First, the preparation of the SEPA provides a focal point for citizen participation in the decision-making process. The SEPA process is public; there may be initial public hearings and later public hearings on the draft EIS, and all the documents are publicly available. Second, land use projects are often opposed because of their environmental effects, and the EIS is a means of crystallizing the discussion of those effects. Third, because

courts can enjoin projects that do not comply with the state SEPA, those laws give opponents a powerful tool to continue their opposition beyond the hearing room of the local city council by moving it into the courtroom.

The process is not without its defects. For one, by focusing so much attention on whether the paperwork discussion of environmental impacts is sufficient, the SEPA process can cause participants to lose sight of the other important issues that underlie the dispute over a particular land use approval. Any subsequent litigation over the project also may focus on whether the EIS adequately addressed a particular impact, rather than on the real concerns of the opponents.

Another problem is generated by the likelihood of litigation over projects for which EISs are prepared. Individuals preparing those documents tend to adopt a defensive posture; it is better to discuss even marginally possible environmental effects in detail than to risk a later finding by a court that this impact has been overlooked. As a result, EISs on controversial projects tend to be lengthy and thus of less use in the actual decision on the project.

Finally, compliance with the SEPA as under NEPA can be expensive, and the developer normally bears that cost.

7. *NEPA.* In Helen Leanne Serassio, Legislative and Executive Efforts to Modernize NEPA and Create Efficiencies in Environmental Review, 45 Tex. Envtl. L.J. 317 (2015), the author argues against agencies creating "encyclopedic" EISs under NEPA which will more than likely not be litigated and offers a number of suggestions to streamline the process:

> Perhaps the most effective action agencies can take to increase efficiencies in the NEPA review process is to get back to the basics with NEPA and halt efforts to make NEPA documents litigation-proof. . . . The vast majority of CEs, EAs, and EISs are not litigated . . . . On average, NEPA lawsuits represent only two-tenths . . . of one percent of more than 50,000 actions that are documented by federal agencies each year under NEPA . . . . Furthermore, when NEPA documents are litigated, the federal government has been successful in the majority of these cases . . . In fact, the cases that the federal government usually lose are those in which the agency failed to follow a procedural step or relied upon flawed data . . . . One possible reason for agencies' encyclopedic NEPA documents is a misunderstanding of judicial interpretation of NEPA review requirements.

Is that advice likely to be carried out if plaintiffs may challenge the adequacy of an EIS?

8. *SEPAs and Planning.* The procedural structure of EISs has within it distinct limitations on the use of the EIS as a planning tool. SEPAs are an "overlay" law; they attach to decisions made by public agencies under other laws — zoning authority, subdivision approval, permit approval, etc. — which the agency administers. This institutional structure means that, unless the underlying decision is broad enough, the EIS may not be a useful tool for planning purposes.

The problem is well illustrated by a 1992 decision of the New York Court of Appeals, *Long Island Pine Barrens Soc'y, Inc. v. Planning Bd.*, 606 N.E.2d 1373 (N.Y. 1992). The plaintiffs were concerned about the impacts of regional development on the aquifer system that provides drinking water for Long Island. They filed suit, claiming that the New York SEPA, known as the State Environmental Quality Review Act, required the preparation of a cumulative EIS for a total of 224 development projects then proposed for the "Central Pine Barrens Region." The court of appeals rejected the claim. It reasoned:

> [T]here is merely a host of Federal, State, and local statutes designating the region as an ecologically sensitive one and mandating the development of adequate land-use controls. Consequently, there is no cohesive framework for relating the 224 projects in issue to each other.

606 N.E.2d at 1379. The projects did share one common element — their location within the Pine Barrens. But this element, said the court, "is an insufficient predicate under the present set of administrative regulations for mandatory cumulative impact analysis." *Id.*

9. *Impacts on Global Warming I.* An emerging issue under the SEPAs is the extent to which EISs must discuss a project's impacts on global warming. There are a number of difficult issues that must be faced in undertaking such an analysis. For example, what is the "baseline" of emissions from which to measure the project's impacts? How does the agency examine "cumulative impacts" in its analysis? What time frame should be used for the analysis? Mitigation measures also will be important. Could an agency require "energy efficient" homes in a subdivision to mitigate potential impacts on global warming?

Various state agencies have issued guidance and regulations on how the analysis must be undertaken. *See, e.g.,* N.Y. Dept. of Envtl. Conservation, Office of Air, Energy, and Climate, Assessing Energy Use and Greenhouse Gas Emissions in Environmental Impact Statements, http://www.dec.ny.gov/docs/administration_pdf/eisghgpolicy.pdf (last visited Nov. 5, 2016); Cal. Natural Resources Agency, Final Statement of Reasons for Regulatory Action, Amendments to the State CEQA Guidelines Addressing Analysis and Mitigation of Greenhouse Gas Emissions Pursuant to SB 97 (Dec. 2009), http://resources.ca.gov/ceqa/docs/Final_Statement _of_Reasons.pdf (last visited Nov. 5, 2016). And plaintiffs have begun alleging that EISs are inadequate in their analysis of impacts related to global warming. *See PT Air Watchers v. State Dep't of Ecology,* 319 P.3d 23 (Wash. Ct. App. 2014) (no EIS needed where Department concluded that the project would decrease the amount of carbon dioxide emitted into the atmosphere); *Center for Biological Diversity v. California Dep't of Fish and Wildlife,* 361 P.3d 342 (Cal. 2015) (project's consistency with meeting statewide goals for reducing emissions was a permissible criterion to use in analyzing the significance of greenhouse gas emissions from a large real estate development).

Regarding the need to consider climate change in development assessment, New York's Community Risk and Resiliency Act requires state agencies to consider climate risks in certain decision-making contexts. *See* Joseph Fornadel, The Community Risk and Resiliency Act: Building on the New York State Legislature's Climate Change Framework, 15 No. 4 New York Zoning Law and Practice Report NL 1 (2015). California has taken a leading role in linking climate change assessment, transportation, and local government planning through incentives that limit the environmental impact assessment requirement for jurisdictions in compliance. In general the relationship between climate change, transportation, and local land use decision making under environmental impact law is addressed in Chapter 11.

10. *Impacts on Global Warming II.* In 2016, the White House provided new guidance on how to work Greenhouse Gas (GHG) analysis into NEPA EIS documents. It:

- Recommends that agencies quantify a proposed agency action's projected direct and indirect GHG emissions, taking into account available data and GHG quantification tools that are suitable for the proposed agency action;
- Recommends that agencies use projected GHG emissions (to include, where applicable, carbon sequestration implications associated with the proposed agency action) as a proxy for assessing potential climate change effects when preparing a NEPA analysis for a proposed agency action;
- Recommends that where agencies do not quantify a proposed agency action's projected GHG emissions because tools, methodologies, or data inputs are not reasonably available to support calculations for a quantitative analysis, agencies include a qualitative analysis in the NEPA document and explain the basis for determining that quantification is not reasonably available;
- Discusses methods to appropriately analyze reasonably foreseeable direct, indirect, and cumulative GHG emissions and climate effects;
- Guides the consideration of reasonable alternatives and recommends agencies consider the short- and long-term effects and benefits in the alternatives and mitigation analysis;
- Advises agencies to use available information when assessing the potential future state of the affected environment in a NEPA analysis, instead of undertaking new research, and provides examples of existing sources of scientific information;
- Counsels agencies to use the information developed during the NEPA review to consider alternatives that would make the actions and affected communities more resilient to the effects of a changing climate;
- Outlines special considerations for agencies analyzing biogenic carbon dioxide sources and carbon stocks associated with land and resource management actions under NEPA;
- Recommends that agencies select the appropriate level of NEPA review to assess the broad-scale effects of GHG emissions and climate change, either to inform programmatic (e.g., landscape-scale) decisions, or at both the programmatic and tiered project- or site-specific level, and to set forth a reasoned explanation for the agency's approach.

Final Guidance for Federal Departments and Agencies on Consideration of Greenhouse Gas Emissions and the Effects of Climate Change in National Environmental Policy Act Reviews, https://www.whitehouse.gov/sites/whitehouse.gov/files/documents/nepa_final_ghg_guidance.pdf (last accessed August 12, 2016).

On local efforts to combat climate change, such as through comprehensive planning and climate action plans, *see* Chapter 11. *See also* Patricia Salkin, 2009 Sustainability and Land Use Planning: Greening State and Local Land Use Plans and Regulations to Address Climate Change Challenges and Preserve Resources for Future Generation, 34 Wm. & Mary Envtl. L. & Pol'y Rev. 121 (2009).

G. HYDRAULIC FRACTURING OR "FRACKING"

A Note on Fracking

1. *What Is Fracking?* Hydraulic fracturing, or "fracking," is the process of drilling and injecting fluid into the ground at a high pressure in order to fracture shale rocks to release the natural gas or oil inside. Shale rocks, or "shales," are fine-grained sedimentary rocks that are often rich sources of petroleum and natural gas. Shales make up large subsurface geological formations, referred to as "shale formations," which can span hundreds of miles.

Although fracking has been commercially practiced in the United States for about 75 years, technological improvements beginning in the late-1990s have made the practice a cost-efficient means to reach otherwise inaccessible mineral deposits. The favorable treatment that oil and gas companies have received from federal and state regulators—in part because of the progressively loud cries of policy advocates calling for a reduction in dependence on foreign oil—has contributed to the rapid expansion of fracking operations across the U.S. *See* http://www.eia.gov/dnav/ng/hist/ngm_epg0_fgs_nus_mmcfa.htm (last visited Nov. 5, 2016). For some reference as to just how rapidly fracking operations have expanded over the past decade, in the year 2000, there were approximately 23,000 hydraulically fractured wells in the United States. By 2015, the number of hydraulically fractured wells was an estimated 300,000. *See* http://www.eia.gov/todayinenergy/detail.php?id=25372 (last visited Nov. 5, 2016).

Entities ranging from energy companies to real estate developers, private individuals, and governments have all taken an interest in increasing the number of fracking operations throughout the United States. It is not only the extraction of the oil and the gas that is valuable, but also the land itself. If zoned to permit fracking, that land can provide valuable oil and gas leases. Problems arise, however, when the entities with monetary interests in potentially lucrative sites encounter adverse entities staunchly opposed to fracking operations. Although financially there may be many reasons to favor additional fracking operations, concerns presented by members of the anti-fracking public have been wide-ranging.

2. *Concerns over Fracking.* Some communities are fearful of the effects that fracking will have on water quality and quantity. Others are convinced that fracking can increase the likelihood of earthquakes. Small, close-knit communities wonder if the fracking industry, dominated by outside interests, will affect the local quality of life. Additional concerns about air quality, the use of explosives during the fracking process, the need to build access roads, the impact on subsidence from lateral drilling, payment for cleanup of former fracking sites, and accidents involving large trucks needed for operations also contribute to the list of worries that fracking advocates must confront. Concerns have manifested themselves in litigation, ordinances, pollution control regulations, community right-to-know laws, occupational health and safety regulation, trade secret issues, antitrust law, and—perhaps most obviously—land use law.

3. *Location, Location.* In the context of land use, the location of shale formations is the source of tension surrounding fracking. Location determines where energy companies can establish their drilling operations. Location, in turn, determines

which lands are valuable, which companies profit, and which cities benefit or suffer from the fracking.

Some U.S. states are home to massive — and massively productive — shale formations, while other states only have parts of shale formations within their borders. A few states have no shale formations at all (or rather, no formations have yet been discovered in those states). Overall, however, more than 30 states overlie shale formations. *See* https://www.eia.gov/energy_in_brief/article/shale_in_the_united_states.cfm (last visited Nov. 5, 2016). Thus, in addition to federal agencies, lawmakers in these states face decisions about how to tackle land use issues that involve the fracking industry.

4. *Regulating Fracking.* Parties on both sides of the fracking debate look to laws and regulations to resolve their issues. For land use attorneys, this process involves creating, interpreting, and reconciling laws and regulations that affect fracking operations. Additionally, a number of vital shale formations span multiple states and multiple localities, such that regulatory action in one region can have a direct impact on other regions (potentially even non-neighboring regions). The Marcellus shale formation, for example — which is the most lucrative and perhaps most important shale formation in the United States — extends through parts of Ohio, West Virginia, Pennsylvania, and southern and central New York. The state and local governments responsible for regulating the lands that overlay these kinds of multi-state, multi-municipality shale formations implement varying approaches that sometimes conflict with one another, or with the goals promulgated by the federal agencies that Congress has authorized to regulate oil and gas production in the United States. The question of "who controls" is, therefore, as prevalent in this area of law as in any other.

Government agencies remain active in responding to concerns about how and where fracking is done. Although a number of robust, longstanding laws relating to the oil and gas industry occupy the regulatory field already, methods used in fracking — e.g., the mix of chemicals and the method of extraction — have motivated zealous anti-fracking organizations and lawmakers to find and use new ways to mitigate the expansion of fracking operations. The problem that both pro- and anti-fracking advocates often encounter, however, is that entities are imbued with limited authority and methods by which they can affect — whether positively or negatively — the expansion of fracking operations, and realms of authority overlap.

For example, some governmental entities have jurisdiction over where fracking takes place; others influence how fracking is done.

5. *Fracking and Multi-Jurisdictional Governance.* Fracking is regulated, or potentially regulated, at the federal, state, and local levels. We first summarize legislation on the subject and then describe litigation that has arisen over several issues in the application of the law including, most centrally, preemption.

Most fracking-specific legislation is promulgated at the state and local level. Current federal laws aimed at regulating fracking focus primarily on regulating the fracking industry, for example, imposing limitations or reporting requirements on companies that engage in fracking operations, or more generally, oil and gas operations. Among the relevant federal statutes are:

(1) 42 U.S.C. §300, the Safe Water Drinking Act, which directs both the EPA and any state with an authorized program to assure that underground injections will be done in such a manner that will "minimize the potentially adverse effect of the injection on the public health." However, the Environmental Policy Act of 2005

amended the Safe Water Drinking Act, to exclude "the underground injection of fluids . . . pursuant to hydraulic fracturing operations related to oil, gas, or geothermal production activities" from those "underground injections" used in assuring safe drinking water. "This is widely referred to as the "Halliburton Loophole," and it was introduced through the Energy Policy Act of 2005;

(2) 42 U.S.C. §§1701–1787, the Federal Land Policy and Management Act of 1976;

(3) 30 U.S.C. §§181–287, the Mineral Leasing Act of 1920;

(4) 42 U.S.C. §7401 et seq., the Clean Air Act;

(5) 42 U.S.C. §9601 et seq., Comprehensive Environmental Response, Compensation, and Liability Act (CERCLA). However, the oil and gas industry is exempted from certain requirements.

The Environmental Protection Agency has delegated its role in overseeing and enforcing safeguards relating to fluid injection into wells associated with oil and gas production to 39 different states under the EPA's Underground Injection Control (UIC) program.

The federal government is generally more concerned with how fracking is done, and less concerned with where fracking is done. States and municipalities usually are much more concerned with where fracking takes place. Texas H.B. 40 (2015) expressly preempts local regulations hoping to ban fracking. SB 809 in Oklahoma had the same purpose. By contrast, the state of Vermont took the opposite approach by becoming the first state to entirely ban fracking. 29 V.S.A. §571.

In states that have taken a stance on fracking somewhere in between the extremes, municipalities will assume the role of promulgating land use regulations that determine the presence or absence of fracking operations. Some cities have enacted ordinances limiting all gas and oil drilling to industrial or quarry zoning districts. Township of Nockamixon, Pa., Ordinance No. 129, §2 (2007). Other municipalities have passed initiatives prohibiting fracking operations from the municipality altogether. Some states and municipalities are also concerned with how fracking is done. In states like California, government agencies are positioned to use environmental permitting requirements to also affect fracking operations. SB-4 (2013) requires oil and gas companies to: (1) expand monitoring and reporting of water use and water quality; (2) conduct analyses of potential engineering and seismic impacts of their operations; and (3) comprehensively disclose chemicals used during fracking and other operations.

The types of legislation or ordinances that are enacted at each level of government determine the legal nature of legal challenges. Communities that ban fracking can expect resistance from energy companies and broader government agencies. In contrast, communities that permit fracking can expect challenges from environmental groups and individuals with interests in nearby properties.

6. *State Preemption.* Preemption debates concerning fracking take place at both the federal and state levels. State level preemption issues (between state and local governments) are much more common than federal level preemption issues (between federal and state governments). There are, however, a few instances where the federal government has encountered preemption challenges in attempting to regulate where fracking is done — on tribal lands and on federal lands.

In March 2015, the Bureau of Land Management adopted its final set of rules to govern fracking well development on federal and Indian tribal areas. The BLM announced:

> There are more than 100,000 oil and gas wells on federally managed lands. Of wells currently being drilled, over 90% use hydraulic fracturing. The rule applies only to development on public and tribal lands and includes a process so that states and tribes may request variances from provisions for which they have an equal or more protective regulation in place. This will avoid duplication while enabling the development of more protective standards by state and tribal governments.

U.S. Dept. of Interior, Interior Department Releases Final Rule to Support Safe, Responsible Hydraulic Fracking Activities on Public and Tribal Lands (Mar. 20, 2015), http://www.blm.gov/wo/st/en/info/newsroom/2015/march/nr_03_20_2015.html (last visited Nov. 5, 2016).

Shortly after the BLM promulgated its measure, a group of western states and energy industry associations challenged the BLM's authority to regulate fracking on federal and Indian lands. The district court held that BLM did not have the authority to regulate hydraulic fracturing on either federal or Indian lands. The court based its reasoning on its inability to find any substantial statutory evidence or rational justification for the BLM's regulatory authority in that area. While the decision was vacated as moot on appeal, it still well illustrates the issues involved:

■ WYOMING V. UNITED STATES DEPARTMENT OF INTERIOR

136 F. Supp. 3d 1317 (D. 2015), vacated and remanded as moot, 2016 WL 385380 (10th Cir. 2016).

ORDER ON MOTIONS FOR PRELIMINARY INJUNCTION . . .

BACKGROUND

On March 26, 2015, the Bureau of Land Management ("BLM") issued the final version of its regulations applying to hydraulic fracturing on federal and Indian lands. 80 Fed. Reg. 16,128–16,222 (Mar. 26, 2015) ("Fracking Rule"). The Fracking Rule's focus is on three aspects of oil and gas development — wellbore construction, chemical disclosures, and water management (*id.* at 16,128 & 16,129) — each of which is subject to comprehensive regulations under existing federal and state law. The rule was scheduled to take effect on June 24, 2015 . . .

For the better part of the last decade, oil and natural gas production from domestic wells has increased steadily. Most of this increased production has come through the application of the well stimulation technique known as hydraulic fracturing (or "fracking") — the procedure by which oil and gas producers inject water, sand, and certain chemicals into tight-rock formations (typically shale) to create fissures in the rock and allow oil and gas to escape for collection in a well. *See* 80 Fed. Reg. at 16,131 (estimating that ninety percent of new wells drilled on federal lands in 2013 were stimulated using hydraulic fracturing techniques). Hydraulic fracturing has been used to stimulate wells in the United States for at least 60 years —

traditionally in conventional limestone and sandstone reservoirs — and meaningful attempts to use the technique to extract hydrocarbons from shale date back to at least the 1970s. *See* U.S. Department of Energy, *How Is Shale Gas Produced?*, at http:// energy.gov/sites/prod/files/2013/04/f0/how_is_shale_gas_produced.pdf (last visited on Nov. 12, 2016). "More recently, hydraulic fracturing has been coupled with relatively new horizontal drilling technology in larger-scale operations that have allowed greatly increased access to shale oil and gas resources across the country, sometimes in areas that have not previously or recently experienced significant oil and gas development." 80 Fed. Reg. 16,128.

Purportedly in response to "public concern about whether fracturing can lead to or cause the contamination of underground water sources," and "increased calls for stronger regulation and safety protocols," the BLM undertook rulemaking to implement "additional regulatory effort and oversight" of this practice. *Id.* at 16,128 & 16,131. In May of 2012, the BLM issued proposed rules "to regulate hydraulic fracturing on public land and Indian land." 77 Fed. Reg. 27,691 (May 11, 2012). The stated focus of the rules was to: (i) provide disclosure to the public of chemicals used in hydraulic fracturing; (ii) strengthen regulations related to well-bore integrity; and (iii) address issues related to water produced during oil and gas operations. *Id.* The BLM reports it received approximately 177,000 public comments on the initial proposed rules "from individuals, Federal and state governments and agencies, interest groups, and industry representatives." 80 Fed. Reg. at 16,131 . . . .

The BLM ultimately published its final rule regulating hydraulic fracturing on federal and Indian lands on March 26, 2015. . . .

DISCUSSION

Petitioners contend the Fracking Rule should be set aside because it is arbitrary, not in accordance with law, and in excess of the BLM's statutory jurisdiction and authority. *See* 5 U.S.C. §706(2)(A) & (C). The Ute Indian Tribe additionally contends the Fracking Rule is contrary to the Federal trust obligation to Indian tribes. . . .

1. Whether BLM Has Authority to Regulate Hydraulic Fracturing . . .

[T]he Court finds that Congress has directly spoken to the issue and precluded federal agency authority to regulate hydraulic fracturing not involving the use of diesel fuels.

Despite having previously disavowed authority to regulate hydraulic fracturing, the BLM now asserts authority to promulgate the Fracking Rule under various statutes: the Federal Land Policy and Management Act of 1976 ("FLPMA"), 43 U.S.C. §§1701–1787; the Mineral Leasing Act of 1920 ("MLA"), 30 U.S.C. §§181–287; the 1930 Right–of–Way Leasing Act, *id.* §§301–306; the Mineral Leasing Act for Acquired Lands, *id.* §§351–360; the Federal Oil and Gas Royalty Management Act of 1982, *id.* §§1701–1759; the Indian Mineral Leasing Act of 1938 ("IMLA"), 25 U.S.C. §§396a–396g; and the Indian Mineral Development Act of 1982 ("IMDA"), *id.* §§2101–2108. 80 Fed. Reg. at 16,217. The State Petitioners and Ute Indian Tribe argue none of these statutes authorize the BLM to regulate hydraulic fracturing activities. . . .

In the Right-of Way Leasing Act, Congress expanded the Secretary's leasing authority to allow leasing of federally owned minerals beneath railroads and other rights of way. 30 U.S.C. §301. Like the MLA, the Right–of–Way Leasing Act grants the Secretary general rulemaking authority to carry out the Act. *Id.* §306. The Mineral Leasing Act for Acquired Lands again extended the provisions of the MLA, including the Secretary's leasing authority, to apply to minerals beneath lands coming into federal ownership and not already subject to the MLA. 30 U.S.C. §§351–52. Although, like the MLA, the Act grants the Secretary rulemaking authority to carry out the purposes of the Act, *id.* §359, the Act simply expanded the BLM's authority to issue and manage leases for the development of specified minerals, including oil and gas. . . . The Fracking Rule's authority section also cites the general rulemaking authority granted by the Federal Oil and Gas Royalty Management Act of 1982 ("FOGRMA"). 30 U.S.C. §1751. FOGRMA, however, simply creates a thorough system for collecting and accounting for federal mineral royalties. *See Shell Oil Co. v. Babbitt,* 125 F.3d 172, 174 (3rd Cir.1997). The general rulemaking authority granted by these ancillary mineral leasing statutes, which is cabined by the purposes of the Acts, cannot be interpreted as authority for comprehensive regulation of hydraulic fracturing.

The Secretary also invokes the statutory authority granted to the BLM by the Indian Mineral Leasing Act and the Indian Mineral Development Act as a basis for the Fracking Rule. These statutes, generally, grant the Secretary broad regulatory jurisdiction over oil and gas development and operations on Indian lands. 25 U.S.C. §§396d, 2107. However, neither the IMLA nor the IMDA delegates any more specific authority over oil and gas drilling operations than the MLA, nor has BLM promulgated separate regulations for operations on Indian lands . . . .

BLM claims the Fracking Rule simply supplements existing requirements for oil and gas operations set out in 43 C.F.R. 3162.3–1 and Onshore Oil and Gas Orders 1, 2 and 7. 80 Fed. Reg. at 16,129. BLM asserts its decades-old "cradle-to-grave" regulations governing oil and gas operations, promulgated pursuant to its MLA §189 authority, already include regulation of hydraulic fracturing, albeit minimally "because the practice was not extensive (or similar to present-day design) when the regulations were promulgated." *(Resp't Br. in Opp'n to Wyoming and Colorado's Mot. for Prelim. Inj.* at 11) (ECF No. 68). Historically, however, BLM's only regulation addressing hydraulic fracturing worked to prevent any additional surface disturbance and impose reporting requirements and did not regulate the fracturing process itself. *See* 43 C.F.R. §3162.3–2(b) ("Unless additional surface disturbance is involved . . . prior approval is not required for routine fracturing or acidizing jobs . . . ; however, a subsequent report on these operations must be filed. . . ."). This requirement makes sense because the MLA expressly authorizes regulation of "all *surface*-disturbing activities . . . in the interest of conservation of *surface* resources." 30 U.S.C. §226(g) (emphasis added). The BLM cites to no other existing regulation addressing hydraulic fracturing. Neither does the BLM cite any specific provision of the mineral leasing statutes authorizing regulation of this underground activity or regulation for the purpose of guarding against any incidental, underground environmental effects. Indeed, the BLM has previously taken the position, up until formulation of the Fracking Rule, that it lacked the authority or jurisdiction to regulate hydraulic fracturing. *See Center for Biological Diversity v. BLM,* 937 F. Supp. 2d 1140, 1156 (N.D.Cal.2013).

When an agency claims to discover in a long-extant statute an unheralded power to regulate "a significant portion of the American economy," [the Court] typically greet[s] its announcement with a measure of skepticism. [The Court] expect[s] Congress to speak clearly if it wishes to assign to an agency decisions of vast "economic and political significance."

Utility Air Regulatory Group v. EPA, —— U.S. ——, 134 S. Ct. 2427, 2444, 189 L.Ed.2d 372 (2014) (quoting *Brown & Williamson*, 529 U.S. at 159, 160, 120 S. Ct. 1291). . . .

Although the Secretary asserts FLPMA delegates to BLM broad authority and discretion to manage and regulate activities on public lands, the BLM has not heretofore asserted FLPMA as providing it with authority to regulate oil and gas drilling operations pursuant to 43 C.F.R. Part 3160. Nothing in FLPMA provides BLM with specific authority to regulate hydraulic fracturing or underground injections of any kind; rather, FLPMA primarily establishes congressional policy that the Secretary manage the public lands under principles of multiple use and sustained yield. At its core, FLPMA is a land use planning statute. *See* 43 U.S.C. §1712; *Rocky Mtn. Oil and Gas Ass'n*, 696 F.2d at 739 ("FLPMA contains comprehensive inventorying and land use planning provisions to ensure that the 'proper multiple use mix of retained public lands' be achieved"); . . . If oil and gas development is allowed, BLM first determines whether the issuance of a particular oil and gas lease conforms to the land-use plan. *Id.* (citing 43 C.F.R. §1610.5–3(a)). The lessee must then obtain BLM approval of an Application for Permit to Drill ("APD") before commencing any "drilling operations" or "surface disturbance preliminary thereto" and comply with other provisions of Part 3160. *See id.*; 43 C.F.R. 3162.3–1(c).

In the meantime, and prior to the enactment of FLPMA, Congress had enacted the Safe Drinking Water Act ("SDWA"). Pub.L. No. 93–523, 88 Stat. 1660 (1974) (codified as amended at 42 U.S.C. §§300f through 300j–26). Part C of the SDWA establishes a regulatory program specifically for the protection of underground sources of drinking water. 42 U.S.C. §§300h through 300h–8. This program requires the Environmental Protection Agency ("EPA") to promulgate regulations that set forth minimum requirements for effective State underground injection control ("UIC") programs "to prevent underground injection which endangers drinking water sources." *Id.* §300h(b)(1). Part C prohibits "any underground injection" without a permit and mandates that a UIC program include "inspection, monitoring, recordkeeping, and reporting requirements[.]" *Id.* §300h(b)(1)(A) & (C). The SDWA defined "underground injection" as "the subsurface emplacement of fluids by well injection." *Id.* §300h(d)(1). *See Legal Envtl. Assistance Found., Inc. v. EPA*, 118 F.3d 1467, 1470 (11th Cir. 1997) ("*LEAF*").

For two decades after the enactment of the SDWA, the EPA took the position that hydraulic fracturing was not subject to the UIC program because that technique for enhancing the recovery of natural gas from underground formations did not, by its interpretation, fall within the *regulatory* definition of "underground injection." *See LEAF*, 118 F.3d at 1471. Responding to a challenge of Alabama's UIC program because it did not regulate hydraulic fracturing activities, the EPA stated it interpreted the definition of "underground injection" as encompassing only those wells whose "principal function" is the underground emplacement of fluids. The EPA had determined that the principal function of gas production wells which are also used for hydraulic fracturing is gas production, not the underground emplacement of fluids. *Id.* The Eleventh Circuit Court of Appeals rejected the EPA's position. Applying the first step in the *Chevron* framework, the *LEAF* court concluded the unambiguous language of the statute made clear that Congress intended for the

EPA to regulate *all* underground injection under the UIC programs, and the process of hydraulic fracturing obviously fell within the plain meaning of the *statutory* definition of "underground injection." *Id.* at 1474–75. Thus, pursuant to the SDWA's cooperative federalism system for regulating underground injection, including hydraulic fracturing, the States and Indian Tribes could assume primary enforcement responsibility for UIC programs, subject to EPA approval and oversight. *See* 42 U.S.C. §300h–1(b), (c) & (e).

Such was the state of the law when Congress enacted the Energy Policy Act of 2005 ("EPAct"), a comprehensive energy bill addressing a wide range of domestic energy resources, with the purpose of ensuring jobs for the future "with secure, affordable, and reliable energy." Pub.L. No. 109–58, 119 Stat. 594 (2005). The EPAct was intended, at least in part, to expedite oil and gas development within the United States . . . . Recognizing the EPA's authority to regulate hydraulic fracturing under the SDWA, the EPAct included an amendment to the SDWA, expressly and unambiguously revising the definition of "underground injection" to *exclude* "the underground injection of fluids or propping agents (other than diesel fuels) pursuant to hydraulic fracturing operations related to oil, gas, or geothermal production activities." EPAct Sec. 322 (codified at 42 U.S.C. §300h(d)(1)(B)(ii)). There can be no question that Congress intended to remove hydraulic fracturing operations (not involving diesel fuels) from EPA regulation under the SDWA's UIC program . . . .

The issue presented here is whether the EPAct's explicit removal of the EPA's regulatory authority over non-diesel hydraulic fracturing likewise precludes the BLM from regulating that activity, thereby removing fracking from the realm of federal regulation. Although the BLM does not claim authority for its Fracking Rule under the SDWA, a statute administered by the EPA, it defies common sense to interpret the more general authority granted by the MLA and FLPMA as providing the BLM authority to regulate fracking when Congress has directly spoken to the issue in the EPAct.

. . . In determining whether Congress has spoken directly to the BLM's authority to regulate hydraulic fracturing under the MLA or FLPMA, this Court cannot ignore the implication of Congress' fracking-specific legislation in the SDWA and EPAct.

2. Whether the Fracking Rule is Arbitrary, Capricious, an Abuse of Discretion or Otherwise Not in Accordance with Law

Even if the BLM had the authority to promulgate the Fracking Rule, the Court is troubled by the paucity of evidentiary support for the Rule. Agency action must be the product of "reasoned decisionmaking" and supported by facts in the record. *Olenhouse,* 42 F.3d at 1575; *see also Michigan v. EPA,* —— U.S. ——, 135 S. Ct. 2699, 2706, 192 L.Ed.2d 674 (2015) . . . The BLM has neither substantiated the existence of a problem this rule is meant to address, identified a gap in existing regulations the final rule will fill, nor described how the final rule will achieve its stated objectives. Rather, the Fracking Rule seems a remedy in search of harm.

The BLM asserts the Fracking Rule is necessary to address concerns raised by the increased technological complexity and expansion of hydraulic fracturing. 80 Fed. Reg. 16,128. Specifically, the final rule raises the risk of groundwater contamination as a primary concern motivating many of its provisions. The rule references and discusses two reports by the National Academy of Sciences issued in 2011 and 2012 identifying "three *possible* mechanisms for fluid migration into shallow drinking-water aquifers that could help explain the increased methane concentrations observed in water wells that existed around shale gas wells in Pennsylvania." *Id.* at 16,194 (emphasis added). The reports indicated that of the three mechanisms, the first (movement of gas-rich solutions within the shale formations up into shallow drinking-water aquifers) was the "least likely possibility," and the third (migration of gases through new or enlarging of existing fractures above the shale formation) is "unlikely." *Id.* The second possible mechanism (contamination from leaky gas-well casings) is the "most likely." *Id.* From this, the BLM determined that "assurances of the strength of the casing are appropriate" but does not discuss how its existing regulations governing well casing are insufficient. *Id.* at 16,193. . . .

While recognizing that many states have regulations in place addressing hydraulic fracturing operations, the BLM determined that the state requirements are not uniform and do not necessarily fulfill BLM's statutory obligations, and further reasoned that "[t]he provisions in this final rule provide for the BLM's consistent oversight and establish a baseline for environmental protection across all public and Indian lands undergoing hydraulic fracturing." 80 Fed. Reg. at 16,130. *See also id.* at 16,133 and 16,154. While the record contains some comparative analyses regarding how the state regulations differ from one another and from the Fracking Rule (*see* DOI AR 0004772, 0007893–94, 0045522–27, 0100575–80), there is no discussion of how any existing state regulations are inadequate to protect against the perceived risks to groundwater. The BLM fails to identify any states that do not have regulations adequate to achieve the objectives of the Fracking Rule, nor does the BLM cite evidence that its rule will be any more effective in practice than existing state regulations protecting water and other environmental values. Indeed, the record supports the contrary. The Court finds a desire for uniformity, in itself, is insufficient. Because the BLM has failed to "examine the relevant data and articulate a satisfactory explanation for its action including a rational connection between the facts and the choice made," the Fracking Rule is likely arbitrary, requiring that it be set aside. *Sorenson Commc'ns, Inc. v. FCC*, 567 F.3d 1215, 1220–21 (10th Cir.2009) (quoting *Motor Vehicle Mfrs. Ass'n of U.S.*, 463 U.S. at 43, 103 S. Ct. 2856) (internal quotation marks omitted).

[The Court then discusses Irreparable Harm]

Whereas Petitioners have demonstrated that a preliminary injunction is necessary to avoid irreparable harm, the issuance of an injunction poses little more than an inconvenience to the BLM's interests. First, neither the BLM nor Respondent–Intervenors can demonstrate that any environmental harm will likely result if the effective date of the Fracking Rule is delayed. The BLM has not identified a single groundwater contamination incident that the Fracking Rule would have prevented, nor offered any analysis measuring, even in estimate form, the risk of environmental harm that the rule purports to prevent. *See Amoco Prod. Co. v. Village of Gambell, AK*, 480 U.S. 531, 545, 107 S. Ct. 1396, 94 L.Ed.2d 542 (1987) (finding the balance of harms tipped in industry's favor when industry had incurred economic costs and movants had failed to show a sufficient likelihood of environmental injury).

To the contrary, the United States Environmental Protection Agency ("EPA") recently released a draft "state-of-the-science assessment" of the available scientific literature and data on the effects of hydraulic fracturing on drinking water resources. U.S. Envtl. Prot. Agency, *Assessment of the Potential Impacts of Hydraulic Fracturing for Oil and Gas on Drinking Water Resources* at Draft ES–1, ES–24 (June 2015). The EPA observed that between 2011 and 2014, as many as 120,000 wells were completed with hydraulic fracturing. *Id.* at ES–5 (estimating 25,000–30,000 new wells were drilled and hydraulically fractured annually in the United States during that time). The EPA also reported that "[a]pproximately 6,800 sources of drinking water for public water systems were located within one mile of at least one hydraulically fractured well during the same period." *Id.* at ES–6. Yet, the EPA identified only three suspected incidents "that have or may have" resulted in impacts to drinking water resources. *Id.* at ES–14 to 15. While the EPA noted there are "mechanisms" by which fracking activities have the *potential* to impact groundwater, the agency "did not find evidence that these mechanisms have led to widespread, systemic impacts on drinking water resources in the United States." *Id.* at ES–6. To the extent there are any potential risks of harm, nearly all hydraulic fracturing operations are already subject to existing state regulations protecting groundwater resources. *See* 80 Fed. Reg. at 16,178 (observing that "[a]ll state laws apply on Federal lands"); *id.* at 16,187 (referencing regulations in California, Colorado, Montana, New Mexico, North Dakota, Oklahoma, Texas, Utah, and Wyoming and acknowledging that more than ninety-nine percent of total well completions on federal lands since 2010 were located in one of these states) . . . .

[T]he Court finds all four factors warranting the issuance of a preliminary injunction weigh in favor of movants, and Petitioners' right to relief is clear and unequivocal

Notes and Comments

1. *The* Wyoming *Decision.* As exemplified in the excerpt above, the federal government has significant authority to regulate the means by which fracking is accomplished. Still, the court in *Wyoming* determined that Congress did not imbue the BLM with the authority to promulgate fracking-specific regulations on certain lands. The decision is consistent with the federal government's largely pro-fracking approach, which relinquishes a fair amount of control over fracking operations to state and local regulatory bodies.

In *Swepi, LP v. Mora County, N.M.,* 81 F. Supp. 3d 1075 (D.N.M. 2015), an energy exploration firm, which had entered into oil-and-gas lease with State of New Mexico, brought an action against a county and its board of county commissioners seeking an injunction to prohibit the board from enforcing a county zoning ordinance proscribing the extraction of oil, natural gas, and other hydrocarbons within the county. The energy exploration firm sought to conduct its activities only on plots of land within Mora County that were owned by the State of New Mexico. In finding that Mora County lacked the authority to enforce its zoning laws on the state lands within the county borders, the court noted that the fact that the "conduct on state lands may affect adjoining county lands" — that "hydrocarbon extraction on state lands may affect the water on the adjoining land" — was not relevant to the court's analysis in determining that the ordinance was unenforceable. *Id.* at 1189.

2. *State Preemption Issues.* States have taken different positions on fracking. Cases are generally initiated by government action at the local level that raises a preemption issue, as local governments — both opposed to and in favor of fracking — often

reject state preemption as an encroachment on their local zoning authority. State preemption litigation is more straightforward. Typically, it involves a state law that is alleged to directly preempt a local ordinance applicable to only local lands. *See City of Longmont v. Colorado Oil & Gas Ass'n*, 369 P.3d 573 (Colo. 2016). There, the Colorado Supreme Court found that the state can preempt local fracking bans by virtue of the state's Oil and Gas Conservation Act if the local bans function to "impede[] the orderly development of Colorado's mineral resources." *Id.* at 581. In Louisiana, the state court of appeals reached a similar conclusion in *St. Tammany Parish v. Welsh*, 194 So. 3d 1108 (La. 2016). The court found that statutory provisions mandating uniformity in local land use and zoning regulations did not apply to the state Commissioner of the Office of Conservation in the exercise of the state's police powers to regulate oil and gas activity.

The Pennsylvania Supreme Court came to the opposite conclusion when asked to determine whether "Act 13" — a law that attempted to adopt uniform statewide zoning requirements to permit fracking in all zoning districts — was constitutional. The high court ruled that, under the "Environmental Rights Amendment" of the state constitution, such an ordinance was unconstitutional, and thus the localities were permitted to enact independent zoning ordinances. *Robinson Twp., Washington County v. Commonwealth of Pennsylvania*, 83 A.3d 901 (Pa. 2013).

New York's highest court went even further interpreting its state's oil and gas law. In *Wallach v. Town of Dryden*, 16 N.E.3d 1188 (2014), the New York Court of Appeals ruled that the state's Oil, Gas and Solution Mining Law did not preempt the use of local zoning laws to ban heavy industry, including oil and gas operations, within municipal borders. The case is set forth in Chapter 16, which addresses preemption as a solution to the question of siting facilities.

In that case, the town of Dryden had amended its zoning ordinance to effectively ban fracking by prohibiting all activities related to oil and gas exploration, extraction, and storage. In drawing a distinction between how fracking is done and where it is done, the court reasoned that the OGSML was most naturally read as preempting only local laws that purport to regulate the actual operations of oil and gas activities, not zoning ordinances that restrict or prohibit certain land uses within town boundaries. The court, however, did not discuss whether state laws might preempt other legitimate zoning methods, like special permit requirements, that are focused more on the means of fracking, rather than the location. Instead, the court's decision seemed to be largely grounded in a traditional Euclidian understanding of zoning. Would the New York law have preempted a city's moratorium on fracking for aesthetic, economic development, or sustainable growth reasons?

The answer is now irrelevant, as the state of New York banned fracking following the release of a 2014 study on the environmental effects of fracking. Thomas Kaplan, Citing Health Risks, Cuomo Bans Fracking in New York State, N.Y. Times (Dec. 17, 2014) .

3. *Nuisance and Trespass.* Preemption is not the only issue implicating land use law in the fracking context. The use of land for fracking can result in tort claims against the fracking companies. This may be a vehicle for influencing land use decisions where state and local laws strongly favor fracking operations. *See Parr v. Aruba Petroleum, Inc.*, 2014 WL 10779139 (Tex. Co. Ct. 2014), where a Texas family prevailed in a private nuisance claim of $3 million over a petroleum company.

15

Urban Redevelopment, Economic Development, and Anticompetitiveness

A. INTRODUCTION

The theme of this chapter is using the land use system to promote economic development in cities and regions. Economic development has long been an element and goal of comprehensive planning as well as an implicit goal of zoning. As urban planning has evolved, economic development has become a central goal of planning in the United States, indeed throughout the world.

1. Economic Development and the Federal Government

Unlike many other areas of land use, the role of the federal government in economic development has been significant. The federal government has long provided the banking, trade, and securities regulation needed to ensure stable, long-term growth. However, much of the actual planning for industrial and commercial development has been left to state and local regulation. Land use planning is central to that effort.

The programs of the federal government most directly affecting local development have been the federal highway program, federal housing subsidies, and grants for community development and other infrastructure. The federal government has also administered programs to encourage small business development, including enterprises for minorities and poor communities. These programs have largely been supplemental to, and supportive of, local planning.

2. The Problem of "Blight"

Local governments have long been involved in promoting economic development. In recent decades, however, a centerpiece of this effort has been the use of its authority to "redevelop" property. Under most redevelopment laws, a city begins by declaring an area "blighted." This finding triggers a series of steps in which the city takes property by eminent domain for redevelopment purposes.

The finding of blight, however, has been abused. Local governments have declared such areas as operating golf courses blighted. In this chapter, we look at one recent case, a 2015 decision by the New Jersey Supreme Court addressing a finding of blight that affected a series of buildings in Hackensack. You must decide for yourself: Was the finding of blight supportable, or did the court overly defer to the local government? In making that decision, bear in mind the consequences of this finding — individual homeowners may well find their property condemned. You will find that "blight" is not an easy term to define.

3. "Public Use" and the Limits of Government Authority

The redevelopment model has largely utilized what is known as "tax-increment financing." Under that model, which was discussed in Chapter 4, a government redevelopment agency freezes property tax levels and then — in conjunction with actors in the private sector — "redevelops" an area. It finances this effort through bonds. Then, when the redevelopment results in increasing property taxes, that incremental "increase" is used to pay off the bonds that financed the venture.

The economic consequences of redevelopment, then, are significant. The most important legal question at the center of this process is the use of eminent domain and, in particular, whether the taking is for a "public use." The use of this term is fraught with controversy, particularly where the government condemns private property for redevelopment and then re-transfers the property into private hands — perhaps to the owner of a "big-box" retail establishment. The Supreme Court's highly controversial decision in *Kelo v. City of New London* (excerpted in Chapter 7) fractured the Court. This chapter includes a second case in which a state court overturned the use of eminent domain to aid the expansion of a raceway. Additionally, the nationwide controversy over *Kelo* led to a deluge of legislation at the state level, a subject briefly explored in the Chapter 7 material on Takings. In this chapter you will read two other state court opinions that construe this legislation to determine what limits now exist on the "public use" requirement in those states.

4. Transportation

The transportation system, of course, plays an important role in how land uses evolve. For example, the growth of the interstate freeway system largely supported the boom in suburbs that began in the 1970s. Some accuse those freeways of causing immense environmental damage, both in the pollution caused by individuals commuting long distances between their suburban homes and their work, and in the deterioration of urban centers.

In recent years, however, a new movement has sprung up advocating "smart growth" principles. Advocates of "smart growth" emphasize containing growth and minimizing its effects, largely through "mixed use" developments. Adoption of smart growth policies would have important effects on land use. For example, it would emphasize the use of transit as a means of moving individuals and it would discourage urban sprawl. At the same time, smart growth advocates press for mixed use development, the antithesis of the separation of uses that underlies Euclidian zoning.

You will read two articles that generally endorse the concept of smart growth. You will then read a third that questions its basic premise. You must decide which view is correct.

5. Anticompetitiveness and Competition

Finally, the chapter examines the problem of anticompetitiveness in the context of land use regulation. Zoning, like subsidies, can be used to encourage economic development, but it can also be used to gain a competitive advantage for private gain. Antitrust law plays a role here, and the discussion focuses on the situation in which a most favored developer and a local government join to protect development against undesired competition.

Also examined is the use of incentives as a means of promoting economic development. The use of such methods, and related changes in the land use system to support economic development, raise a fundamental question of economic freedom and democracy. In the United States, the idea of liberty and competition has remained a paramount consideration. In maximizing locational choice, government policy has permitted suburban office and commercial centers to relocate the city's economic core to suburban edge communities, often leaving destabilized central cities. You can decide for yourself whether such government action is appropriate and constitutional.

B. THE FEDERAL ROLE IN ECONOMIC DEVELOPMENT

For many years, the federal government played a primary role in funding efforts to redevelop blighted property often located in inner cities. For a number of reasons, the federal government's role is now greatly diminished. Nonetheless, to draw any conclusions about the effectiveness of current redevelopment efforts, you need to understand their evolution. Accordingly, the chapter begins with a summary of the past efforts by the federal government. It then turns to the current form of federal involvement, the use of so-called "empowerment zones."

A Note on the Federal Role in Redevelopment

Traditional Urban Renewal. From 1949 until at least 1974, the federal government was heavily involved in redevelopment. The original urban renewal program called for slum removal, with the federal government providing funds to administer the program. The federal grant was the amount necessary to make up the difference between the costs of planning, administration, and land acquisition, and the proceeds from the sale of the cleared land to the ultimate developer. Benjamin B. Quinones, Redevelopment Redefined: Revitalizing the Central City With Resident Control, 27 U. Mich. J.L. Ref. 689, 700-709 (1994).

The program was very costly, as the market for redevelopment on the site of former slums was often not great, and land typically sat empty for long periods awaiting a motivated redeveloper. Prior site residents were displaced. Typically, they were moved into more expensive housing that was, at the same time, often substandard. In some instances, this housing was in the path of the next clearance or highway improvement, and the displacees were usually poor persons of color. *See, e.g., Garrett v. City of Hamtramck*, 335 F. Supp. 16 (E.D. Mich. 1971), *plan ordered*, 357 F. Supp. 925 (E.D. Mich. 1973), *rev'd in part*, 503 F.2d 1236 (6th Cir. 1974) (redevelopment plan targeting removal of African-Americans in community). *See also* Paul Boudreaux, Eminent Domain, Property Rights, and the Solution of Representation Reinforcement, 83 Denver U.L. Rev. 1 (2005) (arguing that takings for private use that harm the poor or those politically disadvantaged should be invalid).

The 1970 Legislation. In an attempt to improve the system, Congress passed the Uniform Relocation Assistance and Real Property Acquisition Policies Act of 1970, 42 U.S.C. §§4601-4655 (2016). This Act promised relocation planning and benefits to compensate displaced persons for the costs of moving and the higher rents or mortgage payments that a move might require. In practice, however, projects were often loosely administered. Adequate relocation payments and proper planning contributed to the costs of acquisition and displacement programs. These costs were quite high.

In response to criticism, Congress again modified the program, re-targeting resources for neighborhood preservation and rehabilitation. The modified redevelopment program provided grants and loans to owners to finance upgrading. It also expanded the geographical areas where rehabilitation could occur, dissipating limited resources as the expanded project areas raised expectations without increased appropriations. Perversely, the law often hastened disinvestment and abandonment.

The Block Grant Program. In 1974, Congress eliminated most categorical aid programs, such as urban renewal and rehabilitation grants and loans. It replaced them with block grants that local government could spend according to local priorities and plans. The block grant program was notable for reallocating federal community development funding away from the traditional cities to the newly eligible suburbs and smaller cities. Alvin Hirshen and Richard T. LeGates, HUD's Bonanza for Suburbia, 39 Progressive 32 (1975). *See generally* James A. Kushner et al. Housing and Community Development Ch. 5 (4th ed. 2011); Peter W. Salsich, Jr., Saving Our Cities: What Role Should the Federal Government Play?, 36 Urb. Law 475 (2004); William H. Simon, The Community Economic Development Movement, 2002 Wis. L. Rev. 377.

Later Developments. Since the 1970s, funding for community development has rapidly declined. With an increased focus on legislative budget deficits, future community development policy must look to different vehicles and strategies. One concept that has dominated public attention is the enterprise zone. The concept of an enterprise zone is that taxes are cut within the geographic zone to attract investment. President Clinton signed into law the Empowerment Zones and

Enterprise Communities Program Omnibus Reconciliation Act of 1993, Pub. L. No. 103-66, §§13301-13303, 107 Stat. 312, 543, *codified at* 26 U.S.C. §§1391-1397f (2016). Most recently, Congress extended the federal tax breaks for enterprise zones through 2016.

In the article below, Professor Wilton Hyman describes the empowerment and enterprise zone programs that were the centerpieces of the Clinton and Reagan urban policies.

■ WILTON HYMAN, EMPOWERMENT ZONES, ENTERPRISE COMMUNITIES, BLACK BUSINESS, AND UNEMPLOYMENT
53 Wash. U.J. Urb. & Contemp. L. 143 (1998)

The Secretary of HUD [the Department of Housing and Urban Development] and the Secretary of the United States Department of Agriculture (USDA) have designated a total of nine empowerment zones, six of which are located in urban areas and three of which are located in rural areas. Businesses that operate in these empowerment zones are eligible for an employment wage credit and increased section 179 first-year depreciation deductions. The empowerment zone employment wage credit provides a tax credit for wages paid to a "qualified zone employee." A qualified zone employee is any person who performs substantially all of his or her services for an employer within the empowerment zone and who has a principal place of residence within the empowerment zone. The credit, which is gradually phased out, is initially equal to twenty percent of qualified zone wages, up to a maximum credit of three thousand dollars per employee. Under the Taxpayer Relief Act of 1997, federally designated empowerment zones are eligible for the wage credit through the year 2007.

The increased section 179 depreciation deductions are allowed if the business is an "enterprise zone business" as defined in section 1397B of the Internal Revenue Code. Under section 179, small businesses can deduct an additional $18,500 in depreciation deductions on depreciable, tangible, personal property when it is purchased and used in the "active conduct . . . of any trade or business. . . ." The provision is elective and applies only to the first year in which businesses use the property in a trade or business. Businesses that satisfy the requirements of section 1397B can also deduct an additional $20,000 under section 179, allowing them to take up to $38,500 in additional first-year depreciation deductions.

The empowerment zones may also issue tax-exempt facilities bonds, which businesses can use for acquiring or constructing an "enterprise zone facility" and any land "functionally related and subordinate" to the facility. An "enterprise zone facility" is any depreciable, tangible property that has as its principal user an enterprise zone business. In addition, empowerment zones are eligible for EZ/EC [Empowerment Zones and Enterprise Communities] Social Service Block Grants in the amount of $40 million for rural empowerment zones and $100 million for urban empowerment zones.

The Secretaries of HUD and the USDA considered for designation as enterprise communities those areas not selected or designated as empowerment zones. There are a total of ninety-five enterprise communities, sixty-five of which are located in urban areas and thirty of which are located in rural areas. Enterprise communities are not eligible for the employer wage credit or increased section 179 first-year depreciation deductions, but they can issue tax-exempt facilities bonds. Enterprise communities can use the proceeds from these bonds to build and renovate structures for use by businesses operating in the enterprise community. Enterprise communities are also eligible for Social Service Block Grants of $3 million, which they can use to fund activities and projects in their communities. . . .

There is at least one potentially negative effect of the EZ/EC program. By requiring businesses to locate within an economically distressed inner-city community in order to receive the EZ/EC benefits, the federal program creates a bias toward the creation of small-scale traditional line black businesses. This occurs because such businesses are more likely to locate within inner-city areas regardless of the EZ/EC incentives, and because the EZ/ECs do not provide special incentives to encourage the creation of emerging line black businesses that locate outside of EZ/ECs. Thus, the EZ/EC program wastes resources because it targets areas that may lack adequate consumer markets or adequately skilled labor, and because the traditional line businesses that are likely to locate within those areas, even in the absence of EZ/EC incentives, will not provide enough jobs to reduce unemployment significantly. . . .

The present EZ/EC incentive program has the potential to create more small-scale minority-owned businesses within the EZ/ECs, despite the fact that these type[s] of businesses may not have a significant impact on reducing minority unemployment. The federal government should respond to this situation by modifying the current EZ/EC program to allow flexibility in the locations where EZ/EC businesses can operate. The federal government should provide the EZ/EC incentives to businesses located inside and outside of the EZ/ECs, provided that they hire EZ/EC residents. . . .

Notes and Comments

1. *Model Cities.* During the 1960s, an initiative called Model Cities was developed as part of President Lyndon Johnson's "Great Society" program. Demonstration Cities and Metropolitan Development Act of 1966, tit. II, 42 U.S.C. §§3301-3313 (1970). *See* Bernard J. Frieden & Marshall Kaplan, The Politics of Neglect (1975); Charles M. Haar, Between the Idea and the Reality (1975). The Model Cities program was designed to expand revitalization programs and concentrate resources in selected neighborhoods, allowing funds to address the full gamut of social as well as physical community needs.

Originally, the initiative called for a few experimental neighborhoods to receive all existing federal urban aid, as well as funds to design new programs aimed at improving neighborhood stability. Although the program was often criticized as ineffective, it was never launched as designed. Instead, funding was cut while demand skyrocketed, as many members of Congress wanted a handful of Model Neighborhoods for their constituents. Frieden & Kaplan, supra, 214-217, 222-224. Indeed, toward the end of the program, cities were allowed to expand such neighborhoods to cover the entire inner city, dissipating limited funding and frustrating unrealistic aspirations. Ultimately, the program was subsumed by §116(a) of the Housing and Community Development Act of 1974, 42 U.S.C. §5316 (2006).

The Model Cities program is just one of many government programs that have failed to generate their promised goals. This pattern of failure, in turn, has led to important political consequences. For example, it has often been cited as an example of the failure of government intervention and provided a justification for a new agenda of redevelopment policies.

2. *The Empowerment Results.* The first round of Empowerment Zones generated $8 billion in additional private investment, with the Detroit zone attracting $2 billion, prompting President Clinton to call for a second round. Clinton Calls for Second Empowerment Zone Round, 23 [Current Developments] Hous. & Dev. Rep. (WGL) 643 (1996). The Empowerment Zones and Enterprise Communities Program were not subject to any audits evaluating whether the program can be termed a success, although some have claimed such success. The enterprise communities expired in 2004. HUD's Initiative for Empowerment Zones and Renewal Communities (EZ/RC), at http://www.hud.gov/offices/cpd/economicdevelop . . . ment/programs/rc/ (last visited Nov. 12, 2016). *See also* Successful Empowerment Zones Can Help City Financial Ratings, Says Standard & Poor's Report, 25 Hous. & Dev. Rep. (West) 557 (1998) (Detroit's general obligation rating increased from BBB to BBB+, and its limited tax general obligation rating increased from BBB- to BBB as a result of its EZ program, which (1) generated $43.8 billion investment, (2) created 2752 jobs, and (3) reduced city unemployment from 11 to 8.7 percent).

For commentary on the enterprise and empowerment zones, *see* Edward J. Blakely, Competitive Advantage for the 21st-Century City: Can a Place-Based Approach to Economic Development Survive in a Cyberspace Age?, 67 J. Am. Plan. Ass'n 133, 139 (2001) (arguing that minority business might be better positioned to locate outside declining central cities); *contra*, Karen Chapple, Foresight or Farsight?: It's the Regional Economy Stupid, 67 J. Am. Plan. Ass'n 142 (2001) (arguing that "place" matters more than ever in the New Economy as investment is lured by a sense of "place"). For an endorsement of the Enterprise Zone program by Atlanta's former mayor, *see* William Campbell, Urban Holism: The Empowerment Zone and Economic Development in Atlanta, 26 Fordham Urb. L.J. 1411 (1999).

3. *Displacement.* The experience for many displacees under federal development and transportation programs has been one of tragedy. Despite the requirement that adequate replacement housing be identified, urban renewal and urban highway projects were routinely approved in earlier years despite the failure to undertake relocation planning. Chester W. Hartman, Relocation: Illusory Promises and No Relief, 57 Va. L. Rev. 745 (1971); Adam P. Hellegers, Eminent Domain as an Economic Development Tool: A Proposal to Reform HUD Displacement Policy, 2001 L. Rev. Mich. St. U. Detroit College L. 901. Even where planning was undertaken, regulations and planning theory too often were violated. For example, in *Tenants & Owners in Opposition to Redevelopment v. HUD*, 406 F. Supp. 1024 (N.D. Cal. 1970), the court rejected, for urban renewal relocation planning, the use of public housing as a planning resource. *See generally* James A. Kushner & Frances E. Werner, Illusory Promises Revisited: Relocation Planning and Judicial Review, 8 Sw. U. L. Rev. 751 (1976).

4. *Promise Zones.* In his 2013 State of the Union address, President Barack Obama discussed an initiative that would designate a number of high-poverty communities as "Promise Zones." The federal government would then partner with and invest in those communities "to create jobs, increase economic security, expand educational opportunities, increase access to quality, affordable housing, and

improve public safety." *See* Fact Sheet: President Obama's Promise Zones Initiative, at https://www.whitehouse.gov/the-press-office/2014/01/08/fact-sheet-president-obama-s-promise-zones-initiative (last visited Oct. 26, 2016). Since then, several rounds of federal action have designated promise zones, with eight new zones announced in 2015.

C. REDEVELOPMENT THROUGH TAX-INCREMENT FINANCING

States have authorized renewal programs that do not depend on federal subsidies. The most popular method is through the use of tax-increment financing, a subject discussed in Chapter 4. To refresh your memory: Under tax-increment-financed (TIF) redevelopment, municipal bonds are sold to finance acquisition of property. Professor Richard Briffault has summarized the TIF idea as follows:

> The theory of TIF is that the revenue growth generated within a territorially defined district is earmarked, for a period of years, to pay for physical infrastructure and other expenditures designed to spur economic growth within that district. By generating new growth, those improvements and expenditures produce the incremental revenues that are used to pay for the program which sparked the growth. TIF is typically presented as self-financing, with its expenditures paid for by the increased revenues resulting from TIF-financed growth, without a tax increase.

Richard Briffault, The Most Popular Tool: Tax Increment Financing and the Political Economy of Local Government, 77 U. Chi. L. Rev. 65, 66 (2010).

Before redevelopment can occur, however, state law usually requires that the local government make a finding that an area is "blighted." The following case addresses that important issue.

■ 62-64 MAIN ST., L.L.C. v. MAYOR & COUNCIL OF CITY OF HACKENSACK
221 N.J. 129, 110 A.3d 877 (2015)

Plaintiffs own five lots in the City of Hackensack on which stood two dilapidated buildings abutted by two poorly maintained and decrepit parking lots. Hackensack designated eleven out of twenty lots in a two-block area as in need of redevelopment, including plaintiffs' five lots. In doing so, the Planning Board made specific findings that those lots met the statutory definitions of blight in *N.J.S.A.* 40A:12A–5(a), (b), and (d). The Hackensack Mayor and Council passed a resolution that adopted the Planning Board's findings.

Plaintiffs filed an action in lieu of prerogative writs in Superior Court, challenging Hackensack's classification of their lots as blighted . . .

I.

In 2006, the Hackensack City Council authorized the City's Planning Board to undertake a preliminary investigation to determine whether a two-block area in

Hackensack's central business district — a mix of commercial and residential uses — should be designated as an area in need of redevelopment. *See N.J.S.A.* 40A:12A–6(a). The targeted two-block area is comprised of fourteen individual properties.

In eight days of hearings between December 2006 and January 2008, the Planning Board took testimony from five witnesses and received evidence, including expert reports and photographs, concerning whether to recommend the two-block area as in need of redevelopment. Ultimately, the Planning Board concluded that five of the fourteen properties were in need of redevelopment, including two properties on Main and Moore Streets acquired by plaintiffs in 1999. Plaintiffs' two properties encompass five lots, where a now defunct auto body repair shop had operated. All five lots are contiguous to one another and are owned by the same individuals through two separate limited liability corporations, each of which is a plaintiff in this case.

Plaintiff 62–64 Main Street, L.L.C., owns Block 205, Lots 4, 5, 6, and 7, a 10,443 square-foot parcel of land, on which sat — at the time of the hearings — two vacant, boarded up, dilapidated buildings with crumbling masonry, which were formerly part of the auto repair business. Behind the buildings is a poorly maintained, partly paved and partly gravel parking lot.

Plaintiff 59–61 Moore Street, L.L.C., owns Block 205, Lot 8, a 4280 square-foot parcel of land on which formerly sat an auto garage, which had been demolished. Currently, the property is used as a paved parking lot, although there are no markings for individual parking spaces, and the pavement is in a deteriorated condition. The parking lot has no landscaping or lighting and encroaches onto the sidewalk.

Plaintiffs intended to build a bank on the five lots, but could not secure site-plan approval from the City's Planning Board or the necessary variances from the City's Board of Adjustment to go forward with their proposals. The denials from those Boards are not at issue in this appeal. Suffice it to say, plaintiffs have treated all five lots as one property for development purposes.

The principal witness for the Planning Board was Janice Talley, a licensed professional planner with H2M Group, the firm retained by the Board to prepare a redevelopment study of the area under investigation. According to Talley and the redevelopment report she authored, the buildings on Lots 4–7 were vacant, dilapidated, and "boarded up due to their unsafe condition." The exterior of the buildings showed "prominent signs of structural deterioration." Notably, plaintiffs refused to give Talley access to make an assessment of the buildings' interior conditions. Talley described the parking lot behind the two buildings as "poorly surfaced" and without lines, lighting, or other necessary improvements.

Talley testified that the decrepit state of the buildings created "unwholesome" living and working conditions and that the buildings were "a detriment to the . . . safety, health and welfare of the community." Talley concluded that Lots 4–7 met the criteria of *N.J.S.A.* 40A:12A–5(a), (b), and (d) for an area in need of redevelopment.

Talley also testified that the current parking area on Lot 8, where the automotive garage once stood, was "crumbling" and "in disrepair." The parking area, she noted, had no defined layout, no lighting, no landscaping, and encroached onto the sidewalk. That encroachment — the lack of separation between the parking area and the sidewalk — posed a threat to pedestrians and rendered it a public-safety danger, in Talley's view. She concluded that Lot 8 met the criteria of *N.J.S.A.* 40A:12A–5(d) for an area in need of redevelopment.

Plaintiffs' expert, Peter Steck, a licensed planner, testified that Lots 4–8 did not satisfy the criteria for an area in need of redevelopment. He explained that the buildings were boarded up and therefore did not pose a danger. According to Steck, the property was in a state of transition, and the buildings were structurally sound, although vacant at the time. He insisted that the condition of Lots 4–8 did not retard the development of properties nearby, such as a new drug store, an automotive parts store, a bank, and a nail salon. Steck maintained that the buildings were not detrimental to the neighborhood and that the unpaved parking areas were similar to others in the neighborhood. He also noted that plaintiffs were appealing the denial of their application to construct a bank on the five lots.

In Steck's opinion, plaintiffs' property should not be considered in need of redevelopment simply because the City desires taller buildings in the area, and that the Board should have taken into account the time it takes to secure the necessary approvals to rehabilitate the property.

In reviewing the validity of the blight declaration in this case, we must remember that plaintiffs treated 62–64 Main Street and 59–61 Moore Street — five contiguous lots — as one property for development purposes. The issue is not whether one isolated lot might have some redeeming features, but whether an "area" is in need of redevelopment. *Levin, supra,* 57 *N.J.* at 539, 274 A.2d 1. For example, where an area in need of redevelopment encompasses a large residential or industrial/commercial area, a municipality may "draw within a blighted area certain houses or buildings which are in good condition" because, to do otherwise, "would be in some instances to defeat the overall legislative purpose, namely, the redevelopment of blighted *areas.*" *Wilson, supra,* 27 *N.J.* at 381, 142 A.2d 837 . . .

B.

We now must assess whether the Hackensack Planning Board and the Mayor and Council properly designated plaintiffs' properties as part of an area in need of redevelopment. More particularly we must decide whether Hackensack's blight determination, based on the statutory criteria in *N.J.S.A.* 40A:12A–5, is supported by substantial evidence in the record. As described earlier, the statutory criteria for blight include buildings that are "substandard," "unsafe," "dilapidated," or "obsolescent," *N.J.S.A.* 40A:12A–5(a); buildings no longer in use for commercial or industrial purposes, abandoned buildings, and buildings that have fallen "into so great a state of disrepair as to be untenantable," *N.J.S.A.* 40A:12A–5(b); and "[a]reas with buildings or improvements which, by reason of . . . faulty arrangement or design . . . are detrimental to the safety, health, morals, or welfare of the community," *N.J.S.A.* 40A:12A–5(d). . . .

62–64 Main Street — Lots 4–7

On Lots 4–7 sat two vacant, boarded up, dilapidated buildings with crumbling masonry — the vestiges of a defunct auto repair business. Plaintiffs denied Talley access to the interior of the buildings. Nevertheless, the buildings' exteriors showed "prominent signs of structural deterioration" and were evidently in a dangerous condition, leading Talley to conclude that the buildings were "a detriment to the . . . safety, health and welfare of the community." Indeed, the roof to one of the buildings collapsed during the appeal of this case, requiring the building to be torn down. Behind the two buildings was a "poorly surfaced" parking lot that did not have lines, lighting, or other necessary improvements.

The Planning Board determined that the decrepit buildings and their decayed parking lot satisfied the criteria for an area in need of redevelopment, focusing on subsections (a), (b), and (d) of *N.J.S.A.* 40A:12A-5. The Board adopted a resolution that explained its findings: the buildings were vacant, in a deteriorated condition, "substandard and unsafe for occupancy," and untenantable, thus meeting the blight criteria for subsections (a) and (b). Moreover, the entirety of the property, including the parking lot, suffered from a faulty arrangement or design under subsection (d).

We hold that substantial evidence in the record supports the Planning Board's findings . . . that Lots 4–7 were part of an area in need of redevelopment. We cannot look separately at the parking lot, which was an integral part of the property, in assessing whether it fits under subsection (d). . . .

59–61 Moore Street — Lot 8

This lot was part of the former auto repair business that encompassed Lots 4–7. An auto garage that once sat on Lot 8 was demolished. The ruins of that property were converted into a parking lot, although one that had no markings for individual parking spaces, no lighting, and no landscaping. The pavement of the parking lot was crumbling and in disrepair and encroached onto the sidewalk. The lack of any visible separation between the parking lot and sidewalk created a public-safety hazard, according to Talley.

In its resolution, the Planning Board determined that the lot's unsightliness and its inefficient use of the parking area — evidenced by its undefined layout — contributed to a greater demand for on-street parking, thereby having "a negative impact on surrounding properties." The Mayor and Council adopted the Board's finding that Lot 8 met the definition of blight under subsection (d) because of its "faulty arrangement [or] design." We hold that substantial evidence in the record supports that finding.

Even if Lot 8, standing alone, did not meet the definition of blight, it still might be properly categorized as part of an area in need of redevelopment. Blight determinations are not viewed in a piecemeal fashion. *Levin, supra,* 57 *N.J.* at 539, 274 *A.2d* 1. The Planning Board's expert testified that Lot 8 could not be redeveloped on its own, and that it could only be redeveloped in conjunction with its neighboring lots. Lot 8 was one of five lots on which an auto repair business operated, and plaintiffs treated Lot 8 as one of five combined lots for development purposes. Thus, the historical and contemplated use of Lots 4–8 was for a single business purpose.

We cannot agree with the Appellate Division that the Planning Board erred by not addressing "the fact that the owners had attempted to obtain approval to develop the properties, and that the proposals were denied." A landowner's desire to develop property "does not militate against [a] blight declaration." *Levin, supra,* 57 *N.J.* at 540, 274 *A.2d* 1. Here, the municipal authorities concluded that the property was unsuitable for the construction of a bank. Plaintiffs unsuccessfully appealed their failed efforts to secure the municipal construction approvals for a bank. In short, plaintiffs' failure to develop the property in accordance with the lawful requirements imposed by Hackensack land-use authorities cannot obscure the reality that the property remains in a state of blight. . . .

Notes and Comments

1. *The Findings of Blight.* Were you convinced by the court's opinion in *62-64 Main Street?* Were the properties really blighted or were they simply underperforming? Did the entire opinion rest on the testimony of the City's redevelopment expert? Did the court give too much deference to the conclusions of the Planning Board? Should an important decision like this one — which will likely result in the condemnation of private property — require a greater evidentiary showing?

In some cases courts reach a different outcome on the issue of blight. In *Sweetwater Valley Civic Ass'n v. City of Nat'l City,* 555 P.2d 1099 (Cal. 1976), the court rejected an attempt to establish a commercial redevelopment project on the site of a profitable golf course. The city's claim that the site was "blighted" was rejected, absent evidence the site had become an economic liability.

Blight designations may be suspicious or manipulated, perhaps more so if a program designed for revitalizing central cities is employed in a suburban community. *See Friends of Mammoth v. Town of Mammoth Lakes Redev. Agency,* 98 Cal. Rptr. 2d 334 (Ct. App. 2000) (little blight in affluent, bucolic golf and ski resort, particularly where the redevelopment plan included an existing golf course); *Walser Auto Sales, Inc. v. City of Richfield,* 635 N.W.2d 391 (Minn. Ct. App. 2001), *aff'd mem.,* 644 N.W.2d 425 (Minn. 2002) (rejecting attempt to classify code-complying structures as substandard and therefore blighted); *Centene Plaza Redev. Corp. v. Mint Properties,* 225 S.W.3d 431 (Mo. 2007) (evidence was insufficient to support finding that area was a social liability or a blighted area)

2. *The "Mark" of a Blight Finding.* A finding of blight is a prerequisite to use of the redevelopment power, and thus a legal term that lawyers may view neutrally. However, perhaps it affects property owners in a more pernicious way:

> [A finding of] [b]light literally adds insult to injury. In addition to the loss of property they portend, blight condemnations constitute a very public, official declaration that one's use and disposition of one's own property is inconsistent with the moral and aesthetic values of the Community and the State. Blight condemnations without a more substantial accompanying harm are not only aestheticism, but a solemn declaration that one is not entitled to the privileges and dignity of property ownership itself.

Andrew Tutt, Blightened Scrutiny, 47 U.C. Davis L. Rev. 1807, 1809–10 (2014).

Another article puts forth a different criticism of a finding of blight: "Too often, this rhetoric provided the framework, and cover, to treat people as movable and land as a market commodity instead of treating both as integral, living components of communities." Amy Laura Cahn, On Retiring Blight as a Policy and Making Eastwick Whole, 49 Harv. C.R.-C.L. L. Rev. 449 (2014). The "rhetoric of blight" is being used "to disenfranchise communities." *Id.*

Are these concerns real or overstated?

3. *The Effectiveness of Tax-Increment Financing.* In an excellent article, Professor George Lefcoe addresses the critiques of tax increment financing. *See* George Lefcoe, Competing for the Next Hundred Million Americans: The Uses and Abuses of Tax Increment Financing, 43 Urb. Law. 427 (2011). Professor Lefcoe points out that most TIF projects are located in the suburbs or gentrifying neighborhoods. TIF would appear to be ineffective in revitalizing blighted neighborhoods or housing the poor. In addition, although many projects are successful, little evidence exists

that the regional tax base is enhanced, only that redeveloping municipalities are able to attract sales and economic activity from neighboring communities. *See* Colin Gordon, Blighting the Way: Urban Renewal, Economic Development, and the Elusive Definition of Blight, 31 Fordham Urb. L.J. 305 (2004).

4. *Targeting the Expenditure.* Remember that large amounts of money are at stake. For example, over a 20-year period, more than $2 billion have been diverted to developers as subsidies for private developments through TIF in the St. Louis region. Joe Wilson, Given a Hammer: Tax-Increment Financing Abuse in the St. Louis Region, 34 St. Louis U. Pub. L. Rev. 83 (2014). Communities may fail to follow statutory obligations to target the expenditure of the "increment," the tax revenue in excess of that amount needed to pay off the bond. Courts generally defer to redevelopment planning. However, they will not sustain the use of bonds, secured by funds earmarked for low- and moderate-income housing, to fund safety-based road improvements, such as building railroad overpasses, when that use is unrelated to providing affordable housing. *Lancaster Redevelopment Agency v. Dibley*, 25 Cal. Rptr. 2d 593 (Ct. App. 1993).

5. *Zombie Properties.* A new type of blight arose in the aftermath of the collapse of the mortgage market in 2008. As the number of foreclosures skyrocketed, individuals moved out of the houses well before the actual foreclosure took place. As a result, so-called "zombie properties" began to appear.

> Zombie properties are properties that have been abandoned in the wake of foreclosure; however, the foreclosure process is never completed. . . . Often, the title owner assumes that the beginning of a foreclosure process signals that the lender (often the bank) is assuming responsibility for the property and that they must immediately vacate the property. This assumption fails to account for the fact that foreclosure processes are rarely timely and often take years to complete by obtaining a judgment of foreclosure and sale; some foreclosure processes are never completed. While the process moves along, the bank . . . will normally pay the taxes on the land . . . but this is often where their involvement ends. As the property continues to degrade, representing potential safety concerns as well as surrounding property value depreciation, this lone property stands in a limbo between life and death–between being owned and cared for and being completely ruined.

Marissa Weiss, Attack of the Zombie Properties, 47 Urb. Law. 485, 485–86 (2015). In some jurisdictions, the problem is severe. For example, one survey indicated that as many as 33,902 homes were vacant in Chicago as of June 2013. Elizabeth Butler, Second Chances for the Second City's Vacant Properties: An Analysis of Chicago's Policy Approaches to Vacancy, Abandonment, & Blight, 91 Chi.-Kent L. Rev 233, 234 (2016). *See also* Georgette Chapman Phillips, Zombie Cities: Urban Form and Population Loss, 11 Rutgers J. L. & Pub. Pol'y 703 (2014).

Some states have responded with legislation. New York's law, enacted in 2016, requires the loan servicer to inspect the property within 90 days of a delinquency, and every 30 days thereafter, to determine if the property is vacant. If the property is vacant, then the loan servicer must maintain it through a series of actions, such a securing windows and doors and providing basic utilities. The company must continue to maintain the property until ownership is transferred. N.Y.R.P.A.P.L. §1308. *See* "Governor Cuomo Signs Sweeping Legislation to Combat the Blight of Vacant and Abandoned Properties," (June 23, 2016) at https://www.governor.ny.gov/

news/governor-cuomo-signs-sweeping-legislation-combat-blight-vacant-and-aban doned-properties (last visited Oct. 26, 2016); Jessica Bacher & Meg Byerly Williams, A Local Government's Strategic Approach to Distressed Property Remediation, 46 Urb. Law. 877, 878 (2014) (suggesting a "comprehensive, strategic approach that local governments can take to remediate distressed properties successfully").

6. *Code Enforcement.* One strategy to stabilize neighborhoods and avoid deterioration to the point of requiring land clearance is enhanced enforcement of a housing conditions code. Although virtually every city has a housing conditions code, those codes are typically enforced on an *ad hoc* basis in response to complaints lodged by a tenant or neighbor.

There are, however, several problems with a systematic code enforcement strategy. Where the economic status of the property owner or of the neighborhood is such that loans cannot be obtained, code enforcement can exacerbate urban problems by causing displacement and, ultimately, abandonment of housing. Additionally, enforcement resources are often limited. Inspectors have little time to engage in proactive inspections rather than simply responding to complaints. One solution is to have all dwellings inspected at the point of sale. *See Butcher v. City of Detroit,* 401 N.W.2d 260 (Mich. 1986), *cert. denied,* 482 U.S. 905 (1987).

A few state courts have ruled that code enforcement can operate as a taking of the landlord's property. *See City of St. Louis v. Brune,* 515 S.W.2d 471 (Mo. 1974) (requirement that unit have a tub or shower connected to hot and cold water was invalid as applied to terminal, deteriorated housing that could not generate sufficient rent to finance repairs and sufficiently extend the life of the building). Most courts, however, have approved of such local initiatives.

7. *Urban Solutions.* Detroit has been plagued with empty buildings and has tried a number of solutions. One was a program of urban "homesteading," under which individuals who did not own the property could occupy and rehabilitate taxdelinquent properties. The homesteader ultimately obtained title through a foreclosure sale. Is this an appropriate approach to blight? Or does it simply create large taking issues? *See Moore v. City of Detroit,* 406 N.W.2d 488 (Mich. Ct. App. 1987) (no taking as the program constitutes a creative alternative to demolition). A later approach involved establishing certain viable areas as "healthy neighborhoods." *See* http://detroitworksproject.com/2011/09/29/detroit-targets-services-to-healthy-neighborhoods/ (last visited Oct. 26, 2016). The city also has pursued a goal of demolishing blighted structures. The city's approach to taking blighted properties is criticized in Yxta Maya Murray, Detroit Looks Toward a Massive, Unconstitutional Blight Condemnation: The Optics of Eminent Domain in Motor City, 23 Geo. J. on Poverty L. & Pol'y 395, 397 (2016) ("The Detroit Blight Removal Task Force . . . prepares the city for an unconstitutional and unjust taking of up to 72,000 structures, but pretends otherwise. . . . "). *See also* Kermit J. Lind, Perspectives on Abandoned Houses in a Time of Dystopia, 24 J. Affordable Housing & Community Dev. L. 121 (2015) (describing various perspectives on abandoned houses in urban neighborhoods and the reactions from those perspectives).

In the worst case, municipalities may be forced to declare bankruptcy as their revenues are insufficient to support the public services and other expenditures required of the city. Between 2007 and 2013, 28 urban municipalities did so. What will these new "minimal cities" look like? How far can cities go in cutting public services? *See* Michelle Wilde Anderson, The New Minimal Cities, 123 Yale L.J. 1118 (2014).

8. *Resilient Cities.* Professor Tony Arnold suggests that cities should be analyzed in terms of their resiliency "in the face of significant and uncertain disturbances," including patterns of distressed properties and fiscal crises. Craig Anthony Arnold, Resilient Cities and Adaptive Law, 50 Idaho L. Rev. 245 (2014). Resilience is the "capacity of a system to withstand or adapt to disturbance while maintaining the same basic structures and functions." If a system's resilience degrades sufficiently, the system may cross the threshold that represents the limits of the system, "pushing the system to suddenly collapse and transform into a new system." *Id.*

Has the blight faced by any American city reached the point where the city's resilience is in doubt? *Compare* J. Peter Byrne, The Rebirth of the Neighborhood, 40 Fordham Urb. L.J. 1505 (2013) (observing that, although since 1972 American cities have lost federal support, "many cities have experienced phenomenal population growth and economic development over the past decade") *with* Kellen Zale, Urban Resiliency and Destruction, 50 Idaho L. Rev. 85, 86 (2014) (arguing that part of resiliency is the power to destroy existing buildings in order to create, that "not every exercise of that right increases the city's resiliency," and that "cities may engage in a tendency to overuse the power to destroy" in certain situations).

D. DISLOCATION AND THE PUBLIC USE REQUIREMENT

Redevelopment can be a catalyst for community renewal, but there are often unavoidable costs. For example, a redevelopment project may cause housing displacement, thereby aggravating a limited, overcrowded housing supply. If the redevelopment is successful, secondary displacement can be generated as private owners upgrade buildings in surrounding streets and neighborhoods. James A. Kushner et al., Housing and Community Development Law ch. 5 (4th ed. 2011). Even where the redevelopment area is racially integrated, displacement may exacerbate community segregation patterns. More fundamentally, redevelopment can take the homes of individuals who were perfectly happy living there, in some cases for many years.

Consequently, the reach of redevelopment power is an important and contested issue. We start out with a note on a highly controversial use of the condemnation power in the City of Detroit. The dispute there gained national attention and highlighted the growing controversy over the "public use" clause in the Fifth Amendment.

A Note on the *Poletown* Case

The City of Detroit was long the center of the American automobile industry. Throughout the 1970s, however, American manufacturers centered there faced competition from a multitude of foreign companies. At the same time, Detroit was suffering from high unemployment and other urban ills.

General Motors Corporation, long a large employer in the region, wanted to expand its manufacturing operations. It could have done so in another state. However, it proposed to build an assembly plant in an area of Detroit commonly known as Poletown. The proposal was enormously controversial in the area, but the City of Detroit supported this effort. Its Economic Development Corporation proposed to exercise its power of eminent domain to acquire the needed property. The action, however, would displace about 4200 people, 1300 homes, as well as businesses and churches.

The litigation reached the Michigan Supreme Court in 1981. The court had to consider whether the use of eminent domain to transfer the property to another private landowner was a "public use" under the Fifth Amendment. In a 5-2 opinion, the court upheld the use of eminent domain. The core of the court's reasoning was:

> In the instant case the benefit to be received by the municipality invoking the power of eminent domain is a clear and significant one and is sufficient to satisfy this Court that such a project was an intended and a legitimate object of the Legislature when it allowed municipalities to exercise condemnation powers even though a private party will also, ultimately, receive a benefit as an incident thereto.
>
> The power of eminent domain is to be used in this instance primarily to accomplish the essential public purposes of alleviating unemployment and revitalizing the economic base of the community. The benefit to a private interest is merely incidental.

Poletown Neighborhood Council v. City of Detroit, 410 Mich. 616, 634, 304 N.W.2d 455, 459 (1981) *overruled by City of Wayne v. Hathcock*, 471 Mich. 445, 684 N.W.2d 765 (2004). The use of eminent domain was then carried out, and the plant was built.

Twenty-three years later — one year before the United States Supreme Court's decision in *Kelo* — the Michigan Supreme Court returned to the same issue. This time a county proposed to use its power of eminent domain to condemn property for the construction of a 1300-acre business and technology park. The park was intended to reinvigorate an economy that was struggling in the area.

The court began its opinion as follows: "We are presented again with a clash of two bedrock principles of our legal tradition — the sacrosanct right of individuals to dominion over their private property . . . and . . . the state's authority to condemn private property for the commonwealth." *City of Wayne v. Hathcock*, 471 Mich. 445, 450, 684 N.W.2d 765, 769 (2004). The court's opinion centered on its previous decision in *Poletown*. The court found, however, that *Poletown* "is most notable for its radical and unabashed departure from the entirety of this Court's pre–1963 eminent domain jurisprudence." *Id.* at 785. Before *Poletown*, said the court, "we had never held that a private entity's pursuit of profit was a "public use" for constitutional takings purposes simply because one entity's profit maximization contributed to the health of the general economy." *Id.* at 786.

Accordingly, concluded the court, *Poletown* was mis-decided:

> Because *Poletown's* conception of a public use — that of "alleviating unemployment and revitalizing the economic base of the community" — has no support in the Court's eminent domain jurisprudence before the Constitution's ratification, its interpretation of "public use" in art. 10, §2 [of the Michigan Constitution] cannot reflect the common understanding of that phrase among those sophisticated in the law at ratification. Consequently, the *Poletown* analysis provides no legitimate support for the condemnations proposed in this case and, for the reasons stated above, is overruled.

684 N.W.2d at 787 (2004).

One year later, the issue reached the United States Supreme Court in a different, even more controversial case. *See Kelo v. City of New London, Connecticut*, 545 U.S. 469 (2005). The *Kelo* case is a principal decision included in the reading on the Takings Clause in Chapter 7. At this point, you should re-read *Kelo* before continuing on to the following materials.

The *Kelo* majority opinion emphasizes that the federal constitution only sets a floor, and that states are free to require more protection. Consider the following opinion, which came out three years before *Kelo*. Does it support that view? Or is an example of a kind of pervasive abuse that concerned the dissenters in *Kelo*?

■ **SOUTHWESTERN ILLINOIS DEVELOPMENT AUTHORITY v. NATIONAL CITY ENVIRONMENTAL, L.L.C.**
768 N.E.2d 1 (Ill. 2002), cert. denied, 537 U.S. 880 (2002)

Justice GARMAN delivered the opinion of the court:

The issue in this case is whether the Southwestern Illinois Development Authority (SWIDA) properly exercised the power of eminent domain to take property owned by National City Environmental, L.L.C., and St. Louis Auto Shredding Company (collectively NCE), and convey that property to Gateway International Motorsports Corporation (Gateway). . . .

SWIDA was created in 1987 by the Illinois General Assembly through passage of the Southwestern Illinois Development Authority Act (the Act) . . . SWIDA is a political entity and municipal corporation whose stated purpose is to "promote industrial, commercial, residential, service, transportation and recreational activities and facilities, thereby reducing the evils attendant upon unemployment and enhancing the public health, safety, morals, happiness and general welfare of this State." . . .

The Act mandates that SWIDA "promote development within the geographic confines of Madison and St. Clair counties." It is the duty of SWIDA to assist in the development, construction, and acquisition of industrial, commercial, housing or residential projects within these counties. A "[c]ommercial project" is defined as "any cultural facilities of a for-profit or non-for-profit type including . . . racetracks . . . [and] parking facilities." . . .

To accomplish the purposes of the Act, the legislature empowered SWIDA to issue bonds for the purpose of acquiring, improving or developing projects, including those established by business entities attempting to locate or expand property within Madison and St. Clair Counties. SWIDA also has the authority to acquire property by condemnation. . . .

In June 1996, SWIDA issued $21.5 million in taxable sports facility revenue bonds. The proceeds of the bonds were lent to Gateway to finance the development of a multipurpose automotive sports and training facility in the region (the racetrack). . . .

The racetrack was developed and has flourished. In 1997, the racetrack had a total attendance of 400,000 at various large and small events. Seating included 25,000 grandstand seats and 25,000 portable seats. In 1998, Gateway increased its seating capacity and desired to increase its parking capacity as well. It called upon SWIDA to use its quick-take eminent domain powers to acquire land to the west of the racetrack for the purposes of expanded parking facilities. The adjacent 148.5 acre tract of land sought was owned by NCE.

NCE operates a metal recycling center in an area of St. Clair County that, until recently, was National City, Illinois. NCE employs 80 to 100 persons full time and has been at its present location since 1975. NCE shred cars and appliances and separates the reusable metals. It disposes of nearly 100,000 cars per year. Nonrecyclable by-products of the process, referred to as "fluff," are deposited in NCE's landfill, located to the east of its recycling center. When this landfill site reaches capacity, NCE plans to expand its landfill operations onto the 148.5 acre tract of land it owns to the east of the current landfill. NCE uses clay and dirt from the 148.5 acre tract to fill and cover fluff in the landfill area currently in use.

In early 1998, Gateway attempted to discuss the purchase of NCE's land with NCE's owner. NCE would not discuss the matter and, initially, Gateway made no offer to purchase the land. Instead, Gateway asked SWIDA to exercise its quick-take eminent domain powers to take the 148.5 acres of land and transfer it to Gateway.

Gateway completed a "Quick-Take Application Packet" and stated that it wanted to use the land as a parking lot for the purpose of increasing the value of Gateway's racetrack. Gateway paid SWIDA an application fee of $2,500, and the sum of $10,000 to be applied toward SWIDA's sliding scale fee of 6% to 10% of the acquisition price of property being condemned. In addition, Gateway agreed to pay SWIDA's expenses, including the acquisition price of the property, and other costs associated with quick-take process.

Approval of the county board is required before SWIDA can use its quick-take eminent domain powers within unincorporated areas of a county. On February 23, 1998, the St. Clair County board adopted a resolution authorizing SWIDA to exercise its quick-take eminent domain authority to acquire the NCE tract of land for Gateway parking. The board noted that dramatic attendance increases could be expected at the racetrack and that it was necessary to create additional parking facilities to adequately serve patrons. The board also found that expansion of the racetrack facilities would enhance the public health, safety, morals, happiness, and general welfare of the citizens of southwestern Illinois by increasing the tax base in the area and generating additional tax revenues. . . .

In an effort to acquire the property through a negotiated sale, [SWIDA Executive Director] Ortbals attended a meeting on March 17, 1998, at which he delivered to NCE a written offer to purchase the property for $1 million. By letter dated March 19, 1998, NCE rejected the $1 million offer but indicated its willingness to meet with SWIDA the week of March 30, 1998, following an expected appraisal of the property. On March 20, 1998, SWIDA made another written offer to NCE to purchase the property for $1 million and advised NCE that SWIDA would initiate proceedings to condemn the property if NCE did not accept the offer by 5 p.m. on March 30, 1998. . . .

The right of a sovereign to condemn private property is limited to takings for a public use. Clearly, private persons may ultimately acquire ownership of property arising out of a taking and the subsequent transfer to private ownership does not by itself defeat the public purpose. However, that principle alone cannot adequately resolve the issues presented in this case. "Before the right of eminent domain may be exercised, the law, beyond a doubt, requires that the use for which the land is taken shall be public as distinguished from a private use." . . .

It may be impossible to clearly delineate the boundary between what constitutes a legitimate public purpose and a private benefit with no sufficient, legitimate public purpose to support it. "We deal, in other words, with what traditionally has been known as the police power. An attempt to define its reach or trace its outer limits is fruitless, for each case must turn on its own facts." . . . "While, from time to time, the courts have attempted to define public use, there is much disagreement as to its meaning." . . . Great deference should be afforded the legislature and its granting of eminent domain authority. However, the exercise of that power is not entirely beyond judicial scrutiny, and it is incumbent upon the judiciary to ensure that the power of eminent domain is used in a manner contemplated by the framers of the constitutions and by the legislature that granted the specific power in question. "Courts all agree that the determination of whether a given use is a public use is a judicial function." . . .

SWIDA contends that the condemnation and taking of NCE's property is sustainable because a public purpose will be served through (1) the fostering of economic development, (2) the promotion of public safety, and (3) the prevention or elimination of blight. Moreover, once the determination is made that one or all of these requirements is satisfied, "possessory use by the public is not an indispensable prerequisite to the lawful exercise of the power of eminent domain." . . .

SWIDA contends that any distinction between the terms "public purpose" and "public use" has long since evaporated and that the proper test is simply to ask whether a "public purpose" is served by the taking. While the difference between a public purpose and a public use may appear to be purely semantic, and the line between the two terms has blurred somewhat in recent years, a distinction still exists and is essential to this case. We agree that these terms are necessarily somewhat loosely defined. However, that does not mean they are indistinguishable. . . .

If this taking were allowed to stand, it may be true that spectators at Gateway would benefit greatly. Developing additional parking could benefit the members of the public who choose to attend events at the racetrack, as spectators may often have to wait in long lines of traffic to park their vehicles and again to depart the facility. We also acknowledge that a public use or purpose may be satisfied in light of public safety concerns. The public is allowed to park on the property in exchange for the payment of a fee. Gateway's racetrack may be open to the public, but not "by right." It is a private venture designed to result not in a public use, but in private profits. If this taking were permitted, lines to enter parking lots might be shortened and pedestrians might be able to cross from parking areas to event areas in a safer manner. However, we are unpersuaded that these facts alone are sufficient to satisfy the public use requirement, especially in light of evidence that Gateway could have built a parking garage structure on its existing property.

We have also recognized that economic development is an important public purpose. . . . SWIDA presented extensive testimony that expanding Gateway's facilities through the taking of NCE's property would allow it to grow and prosper and contribute to positive economic growth in the region. However, "incidentally, every lawful business does this." . . . Moreover, nearly a century ago, [this court] expressed the long-standing rule that "to constitute a public use, something more than a mere benefit to the public must flow from the contemplated improvement." . . .

Entities such as SWIDA must always be mindful of expediency, cost efficiency, and profitability while accepting the legislature's charge to promote development within their defined parameters. However, these goals must not be allowed to overshadow the constitutional principles that lie at the heart of the power with which SWIDA and similar entities have been entrusted. As Justice Kuehn stated in dissent in the appellate court, "If property ownership is to remain what our forefathers intended it to be, if it is to remain a part of the liberty we cherish, the economic by-products of a private capitalist's ability to develop land cannot justify a surrender of ownership to eminent domain." . . .

While the activities here were undertaken in the guise of carrying out its legislated mission, SWIDA's true intentions were not clothed in an independent, legitimate governmental decision to further a planned public use. SWIDA did not conduct or commission a thorough study of the parking situation at Gateway. Nor did it formulate any economic plan requiring additional parking at the racetrack. SWIDA advertised that, for a fee, it would condemn land at the request of "private developers" for the "private use" of developers. In addition, SWIDA entered into a contract with Gateway to condemn whatever land "may be desired . . . by Gateway." Clearly, the foundation of this taking is rooted not in the economic and planning process with which SWIDA has been charged. Rather, this action was undertaken solely in response to Gateway's expansion goals and its failure to accomplish those goals through purchasing NCE's land at an acceptable negotiated price. It appears SWIDA's true intentions were to act as a default broker of land for Gateway's proposed parking plan.

This point is further emphasized by the fact that other options were available to Gateway that could have addressed many of the problems testified to by Pritchett, Ortbals and others. Gateway could have built a parking garage structure on its existing property rather than develop the land owned by NCE. However, when Gateway discovered that the cost of constructing a garage on land it already owned was substantially higher than using SWIDA as its agent to take NCE's property for open-field parking, Gateway chose the easier and less expensive avenue.

As a result of the acquisition of NCE's property, Gateway could realize an estimated increase of $13 to $14 million in projected revenue per year. While we do not deny that this expansion in revenue could potentially trickle down and bring corresponding revenue increases to the region, revenue expansion alone does not justify an improper and unacceptable expansion of the eminent domain power of the government. Using the power of the government for purely private purposes to allow Gateway to avoid the open real estate market and expand its facilities in a more cost-efficient manner, and thus maximizing corporate profits, is a misuse of the power entrusted by the public. . . .

Notes and Comments

1. *Contrasting* Kelo *with* Southwestern Illinois. Are the two cases consistent? What accounts for the different results? How do you explain the Illinois decision in light of the traditional pro-development political and judicial philosophy of that state? Do the facts of *Southwestern Illinois* confirm the fears of the dissenters in *Kelo*? *See also City of Las Vegas Downtown Redev. Agency v. Pappas*, 76 P.3d 1 (Nev. 2003), *cert. denied*, 541 U.S. 912 (2004) (ruling that taking for parking garage that would benefit casinos is a public use).

Would *Southwestern Illinois* have come out differently if the public agency had planned to construct a publicly-owned parking lot or garage and leased it to the race track, or simply charged parking to patrons? For a ruling endorsing the use of tax increment redevelopment to finance an automobile race track, *see State ex rel. Tomasic v. Unified Gov't of Wyandotte County/Kansas City, Kansas*, 962 P.2d 543 (Kan. 1998).

See also Rhode Island Econ. Dev. Corp. v. Parking Co., 892 A.2d 87 (R.I. 2006) (finding that condemnation of an easement to control an airport parking garage and valet service was not for a public purpose where the condemnation was designed to gain control of the garage at a discounted price). Can the state use condemnation power for a public/private venture in which one floor of a five-story building would be devoted to public use? *State ex rel. Washington State Convention & Trade Ctr. v. Evans*, 966 P.2d 1252 (Wash. 1998) (yes for a convention center expansion project, as the agency condemned no more than necessary for the public use).

2. *Social Equity.* Was the sacrifice required of the displaced citizens in *Poletown* fair so as to allow a private corporation to construct its plant? Are the displacees subsidizing the project? Was the blight in the two cases at similar levels? Should it make any difference that Detroit was desperately trying to stimulate a higher level of economic development and was far more distressed than the situation presented in *Southwestern Illinois?*

3. *Economic Development.* What if a town, to protect its tax base and the economic viability of its commercial district, condemned "blighted" commercial buildings adjacent to an automobile dealership to permit the dealer to expand and not leave its location, as it threatened to do? *City of Center Line v. Chmelko*, 416 N.W.2d 401 (Mich. Ct. App. 1987) (invalid taking). Should it even matter that the local government action is intended to prevent jobs in a specific business from leaving the jurisdiction? *Compare City of Jamestown v. Leevers Supermarkets*, 552 N.W.2d 365 (N.D. 1996) (city may condemn downtown parking lots for commercial redevelopment for a supermarket when the public purpose is stimulation of commercial growth and removal of economic stagnation).

According to one lawyer for the City of Detroit in *Poletown*:

> The case represented a great victory for the City during a bleak time. Had we lost the case, General Motors would have constructed this assembly plant in the South. Quite possibly, Chrysler would have followed GM out of Detroit (Chrysler did move its head-quarters to the suburbs, but kept its assembly plant in Detroit). The "domino" effect would have been catastrophic for the City. All the economic benefits of this condem-nation presented at trial were absolutely valid and prophetic.

Letter from William G. Christopher to James A. Kushner, Jan. 21, 1998, at 1.

4. Berman *and* Southwestern Illinois. Is the court in *Southwestern Illinois* incon-sistent with *Berman v. Parker*, 348 U.S. 26 (1954)? In *Berman*, the Supreme Court deferentially endorsed urban renewal land clearance as a public use, even as applied to a nonblighted, commercial structure. Does *Southwestern Illinois* set forth a clear test for determining which projects will pass the "public use" test?

5. *Inevitable "Crony Capitalism"?* Professor Steven Eagle suggests that improper relationships, which he labels "crony capitalism," are endemic to the redevelop-ment process. Steven Eagle, The Perils of Regulatory Property in Land Use Regula-tion, 54 Washburn L.J. 1, 33 (2014) (asserting that "[c]ondemnation for large redevelopment projects naturally lends itself to cozy deals between local officials and favored developers"). Is that true? If so, what is the solution?

As touched on in Chapter 7, in the aftermath of *Kelo* many states adopted legislation designed to alter the operation of the use eminent domain in redevel-opment projects. One article summarized the legislation as follows:

In response to *Kelo*, a total of forty-four states changed their laws: Eleven changed their constitutions, while forty enacted a broad range of statutory changes. The bulk of these changes relate to the meaning of "public use" or "public purpose." Thirty states tightened those definitions to various degrees. Twenty-five states changed their definitions of "blight," requiring a closer connection between the taking and the protection of public health or safety, and diminishing the government's ability to designate large areas as blighted based on the condition of a few properties. Eleven states gave prior owners a right of first refusal to repurchase property that has not been used for the purpose for which it was condemned or that is later sold by the condemnor. Nine states changed the burden of proof in eminent domain cases, either by requiring the government to prove public use or by removing deference from the government's assertions. And two states prohibited transferring condemned property to private parties for any reason, at least for ten years.

Dana Berliner, Looking Back Ten Years After Kelo, 125 Yale L.J. Forum 82, 84–87 (2015).

The following two cases construe post-*Kelo* legislation. Did those laws have a marked effect on the use of eminent domain?

■ READING AREA WATER AUTHORITY v. SCHUYLKILL RIVER GREENWAY ASSOCIATION
100 A.3d 572 (Pa. 2014)

Justice SAYLOR.

The primary question raised is whether a municipal authority may exercise its eminent domain powers to condemn an easement over privately-owned land, where the sole purpose of the easement is to supply a private developer with land to install sewer drainage facilities needed for a proposed private residential subdivision.

The Schuylkill River Greenway Association (the Greenway), a non-profit corporation, owns a strip of land along the west bank of the Schuylkill River in Bern Township, several miles north of the City of Reading. The Greenway and the Township intend to build a public walking/recreational trail on this property as a segment of the larger Schuylkill River Trail. Situated immediately to the west of the Greenway Property is a 58-acre tract owned by Fortune Development, L.P. (Developer), a private developer. Developer seeks to construct a 219-unit adult residential subdivision, known as Water's Edge Village, on this tract.

Water's Edge Village would require access to a clean water supply as well as sanitary sewer and stormwater sewer facilities. As for clean water, a water main passing through Ontelaunee (a municipality on the east side of the Schuylkill River) can potentially connect, underneath the Schuylkill River, with a proposed water main on the west side of the river, and then continue west to Water's Edge Village. For this to occur, however, the west-side main would have to run through the Greenway's property. A similar situation exists with regard to sanitary sewer and stormwater sewer outfall, albeit the water would flow in the opposite direction. In particular, treated sewage would combine with stormwater runoff and flow eastward through the Greenway's property, ultimately discharging into the Schuylkill River. The conduits for the clean water and the sewer outfall could be laid side-by-side within a 50-foot-wide underground space on the Greenway's property, connecting the Schuylkill River and Developer's land.

The Reading Area Water Authority (RAWA), a municipal authority created by the City of Reading, supported Developer's planned development and, to that end, tried to purchase an easement across the Greenway Property so that it could supply water to the proposed development. After negotiations with the Greenway failed to produce an agreement, RAWA adopted a resolution in February 2009, authorizing the use of its eminent-domain powers to condemn a utility easement across the Greenway Property connecting Developer's land with the Schuylkill River. The resolution reflected that the easement was to be condemned at Developer's request and that it would be used for water, sewer, and stormwater purposes specifically to enable Developer to build Water's Edge Village. The resolution also stated that Developer would be responsible for initiating eminent domain proceedings in conjunction with RAWA's solicitor, and would be required to pay all costs associated with such proceedings, including just compensation to the Greenway. The City of Reading then passed a resolution approving the RAWA resolution.

In light of the City's approval, in May 2010 RAWA filed a Declaration of Taking Complaint in the Berks County common pleas court, naming the Greenway as the sole defendant and attaching an appraisal, a bond, and a description of the property to be taken. The Complaint requested a decree condemning a 50-foot-wide easement across the Greenway Property, "to construct, maintain, [and] operate utility lines and appurtenance of a water main to be placed under the Schuylkill River for water, sewer and stormwater purposes," Complaint at ¶ 6, *reprinted in* R.R. 11a, and asked that the court value the easement at $3,500 based on the appraisal. According to the attached exhibits, the water main would travel west from Ontelaunee under the Schuylkill River and continue west through the Greenway Property to Developer's property. The sewer main would travel south from a sewage treatment plant on Developer's property and intersect with a pipe which would drain a stormwater retention basin (also on Developer's property). The sewer main and the stormwater pipe would then combine into a single conduit which would travel east under Developer's property, and then continue east through the Greenway Property, within the same 50-foot-wide strip of land, ultimately emerging through a concrete headwall and discharging the effluent onto a six-foot downward slope covered by riprap.

The Greenway filed preliminary objections, alleging that: the taking was invalid under Pennsylvania's Property Rights Protection Act (PRPA), because it was being accomplished solely for the benefit of private enterprise, *see* 26 Pa.C.S. §204(a) (generally prohibiting the use of eminent-domain powers to take private property "to use it for private enterprise"). . . .

We allowed appeal to consider whether RAWA's actions were legally permissible, particularly in light of recent legislative restrictions on the use of eminent domain to benefit private enterprise . . .

Appellants (the Greenway and the Township) argue generally that the power of eminent domain may only be exercised for a public purpose. They do not challenge the water easement, opting to focus their advocacy on the drainage easement. Appellants observe that this portion of the condemned land exceeds that which is necessary for RAWA's proposed water-supply line. In this respect, they note that RAWA only operates a water-supply system, whereas it condemned an easement large enough to include extensive wastewater outflow facilities — including a pipe, a headwall, grading, and riprap — connected to a private sewage treatment plant and stormwater retention basin on Developer's land. They contend, more particularly, that RAWA may not condemn more land than it needs for water supply solely to enable a private developer to discharge its private sewage and stormwater runoff through a privately built and maintained facility over the land of another. Thus Appellants adopt the position that the drainage easement is being taken for the private use of Developer and, as such, it is not authorized by the Pennsylvania Constitution or the Eminent Domain Code, and is affirmatively prohibited by PRPA. *See* Brief for Appellants at 12. . . .

RAWA proffers that there is a public interest in ensuring that homes have running water and access to a sewer line, and that the taking advances this interest regardless of whether Developer will benefit from the availability of such services through its ability to build and sell fully-functioning homes. So long as there is no evidence of corruption, fraud, or malfeasance by the condemnor, RAWA argues, a condemnation for a public purpose should be upheld. . . .

Under the Constitution, land may only be taken without the owner's consent if it is taken for a public use. The question of what constitutes a public use is highly fact-dependent. . . .

[T]he present case has added complexion because the drainage easement is to be located side-by-side with the water easement, giving the appearance that the two work in tandem. There is also a natural tendency to regard the two functions as intertwined, at least insofar as the sanitary sewer outfall is concerned, since most of the water that enters a residence ultimately leaves the home through its sewer connection. This lends a certain appeal to the concept that the drainage easement is for a public use — particularly as municipal sewer and drainage systems generally constitute a public use. Furthermore, the drainage easement would, according to Developer's plans, ultimately serve 219 homes in an adult-community residential development. This factor also tends to support the view that the drainage easement is intended for at least a limited public use vis-à-vis the prospective purchasers of the residences, regardless of the identity of the party that constructs, owns, and operates the sewer discharge facilities.

The main difficulty, however, is that there is also a significant private overlay to the taking of the drainage easement: it is, as noted, to be acquired at Developer's behest for the sole use of Developer, and at Developer's sole cost. As well, there is no suggestion that the drainage easement is meant to be used for any purpose broader than servicing the subdivision to be built by Developer. Overall, then, the case involves a mix of public and private purposes working in conjunction with one another. With this in mind, a brief discussion of *Kelo v. City of New London, Connecticut*, 545 U.S. 469, 125 S. Ct. 2655, 162 L.Ed.2d 439 (2005), its present application, and its legislative aftermath, will be helpful . . . [The Court then summarized the majority and dissent opinions in *Kelo*.]

The present case is distinguishable from *Kelo* in several respects. First, consistent with the trial court's findings, the taking here has as at least one of its purposes the conferral of a private benefit on a particular, identifiable private party (Developer). . . . Relatedly, there is no evidence of an overall economic development or urban revitalization plan into which this taking fits — above and beyond Developer's own plan for its 58-acre tract.

On the other hand, the scope of the challenged taking is comparatively narrow and, as noted, involves sewer services, which is a more traditional category of public use than the multifaceted, large-scale economic development project at issue in

Kelo . . . It can reasonably be argued, then, that whether the taking presently in issue is "primarily" for a public use or a private benefit is a matter of perspective. . . .

Ultimately, however, we need not decide the constitutional issue because, even if we assume the condemnation can pass Fifth-Amendment scrutiny, to be valid it must also be statutorily permissible. In this regard, it may be observed that, in the wake of *Kelo,* the General Assembly enacted PRPA, which contains a salient, affirmative prohibition on the taking of private property "in order to use it for private enterprise." 26 Pa.C.S. §204(a). . . .

It is possible that a condemnation which satisfies the Constitution's Public Use Clause may also be accomplished so that the property can be used for private enterprise. *Kelo* provides a ready example, as in that case the Supreme Court determined that the taking was for a public use although much of the condemned land was to be used for private enterprise. *See Kelo,* 545 U.S. at 473–74, 125 S. Ct. at 2659 (describing uses for the condemned property under the city's plan, including conference hotel space, retail shopping, a commercial-use marina, and a research and development facility for a pharmaceutical company). . . .

Notably, PRPA was passed as a direct reaction to *Kelo* to curb what legislators perceived as eminent domain abuse, and with the goal of striking a reasonable balance between (a) the need to defend private property rights from takings accomplished for economic development purposes, and (b) the legitimate needs of urban centers to rehabilitate blighted areas imposing substantial, concrete harm upon the public. *See, e.g.,* House Legislative Journal, Nov. 1, 2005, at 2169–72; Senate Legislative Journal, April 25, 2006, at 1552. Whether or not the *Constitution* viewed as merely "ancillary" the benefits to private enterprise ensuing from a plan to use eminent domain to assist in economic development, in the wake of *Kelo* the *Legislature* began to view such benefits as central and wanted to curtail the ability of condemnors to take others' property for such purposes. Against this backdrop, the legislative body elected to phrase the central prohibition broadly in terms of whether the subject property is being condemned "to use it for private enterprise," 26 Pa.C.S. §204(a), rather than "to use it *solely* for private enterprise" — the latter of which, in any event, would have had little effect on the *status quo* since any condemnation accomplished solely for private purposes would likely have failed the constitutional public-use standard.

This observation has particular relevance to the present matter because, in spite of the drainage easement's colorable public-use facet as outlined above, RAWA condemned it, in effect, to allow Developer to occupy and use it for private enterprise — namely, to develop a residential subdivision. . . . We therefore conclude that the condemnation of the drainage easement falls within Section 204(a)'s prohibitive scope. Whatever public benefit may ensue from the drainage easement, it is being taken to be used for private enterprise and, as such, is prohibited by Section 204(a). . . .

■ CITY OF OMAHA v. TRACT NO. 1

778 N.W.2d 122 (Neb. Ct. App. 2010)

CASSEL, Judge. . . .

This is an appeal from a condemnation action. The City negotiated with property owners to acquire a strip of land for the purpose of installing a deceleration lane for traffic that would access a new development which included a building to be occupied by the retailer. The City also sought temporary easements for the purpose of constructing the deceleration lane. After initial negotiations to acquire the real property failed, the City filed a petition in county court to condemn the property.

Haltom filed a "Complaint on Appeal" to appeal this matter to the district court. Haltom alleged four separate causes of action, only one of which is the subject of the instant appeal. In the relevant cause of action, Haltom alleged that §76-710.04 prevented the City from acquiring the property, because the proposed use of the property constituted an "economic and development purpose."

The City then filed a motion for partial summary judgment on three of the four causes of action, including the one pertinent to this appeal.

At the summary judgment hearing, the City adduced evidence regarding the purpose for which the condemned property would be used. This included an affidavit by Charlie Krajicek, the city engineer. His affidavit stated that in his review of the retailer's development plans, he determined that a deceleration lane was necessary for traffic. His specific reasoning was as follows:

> [A]s a result of the anticipated increased traffic on 72nd Street as time elapses and the potential for the slowing of traffic on 72nd Street accessing the new [commercial] facility as traffic proceeded southbound, I determined that it was necessary that a deceleration lane be constructed to handle southbound traffic that would be accessing the new development. . . . [T]he purpose of requiring the deceleration lane was to allow traffic on 72nd Street to proceed in an orderly and efficient fashion and to limit the potential collisions as a result of cars decelerating on the right-of-way.

Krajicek also explained that the decision to acquire the land "was solely the decision of the City . . . and was made by [Krajicek] and those individuals under [his] direct supervision." Krajicek's affidavit also stated that the construction of the deceleration lane had been completed. Haltom did not offer any responsive evidence.

The district court granted the City's motion for partial summary judgment. Later, at the parties' request, the district court dismissed the remaining cause of action. . . .

Haltom assigns, as restated, that the district court erred in failing to determine that the City condemned his property for an economic development purpose. . . .

EFFECT OF §76-710.04

Haltom's sole argument is that §76-710.04 prevents the City from using its eminent domain powers in the instant case.

We first summarize the nature of eminent domain. Eminent domain is defined generally as the power of the nation or a state, or authorized public agency, to take or to authorize the taking of private property for a public use without the owner's consent, conditioned upon the payment of just compensation. . . . The power of eminent domain is a sovereign power which exists independent of the Constitution of Nebraska. . . . The Legislature may delegate the power of eminent domain. . . . The Constitution of Nebraska and legislative enactments pursuant thereto are in no sense a grant of power, but are and should be treated as a limitation of the power of eminent domain.

The Legislature has delegated the power of eminent domain to cities of the metropolitan class, including the City, to acquire property for use as part of a public street pursuant to Neb. Rev. Stat. §14-366 (Reissue 2007). Section 14-366 provides as follows in this regard:

> The city may purchase or acquire by the exercise of the power of eminent domain private property or public property which is not at the time devoted to a specific public use, for the following purposes and uses: (1) For streets, alleys, avenues, parks, recreational areas, park-ways, playgrounds, boulevards, sewers, public squares, market places, and for other needed public uses or purposes authorized by this act, and for adding to, enlarging, widening, or extending any of the foregoing; and (2) for constructing or enlarging waterworks, gas plants, or other municipal utility purposes or enterprises authorized by this act.

. . . Thus, §14-366 specifically allows the City to condemn private property for use as a public street.

However, the Legislature recently subjected the power of eminent domain to an additional limitation. In 2006, after the U.S. Supreme Court determined in *Kelo v. New London*, 545 U.S. 469 (2005), that the transfer of land to a third party for the purpose of furthering a city's economic development plan was a sufficiently public use to permit the exercise of eminent domain, the Nebraska Legislature passed 2006 Neb. Laws, L.B. 924, to prohibit the use of eminent domain "if the taking is primarily for an economic development purpose." This is now codified at §76-710.04.

In pertinent part, §76-710.04 provides as follows:

> (1) A condemner may not take property through the use of eminent domain . . . if the taking is primarily for an economic development purpose.
> (2) For purposes of this section, economic development purpose means taking property for subsequent use by a commercial for-profit enterprise or to increase tax revenue, tax base, employment, or general economic conditions.
> (3) This section does not affect the use of eminent domain for:
> (a) Public projects or private projects that make all or a major portion of the property available for use by the general public or for use as a right-of-way, aqueduct, pipeline, or similar use.

Haltom argues that the deceleration lane primarily served the "economic development purpose" of providing vehicles access to the retailer. He argues that the addition of the deceleration lane will ultimately cause the expansion of the City's property and sales tax bases through providing the retailer's customers easier access to the retailer's parking lot.

However, we conclude that the plain language of §76-710.04 does not prevent the City from acquiring private property for use as a deceleration lane on an existing public road, even though the deceleration lane is contiguous to access to the retailer. Section 76-710.04(1) prohibits the use of eminent domain powers where the taking is "*primarily* for an economic development purpose." (Emphasis supplied.) Absent anything to the contrary, statutory language is to be given its plain meaning, and a court will not look beyond the statute or interpret it when the meaning of its words is plain, direct, and unambiguous. . . . Although the collateral consequences of the addition of a deceleration lane may include some enhancement to economic development, the primary purpose of the deceleration lane clearly is to promote traffic safety and the efficient flow of traffic on the City's streets.

Based on the undisputed evidence, there are four reasons sufficient to dispel Haltom's argument that the deceleration lane was primarily intended to fulfill an "economic development purpose" as defined by §76-710.04(2). First, the City did not take the property primarily "for subsequent use by a commercial for-profit enterprise." The real property was not acquired for the "use" of a commercial enterprise in any traditional sense. The City will be the owner of title to the land, and, because the land will be used as part of a public street, the primary users will be members of the public at large. Second, the City's acquisition of the real property at issue will not serve the primary purpose of "increas[ing] tax revenue" or "tax base." . . . Third, the City's acquisition of the land cannot be construed as primarily serving the purpose of increasing employment. While the construction of a deceleration lane will require the temporary use of labor, the purpose of a deceleration lane is unrelated to the creation of additional jobs. . . . Finally, the use of the property cannot be construed as primarily related to "general economic conditions," because there is no evidence that this affected the City's exercise of its eminent domain powers. The City's engineering department, which decided to acquire the property at issue, did so for reasons entirely unrelated to economic conditions. . . .

We acknowledge that the City's use of eminent domain to acquire land for a deceleration lane may provide an incidental and indirect benefit to the retailer. However, the plain language of §76-710.04 prohibits the exercise of eminent domain only where its *primary* purpose is economic development — not where economic development may be a collateral benefit. Many permissible uses of eminent domain provide collateral benefits to private industry. For example, when land is acquired by eminent domain for the purpose of a public building such as a school, nearby private enterprises, such as convenience stores or restaurants, may also benefit. The use of eminent domain to install utilities can provide collateral benefits to surrounding businesses. There are countless other instances where the exercise of eminent domain indirectly enhances economic development. Therefore, Haltom's argument-which focuses on a collateral consequence of eminent domain as opposed to its primary purpose — is without merit.

CONCLUSION

. . . We . . . conclude that the district court did not err in granting the City's motion for partial summary judgment, because §76-710.04 does not, as a matter of law, prohibit the City from using its eminent domain powers to acquire property for the purpose of constructing a deceleration lane on an existing public road for traffic control and safety purposes.

Notes and Comments

1. Reading *and* City of Omaha. Do you agree with the *Reading* Court that the *Kelo* case is distinguishable on its facts? Was the problem in *Reading* that the public agency didn't create a sufficient plan to avoid the finding that the taking's purpose was to confer a private benefit on an identifiable private party? The Pennsylvania post-*Kelo* legislation contains the phrase "to use it for private enterprise."

How widely does that phrase sweep? Will the interpretation of that phrase result in a flood of litigation?

As to *City of Omaha*: Does it matter that the motivation for the condemnation in *City of Omaha* was traffic needs generated by the retailer? Did the city bifurcate the project to get around the new legislation, with step one being the project approval and step two the traffic improvement necessitated by the project? Had the city used good planning and required the developer to fund the deceleration lane, would the city's use of condemnation be primarily for economic development? If your answer is yes, does the Nebraska court go beyond the dissent in *Kelo* in that the strict public use test is satisfied?

2. *Pretext and Road Building.* In *County of Hawai'i v. C & J Coupe Family Ltd. P'ship*, 242 P.3d 1136 (Haw. 2010), the county's asserted public purpose for a second condemnation instituted due to an agreement between the county and luxury sub-division developer did not demonstrate per se that the county's purpose for condemnation was pretextual. The burden was on the landowner and its insurer to show that the actual purpose of the condemnation was to bestow a private benefit or was a pretext for a primarily private benefit. There was no support in the record that complying with the agreement predominated over the public purpose of building a traffic corridor for the public at large. The court also found that, to overcome the prima facie presumption that condemnation was for a public purpose, a landowner must show that such a finding of public use is manifestly wrong. *See also Town of Matthews v. Wright*, 771 S.E.2d 328, 334 (N.C. Ct. App. 2015) ("The sequence of events leading up to the condemnation bolsters our conclusion that no public use or benefit is served by the condemnation. . . . The evidence shows that Mayor Taylor and some of the Commissioners considered personal conflicts between the Town and the Wrights in making the decision to condemn — rather than considering the public use or benefit of the condemnation.").

3. *Legislative Developments.* As these two cases indicate, *Kelo* unleashed a tsunami of journalistic and public outrage that led to a deluge of state legislation. *See* Me. Rev. Stat. Ann. Tit. 1, §816 (1) (prohibiting use of eminent domain for agriculture, fishing, forestry, residential, commercial, industrial, private office or retail, or for enhancement of tax revenue or transfer to an individual or a for-profit business entity); Neb. Rev. Stat. §76-710.04 (restricting eminent domain designed "primarily for an economic development purpose" with exceptions); Tex. Gov't Code Ann. §2206.001 (prohibiting condemnation for a particular private party nor for economic development unrelated to slum or blight elimination).

In turn, state courts have issued a series of decisions, like *Reading Area Water Auth.* and *City of Omaha*, construing them. As another example, in *State ex rel. Jackson v. Dolan*, 398 S.W.3d 472 (Mo. 2013), the Missouri Supreme Court found that a condemnation to support an expansion of port facilities on other land did not violate the "public use" clause. It did, however, violate a post-*Kelo* statute declaring that no condemning authority "shall acquire private property through the process of eminent domain for solely economic development purposes." Mo. Stats. Ann. §523.271.

In Andrew P. Morriss, Symbol or Substance? An Empirical Assessment of State Responses to *Kelo*, 17 Sup. Ct. Econ. Rev. 237 (2009), the author surveyed the state responses to *Kelo*. The article states that while 46 states adopted legislation, only about half adopted restrictions that were more than symbolic.

4. *Stadiums and Public Purpose.* Using redevelopment to build public stadiums for professional teams is often very controversial and gives rise to legal challenges about whether the "public use" clause is satisfied. *See, e.g., Goldstein v. Pataki*, 516 F.3d 50 (2d Cir. 2008), *cert. denied*, 554 U.S. 930 (2008) (rejecting challenge to redevelopment that included a sports arena and following *Kelo*); *Goldstein v. New York State Urban Dev. Corp.*, 879 N.Y.S.2d 524 (Sup. Ct. App. Div. 2009) (sustaining condemnation of 22 acres allowing a sports arena, thousands of dwelling units, and millions of square feet of office space); *Cascott, L.L.C. v. City of Arlington*, 278 S.W.3d 523 (Tex. Ct. App. 2009) (city's lease of condemned property to professional football team was valid, as the lease did not serve a purely private purpose in violation of state constitution but instead furthered the public purpose of the sports venue project for which the condemnation project was instituted). *See generally* Philip Weinberg, Eminent Domain for Private Sports Stadiums: Fair Ball or Foul?, 35 Envtl. L. 311 (2005).

5. *Revitalization Endangered?* The recent "public use" scholarship has also focused on other, specific aspects of use of the condemnation power. Here are some examples:

a. *Entrepreneurship and Market Process. See* Peter J. Boettke, Christopher J. Coyne and Peter T. Leeson, Takings, 8 Geo. J.L. & Pub. Pol'y 327 (2010) (discussing the harmful hidden effects of redevelopment on entrepreneurship and market process).

b. *Interference with Redevelopment Following Disasters and Other Critical Redevelopment Initiatives. See* John J. Costonis, Narrative as Lawmaking: The Anti-*Kelo* Story, 62 Planning & Envt'l L. 3 (No. 1 Jan. 2010) (arguing that condemnation authority is critical and that anti-*Kelo* rulings and initiatives interfere with redevelopment following disasters).

c. *Tension with Mixed Uses Furthering Diverse and Sustainable Communities. See* Steven J. Eagle, Urban Revitalization and Eminent Domain: Misinterpreting Jane Jacobs, 4 Alb. Gov't L. Rev. 106 (2011) (arguing that the twentieth century proactive government role, through massive redevelopment, is in tension with the mixed uses furthering diverse and sustainable communities that Jane Jacobs championed).

d. *Social Equity Concerns. See* Janet Thompson Jackson, What Is Property? Property Is Theft: The Lack of Social Justice in U.S. Eminent Domain Law, 84 St. John's L. Rev. 63 (2010) (arguing that while not all eminent domain is bad, circumstances exist under which the use of eminent domain is inherently unjust, including the historical and current use of blight as a pretext for the displacement of entire communities of color and economic development condemnations that transfer private property to private interests for profit).

6. *Undercompensation?* Is the problem with use of the eminent domain power that landowners are forced to give up their land without sharing in the land value increase anticipated to be generated by the project? Would most condemnees be satisfied if private economic redevelopment was accompanied by compensation set at an increment above market value?

Professor Christopher Serkin suggests that landowners are undercompensated in eminent domain proceedings. As a result, "the fact of the uncompensated increment means that eminent domain will predictably impose a burden on the condemnee relative to a voluntary transaction." Christopher Serkin, Response Testing the Value of Eminent Domain, 89 Tul. L. Rev. 115, 116 (2014). Does this "uncompensated increment" partially explain the often vehement opposition of landowners to having their property condemned? *See also* Amnon Lehavi and Amir N. Licht, Eminent Domain, Inc., 107 Colum. L. Rev. 1704 (2007) (advocating a choice for landowners facing condemnation of pre-project fair market value or obtaining an interest in the redeveloped project to avoid use of eminent domain); and Mark Seidenfeld, In Search of Robin Hood: Suggested Legislative Responses to *Kelo*, 23 J. Land Use & Envtl. L. 305 (2008) (recommending reform in the form of enhanced compensation).

7. *The End of Redevelopment?* The criticism of *Kelo* and of redevelopment generally might suggest that, rather than incremental amendments trying to tweak the system, states should consider abolishing redevelopment laws entirely. Perhaps surprisingly, at least a couple of states have agreed with that idea. In response to the fiscal crisis affecting the state's budget, the California Legislature—at the governor's urging—passed legislation essentially abolishing redevelopment agencies by redirecting the revenue stream from existing redevelopment. That action brought a deluge of challenges to the law's constitutionality, which the California Supreme Court ultimately rejected. *California Redevelopment Ass'n v. Matosantos,* 53 Cal. 4th 231, 267 P.3d 580 (2011). Arizona likewise abolished redevelopment. *See City of Apache Junction v. Doolittle,* 237 Ariz. 83, 84, 345 P.3d 138, 139 (Ct. App. 2015) ("In May 1999, the Legislature repealed the statute that enabled municipalities to use tax increment financing (TIF) to finance redevelopment projects. . . . ")

Given the problems defining "blight" and the difficulty interpreting the "public use" clause of the Fifth Amendment, is abolition of redevelopment the best solution?

8. The *Kelo* Aftermath. Adding fuel to the fire of criticism of *Kelo* was the aftermath of the redevelopment in New London, Connecticut. As the *Kelo* case details, the plan revolved around a research facility that the pharmaceutical company Pfizer would build. The eminent domain went forward; houses were raised, and Suzette Kelo's house was moved (at private expense). In the end, however, Pfizer merged and, after the merger, decided to withdraw from New London. Patrick McGeehan, Pfizer to Leave City that Won Land-Use Case, N.Y. Times (Nov. 12, 2009) found at http://www.nytimes.com/2009/11/13/nyregion/13pfizer.html?r=0 (last visited Nov. 12, 2016) ("Pfizer said it would pull 1,400 jobs out of New London within two years and move most of them a few miles away to a campus it owns in Groton, Conn., as a cost-cutting measure. It would leave behind the city's biggest office complex and an adjacent swath of barren land that was cleared of dozens of homes to make room for a hotel, stores and condominiums that were never built.").

Does the aftermath change your opinion about the use of eminent domain?

E. TRANSPORTATION PLANNING AND REDEVELOPMENT

Europeans are likely to walk, ride a bicycle, or take public transit for their transportation. In contrast, most Americans rely solely on the automobile. The dramatic difference in these urban designs has its origins in the aftermath of World War II. As the victor with enormous industrial capacity and pent-up demand for consumer goods and housing, America launched a program of sprawling suburbs patterned on automobile travel and low density, single-family homes. In contrast, Europe was decimated by war and suffering from economic chaos. Given limited land available for urban development and the lack of personal automobiles, the only strategy was to build high density apartment blocks linked by train, subway, or bus. The developed pattern became urban villages that were user friendly to transit users, cyclists, and pedestrians.

The excerpts of articles that follow are designed to be provocative. They allow the student to examine the issue of integration of land uses, including transit, with housing, employment, and recreation.

■ EDWARD J. SULLIVAN & JESSICA YEH, SMART GROWTH: STATE STRATEGIES IN MANAGING SPRAWL
45 Urb. Law. 349, 351–54 (2013)

II IDENTIFYING SMART GROWTH CHARACTERISTICS

Smart growth has been described as a mechanism of related policies and land use controls for containing growth and minimizing the effects of growth. Generally, smart growth development is characterized by compact and mixed-use development, and the promotion of a variety of transportation options for a reduction in vehicle-miles traveled (VMT), with the goal of preserving green space and environmentally sensitive areas. Accounting for the increased need for affordable housing in addition to these goals is also an indication of the success of smart growth planning.

A. COMPACT AND MIXED-USE DEVELOPMENT

One attribute of smart growth critical to reducing GHGs [greenhouse gases] is dense, compact development. Density is often inversely related to VMTs, as bigger lot sizes increase the distance between residential and work spaces, requiring residents to travel further. Mixing land uses as opposed to separating them (as is typical under traditional Euclidian zoning) complements high-density development. A range of uses, such as residential and commercial, available within one neighborhood allows residents to access these amenities conveniently and without the use of a vehicle.

Similarly, by maximizing the number of dwelling units or buildable area of a footprint, distances between destination points are reduced, minimizing VMT and GHG emissions because of the shorter distance residents are required to travel, while walking, biking, and public transit become more feasible. Further, mixed-use development in a compact pattern helps preserve open space and reduce sprawl, resulting in cost-savings for the public by reducing the need for publicly funded infrastructure.

B. PROMOTE A VARIETY OF TRANSPORTATION OPTIONS

Street design and layout are integral to smart growth and preventing sprawl. Streets, often improperly regarded as merely a way to move cars, are characterized by "high speed limits, long distances between intersections . . . [and] no sidewalks or bike lanes," which in turn "compels people to drive. . . ." In fact, "complete streets" are identified as multi-function thoroughfares, "designed to serve all modes of travel equally well," including walking, bicycling, and taking transit. Reducing the speed limit, landscaping curb extensions, designating bike lanes, and building shelters for transit users are all ways to maximize the number of people a complete street serves. When used, non-vehicular travel becomes easier and safer, helping to combat high VMTs and excess energy consumption.

However, the benefits of complete streets cannot be realized if streets are connected poorly. Often, transportation planning is done "one project at a time," resulting in inadequate networks of over-crowded streets. Smart growth emphasizes consideration of "macroscale characteristics" and regional needs in roadway planning. Lastly, to promote transit-oriented development (TOD), smart growth proponents recommend coordination between transit and land use agencies, so that transit riders are located near transit centers, street parking is limited, and the investment in public transit does not go to waste. . . .

D. ACCOUNT FOR AFFORDABLE HOUSING

. . . Certain types of growth management regimes can have the effect of exclusionary zoning and displacing low-income persons, especially where a legislative body does not ensure that the housing market is responsive to the needs of the regional population. This may result from growth management development restrictions that drive up property values. However, the impact on housing prices depends on the type of growth management regulations adopted, the land use system, and housing demand. Thus, while growth management programs in certain states may have the effect of making affordable housing less available, successful programs ensure that affordable housing is provided and commensurate with need. . . .

■ JAMES A. KUSHNER, A COMPARATIVE VISION OF THE CONVERGENCE OF ECOLOGY, EMPOWERMENT, AND THE QUEST FOR A JUST SOCIETY
54 U. Miami L. Rev. 301, 309-315 (1998)

The urban poor are a population disproportionately composed of people of color. They are relegated to communities without the tax base to provide safe streets, quality education, or even a semblance of job training and apprenticeship, which could lead to a decent standard of living through secure employment. This is simply unacceptable in the land of a world-class economic and political society. The pattern of community development based upon low-density suburban homes, requiring automobiles for access to employment, is inconsistent with the notion of a just society, if an increasingly significant portion of the population is priced out of that access.

The pattern of development in America's cities also fails to serve the nation's middle class. The suburbs were designed around a $2000 automobile and a house selling for under $10,000. In such a society, a decent wage was earned by the head of the household, while a homemaker was available to supervise and chauffeur children, maintain the home, and serve the family's quest for the pastoral quiet security of the country.

This contrasts sharply with the edge-city village of the twenty-first century. Today, the American suburban family requires a minimum of two cars requiring costly maintenance, insurance, and operation. Where families have two heads of household, both are likely to be employed. . . . The purchase and maintenance of a home is both more costly and time-consuming than desired by modern suburban dwellers. Moreover, automobile use makes living in the suburbs more dangerous for its youth. In fact, the risk of early death is greater in the suburbs than in the central city.[44] . . .

Fair housing can be viewed as a component of what is generally referred to as "sustainable communities." To environmentalists, the term sustainable communities refers to environmental policies of nondegradation and to economic and development decisions that are designed to renew resources and improve air and water quality. On the regional level, sustainable development calls for transit-oriented development patterns, providing for increased trips by pedestrians, bicyclists and transit users, and reduced automobile use. Coincidentally, this is also what many home seekers desire. Sustainable communities envision being able to walk to a village center main street for shopping, along and through attractive parks and pedestrian walkways with bicycle lanes. Ideally, a community should be linked by transit to other transit villages, some of which are higher density with mixed uses of shops, offices, and housing, with vibrant street and cafe life, while others are centers of manufacturing and commerce. . . .

The community of Hellersdorf in Berlin, Germany presents an interesting illustration of a sustainable community at the neighborhood level. Hellersdorf was a socialist suburban village of 130,000 on the northern political boundary of the city of Berlin within the former eastern sector of East Germany. Hellersdorf was not a pretty village, although it was a transit village, lying at the end of an S-Bahn, or surface train line. There was a complete lack of color and foliage in a village of uniformly-drab concrete apartment blocks, each building having at least one flat windowless wall. Hellersdorf had no city services, no telephones, and the apartment units were, like the whole of East Germany, deteriorating and in need of major rehabilitation. A pedestrian-friendly village center was non-existent; by American standards, Hellersdorf lacked even a decent restaurant.

When the Berlin Wall came down in 1989 and millions of East Germans migrated to the West in search of better housing and jobs, a third of Hellersdorf's units were vacated in the exodus. Undoubtedly, if Hellersdorf were located in an American city, it would have become a slum and the market would have awaited its final decline when a developer would purchase the land at low cost, bulldoze the structures, and perhaps redevelop the community for upper-income housing.

Despite the fact that Berlin was greatly overextended in developing its infrastructure to accommodate the relocation of the German capitol from Bonn following the reunification of Germany, and despite a high unemployment rate and a limited municipal budget, the city never hesitated in acting to stabilize one

44. *See* Jane Jacobs, The Death and Life of Great American Cities (1961); James Gerstenzang, Cars Make Suburbs Riskier Than Cities, Study Says, L.A. Times, Apr. 15, 1996, at A1 (Valley ed.) (reporting that more deaths and injuries resulted from cars in suburbs than from guns and drugs in urban settings; in 1995 in the Pacific Northwest, urban deaths occurred at a rate of 16 per 1,000 residents, while the rate was 19.2 in the suburbs; although crime death rates were 10 per 1,000 in cities and only 1 of 1,000 in suburbs, driving death rates were 18.2 per 1,000 in suburbs as compared to 6 of 1,000 in urban settings); Michael E. Lewyn, Are Spread Out Cities Really Safer? (Or, is Atlanta Safer than New York?), 41 Clev. St. L. Rev. 279 (1993).

of its worst neighborhoods. The city planted 15,000 trees, modified building facades to introduce variation and color, and brought in top mural artists to paint attractive varied mural designs on each building. In partnership with a large developer, Berlin rehabilitated the 130,000 housing units and commenced a program to privatize one-quarter of the public housing, offering subsidies to purchasing tenants. The private developer also undertook a massive commercial mixed-use project to build a multi-screen entertainment complex with offices, shops, and restaurants around and over the S-Bahn line.

The Hellersdorf experience demonstrates that, through mixing income groups within public housing, it is possible to bring about the de-stigmatization of neighborhoods. Today, Hellersdorf has a 100% occupancy rate with a waiting list, and each building has families in apartments facing an inner courtyard of new landscaping and modern playground and recreation facilities. Each building has a distinctive and attractive central courtyard. Thus, Hellersdorf has been transformed into a sustainable transit village. Berlin is now more stable and presents an attractive site for private investment, secure that neighborhoods will not be abandoned or investment dishonored.

■ PETER GORDON & HARRY W. RICHARDSON, ARE COMPACT CITIES A DESIRABLE PLANNING GOAL?
63 J. Am. Plan. Ass'n 232 (1997)

The revolution in information processing and telecommunications is accelerating the growth and dispersion of both economic activities and population, possibly moving towards the point where "geography is irrelevant." Yet, at the same time, many planners (and policymakers) advocate "compact cities" as an ideal, in contrast to the reality of "increasingly" spread-out metropolitan development. . . .

Some observers have argued that this is not an unconstrained choice, but influenced by instruments promoting suburbanization, policies such as the preferential income tax treatment of home mortgage interest, subsidies to automobile use, and the ubiquitous interstate highway system. . . .

The policy explanations of United States suburbanization often emphasize the argument that more subsidies are given to auto travel than to public transit. The opposite is true. Federal, state and local expenditures for highways (and parking) were $66.5 billion in 1991; revenues were $53.8 billion (81 percent recovery); federal, state and local expenditures for transit were $20.8 billion, while revenues were $8.8 billion (42 percent recovery). On a per-passenger-mile basis, the auto subsidy was 0.54 cents; the transit subsidy was 54 times as large, 29.42 cents. Moreover, the transit subsidies have been growing faster: the same calculations for 1981 show that the transit subsidy per passenger-mile was then "only" 33 times the auto subsidy.

The absence of congestion pricing and emissions fees is a widely acknowledged problem; it constitutes an implicit subsidy to auto users. While estimates of these costs cover a wide range, the Environmental Defense Fund suggested that air pollution costs per passenger mile in Southern California in 1991 were 3.6 cents and congestion costs were 7.5 cents. Donald Shoup suggested that there may be up to an additional 11 cents per passenger mile of parking subsidies for Los Angeles automobile commuters. In any event, even with these adjustments (and making the extreme assumption that these costs are "subsidies"), the full auto subsidy adds up to little more than 22 cents per passenger mile and still falls short of the transit subsidy.

Many consumer surveys have shown strong preferences for suburban living, and the link between household preferences and preferred spatial patterns is clear: "[in] evaluating the desirability of existing spatial patterns, revealed preferences of consumers, especially when they have persisted as long as they have in the U.S., must be given some weight." . . .

Because the spreading out of cities reduces markets for conventional public transit (especially fixed rail, which is spatially inflexible and usually oriented to downtown), it should surprise no one that the United States transit industry has been in decline for most of the twentieth century. Massive subsidies have not helped; they may have made matters worse. The Congressional Budget Office concluded that "despite more than 25 years of federal assistance, mass transit carries only about 5 percent of people who commute to work. The other 95 percent mostly use automobiles. . . . New federally assisted transit systems have not added to mass transit; instead, they have replaced flexible bus routes with costly fixed-route services to a few downtown areas, while the growth in jobs and population has been in the suburbs and in the smaller cities. At the same time, transit costs are rising: transit fleets in general are greatly underused, and the new transit systems have for the most part added to costs and to unused capacity without attracting riders from cars." A large (and still growing) number of studies echo this finding.

It appears that "neotraditional" neighborhoods, pedestrian pockets, mixed land use developments and other features of the New Urbanism do not make much of a difference. Cervero reports: "Over-all, focusing development near transit and designing communities to be more transit-friendly, by themselves, will have little bearing on people's travel choices." Moreover, Crane has suggested it is possible that neotraditional neighborhoods may increase rather than reduce automobile use, depending on case-by-case empirical considerations, because shorter origin-destination distances reduce the average cost per trip. Cheaper trips mean more *vehicle* trips, and it is conceivable, perhaps more probable than not, that total VMT (vehicle miles traveled) may increase. Thus, neotraditional neighborhoods may neither increase transit use nor reduce auto travel. . . .

High density settlement involves trade-offs between inevitable costs (congestion) and prospective benefits (agglomeration). High-rise buildings exist where they do only because the high costs of erecting and maintaining them were considered to be worth the economies realized through increased accessibility, communication and interaction, and the ease of face-to-face transactions. . . .

For most of the twentieth century, the highway system has been the major force for continued low-density settlement and suburbanization. The barriers of distance continue to "dissolve"; factories and offices continue to move to where employees want to live. Most commuting is now suburb-to-suburb, taking congestion pressures off traditional downtowns and allowing many to drive faster on less congested suburban highways. Suburb-to-central-city commuting continues to diminish. City forms continue to evolve beyond polycentricity to patterns of generalized dispersion. Recent research on the Los Angeles CMSA that compares employment concentrations in the three census years, 1970, 1980, and 1990, shows that all places qualifying as "centers" (based on trip generation densities) accounted for

19 percent of regional employment in 1970, 17 percent in 1980 and only 12 percent in 1990. Also, the number of places qualifying as centers declined from 20 (in 1970) to 12 (in 1990) during a period when the region's employment base grew from 3.6 million to 6.3 million jobs. This dispersion of economic activities, clear-cut in Los Angeles and perhaps evident in other metropolitan areas once the research has been done, is much more radical than implied by the adoption of concepts such as "edge cities," "satellite cities," "polycentricity," and "urban villages."

Rapid advances in telecommunications are now accelerating the decentralization trends set in motion by the advent of the automobile. In 1890, the "effective radius" of U.S. cities was said to be about 2 miles, based largely on pedestrian access. Dyckman reported that this had grown to 8 miles by 1920 because of the development of public transit, to 11 miles by 1950 (the diffusion of automobile ownership), and to 20-24 miles by the 1970s (the construction of urban freeways systems). The centrifugal trends have now accelerated because telecommunications access cannot be measured in terms of geographical distance. The locational choices open to both households and firms have expanded accordingly. In the extreme case, geography might become irrelevant. Peter Drucker suggests that "[o]ffice work, rather than office workers, will do the traveling." Proximity is becoming redundant. . . .

Those who misread these trends do so at considerable cost. For example, Asian real estate investors lost approximately one-half of their $77 billion investment in American cities over the last decade or so by focusing on downtown locations. Americans should not feel too smug, however, because their elected representatives have squandered, in total, even larger sums on dubious downtown renewal schemes. . . .

Notes and Comments

1. *Transit-Based Housing and Sprawl.* While Sullivan and Yeh argue for "smart growth," is it too late for that concept to significantly change land uses in the United State? Does it require effective regional planning? Along the same lines: is the Hellersdorf experience described by Professor Kushner possible to replicate in the United States? Would Gordon and Richardson's thesis be the same if some transit villages were built at densities between 60 and 100 dwelling units per acre as in many European communities? For a general discussion of transit-based housing designed to increase ridership and establish pedestrian villages around transit stops, *see* Michael Bernick & Robert Cervero, Transit Villages in the 21st Century (1997); Hank Dittmar & Gloria Ohland, The New Transit Town: Best Practices in Transit-Oriented Development (2004).

"Sprawl" is a general term, while in actuality a range of density and dispersal patterns exists. *See* George Galster et al., Wrestling Sprawl to the Ground: Defining and Measuring an Elusive Concept, 12 Hous. Pol'y Debate 681 (2001) (offering a conceptual definition considering distinct dimensions of land use patterns — density, continuity, concentration, clustering, centrality, nuclearity, mixed uses, and proximity — with "sprawl" defined as a low value in at least one dimension).

2. *Choosing Transit Priorities.* Transit systems often neglect bus riders, as expensive subway and light-rail projects are funded and designed to serve the more affluent suburban communities. The question of which type of transit is preferable arose in *Darensburg v. Metropolitan Transp. Comm'n*, 636 F.3d 511 (9th Cir. 2011). The

court rejected a challenge to the preference by the San Francisco Bay Area's regional transportation agency to give more funding to rail projects as opposed to local bus projects, even though minority ridership is far higher on local buses. The district court held that plaintiffs had established a prima facie case of disparate impact discrimination only as to the Commission's conduct in disproportionately selecting and allocating funding to rail projects, as opposed to bus projects.

The Ninth Circuit rejected the prima facie case finding. It ruled that, although plaintiffs' statistical evidence shows that minorities make up a greater percentage of the regional population of bus riders than rail riders, it does not necessarily follow that an expansion plan emphasizing rail projects over bus projects will harm minorities. The plaintiffs' theory forecloses altogether the possibility that the Commission could devise *any* rail-centered expansion that could benefit minority transit riders, while the evidence shows that Bay Area minorities already benefit substantially from rail service. In his concurring opinion, Judge Noonan declared that the plaintiffs failed to show any intent or disparate impact from the funding planned.

3. *Modal Splits.* The term "modal splits" describes the methods of trips made by a community's residents. Most Viennese own a transit pass purchased for a few hundred dollars a year, and the average Viennese uses public transit 600 times a year. John Pucher, Urban Travel Behavior as the Outcome of Public Policy: The Example of Modal-Split in Western Europe and North America, 54 J. Am. Plan. Ass'n 509 (1988) (automobile used for 82.3 percent of trips in U.S., 47.6 percent in West Germany, and 38.5 percent in Austria; public transport used for 3.4 percent in U.S., 11.4 percent in West Germany, and 38.5 percent in Austria; bicycle used for 0.7 percent in U.S., 9.6 percent in West Germany, and 38.5 percent in Austria, with walking 10.7 percent in U.S., 30.3 percent in West Germany, and 31.2 percent in Austria).

4. *Parking.* One of the problems with the imbalance between automobiles and public transport is that drivers are provided free roads and free parking, and landowners, including the carless, must pay for it. Donald C. Shoup, The High Cost of Free Parking (2005). In Michael Lewyn, What Would Coase Do? (About Parking Regulation), 22 Fordham Envtl. L. Rev. 89 (2010), the author argues that minimum parking requirements may in fact increase, rather than reduce, congestion, pollution, and greenhouse gas emissions. Thus, they may create, rather than reduce, some of the very harms they were enacted to prevent. This is the case for several reasons. Perhaps most importantly, minimum parking requirements, by artificially increasing the supply of parking, reduce the cost of parking and thus force landowners to not only build parking lots, but also give parking to motorists for free. *See also* Michael Lewyn and Shane Cralle, Planners Gone Wild: The Overregulation of Parking, 33 Wm. Mitchell L. Rev. 613 (2007).

5. *Transportation Plans.* The Clean Air Act requires the adoption of state implementation plans (SIPs) designed to reduce air pollution. The SIPs are partially directed to reducing automobile usage and encouraging alternatives such as carpools and transit, with disincentives such as higher parking and toll costs. Philip Weinberg, Public Transportation and Clean Air: Natural Allies, 21 Envtl. L. 1527 (1991). *See also Conservation Law Found. v. Federal Highway Admin.*, 24 F.3d 1465 (1st Cir. 1994) (Clean Air Act citizen suit is available in challenge to highway construction).

6. *Post-Kelo Consequences.* How will the post-*Kelo* condemnation limitations affect public transport developments? If blight removal is not permitted or is greatly

limited under state law, can transportation planning include transit-oriented development? If a station is planned, can project planning include condemnation to allow adjacent mixed-use, high-density residential neighborhoods? Are communities limited to amending the comprehensive plan or zoning in hopes that a private redeveloper will emerge?

F. ANTICOMPETITIVENESS

Because the promotion of economic development is a centerpiece of contemporary planning, issues of anticompetitiveness necessarily arise in the development and planning process. Indeed, in upcoming years competition among local governments for job development is likely to place anticompetitive behavior even more in the forefront of urban development.

Historically, local government was exposed to federal antitrust liability for zoning and other land use regulation, due to the monopolistic effect of zoning and the fact that the cooperation that often occurs between developers and a city might be characterized as a conspiracy. Later case law and congressional lawmaking have provided local governments with partial immunity from such liability. Nonetheless, some small range of exposure may remain.

The future may see much more concern over intra-regional and inter-regional competition for job development. As competition for jobs and growth increases, greater focus may be placed on the "pirating" of employers to move to new regions. The future emphasis in this field may look to subsidizing business through public infrastructure finance, such as through tax-supported government improvements. Government policy also may emphasize corporate and below-market industrial bonds where government supplies financing at rates lower than the market rate. These subsidies may come under fire as constituting a policy that adversely affects competition by using unfair methods to attract employers.

1. Federal Antitrust Law

By its very nature, the local government power to regulate land use and development carries the potential for exercising anticompetitive or monopoly power. Decisions to restrict growth may favor competing landowners or developers, and the danger of local government complicity in monopolization efforts by politically powerful developers is real. Local government acting in its enterprise (or market participant) capacity as a redevelopment sponsor may also be tempted to restrain competing development to obtain a competitive advantage in the pursuit of tax revenues.

Conspiracies in restraint of trade violate the Sherman Act. 15 U.S.C. §§1-2. Liability requires a conspiracy between local government and a private entity. *See Copperweld Corp. v. Independence Tube Corp.*, 467 U.S. 752 (1984). The conspiracy must be "unreasonable." *Standard Oil Co. v. United States*, 221 U.S. 1, 49 (1911). There does exist, however, an exemption for so-called state action. *Parker v. Brown*, 317 U.S. 341 (1943). Local government is exempt when it acts under state enabling legislation, such as under building codes, outdoor advertising regulation, or zoning. The scope of that exemption is discussed in the next case, *Columbia v. Omni Outdoor Advertising, Inc.*, 499 U.S. 365 (1991).

In addition to the state action exemption, because of tension with the First Amendment, noncriminal organized lobbying to influence public officials in the passage and enforcement of laws to engage in anticompetitive activities is also exempt from antitrust liability. This is the so-called *Noerr-Pennington* doctrine, which applies unless the lobbying is a "sham." *United Mine Workers v. Pennington*, 381 U.S. 657 (1965); *Eastern R.R. Presidents' Conference v. Noerr Motor Freight, Inc.*, 365 U.S. 127 (1961).

■ CITY OF COLUMBIA v. OMNI OUTDOOR ADVERTISING, INC.
499 U.S. 365 (1991)

Justice SCALIA delivered the opinion of the Court.

This case requires us to clarify the application of the Sherman Act to municipal governments and to the citizens who seek action from them.

Petitioner Columbia Outdoor Advertising, Inc. (COA), a South Carolina corporation, entered the billboard business in the city of Columbia, South Carolina (also a petitioner here), in the 1940s. By 1981 it controlled more than 95% of what has been conceded to be the relevant market. COA was a local business owned by a family with deep roots in the community, and enjoyed close relations with the city's political leaders. The mayor and other members of the city council were personal friends of COA's majority owner, and the company and its officers occasionally contributed funds and free billboard space to their campaigns. According to respondent Omni Outdoor Advertising, Inc., these beneficences were part of a "longstanding" "secret anticompetitive agreement" whereby "the City and COA would each use their [*sic*] respective power and resources to protect . . . COA's monopoly position," in return for which "City Council members received advantages made possible by COA's monopoly."

In 1981, Omni, a Georgia corporation, began erecting billboards in and around the city. COA responded to this competition in several ways. . . . Finally (and this is what gives rise to the issue we address today), COA executives met with city officials to seek the enactment of zoning ordinances that would restrict billboard construction. COA was not alone in urging this course; concerned about the city's recent explosion of billboards, a number of citizens, including writers of articles and editorials in local newspapers, advocated restrictions.

In the spring of 1982, the city council passed an ordinance requiring the council's approval for every billboard constructed in downtown Columbia. This was later amended to impose a 180-day moratorium on the construction of billboards throughout the city, except as specifically authorized by the council. A state court invalidated this ordinance on the ground that its conferral of unconstrained discretion upon the city council violated both the South Carolina and Federal Constitutions. The city then requested the State's regional planning authority to conduct a comprehensive analysis of the local billboard situation as a basis for developing a final, constitutionally valid, ordinance. In September 1982, after a series of public hearings and numerous meetings involving city officials, Omni, and COA (in all of which, according to Omni, positions contrary to COA's were not genuinely considered), the city council passed a new ordinance restricting the size, location, and spacing of billboards. These restrictions, particularly those on spacing, obviously benefited COA, which already had its billboards in place; they severely hindered Omni's ability to compete.

In November 1982, Omni filed suit against COA and the city in Federal District Court, charging that they had violated §§1 and 2 of the Sherman Act, 15 U.S.C. §§1, 2,[1] as well as South Carolina's Unfair Trade Practices Act. Omni contended, in particular, that the city's billboard ordinances were the result of an anticompetitive conspiracy between city officials and COA that stripped both parties of any immunity they might otherwise enjoy from the federal antitrust laws. In January 1986, after more than two weeks of trial, a jury returned general verdicts against the city and COA on both the federal and state claims. It awarded damages, before trebling, of $600,000 on the §1 Sherman Act claim, and $400,000 on the §2 claim.[2] The jury also answered two special interrogatories, finding specifically that the city and COA had conspired both to restrain trade and to monopolize the market. . . .

II

In the landmark case of *Parker v. Brown*, 317 U.S. 341 (1943), we rejected the contention that a program restricting the marketing of privately produced raisins, adopted pursuant to California's Agricultural Prorate Act, violated the Sherman Act. Relying on principles of federalism and state sovereignty, we held that the Sherman Act did not apply to anticompetitive restraints imposed by the States "as an act of government."

Since *Parker* emphasized the role of sovereign *States* in a federal system, it was initially unclear whether the governmental actions of political subdivisions enjoyed similar protection. In recent years, we have held that *Parker* immunity does not apply directly to local governments. . . . We have recognized, however, that a municipality's restriction of competition may sometimes be an authorized implementation of state policy, and have accorded *Parker* immunity where that is the case.

The South Carolina statutes under which the city acted in the present case authorize municipalities to regulate the use of land and the construction of buildings and other structures within their boundaries. It is undisputed that, as a matter of state law, these statutes authorize the city to regulate the size, location, and spacing of billboards. . . .

Besides authority to regulate, however, the *Parker* defense also requires authority to suppress competition — more specifically, "clear articulation of a state policy to authorize anticompetitive conduct" by the municipality in connection with its regulation. . . . We have rejected the contention that this requirement can be met

1. Section 1 provides in pertinent part: "Every contract, combination in the form of trust or otherwise, or conspiracy, in restraint of trade or commerce among the several States, or with foreign nations, is declared to be illegal." Section 2 provides in pertinent part: "Every person who shall monopolize, or attempt to monopolize, or combine or conspire with any other person or persons, to monopolize any part of the trade or commerce among the several States, or with foreign nations, shall be deemed guilty of a felony."

2. The monetary damages in this case were assessed entirely against COA, the District Court having ruled that the city was immunized by the Local Government Antitrust Act of 1984, 98 Stat. 2750, as amended, 15 U.S.C. §§34-36, which exempts local governments from paying damages for violations of the federal antitrust laws. . . . Respondent has not challenged that determination in this Court, and we express no view on the matter.

only if the delegating statute explicitly permits the displacement of competition. . . . It is enough, we have held, if suppression of competition is the "foreseeable result" of what the statute authorizes. . . . That condition is amply met here. The very purpose of zoning regulation is to displace unfettered business freedom in a manner that regularly has the effect of preventing normal acts of competition, particularly on the part of new entrants. A municipal ordinance restricting the size, location, and spacing of billboards (surely a common form of zoning) necessarily protects existing billboards against some competition from newcomers.

The Court of Appeals was therefore correct in its conclusion that the city's restriction of billboard construction was prima facie entitled to *Parker* immunity. The Court of Appeals upheld the jury verdict, however, by invoking a "conspiracy" exception to *Parker* that has been recognized by several Courts of Appeals. . . .

There is no such conspiracy exception. The rationale of *Parker* was that, in light of our national commitment to federalism, the general language of the Sherman Act should not be interpreted to prohibit anticompetitive actions by the States in their governmental capacities as sovereign regulators. . . . [T]his immunity does not necessarily obtain where the State acts not in a regulatory capacity but as a commercial participant in a given market. . . . Since it is both inevitable and desirable that public officials often agree to do what one or another group of private citizens urges upon them, such an exception would virtually swallow up the *Parker* rule: All anticompetitive regulation would be vulnerable to a "conspiracy" charge.

Omni suggests, however, that "conspiracy" might be limited to instances of governmental "corruption," defined variously as "abandonment of public responsibilities to private interests," "corrupt or bad faith decisions," and "selfish or corrupt motives." Ultimately, Omni asks us not to define "corruption" at all, but simply to leave that task to the jury. . . .

A conspiracy exception narrowed along such vague lines is similarly impractical. Few governmental actions are immune from the charge that they are "not in the public interest" or in some sense "corrupt." . . . The fact is that virtually all regulation benefits some segments of the society and harms others; and that it is not universally considered contrary to the public good if the net economic loss to the losers exceeds the net economic gain to the winners. *Parker* was not written in ignorance of the reality that determination of "the public interest" in the manifold areas of government regulation entails not merely economic and mathematical analysis but value judgment, and it was not meant to shift that judgment from elected officials to judges and juries. . . .

III

While *Parker* recognized the States' freedom to engage in anticompetitive regulation, it did not purport to immunize from antitrust liability the private parties who urge them to engage in anticompetitive regulation. However, it is obviously peculiar in a democracy, and perhaps in derogation of the constitutional right "to petition the Government for a redress of grievances," U.S. Const., Amdt. 1, to establish a category of lawful state action that citizens are not permitted to urge. Thus, beginning with *Eastern Railroad Presidents Conference v. Noerr Motor Freight, Inc.,* we have developed a corollary to *Parker:* The federal antitrust laws also do not regulate the conduct of private individuals in seeking anticompetitive action from the government. This doctrine, like *Parker*, rests ultimately upon a recognition that the antitrust laws, "tailored as they are for the business world, are not at all appropriate for application in the political arena." That a private party's political motives are selfish is irrelevant: "*Noerr* shields from the Sherman Act a concerted effort to influence public officials regardless of intent or purpose." . . .

Noerr recognized, however, what has come to be known as the "sham" exception to its rule: "There may be situations in which a publicity campaign, ostensibly directed toward influencing governmental action, is a mere sham to cover what is actually nothing more than an attempt to interfere directly with the business relationships of a competitor and the application of the Sherman Act would be justified." . . .

The "sham" exception to *Noerr* encompasses situations in which persons use the governmental *process*—as opposed to the *outcome* of that process—as an anticompetitive weapon. A classic example is the filing of frivolous objections to the license application of a competitor, with no expectation of achieving denial of the license but simply in order to impose expense and delay. . . . A "sham" situation involves a defendant whose activities are "not genuinely aimed at procuring favorable government action" at all, not one "who 'genuinely seeks to achieve his governmental result, but does so *through improper means.*'" . . .

Neither of the Court of Appeals' theories for application of the "sham" exception to the facts of the present case is sound. The court reasoned, first, that the jury could have concluded that COA's interaction with city officials "'was actually nothing more than an attempt to interfere directly with the business relations [sic] of a competitor.'" . . . This analysis relies upon language from *Noerr*, but ignores the import of the critical word "directly." Although COA indisputably set out to disrupt Omni's business relationships, it sought to do so not through the very process of lobbying, or of causing the city council to consider zoning measures, but rather through the ultimate *product* of that lobbying and consideration, viz., the zoning ordinances. The Court of Appeals' second theory was that the jury could have found "that COA's purposes were to delay Omni's entry into the market and even to deny it a meaningful access to the appropriate city administrative and legislative fora." . . . But the purpose of delaying a competitor's entry into the market does not render lobbying activity a "sham," unless (as no evidence suggested was true here) the delay is sought to be achieved only by the lobbying process itself, and not by the governmental action that the lobbying seeks. . . .

Omni urges that if, as we have concluded, the "sham" exception is inapplicable, we should use this case to recognize another exception to *Noerr* immunity—a "conspiracy" exception, which would apply when government officials conspire with a private party to employ government action as a means of stifling competition. . . .

Giving full consideration to this matter for the first time, we conclude that a "conspiracy" exception to *Noerr* must be rejected. . . . As we have described, *Parker* and *Noerr* are complementary expressions of the principle that the antitrust laws regulate business, not politics; the former decision protects the States' acts of governing, and the latter the citizens' participation in government. Insofar as the identification of an immunity-destroying "conspiracy" is concerned, *Parker* and *Noerr* generally present two faces of the same coin. The *Noerr*-invalidating conspiracy alleged here is just the *Parker*-invalidating conspiracy viewed from the standpoint of the private-sector participants rather than the governmental participants. The same factors which, as we have described above, make it impracticable or beyond the purpose of the antitrust laws to identify and invalidate lawmaking that has been infected by selfishly motivated agreement with private interests likewise make it impracticable or beyond that scope to identify and invalidate lobbying that has produced selfishly motivated agreement with public officials. . . .

Notes and Comments

1. *Home Rule.* While some states and units of local government adhere to "Dillon's Rule" (discussed in Chapter 2) under which cities enjoy only specific powers delegated to them through state enabling legislation, an increasing number of local governments enjoy so-called home rule. Under the variations of home rule, communities possess broader police powers, or in the case of charter cities, those powers contained in a locally adopted charter. The local government, however, remains subject to state legislation preempting the exercise of local regulation.

Does *City of Columbia* discriminate against home rule cities? By requiring specific state enabling legislation that authorizes the anticompetitive activity or regulation, does the Court categorize local governments by not recognizing the autonomy of home rule jurisdictions to adopt regulations authorized by the city charter and not in violation of any state legislation?

2. *Anticompetitive Behavior.* The *City of Columbia* decision seems to authorize blanket immunity for anticompetitive actions under zoning ordinances. A later Supreme Court decision, *Federal Trade Comm'n v. Phoebe Putney Health Systems, Inc.,* __ U.S. __, 133 S. Ct. 1003 (2013), found that state laws authorizing a hospital authority did not provide the same kind of anticompetitive authority. The court rejected the court of appeal's conclusion that the Georgia Legislature "must have anticipated" that acquisitions of other hospitals by hospital authorities would produce anticompetitive effects. 133 S. Ct. at 2012. By contrast, in *City of Columbia* the Court said, "the suppression of competition in the billboard market was the foreseeable result of a state statute authorizing municipalities to adopt zoning ordinances regulating the construction of buildings and other structures." *Id.* at 1011.

The authority to engage in anticompetitive conduct through zoning seems well-established, but are there limits? Would a community's desire to retain the vitality of an existing retail area justify the denial of rezoning to commercial use to accommodate potential competitors? Would such anticompetitive legislation violate the Sherman Act? *See G&G Freemont, LLC v. City of Las Vegas,* 2016 WL 4257766 (D. Nev. 2016) (city was immune from liability under *Parker* where "the Las Vegas City Charter confers to the City the power to regulate liquor in a variety of ways" and the legislature "must have reasonably foreseen that the suppression of competition could be a result of these activities"). What if an agency running a convention facility requires lessees to use the convention agency's own employees? *United Nat'l Maint., Inc. v. San Diego Convention Ctr., Inc.,* 766 F.3d 1002, (9th Cir. 2014) (immune where state legislation created a commission that would "manage the use" of the convention center).

Finally, don't forget that, even if a plaintiff can avoid the reach of *City of Columbia,* it still must state a claim for relief under the antitrust laws. *Wooster Indus. Park, LLC v. City of Wooster,* 55 F. Supp. 3d 990, 997 (N.D. Ohio 2014) (plaintiffs' complaint "focuses on possible harm to themselves" but does not allege how the city defendants' actions, in approving a tower that would allow the city to place its telecommunications equipment on it for free, "'harmed *competition* in the relevant market, as the Sherman Act requires.' . . .").

3. *Shams and the Reach of* Noerr-Pennington. How far does the *Noerr-Pennington* doctrine reach? Plainly, most land use lobbying will be protected. For example, in *Harrington v. Hall County Bd. of Supervisors,* 2016 WL 1274534 (D. Neb. 2016), plaintiffs charged individual defendants opposed to a proposed strip club with "creating, promoting, circulating, distributing, copying, publishing, signing and submitting a petition." The court easily found that allegation insufficient.

The *Noerr-Pennington* line of cases recognizes that a defendant will not be immune if the petitioning activity is merely "a sham." The court had quite a workout with this exception in *Hanover 3201 Realty, LLC v. Village Supermarkets, Inc.,* 806 F.3d 162 (3d Cir. 2015). The plaintiff owned land and entered into a deal whereby it would lease land to a supermarket but was required to secure the needed land use and environmental permits for the deal to go through. Defendants, who owned a competing supermarket, undertook a lengthy series of actions challenging the issuance of every permit required. The court of appeal found the plaintiff's allegations of sham sufficient as alleging "indicia of bad faith." 806 F.3d at 181. The court cited numerous allegations of bad faith, including that after initially requesting a hearing, defendants filed an amended request for a hearing five months later whose sole purpose "was to slow down the review process." *Id.* at 181. A dissenting opinion found the allegations insufficient.

4. *The Public Entity as Market Participant.* What if the city is not merely regulating but is acting as a market participant—i.e., engaging in an activity in a market in competition with others in that market? Does *City of* Columbia immunize such action? Neither the *City of Columbia* decision nor the Court's 2013 decision in *Federal Trade Comm'n v. Phoebe Putney Health Sys., Inc.,* discussed above in Note 2, addressed the question.

In *Buena Vista Estates, Inc. v. Santa Fe Solid Waste Mgmt. Agency,* 2016 WL 3574170 (D. N.M. 2016), a county-run agency sold aggregate from its landfill. The county then passed a moratorium that prevented other companies from competing. When the defendants raised *City of Columbia*, the plaintiff argued that the court ought to recognize a "market participant" exception to the immunity established by that case—i.e., the immunity would not apply where the public entity was actually competing in the market. The court refused to recognize such an exception, noting that the sale of aggregate here was "merely a byproduct of Defendants' activity in their regulatory capacity [of running a landfill], rather than Defendants' primary activity." *Id.* at *9.

Should the Supreme Court recognize such a market participant exception?

5. *Corruption and Conspiracy.* What is the dividing line between lobbying and corruption? In *Kearney v. Foley & Lardner, LLP,* 556 F.3d 826 (9th Cir. 2009), the court found that a governmental entity or official may receive immunity in an action brought under the Racketeer Influenced and Corrupt Organizations Act (RICO) for petitioning involved in an eminent domain proceeding. Agents of that litigation may benefit from that immunity as well, where the litigation was protected by the *Noerr-Pennington* doctrine. In contrast, a district court in Massachusetts found that allegations of conspiracy were sufficient to allege a due process violation. Among other acts, the plaintiffs alleged that the defendants refused to even consider the plaintiffs' submissions for a power plant approval "despite repeated reversals by the

state courts." *Brockton Power LLC v. City of Brockton*, 948 F. Supp. 2d 48, 69 (D. Mass. 2013). *See also EDF Renewable Dev., Inc. v. Tritec Real Estate Co., Inc.*, 147 F. Supp. 3d 63 (E.D.N.Y. 2015) (overtly corrupt conduct, such as threatening or bribing a public official, has been ruled as outside *Noerr-Pennington*).

6. *Local Government Immunity.* The Local Government Antitrust Act of 1984 bars the recovery of damages, costs, or attorney's fees against local governments. 15 U.S.C. §35(a) (2016). The 1984 legislation, however, does not entirely eliminate exposure to antitrust litigation for a local government, as injunctive relief remains available as a remedy. The law would not bar a treble damage judgment against private persons who act beyond the cloak of the local government official's action.

2. State Incentives

The focus of the anti-competition cases in the land use field has been on discrimination against disfavored developers. Should the focus shift to inter-regional economic activities? For example, do legal theories exist to challenge the pirating of "rust belt" companies by developing "sun belt" cities? As you read the following case, ask whether it is an example of pirating that should be condemned, or whether it is just good, proactive planning for economic development that should be praised.

■ MAREADY v. CITY OF WINSTON-SALEM
467 S.E.2d 615 (N.C. 1996)

WHICHARD, Justice.

William F. Maready, instituted this action against the City of Winston-Salem, its Board of Aldermen, Forsyth County, its Board of Commissioners, and Winston-Salem Business, Inc. Plaintiff contends that N.C.G.S. §158-7.1, which authorizes local governments to make economic development incentive grants to private corporations, is unconstitutional because it violates the public purpose clause of the North Carolina Constitution. . . .

This action challenges twenty-four economic development incentive projects entered into by the City or County pursuant to N.C.G.S. §158-7.1. The projected investment by the City and County in these projects totals approximately $13,200,000. The primary source of these funds has been taxes levied by the City and County on property owners in Winston-Salem and Forsyth County. City and County officials estimate an increase in the local tax base of $238,593,000 and a projected creation of over 5500 new jobs as a result of these economic development incentive programs. They expect to recoup the full amount of their investment within three to seven years. The source of the return will be revenues generated by the additional property taxes paid by participating corporations. To date, all but one project has met or exceeded its goal.

The typical procedures the City and County observe in deciding to make an economic development incentive expenditure are as follows: A determination is made that participation by local government is necessary to cause a project to go forward in the community. Officials then apply a formula set out in written guidelines to determine the maximum amount of assistance that can be given to the receiving corporation. The amounts actually committed are usually much less than the maximum. The expenditures are in the form of reimbursement to the recipient for purposes such as on-the-job training, site preparation, facility upgrading, and parking. If a proposal satisfies the guidelines as well as community needs, it is submitted to the appropriate governing body for final approval at a regularly scheduled public meeting. If a project is formally approved, it is administered pursuant to a written contract and to the applicable provisions and limitations of N.C.G.S. §158-7.1.

Article V, Section 2(1) of the North Carolina Constitution provides that "[t]he power of taxation shall be exercised in a just and equitable manner, for public purposes only." In *Mitchell v. North Carolina Indus. Dev. Fin. Auth.*, 159 S.E.2d 745 (1968), Justice (later Chief Justice) Sharp, writing for a majority of this Court, stated:

> The power to appropriate money *from* the public treasury is no greater than the power to levy the tax which put the money in the treasury. Both powers are subject to the constitutional proscription that tax revenues may not be used for private individuals or corporations, no matter how benevolent.

In determining whether legislation serves a public purpose, the presumption favors constitutionality. Reasonable doubt must be resolved in favor of the validity of the act. . . .

In exercising the State's police power, the General Assembly may legislate for the protection of the general health, safety, and welfare of the people. It may "experiment with new modes of dealing with old evils, except as prevented by the Constitution." . . . The initial responsibility for determining what constitutes a public purpose rests with the legislature, and its determinations are entitled to great weight. . . .

The enactment of N.C.G.S. §158-7.1 leaves no doubt that the General Assembly considers expenditures of public funds for the promotion of local economic development to serve a public purpose. Under this statute,

> [e]ach county and city in this State is authorized to make appropriations for the purposes of aiding and encouraging the location of manufacturing enterprises, making industrial surveys and locating industrial and commercial plants in or near such city or in the county; encouraging the building of railroads or other purposes which, in the discretion of the governing body of the city or of the county commissioners of the county, *will increase the population, taxable property, agricultural industries and business prospects of any city or county.* These appropriations may be funded by the levy of property taxes pursuant to G.S. 153A-149 and 160A-209 and by the allocation of other revenues whose use is not otherwise restricted by law.

N.C.G.S. §158-7.1(a) (1994) (emphasis added). When making amendments to chapter 158 and adding other provisions designed to promote economic development, the General Assembly mandated: "This act, being necessary for the prosperity and welfare of the State and its inhabitants, shall be liberally construed to effect these purposes." . . . ([A]mending the Constitution to permit cities and counties to issue bonds to finance the public portion of economic development projects and to authorize counties and cities to accept as consideration for a conveyance or lease of property to a private party the amount of increased tax revenue expected to be generated by the improvements to be constructed on the property). The General

Assembly has further demonstrated its commitment to economic development by enacting several other statutes that permit local governments to appropriate and spend public funds for such purposes. These include, *inter alia:*

> *N.C.G.S. §158-8 through -15,* which establish regional economic development commissions and authorize local governments to create or join economic development commissions and to support them with their funds.
>   *N.C.G.S. §160A-209(c),* which provides: "Each city may levy property taxes for one or more of the following purposes . . . : (10b) Economic Development — To provide for economic development as authorized by G.S. 158-12. . . . (17a) Industrial Development — To provide for industrial development as authorized by G.S. 158-7.1."
>   *N.C.G.S. §153A-149(c),* which provides: "Each county may levy property taxes for one or more of the purposes listed in this subsection . . . : (10b) Economic Development — To provide for economic development as authorized by G.S. 158-12. . . . (16a) Industrial Development — To provide for industrial development as authorized by G.S. 158-7.1."

These enactments clearly indicate that N.C.G.S. §158-7.1 is part of a comprehensive scheme of legislation dealing with economic development whereby the General Assembly is attempting to authorize exercise of the power of taxation for the perceived public purpose of promoting the general economic welfare of the citizens of North Carolina.

While legislative declarations such as these are accorded great weight, ultimate responsibility for the public purpose determination rests with this Court. . . . This Court . . . has not specifically defined "public purpose," however; rather, it has expressly declined to "confine public purpose by judicial definition[, leaving]'each case to be determined by its own peculiar circumstances as from time to time it arises.'" As summarized by Justice Sharp in *Mitchell:*

> A slide-rule definition to determine public purpose for all time cannot be formulated; the concept expands with the population, economy, scientific knowledge, and changing conditions. As people are brought closer together in congested areas, the public welfare requires governmental operation of facilities which were once considered exclusively private enterprises, and necessitates the expenditure of tax funds for purposes which, in an earlier day, were not classified as public. Often public and private interests are so co-mingled that it is difficult to determine which predominates. It is clear, however, that for a use to be public its benefits must be in common and not for particular persons, interests, or estates; the ultimate net gain or advantage must be the public's as contradistinguished from that of an individual or private entity. . . .

Plaintiff also argues, and the trial court apparently agreed, that this question falls squarely within the purview of *Mitchell v. North Carolina Industrial Development Financing Authority.* There we held unconstitutional the Industrial Facilities Financing Act, a statute that authorized issuance of industrial revenue bonds to finance the construction and equipping of facilities for private corporations. . . . We find *Mitchell* distinguishable. . . .

[T]he holding in *Mitchell* clearly indicates that the Court considered private industry to be the primary benefactor of the legislation and considered any benefit to the public purely incidental. Notwithstanding its recognition that any lawful business in a community promotes the public good, the Court held that the "Authority's primary function, to acquire sites and to construct and equip facilities for private industry, is not for a public use or purpose." . . . The Court rightly concluded that direct state aid to a private enterprise, with only limited benefit accruing to the public, contravenes fundamental constitutional precepts. . . .

[T]he Court's focal concern in *Mitchell*, . . . the means used to achieve economic growth, has . . . been removed by constitutional amendment. In 1973 Article V, Section 2(7) was added to the North Carolina Constitution, specifically allowing direct appropriation to private entities for public purposes. This section provides:

> The General Assembly may enact laws whereby the State, any county, city or town, and any other public corporation may contract with and appropriate money to any person, association, or corporation for the accomplishment of public purposes only.

N.C. Const. art. V, §2(7). "[U]nder subsection (7) *direct disbursement* of public funds to private entities is a constitutionally permissible *means* of accomplishing a public purpose provided there is statutory authority to make such appropriation." Hence, the constitutional problem under the public purpose doctrine that the Court perceived in *Mitchell* . . . no longer exists. . . .

The majority in *Mitchell* posed the question: "Is it *today* a proper function of government for the State to provide a site and equip a plant for private industrial enterprise?" . . . This explicit recognition of the importance of contemporary circumstances in assessing the public purpose of governmental endeavors highlights the essential fluidity of the concept. While the *Mitchell* majority answered the question in the negative, the passage of time and accompanying societal changes now suggest a positive response. . . .

The General Assembly may provide for, *inter alia*, roads, schools, housing, health care, transportation, and occupational training. It would be anomalous to now hold that a government which expends large sums to alleviate the problems of its citizens through multiple humanitarian and social programs is proscribed from promoting the provision of jobs for the unemployed, an increase in the tax base, and the prevention of economic stagnation.

This Court most recently addressed the public purpose question in *Madison Cablevision v. City of Morganton*. . . . The Court stated that "[t]wo guiding principles have been established for determining that a particular undertaking by a municipality is for a public purpose: (1) it involves a reasonable connection with the convenience and necessity of the particular municipality; and (2) the activity benefits the public generally, as opposed to special interests or persons." . . . Application of these principles here mandates the conclusion that N.C.G.S. §158-7.1 furthers a public purpose and hence is constitutional.

As to the first prong, whether an activity is within the appropriate scope of governmental involvement and is reasonably related to communal needs may be evaluated by determining how similar the activity is to others which this Court has held to be within the permissible realm of governmental action. We conclude that the activities N.C.G.S. §158-7.1 authorizes are in keeping with those accepted as within the scope of permissible governmental action. . . .

As to the second prong of the *Madison Cablevision* inquiry, under the expanded understanding of public purpose, even the most innovative activities N.C.G.S. §158-7.1 permits are constitutional so long as they primarily benefit the public and not a private party. "It is not necessary, in order that a use may be regarded as public, that it should be for the use and benefit of every citizen in the community." . . . Moreover, an expenditure does not lose its public purpose merely because it involves a private actor. Generally, if an act will promote the welfare of a state or a local government and its citizens, it is for a public purpose.

Viewed in this light, section 158-7.1 clearly serves a public purpose. Its self-proclaimed end is to "increase the population, taxable property, agricultural industries and business prospects of any city or county." N.C.G.S. §158-7.1(a). However, it is the natural consequences flowing therefrom that ensure a net public benefit. The expenditures this statute authorizes should create a more stable local economy by providing displaced workers with continuing employment opportunities, attracting better paying and more highly skilled jobs, enlarging the tax base, and diversifying the economy. Careful planning pursuant to the statute should enable optimization of natural resources while concurrently preserving the local infrastructure. The strict procedural requirements the statute imposes provide safeguards that should suffice to prevent abuse. . . .

We therefore hold that N.C.G.S. §158-7.1, which permits the expenditure of public moneys for economic development in incentive programs, does not violate the public purpose clause of the North Carolina Constitution. Accordingly, the decision of the trial court on this issue is reversed. . . .

Notes and Comments

1. *Public Purpose as Public Use?* Does the quote in *Maready* from *Mitchell*, stating that tax revenues may not be used for private individuals or corporations, present the same *Kelo*-like problem but focused on spending? Does the 1973 North Carolina constitutional amendment authorizing contracts for public purposes distinguish spending from condemnation? Should the type of economic incentive at issue in *Maready* be analyzed in the same manner as the redevelopment at issue in *Kelo?*

2. *Challenges from Competitors.* May existing hotels challenge a city subsidy for a new hotel in a redevelopment project, in a revitalization neighborhood or enterprise zone, or at the city's convention center? The issue arose in *1405 Hotel, LLC v. Colorado Economic Dev. Comm'n*, 370 P.3d 309 (Colo. App. 2015). The Colorado Economic Development Commission awarded a tourism subsidy for a new hotel and conference center. Thereafter, the operator withdrew and sold its brand name and management rights to Marriott International. Other hotels then sued arguing that, instead of awarding the money under the previous grant, the Commission must require an application for a new grant. The court of appeal held that the hotels lacked standing to sue. It reasoned that, even if it assumed the new project would cause harm to the existing hotels, the harm was "indirect" because it would result from lawful competition in the tourism marketplace. Do you agree with that reasoning?

3. *The Wide Range of State and Local Economic Incentives.* The types of incentives found in *Maready* are part of a much larger use of economic incentives at the state and local level to attract new development. Those incentives are surveyed in Randle B. Pollard, "Was the Deal Worth It?": The Dilemma of States with Ineffective Economic Incentive Programs, 11 Hastings Bus. L.J. 1 (2015). One type of incentive now used is the "financial incentive":

Financial incentives provide economic value to a business without a reduction of tax liability. These incentives may be grants and other nonrecourse revenue, direct or subsidized loans, financing funded by tax revenue generated from a particular geographic area, known as tax increment financing ("TIF"), municipal bond financing, public utilities reduction, and infrastructure improvements. Grants and other nonrecourse revenue are simply funds from state or local government or quasi-government entities given directly to private businesses while direct and subsidized loans provide private businesses with loans at interest rates at or below market rates. . . .

Id. at 10. Another is the "direct investment incentive" in which "State and local governments with direct investment incentive programs use public funds to make equity investments into privately owned businesses." By using these incentives, "[q]uintessentially, state and local governments become owners of a private business." *Id.* at 12.

4. *Government as Land Developer.* In discussing public agency land developers, Professor George Lefcoe points to the potential danger to a community when the agency offers subsidies to industry or a developer:

[P]rosperous firms are able to buy or lease their sites so cheaply that inquiries can be made about the good judgment or even integrity of local officials. Once a locality does grant land on "give-away" terms, other localities may feel obligated to follow its lead in order to preserve their industrial job bases. Not only do taxpayers suffer, but all the firms that had located in the jurisdiction earlier risk having to compete with newcomers whose rents they have, in effect, subsidized through their own taxes.

George Lefcoe, When Governments Become Land Developers: Notes on the Public-Sector Experience in the Netherlands and California, 51 S. Cal. L. Rev. 165, 169 (1978). *See also* David Schultz, Evaluating Economic Development Takings: Legal Validity Versus Economic Viability, 4 Alb. Gov't L. Rev. 186 (2011) (arguing that the problem with many redevelopment projects is not so much the use of eminent domain but the economic viability of the development project to be undertaken).

5. *Local Government Business Operations.* Is there any constitutional limit to local governments taking over businesses that previously were run as private enterprises? In Cityburgers: Controlling Local Government Profit-Making Activities, 54 Washburn L.J. 105, 109 (2014), Professor John Martinez notes that local governments have responded to the economic crisis that started in 2008 by "rais[ing] additional revenue by providing . . . services through economic enterprises operated for profit." These include retail stores, apartment buildings, gas stations, and liquor stores. *Id. See also* Christopher K. Odinet, Super-liens to the Rescue? A Case Against Special Districts in Real Estate Finance, 72 Wash. & Lee L. Rev. 707, 753 (2015) (citing the use of special taxing districts that "were essentially commandeered by private developers for the purpose of bank-rolling purely private projects" and that "extended far beyond the traditional roles for which they were envisioned.").

6. *Special Legislation?* Is there any limit to singling out individual businesses for incentives when other similar businesses receive no incentives? The Equal Protection Clause comes to mind, but the deferential standard of review applied to such challenges may make such challenges unlikely to succeed. However, in *Moline Sch. Dist. No. 40 Bd. of Educ. v. Quinn*, 403 Ill. Dec. 684, 54 N.E.3d 825 (2016), a different challenge prevailed. A state law exempted leasehold interests at one particular airport from property taxes. The leases were held by a private operator on land owned by a public airport authority. The authority was concerned that the operator would

expand operations at a nearby airport in Iowa rather than at the Illinois airport, and so secured the passage of the state law.

The Illinois Supreme Court first noted that the law contained "no requirement . . . that Elliott Aviation actually use the tax savings to expand in Illinois." 54 N.E.3d at 832. But the "real flaw," said the court, was that the law violated the state constitutional provision against "special legislation" — "there is no reasonable basis for limiting the tax incentives to this particular type of business at this particular facility in this particular part of the state." *Id. Compare Board of Directors of Indus. Dev. Bd. v. All Taxpayers*, 848 So. 2d 740 (La. Ct. App. 2003) (sustaining issuance of revenue bonds for construction of Wal-Mart store over claim it was an unconstitutional donation of public funds for private interests, as the sole donation was in the form of a property tax exemption).

7. *Do State and Local Economic Incentives Work?* The purpose of the incentives, of course, is to generate new growth whose benefits to the state or local government exceed the costs of the incentives. But do they work? There is considerable evidence that they do not. In Stephen Ellis et al., A Game Changer for the Political Economy of Economic Development Incentives, 56 Ariz. L. Rev. 953, 954 (2014), the authors observe that the use economic incentives is "endemic in local government, resulting in the transfer of tens of billions of dollars every year from public coffers to private firms." However, they continue:

> The academic literature points out numerous pitfalls associated with incentive competition, mostly related to ignorance of costs and benefits. It is possible to subsidize the wrong firm — firms that have low value or aren't influenced by the subsidy — or to oversubsidize the right firm. The empirical evidence suggests that offering incentives, in general, does not work.

Id. See also Jeffrey Kleeger, Flexible Development Tools: Private Gain and Public Use, 46 Urb. Law. 377, 279 (2014) ("[E]vidence indicates entities that use TIFs grow slower than those that do not.").

Consider also the following scenario:

> In June of 2014, Leawood, Kansas-based businesses Cbiz Inc. and Mayer Hoffman McCann, PC chose to move their headquarters and 450 employees to the Country Club Plaza in Kansas City, Missouri. This move of just a few miles across the state line triggered incentives from the state of Missouri that could potentially reach a value of over $25 million if the companies meet certain job creation and investment standards in coming years. In an interview . . . the Cbiz Financial Services' Chief Operating Officer said that the company had planned to move to the Country Club Plaza area before going through the application process to receive incentives. Missouri's act of enticing businesses across the state line is far from a one-sided affair. In 2011, AMC Entertainment, Inc. received over $40 million from the state of Kansas in exchange for a commitment to move its corporate headquarters from downtown Kansas City, Missouri to a suburban development just across the state line in Johnson County, Kansas.

Michael T. McGee, The Modern Day Border War: How Kansas Can End Its Economic Development Battle with Missouri in the Kansas City Metropolitan Area, 25-Fall Kan. J.L. & Pub. Pol'y 111 (2015).

Is the use of state and local incentives for economic development an area in need of reform?

16

Siting Unpopular Land Uses and Environmental Justice

A. INTRODUCTION

1. NIMBYs, LULUs, and Related Acronyms

As we have seen from previous chapters in this book, two major developments in current land use practice are (1) the empowerment of third-party groups to participate fully in the regulatory process, as well to institute litigation challenging approvals, and (2) the increasing complexity of that regulatory process. Nowhere are these two developments reflected more clearly than in disputes over the siting of needed land uses that have unquestioned side effects or that pose significant, long-term environmental risks (e.g., prisons, landfills, energy facilities, and hazardous waste or radioactive waste disposal sites). The apparent inability of government to approve such land uses, the so-called siting dilemma, has attracted the attention of legislatures, concerned some courts, appeared in the popular press, and prompted a flood of academic commentary.

It has also added to the lexicon of land use law. The term "NIMBY" (short for "not in my backyard") is now defined by the Oxford Dictionary as "a person who objects to the siting of something perceived as unpleasant or potentially dangerous in their own neighborhood, such as a landfill or hazardous waste facility, especially while raising no objections to similar developments elsewhere." *See* http://oxford dictionaries.com/definition/american_english/Nimby?region=US&q=nimby (last visited August 23, 2016). The acronyms NIMBY and LULU ("locally undesirable land use") have become a regular part of the land use dialogue (e.g., "the neighborhood NIMBYs" or "NIMBYism is rampant"). Other acronyms have been semi-facetiously suggested: NOPE ("not on planet earth"), CAVE ("Citizens Against Virtually Everything"), BANANA ("build absolutely nothing anywhere near anything"), or, from the standpoint of local politicians, NIMTOO ("not in my term of office"). These acronyms should lead you to question what role the public should legitimately play in land use decisions related to undesirable but needed uses.

How serious is the inability to site needed facilities? Over 25 years ago, an article concluded that the NIMBY syndrome "now makes it almost impossible to build or locate vital facilities that the city needs to function." Michael Dear, Understanding and Overcoming the NIMBY Syndrome, 58 J. Am. Plan. Ass'n 288 (1992). The two excerpts reprinted below involving the now-famous Cape Wind project, a proposed energy facility off of Massachusetts, illustrate the extensive legal opposition to that project. Proposals to site solid waste landfills, mental health facilities, jails, and other similar projects can be counted on to generate similar fierce opposition from neighbors. Moreover, recent disputes over energy facilities indicate that the siting issue will remain important for some time to come.

A primary reason for the state of conflict also seems clear: a mismatch between the benefits from such facilities, which accrue to society generally, and the costs, which tend to fall disproportionately on people who reside nearby. Homeowners located near a hazardous waste site will not be interested in arguments that disposal sites are needed for the good of society. Instead, they will be concerned with the risks, or the perceived risks, that the facility will impose upon them and that could reduce their property values.

At the same time, the sheer intensity of local opposition gives one pause: opponents of unwanted facilities exhibit a passion and dedication to their position that is remarkable. What accounts for this fierceness? Professor Michael Gerrard, in his insightful book Whose Backyard and Whose Risk, suggests two principal reasons. The first is perhaps predictable: a dread of the consequences, often unseen and unpredictable, posed by certain kinds of land uses. The second source of the opposition, however, is far less obvious. Gerrard posits that the NIMBY syndrome arises from opposition to "intrusion" into people's lives, intrusion that not only thrusts itself into communities but also seemingly into individual homes. And it is an intrusion without the consent of those upon whom it is inflicted.

Prof. William Fischel, an economist specializing in land use, brings another viewpoint. He sees local opposition as a quite rational response to economic threats. For most homeowners, their homes are the largest single investment in their lives. They respond to perceived threats to this investment, in the form of unwanted nearby land uses, with vigorous opposition intended to protect their investment.

Under the existing land use legal regime, opposition of this nature can make siting such facilities extraordinarily difficult. Opponents can and do use litigation to challenge siting approvals. Even if the litigation is ultimately unsuccessful, the length of time that it may take to resolve the matter in the courts can put a significant financial strain on the applicant. But the pressure that opponents can wield goes far beyond use of the legal system. Because land use remains predominantly a local function, opposition by a large number of local residents sets off political alarm bells among local elected officials. They can count votes and often champion the opposition position.

2. Responses to the Siting Dilemma

If we assume that such facilities must be sited somewhere, the question then becomes how to arrange the legal system so that successful siting can occur. Two general types of solutions have been tried. The first is the most obvious: since the opposition centers at the local government level, the state could preempt the field and make the siting decision itself. Often, preemption is coupled with additional procedures that are tacked onto the siting process in an attempt to resolve disputes over scientific issues or to involve broad segments of the community in the siting decision.

Preemption seems a logical way of ensuring that siting occurs, but it has not proved successful. The intensely political nature of the local opposition means that even if the state preempts the field and thus will make the ultimate decision on siting the project, at least some political pressure from opponents can be aimed at state officials. Moreover, state legislatures are reluctant to preempt local powers over land use, even when a regional or statewide perspective over those decisions seems to make sense. The connection between local government and land use runs deep; it is not easily severed for decisions, such as siting unwanted land uses, that impose costs on local residents. As a result, relatively few jurisdictions have actually attempted to implement a preemption solution to the siting dilemma.

The second type of solution draws on economic theory in an attempt to remedy the mismatch between the benefits of such facilities and the costs imposed. The premise is that citizens who are impacted locally should be compensated for having to bear the costs, whether real or perceived, of siting unwanted facilities in their community. Under this solution, siting legislation should establish a bargaining process in which the community and the facility negotiate and reach agreement on compensation for locating the facility in that community. The Massachusetts siting law, discussed in *Town of Warren v. Hazardous Waste Facility Site Safety Council*, a principal case in this chapter, is the archetype of this approach.

To date, however, approaches of this nature also have not proved particularly successful. While it may be too early to give up on approaches like that tried in Massachusetts, the results are not promising. Indeed, no clear answers have arisen to the siting problem.

This brings us to the last two articles in this chapter that address the NIMBY phenomenon. Perhaps the accepted explanations for NIMBY-like activity, together with the condemnation of those "locals" who oppose facilities that society as a whole needs, miss the point. Robert Lake is quite blunt on the issue. In a revisionist approach to NIMBY, he suggests that attempts to overcome local opposition are not implementing a societal need, but are rather narrow attempts to privilege the use of capital.

In any event, the NIMBY phenomenon continues to generate significant attention. It may even be spreading, as some literature suggests that NIMBY-like citizen activism is increasing in China. Robert V. Perceival & Zhao Huiyu, The Role of Civil Society in Environmental Governance in the United States and China, 24 Duke Envtl. L. & Pol'y F. 141, 146 (2013); Josh Chin, "China Trash Incinerator Sparks Protest," The Wall Street Journal (Sept. 15, 2014). And a book celebrates various cases of NIMBYism throughout the world. Carol Hager & Mary Alice Haddad (eds), Nimby Is Beautiful: Cases of Local Activism and Environmental Innovation Around the World (2015).

3. The Question of Environmental Justice

The siting issue is further complicated by another development, the Environmental Justice movement. The movement started around 1987 with the release of a report by the Commission for Racial Justice of the United Church of Christ. The report, a portion of which is reproduced below, argued that the siting of hazardous waste facilities had occurred almost entirely in areas with minority residents. In short, it raised the issue of whether the siting process, to the extent it *had* been successful in the past, was racially biased. Twenty years later, an "update" on that original report was released.

One important question, then, is why such siting disparities have occurred. Are the disparities due to disproportionate siting targeted at minority communities, or does this phenomenon just reflect market dynamics at work? Discussion over the siting disparities continues to rage in the flood of academic literature that has addressed the issue over the past few years.

Relatively few attempts at solutions to disproportionate siting impacts have been implemented. A presidential executive order directs federal agencies to develop a strategy that identifies and addresses disproportionate adverse environmental effects of its programs on minority and low-income populations. Students will read this order and can determine for themselves whether it is useful and workable. Students can also consider a revisionist line of thinking. Given that the siting crisis has dragged on for so many years, is the siting of certain types of facilities (particularly industrial ones) actually indispensable? Or is the opposition to siting facilities in fact forcing industry to create other, perhaps more environmentally benign alternatives to land disposal, such as recycling, and thus actually improving the environmental performance of industry?

This chapter, then, is a work in progress. It is clear that in many instances, determined local opposition to unwanted land uses has prevented the siting of facilities and that the single-purpose legislation designed to ensure siting has not been successful. What is not clear is the types of solutions, if any, that can respond to this situation.

B. NIMBYS, LULUS, AND NEIGHBORHOOD OPPOSITION

In considering opposition to facility siting, the student must focus on the impact of facilities on third parties, such as neighbors who live in the area, and evaluate what legal rights they should have in siting decisions. The chapter starts out by examining a unique group of statutes that gives neighbors enhanced protections when certain local land use decisions may affect them. Why do they merit those additional protections? We then turn to an outline of a current siting controversy involving an offshore energy facility.

■ EADIE v. TOWN BOARD OF THE TOWN OF NORTH GREENBUSH
854 N.E.2d 464 (N.Y. 2006)

R.S. SMITH, J.

The Town of North Greenbush has rezoned a large area of land to permit retail development. Petitioners seek to annul the rezoning.

FACTS AND PROCEDURAL HISTORY

In September 2003, the Town released a draft generic environmental impact statement (DGEIS), prepared pursuant to address a proposed area-wide rezoning of many parcels of land located near the intersection of routes 4 and 43. The rezoning had been requested by landowners, including John and Thomas Gallogly, who wanted to build retail stores on their property. Retail development was not permitted by the then-existing zoning. . . .

On May 4, 2004, the Town Board held a public hearing on the proposed zoning change at which petitioners, opponents of the change, presented a protest petition pursuant to Town Law §265(1). The petition, if effective, would have required a three-quarters vote of the Town Board to approve the rezoning. Petitioners claim the protest was effective, because it was signed by owners of more than 20% of the land located within 100 feet of the parcels affected by the rezoning, as shown by the Town's tax map. However, not all the land contained in the tax map parcels was affected by the rezoning; some of the land owned by the Galloglys was not rezoned. A "buffer zone" between 200 and 400 feet wide was left between the rezoned portion of the Galloglys' property and the property line. Measuring from the boundary of the rezoned area, the Town determined that petitioners did not own 20% of the land within 100 feet, and that their protest petition was therefore invalid. On May 13, 2004, the Town Board passed the rezoning by a vote of three to two.

. . . [The] Supreme Court granted the article 78 petition and annulled the rezoning on the basis of petitioners' Town Law §265(1) claim . . .

DISCUSSION

I

Under Town Law §265(1), zoning regulations may be amended "by a simple majority vote of the town board, except that any such amendment shall require the approval of at least three-fourths of the members of the town board" in certain circumstances. Petitioners here rely on Town Law §265(1)(b), which requires a supermajority vote where the zoning change is the subject of a written protest presented to the Town Board and signed by "the owners of twenty percent or more of the area of land immediately adjacent to that land included in such proposed change, extending one hundred feet therefrom."

We conclude . . . that the "one hundred feet" must be measured from the boundary of the rezoned area, not the parcel of which the rezoned area is a part. The language of the statute, on its face, points to that result: "land included in such proposed change" can hardly be read to refer to land to which the proposed zoning change is inapplicable.

Fairness and predictability point in the same direction. The interpretation we adopt is fair, because it makes the power to require a supermajority vote dependent on the distance of one's property from land that will actually be affected by the change. Petitioners complain that this allows landowners who obtain rezoning to insulate themselves against protest petitions by "buffer zoning" — i.e., leaving the zoning of a strip of property unchanged, as occurred with the Galloglys' property here. But we see nothing wrong with this. The whole point of the "one hundred feet" requirement is that, where a buffer of that distance or more exists, neighbors beyond the buffer zone are not entitled to force a supermajority vote. If we adopted petitioners' interpretation, such a vote could be compelled by property owners within 100 feet of the boundary of even a very large parcel — though these owners might be far away from any land that would be rezoned.

The interpretation we adopt also makes the operation of the statute more predictable. We see no reason why the right to compel a supermajority vote should change when the boundaries between parcels change — i.e., when parcels are merged or subdivided. Indeed, in this case, petitioners accuse the Galloglys of deeding property to themselves in order to create two parcels and invalidate the protest petition. Whether that was their original intention or not, the Galloglys now argue, and we agree, that such a reconfiguration of property lines, whether done in good faith or bad faith, should have no impact on the Town Law §265(1)(b) issue. . . .

Petitioners rely on Herrington v. County of Peoria, 11 Ill.App.3d 7, 295 N.E.2d 729 (1973), but that case is distinguishable; it did not involve a statute that required measurement of a distance from the land included in the proposed zoning change. The statute in Herrington provided for a protest petition by "the owners of twenty percent of the frontage directly opposite the frontage proposed to be altered" (11 Ill.App.3d at 9, 295 N.E.2d at 730; cf. Town Law §265[1][c]). The holding of Herrington is that the purpose of such a statute cannot be avoided by refraining from rezoning a few feet or inches next to the frontage of the rezoned parcel. The Herrington court distinguished Heaton [v. City of Charlotte, 178 S.E.2d 352 (1971)], saying that the statute in Heaton (which resembles Town Law §265 [1][b]) "appears to have been considered by the court as a legislative declaration, that 'one hundred feet' was a legally sanctioned buffer or barrier insulating the property from the claims of protesters" (11 Ill.App.3d at 13, 295 N.E.2d at 733). We think that the Illinois court correctly characterized the North Carolina's court's interpretation of its statute, and we interpret our statute in the same way.

If a project is large, it can require a multitude of local, state, and federal permits. Most recently, the siting of so-called "wind farms" for use in generating electricity has been the subject of considerable opposition. The most famous of these projects, the so-called Cape Wind project off the coast of Massachusetts, illustrates the avenues available to opposition.

Compare Christian Roselund, Turbines Are Up at Block Island, the First US Offshore Wind Farm (Aug. 24, 2016) at http://cleantechnica.com/2016/08/24/turbines-block-island-first-us-offshore-wind-farm/ (last visited Nov. 12, 2016). "Last Thursday, workers using a boat-mounted crane secured the final 240-foot blade onto a massive wind turbine, anchored to the ocean floor beneath Long Island Sound. With this act the turbine, and four others like it, were completed off the coast of a small island in the sound, known to locals as a tourist destination."

Offshore wind has lagged in the United States. Despite initial siting approval from the state of Massachusetts in 2005, the ambitious 454 MW Cape Wind project has still not broken ground 11 years later due to local opposition, including multiple lawsuits.

■ TOWN OF BARNSTABLE, MASSACHUSETTS V. BERWICK

17 F. Supp. 3d 113, 115–20 (D. Mass. 2014), vacated and remanded sub nom. Town of Barnstable v. O'Connor, 786 F.3d 130 (1st Cir. 2015)

STEARNS, District Judge.

This Complaint is the latest chapter in a long-running saga involving the siting of a wind farm in Nantucket Sound. The dispute pits the Commonwealth of Massachusetts and the diversified energy policy espoused by Governor Deval Patrick against an obdurate band of aggrieved residents of Cape Cod and the Islands. Both sides in the dispute claim the mantle of environmentalism, although for present purposes, plaintiffs have doffed their green garb and draped themselves in the banner of free-market economics. . . .

BACKGROUND

Cape Wind is a for-profit company with plans to develop a wind-powered renewable energy generation facility in federal waters in Nantucket Sound, a triangular-shaped 750 square-mile tract of the Atlantic Ocean bounded by Cape Cod and the Islands of Martha's Vineyard and Nantucket. The proposed wind facility is to consist of 130 horizontal-axis wind turbines dispersed over 24 square miles of open ocean, and is designed to generate 454 megawatts of electricity at peak operation.

In 2001, Cape Wind applied for a permit to build the wind facility on Horseshoe Shoals in the Sound, some five miles from the Cape Cod coastline and roughly 16 miles from the Town of Nantucket. In August of 2002, the U.S. Army Corps of Engineers granted Cape Wind a permit to build a meteorological tower to gather data in preparation for the project. As Judge Tauro presciently predicted in rejecting a suit against the Corps of Engineers' action, this was just "the first skirmish in an eventual battle." *Ten Taxpayers Citizen Grp. v. Cape Wind Assocs., LLC,* 278 F.Supp.2d 98, 99 (D. Mass. 2003). The Alliance, the leading plaintiff in this action, filed a parallel (and equally unsuccessful) lawsuit also challenging the permitting authority of the Corps of Engineers. *See Alliance to Protect Nantucket Sound, Inc. v. U.S. Dep't of the Army,* 288 F. Supp. 2d 64 (D. Mass. 2003), *aff'd,* 398 F.3d 105 (1st Cir. 2005).

In 2005, the Massachusetts Energy Facilities Siting Board approved the construction of two undersea electric transmission cables to connect the proposed wind facility with the regional power grid. The Alliance promptly filed suit protesting the approval. In 2007, the Secretary of the Executive Office of Energy and Environmental Affairs issued a certificate approving Cape Wind's Final Environmental Impact Report. The Ten Taxpayers Group filed a suit in response. The Supreme Judicial Court (SJC) and the Superior Court ultimately dismissed the two lawsuits, separately holding that the Board and the Secretary had each exercised their approval authority appropriately by deferring where necessary to federal jurisdiction. The Town of Barnstable, also a plaintiff in this case, meanwhile filed a lawsuit of its own against the Siting Board. *See Town of Barnstable v. Mass. Energy Facilities Siting Bd.,* 25 Mass. L. Rptr. 375, 2009 WL 1449032 (2009). The Alliance, the Ten Taxpayer Group, and the Town of Barnstable then joined all of their grievances in another Superior Court lawsuit, *Town of Barnstable v. Cape Wind Assocs., LLC,* 27 Mass. L. Rptr. 1111 (2010), followed by another onslaught against the Facilities Siting Board. *See Alliance to Protect Nantucket Sound, Inc. v. Energy Facilities Siting Bd.,* 457 Mass. 663, 932

N.E.2d 787 (2010) (affirming the Siting Board's authority to issue the environmental certificate).

In April of 2010, Kenneth Salazar, the United States Secretary of the Interior, issued a Record of Decision giving federal approval to the Cape Wind project. The Secretary also issued a lease to Cape Wind to operate a wind energy facility on Horseshoe Shoals, effective November 1, 2010. Notwithstanding, as one academic observer has accurately stated, "[d]espite full federal and state approval of the project, CWA has continued to face vehement opposition from local groups."

THE GREEN COMMUNITIES ACT

In 2008, the Massachusetts Legislature passed the Green Communities Act (GCA), Mass. St.2008, ch. 169. Section 83 of the GCA requires Massachusetts electric utilities to solicit long term supply proposals from renewable energy generators. Among the favored suppliers are generators of wind energy like Cape Wind. . . .

THE NATIONAL GRID — CAPE WIND CONTRACT

In December of 2009, National Grid, a competitor of defendant NSTAR, sought approval from the DPU to enter into negotiations with Cape Wind over a long-term energy-supply contract. The parties signed a Power Purchase Agreement (PPA) on May 7, 2010. Plaintiffs allege that the contract prices that National Grid agreed to pay were significantly above the market price for electricity in general and well above the price being charged by other generators of renewable energy in 2010. Compl. ¶ 48. In May of 2010, National Grid submitted two Cape Wind contracts to DPU for approval . . .

Two separate avenues of appeal were taken from DPU's approval of the National Grid contract. The Alliance (along with TransCanada) appealed directly to the SJC [Supreme Judicial Court], asserting, among other claims, that DPU's approval of the contract violated the dormant Commerce Clause. The SJC rebuffed the objections and affirmed DPU's decision, specifically rejecting the dormant Commerce Clause claim. *See Alliance*, 461 Mass. at 174, 959 N.E.2d 413 (noting that "[t]he constitutional challenge advanced by the Alliance and TransCanada fails"). A second group of plaintiffs filed a challenge with the Federal Energy Regulatory Commission (FERC), alleging that the DPU had violated the Supremacy Clause by encroaching on FERC's exclusive prerogative under the Federal Power Act (FPA) to set national wholesale electricity prices. FERC rejected the argument . . .

THE NSTAR — CAPE WIND CONTRACT

. . . DPU had directed NSTAR and other utilities to reopen their Requests for Proposals (RFPs) to take bids from out-of-state generators. Compl. ¶ 53. NSTAR did so and ultimately contracted with three land-based wind generators, Groton Wind, LLC, New England Wind, LLC, and Blue Sky East, LLC. *Id.* ¶ 54. Plaintiffs allege that the price of wind energy from NSTAR's contracts with the three land-based generators was approximately one-half the initial price agreed to by National Grid in its contract with Cape Wind. *Id.* ¶¶ 55–57. NSTAR chose not to enter a contract with Cape Wind. *Id.* ¶ 56. Plaintiffs allege that NSTAR's "refusal" to contract with Cape Wind threatened the very existence of the project because National Grid had secured DPU approval to distribute only half of the wind farm's output (the second

National Grid contract, for the remaining 50% had been rejected by the DPU). *Id.* ¶ 58.

On November 24, 2010, NSTAR filed an application with DPU for approval of a merger between it and Northeast Utilities. . . .

In July of 2011, DOER asked the DPU to stay the merger pending an assessment of its potential impact on consumers . . . On February 15, 2012, NSTAR and DOER entered into a settlement agreement, which included a condition that NSTAR pursue a PPA with Cape Wind on terms that were "substantially the same" as those of the National Grid–Cape Wind contract. . . .

On April 4, 2012, DPU approved the merger between NSTAR and Northeast.

On March 23, 2012, NSTAR and Cape Wind executed a PPA under which NSTAR agreed to purchase energy, capacity, and renewable power certificates from Cape Wind over a 15-year period. Compl. ¶¶ 84 and 86. On March 30, 2012, NSTAR submitted the PPA to DPU for approval. *Id.* ¶¶ 84 and 90. The contract required Cape Wind to comply with the rules of FERC and other government entities, and required Cape Wind to obtain and maintain the requisite permits and approvals from FERC, including wholesale rates clearances. Alliance intervened in the proceedings, which included three public hearings and two evidentiary hearings. On November 26, 2012, DPU approved the PPA. Neither the Alliance nor any other party to the proceedings appealed DPU's final decision to the SJC. On January 14, 2014, over fourteen months after the DPU's decision, plaintiffs filed this case.

Notes and Comments

1. *Protests and Consents.* The statute at issue in *Eadie* falls into a type of enactment that specially empowers a select class of citizens to block a development. The enactments break down into two classes. The first class encompasses the so-called "consent" provisions, which require the written consent of a certain percentage of landowners or residents before a land use change will be allowed. The second type is a "protest" provision, which authorizes certain changes in the normal land use approval process if a percentage of landowners or residents file a written protest to a pending change. Such a protest can result either in a requirement that a supermajority of the local legislative body must approve the pending change before it will be enacted, or an outright veto of that change. *See, e.g., McCarty v. City of Kansas City,* 671 S.W.2d 790 (Mo. Ct. App. 1984) (three-fourths majority vote needed where a neighbor protested); *Tippitt v. City of Hernando,* 780 So. 2d 649 (Miss. Ct. App. 2000) (if protest is signed by 20 percent or more of owners, either of the area of the lots or of those immediately adjacent to the rear within a given number of feet, then two-thirds of all the members of the legislative body must approve it).

The state case law is divided on the validity of these provisions. *Compare Williams v. Bd. of County Commissioners,* 371 Mont. 356, 308 P.3d 88 (2013) (invalidating protest provision which allowed property owners representing 50 percent of the agricultural and forest land in a zoning district to block zoning changes); *with Bourque v. Dettore,* 589 A.2d 815 (R.I. 1991) (rejecting unlawful delegation challenge to statute empowering "owners or occupants of the greater part of the land within two hundred feet" to object). What would you think of a zoning regulation that prohibited the construction of single-family units within one-half mile of a hog confinement facility unless the owner of the land and the owner of the facility signed a "mutual impact easement"? Does this unlawfully delegate zoning power to the owner of the confinement facility? If you owned the confinement facility, would you ever sign such an easement? If not, does the easement provision effectively rezone the property? *See Coffey v. County of Otoe*, 743 N.W.2d 632 (Neb. 2008) (upholding such a provision).

2. *The Nature of Neighbors' Opposition.* Interestingly, neighborhood "veto" provisions first appeared before zoning became widespread. Their purpose was to prevent nuisances:

> Chicago had been using so-called "frontage consent laws" for twenty years as an indirect method for regulating some types of "nuisance" uses. A use could be prohibited on a particular block front if a stipulated percentage of property owners on the street voted to prohibit it. Such "frontage consent" laws had become a routine part of pre-zoning neighborhood planning in Chicago and other cities since at least the 1880s. Frontage consent restrictions on livery stables were adopted by Chicago in 1887. . . .

Richard J. Roddewig, Law As Hidden Architecture: Law, Politics, and Implementation of the Burnham Plan of Chicago Since 1909, 43 J. Marshall L. Rev. 375, 387 (2010).

What is the modern rationale for such rules? A New Jersey court has suggested that their purpose is to give those individuals that would be most affected by a proposed change additional protection against an unwanted or ill-considered change. *Johnson v. Township of Montville*, 264 A.2d 75, 78 (N.J. Super. App. Div. 1970). Why is additional protection of this type needed? An Oklahoma court of appeal found that such provisions serve two purposes: "(1) avoiding the unreasoned and arbitrary exercise of power, and (2) protecting the continuity of property rights." *Homeowners for Fair Zoning v. City of Tulsa*, 123 P.3d 67, 70 (Ok. Ct. App. 2005); *see also Campbell v. Borough of North Plainfield*, 961 A.2d 770, 783 (N.J. Super. Ct. App. Div. 2008) (purpose includes "to better enable property owners to maintain the stability and continuity of zoning regulations . . .") Do these reasons justify such a supermajority provision?

In most situations, consent and protest statutes do not apply. Assuming that they do not, are neighboring property owners entitled to any special procedural protections when they might be affected by a local land use decision? If a quasi-judicial land use decision may affect the neighbors' property, due process arguably entitles them to a hearing before the decision is reached. *See, e.g., Horn v. County of Ventura*, 596 P.2d 1134 (Cal. 1979) (when approval of a tentative subdivision map will constitute a substantial or significant deprivation of the property of other landowners, the affected persons are entitled to reasonable notice and an opportunity to be heard before the approval occurs).

3. *The Forms of NIMBYism.* One recent article summarized the NIMBY phenomenon as follows:

> NIMBY . . . refers to objections by the community about the placement of certain activities or structures in their particular neighborhood. Such NIMBY problems often arise from projects that generate extensive benefits but impose a facility or project that negatively affects the local residents. Examples include when communities use their zoning power to restrict housing for the low income or mentally disabled and the placement of waste disposal facilities.

David Giller, *Implied Preemption and Its Effect on Local Hydrofracking in New York*, 21 J.L. & Pol'y 631, 665 (2013).

The term "NIMBY" has become so well-known that it now appears regularly in the case law, either as an accusation by a defendant or, less often, a description by the court. *See, e.g., Smith Commc'ns, LLC v. Washington Cty., Ark.*, 785 F.3d 1253, 1258–59 (8th Cir. 2015) ("Smith raises various arguments, including that the tower would comply with applicable laws and regulations, that the tower would not affect nearby property values, and that aesthetic objections to the tower are merely generic "NIMBY" (meaning, 'not in my back yard') objections.") There is even a semi-facetious "guide" to NIMBYism. *See* Hillel Aron, A Comprehensive Guide to Every Kind of NIMBY in Los Angeles, Los Angeles Weekly (Aug. 6, 2015) (discussing, among others, "Density NIMBY's," "Bike Lane NIMBYs," "Waze NIMBYs," and "Mega Mansion NIMBYs").

4. *Legitimate Testimony v. "Public Clamor."* Not all objections to projects can correctly be labeled "NIMBY" opposition. Consider the following quote from *T-Mobile South LLC v. City of Jacksonville, Fla.*, 564 F. Supp. 2d 1337, 1348 (M.D. Fla. 2008):

> The Shrewsbury testimony is particularized as to the Proposed Site and expresses the opposition of over twenty-six people to it. The Shrewsburys' testimony makes clear that a significant number of people in the immediate vicinity of the Proposed Site are opposed to its being used to house a cell tower. . . . Full review of the Shrewsburys' testimony makes clear that the Shrewsburys do not simply express a "NIMBY" (Not in My Backyard) perspective, as T-Mobile characterized their testimony. . . . Instead the Shrewsburys testified about legitimate concerns they and their neighbors had regarding construction of a cell tower on the Proposed Site. These concerns were based on aesthetics, in that the trees that T-Mobile claimed would serve as a buffer were no longer there and incompatibility, because the area in which the Proposed Site is located is experiencing significant residential growth.

See also Citizens for the Pres. of Rural Living v. City of San Bernardino, No. G050884, 2015 WL 4554609, at *12 (Cal. Ct. App. July 28, 2015) ("Lazer dismisses the public's and the residents' comments concerning the Project as mere NIMBY-ism (i.e., " 'not in my backyard' statements"), which do not constitute substantial evidence of a fair argument. . . . We disagree. The public comments, when combined with other evidence in the administrative record, support a fair argument of a significant impact to scenic resources.").

If you assume that not all opposition to a facility is unwarranted, is there any way to, as an article put it, "separate the true policy wheat from the NIMBY chaff" in these confrontations? Steven J. Eagle, Securing a Reliable Electricity Grid: A New Era in Transmission Siting Regulation?, 73 Tenn. L. Rev. 1, 27 (2005).

5. *The Cape Wind Project.* The Cape Wind Project has been enormously controversial. Consider the list of required approvals set forth in the *Town of Barnstable* decision. They involve local land use laws, state laws, and federal laws. *See, most recently, Public Employees for Envtl. Responsibility v. Hopper*, 827 F.3d 1077 (D.C. Cir. July 5, 2016) (invalidating environmental impact statement and finding that agency had not complied with the Endangered Species Act in analyzing the Cape Wind Project). Do all the levels of government have distinct interests such that each should retain approval authority? How can we tell whether local views are really

"parochial" or raise concerns so serious that they should be reflected in "veto" authority embedded in law?

Opponents have also been accused of delaying both mixed use urban projects that would implement "smart growth" policies as well as opposing housing for people with handicaps and disabilities. *See* Steve P. Calandrillo, et al., Making "Smart Growth" Smarter, 83 Geo. Wash. L. Rev. 829, 874 (2015) (neighborhood opposition to smart growth "is an older, more pervasive, and more intractable problem"); Susan F. Mandiberg & Richard L. Harris, Alcohol-and Drug-Free Housing: A Key Strategy in Breaking the Cycle of Addiction and Recidivisim, 46 McGeorge L. Rev. 843, 871 (2014) ("Operators of housing and programs for people with handicaps or disabilities are sometimes faced with local agencies, neighborhood groups, and other opponents who use zoning laws and similar barriers to prevent them from locating their facilities as desired."). One recent article argued that the NIMBY movement is costing the United States economy trillions and "[t]he ability of American to flourish is at stake." Christopher Helman & Dan Fisher, "Nimby Nation," Forbes (Aug. 17, 2015).

6. *The Tools of Opposition.* What legal tools are available to neighbors who wish to oppose a particular development? The obvious ones, of course, are appearances before the local decision makers and litigation seeking judicial review of any adverse decision. In some states, the neighbors also may be able to sponsor a referendum that seeks to rescind a quasi-legislative approval. Other approaches are more political in nature. Tim Iglesias, Managing Local Opposition to Affordable Housing: A New Approach to NIMBY, 12 J. of Aff. Housing & Community Dev. L. 78 (2002) ("Opponents' tactics are similarly predictable: distributing flyers; canvassing door to door and holding meetings to organize against the development; circulating petitions to document opposition; demanding meetings with the developer; telling their story to the media; and lobbying local government staff and officials through telephone calls, faxes, e-mails, and private meetings, and at public hearings.").

In opposing a power plant proposed for a low- and middle-income community in San Francisco, the opponents' strategies included developing a community toxics profile, working with city officials to initiate a community health assessment, presenting testimony before the state commission charged with approving the facility, and seeking a temporary moratorium in the siting of new polluting facilities. *See* Clifford Rechtschaffen, Fighting Back Against a Power Plant: Some Lessons From the Legal and Organizing Efforts of the Bayview-Hunters Point Community, 3 Hastings W.-N.W. J. Envtl. L. & Pol'y 407 (1996).

7. *The Purpose of Public Participation.* As noted in Chapter 6 of this casebook, one of the most important developments in land use over the past 25 years has been the participation of third-party groups, such as neighborhood and citizens groups, in the land use process. Procedural requirements in the law have often encouraged this development.

Should such public participation be encouraged, or is enhanced public participation, which often leads to litigation, counterproductive to sound land use decision making? To answer this question, you must consider the purposes that public participation serves. One article identifies two main arguments: (1) public involvement will improve the quality of plans and policies; and (2) direct democratic involvement from the lay public will create more just plans and policies, particularly when decisions affect specific communities or user groups. Carolyn McAndrews & Justine Marcus, Reducing the Negative Effects of Traffic on Communities: Public Engagement, Planners' Engagement, and Policy Change, Planning & Envtl. L 6 (Sept. 2014). *See also* Daniel S. Iacofano, Public Involvement as an Organizational Development Process (1990).

If public participation is principally designed to increase the knowledge base of decision makers before they act, in what types of situations is this purpose likely to be met? Alternatively, if public participation is intended to contribute to the legitimacy of the ultimate decision, will opponents feel that, once a public hearing is held, the final decision is legitimate and thus should be accepted?

Another justification sometimes offered for extensive public participation is that it may build consensus. How likely is it that consensus will occur in such disputes? Consider here the materials in Chapter 10 on mediation as an alternative means of making land use decisions.

8. *Even More Public Participation?* While some argue that citizen opponents have too much power, technology is making available new, expanded avenues of public participation. Professor Lee Ann Fennell highlighted this trend in Crowdsourcing Land Use, 78 Brook. L. Rev. 385 (2013). She observed that "[l]ocal governments have increasingly embraced new technologies like smartphone apps and online interfaces for involving constituents in land use planning and control." Should local governments move in this direction?

Academics and commentators have devoted much attention to the repeated instances of local opposition to proposals for unwanted land uses. The following two excerpts explore both the phenomenon and its causes.

■ MICHAEL B. GERRARD, WHOSE BACKYARD, WHOSE RISK: FEAR AND FAIRNESS IN TOXIC AND NUCLEAR WASTE SITING
99-107 (1994)

Many theories have been offered for the widespread public opposition to HW/RW [hazardous waste/radioactive waste] facilities, but I believe that the reasons can be summed up with two words: *dread* and *intrusion*. These have important implications for the siting dilemma.

Dread Polls confirm that by far the most important reason behind opposition to HW/RW facilities is concern over the impact on health, particularly the health of one's children. This is so not only in the United States but in other societies as well. Many educated people (though few if any of the experts in the field) attribute a large percentage of adult and childhood cancers to hazardous waste sites. Worry about health effects is also at the root of the emergence since about 1980 of thousands of grassroots groups of facility opponents and "toxic victims." . . .

Every era has had its own dreads. The Israelites cast out Moses' sister, Miriam, when she contracted leprosy. Successive civilizations have had ample reason to be terrified of plague, smallpox, and polio, until each was eradicated or controlled. These dreads have manifested themselves in disputes over siting; Louis Pasteur's effort to find a laboratory to develop a rabies vaccine was hampered by residents of Paris who feared they would contract the disease. We now have cancer and AIDS.

Often people who have been exposed to agents that might cause these diseases, or who simply fear such exposure, become preoccupied with health problems. When wastes are the source of these agents, a further layer of revulsion occurs, at least in the view of Freudians. When the waste is burned, as in incinerators, the complex psychological reaction to fire comes into play.

Yet another layer of horror accrues when the waste is radioactive. Since Hiroshima and Nagasaki, fear of nuclear war has become embedded in the culture. . . .

The distinctions drawn by most members of the public [about HW/RW facilities] tend to be rather sharp. . . .

. . . Many people tend to regard them as horribly dangerous, with no meaningful shades of gray between danger and safety; thus most proposed mitigation measures to reduce dangers will sway few minds. . . .

The sociologist Kai Erikson . . . says that toxic emergencies possess two distinguishing characteristics that add to the dread they induce. First they are unbounded and have no frame or end; the "all clear" is never sounded. Second, "they are without form. You cannot apprehend them through the unaided senses; you cannot taste, touch, smell, or see them. That makes them especially ghostlike and terrifying. Moreover, they invert the process by which disasters normally inflict harm. They do not charge in from outside and batter like a gust of wind or a wall of water. They slink in without warning, do no immediate damage so far as one can tell, and begin their deadly work from within. . . ."

Intrusion The insidiousness of their threat is closely related to the second major reason HW/RW facilities are so hated. The facilities themselves are seen as imposed on communities without consent, and once they arrive they do their damage silently. When forced on unwilling localities, the facilities are seen as colossal intrusions, almost as foreign invasions. Attempts to override local siting authority almost invariably backfire and *increase* local opposition, partly by intensifying the community's perception of risk. Some studies have shown that people will accept voluntary risks approximately 1000 times more hazardous than risks they perceive as involuntarily imposed — they will parachute out of an airplane or smoke a cigarette, but they don't want anyone to build a waste plant miles from their house. . . .

This sense of intrusion is magnified when the waste is imported from other areas. The EPA has acknowledged that public opposition is greater when the facilities would accept out-of-state waste. . . .

A concept closely related to intrusion is trust. Opposition is magnified when the community does not trust the people or institutions seeking to place HW/RW in their midst. The political prospects for several proposed HW facilities were severely damaged when it became known that their proposed developers had histories of environmental or other violations. Other proposals were defeated after the public came to believe that the government was negotiating them in secret with corporate sponsors. . . .

Mistrust is often accompanied by despair. The forces behind hazardous facilities are seen not only as evil, but as invincible. As Peter Sandman has said, "Ironically, nearly everyone is impressed by the community's power of opposition — except the community, which sees itself as fighting a difficult, even desperate uphill battle to stop the siting juggernaut. . . ." The sense of intrusion is further magnified if the community feels it is being treated unfairly — if, for example, there is no obvious reason why it is being singled out to be exposed to a waste facility. A sense of random victimization increases the outrage felt by the neighbors. . . .

■ WILLIAM A. FISCHEL, WHY ARE THERE NIMBYS?
77 Land Econ. 144 (2001)

NIMBYs sometimes appear to be irrational in their opposition to projects in the sense that they express far-fetched anxieties or doggedly fight projects whose expected neighborhood effects seem small or even benign. I submit in this note that such anxieties might not be irrational if we consider that most NIMBYs are homeowners, and that homeowners cannot insure their major (and often only) asset against devaluation by neighborhood effects. NIMBYism might better be viewed as a risk-averse strategy. . . .

NIMBYism is weird only if you think solely about the first moment, the rationally expected outcomes from development. NIMBYism makes perfectly good sense if you think about the second moment, the variance in expected outcomes, and the fact that there isn't any way to insure against neighborhood or community-wide decline. . . .

In further support of the idea that the risks of homeownership are the source of the problem, I would point out that both apartment owners and apartment dwellers are rarely NIMBYs, even after accounting for their lower numbers. I don't have numbers on this, but in my ten years experience on a zoning board and my continuous attention to other land-use disputes, it appears that the opposition to land use change is nearly always by homeowners. The only systematic exception is opposition by existing businesses to potential competitors, and even then they usually try to clothe their naked protectionism with appeals to environmental issues that primarily affect homeowners.

Lack of NIMBYism by apartment owners seems strange only if we attribute NIMBYism simply to expected effects of the proposed development rather than the variance of those effects. In absolute dollars, owners of multifamily housing have even more to lose from adverse neighborhood effects than most homeowners. And apartment owners could be pretty effective NIMBYs if they cared to, since they could round up tenants and business allies to oppose the land-use change. But such opposition is rare. The reason is that owners of multifamily homes can spread their risks of ownership much more easily than homeowners. They cannot insure against devaluation of their assets from neighborhood change, but they can divide ownership of rental housing among many owners much more easily by forming a REIT (Real Estate Investment Trust) or some other multi-investor form of ownership.

HOMEOWNERSHIP IS A LOPSIDED ASSET

Homeowners are a major political force in all local decisions, not just land-use regulation. Two-thirds of all American homes are owner occupied, but even this understates the importance of homeowners in local affairs. Homeowners vote in municipal elections fifty percent more than renters do. . . .

An owner-occupied home is a peculiar asset in two respects. The more obvious is that the investor is also the consumer. This dual relationship surely contributes to some of the NIMBY syndrome. Consumers get some surplus from most of the goods in their possession — otherwise they would not long remain in their possession. We should not be surprised that owner-occupants are more attached to the same objects that are for distant investors just so many dollars.

The other peculiarity of homeownership is that it is a high-return, high-risk asset that is held by people who have little ability to diversify that risk. Owning a home is financially attractive because the imputed rent on owner-occupied housing is not taxed and because taxation of capital gains on an owner-occupied home has long been deferrable and is now completely avoidable for most owners. The tax treatment of homes makes it an especially desirable asset during inflationary times. But even in the long run, owning a home — in particular, owning a plot of land on which a home can be built, rebuilt, expanded or simply stay put — has had an excellent average return (Gyourko and Voith 1992).

As with other high-return assets, however, homeownership has a good deal of risk. . . .

Personal Attachments and Reluctance to Trade Also Fan Nimbyism

There are, of course, other reasons that homeowners are touchier about changes in their neighborhood than about other types of financial risks. Living in a home for a long time creates a personal attachment for which changes in the neighborhood are upsetting. And the well-known (but often ignored) "offer/ask" disparity in economics indicates that people who are already in possession of something need to be paid a great deal more when asked to give it up than those same people would offer to pay for the same entitlement if they did not currently possess it. . . . In short, you ask more (to give up something you own) than you offer (to obtain something not already in your possession).

I am inclined to discount at least the first of these sentiments, long-time residence, as a prime mover for NIMBY anxiety, though. My experience observing NIMBYs is that newcomers are at least as inclined to object to changes in their neighborhoods as long-time residents. . . .

The offer-ask disparity is a better explanation but still not entirely satisfying. The problem isn't the concept itself, which has plenty of empirical evidence in support of it. (This is one of the few areas in economics in which psychological experiments have played an important role.) The problem is how to decide what objectors should regard as the status quo of their neighborhood.

Taken at face value, NIMBYism regards the status quo as the current use (or nonuse) of land in their neighborhood. They want it left the way they found it. But I have had little trouble convincing more disinterested observers that a more reasonable status quo is the long-standing zoning rules that apply to the neighborhood. If zoning creates, as I think it does, a sense of entitlement, then that entitlement belongs as much to the owners of the undeveloped parcels as to the owners of homes that were developed under the same rules many years earlier.

In other words, the NIMBYs are not being asked to give something up. They are demanding that someone else give up a right similar to that which they (or their predecessors in title) had themselves exercised to their advantage. . . .

If I'm Right, Why Ain't I Rich?

I have argued that a major — not the only — source of NIMBYism is homeowners' response to uninsured risks. If I am right about this source, and if NIMBYism is responsible for stopping projects that otherwise would raise aggregate land values in the neighborhood, there must be some potential gains from trade that are unexploited. There is room, in other words, for a smart person to initiate a market for home-value insurance.

Here is the insurance contract that would do the trick: In the event that the insured's property does not rise by the amount that it would have had the development not taken place, the insurer will pay the owner the difference at the time the owner of the property (or his heirs or legatees) chooses to sell it. Once this difference is paid, the succeeding owner acquires no further claim for adverse effects of the development on the property.

The reason the purchaser has no further claim after the insurance claim has been paid to the seller is that the purchaser has been compensated for the adverse effect in the form of the lower price of the house. This is why, incidentally, there is no injustice in the mere fact of differing property tax rates to finance schools in different communities. The higher rates are compensated for by lower housing costs, leaving the owner in the high-rate town with more money to pay taxes. . . .

To state the contract's basic terms is to illustrate why such insurance is difficult to write. . . .

WHAT IS THE RIGHT LEVEL OF NIMBYISM?

. . . NIMBYs are not all bad news. Without neighborhood opposition, some projects that devalue their community and neighborhood would get passed. Even local regulators are often unaware of the micro-neighborhood conditions that might be affected by the proposed development. They depend to a large extent on the willingness of neighborhood residents to take the time and expense of testifying about the possible effects. Thus the real trick in dealing with NIMBYs is motivating them to provide information and opposition when it is appropriate to do so, but not further. . . .

Notes and Comments

1. *A Particular Kind of Project.* As the excerpts suggest, certain kinds of projects are almost always opposed by nearby residents. Do these projects share certain general characteristics? Or do different types of proposals for locally unwanted land uses — hazardous waste sites, prisons, group homes, and so forth — raise different questions about the legitimate role of local opposition?

2. *Differentiating LULUs.* Are some locally unwanted land uses even harder to site than others? Will people more readily accept a group home than they will a hazardous waste facility? That conclusion may seem intuitively correct to you. But if you agree, where would you "rank" opposition to distributed energy facilities, such as wind farms? One author suggests that the nature of such facilities compounds the siting problem:

> Many landowners view distributed renewable energy devices as locally undesirable land uses (LULUs). . . .
>
> An ordinance that invites distributed renewables into a municipality can arguably create greater uncertainty for local voters than an ordinance authorizing the siting of a single waste disposal site or power plant. Unlike large-scale, concentrated LULUs, distributed renewables are typically installed at unpredictable locations throughout host communities over time. Individual voters considering whether their town should host a large LULU often already know where it would be sited and thus may have

greater certainty about how it could impact them. In contrast, distributed renewables-friendly ordinances create the risk that any resident could ultimately see a small wind turbine or unsightly solar panel array installed next door. Such broadly distributed risk can make it particularly difficult to build local support for land use controls favoring these devices. . . .

Troy A. Rule, Renewable Energy and the Neighbors, 2010 Utah L. Rev. 1223, 1235-36.

    3. *Dread and Intrusion.* The excerpt from the Gerrard book traces the formation of public opposition to two sources: "dread" and "intrusion." Gerrard cites a variety of cultural forces and psychology (e.g., reactions to the use of fire), and suggests that each era "has its own dreads." For example, community opposition to fracking may result from the possibility that fracking could cause seismic activity and earthquakes. Erik Lange, Local Control of Emerging Energy Sources: A Due Process Challenge to Disparate Treatment by States, 64 Case W. Res. L. Rev. 619, 687 (2013). A recent article categorized this type of reaction as "amygdala politics":

> The fear circuitry of the brain can override reason. Neurobiologist Dean Buanomano calls this "amygdala politics," and warns that "we should be most concerned about how vulnerabilities in our fear circuits are exploited by others." Indeed, the brain's fear circuitry (the amygdala) has greater influence on the brain's reasoning centers (the cortex) than the cortex has on the amygdala, allowing emotion to override reason in decision-making when emotion is invoked. Appeals to fear, then, can be effective tools in the battle over public opinion. In particular, local NIMBY (not in my backyard) opposition to fracking seems consistent with amygdala politics. The probability that one's drinking water well will be contaminated by fracking nearby may be low, but the harm (if it does occur) is great, invoking the brain's fear centers. Furthermore, even if the probability of contamination is low, the fear is real, and NIMBY opposition may be entirely rational.

David B. Spence, Responsible Shale Gas Production: Moral Outrage vs. Cool Analysis, 25 Fordham Envtl. L. Rev. 141, 183 (2013).

    Do these sources mean that opposition to facilities based upon a currently prominent "dread" cannot be overcome?

    Consider another set of laws, also discussed in Chapter 11, that might be categorized as "land use" laws: those which prohibit convicted sex offenders from living in certain areas. *See Nieves v. Pennsylvania Bd. of Probation and Parole,* 995 A.2d 412, 420 (Pa. Commw. Ct. 2010), *aff'd,* 33 A.3d 1260 (2011) ("enactment of local ordinances restricting where paroled sex offenders and sexually violent predators could reside, sometimes referred to as NIMBY ('Not in My Backyard') ordinances . . ."). In a 2006 article, the author argues that such laws—which are certainly based on a form of "dread"—violate the concept of collectivism founded in the constitution that is fundamental to American society: "This expansion [of laws preventing convicted sex offenders from living in prescribed areas], will come at the expense of the nation's collectivist tradition, for while the individuals targeted by the laws are despised and feared, they ineluctably also constitute part of the 'people[]' with whom all Americans must 'swim.'" Wayne A. Logan, Constitutional Collectivism and Ex-Offender Residence Exclusion Laws, 92 Iowa L. Rev. 1, 2 (2006). The author suggests that these laws "share an obvious common motivation with other types of Not in My Backyard ("NIMBY") legislation, which seek to deflect activities with adverse community impacts (especially environmental) to other jurisdictions." *Id.* at 10.

Do you agree, or are these laws distinguishable from the "usual" NIMBY situation?

4. *Trust, Deference, and More Intrusion.* Local opposition can legally be overcome by either state preemption or legislation controlling placement of facilities. David Giller, Implied Preemption and Its Effects on Local Hydrofracking Bans in New York, 21 J.L. & Pol'y 631, 655-56 (2013). But these two solutions have been used only infrequently. Does the idea of intrusion emphasized by Professor Gerrard explain why the political system, faced with evidence that many land use problems are regional in nature and cannot be dealt with locally, has resisted taking control of land use powers away from local government?

5. *Property Values and Efficiency.* Professor Fischel presents an economic explanation (and justification) for the NIMBY phenomenon. *See also* William A. Fischel, How Home Values Influence Local Government Taxation, School Finance, and Land-Use Policies (2001). The phenomenon is simply a form of wealth protection. Homeowners, guided by concern for the value of their homes, make political decisions that are more efficient than those that would be made at higher government levels.

Does this theory capture the entirety of local opposition? Or is part of that opposition irrational, the "dread" pointed to by Professor Gerrard? Interestingly, Professor Fischel's theory seems to suggest that from an economic perspective, local opposition is not totally a "bad" thing.

6. *The Opponents' Perspective.* By their nature, siting decisions present problems of collective action. The benefits of approving land uses such as hazardous waste treatment facilities may well be substantial. Those benefits, however, are spread among a variety of beneficiaries of that site. Individually, each of these beneficiaries has little incentive to participate in an individual siting decision. In contrast, opponents of the project, such as those that live near a site, may feel (rightly or wrongly) that the project will impose specific, large costs upon them. They have a great incentive to organize for the purpose of opposing the project. Thus, even projects with net public benefits may be blocked. *See generally* Mancur Olson, The Logic of Collective Action — Public Goods and the Theory of Groups (1965).

7. *The Developer's Perspective.* In an early, influential book on facility siting, the authors posited that siting proposals follow a set pattern or model:

> In the first stage, the developer makes a series of technical choices with his engineer, market analysts, and lawyers. He typically has no interaction with local government nor those who would be affected by his decisions. . . .
>
> The developer then announces his technology and site package to the public. If he mentions alternatives, they seem factitious. He appears to approach the public with a single firm decision camouflaged behind impossible alternatives. His strong position sets the stage for conflict.
>
> Now the permitting process begins. . . . People with strong concerns about the project and those who don't thoroughly understand it approach this opportunity defensively. They have no reason to expect the developer to change his mind, alter his project, choose another site, or heed the public's concern. In fact, they perceive themselves as having power only to delay or stop the project — because the developer has taken an apparently firm position, they must likewise be intransigent in order to protect themselves.

Michael O'Hare, Lawrence Bacow, & Debra Sanderson, Facility Siting and Public Opposition, 6-7 (1983).

Does the model imply that a developer should be required to discuss a project with interested parties *before* deciding to propose it? Even if such a step is not required, would you recommend to your client that it do so? *See* Tim Iglesias, Managing Local Opposition to Affordable Housing: A New Approach to NIMBY, 12 J. Affordable Hous. & Community Dev. L. 78 (2002) (describing a proactive and collaborative process for "managing local opposition" to affordable housing projects). As you will see later in this chapter, the literature on environmental justice emphasizes that members of the public affected by projects *must* be given a chance to participate in the approval process.

One report seems to advocate a slightly different approach: "If your project does not need re-zoning or government money that is tied to neighborhood support, telling the neighborhoods too far in advance only gives them more time to be mad and angry." Michael Allen (compiler), "Getting Beyond NIMBY: Advice from a Non-Profit Developer," in Getting to Yes: Lessons in *Yes* in My Back Yard (2003) 16. The article continues that the developer of a housing project for homeless men has "learned that the more time an opposing neighborhood has to learn about the project, the longer they have to create more opposition." *Id.* Do you agree?

8. *Siting and Political Theory.* One theory of public decision making that has received much attention in the academic literature is "public choice" theory. Essentially (and in much abbreviated form), public choice theory posits that government decision making has much in common with the operation of a market: "[G]overnment is merely a mechanism for combining private preferences into a social decision." Daniel A. Farber & Philip P. Frickey, Law and Public Choice 44 (1991). The theory posits that participants in that process are motivated by self-interest, much like private participants in a market. "A central tenet of public choice theory is that organized groups enjoy greater influence in the regulatory market-place than individual voters because the group's greater aggregate benefits from a given regulatory good enable it to outbid the individual vote." Felix Mormann, Clean Energy Federalism, 67 Fla. L. Rev. 1621, 1676 (2015).

If you employ public choice theory to analyze the siting phenomenon, what will your conclusion be regarding whether government regulation of the sites chosen will be excessive or insufficient?

A competing political theory is known as "civic republicanism." Instead of the individualistic approach found in public choice theory, civic republicanism posits the idea that "the elusive voice of the public good, momentarily audible above the din of power politics, carries the day." Amy Sinden, In Defense of Absolutes: Combating the Politics of Power in Environmental Law, 90 Iowa L. Rev. 1405, 1447 (2005). *See* David J. Arkush, Direct Republicanism in the Administrative Process, 81 Geo. Wash. L. Rev. 1458, 1482 (2013) ("'civic republicanism' holds that public policy should derive not from the mere aggregation of private preferences, but rather from a deliberative discourse that, to the extent possible, produces consensus regarding the public good").

How would those championing civic republicanism view the local opposition to siting found in the NIMBY syndrome? *See* Peter Margulies, Building Communities for Virtue: Political Theory, Land Use Policy, and the "Not in My Backyard" Syndrome, 43 Syracuse L. Rev. 945, 947 (1992) (suggesting that such opposition "compromise[s] the civic republican account of community service as a public commitment shared by all").

C. RESPONSES TO THE SITING DILEMMA

The following materials address two possible responses to the siting dilemma.

■ WALLACH v. TOWN OF DRYDEN
16 N.E.3d 1188 (N.Y. Ct. App. 2014)

GRAFFEO, J.

We are asked in these two appeals whether towns may ban oil and gas production activities, including hydrofracking, within municipal boundaries through the adoption of local zoning laws. We conclude that they may because the supersession clause in the statewide Oil, Gas and Solution Mining Law (OGSML) does not preempt the home rule authority vested in municipalities to regulate land use. . . .

I.

Respondent Town of Dryden is a rural community located in Tompkins County, New York . . . . Despite the fact that oil and gas drilling has not historically been associated with Dryden, its location within the Marcellus Shale region has piqued the interest of the natural gas industry.

The Marcellus Shale formation covers a vast area across sections of a number of states, including New York, Pennsylvania, Ohio and West Virginia. Natural gas — primarily methane — is found in shale deposits buried thousands of feet below the surface and can be extracted through the combined use of horizontal drilling and hydrofracking. To access the natural gas, a well is drilled vertically to a location just above the target depth, at which point the well becomes a horizontal tunnel in order to maximize the number of pathways through which the gas may be removed. The process of hydraulic fracturing — commonly referred to as hydrofracking — can then commence. Hydrofracking involves the injection of large amounts of pressurized fluids (water and chemicals) to stimulate or fracture the shale formations, causing the release of the natural gas (*see generally* U.S. Dept. of Energy, *Natural Gas from Shale: Questions and Answers* [Apr. 2013], at http://www.energy.gov/sites/prod/files/2013/04/f0/complete_brochure.pdf [last visited June 18, 2014]).

In 2006, petitioner Norse Energy Corp. USA (Norse), through its predecessors, began acquiring oil and gas leases from landowners in Dryden for the purpose of exploring and developing natural gas resources . . . . After holding a public hearing and reviewing a number of relevant scientific studies, the Town Board unanimously voted to amend the zoning ordinance in August 2011 to specify that all oil and gas exploration, extraction and storage activities were not permitted in Dryden. . . .

II.

. . . Our analysis begins with a review of the source of municipal authority to regulate land use and the limits the State may impose on this power. Article IX, the "home rule" provision of the New York Constitution, states that "every local government shall have power to adopt and amend local laws not inconsistent with the provisions of this constitution or any general law . . . except to the extent that the legislature shall restrict the adoption of such a local law" (N.Y. Const., art. IX, §2[c][ii]) . . . . As a fundamental precept, the legislature has recognized that the local regulation of land use is "[a]mong the most important powers and duties granted . . . to a town government" (Town Law §272–a [1][b]). . . .

That being said, as a political subdivision of the State, a town may not enact ordinances that conflict with the State Constitution or any general law (*see* Municipal Home Rule Law §10 [1][i], [ii]). . . .

Norse and CHC . . . claim . . . that the state legislature has clearly expressed its intent to preempt zoning laws of local governments through the OGSML's "supersession clause," which reads:

> The provisions of this article [i.e., the OGSML] shall supersede *all local laws or ordinances relating to the regulation of the oil, gas and solution mining industries;* but shall not supersede local government jurisdiction over local roads or the rights of local governments under the real property tax law. (ECL 23–0303[2] [emphasis added]).

According to Norse and CHC, this provision should be interpreted broadly to reach zoning laws that restrict, or, as presented here, prohibit oil and gas activities, including hydrofracking, within municipal boundaries.

[O]ur decision in *Matter of Frew Run Gravel Prods. v. Town of Carroll,* 71 N.Y.2d 126, 524 N.Y.S.2d 25, 518 N.E.2d 920 (1987) . . . articulated the analytical framework to determine whether a supersession clause expressly preempts a local zoning law. There, we held that this question may be answered by considering three factors: (1) the plain language of the supersession clause; (2) the statutory scheme as a whole; and (3) the relevant legislative history. The goal of this three-part inquiry, as with any statutory interpretation analysis, is to discern the legislature's intent. . . .

(1) PLAIN LANGUAGE

The first factor in assessing whether a supersession provision preempts local control over land use requires us to examine the words of the clause itself. And because the text of a statutory provision "is the clearest indicator of legislative intent" (*Matter of DaimlerChrysler Corp. v. Spitzer,* 7 N.Y.3d 653, 660, 827 N.Y.S.2d 88, 860 N.E.2d 705 [2006]), this factor is most important. . . .

. . . ECL 23–0303(2) is most naturally read as preempting only local laws that purport to regulate the actual operations of oil and gas activities, not zoning ordinances that restrict or prohibit certain land uses within town boundaries. Plainly, the zoning laws in these cases are directed at regulating land use generally and do not attempt to govern the details, procedures or operations of the oil and gas industries. Although the zoning laws will undeniably have an impact on oil and gas enterprises . . . "this incidental control resulting from the municipality's exercise of its right to regulate land use through zoning is not the type of regulatory enactment relating to the [oil, gas and solution mining industries] which the Legislature could have envisioned as being within the prohibition of the statute" (*Frew Run,* 71 N.Y.2d at 131, 524 N.Y.S.2d 25, 518 N.E.2d 920).

Nevertheless, Norse and CHC, relying on the secondary clause in the OGSML's supersession provision — preserving "local government jurisdiction over local roads or the rights of local governments under the real property tax law" (ECL 23–0303[2]) — contend that the operative text cannot be limited to local laws that purport to regulate the actual operations of oil and gas companies. They submit that the secondary clause's exemption of local jurisdiction over roads and taxes makes sense only if the preemptive span of the operative text is broader than we have allowed because roads and taxes are not associated with "operations." Consequently, they argue that there would have been no need for the legislature to exclude them from the operative language if supersession was limited to local laws aimed at oil and gas operations.

We find this textual argument misplaced because local regulation of roads and taxes can fairly be characterized as touching on the operations of the oil and gas industries and would have been preempted absent the secondary savings clause. The state legislature's decision to preserve "local government jurisdiction over local roads" was appropriate given the heavy truck and equipment traffic typically associated with oil and gas production, including water and wastewater hauling. Local laws dictating the number of daily truck trips or the weight and length of vehicles bear directly on industry operations and would otherwise be preempted absent the secondary clause. . . .

Indeed, it is instructive to compare the OGSML's supersession clause to other statutes that clearly preempt home rule zoning powers. Unlike ECL 23–0303(2), such provisions often explicitly include zoning in the preemptive language employed by the legislature (*see e.g.* ECL 27–1107 [prohibiting municipalities from requiring "any approval, consent, permit, certificate or other condition including conformity with local zoning or land use laws and ordinances" for the siting of hazardous waste facilities]; Mental Hygiene Law §41.34[f] ["A community residence established pursuant to this section and family care homes shall be deemed a family unit, for the purposes of local laws and ordinances"]; Racing, Pari–Mutuel Wagering and Breeding Law §1366 ["Notwithstanding any inconsistent provision of law, gaming authorized at a location pursuant to this article shall be deemed an approved activity for such location under the relevant city, county, town, or village land use or zoning ordinances, rules, or regulations"]).

Further, the legislative schemes of which these preemption clauses are a part typically include other statutory safeguards that take into account local considerations that otherwise would have been protected by traditional municipal zoning powers (*see e.g.* ECL 27–1103[2][g] [requiring the Department of Environmental Conservation to consider the "impact on the municipality where the facility is to be sited in terms of health, safety, cost and consistency with local planning, zoning or land use laws and ordinances"]; Mental Hygiene Law §41.34[c] [allowing municipalities a means of objecting to the placement of community residential facilities]; Racing, Pari–Mutuel Wagering and Breeding Law §1320[2] [mandating the consideration of local impacts and community support in the siting of gaming facilities]). Norse and CHC are unable to point to any comparable measures in the OGSML that account for the salient local interests in the context of drilling and hydrofracking activities.

In sum, the plain language of ECL 23–0303(2) does not support preemption with respect to the Towns' zoning laws.

(2) STATUTORY SCHEME

The second factor relevant to discerning whether a supersession clause preempts local zoning powers involves an assessment of the clause's role in the statutory framework as a whole. We therefore turn to the OGSML — article 23 of the Environmental Conservation Law.

The stated purposes of the OGSML are fourfold: (i) "to regulate the development, production and utilization of natural resources of oil and gas in this state in such a manner as will prevent waste"; (ii) "to authorize and to provide for the operation and development of oil and gas properties in such a manner that a greater ultimate recovery of oil and gas may be had"; (iii) to protect the "correlative rights of all owners and the rights of all persons including landowners and the general public"; and (iv) to regulate "the underground storage of gas, the solution mining of salt and geothermal, stratigraphic and brine disposal wells" (ECL 23–0301).

In furtherance of these goals, the OGSML sets forth a detailed regime under which the New York State Department of Environmental Conservation is entrusted to regulate oil, gas and solution mining activities and to promulgate and enforce appropriate rules. . . .

Based on these provisions, it is readily apparent that the OGSML is concerned with the Department's regulation and authority regarding the safety, technical and operational aspects of oil and gas activities across the State. The supersession clause in ECL 23–0303(2) fits comfortably within this legislative framework since it invalidates local laws that would intrude on the Department's regulatory oversight of the industry's operations, thereby ensuring uniform exploratory and extraction processes related to oil and gas production . . . . [W]e perceive nothing in the various provisions of the OGSML indicating that the supersession clause was meant to be broader than required to preempt conflicting local laws directed at the technical operations of the industry. . . .

Nothing in the legislative history undermines our view that the supersession clause does not interfere with local zoning laws regulating the permissible and prohibited uses of municipal land. . . .

In sum, application of the three *Frew Run* factors — the plain language, statutory scheme and legislative history — to these appeals leads us to conclude that the Towns appropriately acted within their home rule authority in adopting the challenged zoning laws.

■ TOWN OF WARREN v. HAZARDOUS WASTE FACILITY SITE SAFETY COUNCIL
466 N.E.2d 102 (Mass. 1984)

O'CONNOR, Justice.

In these appeals by the town of Warren and numerous citizen interveners, we consider the constitutionality of St. 1980, c. 508, An Act further regulating the disposal of hazardous waste materials, and the enforceability of town by-laws that would exclude certain hazardous waste facilities from the town. . . .

In 1979 the Legislature established a special commission to "investigate alternative procedures to be utilized by the authorities in granting local and state approval of sites for hazardous waste facilities," and to propose appropriate legislation. St. 1979, c. 704, 4. Draft legislation was submitted by the commission and on July 15, 1980, the Legislature enacted St. 1980, c. 508. The statute's preamble recited that the Legislature's purpose was "to immediately encourage and expedite the process of development of hazardous waste treatment and disposal facilities which provide adequate safeguards to protect the public health, safety, and environment of the commonwealth."

To achieve that purpose, St. 1980, c. 508, §8, inserted in the general laws of the Commonwealth the Massachusetts Hazardous Waste Facility Siting Act (Siting Act), codified as G.L. c. 21D. The Siting Act created the council, which monitors and implements the siting process. G.L. c. 21D, §4.

A developer proposing to construct, maintain, and operate a hazardous waste facility initiates the siting process by submitting a notice of intent to the council and to various other State agencies. The notice may, but need not, propose specific sites. If specific sites are proposed, the notice must be submitted to the communities in which those sites are located. The notice must include, among other items, information about the hazardous wastes that would be treated, the procedures to be used, and any proposed sites. Also, the notice must include preliminary specifications and architectural drawings of the proposed facility. Following the receipt of a completed notice of intent, the council has fifteen days to determine whether the proposal is "feasible and deserving of state assistance." G.L. c. 21D, §7. If the developer has not proposed specific sites, or has done so but is willing to accept alternatives, the council solicits suggestions of sites from various described persons. If more than three sites are suggested, the council reduces the potential sites to three, including the developer's suggested site, if any. G.L. c. 21D, §9.

Within thirty days after receiving either a notice of intent naming a potential site within its borders or, in the case of a site named during the site suggestion period, notice that a site within its borders is on the final list of suggested sites, each community in which such a site is located, referred to in the statute as a "host" community, is required to establish a local assessment committee. The local assessment committee is made up of representatives of the host city or town and may also include representatives of abutting communities. G.L. c. 21D, §5.

The developer must then submit to the council and to the Secretary of the Executive Office of Environmental Affairs a preliminary project impact report for each site under consideration. The report shall consist of (1) the environmental impact report required by G.L. c. 30, 62-62H, to be reviewed by the secretary, and (2) a social and economic appendix, to be reviewed by the council. G.L. c. 21D, §10. The special commission that drafted the Siting Act expressed the hope that the preliminary report would provide the basis for negotiation of a siting agreement between the developer and the host community. 1980 House Doc. No. 6756, at 22.

No facility can be constructed unless a siting agreement has been established by the developer and the host community. G.L. c. 21D, §12. The siting agreement results from negotiations between the local assessment committee and the developer and specifies the terms and conditions under which the facility will be constructed and operated. G.L. c. 21D, §§12 and 13. The agreement is a "nonassignable contract binding upon the developer and the host community, and enforceable against the parties in any court of competent jurisdiction." G.L. c. 21D, §12. A local assessment committee may request technical assistance grants from the council to pay costs incurred in the siting process. G.L. c. 21D, §11.

Sixty days after the determination by the council and the secretary that the preliminary project report is in compliance with the law, if an impasse in negotiations exists, the council may require the local assessment committee and the developer to submit the issues in dispute to final and binding arbitration. Such arbitration is to be conducted in accordance with the provisions of G.L. c. 251, including the provisions for judicial review of an arbitration decision. G.L. c. 21D, §15.

Upon the establishment of a siting agreement, the developer must prepare a final project impact report which incorporates the provisions of the siting agreement. If the secretary and the council find that the final project impact report is in compliance with all applicable provisions of law, the council may then declare that the siting agreement is operative and is to be given full force and effect. G.L. c. 21D, §10. The siting agreement is the final goal of the Siting Act, G.L. c. 21D, which, as we have said, was inserted in the general laws by St. 1980, c. 508, §8. It was designed, at least in part, to mitigate local resistance to the siting of hazardous waste facilities. 1980 House Doc. No. 6756, at 13.

Other sections of St. 1980, c. 508 have a similar purpose. For instance, 2A of St. 1980, c. 508 amended G.L. c. 21C, §7, to provide that the Department of Environmental Quality Engineering "shall grant a license to construct, maintain and operate a [hazardous waste] facility on a site if it determines that said construction, maintenance, and operation does not constitute a significant danger to public health, public safety, or the environment, does not seriously threaten injury to the inhabitants of the area or damage to their property, and does not result in the creation of noisome or unwholesome odors." That determination is subject to judicial review. G.L. c. 21C, §11. General Laws c. 111, §150B, was inserted by §4 of St. 1980, c. 508, to provide that no hazardous waste facility may be operated unless the local board of health has determined that its operation will impose "no significantly greater danger to the public health or public safety from fire, explosion, pollution, discharge of hazardous substances, or other construction or operational factors than the dangers that currently exist in the conduct and operation of other industrial and commercial enterprises in the commonwealth not engaged in the treatment, processing or disposal of hazardous waste, but utilizing processes that are comparable." Any person aggrieved by the board of health action may appeal its decision to the Superior Court.

The Legislature's desire to decrease local resistance to hazardous waste facilities was accompanied by a determination not to permit towns and cities to exclude such facilities from within their borders altogether. . . . In short, the Legislature sought, by means of St. 1980, c. 508, to facilitate the siting of safe facilities for the disposal and treatment of the wastes generated by schools, hospitals, government, and industry in Massachusetts by denying municipalities the right to veto facilities outright. In return, however, the Legislature established a means of involving affected municipalities in the siting process at the earliest possible moment, making available to them the legal, technical, and financial resources necessary for effective participation in that process, and allowing them significant control over the siting of a facility. . . .

Notes and Comments

1. *Why Not Preemption?* The *Town of Dryden* case illustrates a recurring question: whether the state legislature should intervene to preempt local decisions over projects that implicate important societal interests. Perhaps the most obvious response to local obstructionism of the NIMBY variety is to remove the decision from the hands of the local jurisdiction and place it at the regional or state level. A number of

jurisdictions have taken the preemption approach. *See, e.g., Residents Opposed to Kittitas Turbines v. State Energy Facility Site Evaluation Council,* 197 P.3d 1153 (Wash. 2008) (Energy Facility Site Locations Act authorized Council to preempt county land use decisions regarding wind turbine project). In many situations, however, the state law is simply not clear about whether it is preempting local land use authority, so state appellate courts like the New York Court of Appeals in *Town of Dryden* must consider this issue. *See United Water New Jersey, Inc. v. Borough of Hillsdale,* 438 N.J. Super. 309, 103 A.3d 309 (App. Div. 2014) (Borough was preempted from applying its land use approval requirements to a dam improvement project); *State ex rel. Morrison v. Beck Energy Corp.,* 143 Ohio St. 3d 271, 37 N.E.3d 128 (2015) (state has sole authority over permitting, location, and spacing of oil and gas wells); *City of Longmont v. Colorado Oil & Gas Ass'n,* 369 P.3d 573 (Colo. 2016) (city's ban on fracking was preempted by state law); Robinson Twp. v. Pennsylvania, 83 A.3d 901, 913 (Pa. 2013) (rejecting preemption of local regulation of fracking).

Even where it is very clear that local governments are preempted, however, certain types of facilities (such as hazardous waste facilities) still have great difficulties getting sited. Why? Consider what other avenues of opposition are available to a local government whose local zoning power has been preempted. Most importantly, remember that local government officials may not be without political influence at the state level, both in the legislature and before administrative agencies involved in the siting process. Is it possible that preemption only serves to intensify local opposition? Are such proposals more likely to work for some types of "unwanted" land uses (perhaps correctional facilities) than others (hazardous waste sites)?

2. *If Preemption, Where?* If there is preemption, is state law preemption sufficient, or should federal preemption occur? Does the deregulation of the electric industry mean that federal intervention in the siting process is needed to ensure the free flow of electricity across state lines? Is broader preemption necessary? How do we decide which industries merit preemption?

Numerous articles have suggested that some greater level of state preemption is needed in the energy field. *See, e.g.,* Uma Outka, Intrastate Preemption in the Shifting Energy Sector, 86 U. Colo. L. Rev. 927, 929-30 (2015) ("Most of the literature on renewable energy reflects a common ideal: a federalism model that will more effectively promote rapid policy and infrastructure development."). For example, some argue that the siting of facilities to refine gasoline should be federally preempted. Alastair Walling, Exposed Refineries, Price-Gouging, and the Gas Crisis That Never Was, 20 Nat. Res. & Env't 55, 56 (2006) (discussing problems siting refineries). *See also* Joshua P. Fershee, Misguided Energy: Why Recent Legislative, Regulatory, and Market Initiatives Are Insufficient to Improve the U.S. Energy Infrastructure, 44 Harv. J. on Legis. 327, 361 (2007) (arguing for exclusive federal transmission siting); Patricia E. Salkin and Ashira Pelman Ostrow, Cooperative Federalism and Wind: A New Framework for Achieving Sustainability, 37 Hofstra L. Rev. 1049, 1052 (2009) ("more centralized regulation is desirable" for siting wind energy facilities).

3. *If Preemption, How?* Traditionally, preemption — whether by the federal government over states, or states over local governments — tended to be viewed as "all or nothing." Now, however, more nuanced forms of preemption are appearing. Consider, for example, the issue that arose in *California Wilderness Coalition v. U.S. Dep't of Energy,* 631 F.3d 1072 (9th Cir. 2011). Under the Energy Policy Act of 2005, Congress has provided for preemption of electric transmission line siting under

fairly limited circumstances. Additionally, in setting transmission corridors, the Secretary of Energy must "consult" with the states. The court held that the consultation was insufficient. Can it be realistically expected that, by statutory command, a federal agency and states will develop the kind of workable relationship that true consultation requires?

Additionally, the Federal Energy Regulatory Commission (FERC) may approve transmission facilities in a "national interest electric transmission corridor" when a state entity has "withheld" approval for more than one year. 16 U.S.C. §824p(b)(1)(C)(i). FERC defined "withheld" to include "denial." Do you agree? In *Piedmont Envtl. Council v. FERC,* 558 F.3d 304 (4th Cir. 2009), a panel of the Fourth Circuit Court of Appeal, over a dissent, ruled that the term "withheld approval for more than 1 year" did not include a denial within the one-year deadline.

A recent article suggests a different approach for energy facilities: "disaggregating preemption." Rather than wholesale "yes or no" decisions on preemption, courts and legislatures would take a nuanced approach. They "would recognize the different components of a regulatory scheme — such as land use versus technological requirements — and consider which level of government might best exercise authority over each domain." Hannah J. Wiseman, 40 Harv. Envtl. L. Rev. 293, 297 (2016). Is this a better approach, or will it just produce a confusing overlap of dual regulation?

4. *Compensated Siting: The Academic Proposals.* Locals fighting unwanted facilities often see themselves as bearing the costs of such facilities but receiving few benefits. *See* David B. Spence, The Political Economy of Local Vetoes, 93 Tex. L. Rev. 351, 352 (2014) ("[A]ttempts by local governments to veto local development are essentially fights over the distribution of costs and benefits of development."). The compensated siting approach responds to this insight. It was set forth in several leading academic articles and then implemented in the Massachusetts Hazardous Waste Facility Siting Act, which was described in the *Town of Warren* case. *See* Lawrence S. Bacow & James R. Milkey, Overcoming Local Opposition to Hazardous Waste Facilities: The Massachusetts Approach, 6 Harv. Envtl. L. Rev. 265, 275 (1982). The authors posit that requiring compensation should encourage discussions between the community and the developer, promote efficiency by allowing projects to proceed only if their social benefits outweigh their social costs, and create an incentive for the developer to minimize costs. *Id.* at 275-276. *See also* Susan Lorde Martin, Wind Farms and NIMBYs: Generating Conflict, Reducing Litigation, 20 Fordham Envtl. L. Rev. 427, 465 (2010) ("the idea of paying potential NIMBYs is a good one").

What practical difficulties can you foresee in the implementation of compensated siting? Consider, for example, whether it is easy to determine the boundaries of the appropriate "community" that should be compensated. Should the lines be drawn solely on the basis of the jurisdictional boundaries of local governments? *See* Daniel C. Esty, Revitalizing Environmental Federalism, 95 Mich. L. Rev. 570, 597 (1996) (arguing that the sphere of affected interests may expand or contract depending on an evolving definition of community).

Another question is the function of compensation. Is the purpose to compensate members of the community for the "damage" caused by siting the facility (that is, to compensate for the reduction in property values caused when the facility is sited in that community)? Alternatively, is it to increase the number and effectiveness of so-called mitigation measures, which might lessen the risks posed by the facility? Or is compensation intended simply to act as an incentive by enticing members of the community to accept the facility?

5. *Compensated Siting: The Experience.* Although much-heralded as the solution to the siting dilemma, "negotiated compensation" has had only limited success in siting facilities. In Massachusetts, the siting law has not provided the results envisioned. *See* Mary R. English, The Search for Political Authority in Massachusetts' Toxic Waste Management Law, 16 B.C. Envtl. Aff. L. Rev. 39, 41 (1988). The federal Low-Level Radioactive Waste Policy Act Amendments of 1985 include a provision allowing the imposition of surcharges to be used to mitigate the impact of the waste disposal facilities on the host state. 42 U.S.C. §2021e(d)(2)(E)(i) (2012). To date, however, no new facilities have been sited under the law despite significant efforts. A Wisconsin law, which relies on compensation, negotiation, and arbitration to site facilities, has shown some success. Vicki Been, Compensated Siting Proposals: Is it Time to Pay Attention?, 21 Fordham Urb. L.J. 787, 821 (1994) (by the end of 1993, siting agreements had been reached for 5 hazardous waste sites and 41 solid waste sites in Wisconsin).

What is the problem with the theory? One article identifies a series of flaws in the Massachusetts approach. Among them, according to the author, were that (1) the compulsory nature of negotiations imparted a strong adversarial cast to the negotiating sessions; (2) the Siting Council was not perceived as neutral and was seldom an effective broker between communities, developers, and agencies; and (3) the law focused too narrowly on compensation as the centerpiece of the negotiating agenda. Michael Wheeler, Negotiating NIMBYs: Learning from the Failure of the Massachusetts Siting Law, 11 Yale J. on Reg. 241, 273-280 (1994). If the article's conclusions are accepted, will it be easy to remedy these flaws by amending the legislation?

6. *Dispersion.* Some states have attempted to solve the problem of siting group homes, hazardous waste facilities, and other unwanted land uses by passing statutes. One approach is to ensure that such homes are not unduly concentrated. In New York, municipalities may refuse to permit a group home for the mentally disabled if establishing the facility "would result in such a concentration of community residential facilities . . . that the nature and character of areas within the municipality would be substantially altered." N.Y. Mental Hyg. Law §41.34(c)(1)(C).

Can this type of dispersion solution solve all siting problems? For example, do we want more landfills and hazardous waste sites that are spread out among the areas that they serve, or are there strong reasons for siting fewer facilities on more targeted sites? Will the knowledge that other, similarly situated localities will also suffer the same "fate" cause local opposition to a facility to subside? *See* Daniel R. Mandelker, Housing Quotas for People with Disabilities, 43 Urb. Law 915, 930-31 (2011) (criticizing dispersion requirements).

7. *Safety, Compensation, and "Bribery."* Compensation systems assume that, through bargaining, doubts about the safety of a facility may be resolved. *See* Douglas J. Amy, The Politics of Environmental Mediation 190 (1987) ("The assumption of the state-mandated mediation process in Massachusetts is that health risks should be negotiable — that the developers can economically compensate the local citizens for any increase in health risks. Thus, the mediation process attempts to portray health as simply another interest, one to which a price can be attached, and one that can be bargained over like any other commodity."). If local citizens will never feel completely safe about a project, however, consider how they will react to suggestions

942   16 ■ Siting Unpopular Land Uses and Environmental Justice

that they should accept the project in any event and, in return, receive some sort of payment for that acceptance. Will they view it as a kind of "bribery," thus adding a moral dimension to the opposition?

At the least, certainly some sort of emotional reaction on their part is probable. *See* Sean F. Nolon, Negotiating the Wind: A Framework to Engage Citizens in Siting Wind Turbines, 12 Cardozo J. Conflict Resol. 327, 353 (2011) ("Since dealing with local opposition involves emotional as well as rational engagement, any process must address the emotions associated with the proposed action."); Eduardo M. Peñalver, Land Virtues, 94 Cornell L. Rev. 821, 846 (2009) ("Monetary payments may help to overcome concerns about declining property values, but they do little to assuage fears about the in-kind impacts of development or about unfairness. This may help to explain why in-kind compensation offers, efforts to mitigate the actual impact of the facility, and attempts to increase the perceived legitimacy of siting procedures, have proved relatively successful at overcoming local opposition to proposed LULUs.").

A study of siting a nuclear waste repository in Switzerland reached a different conclusion regarding compensation. While half of the respondents who were not offered compensation agreed to have the facility built within their locality, the level of acceptance dropped to one quarter among those offered amounts from $2175 to $6525. The authors of the study tested to see if the acceptance level declined because the recipients now inferred from the compensation that the harm from the facility was greater, but the data did not support this hypothesis. Instead, they concluded, "public spirit"—altruistic motivations to accept the project from a sense of civic duty—declined when compensation was offered. Emad H. Atiq, Why Motives Matter: Reframing the Crowding Out Effect of Legal Incentives, 123 Yale L.J. 1070, 1083 (2014) (citing Bruno S. Frey & Felix Oberholzer-Gee, The Cost of Price Incentives: An Empirical Analysis of Motivation Crowding-Out, 87 Am. Econ. Rev. 746 (1997)).

8. *NIMBY Reconsidered.* The term "NIMBY" has taken on negative connotations suggesting the need for a solution to overcome self-centered local objections. One of the authors of this book has argued that the term serves to mask real concerns that local homeowners and citizens have about negative externalities:

> [U]sing the pejorative term "NIMBY" to label property owners who seek to protect themselves from negative externalities needlessly suggests that they are less worthy of respect and protection than property owners who seek to advance their self-interest by exploiting property in a way that may impose negative externalities on the community. There is no *a priori* reason to favor property owners whose interests are served by developing property over property owners whose interests are served by community protection. The Constitution protects the interests of property owners but it also protects the interests of citizens in the benefits of representative government.

John D. Echeverria, The Costs of *Koontz*, 39 Vt. L. Rev. 573, 604 (2015). *See also* Patrick Devine-Wright, Renewable Energy and the Public: From NIMBY to Participation, xxiii (2011) ("[M]any local scientists have argued that the NIMBY concept is a misleading, inaccurate and pejorative way of understanding local objections . . . ."). Is the hue and cry over "NIMBYism" an overreaction?

Additionally, a new body of literature is directed at "localism." *See* Richard C. Schragger, The Limits of Localism, 100 Mich. L. Rev. 371, 382 (2001) ("Scholars and policy-makers have increasingly advocated the proliferation of lawmaking authority down to the neighborhood and block level. This body of work calls for deference to local decisions addressing the quality of life on streets and in particular neighborhoods, and suggests that norms of street (and other behavior) be set locally"); Nadav Shoked, The New Local, 100 Va. L. Rev. 1323, 1327, 1329 (2014) (while the city used to be the lowest level of government responsible for planning, the "new local" invests power in groups of citizens and is "smaller than existing levels of local government").

Is this theory inconsistent with the idea that a "solution" to NIMBY behavior is required? Doesn't this theory require acceptance of local control, even when it opposes facilities that might be needed regionally?

D. JUSTICE AND SITING DECISIONS

It may seem that the siting process has been unsuccessful and that arranging the legal structure to ensure more successful siting outcomes is very difficult. The problem, however, is even more complicated than the material above suggests. In recent years, a movement has emerged, often labeled the "environmental justice" movement, which has added a new voice to the debate. Environmental justice advocates point to evidence that the environmental impacts of facilities that have been sited have fallen overwhelmingly on persons of color. The debate on this issue is summarized in the following materials.

■ COMMISSION FOR RACIAL JUSTICE (UNITED CHURCH OF CHRIST), TOXIC WASTES AND RACE IN THE UNITED STATES: A NATIONAL REPORT ON THE RACIAL AND SOCIO-ECONOMIC CHARACTERISTICS OF COMMUNITIES WITH HAZARDOUS WASTE SITES
xi-xv, 13 (1987)

[T]he United Church of Christ Commission for Racial Justice decided, in 1986, to conduct extensive research on the relationship between the location of sites containing hazardous wastes and the racial and socio-economic characteristics of persons living in close proximity to those sites. . . .

MAJOR FINDINGS

This report presents findings from two cross-sectional studies on demographic patterns associated with (1) commercial hazardous waste facilities and (2) uncontrolled toxic waste sites. The first was an analytical study which revealed a striking relationship between the location of commercial hazardous waste facilities and race. The second was a descriptive study which documented the widespread presence of uncontrolled toxic waste sites in racial and ethnic communities throughout the

United States. Among the many findings that emerged from these studies, the following are most important:

DEMOGRAPHIC CHARACTERISTICS OF COMMUNITIES WITH COMMERCIAL HAZARDOUS WASTE FACILITIES

- Race proved to be the most significant among variables tested in association with the location of commercial hazardous waste facilities. This represented a consistent national pattern.
- Communities with the greatest number of commercial hazardous waste facilities had the highest composition of racial and ethnic residents. In communities with two or more facilities or one of the nation's five largest landfills, the average minority percentage of the population was more than three times that of communities without facilities (38 percent vs. 12 percent).
- In communities with one commercial hazardous waste facility, the average minority percentage of the population was twice the average minority percentage of the population in communities without such facilities (24 percent vs. 12 percent).
- Although socio-economic status appeared to play an important role in the location of commercial hazardous waste facilities, race still proved to be more significant. This remained true after the study controlled for urbanization and regional differences. Incomes and home values were substantially lower when communities with commercial facilities were compared to communities in the surrounding counties without facilities.
- Three out of the five largest commercial hazardous waste landfills in the United States were located in predominantly Black or Hispanic communities. These three landfills accounted for 40 percent of the total estimated commercial landfill capacity in the nation.

DEMOGRAPHIC CHARACTERISTICS OF COMMUNITIES WITH UNCONTROLLED TOXIC WASTE SITES

- Three out of every five Black and Hispanic Americans lived in communities with uncontrolled toxic waste sites.
- More than 15 million Blacks lived in communities with one or more uncontrolled toxic waste sites.
- More than 8 million Hispanics lived in communities with one or more uncontrolled toxic waste sites.
- Blacks were heavily over-represented in the populations of metropolitan areas with the largest number of uncontrolled toxic waste sites. . . .

MAJOR CONCLUSIONS AND RECOMMENDATIONS

The findings of the analytical study on the location of commercial hazardous waste facilities suggest the existence of clear patterns which show that communities with greater minority percentages of the population are more likely to be the sites of such facilities. The possibility that these patterns resulted by chance is virtually impossible, strongly suggesting that some underlying factor or factors, which are related to race played a role in the location of commercial hazardous waste facilities.

Therefore, the Commission for Racial Justice concludes that, indeed; race has been a factor in the location of commercial hazardous waste facilities in the United States.

The findings of the descriptive study on the location of uncontrolled toxic waste sites suggest an inordinate concentration of such sites in Black and Hispanic communities, particularly in urban areas. This situation reveals that the issue of race is an important factor in describing the problem of uncontrolled toxic waste sites. . . .

RESULTS

This section summarizes the major findings of both studies: the analysis of race and the location of commercial hazardous waste facilities and the descriptive study on the racial composition of communities with uncontrolled toxic waste sites. The first study found that the group of residential ZIP code areas with the highest number of commercial hazardous waste facilities also had the highest mean percentage of residents who belong to a racial and ethnic group. Conversely those residential ZIP codes with no waste facilities had a lower proportion of racial and ethnic residents. . . .

The descriptive study, which focused on closed or uncontrolled toxic waste sites, found their presence in American communities to be highly pervasive. This study found that more than half of the population in the United States lived in residential ZIP code areas with one or more uncontrolled toxic waste sites. The study also found that three out of every five Black and Hispanic Americans lived in communities with uncontrolled toxic waste sites. This figure represents more than 15 million Blacks and 8 million Hispanics. Approximately 2 million Asian/Pacific Islanders and 700,000 American Indians lived in such communities.

■ ROBERT D. BULLARD ET AL., EXECUTIVE SUMMARY, TOXIC WASTES AND RACE AT TWENTY 1987-2007
(February 2007) 1-2

INTRODUCTION

In 1987, the United Church of Christ Commission for Racial Justice released its groundbreaking study *Toxic Wastes and Race in the United States*. The report was significant because it found race to be the most potent variable in predicting where commercial hazardous waste facilities were located in the U.S., more powerful than household income, the value of homes and the estimated amount of hazardous waste generated by industry.

This year, the United Church of Christ Justice and Witness Ministries commissioned a new report as part of the twentieth anniversary of the release of the 1987 report. The 2007 *Toxic Wastes and Race at Twenty* report uses 2000 census data. . . .

KEY FINDINGS

The application of these new methods, which better determine where people live in relation to where hazardous sites are located, reveals that racial disparities in the distribution of hazardous wastes are greater than previously reported. In fact, these methods show that people of color make up the majority of those living in host neighborhoods within 3 kilometers (1.8 miles) of the nation's hazardous waste facilities. Racial and ethnic disparities are prevalent throughout the country.

NATIONAL DISPARITIES

More than nine million people (9,222,000) are estimated to live in circular host neighborhoods within 3 kilometers of the nation's 413 commercial hazardous waste facilities. More than 5.1 million people of color, including 2.5 million Hispanics or Latinos, 1.8 million African Americans, 616,000 Asians/Pacific Islanders and 62,000 Native Americans live in neighborhoods with one or more commercial hazardous waste facilities.

Host neighborhoods of commercial hazardous waste facilities are 56% people of color whereas nonhost areas are 30% people of color. Percentages of African Americans, Hispanics/Latinos and Asians/Pacific Islanders in host neighborhoods are 1.7, 2.3 and 1.8 times greater (20% vs. 12%, 27% vs. 12%, and 6.7% vs. 3.6%), respectively. Poverty rates in the host neighborhoods are 1.5 times greater than nonhost areas (18% vs. 12%).

NEIGHBORHOODS WITH CLUSTERED FACILITIES

Neighborhoods with facilities clustered close together have higher percentages of people of color than those with nonclustered facilities (69% vs. 51%). Likewise, neighborhoods with clustered facilities have disproportionately high poverty rates. Because people of color and the poor are highly concentrated in neighborhoods with multiple facilities, they continue to be particularly vulnerable to the various negative impacts of hazardous waste facilities.

EPA REGIONAL DISPARITIES

Racial disparities for people of color as a whole exist in nine out of 10 U.S. EPA regions (all except Region 3). Disparities in people of color percentages between host neighborhoods and nonhost Areas are greatest in: Region 1, the Northeast (36% vs. 15%); Region 4, the southeast (54% vs. 30%); Region 5, the Midwest (53% vs. 19%); Region 6, the South (63% vs. 42%); and Region 9, the southwest (80% vs. 49%). For Hispanics, African Americans and Asians/Pacific Islanders, statistically significant disparities exist in the majority or vast majority of EPA regions. The pattern of people of color being especially concentrated in areas where facilities are clustered is also geographically widespread throughout the country.

STATE DISPARITIES

Forty of the 44 states (90%) with hazardous waste facilities have disproportionately high percentages of people of color in circular host neighborhoods within 3 kilometers of the facilities. States with the 10 largest differences in people of color percentages between host neighborhoods and nonhost areas include (in descending order by the size of the differences): Michigan (66% vs. 19%), Nevada (79% vs. 33%), Kentucky (51% vs. 10%), Illinois (68% vs. 31%), Alabama (66% vs. 31%), Tennessee (54% vs. 20%), Washington (53% vs. 20%), Kansas (47% vs. 16%), Arkansas (52% vs. 21%) and California (81% vs. 51%). Thirty-five states have socioeconomic disparities, i.e., in poverty rates. In these states, the average poverty rate in host neighborhoods is 18% compared to 12% in nonhost areas.

METROPOLITAN DISPARITIES

In metropolitan areas, where four of every five hazardous waste facilities are located, people of color percentages in hazardous waste host neighborhoods are significantly greater than those in nonhost areas (57% vs. 33%). Likewise, the nation's metropolitan areas show disparities in percentages of African Americans, Hispanics/Latinos and Asians/Pacific Islanders, 20% vs. 13%, 27% vs. 14% and 6.8% vs. 4.4%, respectively. Socioeconomic disparities exist between host neighborhoods and nonhost areas, with poverty rates of 18% vs. 12%, respectively. One hundred and five of the 149 metropolitan areas with facilities (70%) have host neighborhoods with disproportionately high percentages of people of color, and 46 of these metro areas (31%) have majority people of color host neighborhoods.

CONTINUING SIGNIFICANCE OF RACE

In 1987, *Toxic Wastes and Race in the United States* found race to be more important than socioeconomic status in predicting the location of the nation's commercial hazardous waste facilities. In 2007, our current study results show that race continues to be a significant and robust predictor of commercial hazardous waste facility locations when socioeconomic factors are taken into account. . . .

Notes and Comments

1. *The Issue of Environmental Justice and Land Use.* The excerpts from the two reports give you a sense of the empirical research about siting patterns. Those reports spawned a very large environmental justice movement supported by a lot of academic literature. The Environmental Protection Agency defines "environmental justice" as "the fair treatment and meaningful involvement of all people regardless of race, color, national origin, or income, with respect to the development, implementation, and enforcement of environmental laws, regulations, and policies." *See* https://www.epa.gov/environmentaljustice (last visited Oct. 26, 2016). A wide variety of environmental and land use laws fall under that definition. It is clear, however, that the siting of facilities such as hazardous waste sites, solid waste disposal sites, airports, etc. fall under the rubric of land use decisions.

2 *Other Evidence.* A variety of studies and articles have addressed the environmental justice issue. *See, e.g.,* U.S. General Accounting Office, Siting of Hazardous Waste Landfills and Their Correlation with Racial and Economic Status of Surrounding Communities (1983) (concluding that a majority of residents in the communities containing three of the four hazardous waste landfills in the EPA's Region IV were African-American). A study of Superfund sites in Florida found that blacks and Hispanics are more likely than whites to live near Superfund sites in that state, and that these patterns persist when other variables (housing values, income, percentage of manufacturing employment, urbanization) are controlled. The author concludes that race and ethnicity are the most salient factors in predicting the location of hazardous waste sites. *See* Paul Stretesky & Michael J. Hogan, Environmental Justice: An Analysis of Superfund Sites in Florida, 45 Soc. Probs. 268-287

(1998). Other influential articles broadened the analysis from pure siting decisions to suggest that environmental laws generally have distributed risks unfairly upon minority populations. *See, e.g.,* Richard J. Lazarus, Pursuing "Environmental Justice": The Distributional Effects of Environmental Protection, 87 Nw. U.L. Rev. 787 (1993).

A number of individuals have seen large environmental justice implications in the causes of, and the governmental response to, the damage caused by Hurricane Katrina to New Orleans and the provision of contaminated water in Flint, Michigan. *See, e.g.,* Leslie G. Fields, One Heckuva Snafu: The Environmental Justice Implications of Katrina, 33 Fall Hum. Rts. 5 (2006); Robert D. Bullard and Beverly Wright (eds.), Race, Place, and Environmental Injustice After Hurricane Katrina (2009); Catherine Millas Kaiman, Environmental Justice and Community Based Reparations, 39 Seattle U. L. Rev. 1327 (2016) ("As has been recently illustrated by Michigan's state action of providing lead-contaminated water *for over a year* to residents of Flint, Michigan, environmental injustices at the hands of local, state, and federal governments are, unfortunately, all too common.").

3. *Some Revisionism.* The initial round of environmental justice literature in turn produced some revisionist writing. In one article, Professor Lynn E. Blais suggested that the political and market determinations leading to the distribution of risks through siting of facilities may reflect rational and legitimate preferences of individuals. Lynn E. Blais, Environmental Racism Reconsidered, 75 N.C. L. Rev. 75, 81 (1996). Others have re-analyzed the data available on siting and reached somewhat different conclusions than those in the "first wave" of literature on environmental justice. *See, e.g.,* Terence J. Centner, Environmental Justice and Toxic Releases: Establishing Evidence of Discriminatory Effect Based on Race and Not Income, 3 Wis. Envtl. L.J. 119 (1996); Christopher Boerner, Environmental Justice? (1994).

Nonetheless, much of the academic literature considers the empirical question settled as demonstrating the siting disparities and impacts on minority populations. For explanation, Professor Alice Kaswan summarizes:

> Public light on distributional justice prompted numerous empirical assessments on the distribution of undesirable facilities and land uses. These studies largely confirmed that undesirable land uses are unevenly distributed. Racial minorities, particularly African-Americans and Latinos, experience the greatest disproportionate impact. Income is also correlated with undesirable facilities, but less strongly than race.

Alice Kaswan, Environmental Justice and Environmental Law, 24 Fordham Envtl. L. Rev. 149, 151 (2013)

4. *An Ethical Issue.* Perhaps the debate over the numbers obscures a larger point. In a recent article, the authors assert that the issue is not simply the equitable distribution of environmental burdens and benefits. Rather, "the principles of environmental justice are grounded in the realm of ethics." Julia C. Rinne and Carol E. Dinkens, Environmental Justice: Merging Environmental Law and Ethics, 25 WTR Nat. Resources & Env't 3 (2011). They suggest that, regardless of cause, "poor and minority communities appear to bear a disproportionate burden of the environmental hazards associated with landfills and other polluting land uses." *Id.* at 5. They then set out a series of "ethical issues," such as, "Once the decision is made to burden a certain community with an environmental hazard, the ethical analysis shifts to how the community should participate in the decision-making process." *Id.*

Does viewing the issue of environmental justice in terms of "ethics" suggest solutions to the debate over the empirical evidence? Is it helpful in determining the procedures and substantive criteria to be used in approving a particular facility?

5. *Harm from NIMBYism.* Is there a relationship between the NIMBY phenomenon, discussed above in this chapter, and the question of environmental justice? Professor Bullard has argued that the victims of NIMBY are minority communities:

> [T]he cumulative effect of not-in-my-backyard (NIMBY) victories by environmentalists appears to have driven the unwanted facilities toward more vulnerable groups. Black neighborhoods are especially vulnerable to the penetration of unwanted land uses. . . . NIMBY, like white racism, creates and perpetuates privileges for whites at the expense of people of color.

Robert D. Bullard, Dumping in Dixie: Race, Class, and Environmental Quality 46, 108 (1990).

Professor Michael Gerrard has suggested that the consequences of the NIMBY movement are more variable. Michael R. Gerrard, The Victims of NIMBY, 21 Ford. Urb. L.J. 495, 497 (1994). He concluded that local opposition has numerous and complex impacts that vary considerably depending on the nature of the facility that is opposed. For example, he found that opposition to waste disposal facilities "has not generally increased the siting of new landfills and incinerators in minority communities, but it has perpetuated the existence of old, substandard disposal units in those communities." *Id.* at 521. At the same time, it has spurred efforts to recycle and to reduce the creation of waste.

Given the extensive debate over the existence and extent of injustice in the land use siting process, it should come as no surprise that devising solutions that address the issue will not be simple.

A Note on the Response of Federal Law to Environmental Justice Issues

1. *The Executive Order.* A primary response was President Clinton's issuance of Executive Order No. 12898, 59 Fed. Reg. 7629 (1994), entitled Federal Actions to Address Environmental Justice in Minority Populations and Low-Income Populations:

> **§1-103.** *Development of Agency Strategies.* (a) Except as provided in section 6-605 of this order, each Federal agency shall develop an agency-wide environmental justice strategy, as set forth in subsections (b)-(e) of this section that identifies and addresses disproportionately high and adverse human health or environmental effects of its programs, policies, and activities on minority populations and low-income populations. The environmental justice strategy shall list programs, policies, planning and public participation processes, enforcement, and/or rule-makings related to human health or the environment that should be revised to, at a minimum: (1) promote enforcement of all health and environmental statutes in areas with minority populations and low-income populations; (2) ensure greater public participation; (3) improve research and data collection relating to the health of and environment of minority populations and low-income populations; and (4) identify differential patterns of consumption of natural resources among minority populations and low-income populations. In

addition, the environmental justice strategy shall include, where appropriate, a time-table for undertaking identified revisions and consideration of economic and social implications of the revisions.

2. *The Importance of the Executive Order.* The difficulty of securing judicial relief has led plaintiffs pursuing environmental justice issues to rely on administrative and statutory solutions, such as the executive order signed by President Clinton. The executive order is particularly important, for it constitutes governmental recognition that inequities exist in the distribution of risks. Do you think that the processes called for in the order are likely to be effective?

3. *Civil Rights Laws.* In addition to the executive order, the environmental justice problem appeared to call for a response rooted in the civil rights laws. The federal Environmental Protection Agency issued an interim guidance on how it would respond to complaints, filed under Title VI of the 1964 Civil Rights Act, that state or local agencies issuing EPA-funded permits cause discriminatory effects. In 1998, EPA released the Revised Draft Guidance for Investigating Title VI Administrative Complaints Challenging Permits. The Guidance took a broad approach to disparate impact, examining all the circumstances of the particular siting action, including cumulative environmental impacts from the permitting of other facilities. Under the Interim Guidance, if EPA made a finding of "disparate impact," the state agency would bear the burden of showing that the impact does not exist, of mitigating the impact, or of justifying it. But the Interim Guidance has never been finalized.

4. *Litigation under Title VI?* Behind all of this controversy a large issue loomed: would private citizens have a cause of action to enforce Title VI? In *Alexander v. Sandoval*, 532 U.S. 275 (2001), the Court held that no private right of action existed to enforce disparate-impact regulations pursuant to Section 602 of Title VI, 42 U.S.C. §2000e. That left one theory possibly available to plaintiffs seeking to use Title VI to enforce the disparate-impact regulations in a private case: to argue that a cause of action existed under Section 1983 of the Civil Rights Act. However, in *South Camden Citizens in Action v. New Jersey Dep't of Envtl. Protection*, 274 F.3d 771 (3d Cir. 2001), the Third Circuit held that plaintiffs cannot maintain an action under §1983 for disparate impact discrimination in violation of Title VI and its implementing regulations.

5. *Litigation Alleging Intentional Discrimination.* Some cases have attempted to show intentional discrimination in siting decisions. But that standard is quite difficult to meet.

One important decision was *East Bibb Twiggs Neighborhood Ass'n v. Macon-Bibb County Planning & Zoning Comm'n*, 706 F. Supp. 880 (M.D. Ga. 1989), *aff'd*, 896 F.2d 1264 (11th Cir. 1989) (rejecting challenge that racial discrimination motivated the siting of a landfill in an area where a majority of citizens was black). *See also R.I.S.E. v. Kay*, 768 F. Supp. 1144 (E.D. Va. 1991), *aff'd*, 977 F.2d 573 (4th Cir. 1992) (plaintiff failed to establish that placement of landfill in a predominantly black area resulted from intentional discrimination in violation of the Equal Protection Clause); *Bean v. Southwestern Waste Mgmt. Corp.*, 482 F. Supp. 673 (S.D. Tex. 1979), *aff'd*, 782 F.2d 1038 (5th Cir. 1986) (plaintiffs did not establish a substantial likelihood of proving that the grant of a permit had been motivated by purposeful racial discrimination).

In short, even in those instances where plaintiffs may be able to allege a cause of action, the substantive law is a large obstacle. *See, e.g.*, Daniel A. Farber, Disaster Law and Inequality, 25 Law & Ineq. 297, 309 (2007) ("Environmental justice advocates have hit something of a dead end in their efforts to find a legal remedy for . . . harm resulting from exposure to toxic substances."); Mihaela Popescu and Oscar H. Gandy, Jr., Whose Environmental Justice? Social Identity and Institutional Rationality, 19 J. Envtl. L. & Litig. 141 (2004) (noting that the Supreme Court's *Sandoval* decision, discussed in *South Camden*, "has seriously limited the available opportunities for minorities to argue their claims for environmental justice.").

6. *The National Environmental Policy Act.* Federal agencies have begun implementing a variety of process changes to address environmental justice concerns generally. In particular, environmental impact statements prepared under the National Environmental Policy Act, 42 U.S.C. §4321 et seq., have begun analyzing the environmental justice impacts of decisions by federal agencies that have land use implications. Some plaintiffs have argued in litigation that environmental justice analyses in such statements are inadequate.

However, while courts have considered such claims, there have been no outstanding successes for the plaintiffs. *See, e.g., Coalition for Health Ports v. U.S. Coast Guard,* 2015 WL 7460018, at 26 (S.D.N.Y. 2015) ("[T]he Coast Guard did take a 'hard look' at the project's environmental justice impacts . . . .[T]he Coast Guard devoted an entire chapter to environmental justice impacts and complied not only with its own methodology but with CEQ [federal Council on Environmental Quality] guidance as well."); *Crenshaw Subway Coalition v. Los Angeles County Metro. Transp. Auth.,* 2015 WL 6150847, at 30-31 (C.D. Cal. 2015) (while the Federal Transportation Administration "fails to compare the population affected by the [light-rail line extension] Project with the population of Los Angeles County or any other unaffected population," and that failure "might have led the court to conclude that the FTA's analysis was insufficient," the agency did that comparison elsewhere in the administrative record).

Can analyses in environmental impact statements provide the basis for meaningful change?

Some states and localities have also begun to make changes in their land use siting decisions and in their planning to specifically address environmental justice.

■ CITY OF BROCKTON v. ENERGY FACILITIES SITING BOARD (NO. 1)
469 Mass. 196, 14 N.E.3d 167 (2014)

BOTSFORD, J.

Brockton Power Company LLC (Brockton Power, or company) filed a petition . . . with the Energy Facilities Siting Board (board) to construct and operate a 350-megawatt combined-cycle energy generating facility (facility) powered by natural gas and ultra-low sulfur distillate (ULSD) on a 13.2-acre lot in the city of Brockton (city). After extensive hearings, the board approved Brockton Power's petition, with conditions. . . .

On appeal the interveners argue that the board (1) failed to adopt and apply the 2002 environmental justice policy that is a binding environmental protection policy of the Commonwealth . . . We affirm the decision of the board.

Section 69J ¼ requires the board to conduct an evidentiary hearing on a petition to construct a generating facility within 180 days of filing, and to approve a petition within one year of filing if it "determines that the petition meets the following requirements: (i) the description of the proposed generating facility and its environmental impacts are substantially accurate and complete; (ii) the description of the site selection process used is accurate; . . . (iii) the plans for the construction of the proposed generating facility are consistent with current health and environmental protection policies of the commonwealth and with such energy policies as are adopted by the commonwealth for the specific purpose of guiding the decisions of the board; [and] (iv) such plans minimize the environmental impacts consistent with the minimization of costs associated with the mitigation, control, and reduction of the environmental impacts of the proposed generating facility." G.L. c. 164, §69J ¼, fourth & fifth pars. . . .

1. *Environmental justice policy.* The interveners argue that the board erred by failing properly to apply the Commonwealth's environmental justice (EJ) policy, as promulgated by the predecessor to the Executive Office of Energy and Environmental Affairs (EOEEA). The resolution of this issue requires a two-part analysis: whether the EJ policy is among the factors the board must consider under §69J ¼ (and is therefore subject to our review); and if so, whether the board correctly applied the policy to Brockton Power's petition.

The EJ policy states: "Environmental justice is based on the principle that all people have a right to be protected from environmental pollution and to live in and enjoy a clean and healthful environment. Environmental justice is the equal protection and meaningful involvement of all people with respect to the development, implementation, and enforcement of environmental laws, regulations, and policies and the equitable distribution of environmental benefits." The EJ policy defines "[e]qual [p]rotection" to mean "that no group of people, because of race, ethnicity, class, gender, or handicap bears an unfair share of environmental pollution from industrial, commercial, state and municipal operations or have limited access to natural resources, including greenspace (open space) and water resources." An "[e]nvironmental [j]ustice [p]opulation" is defined as "a neighborhood whose annual median household income is equal to or less than [sixty-five] percent of the statewide median or whose population is made up [of twenty-five] percent [m]inority, [f]oreign [b]orn, or [l]acking [e]nglish [l]anguage [p]roficiency." Brockton Power's proposed project site was within one-half mile of EJ communities to the west, north, and northeast.

The EJ policy directs agencies within the EOEEA to "develop their own strategies to proactively promote environmental justice in all neighborhoods in ways that are tailored to the specific mission of each agency . . . . [EOEEA] agencies shall identify and promote agency-sponsored projects, funding decisions, rulemakings or other actions intended to further environmental justice in the Commonwealth." The EJ policy also mandates specific agency action in two areas: enhanced public participation in EJ communities and, in certain circumstances, enhanced substantive review of new projects in EJ communities when a proposed generating facility exceeds thresholds established by the Massachusetts Environmental Policy Act, G.L. c. 30, §§61–62H (MEPA).

With respect to public participation, the EJ policy mandates that "all [EOEEA] agencies shall have an inclusive, robust public participation program that focuses agency resources on outreach activities that enhance public participation opportunities for agency activities that potentially affect EJ populations." The policy calls for "enhanced public participation" through "use of alternative media outlets such as community or ethnic newspapers . . . and translation of materials or interpretation services at public meetings" in cases where a project exceeds Environmental Notification Form (ENF) thresholds for "air, solid and hazardous waste . . . or wastewater and sewage sludge treatment and disposal" as determined by the Secretary of EOEEA (Secretary) under MEPA and its implementing regulations, and the project site is within one mile (or, in the case of air emissions, five miles) from an EJ population.

In addition to these procedural requirements, the EJ policy substantively provides for enhanced analysis and review of "impacts and mitigation" in relation to projects that meet two conditions: (1) the project exceeds "a mandatory EIR [environmental impact report] threshold for air, solid and hazardous waste . . . , or wastewater sewage sludge treatment and disposal"; and (2) the project is located within one mile of an EJ population, or within five miles for projects exceeding the EIR threshold for air. "Enhanced analysis . . . may include analysis of multiple air impacts; data on baseline public health conditions within affected EJ [p]opulation; analysis of technological, site planning, and operational alternatives to reduce impacts; and proposed on-site and off-site mitigation measures to reduce multiple impacts and increase environmental benefits to the affected EJ [p]opulation."

The project at issue here, construction of Brockton Power's facility, was subject to mandatory MEPA review. In conducting that review, the Secretary certified that because the project exceeded the ENF threshold for air and is located within five miles of an EJ community, it was subject to enhanced public participation under the EJ policy. However, the Secretary also certified that the project did not exceed the mandatory EIR threshold for air pollutants, and therefore was not subject to enhanced review under the EJ policy.

The board addressed the EJ policy in its decision, interpreting it to provide for both "enhanced analysis" and additional procedures during a review of a petition filed with the board pursuant to §69J ¹/₄. The board concluded, however, that the EJ policy's enhanced analysis provisions applied only to §69J ¹/₄ petitions that propose a generating facility that would exceed the EIR threshold for air emissions. Because the Secretary's MEPA certification had determined that the facility's expected emissions did not exceed this threshold, the board found that the policy, as applied to Brockton Power's petition, was limited to additional procedures, namely, "enhanced outreach and public participation" during the board's review process.

Before turning to the interveners' claims, however, we first discuss whether the board's interpretation and application of the EJ policy in its decision is subject to our review at all. The board, joined by Brockton Power, contends that judicial review of this aspect of its decision is not available, because the EJ policy states that it "is intended only to improve the internal management of [EOEEA] agencies" and expressly disclaims the creation of "any right, benefit, or trust responsibility, substantive or procedural, enforceable at law or equity," as well as "any right to judicial review involving compliance or noncompliance" with the policy.

The board's contention fails. As the board recognized in its decision, §69J ¹/₄, fifth par., requires the board to determine whether "plans for the construction of the proposed generating facility are consistent with current health and environmental protection policies of the commonwealth and with such energy policies as are adopted by the commonwealth for the specific purpose of guiding the decisions of the board," and also that the EJ policy is among the "environmental protection policies of the Commonwealth." It follows, therefore, that the board's application of the EJ policy is subject to judicial review as part of the court's consideration whether the board's decision meets the requirements of §69J ¼, fifth par . . . . The standard of review is that set out in §69P, namely, whether the board's application "was supported by substantial evidence of record in the board's proceedings; and was arbitrary, capricious or an abuse of discretion."

The interveners' claims concerning the EJ policy, however, fail on the merits. As mentioned, the Secretary certified that the proposed facility did not exceed the mandatory EIR threshold under MEPA for air pollutants. Under the express language of the EJ policy, therefore, Brockton Power's petition was not subject to "enhanced analysis." The interveners do not challenge the Secretary's determination under MEPA, nor do they argue that the board failed to meet the EJ policy's procedural requirements. In the context of this case, we cannot accept the interveners' contention that, independent of a triggering MEPA threshold for enhanced analysis, the EJ policy required the board to apply unspecified "substantive equal protection" principles to its review of Brockton Power's proposed facility and that the board's failure to do so rendered its decision arbitrary, capricious, or an abuse of the board's discretion. The interveners do not point to a specific or affirmative requirement in the EJ policy to do so, and we have found none. . . .

■ ENVIRONMENTAL JUSTICE ELEMENT, CITY OF JURUPA (CALIFORNIA) AREA PLAN (2014)

GOAL:

An open and transparent public process that improves the quality of life relative to a cleaner and healthier environment. . . .

OBJECTIVE EJ-1:

Meaningful participation in the public process by all members of the community.

Policies:

EJ-1.1: Ensure that affected residents have the opportunity to participate in decisions that impact their health.

EJ-1.2: Facilitate the involvement of residents, businesses and organizations in all aspects of the planning process.

EJ-1.3: Utilize culturally appropriate approaches to public participation and involvement.

EJ-1.4: Schedule public meetings on key issues affecting the public at times and locations most convenient to community members.

EJ-1.5: Utilize a variety of communication techniques and social media tools to convey information to the public.

EJ-1.6: Provide translation and interpretation services at public meetings on issues affecting populations whose primary language is not English. Translation time should not be taken from the person's time limit for comments.

EJ-1.7: Support efforts to raise the public's awareness of the importance of a healthy environment and physical activity. EJ-1.8: Educate decision makers and the general public on the principles of environmental justice.

EJ-1.9: Consult with Native American Tribes early in the process on issues that could affect culturally significant areas.

EJ-1.10: Collaborate with and among public agencies to leverage resources, avoid duplication of effort and enhance the effectiveness of public participation.

EJ-1.11 Identify those areas of the City most vulnerable to environmental hazards through CalEnviroScreen, the Environmental Justice Screening Model (EJSM) or other model. . . .

Notes and Comments

1. *Attacking Distributional Inequities.* Assuming that, at its core, environmental justice in part concerns distributional inequities in the siting of unwanted land uses, the question becomes how to frame a response to that problem. As you can surmise from what you have studied in this book, crafting a response is not simple despite the deluge of academic literature on the subject. One article suggested that the response to environmental injustice in the land use context has taken five forms, "each with corresponding conceptions of, or ways of thinking about, the environmental justice problem":

> (1) to study the evidence and causes of the distribution of environmental hazards and LULUs (evidentiary conceptions); (2) to organize politically against proposed or existing LULUs (power conceptions); (3) to vindicate the constitutional, statutory, or common-law rights of those affected disproportionately by environmental hazards or LULUs (legal conceptions); (4) to heighten enforcement of environmental laws (environmental conceptions); and (5) to seek or rely on market mechanisms to address the distribution problem (economic conceptions).

Craig Anthony (Tony) Arnold, Land Use Regulation and Environmental Justice, 30 Envtl. L. Rep. 10395 (2000). In Joshua Glasgow, Not in Anybody's Backyard? The Non-Distributive Problem with Environmental Justice, 13 Buff. Envtl. L.J. 69, 108 (2005), the author breaks down suggested remedies for the environmental justice problem into three categories: (1) the "equal protection" model requiring regions to accept their fair share of pollution; (2) the "due process" model calling for increased public participation in the siting process; and (3) the "property" model calling for compensation to those who suffer harms.

Into which categories do the City of Brockton and Jurupa policies fall? Is the real problem that the idea of environmental justice is extremely broad? Doesn't the environmental justice movement call into question the very foundation of the current land use system with respect to the consequences of siting decisions?

2. *Administrative Participation as a Tool.* Some have suggested that environmental justice has to begin at the administrative level and have urged that new voices must be heard. The National Academy of Public Administration studied the connection between environmental justice and land use controls. National Academy of Public Administration, Addressing Community Concerns: How Environmental Justice Relates to Land Use Planning and Zoning (July 2003). Among its recommendations, the report suggests that local governments must make a greater outreach to affected citizens in the community:

> Local governments should help residents of low-income and people-of-color communities participate in planning and zoning decisions and ensure that their concerns are integrated into planning and zoning documents. This help may include translating relevant materials into other languages, using different places and times for public meetings to facilitate public participation and enable citizens to keep their regular work-day commitments, taking extra steps for outreach to communities unaccustomed to participating in government decisions, establishing ongoing partnerships with community organizations, facilitating dialogues on a continuing basis, and placing notices in publications or other media formats that are more likely to reach residents of low-income or people-of-color communities.

Id. at 22.

As the *City of Brockton* case demonstrates, some states have addressed the participation issue. For example, in Connecticut, if an applicant seeks a permit from the Connecticut Department of Energy and Environmental Protection or that state's Siting Council for a facility in an "Environmental Justice community," it must file a "meaningful public participation plan" with the agency. Conn. Gen. Stat. Ann. §22a-20a(b). *See also* Steven Bonorris and Nicholas Targ, Environmental Justice in the Laboratories of Democracy, 25 Fall Nat. Resources & Env't 44 (2010) (discussing what it terms the "Public Participation Practices Model" of implementing environmental justice).

The EPA has also adopted a policy to "Facilitate Meaningful Community Engagement in Planning and Land Use Decisions" as part of its environmental justice strategy. It states that "[p]lanners and community-based organizations can use interactive, customizable strategies to engage low-income, minority, tribal, and overburdened residents who face barriers to participation, are not traditionally involved in public processes, or are particularly affected by development proposals." Environmental Protection Agency, Creating Equitable, Healthy, and Sustainable Communities: Strategies for Advancing Smart Growth, Environmental Justice, and Equitable Development (2013).

3. *The Newark Ordinance.* In 2016, Newark, New Jersey passed what some pronounced a "first in the nation" environmental justice ordinance. The law, known as the "Environmental Justice and Cumulative Impact Ordinance," requires the city to prepare a Natural Resource Index (NRI) detailing existing environmental, health, demographic, and land use information. The index would serve as a "baseline" for analyzing new development applications. Then, applicants for major

commercial or industrial uses would have to use the NRI to prepare an "Environmental Review Checklist" on the proposed project. The city's Environmental Commission can then prepare an "opinion" and submit its recommendation to the Planning Board or the Zoning Board of Adjustment. *See* https://newark.legistar .com/LegislationDetail.aspx?ID=2770971&GUID=D0C566D0-463A-482D-A4AC-78884351DA79&FullText=1 (last visited Oct. 26, 2016).

How helpful are the procedural steps in the City of Brockton, Jurupa, and Newark enactments in ensuring environmental justice in siting decisions?

4. *State Anti-Discrimination Statutes.* California Government Code §11135 states:

> No person in the State of California shall, on the basis of race, national origin, ethnic group identification, religion, age, sex, sexual orientation, color, genetic information, or disability, be unlawfully denied full and equal access to the benefits of, or be unlawfully subjected to discrimination under, any program or activity that is conducted, operated, or administered by the state or by any state agency, is funded directly by the state, or receives any financial assistance from the state.

In *Comunidad En Accion v. Los Angeles City Council*, 162 Cal. Rptr. 3d 423 (Ct. App. 2013), plaintiffs challenged the siting of solid waste facilities in a predominantly Latino neighborhood, alleging a violation of §11135. The court rejected the claim on the basis that no state funding was involved in the particular city agency involved. A dissent disagreed, finding that "[a]t a time when federal state and local governments are calling for increased vigilance to stop imposing disproportional environmental burdens on lower income communities, the majority discards a potential tool for the enhancement of environmental justice."

Will this type of statute be useful in ensuring that land use decisions do not disproportionately impact lower income communities?

5. *The Usefulness of Policies.* From the materials presented above you can discern that policies concerning environmental justice have been adopted at all levels of government. How effective are they? Consider the following conclusion:

> In our research, we have found that policies on environmental justice, generally, are more effective at recognizing the plight of minority and low-income communities in regards to adverse environmental conditions than they are at actually addressing the problem. By creating a policy on environmental justice, a state's policymakers not only publicly recognize the plight of traditionally disempowered groups, but affirmatively take a stance on the side of protecting these communities. The provisions of environmental justice policies are most often incapable of actually addressing the problem at hand, essentially making these policies more symbolic than authentic.

Tonya Lewis & Jessica Owley, Symbolic Politics for Disempowered Communities: State Environmental Justice Policies, 29 BYU J. Pub. L. 183, 186 (2014). Assuming this statement is accurate, what further steps would you suggest? For example, would federal preemption of certain decisions help attain environmental justice in siting decisions?

6. *Future Directions of the Movement.* Commentators continue to evaluate the effectiveness and future of the environmental justice movement. For example, Professor Gauna has suggested that "[p]erhaps the most important contribution the environmental justice movement has made . . . has been to bring to the surface the potential conflict between efficiency and equity and the complicated interplay

between the two principles." Eileen Gauna, An Essay on Environmental Justice: The Past, the Present, and Back to the Future, 42 Nat. Res. J. 701, 706 (2002). As she develops the argument, the "willingness to pay" criterion is the foundation upon which efficiency is measured and resources allocated. However, she continues, "it does not necessarily follow that environmental necessities that affect public health can or should be distributed this way. Everyone, regardless of their wealth, should be able to breathe clean air and drink uncontaminated water." *Id.*

Do you see any way the principles of efficiency and equity can be reconciled, or at least co-exist?

Another author has also suggested where the environmental justice movement should head:

> [T]hose of us concerned with environmental justice should focus more attention on housing integration as an ultimate goal. We must at least acknowledge that, in some instances, exit and integration may be the best option for residents of particularly environmentally beleaguered, racially segregated communities. [Previously] I, like many who have been working as environmental justice advocates, have been animated by a vision of community empowerment for residents of poor communities of color. This vision tends to translate into the espousal of remedies aimed at preserving existing communities — "community preservationist" remedies. . . .

Rachel Godsil, Environmental Justice and the Integrationist Ideal, 49 N.Y. L. Sch. L. Rev. 1109, 1111-12 (2004-05).

What implications would these views have for land use law? Where do you see the movement for environmental justice heading in terms of land use?

17

Protection of Cultural and Aesthetic Values

A. INTRODUCTION

This chapter examines the use of land use regulatory tools to protect cultural and aesthetic values. The material includes regulation to preserve historic buildings and sites, and regulation of the design, color and architectural form of new building development. It also addresses other types of aesthetic regulation relating to subjects such as signs, junkyards, fences, scenic views, landscapes, and tree and vegetation protection. Like other areas of land use regulation, the subjects covered in this chapter are marked with controversy, as local governments throughout the nation balance the benefits of regulation with the burdens imposed by these restrictions on individual freedoms and private property rights.

1. Review and Synthesis

In many ways the issues that arise in aesthetic regulation constitute a review of subjects covered previously in this casebook. The following subjects studied in previous chapters are directly relevant:

- Aesthetic regulation is imposed through tools that you learned about in Chapter 2. They include special permits required for any change in an historic property, the use of overlay and special zoning districts, and site plan review techniques, as well as application of zoning restrictions, performance standards, and mitigating conditions.

- State law issues that often are involved in aesthetic regulation relate to a city's legal authority to enact the particular program, and state and local law procedural questions. They also involve the same federal constitutional issues that often arise in zoning cases: substantive due process, equal protection, and First Amendment claims. All of these are addressed in Chapters 7 and 8.
- Historic preservation litigants in particular often raise takings claims, and the leading case on the applicability of the takings clause in this context is *Penn Central v. City of New York*, which you read in Chapter 7.
- Aesthetic regulation can take the form of conditions placed on project approvals. Conditions of this type may be subject to the "*Nollan-Dolan*" constitutional analysis covered in Chapter 7.
- Regulation of billboards raises free expression issues, and the leading case is *Metromedia Inc. v. City of San Diego*, 453 U.S. 490 (1981), another case you read in Chapter 8.
- As you learned in Chapter 10, many communities today are subject to recorded covenants administered by a homeowners association. These covenants often allow the association to regulate the aesthetic features of a development, such as the color used to paint the outside of the units or the types of architectural improvements that an individual owner may construct. Disputes over these types of regulations are normally private rather than public, as they concern the contractual terms enforced by the covenant. However, as the proliferation of homeowners associations continues and their powers expand, questions are being raised if some of these restrictions may be subject to constitutional constraints. According to an estimate of The Community Associations Institute, HOAs governed almost 26.2 million American homes and 68 million residents in 2015. National and State Statistical Review for 2015, Community Associations Institute (2015), at https://www.caionline.org/AboutCommunityAssociations/Pages/StatisticalInformation.aspx (last visited Oct. 26, 2016).

2. The Rationale for Aesthetic Regulation

Village of Euclid v. Ambler Realty, covered in Chapter 2, presented the original purpose of land use regulation as principally to prevent nuisance-like conflicts. As regulation evolved through the twentieth century, the regulatory system expanded to recognize many other goals, such as ensuring a variety of housing types, promoting economic development, and protecting the environment. Today, planning and zoning controls also are directed at promoting largely aesthetic values. Aesthetic restrictions on land use and development that regulate the visual environment are now quite commonplace. Since such controls are sometimes perceived to be intrusive on individual freedom and restrictive of private property rights, they may also be highly controversial.

Perhaps a good starting point is the question whether aesthetic regulation is a qualitatively different extension of the field of land use regulation. Answering this question requires the identification of the public purposes sought to be furthered by aesthetic restrictions on land use and development.

■ JOHN J. COSTONIS, ICONS AND ALIENS: LAW, AESTHETICS, AND ENVIRONMENTAL CHANGE
15-19, 76-79 (1989)

THE CASE FOR LEGAL AESTHETICS

[W]e are condemned to come to terms with aesthetics, whether we like it or not. Aesthetics considerations are ubiquitous, "underl[ying] *all* zoning, usually in combination with other factors with which they are interwoven," as one judge has accurately observed. Lawmakers therefore must attend to these considerations unless they are prepared to shut down land use regulation in its entirety. To suppose, moreover, that the other values advanced by land use controls are hard, coherent, objective, nonmanipulable, and fully accessible to economics or any other form of analysis is to substitute one kind of tooth fairy logic for another. . . .

If there is a case to be made for legal aesthetics, it must be centered in legal aesthetics' role as a regulator of change in the symbolic environment. Legal aesthetics does for the social system what homeostatic agents do for the human body. Physical health requires the maintenance of key biological constancies within the body. When they go out of balance, biological indicators signal the danger and homeostatic agents swing into action to re-establish equilibrium. Individuals and groups, too, must cope with the threats to their personal and social identity that icon-menacing aliens present. They expect that aesthetics measures will function in a socially homeostatic fashion by precluding, or at least minimizing, the shock of the alien.

The case is not a simple one to make, however. . . .

Little can be said about legal aesthetics in one breath that cannot plausibly be denied in the next. Hence, the necessity of thinking as clearly about legal aesthetics' purpose as this elusive topic allows. The government should not set in motion programs capable of generating such far-flung and contradictory results absent the focused vision of the program's ends and means as envisaged by the substantive due process doctrine. For legal aesthetics, unfortunately, that vision remains blurred to this day. For example, many judges embarrass us and themselves in their clumsy attempts to found legal aesthetics' public purpose in beauty. Those who insist that the government may zone "solely for aesthetics" don't even try. Their formula calls to mind the nineteenth-century Romantics' rallying cry, "art for art's sake," as well as Keats's "'Beauty is truth, truth beauty,' — that is all/Ye know on earth, and all ye need to know."

Aside from confusing metaphysics with law, these judges beg the question. Even assuming — as I do not — that beauty can be defined for legal purposes, judges are still obligated by the substantive due process doctrine to identify the governmental purpose advanced by measures enacted in beauty's name. Those who attempt this step often sink even further into the mire as, from time to time, the moral theory of art creeps into their discourse. A favorite of Plato and John Ruskin, the claim is that good art makes good citizens, and vice versa. Unfortunately, the theory was praised by Hitler as well, who banished the Bauhaus School from Germany lest it corrupt the Third Reich. The asserted linkage between art and civic virtue is simply too problematic, moreover, to serve as a persuasive justification for aesthetics regulation. . . .

Other judges take refuge in the assertion that beauty's preservation increases property values. Sometimes the facts support the assertion, as in the case of gentrifying areas designated as historic districts. But the facts often cut the other way as well. My own studies in Chicago document that, depending upon the building in question, landmark designation can severely diminish a structure's value and its resulting tax yield to the city. . . .

Fortunately, encouraging signs can be detected in more recent judicial opinions intimating a shift from a beauty- to a stability-based rationale for legal aesthetics. Illustrative is the statement of a District of Columbia court contained in its ruling on a controversy concerning the proposed demolition of Washington's Willard Hotel, a National Register of Historic Places entrant: "The retention of fine architecture, especially in the capitol city of a relatively young country such as ours, lends a certain stability and cultural continuity, which can only contribute over the years to national substance." To like effect is the comment of a Michigan judge in a 1972 opinion sustaining a municipal sign ordinance: "The modern trend is to recognize that a community's aesthetic well-being can contribute to urban man's psychological and emotional stability. . . . We should begin to realize . . . that a visually satisfying city can stimulate an identity and pride which is the foundation for social responsibility and citizenship."

Similar movement is evident on the legislative and administrative fronts, perhaps most clearly in the field of historic preservation. While various statutory or administrative texts could be cited, none better reflects this movement than the following excerpt from a 1981 United States Department of the Interior policy directive: "The historic buildings in a community are tangible links with the nation's past that help provide a sense of identity and stability that is often missing in this era of constant change. . . . Preservation is an anchor that keeps communities together and re-establishes pride and economic vitality." The reformulation of legal aesthetics' goals suggested in these excerpts . . . affords a cogent response to the substantive due process objection.

Notes and Comments

1. *Law, Zoning, and Aesthetics.* Professor Costonis argues that other values advanced by land use regulation are not too unlike aesthetics interests, that is, they are not necessarily "hard, coherent, objective, and nonmanipulable." Do you see qualitative differences between those values and the value of aesthetics? Hasn't zoning always been concerned with "the look of things"? How about restrictions on lot size, height, yards, frontage, setbacks, bulk, lot coverage, and fences? Are these restrictions ordinarily established by analysis of scientific data, and are they enacted to protect public health and safety? These zoning restrictions clearly shape a desired form of the visual environment and may relate only derivatively (through their impact on the visual environment) to protecting the character of the area and property values.

2. *Judicial Evolution of Aesthetic Doctrine.* The judicial attitude toward aesthetic restrictions can be described as evolving through three different stages or periods. Early court decisions usually held as a matter of substantive due process that visual beauty was an inherently arbitrary and capricious standard for police power regulation. *See, e.g., Spann v. City of Dallas,* 235 S.W. 513, 516 (Tex. 1921) ("it is

not the law . . . that a man may be deprived of the lawful use of his property because his tastes are not in accord with those of his neighbors").

Gradually the judicial attitude toward aesthetic regulation changed as many courts approved regulation for aesthetic purposes, but only if, in addition to aesthetics, the regulation also served some other derivative and legitimate public purpose, such as promoting tourism, regulating traffic safety, or protecting property values. *See, e.g., General Outdoor Advertising Co. v. Indianapolis*, 172 N.E. 309, 312 (Ind. 1930) (while "aesthetic or artistic considerations alone are not considered sufficient to warrant the exercise of the police power," "aesthetic considerations enter in to a great extent as an auxiliary consideration").

The judicial movement toward recognition of aesthetic regulation was greatly bolstered by the Supreme Court's opinion in *Berman v. Parker*, 348 U.S. 26 (1954). In that case the Court declared, "It is within the power of the legislature to determine that the community should be beautiful as well as healthy, spacious as well as clean, well balanced as well as carefully controlled." 348 U.S. at 33. That case, though influential, was an eminent domain case and did not expressly sanction visual beauty as a standard for police power regulation. By the late 1960s, however, an increasing number of state courts were ruling that aesthetics alone is a sufficient basis for land use regulation. *See, e.g., State v. Smith*, 618 S.W.2d 474, 477 (Tenn. 1981) ("We are therefore of the opinion that in modern society aesthetic considerations may well constitute a legitimate basis for the exercise of the police power"). *See generally* Elizabeth A. Garvin & Glen S. LeRoy, Design Guidelines: The Law of Aesthetic Controls, Land Use L. & Zoning Dig. 3, 5, (April 2003) (listing 37 states as authorizing regulation based on aesthetics alone).

This recent body of case law now establishes the so-called modern aesthetic doctrine, sanctioning regulation of land use for "aesthetics alone." The court decisions, however, often have left undecided the constitutionally permissible scope and limits of aesthetic regulation. Could a state legislature, for example, mandate that everyone wear powder blue jackets with red and white stars on the Fourth of July? Is there "anything" that arguably does not affect the public interest?

3. *The Rational of Modern Aesthetic Doctrine.* Professor Costonis suggests that the visual environment can be thought of as a stage "rich in icons invested with and broadcasting our deepest religious, artistic, social, and personal commitments." If so, does that idea justify aesthetic regulation and advance a coherent principle around which a legal regime of aesthetic regulation may be fashioned? Can a community's aesthetic well-being contribute to "man's psychological and emotional stability" and stimulate an identity and pride, "which is the foundation for social responsibility and citizenship"? In this view aesthetic regulation furthers the public interest by preventing harm to "our symbolic environment."

Picking up on this theme, courts in modern aesthetic doctrine cases often have ruled that aesthetic regulation promotes the happiness, comfort, and general welfare of persons in the community. These are cases where aesthetics is found to be linked with derivative human values related to existing features of the visual environment selected for protection. *See, e.g., Sun Oil Co. v. City of Madison Heights*, 199 N.W.2d 525, 529 (Mich. App. 1972) (aesthetic regulation linked with "urban man's psychological and emotional stability"); *Village of Hudson v. Albrecht, Inc.*, 458 N.E.2d 852, 856 (Ohio 1984) (aesthetics linked with "citizens' happiness, comfort and general well-being"); *State v. Miller*, 416 A.2d 821, 824 (N.J. 1980) (aesthetics linked with "psychological and emotional stability and well-being" as well as "civic pride").

Is this the legitimizing rational for modern aesthetic regulation?

4. *A Harm Prevention Rationale?* Modern cases seem always to sanction only "aesthetics in context," preventing harm to existing features of the visual environment that are thought to reasonably promote the general welfare, and not regulating "something" as an isolated work of art that would necessarily involve promoting some official standard of visual beauty. Even landmark preservation restrictions seem to share this rationale. *See* Edward H. Ziegler, *Visual Environment Regulation and Derivative Human Values; The Emerging Rationale Basis for Modern Aesthetic Doctrine,* 9 Zoning & Plan. L. Rep. 17 (1986) (suggesting that court decisions adopting modern aesthetic doctrine often embrace the rationale of preventing substantial harm to existing features of the visual environment and related derivative human values). The author suggests that this "harm prevention rationale" has the potential for imposing a greater degree of discipline on aesthetic regulation. It can do so by requiring intelligible standards derived from those features of the visual environment selected for protection, and by requiring that regulation as applied prevent substantial harm to those features of the visual environment sought to be preserved. He summarizes:

> The doctrine as restated would shift the attention of legislators, administrators, and the courts away from the futile search for visual standards of beauty or ugliness. Instead, the doctrine as restated would focus on the cogency of a claim that certain features of the visual environment relate to widely shared stability-identity values, the identification and articulation of those specific features of the visual environment sought to be protected, the clarity of regulatory standards derived therefrom, and the extent to which regulation unnecessarily restricts private rights in preventing substantial harm to those existing features of the environment protected by regulation.

Id. at 19.

Do you agree? Are early court decisions disapproving of "visual beauty" as a standard for regulation still "good law"? Keep this rationale in mind as we examine various forms of aesthetic regulation throughout this chapter. If this is the rationale, might municipalities be only subject to the task that they hire good planners, rather than stupid staff, as was famously distinguished by Justice Scalia in *Lucas?*

5. *Challenging Issues in Aesthetic Regulation: Colors.* Judicial endorsement of aesthetic regulation, even in recent court decisions, continues to be somewhat cautious, and with good reason. Aesthetic regulation conflicts with strongly held cultural values of individuality, pluralism, and diversity. The central question is how far aesthetic regulation should legitimately extend. Let us assume that a certain type of development is in such aesthetic conflict with others in an area that a city may legitimately deny it. Perhaps property values in the area, as a whole, are bolstered by such a decision. However, once we proceed down that slippery aesthetic slope, where does it stop?

Take, for example, regulating the colors that houses may be painted. Opponents argue, with some justification, that the public interest involved in such decisions is so small (or even nonexistent) that the regulation should not stand under the police power. Furthermore, some of the citizens painting in loud colors may claim a cultural or even quasi-political motive for their color choice, as the use of loud colors is commonplace in countries from which they immigrated to the United States. Are there First Amendment rights, at least in this community, that the proposed ordinance violates? *See* Mariana Valverde, The Ethic of Diversity: Local Law and the Negotiation of Local Norms, 33 Law & Soc. Inquiry 895 (2008); Lindsay Nash, Expression By Ordinance: Preemption and Proxy in Local Legislation, 25 Geo. Immigr. L.J. 243 (2011).

6. *A Possible Framework for Analysis: The Visual Environment.* Another example is protection of views. If aesthetics alone is a legitimate goal of the exercise of the police power, then protection of views arguably falls within that goal. Recall the Supreme Court's discussion in the *Nollan* case, covered in Chapter 7, which appeared to endorse the legitimacy of protecting ocean views. But should one person's property enjoyment be restricted simply because her property is situated at a lower height than other property, and those residing higher up wish to preserve their views? What is the legitimate and permissible scope of the general welfare goals and purposes that aesthetic regulation of the visual environment may support? *See* 2 Edward H. Ziegler, Rathkopf's The Law of Zoning & Planning §16:8 (4th ed. 2005 & Supp. 2016). Therein, the author suggests the following framework for adjudging the validity of a regulation under modern aesthetic doctrine. Aesthetic regulation, under this analysis would be held valid where:

> There is a reasonable basis to believe that those features of the visual environment selected for protection reflect widely shared human meanings and associations that the regulation is intended to preserve;
> There exist reasonably intelligible standards for regulation derived from those existing features of the visual environment selected for protection; and
> The regulation as applied is reasonably related to preventing substantial harm to those features of the visual environment selected for protection.

Do the following court decisions holding aesthetic regulation invalid support this suggested framework for analysis? *See Route 22 Properies v. Town Bd. of Town of Southeast,* 767 N.Y.S.2d 813 (A.D. 2003) (denial of sign permit held arbitrary and capricious since finding that sign would, under the ordinance, be "ugly" or "offensive" had no rational basis related to existing character of the area); *Gibson v. Sussex County Council,* 877 A.2d 54 (Del. Ch. 2005) (holding that denial of permit for three-unit townhome was arbitrary and capricious since townhomes were common in the area and the area in question had no distinctive harmony in building design); *MCC Outdoor v. Town of Franklinton Bd. of Comm'rs,* 620 S.E. 794 (N.C. Ct. App. 2005) (finding of incompatibility of billboard held arbitrary where the area in question was commercial with extensive existing businesses and signs); *Kosalka v. Town of Georgetown,* 752 A.2d 183 (Me. 2003) (the standard "conserve natural beauty" is not a constitutionally permissible standard for review of new development); *City of Nichols Hills v. Richardson,* 939 P.2d 17 (Okla. Ct. Crim. App. 1997) (holding unreasonable aesthetic regulation prohibiting parking of pick-up trucks in residential area between 2:00 A.M. and 5:00 A.M.).

7. *The First Amendment.* Perhaps the most important critique of aesthetics control, even at the community association/private government level, is that it may conflict with First Amendment rights. *See* Darrel C. Menthe, Aesthetic Regulation and the Development of First Amendment Jurisprudence, 19 B. U. Pub. Int. L.J. 225, 260 (2010). The article concludes that "[t]he time may have come to start talking seriously about putting the first amendment back in balance with other freedoms" and cites *United States v. Stevens,* 559 U.S. 460 (2010). In *Stevens,*

an animal cruelty case, the Court criticized the government's assertion that "(w)hether a given category of speech enjoys First Amendment protection depends upon a categorical balancing of the value of the speech against its societal costs." The Court warned: "As a free-floating test for First Amendment coverage, that sentence is startling and dangerous."

Has the evolution of the notion that aesthetics protection falls within the police power of the state been expanded too far? In *Discount Inn v. City of Chicago*, 803 F.3d 317, 326-27 (7th Cir. 2015), a challenge to a weed control ordinance, Judge Posner in his eloquent way posed the balancing act:

> We must be careful not to impose a minimal standard of "expressiveness" for determining when an object is art and therefore protected by the First Amendment from government prohibition or destruction. In 1917 Marcel Duchamp exhibited a urinal that he called "Fountain"—it is a famous work of art, though Duchamp had not designed, built, altered, or decorated the urinal. But Discount Inn does not claim to have added *anything* to the weeds that grow on its lots—not even a name. Allowing weeds to grow tall cannot, in and of itself, be regarded as creating works of art.

He concluded:

> Taken to its logical extreme, the plaintiff's defense of the weed would preclude any efforts by local governments to prevent unsightly or dangerous uses of private property. Homeowners would be free to strew garbage on their front lawn, graze sheep there, and broadcast Beethoven's Fifth Symphony 24 hours a day through outdoor loudspeakers—all in the name of the First Amendment.

Id. at 327.

B. HISTORIC PRESERVATION REGULATION

The rationale for historic preservation, while aesthetic in nature, is less controversial. Academics and others have postulated that societal benefits, both monetary and psychological, accrue from preserving historic sites. Furthermore, a societal consensus seems to support historic regulation; increasingly, even small communities are concerned about preserving the best of their past for future generations. Indeed, the country is in the midst of a long-term historic preservation "boom." One statistic can give you a sense of the growth. In 1957, about 11 communities in the Southeast and Northeast had enacted historic preservation ordinances. By 1983, there were between 8000 and 10,000 historic preservation commissions throughout the entire country. American Planning Ass'n, Preparing a Historic Preservation Ordinance (1983). In the last 30 years, these efforts have continued to grow.

A problem here is the cost involved. When historic districts are created, the concept of "reciprocity of advantage," which underlies the judicial acceptance of zoning, applies. Individual properties benefit from the ambience of the entire district, and burdens as well as benefits are reciprocal. Designation of individual historic landmarks, however, may be quite different. Requiring the preservation of an individual structure can impose significant, specific costs on individual landowners, arguably without the corresponding reciprocity normally found in zoning ordinances. In this respect, the facts in the *Penn Central* case, discussed in Chapter 7, may be somewhat atypical, for in that case the plaintiff admitted for purposes of the litigation that it could earn a reasonable return on the railroad station as it then existed. In many cases, the ability to fashion a productive use of a specific "landmarked" property can be difficult; the nature of the property and the inability to make changes in it rule out many uses that would otherwise be appropriate for such property.

These issues often play out when the owner seeks to demolish the building. Demolition may be delayed while the subject is studied, historic preservation officers are consulted, and efforts are made to find alternative uses for the building. At the same time, even when these efforts are exhausted, some laws allow demolition of a historically landmarked structure only if the owner can meet a somewhat stringent statutory standard, such as showing that no economically viable use for the property as it now stands is possible.

Historic preservation, then, is one of those areas of land use regulation where private property rights are often in dramatic conflict with regulation. Is historic preservation "almost communism," as the mayor of one small Florida town with an historic preservation ordinance opined? Or is it, as the local newspaper responded, a "well-conceived idea call[ing] for protecting the city against encroaching development, preserving its historic buildings and enhancing the local economy"? Opinion, Don't Tear Down Town History, Orlando Sentinel at K4 (June 21, 1998). Even if it is a great idea to preserve a particular building, the question is always who should pay for the destruction of the building owner's use opportunities, and regulation (as opposed to eminent domain by taking a negative easement) typically puts that burden on the owner whose property is selected for protection.

We now have good examples of how historic preservation can be coupled with economic vitality and tourism. Not every historic building will become an economic success story, but the economic potential of historic preservation exists in some places. Still, while some European countries have made historic preservation a government priority and funded it, the United States has not done so. Indeed, in recent years funding for preservation at the federal level has declined. *See, generally,* Rebecca Birmingham, Smash or Save: New York City Landmarks Preservation Act and New Challenges to Historic Preservation, 19 J. L. & Pol'y 271 (2010) (discussing need for regulatory reform and increased economic support for building owners); Jennifer Kuntz, A Guide to Solar Panel Installation at Grand Central Terminal: Creating a Policy of Sustainable Rehabilitation in Local and National Rehabilitation Law, 10 Vt. J. Envtl. L. 315 (2009) (discussing policies and issues related to the sustainable rehabilitation of historic buildings). Preservationists also have sought private funding.

Efforts by those in charge of historical sites are understandable. Still, these are *historic* sites. At some point, do intrusions by modern economic interests reach a level that is inconsistent with the purpose of preserving the site? Yet it has been suggested, to avoid the pitfalls of changing public opinion and changing public finances, that the law endow historic buildings and other inanimate historic objects with independent legal rights to preservation and a damage-free existence, and that these rights be enforced by appointed legal guardians. *See* Nathaniel Guest, Putting

History on a Stone Foundation: Toward Legal Rights for Historic Properties, 18 Temp. Pol. & Civ. Rts. L. Rev. 699 (2009).

Historic preservation ordinances thus present a range of issues. The initial question is: what is the rationale for protecting historical landmarks? Also, can the law translate aesthetic goals into legal standards for building preservation? From a legal standpoint, you need to consider the criteria for designation of property as an historical landmark as well as the consequences of "landmarking" — that is, how that designation affects the owner's right to use the property. The New York Court of Appeals decision in *Teachers Ins. & Annuity Ass'n v. City of New York* is a classic case that introduces you to these questions.

■ TEACHERS INSURANCE & ANNUITY ASSOCIATION OF AMERICA v. CITY OF NEW YORK
623 N.E.2d 526 (N.Y. 1993)

KAYE, Chief Judge.

At issue on this appeal is the statutory authority of the Landmarks Preservation Commission to landmark the interior of the Four Seasons restaurant in Manhattan.

Appellant, Teachers Insurance and Annuity Association of America (TIAA), owner of the building that houses the restaurant, argues that the Commission has exceeded its authority under the New York City Landmarks Law. . . .

I.

In 1959, the Four Seasons restaurant opened on the first two floors of the newly constructed Seagram Building on Park Avenue in New York City. The building, designed by the German architectural master Ludwig Mies van der Rohe, is the sole example of his work in New York City. The celebrated American architect Philip Johnson, who assisted Mies van der Rohe in the building design, created the restaurant interior. Both the building exterior and the restaurant interior—which reflects and complements the building's modular design and architectural innovation have been acclaimed as quintessential expressions of the International style. No one disputes their special historical and aesthetic interest.

When TIAA purchased the building from Joseph E. Seagram & Sons in 1980, the portions of the ground and first floors occupied by the restaurant were subject to a 25-year lease that will expire in 1999. By agreement with Seagram, appellant must use its best efforts to continue to lease the space for restaurant use. If it cannot, Seagram has an option until 2025 to find a suitable restaurant tenant. TIAA also agreed to propose the building for landmarking when it became eligible.

In December 1987, appellant proposed the designation of the Seagram Building, including the building lobby and outdoor plaza. Prior to the public hearings before the Commission, and without consulting appellant, the restaurant operators themselves proposed to the Commission that the restaurant interior also be considered for landmark status. The Commission then added that proposal to the calendar and in May and July 1988 conducted public hearings.

Dozens of witnesses and letters before the Commission from prominent architects, artists, community leaders and others supported the designation of the Four

Seasons interior. TIAA, several commercial real estate interests and architect Paul Byard opposed the designation.

In October 1989, the Commission unanimously landmarked the building, outdoor plaza, building lobby and the Four Seasons interior. Noting the particular architectural features of the restaurant, including its distinctive design, integral relation to the building architecture and innovative use of new technologies, the Commission found that the restaurant interior "has a special character, special historical and aesthetic interest and value as part of the development, heritage and cultural characteristics of New York City" and that "the Interior is one which is customarily open and accessible to the public, and to which the public is customarily invited." The restaurant designation accords landmark status to the entrance lobby, Grill Room, Pool Room and balcony dining rooms, and includes the marble pool, walnut bar, wall surfaces, floor surfaces, ceiling surfaces, doors, railings, metal draperies and two hanging metal sculptures commissioned by Johnson from the artist. The Board of Estimate, after its own public hearings, approved those designations. . . .

II.

Responding to the loss of a number of its more significant buildings, New York City in 1965 enacted its first historic preservation statute (Administrative Code of City of NY, ch. 8-A [now tit. 25, ch. 3]; *see,* Pyke, Landmark Preservation, at 15 [1969]) for the "protection, enhancement, perpetuation and use of improvements and landscape features of special character or special historical or aesthetic interest or value" (Administrative Code §25-301[b]). In 1973, the Landmarks Law was amended to expand the Commission's jurisdiction by authorizing designation of interior landmarks and by charging the Commission with promoting the use of interior landmarks "for the education, pleasure and welfare of the people of the city" (Administrative Code §25-301[b][g]). . . .

PUBLIC OPENNESS REQUIREMENT

The Commission is authorized to landmark an interior 30 or more years old that is "customarily open or accessible to the public, or to which the public is customarily invited, and which has a special historical or aesthetic interest or value as part of the development, heritage or cultural characteristics of the city, state or nation" (Administrative Code §25-302[m]; §25-303[a][2]). . . .

TIAA's principal argument is that the Landmarks Law must be read to require that interiors subject to landmarking have a "distinctively public character" to bring them within the Commission's jurisdiction. An "ordinary commercial space" that has not been dedicated to public use, TIAA argues, cannot be landmarked over the owner's objection.

At the outset, we note that nothing in the Landmarks Law requires an owner's consent as a prerequisite to designation. While other jurisdictions have required owner consent, the New York City legislature, significantly, has not. Administrative Code §25-313(a) provides only that the owner is entitled to notice of the public hearing, and indeed, failure to give such notice does not invalidate a designation. So long as the statutory criteria are satisfied, the Commission may make a valid designation over an owner's objection . . .

. . . [U]rging "strict construction" of the statute, TIAA asks us to distinguish between a restaurant and "inherently" public interiors, such as railroad stations, lobbies and theaters, which are intrinsically dedicated to public use by their public assemblage purpose. Appellant asserts that the Four Seasons interior has no distinctively public purpose, pointing out that Seagram had considered such uses as an automobile showroom and art gallery before outfitting the space to accommodate the restaurant, and that permitting designations such as this will adversely impact the real estate and economy of New York City.

We reject TIAA's asserted distinction, which on its face is a difficult one. No less than a theater, which generally requires a ticket for public entry, a restaurant by the very nature of its business invites the general public to enter (*see, Weinberg v. Barry*, 634 F. Supp. 86, 93 [D.D.C.]). But even if we might agree that it would be prudent policy to adopt the distinction appellant suggests, the argument suffers a more fundamental flaw: the proffered distinction is nowhere part of the unambiguous statute we are obliged to enforce as the City legislature has written it.

The threshold requirement prescribed by the legislature is that an interior be "customarily open or accessible to the public, or [a place] to which the public is customarily invited." The crux of this provision is *customary* openness, accessibility, invitation to the public — words that are readily understood to require usual, ordinary or habitual (rather than rare or occasional) availability to the general public. The legislature did not also specify that an interior must be intended as a place of assemblage — adding an additional dimension to customary public availability — as it might well have done if that were the intention. Consistent with the letter and purpose of the Landmarks Law, the relevant inquiry thus becomes an objective one of whether the interior is habitually open or accessible to the public at large. An interior to which the general public is usually invited, regardless of its intended purpose, falls within the ambit of the statute. . . .

Applying this interpretation, unquestionably the Commission's determination that the Four Seasons "customarily" invites the public is not arbitrary or capricious. The restaurant interior having been provided for the enjoyment of New York City's residents and visitors since it opened more than three decades ago, the Commission now may seek to preserve it for others (*see*, Administrative Code 301[b]). . . .

DESIGNATED INTERIOR ITEMS

Even if the designation was authorized, appellant argues, items appurtenant to the interior of the restaurant cannot properly be included in the designation. We find no such limitation in the Landmarks Law.

The City does not challenge appellant's assertion that the Commission's jurisdiction over interior landmark designations extends only to "interior architectural features," defined as the "architectural style, design, general arrangement and components of an interior, including, but not limited to, the kind, color and texture of the building material and the type and style of all windows, doors, lights, signs and other fixtures appurtenant to such interior" (Administrative Code §25-302[*l*]). Emphasizing the word "other," appellant argues that the Commission's jurisdiction extends only to items that qualify as fixtures at common law, and it specifically challenges designation of the hanging sculptures, walnut bar, metal draperies, decorative metal railings and ceiling panels.

We need not pass on whether the designated items are fixtures because the Landmarks Law does not limit the Commission's jurisdiction to fixtures. The language of the statute unambiguously states that interior architectural features are composed of the "architectural style, design, general arrangement and components of an interior" (Administrative Code §25-302[*l*]). We agree with the Appellate Division's construction of the statute that, in authorizing the Commission to designate items appurtenant to an interior, the legislation does not distinguish between personality and realty.

We defer to the expertise of the Commission in its application of the provision. The Commission found that each of the designated items was created and installed at Philip Johnson's direction as an integral element of the design of the interior. Other items specially created or chosen for the restaurant, although mentioned in the designation report, were not designated by the Commission. As demonstrated by the items chosen for designation, the Commission has drawn a rational distinction between items integral to the design of the interior space, and items that merely enhance the restaurant's ambiance. . . .

Accordingly, the order of the Appellate Division should be affirmed, with costs.

SIMONS, TITONE, HANCOCK and BELLACOSA, J J., concur, SMITH and LEVINE, J J., taking no part.

Notes and Comments

1. *Preservation of Historic or Distinctive Buildings, Structures, or Sites.* Courts have upheld preservation controls to protect a wide range of human values, usually related to heritage, culture, and education but also to tourism, economic development, and the protection of the character of an area and property values. *See, generally,* Preserving Cultural Landscapes in America (Arnold R. Alamen & Robert Z. Melnick eds., 2000). On the basis for preservation controls, *see* Ernest Freund, Standards of American Legislation 115–16 (2d ed. 1965):

> It is undesirable to force by law upon the community standards of taste which a representative body may happen to approve of. . . . But it is a different question whether the state may not protect the works of nature or the achievements of art or the associations of history from being willfully marred. In other words, emphasis should be laid upon the character of the place as having an established claim to consideration and upon the idea of disfigurement as distinguished from the falling short of some standard of beauty.

There are more than 33,000 landmark properties in New York City. The total number of protected sites also includes 1347 individual landmarks, 117 interior landmarks, and 10 scenic landmarks. Landmarks Preservation Comm'n, About the Landmarks Preservation Commission, *see* http://www.nyc.gov/html/lpc/html/about/about.shtml (last visited June 10, 2016).

Preservation of "cultural heritage" is an issue for international law as well. *See* Lakshman Guruswamy et al., Protecting the Cultural and Natural Heritage: Finding Common Ground, 7 Buff. Envtl. L.J. 47 (2000) ("[T]he reasons for protecting biological diversity apply with even greater force to the cultural heritage. While species and animals facing extinction can reproduce themselves and be raised in captivity, cultural resources are not capable of such renewal."). The Buddhas of Bamiyan were destroyed by the Taliban in 2001. In Palmyra, the Islamic State destroyed the Lion of Al-lāt, the temples of Bel and Baalshamin, the Arch of Triumph, and other sites. These actions led to international condemnation and the search for some international legal rationale for a proper response.

Preservation today has many subspecialties and applications, among them: sacred Native American sites, historical trails, ancient lights, unobstructed views, waterfronts, and cultural activities.

2. *How Old Is Historic: The Over and Under Distinction.* In *Metropolitan Dade County v. P.J. Birds, Inc.*, 654 So. 2d 170 (Fla. Dist. Ct. App. 1995), the court considered the county's designation of the "Parrot Jungle and Gardens," a unique tourist attraction which opened in 1936, as an historic site. The Dade County ordinance divided property into "over fifty" and "under fifty" categories. The ordinance declared that "properties that have achieved significance within the last fifty years, will not normally be considered for designation" as historic. However, the "under fifty" properties will quality if they "are integral parts of districts that do meet the criteria" or are "of exceptional importance." *Id.* at 173.

How important is age to determining whether a property is of historic significance? Is the "over fifty" and "under fifty" line arbitrary? What if, at the time it was built, a structure was "futuristic" to begin with (for instance, the famous Seattle Space Needle)? Should that characteristic affect whether it can be designated as "historic"? How about culturally or socially distinctive?

At the same time, historic property designations seek to preserve property into the foreseeable future, if not in perpetuity. Is it possible to design systems that provide for such long-term protection? *See* Jess R. Phelps, Preserving Perpetuity?: Exploring The Challenges of Perpetual Preservation in an Ever-Changing World, 43 Envtl. L. 941 (2013).

3. *Private Property and Public Areas: The Inside and Outside Distinction.* When historic preservation is mentioned, the layperson often thinks of the outside facade of the building. As the *Teachers Ins.* case demonstrates, however, both the outside and the inside of a building can be landmarked. Whether the agency has authority to include both parts in the landmark designation depends upon its statutory authority. *See, e.g., United Artists' Theater Circuit, Inc. v. City of Philadelphia*, 635 A.2d 612, 622 (Pa. 1990) ("[t]he Historical Commission is not explicitly authorized by statute to designate the interior of the building as historically or aesthetically significant").

It may be more likely that the designation of the inside of a building as a landmark will interfere with the actual use of the building, a factor that can be critical where the designation is challenged on freedom of religion grounds. *See The Society of Jesus of New England v. Boston Landmarks Comm'n*, 564 N.E.2d 571, 573 (Mass. 1990) (designation of interior of church as a landmark violated state constitution because "[t]he configuration of the church interior is so freighted with religious meaning that it must be considered part and parcel of the Jesuits' religious worship"). Or, more mundanely, interior designation may affect the ability of an owner to introduce design alterations allegedly necessitated by changes in taste. *See* Robin Pogrebin, Landmarks Commission Rejects Plan to Change Interior of Four Seasons, N.Y. Times (May 19, 2015). The owner, frustrated by the Landmarks Commission's refusal to allow what he considered minor changes, said, "Their lease is up in July (2016), so they're out." "If something was designed in 1958 and it's not as functional in 2015, you ask for a change," he continued. "I'm going to restore the

Four Seasons back to its glory. I love the guys [speaking of the former restaurateurs] but their time has passed, and sometimes something great needs to go." In July 2016, the Four Seasons Restaurant closed. A new restaurant is to take over the space but will make no major design changes to the rooms. Jeff Gordinier, "A Little Old, a Little New for the Four Seasons Space," N.Y. Times (May 17, 2016).

Designating an interior for landmark status does not guarantee that the public will benefit by getting to visit it. *See* Nicholas Caros, Interior Landmarks Preservation and Public Access 40 (April 24, 2016), at http://papers.ssrn.com/sol3/papers.cfm?abstract_id=2769689 (last visited Nov. 12, 2016) (concluding that "today, some of New York's most celebrated interior landmarks are closed off to the public, the very group for whose benefit the spaces have been protected").

4. *Preservation by Zoning and Subdivision Laws.* Historic preservation laws often use the regulatory tools covered in Chapter 2. For example, a city might enact an "overlay" historic zone over its existing zoning. This type of zone creates additional protections for buildings in the district. *See Heithaus v. Planning & Zoning Comm'n of the Town of Greenwich*, 779 A.2d 750 (Conn. 2001) (upholding denial of historic overlay zone application and discussing application of historic protection regulation to a particular house).

Subdivision laws also may be pertinent. Could a city deny an application for development approval under its subdivision laws on the grounds that the subdivision would impair a historic district's "streetscape," where the state subdivision statute in question mentions specific factors such as water, drainage, sewage, etc., but does not mention effects on historic preservation efforts? *See Smith v. Zoning Bd. of Appeals of the Town of Greenwich*, 629 A.2d 1089, 1097 (Conn. 1993), *cert. denied*, 510 U.S. 1164 (1994) ("The defendants argue that public health and safety includes protecting the environment, which, in turn, includes historic preservation. We agree with defendants.").

5. *Historic Districts: Landmarks, Overlays, and Special Districts.* While some cities denote landmarks on a case-by-case basis, others have designed entire areas as "historic districts." New Orleans, for example, has designed the historic Vieux Carré section of the city (popularly known as the French Quarter) as a historic district. *See Maher v. City of New Orleans*, 516 F.2d 1051 (5th Cir. 1975), *cert. denied*, 426 U.S. 905 (1976) (upholding the ordinance). Some cities, like Corning, New York, and Park City, Utah, have designated their downtown commercial district as historic. Others, like Georgetown in Washington, D.C., and Annapolis, Maryland, include both the commercial district and the surrounding area. New York State now has more than 175 local district preservation laws or ordinances. The first one dates to 1962 in Schenectady created to protect the Stockade Historic District. N.Y. Dept. of State, Legal Aspects of Municipal Historic Preservation (James A. Coon Government Technical Series, reprint 2011).

In historic districts, the local agency's powers will likely extend beyond the buildings to preserving the entire ambiance of the district. Thus, in *Globe Newspaper Co. v. Beacon Hill Architectural Comm'n*, 659 N.E.2d 710 (Mass. 1996), the Supreme Judicial Court of Massachusetts concluded that the defendant commission's enabling legislation authorized it to regulate newsracks as an "exterior architectural feature" of a "structure" in the Beacon Hill area of Boston. *See Scully-Bozarth Post # 1817 of Veterans of Foreign Wars of U.S. v. Planning Bd. of City of Burlington*, 827 A.2d 1129 (App. Div. 2003) (upholding denial of permit for "tank memorial" on association's lawn based on historic design criteria for area); *Conner v. City of Seattle*, 223

P.3d 1201 (Wash. App. 2009) (upholding designation of entire residential site, not just building). *See also* Garreth A. DeVoe, *A Tale of Two Cities' Preservation Laws*, 50 Real Prop. Tr. & Est. L.J. 113, 130 (2015) (discussing the preservation systems for the French Quarter and Charleston, South Carolina, and concluding that "while South Carolina enacted historic preservation laws before Louisiana, South Carolina appears prone to exempt specific properties at the risk of diluting its historic architecture.").

6. *Historic Districts: State and Local Procedures.* Historic preservation statutes may lay out extensive procedures that must precede designation of historic districts. These often include an investigation and preparation of a report by experts in the field. *See Russell v. Town of Amite City*, 771 So. 2d 289 (La. Ct. App. 2000) (designation of Amite Historic Preservation District invalidated because of failure to follow the required procedures). Historic district designations are usually upheld today under deferential standards for judicial review of legislative or administrative actions. Often their legality is strengthened if they are part of a comprehensive plan. *See, e.g., Ely v. City Council of City of Ames*, 787 N.W.2d 479 (Iowa Ct. App. 2010) (landmark designation); *Baltimore v. Street Parking Co., LLC v. Mayor & City Council of Baltimore*, 194 Md. App. 569, 5 A.3d 695 (2010) (same).

7. *New Construction in Historic Districts.* Historic preservation laws also must contend with applications to construct new buildings in areas designated as historic. The obvious criterion here is compatibility with the existing environment. For example, the District of Columbia Historic Landmark and Historic District Protection Act of 1978 declares that a permit for new construction shall be issued unless the Mayor "finds that the design of the building and the character of the historic district . . . are incompatible." *See District Intown Properties, Ltd. v. District of Columbia Dep't of Consumer & Regulatory Affairs*, 680 A.2d 1373, 1378 (D.C. App. 1996) ("In contrast to other. . . . Provisions, which expressly authorize the Mayor to consider unreasonable economic hardship . . . when evaluating applications for permits to demolish, Section 5-1007, which deals with permits for new construction, makes no mention at all of economic hardship").

8. *Invalid if Unreasonable as Applied.* As with other types of land use restrictions, preservation controls may be held constitutionally invalid where the purpose for regulation would not be furthered under the particular circumstances of the case. For example, in *Norton v. City of Danville*, 602 S.E.2d 126 (Va. 2004), the court found unreasonable the city's requirement that a homeowner replace a glass-paned door with a wooden door to maintain a house's historic condition. No witnesses or exhibits showed that the house originally had a wooden door, and the city admitted it did not know what type of door was originally on the house, and the house had other glass-paned doors visible from the street). *See also Billy Graham Evangelistic Ass'n v. City of Minneapolis*, 653 N.W.2d 638 (Minn. Ct. App. 2002) (historic district boundary held arbitrary and capricious under designation criteria).

9. *Replacement and Demolition.* Where a landowner owns a property designated a landmark or included in a historic district, conflict about the effect of the landmark designation often arises when the landowner seeks to change the property. The flash point may be a request to modify the building or to demolish it.

In the case of a modification, the ultimate question is whether a requirement that the building be maintained constitutes a taking under a standard that looks at whether the owner has an economically viable existing use of the property. *See, e.g., Conner v. City of Seattle*, 223 P.3d 1201 (Wash. App. 2009) (rejecting taking claim as owner had reasonable use); *BSW Dev. Grp. v. City of Dayton*, 699 N.E.2d 1271 (Ohio 1998) (no taking because the building was structurally sound and two-thirds of the building had been used by two different businesses for several years just before denial of the demolition permit); *Harris v. Old King's Highway Reg'l Historic Comm'n*, 658 N.E.2d 972 (Mass. 1996) (upholding denial of certificate to convert the garage on a residential property in the historic district to a shed or studio).

The situation when an owner seeks to demolish a building is more complicated, since the entire structure would vanish. Litigation over proposed demolitions centers on whether the proper procedures have been followed (including, often, consultation with historic preservation officials). *See Saratoga Springs Pres. Found. v. Boff*, 110 A.D.3d 1326 (App. Div. 2013) (upholding demolition permit and rejecting charge that landowner did not sufficiently show plans for the property's use). If the procedures have been followed, the principal remaining question is whether officials have the right to deny a demolition permit. *See Donovan v. City of Deadwood*, 538 N.W.2d 790, 793 (S.D. 1995) ("SDCL 1-19B-27 provides that historic properties may be demolished after 180 days notice given to the historic preservation commission and during that 180 day period, the commission may negotiate with the owner in an effort to find a means of preserving the property. However, at the conclusion of the 180 days, the owner of historic property may raze the property."); *Friends of Bethany Place, Inc. v. City of Topeka*, 307 P.3d 1255 (2013) (Before issuing permit for a project which will encroach upon, damage, or destroy historic property, governing body must establish that no feasible and prudent alternatives exist and that all possible planning has been done to minimize harm to the historic property).

A related question is the legal significance of a change in ownership of the designated property.

■ LAKE OSWEGO PRESERVATION SOCIETY v. CITY OF LAKE OSWEGO
379 P.3d 462, 360 Or. 115 (2016)

BALMER, C. J.

I. FACTUAL AND PROCEDURAL BACKGROUND

Since 1973, with the passage of Senate Bill (SB) 100, the system of land use planning and development in Oregon has been governed by a comprehensive statutory scheme . . . . Pursuant to that scheme, codified in ORS chapter 197, individual cities and counties across the state are responsible for adopting local comprehensive plans, zoning land, administering land use regulations, and handling land use permits, all in accordance with mandatory Statewide Planning Goals and Guidelines set by the Oregon Land Conservation and Development Commission (LCDC) . . . Statewide Planning Goal 5 requires local governments to identify and designate historically significant properties, and where appropriate, protect those properties long-term by regulating their use and development . . .

The 1995 passage of the statute at issue in this case, ORS 197.772, created an anomaly in one part of that comprehensive system. Whereas the statewide scheme for land use planning and development under SB 100 requires local governments to utilize a holistic approach that balances a variety of considerations when making land use planning decisions, ORS 197.772 specifically requires that with respect to local historic designations, property owners have the right to refuse a request to designate their property as historic, and in some cases, to remove historic designations already in place. Noting that fundamental inconsistency, petitioner, the Lake Oswego Preservation Society (LOPS), contends that the designation removal provision in that statute, set out in ORS 197.772(3), was intended to provide a specific remedy to a limited group of property owners and that in light of its broader statutory and regulatory context, we should interpret that provision narrowly in a way that preserves Oregon's well-established system under Goal 5 of designating and regulating historic properties in order to protect them from alteration or demolition. Respondent, the Mary Cadwell Wilmot Trust (the Trust) — the owner of the property whose designation is at issue here — argues that the effect of ORS 197.772(3) was intended to be more fundamental and that, as a result of that provision, any owner of a property upon which an historic designation was imposed may remove that designation, and any accompanying land use restrictions, at any time, regardless of whether that owner acquired the property decades later and with the designation already in place.

A. The Designation of the Carman House

. . . Located in Lake Oswego, the property was originally part of a pioneer homestead, created by one of the first Donation Land Claim grants in the state. The main structure on the property, the Carman House, was built circa 1856. Because the Carman House and the lot on which it sits have been subject to relatively few modifications, the property is considered a rare and valuable example of a territorial Oregon residence.

. . . . The issue of the property's status as an historic landmark first arose in the late 1980s, when the city of Lake Oswego began developing its inventory of local historic properties as required by Goal 5 of Oregon's land use planning scheme . . . . As a result of that inventory review, the city determined that the Carman House and the property immediately surrounding it constituted an historic "farm complex" under the city's Historic Resource Protection Plan (1989) and that it should be designated as a landmark under the city's municipal code.

In 1990, as a result of that determination, both the lot containing the Carman House and an adjoining parcel of land were added to the city's Landmark Designation List and, as a consequence, became subject to certain restrictions on their use and development pursuant to the city's local historic preservation ordinance. *See* Lake Oswego Municipal Code (LOC) 58.020–58.135 (1990) (setting out limitations on demolition, moving, or exterior alteration of properties on Landmark Designation List).

At the time, the city could designate a property as historic, and subject it to special land use requirements, without the property owner's consent. . . . A property owner did have the right to be notified of the city's decision to designate a property, however, and could challenge that decision through a quasi-judicial post-designation process. LOC 58.025 (1990). Using that mechanism, in 1990, Richard Wilmot, one of the owners of the Carman House at that time, objected to the historic farm complex designation. Wilmot argued that the designation was improper for several reasons, including that the city had failed to account adequately for the economic impact of designation and that it should have considered the Carman House separately from the adjoining parcel that it had included as part of the historic farm complex. In the alternative, Wilmot argued that because only the Carman House had historic value, any landmark designation should be limited to the house and a smaller parcel of land immediately surrounding it.

[In a later proceeding the city determined that the historic designation should be retained on the Carman House.] Despite his earlier objections, Wilmot did not challenge the city's decision . . .

Not long after the city decided to retain the Carman House on its historic landmark list, the Oregon legislature passed a variety of measures relating to the protection of historic properties under the state's comprehensive planning scheme. One of those measures, enacted in 1995, established the owner consent requirements for local historic designations that are at issue here. *See* Or Laws 1995, ch 693, §21, *codified as* ORS 197.772. That law provided that local governments must allow "a property owner" whose property is under consideration for local historic designation to refuse the designation. ORS 197.772(1). It also included a removal provision for properties already designated, which provided that "a property owner" may "remove from the property a historic property designation that was imposed on the property by the local government." ORS 197.772(3). Despite objecting to the city's designation of his property in 1990, Wilmot never sought the removal of the historic farmhouse designation . . .

B. THE TRUST SEEKS THE REMOVAL OF THE HISTORIC DESIGNATION

In 2013, the Trust began its effort to remove the historic designation from the Carman House property in order to facilitate its subdivision and redevelopment. Although the city's Historic Resource Advisory Board initially denied that request, the City Council, following a public hearing on the issue, overturned that decision. In its written opinion, the City Council concluded that the right to remove a local historic designation under ORS 197.772(3) applies to any owner of a property on which an historic designation was "imposed." The City Council stated its view that because the designation was "imposed" on the Carman House in 1990, its present owners were entitled by law to remove it from the city's Landmark Designation List. Accordingly, the city approved the Trust's request. . . .

II. ANALYSIS

A. STATUTORY TEXT

ORS 197.772 provides:

(1) Notwithstanding any other provision of law, a local government shall allow a property owner to refuse to consent to any form of historic property designation at any point during the designation process. Such refusal to consent shall remove the property from any form of consideration for historic property designation under ORS 358.480 to 358.545 or other law except for consideration or nomination to the National Register of Historic Places pursuant to the National Historic Preservation Act of 1966, as amended (16 U.S.C. 470 et seq.).

(2) No permit for the demolition or modification of property removed from consideration for historic property designation under subsection (1) of this section shall be

issued during the 120–day period following the date of the property owner's refusal to consent.

(3) A local government shall allow a property owner to remove from the property a historic property designation that was imposed on the property by the local government.

. . . Urging us to interpret the term "a property owner" in its broadest possible sense, the Trust emphasizes the fact that the legislature chose to use the indefinite article "a" as a determiner rather than the definite article "the" in that phrase. That word choice, the Trust suggests, unambiguously shows that the legislature intended ORS 197.772(3) to apply to *all* property owners, including successors-in-interest like the Trust. . . .

On the other hand, the use of the article "a" as a determiner does not always mean that the referenced noun is unspecified in the most generic sense. For example, "a" may also be used quantitatively. *See Webster's* at 1 ("a" may be used "to suggest a limitation in number"). As a result, "a" may simply signal that the specified noun is one of a particular class, whether that class is defined by a subsequent restrictive clause or other modifier, *id.* or is implied more generally by the context in which the phrase appears . . . When used in that manner, the determiner "a" indicates that the noun that follows is one unspecified member of a limited group . . .

[T]he text of ORS 197.772(3) does not, on its own, compel any particular interpretation of the term "a property owner." Although the use of the indefinite article "a" in that provision could be read as synonymous with "any," there is at least one other plausible way in which to read the same words. That variation highlights the fact that, while grammatical "rules" are helpful in statutory interpretation, they are often subject to qualification and should not be applied mechanically in seeking to discern the meaning of a provision. . . .

B. LEGISLATIVE AND REGULATORY CONTEXT

. . . A central aspect of [the statute's legislative and regulatory] context, and one particularly pertinent here, was the requirement, as part of Oregon's comprehensive land use planning process, that local governments create and implement comprehensive development plans and local land use regulations to protect historically significant properties . . . .

As noted above, pursuant to Statewide Planning Goal 5, local governments were required to inventory all historic properties, analyze the potential uses and conflicts as to the use of those properties, and adopt measures, usually in the form of local land use ordinances, to ensure that those properties were appropriately protected in light of economic, social, environmental, and energy considerations . . . . Thus, in implementing Goal 5, local governments were obligated to not only identify historically significant properties, but also to ensure that those properties would be preserved for future generations . . . It was pursuant to that process that the Carman House was identified, added to the city of Lake Oswego's Landmark Designation List, and made subject to certain land use restrictions.

One of the defining features of the Goal 5 program, and the feature of greatest concern to legislators when they revisited the issue in 1995, was that the process for designating properties was largely involuntary from the property owner's standpoint. . . .

As in other states, Oregon's approach to historic preservation included proactively identifying and designating properties as a precursor to the application of general restrictions on use and development. . . .

That approach to historic preservation also had the benefit of ensuring long-term stability. Once a property was designated as historic, it ordinarily remained so, regardless of any future owner's preference, as long as it continued to meet the specified criteria for designation. . . .

The downside of that approach, however, was that the imposition of an historic designation could interfere with the investment-based expectations of the owner who suddenly became subject to restrictions on the use and enjoyment of its property . . . .

Thus, while Oregon's system of designating and regulating historic properties under Goal 5 was similar to other land use planning in that it elevated certain public interests over individual landowner preferences, it tended to impose the costs of those benefits to an even greater extent on specific landowners. . . .

Pointing to the comprehensive nature of Oregon's statewide historic preservation program under Goal 5 and the many benefits of that system, LOPS and *amici* argue that that context strongly undercuts any interpretation of ORS 197.772(3) that would allow subsequent owners to use that provision to unilaterally opt out of designation decades later. They contend that because the overwhelming majority of historically significant properties in Oregon were designated before ORS 197.772 was enacted in 1995, and therefore likely had designations put in place regardless of their owners' desires at the time, creating a removal right that would run to successors-in-interest would fundamentally and permanently destabilize the entire system of historic preservation in Oregon. Most of the state's historic properties would be perpetually at risk of being de-listed and, thus, subject to modification or demolition with little warning and no consideration of the broader impact of that decision.

Acknowledging that impact, the Trust responds that because the text of ORS 197.772(3) is inherently at odds with Goal 5, the only way to interpret that provision is as a substantial abrogation of that program. . . .

The mere fact that ORS 197.772 is in tension with Goal 5, however, does not answer the question of how far the legislature intended to go in cutting back the scope of existing local preservation programs created pursuant to that goal, or the extent to which the legislature intended to limit the effect of historic designations that were already in place. Rather, even if the right to refuse consent in ORS 197.772(1) decreases the number of new designations, the impact of the removal right in ORS 197.772(3) on existing designations and preservation programs depends in substantial part on how one reads that provision. If one interprets the right to remove an historic designation as applying to *any* owner of a property on which a designation was ever "imposed," the result could be, as LOPS contends, that most, if not all, of Oregon's historic properties are at risk of having their designations, and the protections that accompany that status, removed at any time. If, however, the right to remove a designation applies only to those owners who owned their properties at the time of designation, the long-term impact of ORS 197.772(3) is more limited. Although some of those owners may still opt out, the number of properties eligible for de-listing is smaller and would tend to decrease over time as historic properties change hands.

Contrary to the Trust's assertions, nothing about the context of ORS 197.772(3) suggests that the legislature intended to eliminate local governments' use of historic designations to protect and preserve historic properties long-term and therefore meet their obligations under Goal 5. Rather, what that context shows is that the legislature sought to adjust that existing framework to strike a more equitable balance between the countervailing interests of historic preservation and property rights. . . .

In light of that context, and the absence of any evidence suggesting that the legislature intended to dismantle the established statutory and regulatory framework for the protection of historic properties under Goal 5, we are hesitant to construe ORS 197.772(3) in a manner that would lead to such a result . . . . Rather, considering the legislature's expression of support for *both* the use of local land use regulations to preserve historic properties and for the protection of property owners' economic interests, the most plausible interpretation of ORS 197.772(3) is one that furthers both of those objectives.

Finally, additional context supporting LOPS's interpretation of ORS 197.772(3) can be found in the dramatically different way that historic designation affects property owners, depending on when they acquired their property. As noted, when an historic designation is placed on a property for the first time, that action ordinarily triggers the application of legal restrictions — often in the form of local land use and zoning ordinances — on the owner's ability to use and develop that property. . . .

Such concerns are muted, however, when historic designation is enforced against an owner who acquired its property with the designation already in place, and who therefore had actual or constructive notice of such restrictions from the outset . . . At that point, to the extent that a previous designation may have diminished the property's value, that diminution is reflected at the time of transfer, and therefore, informs not only the reasonable expectations of the successor . . . but the actual contents of the bundle of property rights that the successor obtains at that time. . . .

As a result, whatever harm an owner may suffer as a result of the imposition of an historic designation, that harm does not flow to its successor-in-interest, who acquires the property with notice of the designation and, most likely, at a price or valuation that reflects that designation. Under those circumstances, the ability to remove a previously-imposed designation at will would constitute a windfall for the successor. . . .

As the foregoing analysis demonstrates, while the text of ORS 197.772(3) is ambiguous, the most plausible reading of that provision, when read in context, is one that furthers both the objective of historic preservation generally and the goal of ensuring that historic designations are not placed on properties against an owner's wishes. Considering the text against that background, we conclude that the legislature most likely did not intend ORS 197.772(3) to apply to *all* owners of designated properties, but instead to members of a more specific class: those who owned their property at the time that the designation was placed on the property. . . .

III.   APPLICATION

. . . For the reasons discussed, we agree with LUBA that the right to remove an historic designation under ORS 197.772(3) applies only to those owners who held title when a local historic designation was first imposed and not to those whose property was already designated at the time they acquired it. Because the Trust acquired the Carman House property after it was designated, it does not qualify as "a property owner" within the meaning of ORS 197.772(3). As a result, the Trust cannot use ORS 197.772(3) to remove the historic designation from the Carman House now.

Notes and Comments

1 *The Effect of the State Law.* Do you see how the outcome in *Lake Oswego* is affected by Oregon's unique state land use system? Note also that Oregon is one of the few states that regulate a municipality's designation and protection of historical resources.

2. *The National Historic Preservation Act.* The principal federal legislation in this field is the National Historic Preservation Act, 16 U.S.C. §§470-470w-6 (2000), recently moved to 54 U.S.C. §§300101-300321 for better organization of statutes related to the National Park Service. Originally enacted in 1966 the act established the National Register of Historic Places, a federally compiled list of historic and cultural resources, as well as a national register including sites of state and local significance. It also established the Advisory Council of Historic Preservation, which provides information on historic properties to federal agencies.

The rationale for the statute is laid out in its findings:

(b) The Congress finds and declares that—

(1) the spirit and direction of the Nation are founded upon and reflected in its historic heritage;

(2) the historical and cultural foundations of the Nation should be preserved as a living part of our community life and development in order to give a sense of orientation to the American people;

(3) historic properties significant to the Nation's heritage are being lost or substantially altered, often inadvertently, with increasing frequency;

(4) the preservation of this irreplaceable heritage is in the public interest so that its vital legacy of cultural, educational, aesthetic, inspirational, economic, and energy benefits will be maintained and enriched for future generations of Americans;

(5) in the face of ever-increasing extensions of urban centers, highways, and residential, commercial, and industrial developments, the present governmental and nongovernmental historic preservation programs and activities are inadequate to insure future generations a genuine opportunity to appreciate and enjoy the rich heritage of our Nation;

(6) the increased knowledge of our historic resources, the establishment of better means of identifying and administering them, and the encouragement of their preservation will improve the planning and execution of Federal and federally assisted projects and will assist economic growth and development; and

(7) although the major burdens of historic preservation have been borne and major efforts initiated by private agencies and individuals, and both should continue to play a vital role, it is nevertheless necessary and appropriate for the Federal Government to accelerate its historic preservation programs and activities, to give maximum encouragement to agencies and individuals undertaking preservation by private means, and to assist State and local governments and the National Trust for Historic Preservation in the United States to expand and accelerate their historic preservation programs and activities.

Most significantly, Section 106 requires that federal agencies must seek comments from the Advisory Council before they take any action that may affect property either on, or eligible for inclusion on, the National Register of Historic Places. The section, however, is procedural rather than substantive in nature. Once the comments are received and the review process is complete, the federal agency maintains full discretion to take whatever action it wishes with respect to the historic resource.

Based on your review of the findings of the National Historic Preservation Act, what is the most compelling reason for its passage?

3. Other Federal Laws Affecting Historic Preservation. There are other federal laws that affect historic preservation. Perhaps the most important of these is §4(f) of the Department of Transportation Act, 49 U.S.C. §303 (2000). This section bars federal agencies from approving or funding a transportation project that requires the use of an historic site unless (1) there is no feasible and prudent alternative to the action, and (2) the project includes all possible planning to minimize harm to the site. The statute has been the source of a cause of action in cases involving construction of urban freeways. *See generally* Joseph F. C. DiMento & Cliff Ellis, Changing Lanes: Visions and Histories of Urban Freeways (MIT Press 2013). Other important federal laws affecting the preservation of historic resources include the tax codes, which provide incentives for the rehabilitation of buildings designated as landmarks. The Economic Recovery Tax Act of 1981 authorized an investment tax credit for rehabilitation of historic structures. *See* Robert F. Mann, Tax Incentives for Historic Preservation: An Antidote to Sprawl, 8 Widener L. Symp. J. 207 (2002).

Another federal law touching on historic preservation is the Native American Grave Protection and Repatriation Act ("NAGPRA"), 25 U.S.C. §3001 *et seq.* Applying only to federal lands, NAGPRA requires anyone who discovers "Native American cultural items" to notify the public land manager. The discoverer must also "cease the activity [and] make a reasonable effort to protect the items discovered before resuming the activity. . . ." 25 U.S.C. §3002(d)(1). *See also Yankton Sioux Tribe v. U.S. Army Corps of Engineers,* 194 F. Supp. 2d 977 (D.S.D. 2002) (dispute over remains discovered on shore of a lake behind a dam in South Dakota). *See also* the Archaeological Resources Protection Act, 16 U.S.C. §470aa , and the Archeological and Historic Preservation Act of 1974, 16 U.S.C. §§469-469c.

4. Conservation Districts. Municipalities in three dozen states have also created conservation districts that are distinct from historic districts. "By regulating features such as architectural style, roof angle, and maximum eave overhang, conservation districts purport to protect 'neighborhood character' or 'cultural stability.'" Anika S. Lamar, Zoning as Taxidermy: Neighborhood Conservation Districts and the Regulation of Aesthetics, 90 Ind. L.J. 1525 (2015). Criticizing these extensions of the police power, Professor Lemar argues that the ordinances are exclusionary and overly restrictive. She cites municipal restrictions on vinyl siding, on housing type limiting it to High Tudor, and on those regulating "the rhythm of solids to voids in the facade." For a summary of some regulatory tools that can be used to create conservation zones, *see* Gerald Korngold, Private Land Use Arrangements: Easements, Real Covenants and Equitable Servitudes (3d ed. Juris Pub. 2016).

5. Listing Lands. In *Rayellen Res., Inc. v. NM Cultural Prop. Review Bd.,* 319 P.3d 639 (NM 2014), the New Mexico Supreme Court held that a decision of the New Mexico Cultural Properties Review Committee to list Mount Taylor as a cultural property under the New Mexico Cultural Properties Act did not violate due process guarantees or statutory requirements. It further held that the Cebolleta Land Grant common lands are not state land for purposes of the Cultural Properties Act, while rejecting claims that the listing violates protections against the establishment of religion. *See* Ann Berkley Rodgers, Presentation to Land Grants Committee of New Mexico Legislature 1 (Nov. 13, 2014), at https://www.nmlegis.gov/handouts/ LGC%20111314%20Item%201%20Some%20implications%20of%20the%20Cultural% 20Properties%20court%20decision.pdf (last visited Oct. 26, 2016):

> The role that prominent natural features play in the lives of the people who have made New Mexico their home for centuries is a hallmark of the culture in the state. What other cultures may imbue in buildings and structures, such as the Taj Mahal, the Statue of Liberty, or even Mount Vernon, the people of New Mexico have long found in the mountains and mesas that have framed our lives and our forbearers for centuries. Now there is no question as to whether these features can be given the respect under law that the people give to them as a matter of course.

C. ARCHITECTURAL AND DESIGN REVIEW

Once regulation for aesthetic purposes was found to be within the police power, some local jurisdictions seized the opportunity to regulate architectural design. This type of regulation often raises constitutional claims.

■ ANDERSON v. CITY OF ISSAQUAH
851 P.2d 744 (Wash. Ct. App. 1993)

KENNEDY, Judge.

Appellants M. Bruce Anderson, Gary D. LaChance, and M. Bruce Anderson, Inc. (hereinafter referred to as "Anderson"), challenge the denial of their application for a land use certification, arguing, *inter alia*, that the building design requirements contained in Issaquah Municipal Code (IMC) 16.16.060 are unconstitutionally vague. . . .

FACTS

Anderson owns property located at 145 N.W. Gilman Boulevard in the City of Issaquah (City). In 1988, Anderson applied to the City for a land use certification to develop the property. The property is zoned for general commercial use. Anderson desired to build a 6800 square foot commercial building for several retail tenants.

After obtaining architectural plans, Anderson submitted the project to various City departments for the necessary approvals. The process went smoothly until the approval of the Issaquah Development Commission (Development Commission) was sought. This commission was created to administer and enforce the City's land use regulations. It has the authority to approve or deny applications for land use certification.

Chapter 16.16.060 of the IMC enumerates various building design objectives which the Development Commission is required to administer and enforce. Insofar as is relevant to this appeal, the Development Commission is to be guided by the following criteria:

IMC **16.16.060(B)**. RELATIONSHIP OF BUILDING AND SITE TO ADJOINING AREA.

1. Buildings and structures shall be made compatible with adjacent buildings of conflicting architectural styles by such means as screens and site breaks, or other suitable methods and materials.
2. Harmony in texture, lines, and masses shall be encouraged. . . .

IMC **16.16.060(D)**. BUILDING DESIGN.

1. Evaluation of a project shall be based on quality of its design and relationship to the natural setting of the valley and surrounding mountains.
2. Building components, such as windows, doors, eaves and parapets, shall have appropriate proportions and relationship to each other, expressing themselves as a part of the overall design.
3. Colors shall be harmonious, with bright or brilliant colors used only for minimal accent.
4. Design attention shall be given to screening from public view all mechanical equipment, including refuse enclosures, electrical transformer pads and vaults, communication equipment, and other utility hardware on roofs, grounds or buildings.
5. Exterior lighting shall be part of the architectural concept. Fixtures, standards and all exposed accessories shall be harmonious with the building design.
6. Monotony of design in single or multiple building projects shall be avoided. Efforts should be made to create an interesting project by use of complimentary details, functional orientation of buildings, parking and access provisions and relating the development to the site. In multiple building projects, variable siting of individual buildings, heights of buildings, or other methods shall be used to prevent a monotonous design.

As initially designed, Anderson's proposed structure was to be faced with off-white stucco and was to have a blue metal roof. It was designed in a "modern" style with an unbroken "warehouse" appearance in the rear, and large retail style windows in the front. The City moved a Victorian era residence, the "Alexander House," onto the neighboring property to serve as a visitors' center. Across the street from the Anderson site is a gasoline station that looks like a gasoline station. Located nearby and within view from the proposed building site are two more gasoline stations, the First Mutual Bank Building built in the "Issaquah territorial style," an Elk's hall which is described in the record by the Mayor of Issaquah as a "box building," an auto repair shop, and a veterinary clinic with a cyclone fenced dog run. The area is described in the record as "a natural transition area between old downtown Issaquah and the new village style construction of Gilman [Boulevard]."

The Development Commission reviewed Anderson's application for the first time at a public hearing on December 21, 1988. Commissioner Nash commented that "the facade did not fit with the concept of the surrounding area." Commissioner McGinnis agreed. Commissioner Nash expressed concern about the building color and stated that he did not think the building was compatible with the image of Issaquah. Commissioner Larson said that he would like to see more depth to the building facade. Commissioner Nash said there should be some interest created along the blank back wall. Commissioner Garrison suggested that the rear facade needed to be redesigned.

At the conclusion of the meeting, the Development Commission voted to continue the hearing to give Anderson an opportunity to modify the building design.

On January 18, 1989, Anderson came back before the Development Commission with modified plans which included changing the roofing from metal to tile, changing the color of the structure from off-white to "Cape Cod" gray with "Tahoe" blue trim, and adding brick to the front facade. During the ensuing discussion among the commissioners, Commissioner Larson stated that the revisions to the front facade had not satisfied his concerns from the last meeting. In response to Anderson's request for more specific design guidelines, Commissioner McGinnis stated that the Development Commission had "been giving direction; it is the applicant's responsibility to take the direction/suggestions and incorporate them into a revised plan that reflects the changes." Commissioner Larson then suggested that "[t]he facade can be broken up with sculptures, benches, fountains, etc." Commissioner Nash suggested that Anderson "drive up and down Gilman and look at both good and bad examples of what has been done with flat facades."

As the discussion continued, Commissioner Larson stated that Anderson "should present a [plan] that achieves what the Commission is trying to achieve through its comments/suggestions at these meetings" and stated that "architectural screens, fountains, paving of brick, wood or other similar method[s] of screening in lieu of vegetative landscaping are examples of design suggestions that can be used to break up the front facade." Commissioner Davis objected to the front facade, stating that he could not see putting an expanse of glass facing Gilman Boulevard. "The building is not compatible with Gilman." Commissioner O'Shea agreed. Commissioner Nash stated that "the application needs major changes to be acceptable." Commissioner O'Shea agreed.

Commissioner Nash stated that "this facade does not create the same feeling as the building [e]nvironment around this site." Commissioner Nash continued, stating that he "personally like[d] the introduction of brick and the use of tiles rather than metal on the roof." Commissioner Larson stated that he would like to see a review of the blue to be used: "Tahoe blue may be too dark." Commissioner Steinwachs agreed. Commissioner Larson noted that "the front of the building could be modulated [to] have other design techniques employed to make the front facade more interesting."

With this, the Development Commission voted to continue the discussion to a future hearing.

On February 15, 1989, Anderson came back before the Development Commission. In the meantime, Anderson's architects had added a 5-foot overhang and a 7-foot accent overhang to the plans for the front of the building. More brick had been added to the front of the building. Wood trim and accent colors had been added to the back of the building and trees were added to the landscaping to further break up the rear facade.

Anderson explained the plans still called for large, floor to ceiling windows as this was to be a retail premises: "[A] glass front is necessary to rent the space. . . ." Commissioner Steinwachs stated that he had driven Gilman Boulevard and taken notes. The following verbatim statement by Steinwachs was placed into the minutes:

"My General Observation From Driving Up and Down Gilman Boulevard."
    I see certain design elements and techniques used in various combinations in various locations to achieve a visual effect that is sensitive to the unique character of our Signature Street. I see heavy use of brick, wood, and tile. I see minimal use of stucco. I see colors that are mostly earthtones, avoiding extreme contrasts. I see various methods used to provide modulation in both horizontal and vertical lines, such as gables, bay windows, recesses in front faces, porches, rails, many vertical columns, and breaks in roof lines. I see long, sloping, conspicuous roofs with large overhangs. I see windows with panels above and below windows. I see no windows that extend down to floor level. This is the impression I have of Gilman Boulevard as it relates to building design.

    Commissioner Nash agreed stating, "[T]here is a certain feeling you get when you drive along Gilman Boulevard, and this building does not give this same feeling." Commissioner Steinwachs wondered if the applicant had any option but to start "from scratch." Anderson responded that he would be willing to change from stucco to wood facing but that, after working on the project for 9 months and experiencing total frustration, he was not willing to make additional design changes.
    At that point, the Development Commission denied Anderson's application, giving four reasons:

1. After four [sic] lengthy review meetings of the Development Commission, the applicant has not been sufficiently responsive to concerns expressed by the Commission to warrant approval or an additional continuance of the review.
2. The primary concerns expressed relate to the building architecture as it relates to Gilman Boulevard in general, and the immediate neighborhood in particular.
3. The Development Commission is charged with protecting, preserving and enhancing the aesthetic values that have established the desirable quality and unique character of Issaquah, reference IMC 16.16.010C.[3]
4. We see certain design elements and techniques used in various combinations in various locations to achieve a visual effect that is sensitive to the unique character of our Signature Street. On Gilman Boulevard we see heavy use of brick, wood and tile. We see minimal use of stucco. We see various methods used to provide both horizontal and vertical modulation, including gables, breaks in rooflines, bay windows, recesses and protrusions in front face. We see long, sloping, conspicuous roofs with large overhangs. We see no windows that extend to ground level. We see brick and wood panels at intervals between windows. We see earthtone colors avoiding extreme contrast.

    Anderson, who by this time had an estimated $250,000 into the project, timely appealed the adverse ruling to the Issaquah City Council (City Council). After a lengthy hearing and much debate, the City Council decided to affirm the Development Commission's decision by a vote of 4 to 3. . . .

------

3. IMC 16.16.010(C) provides that one of the purposes of the code is "[to] protect, preserve and enhance the social, cultural, economic, environmental and aesthetic values that have established the desirable quality and unique character of Issaquah[.]"

Discussion . . .

3. CONSTITUTIONALITY OF IMC 16.16.060 (BUILDING DESIGN PROVISIONS)

[A] statute which either forbids or requires the doing of an act in terms so vague that men [and women] of common intelligence must necessarily guess at its meaning and differ as to its application, violates the first essential of due process of law. . . .

Looking first at the face of the building design sections of IMC 16.16.060, we note that an ordinary citizen reading these sections would learn only that a given building project should bear a good relationship with the Issaquah Valley and surrounding mountains; its windows, doors, eaves and parapets should be of "appropriate proportions," its colors should be "harmonious" and seldom "bright" or "brilliant," its mechanical equipment should be screened from public view; its exterior lighting should be "harmonious" with the building design and "monotony should be avoided." The project should also be "interesting." IMC 16.16.060(D)(1)-(6). If the building is not "compatible" with adjacent buildings, it should be "made compatible" by the use of screens and site breaks "or other suitable methods and materials." "Harmony in texture, lines, and masses [is] encouraged." The landscaping should provide an "attractive . . . transition" to adjoining properties. IMC 16.16.060(B)(1)-(3).

[We] conclude that these code sections "do not give effective or meaningful guidance" to applicants, to design professionals, or to the public officials of Issaquah who are responsible for enforcing the code. . . . Although it is clear from the code sections here at issue that mechanical equipment must be screened from public view and that, probably, earth tones or pastels located within the cool and muted ranges of the color wheel are going to be preferred, there is nothing in the code from which an applicant can determine whether his or her project is going to be seen by the Development Commission as "interesting" versus "monotonous" and as "harmonious" with the valley and the mountains. Neither is it clear from the code just what else, besides the valley and the mountains, a particular project is supposed to be harmonious with, although "[h]armony in texture, lines, and masses" is certainly encouraged. IMC 16.16.060(B)(2).

In attempting to interpret and apply this code, the commissioners charged with that task were left with only their own individual, subjective "feelings" about the "image of Issaquah" and as to whether this project was "compatible" or "interesting." The commissioners stated that the City was "making a statement" on its "signature street" and invited Anderson to take a drive up and down Gilman Boulevard and "look at good and bad examples of what has been done with flat facades." One commissioner drove up and down Gilman, taking notes, in a no doubt sincere effort to define that which is left undefined in the code.

The point we make here is that neither Anderson nor the commissioners may constitutionally be required or allowed to guess at the meaning of the code's building design requirements by driving up and down Gilman Boulevard looking at "good and bad" examples of what has been done with other buildings, recently or in the past. We hold that the code sections here at issue are unconstitutionally vague on their face. The words employed are not technical words which are commonly understood within the professional building design industry. Neither do these words have a settled common law meaning.

As they were applied to Anderson, it is also clear the code sections at issue fail to pass constitutional muster. Because the commissioners themselves had no objective guidelines to follow, they necessarily had to resort to their own subjective "feelings." The "statement" Issaquah is apparently trying to make on its "signature street" is not written in the code. In order to be enforceable, that "statement" must be written down in the code, in understandable terms. *See, e.g., Morristown Road Assocs. v. Mayor & Common Council & Planning Board*, 163 N.J. Super. 58, 394 A.2d 157 (1978). The unacceptable alternative is what happened here. The commissioners enforced not a building design code but their own arbitrary concept of the provisions of an unwritten "statement" to be made on Gilman Boulevard. The commissioners' individual concepts were as vague and undefined as those written in the code. This is the very epitome of discretionary, arbitrary enforcement of the law. . . .

Conclusion

. . . We order that Anderson's land use certification be issued, provided however, that those changes which Anderson agreed to through the hearing before the City Council may validly be imposed.

Grosse and Scholfield, JJ., concur.

Notes and Comments

1. *Design Review of New Buildings.* Design review of new building development is now widespread both in commercial districts and in residential areas. These review ordinances generally attempt to assure that new buildings are visually compatible and harmonious with an area's existing design scheme. As summarized in Anika Singh Lemar, Zoning as Taxidermy: Neighborhood Conservation Districts and the Regulation of Aesthetics, 90 Ind. L.J. 1525, 1526–27 (2015), such ordinances can promote a variety of design types:

> These ordinances establish design standards and oftentimes entrust an appointed board or commission with the review of the proposed design of a building, including choice of building materials, roof lines, siting and orientation, and scale. For example, a neighborhood conservation district in Phoenix, Arizona, requires all commercial buildings to be built with traditional agrarian materials, such as adobe. Another such district in the Avon Hill neighborhood of Cambridge, Massachusetts, expressly prohibits the use of vinyl siding and requires a local commission to consider the "site layout" of accessory buildings when determining whether to permit their construction. A design review ordinance in Noank, Connecticut, requires the local zoning commission to consider "the rhythm of solids to voids in the facade" and the "[r]hythm of spacing of buildings on the street" when determining whether to allow issuance of a building permit. And a district in Dallas requires all new construction to be limited to single-family High Tudors, of the type that were commonly built in that neighborhood in the 1920s.

Public purposes furthered by these controls can include protecting the character and property values of the area, as well as economic development and tourism, all of which are thought to be related to the particular or distinctive "sense of place" created by the visual building scheme that exists in the area. These aesthetic controls usually are implemented by some form of site plan review in an overlay or special zoning district. Courts generally have upheld this type of aesthetic regulation. *See, e.g., Richmond Co., v. City of Concord*, 821 A.2d 1059 (N.H. 2003) (upholding denial of site plan for retail shopping center); *Georgia Manufactured Hous. Ass'n, Inc. v. Spalding County, Ga.*, 148 F.3d 1304 (11th Cir. 1998) (upholding roof design standard for manufactured housing in residential area); *Breneric Assoc.'s v. City of Del Mar*, 81 Cal. Rptr. 2d 324 (Cal. Ct. App. 1998) (upholding denial of permit to construct two-story structure and glass-paneled roof deck as addition to existing home under compatibility design ordinance).

2. *"Pleasing" or an "Affront"?* In *Reid v. Architectural Bd. of Review*, 192 N.E.2d 74 (Ohio 1984), the Ohio Supreme Court upheld denial of a permit to build a home in an existing neighborhood under the terms of a review ordinance which allowed permit denial when the proposed construction would not maintain the "high character of community development" or "protect real estate from impairment or destruction of value." 148 N.E.2d at 76. The proposed house was a single story, flat-roofed complex of 20 modules arranged in a loosely formed "U" and entirely screened from the street in front by a wall ten feet high. From the street, the proposed structure would not be identifiable as a residence. The neighborhood consisted of "dignified, stately and conventional structures, all two and one-half stories high." The majority upheld a review board finding that the design of the house would harm property values in the area. The court further noted:

> [T]he evolving trend has been to grant aesthetic considerations a more significant role. We believe that this is the correct approach as the appearance of a community relates closely to its citizens' happiness, comfort and general well-being. Accordingly, it is our finding that there is a legitimate governmental interest in maintaining the aesthetics of the community. . . .

192 N.E. 2d at 77–78.

The dissent would have none of it:

> What is aesthetically pleasing to one individual is an affront to the senses of another. . . .
>
> This zoning case has now placed us in the era of Orwell's "1984" where Big Brother tells us what to do and think in a realm that is protected by the constitutional right of privacy under the first Amendment. . . .
>
> If a zoning code regulation or restriction devoted solely to aesthetic considerations, as in this case, can be bootstrapped to the status of lawfulness by merely adding a provision somewhere in the zoning code that the purpose of the zoning regulation is to protect real estate "from impairment or destruction of value," then any zoning code provision, no matter how absurd, unreasonable or confiscatory can be given the aura of lawfulness.

Id. at 80–81. Who has the better of the argument?

It might interest you to know that in China's building tradition many affluent neighborhoods were built with front-walled courtyards that screen the houses from the street (like the proposed house in the *Reid* case above). To better integrate affluent homes into the streetscape and promote social cohesion, this pattern of neighborhood development is now illegal in China. It is also illegal in most neighborhoods in this country through zoning setback and fence restrictions.

3. *Aesthetics, Standards, and Subjectivity.* As the *Anderson v. City of Issaquah* case makes clear, standards for design review may have to be, at least in some states, reasonably intelligible to avoid a successful constitutional vagueness challenge. Courts, however, often have upheld design review decisions based on ordinance standards requiring only that new development be "compatible" or "in harmony with" existing development. In these cases, courts typically make clear that these rather vague standards derive their meaning from the observable features of the visual environment that exists in the particular area or from background documents or more particular identifiable review criteria. *See, e.g., A-S-P Assoc.'s v. City of Raleigh,* 258 S.E.2d 444 (N.C. 1979); *Goldman v. Shefftz,* 2009 WL 27310 (Mass. Land Ct. 2009) (holding that denial of permit was reasonable, as proposed house would be out of scale for its location, would interfere with light and view of the neighboring owner, and would have created a 93-foot long wall when viewed from that property).

In *Novi v. City of Pacifica,* 215 Cal. Rptr. 439 (Cal. App. 1985) a California appellate court upheld the application of an ordinance that prohibited development if it would be detrimental to the "general welfare" or if "there is insufficient variety in the design of the structure and grounds to avoid monotony in the external appearance" of a proposed development. The court rejected a vagueness claim, noting that the "variety" standard took its meaning from the obvious legislative intent to avoid the sameness of "ticky-tacky" little boxes. The court stated that, in this particular case, denial of the application prohibited a 48-unit condominium project consisting of eight four-story buildings. A permit would have been granted had the developer complied with the mitigation requirements of avoiding "linear monotony and massive bulky appearance" and redesigning the project to achieve "a small scale village atmosphere" characteristic of the city. The court found that the developer clearly understood these requirements, but "deliberately chose to litigate rather than mitigate." 215 Cal. Rptr. at 443.

Under this type of review ordinance, which apparently allows the city to prohibit any visually "boring" development project, is the design of a project simply turned over to the city?

4. *Building Size, Bulk, Materials, and Color, etc.* Design review ordinances can regulate any number of aspects of building development. Height, bulk, style, color, roof type and slope, windows and door style, placement, and orientation, porches, mailboxes, lighting fixtures, gates, fences, external materials and surfaces, as well as other aspects of building design may all be within the scope of city regulation. *See, e.g., Country Club Estates v. Town of Loma Linda,* 281 F.3d 723 (8th Cir. 2002) (upholding ordinance requiring minimum of 1800 square feet of above-ground living space to protect aesthetic character of residential area); *Village of Hudson v. Albrecht, Inc.,* 458 N.E.2d 852 (Ohio 1984) (upholding decision requiring plate glass windows instead of solid aggregate panels for front of retail store in commercial plaza).

Is it possible for local governments to decide, in a non-arbitrary way, whether excessive use of colors on houses is against the public interest? Some design schemes have an official "color pallet" from which an owner can select a permitted color. One person's ugly color is another's fount of beauty (or, perhaps more pragmatically, another's attempt to distinguish his business from other businesses). *See* Jennifer Brett, Yellow Store Sparks Talk of Color Codes in Pinellas Park, St. Petersburg Times, at 10 (Jan. 19, 1997) (while critic found that a pet store painted marigold yellow "looks like a radiation sign" from a distance, the owner declared that "[w]hen I tell people I'm in the yellow building, they know what building I'm in").

5. *Invalid If Unreasonable as Applied.* As with historic preservation restrictions, design restrictions are held invalid if the restriction as applied fails to further the asserted aesthetic purpose for the restriction. *See, e.g., Lodge Hotel Inc. v. Town of Erwin Planning Bd.,* 62 A.D.3d 1257, 87 N.Y.S.2d 803 (4th Dept. 2009) (holding that denial of permit for retail store based on "inconsistent appearance" was unreasonable because landscaping incorporated in site plan adequately screened inconsistent features from public view); *Gibson v. Sussex County Council,* 877 A.2d 54 (Del. Ch. 2005) (holding invalid denial of permit for three unit townhome since some townhomes were already located in the area and the area, as a whole, had no distinctive residential design scheme); *Hankins v. Borough of Rockleigh,* 150 A.2d 63 (App. Div. 1959) (holding invalid "early American" design compatibility scheme since area in question had no distinctive architectural style); *Bourgeois v. Parish of St. Tammany,* 628 F. Supp. 159 (E.D. La. 1986) (holding aesthetic basis for exclusion of mobile home from area was arbitrary and capricious since even more unsightly or visually offensive stick-built housing, such as "tar paper shacks," could be built in the area).

6. *The Limits of Modern Aesthetic Regulation?* The "unreasonable as applied" standard for aesthetic regulation mentioned above, as well as possible "vagueness" claims, suggest a possible formulation of due process limitations on the permissible scope of modern aesthetic regulation. Perhaps the reasonableness, if not the objectivity, of aesthetic regulation under a rationale of "associational dissonance" could be rooted in two factors: (1) the potential for articulating the specific features of the visual environment intended to be protected by regulation, and (2) the ability of reasonably competent planning staffs to draft intelligible standards derived from those features, such as bulk, height, scale, topography, and building materials, etc. It could also be grounded in the requirements, articulated in a number of court decisions, that regulation reflect a widespread pattern of community preference and that regulation prevent some substantial harm to those features of the visual environment selected for protection. 2 Edward H. Ziegler, Rathkopf's The Law of Zoning & Planning §16:8 (4th ed. 2005 & Supp. 2016). *See, e.g., Sackson v. Zimmerman,* 478 N.Y.S.2d 354 (App. Div. 1984) (holding denial of subdivision approval arbitrary and capricious since the building of an additional house on a lot with large mansion would not have substantial impact on aesthetics in the area); *Village of Hempstead v. SRA Realty Corp.,* 611 N.Y.S.2d 442 (Sup. Ct. 1994) (holding prohibition of sheet metal security gate arbitrary and capricious since city failed to show gate would do substantial harm to visual environment of area); *Castle Properties Co. v. Ackerson,* 558 N.Y.S.2d 334 (App. Div. 1990) (holding arbitrary and capricious a requirement that fountains be installed at an office/warehouse site since city failed to show fountain installation was necessary to prevent substantial harm to visual character of the area).

7. *Design Controls from the Ground Up?* Design controls can be imposed on new development through covenants placed on a tract of land by a city, a developer, or some other entity. Most regulatory design review schemes, however, operate to prevent "associational dissonance" with respect to an already developed or developing area. In such cases, aesthetic controls ordinarily are based on existing features of the already built, or developing, environment.

May a city impose regulatory aesthetic controls on new buildings in an *undeveloped* area, to promote some officially approved design scheme (perhaps New Urbanism) as found in a neighborhood "vision plan"? Would community involvement in the formulation of the vision plan provide a "rational basis" for imposition of the aesthetic controls? This is an unanswered question, although some court decisions suggest support for upholding regulation based on such plans. *See, e.g., Coscan Washington, Inc. v. Maryland-National Capital Park & Planning Comm'n,* 590 A.2d 1080 (Md. App. 1992) (upholding aesthetic conditions based on subarea design plan which called for encouragement of wood, stucco, stone, and brick and the discouragement of vinyl and aluminum siding as reasonably related to the quality of housing in the area and protecting the approach to and vista from a nearby historical site); and *Board of County Comm'rs of Teton County v. Crow,* 65 P.2d 720 (Wyo. 2003) (upholding maximum 8000 square feet habitable space restriction on size of new single-family dwellings to protect visual character of the area based, in part, on "Community Vision" plan that reflected citizen opinions within the community).

8. *Aesthetics and Individual Freedom.* In a series of articles, Professor Joseph Sax explored the origins of the idea that the government bears responsibility to conserve artifacts of historic or aesthetic value. *See* Joseph L. Sax, Heritage Preservation as Public Duty: The Abbé Gregoire and the Origins of an Idea, 88 Mich. L. Rev. 1142 (1990); Joseph L. Sax, Is Anyone Minding Stonehenge? The Origins of Cultural Property Protection in England, 78 Cal. L. Rev. 1543 (1990). In the Michigan article he notes the seeming oddity of a shared "cultural heritage" in a country that celebrates limited government:

> As uncontroversial as heritage preservation may appear when one thinks of historic monuments and artistic masterworks, the idea of an officially designated culture seems greatly at odds with modern sensibilities. The very idea of government involving itself in cultural life raises the unwelcome specter of censorship on the one side and official propaganda on the other. In addition, there is the more general question of cultural policy as a tool of a paternalistic state that aspires to make its citizens good, a notion that has lost all cachet in our time. In short, state cultural policies appear to be out of harmony with modern ideas about the role of government. Nonetheless, they flourished. Obviously, there is some very strong attraction to the idea of a common heritage: a people and a community bound together in some shared enterprise with shared values.

88 Mich. L. Rev. at 1142.

Have the courts sufficiently confronted the specter of propaganda and censorship in generally affirming aesthetic-based regulation? Keep in mind, however, that even First Amendment protected speech rights are not unlimited. Do aesthetic "associational dissonance" controls function as somewhat unique time, place, and manner restrictions on symbolic expression, and simply operate to keep "the pig out of the parlor" in the best tradition of Euclidean zoning? On the other hand, is free expression limited to situations where no one can take offense? *See generally* Darrel C. Menthe, Aesthetic Regulation and the Development of First Amendment Jurisprudence, 19 B.U. Pub. Int. L.J. 225, 260 (2010) (suggesting some reassessment of the First Amendment limits on aesthetic regulation).

Could New York City ban a "mosque" from locating near ground zero? What if it is out of harmony with the building character of the area? May the "character of an area" be defined without reference to visual objects? How about the historic preservation of areas because of past events, like Gettysburg or Valley Forge? Religious land uses may receive some extra measure of protection from design controls under the Religious Land Use and Institutionalized Persons Act and also possibly under the First Amendment Free Exercise clause. *See* Shelly Ross Saxer, Assessing RLUI-PA's Application to Building Codes and Aesthetic Land Use Regulation, 2 Alb. Gov't L. Rev. 623 (2009).

9. *The House as a First Amendment Castle.* Aside from land uses involving traditional vehicles of communication and expression, such as conduct involving signs, books, movies and, perhaps, dancing, courts generally have not granted First Amendment protection to "conduct" involving simply land use and building development. Should there be First Amendment protection for the exterior design of a private, single-family house? One academic has made the argument, analogizing its design to the protection given to signs in *City of Ladue v. Gilleo*, 512 U.S. 43 (1994). He argues:

> Architecture is entitled to First Amendment protection; in the case of a single-family house, it is entitled to the same protection as Ms. Gilleo was given in posting her sign. The exterior design of the house is speech; it can be read by its viewers. The land-owner's choice of an exterior design cannot be suppressed simply because a municipality finds it grotesque or appalling or unsightly. If that is the objection, then the viewers must simply turn their heads.

John Nivala, Constitutional Architecture: The First Amendment and the Single Family House, 33 San Diego L. Rev. 291, 339 (1996).

In this view, what would not be protected expression? Would state laws banning "spite fences" be unconstitutional?

10. *A Design in the Form of a Human Hand.* How about "spite houses"? A city councilman in Utah, Mark Easton, had a beautiful view of the mountains, until a new neighbor purchased the lot below his house and built a large new home. The new home was 18 inches higher than the ordinances would allow, so Easton, upset about his lost view, went to the city to make sure they enforced the zoning height restriction. The new neighbor had to drop the roof line, at enormous expense. Recently, Easton called the city zoning office again, and informed them that his new neighbor had installed some vents on the backside of his home facing Easton's house. The zoning inspector arrived late in the afternoon. It may have been the fading light, but the vents seemed to be designed in the form of a large human hand and seemed to display a distinctly obscene finger gesture towards Easton's house.

Are the new vents an "attention attracting device"? As city attorney, what are the possibilities for making Easton's new neighbor perform a costly "do over" again? *See* Maria Villasenor, "Is It Art or the One-Finger Salute," Salt Lake Tribune (Aug.16, 2006).

■ HUGO MARTIN, HUE AND CRY OVER COLORS OF HOMES IN SOUTH GATE: WHILE THE COUNCIL CONSIDERS BANNING LOUD PAINT JOBS, OTHERS DEFEND THEM AS A TRADITION BROUGHT FROM LATIN AMERICA
L.A. Times, at B1 (Sept. 22, 1998)

Since Hermila Sanchez and her husband, Miguel, painted their beige South Gate home a light turquoise with white trim, they have noticed some passing neighbors giving the small stucco house disapproving looks.

"I say if they don't like it they can come help us paint it another color," Hermila Sanchez said good-naturedly from her front porch.

Her neighbors may not have a say in the color, but the city of South Gate soon may. This predominantly Latino, blue-collar city in southeast Los Angeles County is considering imposing the kind of color and design restrictions that are usually found only in affluent communities. . . .

At the request of Mayor Henry Gonzalez, the South Gate City Council will vote today on creating a citywide program that limits the colors of homes and businesses to a designated few — most likely not to include the turquoise of the Sanchez home, or the maroon, orange and purple that also dot the landscape.

Gonzalez said the proposed restrictions were prompted by several complaints from residents about garish colors on businesses and homes around the city.

"People are saying, 'It looks like hell,'" he said.

Many homes in this town of 93,000 can best be described as the colors of sorbet: lime green, peach, raspberry and banana yellow. An automotive shop that has drawn the mayor's ire is bright purple with white trim.

But the politics of color may turn into a cultural debate. Many of the property owners who have chosen the lively hues for their homes and businesses may be carrying over a tradition from Mexico or other Latin American countries where vivid colors are embraced and are an expression of individuality.

"It's part of our cultural identity," said Leo Limon, a local artist and co-chairman of the Aztlan Cultural Arts Foundation in Los Angeles. "It's the colors of feathers and birds and trees, and the Latino population sees that and uses that." . . .

Gonzalez said he will ask the council to consider restricting homes and businesses to three or four colors. The city's code enforcement unit would enforce the restrictions, which would apply only when a structure is repainted or rebuilt, he said.

To avoid imposing a financial hardship, Gonzalez said he will ask the city to provide grants to subsidize the cost of the paint and labor.

"I don't want to create a burden, but I want a consistent [color] code where everybody knows what it is," he said. . . .

But most of the dozen or so homeowners and merchants who were interviewed last week said the bright colors they chose for their homes and businesses are a personal expression that should not be restricted by government. . . .

Antonio Rubio, a mechanic and longtime Los Angeles resident, owns that purple, two-story auto shop on the corner of Southern and California avenues that has drawn the ire of Gonzalez and other city officials. Rubio said he painted the building purple about three months ago to grab the attention of potential customers on the nearby busy intersection.

"This is a place where we paint cars and sell exotic rims," he said in Spanish. "The color of the building should be exotic."

———————————————

Some local communities attempt to maintain or develop a village character by regulating the number of same use facilities in an area of town or by regulating out formula establishments, including restaurants and coffee shops. Are such ordinances valid uses of the police power or infringements on business rights?

■ MEAD SQUARE COMMONS, LLC v. VILLAGE OF VICTOR

97 A.D.3d 1162 (N.Y. App. Div. 2012)

.... Plaintiff commenced this action seeking injunctive relief and a declaration that section 170-13(C)(1) of defendant's Zoning Ordinance (Ordinance) is unlawful, invalid and unenforceable. That section prohibits the operation of a "Formula fast-food restaurant" (FFFR) in defendant's "Central Business District" (§170-13[C][1][d]; *see* Ordinance §§50-12, 170-3[B]). An FFFR is defined in section 170-13(C)(1)(b) as "[a]ny establishment, required by contract, franchise or other arrangements, to offer two or more of the following: [1] Standardized menus, ingredients, food preparation, and/or uniforms[;] [2] Prepared food in ready-to-consume state[;] [3] Food sold over the counter in disposable containers and wrappers[;] [4] Food selected from a limited menu[;] [5] Food sold for immediate consumption on or off premises[;] [6] Where customer pays before eating." The stated purpose of section 170-13(C)(1)(a) is "to maintain [defendant's] . . . unique village character, the vitality of [its] commercial districts, and the quality of life of [its] residents."[1]

Plaintiff, a limited liability company that owns real property in the Central Business District, challenges the validity of Ordinance §170-13 because plaintiff seeks to lease commercial space for a Subway restaurant, which qualifies as an FFFR under the Ordinance. In its complaint, plaintiff alleges that section 170-13 is unconstitutional because it "is based solely upon the ownership or control of the restaurant owner and not upon the characteristics of the use itself." Plaintiff further alleges that section 170-13 should be declared invalid because it "excessively regulates the details" of plaintiff's business operation. Plaintiff moved for summary judgment, and defendant cross-moved for summary judgment dismissing the complaint. Supreme Court denied plaintiff's motion and granted defendant's cross motion.

Relying largely on *Matter of Dexter v Town Bd. of Town of Gates* (36 N.Y.2d 102 [1975]), plaintiff contends that the court erred in rejecting its allegation that Ordinance §170-13 improperly regulates the ownership rather than the use of property within the Central Business District. We reject that contention. In *Dexter,* the Town Board resolved to rezone 12 acres of land from a residential classification to a commercial classification to permit the construction of a supermarket (*see id.* at 104). The resolution was conditioned, however, upon a specified corporation developing the land and constructing the supermarket, which suggested that the site would revert back to its former classification if that corporation did not develop

---

1. Editor's note: The Village of Victor ordinance reads as follows:

A Formula Fast-Food Restaurant is defined under section 170-13(C)(1)(b) of the Village Code as follows:

FORMULA FAST-FOOD RESTAURANT

Any establishment, required by contract, franchise or other arrangements, to offer two or more of the following:

[1] Standardized menus, ingredients, food preparation and/or uniforms.
[2] Prepared food in ready-to-consume state.
[3] Food sold over the counter in disposable containers and wrappers.
[4] Food selected from a limited menu.
[5] Food sold for immediate consumption on or off premises.
[6] Where customer pays before eating.

the property (*see id.* at 106). The Court of Appeals held that such a condition was invalid based upon its "lack of adherence to the fundamental rule that zoning deals basically with land use and not with the person who owns or occupies it" (*id.* at 105; *see Matter of St. Onge v Donovan,* 71 N.Y.2d 507, 514-517 [1988]). The fundamental rule referred to in *Dexter* is in essence a "prohibition against *ad hominem* zoning decisions" (*Village of Valatie v Smith,* 83 NY2d 396, 403 [1994]; *see St. Onge,* 71 N.Y.2d at 514-517).

Here, unlike in *Dexter,* the challenged Ordinance section does not single out a particular property owner for favorable or unfavorable treatment .... Rather, all property owners in the Central Business District are treated the same under section 170-13 inasmuch as all property owners are prohibited from operating an FFFR ... Contrary to plaintiff's related contention, we conclude that section 170-13 regulates the use, not the ownership, of the subject property. Indeed, plaintiff is not an FFFR, nor does it seek to operate an FFFR. Instead, plaintiff is a property owner that seeks to rent commercial space to an FFFR. Thus, it is plaintiff's use of the property that is being regulated, and its ownership status is irrelevant.

We further conclude that the court properly determined that Ordinance §170-13 does not improperly regulate the manner of plaintiff's business operations ... We note that plaintiff failed to preserve for our review any contention that there is no rational basis for distinguishing between FFFRs and non-FFFRs that meet two or more of the criteria set forth in section 170-13 because it did not advance that contention in

Notes and Comments

1. *Basis for Regulation.* Might a stronger basis for regulation be based on health considerations as addressed in Chapter 11? Or might a formula fast-food restaurant under the Village definition serve healthy food?

2. *Parsley on the Pig?* There are very different views of the impact and value of formula business regulations. Below is an exchange at the Mendocino County California Planning Commission on August 18, 2016:

> David Roderick ... addressed Hopland's difficulties in attracting a grocery store. When the Hopland Superette closed, he said, "it looked like a Soviet-era grocery store with one can of something nobody wanted to buy." He said that a Nugget outlet, a small chain he characterized as "a high-value operator," was a possibility for Hopland, and concluded that "if those people are shut out, that shuts out Hopland." ... Bill Taylor .... stated his opinion that the ordinance's focus on aesthetics allowed unsightly chain stores to "put a little parsley on the pig."

Sarah Reith, Community Character to be Codified in November, Willits News, (Aug. 23, 2016), at http://www.willitsnews.com/general-news/20160823/community-character-to-be-codified-in-november (last visited Nov. 6, 2016).

D. MANSIONIZATION

Under what rationale can municipalities manage what has come to be known as mansionization? This is the building of homes, sometimes called "McMansions," that dwarf their neighbors. One more formal definition was offered by a study commissioned by the Metropolitan Washington Council of Governments: "mansio-nization is formally defined as 'replacing (or constructing additions to) small dwell-ings within established neighborhoods with significantly larger homes,' and is synonymous with residential infill development." Paul J. Weinberg, Mansionization and Its Ordinances: How's That Working Out for You?, 36 No. 2 Zoning & Plan. L. Rep. 1 (2013). Is the rationale one of traditional health and safety — e.g., requiring emergency vehicle access to the property, deprivation of sunshine and light to neighbors? Of aesthetics? Of cultural or historic preservation? Of some combina-tion? *See* Emily Alpert Reyes, "L.A. Takes a Step Toward Tighter Rules to Curb Mansionization," L.A. Times (July 14, 2016)

Among the regulatory tools to address the phenomenon are set back require-ments, floor area ratios, cubic footage regulations, and plan review requirements for homes over a certain size. *See also* Paul Weinberg, Zoning for Aesthetics — Who Deci-des What Your House Will Look Like?, 28 No. 9 Zoning & Plan. L. Rep. 1 (2005).

Timing of attempts to regulate is important, as rights might vest or other obstacles to application of proposed rules may exist. *See Association of Friends of Sagaponack v. Zoning Bd. of Appeals of the Town of Southampton*, 287 A.D.2d 620, 731 N.Y.S.2d 851 (2001). A proposed 29-bedroom, 40-bathroom, 55,000-square-foot home with a 75-car garage and a 10,000-square-foot playhouse on a 63-acre tract led to the adoption of an ordinance limiting houses to 20,000 square feet. The ordinance came too late to prevent this proposal as the court found the owner had a vested right to complete his house.

E. SIGN AND BILLBOARD REGULATION

Regulation of signs and billboards is now commonplace. Many jurisdictions regulate signs to be uniform and non-intrusive. What is the rationale for precluding signs that are larger in size or that are lit in a certain way? Consider carefully the justifications put forth by the town in the following case.

■ ASSELIN v. TOWN OF CONWAY
628 A.2d 247 (N.H. 1993)

JOHNSON, Justice.

Michael Asselin, doing business as Mario's restaurant; Barlo Signs, Inc.; and Cardiff & Company (hereinafter Cardiff) appeal from a judgment in Superior Court (*O'Neil*, J.) upholding the validity of the sign illumination provision of the Conway zoning ordinance. . . .

Nestled in the Mount Washington Valley, Conway historically has been a tourist destination for activities in the White Mountain National Forest. Route 16 links the villages of Conway and North Conway and offers striking views of the mountains and ledges to the west. Substantial commercial development, primarily along this high-way, has rendered part of the town a shoppers' Mecca. Hundreds of signs draw tourists in the day and evening hours to the shopping centers, lodging facilities, and restaurants clustered in the villages of Conway and North Conway and lining Route 16.

The town passed its first zoning ordinance in 1982, requiring all property owners, with certain exceptions, to obtain a permit from the town zoning officer before erecting a sign. Since 1982, the ordinance has banned signs "illuminated from within," but has allowed the use of signs illuminated by external lights.

Michael Asselin is a town resident who owned Mario's restaurant on Route 16 in North Conway. In December 1988, Asselin acquired a permit to erect an *externally* lit sign. Barlo Signs, Inc. leased to Asselin a sign for Mario's restaurant capable of *internal* illumination. The town notified Asselin that the sign's internal lighting violated the zoning ordinance, and the ZBA denied him permission to use an internally lit sign. Asselin and Barlo Signs, Inc. (hereinafter the Asselin plaintiffs) appealed the ZBA's decision pursuant to RSA 677:4 (1986). The trial court found the sign illumination provision valid and upheld the ZBA's decision.

The trial court's consideration of the Asselin plaintiffs' claims was consolidated with the town's petition for a temporary injunction against Cardiff. Cardiff owns the Indian Head Village Plaza shopping center on Route 16 in North Conway. In February 1990, the town issued Cardiff a permit to erect a sign described in the permit application as externally lit. The two faces of the sign are translucent, and lights in the sign's supporting posts can shine against mirrored surfaces that reflect the light out through the sign faces. Cardiff was convicted in district court in June 1990 of five violations of the sign illumination provision but failed to file a timely appeal. The town petitioned the superior court to enjoin Cardiff from using the lights within the posts to illuminate the sign, and that action was consolidated with the Asselin plaintiffs' action. Following a hearing on the merits, the trial court issued an injunction. . . .

We next consider whether the State zoning enabling act authorized the town to pass the sign illumination provision solely to promote aesthetic values, including preserving scenic vistas, discouraging development from competing with the natural environment, and promoting the character of a "country community." The State zoning enabling act grants municipalities broad authority to pass zoning ordinances for the health, safety, morals, and general welfare of the community. *See* RSA 674:16, I (1986 & Supp. 1992); *Britton v. Town of Chester*, 134 N.H. 434, 441, 595 A.2d 492, 496 (1991) . . .

> The concept of the public welfare is broad and inclusive. The values it represents are spiritual as well as physical, aesthetic as well as monetary. It is within the power of the legislature to determine that the community should be beautiful as well as healthy, spacious as well as clean, well-balanced as well as carefully patrolled.

Berman v. Parker, 348 U.S. 26, 33 (1954) (citation omitted). Consistent with this expansive view, we have held that towns may consider, at least among other factors, "aesthetic values, such as preserving rural charm," when passing zoning regulations under State law. *Town of Chesterfield v. Brooks*, 126 N.H. 64, 69, 489 A.2d 600, 604 (1985); *see also* RSA 674:17, II (1986). We now conclude that municipalities may validly exercise zoning power *solely* to advance aesthetic values, because the preservation or enhancement of the visual environment may promote the general welfare. *See* RSA 674:16, I; *Opinion of the Justices*, 103 N.H. 268, 270, 169 A.2d 762, 764 (1961). We hold that the town in this case has not exceeded its authority under RSA 674:16 by relying exclusively on the promotion of aesthetic values for its exercise of zoning power.

The next issue is whether the Conway sign illumination provision is a reasonable exercise of the town's police power. *See* N.H. CONST. pt. I, arts. 2, 12. . . .

. . . The parties challenging the provision in this case argue that it unreasonably burdens "all" sign users and "many" manufacturers. The appropriate inquiry for reviewing this *substantive due process* claim is whether the claimants proved that the provision constitutes a restriction on property rights that is not rationally related to the town's legitimate goals.

. . . The town passed the provision for legitimate purposes, including preserving scenic vistas, discouraging development from competing with the natural environment, and "promoting community character." The community character sought to be promoted is that of a "country community . . . accustomed to having small hanging signs," or a "business community that operated mostly during the daylight hours, not in the evening." There is support for the trial court's finding that "the natural appeal and general atmosphere of the area could well be negatively affected by the unregulated use of nighttime lighting." It is reasonable to infer that the scenic vistas sought to be preserved by the town include the splendor of mountains at twilight and the brilliance of stars at night. Ronald Fleming, an expert witness experienced in planning for the preservation and enhancement of visual environments, testified that . . . internally illuminated signs appear as "disconnected squares of light" at dusk and at night, and that the "overall effect" of "an internally-lit sign is to create a visual block that is seen at some great distance sort of bobbing at the windshield," while external lights "soften the impact" of signs in the darkness. The evidence supports a finding that the restriction on internally lighted signs is rationally related to the town's legitimate, aesthetic goals of preserving vistas, discouraging development that competes with the natural environment, and promoting the character of a "country community."

Furthermore, the evidence supports the finding that the provision does not place oppressive burdens on the private rights of affected businesses. We note that there is no merit to the position that the ordinance impairs the freedom of expression; the provision is merely a content-neutral restriction on one of the myriad ways in which outdoor messages may be conveyed at night. *See State v. Comley,* 130 N.H. 688, 691-92, 546 A.2d 1066, 1068 (1988); *see also Metromedia, Inc. v. San Diego,* 453 U.S. 490, 516 (1981). The provision allows every business owner to erect a sign that may be effectively illuminated. The evidence reflects that a number of manufacturers are capable of constructing signs fit for external lights, and that signs with external lights may be less expensive. We hold that the trial court did not err in finding the provision valid because it is a reasonable regulation consistent with the due process requirements of our Constitution. . . .

Notes and Comments

1. *"Disconnected Squares of Light" at Dusk.* In upholding the regulation, the court relied on testimony by an expert witness regarding the aesthetic problems that internally illuminated signs pose. He testified that internally lit signs appear as "disconnected squares of light" at dusk and the effect is to create a visual block that is seen at some great distance "sort of bobbing at the windshield." Does this testimony provide a firm enough basis to differentiate internal from external lights? Courts tend to show some deference to local regulatory judgments even when

ordinances are directed at forms of protected speech like signs. *See, e.g., E & J Equities, LLC v. Board of Adjustment of the Twp. of Franklin,* __ A.3d __, 2016 WL 4916964 (N.J. 2016) (record provided no basis for differentiating between three static billboards, which were allowed, and digital billboards, which were not); *Township of Exeter v. Zoning Hearing Bd. of Exeter Twp.,* 911 A.2d 201 (Pa. Commw. Ct. 2006) (holding that ban on large signs below industry standard furthered purposes of aesthetics and traffic safety).

2. *Pervasiveness of Sign Controls.* Nearly every community in this country has enacted some form of sign control. There is a lot to regulate. New York's guidance document on sign control is 66 pages long. N.Y. Dept. of State, Municipal Control of Signs (James A. Coon Government Technical Series, reprint 2015), at http://www.dos.ny.gov/lg/publications/Municipal_Control_of_Signs.pdf (last visited Nov. 6, 2016). These regulations, though based in part on traffic or pedestrian safety, are largely motivated by aesthetic considerations. Historic districts and certain commercial and neighborhood zoning districts usually give special treatment to the nature and type of allowed signs. Signs may be defined as simply "any attention attracting device" used for commercial purposes or to convey a message. Restrictions can apply to nearly any item, structure, or device on site and visible from the street.

While signs (because of their messages) are a form of "speech" protected by the First Amendment, the courts grant local communities considerable discretion in regulating the time, place, and manner of sign usage, including banning altogether certain types of signs, such as free-standing, overhanging, and backlit signs, etc. Courts have upheld a variety of types of sign controls, including, among other things, restrictions on height, size, color, lighting, movement, and manner of display and support. *See, e.g., Prime Media, Inc. v. City of Brentwood, Tenn.,* 389 F.3d 814 (6th Cir. 2005) (upholding size and height restrictions for billboards of 120 square feet and 6 feet respectively); *Kroll v. Steere,* 759 A.2d 541 (Conn. Ct. App. 2000) (upholding restriction of one square foot on size of most signs); *Salib v. City of Mesa,* 133 P.3d 756 (Ariz. App. 2006) (upholding restriction on commercial sign of no more than 30 percent of window space).

3. *The Effect of* Reed v. Town of Gilbert. The Supreme Court's 2015 decision in *Reed v. Town of Gilbert,* 576 US _, 135 S. Ct. 2218 (2015), is covered in detail in Chapter 8. Here is the key reasoning that applies to the concerns with aesthetics.

> That is why we have repeatedly considered whether a law is content neutral on its face *before* turning to the law's justification or purpose . . . . Because strict scrutiny applies either when a law is content based on its face or when the purpose and justification for the law are content based, a court must evaluate each question before it concludes that the law is content neutral and thus subject to a lower level of scrutiny.
>
> The Court of Appeals and the United States misunderstand our decision in *Ward* as suggesting that a government's purpose is relevant even when a law is content based on its face. That is incorrect. . . .
>
> The Town seizes on this reasoning [of the Court of Appeals regarding content neutrality], insisting that "content based" is a term of art that "should be applied flexibly" with the goal of protecting "viewpoints and ideas from government censorship or favoritism." Brief for Respondents 22. In the Town's view, a sign regulation that "does not censor or favor particular viewpoints or ideas" cannot be content based. *Ibid.* The Sign Code allegedly passes this test because its treatment of temporary directional signs does not raise any concerns that the government is "endorsing or suppressing

'ideas or viewpoints,'" *id.,* at 27, and the provisions for political signs and ideological signs "are neutral as to particular ideas or viewpoints" within those categories. *Id.,* at 37. . . .

[A] speech regulation targeted at specific subject matter is content based even if it does not discriminate among viewpoints within that subject matter. *Ibid.* For example, a law banning the use of sound trucks for political speech — and only political speech — would be a content-based regulation, even if it imposed no limits on the political viewpoints that could be expressed. See *Discovery Network, supra,* at 428, 113 S. Ct. 1505. The Town's Sign Code likewise singles out specific subject matter for differential treatment, even if it does not target viewpoints within that subject matter. Ideological messages are given more favorable treatment than messages concerning a political candidate, which are themselves given more favorable treatment than messages announcing an assembly of like-minded individuals. That is a paradigmatic example of content-based discrimination.

. . . Because the Town's Sign Code imposes content-based restrictions on speech, those provisions can stand only if they survive strict scrutiny . . . Thus, it is the Town's burden to demonstrate that the Code's differentiation between temporary directional signs and other types of signs, such as political signs and ideological signs, furthers a compelling governmental interest and is narrowly tailored to that end. *See ibid.*

The Town cannot do so. It has offered only two governmental interests in support of the distinctions the Sign Code draws: preserving the Town's aesthetic appeal and traffic safety. Assuming for the sake of argument that those are compelling governmental interests, the Code's distinctions fail as hopelessly underinclusive.

Starting with the preservation of aesthetics, temporary directional signs are "no greater an eyesore," *Discovery Network,* 507 U. S., at 425, than ideological or political ones. Yet the Code allows unlimited proliferation of larger ideological signs while strictly limiting the number, size, and duration of smaller directional ones. The Town cannot claim that placing strict limits on temporary directional signs is necessary to beautify the Town while at the same time allowing unlimited numbers of other types of signs that create the same problem. . . .

The Town has ample content-neutral options available to resolve problems with safety and aesthetics. For example, its current Code regulates many aspects of signs that have nothing to do with a sign's message: size, building materials, lighting, moving parts, and portability. See, *e.g.,* §4.402(R). And on public property, the Town may go a long way toward entirely forbidding the posting of signs, so long as it does so in an evenhanded, content-neutral manner.

Justice Alito's concurring opinion gives specific examples, and thus is likely to be widely used by practicing attorneys:

As the Court shows, the regulations at issue in this case are replete with content-based distinctions, and as a result they must satisfy strict scrutiny. This does not mean, however, that municipalities are powerless to enact and enforce reasonable sign regulations. I will not attempt to provide anything like a comprehensive list, but here are some rules that would not be content based:

Rules regulating the size of signs. These rules may distinguish among signs based on any content-neutral criteria, including any relevant criteria listed below.

Rules regulating the locations in which signs may be placed. These rules may distinguish between free-standing signs and those attached to buildings.

Rules distinguishing between lighted and unlighted signs.

Rules distinguishing between signs with fixed messages and electronic signs with messages that change.

Rules that distinguish between the placement of signs on private and public property.

Rules distinguishing between the placement of signs on commercial and residential property.

Rules distinguishing between on-premises and off-premises signs.

Rules restricting the total number of signs allowed per mile of roadway.

Rules imposing time restrictions on signs advertising a one-time event. Rules of this nature do not discriminate based on topic or subject and are akin to rules restricting the times within which oral speech or music is allowed.[footnote omitted]

   . . . [G]overnment entities may also erect their own signs consistent with the principles that allow governmental speech . . . . They may put up all manner of signs to promote safety, as well as directional signs and signs pointing out historic sites and scenic spots.

4. *Problematic Constitutional Issues in Sign Regulation.* The rationale for the sign code in *Reed v. Town of Gilbert* was both safety and aesthetics. However, city sign controls may be held to violate the First Amendment on a variety of grounds. Regulation must generally be content neutral, not favor commercial signs over noncommercial signs, and be narrowly tailored to achieve their purpose, and the regulation as applied must leave open ample alternative avenues for the expression involved. What does *Reed* add to our understanding of the test for content neutrality? *See* Brian J. Connolly & Alan C. Weinstein, Sign Regulation After Reed: Suggestions for Coping with Legal Uncertainty, 47 Urban Law. 569 (2015).

Earlier cases included *Nichols Media Group v. Town of Babylon*, 365 F. Supp. 2d 295 (E.D. N.Y. 2005) (exemptions based on content held unconstitutional); *KH Outdoor v. City of Trussville*, 458 F.3d 1261 (11th Cir. 2006) (ordinance favoring commercial signs held unconstitutional); *McFadden v. City of Bridgeport*, 422 F. Supp. 2d 659 (N.D. W.Va. 2006) (ordinance prohibiting posting of political and temporary signs more than 30 days before and 48 hours after event or election held unconstitutional).

5. *The Impact of Reed. Reed's* impact will likely play out in various challenges to an aesthetics rationale for sign regulation as laid out in Chapter 8. Query, for example, as to the effect of *Reed* on:

(1) Conflicts between expression and highway beauty, which was addressed before *Reed* in *World Wide Rush, LLC v. City of Los Angeles*, 606 F.3d 676 (9th Cir. 2010), in which the Court of Appeals held inter alia that content-neutral exceptions to a freeway facing sign ban did not undermine the city's substantial interests in aesthetics;

(2) Banners and signs on highway overpasses, *Luce v. Town of Campbell*, 113 F. Supp. 3d 1002 (W.D. Wis. 2015), in which the court concluded that the ordinance was content-neutral, as required for an ordinance to be a valid time, place, and manner restriction of speech under the First Amendment, made no reference to content of speech, and was indifferent to any specific message or viewpoint; and

(3) Outdoor advertising for aesthetic and safety purposes, *CBS Outdoor, Inc. v. City of New York*, 50 Misc. 3d 283, 16 N.Y.S.3d 411 (Sup. 2015), where the court found

municipal regulation of outdoor advertising for aesthetic and safety purposes is an exercise of the municipality's police power.

Justice Alito provides some rules that would not be content-based. Can you think of others? Put yourself in the role of a First Amendment absolutist, can you devise scenarios where some of his rules would be cover for content discrimination?

Discretionary permit systems for sign display are particularly vulnerable to constitutional challenge as impermissible prior restraints. *See, e.g., Lamar Advertising Co. v. City of Douglasville, Ga.,* 254 F. Supp. 2d 1321 (N.D. Ga. 2003) (there must be reasonably specific and objective criteria for sign permit processing to avoid the potential for content-based decisions).

Ideological signs, and even some on-site commercial signs, probably cannot be banned in any residential area. *See, e.g., Ladue v. Gilleo,* 512 U.S. 43 (1994) (holding ordinance unconstitutional which banned a variety of noncommercial signs in residential area); and *Linmark Assoc.'s, Inc. v. Township of Willingboro,* 431 U.S. 85 (1977) (holding unconstitutional a ban on on-site commercial "for sale" sign in residential area).

6. *Amortization or Compensation.* As discussed in the Note on Nonconforming Uses in Chapter 2, a city that enacts a ban on existing billboards may face a taking claim. *See Odegard Outdoor Advertising, LLC v. Board of Zoning Adjustment of Jackson County,* 6 S.W.3d 148, 150 (Mo. 1999) ("the zoning authority is faced with the choice of allowing the property owners to continue the nonconforming use or compensating the property owner for the value of the taken use"). It may avoid the taking claim by allowing the owner a reasonable time in which to use the billboard and amortize its costs. A steady stream of litigation concerns the sufficiency of the amortization period provided. *See, e.g., Outdoor Graphics, Inc. v. City of Burlington,* 103 F.3d 690 (8th Cir. 1997) (five-year amortization period was sufficient). Some jurisdictions, however, require payment for any billboard that is outlawed. *See Eller Media Co. v. Montgomery County,* 795 A.2d 728 (Md. Ct. Sp. App. 2002) (amortization period could not be used where Maryland statute declared that a city or county "shall pay the fair market value of an outdoor advertising sign removed or required to be removed by the county or municipality").

F. LANDSCAPES, VIEWS, TREES, LAWNS, FENCES, TRUCKS, TRAILERS, AND BOATS

■ WEBSTER v. TOWN OF CANDIA
778 A.2d 402 (N.H. 2001)

DALIANIS, J.

... [P]laintiffs Kenneth Webster and Margaret Demos as Trustees of the Kenneth Webster Trust, and Winthrop Sargeant (Webster plaintiffs), appeal the Superior Court's (*Galway,* J.) order affirming the decision of the Town of Candia Planning Board (planning board) denying their application to remove trees from Libbee Road, a designated scenic road. Plaintiff Julee Sanderson, as Trustee of Candia Rangeway Realty Trust (*Sanderson*), appeals the Superior Court's (*Abramsom,* J.) order affirming the planning board's decision denying her application to remove trees from Libbee Road. Sanderson also appeals the Superior Court's (*Coffey*, J.) order denying her motion for reconsideration. We affirm. . . .

1. CONSTITUTIONALITY OF SCENIC ROAD STATUE

The plaintiffs assert that RSA 231:158 (1993), prohibiting cutting trees or destroying stone walls on designated scenic roads absent permission from the planning board (or other "official municipal body"), is impermissibly vague and thus void under the New Hampshire Constitution. . . .

RSA 231:158 provides, in pertinent part:

> Upon a road being designated as a scenic road as provided in RSA 231:157, any repair, maintenance, reconstruction, or paving work done with respect thereto by the state or municipality . . . shall not involve the cutting, damage or removal of trees [of a particular circumference], or the tearing down or destruction of stone walls, or portions thereof, except with the prior written consent of the planning board, or any other official municipal body designated by the meeting [of the town voters] to implement the provisions of this subdivision. . . .

RSA 231:158, II. . . .

The warrant articles by which the town voted to designate Libbee Road as scenic specify that the purpose of so doing was to "protect[] and enhanc[e] . . . the scenic beauty of Candia." *See also N.H.S. Jour.* 708 (1971) (purpose of scenic road statute is to "encourage the tourist attractiveness of our scenic roads in our towns and . . . permit the retention of trees and stone walls so characteristic of our New England scenery"). In context then, RSA 231:158 informs a developer that any plan to cut trees or remove stone walls from a designated scenic road must not destroy the "scenic beauty" of the road. This is sufficient notice to developers of the relevant standards.

The legislature would have been hard pressed to define the concept of "scenic beauty" more specifically. *See Finks v. Maine State Highway Commission*, 328 A.2d 791, 796 (Me. 1974). We agree with the Maine Supreme Judicial Court and the New Jersey Supreme Court that:

> The Act contemplates that there is a certain basic beauty in natural terrain and vegetation unspoiled by the hands of man, which it proposes to recapture or maintain. Although the extent to which each individual finds a specific landscape beautiful must be determined by a subjective test, this does not denote that there is no catholic criterion for the ascertainment of whether *any scenic beauty* exists in a given panorama. "Scenic beauty" is concerned with such manifold possible situations that it does not lend itself to a more specifically detailed descriptive statement. A tabulation of the various possible elements constituting scenic beauty is well-nigh impossible.

Id. (quoting *Wes Outdoor Advertising Company v. Goldberg*, 55 N.J. 347, 262 A.2d 199, 202 (1970)).

Moreover, the concept of "scenic beauty[]," although more generally used in a subjective sense, connotes, in terms of [the scenic road statute], a sufficiently definite concrete image . . . to furnish in and of itself an adequate standard." *Id.* . . .

Affirmed.

Notes and Comments

1. *Authority to Consider Aesthetics.* The local agency must be authorized to regulate for aesthetic purposes. That authorization can come from state zoning enabling legislation or other types of state land use law. *See In re Denio*, 608 A.2d 1166, 1168 (Vt. 1992) ("the conditions were based on the Board's finding, under 10 V.S.A. §6086(a)(8), that, in the absence of adherence to the conditions, the subdivision would adversely affect the aesthetics of the surrounding area").

Local governments employ a variety of means to implement aesthetic regulation. Cities may use overlay or special zoning districts and typically utilize some form of site plan review. *See, e.g., Franchise Developers, Inc. v. City of Cincinnati*, 505 N.E.2d 966 (Ohio 1987) (city validly disapproved a permit to construct a "Burger Chef" restaurant in an overlay "environmental quality-urban design zone district"); *People v. Novie*, 976 N.Y.S.2d 636 (App. 2013) (upholding local village tree preservation law which required a permit to cut certain trees).

2. *Scenic Beauty.* In the *Webster* case above, the Supreme Court of New Hampshire concludes that the phrase "scenic beauty" is not so vague as to be unconstitutional, at least, with respect to state administrative implementation through state scenic road designations. In a later case, *Kosalka v. Town of Georgetown*, 752 A.2d 183 (Me. 2003), the Maine Supreme Court held a local zoning ordinance unconstitutionally vague that provided, as a standard for zoning board approval of shoreline development, that a project "conserve natural beauty." The court ruled that this standard did not provide any guidance to a developer or the zoning board involved as to "how much conservation is necessary." Are these cases reconcilable?

As the town's attorney, how could you redraft this *Kosalka* ordinance to accomplish the same purpose? How about a site plan review process that uses a simple "natural disturbance" percentage limitation (50 percent or less?) for development of shoreline lots as well as a standard that requires project design to minimize, to the extent feasible, harm to the natural environment? Would these changes remove the problematic issue of "beauty" from the equation?

3. *Protection of Landscapes and Views.* Use of zoning to protect landscapes and scenic views is not uncommon today. It is also being applied to prohibit wind turbines and solar collectors. *See* LaVonda Reed-Huff, Dirty Laundry, Dirty Dishes, and Windmills: A Framework for Regulation of Clean Energy Devices, 40 Envtl. L. 859 (2010); Adam Sherwin, Sighting Wind Energy Facilities in Vermont: Finding the Right Balance Between Social Benefits and Aesthetic Burden, 17 Buff. Envtl. L.J. 1 (2010). Indian tribes have objected that energy projects can adversely impact landscapes that have cultural or religious significance for the tribes. *See* Allison M. Dussias, Room For a (Sacred) View? American Indian Tribes Confront Visual Desecration Caused by Wind Energy Projects, 38 Am. Indian L. Rev. 333 (2013-14).

This form of preservation can be implemented directly by zoning restrictions or through some form of site plan review. In California, for example, Malibu and Monterey County have adopted view protection ordinances as "scenic corridor" regulatory programs. The City of Denver uses a "line of site" restriction to protect the view of the Rocky Mountains from all of its city parks. *See Landmark Land Co., Inc. v. City & County of Denver*, 728 P.2d 1281, 1284 (Colo. 1986) (holding that, in the context of Denver, a city whose civic identity is associated with its connection with the mountains, preservation of the view of the mountains is within the lawful scope of the police power); *Ross v. City of Rolling Hills Estates*, 238 Cal. Rptr. 561 (Ct. App.

1987) (view protection ordinance held not unconstitutionally vague). And in a case where on its face aesthetics concerns confronted federal telecommunication policy, *PI Telecom Infrastructure, LLC v. City of Jacksonville*, 104 F. Supp. 3d 1321 (M.D. Fla. 2015), the court found that substantial evidence supported the city's ruling unanimously denying PI Telecom's application to site a cell tower. The documented visibility of a proposed cell tower from a public park, which, by ordinance, the city was trying to protect and keep pristine, rose above mere generalized concerns regarding aesthetics. In addition, the company did not demonstrate that it adequately explored alternative sites to remedy the service gap.

Courts will also make judgments on application of standards. *See Rockville Haven, LLC v. Town of Rockville*, 394 S.C. 1, 714 S.E.2d 277 (2011), involving denial of a permit to construct a dock and walkway. The Supreme Court of South Carolina held that evidence failed to establish that a rural and scenic view would be impeded by construction of the dock and walkway.

4. *Alternatives?* The decision in *In re Goddard College Conditional Use*, Goddard College 2014 VT 124, 111 A.3d 1285 (Vt. 2014) is based on Act 250 of Vermont, covered in Chapter 9. There, the court addressed application of a criterion under Act 250, concluding that Criterion 8 requires that a project "not have an undue adverse effect to the scenic or natural beauty of the "area" or "aesthetics." Neighboring residents to the college challenged the grant of an Act 250 permit to build a central wood chip boiler system. They complained that "missing from the lower court's analysis" was an indication that the college or the court "thoroughly review[ed]" mitigating steps, "including relocation within the project tract."

The Supreme Court of Vermont addressed "the narrow issue of the third factor in the undue-impact analysis: whether the college failed to take reasonable and generally available mitigating steps to improve the harmony of the proposed project with its surroundings in a way that makes the project's impacts unduly adverse." *Id.* at 1287. The court upheld the application of the reasonable alternative analysis and ruled against the plaintiff on the substantive issue of aesthetics. The court further explained, "Assuming without deciding that the court can consider proposed alternative siting as a reasonable mitigating measure in the undue-impact analysis, neighbor in this case failed to produce any competent evidence to support an alternative siting argument." *Id.* at 1288.

5. *Low Density Landscape Protection.* Landscape protection is also undertaken by enactment of very low density restrictions on development. *See, e.g., Ada County v. Henry*, 668 P.2d 994 (1983) (60-acre lot size upheld to protect rural character of area); *Wilson v. McHenry County*, 416 N.E.2d 426 (Ill. App. 1981) (120-acre lot size upheld to protect rural character of area).

In *Barancik v. County of Marin*, 872 F.2d 834 (9th Cir. 1988) a federal court of appeals rejected both due process and taking claims in upholding a 60-acre per dwelling requirement enacted to protect the Nicasio Valley as a "jewel" in California's "beautiful rural landscape." The restriction sought to preserve ranching and agricultural uses in the valley and "the open spacious feeling" of western Marin County. Upholding the constitutionality of the density restriction, both on its face and as applied, the court observed:

> The cowboy and the farmer may be friends as the song has it, but not the rancher and the urban commuter, at least not if commuters, with the roads they need and the cars they drive and the tastes they have, begin to predominate in the countryside. Marin's

zoning no doubt preserves a bucolic atmosphere for the benefit of a portion of the population at the expense of those who would flow into the county if there was no zoning. The Constitution lets that decision be made by the legislature.

See Committee for Reasonable Regulation of Lake Tahoe v. Tahoe Reg'l Planning Agency, 311 F. Supp. 2d 972 (D. Nev. 2004). A citizens group brought an action challenging the Tahoe Regional Planning Agency's (TRPA) adoption of a scenic review ordinance regulating the appearance of residential housing on littoral and shoreland properties in the Lake Tahoe basin. The court held that TRPA was authorized to adopt a scenic review ordinance; that the ordinance did not constitute a regulatory taking; and that it did not facially violate the First Amendment.

Can landscape preservation zoning be used as an urban planning tool to curb urban sprawl?

6. *Tree and Vegetation Protection.* Zoning today is often used to preserve trees and natural vegetation and wildlife habitat. Some communities have "landmark" or "champion" tree preservation restrictions. Ordinance performance standards that limit site disturbance also are commonly used today to protect trees and natural vegetation. *See Chrin Bros., Inc. v. Williams Tp. Hearing Bd.*, 815 A.2d 1179 (Pa. Commw. Ct. 2003) (upholding zoning ordinance restricting clear cutting on slopes greater than 15 percent, prohibiting clear cutting on tracts larger than two acres, and requiring at least 30 percent of forest canopy be preserved on tracts larger than two acres); *Wonders v. Pima County*, 89 P.3d 810 (Ariz. App. Ct. 2004) (upholding constitutionality of county's native plant preservation ordinance as applied to subdivision development). *See generally* 2 Edward H. Ziegler, Rathkopf's The Law of Zoning & Planning §20 (4th ed. 2005 and Supp. 2012) (citing and discussing tree and vegetation preservation cases).

Would an impact fee system for tree replacement in a neighborhood be constitutional under the *Nollan* and *Dolan* nexus analysis discussed earlier in Chapter 4? *See Mira Mar Dev. Corp. v. City of Coppell*, 421 S.W.3d 74 (Tex. App. 2013) (applying constitutional "nexus/ rough proportionality" test for exactions to city's assessment of $34,500 "tree retribution fee.")

7. *Landscaping, Lawns, and Fences.* A number of court decisions have upheld ordinance requirements relating to landscaping and lawns, both as applied to commercial and residential areas. *See, e.g., Parking Ass'n of Georgia, Inc. v. City of Atlanta*, 450 S.E.2d 200 (1994) (upholding imposition of affirmative landscaping, one tree for every eight parking spaces, on existing parking lots in commercial areas); *Kucera v. Lizza*, 69 Cal Rptr. 2d 582 (Cal. App. 1997) (upholding height restriction on vegetation to protect scenic views). Lawn maintenance ordinances that require the cutting of lawns and removal of weeds have also been upheld. *See, e.g., Rose v. Board of Zoning Adjustment Platte County*, 68 S.W.2d 507 (Mo. Ct. App. 2001) (upholding lawn maintenance ordinance but remanding for finding on whether natural wooded area was a protected nonconforming use).

Courts have upheld various types of aesthetic zoning restrictions on fences. Ordinances may ban a front yard fence, regulate fence height, or prohibit certain types of fences. *See, e.g., Smyrna v. Parks*, 242 S.E.2d 73 (Ga. 1978) (upholding ban on chain-link or woven wire fences but allowing picket and split rail fences to protect aesthetics of the area); *Westminster Homes, Inc. v. Town of Cary Zoning Bd. of Adjustment*, 554 S.E.2d 634 (N.C. 2001) (upholding condition imposed on permit that fencing and landscaping serve as an architecturally compatible fence and as a buffer providing optical and acoustical screening).

8. *Junk Cars, Trucks, Trailers, and Boats.* Zoning restrictions often control the placement, parking, and storage of junk cars, or even operable trucks, trailers, motorhomes, or boats in residential neighborhoods, often simply banning their overnight parking or their storage on a lot if they can be seen from a public street. *See, e.g., Town of Manitowish Waters v. Malouf,* 316 Wis. 2d 357, 763 N.W.2d 249 (Wis. App. 2008) (upholding limit on number of vehicles that could be parked outdoors in residential areas); *Kuvin v. City of Coral Gables,* 45 So. 3d 836 (Fla. App. 2010) (upholding ban in residential area on overnight street parking of trucks, and on off-street parking except in enclosed garage); *Whaley v. Dorchester County Zoning Bd. of Appeals,* 524 S.E.2d 404 (S.C. 1999) (upholding ban on long-term parking of commercial vehicles in a residential area); *Johnson v. Village of Morton,* 352 N.E.2d 456 (Ill. App. 1976) (upholding ban on outside storage of campers and recreation vehicles).

Is a commercial truck "associationally dissonant" with the residential character of a neighborhood? What if the ordinance banned the parking of "motor boats" but not sailboats? *See City of Nichols Hills v. Richardson,* 939 P.2d 17 (Okla. Ct. Crim. App. 1997), wherein the court overturned a conviction under an ordinance that banned the parking of pickup trucks, but not passenger vehicles, in the driveway of private residences between 2:00 and 5:00 A.M., on the grounds that an "ugly, rusted or offensive" vehicle could legally be parked during that period, while a brand new pickup truck could not. The court concluded: "The obvious contradiction belies the City's claim that it has enacted the ordinance to protect the aesthetic integrity of the community."

9. *Aesthetic Regulation Versus Private Property Rights.* Political battles over aesthetic regulation are sometimes portrayed as contests between the "public interest" concerns of citizen activists and the self interest of individual owners of private property. Is this an accurate view of the political dynamic involved in the enactment of aesthetic controls? Who are the primary beneficiaries of these controls?

For scholarly articles on aesthetic regulation, *see* Meg Stevenson, Aesthetic Regulations: A History, 35 Real Est. L.J. 519 (2007); Stephen M. Judge, Codex Imaginarius: Visual Codes in Land Use Planning and Aesthetic Regulation, 81 Notre Dame L. Rev. 1595 (2006); Kenneth Pearlman et al., Beyond the Eye of the Beholder Once Again, 38 Urban Law. 1119 (2006).

Table of Cases

Principal cases are indicated by italics. Alphabetization is letter-by-letter ("Newport" precedes "New Smyrna Beach").

Table of Secondary Authorities

Index